FASHION NOW 2

i-D selects 160 of its favourite fashion designers from around the world

EDITED BY TERRY JONES & SUSIE RUSHTON

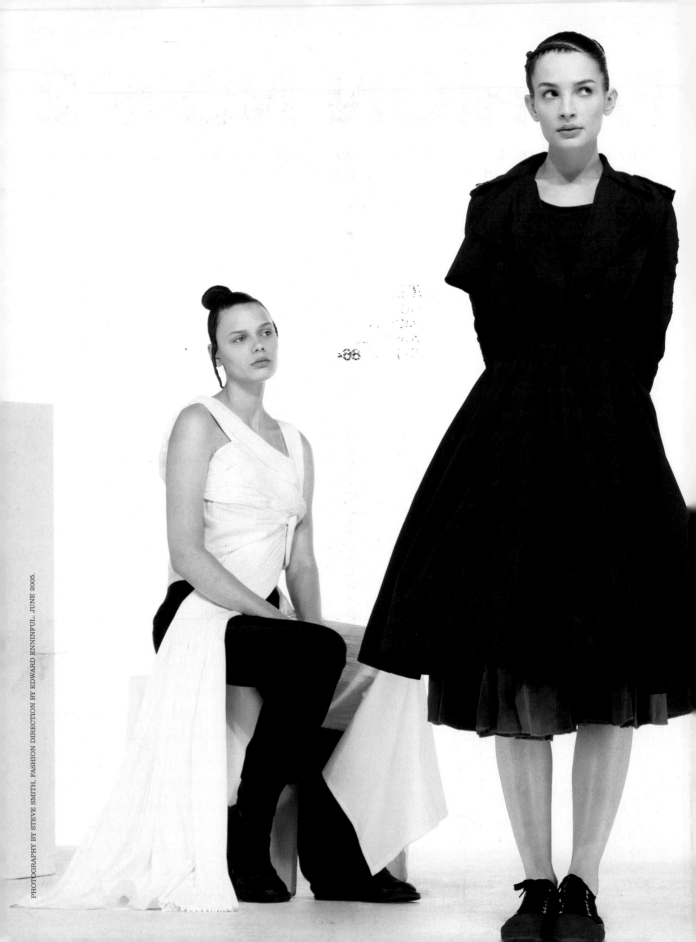

PHOTOGRAPHY BY STEVE SMITH. FASHION DIRECTION BY EDWARD ENNINFUL. JUNE 2005.

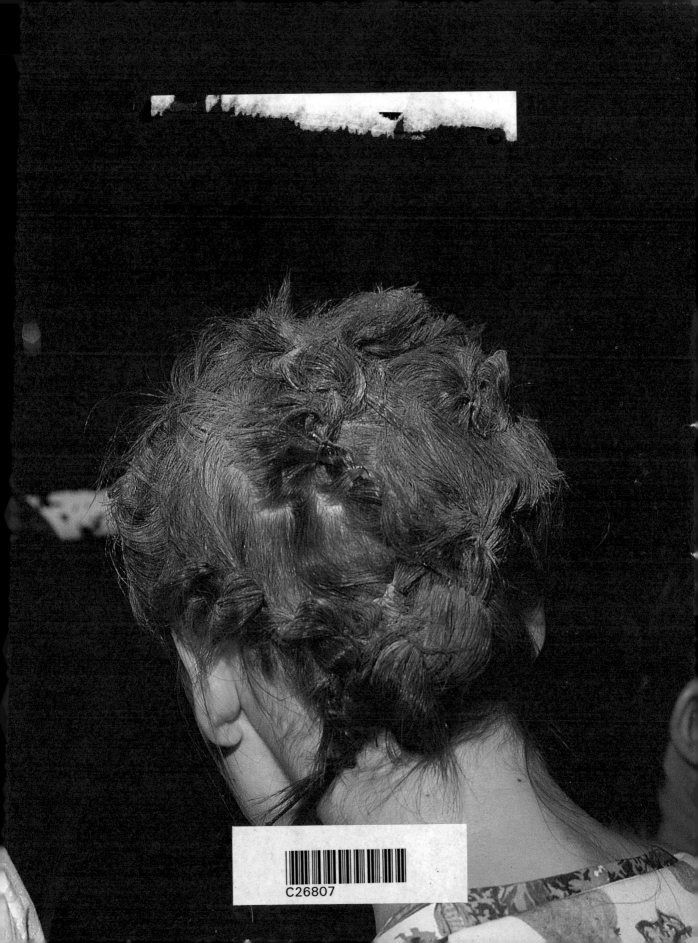

FASHION NOW 2

i-D selects 160 of its favourite fashion designers from around the world

EDITED BY TERRY JONES & SUSIE RUSHTON

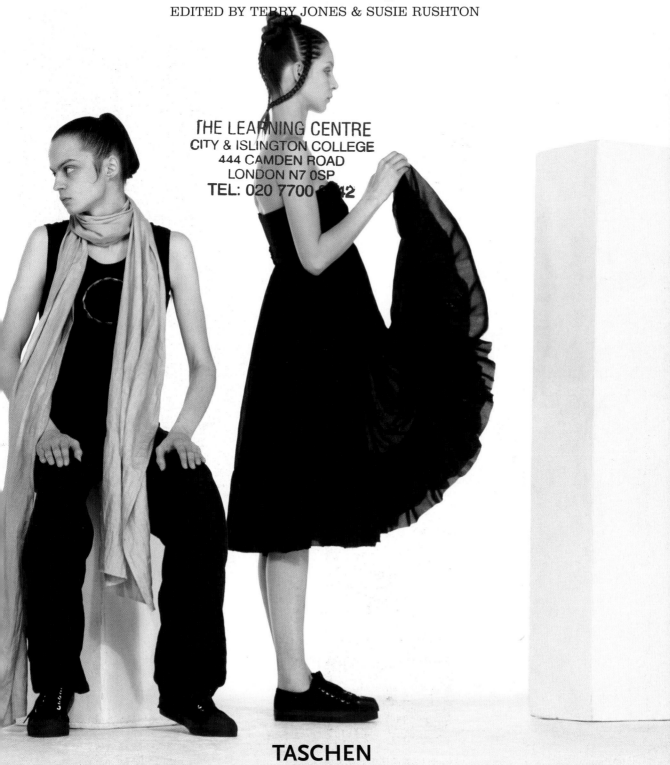

TASCHEN

Very Special thanks to..

EMPORIO ARMANI

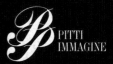
DIESEL

DOLCE & GABBANA

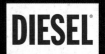
GIUSEPPE ZANOTTI DESIGN

GUESS
J E A N S

PITTI
IMMAGINE

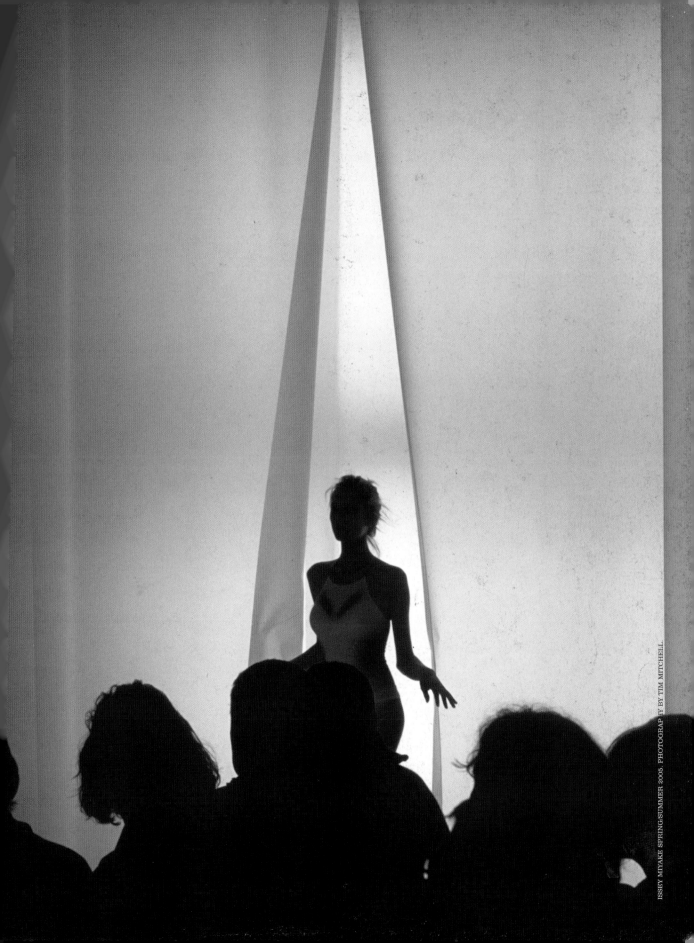

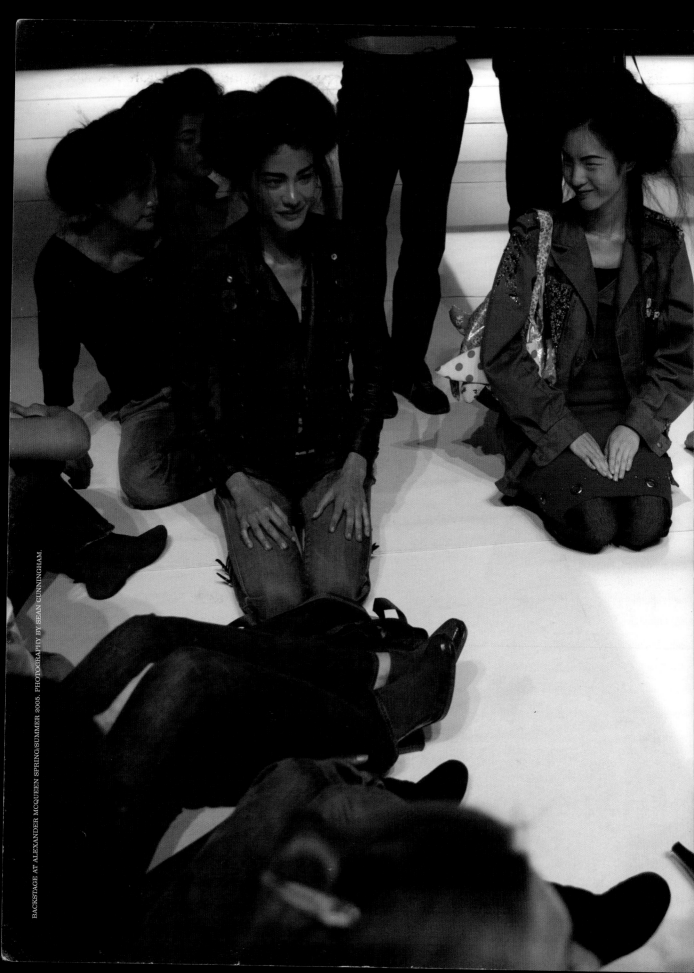

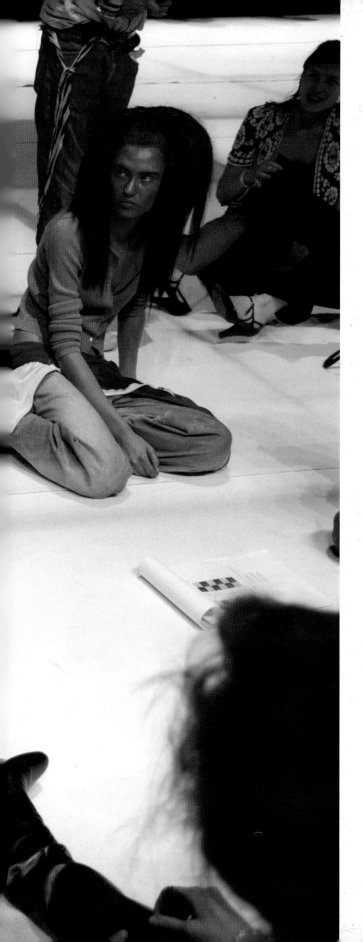

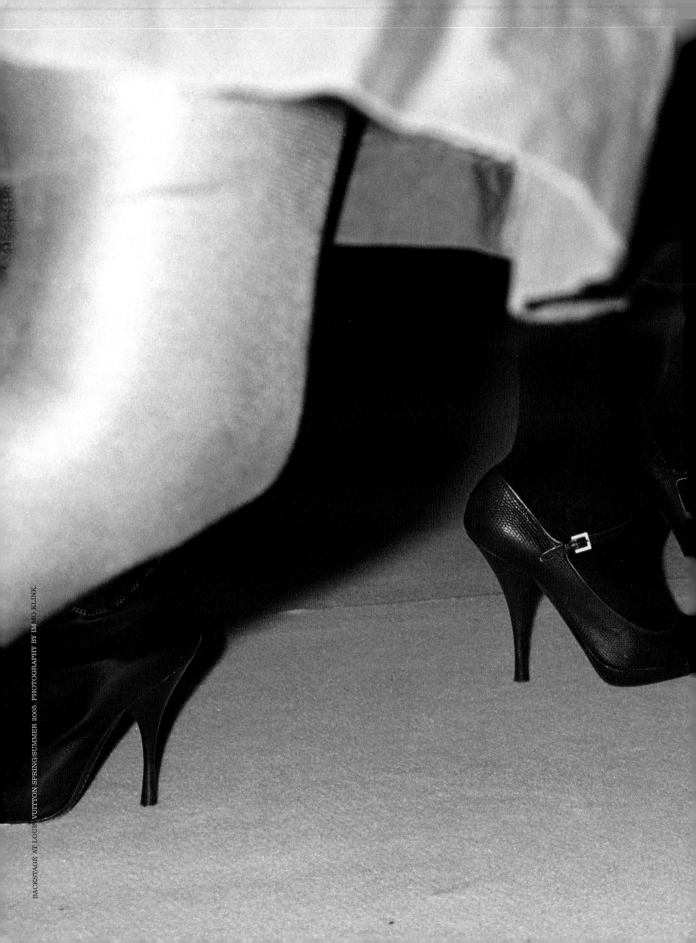

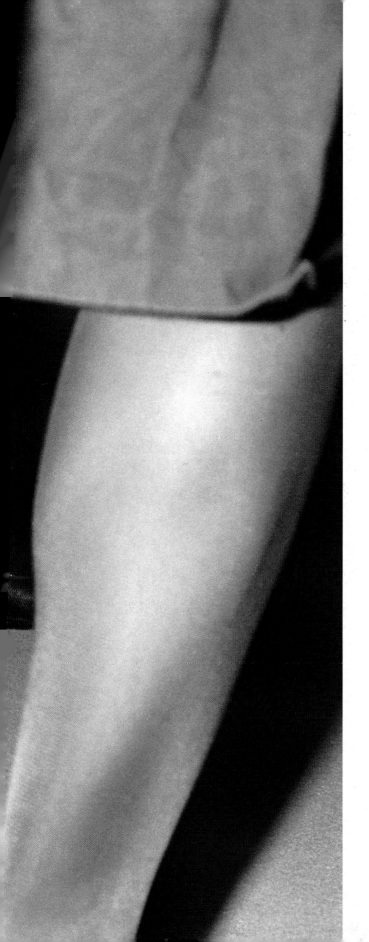

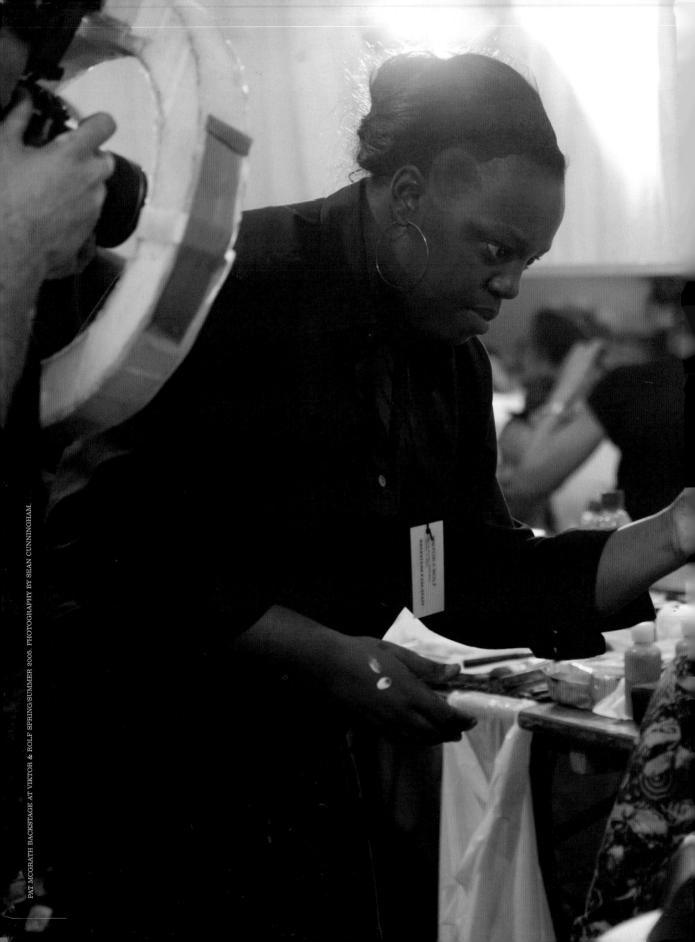

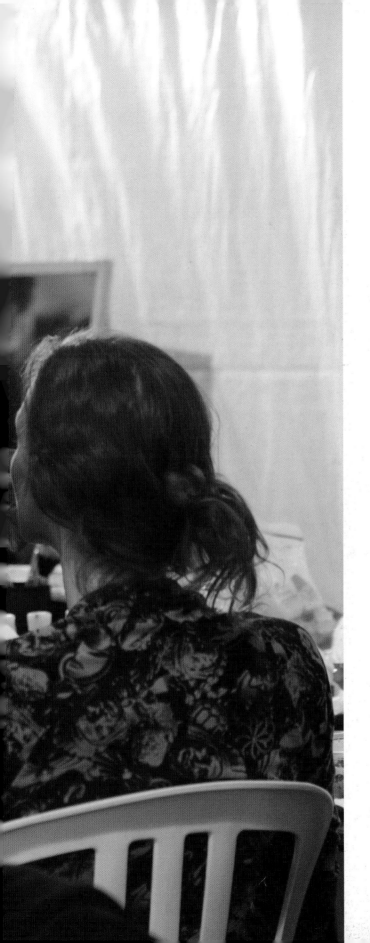

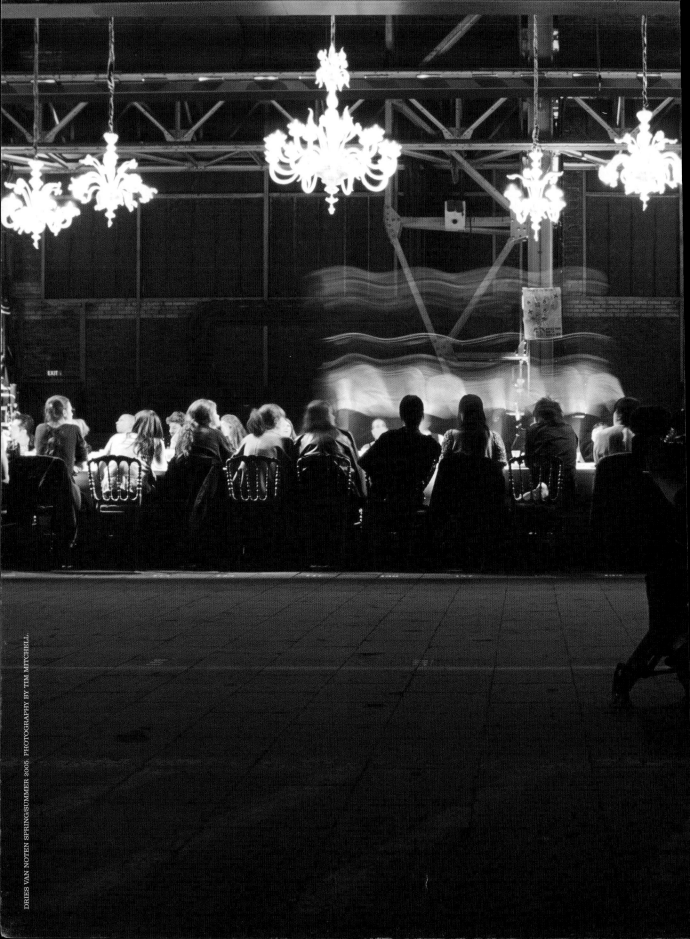

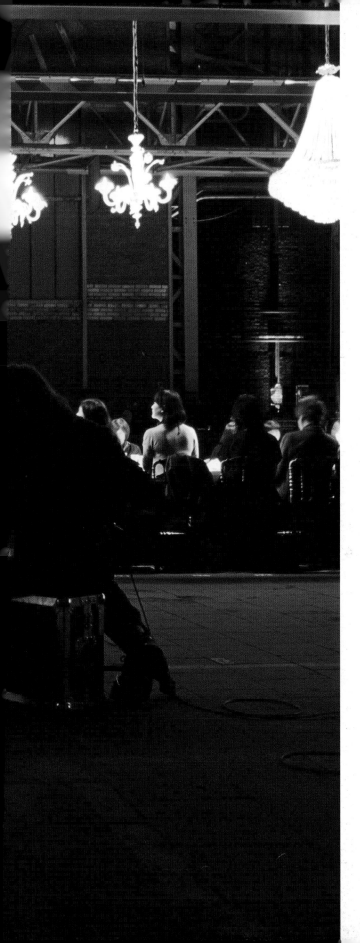

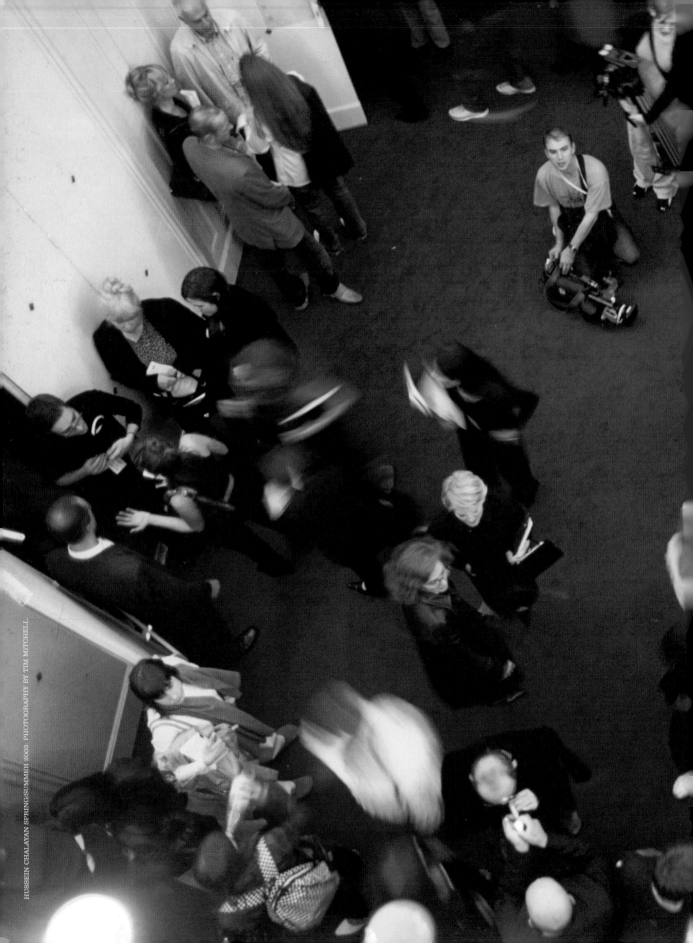

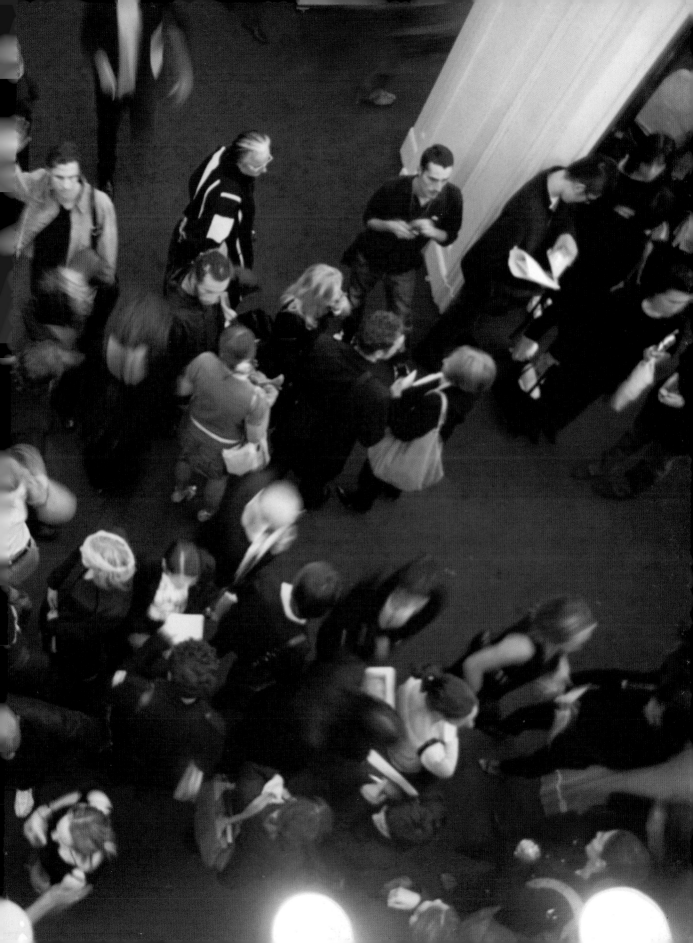

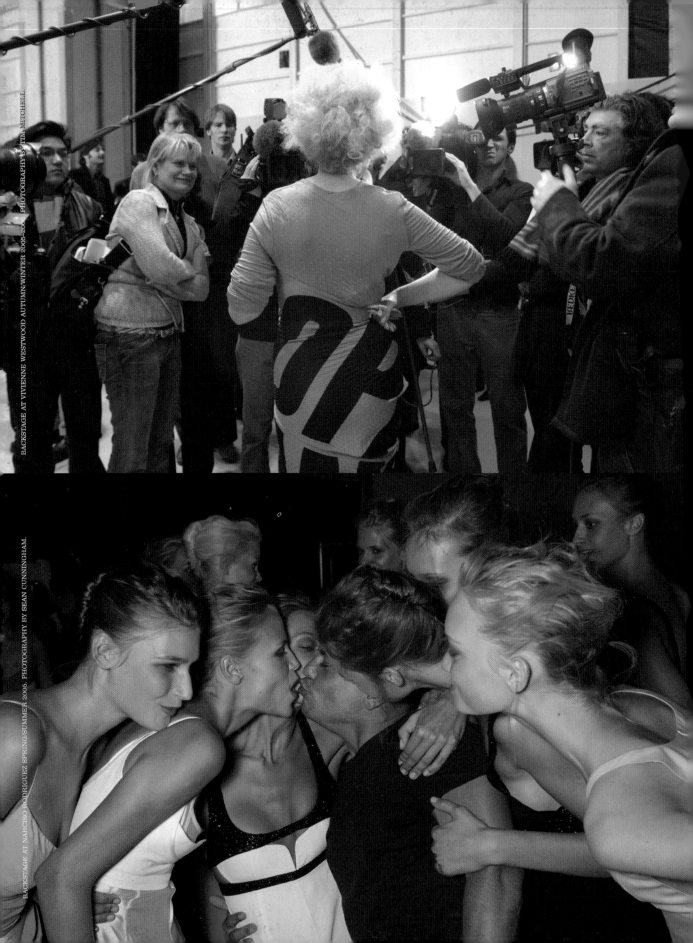

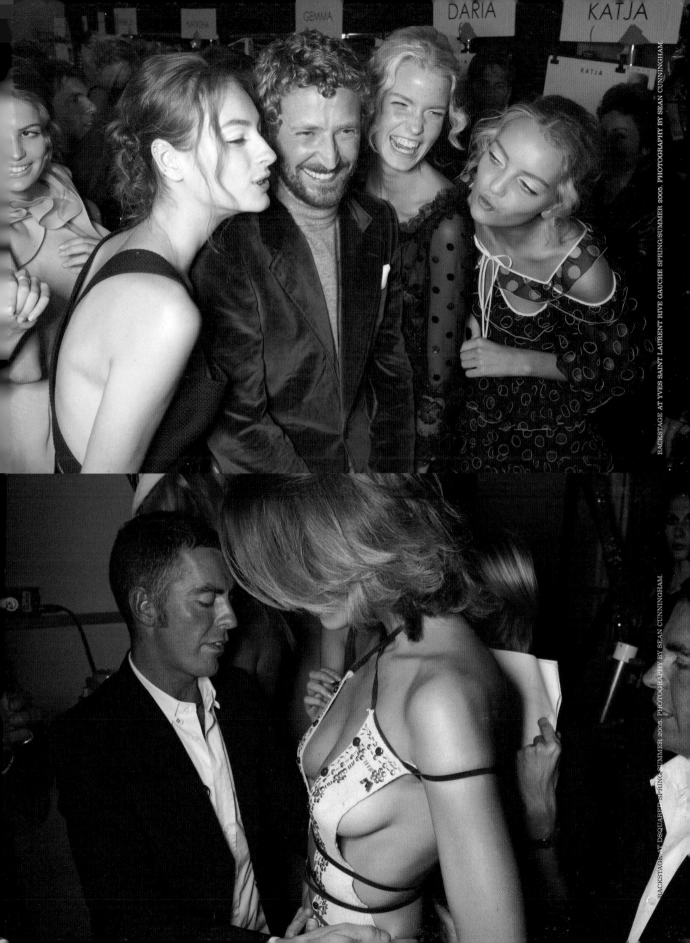

GEMMA DARIA KATJA

KATJA

BACKSTAGE AT YVES SAINT LAURENT RIVE GAUCHE SPRING/SUMMER 2005. PHOTOGRAPHY BY SEAN CUNNINGHAM.

BACKSTAGE AT DSQUARED SPRING/SUMMER 2005. PHOTOGRAPHY BY SEAN CUNNINGHAM.

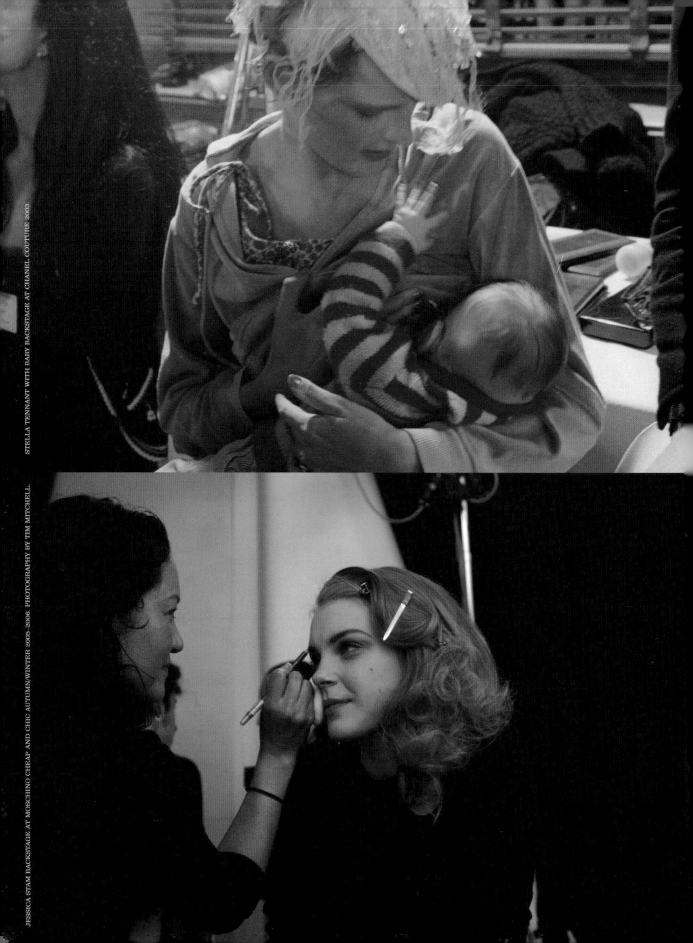

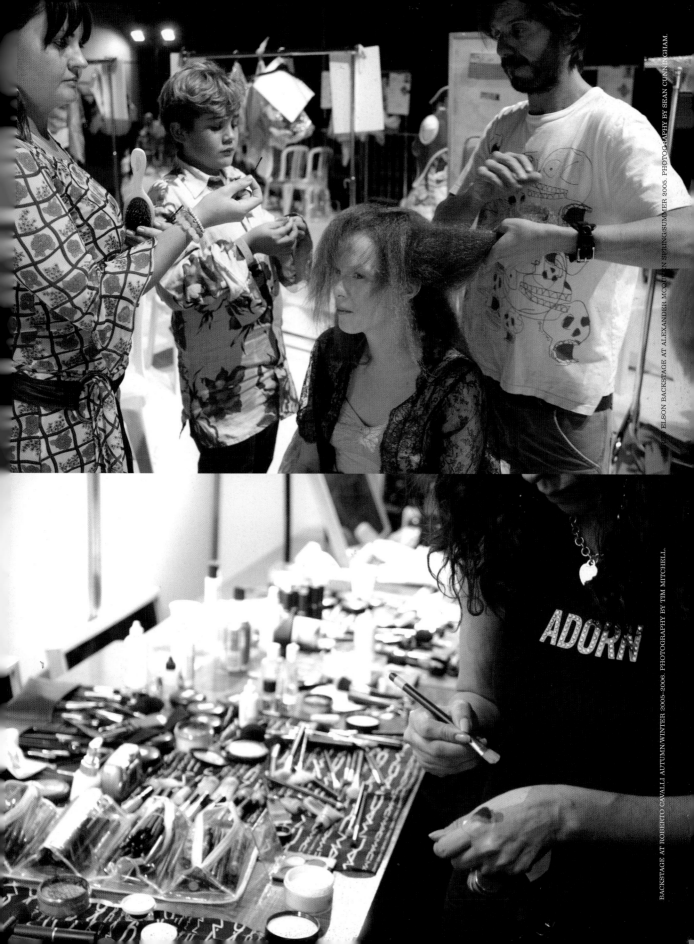

... ELSON BACKSTAGE AT ALEXANDER MCQUEEN SPRING/SUMMER 2005. PHOTOGRAPHY BY SEAN CUNNINGHAM.

BACKSTAGE AT ROBERTO CAVALLI AUTUMN/WINTER 2005–2006. PHOTOGRAPHY BY TIM MITCHELL.

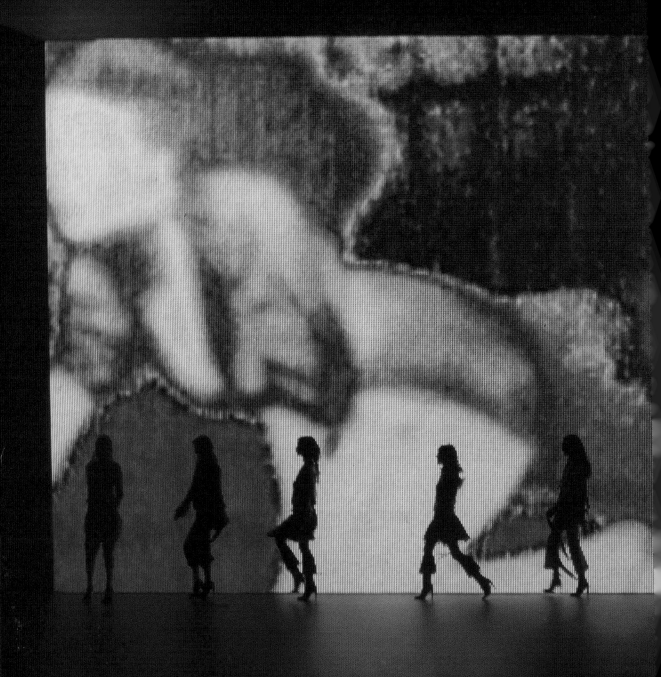

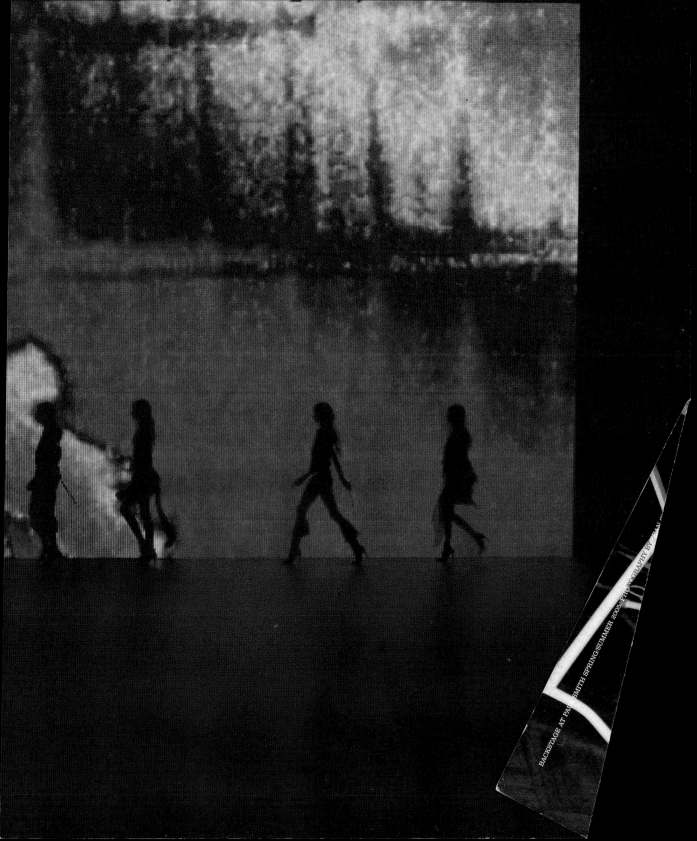

BACKSTAGE AT PAUL SMITH SPRING/SUMMER 2005 · PHOTOGRAPHY BY FRAN

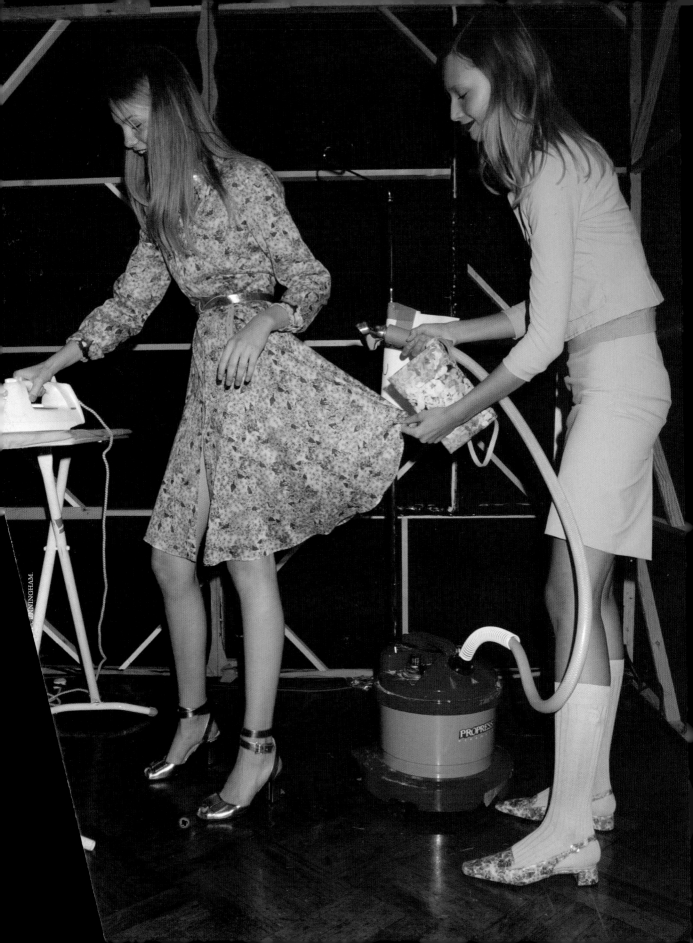

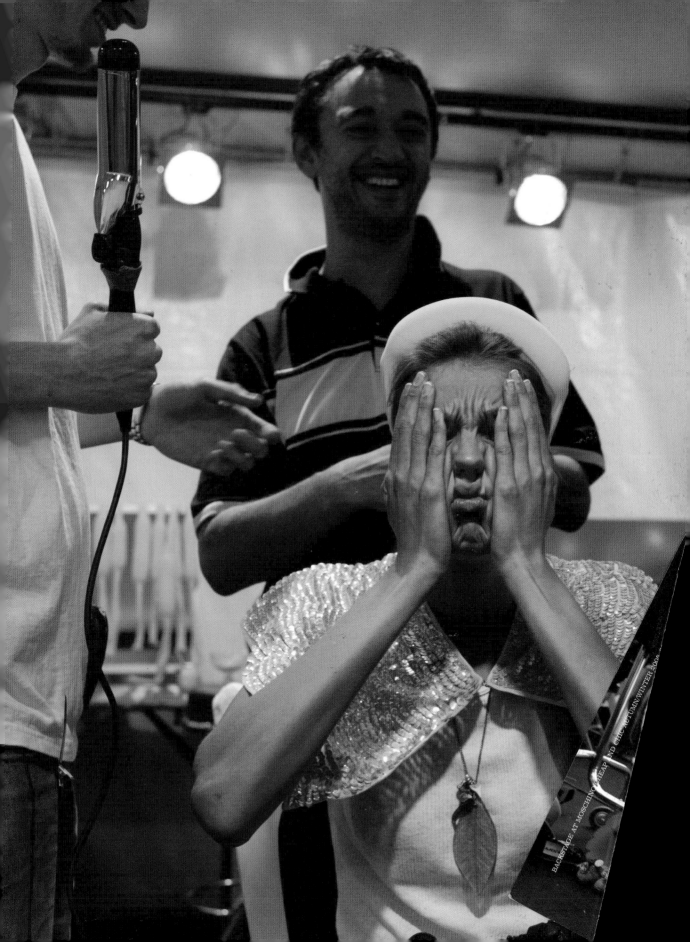

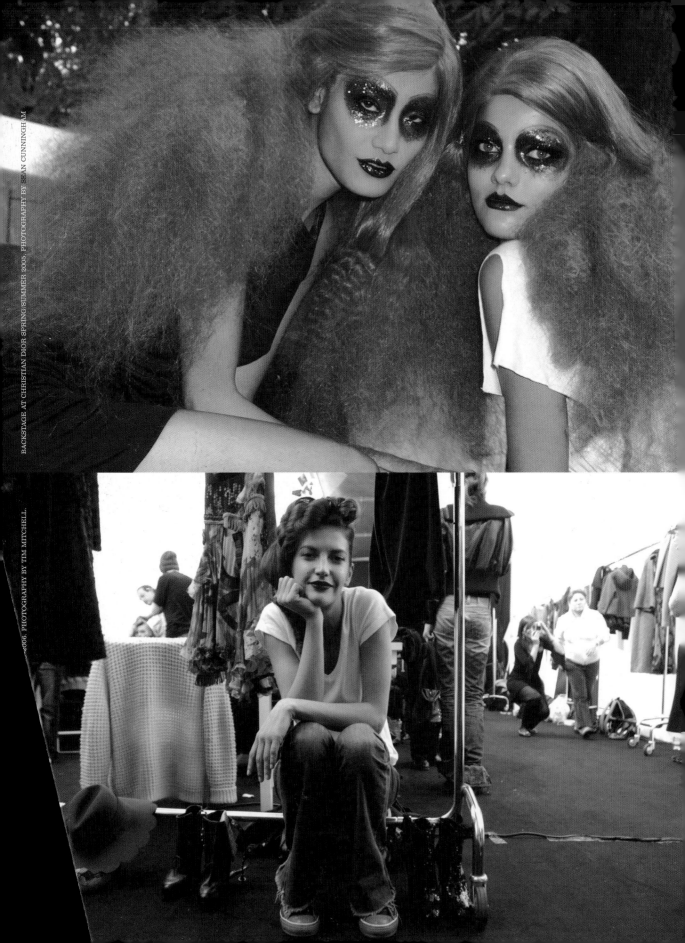

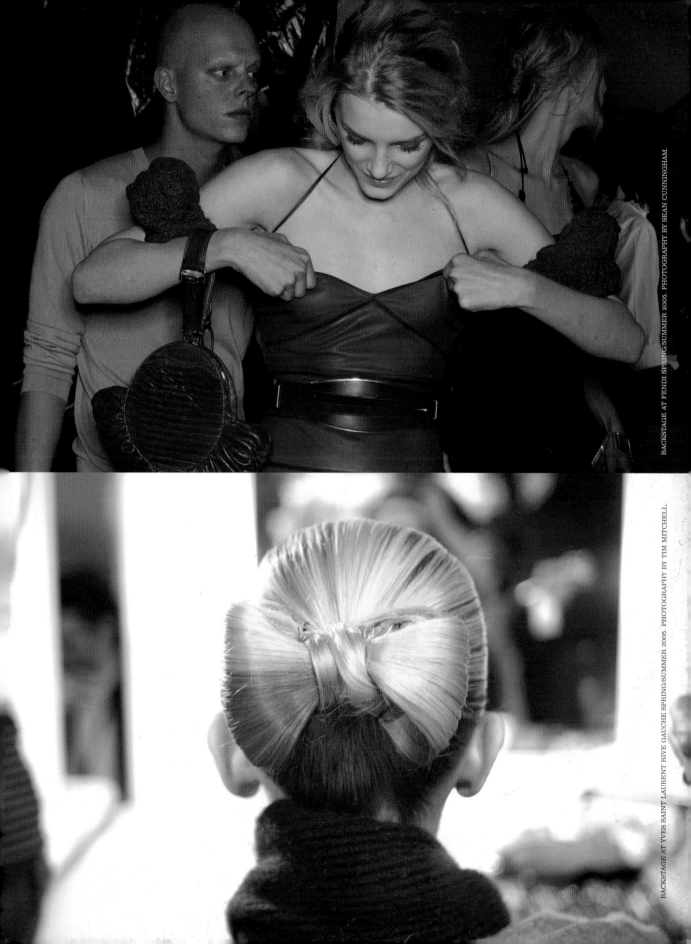

BACKSTAGE AT FENDI SPRING/SUMMER 2005. PHOTOGRAPHY BY SEAN CUNNINGHAM.

BACKSTAGE AT YVES SAINT LAURENT RIVE GAUCHE SPRING/SUMMER 2005. PHOTOGRAPHY BY TIM MITCHELL.

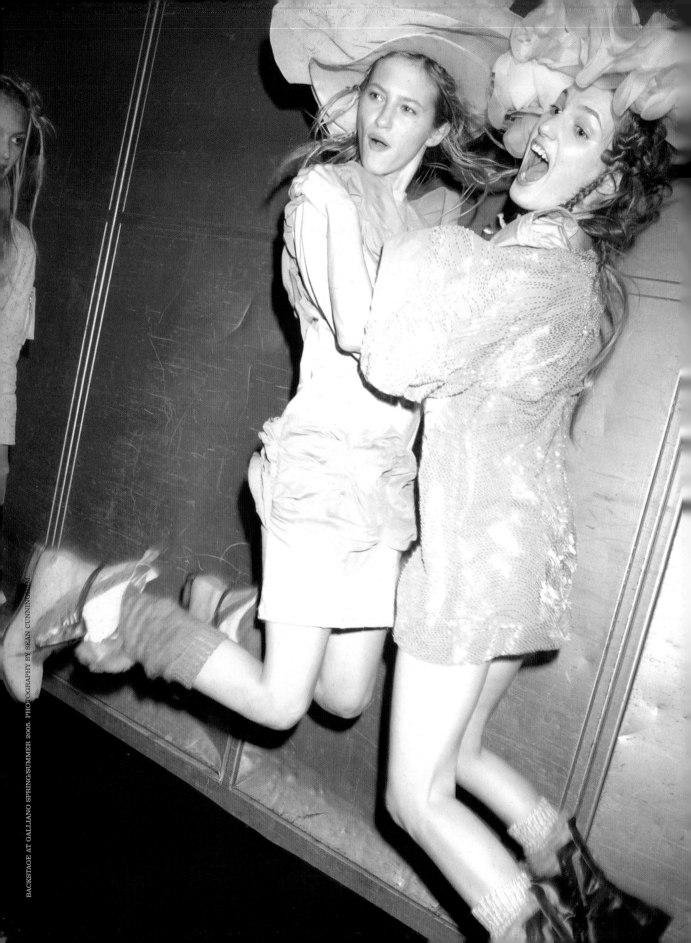

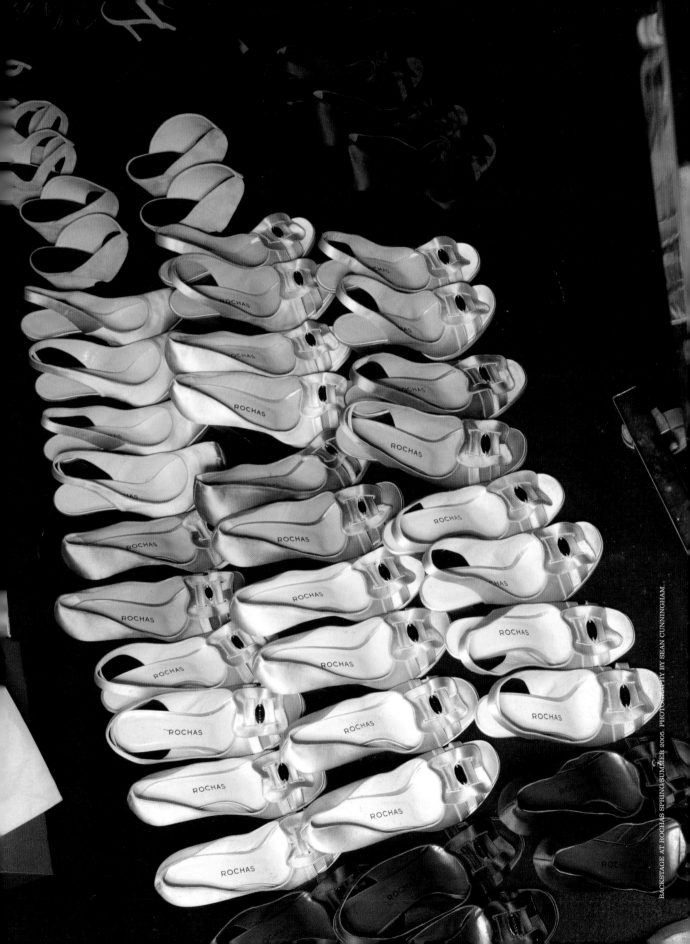

BACKSTAGE AT ROCHAS SPRING/SUMMER 2005. PHOTOGRAPHY BY SEAN CUNNINGHAM.

FOREWORD

"The 21st century didn't start in 2000, it starts now, at a time of uncertainty," says Raf Simons, a designer who continually reflects the Zeitgeist in his work. Each year, more designers are added to the international fashion calendars. Today, Paris, Milan, New York and London are still the fashion show capitals of the world, but many other cities are also creating successful showcase events which give chances to future talents. In 2005, the Hyères competition in the south of France celebrated its 20th anniversary and the International Talent Support in Trieste, Italy staged its fourth contest. More fashion colleges are producing more students who enter an industry which continues to grow every year.

There is also no doubting the importance of emerging economies, where consumers are buying fashion as a way to express newfound success. Global distribution and branding have grown; manufacturing is changing rapidly, with more companies sourcing their suppliers where labour is cheaper. Value for money and credibility are major considerations for any designer today and the fashion-buying customer is better informed than at any other time in history.

So, as consumers of fashion we have an important role to play. Limited edition or purchased from a 'secret' sale, hand-crafted by artisans or produced in multiple – the items we choose to buy and wear are a reflection of our personal ethics and choices. Today we are given so much information about fashion, yet we rarely ask where it's made. It is not enough to know the source of the idea. We should know which animal we are wearing, whether it suffered for our sake and how it was farmed. Several companies are paving the way for an organic movement inside the fashion industry.

In the future, the craft of fashion could be endangered by a market economy focused on price alone. Perhaps counterfeit designer goods fuel the desire to own the real thing, but we need to address how the fakes, too, are manufactured: How old is the person who made that handbag? Did they get a proper meal this week? We have the power to change this in our wallets. How we buy fashion could force change in the future of consumption and manufacture. This is one of the greatest challenges facing fashion: when fur-wearing editors are targeted by animal rights protesters, this is only the most tabloid-friendly side of the issue.

If it didn't change with the times, it wouldn't be fashion. Susie Rushton's introduction, which considers the power struggle between individual designers and brands, and the inclusion of more brands in this book, reflect recent shifts in the industry, as does Glenn Waldron's essay that looks at the exponential growth of designer menswear.

There are more fashion boutiques, department stores and retail outlets than ever, more people entering fashion institutions that fuel the industry around the world and more TV-time and news coverage that is hungry for a glimpse of glamour. Constantly redefined, fashion captures the moment and reflects a couple of seasons – and these visual impressions make the memory of that day, that month, that year, a living proof that we kept our eyes open, for a split second.

VORWORT

„Das 21. Jahrhundert begann nicht im Jahr 2000, sondern es beginnt jetzt. In einer Zeit der Ungewissheit", sagt Raf Simons, der als Designer stets den Zeitgeist reflektiert. Jedes Jahr werden mehr Designer in den internationalen Modekalender aufgenommen. Paris, Mailand, New York und London sind bis heute die Welthauptstädte der Modenschauen, aber auch viele andere große und kleinere Städte veranstalten erfolgreich Präsentationen, die zukünftigen Talenten Chancen geben. 2005 feierte etwa der Wettbewerb von Hyères in Südfrankreich sein 20-jähriges Jubiläum, während der International Talent Support im italienischen Triest seinen vierten Wettbewerb durchführte. Immer mehr Modeschulen sorgen für immer mehr Studierende, die in eine kontinuierlich wachsende Branche einsteigen.

Zweifellos wichtig sind Länder mit aufstrebender Wirtschaft, in denen Konsumenten Mode kaufen, um ihren soeben verzeichneten Erfolg zum Ausdruck zu bringen. Globale Vertriebsstrukturen und internationale Marken haben sich etabliert; die Fertigung verändert sich rasch, da immer mehr Firmen sich ihre Zulieferer dort suchen, wo Arbeit billig ist. Geldwerte Qualität und Glaubwürdigkeit sind heute die zentralen Faktoren für jeden Designer, und der Kunde ist besser informiert denn je.

Als Modekonsumenten spielen wir eine wichtige Rolle. Ob limitierte Auflage oder Schnäppchen aus einem „geheimen" Ausverkauf, ob von Künstlern handgefertigt oder aus der Massenproduktion – das Kleidungsstück, das wir kaufen und tragen, reflektiert unsere persönlichen Überzeugungen. Wir erhalten heute so viele Informationen zum Thema Mode, fragen aber dennoch selten danach, wo etwas produziert wurde. Dabei genügt es nicht, nur die Quelle der Idee zu kennen. Wir sollten auch wissen, was für ein Tier wir tragen und ob es für unsere Schönheit leiden musste, wie es gezüchtet wurde. Einige Unternehmen fungieren als Wegbereiter des Natur- und Umweltschutzes innerhalb der Modeindustrie.

In Zukunft könnte das Modehandwerk von einer Marktwirtschaft gefährdet sein, die sich allein am Preis orientiert. Vielleicht fördern nachgemachte Designerwaren das Verlangen danach, das Original zu besitzen. Wir müssen uns auch dafür interessieren, wie die Imitate produziert wurden: Wie alt ist derjenige, der die falsche Tasche genäht hat? Hat er in dieser Woche genug zu essen bekommen? Mit Hilfe unserer Geldbörsen haben wir die Macht, einen Wandel zu bewirken. Die Art, wie wir Mode kaufen, kann tatsächlich etwas daran ändern, wie in Zukunft konsumiert und produziert wird. Darin besteht eine der größten anstehenden Herausforderungen für die Modebranche. Denn wenn pelztragende Journalistinnen von Tierschützern attackiert werden, ist das nur der Aspekt dieses Themas, der den meisten Wirbel in der Boulevardpresse verspricht.

Wenn sie sich nicht im Lauf der Zeiten verändern würde, wäre sie keine Mode mehr. Susie Rushtons Einführung, die den Machtkampf zwischen individuellen Designern und Marken thematisiert, und die Einbeziehung von mehr Labels in dieses Buch spiegeln den gegenwärtigen Umschwung in der Branche. Das gilt auch für Glenn Waldrons Überlegungen zum exponentiellen Wachstum der Designermode für Männer.

Es gibt mehr Modeboutiquen, Kaufhäuser und Textileinzelhändler denn je, auch mehr Leute, die sich in Modeinstitutionen als Nachwuchs für die Industrie auf der ganzen Welt ausbilden lassen, und mehr Fernsehminuten und Presseberichte, die nach ein wenig Glamour lechzen. Weil sich die Mode ständig neu definiert, können wir nur eine Momentaufnahme liefern und ein paar Saisons abdecken – diese visuellen Impressionen machen die Erinnerung an jenen Tag, jenen Monat, jenes Jahr aus, als sicherer Beweis dafür, dass wir die Augen offen gehalten haben, zumindest für einen Sekundenbruchteil.

PREFACE

« Le XXIe siècle n'a pas commencé en l'an 2000. Il démarre aujourd'hui en des temps d'incertitude », affirme Raf Simons, un créateur qui puise toujours son inspiration dans l'esprit du siècle. Chaque année voit défiler toujours plus de créateurs dans le calendrier de la mode. Aujourd'hui, Paris, Milan, New York et Londres restent les capitales mondiales de la mode, mais de nombreuses autres villes organisent avec succès des manifestations qui donnent leur chance aux talents de demain. En 2005, le concours de Hyères fête son 20e anniversaire et International Talent Support à Trieste en Italie son quatrieme. De plus en plus d'écoles de mode produisent un nombre croissant de diplômés pour alimenter un marché qui grossit chaque année.

Il ne faut pas non plus négliger l'importance des économies émergentes, où les consommateurs achètent de la mode comme un moyen d'expression de leur nouveau succès. Les réseaux de distribution mondiale et le branding se développent ; l'industrie de production évolue rapidement et toujours plus d'entreprises et de créateurs indépendants travaillent avec des fournisseurs qui se trouvent là où la main-d'œuvre coûte moins cher. Aujourd'hui, le rapport qualité-prix et la crédibilité représentent des considérations majeures pour tout créateur car le client acheteur de mode est mieux informé qu'à n'importe quelle autre période de l'histoire.

En tant que consommateurs de mode, nous avons là un rôle important à jouer. Proposés en édition limitée ou achetés lors d'une vente confidentielle, fabriqués à la main par des artisans ou produits en masse, les articles que nous décidons d'acheter et de porter reflètent notre éthique et nos choix personnels. Aujourd'hui, nous sommes submergés d'informations sur la mode, mais on se demande rarement où les vêtements sont fabriqués. Connaître l'origine d'une idée ne suffit plus. Nous devrions savoir quel animal nous portons, s'il a souffert pour nous embellir ou comment il a été élevé. Au sein de l'industrie de la mode, plusieurs entreprises ouvrent la voie d'une tendance au bio.

A l'avenir, l'art de la mode pourrait être menacé par une économie de marché obsédée par les prix. Certes, les produits de contrefaçon alimentent peut-être le désir de posséder un original, mais nous devons aussi nous demander comment ces faux sont produits : quel âge a la personne qui a fabriqué cet ersatz de sac de créateur ? A-t-elle suffisamment mangé cette semaine ? Nos portefeuilles ont le pouvoir de changer cet état de fait. Notre façon d'acheter la mode pourrait entraîner des changements dans l'avenir de la consommation et de la production. C'est l'un des plus grands défis que la mode devra relever : quand les journalises qui portent de la fourrure deviennent la cible des défenseurs des droits des animaux, ce n'est que la face la plus médiatique du problème.

Si la mode n'évoluait pas au fil du temps, ce ne serait plus la mode. L'introduction de Susie Rushton, qui évoque la lutte de pouvoir entre les marques et les créateurs indépendants, ainsi que les marques supplémentaires ajoutées dans ce volume, reflètent les récentes modifications du marché, comme le fait le texte de Glenn Waldron sur la croissance exponentielle dont bénéficie la mode pour homme.

Il n'y a jamais eu autant de boutiques, de grands magasins et de points de vente, plus d'étudiants entrant dans les écoles de mode pour alimenter le marché mondial et plus de couverture médiatique dans la presse et à la télévision, à la recherche d'une touche de glamour. Alors que la mode est dans un état de constante redéfinition, nous pouvons saisir le parfum du moment et refléter quelques saisons : ces impressions visuelles sont le souvenir d'un jour, d'un mois ou d'une année, preuve incontestable que nous avons gardé les yeux ouverts, ne serait-ce qu'un quart de seconde.

TERRY JONES
Creative Director & Editor-in-Chief, i-D magazine

FASHION DESIGNERS, FASHION BRANDS

What's in a name? Why do we prize the jacket stitched with a label bearing the name of a famous designer, over that with an unknown provenance? Why do we treat fashion designers as cultural weathervanes? They rank among the most influential and adulated individuals in modern society. Yet, at the time of writing, at a corporate level at least, the relationship between a designer and his or her brand has never been so uncertain. The century of the superstar couturier now behind us – with Paul Poiret, a bona fide dictator of fashionable silhouettes, working at its dawn and Tom Ford, the ultimate celebrity designer, reigning at its dusk – and it's not yet clear what kind of rôle 'personality' designers will play in the future of fashion. It seems that the traditional role of designer as sole author and cultural oracle might be under threat from the might of commercially 'safe' faceless brands.

After all, now that stars from the worlds of music and film are loaning their names to fashion brands, it could be argued that the archetypal 'famous fashion designer', as portrayed by the likes of Coco Chanel and Calvin Klein, will be succeeded by the celebrity brand. Sounds unlikely? Consider the fact that an increasing number of established houses – most of them owned by the giant luxury goods conglomerates such as LVMH and the Prada Group, which transformed the face of fashion in the late '90s – are currently preferring to appoint lesser-known designers as their chiefs, promote internally, or rely on a team of anonymous 'studio' designers to produce collections. The visible 'face' of a brand is now often an actress whose fame far outstrips that of any designer. Today, no fashion brand is complete without a celebrity from the worlds of film or music to star in its ad campaigns: times have changed, it goes without saying, since Coco Chanel and Yves Saint Laurent posed in advertisements for their own perfumes (Karl Lagerfeld, who personally promoted his H&M collection of 2004, being one rare exception).

A number of momentous events have conspired to change the shape of fashion's landscape. The exit of iconic designers such as Helmut Lang and Jil Sander (in 2005 and 2004 respectively) from their own brands, not to mention Tom Ford's momentous departure from Gucci (in 2004), signalled a new phase in the evolution of the modern fashion system. In the mid-'90s, a well-known, much-hyped young designer was the highly prized asset of many a fashion house. Now fashion graduates and established brands both take a more prudent view, with the former carefully pacing their careers and the latter preferring to concentrate their resources on improving bestselling products. In very recent history, 'revived' houses – or in industry shorthand, those who want to 'do a Burberry' – have often concentrated on building up a solid accessories business to underpin their ambitions, rather than place a prodigal talent at their helm: witness the rise to fashionable credibility of companies such as Mulberry, Alfred Dunhill and Bottega Veneta. Of course, there have always been a handful of fashion labels that, despite high-profile success, have never pushed the celebrity of their chief designer for marketing purposes: Maison Martin Margiela and MaxMara are just two houses that have steadfastly refused to court personal publicity for their designers. Perhaps their unconventional stance will provide a new template for the future.

Are we looking toward a future of faceless fashion brands? Somehow, this is a joyless prospect for a craft so intimately engaged with authorship, personality and allure. Despite recent shifts within the industry, there remains a strong case for a figurehead designer at the helm of a brand. Certain brands seem to share a DNA with their chief designer. Each and every season at fashion shows by Balenciaga, Prada and Comme des Garçons, for example, an unique creative view and a clear single-mindedness is revealed. Brands such as these are guided by individuals – incidentally, none of whom are known for their love of the limelight – who, while they will each credit the supportive work of their studios, are nonetheless pivotal to the continued success of their brands.

Beyond the boundaries of high fashion, meanwhile, the big 'name' fashion designer remains highly prized by mass market fashion chains, corporate sportswear brands, mail order catalogues and even airlines. Sports giants such as Adidas and Puma, for example, know the value of hiring Alexander McQueen, Yohji Yamamoto or Mihara Yasuhiro to design special collections.

And among many grand fashion houses, there are happy collaborations between a status brand and a revered designer. Take Marc Jacobs at Louis Vuitton and Alber Elbaz at Lanvin: both brands have been utterly transformed under the direction of these two men, who have finally found their perfect creative and corporate partners. Similarly, it's impossible to imagine the brands that Karl Lagerfeld, Hedi Slimane, John Galliano and Nicolas Ghesquière create, without their headstrong designers. Another crucial issue that is driving change today is the question of succession: a generation of virtuoso designers are now nearing retirement age. Who or what replaces them will define the structure of the fashion industry over the next decade and beyond.

So it seems that fashion is at a crossroads. This current state of flux – with every few months bringing a new appointment and a new retirement – has had a direct impact on the way in which we've put together FASHION NOW 2. In the book's first incarnation, published in 2002, designers were entered under their own names, and ordered alphabetically according to surname. This time around, they're listed under the brands they create, with eponymous labels taking primacy. This is not to devalue the rôle of the designer. In part, it is intended to ease navigation of the book, and put all working designers, world-famous and publicity-shy, on something approaching an equal footing. For better or worse, this is also a symptom of the aforementioned dynamic in the industry, where designers come and go with increasing frequency, but brands, for the moment at least, remain. Of course, there are numerous designers who have had the vision to build independent businesses within the fashion industry. Those companies, such as Comme des Garçons, Dries Van Noten, Dolce & Gabbana, Paul Smith and Giorgio Armani, control their own destiny, market forces allowing. And fortunately, a new generation of younger designers – based in cities from New York to Buenos Aires, in addition to traditional seedbeds for talent such as London – are also choosing to found brands under their own names, although perhaps with more of a sense of caution than those that went before them. In this book their unfamiliar brand-names, and their responses to our Q+A interview, sit alongside those of the most revered houses in Paris fashion, the biggest sportswear companies in the world and the most popular denim labels, to create a snapshot of what i-D believes is fashion, now.

MODEDESIGNER UND MODEMARKEN

Was steckt in einem Namen? Warum schätzen wir eine Jacke, in die das Etikett eines berühmten Designers eingenäht ist, mehr als ein Stück unbekannter Herkunft? Warum kümmern uns die Gedanken und Wertvorstellungen von Modeschöpfern, als seien diese kulturelle Wetterfahnen? Modedesigner rangieren unter den einflussreichsten und am meisten umschmeichelten Individuen unserer modernen Gesellschaft. Während wir dieses Buch schreiben, ist, zumindest was die Modefirmen betrifft, die Beziehung zwischen einem Designer und seiner Marke so ungewiss wie noch nie. Das Jahrhundert der Superstars unter den Couturiers liegt hinter uns – Paul Poiret, ein echter Diktator der modischen Silhouetten, markiert seinen Beginn, der ultimative Promi-Designer Tom Ford sein Ende. Und noch ist nicht klar, welche Rolle Designerpersönlichkeiten in Zukunft spielen werden. Es scheint, als sei die Rolle des Modeschöpfers als alleiniger Autor und kulturelles Orakel durch die Macht kommerziell erfolgversprechender gesichtsloser Marken gefährdet.

Schließlich könnte man angesichts der Stars aus der Musik- und Filmbranche, die ihre Namen für Modemarken hergeben, argumentieren, dass auf den Archetyp des berühmten Modeschöpfers – wie Coco Chanel oder Calvin Klein es waren – nun Promi-Labels folgen, bei denen jede Kollektion mit einer vorher ausgehandelten MTV-Kooperation herauskommt. Das erscheint Ihnen unwahrscheinlich? Dann denken Sie doch bitte an die große Zahl etablierter Modehäuser – die meisten im Besitz großer Luxusartikel-Konzerne wie LVMH oder Prada Group, die das Antlitz der Mode in den späten 1990er Jahren verändert haben –, die nun bevorzugt unbekanntere Designer verpflichten oder sich für ein Team von anonymen Atelierdesignern entscheiden, die dann ihre Kollektionen produzieren. Das so überaus wichtige Gesicht einer Marke kann schließlich auch von einer berühmten Schauspielerin stammen, deren Ruhm den eines Designers immer übersteigt. Heute kommt keine Modemarke ohne Promis aus der Film- oder Musikwelt bei ihren Werbekampagnen aus. Zweifellos haben sich die Zeiten geändert, seit Coco Chanel und Yves Saint Laurent in Anzeigen für ihre eigenen Parfums posierten. (Karl Lagerfeld bildete da in den Anzeigen für seine Kollektion bei H&M 2004 eine bemerkenswerte Ausnahme.)

Eine Reihe folgenschwerer Ereignisse wirkte zusammen und veränderte die Modelandschaft. Der Ausstieg von Design-Ikonen wie Helmut Lang und Jil Sander (2004 bzw. 2005), die sich von ihren eigenen Marken trennten, gar nicht zu reden von Tom Fords Weggang bei Gucci (2004), signalisierte eine wenn auch vielleicht nur vorübergehende neue Ära in der Evolution des modernen Modezirkus. Mitte der 1990er Jahre war ein bekannter, gehypter junger Designer oder eine Designerin noch eine Art heiliger Gral für jedes Label. Heute agieren sowohl die frischgebackenen Absolventen der Modeschulen wie auch die etablierten Marken besonnener: Erstere planen die Entwicklung ihrer Karriere sorgsamer, letztere konzentrieren ihre Ressourcen eher darauf, etablierte Bestseller weiterzuentwickeln. In allerjüngster Vergangenheit konzentrierten sich wiederbelebte Marken – oder, wie man in der Branche sagt: Leute, die einen Burberry machen wollen – oft auf den Aufbau eines soliden Accessoire-Geschäfts, um ihre Ambitionen zu unterstreichen, anstatt ein verschwenderisches junges Talent ans Ruder zu lassen. Das kann man etwa am Zuwachs modischer Glaubwürdigkeit von Unternehmen wie Mulberry, Alfred Dunhill oder Bottega Veneta sehen. Natürlich gibt es immer eine Handvoll Marken, die trotz größter Erfolge nie die Prominenz ihrer Chefdesigner zu PR-Zwecken vermarktet haben: Maison Martin Margiela und Max Mara sind nur zwei, die sich gegen personenbezogene Publicity ihrer Modeschöpfer stets verwahrten. Vielleicht wird diese unkonventionelle Haltung ja in Zukunft zum neuen Vorbild.

Stehen wir also am Beginn einer Zeit gesichtsloser Modemarken? Irgendwie scheint das eine freudlose Aussicht für ein Handwerk, das so viel mit Persönlichkeit und individueller Anziehungskraft zu tun hat. Trotz der jüngsten Entwicklung stehen die Chancen für Designer, die eine Marke als Galionsfigur führen, nicht schlecht. Einige Labels scheinen sogar die DNA mit ihren Chefdesignern zu teilen. So kommt etwa bei jeder einzelnen Schau von Balenciaga, Prada und Comme des Garçons unverwechselbare Kreativität und klare Zielstrebigkeit zum Ausdruck. Solche Marken werden von Individualisten geführt – von denen übrigens bekanntermaßen niemand gern im Rampenlicht steht –, die zwar die Unterstützung ihrer Ateliers durchaus anerkennen, aber dennoch selbst Dreh- und Angelpunkt für den anhaltenden Erfolg ihrer Marke sind.

Außerhalb der Haute Couture sind die klingenden Namen unter den Designern nach wie vor hoch geschätzt, etwa bei den großen Ketten, Sportartikelherstellern, Versandhäusern und sogar Fluglinien. Giganten auf dem Sportmarkt wie Adidas und Puma wissen, welchen Wert es hat, Alexander McQueen, Yohji Yamamoto oder Mihara Yasuhiro für Sonderkollektionen zu engagieren.

Auch bei den angesehensten Modehäusern gibt es viele gelungene Kooperationen von etablierten Marken und geachteten Designern. Man denke nur an Marc Jacobs und Louis Vuitton oder Alber Elbaz und Lanvin: Beide Marken wurden unter der Leitung der Männer, die dort offenbar ihre perfekten kreativen und kommerziellen Partner gefunden haben, von Grund auf umstrukturiert. Genauso wenig vermag man sich die Marken von Karl Lagerfeld, Hedi Slimane, John Galliano und Nicolas Ghesquière ohne ihre eigenwilligen Designer vorzustellen. Ein weiteres wichtiges Thema, das heute zwangsläufig für Veränderung sorgt, ist die Frage der Nachfolge: eine Generation virtuoser Designer nähert sich inzwischen dem Pensionsalter. Wer oder was ihnen folgt, wird die Struktur der Modeindustrie in den nächsten Jahrzehnten und darüber hinaus bestimmen.

Wie es scheint, steht die Mode also am Scheideweg. Die gegenwärtige Fluktuation – mit einer Neuernennung und einem Rückzug alle paar Monate – nahm direkten Einfluss auf unsere Zusammenstellung für FASHION NOW 2. Im ersten 2002 veröffentlichten Band listeten wir die Designer unter ihren eigenen Namen auf und sortierten sie alphabetisch nach ihren Nachnamen. Dieses Mal haben wir sie nach ihren Marken geordnet, wobei die Labels, die den Namen der Designer tragen, Vorrang hatten. Das soll die Bedeutung der Modeschöpfer nicht schmälern. Zum einen möchten wir damit die Orientierung im Buch erleichtern, zum anderen alle Designer, die weltberühmten, aber auch jene, die das Licht der Öffentlichkeit scheuen, irgendwie auf eine Stufe stellen. Jede und jeder ist unter dem Namen des Labels gelistet, bei dem die von ihr oder ihm entworfenen Kleider verkauft werden. Das mag man gut oder schlecht finden, aber es ist symptomatisch für die aktuelle Rekrutierungspolitik in der Branche, wo Designer in immer kürzeren Intervallen kommen und gehen, die Marken aber, zumindest im Moment jedenfalls, bleiben. Natürlich gibt es zahlreiche Designer, die sich vorgenommen haben, eigene unabhängige Firmen unter ihrem Namen aufzubauen. Comme des Garçons, Dries van Noten, Dolce & Gabbana, Paul Smith und Giorgio Armani lenken ihr Schicksal – soweit die Kräfte des Marktes es erlauben – selbst. Und zum Glück entscheidet sich auch eine neue Generation jüngerer Designer – aus Städten von New York bis Buenos Aires und nicht nur aus den traditionellen Talentschmieden wie London – für die Gründung von Labels, die den eigenen Namen tragen. Auch wenn sie etwas vorsichtiger zu Werke gehen als ihre Vorgänger. In diesem Buch stehen sie mit ihren noch unvertrauten Markennamen und den Antworten auf unseren Interviewfragebogen neben den angesehensten Pariser Modehäusern, den größten Sportmodeherstellern der Welt und den beliebtesten Jeanslabeln. Damit geben wir von i-D Ihnen einen Überblick in Sachen Mode. Jetzt.

CRÉATEURS ET MARQUES DE MODE

Quelle est l'importance d'un nom ? Pourquoi préférons-nous une veste dessinée par un créateur célèbre à tout autre modèle de provenance inconnue ? Pourquoi évaluons-nous les pensées et les valeurs des créateurs de mode comme s'ils étaient les nouvelles girouettes de la culture ? Les créateurs de mode comptent parmi les individus les plus influents et les plus adulés de la société moderne. Aujourd'hui, du moins au niveau corporate, la relation entre le créateur et sa marque n'a pourtant jamais été si incertaine. Le siècle du couturier superstar est désormais derrière nous (de Paul Poiret, authentique dictateur des silhouettes à la mode au début du siècle dernier, à Tom Ford, célébrité de la mode par excellence régnant à la fin du siècle), mais on ne sait pas encore vraiment quel rôle joueront les créateurs « célèbres » dans l'avenir de la mode. Il semble que la position du créateur en tant qu'unique auteur de sa production et oracle culturel soit remise en cause par la puissance des marques sans visage et commercialement « sûres ».

Après tout, maintenant que les stars de la musique et du cinéma prêtent leurs noms à des marques de mode, on peut penser que l'archétype du « couturier célèbre », tel qu'illustré par Coco Chanel et Calvin Klein, cédera sa place aux marques célèbres, où chaque collection sera livrée clé en main, avec produits dérivés négociés à l'avance pour MTV. Cela semble-t-il si improbable ? Pas vraiment, si l'on considère qu'un nombre croissant de maisons bien établies – la plupart d'entre elles appartenant aux géants du luxe tels que LVMH et le groupe Prada, un phénomène qui a transformé le visage de la mode à la fin des années 90 – préfèrent recruter des créateurs quasi inconnus ou développent des promotions en interne plutôt que d'aller dénicher de nouveaux talents, voire optent pour toute une équipe de créateurs pour produire leurs collections. Après tout, le « visage » si important de la marque peut être celui de l'actrice connue qui pose pour sa campagne publicitaire : c'est évident, les temps ont bien changé depuis l'époque où Coco Chanel et Yves Saint Laurent apparaissaient dans les publicités de leurs propres parfums (Karl Lagerfeld, qui a posé dans les publicités de sa collection H&M en 2004, constituant l'une des rares et mémorables exceptions de ces dernières années).

Plusieurs bouleversements semblent avoir conspiré pour transformer le paysage de la mode. Le fait que des créateurs cultes, tels que Helmut Lang et Jil Sander, aient quitté leurs propres marques (respectivement en 2005 et 2004), sans mentionner le départ de Tom Ford de chez Gucci (en 2004), annonce une nouvelle phase, quoique temporaire, dans l'évolution du système moderne de la mode. Au milieu des années 90, le Saint-Graal de toute maison de mode consistait à recruter un jeune créateur connu et branché. Aujourd'hui, les diplômés en mode comme les marques établies paraissent plus avertis, les premiers entamant leurs carrières avec plus de prudence et les secondes préférant orienter leurs efforts sur l'amélioration de leurs best-sellers. Dernièrement, les marques « ressuscitées », ou comme on le dit dans la mode, ceux qui veulent « faire un Burberry », se sont souvent concentrées sur la création d'une solide collection d'accessoires pour étayer leurs ambitions, plutôt que de nommer un talent prodigue à la direction de la création : en témoigne l'ascension vers la crédibilité d'entreprises telles que Mulberry, Alfred Dunhill et Bottega Veneta. Bien sûr, il y a toujours eu une poignée de griffes qui, malgré leur succès, n'ont jamais mis en valeur la célébrité de leur styliste principal à des fins marketing : Maison Martin Margiela et MaxMara ont tous deux refusé de faire la publicité personnelle de leurs créateurs. Leur position à contre-courant fournira peut-être un nouveau modèle pour le futur.

L'avenir appartient-il aux marques sans visage ? Sous un certain angle, c'est une perspective un peu déprimante pour un art si intimement lié à la personnalité et à l'allure. En dépit des événements récents, on compte encore de nombreux exemples de créateurs hissés au rang de figures de proue d'une marque. Certaines griffes semblent partager le même ADN que leur styliste. Chaque saison aux défilés de Balenciaga, Prada ou Comme des Garçons, une créativité individuelle et un état d'esprit clairement unique se révèlent. Ces marques sont guidées par des individus – d'ailleurs, aucun d'eux n'est réputé pour son amour des feux de la rampe – qui, bien qu'ils ne manquent jamais de créditer le travail de leurs ateliers, ont néanmoins le dernier mot. Car sans leur leadership, il ne resterait plus rien d'autre que des vêtements.

Au-delà des frontières de la mode de luxe, le nom d'un créateur reste très apprécié par les grandes chaînes d'habillement, les marques commerciales de sportswear, les catalogues de vente par correspondance et même les compagnie aériennes. Par exemple, les géants du sport tels que Adidas et Puma connaissent la valeur du recrutement d'un Alexander McQueen, Yohji Yamamoto ou d'un Mihara Yasuhiro pour dessiner des collections spéciales.

Au sein de nombreuses grandes maisons, il existe des collaborations heureuses entre une marque établie et un créateur adulé. Prenez Marc Jacobs chez Louis Vuitton et Alber Elbaz chez Lanvin : ces deux marques ont été radicalement transformées sous l'impulsion de ces deux hommes, qui ont fini par trouver leurs partenaires créatifs et corporate idéaux. De même, il est impossible d'imaginer les marques pour lesquelles travaillent Karl Lagerfeld, Hedi Slimane, John Galliano et Nicolas Ghesquière sans leurs impétueux stylistes. Les questions de succession représentent un autre problème crucial motivant les changements actuels : toute une génération de virtuoses approche en effet l'âge de la retraite. Qui ou quoi les remplacera va définir la structure de l'industrie de la mode au cours de la prochaine décennie, et même au-delà.

Il semble donc que la mode soit à un carrefour. La situation actuelle du flux, où l'on annonce tous les deux mois une nouvelle embauche ou un énième départ en retraite, influence directement la façon dont nous avons présenté FASHION NOW 2. Dans le premier opus publié en 2002, les créateurs étaient entrés sous leurs propres noms et classés par ordre alphabétique en fonction de leur nom de famille. Cette fois-ci, ils sont répertoriés selon les marques pour lesquelles ils travaillent, leur griffe éponyme étant davantage mise en avant. Il n'est pas ici question de dévaluer le rôle du créateur. Ce classement vise en partie à faciliter le repérage du lecteur et à mettre tous les créateurs en exercice sur un pied d'égalité, qu'ils soient mondialement connus ou fuient la publicité. Chacun d'eux est répertorié en fonction de la griffe sous laquelle ses créations sont vendues. Pour le meilleur ou pour le pire, c'est également un symptôme de l'actuelle dynamique de recrutement dans la mode, où le rythme de rotation des créateurs se fait de plus en plus fréquent, mais les marques demeurent, du moins pour le moment. Evidemment, de nombreux créateurs ont compris très tôt qu'ils avaient tout intérêt à bâtir des entreprises indépendantes sous leur propre nom : Comme des Garçons, Dries Van Noten, Dolce & Gabbana, Paul Smith et Giorgio Armani contrôlent leur propre destin en fonction du rapport de forces en jeu sur le marché. Heureusement, une nouvelle génération de créateurs, venus de New York à Buenos Aires, en plus des terreaux de talents habituels tels que Londres, choisissent aussi de créer des marques éponymes, sans doute plus motivés par la prudence que ne l'étaient leurs prédécesseurs. Dans ce livre, les noms étranges de leurs griffes et leurs réponses à nos interviews côtoient ceux des plus grandes maisons parisiennes, des plus grosses entreprises de sportswear du monde et des griffes de jean les plus populaires, pour vous offrir un sondage complet de ce que i-D considère comme la mode d'aujourd'hui.

SUSIE RUSHTON
Editor, Fashion Now 2

MEN'S FASHION NOW

"Men reading fashion magazines/Oh, what a world it seems we live in…" Rufus Wainwright

The relationship between fashion and the modern male – the mythical 'man in the street' – has always been a curious one. For many years, the pair existed in a state of mutual distrust. Like two jealous suitors eyeing each other across a smoky room, men and fashion did not get on. Of late, however, something has shifted. Slowly but surely, a friendship has been struck – at first mildly flirtatious, later vaguely indecent – and suddenly, it seems that men and fashion more than get on. Men and fashion are positively in love.

From the significant number of menswear shows filling up the Milan and Paris schedules to the increasing percentage of serious fashion students at serious fashion colleges opting to study traditional tailoring techniques, interest in the genre has exploded. Whilst it could be argued that the womenswear market is moving through a period of creative and commercial stagnation, men's fashion has become the focus for renewed artistic and financial investment. Indeed, evidence of the burgeoning romance between men and fashion is everywhere; major fashion houses aggressively woo a new male customer base; leading designers race to add menswear lines to their expanding empires (Alexander McQueen, Hussein Chalayan, Nicolas Ghesquière for Balenciaga, Véronique Branquinho…); photographers, stylists and editors establish a bright new aesthetic, encompassing influences from Bruce Weber to Wolfgang Tillmans; major publishing houses incubate new men's glossies… The list goes on.

At the same time, many of the industry's most singular talents are also receiving their dues. Raf Simons, the most celebrated menswear designer working independently today, himself celebrates his tenth anniversary (with a major retrospective in 2005). Similarly, Giorgio Armani, another designer who helped to define the male silhouette (albeit decades before), reaches his thirty-year mark. Meanwhile, the shadow of Helmut Lang – an essential influence for the current menswear moment and a designer who radically chose to show his men's fashion on the same catwalk as his womenswear – looms large. Men's fashion, it seems, is no longer the bridesmaid – or the rather embarrassed page boy – to women's collections, a footnote to the 'real business of fashion'. It has seized its own unique moment, created its own unique path.

Whilst womenswear trends are documented and disposed of at an increasingly frenetic rate, making the ideas they propose seem ever more disposable, ever more hollow, menswear continues to evolve at its own distinct pace. Historically, this has been perceived as 'dragging behind', adopting trends at least a good season after the fact. But the steadiness of evolution within menswear (itself reflecting perhaps a certain sense of natural reticence within the male disposition) now feels like a distinct advantage. Working within a tighter frame of reference and at a less hectic, less alarming rate of change, the sector has been able to develop a clearer, more considered sense of identity. To focus, perhaps, on the substance of 'style' over the transient nature of 'fashion'.

So what is shaping this new menswear identity? The sweaty thrash of the moshpit and the low throb of the guitar are an obvious place to start. The influence of rock 'n' roll on the form, fit and attitude of contemporary menswear is considerable. From the multitude of musical heroes inspiring Raf Simon's beautiful, challenging designs (Kraftwerk, the Manic Street Preachers, Peter Saville et al) to the razor-sharp, Bowie-inspired silhouette of Hedi Slimane for Dior Homme, a trainspotterish musical youth seems to be essential training for any successful menswear designer. One need look no further than the perfectly-tailored look of current pop darling, Franz Ferdinand, or indeed of the re-born Morrissey, to see how the music industry is returning the compliment.

Similarly, ideas of process, craftsmanship and tradition weigh heavily on the current menswear movement (qualities that are stealthily seeping back into womenswear also, as fashion houses look to their couture pasts for inspiration). In part, a response to the history of menswear – to the esteemed heritage of Savile Row tailors and to the continued role of the suit within men's fashion – this emphasis works to further differentiate menswear from the 'frivolity and frippery' of its female counterparts. Ideas that lend an air of 'authenticity' or 'realness' to the business of fashion. Or – to put it more crudely – make straight men feel more comfortable buying fancy clothes.

Quirky Norwegian Siv Støldal – who alongside the likes of Peter Jensen, Kim Jones, Cloak and Number (N)ine represents a new generation of emerging menswear talent – is typical in her respect for heritage and tradition. She is also typical of this peer group in her desire to somehow subvert it. "I am fascinated by a garment's history," she explains, in her entry to this book. "I'm excited when I discover old clothing worn by my ancestors, something that still holds onto their character. These things help me unlock the past and I try to honour their history and translate them into the present." Likewise, Maison Martin Margiela, whose attention to form and fit has been highly influential for many of the new breed, similarly describe their work as "a continuation and the deepening of our creativity, technical experience, collaboration and craft."

Indeed as this current menswear moment has progressed, another long-time Margiela principle has also taken hold; the idea of creative collaboration. The past few years have seen a growing number of highly successful hook-ups between the most unlikely of brands, joining the dots between streetwear and high fashion; Fred Perry and Comme des Garçons, Junya Watanabe and Levi's, Timothy Everest and Kim Jones, and then – for members of the hip-hop fraternity at least, the most irresistible of them all – Adidas and Yohji Yamamoto, in the slippery, Lycra-clad form of Y-3. Couplings that have broadened fashion's scope beyond the catwalk and the boutique towards a wider mainstream audience.

Yet for all the early-Noughties talk of the explosion in menswear (and in its 'little brother' industries of accessories and cosmetics) leading to the so-called 'feminisation' of men, there is little evidence of this happening. Or not in an obvious, broadsheet comment-worthy way, at least. In 2005, discussion of menswear has moved beyond talk of a sarong-ed David Beckham (and all the label-addicted crassness that the late '90s represented) towards a more comfortable – and considered – appraisal of the role of men's fashion. As the sector continues to grow in respect and recognition, the love affair looks set to continue.

MEN'S FASHION HEUTE

„Männer, die Modemagazine lesen/Oh, in was für einer Welt wir doch leben …" Rufus Wainwright

Das Verhältnis des modernen Mannes – des mythischen „Mannes von der Straße" – zur Mode war schon immer seltsam. Jahrelang herrschte zwischen den beiden ein Zustand gegenseitigen Misstrauens. Wie zwei eifersüchtige Kavaliere, die einander über einen verrauchten Raum hinweg mustern, kamen Mann und Mode nicht miteinander zurecht. In letzter Zeit jedoch hat sich etwas bewegt. Langsam, aber sicher keimte eine Freundschaft auf – zunächst vorsichtig flirtend, später ein wenig anstößig –, und plötzlich scheint es, dass Männer und Mode mehr als miteinander aus-kommen. Männer und Mode scheinen einander zu lieben.

Die Begeisterung für das Thema ist geradezu explosionsartig gewachsen, angefangen bei der beträchtlichen Zahl der Herrenmodeschauen in den offiziellen Kalendern von Mailand und Paris bis hin zu dem stetig wachsenden Männeranteil unter den Studierenden an den seriösen Mode-schulen, die sich für die traditionellen Techniken des Schneiderhandwerks entscheiden. Nun könnte man argumentieren, dass der Markt für Damenmode gerade eine Phase kreativer und kom-merzieller Stagnation durchlebt, während die Herrenmode im Mittelpunkt des Interesses steht – sowohl für erneuerte künstlerische wie auch für finanzielle Investitionen. Und in der Tat trifft man überall auf Beweise der knospenden Romanze zwischen Männern und Mode. Große Modehäuser werben aggressiv um einen neuen männlichen Kundenstamm; führende Designer wetteifern um die Ergänzung ihrer Modeimperien durch Herrenlinien (Alexander McQueen, Hussein Chalayan, Nicolas Ghesquière für Balenciaga, Véronique Branquinho …); Fotografen, Stylisten und Journa-listen etablieren eine neue Ästhetik, die Einflüsse von Bruce Weber bis Wolfgang Tillmans ein-schließt; die großen Zeitschriftenverlage denken sich neue Hochglanzmagazine für Männer aus … Und so weiter und so fort.

Gleichzeitig tragen aber auch die hervorragendsten Talente der Modebranche ihr Scherflein bei. Raf Simons, der gegenwärtig berühmteste unabhängige Herrenmode-Designer, feiert gerade zehn-jähriges Jubiläum (mit einer großen Retrospektive 2005). Ein anderer, der half, die männliche Sil-houette (wenn auch Jahrzehnte früher) neu zu definieren, nämlich Giorgio Armani, steuert auf die Dreißig-Jahr-Marke zu. Zugleich ragt der Schatten von Helmut Lang – der die gegenwärtige Bewe-gung auf dem Markt für Männermode entscheidend geprägt hat und den radikalen Entschluss fasste, Herren- und Damenmode gleichzeitig auf den Catwalk zu bringen – drohend auf. Die Män-nermode, so scheint es, ist nicht länger die Brautjungfer oder der verlegene Page der Damenkol-lektionen, eine Fußnote des „wahren" Modebusiness. Sie hat vielmehr ihre einzigartige Chance genutzt und sich ihren eigenen Weg gebahnt.

Und während die Trends bei den Damen immer hektischer dokumentiert und verworfen wer-den, was die Ideen selbst umso vergänglicher, ja geradezu wertlos erscheinen lässt, entwickelt sich die Herrenmode kontinuierlich in ihrem selbst gewählten Tempo. In der Vergangenheit nahm man das oft als „Hinterherhinken" wahr, wenn Trends frühestens eine gute Saison später aufgegriffen wurden. Doch die Beständigkeit der Evolution innerhalb der Männermode (die vielleicht einer gewissen natürlichen Zurückhaltung des männlichen Geschlechts entspricht) erscheint inzwi-schen als klarer Vorteil. Das Arbeiten in einem festeren Bezugsrahmen und mit einer weniger hek-tischen, weniger alarmierenden Neuerungsfrequenz ermöglichte eine klarere, sorgsamere Identi-tätsfindung. Vielleicht kann man sich so eher darauf konzentrieren, was *Stil* ausmacht, als auf die ach so vergängliche *Mode*.

Was genau macht aber nun die neue Herrenmode aus? Das verschwitzte Toben im Mosh Pit und das tiefe Dröhnen einer Gitarre sind ein guter Ausgangspunkt. Der Einfluss des Rock 'n' Roll auf

Form, Sitz und Anmutung der aktuellen Männermode ist beträchtlich. Von der Vielzahl musikalischer Helden, die Raf Simons zu seinen wundervollen, herausfordernden Entwürfen inspirierten (Kraftwerk, The Manic Street Preachers, Peter Saville u. a.), bis hin zur rasiermesserscharfen Bowie-artigen Silhouette von Hedi Slimane für Dior Homme – eine musikverrückte Jugend im Trainspotting-Stil scheint unverzichtbare Voraussetzung für jeden erfolgreichen Herrenmode-Designer zu sein. Man braucht eigentlich gar nicht weiter zu suchen als bis zum handwerklich perfekten Look derzeitiger Pop-Darlings wie Franz Ferdinand oder Morrissey, um festzustellen, dass die Musikindustrie das Kompliment zurückgibt.

Ähnlich ist es mit den Vorstellungen von der Entstehung, der Handwerkskunst und der Tradition, die im gegenwärtigen Herrenmode-Movement großes Gewicht haben (diese Qualitäten stehlen sich nach und nach auch in die Damenmode zurück, weil die Modehäuser in ihrer Couture-Vergangenheit nach Inspirationen suchen). Als Reaktion auf die Geschichte der Herrenkleidung – auf das geschätzte Vermächtnis der Schneider aus der Savile Row und auf die anhaltende Bedeutung des Anzugs in der Männermode – sorgt diese Ausrichtung für eine noch stärkere Abkehr von „Frivolität und Flitter" des weiblichen Gegenstücks. Das Ganze verleiht dem Mode-Business Authentizität und Echtheit. Oder, um es drastischer auszudrücken: Es gibt Hetero-Männern ein besseres Gefühl, wenn sie ausgefallene Sachen kaufen. Die eigenwillige Norwegerin Siv Støldal, die neben Leuten wie Peter Jensen, Kim Jones, Cloak und Number (N)ine eine neue Generation nachwachsender Herrenmode-Talente repräsentiert, ist mit ihrer Achtung vor Althergebrachtem die Regel, nicht die Ausnahme. Auch in ihrem Wunsch, diese Tradition dennoch irgendwie zu untergraben, ist sie eine typische Vertreterin dieser Gruppe. „Ich bin fasziniert von der Geschichte mancher Kleidungsstücke", erklärt sie im Interview für dieses Buch. „Ich finde es aufregend, wenn ich alte Sachen finde, die meine Vorfahren getragen haben, etwas, das noch ihren Charakter ausdrückt. Solche Dinge helfen mir, die Vergangenheit zu entschlüsseln, und ich versuche, ihre Geschichte in Ehren zu halten und sie zugleich in die Gegenwart zu übersetzen." Ähnliches gilt für das Haus Martin Margiela, dessen Augenmerk auf Schnitt und Passform viele der neuen Generation stark beeinflusste. Auch hier beschreibt man die eigene Arbeit als „ein Kontinuum und die Vertiefung unserer Kreativität, unserer technischen Erfahrung, Zusammenarbeit und Handwerkskunst".

Im Verlauf der gegenwärtigen Entwicklung in der Herrenmode hat sich ein weiteres langjähriges Margiela-Prinzip bewährt: die Idee der kreativen Zusammenarbeit. In den letzten paar Jahren konnte man eine wachsende Zahl äußerst erfolgreicher Zusammenschlüsse von den unwahrscheinlichsten Marken erleben, die Gemeinsamkeiten von Streetwear und Haute Couture zutage brachten: Fred Perry und Comme des Garçons, Junya Watanabe und Levi's, Timothy Everest und Kim Jones sowie nicht zuletzt – und zumindest für die Hiphop-Fans das unwiderstehlichste Paar – Adidas und Yohji Yamamoto in der glitschigen, Lycra-geprägten Form von Y-3. Diese Paarungen haben die Reichweite der Mode über Laufsteg und Designerboutique hinaus vergrößert in Richtung einer breiteren Mainstream-Klientel.

All jene, die die explosionsartige Entwicklung der Männermode (und ihres „kleinen Bruders", der Accessoire- und Kosmetikindustrie) schon vorab schlecht geredet haben, indem sie vor der so genannten Feminisierung der Männer warnten, muss die Realität enttäuschen. Es gibt nämlich kaum Hinweise darauf. Zumindest nicht offensichtlich auf breiter Front und damit der Rede wert. Im Jahr 2005 geht die Diskussion über Herrenmode über David Beckham in einem Sarong (und die ganze labelbesessene krasse Dummheit der späten Neunziger) hinaus und richtet sich auf die erfreulichere – und überlegte – Selbsteinschätzung. Nachdem Anerkennung und Beachtung dieses Bereichs wachsen, scheint es mit der Liebesaffäre wohl weiter zu gehen.

LA MODE MASCULINE AUJOURD'HUI

«Des hommes lisant des magazines de mode/Oh, dans quel monde vivons-nous …» Rufus Wainwright

La mode et le mâle moderne, le mythique «homme de la rue», ont toujours entretenu une étrange relation. Pendant de nombreuses années, les deux coexistaient dans un rapport de méfiance mutuelle. Tels deux soupirants jaloux s'épiant en chiens de faïence à travers une pièce enfumée, les hommes et la mode ne s'entendaient pas. Toutefois, les choses ont changé récemment. Lentement mais sûrement, une relation s'est nouée: le petit flirt amical a dégénéré en liaison sulfureuse et soudain, on dirait que les hommes et la mode s'entendent à merveille. En fait, ils sont même fous amoureux.

Du nombre important de défilés masculins lors des semaines de la mode de Milan, Paris au pourcentage croissant d'étudiants sérieux, inscrits dans des écoles de mode tout aussi sérieuses, en vue de se former aux techniques traditionnelles de la couture, l'intérêt pour le genre a explosé. Alors qu'on peut affirmer sans se tromper que le marché de la mode féminine traverse actuellement une période de stagnation créative et commerciale, la mode pour homme accapare le renouveau des investissements artistiques et financiers. En effet, on trouve partout des preuves de l'idylle naissante entre les hommes et la mode: les grandes maisons courtisent de façon offensive une nouvelle clientèle masculine et les grands créateurs se ruent pour ajouter des lignes masculines à leurs empires en pleine expansion (Alexander McQueen, Hussein Chalayan, Nicolas Ghesquière pour Balenciaga, Véronique Branquinho...); les photographes, les stylistes et les journalistes de mode définissent une nouvelle esthétique brillante qui réunit diverses influences, de Bruce Weber à Wolfgang Tillmans, et les principales maisons d'éditions préparent de nouveaux magazines pour homme…

Parallèlement, la plupart des talents les plus singuliers de l'industrie reçoivent également leur dû. Raf Simons, le créateur pour homme indépendant aujourd'hui le plus apprécié, célèbre le dixième anniversaire de sa griffe (avec une grande rétrospective en 2005). De même, Giorgio Armani, autre créateur qui a contribué à définir la silhouette masculine (bien que cela fasse déjà plusieurs décennies), approche de ses trente ans de carrière. L'ombre de Helmut Lang plane toujours, une influence essentielle de la mode masculine actuelle et un créateur qui a pris la décision radicale de présenter ses collections pour homme et pour femme dans un même défilé. La mode pour homme ne serait donc plus la demoiselle d'honneur, ou plutôt le jeune page gêné, des collections pour femme, ni un simple post-scriptum du «vrai business de la mode». Elle a su saisir son heure et se frayer un chemin.

Alors que les tendances de la mode féminine sont documentées, puis oubliées à un rythme toujours plus frénétique, ce qui rend les idées qu'elles proposent d'autant plus jetables et creuses, la mode pour homme continue d'évoluer à son propre rythme. Auparavant, on avait l'impression qu'elle restait «à la traîne», adoptant les tendances avec au moins une bonne saison de retard. Mais l'évolution stable de la mode masculine (qui reflète peut-être une réticence naturelle propre à la masculinité) apparaît désormais comme un avantage distinct. Travaillant au sein d'un cadre de référence plus étroit et à un rythme de changement moins bousculé, le secteur a réussi à se forger une identité plus claire et plus étudiée. Probablement pour se concentrer sur la substance du «style» plutôt que sur la nature éphémère de la «mode».

Comment cette nouvelle identité de la mode pour homme se forme-t-elle? La foule en sueur collée à la scène de et le crachat des guitares dans les concerts, rock constituent un point de départ évident. Le rock exerce une influence considérable sur les formes, les coupes et l'attitude de la mode masculine contemporaine. De la multitude de héros musicaux inspirant les superbes créations dérangeantes de Raf Simons (Kraftwerk, les Manic Street Preachers, Peter Saville etc.) à la silhouette au rasoir de Hedi Slimane pour Dior Homme, influencée par Bowie, une jeunesse accro de musique et de drogue s'avère une étape de formation incontournable dans la carrière de tous les créateurs pour homme qui réussissent. Pas besoin de chercher plus loin que le look soigné des chouchous actuels de la pop, Franz Ferdinand ou du Morrissey ressuscité, pour comprendre comment l'industrie de la musique leur retourne le compliment.

De même, les idées de processus, d'artisanat et de tradition pèsent lourd dans le mouvement actuel de la mode masculine (des qualités qui filtrent furtivement dans la mode pour femme car les maisons de mode se tournent vers leurs archives en quête d'inspiration). En partie grâce à l'histoire de la mode pour homme, de l'illustre héritage des tailleurs de Savile Row au rôle indétrônable du costume au sein de la mode masculine, cette approche permet d'encore mieux différencier la mode pour homme de la « frivolité » de son homologue féminine. Des idées qui apportent un air « d'authenticité » et de « vérité » au business de la mode, ou pour parler plus franchement, qui permettent aux hommes hétérosexuels d'être plus à l'aise lorsqu'ils achètent des vêtements haut de gamme.

L'étrange Norvégienne Siv Støldal, aux côtés de Peter Jensen, Kim Jones, Cloak et Number (N)ine, incarne une nouvelle génération de créateurs pour homme qui respecte typiquement l'histoire et la tradition. Comme son groupe de pairs, elle cherche à en proposer une version subversive. « Je suis fascinée par l'histoire des vêtements », explique-t-elle dans ce livre. « J'adore retrouver les vieux vêtements portés par mes ancêtres, ces affaires qui ont gardé quelque chose de leur caractère. Ces choses m'aident à déverrouiller le passé et j'essaie d'honorer leur histoire et de la traduire pour le temps présent ». De même, Maison Martin Margiela, dont l'attention portée à la forme et à la coupe a largement influencé la plupart des créateurs de cette nouvelle génération, décrit son travail comme « la continuation et l'approfondissement de notre créativité, de notre expérience technique, de notre collaboration et de notre art ».

Alors que cette phase actuelle de la mode masculine se poursuit, un autre vieux principe de Margiela a pris racine : l'idée de la collaboration créative. Ces dernières années ont vu un nombre croissant de coopérations couronnées de succès entre les marques les plus improbables, créant un pont entre le streetwear et la mode de luxe : Fred Perry et Comme des Garçons, Junya Watanabe et Levi's, Timothy Everest et Kim Jones, puis la plus irrésistible de toutes, du moins pour les membres de la confrérie hip-hop, Adidas et Yohji Yamamoto sous la forme des tennis Y-3 en Lycra et sans lacets... Autant d'associations qui ont étendu l'influence de la mode au-delà du podium et de la boutique vers un public plus large et moins averti.

Malgré tous les débats des premières années 00 autour de l'explosion de la mode masculine (et de ses « petits frères » : accessoires et produits cosmétiques) qui mènerait soi-disant à la « féminisation » des hommes, on trouve peu d'exemples de cette théorie. Du moins pas assez de preuves pour satisfaire un tribunal. En 2005, le débat sur la mode pour homme a su aller au-delà des discussions autour d'un David Beckham en sarong (et de l'obsession crasse pour les griffes que représentait la fin des années 90) pour évoluer vers une évaluation plus confortable, et plus étudiée, du rôle de la mode pour homme. Alors que le secteur continue de gagner en respect et en reconnaissance, l'histoire d'amour entre les hommes et la mode semble bien partie pour durer.

GLENN WALDRON
Editor, i-D magazine

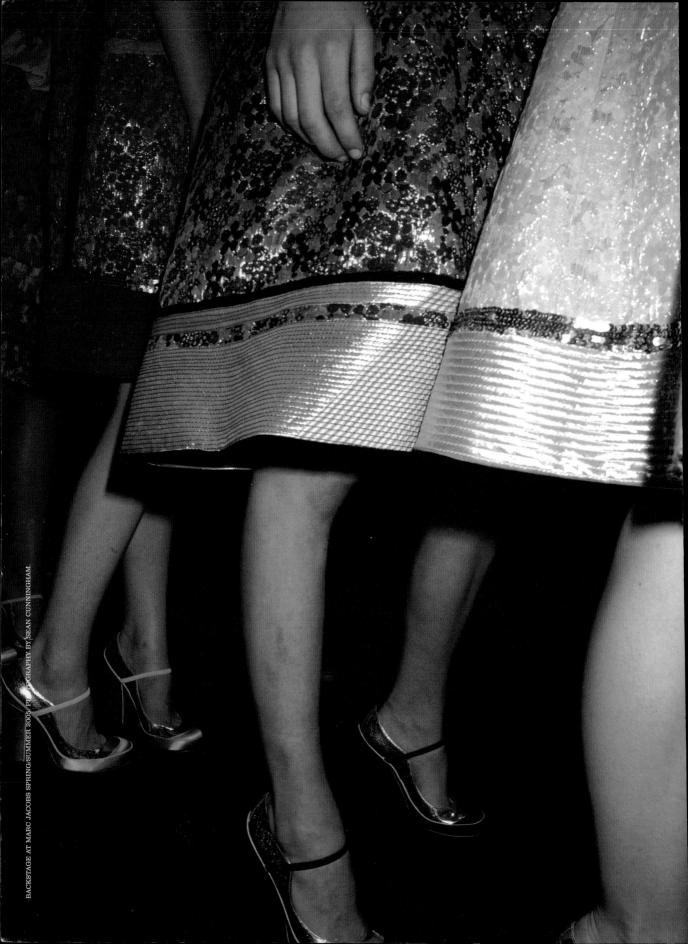

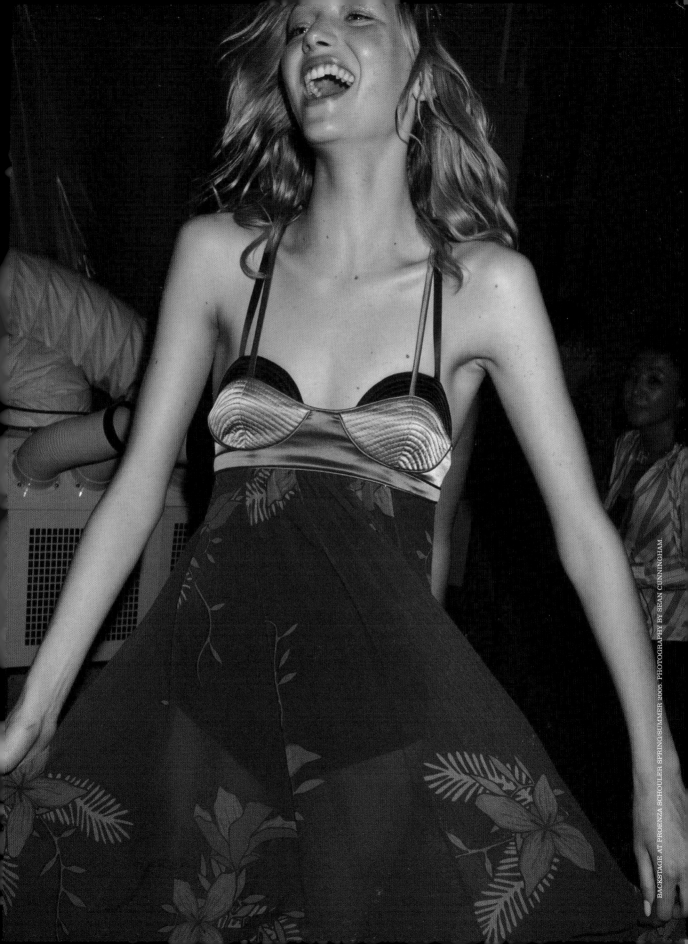

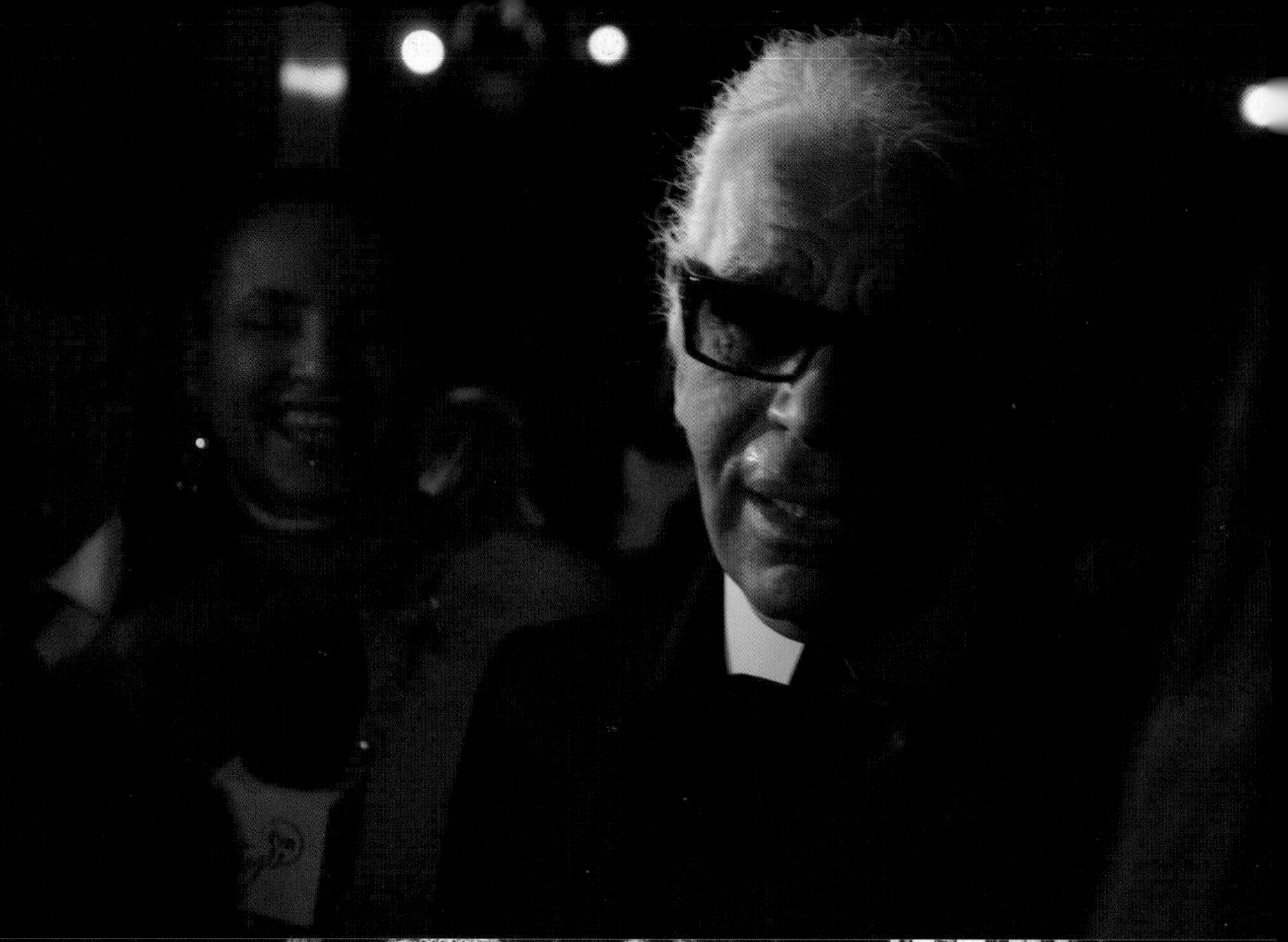

KARL LAGERFELD BACKSTAGE AT CHANEL AUTUMN/WINTER 2005–2006. PHOTOGRAPHY BY TIM MITCHELL.

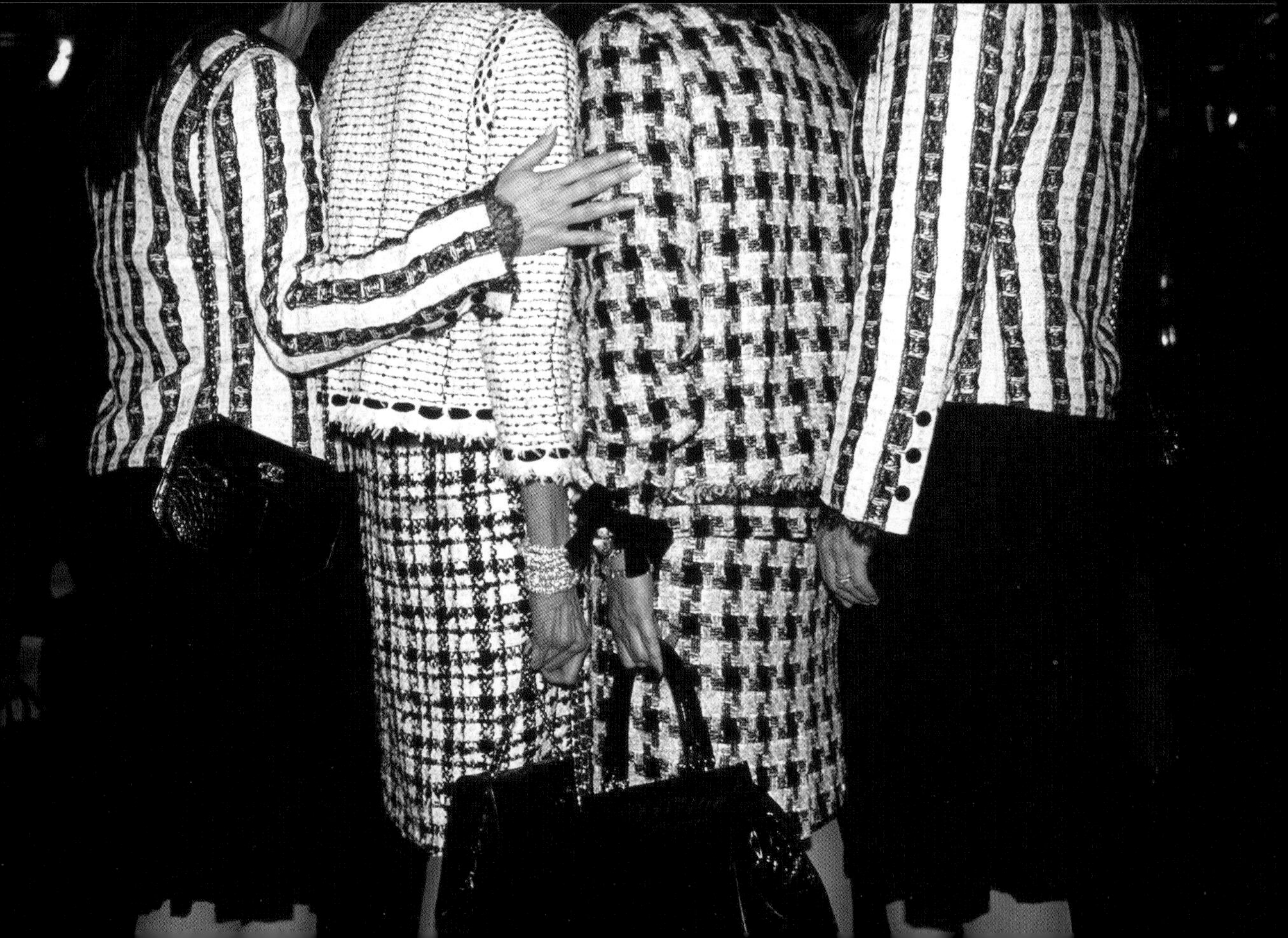

CHANEL AUTUMN/WINTER 2005–2006. PHOTOGRAPHY BY TIM MITCHELL.

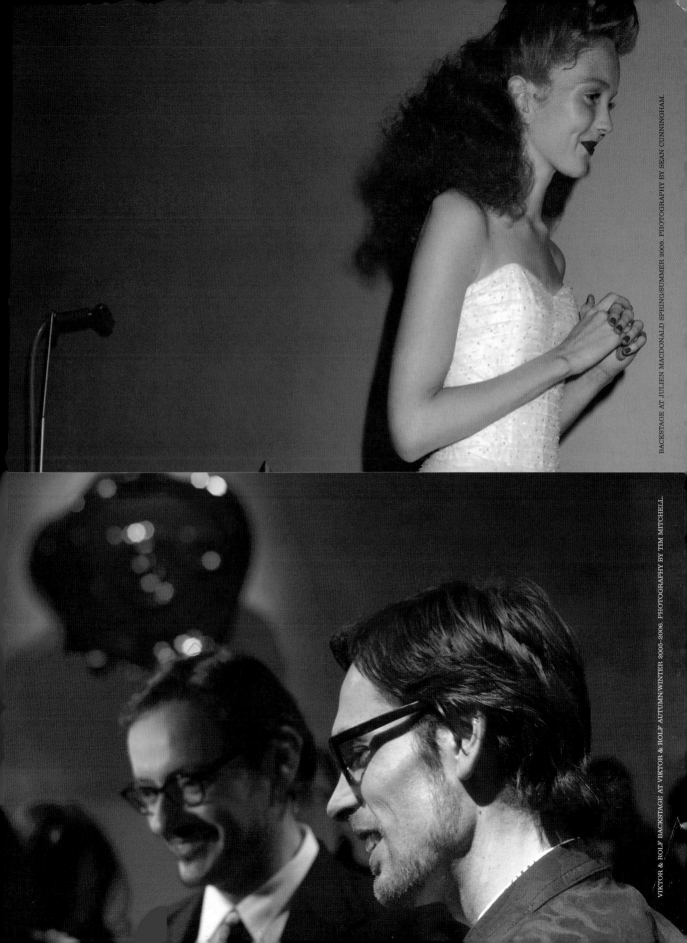

BACKSTAGE AT JULIEN MACDONALD SPRING/SUMMER 2005. PHOTOGRAPHY BY SEAN CUNNINGHAM.

VIKTOR & ROLF BACKSTAGE AT VIKTOR & ROLF AUTUMN/WINTER 2005-2006. PHOTOGRAPHY BY TIM MITCHELL.

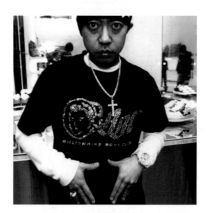

A BATHING APE
"Ape shall never kill Ape" NIGO

A Bathing Ape has thrived on exclusivity since its conception in 1993. Hip-hop inspired baggies, urban camouflage prints and playful simian motifs are all signatures for the label, which is affectionately known to its disciples as BAPE. The longevity of the brand is impressive: in the ephemeral world of streetwear, 12 years is a long time. The secret to the success of A Bathing Ape, the brainchild of Japanese designer Nigo, is ruthlessly limited editions and an almost mythological inaccessibility. (Outside of Japan, the brand is only available in two direct-management stores in the UK and, since 2005, the US.) Nigo studied fashion at the Bunka Fashion College in 1988 and the young entrepreneur now has his jewel-adorned fingers in a variety of pies, including a record label (which grew out of his collaboration with James Lavelle, founder of Mo' Wax), art gallery, café/restaurant, hair salon, toy division (think *Planet of the Apes*) and TV show. Perhaps it is through the continual diversification of the brand that Nigo has managed to retain BAPE's underground mystique, despite advertising tie-ins with multinationals such as Pepsi, Sony and Adidas. The name A Bathing Ape derives from a Japanese expression meaning 'to bathe in lukewarm water', and is intended as a comment on the sheltered and shallow nature of Japanese youth culture. The irony, however, is apparently lost on the swelling army of BAPE followers, whose uniform is head-to-toe 'APECAMO'. And with a clutch of A-list clients such as The Beastie Boys, Futura 2000 and Pharrell Williams on his side, the Ape looks set for worldwide domination, King Kong style.

A Bathing Ape setzt seit seiner Gründung 1993 auf Exklusivität. Vom Hip-Hop inspirierte Baggypants, urbane Camouflage-Muster und verspielte Affenmotive sind die Markenzeichen dieses Labels, das seine Fans liebevoll BAPE nennen. Die Ausdauer der Marke ist schon ziemlich beeindruckend, denn in der schnelllebigen Welt der Streetwear sind zwölf Jahre eine lange Zeit. Das Erfolgsgeheimnis von A Bathing Ape, der Erfindung des japanischen Designers Nigo, sind die gnadenlos limitierten Stückzahlen und die schon legendär schwierige Erhältlichkeit. (Außerhalb Japans werden die Sachen nur in zwei eigenen Läden in Großbritannien sowie seit 2005 auch in den USA verkauft.) Nigo machte 1988 seinen Abschluss am Bunka Fashion College und hat als Jungunternehmer seine reich beringten Finger in allen möglichen Geschäften: einem Plattenlabel (entstanden aus seiner Zusammenarbeit mit James Lavelle, dem Gründer von Mo' Wax), einer Kunstgalerie, einem Café-Restaurant, einem Friseursalon, in der Spielzeugbranche (inspiriert vom „Planet der Affen") sowie in einer Fernsehsen-

dung. Und vielleicht ist es gerade dieser permanenten Diversifikation der Marke zu verdanken, dass Nigo es geschafft hat, den anarchistischen Charme von BAPE zu bewahren – trotz Werbekooperationen mit Weltmarken wie Pepsi, Sony und Adidas. Der Name „A Bathing Ape" ist übrigens die englische Entsprechung einer japanischen Redewendung, die so viel bedeutet wie „Warmduscher" und als Kritik an der behüteten, in ihren Ansprüchen eher seichten japanischen Jugend zu verstehen ist. Diese Ironie scheint die ständig wachsende Menge der BAPE-Fans jedoch kalt zu lassen – sie kleiden sich von Kopf bis Fuß in „APECAMO". Angesichts einer Liste höchst prominenter Kunden wie The Beastie Boys, Futura 2000 und Pharrell Williams scheint der Affe für die Weltherrschaft à la Kingkong bestens gerüstet.

Depuis sa création en 1993, A Bathing Ape prospère sur la vague de l'exclusivité. Baggies d'inspiration hip-hop, imprimés camouflage urbains et motifs simiens rigolos sont autant de signatures de la griffe, affectueusement surnommée BAPE par ses disciples. Sa longévité est impressionnante : en effet, dans le monde éphémère du streetwear, 12 ans c'est long. Invention du créateur japonais Nigo, le secret du succès d'A Bathing Ape repose sans pitié sur les éditions limitées et une inaccessibilité presque mythique (en dehors du Japon, la marque n'est disponible que dans deux boutiques directement gérées par la griffe au Royaume-Uni, et depuis 2005 aux Etats-Unis). Depuis sa formation en mode au Bunka Fashion College en 1988, le jeune entrepreneur a plongé ses doigts bagousés dans divers domaines, notamment un label de musique (né de sa collaboration avec James Lavelle, fondateur de Mo' Wax), une galerie d'art, un café-restaurant, un salon de coiffure, une ligne de jouets (largement inspirée du film « La Planète des Singes ») et une émission de télé. C'est peut-être grâce à l'incessante diversification de sa marque que Nigo réussit à préserver la mystique underground de BAPE, en dépit de liens publicitaires avec des multinationales telles que Pepsi, Sony et Adidas. Le nom « A Bathing Ape » vient d'une expression japonaise qui signifie « se baigner dans de l'eau tiède », ici utilisée comme un commentaire sur la tendance surprotégée et superficielle de la culture jeune au Japon. Toutefois, l'ironie du nom a tendance à se perdre face à l'armada croissante des disciples de BAPE, vêtus de la tête aux pieds de l'uniforme « APECAMO ». Et avec quelques clients VIP tels que les Beastie Boys, Futura 2000 et Pharrell Williams, le « Singe » semble bien parti pour dominer le monde, comme King Kong.

NANCY WATERS

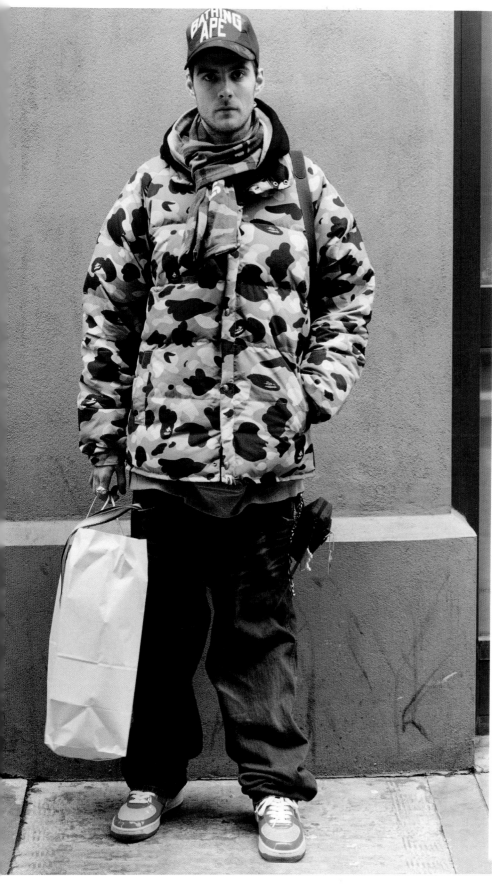

What are your signature designs? The logo of A BATHING APE and the APE CAMOU-FLAGE pattern What is your favourite piece from any of your collections? I like all the items How would you describe your work? Fun amusement What's your ultimate goal? I do not set a goal What inspires you? MY LIFE Can fashion still have a political ambition? No, I don't think so Who do you have in mind when you design? About myself Is the idea of creative collaboration important to you? Yes, I guess it is important Who has been the greatest influence on your career? Pharrell Williams How have your own experiences affected your work as a designer? Yes, all experiences have been affecting my work Which is more important in your work: the process or the product? Both Is designing difficult for you, if so, what drives you to continue? It is not difficult – as all is inspi-ration and casual ideas Have you ever been influenced or moved by the reaction to your designs? Nothing in particular crosses my mind as an answer to this What's your defi-nition of beauty? Nothing in particular What's your philosophy? APE SHALL NEVER KILL APE What is the most important lesson you've learned? Nothing in particular.

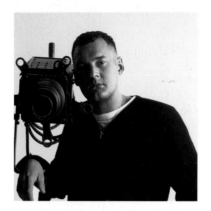

ADIDAS

"Personality is what gives life to design" MICHAEL MICHALSKY

"Now the Adidas I possess for one man is rare/Myself homeboy got 50 pair/Got blue and black 'cause I like to chill/And yellow and green when it's time to get ill." When Run DMC wrote rhymes about their trainers, no one could comprehend the speed at which said trainers would jump into the stratosphere. Right now, Adidas has grown into one of the biggest brands in the world, and all that from an acorn planted in a brain of the sports-obsessed German, Adi Dassler. After the First World War, Dassler started designing track shoes out of 'found' materials. Come the mid-'20s, he was sticking spikes through the soles of his shoes to improve grip and by 1948 Dassler had come up with the idea of splicing his first name and surname together forming the brand name known today. In 1949, Adidas registered their distinctive triple-striped logo, and when the Adidas-wearing German team smashed their winning goal to the back of Hungary's net in the 1954 World Cup final, the brand's legend was secured. In '71, the 'Fight Of The Century' between Muhammad Ali and Joe Frazier saw both heavyweights wearing boxing boots specially developed by Adi Dassler. For a while, the brand's profile was lowered, until being resurrected by music fans in the early '80s who imitated the dress of their pop idols The Stone Roses and The Happy Mondays. The Gazelle, in particular, became an object of lust when Madonna lounged on a chaise longue in the video for Rain, prompting Camden Market to start a bidding war on the then rare product. Today, collaborations with Missy Elliott and Yohji Yamomoto have changed the way sportswear is perceived; in 2005 a new partnership was made with Stella McCartney, the same year that would have marked the 100th birthday of the late Adi Dassler. Michael Michalsky (photographed above) is global creative director of Adidas.

„Now the Adidas I possess for one man is rare/Myself homeboy got 50 pair/Got blue and black 'cause I like to chill/And yellow and green when it's time to get ill." Als Run DMC diese Zeilen über seine Turnschuhe reimte, war noch nicht absehbar, in welchem Tempo eben diese Kleidungsstücke alle Rekorde brechen würden. Inzwischen ist Adidas eine der größten Marken der Welt. Begonnen hat alles mit einer Idee des sportverrückten Deutschen Adi Dassler. Nach dem Ersten Weltkrieg begann Dassler aus Abfallmaterialien, die er in seiner von Zerstörung geprägten Umgebung fand, Laufschuhe zu fertigen. Mitte der 1920er Jahre hatte er den Einfall, Stollen an den Sohlen seiner Schuhe zu befestigen, um für mehr Halt zu sorgen. 1948 schließlich hatte Dassler die Idee, seine Vornamen mit der Hälfte seines Nachnamens zu verbinden und so den bis heute bekannten Markennamen zu kreieren. 1949 wurden die berühmten drei Streifen als Logo registriert. Als die von Adidas ausgerüstete deutsche Nationalmannschaft 1954 im Finale der Fußballweltmeisterschaft das entscheidende Tor gegen Ungarn schoss, war der Grundstein zu einer Legende gelegt. Beim so genannten Jahrhundertkampf 1971 zwischen Muhammad Ali und Joe Frazier

trugen beide Boxer spezielle, von Adi Dassler entwickelte Boxstiefel. Danach wurde es eine Zeit lang stiller um die Marke, bis Anfang der 1980er Jahre Musikfans ihre Idole von The Stone Roses und The Happy Mondays imitierten und so für eine Neubelebung sorgten. Das Modell Gazelle wurde zum Objekt der Begierde, nachdem Madonna sich damit in dem Video zu „Rain" auf einer Chaiselongue geräkelt hatte. Als Folge brach insbesondere auf dem Londoner Flohmarkt Camden Market eine regelrechte Hysterie um die damals schwer zu findenden Schuhe aus. Kooperationen mit Missy Elliott und Yohji Yamamoto haben das Bild von Sportswear nachhaltig verändert. 2005 ging Adidas eine neue Partnerschaft mit Stella McCartney ein. Im selben Jahr wäre Adi Dassler 100. Jahre alt geworden. Michael Michalsky (Bild oben) ist heute Global Creative Director von Adidas.

« Now the Adidas I possess for one man is rare/Myself homeboy got 50 pair/Got blue and black cause I like to chill/And yellow and green when it's time to get ill »… A l'époque où Run DMC écrit quelques rimes sur ses baskets préférées, personne n'aurait pu deviner à quelle vitesse lesdites chaussures allaient devenir un succès interplanétaire. Aujourd'hui l'une des plus grandes marques mondiales, la petite graine d'Adidas avait germé dans le cerveau d'Adi Dassler, un Allemand obsédé de sport. Après la Première Guerre mondiale, Dassler commence à créer des chaussures de course en recyclant des objets de récupération trouvés dans son quartier digne de l'Apocalypse. Au milieu des années 20, il insère des picots dans les semelles de ses chaussures pour améliorer leur adhérence. En 1948, Adi Dassler coupe son prénom et son nom en deux et réunit les deux syllabes qui formeront le nom de la marque qu'on connaît aujourd'hui. En 1949, Adidas fait breveter son célèbre logo aux trois bandes. Quand l'équipe de foot d'Allemagne, vêtue en Adidas, marque le but de la victoire contre les Hongrois lors de la finale de la Coupe du Monde 1954, la marque entre enfin dans la légende. En 1971, le « Combat du Siècle » opposant Muhammad Ali à Joe Frazier voit deux poids lourds arborer des chaussures de boxe spécialement conçues par Adi Dassler. Pendant un temps, la marque fait profil bas avant d'être ressuscitée et plébiscitée par les fans de musique du début des années 80, qui aiment à imiter leurs idoles pop comme les Stone Roses et les Happy Mondays. En particulier la Gazelle, qui devient un objet de convoitise dès qu'on la repère aux pieds d'une Madonna en chaise longue dans son clip Rain, incitant le marché de Camden à se lancer dans une guerre d'enchères sur ce produit alors très rare. Aujourd'hui, des collaborations avec Missy Elliott et Yohji Yamamoto transforment la façon dont le sportswear est perçu ; en 2005, Adidas conclut un nouveau partenariat avec Stella McCartney, une année qui aurait également marqué le centenaire de feu Adi Dassler. Michael Michalsky est directeur de la création d'Adidas.

BEN REARDON

PORTRAIT BY KARL LAGERFELD. PHOTOGRAPHY BY CHRISTIAN WITKIN, STYLING BY SONJA. MODEL. SEAN PAUL. NOVEMBER 2003.

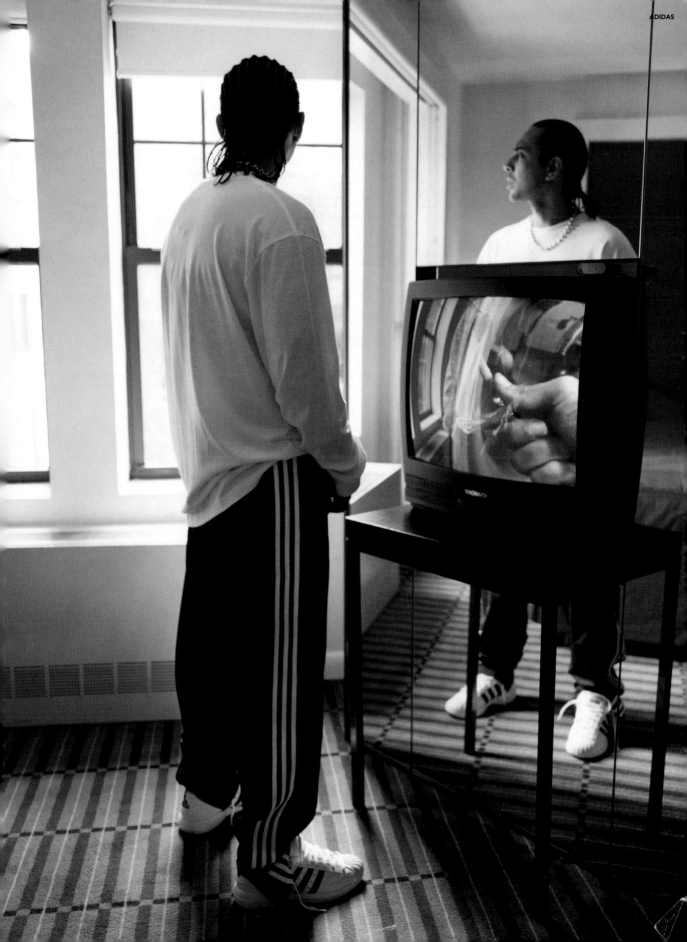

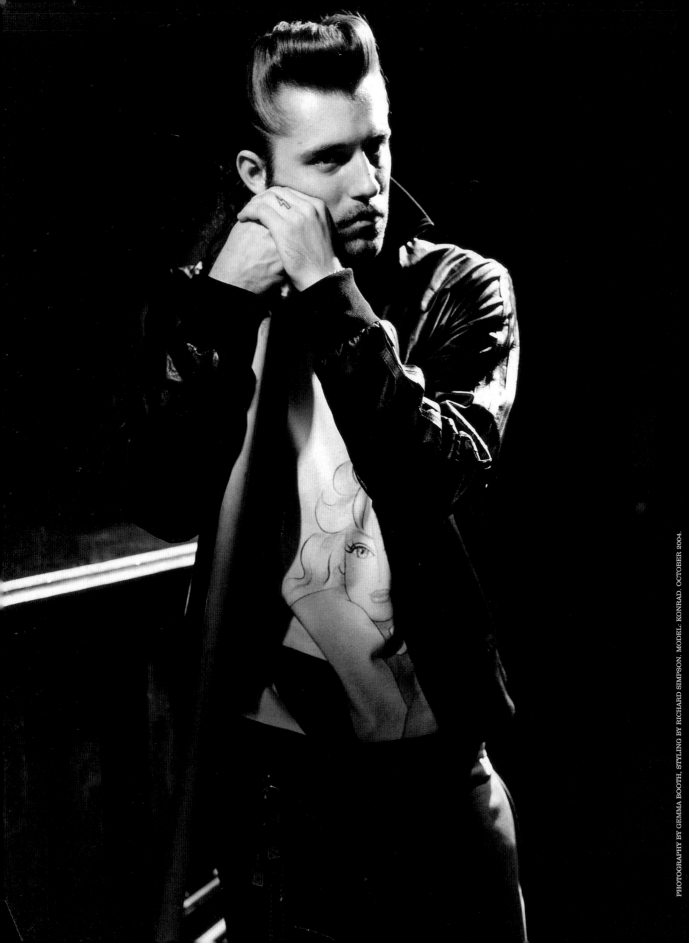

PHOTOGRAPHY BY GEMMA BOOTH. STYLING BY RICHARD SIMPSON. MODEL: KONRAD. OCTOBER 2004.

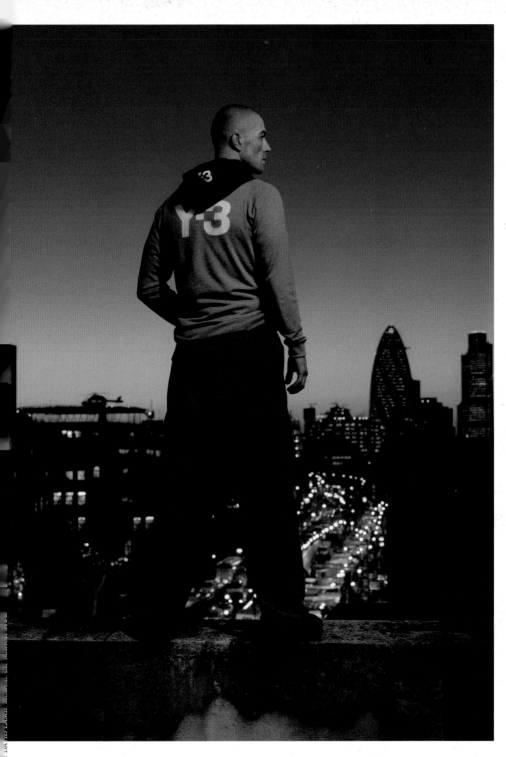

What are your signature designs? Real products for real people... they must always look different on different people **What is your favourite piece from any of your collections?** Superkegler Ostrich, celebrating Adi Dassler's 100th birthday **How would you describe your work?** I am the conductor of an orchestra of musicians from different cultures and different music styles **What's your ultimate goal?** Create product that appeals to everyone... a true people's brand not excluding anyone **What inspires you?** Music, music, music... clubbing, clubbing, clubbing... photography, photography, photography **Can fashion still have a political ambition?** Definitely... depending how you wear it and what **Who do you have in mind when you design?** When I design I take on different personalities depending on which of Adidas' divisions I design for **Is the idea of creative collaboration important to you?** Very important, as it opens your mind and lets you step out of your box in a very comfortable manner **Who has been the greatest influence on your career?** My mother and Karl Lagerfeld... my mother developed my interest in fashion and how to mix it, and an article on Karl in a German magazine I read when I was 13 made me become a designer **How have your own experiences affected your work as a designer?** As I am also responsible for Adidas performance products, my experience when using them for sport goes into them **Which is more important in your work: the process or the product?** In my life product is king **Is designing difficult for you, if so, what drives you to continue?** It comes very natural for me as I don't really see it as a job but an attitude to life **Have you ever been influenced or moved by the reaction to your designs?** Not really as I know stuff like that is very subjective and I am doing a job **What's your definition of beauty?** Beauty lies in the eye of the beholder and is really a combination of a lot of different things **What's your philosophy?** Life is a party and if you are clever you take money at the door **What is the most important lesson you've learned?** People are people.

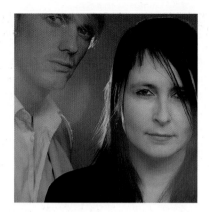

AF VANDEVORST
"Fashion is a language"

AF Vandevorst, the Belgian design duo of An Vandevorst (born 1968) and Filip Arickx (born 1971), view fashion as nothing less than a way to communicate the inner workings of the mind. The husband-and-wife design team met in 1987 at the Royal Academy in Antwerp. On graduating, Vandevorst worked as assistant to Dries Van Noten. Meanwhile Arickx, who worked for Dirk Bikkembergs for three years as a teenager, completed military service after leaving the Academy, and then worked as a freelance designer and stylist. Together they established their own label in 1997, and presented their first collection in Paris for autumn/winter 1998. The label quickly came to the attention of both the fashion press and establishment; after only their second collection they were awarded Paris Fashion Week's Venus de la Mode award for 'Le Futur Grand Créateur', a prestigious prize for newcomers. For the spring/summer and autumn/winter 2000 seasons the pair were invited to design the Ruffo Research collection, an opportunity periodically offered to young designers by the Italian leather house Ruffo. AF Vandevorst clothes convey a slouchy confidence, and a version of femininity that evokes a sexy yet intellectual cool. Traditional clothing (horse riding equipment, kimonos, frock coats) is often referenced, reworked and refined until it sits slightly left-of-centre; a medical-style red cross is their enduring symbol. For collection themes, they often favour the unexpected, as for autumn/winter 2003, when honey bees provided inspiration. Following no set colour palette, AF Vandevorst stray from muted tones into brights. Recently the label has expanded to encompass footwear, accessories and lingerie, and they continue to present catwalk shows during the Paris collections.

Für das belgische Designerduo An Vandevorst (Jahrgang 1968) und Filip Arickx (Jahrgang 1971) ist Mode nichts Geringeres als eine Möglichkeit, die Vorgänge des Geistes sichtbar zu machen. Das Ehepaar lernte sich 1987 an der Königlichen Akademie in Antwerpen kennen. Nach ihrem Abschluss arbeitete Vandevorst zunächst als Assistentin für Dries van Noten. Arickx hatte schon als Teenager drei Jahre lang bei Dirk Bikkembergs gejobbt und absolvierte nach der Akademie erst einmal seinen Wehrdienst. Anschließend arbeitete er als freischaffender Designer und Stylist. Das gemeinsame eigene Label gründeten die beiden 1997. Ihre erste Kollektion, Herbst/Winter 1998, präsentierten sie in Paris. Rasch gewannen sie die Aufmerksamkeit sowohl der Presse als auch des Fashion Establishments. So wurden sie bereits für ihre zweite Kollektion im Rahmen der Pariser Modewoche mit der Vénus de la Mode als „Le Futur Grand Créateur" ausgezeichnet, einem prestigeträchtigen Preis für Newcomer. Für Frühjahr/Sommer sowie Herbst/Winter 2000 erhielt das Paar den Auftrag, die Kollektion für Ruffo Research zu entwerfen. Der italienische Lederwarenhersteller Ruffo bietet

jungen Designern regelmäßig diese Gelegenheit. Die Entwürfe von AF Vandevorst drücken lässiges Selbstvertrauen aus, zugleich wirken sie auf eine Weise feminin, die sexy, aber zugleich intellektuell und cool rüberkommt. Funktionale Sachen (Reitkleidung, Kimonos, Gehröcke) werden oft zitiert, umgearbeitet und leicht verfremdet. Symbol des Labels ist seit jeher ein rotes Kreuz wie im medizinischen Bereich. Als Themen ihrer Kollektionen wählen die Designer oft Ungewöhnliches, wie die Bienen im Herbst/Winter 2003. Was die Farben angeht, ist man bei AF Vandevorst völlig ungebunden und bedient sich mal bei den gedämpften und mal bei den kräftigen Tönen. Kürzlich wurde die Produktpalette des Labels um Schuhe, Accessoires und Dessous erweitert. Präsentiert werden die Kollektionen weiterhin bei den Schauen in Paris.

AF Vandevorst, le duo de créateurs belges formé par An Vandevorst (née en 1968) et Filip Arickx (né en 1971), considère la mode comme rien de moins qu'un moyen de révéler les rouages cachés de l'esprit. Aujourd'hui mariés, ils se sont rencontrés en 1987 à l'Académie Royale d'Anvers. Une fois diplômée, An Vandevorst travaille comme assistante pour Dries Van Noten, tandis que Filip Arickx, qui avait fait ses classes pendant trois ans auprès de Dirk Bikkembergs, effectue son service militaire après avoir quitté l'Académie et avant de travailler comme créateur et styliste en free-lance. Ensemble, ils fondent leur propre griffe en 1997 et présentent une première collection à Paris lors des défilés automne/hiver 1998. Leur travail attire rapidement l'attention de la presse et du monde de la mode ; dès leur deuxième collection, le duo reçoit le prix du Futur Grand Créateur des Vénus de la Mode, récompense prestigieuse décernée aux nouveaux talents pendant la Semaine de la Mode de Paris. Pour les saisons printemps/été et automne/hiver 2000, ils sont invités à dessiner la collection Ruffo Research, une opportunité que le grand maroquinier italien Ruffo offre régulièrement aux jeunes créateurs. Des vêtements AF Vandevorst émanent une confiance désinvolte et une féminité originale témoignant d'une attitude cool, sexy mais néanmoins intello. Les collections font souvent référence aux costumes traditionnels (tenues d'équitation, kimonos, fracs), retravaillés et raffinés jusqu'à leur conférer une asymétrie légèrement décalée sur la gauche, avec une croix rouge d'inspiration médicale comme symbole récurrent. Pour les thèmes de leurs collections, ils privilégient souvent l'inattendu, comme pour la saison automne/hiver 2003 inspirée par les abeilles. Ne suivant aucune palette de couleurs prédéfinie, AF Vandevorst vagabonde des tons les plus neutres aux plus vifs. Récemment, la griffe s'est enrichie pour inclure des chaussures, des accessoires et de la lingerie. Le duo continue à présenter ses collections pendant les défilés parisiens.

LIZ HANCOCK

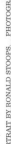

PORTRAIT BY RONALD STOOPS.   PHOTOGRAPHY BY JENNIFER TZAR, STYLING BY PATTI WILSON.   MODEL: LILY COLE, FEBRUARY 2004

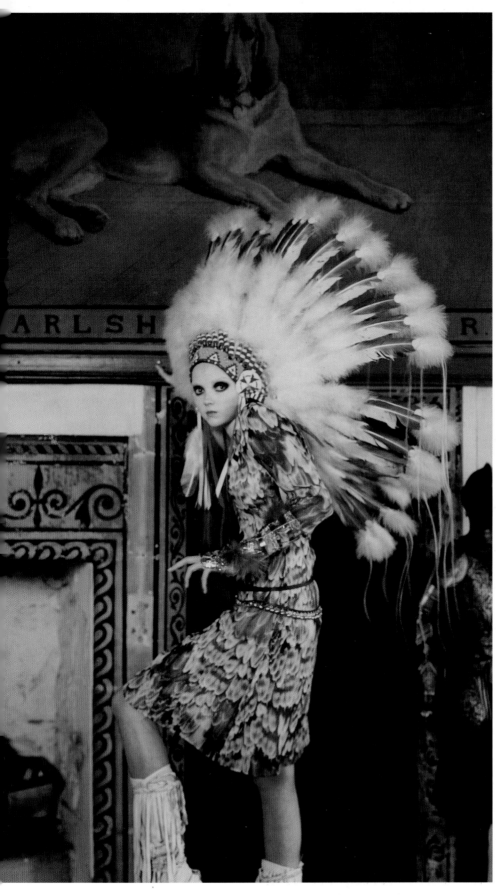

What are your signature designs? Assembling by studding, classics with a twist, contrast, humour, leather applications **What is your favorite piece from any of your collections?** Every piece we've made has a specific meaning for us. Every garment we've designed was or is important for the evolution and development of the next one **How would you describe your work?** The research in the world of AF Vandevorst and the challenge of pushing back frontiers and opening new horizons **What's your ultimate goal?** The freedom to keep on exploring and expanding our universe and all of this in collaboration with people who are stimulated to work with the two of us **What inspires you?** Every emotion and situation. As long as it encourages us to take a decision or a certain position **Can fashion still have a political ambition?** Yes, fashion is a language **Who do you have in mind when you design?** Our own generation **Is the idea of creative collaboration important to you?** Yes, because it can lead to an energetic interchange **Who has been the greatest influence of your career?** Our own attitude **How have your own experiences affected your work as a designer?** Our work is a reflection of our own experiences **Which is more important in your work: the process or the product?** The process, which leads in the end to satisfaction with the result **Is designing difficult for you? If so, what drives you to continue?** Designing is like writing a book: the words come out fluidly but to put them in the right context is not always that easy **Have you ever been influenced or moved by the reaction to your designs?** It's a valuable experience **What's your definition of beauty?** Beauty lies in the unexpected **What's your philosophy?** Open-mindedness **What is the most important lesson you've learned?** A rolling stone gathers no moss.

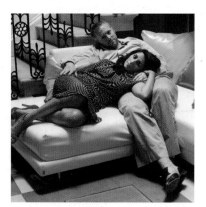

AGENT PROVOCATEUR

"Girls, girls, girls: sex kittens, sex bombs, seductresses, naughty girls, secretaries, schoolgirls and Kate Moss"

SERENA REES & JOSEPH CORRE

From Soho to Vegas, Agent Provocateur is first stop for connoisseurs of sexy lingerie. Since founding their company in 1994, AP inventors Serena Rees and Joseph Corre have transformed the underwear market with their seductive and nostalgic designs. It's hot tabloid news when a celebutant goes shopping in one of their boudoir-esque stores, not least because purchases might include crotchless panties, sequin pasties or fluffy high-heeled slippers. We will probably never find out, however, because the AP shopgirl, cute as a cupcake in her baby pink button-up shirtdress (designed by Vivienne Westwood, who happens to be Joseph's mum) is sworn never to reveal her VIP dressing room secrets. Married couple Rees (born 1968) and Corre (born 1969) design an entire range of fit-for-a-glamour-goddess lingerie plus accessories, jewellery, lipsmacking leather pieces, shoes and stockings. An award-winning perfume made its debut in 2000, closely followed by a wealth of bathroom and bedroom fancies – candles, lotions and even a nipple balm. Famed for the racy window displays in their boutiques, and an equally welcoming retail website, Agent Provocateur's passion is evident in everything they do. And the Provocateur product is not just on display in the most interesting bedrooms: it was included in the V&A's Cutting Edge exhibition in 1997 and also 'The Inside Out' show at The Design Museum in 2000. Whether it's their adult-rated commercials, music projects such as their well-received CD, Peep Show, of 2004, or collaborations with Marks & Spencer and Tate Modern, AP is always about sexual liberation conducted, of course, all in the best possible taste.

Ob in Soho oder Las Vegas, Agent Provocateur ist die erste Adresse für die Liebhaber von sexy Dessous. Seit der Gründung von Agent Provocateur 1994 haben deren Erfinder Serena Rees und Joe Corre den Markt für Wäsche mit ihren verführerischen und nostalgischen Entwürfen regelrecht umgekrempelt. Der Boulevardpresse ist es jedes Mal eine Schlagzeile wert, wenn ein Neo-Promi in einem ihrer Läden im Boudoirstil einkauft. Und das nicht nur, weil die Person Slips ohne Schritt, Pasties mit Pailletten oder flauschige High-Heel-Pantöffelchen erworben haben könnte. Genaueres werden wir wohl nie erfahren, weil die Verkäuferinnen bei AP – selbst zuckersüße Erscheinungen in ihren zugeknöpften babyrosa Hemdblusenkleidern (ein Entwurf von Vivienne Westwood, die zufällig Joes Mum ist) – darauf eingeschworen sind, ihre Geheimnisse aus der VIP-Umkleide niemals preiszugeben. Das Ehepaar Rees-Corre (sie Jahrgang 1968, er Jahrgang 1969) entwirft inzwischen ein ganzes Lingerie-Sortiment, das jeder Diva gerecht wird, dazu Accessoires, Schmuck, scharfe Ledersachen, Schuhe und Strumpfwaren. Ein inzwischen preisgekröntes Parfum kam 2000 auf den Markt, bald gefolgt von reichlich hübschen Kleinigkeiten für Bad und Boudoir –

Kerzen, Lotionen und sogar eine Brustwarzencreme. Das Label ist berühmt für die gewagte Schaufensterdeko seiner Boutiquen und für die ebenso ansprechende Seite des Online-Stores. Leidenschaft prägt einfach alles, was Agent Provocateur macht. Und man findet die Produkte nicht nur in den aufregendsten Schlafzimmern: 1997 waren sie in der Ausstellung „Cutting Edge" des Victoria & Albert Museums zu sehen, 2000 bei „Inside Out" im Design Museum in London. Ob bei der nicht jugendfreien Werbung, bei Musikprojekten wie der erfolgreichen CD „Peep Show" (2004) oder bei Kooperationen mit Marks & Spencer und der Tate Modern – AP steht immer im Dienste der sexuellen Befreiung, allerdings auf die denkbar geschmackvollste Weise.

De Soho à Las Vegas, Agent Provocateur est la marque de prédilection des amateurs de dessous sexy. Depuis qu'ils ont fondé leur entreprise en 1994, Serena Rees et Joe Corre, les inventeurs d'AP, ont révolutionné le marché de la lingerie grâce à leurs créations séduisantes et nostalgiques. Quand une star en devenir est repérée en train de faire du shopping dans l'un de leurs boudoirs, elle est sûre de faire la une des tabloïds anglais, qui la soupçonneront d'avoir acheté des culottes sans fond, des cache-tétons à paillettes ou des mules en peluche à talons aiguilles. Mais on n'en apprendra sans doute jamais plus, car la vendeuse d'AP, toute appétissante dans sa robe-chemisier rose layette boutonnée de haut en bas (une création de Vivienne Westwood, qui se trouve être la maman de Joe) a juré de ne jamais révéler les secrets de la salle d'essayage VIP. Les époux Serena Rees (née en 1968) et Joe Corre (né en 1969) conçoivent ainsi une gamme complète de lingerie destinée aux déesses du glamour, mais aussi des accessoires, des bijoux, d'irrésistibles créations en cuir, des chaussures et des bas. En l'an 2000, ils ont lancé un parfum maintes fois primé, rapidement suivi par une profusion de fantaisies pour la salle de bains et la chambre : des bougies, des crèmes et même un baume bouts de seins. Réputé pour les vitrines aguicheuses de ses boutiques et pour son site Web tout aussi accueillant, le duo Agent Provocateur investit une passion évidente dans tout ce qu'il entreprend. Et on ne retrouve pas son travail que dans les chambres à coucher les plus folles : il a été présenté dans le cadre de l'exposition «Cutting Edge» du Victoria & Albert Museum de Londres en 1997, ainsi qu'à l'exposition itinérante «The Inside Out» du Design Museum en l'an 2000. Que ce soit dans ses publicités interdites aux moins de 18 ans, ses projets musicaux tels que le CD «Peep Show», bien accueilli en 2004, ou ses collaborations avec Marks & Spencer et le musée Tate Modern, AP parle toujours d'une libération sexuelle menée, bien évidemment, dans le respect du meilleur goût possible.

TERRY NEWMAN

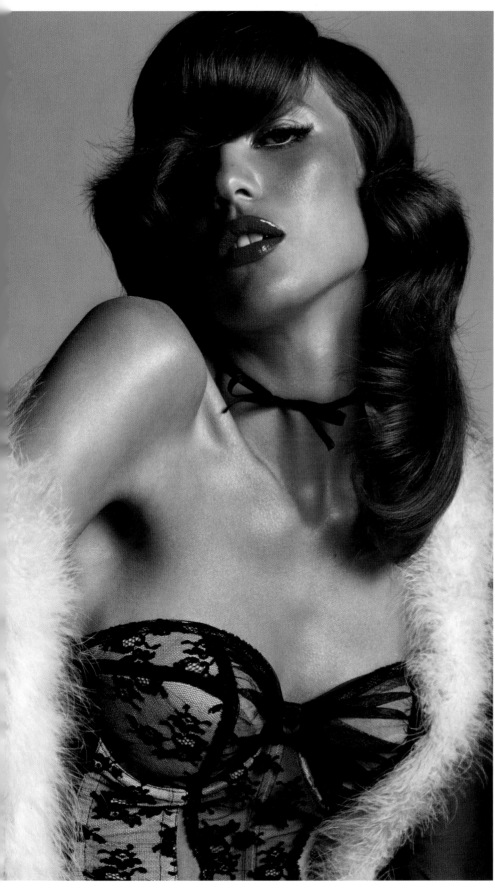

What are your signature designs? Our signature is the introduction of colour and fashion fabrics into lingerie. We're constantly changing and offering new styles all year round, not just collections twice a year. We lead where others follow **What are your favourite pieces from any of your collections?** We love all of the collections, we never put anything in that we don't personally believe in. We don't really have favourites, they change day to day with our moods **How would you describe your work?** Hard and sexy **What's your ultimate goal?** To continue working in an honest way – do only what you believe in **What inspires you?** A great arse **Can fashion still have a political ambition?** At certain points in time fashion has been about joining a gang and the gang's objective can be political **Who do you have in mind when you design?** Girls, girls, girls: sex kittens, sex bombs, seductresses, naughty girls, secretaries, schoolgirls and Kate Moss **Is the idea of creative collaboration important to you?** In our position it is vital – we have both a male and female point of view **What has been the greatest influence on your career?** The quest for excellence in one's technique **How have your own experiences affected your work as designers?** Previous disappointments by discovering dreadful undies on various different sexual escapades **Is designing difficult for you?** No **Have you ever been influenced or moved by the reaction to your designs?** At parties girls are constantly lifting their skirts and tops to show us their undies **What's your definition of beauty?** A fantastic mind. A brilliant smile. A great arse **What's your philosophy?** To only sell what we personally like and not blab about who wears our knickers **What is the most important lesson you've learned?** It's okay to make mistakes, but don't make the same mistake twice.

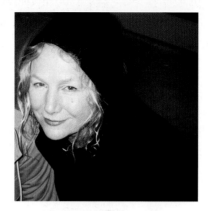

AGNÈS B.

"I love to meet someone who shows me his jacket and says: "Look at it, it's all worn, I have been wearing it for 6 years!"

Believing that things do not have to be complicated to be beautiful, agnès b. designs clothes, simply, rather than high fashion. Shying away from global business practices, her outlook is alluringly fresh. Her style might be summed up as modern, crisp and definite. Born in Versailles (1941) as Agnès Trouble, she studied at Paris' Ecole Nationale Supérieure des Beaux-Arts before starting work as a junior editor for French Elle. From here she assisted the designer Dorothée Bis as a stylist and worked as a freelance designer before opening her own Parisian boutique in 1975. A tonic for any wardrobe, agnès b. designs are intended to make one feel good within one's own skin. Her tailoring creates an air of unadulterated elegance, while her simple angular cuts ensure timelessness. A true lover of people rather than fashion, she neither shops nor attends catwalk shows, choosing instead to find inspiration in 'people watching', a trait she describes as very French. From her popular snap cardigan to her press-studded cotton jackets there's something resolutely personal in agnès b. designs. She'll remake a piece from a past season if a customer requests it, reiterating her belief that people are more important than the clothes. With over 118 boutiques around the world, agnès b.'s business has grown without advertising. Her collections include clothes and accessories for all – maternity, babies and teenagers included. She is also a photographer, film producer and avid art collector. With two art galleries, a modern art magazine and a cinema production company of her own, agnès b. has got her finger on the pulse of the creative world.

Gemäß der Überzeugung, dass etwas nicht kompliziert sein muss, um schön zu sein, entwirft agnès b. lieber schlichte Sachen als Haute Couture. Abgestoßen von den internationalen Geschäftspraktiken, verfolgt sie einen verlockend unorthodoxen Ansatz. Man könnte ihren Stil als modern, frisch und zielstrebig charakterisieren. Unter dem Namen Agnès Trouble 1941 in Versailles geboren, studierte sie an der Pariser Ecole nationale supérieure des Beaux Arts, bevor sie bei der französischen Elle als Jungredakteurin begann. Von dieser Position aus assistierte sie der Designerin Dorothée Bis als Stylistin und arbeitete als freie Designerin, bevor sie 1975 ihre eigene Boutique in Paris eröffnete. Ihre Kleider sind das reinste Tonikum für jede Garderobe, denn die Entwürfe sind so gestaltet, dass man sich in seiner eigenen Haut wohl fühlt. Sie erzeugen ein Flair unverfälschter Eleganz, die schlichten eckigen Schnitte garantieren Zeitlosigkeit. Die Designerin macht sich mehr aus Menschen als aus Mode und geht daher weder shoppen, noch besucht sie Modenschauen. Ihre Inspirationen holt sie sich lieber beim „Menschen beobachten", einer Passion, die sie als typisch französisch empfindet. Angefangen bei ihrer beliebten Jacke mit Druckknöpfen (Cardigan Pression) bis hin zu nietenbesetzten Baumwolljacken haben die Kreationen von agnès b. etwas absolut Persönliches. Und wenn ein Kunde es wünscht, fertigt sie auch ein Stück aus einer älteren Kollektion noch einmal. Mit inzwischen 118 Filialen weltweit ist das Geschäft von agnès b. ohne jegliche Werbung beträchtlich gewachsen. Ihre Kollektionen umfassen Kleider und Accessoires vom Baby bis zum Teenager. Die Modeschöpferin ist außerdem als Fotografin, Filmproduzentin und leidenschaftliche Kunstsammlerin tätig. Mit zwei Galerien, einer Zeitschrift für moderne Kunst und einer eigenen Filmproduktionsfirma hat agnès b. ihre Finger wahrlich am Puls der Kreativität.

Convaincue que les choses n'ont pas besoin d'être compliquées pour être belles, agnès b. dessine des vêtements, tout simplement, plutôt que des créations d'avant-garde. Elle fuit les grands groupes mondiaux et propose une vision qui séduit par sa fraîcheur. Son style peut être considéré comme moderne, précis et univoque. Née à Versailles (1941) sous le nom d'Agnès Trouble, elle étudie à l'Ecole Nationale Supérieure des Beaux-Arts de Paris avant de travailler comme journaliste junior pour le Elle français. Ensuite, elle assiste Dorothée Bis en tant que styliste et travaille comme créatrice free-lance avant d'ouvrir sa propre boutique parisienne en 1975. Tel un tonique énergisant pour toute garde-robe, les créations agnès b. sont conçues pour que ceux qui les portent se sentent bien dans leur peau. Ses tailleurs dégagent une impression d'élégance pure, avec des coupes simples et angulaires qui ne sont pas près de se démoder. Aimant plus les gens que la mode, elle ne fait pas les boutiques et n'assiste à aucun défilé, préférant puiser son inspiration dans « l'observation des autres », une attitude qu'elle considère comme très française. De son célèbre cardigan à ses vestes de coton à boutons-pression, on distingue quelque chose de résolument personnel dans ses créations. Si un client le lui demande, elle n'hésitera pas à reproduire une pièce d'une saison passée, réitérant sa conviction selon laquelle les personnes comptent plus que les vêtements. Avec 118 boutiques à travers le monde, l'entreprise d'agnès b. s'est développée sans publicité. Ses collections proposent des vêtements et des accessoires pour tous, y compris les femmes enceintes, les bébés et les adolescents. Elle est également photographe, productrice de films et une avide collectionneuse d'art. Avec deux galeries d'art, un magazine d'art moderne et sa propre société de production cinématographique, agnès b. a toujours le doigt sur le pouls du monde créatif.

HOLLY SHACKLETON

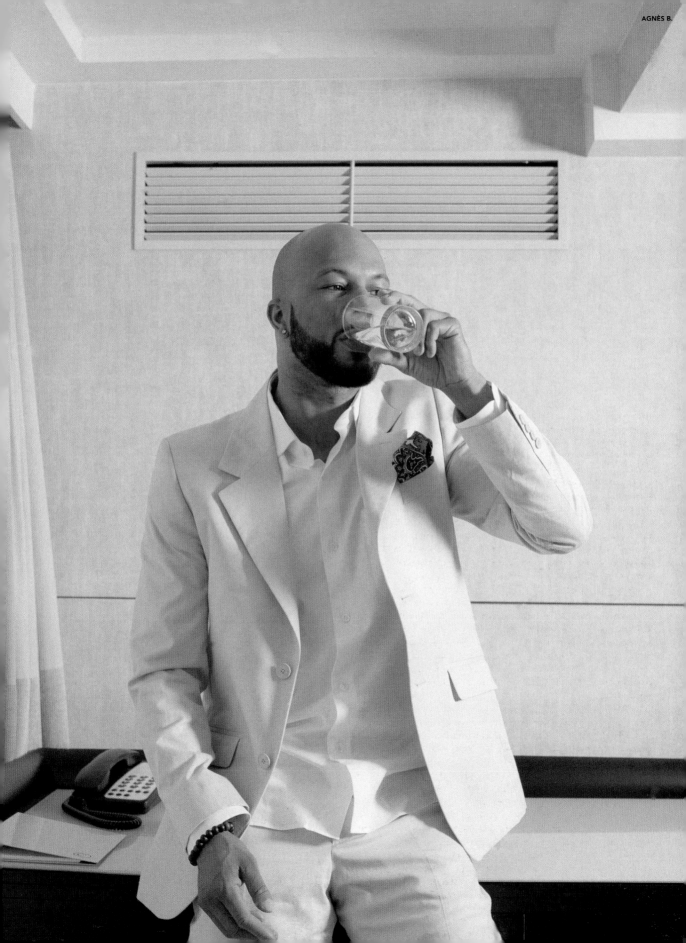

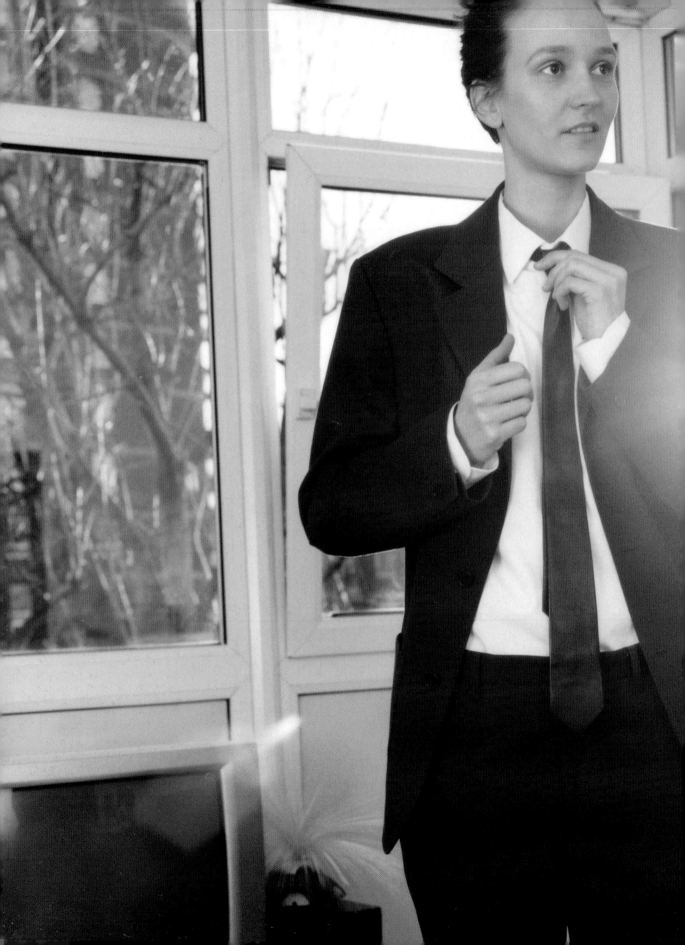

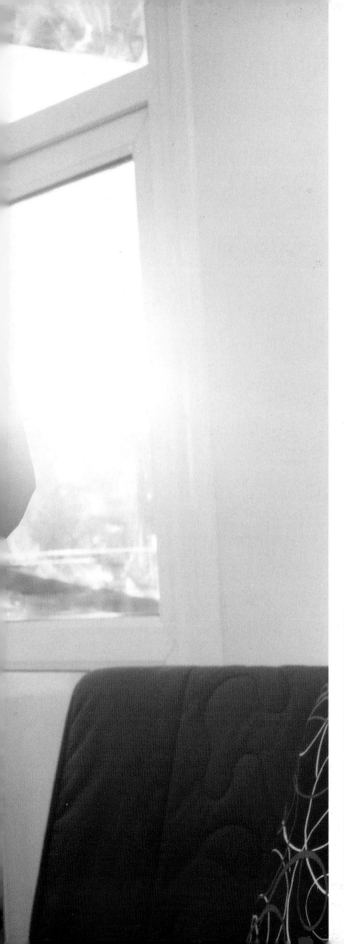

What are your signature designs? The 'snap cardigan' created in 1979, the 'fifre' leather jacket, the wrinkled cotton voile petticoat or skirt **What is your favourite piece from any of your collections?** The one I just did **How would you describe your work?** Exciting, amusing, light, heavy, intense, too much, too cool and never ending! **What is your ultimate goal?** To be where I am, doing my best for love and peace **What inspires you?** I like to watch people in the street, because people astonish me and it can be positive and negative **Can fashion still have a political ambition?** How could it have? But T-shirts have always been and still are a great medium for affirming art, humour and political ideas **Who do you have in mind when you design?** A lot of people! It can be Marilyn or Jackie Kennedy, peasants or artists, Cocteau or my friends **Is the idea of creative collaboration important to you?** I design everything myself, I don't have a studio, but I like very much to collaborate with my team and with the artists on their agnès b. T-shirts **Who has been the greatest influence on your career?** The many people around me with their happiness to be alive, their courage and their good humour **How have your own experiences affected your work as a designer?** I can put myself in any of the times of my life and I think it's great luck! I think I am working with all these feelings. I have very clear memories from the age of two **Which is more important in your work: the process or the product?** The product depends on the process, you can't separate them, and of course it's important to succeed in creation **Is designing difficult for you, and if so, what drives you to continue?** I don't have and never had creative difficulties. I enjoy doing my work and I am quick! Dressing the models for the show is for me like playing with dolls (for men and women) which is the finale of the designs for the season **Have you ever been influenced or moved by the reaction to your designs?** I love to meet someone I don't know who shows me his jacket and says: "Look at it, it's all worn, I have been wearing it for 6 years!" **What's your definition of beauty?** From the encyclopédie Diderot et d'Alembert — completed in the 18th century, "la beauté est une sensation de rapports agréables…": beauty is a sensation of agreeable rapports… **What's your philosophy?** Love them all! **What is the most important lesson you've learned?** Caring for others, and I keep learning.

PHOTOGRAPHY BY ISABEL AND HATTIE, STYLING BY CHARLES ADESANYA, APRIL 2005.

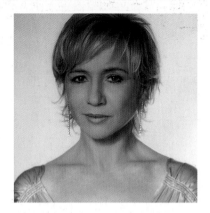

ALBERTA FERRETTI

"I try to transform a dream's magic into reality"

As a woman famed for her fragile little dresses blown together from raw-edged chiffon, appliquéd ribbon and intricate rivulets of beading, Alberta Ferretti is an unlikely player in the boardroom wars of the world's luxury goods groups. Yet Aeffe SpA, the company she founded in 1980 with her brother Massimo as chairman, now owns the controlling stake in Moschino and brokered production and distribution deals with Jean Paul Gaultier (1994) and Narciso Rodriguez (1997). As well as Alberta Ferretti and her successful diffusion line, Philosophy di Alberta Ferretti, Aeffe owns swimwear/lingerie label Velmar and shoemaker Pollini. Born in 1950 in Cattolica, Italy, Ferretti is the daughter of a dressmaker and was raised assisting in her mother's atelier. Not for her the sharp, tight and angular silhouettes of the male Parisian couturiers. Ferretti was inspired instead by a lyrical femininity and fluidity as celebrated in the Fellini movies being made around Cattolica in the 1950s. At the age of 18, Ferretti opened a boutique in her hometown and in 1974 unveiled her own label. 1980 saw Alberta and Massimo go into business together. Alberta Ferretti's debut on the catwalk in Milan came in 1981 with sheer, ethereal chiffons and pin-tucked satin dresses. In 1994 Aeffe annexed the medieval village of Montegridolfo as its Italian headquarters and more than a decade later her collections look as relevant today as they did when Ferretti first proposed delicate, romantic but modern fashion for the new bohemian woman.

Diese Frau, die für ihre zarten Kleidchen aus ungesäumtem Chiffon mit applizierten Bändern und raffinierten Perlenstickereien bekannt ist, kann man sich als Kämpferin auf dem Schlachtfeld der Luxuswarenkonzerne kaum vorstellen. Dabei besitzt Aeffe SpA, die 1980 mit Bruder Massimo als Geschäftsführer gegründete Firma, inzwischen die Mehrheit bei Moschino und blickt auf Produktions- und Vertriebskooperationen mit Jean Paul Gaultier (1994) und Narciso Rodriguez (1997) zurück. Neben dem Label Alberta Ferretti und der erfolgreichen Nebenlinie Philosophy di Alberta Ferretti gehört Aeffe auch noch das Bademoden- und Dessoushaus Velmar sowie die Schuhmarke Pollini. Ferretti kam 1950 im italienischen Cattolica als Tochter einer Schneiderin zur Welt und half schon in ihrer Kindheit im mütterlichen Atelier. Die scharfen, harten und geometrischen Silhouetten der Pariser Couturiers waren noch nie ihre Sache. Ferretti ließ sich stattdessen von einer lyrischen Weiblichkeit und den weichen Konturen inspirieren, wie sie in den Fellini-Filmen gefeiert wurden, die man in den 1950er Jahren in der Gegend um Cattolica drehte. Mit 18 eröffnete Ferretti in ihrer Heimatstadt einen Laden, 1974 präsentierte sie ihr eigenes Label. 1980 schließlich taten sich die Geschwister Alberta und Massimo geschäftlich zusammen. Ihr Debüt auf dem Laufsteg gab Alberta 1981 in Mailand mit hauchdünnen ätherischen Chiffonkleidchen und mit Stecknadeln gerafften Satinroben. 1994 erkor Aeffe das mittelalterliche Städtchen Montegridolfo zu seinem Firmensitz in Italien. Mehr als ein Jahrzehnt später sind die Kollektionen immer noch so bedeutend wie damals, als Ferretti erstmals zarte, romantische, aber durchaus moderne Mode für die neue Frau der Bohème vorstellte.

Réputée pour ses délicates petites robes en mousseline de soie aux finitions brutes, applications de rubans et rivières de perles très élaborées, Alberta Ferretti fait figure de personnage improbable au sein des guerres que se livrent les conseils d'administration des grands groupes de luxe mondiaux. Pourtant, Aeffe SpA, l'entreprise qu'elle fonde en 1980 avec son frère Massimo au poste de président, possède aujourd'hui une part majoritaire dans la société Moschino et a conclu des accords de production et de distribution avec Jean Paul Gaultier (1994) et Narciso Rodriguez (1997). Aux côtés de la griffe Alberta Ferretti et de sa ligne à succès Philosophy di Alberta Ferretti, Aeffe possède la marque de maillots de bain et de lingerie Velmar, ainsi que le fabricant de chaussures Pollini. Fille de couturière, Alberta Ferretti est née en 1950 à Cattolica en Italie et grandit dans l'atelier de sa mère dont elle est aussi l'assistante. Les silhouettes acérées, angulaires et restreintes des couturiers parisiens ne la séduisent pas. Elle s'inspire au contraire de la féminité lyrique et de la fluidité célébrées dans les films que Fellini tourne dans la région de Cattolica dans les années 1950. A 18 ans, Alberta Ferretti ouvre une boutique dans sa ville natale avant de lancer sa propre griffe en 1974. En 1980, Alberta et Massimo s'associent en affaires. Pour son premier défilé à Milan en 1981, Alberta Ferretti présente des robes transparentes et aériennes en mousseline de soie et en satin nervuré. En 1994, Aeffe installe son siège italien dans le village médiéval de Montegridolfo. Dix ans plus tard, ses collections semblent toujours autant d'actualité qu'à l'époque où la créatrice proposait pour la première fois sa mode délicate, romantique mais néanmoins moderne à l'intention des nouvelles bohémiennes. JAMES SHERWOOD

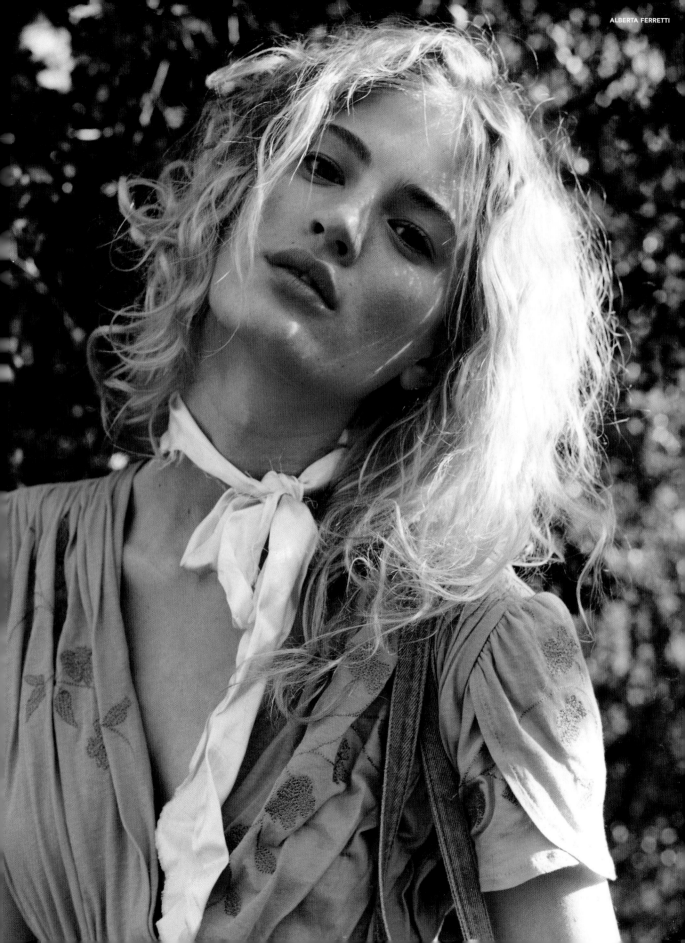

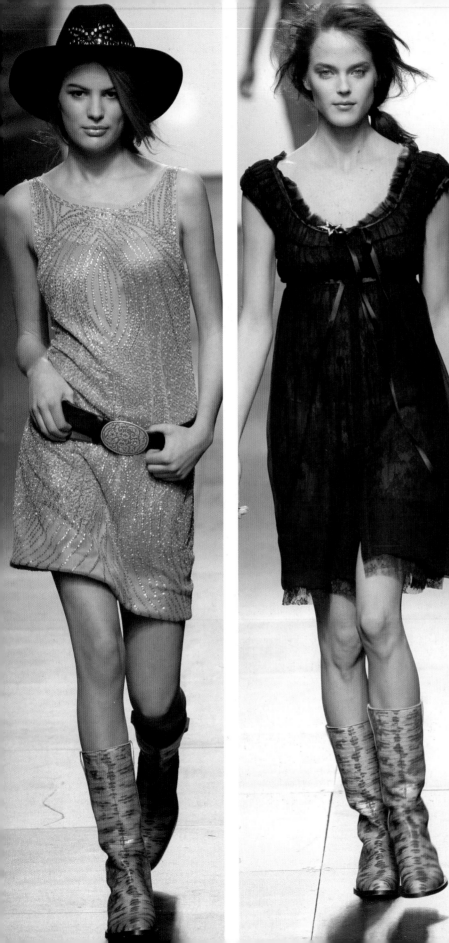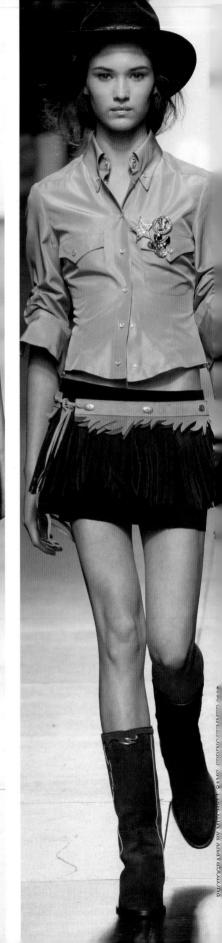

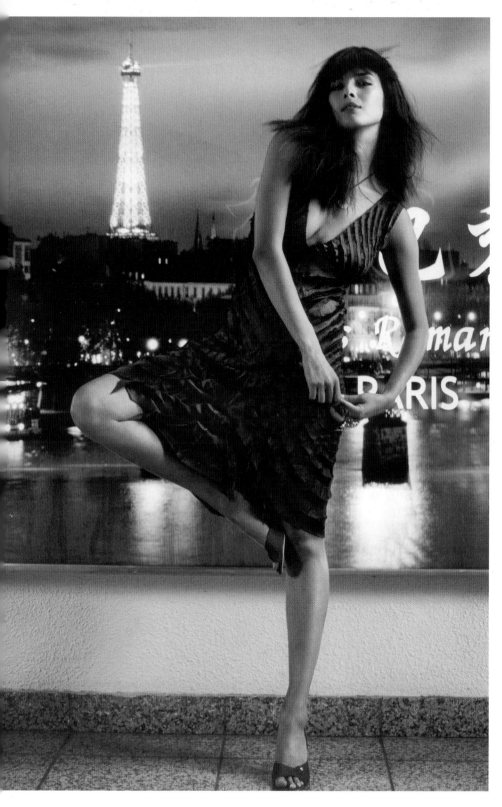

What are your signature designs? Lightness What is your favourite piece from any of your collections? The one that best represents my style How would you describe your work? Challenging, stimulating, satisfying What's your ultimate goal? To create a dress like the Intarsia dresses of my Alberta Ferretti autumn/winter 2004 collection. Like the one that Scarlett Johansson wore for the Oscars in 2004 What inspires you? Emotions Can fashion still have a political ambition? Particular styles in dressing can underline belonging to a group with a specific and identifiable ideology. Only in that sense can we say that fashion has political ambitions Who do you have in mind when you design? Not a specific person, but I try to transform a dream's magic into reality Is the idea of creative collaboration important to you? Yes, as working with the others is essential to moving forward Who has been the greatest influence on your career? Myself: from the endless challenges I face to the effort I make to improve myself and reach new goals How have your own experiences affected your work as a designer? I decided to become a designer watching my mother working in her atelier and there I started loving fabrics and dresses, draped carefully following the harmony and proportions of the feminine silhouette Which is more important in your work: the process or the product? There is no outcome without process, elaborating without producing is sterile. The result really only comes from the union of these two phases Is designing difficult for you, and if so, what drives you to continue? No, designing is my passion. It's almost a necessity, keeping the creativity alive Have you ever been influenced or moved by the reaction to your designs? I consider the opinion of others, but it is fundamental to maintain my concept of elegance, femininity and sensuality What's your definition of beauty? In my opinion beauty is the harmony created by the dress and the woman who wears it What's your philosophy? In addition to my younger line, I try to emphasise the personality and elegance of women What is the most important lesson you've learned? Everyday life is full of lessons. All of them are important. There is always something to learn.

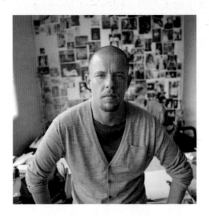

ALEXANDER MCQUEEN

"There is still a lot I want to achieve.
There isn't any room for complacency in this head!"

The Gothic sensibility of a Brothers Grimm fairytale is closer in spirit to Alexander McQueen's clothing than the fetish, gore and misogyny he's been accused of promoting. However dark McQueen's design, it still achieves a femininity that has seduced everyone from Björk to the Duchess of Westminster. McQueen's rise to power is a fashion fairytale all of its own. The East End taxi driver's son, born in 1969, is apprenticed to the Prince of Wales' tailor Anderson & Sheppard on Savile Row where he infamously scrawls obscenities into the linings of HRH's suits. He works with Romeo Gigli, theatrical costumers Angels & Bermans and Koji Tatsuno before Central Saint Martins MA course director Bobby Hilson suggests he enrol. His 1992 'Jack the Ripper' graduation collection thrills members of the British fashion press, none more so than Isabella Blow who buys the entire collection and adopts McQueen as one of her protégés. McQueen's bloodline of angular, aggressive tailoring is inherited from MGM costume designer Adrian, Christian Dior and Thierry Mugler. His 'Highland Rape' and 'The Birds' collections used Mr Pearl corsetry to draw in the waist and exaggerate square shoulders and sharp pencil skirts. Brutality tempered by a lyricism characterises the McQueen style. By 1996 he was named British Designer of the Year. 1996 also saw McQueen replace John Galliano as head of Givenchy haute couture. But by 2001 the Gucci Group had acquired a controlling stake in McQueen's own label and the designer left both Givenchy and LVMH. Since then, McQueen's eponymous label has dazzled Paris with bittersweet theatrical presentations. 2003 saw the launch of his first perfume, Kingdom, and a bespoke menswear collection produced by Savile Row tailor Huntsman; in 2004 his men's ready-to-wear was shown in Milan for the first time.

Die Kleidung von Alexander McQueen entspricht in ihrem Geist eher dem schauerlichen Reiz eines Märchens der Gebrüder Grimm als dem Fetischcharakter, der Blutrünstigkeit und der Frauenfeindlichkeit, die man ihm vorwirft. Wie düster die Entwürfe McQueens auch sein mögen, er erzielt damit dennoch eine Weiblichkeit, die Frauen angefangen bei Björk und bis hin zur Herzogin von Westminster ansprach. McQueens Aufstieg zur Macht ist für sich genommen schon ein Märchen. Der Sohn eines Taxifahrers aus dem Londoner East End wurde 1969 geboren und absolvierte seine Lehre beim Schneider des Prince of Wales, Anderson & Sheppard, in der Savile Row. Dort kritzelte er heimlich Obszönitäten in das Futter der Anzüge Seiner Königlichen Hoheit. Anschließend arbeitet er mit Romeo Gigli sowie den Kostümbildnern Angels & Berman und Koji Tatsuno, bevor ihm der Leiter des Magisterstudienganges Bobby Hilson vorschlug, sich am Central Saint Martins zu immatrikulieren. Mit seiner Abschlusskollektion „Jack the Ripper" entzückte er 1992 die britische Modepresse wie auch Isabella Blow, die die gesamte Kollektion kaufte und McQueen als Protegé unter ihre Fittiche nahm. McQueens kantige, geradezu aggressive Form der Schneiderei hat ihre Wurzeln beim MGM-Kostümdesigner Adrian, bei Christian Dior und

Thierry Mugler. Für seine Kollektionen ‚Highland Rape' und „The Birds" benutzte er Korsetts von Mr Pearl, um die Taillen zu verschmälern und so die eckigen Schultern wie auch die scharf geschnittenen Bleistiftröcke zu betonen. Durch einen lyrischen Charakter gemäßigte Brutalität zeichnet McQueens Stil aus. 1996 wurde er British Designer of the Year und trat die Nachfolge von John Galliano als Chef der Haute Couture bei Givenchy an. 2001 hatte der Gucci-Konzern allerdings schon die Kontrollmehrheit an McQueens eigenem Label erworben, und so verließ der Designer Givenchy und LVMH. Seit damals hat McQueen mit dem nach ihm benannten Label Paris schon mehrfach mit bittersüßen, theatralischen Präsentationen verwirrt. 2003 wurde mit Kingdom sein erstes Parfum lanciert sowie eine Maßkollektion für Herren, produziert vom Savile-Row-Schneider Huntsman. Seine erste Prêt-à-porter-Kollektion für Herren war 2004 in Mailand zu sehen.

Souvent accusé de faire la promotion du fétichisme, d'un certain côté gore et de la misogynie, la mode d'Alexander McQueen est pourtant plus proche de la sensibilité gothique d'un conte de Grimm. Quelle que soit l'importance du côté obscur de McQueen dans son travail, il propose toujours une féminité qui séduit le plus grand nombre, de Bjork à la Duchesse de Westminster. En fait, la montée en puissance de McQueen relève du conte de fées. Né en 1969 d'un père chauffeur de taxi dans l'East End, il commence son apprentissage à Savile Row chez Anderson & Sheppard, tailleurs du Prince de Galles, où l'on raconte qu'il gribouillait des obscénités dans les doublures des costumes de Son Altesse Royale. Il travaille ensuite avec Romeo Gigli, les costumiers de théâtre Angels & Bermans ainsi que pour Koji Tatsuno, avant de suivre un cursus à Central Saint Martins sur les conseils de Bobby Hilson, son directeur d'études. En 1992, sa collection de fin d'études « Jack the Ripper » ravit les journalistes de mode britanniques et en particulier Isabella Blow qui, en achetant l'intégralité de sa collection, fait entrer McQueen dans le cercle de ses protégés. Les coupes signature de McQueen, viscéralement angulaires et brutales, lui ont été inspirées par Adrian, costumier de la MGM, par Christian Dior et Thierry Mugler. Ses collections « Highland Rape » et « The Birds » utilisaient des corsets de M. Pearl pour cintrer la taille et exagérer les épaules carrées et les jupes droites aux lignes sévères. La brutalité tempérée par le lyrisme, tel est le style McQueen. En 1996, il remporte le prix de British Designer of the Year. La même année, il est nommé directeur de la création haute couture chez Givenchy, où il succède à John Galliano. Mais en 2001, le Groupe Gucci acquiert une part majoritaire dans la propre griffe du créateur, qui décide de quitter Givenchy et LVMH. Depuis, la griffe éponyme de McQueen ne cesse d'éblouir le tout – Paris à travers des présentations grandiloquentes au style doux-amer. En 2003, le créateur lance son premier parfum, Kingdom, ainsi qu'une collection pour homme « à façon » produite par le tailleur Huntsman de Savile Row ; en 2004, il présente pour la première fois sa ligne de prêt-à-porter pour homme à Milan.

JAMES SHERWOOD

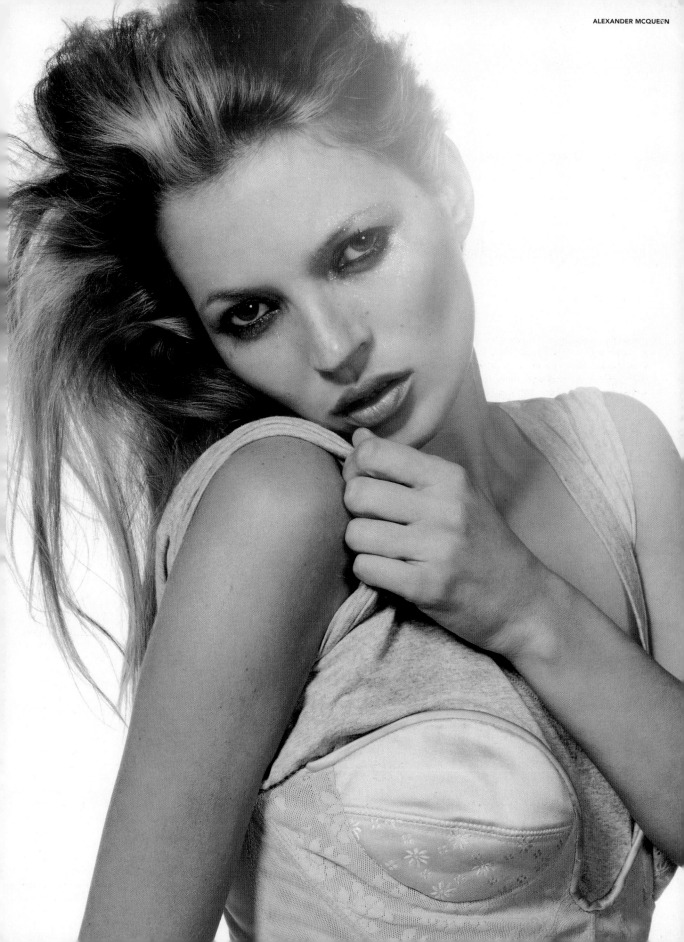

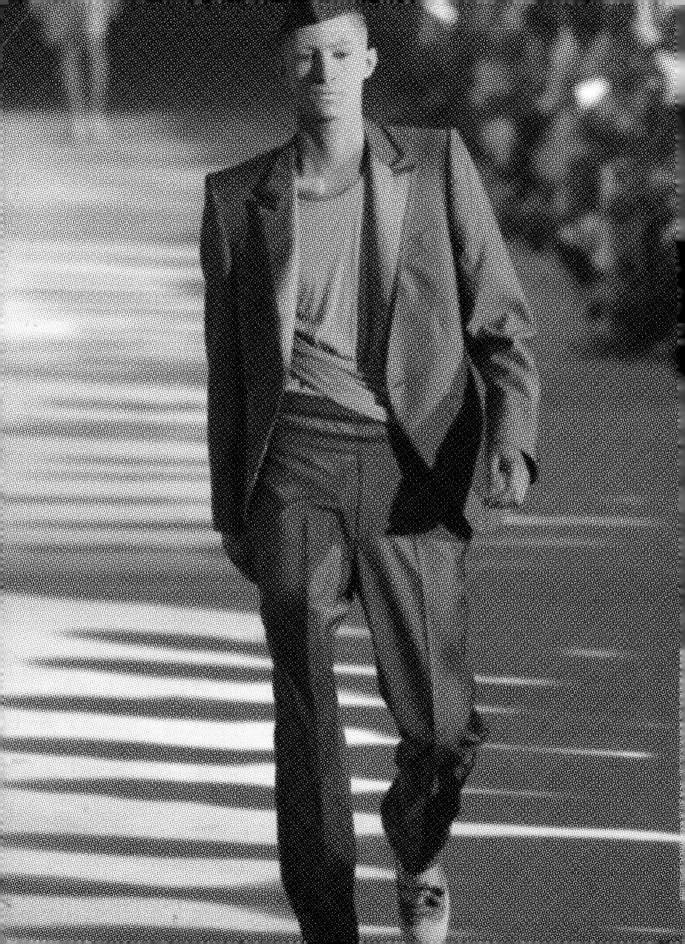

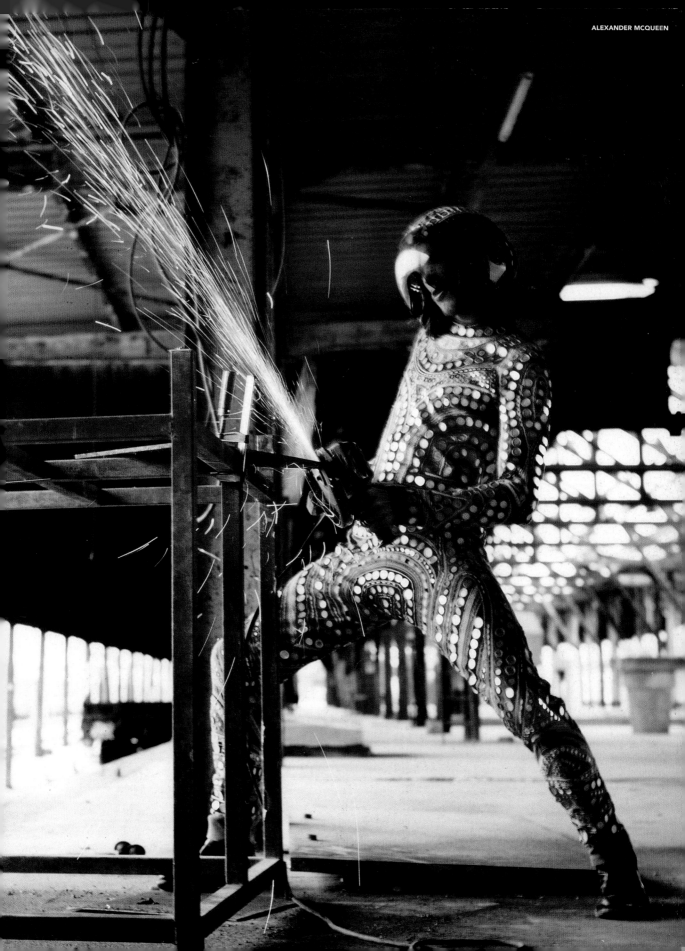

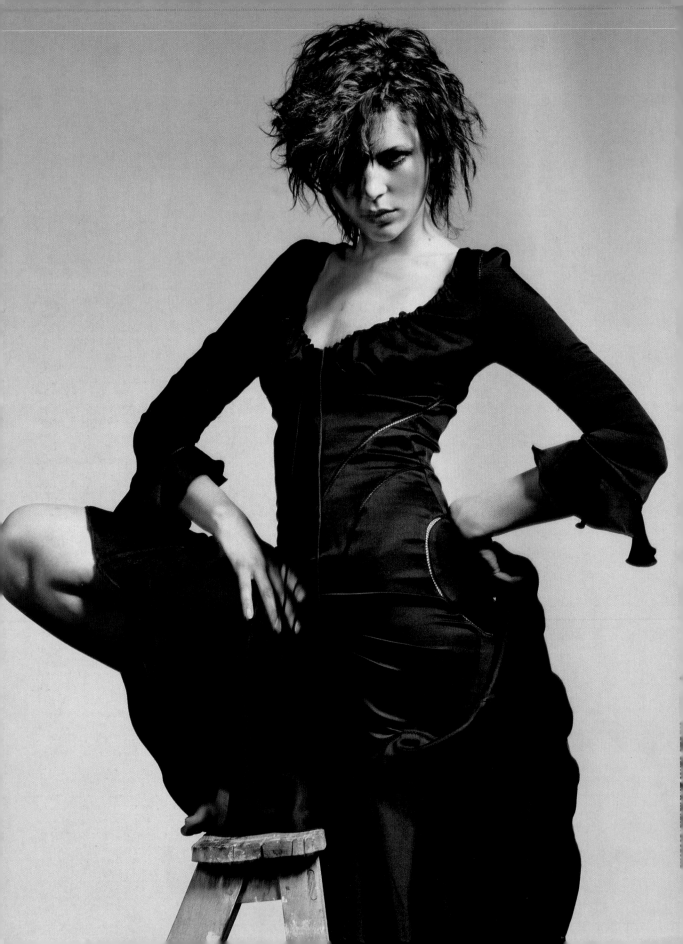

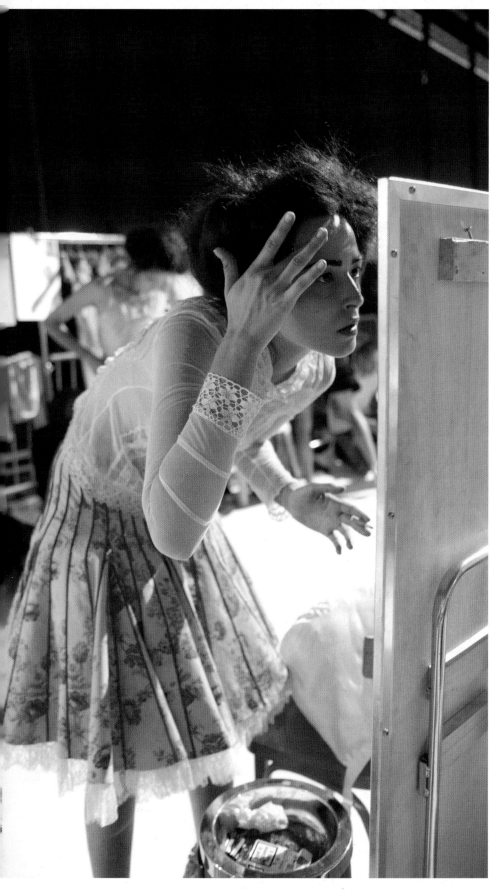

What are your signature designs? Signature pieces include the bumster, the frock coat, anything trompe-l'œil **What is your favourite piece from any of your collections?** The wooden fan kilts from spring/summer 1999, the red slide dress from spring/summer 2001, the jellyfish dress from autumn/winter 2002 **How would you describe your work?** Electric, eccentric **What's your ultimate goal?** To offer haute couture pieces as an integral part of the ready-to-wear collection **What inspires you?** I find a multitude of influences inspiring – homeless to the rich, vulgar to the common **Can fashion still have a political ambition?** Because fashion is so indicative of the political and social climate in which we live, what we wear will always be a symptom of our environment **Who do you have in mind when you design?** A strong independent woman who loves and lives fearlessly in equal measure **Is the idea of creative collaboration important to you?** Collaborations give me the opportunity to work with peers who I admire, as well as pushing myself creatively. What's the point otherwise? **Who has been the greatest influence on your career?** Anyone I come into contact with and find a connection with **How have your own experiences affected your work as a designer?** Working with the atelier at Givenchy showed me the possibilities that only haute couture can give a designer, where craftsmanship suddenly becomes state of the art **Which is more important in your work: the process or the product?** Design development allows you to make mistakes; without screwing up once in a while you can't ever move forward **Is designing difficult for you, if so, what drives you to continue?** I enjoy putting the whole picture together – from the initial design phase to the shows and the stores. It's rewarding to see the entire concept work in unison. There is still a lot I want to achieve, my mind works very quickly and there isn't any room for complacency in this head! **Have you ever been influenced or moved by the reaction to your designs?** When I watched Shalom Harlow being spray painted as the finale of my spring/summer 2000 show I was very moved. She was so poetic and elegant that I could hear the audience gasp – it really moved me to hear such an immediate reaction to my work **What's your definition of beauty?** An image that combines opposing or unusual aesthetics **What's your philosophy?** To make a piece that can transcend any trend and will still hold as much presence in 100 years' time, when you find it in an antique store, as when you bought it in my store yesterday **What is the most important lesson you've learned?** How trust really works.

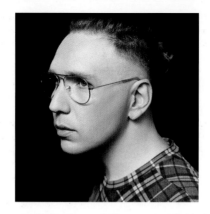

ALEXANDRE HERCHCOVITCH

"I am too emotional sometimes, but I
rationally think about shape"

Latex from the Amazon jungle, bold splashes of colour, hectic prints allied to an often austere silhouette: all of these are signatures for Brazil's most prolific designer, Alexandre Herchcovitch. Of Romanian and Polish extraction but born in São Paulo, the designer knew at the age of ten what he wanted to do with his life. While attending a local Jewish orthodox school he made clothes and often dressed his mother, who ran a lingerie factory. The fashion training that followed was completed at the Catholic institution Santa Marcelina College of Arts, also in his home city. Herchcovitch wasted no time launching an eponymous line, which was first conceived and shown in Brazil in 1993. More recently his designs have been seen on the runways of London, Paris and New York. His spring/summer 2005 collection marked his debut in Manhattan where he transformed the catwalk into a bright, floral maze that clashed appropriately with his eclectic prints and colourful designs. Inspired by politics and art, Herchcovitch's unique Brazilian flavour is mixed with myriad influences which result in complex clothes for people who are not shy of making a statement. For example: a tailored jacket may look straightforward when viewed from the front, but a cascade of colourful fabric ruffles dance down its back, finishing in a floor-sweeping train. This kind of outfit illustrates his philosophy of producing wearable art for both men and women. However, Herchcovitch is savvy enough to know that flamboyance isn't for everyone, so simpler separates also feature in his collections. In addition to his menswear and womenswear lines, he also produces four denim collections a year, has two stores in São Paulo and boasts a handful of partnerships with major companies, including Converse.

Latex aus dem Dschungel des Amazonas, kräftige Farbtupfer, aufregende Muster, verbunden mit einer oft nüchternen Silhouette: Das sind die Charakteristika des produktivsten brasilianischen Designers. Der in São Paulo geborene Alexandre Herchcovitch ist rumänisch-polnischer Abstammung und wusste schon im Alter von zehn Jahren, was er einmal werden wollte. Noch während er die örtliche jüdisch-orthodoxe Schule besuchte, entwarf er eigene Teile und kleidete seine Mutter ein, die eine Dessousfirma führte. Sein Modestudium absolvierte er am katholischen Santa Marcelina College of Arts in seiner Heimatstadt. Danach verlor Herchcovitch keine Zeit und lancierte zunächst 1993 in Brasilien eine eigene, nach ihm benannte Modelinie. In jüngster Zeit waren seine Kollektionen aber auch auf den Catwalks von London, Paris und New York zu sehen. Mit der Kollektion Frühjahr/Sommer 2005 gab er sein Debüt in Manhattan. Aus diesem Anlass verwandelte er den Laufsteg in ein fröhliches Pflanzenlabyrinth, das sich wie gewünscht mit seinen eklektischen Mustern und farbenfrohen Designs „biss". Inspiriert von Politik und Kunst, kombiniert Herchcovitch sei-

nen typisch brasilianischen Geschmack mit Myriaden von Einflüssen. Das ganze resultiert in komplexen Kleidern für Leute, die sich nicht scheuen, mit ihrer Kleidung ein Statement abzugeben. Die auf Figur geschnittene Jacke etwa mag von vorn ganz normal aussehen, allerdings ergießt sich über ihre Rückseite ein Wasserfall bunter Rüschen, die in einer bodenlangen Schleppe auslaufen. Diese Art Outfit verkörpert seine Auffassung von Mode als tragbare Kunst für Damen und Herren. Herchcovitch ist jedoch klug genug zu wissen, dass Extravaganz nichts für Jedermann ist, und präsentiert deshalb in seinen Kollektionen auch schlichtere Einzelteile. Zu den Linien für Damen und Herren kommen noch vier Jeanskollektionen pro Jahr, die er in zwei eigenen Läden in São Paulo verkauft sowie über eine Handvoll Kooperationen mit größeren Unternehmen wie Converse vertreibt.

Latex de la jungle amazonienne, éclaboussures colorées et audacieuses, imprimés désordonnés, conjugués à une silhouette souvent austère : telles sont les signatures d'Alexandre Herchcovitch, le créateur le plus prolifique du Brésil. D'origine roumaine et polonaise mais né à São Paulo, il sait dès l'âge de dix ans ce qu'il compte faire de sa vie. Encore élève de l'école juive orthodoxe de son quartier, il crée déjà ses propres vêtements et habille souvent sa mère, qui dirige une usine de lingerie. Il entame ensuite sa formation en mode au Santa Marcelina College of Arts, une institution catholique de sa ville natale. Herchcovitch n'attend pas longtemps avant de lancer sa ligne éponyme, conçue et présentée pour la première fois au Brésil en 1993. Dernièrement, on a pu admirer ses créations sur les podiums de Londres, Paris et New York. Sa collection printemps/été 2005 marque ses débuts à Manhattan : il transforme le podium en un labyrinthe floral vivant, en parfaite résonance avec ses imprimés éclectiques et ses créations colorées. Inspiré tant par la politique que par l'art, Herchcovitch mêle sa vibration brésilienne unique à une myriade d'influences pour produire des vêtements complexes, destinés à tous ceux qui n'ont pas peur d'exprimer leur personnalité. Par exemple, une veste de tailleur peut sembler toute simple vue de face, mais, vue de dos, elle arbore une cascade dansante de volants colorés prolongée d'une traîne balayant le sol. Ce genre de tenue illustre parfaitement la philosophie du créateur, qui cherche à proposer des œuvres d'art portables par les hommes comme les femmes. Mais Herchcovitch connaît assez bien son métier pour savoir que la flamboyance ne convient pas à tout le monde; et ses collections proposent donc aussi des séparés plus faciles à porter. Outre ses lignes pour homme et pour femme, il produit également quatre collections en denim chaque année, possède deux boutiques à São Paulo et revendique plusieurs partenariats avec de grandes entreprises telles que Converse. SIMON CHILVERS

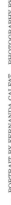

What are your signature designs? The way I work with contrasts of shape, texture, fabric weight and colour **What is your favourite piece from any of your collections?** A dress with a tail turns into a jumpsuit with an apron (autumn/winter 1988); patchwork dress with aluminum chains inserted (spring/summer 2002); a T-shirt with a Pomba-Gira (an African-Brazilian goddess from Umbanda, she's a bit of a devil-woman spring/summer 1995); unisex skirt with legs of trousers attached, later called 'skousers' (autumn/winter 1996); black ruffled rubber dress (autumn/winter 2004); natural rubber with colourful flowers round dress (spring/summer 2005) **How would you describe your work?** A formal research on clothes-making, and a way to express my emotions, thoughts and criticise society from a very personal point of view **What's your ultimate goal?** I am working as a director in a fashion university in São Paulo, Brazil, called FMU and being part of an exhibition at the Metropolitan Museum in New York called 'Wild – Fashion Untamed' with two rubber dresses **What inspires you?** My own daily life, my own work, my family and friends and people on the streets **Can fashion still have a political ambition?** It must, especially at times when it seems to move away from politics **Who do you have in mind when you design?** It is a bit of a mess. I am too emotional sometimes, but I rationally think about shape and how to make what I am designing **Is the idea of creative collaboration important to you?** Yes, it's extremely important. I don't work alone, I don't create alone, I listen to everyone I trust and who are around me, working for me, unanimity makes people blind and stupid, we always need other people! **Who has been the greatest influence on your career?** When I was a teenager, Boy George was a great influence on me, and I think that his attitude towards fashion and sexuality drove me to the vision I have of fashion **How have your own experiences affected your work as a designer?** A lot, especially the ones of my adolescence: studying in a Jewish orthodox school, being a Boy George fan, the support my mother gave to me when I decided to be a designer, etc **Which is more important in your work: the process or the product?** Without doubt, both of them, but I still believe that the idea is the starting point. Without a good idea there can't be either a process or a final product **Is designing difficult for you, if so, what drives you to continue?** No, designing is not difficult for me at all! **Have you ever been influenced or moved by the reaction to your designs?** Sometimes… **What's your definition of beauty?** Something that challenges the imagination of the viewer **What's your philosophy?** Fashion is a language that people use to communicate with and hide from each other **What is the most important lesson you've learned?** That I must carry on with my own beliefs, always.

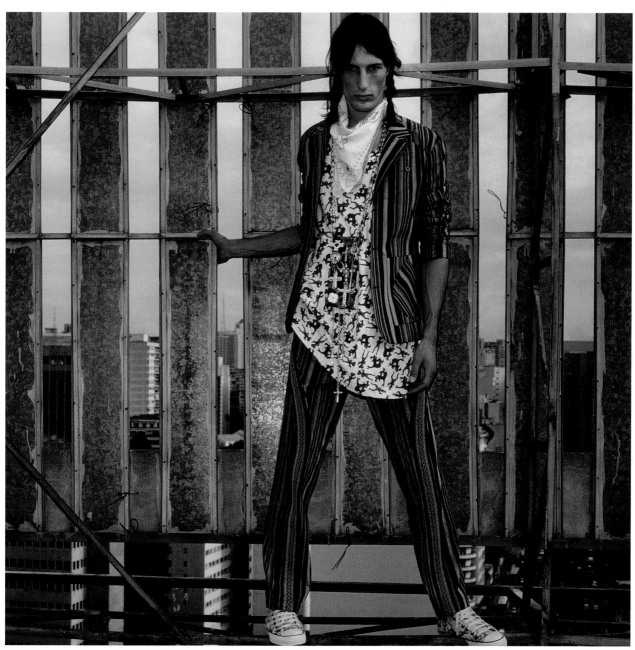

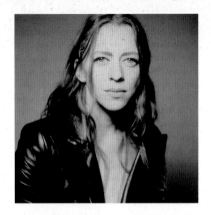

ANN DEMEULEMEESTER

"Fashion has a reason 'to be' because in fashion you can find new kinds of expressions about human beings"

Ann Demeulemeester once told an interviewer that women are not like Barbie dolls, and that she finds a subtle femininity in men most pleasing. Inevitably, then, her own designs for both sexes are far removed from the types of clothing in which bimbos and himbos might typically attire themselves. Hers is a far more personal, subtle and emotional aesthetic, one frequently, and lazily, labelled as androgynous, but which could more accurately be termed as romantically modernist. Born in Belgium, in 1959, Demeulemeester went on to study at Antwerp's Royal Academy, from which she graduated in 1981, as part of the now-legendary Antwerp Six group of designers. In 1985 she launched her own label, along with her husband Patrick Robyn – a man she has cited as her biggest influence – and made her womenswear debut in Paris in 1992. By 1996 she would also be designing menswear collections. Given her long-entrenched fondness for the colour black (she has mainly clad herself in black, since her Patti Smith-loving teens) along with the severity of her earlier work, with its wilfully unfinished look, she became known as a key figure of the deconstruction era of fashion during the late '80s and early '90s. Avoiding the fickle whims and fads of the fashion industry, Demeulemeester has subsequently carved out her own unique niche, not to mention a loyal fan-base which continues to grow. Not surprisingly, the designer now also creates extremely successful shoe and accessory lines, and her collections are sold in over 30 countries around the world. She continues to champion clothing that favours high quality, natural materials – leather, wool and flannels – over less covetable synthetic fabrics, and her poetic mix of edgy rebellion with sensuality, plus slick tailoring with softer layers, creates an ever-intriguing design proposition.

Ann Demeulemeester erklärte einmal in einem Interview, dass Frauen keine Barbiepuppen seien und sie eine Spur Weiblichkeit an Männern schätze. Folglich sind auch ihre Entwürfe für beide Geschlechter weit von der Art Kleidung entfernt, die Lieschen Müller und ihr männliches Pendant üblicherweise tragen. Sie besitzen eine sehr viel individuellere, raffiniertere und emotionalere Ästhetik, die oft aus Bequemlichkeit mit dem Etikett „androgyn" versehen wird. Dabei wäre romantisch-modernistisch viel treffender. Die 1959 in Belgien geborene Demeulemeester studierte an der Königlichen Akademie in Antwerpen, wo sie 1981 als Mitglied des heute legendären Designerteams Antwerp Six ihren Abschluss machte. Ihr eigenes Label präsentierte sie 1985 gemeinsam mit ihrem Ehemann Patrick Robyn – den sie ihren wichtigsten Einfluss von außen nennt. Ihr Damenmoden-Debüt in Paris gab sie 1992. Ab 1996 entwarf sie auch Herrenkollektionen. Ihre lang gehegte Liebe zur Farbe Schwarz (seit ihrer Begeisterung für Patti Smith im Teenageralter kleidet sie sich hauptsächlich schwarz) sowie die Strenge der

frühen Arbeiten mit ihrem absichtlich unfertigen Aussehen machten sie zu einer Schlüsselfigur der dekonstruktivistischen späten 1980er und frühen 1990er Jahre. Demeulemeester mied die kurzlebigen Launen und Marotten der Modeindustrie und schuf sich stattdessen bald eine einzigartige Nische im Markt. Von ihrer treuen, ständig wachsenden Fangemeinde ganz zu schweigen. Deshalb überrascht es auch nicht, dass die Designerin inzwischen außerdem äußerst erfolgreich Schuhe und Accessoires entwirft und ihre Kollektionen in mehr als dreißig Ländern weltweit verkauft. Dabei gibt sie weiterhin einer Mode hoher Qualität den Vorzug, meist aus natürlichen Materialien – Leder, Wolle und Flanell –, kaum einmal aus synthetischen Stoffen. Mit ihrem poetischen Mix aus dezidierter Rebellion und Sinnlichkeit sowie eleganter Schneiderkunst und weichem Lagenlook gelingt ihr ein immer wieder ansprechendes designerisches Statement.

Un jour, Ann Demeulemeester a déclaré dans une interview que les femmes n'étaient pas des poupées Barbie et qu'elle adorait les hommes un peu féminins. Ses créations pour les deux sexes n'ont donc strictement rien à voir avec l'attirail dont se parent généralement les bimbos, hommes ou femmes. Son esthétique, qui se veut avant tout personnelle, subtile et émotionnelle, est souvent étiquetée d'androgyne par les journalistes paresseux, alors qu'elle relève davantage d'un certain romantisme moderne. Née en 1959 en Belgique, Ann Demeulemeester étudie la mode à l'Académie Royale d'Anvers dont elle sort diplômée en 1981, membre d'une promotion de créateurs désormais légendaires : les Antwerp Six. Elle lance sa propre griffe en 1985 avec son mari Patrick Robyn, qu'elle considère comme sa principale influence, et présente son premier défilé pour femme en 1992 à Paris. En 1996, elle commence à dessiner des collections pour homme. Etant donné sa prédilection pour le noir (depuis sa passion adolescente pour Patti Smith, elle ne porte quasiment que du noir) et l'austérité de ses premières créations aux finitions délibérément brutes, elle émerge comme un personnage clé de l'ère déconstructionniste de la fin des années 80 et du début des années 90. Fuyant le grand cirque des médias et de l'industrie de la mode, Ann Demeulemeester s'est imposée sur un marché de niche et revendique un nombre de fans sans cesse croissant. Rien d'étonnant à ce que les lignes de chaussures et d'accessoires qu'elle s'est mise à dessiner remportent un tel succès, ni à ce que ses collections soient vendues dans plus de 30 pays à travers le monde. Elle continue à défendre une mode privilégiant les matières naturelles de qualité supérieure (cuir, laine et flanelles) aux tissus synthétiques moins précieux. Son mélange poétique de rébellion décalée et de sensualité, conjugué à des coupes parfaites et des superpositions de tissus plus douces, produit une mode créative et toujours intrigante.

JAMES ANDERSON

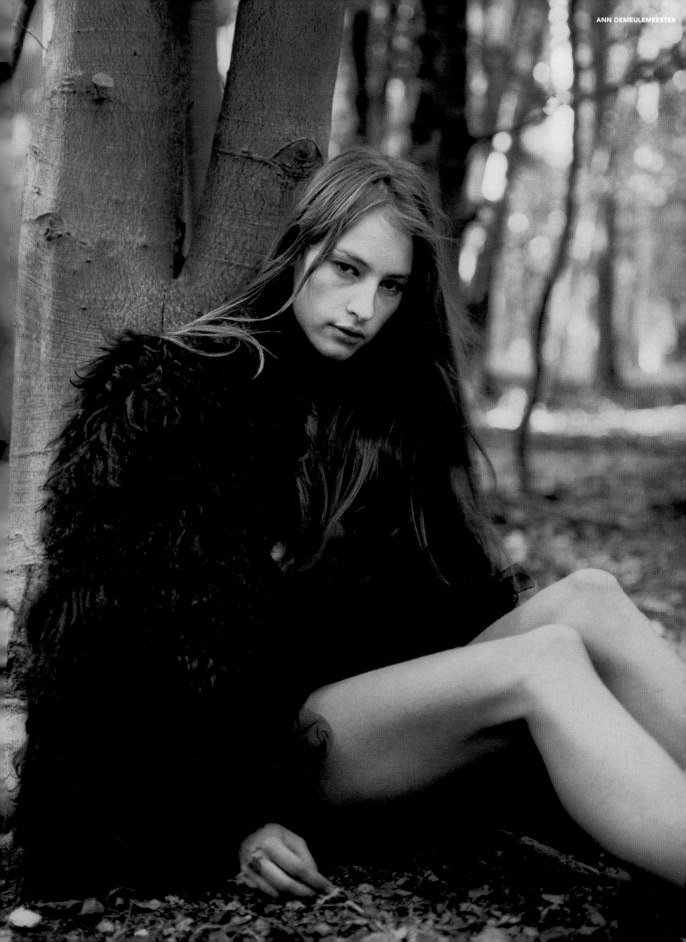

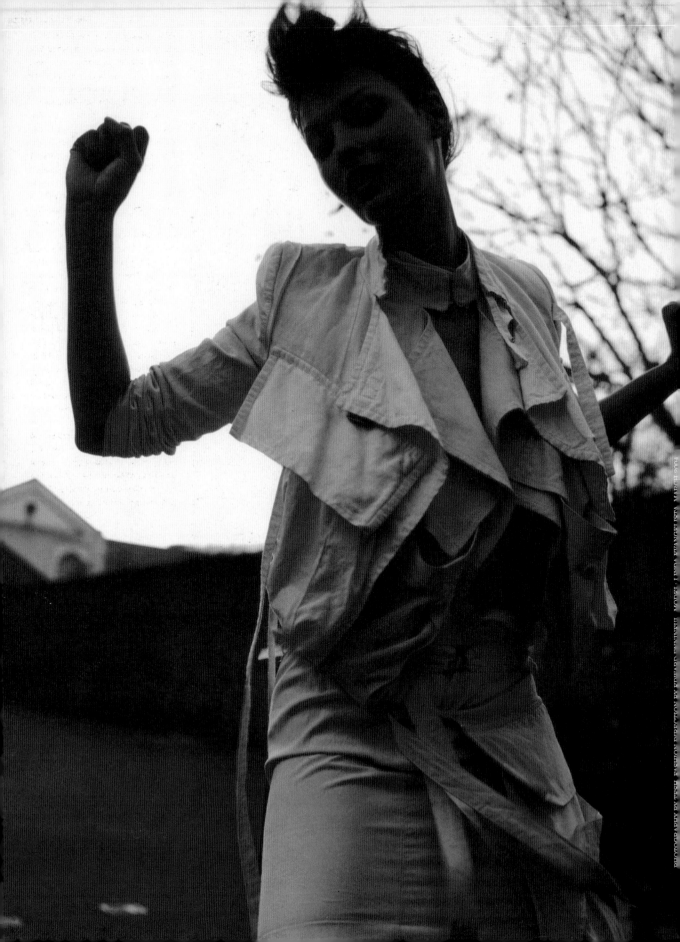

PHOTOGRAPHY BY TESH. FASHION DIRECTION BY EDWARD ENNINFUL. MODEL: JEREMY SANTUCCI. LEVI'S FUNCTION 1 — JACKET. MARC JACOBS 2006.

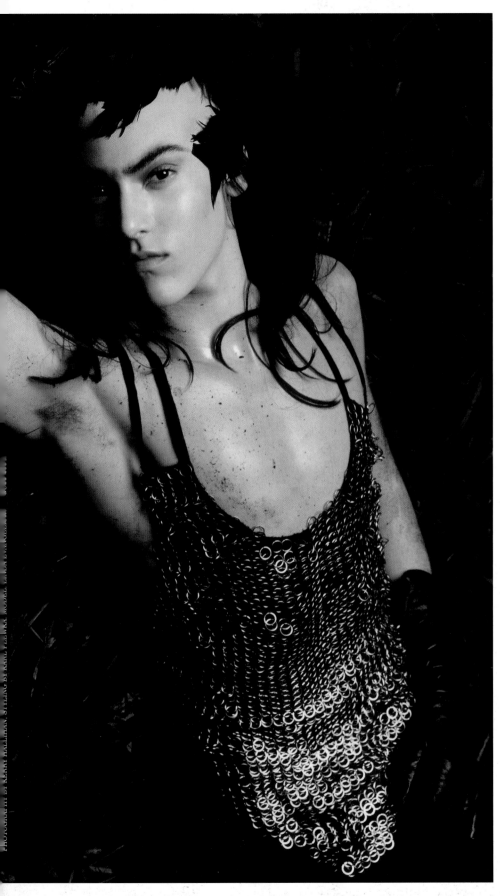

What are your signature designs? My aim is that all my designs wear my signature **What is your favourite piece from any of your collections?** Too many to sum up… **How would you describe your work?** As a never ending search **What's your ultimate goal?** To live every moment to the fullest **What inspires you?** Inspiration is very difficult to define, I think it is somehow given to you **Can fashion still have a political ambition?** Fashion has a reason "to be" because in fashion you can find new kinds of expressions about human beings **Who do you have in mind when you design?** Somebody I would love to meet **Is the idea of creative collaboration important to you?** Yes, I think it's part of my job **Who has been the greatest influence on your career?** My partner in life and work **How have your own experiences affected your work as a designer?** Everything that I have experienced in the 44 years that lie behind me has made me into the person I am now and that's my working tool **Which is more important in your work: the process or the product?** Both **Is designing difficult for you, if so, what drives you to continue?** Yes, it is. What drives me is my never ending will to give the best of myself **Have you ever been influenced or moved by the reaction to your designs?** It's the communication, it is what keeps me going on **What's your definition of beauty?** Beauty is constantly redefined, it is the joy that you feel when you discover it **What's your philosophy?** Get the maximum out of life **What is the most important lesson you've learned?** Stay true to yourself.

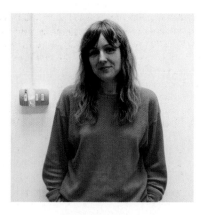

ANN-SOFIE BACK

"My designs are about other designs that are perceived as being better than my designs"

Ann-Sofie Back, who was born in Sweden in 1971, is one of the most subversive fashion designers working in London today. She is also one of the city's most promising. Uncomfortable with conventional idea of 'glamour' or 'femininity', Back confronts the clichés of fashion (frills, cinched waists, luxury fabrics) by transforming them with her uniquely off-kilter – yet nonetheless elegant – sense of construction. And, where others might shudder at the thought of an embarassing fashion 'mistake', Back celebrates them; for example, two recurring emblems in Back's collections include padded bra cups and shoulder pads that show through, as if by accident, her carefully-selected 'everyday' fabrics. At her catwalk shows she eschews the perfect beauty of professional models in favour of quirky-looking friends and acquaintances. Back is also fascinated by mediocrity, which she attributes to her youth in Stenhamra, a particularly nondescript suburb of Stockholm. Following a BA in fashion design at Beckman's College of Design in Sweden, Back moved to London to study at Central Saint Martins, completing the fashion MA course in 1998. She then worked as a designer for Joe Casely-Hayford in London and various brands in Sweden while also styling fashion shoots for magazines including Self Service and Purple. She also styled the spring/summer 2001 campaign for Miu Miu. In October 2001 she launched her own label with a show at the Purple Institute in Paris and after four seasons in France, moved her show to London Fashion Week; in 2005 she was accepted onto the official show schedule. Back has numerous stockists in Japan and a string of other high-profile stores around the world. In 2005 she introduced a second, more casual line, called 'BACK'. Her work has also been included in numerous exhibitions, including the 'Reshape' show at the 2003 Venice Biennale.

Die 1971 in Schweden geborene Ann-Sofie Back ist wohl eine der subversivsten Designerinnen, die derzeit in London arbeiten. Zweifellos ist sie auch eine der besonders viel versprechenden. Mit den konventionellen Vorstellungen von Glamour oder Weiblichkeit hat sie nichts am Hut, stattdessen greift Back Modeklischees (Rüschen, gegürtete Taillen, lxuriöse Stoffe) auf und transformiert sie mit ihrem einzigartig schrägen Gespür für Schnitte. Und wo andere sich bei dem Gedanken an einen peinlichen modischen Fehler schütteln, da feiert Back genau diesen Aspekt. Das gilt beispielsweise für die in Backs Kollektionen immer wieder auftauchenden Elemente gepolsterter BH und Schulterpolster, die wie aus Versehen sichtbar sind. Dazu kommen noch die sorgsam gewählten, scheinbar alltäglichen Stoffe. Bei ihren Catwalk-Shows gibt die Designerin eigenwillig aussehenden Freunden und Bekannten den Vorzug vor der perfekten Schönheit professioneller Models. Back ist auch fasziniert von Mittelmäßigkeit, was sie selbst ihrer Jugend in Stenhamra, einem besonders gesichtslosen Vorort von Stockholm, zuschreibt. Nach einem Bachelor-Studium in Modedesign am schwedischen Beckman's College of Design zog Back nach London, um am Central Saint Martins weiter zu studieren. 1998 machte sie dort ihren Master in

Mode. Anschließen arbeitete sie als Designerin für Joe Casely-Hayford in London sowie für diverse Labels in Schweden. Nebenher machte sie noch das Styling bei Modeaufnahmen für Zeitschriften wie Self Service und Purple. Auch für die Werbekampagne für Frühjahr/Sommer 2001 von Miu Miu war sie als Stylistin verantwortlich. Im Oktober 2001 präsentierte Back ihr eigenes Label mit einer Schau am Purple Institute in Paris. Nach vier Saisons in Frankreich wechselte sie mit ihren Schauen zur London Fashion Week, wo sie seit 2005 Teil des offiziellen Veranstaltungskalenders ist. Back arbeitet mit zahlreichen Einzelhändlern in Japan zusammen und mit einer Auswahl anderer anspruchsvoller Läden im Rest der Welt. 2005 führte sie eine zweite, etwas legerere Linie namens „BACK" ein. Ihre Arbeiten wurden bereits bei zahlreichen Ausstellungen gezeigt, etwa 2003 im Rahmen von „Reshape" bei der Biennale von Venedig.

Née en 1971 en Suède, Ann-Sofie Back est l'une des créatrices les plus subversives actuellement en exercice à Londres, mais c'est aussi l'une des plus prometteuses de la ville. Mal à l'aise avec les idées conventionnelles du « glamour » ou de la « féminité », Ann-Sofie Back affronte les clichés de la mode (fanfreluches, tailles cintrées, tissus luxueux) et les transforme grâce à son sens unique et détraqué de la construction tout en préservant une certaine élégance. Alors que les autres frémissent à l'idée de commettre une embarassante « erreur » de mode, Ann-Sofie Back les célèbre : par exemple, deux emblèmes récurrents de ses collections incluent les bonnets de soutien-gorge rembourrés et les épaulettes qui transpercent, comme par accident, ses tissus « quotidiens » soigneusement sélectionnés. Pour ses présentations, elle évite de recourir à la beauté parfaite des mannequins professionnels, préférant faire défiler les physiques étranges de ses amis et relations. Ann-Sofie Back est également fascinée par la médiocrité, une passion qu'elle attribue à sa jeunesse passée à Stenhamra, une banlieue de Stockholm absolument quelconque. Après l'obtention d'un BA en création de mode au Beckman's College of Design de Suède, elle s'installe à Londres pour étudier à Central Saint Martins, où elle décroche un MA en mode en 1998. Elle travaille ensuite comme créatrice pour Joe Casely-Hayford à Londres et d'autres marques en Suède, tout en faisant du stylisme sur les shootings photo de magazines tels que « Self Service » et « Purple ». Elle a également mis en style la campagne printemps/été 2001 de Miu Miu. En octobre 2001, elle lance sa propre griffe lors d'un défilé donné au Purple Institute de Paris. Après quatre saisons passées en France, elle décide de défiler à la London Fashion Week, où elle est acceptée dans le calendrier officiel des collections en 2005. Ann-Sofie Back compte de nombreux stockistes au Japon et ses créations sont également distribuées par plusieurs boutiques de luxe à travers le monde. En 2005, elle lance une seconde ligne plus décontractée baptisée « BACK ». Son travail a aussi été présenté dans le cadre de nombreuses expositions, notamment lors du show « Reshape » de la Biennale de Venise 2003. SUSIE RUSHTON

What are your signature designs? The bra cup T-shirts, the belt chinos, the sweater bags, label T-shirts and the tromp l'œil prints What is your favourite piece from any of your collections? All of the above How would you describe your work? Easy to wear. Surprisingly versatile and simple What's your ultimate goal? I don't have an ultimate goal as such. I would like to find a business/design partner. I would like to find alternative ways of working within the fashion industry that are more creative and collaborative. I want my new casual line BACK to be like GAP What inspires you? How we aspire to be better than we are through clothes, the way we lie and confuse through our dress. Fashion clichés and my own prejudice about people. My

designs are about other designs that are perceived as being better than my designs Can fashion still have a political ambition? I don't know, but I think fashion's ambition should be to get more respect, as a creative medium and as a business. There is nothing as personal and socially/culturally interesting as fashion, nothing as visible and nothing that all people have to care about, even the people who say they don't. You can't ignore it Who do you have in mind when you design? I know who it isn't for. It's not for a strong, individual woman in her 30s. Who the fuck is that person? Has anyone ever met her? I want weak-minded people with large wallets to buy my clothes Is the idea of creative collaboration important to you? Yes, but it has to be a very particular

kind of person Who has been the greatest influence on your career? It's not who, it's the place where I grew up How have your own experiences affected your work as a designer? The lack of interest and knowledge about art and culture in the suburb of Stenhamra, the small-town ignorance and prejudice and the conformity of Sweden in general. Where I grew up has shaped my whole outlook on fashion. It is the reason why I design and it is the reason why it looks the way it does. Initially I fled from it, now I celebrate it Which is more important in your work: the process or the product? They are equally important Is designing difficult for you, if so, what drives you to continue? Yes, very difficult. I'm very stubborn, I think what I do is very good,

I think my designs say something different to what I see other people do and I'm also extremely stupid Have you ever been influenced or moved by the reaction to your designs? I'm not sure, I can be surprised or embarrassed by reactions but I don't know how much it is actually influencing me What's your definition of beauty? It's important that I don't have one, beauty is not something I find important, or it probably is important because it isn't. I find beauty boring, I find interesting more beautiful than beautiful. But come to think of it, I can't stand interesting, so final verdict, boring is beautiful What's your philosophy? It's good to be wrong What is the most important lesson you've learned? Business is fun!

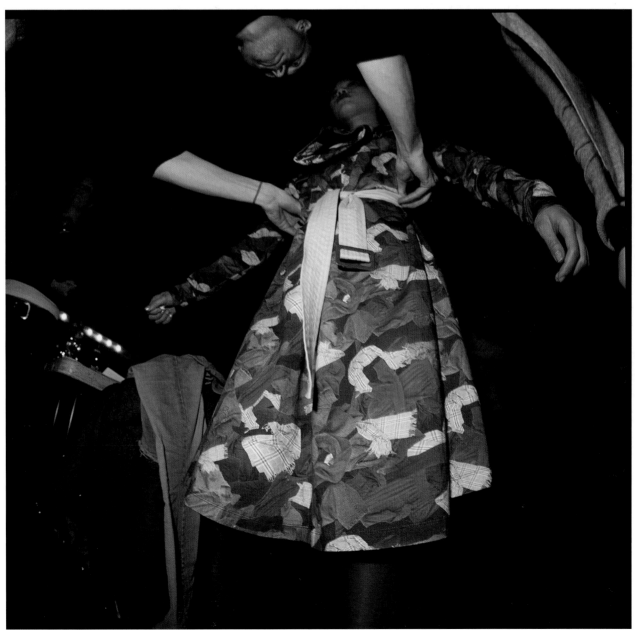

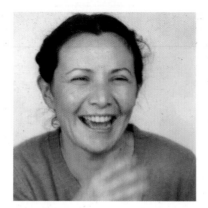

ANNA MOLINARI

"I believe in the power of contradiction"

ROSSELLA TARABINI

Rossella Tarabini (born 1968), daughter of the Blumarine designer Anna Molinari and designer of the collection that takes her mother's name, has an affinity with London. Its street life, the punks on the Kings Road in the '70s, and glamorous Mayfair nights all served as inspiration for her autumn/winter 2005 collection. Tarabini's creations are a mirror to her interests and experiences, and each of her collections tells a story, whether it be of a Russian princess or a rock singer. Her designs range from flirty florals to sophisticated chic – sometimes laced with a darker edge – in chiffon, ruching and lace. Overall, the line has a more eclectic and experimental feel in comparison to the more established Blumarine label. Born in Carpi, Italy, Tarabini is the eldest daughter of Anna Molinari and her husband Gianpaolo Tarabini. When she was nine years old, her mother and father started Blumarine. Raised in the world of fashion, it was only natural that she should follow in her mother's footsteps. Tarabini studied arts at Modena's Liceo Linguistico before going to Bologna University. In 1994, after a stay in London, she started working on the Blumarine ad campaigns as an art director. The following year, aged just 26, she began to design a new collection for the family-run fashion house, named Anna Molinari. Recently, Tarabini has resumed her former role as art director of the Blumarine campaigns, while continuing to work on Anna Molinari and another of the company's ultra-feminine brands, Blugirl.

Die 1968 geborene Rossella Tarabini ist die Tochter der Blumarine-Designerin Anna Molinari. Sie entwirft die Kollektion, die den Namen ihrer Mutter trägt, und hat eine starke Affinität zu London. Die Atmosphäre in den Straßen, die Punker auf der Kings Road in den 1970er Jahren und die glamourösen Nächte in Mayfair – all das diente ihr als Inspiration für ihre Kollektion Herbst/Winter 2005. Tarabinis Kreationen spiegeln ihre Interessen und Erfahrungen wider. Außerdem erzählt sie mit ihren Kollektionen Geschichten, sei es von einer russischen Prinzessin, sei es von einem Rockstar. Die Entwürfe reichen von flatternd-floral bis hin zu klassenbewusstem Chic – manchmal mit einem dunkleren Unterton – aus Chiffon, Rüschen und Spitze. Insgesamt erscheint die Linie im Vergleich zum älteren und stärker etablierten Label Blumarine eher eklektisch und experimentierfreudig. Tarabini wurde als älteste Tochter von Anna Molinari und Ehemann Gianpaolo Tarabini auf Capri geboren. Als sie neun Jahre alt war,

gründeten die Eltern Blumarine. Und nachdem sie quasi in der Welt der Mode aufwuchs, war es ganz normal, dass sie in die Fußstapfen der Mutter trat. Tarabini studierte zunächst Kunst am Liceo Linguistico in Modena, bevor sie in Bologna die Universität besuchte. Nach einem Londonaufenthalt begann sie 1994 bei Blumarine als Art Director für die Werbekampagnen. Im darauf folgenden Jahr entwarf sie mit gerade 26 Jahren eine neue Kollektion namens Anna Molinari für das Modehaus im Besitz ihrer Familie. Kürzlich nahm Tarabini die ehemalige Position des Art Director für die Werbekampagnen wieder ein. Sie designt jedoch weiterhin für Anna Molinari sowie für Blugirl, eine weitere ultra-feminine Marke des Unternehmens.

Rossella Tarabini (née en 1968), fille d'Anna Molinari, la styliste de Blumarine, et créatrice de la collection qui porte le nom de sa mère, semble avoir de grandes affinités avec Londres. Les rues de la ville, les punks de Kings Road dans les années 70 et les nuits glamour de Mayfair lui ont inspiré sa collection automne/hiver 2005. Les créations de Rossella Tarabini reflètent ses centres d'intérêt et ses expériences. Elle utilise ses collections pour raconter des histoires, que ce soit celle d'une princesse russe ou d'une chanteuse de rock. Son travail oscille entre imprimés floraux séduisants et élégance chic et classe, parfois avec un côté plus sombre, à travers des vêtements qui font la part belle à la mousseline, aux ruchés et à la dentelle. En général, sa ligne se veut plus éclectique et plus expérimentale que la griffe Blumarine, plus ancienne et déjà bien établie. Née à Carpi en Italie, Rossella Tarabini est la fille aînée d'Anna Molinari et de son mari Gianpaolo Tarabini. Elle a neuf ans quand ses parents créent Blumarine. Elevée dans l'univers de la mode, c'est tout naturellement qu'elle décide de suivre les traces de sa mère. Après des études artistiques au Liceo Linguistico de Modène, elle s'inscrit à l'Université de Bologne. De retour d'un séjour à Londres en 1994, elle travaille sur les campagnes Blumarine en tant que directrice artistique. L'année suivante, à 26 ans seulement, elle commence à dessiner une nouvelle collection pour l'entreprise familiale, qu'elle baptise Anna Molinari. Récemment, Rossella Tarabini a repris son ancien poste de directrice des campagnes Blumarine, tout en continuant à travailler pour Anna Molinari et pour Blugirl, une autre marque ultra-féminine de la maison.

KAREN LEONG

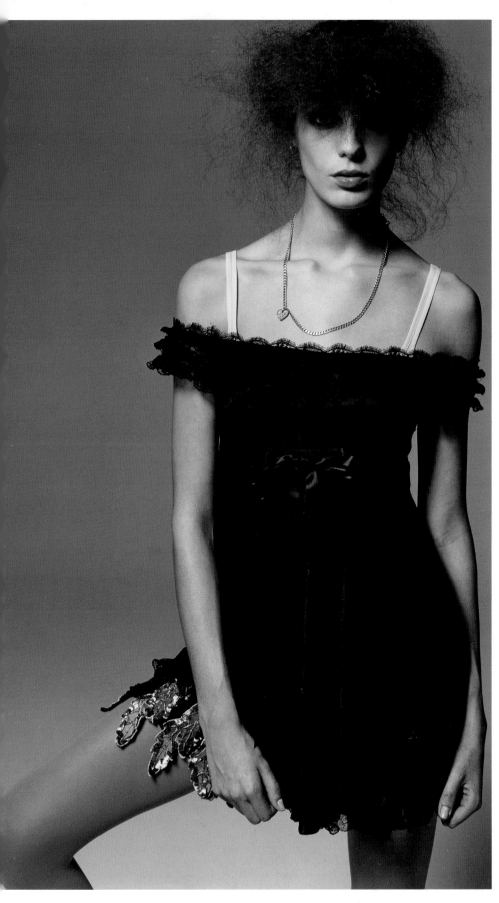

What are your signature evening dresses and **favourite piece from** I like the pieces from 2005 collection. The vi the blue one with tulle, both worn by Karen Elson **How would you describe your work?** I believe in the power of contradiction. I think that from unfinished thinking, new energy spark off. I don't like "precise", "polished" – I find confusion much more interesting **What's your ultimate goal?** Try to dress all the people I like and admire **What inspires you?** Beautiful details **Who do you have in mind when you design?** Usually I start to build my fairytales, then I think what the character could wear. It's not somebody real, it's somebody totally invented **Is the idea of creative collaboration important to you?** The idea of collaboration is always important for me, I believe it is a team work! **Who has been the greatest influence of your career?** I have been influenced by lots of people and I will need an entire page to thank everybody **How have your own experiences affected your work as a designer?** I think a lot. You can always see what is going on in my private life from the catwalk **Which is more important in your work: the process or the product?** The process for sure, without any doubt **Is designing difficult for you. If so, what drives you to continue?** Design is difficult because I always try to show a little bit about myself. I continue just for passion **Have you ever been influenced or moved by the reaction to your designs?** Yes, I have been influenced because I am a human being and criticism always affects you, but I have learnt to listen only to people I trust and esteem **What is your definition of beauty?** Beauty is in the eyes of the beholder **What's your philosophy?** My philosophy is to keep in touch with myself and to show just what I like **What is the most important lesson you've learned?** Not to be arrogant, to be loyal to myself and to have a normal life!

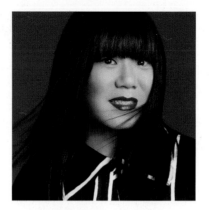

ANNA SUI

"People who go to my fashion shows
kinda go to a rock concert"

Anna Sui's singularity lies in her ability to weave her own passions into her work. Her creations are intricate pastiches of vintage eras and knowing nods to music and popular culture – from '60s Portobello to downtown rockers and B-Boys. Her love of fashion began early. Growing up in a sleepy suburb of Detroit, Sui (born 1955) spent her days styling her dolls and collating her 'genius files', a source book of magazine clippings that she continues to reference today. In 1972, she began studying at Parsons School of Design in New York, where she became a regular on the underground punk scene and where she met photographer Steven Meisel, a long-time friend and collaborator. Sui spent the remainder of the '70s designing for a string of sportswear companies. Then, in 1980, she presented a six-piece collection at the Boutique Show, receiving an immediate order from Macy's. Sui made her runway debut proper in 1991; the collection was a critically-acclaimed homage to her heroine, Coco Chanel. And by the early '90s, her self-consciously maximalist look was helping to pave the way for designers like Marc Jacobs, sparking a revival in the New York fashion scene. In 1993, she won the CFDA Perry Ellis Award for New Fashion Talent. Sui encapsulated the grunge spirit of the times, with Smashing Pumpkins guitarist James Iha – a close friend – appearing in her winter 1995 'California Dreaming' show, and Courtney Love famously adopting Sui's classic baby-doll dresses. Nowadays, Sui has stores in New York, LA, Tokyo and Osaka, and has added denim, sportswear, shoes and accessories to her brand. Her kitsch cosmetics and best-selling fragrances, with distinctive rose-embossed packaging, have all helped to establish her as an important designer and shrewd business woman with an eccentric spirit and limitless sense of fun.

Anna Suis Einzigartigkeit liegt darin begründet, dass sie spielerisch ihre eigenen Leidenschaften in ihre Arbeit hineinwebt. Ihre Kreationen sind aufwändige Imitationen von Vintage vergangener Epochen und Anspielungen auf Musik und Popkultur – vom Portobello der 1960er Jahre bis zu den Downtown Rockers und B-Boys. Ihre Liebe zur Mode entwickelte sich früh. Während ihrer Kindheit in einem verschlafenen Vorort von Detroit verbrachte die 1955 geborene Sui viel Zeit mit dem Stylen ihrer Puppen und den Anlegen ihrer „Genius Files", einer Sammelmappe mit Zeitungsausschnitten, auf die sie bis heute zurückgreift. 1972 begann sie ihr Studium an der Parsons School of Design in New York, wo sie treues Mitglied der Underground-Punk-Szene wurde und den Fotografen Steven Meisel kennen lernte, der ihr langjähriger Freund und Kollege werden sollte. Den Rest der 1970er Jahre verbrachte Sui mit dem Designen von Sportswear für diverse Firmen. 1980 präsentierte sie dann auf der Boutique Show eine sechsteilige Kollektion, die sofort von Macy's geordert wurde. Ihr offizielles Laufsteg-Debüt gab Sui schließlich 1991. Ihre damalige, von den Kritikern gefeierte Kollektion war eine Hommage an ihr Idol Coco Chanel. Ihr selbstbewuss-ter maximalistischer Look bahnte Anfang der 1990er Jahre Designern wie Marc Jacobs den Weg und sorgte für eine Neubelebung der New Yorker Modeszene. 1993 gewann sie den Perry Ellis Award for New Fashion Talent der CFDA. Sui griff den Grunge-Stil der damaligen Zeit auf, insbesondere als der Gitarrist der Smashing Pumpkins James Iha – ein enger Freund der Designerin – in ihrer Schau „California Dreaming" im Winter 1995 auftrat und Courtney Love öffentlichkeitswirksam Suis klassische Babydoll-Kleider für sich entdeckte. Heute betreibt Sui eigene Läden in New York, LA, Tokio und Osaka und hat ihr Programm um Jeans, Sportswear, Schuhe sowie Accessoires erweitert. Nicht zuletzt haben ihre kitschig gestalteten Kosmetika und bestens verkäuflichen Düfte mit der typischen rosenverzierten Verpackung dazu beigetragen, sie als wichtige Designerin und kluge Geschäftsfrau mit exzentrischem Geschmack und grenzenlosem Sinn für Humor zu etablieren.

La singularité d'Anna Sui réside dans son talent ludique à intégrer ses propres passions dans son travail. Ses créations sont autant de pastiches élaborés des époques vintage que des clins d'œil entendus à la musique et à la culture pop, du Portobello des années 60 aux B-Boys d'aujourd'hui. Elle tombe amoureuse de la mode dès son plus jeune âge. Elevée dans une triste banlieue de Detroit, Anna Sui (née en 1955) passe ses journées à habiller ses poupées et à compiler ce qu'elle appelle ses « genius files », un album de photos découpées dans les magazines de mode qu'elle continue à documenter aujourd'hui. En 1972, elle entame des études à la Parsons School of Design de New York, où elle fraye avec la scène punk underground et rencontre le photographe Steven Meisel, qui deviendra son ami et collaborateur. Jusqu'à la fin des années 70, Anna Sui occupe plusieurs postes de styliste dans le sportswear. Puis, en 1980, elle présente au Boutique Show une petite collection de six pièces immédiatement achetée par Macy's. Anna Sui fait ses véritables débuts lors d'un premier défilé en 1991, avec une collection créée en hommage à son héroïne Coco Chanel et plébiscitée par la critique. Au début des années 90, son look délibérément maximaliste ouvre la voie à des créateurs tels que Marc Jacobs et déclenche le renouveau de la mode new-yorkaise. En 1993, elle remporte le prix Perry Ellis décerné aux nouveaux talents par le CFDA. Anna Sui saisit parfaitement l'esprit grunge de l'époque: son grand ami James Iha, guitariste des Smashing Pumpkins, défile pour sa collection « California Dreaming » de l'hiver 1995 et Courtney Love adopte ses petites robes de baby doll. Aujourd'hui, Anna Sui possède des boutiques à New York, Los Angeles, Tokyo et Osaka. Sa marque s'est enrichie d'une ligne de pièces en denim, d'une gamme sportswear, de chaussures et d'accessoires. Dans leurs flacons roses originaux, ses produits de maquillage kitsch et ses parfums à succès ont contribué à faire d'elle une créatrice qui compte, une femme d'affaires avisée à l'esprit excentrique et au sens de l'humour illimité. AIMEE FARRELL

PORTRAIT BY JOSHUA JORDAN. PHOTOGRAPHY BY YELENA YEMCHUK, STYLING BY SORAYA DAYANI. MODEL: JP OCTOBER 2004.

What are your signature designs? When people think of my clothes they think romantic and feminine with a lot of embellishment. I love folkloric and vintage, so there's all those elements thrown in. Then there's always rock 'n' roll What is your favourite piece from any of your collections? A trompe l'oeil print dress I did for spring 2001 How would you describe your work? My favourite thing is discovering something, absorbing it and then putting it into my collection and showing it off to everybody. People who go to my fashion shows kinda go to a rock concert, as I like to take them on a journey, an escapist journey. It's a fantasy, something that they are going to have fun with What's your ultimate goal? This is it! I like making beautiful clothes. I'm the ultimate consumer, so there's nothing better than to be able to do products that I love, plus cosmetics and perfumes What inspires you? I'm fortunate that I can find inspiration in anything I'm currently interested in and incorporate it into my work. Books I read, places I travel, exhibitions I see, music I listen to Can fashion still have a political ambition? I imagine it could – but that's not my intention. Perhaps I'm past the stage of being rebellious. It is possible to be really rebellious with fashion but usually it's a younger person who feels they need to make their statement that way. It's not an issue that I aspire to Who do you have in mind when you design? Again, there's always the selfish consumer in me Is the idea of creative collaboration important to you? Yes, naturally fashion involves collaboration. I collaborate with fabric houses and print companies. I'm proud of the beautiful knitwear I've developed with James Coviello for my show. Erickson Beamon and I think up fun ideas for jewellery. I'm lucky to have wonderful licensee products: perfume, cosmetics, shoes, hose, sunglasses Who has been the greatest influence on your career? My parents. I think I got my creative and artistic side from my mother and the practical and logical side from my father. If I didn't have that combination, I wouldn't be able to do what I'm doing How have your own experiences affected your work as a designer? Every experience I have could show up in my work Which is more important in your work: the process or the product? I learned a long time ago that designing is a process which doesn't come overnight – you have to develop it to get the end result that you want. The more you develop your craft, the more the product becomes the ideal product and the thing that you were aiming for Is designing difficult for you. If so, what drives you to continue? It's difficult and you are never happy. But that's part of the creative process Have you ever been influenced or moved by the reaction to your designs? The biggest compliment I've ever had was when a man who didn't really even know that much about fashion came up to me and said, 'You know, my wife looks her most beautiful when she wears a dress she bought from you eight years ago.' That really means something because it's heartfelt. An old dress that makes her feel happy every time she wears it. I mean, what more could you ask for? What's your definition of beauty? There are so many levels of beauty. There's the ideal beauty, but that's not always the most attractive thing. I think there's beauty in almost everything, if you look in a certain way What's your philosophy? Live your dream What is the most important lesson you've learned? That the world is a much bigger place than just fashion.

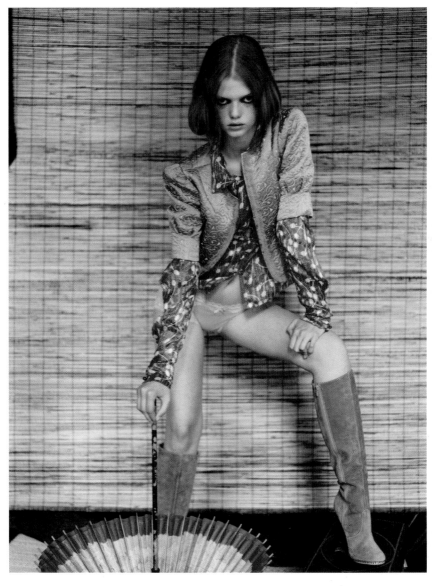

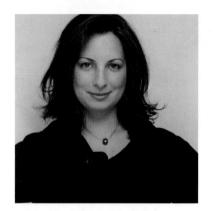

ANNE VALÉRIE HASH

"I work on the cut"

Anne Valérie Hash is a thoroughly modern couturière. Known for her virtuoso cutting skills, Hash transforms pieces of classic men's tailoring into elegant and unusual womenswear. For example, a man's white shirt is upended to become a sculpted blouse, or pleated pinstriped trousers are deconstructed to become a strapless dress. Hash, who was born in Paris in 1971, was one of the first of a younger generation of designers to be invited to show during haute couture week, despite being unable to fulfil all the traditional requirements for full qualification as an haute couture house. She made her debut in July 2001. Before this, Hash had studied at both the Ecole des Arts Appliqués Duperré (1992) and the prestigious Ecole de la Chambre Syndicale de la Couture Parisienne (1995). She also completed internships at Nina Ricci, Chloé, Christian Lacroix and Chanel – the latter a particularly high point for Hash, who has been constantly re-reading the biography of Coco Chanel since the age of 18. From her first collection, Hash has demonstrated how the refined handcraft techniques of haute couture can be applied to an aesthetic that has more in common with Martin Margiela than Valentino. In recent seasons, Hash has softened her androgynous look to allow for the inclusion of more obviously romantic pieces such as layered tulle dresses. However, the skeleton of her garments – their bindings, linings and seams – remain deliberately exposed, the result of her investigations into tailoring. In collaboration with the photographer Michelangelo Batista, Hash is also known for producing extremely beautiful catalogues, which each season star an iconic 'androgynous' model such as Guinevere Van Seenus, Stella Tennant or Erin Wasson. Her clothes are now stocked by stores including Browns Focus and Liberty in London and Louis Boston and Nordstrom in America.

Anne Valérie Hash ist eine durch und durch moderne Couturière. Berühmt für ihre virtuosen Schnitte, transformiert sie Kleidungsstücke aus der klassischen Herrenschneiderei zu eleganter und außergewöhnlicher Damenmode. Da wird beispielsweise ein weißes Herrenhemd zur skulpturalen Bluse umgestülpt oder eine Nadelstreifenhose mit Bügelfalte zum schulterfreien Kleid umgeschneidert. Die 1971 in Paris geborene Hash war eine der Ersten einer jüngeren Designergeneration, die man einlud, bei der Haute-Couture-Woche zu präsentieren, auch wenn sie nicht alle traditionellen Anforderungen erfüllte, um als echtes Haute-Couture-Haus zu gelten. Ihr Debüt gab sie im Juli 2001. Zuvor hatte Hash sowohl an der Ecole des Arts Appliqués Duperré (1992) als auch an der angesehenen Ecole de la Chambre Syndicale de la Couture Parisienne (1995) studiert. Sie absolvierte auch Praktika bei Nina Ricci, Chloé, Christian Lacroix und Chanel. Wobei Chanel einen besonderen Höhepunkt für Hash darstellte, weil sie sich schon seit ihrem 18. Lebensjahr intensiv mit Coco Chanels Biografie auseinan-

dergesetzt hatte. Bereits mit ihrer ersten Kollektion bewies die Designerin, dass die raffinierten handwerklichen Techniken der Haute Couture sich auf eine Ästhetik anwenden lassen, die mehr mit Martin Margiela als mit Valentino verbindet. In den letzten Saisons hat Hash ihren androgynen Look etwas abgemildert und sich auch eindeutig romantische Kreationen wie mehrlagige Tüllkleider gestattet. Das Gerüst ihrer Kleidung – Einfassungen, Futter und Säume – bleibt jedoch bewusst sichtbar, sozusagen als Ergebnis ihrer Recherchen in der hohen Schneiderkunst. Hash ist auch bekannt für ihre in Zusammenarbeit mit dem Fotografen Michelangelo Batista produzierten wunderschönen Kataloge, in denen pro Saison jeweils eine androgyne Model-Ikone wie Guinevere van Seenus, Stella Tennant oder Erin Wasson im Mittelpunkt steht. Ihre Entwürfe werden inzwischen u. a. bei Browns Focus und Liberty in London sowie bei Louis Boston und Nordstrom in den USA geführt.

Anne Valérie Hash est une couturière résolument moderne. Réputée pour ses coupes virtuoses, elle transforme les pièces du costume classique pour homme en vêtements pour femme élégants et insolites. Par exemple, elle renverse une chemise blanche masculine pour la transformer en un sculptural chemisier, ou déconstruit un pantalon mille-raies à pinces pour en faire une robe bustier. Née en 1971 à Paris, Anne Valérie Hash figure parmi la nouvelle génération de créateurs invités à défiler pendant la semaine de la haute couture, bien qu'elle ne soit pas en mesure de satisfaire à tous les critères traditionnels requis pour être officiellement qualifiée de styliste de haute couture. Elle fait ses débuts en juillet 2001, après avoir étudié à l'Ecole des Arts Appliqués Duperré (1992) et dans la prestigieuse Ecole de la Chambre Syndicale de la Couture Parisienne (1995). Elle effectue également des stages chez Nina Ricci, Chloé, Christian Lacroix et surtout Chanel, grande source d'inspiration pour elle, qui depuis l'âge de 18 ans ne cesse de relire la biographie de Coco Chanel. Depuis sa première collection, Anne Valérie Hash démontre comment les techniques artisanales raffinées de la haute couture peuvent être appliquées à une esthétique plus proche de Martin Margiela que de Valentino. Ces dernières saisons, elle a atténué son look androgyne pour permettre l'introduction de pièces franchement plus romantiques, telles que ses robes composées de plusieurs couches de tulle. Toutefois, l'ossature de ses vêtements (leurs points de liage, leurs doublures et leurs coutures) reste délibérément exposée, en conséquence de ses recherches sur la coupe. En collaboration avec le photographe Michelangelo Batista, Anne Valérie Hash produit des catalogues absolument magnifiques, qui chaque saison mettent en scène un mannequin « androgyne » ultra-célèbre comme Guinevere Van Seenus, Stella Tennant ou Erin Wasson. Ses créations sont aujourd'hui vendues par Browns Focus et Liberty à Londres, et par Louis Boston et Nordstrom aux Etats-Unis, entre autres. SUSIE RUSHTON

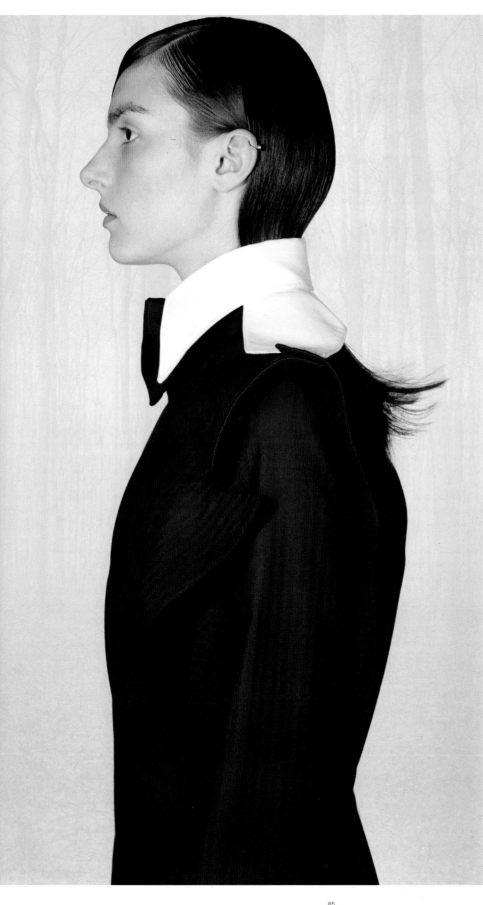

What are your signature designs? A pant-dress mixture of femininity and masculinity **What is your favourite piece from any of your collections?** Lace dress, it is my contradiction **How would you describe your work?** I work on the cut **What's your ultimate goal?** Jocker **What inspires you?** My muse Lou Lisa Lesage was 10 years old when we started my work and she is now almost 13. She inspires me. We work as we play **Can fashion still have a political ambition?** Yes, to start with pants for women were a revolution. To stop wearing the corset was also a new way to see women. The best example is the tiny shoes that the Chinese women had to wear during the last century in order to get married — we used to teach them that small feet were more precious! **Who do you have in mind when you design?** It depends on the season **Is the idea of creative collaboration important to you?** Yes, I love to collaborate with different illuminated spirits **Who has been the greatest influence on your career?** Fontana the artist **How have your own experiences affected your work as a designer?** It is not so clear yet **Which is more important in your work: the process or the product?** The product is the result of the process, the product is what you see at the end **Is designing difficult for you. If so what drives you to continue?** My team **Have you ever been influenced or moved by the reaction to your designs?** Each season I move to another reflection **What's your definition of beauty?** The heart hides the absolute beauty **What's your philosophy?** CUT **What is the most important lesson you've learned?** To stay simple — I could die any minute — so stay calm and enjoy being alive. To do what I love.

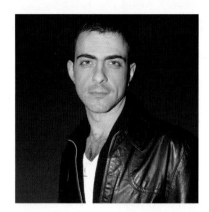

ANTONIO BERARDI

"My work is not for shy, retiring wall-flowers,
it's about tits and arse"

When Antonio Berardi comissioned his own perfume as a gift to the audience of his 1994 graduation show, it was clear that this was a fashion student with his sights set sky-high. Born in Grantham, UK, in 1968 to Sicilian parents, Berardi credits many design influences to his Italian roots: hourglass figures are his preferred silhouette and he constantly references Catholic symbolism in collections. A job assisting at John Galliano's studio was a solid training ground while he tried to land a place on the BA fashion course at Central Saint Martins; he was finally accepted onto the course in 1990, after his third application. On leaving college, Berardi quickly rose to fame. His degree collection was bought by Liberty and A La Mode in London, Kylie Minogue modelled for his first official show and Philip Treacy and Manolo Blahnik designed accessories. His signature tailored leather trouser suits and sheer chiffon dresses, often embellished with crystals, punchwork or hand-painted flowers, were shown at spectacular themed presentations. By his fourth collection, for autumn/winter 1997, Berardi had found an Italian backer, Givuesse. In 1999 he moved from the London catwalks to Milan. The following year, Extè appointed Berardi head designer and also began to produce his eponymous line. The partnership ended in autumn 2001 and a new Italian backer, Gibo, stepped in to provide Berardi with financial security. He now has a second line, called 2die4, and myriad stockists around the world, including a substantial client list in Russia. Berardi is a designer fascinated by technical achievement and his showstopping pieces – a coat decorated with dozens of tiny lightbulbs that illuminate to form a crucifix, say – support his view that, in the pursuit of glamour, nothing is impossible.

Schon als Antonio Berardi sein eigenes Parfüm als Geschenk für die Zuschauer seiner Studienabschluss-Show 1994 verteilen ließ war klar, dass es sich bei ihm um einen Absolventen mit himmelhohen Ambitionen handelte. Im britischen Grantham als Sohn sizilianischer Eltern geboren, verdankt Berardi seinen italienischen Wurzeln viele designerische Einflüsse: So ist die Sanduhr seine Lieblingssilhouette, und er verwendet in seinen Kollektionen immer wieder Symbole des Katholizismus. Ein Assistentenjob in John Gallianos Atelier war die richtige Spielwiese, während er sich um einen Studienplatz am Central Saint Martins bemühte. Nach seiner dritten Bewerbung wurde er schließlich 1990 aufgenommen. Nach dem Studium gelangte er rasch zu Ruhm. Liberty und A La Mode aus London kauften seine Abschlusskollektion, Kylie Minogue modelte bei seiner ersten offiziellen Show, Philip Treacy und Manolo Blahnik entwarfen die Accessoires. Seine Markenzeichen – perfekt geschneiderte Hosenanzüge aus Leder und durchsichtige Chiffonkleider, oft mit Kristallen, Stanzarbeiten oder handgemalten Blumen verziert – wurden bei spektakulären themenbezogenen Präsen-

tationen vorgeführt. Für seine vierte Kollektion, Herbst/Winter 1997, hatte Berardi mit Givuesse einen italienischen Finanzier gefunden. 1999 tauschte er die Londoner gegen die Mailänder Laufstege. Im darauf folgenden Jahr wurde Berardi Chefdesigner von Extè und begann auch eine nach ihm benannte Linie zu produzieren. Diese Partnerschaft endete im Herbst 2001, und mit Gibo trat ein neuer italienischer Mentor auf den Plan, der Berardi finanzielle Sicherheit gewährte. Inzwischen entwirft er mit 2die4 eine zweite eigene Linie und beliefert unzählige Einzelhändler weltweit, darunter auch eine beträchtliche Anzahl in Russland. Als Designer faszinieren Berardi alle technischen Errungenschaften. Seine Aufsehen erregenden Kreationen – etwa ein mit Dutzenden kleiner Glühbirnen verzierter Mantel, die in Form eines Kruzifixes leuchten – bestätigen seine Ansicht, dass im Streben nach Glamour nichts unmöglich ist.

Quand en 1994 Antonio Berardi commande un parfum à son nom pour l'offrir au public de son défilé de fin d'études, tout le monde s'accorde à dire que cet étudiant-là ne manque pas d'ambition. Né en 1968 de parents siciliens à Grantham en Angleterre, Berardi est largement influencé par ses racines italiennes : il affectionne particulièrement les silhouettes en forme de sablier et fait constamment référence aux symboles du catholicisme dans ses collections. Son expérience en tant qu'assistant dans l'atelier de John Galliano lui offre une solide base de formation tandis qu'il tente d'obtenir une place au cours de mode de Central Saint Martins, où il est finalement accepté en 1990 au bout d'une troisième candidature. Une fois diplômé, Berardi rencontre vite la célébrité. Sa collection de fin d'études est achetée à Londres par Liberty et la boutique de luxe A La Mode, Kylie Minogue défile pour sa première collection officielle tandis que Philip Treacy et Manolo Blahnik dessinent ses accessoires. Son célèbre tailleur-pantalon en cuir et ses robes en mousseline de soie ultra-fine, souvent ornées de cristaux, de perforations ou de fleurs peintes à la main, sont présentés à l'occasion de défilés thématiques spectaculaires. Pour sa quatrième collection automne/hiver 1997, Berardi fait appel à un important financier italien, Givuesse. En 1999, il délaisse les podiums londoniens pour Milan et devient, l'année suivante, directeur de la création chez Extè, qui produit également sa ligne éponyme. Ce partenariat prend fin à l'automne 2001 et Berardi retrouve un soutien financier auprès d'un autre italien, Gibo. Il dessine aujourd'hui une seconde ligne baptisée 2die4, et compte des myriades de stockistes dans le monde, dont un important marché en Russie. Berardi est fasciné par les exploits techniques, comme le prouve par exemple son manteau décoré de dizaines d'ampoules minuscules qui s'illuminent pour former un crucifix... autant de pièces extravagantes qui viennent étayer sa vision selon laquelle, dans la poursuite du glamour, tout est permis.

SUSIE RUSHTON

What are your signature designs? Anything which enhances the female form. Sexy tailoring juxtaposed with the lightest of chiffon **What is your favorite piece from any of your collections?** A bobbin-lace dress with no seams that took 14 women three months to make, and 45 minutes to put on, as it was laced up with threaded bone bobbins **How would you describe your work?** My work is not for shy, retiring wall-flowers, it's about tits and arse, with a little historical reference for good measure. I was born in England of Sicilian parents, so I tend to mix hard tailoring with sensual frou-frou, it kinda sums me up **What's your ultimate goal?** To invent that which hasn't yet been invented in clothing **What inspires you?** My friends and family. I love to analyse the way they affect me emotionally and the way they affect my everyday life; throw music, film, clubs and holidays into the soup, and "Bob's your uncle." **Can fashion still have a political ambition?** For some maybe, any designer can make a statement, but it takes one hell of a lot of money, advertising and luck to make fashion into a movement, political or otherwise. (Not to mention having friends in high places.) Then consider the fact that people's perception of fashion changes every six months, how politically incorrect is that? **Who do you have in mind when you design?** What haven't I done yet, and what's inspired me of late, whether it's a book I'm reading, a film I've seen, an exhibition or a great conversation that has made my mind race **Is the idea of creative collaboration important to you?** A lethal injection of collaborative creativity is one of the most inspiring of drugs. I love a challenge, and I subscribe to the idea that two minds are better than one **Who has been the greatest influence of your career?** Both my mother and my sister Piera – two of the most inspiring women who have totally shaped my career and my sense of being. I am eternally grateful and constantly inspired **How have your own experiences affected your work as a designer?** Emotion and growth, spiritually, mentally and physically, shape me, and as a consequence these experiences affect what I do **Which is more important in your work: the process or the product?** Both, the process is the fantasy, the product is the reality **Is designing difficult for you? If so, what drives you to continue?** Not at all. Sometimes I complicate matters by having too many ideas, and not being focused. My drive is the process of realising everything that comes into my head **Have you ever been influenced or moved by the reaction to your designs?** To have people come backstage after a show in tears is perhaps one of the most moving reactions I have ever had. It actually moved me to tears **What's your definition of beauty?** Anything that leaves me lost for words or with a lump in my throat **What's your philosophy?** To always follow your dreams and not let anyone stand in your way **What is the most important lesson you've learned?** That you are only as good as your last collection.

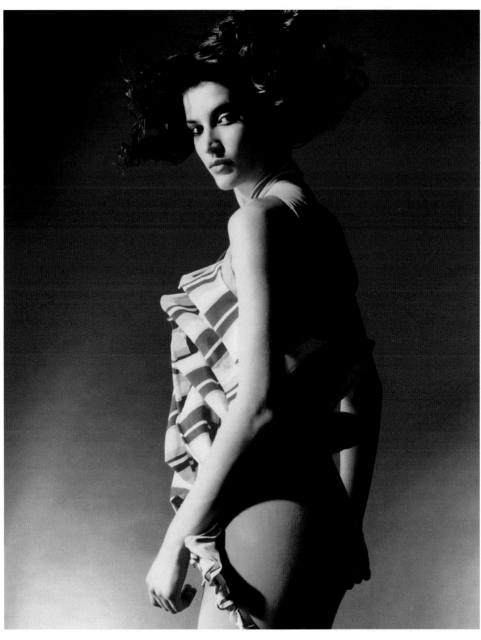

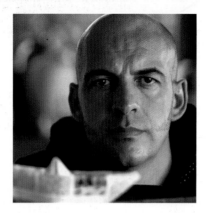

ANTONIO MARRAS

"Every single piece is a piece of my heart"

Since 2003 Antonio Marras has been in the limelight as artistic director of womenswear for Kenzo – an appointment, perhaps, that reflects the sense of tradition that was so important to Kenzo Takada when he was designing his eponymous line. Although Marras's first collection under his own name was launched as recently as 1999, with 2002 seeing his first men's ready-to-wear collection, he is already established as an international designer in his own right. He remains firmly based in his native Sardinia, working with his extended family in Alghero, where the locality and culture have a strong influence on his design. It is here that Marras (born 1961) pulls together his cut-and-paste aesthetic. This is characterised by his high standard of craftsmanship (laborious and highly detailed embroidery), random destruction (holes burned in fine fabrics), extravagant brocades sitting cheek-by-jowl with an unfinished hem, deconstructed shapes with vintage fabrics and a wide repertoire of what Marras calls "mistreatments": tearing, matting, staining, encrusting with salt, and so on. Marras takes this approach to its logical conclusion, creating a range of off-the-peg one-offs made from the material scraps saved in making his main line, the kind of scraps he grew up surrounded by in his father's fabrics shop. Lacking any formal training, it took a Rome-based entrepreneur to spot Marras's potential, allowing him to launch a career as a designer in 1988. That same year he won the Contemporary Linen Prize for a wedding dress and worked freelance for a number of companies whose collections he infused with his love of Mediterranean costume. Certainly, handcrafting is where Marras's heart lies and his philosophy of mend and make-do is applied to all the collections he designs.

Seit 2003 steht Antonio Marras als Artistic Director der Damenmode bei Kenzo im Rampenlicht – eine Besetzung, die vielleicht das Traditionsbewusstsein widerspiegelt, das Kenzo Takada beeinflusste, als er das nach ihm benannte Label gründete. Auch wenn Marras eine Kollektion unter eigenem Namen erst 1999 startete – die Prêt-à-porter-Linie für Herren folgte 2002 –, gilt er bereits als international etablierter, eigenständiger Designer. Seiner Heimat Sardinien bleibt er eng verbunden, und er arbeitet auch weiterhin mit Familienangehörigen in Alghero zusammen. Diese Region und ihre Kultur üben einen starken Einfluss auf seine Entwürfe aus. Der 1961 geborene Marras bezieht von dort seine Cut & Paste-Ästhetik. Diese ist wiederum geprägt von hohem handwerklichem Niveau (wie arbeitsintensive und äußerst detailreiche Stickereien), zufälliger Dekonstruktion (wie in kostbare Stoffe gebrannte Löcher), extravaganten Brokaten neben unfertigen Säumen, dekonstruierten Formen aus Vintage-Stoffen und einem großen Repertoire so genannter „Mistreatments": reißen, mattie-

ren, verflecken, mit Salz verkrusten usw. Marras führt seinen Ansatz zu einer logischen Konsequenz und kreiert eine Reihe von Prêt-à-porter-Unikaten aus Materialresten, die beim Designen seiner Hauptlinie übrig bleiben. Das sind Reste, wie sie ihn in seiner Kindheit im Stoffgeschäft seines Vaters umgaben. Obwohl er keine traditionelle Ausbildung hat, erkannte ein römischer Unternehmer sein Potential und ermöglichte ihm 1988 den Beginn seiner Designerkarriere. Im selben Jahr gewann er den Contemporary Linen Prize für ein Hochzeitskleid und war bereits als freier Mitarbeiter für eine Vielzahl von Unternehmen tätig, deren Kollektionen er mit seinem Faible für die Mittelmeertrachten prägte. Natürlich gehört sein Herz auch der handwerklichen Kunstfertigkeit, und seine Philosophie des Flickens und Improvisierens findet in all seinen Kollektionen ihren Niederschlag.

Depuis 2003, Antonio Marras occupe les feux de la rampe en tant que directeur artistique des lignes pour femme de Kenzo : un poste qui reflète sans doute le sens de la tradition auquel Kenzo Takada accordait tant d'importance quand il concevait lui-même sa ligne éponyme. Bien que Marras ait lancé sa propre griffe en 1999 seulement et sa première collection de prêt-à-porter pour homme en 2002, il s'était déjà imposé comme un styliste international à part entière. Il refuse de quitter sa Sardaigne natale, travaillant avec sa grande famille à Alghero, village dont la culture influence considérablement ses créations. C'est là que Marras (né en 1961) élabore son esthétique du « couper/coller », caractérisée par son immense savoir-faire artisanal (broderies méticuleuses fourmillant de détails), une destruction aléatoire (trous brûlés dans des tissus de luxe), des brocarts extravagants côtoyant des ourlets non finis, des formes déconstruites coupées dans des tissus vintage et un vaste répertoire de ce que Marras appelle des « maltraitances » : déchirures, feutrage, taches, incrustations au sel, etc. Antonio Marras adopte cette approche jusqu'à sa conclusion logique, créant une palette de pièces uniques mais prêtes à porter, taillées dans les coupons de tissu qu'il récupère en créant sa ligne principale : le genre de chutes au milieu desquelles il a grandi dans le magasin de tissus de son père. Sans formation préalable, c'est un entrepreneur romain qui détecte le premier tout le potentiel de Marras, l'aidant à se lancer dans une carrière de styliste en 1988. La même année, il remporte le prix Contemporary Linen pour une robe de mariée et travaille en free-lance pour de nombreuses maisons, insufflant à leurs collections son amour du costume méditerranéen. C'est sans doute pour l'artisanat que bat le cœur de Marras, et sa philosophie du « rien ne se perd, tout se transforme » transparaît dans toutes les collections qu'il dessine.

JOSH SIMS

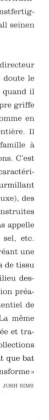

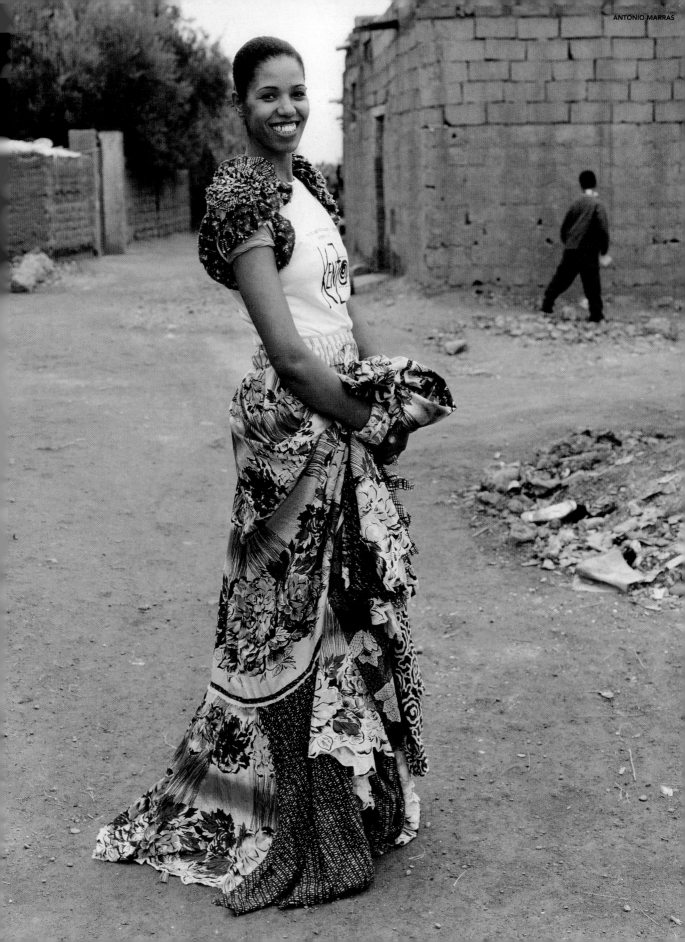

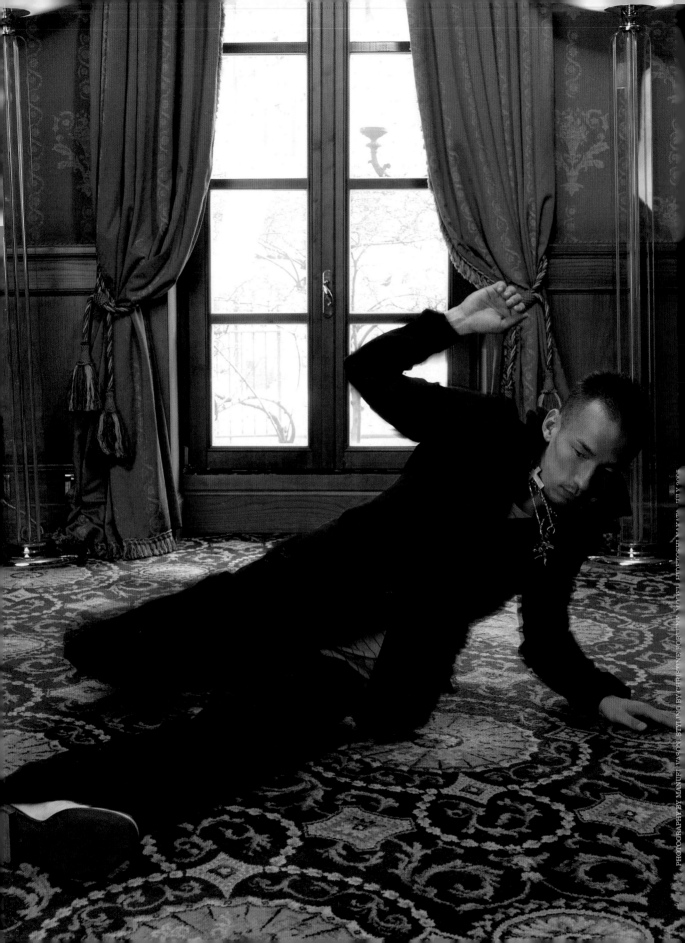

PHOTOGRAPHY BY MANUEL YASONI STYLING BY CHRISTINE ROEHRING MODEL HIDETOSHI YAZATA JULY 2005

What are your signature designs? Uniqueness, character and soul. A big part of every Antonio Marras collection is made of customised vintage pieces or handmade pieces **What is your favourite piece from any of your collection?** I can't answer, as we say in Italy every single piece is "piezze 'e cuore" (a piece of my heart). They all are beloved sons **How would you describe your work?** A big good luck! I can do a job that sums up all my passions: cinema, literature, photography, art, etc. **What's your ultimate goal?** I always work for today, I never think about tomorrow **What inspires you?** Everything and nothing: a word that a friend told me on the phone, my grandmother's photo, an old child shoe found on a market **Can fashion still have a political ambition?** Yes, of course! Everything is politics: choose to wear a particular T-shirt, decide not to wear furs, broach certain matters. Deciding how to live is politics **Who do you have in mind when you design?** I don't think, I go into a kind of trance **Is the idea of creative collaboration important to you?** It's essential! **Who has been the greatest influence on your career?** A very little big Sardinian artist aged 85. She's called Maria Lai **How have your own experiences affected your work as a designer?** To me, private and working experiences are one single thing, they influence each other, there are no bounds or limits between them **Which is more important in your work: the process or the product?** They are both important! Of course, creative process is much more stimulating, alluring, full of pains, doubts, hesitations and then determinations and passions. When the collection is ready and everything is over, I'm already thinking about something else! **Is designing difficult for you, if so, what drives you to continue?** Yes, it's difficult, but it is the only thing I love to do! **Have you ever been influenced or moved by the reaction to your designs?** I don't think so! **What's your definition of beauty?** What said my son Efisio when he was four years old: what is beautiful, is beauty **What's your philosophy?** If it has to be, let it be! That means, never half-measures **What is the most important lesson you've learned?** Never take something for granted.

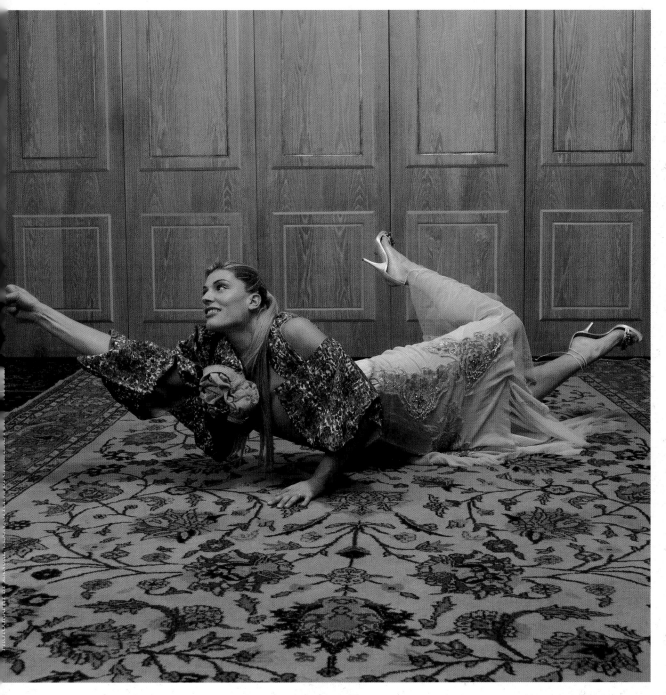

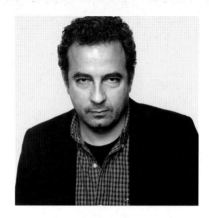

APC

"What inspires me is whatever helps you
to get away from mental pollution" JEAN TOUITOU

You'll never see an APC creation waltzing down a catwalk accessorised with a pair of horns. Instead, the subtle fashion brand has a coded elegance that attracts discerning customers drawn to APC's perfect jeans, shrunken blazers, sunglasses and radical T-shirts. In addition to clothing, there's the treasure trove of APC 'things' on offer each season: guitar plectrums, books (such as their edition of Charles Anastase illustrations), shaving oil, candles, olive oil. And it's all the brainchild of Jean Touitou, who was born in Tunis in 1951 and graduated from the Sorbonne in Paris with a history degree and no intention whatsoever of becoming a fashion designer. It was entirely by accident that he landed his first job with Kenzo, which was followed by gigs at agnès b. and Irié before finally deciding to go his own way in 1987 with the launch of APC (Atelier de Production et de Création). Touitou began with menswear, and quickly followed with a womenswear collection debuting the year after. In 1991 the first APC shop opened in Japan and today the company has stores in Hong Kong, New York, Berlin and Paris, plus a comprehensive online service. Collaboration is important to Touitou and over the years he has partnered Margiela, Martine Sitbon, Eley Kishimoto and Gimme 5 for innovative limited edition projects. Jessica Ogden designs a childrenswear line and, since 2004, also the mini Madras collection of beachwear inspired by Indian textiles. The company also has a music division; Marc Jacobs and Sofia Coppola, among others, have put their names to compilations on the APC music label and dance albums, punk-jazz and French-Arabic CDs have all been released to further express the brand's originality.

Sie werden nie eine Kreation von APC auf dem Laufsteg vorgeführt bekommen, die als Accessoire mit einem Paar Hörner versehen ist. Stattdessen propagiert diese feinsinnige Modemarke eine verschlüsselte Eleganz, die aufmerksame Kunden mit perfekten Jeans, kleinen Blazern, Sonnenbrillen und radikalen T-Shirts anzieht. Neben Kleidern gibt es bei APC in jeder Saison auch noch eine Art Schatzkiste mit den verschiedensten Dingen: Gitarrenplektren, Bücher (etwa die firmeneigene Edition von Charles Anastases Illustrationen), Rasieröl, Kerzen, Olivenöl. Das sind alles die Ideen von Jean Touitou, der 1951 in Tunis geboren wurde, an der Pariser Sorbonne einen Abschluss in Geschichte machte und nie vorhatte, Modedesigner zu werden. Sein erster Job bei Kenzo war ein absoluter Zufall. Danach folgten Engagements bei agnès b. und Irié, bevor er sich 1987 entschloss, eigene Wege zu gehen und APC (Atelier de Production et de Création) gründete. Touitou begann mit Herrenmode, gab aber schon ein Jahr später mit

einer Kollektion sein Debüt in der Damenmode. 1991 eröffnete der erste APC-Laden in Japan. Inzwischen besitzt die Firma eigene Geschäfte in Hongkong, New York, Berlin und Paris sowie einen umfassenden Online-Shop. Kooperation ist Touitou ungeheuer wichtig, und so hat er im Laufe der Jahre bereits mit Margiela, Martine Sitbon, Eley Kishimoto und Gimme 5 im Rahmen von innovativen Projekten mit limitierten Auflagen zusammengearbeitet. Jessica Ogden entwirft die Kinderkollektion und seit 2004 auch die von indischen Textilien inspirierte kleine Madras-Linie für Beachwear. Zum Unternehmen gehört auch eine Musikabteilung. Unter anderem haben Marc Jacobs und Sofia Coppola Compilations beim Musiklabel APC veröffentlicht. Dance-Alben, Punk-Jazz und CDs mit franco-arabischer Musik unterstreichen allesamt die Originalität der Marke.

On ne verra jamais une création APC valser toutes griffes dehors le long d'un podium. Au contraire, la mode subtile que propose cette marque se distingue par son élégance codée qui attire les clients les plus exigeants, séduits par ses jeans parfaitement coupés, ses petits blazers, ses lunettes de soleil et ses T-shirts à slogan. Outre les vêtements, APC propose chaque saison ses dernières «trouvailles»: médiators de guitare, livres (tels que l'édition APC des illustrations de Charles Anastase), huile de rasage, bougies ou huile d'olive. Des idées tout droit sorties du cerveau de Jean Touitou, né en 1951 à Tunis. Diplômé de la Sorbonne en histoire, il n'a jamais cherché à devenir styliste. C'est donc par pur hasard qu'il se retrouve chez Kenzo, avant de partir travailler chez agnès b. et Irié. Il finit par lancer sa propre griffe en 1987 et la baptise APC (Atelier de Production et de Création). Touitou propose d'abord une ligne pour homme, rapidement suivie d'une collection pour femme au début de l'année suivante. En 1991, la première boutique APC ouvre ses portes au Japon. Aujourd'hui, l'entreprise possède des points de vente à Hong Kong, New York, Berlin et Paris, sans oublier son service de vente sur Internet. La collaboration revêt beaucoup d'importance aux yeux de Jean Touitou, qui au fil des années s'est associé à Margiela, Martine Sitbon, Eley Kishimoto et Gimme 5 pour travailler sur des projets innovants en édition limitée. Jessica Ogden, qui dessine la ligne pour enfant d'APC, conçoit également depuis 2004 la collection de maillots de bain à mini-carreaux Madras, inspirée des textiles indiens. L'entreprise s'est également diversifiée dans la musique: Marc Jacobs et Sofia Coppola, entre autres, ont proposé leurs titres sur les compilations du label d'APC dont les albums électro, punk-jazz et franco-arabes ont tous été commercialisés afin d'exprimer la grande originalité de la marque.

TERRY NEWMAN

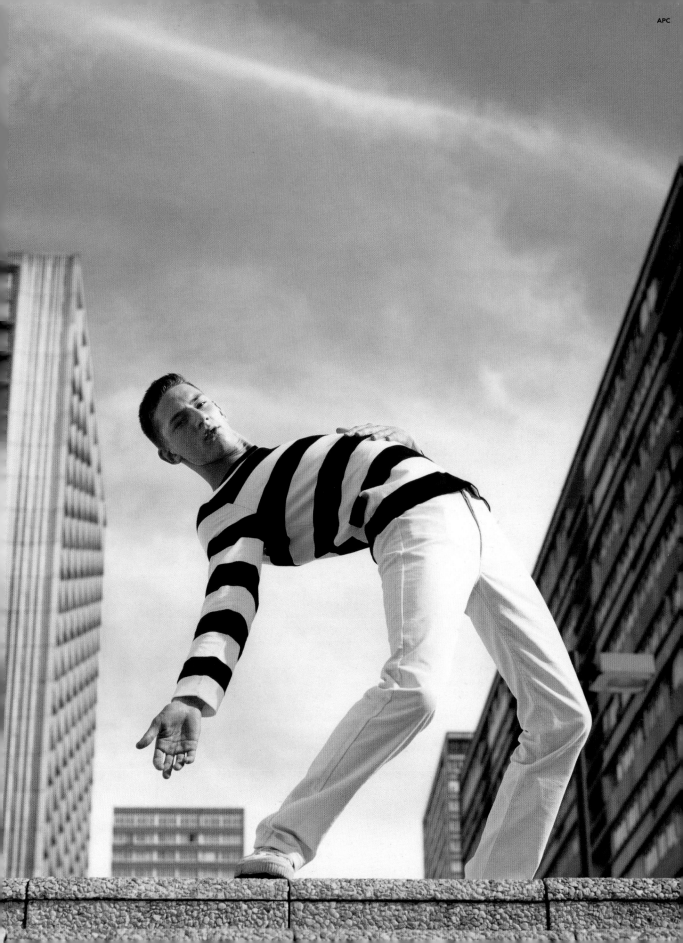

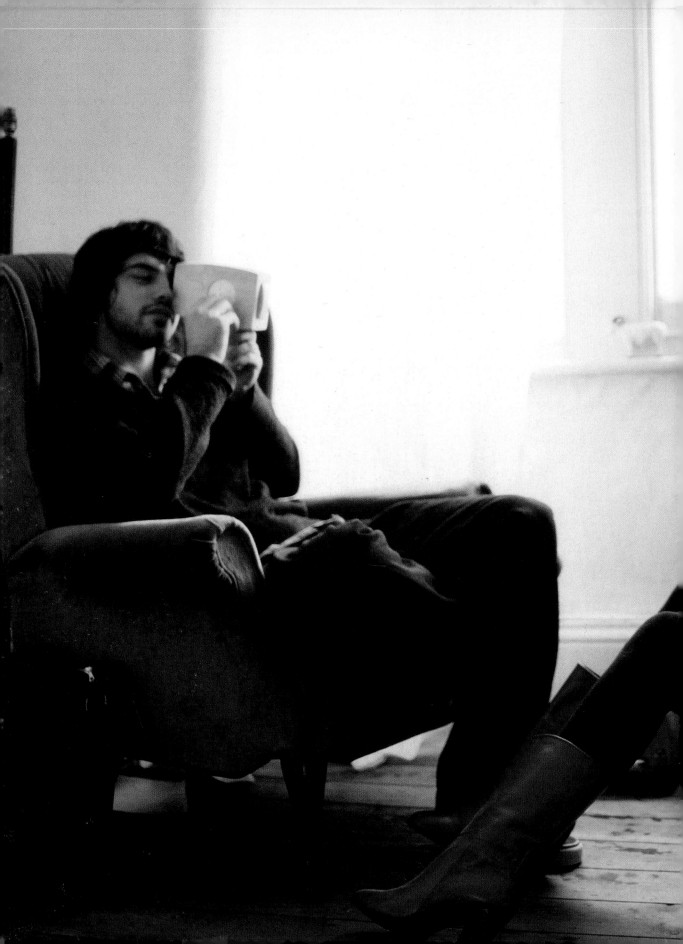

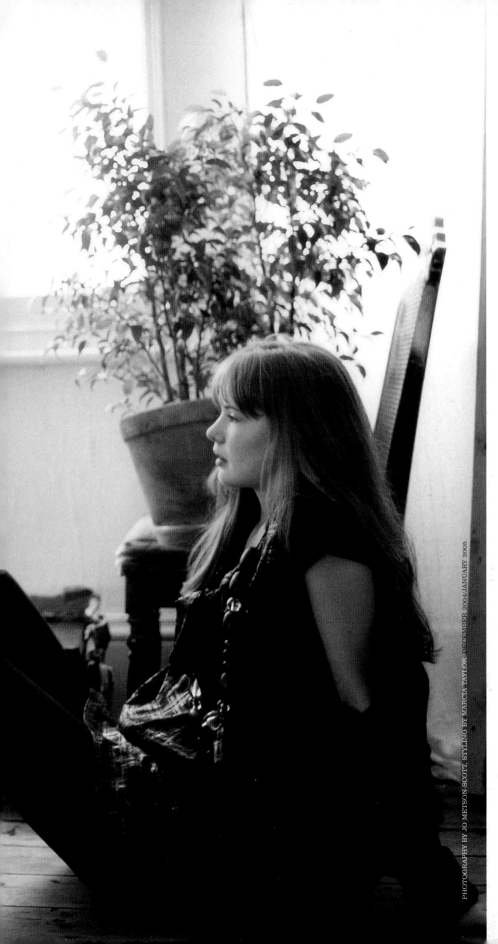

PHOTOGRAPHY BY JO METSON-SCOTT, STYLING BY MARCIA TAYLOR. DECEMBER 2004/JANUARY 2005.

What are your signature designs? My signature is to make the signature hard to see, but yet noticeable **What is your favourite piece from any of your collections?** This varies every day, otherwise fashion would not exist **How would you describe your work?** It's like putting a team together, be a bit of a guru/dictator/father/entertainer in design and business **What's your ultimate goal?** Tee off at 2:00 p.m. on Fridays and read and write on Saturdays **What inspires you?** Not the Mercer Hotel lobby during fashion week, not dog shit in Paris street, not French diplomacy asking for Hamas help to release hostages, not being served by lumpen proletariat in any New York shop, what inspires me is whatever helps you to get away from mental pollution **Can fashion still have a political ambition?** Never had, never will. Sorry, but this question makes me laugh again **Who do you have in mind when you design?** Nobody **Is the idea of creative collaboration important to you?** Of course. C'est même vital **Who has been the greatest influence on your career?** Alvar Aalto **How have your own experiences affected your work as a designer?** I cannot be my own shrink, on top of that, I just fired mine **Which is more important in your work: the process or the product?** The product **Is designing difficult for you, if so, what drives you to continue?** Once you decide that suicide is not an option, you just keep going **Have you ever been influenced or moved by the reaction to your designs?** I am influenced by my own reactions, when I see actual products in actual shops **What's your definition of beauty?** I am no philosopher, I cannot develop a concept about that, please check on Hegel or Kant. I work on precepts, not on concepts **What's your philosophy?** No philosophy **What is the most important lesson you've learned?** I do not remember.

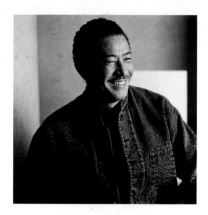

A-POC

"Making things happen is a natural
extension of myself" ISSEY MIYAKE

Issey Miyake interrogates cloth with the same intellectual rigour as an architect mapping a structure. Born in Hiroshima in 1938, Miyake was among the first wave of Japanese designers to revolutionise Paris fashion, making his debut in 1973. After studying graphic design at Tama Art University, Miyake first moved to Paris in 1964 to work for Guy Laroche, followed by Givenchy. After a stint with Geoffrey Beene, Miyake returned to Tokyo and founded the Miyake Design Studio in 1970. Miyake's work plays on the tension between body and cloth, padding, pleating and layering fabrics to create otherworldly shapes; he has experimented with fabric origami using permanent creasing, crimping and pleating. Rejecting the conventions of Western tailoring, the designer eradicated fastenings, introduced laser cutting and began experimenting with garments shaped from a single piece of cloth. In 1986, Miyake started one of the greatest collaborations in fashion when Irving Penn began to chronicle his collections. In 1988 Miyake started work on the concept for a new label, Pleats Please. Launched in 1993, the simple shapes in pleated polyester earned Miyake the Légion d'Honneur and an Honorary Doctorate from London's Royal College of Art. Since 1999, Issey Miyake's eponymous line has been designed by Naoki Takizawa while Miyake and his assistant Dai Fujiwara dedicate their creativity to A-POC (A Piece of Cloth). A-POC was unveiled in Paris in 1998 when 23 models appeared on the catwalk all connected by one tube of fabric. Of A-POC, Miyake declares: "I have endeavoured to make fundamental changes to the system of making clothes. Think: a thread goes into a machine that in turn, generates complete clothing using the latest computer technology and eliminates the usual needs for cutting and sewing the fabric."

Issey Miyake behandelt Stoff mit der gleichen intellektuellen Strenge wie ein Architekt, der einen Bauplan zeichnet. Geboren wurde er 1938 in Hiroshima. Später gehörte er zur ersten Welle japanischer Designer, die die Pariser Modeszene revolutionieren sollten. Sein Debüt gab er 1973. Nach dem Grafikdesign-Studium an der Tokioter Tama Art University kam Miyake 1964 erstmals nach Paris, um dort zunächst für Guy Laroche, später für Givenchy zu arbeiten. Nach einem Zwischenspiel bei Geoffrey Beene kehrte Miyake nach Tokio zurück und gründete dort 1970 das Miyake Design Studio. Seine Arbeiten spielen mit der Spannung zwischen Körper und Stoff. Durch das Wattieren, Falten und Schichten von Stoffen erzielt er geradezu weltfremde Silhouetten. Miyake experimentierte mit Origami aus Stoff, den er dauerhafte knitterte, kräuselte oder plissierte. Über die Regeln der westlichen Schneiderkunst setzte sich der Designer hinweg, indem er auf Befestigungen verzichtete, den Laserschnitt einführte und Versuche mit Kleidern aus einem einzigen Stoffstück unternahm. 1986 begann er eines der großartigsten Gemeinschaftsprojekte der Modegeschichte, als Irving Penn anfing, seine Kollektionen zu dokumentieren. 1988 begann er am

Konzept für das neue Label Pleats Please zu arbeiten. Die 1993 vorgestellten schlichten Silhouetten aus plissiertem Polyester brachten Miyake in die Légion d'Honneur und bescherten ihm die Ehrendoktorwürde des Londoner Royal College of Art. Seit 1999 wird die nach ihm benannte Linie von Naoki Takizawa designt, während Miyake und sein Assistent Dai Fujiwara ihre Kreativität A-POC (A Piece of Cloth) widmen. Das Projekt wurde 1998 in Paris vorgestellt, als 23 mit einem einzigen Stoffschlauch verbundene Models auf den Laufsteg traten. Miyakes Erklärung dazu: „Ich habe mich bemüht, das System der Kleiderproduktion fundamental zu ändern. Stellen Sie sich vor, ein Faden wird in eine Maschine eingespeist, die daraus ein fertiges Kleidungsstück macht und die üblicherweise notwendigen Schritte, das Zuschneiden und Nähen des Stoffes, überflüssig macht."

Issey Miyake approche le tissu avec la même rigueur intellectuelle qu'un architecte qui dessine un plan. Né en 1938 à Hiroshima, Miyake fait partie de la première vague de stylistes japonais qui révolutionne la mode parisienne lors de ses débuts très remarqués en 1973. Après des études de graphisme à la Tama Art University, Issey Miyake s'installe à Paris en 1964 où il travaille pour Guy Laroche, puis pour Givenchy. Après un petit détour par New York chez Geoffrey Beene, Miyake revient à Tokyo et fonde son Miyake Design Studio en 1970. Son travail joue sur les tensions entre le corps et le vêtement, rembourrant, plissant et superposant les tissus pour produire des formes d'un autre monde. Miyake expérimente la technique de l'origami en chiffonnant, en texturant et en plissant le tissu de façon permanente. Rejetant les conventions de la mode occidentale, il se débarrasse des boutons et autres attaches, introduit la coupe au laser et commence à créer des vêtements coupés dans une seule et même pièce de tissu. En 1986, quand Irving Penn décide de faire la chronique de ses collections, Miyake se lance dans l'une des collaborations les plus géniales que la mode ait jamais connue. En 1988, il souhaite approfondir le concept à travers une nouvelle griffe, Pleats Please, qu'il finira par lancer en 1993. Ces formes simples en polyester plissé lui valent la Légion d'Honneur et un doctorat honorifique du Royal College of Art de Londres. Depuis 1999, Naoki Takizawa dessine la ligne éponyme d'Issey Miyake tandis que ce dernier, assisté de Dai Fujiwara, investit toute sa créativité dans A-POC (A Piece of Cloth). La première présentation d'APOC a lieu en 1998 sur les podiums parisiens, qui voient défiler 23 mannequins tous reliés par un même tube de tissu. A propos d'A-POC, Miyake déclare : « J'ai tout fait pour transformer fondamentalement le système de fabrication des vêtements. Imaginez : on insère un fil dans une machine qui produit en retour un vêtement complètement fini à l'aide de la technologie informatique la plus récente, et qui élimine les étapes habituelles de découpe et de couture ».

JAMES SHERWOOD

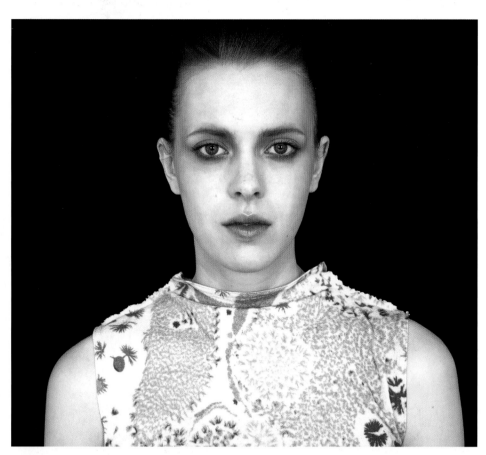

What's your favourite piece from any of your collections? Always whatever piece I am working on **How would you describe your work?** A-POC is the innovative process of making reality **What's your ultimate goal?** It is that our work will be a part of our daily lives and be of use. To realise it, we are just trying to establish the method and system **What inspires you?** Life **Who do you have in mind when you design?** People **Is the idea of creative collaboration important to you?** Sometimes important. Sometimes dangerous **What has been the greatest influence on your career?** People, nature and technologies **How have your own experiences affected your work as a designer?** I am a part of my past, but I look to the future **Which is more important in your work: the process or the product?** Both **Is designing difficult for you?** Making things is a natural extension of myself **Have you ever been influenced or moved by the reaction to your designs?** I always learn from other people **What's your definition of beauty?** Joy **What's your philosophy?** Advancing **What is the most important lesson you've learned?** Honesty.

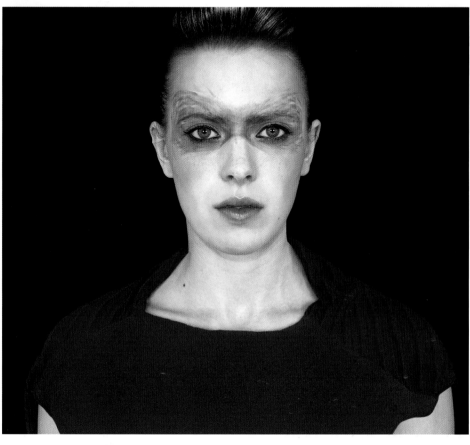

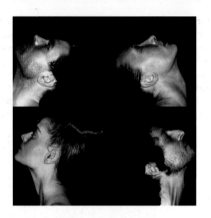

AS FOUR

"As one, as all. As all, as one"

In the beginning there was chaos. Then in the mid-'90s, Adi, from Israel, met Ange, from Tajikistan, at fashion school in Germany and they moved to New York to become stylists. They're the girls. Then Kai, a former model from Germany whose house burned down, met Gabi, a Lebanese designer who was working for mainstream fashion labels including Kate Spade. They're the boys. Together they made As Four, if you don't count Powder, the white dog who never leaves their side. Almost immediately, the flashy quartet became the centre of New York's avant-garde and a cult following mushroomed not unlike their organic, ambiguously shaped clothes. The four staged their first show using tiny mechanised hula dolls, all dressed in miniature As Four clothes and spinning in circles to the sound of Wagner. From then on the circle and its various elliptical permutations have become synonymous with As Four, whose ubiquitous 'disc bags' have even appeared on 'Sex and the City'. As Four make not just fashion but wearable sculpture – in equal parts outré and classic, spanning leather to silk charmeuse. The shapes and silhouettes they make often look entirely new even to the most jaded fashion eyes; dresses, tops and pants flutter here and hug there, constantly shifting with the wearer's body. It wasn't long before Björk became a big fan, scooping up their futuristic fashions as often as she could. But 2004 was a struggle for As Four. The tightness of the group, which had been their good fortune, began to chafe. Adi was first to move out from the silver-painted Chinatown apartment. Kai followed. Then Ange and Gabi eloped in a last-ditch effort to keep the family together. It still is.

Am Anfang war das Chaos. Dann begegneten sich Anfang der 1990er Jahre Adi aus Israel und Ange aus Tadschikistan an einer Modeschule in Deutschland. Sie beschlossen, zusammen nach New York zu gehen und dort Stylisten zu werden. Das sind die beiden Mädchen. Dann traf Kai, ein ehemaliges Model aus Deutschland, dessen Haus gerade abgebrannt war, einen libanesischen Designer namens Gabi, der für Mainstream-Labels wie Kate Spade arbeitete. Das sind die beiden Jungs. Zusammen gründeten sie As Four. Powder, der weiße, nie von ihrer Seite weichende Hund, wurde nicht eingerechnet. Fast sofort avancierte das fetzige Quartett zum Mittelpunkt der New Yorker Avantgarde, und ihren organischen, mehrdeutig geschnittenen Kleidern nicht unähnlich, erwuchs ihnen eine Gefolgschaft, bis sie Kultstatus genossen. Bei ihrer ersten Modenschau präsentierten die vier ihre Modelle an winzigen, mechanischen Hula-Puppen, die As-Four-Sachen in miniature trugen und sich zu Wagnerklängen drehten. Seit damals sind der Kreis und seine elliptischen Variationen sozusagen Synonym für das Label. Die allgegenwärtigen Disc Bags waren sogar in „Sex and the City" zu sehen. As Four macht nicht einfach Mode, sondern tragbare Skulpturen – so aus-

gefallene wie klassische, aus Materialien von Leder bis Seidencharmeuse. Die Schnitte und Silhouetten wirken oft selbst für übersättigte Augen völlig neuartig. Kleider, Tops und Hosen flattern hier und schmiegen sich dort an, in permanenter Veränderung und Anpassung an den Körper ihrer Trägerin. Schon bald wurde die Sängerin Björk zu einem großen Fan und sicherte sich so oft wie möglich die futuristischen Entwürfe der Gruppe. Im Jahr 2004 hatte As Four allerdings zu kämpfen. Der Zusammenhalt, bis dato ihr Glück, begann zu bröckeln. Adi war die erste, die das silberfarbene Apartment in Chinatown verließ. Dann folgte Kai. Schließlich brannten Ange und Gabi, in einem letzten Versuch, die Familie zusammenzuhalten, durch. Bis jetzt ist es ihnen gelungen.

Au commencement régnait le chaos. Puis au milieu des années 90, l'Israélienne Adi rencontre Ange du Tadjikistan dans une école de mode en Allemagne et elles s'installent ensemble à New York pour devenir stylistes. Voilà pour les filles. Enfin Kai, ancien mannequin allemand dont la maison venait d'être incendiée, rencontre Gabi, un créateur libanais qui travaillait pour des marques de grande diffusion telles que Kate Spade. Voilà pour les garçons. Tous les quatre, ils créent As Four, si on exclut Powder, le chien blanc qui ne les quitte jamais d'une semelle. Presque tout de suite, ce voyant quartett s'impose au cœur de l'avant-garde new-yorkaise et leurs fans poussent comme des champignons, à l'instar de leurs créations instinctives aux formes ambiguës. Ils présentent leur premier défilé sur de minuscules poupées mécaniques dansant le tamouré sur une musique de Wagner, toutes habillées de vêtements As Four miniatures. Dès lors, le cercle et ses diverses permutations elliptiques sont devenus synonymes d'As Four : leurs fameux sacs en forme de disque ont même fait une apparition dans la série « Sex & The City ». As Four ne produit pas que de la mode, mais des sculptures portables, qu'elles soient outrées ou classiques, coupées dans du cuir ou de la charmeuse de soie. Les formes et les silhouettes d'As Four semblent souvent entièrement inédites, même aux yeux des pires blasés de la mode ; robes, tops et pantalons sont à la fois fluides et ajustés, se transformant constamment en fonction du corps de ceux qui les portent. Björk devient rapidement l'une de leurs plus grandes fans et arbore volontiers leurs créations futuristes, dès qu'elle en a l'occasion. Mais en 2004, les choses se corsent pour As Four. Les liens solides qui avaient porté chance au groupe commencent à se déliter. Adi est le premier à quitter leur appartement de Chinatown peint à la bombe argentée. Kai suit peu de temps après. Puis vient le tour d'Ange et de Gabi, dans un ultime effort pour ressouder la famille. Ainsi le groupe a-t-il pu survivre.

LEE CARTER

What are your signature designs? All our creations are signature designs for us **What is your favourite piece from any of your collection?** No favourite. All is favourite **How would you describe your work?** True, original. Beautiful, timeless **What's your ultimate goal?** To As Fourize more people **What inspires you?** People, ageing, love, our moods **Can fashion still have a political ambition?** Fashion is politics. What you wear reflects how you feel **Who do you have in mind when you design?** Us and them **Is the idea of the creative collaboration important to you?** Very important. It is the basis of As Four. As One As Four, As Four As One. Four is more **Who has been the greatest influence of your career?** All the great people around us. This wonderful place we live in **How have your own experiences affected your work as a designer?** You cry, you laugh, you love, you learn **Which is more important in your work: the process or the product?** The process is as important as the product **Is designing difficult for you? If so, what drives you to continue?** It is not difficult. It is a challenge. It is natural and exciting **Have you ever been influenced or moved by the reaction to your designs?** Always **What's your definition of beauty?** Balance, truth, love and individuality **What's your philosophy?** As one, as all. As all, as one **What is the most important lesson you've learned?** To be yourself as one. To be yourself as four.

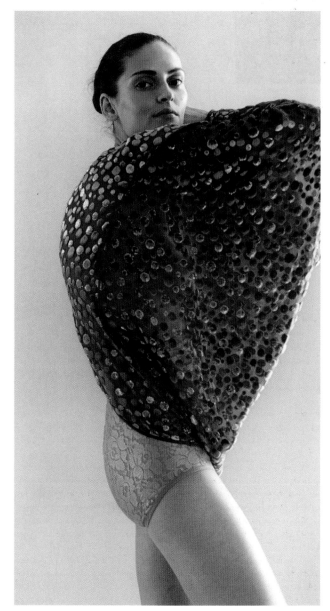
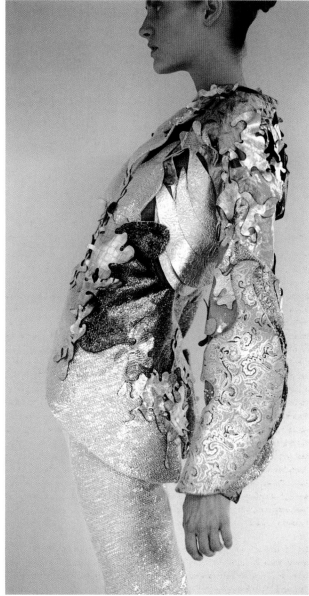

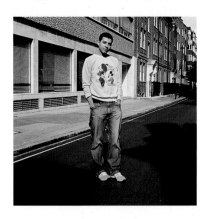

ASHISH

"Ambition and my love for fashion drive me to continue"

"Anything with sequins on it" is how young London-based designer Ashish Gupta defines his signature look. Add to this glittery starting point bold prints, acid shades, retro sportswear and Americana, and the lively appeal of one of fashion's most vibrant fledgling labels is clear. Born in Delhi, India in 1973, Gupta fell in love with fashion at the age of 10, thanks to a grandmother who knitted and a glamorous mother whose westernised approach to style gave the budding designer access to British fashion magazines. Schooled in fine art in India before heading West in the mid-'90s, he studied fashion design at Middlesex University, during which time he trained under the flamboyant queen of print, Zandra Rhodes. He completed an MA in fashion at Central Saint Martins in 2000. Only a year later his designs, under the label Ashish, were being sold in London boutique Browns Focus. In 2002 he was invited to show as part of the GenArt platform for newcomers in New York. Gupta returned to London to show off-schedule for autumn/winter 2004 and by the following season had bagged himself a sponsorship and a place on the official calendar. The neon scissor-print coat, rainbow tights and spangly gold shoes which opened that show are typical of his bold approach. Each piece is handcrafted, with beading and embroidery completed in India, ensuring precious results. Gupta has an eclectic celebrity following that includes Jerry Hall, Mena Suvari and Alison Goldfrapp. The future, quite literally, is bright.

„Alles mit Pailletten dran", beschreibt der junge, in London lebende Designer Ashish Gupta seinen Stil. Zu diesem Glitzern stelle man sich noch kräftige Muster, grelle Farbtöne, Sportswear und Americana im Retrostil vor – und fertig ist der lebenslustige Appeal von einem der frischesten jungen Labels der Modeszene. Der 1973 in Delhi geborene Gupta entdeckte mit zehn sein Faible für Mode. Schuld daran waren eine strickende Großmutter und eine bezaubernde Mutter, deren westlich beeinflusster Geschmack dem späteren Designer Zugang zu britischen Modemagazinen gewährte. In Indien erhielt Gupta eine künstlerische Ausbildung, bevor er Mitte der 1990er Jahre in den Westen kam und an der Universität von Middlesex Modedesign studierte, u. a. bei Zandra Rhodes, der extravaganten Königin der Muster. Seinen Master im Fach Mode machte er im Jahr 2000 am Central Saint Martins. Nur ein Jahr später wurden seine Entwürfe bereits unter dem Label „Ashish" in der Londoner Boutique Browns Focus verkauft. 2002 lud man ihn ein, in New York zu präsentieren, und zwar im Rahmen

der GenArt, einem Forum für Newcomer. Nach London zurückgekehrt, zeigte Gupta seine Kollektion Herbst/Winter 2004 außerhalb des offiziellen Kalenders. Schon eine Saison später hatte er einen Sponsor und einen Platz im Show-Kalender sicher. Der neonfarbene Scherenschnittmantel, die Regenbogenstrümpfe und goldenen Spangenschuhe, mit denen er jene Schau eröffnete, sind typisch für sein selbstbewusstes Auftreten. Jedes seiner Stücke ist handgefertigt, Perlenbesatz und Stickereien werden in Indien vollendet, was prächtigste Ergebnisse garantiert. Guptas Gefolgschaft ist eine bunte Promi-Mischung, zu der Jerry Hall, Mena Suvari und Alison Goldfrapp gehören. Die Zukunft ist, jedenfalls wenn es nach Ashish Gupta geht, strahlend schön.

« Il faut que ça brille ! » : voilà comment le jeune créateur londonien Ashish Gupta définit son look signature. Ajoutez à ce brillant point de départ des imprimés audacieux, des couleurs acidulées, un sportswear rétro et des références à l'attirail cow-boy, et l'attrait de l'une des bébés griffes les plus vibrantes de la mode ne fait plus aucun doute. Né en 1973 à New Delhi en Inde, Gupta tombe amoureux de la mode dès l'âge de 10 ans grâce à une grand-mère tricoteuse et une mère glamour dont l'approche occidentalisée permet au futur créateur de découvrir les magazines de mode anglais. Il étudie les beaux-arts en Inde avant de partir en Occident au milieu des années 90. Il suit un cursus en mode à l'université de Middlesex, période pendant laquelle il est formé par Zandra Rhodes, la flamboyante reine de l'imprimé. En l'an 2000, il décroche un Master en mode à Central Saint Martins. A peine un an plus tard, ses créations sont déjà en vente dans la boutique Browns Focus de Londres, sous la griffe « Ashish ». En 2002, il est invité à New York pour présenter son travail dans le cadre de GenArt, une plateforme dédiée aux nouveaux talents. Gupta revient à Londres pour présenter sa collection automne/hiver 2004 dans le cadre du circuit « off » de la Fashion Week. Dès la saison suivante, il se trouve un sponsor et une place dans le calendrier officiel des défilés. Le manteau fluo avec imprimés de ciseaux, les collants arc-en-ciel et les chaussures dorées et pailletées qui ouvrent ce défilé sont typiques de son audace créative. Chaque pièce est confectionnée à la main avec des perles et des broderies réalisées en Inde, ce qui garantit un résultat très « objet précieux ». Gupta compte des célébrités éclectiques parmi ses fidèles, notamment Jerry Hall, Mena Suvari et Alison Goldfrapp. Il semble, littéralement, promis à un brillant avenir.

SIMON CHILVERS

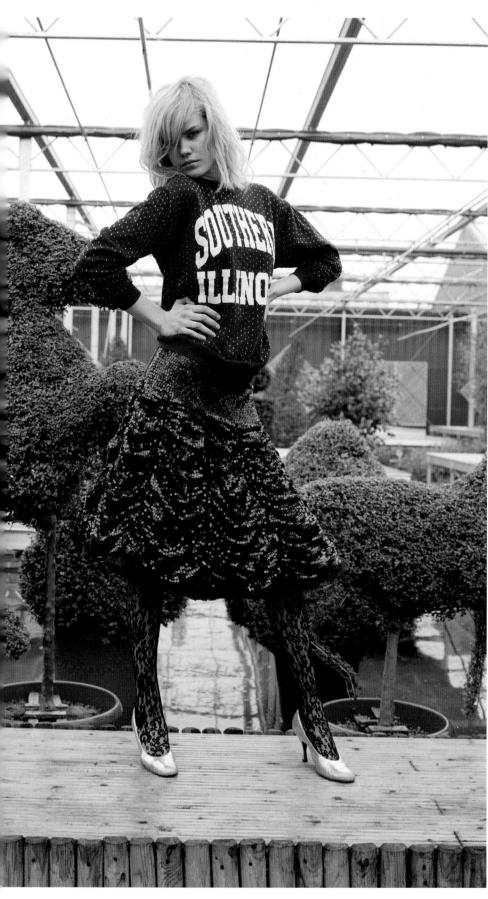

What are your signature [...]
with colour and seq[...]
favourite piece from any[...]
It changes every seas[...]
describe your work? Han[...]
with a sense of humour [...] **What's [...]
goal?** To be able to continue doing what I am
doing **What inspires you?** Travelling, people,
street culture, big cities, nightlife, music,
films, friends, markets, love and life **Can
fashion still have a political ambition?** Yes
because fashion and politics are interlinked
through sex, money, power, status, ethics
Who do you have in mind when you design?
My friend Nadine **Is the idea of creative
collaboration important to you?** Yes, two brains
are (sometimes) better than one **Who has
been the greatest influence on your career?** My
mother **How have your own experiences
affected your work as a designer?** Experiences
either inspire, or teach you to know better
next time **Which is more important in your
work: the process or the product?** The process
because it leads to the product **Is designing
difficult for you, if so, what drives you to
continue?** It's not difficult, but it's hard work,
and it can be exhausting. Ambition and my
love for fashion make me continue **Have you
ever been influenced or moved by the reaction to your designs?** Not really influenced,
certainly moved **What's your definition of
beauty?** Something that cannot be defined
What's your philosophy? If you're not enjoying
it, it's probably not worth doing **What is the
most important lesson you've learned?** Never
have your pictures taken while naked.

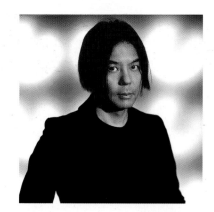

ATSURO TAYAMA

"I've learned that I can destroy a dress beautifully"

Paris-based designer Atsuro Tayama (born in Kumamoto, Japan in 1955) is not one to seek out the limelight and his tranquil nature is reflected in the thoughtful clothing he creates. Yet he is one of the most prolific working in fashion today. Shortly after graduating from the Bunka Fashion College, Tokyo, in 1975, he was awarded the Pierre Cardin Fashion Prize and immediately became an assistant designer at Yohji Yamamoto's Y's Company, where he remained until 1982. At the end of his time working for Yamamoto, from 1978-82, Tayama had ascended to the position of director of European Operations. He founded his own firm, MT company, in 1982 in Tokyo and showed his first collection under the A/T label; 1991 Tayama was invited to join the official schedule of the Paris ready-to-wear collections. His connection with French fashion was further strengthened between 1990 and 1994 when he worked as the chief designer of Cacharel. He then signed agreements with World Co., Ltd to design several lines including Indivi, OZOC (a music- and streetwear-inspired brand) and Boycott, a menswear brand. In 1999 he launched Atsuro Tayama Green Label.

Der 1955 im japanischen Kumamoto geborene und heute in Paris lebende Atsuro Tayama ist kein Mensch, der das Rampenlicht sucht. Sein stilles Wesen kommt auch in seinen gedankenvollen Kreationen zum Ausdruck. Dennoch ist er eine der produktivsten Kräfte in der heutigen Modeszene. Nach seinem Abschluss am Tokioter Bunka Fashion College 1975 erhielt er den Pierre Cardin Fashion Prize und wurde umgehend Assistant Designer bei Yohji Yamamotos Y's Company, wo er bis 1982 blieb und zum Schluss die Position des Director of European Operations innehatte. Seine eigene Firma, MT Company, gründete er 1982 in Tokio. Die erste Kollektion präsentierte er anschließend unter dem Label A/T. 1991 lud

man ihn zur Teilnahme am offiziellen Programm der Pariser Prêt-à-porter-Schauen ein. Die Verbindung zur französischen Modeszene wurde zwischen 1990 und 1994 weiter intensiviert, weil er in diesem Zeitraum als Chefdesigner bei Cacharel tätig war. Dann unterzeichnete Tayama eine Vereinbarung mit der World Co. Ltd. über die Kreation verschiedener Linien, darunter Indivi, OZOC (ein von der Musikszene und der Streetwear inspiriertes Label) sowie die Herrenmarke Boycott. 1999 kam schließlich Atsuro Tayama Green Label auf den Markt.

Aujourd'hui installé à Paris, le créateur Atsuro Tayama (né en 1955 à Kumamoto au Japon) n'est pas du genre à vouloir briller sous les feux de la rampe et cette nature tranquille se reflète dans les vêtements réfléchis qu'il dessine. Il reste néanmoins l'un des créateurs les plus prolifiques de la mode actuelle. Peu de temps après l'obtention de son diplôme du Bunka Fashion College de Tokyo en 1975, il remporte le prix Pierre Cardin et devient immédiatement assistant de Yohji Yamamoto pour Y's Company, où il reste jusqu'en 1982. Pendant ces quatre années passées chez Yamamoto, entre 1978 et 1982, Tayama se hisse au poste de directeur des opérations européennes. En 1982, il fonde sa propre entreprise à Tokyo, MT Company, et présente sa première collection sous la griffe A/T; en 1991, Tayama est invité à rejoindre le calendrier officiel des collections parisiennes de prêt-à-porter. Sa relation avec la mode française est encore renforcée entre 1990 et 1994, alors qu'il occupe les fonctions de styliste principal chez Cacharel. Il signe ensuite des accords avec World Co., Ltd pour dessiner plusieurs lignes, notamment Indivi, OZOC (marque inspirée du streetwear et de l'univers de la musique) et Boycott, une griffe pour homme. En 1999, il lance Atsuro Tayama Green Label.

SUSIE RUSHTON

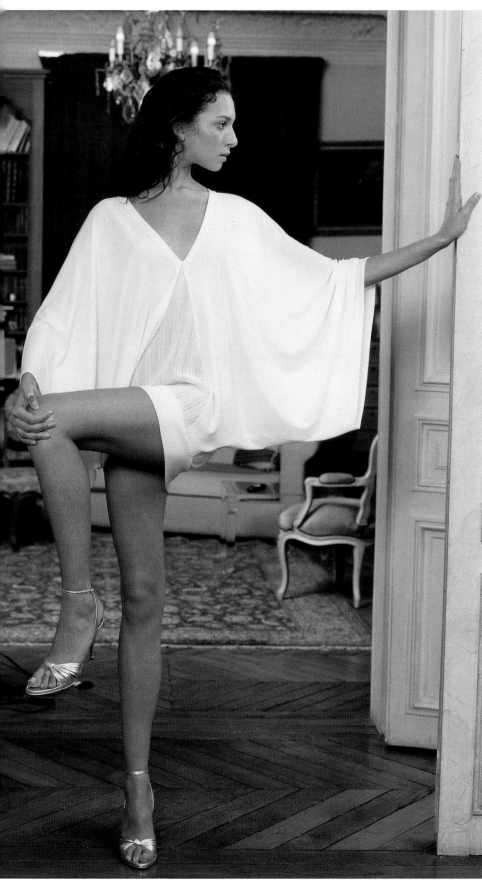

What are your signature designs? It's about mixing or combining. Combining feminine and masculine, East with West. (That's because I'm Japanese.) Natural and artificial, beauty and destruction **What is your favourite piece from any of your collections?** Incomplete jackets and dresses which I continue making or completing **How would you describe your work?** A clergyman who creates fashion **What's your ultimate goal?** I don't have goals. It's all a process. For me, a finished line is yet another beginning **What inspires you?** A mixture of all feelings, such as confidence and anxiety **Can fashion still have a political ambition?** It depends on each designer. Personally I don't place a political ambition on my design **Who do you have in mind when you design?** I only think about clothing **Is the idea of creative collaboration important to you?** Yes, collaboration is important and necessary. I collaborate with my staff **Who has been the greatest influence on your career?** My first collection in Paris **How have your own experiences affected your work as a designer?** All my experiences affect my work. Connecting with people as well as solitude, sad as well as happy experiences **Which is more important in your work: the process or the product?** Both of them **Is designing difficult for you, if so, what drives you to continue?** Designing brings me joy. Nevertheless it is difficult to maintain the environment where I can continue to design **Have you ever been influenced or moved by the reaction to your designs?** I have been influenced by the reaction to each collection **What's your definition of beauty?** Les belles choses ont une ame... **What's your philosophy?** Continuation is everything **What is the most important lesson you've learned?** I've learned that I can destroy a dress beautifully.

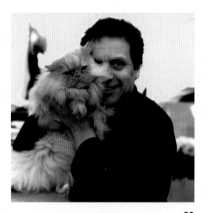

AZZEDINE ALAÏA

"Perfection is never achieved, so you need to go on working"

Azzedine Alaïa's place in the design hall of fame is guaranteed – his signature being the second skin that he creates when challenging the boundaries of flesh and fabric. Alaïa was born in Tunisia in the '40s to wheat-farming parents. A French friend of his mother's fed Alaïa's instinctive creativity with copies of Vogue and lied about his age to get him into the local Ecole des Beaux-Arts to study sculpture – a discipline in which he didn't excel, but that he would put to good use in the future. After spotting an ad for a vacancy at a dressmaker's, Alaïa's sister taught him to sew and he started making copies of couture dresses for neighbours. Soon afterwards, he went to Paris to work for Christian Dior, but managed only five days of sewing labels before being fired. Alaïa moved to Guy Laroche, where for two seasons he learned his craft while earning his keep as housekeeper to the Marquise de Mazan. In 1960, the Blegiers family snapped up Alaïa, and for the next five years he was both housekeeper and dressmaker to the Countess and her friends, mixing with glamorous Paris society; a clientele that followed him when he started out on his own. His first ready-to-wear collection for Charles Jourdan in the '70s was not well received, but eventually fashion editors tuned into Alaïa's modern elegance – something that would eventually come to define body conscious aesthetics a decade later. Worldwide success followed with exhibitions, awards, supermodel disciples and the power to command an audience outside of the catwalk schedule: Alaïa shows when he wants, regardless of the round of timetabled international fashion weeks, and editors never miss it. In 1998, he published a book of photographs of his creations, entitled 'Alaïa' and in 2000, he joined forces with the Prada Group. The same year, he was honoured with a solo exhibition at the New York Guggenheim. In October 2004 he opened his very own hotel (5 rue de Moussy) adjoining the Alaïa headquarters in Paris.

Ein Platz in der Hall of Fame der Designer ist Azzedine Alaïa bereits sicher – dank seines Markenzeichens, der zweiten Haut, mit der er die Grenzen zwischen Körper und Stoff aufzuheben scheint. Geboren wurde der tunesische Bauernsohn in den 1940er Jahren. Eine französische Freundin seiner Mutter förderte seine angeborene Kreativität mit Ausgaben der Vogue und mogelte bei seinem Alter, um ihn an der Kunstakademie von Tunis im Fach Bildhauerei unterzubringen. Er erwies sich zwar nicht als überragender Student, doch sollte ihm diese Ausbildung in der Zukunft noch von Nutzen sein. Weil ihn die Anzeige für eine freie Stelle in einer Schneiderei interessierte, ließ er sich von seiner Schwester das Nähen beibringen und kopierte schon bald Haute-Couture-Kleider für die Frauen der Nachbarschaft. Kurz darauf ging er nach Paris, um für Christian Dior zu arbeiten, dort nähte er allerdings gerade mal fünf Tage lang Etiketten ein, bevor man ihn feuerte. Daraufhin wechselte Alaïa zu Guy Laroche, wo er zwei Saisons lang sein Handwerk lernte und sich seinen Lebensunterhalt als Haushälter der Marquise de Mazan verdiente. 1960 engagierte ihn die Familie Blegiers, bei der er fünf Jahre lang Haushälter und Hausschneider für die Comtesse und ihre Freundinnen sein sollte und auch Zugang zur Glamour-Gesellschaft von Paris fand. Diese

Klientel hielt ihm weiter die Treue, als er sich schließlich selbstständig machte. Seine erste Prêt-à-porter-Kollektion für Charles Jourdan in den 1970er Jahren kam nicht besonders gut an, doch irgendwann hatten sich die Modejournalisten an Alaïas moderne Eleganz gewöhnt. Sein Stil nahm die figurbetonte Ästhetik des darauf folgenden Jahrzehnts vorweg. Der weltweite Erfolg wurde von Ausstellungen, Preisen, treu ergebenen Supermodels und der Macht begleitet, ein Publikum auch abseits des offiziellen Modenschau-Kalenders zu finden. Alaïa präsentiert seine Entwürfe, wann es ihm passt, und ignoriert einfach die exakt terminierten internationalen Modewochen. Die Journalisten sind trotzdem immer da. 1998 veröffentlichte der Designer einen Band mit Fotos seiner Kreationen unter dem Titel „Alaïa". Im Jahr 2000 begab er sich unter die Fittiche des Prada-Konzerns. Im selben Jahr ehrte das New Yorker Guggenheim Museum ihn mit einer Einzelausstellung. Sein Hotel in der Pariser Rue de Moussy Nummer 5, gleich neben der Alaïa-Zentrale, wurde im Oktober 2004 eröffnet.

Défiant les frontières qui séparent la chair du tissu, les créations « seconde peau » qui distinguent le travail d'Azzedine Alaïa lui garantissent une place de choix dans l'Olympe de la mode. Alaïa est né dans les années 1940 en Tunisie de parents cultivateurs de blé. Sa créativité instinctive se nourrit des exemplaires de Vogue d'une amie française de sa mère, qui mentira sur son âge pour le faire entrer à l'Ecole des Beaux-Arts de la région. Il y étudie la sculpture, discipline dans laquelle il n'excelle pas particulièrement mais qu'il utilisera à bon escient par la suite. Après avoir repéré une offre d'emploi chez un couturier, la sœur d'Alaïa lui apprend à coudre et il commence à copier les robes haute couture pour ses voisines. Peu de temps après, il s'installe à Paris pour travailler chez Christian Dior, mais se fait mettre à la porte après cinq jours passés à coudre des étiquettes. Alaïa travaille ensuite pour Guy Laroche, chez qui il se forme au métier pendant deux saisons tout en gagnant sa vie en tant qu'intendant de la marquise de Mazan. En 1960, la famille Blegiers embauche Alaïa et pendant cinq ans, il est à la fois l'intendant et le couturier de la comtesse et de ses amis, se mêlant à la haute société parisienne, une clientèle qui le suivra lorsqu'il lancera sa propre griffe. Dans les années 70, sa première collection de prêt-à-porter pour Charles Jourdan n'est pas bien accueillie, mais les journalistes de mode s'intéressent tout de même à l'élégance moderne d'Alaïa, qui finira par définir l'esthétique du « body consciousness » une décennie plus tard. Le succès mondial s'ensuit grâce à des expositions, des récompenses, le soutien des plus grands top models et le pouvoir de séduire le public même en dehors du calendrier officiel : Alaïa présente ses collections quand ça lui chante, sans se soucier de l'agenda mondial des semaines de la mode, et la presse ne rate pas un seul de ses défilés. En 1998, il sort un livre de photos de ses créations intitulé « Alaïa », puis en l'an 2000, il s'associe au Groupe Prada. La même année, le musée Guggenheim de New York lui consacre toute une exposition. En octobre 2004, il ouvre son propre hôtel (5, rue de Moussy), juste à côté du siège social parisien d'Alaïa.

JAMIE HUCKBODY

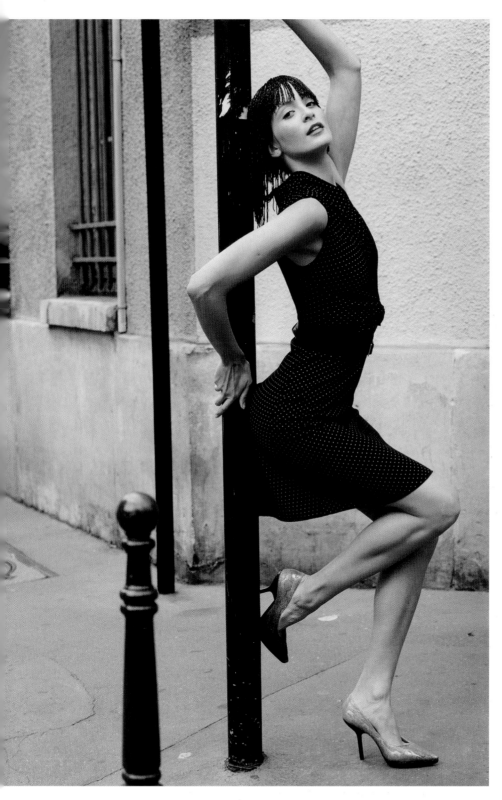

What is your favourite piece from any of your collections? I'm still waiting for that feeling. I always doubt **How would you describe your work?** It's not me but only journalists who can describe my work **What's your ultimate goal?** Only the future will tell us **What inspires you?** Women **What do you have in mind when you design?** How and when shall I finish it **Is the idea of creative collaboration important to you?** Always **What has been the greatest influence on your career?** Art, sculpture, design, paintings **Which is more important in your work: the process or the product?** The process **Is the designing difficult for you. If so, what drives you to continue?** What drives me to continue is the pleasure to keep on learning. In other words, perfection is never achieved so you need to go on working **Have you ever been influenced or moved by the reaction to your designs?** Always – emotion is very important **What's your philosophy?** Overall integrity.

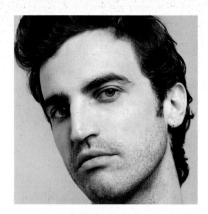

BALENCIAGA

"The history of the house is incredible, which means I can work with a lot of freedom" NICOLAS GHESQUIÈRE

When the great Cristobal Balenciaga closed the doors of his couture house in 1968 he lamented, "There is no one left worth dressing." For decades the house lay dormant until 26-year-old Frenchman Nicolas Ghesquière was appointed creative director of Balenciaga in 1997 after the departure of Josephus Thimister. Since 1995, Ghesquière had quietly freelanced for Balenciaga's licences. Three years later, Ghesquière won the Vogue/VH1 Avant Garde Designer of the Year Award, followed by the CFDA womenswear Designer of the Year title in 2001. Suzy Menkes of The International Herald Tribune called him "the most intriguing and original designer of his generation". Though relatively unknown when he was appointed to Balenciaga, Ghesquière's is a life in fashion. He won work placements at agnès b. and Corinne Cobson while still at school in Loudon, central France. At 19, he became an assistant designer to Gaultier and then Mugler, before a brief tenure as head designer at Trussardi. But his great achievement has been his revival of Balenciaga. His green silk crop combat pants for spring/summer 2002 were the most copied garment of the season and Neoprene mini skirts and dresses for spring/summer 2003 kept Balenciaga on the edge, creatively and commercially. In 2002 a menswear line was launched, a year after the house of Balenciaga was bought by the Gucci Group. For autumn/winter 2005 he showed A-line leather dresses trimmed with pale ostrich feathers and sleek tailoring fitted with chrome fastenings. Former Gucci CEO Domenico De Sole has said: 'Balenciaga has one fantastic asset. He's called Nicolas Ghesquière'.

Als der große Cristobal Balenciaga 1968 die Tore seines Couture-Hauses schloss, klagte er: „Es gibt niemanden mehr, der es wert wäre, eingekleidet zu werden." Danach lag das Modehaus jahrzehntelang in einer Art Dornröschenschlaf, bis der Franzose Nicolas Ghesquière 1997 nach dem Weggang von Josephus Thimister Chefdesigner von Balenciaga wurde. Bereits ab 1995 hatte Ghesquière im Stillen als freier Mitarbeiter für Balenciagas Lizenzmarken entworfen. Drei Jahre später gewann er den Avant Garde Designer of the Year Award von Vogue und VH1, 2001 folgte der Titel Designer of the Year für seine Damenmode, gestiftet von der CFDA. Suzy Menkes von der International Herald Tribune nannte ihn „den faszinierendsten und originellsten Designer seiner Generation". Auch wenn er bei seiner Verpflichtung für Balenciaga noch relativ unbekannt war, drehte sich doch auch bis dahin schon sein ganzes Leben um Mode. Bereits während seiner Schulzeit im französischen Loudon ergatterte er Praktikumsplätze bei agnès b. und Corinne Cobson. Mit 19 assistierte er Gaultier, anschließend Thierry Mugler, dann folgte ein kurzes Intermezzo als Chefdesigner bei Trussardi. Seine größte Leistung bis dato ist jedoch die Wiederbelebung von Balenciaga. Die abgeschnittenen Army-Hosen aus grüner Seide für Frühjahr/Sommer 2002 gehörten zu den meistkopierten Kleidungsstücken der Saison. Die Miniröcke und -kleider aus Neopren für Frühjahr/Sommer 2003 sorgten dafür, dass Balenciaga führend blieb – kreativ wie kommerziell. 2002 wurde erstmals eine Herrenkollektion präsentiert, ein Jahr später kaufte der Gucci-Konzern Balenciaga. Im Herbst/Winter 2005 zeigte er Lederkleider in A-Form mit hellem Straußenfederbesatz, schmaler Silhouette und Verschlüssen aus Chrom. Der ehemalige CEO von Gucci, Domenico De Sole, sagte einmal: „Balenciaga besitzt einen phantastischen Aktivposten. Er heißt Nicolas Ghesquière."

Quand le grand Cristobal Balenciaga ferme sa maison en 1968, il déplore que « plus personne ne mérite d'être habillé ». Pendant plusieurs décennies, la griffe semble plongée dans un sommeil de Belle au bois dormant jusqu'à ce que Nicolas Ghesquière, un jeune Français de 26 ans, soit nommé directeur de la création de Balenciaga en 1997, après le départ de Josephus Thimister. Depuis 1995, Ghesquière travaillait tranquillement comme styliste free-lance pour les collections sous licence de Balenciaga. Trois ans plus tard, il remporte le prix d'Avant Garde Designer of the Year décerné par Vogue et la chaîne VH1, puis le titre de Womenswear Designer of the Year du CFDA en 2001. Suzy Menkes de l'International Herald Tribune le considère alors comme « le créateur le plus fascinant et le plus original de sa génération ». Presque inconnu lorsqu'il a pris ses fonctions chez Balenciaga, Ghesquière revendiquait déjà un beau parcours dans la mode. Il avait suivi des stages chez agnès b. et Corinne Cobson alors qu'il était encore lycéen à Loudon dans le centre de la France. A 19 ans, il devient assistant-styliste chez Gaultier puis chez Mugler, avant de travailler pendant une brève période comme styliste principal chez Trussardi. Mais la renaissance de Balenciaga reste sa plus grande réalisation. Le treillis-pantacourt en soie verte de sa collection printemps/été 2002 devient le vêtement le plus copié de la saison ; quant aux minijupes et robes en néoprène du printemps/été 2003, elles placent Balenciaga au pinacle de la mode, tant sur le plan créatif que commercial. En 2002, Balenciaga lance une ligne pour homme, un an après le rachat de la maison par le groupe Gucci. Pour l'automne/hiver 2005, il présente des robes trapèze en cuir, ornées de plumes d'autruche aux couleurs pâles, ainsi que des tailleurs épurés dotés d'attaches en chrome. Domenico De Sole, ancien P-DG de Gucci, a un jour déclaré : « Balenciaga possède un atout fantastique. Il s'appelle Nicolas Ghesquière ». JAMES SHERWOOD

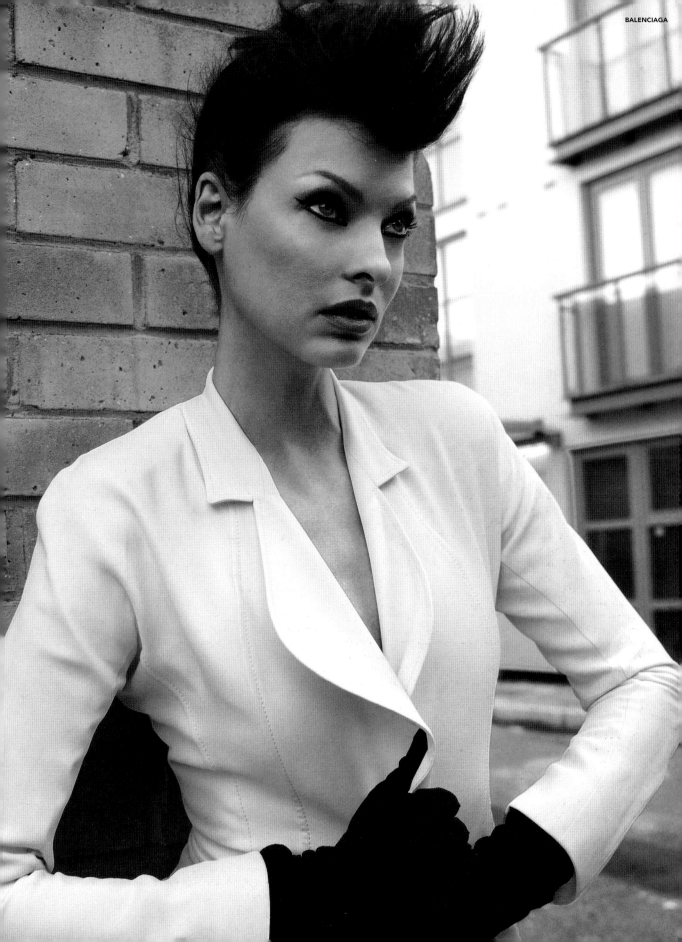

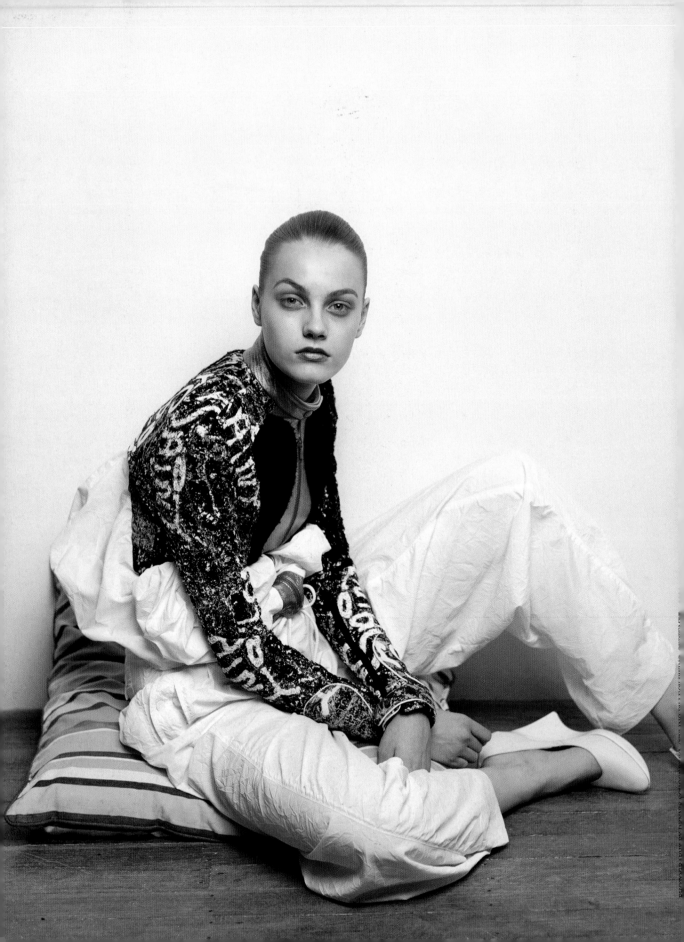

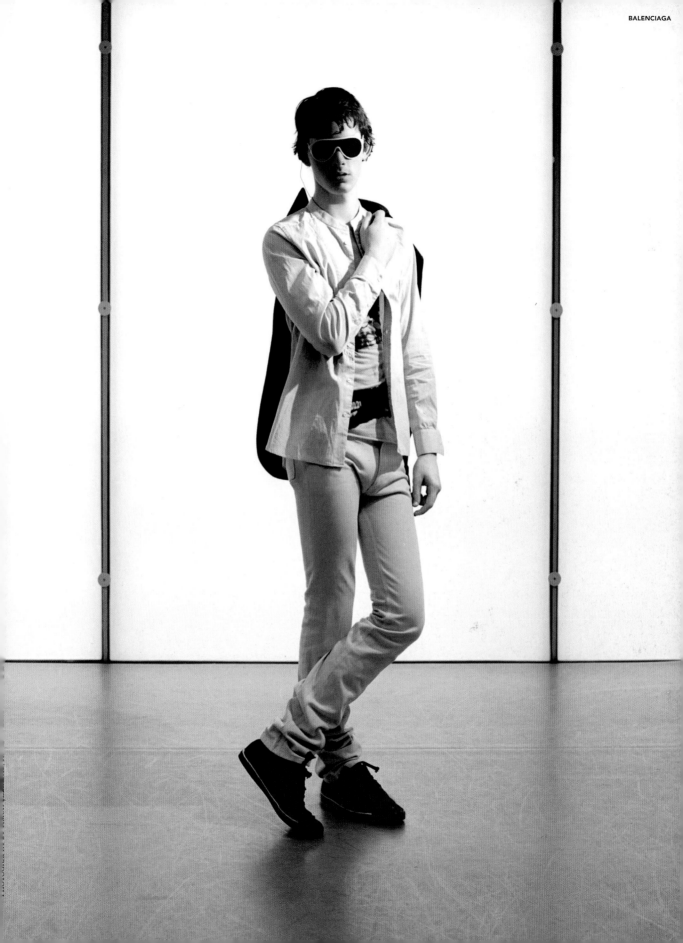

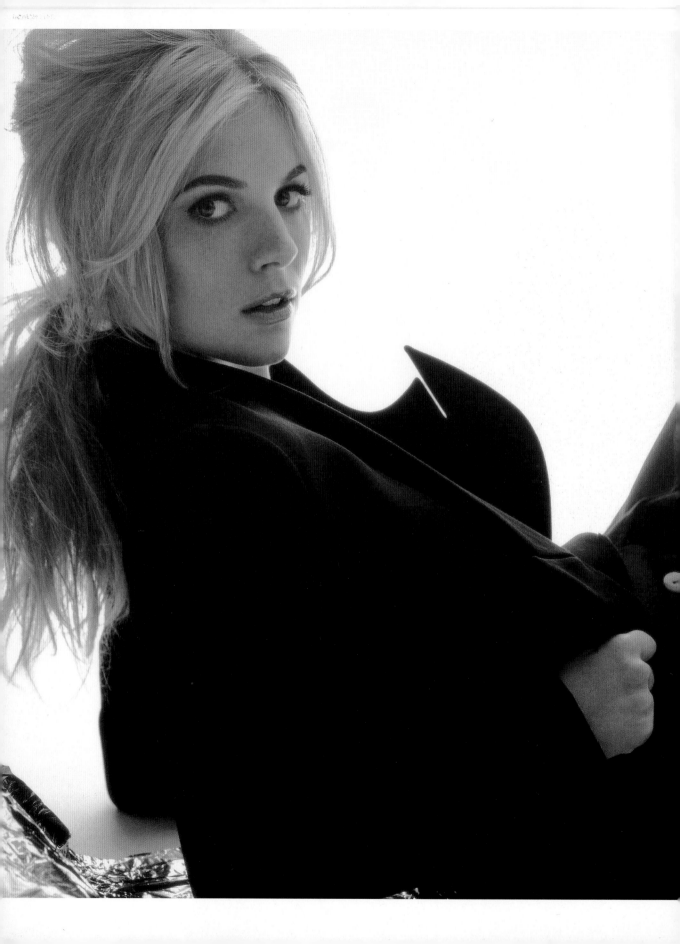

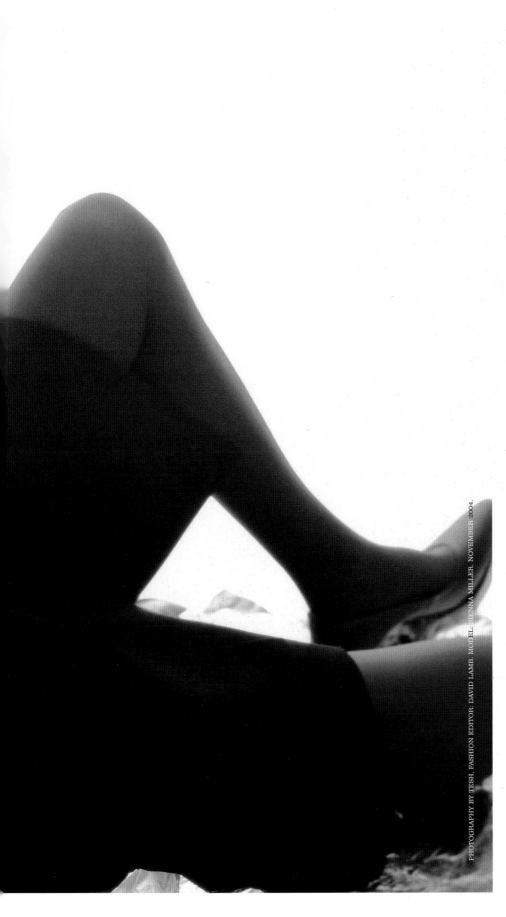

What are your signature designs? I can't define what I do and I don't really want to. If people interpret this or that in a certain way, it's fine. It's done for that reason – to be open **How would you describe your work?** What I do is always because of last season, not a reaction against it. I always want to find a surprising way to go, but beneath that I want to try and say the same things **What's your ultimate goal?** I've never really wanted to be famous. That, for me, is not the intention **What inspires you?** I'm an 1980s child, so it's completely natural for me to be inspired by that decade. I've always used those references. I think, in a way, you always have to use the same thing in fashion, but you must find a new way to tell it **Who do you have in mind when you design?** Any girl who puts on Balenciaga is a muse. I don't like to think of one in particular when I'm designing **How have your own experiences affected your work as a designer?** The history of the house is incredible, which means I can work with a lot of freedom. Cristobal Balenciaga discovered so many things, was so inventive, it's astonishing. I can work on something and then look back through the archives and find it already. I am very respectful of Balenciaga, but this is another time and it is my vision of what Balenciaga is now **What's your philosophy?** For me it's about evolution, not revolution **What is the most important lesson you've learned?** If you want to be happy, then keep yourself a little hidden.

PHOTOGRAPHY BY TESH. FASHION EDITOR: DAVID LAMB. MODEL: SIENNA MILLER. NOVEMBER 2004.

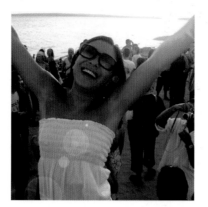

BARBARA BUI

"A designer must be open-minded.
You can't withdrew into yourself"

With an academic background in English literature and a passion for theatre, there is every chance we may never have seen a Barbara Bui creation step out onto the catwalk. Born in Paris in 1957, her first venture in fashion came in 1983 with the opening of the boutique, Kabuki – the name is testimony to her admiration for the traditional Japanese performance art – a joint venture with her business partner William Halimi. Originally a retailer of other designers' collections, Bui started to introduce pieces of her own work into the boutique and only four years later, in 1988, she presented her first collection to the international fashion press and her main line was born. In the same year, she opened the first Barbara Bui shop in Paris. Strength and elegance have been at the heart of her work from the beginning. The use of delicate embroidery against block tonal leather emphasizes the feminine qualities that Bui admires. By 1998 a diffusion line, Barbara Bui Initials, was taking the classic style of her mainline and translating it into daywear. In 1999 she temporarily moved her show from Paris to New York before, for a period, removing her collections from the catwalk altogether. Her preference for alternative forms of presentation led to a successful collaboration with David Bailey, a photographer she felt was able to communicate the ethos of her designs. However, 2004 saw a return to the Paris runways with a show of her signature leather, furs and heels. Today Bui presides over four collections (her main line, diffusion, menswear and a shoe range) with shops in Paris, Milan and New York.

Bedenkt man ihre akademische Ausbildung in englischer Literatur und ihre Liebe zum Theater, hätte es eigentlich gut passieren können, dass nie eine Kreation von Barbara Bui auf den Laufsteg gekommen wäre. Ihren ersten Auftritt in der Modebranche hatte die 1957 in Paris geborene Bui 1983, als sie zusammen mit ihrem Geschäftspartner William Halimi die Boutique Kabuki eröffnete. Der Name ist ein Verweis auf ihre Bewunderung für diese traditionelle japanische Theaterform. Ursprünglich wurden dort die Kollektionen anderer Designer verkauft, doch dann begann Bui auch eigene Entwürfe anzubieten. Nur vier Jahre später, 1988, präsentierte sie der internationalen Modepresse ihre erste Kollektion, und ihre Hauptlinie war geboren. Noch im selben Jahr eröffnete sie den ersten Barbara-Bui-Laden in Paris. Kraft und Eleganz haben ihre Arbeit von Beginn an geprägt. Die Kombination von zarter Stickerei mit grobem Leder

unterstreicht die weiblichen Eigenschaften, die Bui schätzt. Ab 1998 griff sie in der Nebenlinie Barbara Bui Initials den klassischen Stil ihrer Hauptlinie auf und übertrug ihn auf Mode für jeden Tag. 1999 verlegte die Designerin ihre Schauen von Paris nach New York, bevor sie sie für einen gewissen Zeitraum ganz vom Laufsteg nahm. Ihre Vorliebe für alternative Präsentationsformen führte sie zur erfolgreichen Zusammenarbeit mit David Bailey, der ihrer Ansicht nach als Fotograf das Ethos ihrer Entwürfe optimal zum Ausdruck bringen konnte. Dennoch kehrte sie 2004 auf die Laufstege von Paris zurück, und zwar mit ihren Markenzeichen Leder, Pelz und High Heels. Heute herrscht Bui über vier Kollektionen (ihre Hauptlinie, die Nebenlinie, Herrenmode und Schuhe) sowie Läden in Paris, Mailand und New York.

Avec ses études universitaires en littérature anglaise et sa véritable passion pour le théâtre, on a bien failli ne jamais admirer le travail de Barbara Bui sur le podium des défilés. Née à Paris en 1957, elle se lance dans la mode en 1983 en ouvrant la boutique Kabuki (un nom choisi en hommage au théâtre traditionnel japonais), épaulée par son partenaire en affaires William Halimi. La boutique propose d'abord les collections d'autres créateurs, mais Barbara Bui ne tarde pas à y présenter ses propres créations. Quatre ans plus tard, en 1988, elle présente sa toute première collection à la presse internationale : sa ligne principale est née. La même année, elle ouvre la première boutique Barbara Bui à Paris. Force et élégance caractérisent son travail depuis ses débuts. L'application de broderies délicates sur du cuir monochrome exprime toutes les qualités féminines que Barbara Bui admire. En 1998, la ligne secondaire Barbara Bui Initials reprend le style classique de sa première ligne pour le transformer en tenues de jour. En 1999, elle transfère temporairement son showroom de Paris à New York, avant de fuir les défilés pendant une certaine période. En effet, elle préfère présenter son travail de façon moins formelle, ce qui a donné lieu à une collaboration très réussie avec David Bailey, un photographe capable, selon elle, de communiquer l'esprit de ses créations. Mais en 2004, on la retrouve sur les podiums parisiens avec un défilé présentant ses célèbres cuirs, fourrures et chaussures à talon. Aujourd'hui, Barbara Bui dirige quatre collections (sa ligne principale, sa ligne secondaire, une collection pour homme et une gamme de chaussures), avec des boutiques à Paris, Milan et New York.

WILL FAIRMAN

PORTRAIT BY CARLOS PUIG.   PHOTOGRAPHY BY STEVE SMITH.   STYLING BY DAVID LAMB.   MODEL: ASTA MARCH 2003

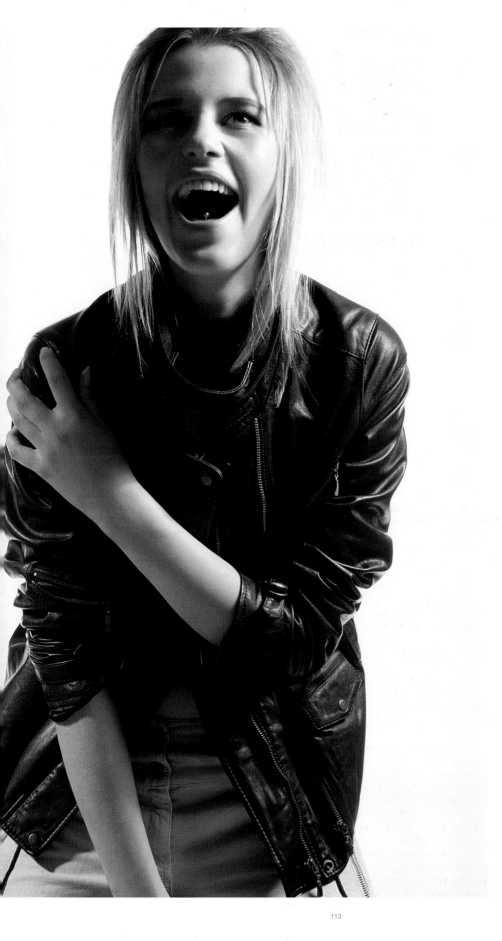

What are your signature designs? They balance elegant simplicity with the freedom of rock'n'roll romanticism **What is your favourite piece from any of your collections?** For years I've adored trousers. Now I have a new passion: the dress **How would you describe your work?** Giving expression to a womanhood at once touching and true, fragile and fearless **What inspires you?** Encounters. Films. Music. Things percolating through my mind. Moments of grace. Women in general. Cities. Soaking in the natural environment. A kaleidoscope of impressions real or imaginary, experience and daydream **Can fashion still have a political ambition?** Of course. Fashion can convey declared or subliminal messages **Who do you have in mind when you design?** Actresses who are moving by their evident duality, such as Romy Schneider or Emma Thompson **Is the idea of creative collaboration important to you?** Of course, with my staff and in encounters with people from different worlds such as the music world. In fashion, a designer must be open-minded. You can't withdraw into yourself **What has been the greatest influence on your career?** An Yves Saint Laurent exhibition at the very beginning of my career **How have your own experiences affected your work as a designer?** I experience wounds or joy as a person – these can be private or social experiences – and they find expression in my work. There is always a mix of the private and the communal in my work **Which is more important in your work: the process or the product?** The 'process' justifies the product. The product justifies the 'process' **Is designing difficult for you and, if so, what drives you to continue?** It's always difficult but there are magical moments when everything is suddenly clear and self-evident. These are the moments one is always looking for. They're the reason why I go on **Have you ever been influenced or moved by the reaction to your design?** Yes, when the reaction is good and one is carried on a wave of other people's trust. When the reactions are critical, often you must simply persist, trying to become more convincing, more mature **What's your definition of beauty?** Simplicity of being: an innate beauty that is not dependent on the beholder **What's your philosophy?** Don't be impatient **What is the most important lesson you've learned?** Be demanding and trust your intuitions.

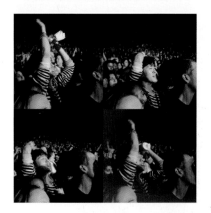

BENJAMIN CHO

"Everything is difficult for me. Designing is the easiest part"

Benjamin Cho is the fashion school drop-out with all of Manhattan at his feet. Born in Cambridge, Massachusetts, in 1976, the son of an opera singer and scientist, Cho was raised in California but settled in New York after he began studying fashion at Parsons School of Design in 1994. He stayed there for almost two years before dropping out to concentrate on his own design work, showing a debut collection to rave reviews in 1999. Cho places much emphasis on labour-intensive techniques, which are an intrinsic aspect of his work. He takes relatively simple skills – lacing, braiding, ruching – and uses them for sensuous evening wear, creating the complex and dramatic effects that have become a trademark of his easily recognisable work. Cho possesses more of a European rather than an American aesthetic sensibility; he is at the forefront of a generation of less-established, avant-garde New York and Los Angeles-based designers whose clothes are directional, unconventional and stand out in the largely commercially-driven American fashion scene. Cho's distinctive work has attracted the attention of celebrities, many of whom are now loyal clients, such as actresses Milla Jovovich and Claire Danes. In spring 2002, following 9/11 and the subsequent cancellation of Cho's New York Fashion Week show, he was invited by American Vogue to present his collection alongside ten other young designers, an invitation that helped to gain international recognition for his talent. For autumn/winter 2005 Cho presented a romantic collection of voluminous pieces where black satin skirts were tied at the waist with outsized bows and a pale pink dress ballooned to completely cocoon the wearer.

Benjamin Cho hat sein Modestudium zwar abgebrochen, dennoch liegt ihm ganz Manhattan zu Füßen. Geboren wurde er 1976 als Sohn einer Opernsängerin und eines Wissenschaftlers in Cambridge, Massachusetts. Er wuchs in Kalifornien auf und zog 1994 nach New York, um an der Parsons School of Design zu studieren. Das tat er auch knapp zwei Jahre lang, brach dann die Ausbildung ab, um sich auf seine eigenen Entwürfe zu konzentrieren, und präsentierte 1999 eine Debütkollektion, die die Kritiker hinriss. Cho legt viel Gewicht auf arbeits-aufwändige Techniken, die seine Arbeit prägen. Er verwendet relativ einfache Dekors wie Spitzen, Borten und Rüschen für sinnliche Abendmode und erzielt damit komplizierte, dramatische Effekte, die zu Markenzeichen seiner leicht erkennbaren Kreationen avancierten. Chos ästhetisches Empfinden wirkt eher europäisch als amerikanisch, und er gehört zu den Vorreitern einer neuen Gene-ration von wenig etablierten, avantgardistischen Designern mit Sitz in New York oder Los Angeles, deren zielstrebige, unkonventionelle Kleider sich von der

größtenteils kommerziell ausgerichteten amerikanischen Modeszene deutlich abheben. Seine unverwechselbaren Kreationen haben Cho die Aufmerksamkeit zahlreicher Prominenter gesichert, von denen inzwischen viele zu treuen Kun-den geworden sind, wie z.B. die Schauspielerinnen Milla Jovovich und Claire Danes. Im Frühjahr 2002 erhielt Cho nach den Anschlägen vom 11. September 2001 und der daraufhin abgesagten Schau im Rahmen der New York Fashion Week eine Einladung der amerikanischen Vogue. Gemeinsam mit zehn anderen jungen Designern zeigte er dort seine Kollektion und erntete dabei internatio-nale Anerkennung für sein Talent. Für Herbst/Winter 2005 zeigte Cho eine romantische Kollektion voluminöser Entwürfe: Schwarze Satinröcke wurden in der Taille von überdimensionalen Schleifen gehalten, und blassrosa Kleider bauschten sich so stark, dass sie ihre Trägerinnen komplett verhüllten.

Bien qu'il ait interrompu ses études de mode, Benjamin Cho n'en a pas moins tout Manhattan à ses pieds. Né en 1976 à Cambridge dans le Massachusetts, fils d'une chanteuse d'opéra et d'un scientifique, Cho grandit en Californie mais s'installe à New York en 1994 pour étudier la mode à la Parsons School of Design. Il y passe presque deux ans avant de se consacrer à ses propres créa-tions. En 1999, il présente une première collection saluée par une critique una-nime. Cho privilégie une couture qui nécessite de nombreuses heures de travail, un aspect intrinsèque de son style. Il utilise des techniques relativement simples – dentelle, tresses, ruchés – pour créer des tenues de soirée voluptueuses aux effets complexes et théâtraux désormais très reconnaissables. La sensibilité esthétique de Benjamin Cho est plus européenne qu'américaine ; il est l'une des figures de proue de cette génération de créateurs avant-gardistes peu établis qui travaillent à New York et Los Angeles et dont les vêtements anticonformistes définissent la tendance par contraste avec le reste de la mode américaine, essen-tiellement motivée par la rentabilité commerciale. Le travail original de Cho attire l'attention de clients célèbres et fidèles, notamment les actrices Milla Jovo-vich et Claire Danes. Au printemps 2002, alors que les attentats terroristes du 11 septembre 2001 entraînent l'annulation des défilés de la New York Fashion Week, le Vogue américain lui propose de présenter sa collection aux côtés de dix autres jeunes créateurs, une invitation qui lui permet de faire reconnaître son talent sur la scène internationale. Pour l'automne/hiver 2005, Benjamin Cho pré-sente une collection romantique composée de pièces volumineuses, avec des jupes en satin noir pincées à la taille par de gros nœuds et une robe rose pâle ballonnante qui forme un cocon autour de celle qui la porte.   LESLEY ARFIN

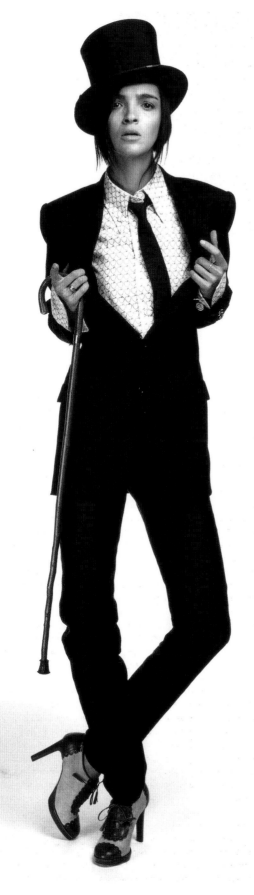

What are your signature [...] signatures. Unique to [...] have fathered. Especia[...] Bunnie **What is your fa[...] your collections?** I m[...] affection for any of them at this poi[...] still conjuring a favourite. **How would you describe your work?** Aggressive, alternative, ChoCD, depressed, ecstatic, gentle, heartfelt, idiosyncratic, nerdy, ostracised, progressive, sweating, vegetarian. That is in no particular order... well, alphabetical perhaps **What's your ultimate goal?** Calling the wild kestrel and having it swoop over and land on my hand. And vice versa **What inspires you?** Profound sadness of a pitiful few. Or pitiless few. Beautiful fews. A beautiful fuse **Can fashion still have a political ambition?** It had better or I'm outta here! I could not keep going if I did not believe this. **Who do you have in mind when you design?** Absolutely no-one. Except for myself... me and my multiple personalities, which accounts for a pretty large number. "One singular sensation..." **Is the idea of creative collaboration important to you?** I wish. I always try to refrain from collaboration, although it is tempting to me in a romantic sense. It would be important if somebody cared enough. But I don't expect anyone to **Who has been the greatest influence on your career?** Tara Sinn, Brian Degraw, Morrissey, and, with much resistance, my father **How have your own experiences affected your work as a designer?** Overwhelmingly so. I have an acute disdain for creating anything which smells of retro, ethnic, or anything derivative in that sense. The experiences and all the intangibles are all I have to draw upon. Alone **Which is more important in your work: the process or the product?** Ultimately it is all a constant process **Is designing difficult for you, if so, what drives you to continue?** Everything is difficult for me. Designing, however, is the easiest part. The rest of life is what wrings me **Have you ever been influenced or moved by the reaction to your designs?** Sure. But I get moved by plenty of things **What's your definition of beauty?** Complicated hearts, untouchables, serendipity, sharp wits, croc-less tears, Oliver Payne **What's your philosophy?** The image of the Virgin Mary will appear in your grilled cheese sandwich and start to cry. Then you will realise that it is not Mary and is actually a notable homosexual, who is actually bisexual, and he is crying and then you will understand that "it" was all a hoax and there is no God. We are all fish, we cannot swim in sand, and we all drown **What is the most important lesson you've learned?** Accepting some of the ugliness buys some time.

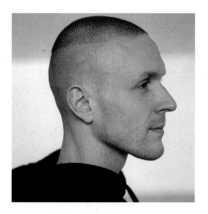

BERNHARD WILLHELM

"The most important lesson I've learned is, be kind"

Since graduating from Antwerp's Royal Academy back in 1998, Bernhard Willhelm has grown to become an icon and even an institution. Lamented by some, ridiculed by others, his voice is so strong, so extreme and so challenging. Like his mentor/tutor Walter Van Beirendonck, Willhelm's vision is unflappable and at times alienating to mass consumerism, but to challenge, confound and raise questions is surely Willhelm's point; at the end of the day, isn't fashion without a concept just clothes? Willhelm's catalogues can stand alongside art books. His Paris shows are performance pieces (a recent catwalk show ended with a parade of models bouncing on space hoppers) and his key pieces are instantly collectable artefacts. A German living in Antwerp, Willhelm references traditional folklore and fairytales, but not in a romantic, wistful way. His style is brash, playful and in your face: his day-glo dinosaur print has been a high point of his career so far. When Butt Magazine tore up the magazine rulebook in 2001, they chose Willhelm in tightie whities and a handle bar moustache to visually represent everything they stand for – fun fashion and fags. Proving he wasn't a one-trick show pony, in 2002, along with support from Tara Subkoff of Imitation of Christ and Sybilla, Willhelm enrolled as head designer at Roman couture brand Capucci. He instantly re-invigorated the house, giving edge, sporty energy and a refined touch to the label. With a newly realised shoe line and capsule collections for Yoox.com, Bernhard Willhelm is one of fashion's true gems.

Seit seinem Abschluss an der Königlichen Akademie von Antwerpen im Jahr 1998 ist Bernhard Willhelm zu einer Ikone, wenn nicht gar zu einer Institution geworden. Manche beklagen, andere belächeln das, aber seine Aussage ist stark, extrem und herausfordernd. Wie sein Mentor und Tutor Walter van Beirendonck hat auch Willhelm eine unerschütterliche Vision, die für Vertreter des Massengeschmacks manchmal befremdlich wirken mag. Es ist jedoch seine erklärte Absicht, zu provozieren, zu verwirren und Fragen aufzuwerfen. Und liefert letztlich Mode ohne Konzept nichts anderes als bloß Kleider? Die in Paris veranstalteten Schauen sind Performances (bei seiner letzten endete der Catwalk mit einer Parade der Models auf Hüpfbällen), und seine Schlüsselkreationen sind Kunstobjekte mit sofortigem Sammlerwert. Als Deutscher, der in Antwerpen lebt, stellt Bernhard Willhelm Bezüge zu traditioneller Folklore und zu Märchen her, allerdings nicht auf romantisch-sehnsüchtige Weise. Sein Stil ist frech, ver-

spielt und unmittelbar: sein leuchtender Dinosaurierdruck bildet einen Höhepunkt seiner bisherigen Karriere. Als das Magazin Butt 2001 mit allen Regeln des Zeitschriftengeschäfts brach, ließ es Willhelm in enger weißer Unterhose und mit Schnurrbart optisch repräsentieren, wofür es steht – Spaß, Mode und Schwule – Fun, Fashion and Fags. Zum Beweis dafür, dass er kein Zirkuspferd ist, das nur ein einziges Kunststück beherrscht, ließ sich Willhelm 2002 mit der Unterstützung von Tara Subkoff (Imitation of Christ) und Sybilla als Chefdesigner des längst verblassten römischen Couture-Hauses Capucci verpflichten. Er belebte die Marke sofort neu, gab ihr wieder Ecken und Kanten, frische Energie und Raffinesse. Mit einer neuen Schuhlinie und Minikollektionen für Yoox.com erweist sich Bernhard Willhelm als ein wahres Modejuwel.

Depuis qu'il a décroché son diplôme de l'Académie Royale d'Anvers en 1998, Bernhard Willhelm est devenu une véritable icône, voire une institution. Lamentable aux yeux de certains, ridicule pour d'autres, son style est marqué, extrême et provocant. A l'instar de son mentor et professeur Walter Van Beirendonck, Willhelm propose une vision flegmatique et parfois aliénante du consumérisme de masse, mais il cherche avant tout à provoquer, à confondre et à soulever des questions; finalement, une mode sans concept ne se réduirait-elle pas au simple vêtement? Ses défilés parisiens relèvent de la véritable performance (il a clôturé son dernier défilé avec une parade de mannequins sautant sur d'énormes ballons gonflables) et ses pièces signature deviennent immédiatement des «collectors». Cet Allemand installé à Anvers fait souvent référence au folklore traditionnel et aux contes de fées, mais sans la moindre nostalgie romantique. Il se distingue par son style effronté, ludique et choquant: à ce jour, son imprimé dinosaure fluorescent constitue sans doute le point fort de sa carrière. Quand le magazine Butt part en dissidence en 2001, il choisit de faire poser Bernhard Willhelm en slip kangourou blanc et moustaches à la gauloise pour incarner visuellement ses centres d'intérêt: gays et mode décalée. Pour démontrer qu'il a plus d'une corde à son arc, soutenu par Tara Subkoff d'Imitation of Christ et par Sybilla, Willhelm devient en 2002 styliste principal de Capucci, une marque romaine tombée en désuétude. Il lui redonne immédiatement un nouveau souffle en apportant son côté branché, son énergie sport et sa touche de raffinement. Avec une toute nouvelle ligne de chaussures et des mini-collections pour Yoox.com, Bernhard Willhelm est un petit bijou de la mode.

BEN REARDON

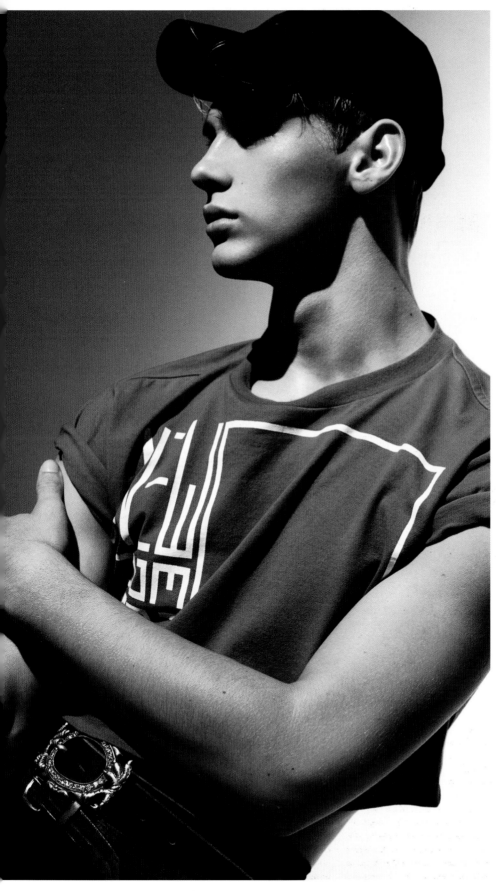

What are your signature designs? You decide **What is your favourite piece from any of your collections?** The pieces I wear myself **How would you describe your work?** WUNDER-SCHÖN **What's your ultimate goal?** The next collection **What inspires you?** Laziness **Can fashion still have a political ambition?** No. It's not ambitious enough **Who do you have in mind when you design?** An idea, never a person **Is the idea of creative collaboration important to you?** My team is everything **Who has been the greatest influence of your career?** My business partner Jutta Kraus **How have your own experiences affected your work as a designer?** I keep on cooking **Which is more important to you: the process or the product?** Both, it has the same value **Is designing difficult for you? If so, what drives you to continue?** If the drive is not there, you forget about this job **Have you ever been influenced or moved by the reaction to your designs?** Yes, my mother is still complaining **What's your definition of beauty?** Chaos (let's not be emotional about it) **What's your philosophy?** Forget about Philosophy **What is the most important lesson you've learned?** Be kind.

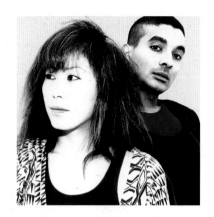

BLAAK

"Seeing your clothes on a person validates your work"

AARON SHARIF & SACHIKO OKADA

Blaak is Aaron Sharif and Sachiko Okada. Founded in 1998, they initially showed with Fashion East, an initiative supporting new British talent, and were awarded New Generation show sponsorship the following season. Blaak's collections were sold to Browns, Liberty, Colette and Barneys before the duo had even graduated from Central Saint Martins, where they had met while studying for a BA in fashion design. While Okada's future in fashion seemed destined (her mother was a weaver in Sweden), Sharif initially studying anthropology, fashion journalism and photography, before being persuaded by one of his tutors to turn his hand to fashion design. After four years of showing their collections in London, they successfully debuted in Paris in 2004. Regardless of their choice of fashion week, Blaak retain their individualism. Their contemporary street style creations are a result of their own instincts and passions, unmoved by popular trends. Drawing from a wealth of world cultures, they reinterpret tribal influences and traditions. In addition to their successful menswear and womenswear, a Blaak shoe collection is also in the pipeline. The pair also now teach at Central Saint Martins. Blaak are also passionate about film. In early 2004, the 'Blaak Broken Logo' installation (in collaboration with graphic firm Saturday) was shown in London, Paris, Tokyo, and Melbourne.

Blaak, das sind Aaron Sharif und Sachiko Okada. 1998 gegründet, präsentierte sich das Label im Rahmen von Fashion East, einer Initiative zur Förderung britischer Talente. Dort erhielt man den Preis New Generation zum Sponsoring der Schau in der darauf folgenden Saison. Noch bevor das Designerduo seine Abschlüsse am Central Saint Martins gemacht hatte, verkaufte es seine Kollektionen bereits an Browns, Liberty, Colette und Barneys. Kennen gelernt haben sich die beiden während ihres Bachelor-Studiums im Fach Modedesign. Und während Okadas Zukunft im Bereich Mode schicksalhaft vorgezeichnet schien (ihre Mutter arbeitete in Schweden als Weberin), passierte das bei Sharif eher zufällig. Nach kurzen Versuchen in den Fächern Anthropologie und Modejournalismus bzw. -fotografie ließ er sich von einem seiner Tutoren zum Wechsel in Richtung Modedesign überreden. Nachdem sie ihre Kollektionen vier Jahre lang in London gezeigt hatten, gaben die beiden 2004 erfolgreich ihr Debüt in Paris. Der Umzug von London nach Paris ist auch auf die Abneigung der beiden Designer gegen jede Art von Stillstand zurückzuführen. Und trotz der regelmäßigen

Teilnahme an der Fashion Week hat sich Blaak seinen Individualismus bewahrt. Die zeitgemäßen Kreationen im Street Style sind Ergebnis des eigenen Instinkts und der persönlichen Vorlieben, unabhängig von populären Trends. Man bedient sich beim Reichtum der Weltkulturen und interpretiert die Einflüsse und Traditionen diverser Naturvölker neu. Als Ergänzung der erfolgreichen Herren- und Damenmode ist eine Blaak-Schuhkollektion gerade in Vorbereitung. Das Paar lehrt inzwischen auch selbst am Central Saint Martins und engagiert sich außerdem im Bereich Film. So war von Februar bis Mai 2004 die Installation „Blaak Broken Logo" (in Zusammenarbeit mit der Grafikagentur Saturday) in London, Paris, Tokio und Melbourne zu sehen.

Fondée en 1998 par Aaron Sharif et Sachiko Okada, la griffe Blaak défile pour la première fois grâce à Fashion East, projet de soutien aux jeunes talents britanniques, et remporte le mécénat New Generation pour la saison suivante. Les collections Blaak sont achetées par Browns, Liberty, Colette et Barneys avant même que le duo de créateurs ne sorte diplômé de Central Saint Martins, où ils se sont rencontrés au cursus de BA en mode. Alors que le destin de Sachiko Okada dans la mode semble tout tracé (sa mère était tisseuse en Suède), celui d'Aaron Sharif paraît plus accidentel. Après avoir étudié brièvement l'anthropologie, le journalisme et la photographie de mode, l'un de ses professeurs finit par le convaincre de se réorienter vers la création de mode. Le duo présente ses collections à Londres pendant quatre ans et fait des débuts couronnés de succès à Paris en 2004. La décision de quitter les podiums londoniens à la faveur de Paris repose sur leur aversion pour l'inertie. Peu importent les semaines de la mode qui voient défiler Blaak, la griffe exprime l'individualisme de ses créateurs. Leurs créations contemporaines inspirées de la rue résultent de leurs propres instincts et passions, insensibles aux tendances du moment. S'inspirant de toutes les cultures du monde, ils réinterprètent les influences et les traditions tribales. Outre des collections à succès pour homme et pour femme, Blaak compte également sortir une ligne de chaussures. Le duo enseigne aujourd'hui à Central Saint Martins tout en se passionnant pour le cinéma. De février à mai 2004, leur installation « Blaak Broken Logo » (réalisée en collaboration avec les graphistes de Saturday) voyage de Londres à Paris, jusqu'à Tokyo et Melbourne.

KAREN LEONG

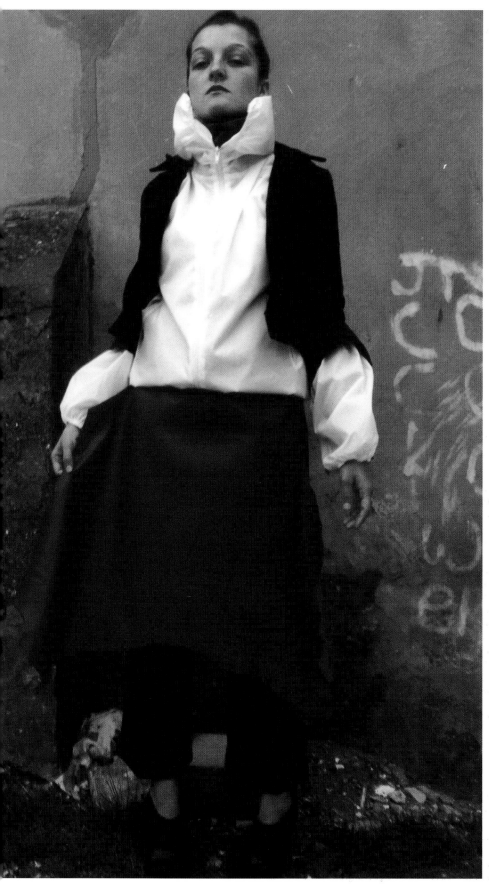

What are your signatur[...] without constraint and [...] is your favourite piece [...] collections? Autumn/win[...] the first collection wh[...] at Saint Martins **How would you describe your work?** Pushing our own boundaries – a single thought through chaos **What's your ultimate goal?** Freedom through self-expression **What inspires you?** The experiences of circumstances and the result of these situations **Can fashion still have a political ambition?** Fashion is a result of what is happening. Hence political meaning can be decoded from what people wear, but not sure about political ambition **Who do you have in mind when you design?** Me, myself and I **Is the idea of creative collaboration important to you?** Blaak is a collaboration, by working with people outside Blaak in different areas we're given the opportunities to broaden our understanding in these areas and that gives Blaak a new dimension. Collaborating with Saturday for our logo and Twin studio for the video has been very successful, at the moment we are working with musicians from around the world on a new project **Who has been the greatest influence on your career?** Understanding that sometimes it's better to go through all experiences, be they good or bad. To realise that we are the greatest influence on what we do **How have your own experiences affected your work as a designer?** Everything we do affects our work. The collection is a result of the decisions and the paths we experience at the time, the feeling and the reaction towards it **Which is more important in your work: the process or the product?** Both. Without good process there will be no good product. And product is what we present. It has to be able to speak for itself **Is designing difficult for you, if so, what drives you to continue?** Everything in life is difficult but achievable. Without challenging life, you are only allowing yourself to be a spectator of life **Have you ever been influenced or moved by the reaction to your designs?** Always – be they positive or negative, a reaction is far better than indifference. Creating a collection is one third, seeing your clothes on a person validates your work. Selling our first collection to Browns at the time gave us so much **What's your definition of beauty?** Individuality through a strong mind **What's your philosophy?** Sometimes when you lose, you win, and sometimes when you win, you lose. There is a reason for everything and everything is for a reason **What is the most important lesson you've learned?** A problem shared is a problem halved.

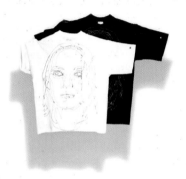

BLESS

"We don't design things we would not
need if we were the client" DESIRÉE HEISS & INES KAAG

Whether Bless counts as a fashion label at all is a moot point. Preferring to describe their venture as 'a project that presents ideal and artistic values to the public via products', Desirée Heiss (born 1971) and Ines Kaag (born 1970) formed Bless in 1995, positioning themselves as a collaborative experiment in fashion. The business is spilt between two European capitals: Heiss, who graduated from the University of Applied Arts in Vienna in 1994, is based in Paris, while Kaag, who graduated from the University of Arts and Design in Hanover in 1995, is based in Berlin. The two met by chance when their work was shown adjacently at a Paris design competition. The Bless modus operandi is to re-invent existing objects to produce new garments and accessories which are released in quarterly limited editions and are available through subscription. Their work has included fur wigs for Martin Margiela's autumn/winter 1997 collection, customisable trainers for Jean Colonna, and the creation of 'Human-Interior-Wear' for Levi's. While these all function as wearable garments, many of their products cross entirely into the realm of art. 'Embroidered Flowers', for instance, is a series of photographic prints, while their 'Hairbrush Beauty-Product' (a brush with human hair for bristles) is closer to the work of Joseph Beuys or Marcel Duchamp than any fashion designer. Consequently, when the 'Bless Shop' goes on tour, it visits Europe's alternative galleries, rather than department stores. Heiss and Kaag's success is in providing a unique comment on fashion that can also (usually) be worn.

Ob man Bless überhaupt zu den Modelabels zählen kann, ist umstritten. Desirée Heiss (Jahrgang 1971) und Ines Kaag (Jahrgang 1970) bezeichnen ihr Unternehmen lieber als „ein Projekt, das der Öffentlichkeit mittels Produkten ideelle und künstlerische Werte präsentiert". Sie gründeten Bless 1995 und positionierten sich selbst als kollaboratives Modeexperiment. Das Unternehmen ist auf zwei europäische Hauptstädte aufgeteilt: Heiss, die 1994 ihren Abschluss an der Wiener Universität für angewandte Kunst machte, ist in Paris stationiert, während Kaag, die an der Fachhochschule für Kunst und Design in Hannover studiert hat, von Berlin aus arbeitet. Kennen gelernt haben sich die beiden per Zufall, als ihre Arbeiten bei einem Pariser Designwettbewerb nebeneinander ausgestellt waren. Das Konzept von Bless besteht darin, bereits existierende Objekte neu zu erfinden. Diese Kleidungsstücke oder Accessoires werden vierteljährlich in limitierten Auflagen an Abonnenten verkauft. Zu ihren bisherigen Arbeiten gehören Pelzperücken für Martin Margielas Kollektion Herbst/Winter

1997, „verstellbare" Turnschuhe für Jean Colonna und eine Kreation namens „Human Interior Wear" für Levi's. Die genannten Produkte lassen sich alle tragen, während viele andere reine Kunstobjekte sind. So etwa die Fotoserie „Embroidered Flowers". Mit ihrem „Hairbrush Beauty-Product" (einer Art Bürste mit „Borsten" aus Menschenhaar) nähern sich Heiss und Kaag mehr als jeder andere Modedesigner den Arbeiten von Joseph Beuys oder Marcel Duchamp an. Da ist es nur folgerichtig, dass man den „Bless Shop" auf Tour eher in Europas alternativen Galerien als in Kaufhäusern antrifft. Der Erfolg des Labels liegt wohl darin begründet, dass es einzigartige Kommentare zur Mode abgibt, die man (meistens) sogar anziehen kann.

Peut-on vraiment considérer Bless comme une marque de mode? Desirée Heiss (née en 1971) et Ines Kaag (née en 1970) décrivent plutôt leur association comme « un projet présentant au public des valeurs idéales et artistiques par le biais de produits ». Elles créent Bless en 1995 dans l'optique d'une collaboration expérimentale autour de la mode. Leur activité se divise entre deux capitales européennes : Desirée Heiss, diplômée de l'Université des Arts appliqués de Vienne en 1994, travaille à Paris, tandis qu'Ines Kaag, diplômée de l'Université des Arts et du Design de Hanovre en 1995, est installée à Berlin. Elles se sont rencontrées par hasard à Paris lors d'un concours de design où leurs travaux respectifs étaient présentés côte à côte. Le modus operandi de Bless consiste à réinventer les objets existants pour produire de nouveaux vêtements et accessoires, commercialisés chaque trimestre en édition limitée et uniquement sur abonnement. Entre autres, elles ont créé des perruques en fourrure pour la collection automne/hiver 1997 de Martin Margiela, des survêtements personnalisables pour Jean Colonna et travaillé sur un concept de « Human-Interior-Wear » pour Levi's. Bien que toutes ces pièces soient portables, la plupart de leurs produits s'apparentent entièrement au domaine de l'art. Par exemple, « Embroidered Flowers » est une série d'impressions photographiques, tandis que leur « Hairbrush Beauty-Product » (une brosse en cheveux humains) relève davantage du travail de Joseph Beuys ou de Marcel Duchamp que de la pure création de mode. Quand le « Bless Shop » part en tournée, il préfère donc faire étape dans les galeries d'art alternatives d'Europe plutôt que dans les grands magasins. Le succès de Desirée Heiss et d'Ines Kaag repose avant tout sur leur approche unique d'une mode que l'on peut aussi porter, la plupart du temps. MARK HOOPER

What are your signature designs? All-day-life-necessities combined with products that one can't categorise at all, because they didn't exist, in our experience, before What is your favourite piece from any of your collections? Always the unknown new piece for the next collection How would you describe your work? Our work is more a life concept than a job, since we follow our personal needs with our work and the other way around. We try to satisfy ourselves and the people we work and live with. The reactions to our different activities often turn out to become a friendship, a future collaboration, a business relationship or lead us to other new projects, so it's more a process we are acting in than a defined work What's your ultimate goal? Maybe to design a car What inspires you? Needs, lacks and questions Can fashion still have a political ambition? Do you want to be dressed sexy? Why? Does he/she love (desire) you if you are not? Do your business partners take you seriously, when you are? Do you take yourself seriously, when you are? Do you feel comfortable in your clothes? Does a stylist want to wear the clothes that are used for the story? If yes, are they unexpected? If not, are they desirable clothes, or too spectacular to wear? Would a businessman ever wear a Palestinian scarf, because he likes the colours and the material? How many models wear in real life the clothes they present on the catwalk and if yes, to what occasions and for what reasons? Fashion can still have a political ambition, but it is unfashionable at the moment. Wear and don't care. But if you care it's okay Who do you have in mind when you design? Ourselves or a client that came to us with a specific demand. We don't design things we would not need if we were the client Is the idea of creative collaboration important to you? It's the base Who has been the greatest influence on your career? Morihei Ueshiba (aikido), Martin Margiela (fashion) & Yasmine Gauster (business survival support and humanity) How have your own experiences affected your work as a designer? Our sensitivity of attraction changed. We are less interested in simple decorative elements, but are more into redefining and re-contextualising usual products Which is more important in your work: the process or the product? Both, depending on the project Is designing difficult for you, if so, what drives you to continue? Sometimes it's even very easy. The problem is not the designing in the sense of developing an idea, but the finalisation, distribution and marketing of it. What drives us to continue is the constant challenge that there is always something to do for the next project and the fact that we need to do what we do Have you ever been influenced or moved by the reaction to your designs? It always moves you to get reactions, whatever nature they are and it definitely influences temporary moods What's your definition of beauty? A very personal notion of feeling astonished and happy if you suddenly see or feel it What's your philosophy? Bless fits every style What is the most important lesson you've learned? To be patient.

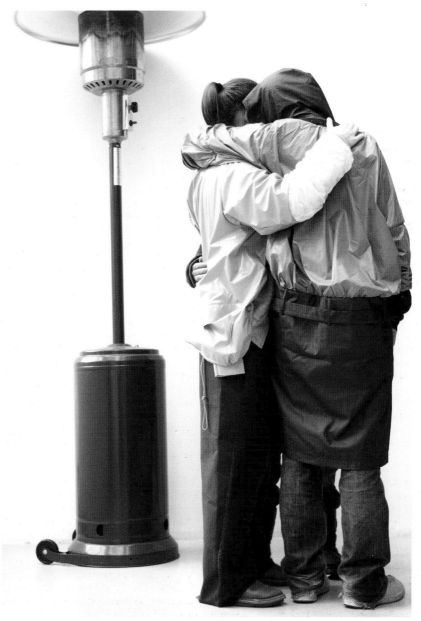

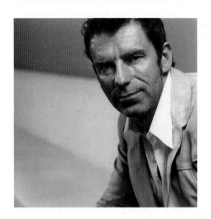

BOTTEGA VENETA

"At the end of every cycle there is a desire to move on"

TOMAS MAIER

Bottega Veneta's pedigree in fine leathergoods makes it a world-leader in its field. Founded in Vicenza, Italy, in 1966, the house quickly became the choice of the Studio 54 crowd; Andy Warhol bought his Christmas presents at the New York store. At that time, Bottega was a family company designed and run by husband and wife team Vittorio and Laura Moltedo, and it was famed for its hand-made, super-soft bags created from signature 'intrecciato' woven leather. Following this heyday Bottega looked like being consigned to fashion history until the intervention of two forces: one, the Gucci Group, which in 2001 spent $60m on acquiring two thirds of the company, giving it the financial clout to undergo an extensive re-launch. The other was the appointment of Tomas Maier as creative director; previously in the company's recent history, British designer Giles Deacon had been head designer. Maier's revamp has included BV's Milan headquarters, its stationery, staff and uniforms. Collections, too, have returned to a more sophisticated aesthetic and have been extended to cover lap-top cases, shoes in exotic leathers, cashmere knits and homeware ranges. The focus, Maier has stated, is to remain on accessories and niche products. Miami-based, German-born (1958) Maier trained at the Chambre Syndicale de la Haute Couture in Paris and has a long history as a luxury goods designer – including nine years as designer of womenswear for Hermès and, in 1998, the launch of his own collection – and is now being tipped as a man to watch.

Bottega Venetas langjähriger Ruf als Hersteller feinster Lederwaren machte die 1966 im italienischen Vicenza gegründete Firma zu einer der internationalen Marktführerinnen. Bald kauften die Leute vom Studio 54 dort. Andy Warhol erledigte seine Weihnachtseinkäufe im New Yorker Laden. Das vom Ehepaar Vittorio und Laura Moltedo erdachte und geführte Familienunternehmen war berühmt für seine handgefertigten, superweichen Taschen aus dem typisch eingeflochtenen (intrecciato) Leder. Nach dieser Blütezeit schien es zunächst, als wäre Bottega bald nur noch Modegeschichte, doch dann traten zwei Kräfte auf den Plan: zum einen die Gucci-Gruppe, die 2001 für 60 Millionen Dollar zwei Drittel des Unternehmens erwarb und diesem damit einen umfassenden Relaunch ermöglichte; zum anderen die Ernennung von Tomas Maier zum Creative Director. Maiers Großreinemachen umfasste einfach alles – auch den Firmensitz in Mailand, Briefpapier, Personal und dessen Outfits. Bei den Kollek-

tionen kehrte man zu einer edleren Ästhetik zurück und erweiterte die Produktpalette um Laptophüllen, Schuhe aus exotischen Ledersorten, Kaschmirschals und Heimtextilien. Dabei ist es allerdings Maiers erklärtes Ziel, bei Accessoires und Nischenprodukten zu bleiben. Der in Miami lebende, 1958 in Deutschland geborene Maier hat am Chambre Syndicale de la Haute Couture in Paris gelernt und besitzt langjährige Erfahrung als Designer von Luxusartikeln. Dazu gehören u. a. neun Jahre als Designer für Damenmode bei Hermès und die erste eigene Kollektion 1998. Heute gilt er in der Branche als ein Mann, den man unbedingt im Auge behalten sollte.

Grâce à son immense savoir-faire, le maroquinier de luxe Bottega Veneta est devenu l'un des leaders mondiaux dans son domaine. Fondée en 1966 à Vicence en Italie, la maison s'impose rapidement comme le choix de prédilection des habitués du Studio 54 : Andy Warhol avait l'habitude d'acheter ses cadeaux de Noël dans la boutique de New York. L'entreprise est alors une affaire familiale créée et dirigée par les époux, Vittorio et Laura Moltedo, qui proposent des sacs ultra-souples faits à la main et coupés dans le cuir tressé « intrecciato » qui a fait la gloire de la maison. A la fin de cet âge d'or, Bottega Veneta semble voué à sombrer dans les oubliettes de la mode jusqu'à l'intervention de deux puissantes forces : d'abord le groupe Gucci, qui en 2001 investit 60 millions de dollars pour s'octroyer les deux tiers de l'entreprise et lui offrir ainsi le poids financier nécessaire pour être relancée sur le marché, et ensuite le recrutement de Tomas Maier à la direction de la création, en remplacement du styliste anglais Giles Deacon. Maier ira même jusqu'à transformer le siège milanais de l'entreprise, son papier à lettres et l'uniforme de ses employés. Les collections reviennent alors à une esthétique plus sophistiquée et s'enrichissent de housses d'ordinateurs portables, de chaussures taillées dans des cuirs exotiques, de pulls en cachemire et de gammes d'articles pour la maison, l'intention déclarée de Maier consistant à rester spécialisé sur les accessoires et les produits de niche. Né en 1958, le styliste allemand Tomas Maier vit aujourd'hui à Miami. Il a suivi une formation à la Chambre Syndicale de la Haute Couture de Paris et revendique une longue expérience de création dans l'industrie du luxe : il a notamment travaillé pendant neuf ans comme styliste pour femme chez Hermès, et lancé sa propre collection en 1998. On le considère aujourd'hui comme un talent à suivre de très près.

JOSH SIMS

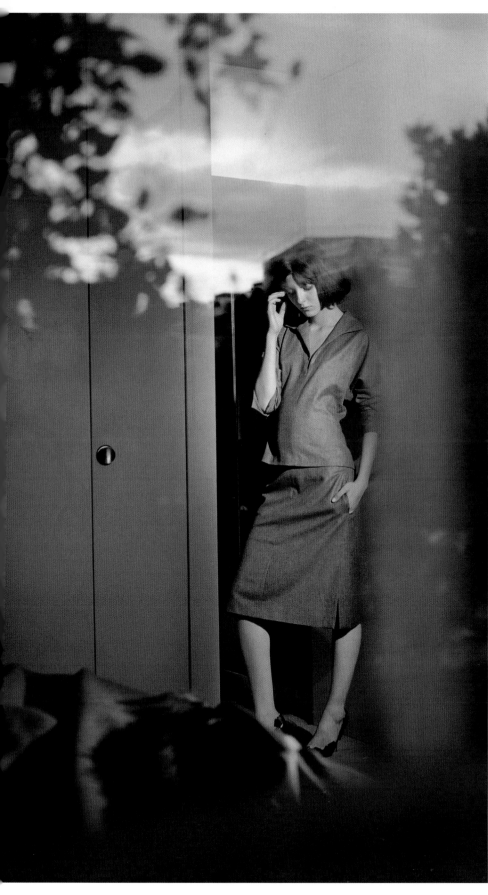

What are your signature designs? Casual low key luxury **What is your favourite piece from any of your collections?** My surf shorts, my Bottega Cabat **How would you describe your work?** A combination of design, material and colour research, to fulfil a desire for beauty and function **What's your ultimate goal?** Underlining personality rather than the opposite **What inspires you?** Anything around me and everything that I have stored in my brain **Can fashion still have a political ambition?** Fashion is a reflection of our time and many times an indicator of human sensibility **Who do you have in mind when you design?** Nobody in particular because my motto is everybody different – please! **Is the idea of creative collaboration important to you?** Absolutely and everyday of my life **Who has been the greatest influence on your career?** A group of people I encountered in my life as well as my family and upbringing **How have your own experiences affected your work as a designer?** Very much for having worked in so many different categories, areas and countries **Is designing difficult for you, if so, what drives you to continue?** It is not because at the end of every cycle there is a desire to move on **Have you ever been influenced or moved by the reaction to your designs?** I am interested in reactions but I can judge the result by myself **What's your definition of beauty?** It's when everything comes together – harmony **What's your philosophy?** There is always room for improvement **What is the most important lesson you've learned?** Passion and patience go together.

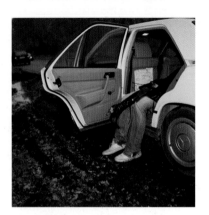

BOUDICCA

"Our work reflects the modern paranoias of human life, the beauty and the vanity of modern life, the anger of another, the fake lies that we are told and the real truths we forget"

ZOWIE BROACH & BRIAN KIRBY

Zowie Broach and Brian Kirby work (and live) together as Boudicca. The label takes its name from the rebel Iceni queen who rose up against the Romans in Britain. A similarly rebellious streak permeates Boudicca's design and has led to Broach and Kirby gaining a non-conformist reputation within the fashion industry. Although they don't see themselves as 'fashion rebels', the aesthetics of revolution and change, together with the 'uniforms' of global capitalism have been frequent reference points within Boudicca's womenswear collections. Much time and effort is spent on each ready-to-wear garment, making their clothes a kind of politico couture. Their backgrounds are just as unconventional as their output: Brian Kirby grew up in Manchester, where he trained to be a mechanic, later studying fashion and completing an MA at the Royal College of Art, London, in 1994. Zowie Broach grew up between various seaside towns in the West Country, studied at Middlesex (graduating 1989), then becoming a stylist and video director. They met on a windswept beach in Rimini in 1996. At home on catwalks, stages and galleries alike, Boudicca's work has included a collaboration with Turner Prize winning artist Gillian Wearing in 2000, and more recently, international collaborations in the fields of opera, film, architecture and art. In 2004 Boudicca was chosen by Rei Kawakubo to appear in her Dover Street Market store, and by Alexander McQueen for the book 'Fashion Cream'. In 2005, having been a regular fixture on the London calendar since spring/summer 1998, Boudicca made their debut at New York Fashion Week.

Zowie Broach und Brian Kirby von Boudicca sind beruflich wie privat ein Team. Seit Frühjahr/Sommer 1998 ist das Label fixer Bestandteil des Londoner Modenschau-Kalenders. Der Name Boudicca stammt übrigens von einer keltischen Iceni-Königin, die sich gegen die Herrschaft der Römer in Britannien auflehnte. Ähnlich rebellisch ist der Grundtenor von Boudiccas Design, das Broach und Kirby innerhalb der Branche den Ruf von Nonkonformisten eintrug. Auch wenn die beiden sich selbst nicht als Moderebellen betrachten, finden sich in ihren Damenkollektionen oft Bezüge zur Ästhetik von Revolution und Umbruch, aber auch zu den „Uniformen" des globalen Kapitalismus. Auf jedes Prêt-à-porter-Stück wird jedoch viel Zeit und Mühe verwendet, so dass man die Sachen als „Politico-Couture" bezeichnen könnte. Der biografische Hintergrund der beiden Designer ist genauso unkonventionell wie ihre Entwürfe: Brian Kirby wuchs in Manchester auf, wo er zunächst eine Ausbildung als Mechaniker machte; 1994 schloss er sein Modestudium mit einem Master am Royal College of Art in London ab. Zowie Broach wuchs in verschiedenen Küstenstädten von West Country

auf, studierte in Middlesex (wo sie 1989 ihren Abschluss machte) und arbeitete zunächst als Stylistin und Videoregisseurin. Kennen gelernt haben sich die beiden 1996 an einem windigen Strand in Rimini. Inzwischen ist Boudicca auf Laufstegen, Bühnen und in Galerien gleichermaßen zu Hause. Im Jahr 2000 arbeitete man mit dem Künstler Gillian Wearing zusammen, der bereits mit dem Turner-Preis ausgezeichnet wurde. In jüngerer Vergangenheit gab es außerdem Kooperationen auf den Gebieten Oper, Film und Architektur. 2004 lud Rei Kawakubo Boudicca auf ihren Dover Street Market ein. Alexander McQueen nahm das Label in sein Buch „Fashion Cream" auf. Der heiß ersehnte erste Boudicca-Duft kam 2005 auf den Markt.

Zowie Broach et Brian Kirkby travaillent (et vivent) ensemble sous le nom de Boudicca. Griffe de mode et rendez-vous régulier des défilés londoniens depuis le printemps/été 1998, Boudicca est également le nom d'une reine de la tribu des Iceni qui s'était rebellée contre les Romains en Grande-Bretagne. Une rébellion similaire habite les créations de Boudicca, conduisant Zowie Broach et Brian Kirkby à se forger une réputation d'anticonformistes au sein du monde de la mode. Bien qu'ils ne se considèrent pas comme des «rebelles de la mode», l'esthétique de la révolution et du changement, associée à leurs «uniformes» du capitalisme mondial, revient souvent sous forme de référence dans les collections pour femme de Boudicca. Le duo investit beaucoup de temps et d'efforts dans chaque pièce de prêt-à-porter, ce qui transforme leur mode en une sorte de «couture politique». Leur parcours est aussi inattendu que leur production : Brian Kirkby a grandi à Manchester, où il a suivi une formation de mécanicien avant d'étudier la mode et d'obtenir un MA du Royal College of Art de Londres en 1994. Zowie Broach a grandi entre plusieurs villes de la côte du sud-ouest de l'Angleterre, a étudié à Middlesex (diplômée en 1989), puis est devenue styliste et vidéaste. Ils se sont rencontrés en 1996 à Rimini sur une plage balayée par le vent. Tout aussi à l'aise sur les podiums et les scènes de théâtre que dans les galeries d'art, Boudicca a collaboré en l'an 2000 avec l'artiste Gillian Wearing, lauréat du Turner Prize. Plus récemment, ils se sont également investis dans des collaborations internationales dans les domaines de l'opéra, du cinéma, de l'architecture et de l'art. En 2004, Rei Kawakubo a demandé au duo Boudicca de présenter ses créations dans sa boutique du Dover Street Market, et Alexander McQueen les a sollicités pour une participation au livre «Fashion Cream». En 2005, Boudicca a enfin lancé son parfum très attendu.

JO-ANN FURNISS

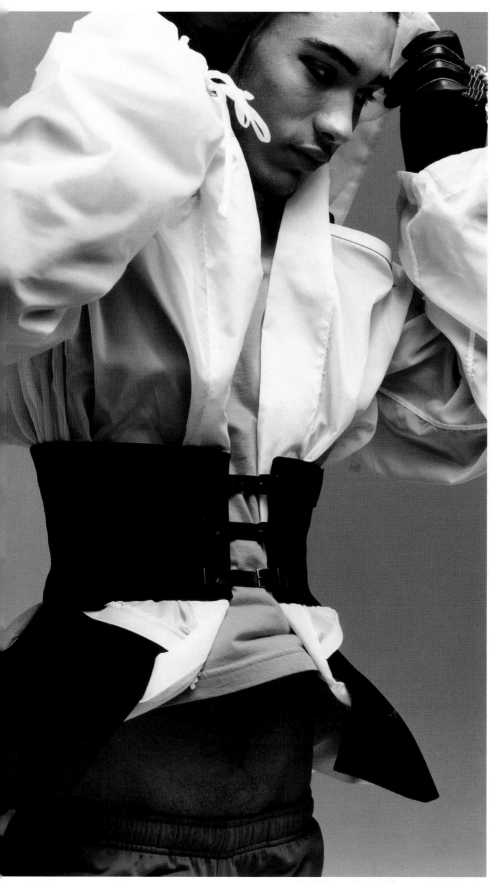

What are your signature designs? A constant evolution between Light & Dark, Hot & Cold, Hard & Soft, Right & Wrong, Day & Night, Male & Female, Rich & Poor, Fast & Slow, Now & Never, Forever & Ever **What is your favourite piece from any of your collections?** There is an ongoing narrative within our work, which makes it very difficult to isolate one specific piece **How would you describe your work?** An exploration and documentary of ourselves and the world we live in. The collections from Boudicca are stories, short scenes from films that at times are simple and reference the obvious, at others become complex and ill fitting. The modern paranoias of human life, the beauty and the vanity of modern life, the anger of another, the fake lies that we are told and the real truths we forget **What's your ultimate goal?** To be able to answer this question **What inspires you?** Knowing that our inspirations are ever evolving – and that everything in life is open to investigation **Can fashion still have a political ambition?** Yes – clothing throughout history has been used as a vehicle for Association/ Revolution/ Acceptance/ Symbolism/ Protest **Who do you have in mind when you design?** Likeminded people **Is the idea of creative collaboration important to you?** We are a creative collaboration **Who has been the greatest influence on your career?** Our own bloody mindedness – our alter egos **How have your own experiences affected your work as a designer?** There is no escape from the influences that effect you. Every experience within one's lifetime becomes embedded within the manifesto **Which is more important in your work: the process or the product?** The process creates the product and the product pays homage to the process **Is designing difficult for you, if so, what drives you to continue?** All things are possible, so long as we demonstrate with patience, stubbornness and faith **Have you ever been influenced or moved by the reaction to your designs?** To have made someone remember that they missed tenderness, and how that was crucial to their life **What's your definition of beauty?** With every breath… you have power to give life, to have life, to be still and to have an opinion, to change another and to create, and to believe **What's your philosophy?** To strive for that which you do not fully understand – for confusion is the generator **What is the most important lesson you've learned?** Find your own prophets. Turn nightmares into dreams and confront the darkness – it becomes illuminated with victory.

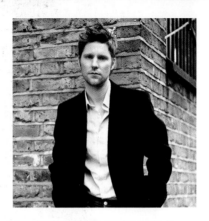

BURBERRY

"I'm a very down-to-earth designer"

CHRISTOPHER BAILEY

Yorkshire-born Christopher Bailey has become something of a household name, thanks to his sterling work as creative director of Burberry, the British company he joined back in 2001. Yet Bailey (born 1971) is far from an overnight sensation, having previously notched up impressive fashion credentials. On completing a Master's degree at the Royal College of Art in London (1994), Bailey worked in New York for Donna Karan from 1994 to 1996, before being hired by Tom Ford as a senior designer of womenswear at Gucci in Milan, from 1996 to 2001. At Burberry, Bailey is responsible for the direction of all product lines, as well as the definition of the company's overall image and seasonal advertising concepts. His flagship collection is the forward-thinking Prorsum lines for men and women that are presented in Milan to consistently rave reviews and from which he has banished almost all trace of the hallmark Burberry check. An unerring eye for clear, bright colour and subtle innovations in tailoring have emerged as key to both menswear and womenswear collections. Developing his codes gradually, Bailey is concerned with longevity, rather than resting on the corporate laurels. Nonetheless, the designs he has produced respectfully acknowledge the Burberry heritage (the company was founded in 1856). For example, he has made no secret of his admiration for their classic gabardine trenchcoat, which for autumn/winter 2004 he abbreviated into capes, for both men and women. Renowned for his hands-on approach to design and an enthusiasm for the details, he continues to propel the brand into the 21st century with his customary passion, enthusiasm and cheerful demeanour. In acknowledgement of his many successes, the Royal College of Art awarded Bailey an Honorary Fellowship in 2003.

Der aus Yorkshire stammende Christopher Bailey ist inzwischen selbst zu einer Art Markenzeichen avanciert. Zu verdanken hat er das seiner soliden Arbeit als Creative Director für das britische Modehaus Burberry, in das er 2001 eintrat. Bailey (Jahrgang 1971) wurde jedoch keineswegs über Nacht zum Star, sondern erwarb sich zunächst eindrucksvolle Referenzen. Nachdem er 1994 sein Studium am Londoner Royal College of Art mit dem Mastertitel abgeschlossen hatte, arbeitete er bis 1996 für Donna Karan in New York. Dann warb ihn Tom Ford als Senior Designer für die Damenmode bei Gucci ab, so dass er von 1996 bis 2001 in Mailand tätig war. Bei Burberry ist Bailey für die Leitung aller Produktlinien ebenso verantwortlich wie für das Image der Marke und die Werbekonzepte der jeweiligen Saison. Seine Flagschiffkollektion ist die zukunftsorientierte Prorsum-Linie für Damen und Herren. Wenn diese in Mailand präsentiert wird, erntet er regelmäßig hymnische Kritiken. Das typische Burberry-Karo ist daraus übrigens fast vollständig verbannt. Sein unfehlbarer Blick für klare, leuchtende Farben und raffinierte handwerkliche Innovationen hat sich als Erfolgskriterium für die Herren- wie für die Damenkollektionen herauskristallisiert. Bailey, der seine Stile schrittweise entwickelt, hat eher die Langlebigkeit seiner Entwürfe im Sinn, anstatt sich auf den Lorbeeren seines Hauses auszuruhen. Dennoch spricht aus seinen Kreationen die respektvolle Anerkennung des Vermächtnisses von Burberry (die Firma wurde bereits 1856 gegründet). So macht er kein Geheimnis aus seiner Bewunderung für den klassischen Trenchcoat aus Gabardine, den er für die Kollektion Herbst/Winter 2004 zu Capes für Damen und Herren abwandelte. Bailey ist bekannt für seine pragmatische Einstellung zum Thema Design und für seine Detailversessenheit. So führt er die Traditionsmarke weiter ins 21. Jahrhundert – mit gewohnter Leidenschaft, Enthusiasmus und einer optimistischen Grundhaltung. Als Anerkennung für seine diversen Leistungen wurde Bailey 2003 vom Royal College of Art ein Honorary Fellowship verliehen.

Né en 1971 dans le Yorkshire, Christopher Bailey est aujourd'hui un nom connu de tous les Anglais grâce au travail remarquable qu'il a accompli à la direction de la création de Burberry, maison britannique qu'il a rejointe en 2001. Pourtant, Bailey n'a rien d'une star éphémère dans la mesure où son CV affichait déjà d'impressionnantes références dans le domaine de la mode. Après avoir décroché son Master au Royal College of Art de Londres (1994), Bailey travaille à New York pour Donna Karan entre 1994 et 1996, avant d'être embauché par Tom Ford chez Gucci à Milan, où il occupera le poste de styliste senior des collections pour femme de 1996 à 2001. Chez Burberry, Bailey ne se contente pas de superviser toutes les lignes de produits, il développe également l'image de la maison et ses concepts publicitaires saisonniers. Sa collection phare inclut les lignes visionnaires Prorsum pour homme et femme qu'il a entièrement dépouillées des fameux carreaux Burberry, un travail salué par une critique unanime lors de chaque défilé milanais. Son œil aiguisé pour les couleurs claires et vives et ses innovations subtiles en matière de coupe distinguent aujourd'hui ses collections pour homme comme pour femme. Bien que Bailey impose progressivement ses propres codes, il cherche aussi à faire durer la marque Burberry sans se reposer sur ses lauriers. Ses créations rendent néanmoins un respectueux hommage à l'héritage de cette maison fondée en 1856. Par exemple, il n'a jamais caché son admiration pour le fameux trench-coat Burberry, un classique qu'il a raccourci sous forme de cape pour homme et femme lors de la saison automne/hiver 2004. Réputé pour son approche pratique de la création et pour sa passion du détail, il continue à propulser Burberry dans le XXe siècle, animé d'une passion et d'un enthousiasme qui sont aujourd'hui devenus sa marque de fabrique. En reconnaissance de ses nombreux succès, le Royal College of Art lui a décerné un doctorat honorifique en 2003.

JAMES ANDERSON

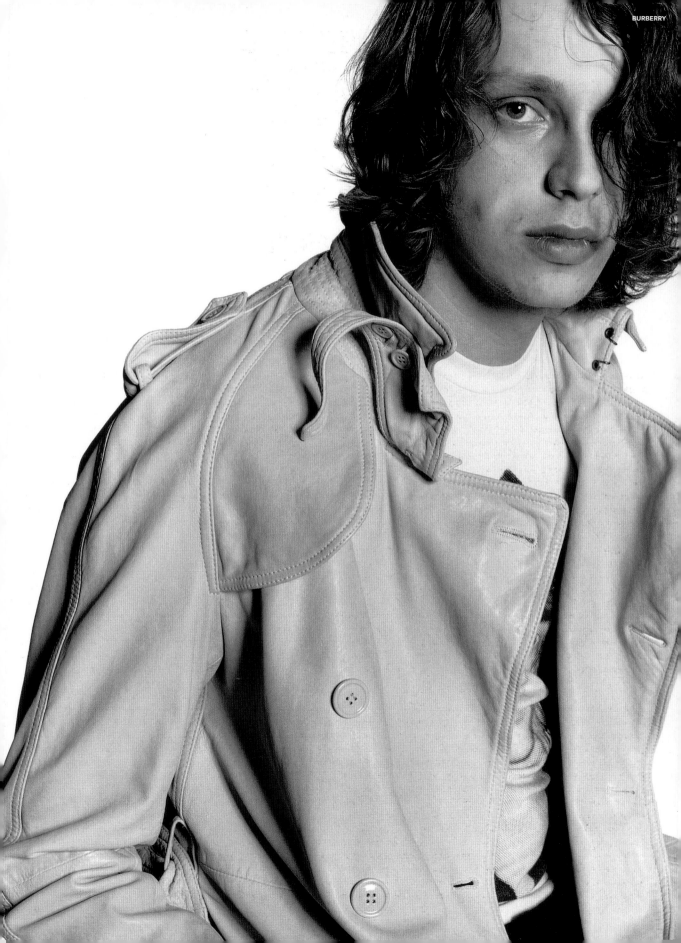

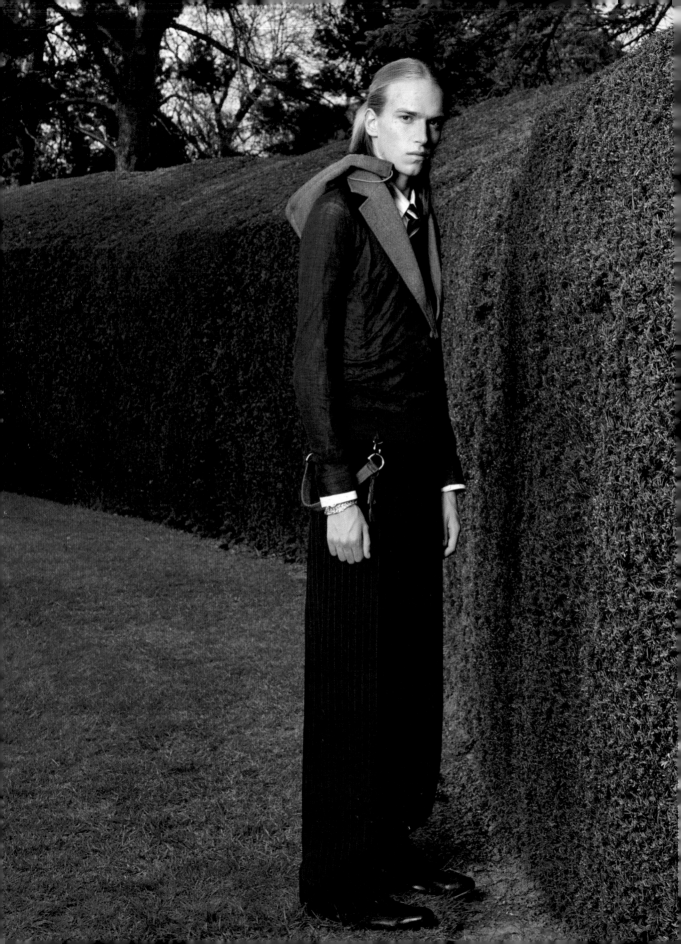

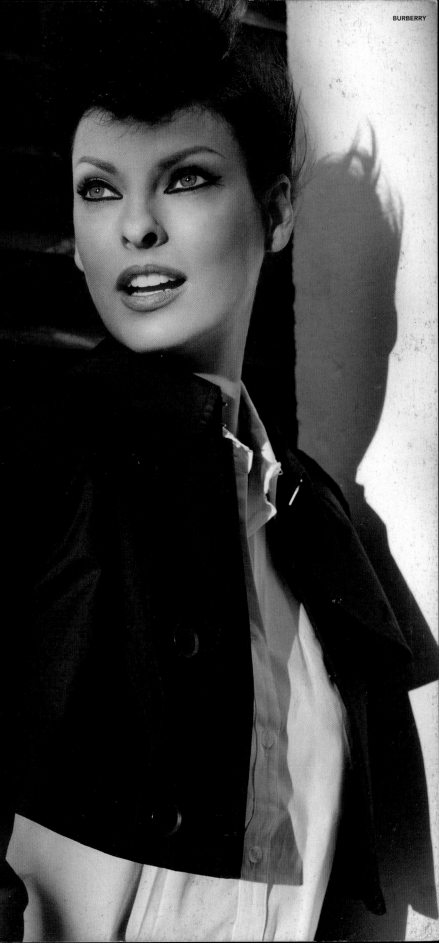

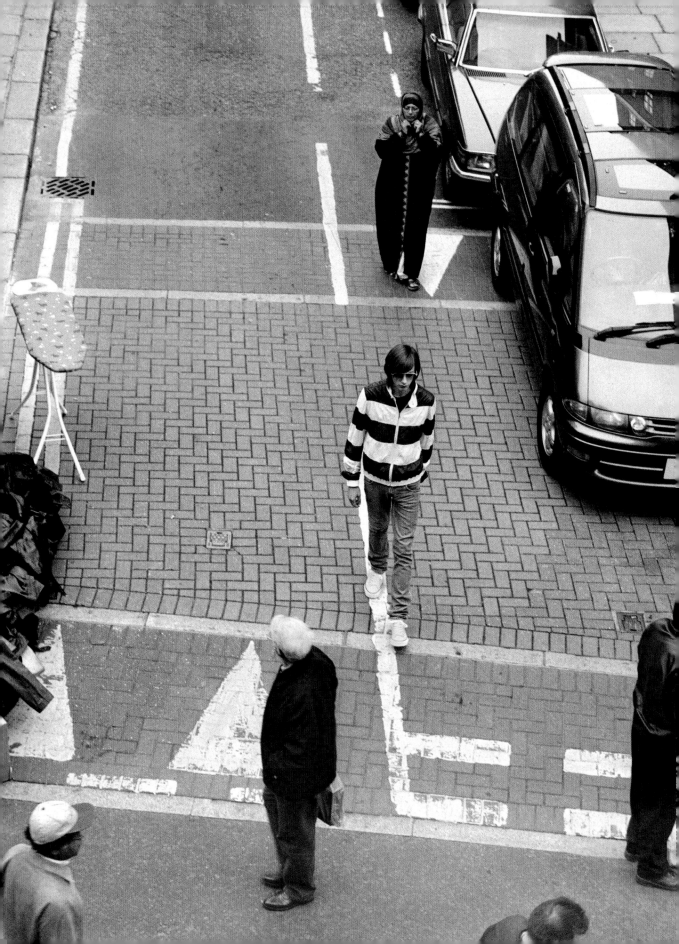

What are your signature designs? I'm a very down-to-earth designer in the sense that I love that mix of really classic, traditional, historical design with real fashion. I love fashion for its throwaway of-the-moment value, but I enjoy mixing it with something that's really thought about. That's what makes my role at Burberry particularly exciting **What's your favourite piece from any of your collections?** In terms of this company, without it sounding clichéd, I really love the trenchcoat. Obviously it's not something I designed, but it's an incredible piece: completely genderless, crossing all the different age groups and inspiring so many people and designers. It's a classic staple. Anything that I have designed I'm bored of; anything that is a trenchcoat for me is good **How would you describe your work?** It's very considered. I hate anything slapdash **What's your ultimate goal?** To always enjoy my work. I dread boredom. If I ever sensed that I was getting bored of my job, it would just

be the end for me **What inspires you?** It comes in so many guises that it's impossible to say. I love architecture, I love design, I love art, I love people and I love eating. For me, inspiration is really about keeping your mind open and never getting jaded **Who do you have in mind when you design?** I don't have one particular person. It's much more about an attitude and a spirit and character than an actual person. It's nice if you can find somebody – it's my dream to discover a muse. I would love an ideal person who personifies everything I'm thinking, but I don't think that person will ever exist **Is the idea of creative collaboration important to you?** I love working with people who share my sense of passion – I'm a very upbeat person and my natural spirit is cheerful. For me it's a pleasure working with enthusiastic, passionate, happy people. I also like working with people who have a very strong will and strong mind, because it's a challenge – but it's a huge frustration as well **Who has**

been the greatest influence on your career? The little person inside my body who tells me what to do. Whenever I've made any major decisions, I've always completely relied on that little voice. Even when I decided to leave Gucci and everybody without fail told me I was crazy, that little voice kept saying 'it's time, you need to move on'. I was going to nothing and I certainly didn't have this role here, but I did it anyway **Which is more important in your work: the process or the product?** The process – once you've got to the product, you're kind of over it **Is designing difficult for you and, if so, what drives you to continue?** The actual process of designing isn't difficult, but the process of designing something that fulfils all the criteria it needs to fulfil is very difficult. Fashion is functional, practical, emotional, commercial and aesthetic: there are so many things to take into consideration. Also, I have two agendas – my personal agenda when designing and

then the company's one as well **Have you ever been influenced or moved by the reaction to your designs?** I guess every time and never. It's always a great feeling when someone tells you that they love it and it's always depressing when someone doesn't like what you've done. It's important in both instances to say okay, that was then and now we're on other things **What's your definition of beauty?** It's got nothing to do with fashion or clothes. It's really somebody's inner self. For me, a beautiful person is someone with kindness and happiness, a good spirit and a good soul **What's your philosophy?** Enjoy everything that you do. It's important to be happy. If tomorrow I became jaded and bored in this job and wanted to go back to filling shelves in a supermarket, which I used to do and loved, then I would do that… Listen to me sounding like I want to work at Tesco! **What is the most important lesson you've learned?** Listen to your heart. It's never wrong.

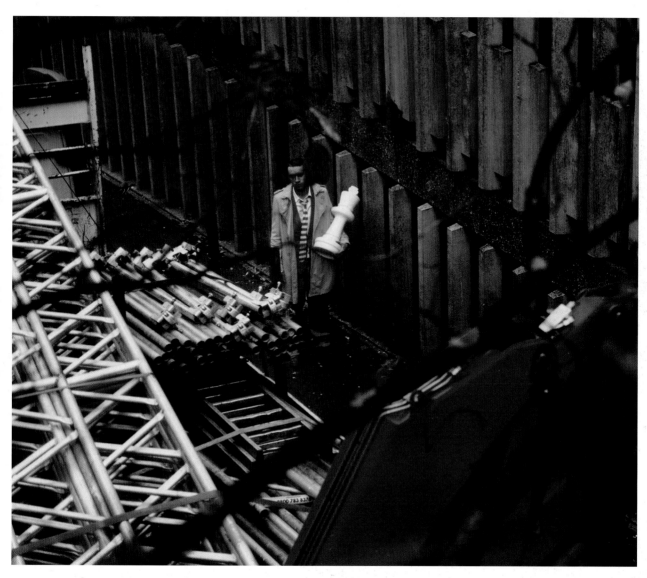

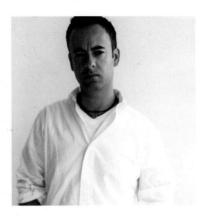

CALVIN KLEIN

"I really enjoy translating an idea into real product — it's energising" FRANCISCO COSTA

It's hard to imagine a young Francisco Costa growing up in the small Brazilian town where he was born (even to a family already rooted in fashion) and having even an inkling of the career he has now – a career which, in some ways, is only just starting. In the early '90s, the diminutive and cherubic immigrant arrived in New York as bright-eyed in the big city as any who had come before. He set about learning English and enrolled at the Fashion Institute of Technology, where he won the Idea Como/Young Designers of America award. After graduation, he was recruited to design dresses and knits for Bill Blass. But fate soon swept Costa towards his first big break when Oscar de la Renta asked him to oversee the signature and Pink Label collections of his own high-society house, plus Pierre Balmain haute couture and ready-to-wear. In 1998, at Tom Ford's bidding, Costa decamped for the red-hot Gucci studio where he served as senior designer of eveningwear, a position in which he was charged with creating the custom designs for both high-rolling clients and high-profile celebrities. This is where Costa cut his teeth, acquiring the skills required to direct a major label, as he would soon do, returning to New York in 2002 to work for Calvin Klein. Here he assumed the role of creative director of the women's collections, where he remains today. Costa's first marquee Calvin Klein collection was shown in the autumn of 2003, following the departure of the namesake designer (and, as the man who invented designer denim and who, in 1968, founded one of New York's mega-brands, Klein was hardly the easiest act to follow). Costa's debut drew rave reviews across the board for its seamless integration of the label's signature minimalism with a deft vision of how fashion looks now.

Man kann sich den jungen Francisco Costa kaum vorstellen, wie er in seiner kleinen brasilianischen Heimatstadt (wenn auch als Kind einer Familie, die bereits mit Mode zu tun hat) aufwächst und noch keinen Schimmer von seiner späteren Karriere hat. Wobei diese Karriere genau genommen erst der Anfang ist. Zu Beginn der 1990er Jahre kam er als kleiner, unschuldiger Immigrant so blauäugig wie viele andere in die Großstadt New York. Er machte sich daran, Englisch zu lernen, und schrieb sich am Fashion Institute of Technology ein, wo er später den Preis Idea Como/Young Designers of America gewann. Nach dem Studium bot sich ihm die Möglichkeit, bei Bill Blass Kleider und Strickwaren zu entwerfen. Das Schicksal bescherte Costa jedoch schon den ersten Durchbruch, als Oscar de la Renta ihm die nach ihm benannte Kollektion Oscar de la Renta und Pink Label seines High-Society-Modehauses sowie die Haute Couture und die Prêt-à-porter-Linie von Pierre Balmain anvertraute. 1998 folgte Costa dem Ruf von Tom Ford und wechselte in das damals absolut heiße Atelier von Gucci, wo er als Chefdesigner der Abendmode fungierte. In dieser Position war er für

die maßgefertigten Kreationen sowohl der betuchtesten Kunden als auch der Super-Promis verantwortlich. Costa verdiente sich seine Sporen und eignete sich die Fähigkeiten an, die man braucht, um ein großes Label zu führen, was er auch bald tun sollte, denn 2002 kehrte er nach New York zurück, um für Calvin Klein zu arbeiten. Hier übernahm er den Posten des Creative Director für alle Damenkollektionen, den er bis heute innehat. Costas erste unverkennbare Calvin-Klein-Kollektion wurde im Herbst 2003 gezeigt. Das war unmittelbar nach dem Ausscheiden des namengebenden Designers (der die Designerjeans erfunden und 1987 eines der New Yorker Mega-Labels gegründet hatte), in dessen Fußstapfen zu treten sicher keine leichte Aufgabe war. Costas Debüt erhielt durchweg Bombenkritiken für die nahtlose Integration des für die Marke so typischen Minimalismus in eine überzeugende Vision dessen, was Mode heute ausmacht.

Elevé dans sa petite ville natale du Brésil (au sein d'une famille déjà établie dans la mode), le jeune Francisco Costa ne pouvait sans doute pas imaginer la carrière qu'il a aujourd'hui et qui, sous certains aspects, ne fait que commencer. Au début des années 90, ce minuscule immigrant au visage chérubin débarque à New York, les yeux pleins d'étoiles, à l'instar de tous ceux qui ont découvert la ville avant lui. Il apprend l'anglais et s'inscrit au Fashion Institute of Technology, où il remporte le prix «Idea Como/Young Designers of America». Une fois diplômé, il dessine des robes et des pièces en maille pour Bill Blass. Mais le destin s'apprête à lui offrir sa première grande réussite : Oscar de la Renta lui demande de superviser sa collection signature et la griffe Pink Label de sa maison, si prisée par la haute société, ainsi que les lignes haute couture et prêt-à-porter de Pierre Balmain. En 1998, Tom Ford invite Costa à venir travailler dans l'atelier ultra-branché de Gucci en tant que styliste senior des tenues de soirée, où il est en charge des créations personnalisées sur mesure pour les clients les plus prestigieux et autres célébrités de premier plan. C'est là que Costa forge son style, acquérant les compétences requises pour diriger une grande marque, ce qu'il fera d'ailleurs rapidement en revenant à New York pour travailler chez Calvin Klein en 2002. Il y devient directeur de la création des collections pour femme, un poste qu'il occupe encore aujourd'hui. La première collection de Costa pour Calvin Klein est présentée à l'automne 2003, après le départ du fondateur de la maison (pas évident de reprendre le flambeau de l'homme qui a inventé le jean de créateur et fondé l'une des mégamarques new-yorkaises dès 1987). Les débuts de Costa suscitent les éloges de la critique, qui sait reconnaître son talent à fusionner le minimalisme signature de la griffe avec une vision habile de ce qu'est la mode aujourd'hui. LEE CARTER

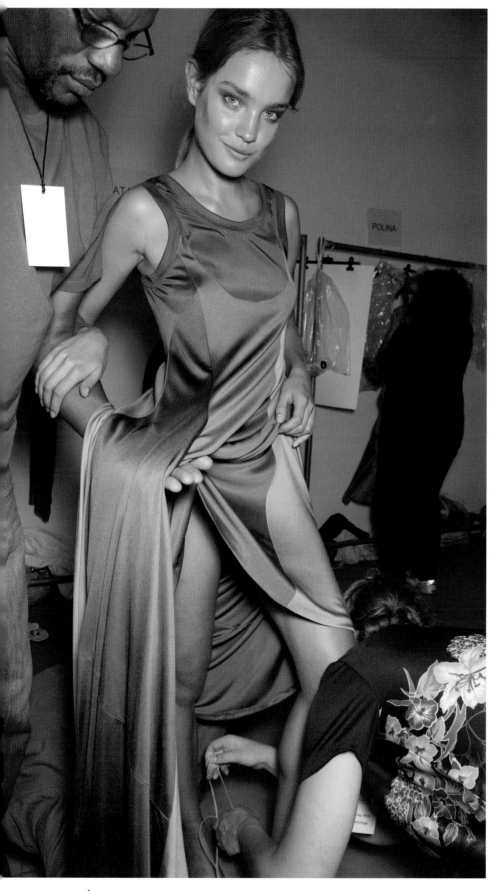

What is your favourite piece from any of your collections? Look #36 from the spring/ summer 2005 show because it embodies two worlds. It's understated, but also eccentric. It's based on the simplicity of a T-shirt pattern, but it has volume & colour **How would you describe your work?** Eclectic, but consistent **What's your ultimate goal?** To be completely satisfied **What inspires you?** Nature, art, people, film, books, books, books **Can fashion still have a political ambition?** Yes, the more complicated & convoluted the world gets, the more influenced we are by our environment & international relations. We're much more likely to make a statement based upon where we live **Who do you have in mind when you design?** She is a confident individual with an ageless beauty. But, ultimately, I design for the consumer, and she is constantly evolving and so must each collection **Is the idea of creative collaboration important to you?** Yes, I believe very much in a free exchange of ideas and inspirations. We each absorb influences from all areas of our world and our environment and process them in different ways **Who has been the greatest influence on your career?** There is not one specific person. Again, I think as we go along working with different people, we absorb and learn from each of them and move on **How have your own experiences affected your work as a designer?** Definitely. Your own experiences are very telling. It is what you have learned and the way you choose to live **Which is more important in your work: the process or the product?** The product, although I love the process. The product is what gets represented – very few people want to know about process **Is designing difficult for you, if so, what drives you to continue?** Designing is the easiest thing for me. I really enjoy translating an idea into a real product – it's energising **Have you ever been influenced or moved by the reaction to your designs?** Yes, because a reaction – good or bad – creates momentum to further or improve an idea **What's your definition of beauty?** All elements in balance. Perfection of integration. Person: confidence. Object: proportion **What's your philosophy?** Be positive **What is the most important lesson you've learned?** Trust yourself.

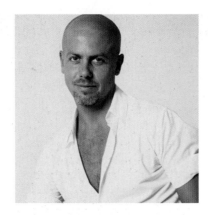

CALVIN KLEIN

"It's really amazing when you see your designs on the streets"
ITALO ZUCCHELLI

When Calvin Klein stepped down in 2003, Italo Zucchelli assumed the role of design director of the brand's menswear collections, following four seasons working directly with Klein. The spring/summer 2004 collection, shown in 2003, was Zucchelli's first. Zucchelli is a graduate of the Polimoda School of Fashion Design in Florence (1988), although he also previously attended courses for two years at the Architecture University, also in Florence. Prior to being recruited by Calvin Klein, he spent two years as menswear designer for Jil Sander; then a spell as designer at Romeo Gigli. Born 6 April 1965, he grew up near the Italian coastal town of La Spezia. Zuchelli recalls that his first glimpse into the world of Calvin Klein was provided in 1982, with a men's underwear advertisement that starred Olympic pole-vault athlete Tom Hintnaus. Zucchelli's designs encapsulate the spirit of Calvin Klein's sexy, American philosophy; an aesthetic inspired by the human form and the idea of designing clothes that relate directly to the body in a sophisticated and effortless manner. The simplicity and purity of the brand's design roots is a discipline in itself, one which Zucchelli deploys with a certain European panache, and inherent sense of sophisticated cool that has not only met with critical acclaim, but is an honest continuation of the Calvin Klein brand philosophy. Zucchelli lives and works in New York City.

Als Calvin Klein sich 2003 zurückzog, übernahm Italo Zucchelli den Posten des Design Director für die Herrenkollektionen, nachdem er vier Saisons lang eng mit Klein persönlich zusammengearbeitet hatte. Zucchellis Debüt war die 2003 präsentierte Kollektion Frühjahr/Sommer 2004. Zucchelli ist Absolvent der Polimoda Schule für Modedesign in Florenz (1988), studierte zuvor jedoch ebenfalls in Florenz zwei Jahre lang Architektur. Bevor er von Calvin Klein engagiert wurde, hatte er zwei Jahre lang Herrenmode für Jil Sander entworfen und anschließend als Designer bei Romeo Gigli gearbeitet. Geboren wurde er am 6. April 1965, aufgewachsen ist er in der Nähe der italienischen Hafenstadt La Spezia. Zucchelli erinnert sich, dass er den ersten Eindruck von der Welt Calvin Kleins einer Werbung für Herrenunterwäsche von 1982 verdankte, die den

olympischen Stabhochspringer Tom Hintnaus zeigte. Zucchellis Entwürfe verkörpern den Geist von Calvin Kleins verführerischer amerikanischer Philosophie; eine Ästhetik, die vom menschlichen Körper inspiriert ist und von der Vorstellung, Mode zu designen, die auf raffinierte und zugleich mühelose Weise in unmittelbarem Bezug zum Körper steht. Die Schlichtheit und Reinheit der designerischen Ursprünge des Labels sind eine Disziplin für sich, die Zucchelli mit einer gewissen europäischen Überlegenheit absolviert. Dazu kommt sein angeborenes Gespür für exquisite Coolness, die nicht nur für Lob bei den Kritikern sorgte, sondern echte Kontinuität in der Markenphilosophie von Calvin Klein bedeutet. Zucchelli lebt und arbeitet in New York.

Depuis que Calvin Klein a pris sa retraite en 2003, Italo Zucchelli assume le rôle de directeur de la création des collections pour homme de la marque, après quatre saisons de collaboration directe avec Klein. Présentée en 2003, la collection printemps/été 2004 est la première signée par Zucchelli. Bien qu'il ait également suivi des études d'architecture à l'université de Florence, Italo Zucchelli est diplômé de la Polimoda School of Fashion Design de la même ville (1988). Avant d'être recruté par Calvin Klein, il passe deux ans chez Jil Sander en tant que styliste pour homme, puis travaille pendant une brève période pour Romeo Gigli. Né le 6 avril 1965, il grandit près de la ville côtière italienne de La Spezia. Zuchelli découvre pour la première fois l'univers de Calvin Klein en 1982, grâce à une publicité de sous-vêtements pour homme de la marque où apparaît le champion olympique de saut à la perche Tom Hintnaus. Les créations de Zucchelli réussissent à saisir la philosophie américaine et sexy, propre à l'esprit Calvin Klein ; son esthétique s'inspire de la forme humaine, et de l'idée qui consiste à créer de manière sophistiquée et facile des vêtements qui entretiennent une relation directe avec le corps. La simplicité et la pureté des racines créatives de la marque sont une véritable discipline en soi, que Zucchelli déploie avec son panache très européen et son sens inné du cool sophistiqué, lequel est non seulement plébiscité par la critique, mais constitue également une continuation honnête de la philosophie Calvin Klein. Zucchelli vit et travaille à New York.

DAVID LAMB

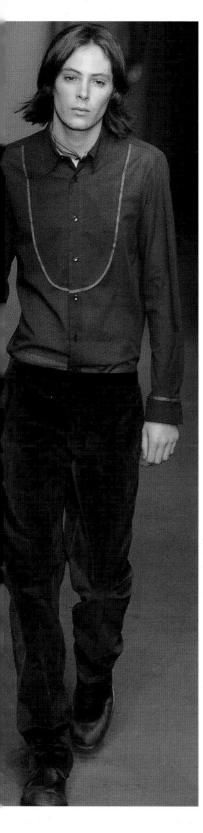
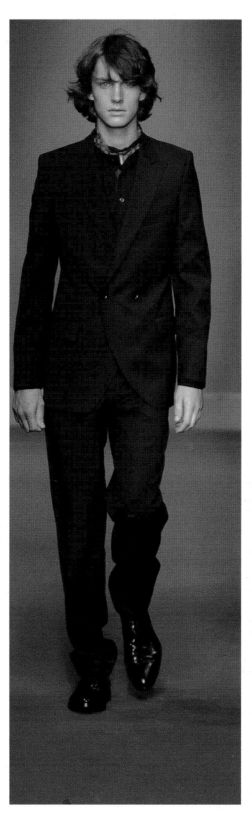
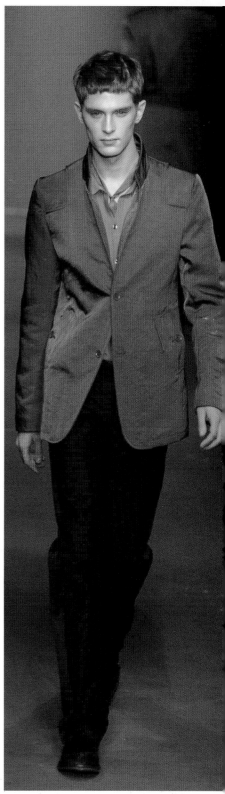

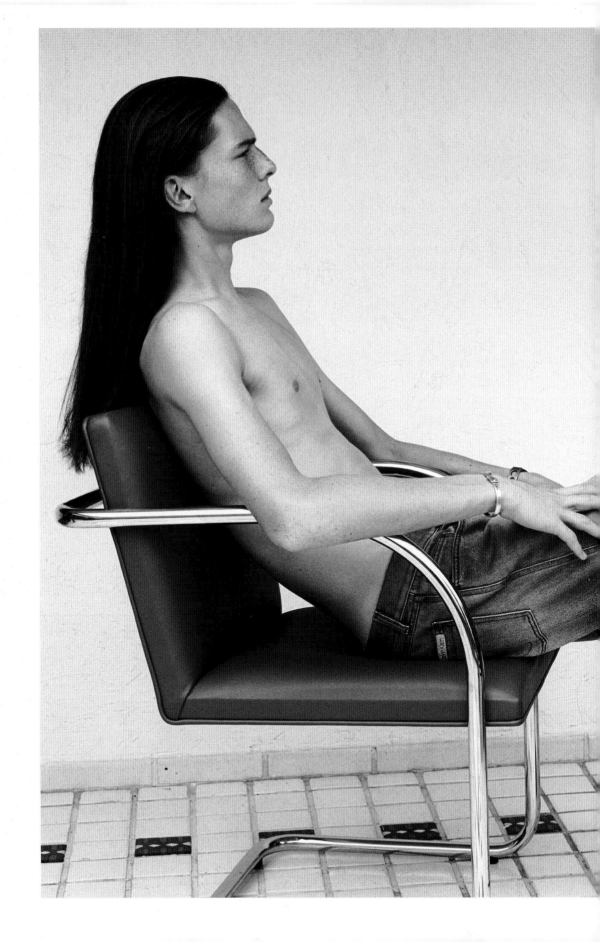

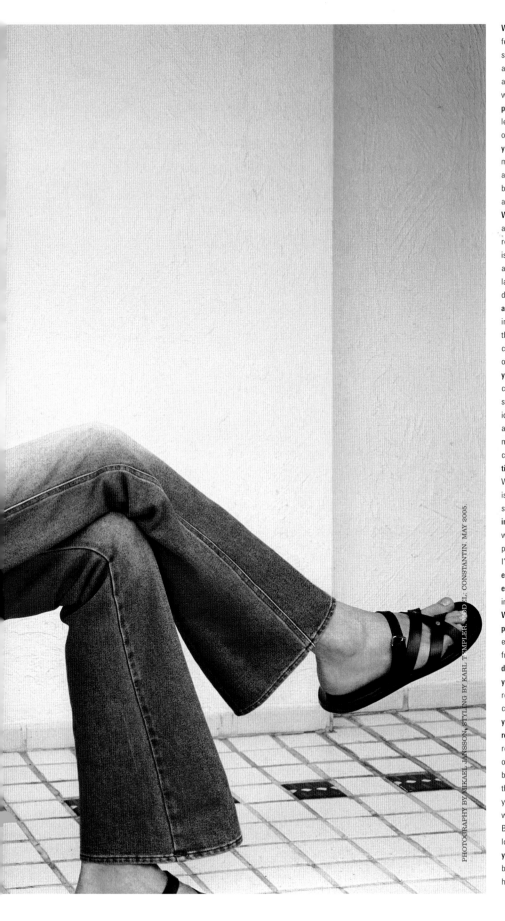

PHOTOGRAPHY BY MIKAEL JANSSON, STYLING BY KARL TEMPLER. MODEL: CONSTANTIN. MAY 2005.

What are your signature designs? The perfect leather jacket, a sharp-cut blazer, a skinny sexy pant, a multi-seamed shirt with a complicated construction, a wearable accessory (such as a bag-belt, or a bag worn under clothes) **What is your favourite piece from any of your collections?** A perfect leather jacket with leather-covered studs on the shoulders. **How would you describe your work?** Genuine, playful, sexy and masculine **What's your ultimate goal?** To live a full life, surrounded by people I love, and be able to do my job with the same integrity and passion I have put in since I started **What inspires you?** Inspiration can be anywhere, in a song, a smell. Seeing and realising the inspiration is a soul quality. It is something that happens at another level and comes to you almost magically, and is later translated into an object or a simple detail **Can fashion still have a political ambition?** In the past, politics has been influential and reflected in fashion, like the punk movement. Today, so much has changed, and it seems a bit pretentious and out of place to introduce politics **Who do you have in mind when you design?** It is a combination of an impalpable inspiration, a sort of character or persona that I like to identify with at the beginning of the process and what I would like to wear at the moment – and the needs of the ideal final consumer **Is the idea of creative collaboration important to you?** Yes, very much so. Working with a design team, collaboration is critical and the resulting creativity is stimulating **Who has been the greatest influence on your career?** My grandmother, who inspired and encouraged me with her passion for life and beauty. I'm doing what I'm doing, thanks to her **How have your own experiences affected your work as a designer?** My experiences and what I go through in life naturally translate into what I do. **Which is more important in your work: the process or the product?** I love the process. I enjoy it very much. The best product comes from the most enjoyable process. **Is designing difficult for you, if so, what drives you to continue?** It's not difficult at all. I really love it because it's one of the most creative stages of the whole process **Have you ever been influenced or moved by the reaction to your designs?** Of course. It's really amazing when you see your designs on the streets, worn by actual people, because it's the moment when you realise that somebody somehow related to what you did **What's your definition of beauty?** One word: love **What's your philosophy?** Integrity. Be honest with yourself and the ones you love **What is the most important lesson you've learned?** Believe in your own dreams, because they can come true – but you still have to work hard.

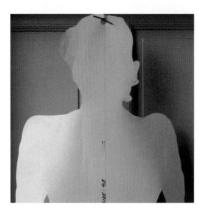

CAROL CHRISTIAN POELL

"I've learned that not everything sells"

Carol Christian Poell is one of the only avant-garde designers living and working in Milan. In a city that prides itself on the successful marriage of commerce and creativity, Poell (born in Linz, Austria in 1966) is something of an anomaly. 'Curious' is perhaps the most appropriate adjective for this designer, whose presentations (he never offers conventional catwalk shows) ask as many questions as they offer solutions. Poell became interested in fashion at an early age, helping out in his stepfather's clothes factory from the tender age of eight. After graduating from Milan's Domus Academy, Poell showed his first menswear collection for autumn/winter 1994, immediately provoking enthusiastic reactions with his unique vision. His particular talent is an ability to challenge established ideas – for example, his use of human hair as an alternative to wool – combined with unrivalled tailoring skills. Since 1999, he has put these to good use by also presenting a womenswear collection; his women's trousers, in particular, are much sought-after. Poell's designs can often be perceived as quite simple – many of them are long, lean examples of precision tailoring – but that would be to ignore his immense craftsmanship. Poell doesn't design collections in the usual sense, preferring to work on individual garments, working and reworking them with such attention to detail that they become faultless and timeless.

Carol Christian Poell ist einer der wenigen Avantgarde-Designer, die in Mailand leben und arbeiten. In einer Stadt, die so stolz auf ihre erfolgreiche Einheit von Kommerz und Kreativität ist, stellt der 1966 im österreichischen Linz geborenen Poell eine echte Ausnahmeerscheinung dar. „Neugierig" ist der Begriff, mit dem sich dieser Designer vielleicht am besten charakterisieren lässt. Seine Präsentationen (er liefert nie konventionelle Catwalk-Shows ab) stellen ebenso viele Fragen, wie sie Antworten geben. Poells Interesse für Mode wurde schon früh geweckt. Bereits im zarten Alter von acht Jahren half er in der Kleiderfabrik seines Stiefvaters mit. Nach dem Abschluss an der Mailänder Domus-Akademie zeigte Poell seine erste Herrenkollektion für Herbst/Winter 1994 und rief mit seinen einzigartigen Visionen sofort enthusiastische Reaktionen hervor. Seine

besondere Begabung besteht darin, etablierte Ideen in Frage zu stellen – beispielsweise durch die Verwendung von Menschenhaar anstelle von Wolle –, sowie in unvergleichlichen handwerklichen Fähigkeiten. Seit 1999 nutzt er seine Schneiderkunst auch für eine Damenkollektion, aus der insbesondere die Hosen heiß begehrt sind. Poells Kreationen wirken oft ganz simpel – viele sind lange, schmale Beispiele präzisester Maßschneiderei – und lassen seine immense Kunstfertigkeit erst auf den zweiten Blick erkennen. Poell produziert keine Kollektionen im herkömmlichen Sinn, sondern bevorzugt die Arbeit an individuellen Einzelstücken, die er mit großer Liebe zum Detail so lange umarbeitet, bis sie so makel- wie zeitlos sind.

Carol Christian Poell est l'un des rares créateurs d'avant-garde qui vit et travaille à Milan. Dans cette ville qui se flatte d'incarner la réussite du mariage entre commerce et créativité, Poell (né en 1966 à Linz en Autriche) fait vraiment figure d'anomalie. « Curieux » est sans doute l'adjectif qui décrit le mieux ce designer dont les présentations posent autant de questions qu'elles apportent de réponses (il n'a jamais présenté de défilé traditionnel). Très tôt, Poell commence à s'intéresser à la mode en aidant son beau-père dans son usine de vêtements. Une fois diplômé de la Domus Academy de Milan, Poell présente une première collection pour homme automne/hiver 1994 qui, grâce à son approche unique, suscite immédiatement beaucoup d'enthousiasme. Son talent particulier réside dans sa capacité à remettre en question les idées reçues – par exemple en utilisant des cheveux humains en alternative à la laine – ainsi que dans ses compétences inégalées en matière de coupe. Depuis 1999, il applique ce potentiel à la mode féminine et ses pantalons pour femme sont aujourd'hui très recherchés. Le style de Poell est souvent considéré comme assez simple, avec ses vêtements longs et près du corps pourtant parfaitement coupés, mais cette simplicité-là doit beaucoup à son immense savoir-faire. Poell ne dessine pas de « collections » à proprement parler ; il préfère travailler et retravailler chaque vêtement en portant une grande attention aux détails afin d'aboutir à des pièces parfaites et intemporelles.

MARCUS ROSS

What are your signature designs? I don't have any How would you describe your work? Undecided What's your ultimate goal? To continue What inspires you? Problems Can fashion still have a political ambition? If political means power and money, yes What do you have in mind when you design? A jacket, a shirt... Is the idea of creative collaboration important to you? Yes, when necessary What has been the greatest influence on your career? Coincidence How have your own experiences affected your work as a designer? Questioning myself in my work Which is more important in your work: the process or the product? The process of producing the product Is designing difficult for you and, if so, what drives you to continue? Yes – I don't know Have you ever been influenced or moved by the reaction to your designs? Impossible not to be What's your definition of beauty? Beauty cannot be defined What's your philosophy? To doubt What is the most important lesson you've learned? Not everything sells.

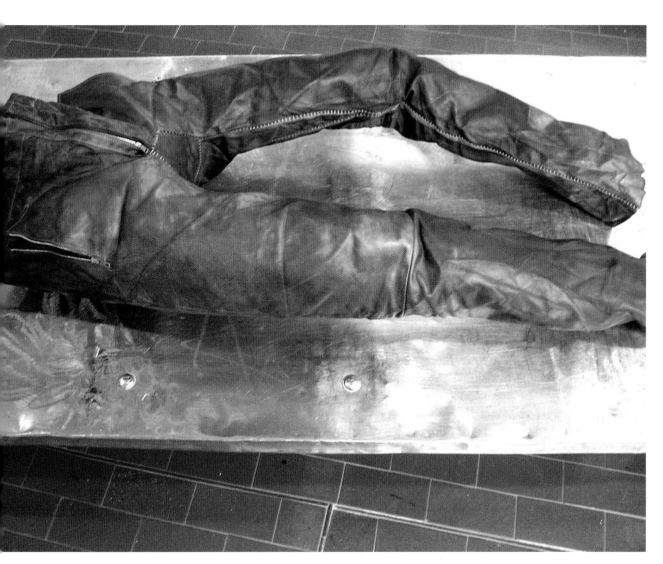

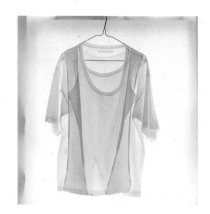

CAROLA EULER

"I try to be a clever pattern cutter and the
struggle with that can keep me going for a while"

Carola Euler (born 1976) chose the menswear option for her Art Foundation course at the London College of Fashion in 1999 simply because so many other students were opting for womenswear. Euler says she found men's fashion more 'exclusive'. Fast forward six years and the German-born designer presented her MA menswear collection at the Central Saint Martins show in March 2005 to a rapt reception from London stylists. Standout pieces from that show were her baby-blue knits with scoop necklines, a hip-hugging all-white denim ensemble and layers of Euler's favourite white jersey, which was cut into sporty, slouchy T-shirts and put with matching baseball caps. By that time, Euler had already notched up an impressive CV that included stints working as a pattern cutter and studio assistant at Frank Leder, Alexander McQueen, Alfred Dunhill, Jonathan Saunders and Raf Simons. In fact, Euler's first foray into menswear was sewing a fleece shirt for her boyfriend at the age of 14. She took numerous sewing classes and after school in Germany studied dressmaking and tailoring, moving to London 1999 to continue her fashion education. Since 2003 Euler has created her own collection, which is sold at B-Store in London.

Die 1976 geborene Carola Euler entschied sich 1999 im Rahmen ihres Art-Foun-dation-Studiums am London College of Fashion für Herrenmode. Und zwar aus dem einfachen Grund, weil so viele Kommilitonen für die Damenmode optierten. Euler empfand Männermode außerdem als exklusiver. Spulen wir sechs Jahre im Schnelldurchlauf vor, dann sehen wir die in Deutschland geborene Designerin im März 2005 die Abschlusskollektion ihres Master-Studiums am Central Saint Martins präsentieren, die von Londons Stylisten mit Verzückung aufgenommen wurde. Herausragende Stücke aus dieser Schau waren ihre babyblauen Strick-sachen mit rundem Ausschnitt, ein die Hüften umspielendes Jeans-Ensemble in Weiß und viele Schichten von Eulers weißem Lieblingsjersey, der zu sportlich-lässigen T-Shirts geschnitten und mit dazu passenden Baseballcaps getragen

wurde. Zu diesem Zeitpunkt hatte Euler bereits eine eindrucksvolle Laufbahn hinter sich, mit Erfahrungen als Zuschneiderin und Atelierassistentin bei Frank Leder, Alexander McQueen, Alfred Dunhill, Jonathan Saunders und Raf Simons. Eulers allererster Versuch auf dem Gebiet der Herrenmode war übrigens ein Fleece-Shirt, das sie im Alter von 14 Jahren für ihren damaligen Freund nähte. Später besuchte sie diverse Nähkurse und studierte nach ihrem Schulabschluss in Deutschland Modedesign. 1999 zog sie nach London, um ihre Ausbildung dort fortzusetzen. Seit dem Jahr 2003 produziert Euler eine eigene Kollektion, die im Londoner B-Store verkauft wird.

En 1999, si Carola Euler (née en 1976) opte pour le cours de mode masculine du London College of Fashion, c'est simplement parce que la plupart des étudiants choisissent la mode féminine. Carola Euler trouve alors la mode pour homme plus « luxueuse ». Six ans plus tard, la créatrice allemande décroche son MA en présentant sa collection de fin d'études lors du défilé de Central Saint Martins en mars 2005, pour le plus grand bonheur des stylistes de Londres. Les pièces les plus remarquées incluent ses pulls bleu layette à col bateau, un ensemble en denim tout blanc moulant aux hanches et une profusion du jersey blanc qu'elle affectionne particulièrement, coupé sous forme de t-shirts sport très souples, coordonnés à des casquettes de baseball. A ce stade, la créatrice affiche déjà un impressionnant CV avec plusieurs expériences dans la coupe de patrons et l'as-sistanat en atelier chez Frank Leder, Alexander McQueen, Alfred Dunhill, Jona-than Saunders et Raf Simons. En fait, sa première incursion dans la mode mas-culine remonte à l'âge de 14 ans, quand elle a cousu une chemise en polaire pour son petit ami. Elle a suivi de nombreux cours de couture et après le lycée, elle étudie la couture et la coupe en Allemagne avant de partir pour Londres en 1999 afin de poursuivre sa formation en mode. Depuis 2003, Carola Euler dessine sa propre collection, vendue dans la boutique B-Store de Londres. SUSIE RUSHTON

What are your signature designs? I'm only working on my third collection, it's too early to say… but I certainly can't help myself but using cheap white T-shirt jersey again and again. It's so versatile and you can do cool things with it, it's just a never-ending story really… **What is your favourite piece from any of your collections?** There are quite a few, I usually like most of my collections otherwise I wouldn't do it. But there's one piece, a slouchy hand-knitted cardigan with half set-in half raglan sleeves, droopy epaulettes and a width-varying ribbed shawl collar that my heart is very fond of. My mum knitted it for my first collection – she's a wizard with the needles! (That woman can knit whole castles if you ask her to but she will also insist on explaining how it's done so "The next time you can do it yourself!" Bless her.) **How would you describe your work?** I wouldn't. I just make it. Describing is your job, isn't it? **What's your ultimate goal?** Do a little more living and a little less surviving **What inspires you?** Anything really. Music, films, sitting on a bus watching the people outside. A single photograph once inspired a whole collection. I also try to be a clever pattern cutter and the struggle with that can keep me going for a while **Can fashion still have a political ambition?** Maybe, but not in my department. Personally I find it a bit dated. Fashion is a consumer product, an enjoyable one, but a product **What do you have in mind when you design?** A total look, an atmosphere, a mood, a piece of music **Is the idea of creative collaboration important for you?** Very. A great collection is never one person's achievement! It's the result of a great team behind it **What has been the greatest influence on your career?** Having no money. It eats you and it feeds you **How have your own experiences affected your work as a designer?** Growing up in a small town in Germany definitely made me want to go "out there" and do something "glamorous" (ha ha, little did I know…) that "will show them", especially after a three-year tailoring apprenticeship with some "old-school" ladies as teachers. I learnt a great deal of technical skill that comes in very handy now and often informs my work **Which is more important in your work: the process or the product?** Both. If you don't like the process it kills you. I need the ups and downs, the excitement, the fun and the tears, all of it. That's why my product is what it is. And when I can hold it up and say "Yep, that's it!", I have this elevating feeling of accomplishment **Is design-**ing difficult for you, if ⌷ continue? Designing, ⌷ documenting my ide⌷ I am happy with, ye⌷ **Have you ever been ⌷ the reactions to your design⌷** I want my clothes to be worn and the fact that there are people out there who go and buy my clothes, something that I designed and made, is really amazing. I want to know if my work is appreciated and ultimately "of use". I'm like a child that needs a pat on the shoulder after it has done its homework **What's your definition of beauty?** Beautiful is somebody who doesn't long to be somebody else **What's your philosophy?** Links liegenlassen, rechts aufstellen! (Danke Björn) **What's the most important lesson you've learned?** You are what you think of yourself.

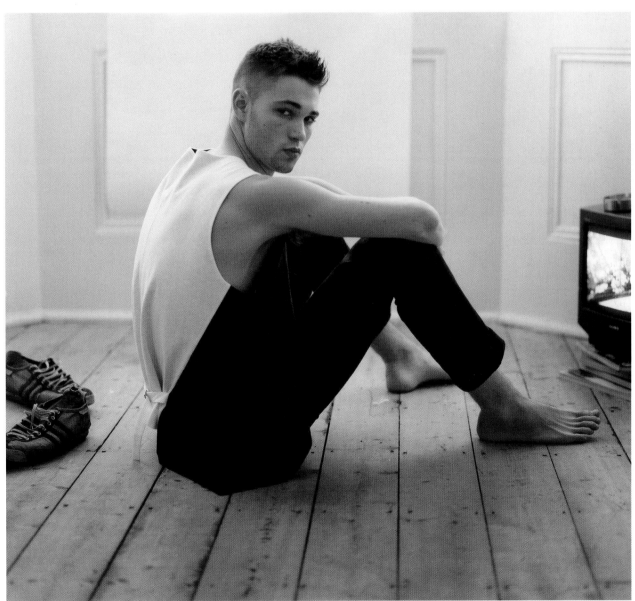

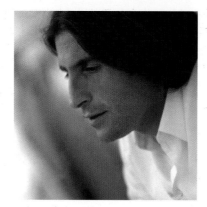

CÉLINE

"My goal is to create something that women feel they really need"
ROBERTO MENICHETTI

Like any major fashion name, deluxe LVMH brand Céline has kept its A-list status by marketing the kind of must-have products that spawn waiting lists from Manhattan to Milan. But, uncharacteristically enough, when the first Céline boutique opened in Paris in 1945, its focus was on hard-wearing children's shoes. It wasn't until 1959 that a womenswear initiative was launched and it was another three years later that the famous three horse-bit link started to adorn shoes, accessories and, of course, handbags. Céline finery has adorned the most chic ladies ever since. In 1998, the American Michael Kors was appointed chief designer of the ready-to-wear womenswear line – the first ever – and in 1999 he went onto become the company's creative director. Under his leadership, Céline became renowned for super-charged, ultra-luxurious womenswear. When the private-jet set needed something to go with their diamonds, their first stop was Céline. And it was a recipe for success: sales in the brand's 100 stores worldwide shot up to a record high. April 2004 saw Kors' contract come to an end and new designer Roberto Menichetti step into his shoes. Menichetti, who was first discovered by Claude Montana, has an impressive career history that includes both Jil Sander and an artistic director role at Burberry. His own label, Menichetti, launched in New York in February 2004, and his first collection for Céline hit the stores for spring/summer 2005; Menichetti has set tongues wagging with his experimental and streamlined vision of what the Céline customer should be wearing – a dramatic departure from Kors's glamour-puss aesthetic.

Wie jede andere größere Modemarke hat sich auch das Luxuslabel Céline des LVMH-Konzerns seinen Spitzenstatus gesichert, indem es die Art von Must-Haves vermarktet, die von Manhattan bis Mailand für Wartelisten sorgen. Ziemlich untypisch ist allerdings, dass die erste 1945 in Paris eröffnete Céline-Boutique hauptsächlich robuste Kinderschuhe verkaufte. Erst 1959 wurde Damenmode lanciert. Danach dauerte es noch drei weitere Jahre, bis das berühmte dreiteilige Pferdezaumzeug Schuhe, Accessoires und natürlich Handtaschen zierte. Seit damals schmückt Céline die chicsten Damen. 1998 wurde der Amerikaner Michael Kors zunächst Chefdesigner der ersten Prêt-à-porter-Damenlinie des Hauses, ein Jahr später folgte sein Aufstieg zum Creative Director des Unternehmens. Unter seiner Leitung wurde Céline für seine superteure, ultraluxuriöse Damenmode berühmt. Wenn der Privat-Jet-Set etwas Passendes zu neuen Juwelen suchte, war Céline die erste Adresse. Dies war das Erfolgs-

rezept des Labels: Die Verkaufszahlen in den hundert eigenen Läden in aller Welt erreichten Rekordhöhen. Im April 2004 endete der Vertrag von Kors, und der neue Designer Roberto Menichetti trat in seine Fußstapfen. Menichetti, den Claude Montana entdeckt hatte, blickte damals bereits auf eine eindrucksvolle Karriere zurück, mit Stationen bei Jil Sander und Burberry, wo er Artistic Director gewesen war. Das eigene Label namens Menichetti präsentierte er im Februar 2004 in New York, seine erste Kollektion für Céline war Frühjahr/Sommer 2005. Mit seiner experimentellen und zugleich modernisierten Vision vom Outfit der Céline-Kundinnen sorgte er für viel Gerede, stellte es doch einen radikalen Bruch mit der Glamour-Häschen-Ästhetik eines Michael Kors dar.

Comme tout grand nom de la mode, Céline, marque de luxe du groupe LVMH, a préservé son statut haut de gamme en proposant le genre de « must » qui génère des listes d'attente de Manhattan jusqu'à Milan. Pourtant, quand la première boutique Céline a ouvert ses portes à Paris en 1945, la maison ne vendait alors que des chaussures pour enfant ultra-résistantes à l'usure. Ce n'est qu'en 1959 que la marque se diversifie dans le féminin, et il faut attendre encore trois ans pour commencer à voir le célèbre mors de cheval apparaître sur les chaussures, les accessoires et, bien sûr, les sacs à main. Depuis, Céline accessoirise les femmes les plus élégantes. En 1998, le créateur américain Michael Kors est nommé styliste principal de la toute première ligne de prêt-à-porter féminin, puis devient directeur de la création de toutes les lignes de la maison en 1999. Sous sa direction, la griffe Céline devient réputée pour ses créations féminines très chargées et archi-luxueuses. Quand un membre de la jet-set cherche une tenue pour accompagner ses diamants, il commence toujours son shopping chez Céline. C'est la vraie recette du succès : les ventes de la marque dans ses 100 boutiques à travers le monde atteignent des records. En avril 2004, Kors termine son contrat, remplacé par le nouveau créateur Roberto Menichetti. Ce dernier, découvert par Claude Montana, revendique une impressionnante carrière chez Jil Sander et comme directeur de la création chez Burberry. Sa griffe éponyme lancée à New York en février 2004 et sa première collection pour Céline débarquent en magasin pour le printemps/été 2005 ; Menichetti fait jaser en proposant une vision expérimentale et épurée de ce que la cliente Céline devrait porter, opérant un tournant radical par rapport à l'esthétique de minette glamour prisée par Kors.

TERRY NEWMAN

SPRING/SUMMER 2005 BACKSTAGE. PHOTOGRAPHY BY SEAN CUNNINGHAM

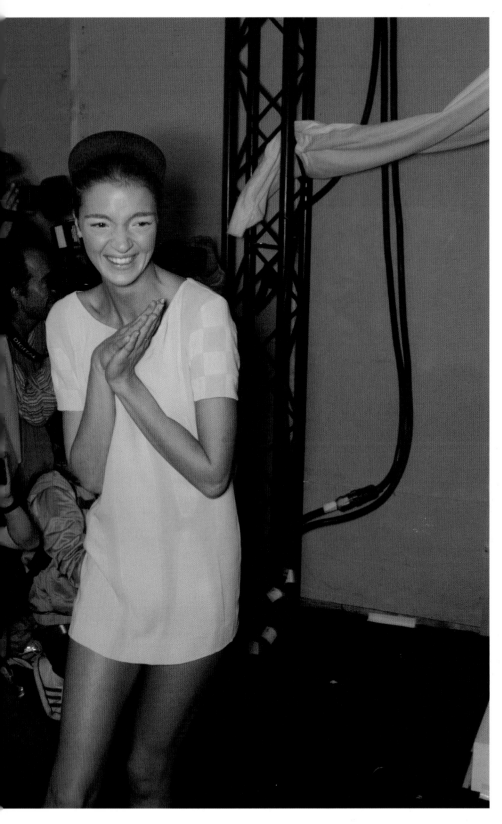

What are your signature designs? Positive How would you describe your work? I am creating for Céline a Parisian attitude to dressing a woman What's your ultimate goal? To create something that women feel they really need, something that makes them feel modern and feminine What inspires you? If you look profoundly into things it is difficult to choose one thing only Can fashion still have a political ambition? Yes. For example the 21st century represents a bridge or a passage between the past and the future, the old era and the new, from a more rational time to a time of the senses and sensibility Who do you have in mind when you design? A representation is created by a succession of many things that somehow create an image. I believe in a dynamic life and creativity and therefore prefer the movement that a summary of words, images, symbols, etc. can create. It respects the continual evolution of things Is the idea of creative collaboration important to you? Yes How have your own experiences affected your work as a designer? There has been a lot of movement in the last years, but confined between who is copying and who is actually creating and anticipating the trends. This does not have to be a negative thing but can create the need for great change, which I believe it has. It is time for an accelerated move forward Which is more important in your work: the process or the product? Both are important Is designing difficult for you, if so, what drives you to continue? No, it is not. The design for the future connects more with the five senses than rational thinking. The touch, feel, visual, smell and taste of things around us are important. All of these things combined, the sensation these things give and more importantly the selection of these things will be the synthesis that creates style and this is what drives me What's your definition of beauty? Beauty is hope. I see the new generation that are children now, how they interact with each other and the world What's your philosophy? There is always room for diversity What is the most important lesson you've learned? Team work is essential to ensure the designer's vision.

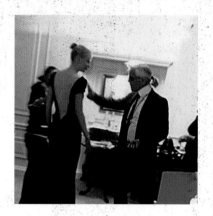

CHANEL

"I am inspired by everything. There is only one rule: eyes open!"

KARL LAGERFELD

A legendary name in fashion, Chanel is today synonymous both with its founder, Gabrielle "Coco" Chanel and its artistic director since 1983, Karl Lagerfeld. Chanel herself – who was born in an orphanage, was self-taught and who first established her house in 1913 – is perhaps the most important fashion designer of the 20th century. Her pioneering use of sportswear for high fashion in the '20s, her little black dresses, her costume jewellery, taste for suntanning and appropriation of male dress are the stuff of fashion legend. Her Chanel No. 5 perfume (invented in 1921), is a confirmed 'classic', as are her softly-structured tweed suit and quilted leather handbags (both developed in the '50s). When Chanel died in 1971 she left a rich legacy of house codes which are today boldly reinvented by Karl Lagerfeld. Mademoiselle's favourite pearls turn up, outsized, as little evening bags; tweed is transformed into fluffy leggings and matching berets; a love of the sporty, outdoors life is expressed via Chanel-branded snowboards and surfboards. At Chanel, Lagerfeld heads up one of Paris' few remaining haute couture salons; in July 2002 the company, which is owned by the Wertheimer family, secured the future of its couture business by acquiring five specialist workshops, including Lesage, the prestigious embroidery company. Chanel is today nothing if not a commercial powerhouse and in December 2004 the company opened a multi-floored new store in the Ginza shopping district of Tokyo that includes a restaurant, Beige Tokyo, and a glassy façade fitted with twinkling lights that resemble the brand's famous tweed. In May 2005 the Metropolitan Museum of Art in New York opened an exhibition devoted to Chanel's historic innovations, featuring designs by both the house founder and its present incumbent. Despite this grand heritage, what Coco and Lagerfeld have in common above all is relish for the present times and for the future. As Chanel herself once said, "I am neither in the past nor avant-garde. My style follows life." [Also see Lagerfeld Gallery]

Der Name Chanel ist legendär in der Modebranche heute gleichermaßen als Synonym für seine Gründerin Gabrielle „Coco" Chanel wie für den künstlerischen Direktor seit 1983, Karl Lagerfeld. Die in einem Waisenhaus aufgewachsene Coco Chanel war Autodidaktin, gründete ihr Modehaus im Jahr 1913 und ist die vielleicht wichtigste Designerin des 20. Jahrhunderts. Ihr pionierhaftes Einbringen von Sportswear in die Haute Couture in den 1920er Jahren, ihre kleinen Schwarzen, ihr Modeschmuck und die Verwendung von typisch männlichen Stilattributen – all das ist längst in die Modegeschichte eingegangen. Ihr 1921 kreierter Duft Chanel No. 5 gilt als absoluter Klassiker, ebenso wie das weich strukturierte Tweedkostüm und die gesteppte Lederhandtasche (beides Entwürfe aus den 1950er Jahren). Als Chanel 1971 starb, hinterließ sie ein reiches Vermächtnis, das Karl Lagerfeld bis heute entschieden neu interpretiert. So kommen beispielsweise Mademoiselles Lieblingsperlen überdimensioniert zu einem neuen Auftritt als Abendtäschchen. Tweed wird zu flauschigen Leggings und dazu passenden Beretten verarbeitet. Die Vorliebe für sportliche Aktivitäten

im Freien findet ihren Ausdruck in Snow- und Surfboards mit Chanel-Logo. Lagerfeld steht einem der wenigen noch verbliebenen Pariser Haute-Couture-Salons vor. Im Juli 2002 sicherte das Unternehmen, das sich im Besitz der Familie Wertheimer befindet, die Zukunft seines Couture-Geschäfts, indem es fünf Spezialmanufakturen, darunter die berühmte Spitzenfabrik Lesage, aufkaufte. Chanel ist heute kommerziell überaus erfolgreich. Im Dezember 2004 eröffnete man einen mehrstöckigen neuen Laden im Tokioter Shopping-Viertel Ginza mit eigenem Restaurant – Beige Tokyo – und einer Glasfassade, die mit ihren blinkenden Lichtern an den berühmten Tweed der Marke erinnert. Das New Yorker Metropolitan Museum of Art eröffnete im Mai 2005 eine Ausstellung, die Kreationen der Unternehmensgründerin wie auch des gegenwärtigen Firmenchefs zeigt. Trotz dieses großartigen Erbes haben Coco und Lagerfeld vor allem eines gemein: die Lust an der Gegenwart und der Zukunft. Oder, wie Chanel es selbst formulierte: „Ich stecke weder in der Vergangenheit fest, noch bin ich Avantgarde. Mein Stil folgt einfach dem Leben." [Siehe auch Lagerfeld Gallery]

Imposante figure de la mode, la maison Chanel est aujourd'hui à la fois synonyme de sa fondatrice Gabrielle « Coco » Chanel et de son directeur artistique depuis 1983, Karl Lagerfeld. Née dans un orphelinat et entièrement autodidacte, Gabrielle Chanel, qui a ouvert sa maison en 1913, est sans doute la créatrice de mode la plus importante du XXᵉ siècle. Son utilisation révolutionnaire du sportswear appliqué à la haute couture dans les années 20, ses petites robes noires, ses bijoux fantaisie et son appropriation des tenues masculines constituent l'étoffe dont on tisse les légendes. Son parfum Chanel N° 5 (inventé en 1921) est désormais un « classique » incontesté, tout comme ses tailleurs en tweed souples et ses sacs à main en cuir matelassé (deux modèles créés dans les années 50). Quand Coco Chanel meurt en 1971, elle laisse un riche héritage de codes aujourd'hui revisités avec audace par Karl Lagerfeld : les perles préférées de Mademoiselle font un retour géant sous la forme de petits sacs de soirée, le tweed réapparaît sur des leggings pelucheux avec bérets coordonnés, sa passion du sport et du plein air s'expriment, via les snowboards et les surfs griffés Chanel. Chez Chanel, Lagerfeld dirige l'un des derniers salons de haute couture parisiens ; en juillet 2002, l'entreprise qui appartient à la famille Wertheimer a sécurisé l'avenir de son activité haute couture en rachetant cinq ateliers spécialisés, dont Lesage, prestigieux maître des broderies. Aujourd'hui, la maison Chanel remporte un immense succès commercial : en décembre 2004, elle a ouvert une nouvelle boutique dans le quartier de Ginza à Tokyo, avec un restaurant, Beige Tokyo, et une façade de verre dont les lumières clignotantes rappellent le fameux tweed de la griffe. En mai 2005, le Metropolitan Museum of Art de New York a inauguré une exposition, avec des créations de la fondatrice comme de son héritier au trône. En dépit d'un legs aussi grandiose, ce que Coco et Lagerfeld ont en commun, c'est avant tout le goût du présent et du futur. Comme Coco Chanel dit : « Je ne suis ni du passé, ni d'avant-garde. Ma mode suit la vie ». [Voir aussi Lagerfeld Gallery] SUSIE RUSHTON

SPRING/SUMMER 2005 BACKSTAGE. PHOTOGRAPHY BY SEAN CUNNINGHAM

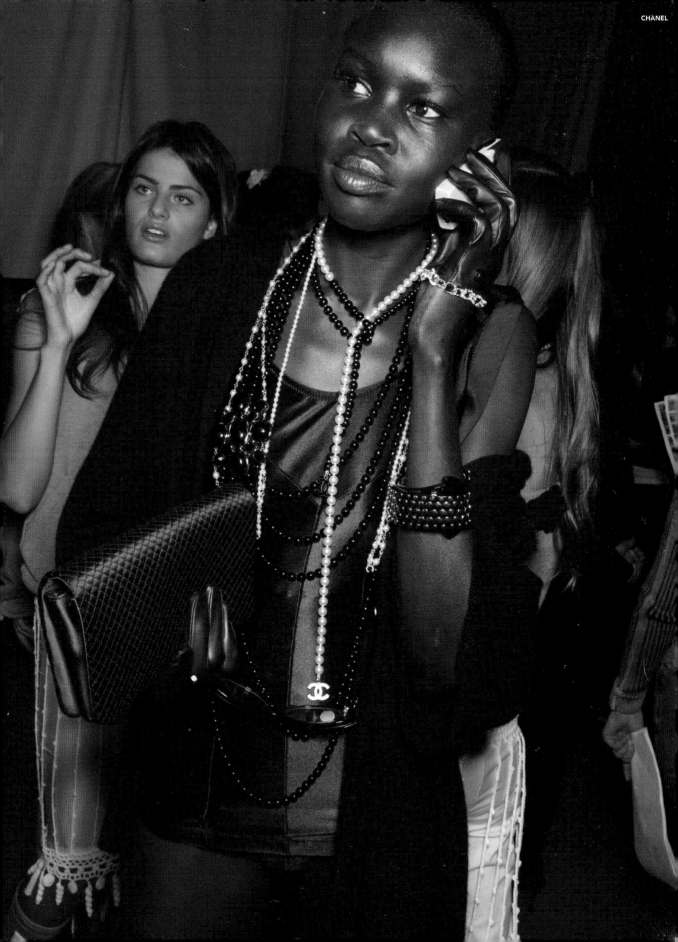

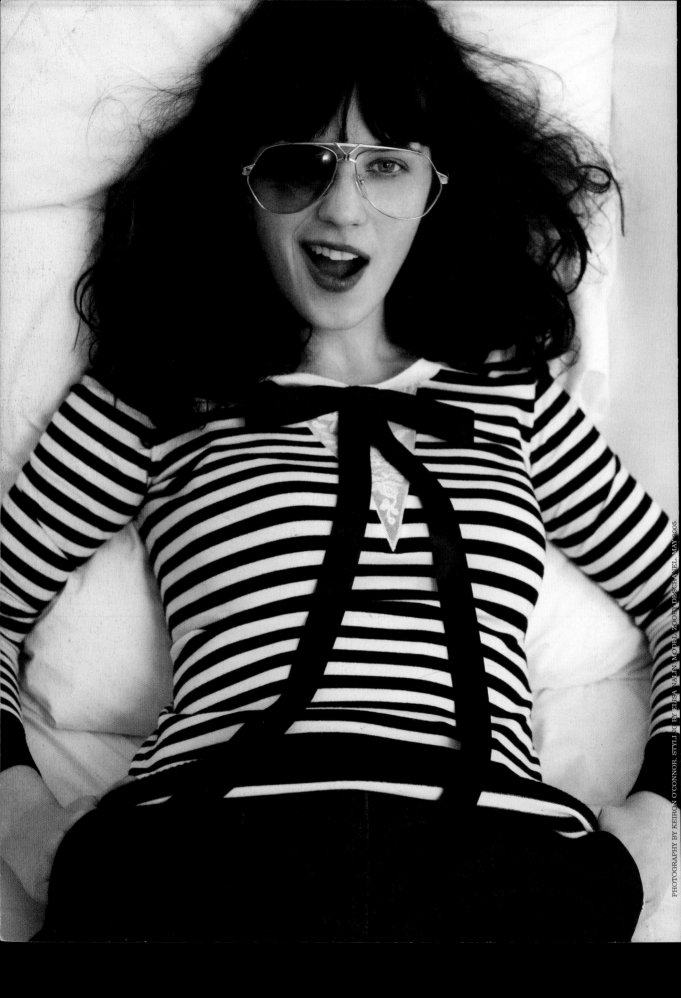

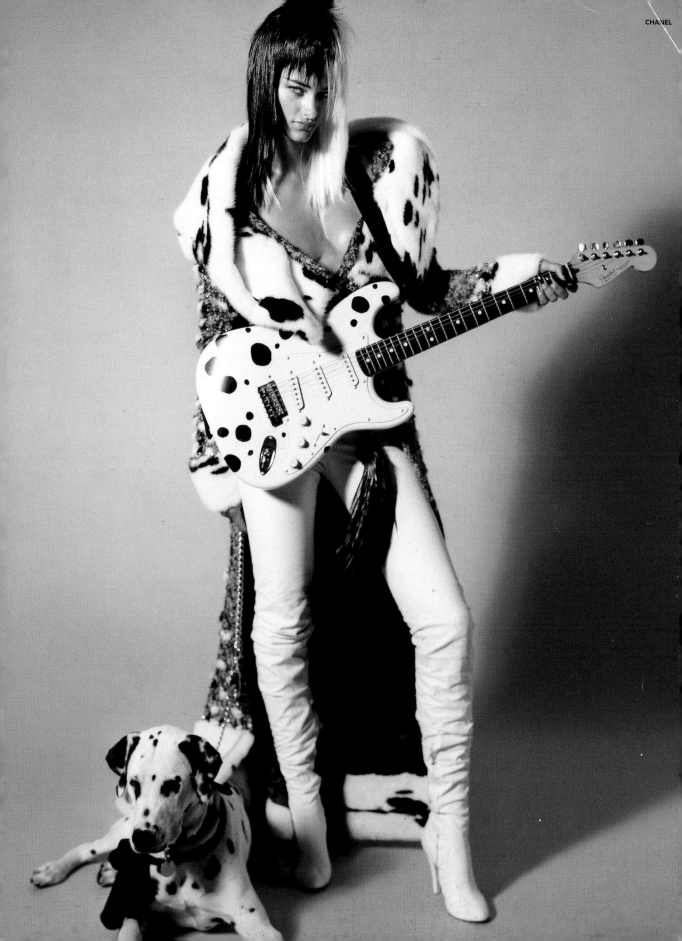

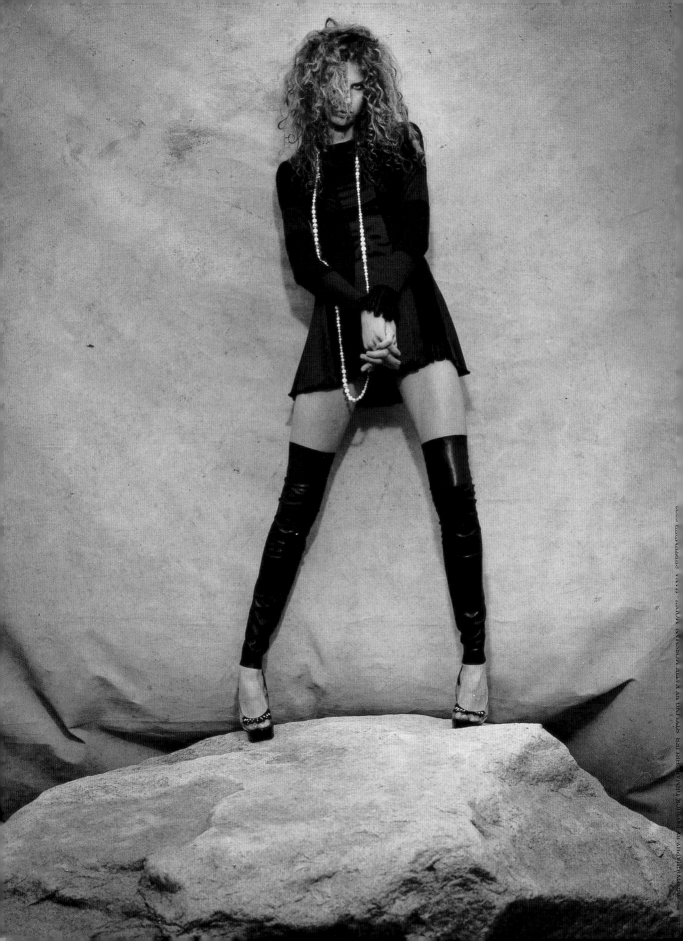

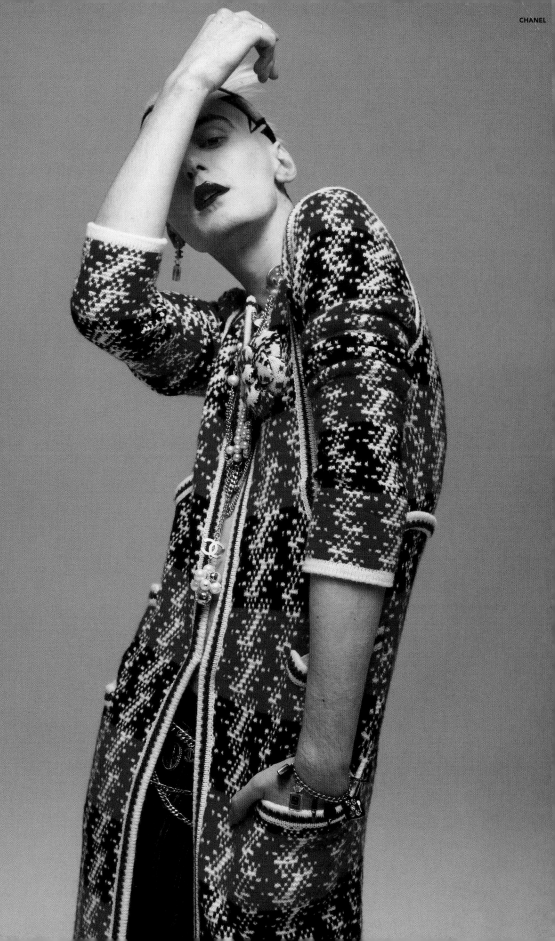

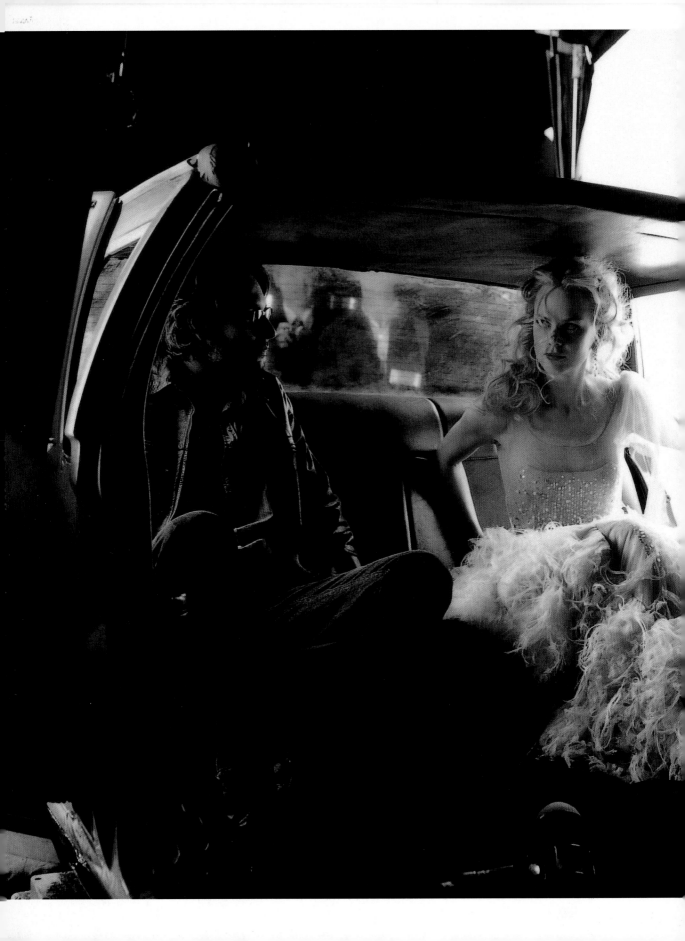

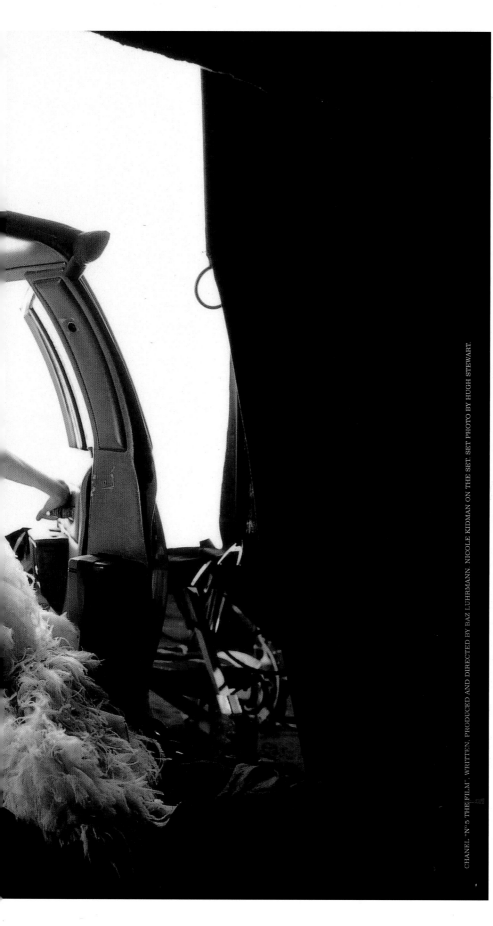

CHANEL "N° 5 THE FILM". WRITTEN, PRODUCED AND DIRECTED BY BAZ LUHRMANN. NICOLE KIDMAN ON THE SET. SET PHOTO BY HUGH STEWART.

What are your signature designs? Every detail and look that makes identification instantly possible **What is your favourite piece from any of your collections?** Pieces from the next collection **How would you describe your work?** I remember Voltaire's line: Everything that needs an explanation or description is not worth it **What's your ultimate goal?** The next collections **What inspires you?** Everything – there should be only one rule: eyes open!! **Can fashion still have a political ambition?** Should it? It should reflect it... **Who do you have in mind when you design?** Several women, never and always the same, women who change with the times and are interested in what is going on – not only in fashion **Is the idea of creative collaboration important to you?** Difficult to do without **Who has been the greatest influence on your career?** The events we have all gone through, changes in the times **How have your own experiences affected your work as a designer?** Difficult to analyse – and I am not sure one should think about what makes the past what it became... **Which is more important in your work: the process or the product?** Both are very important **Is designing difficult for you, if so, what drives you to continue?** No. I love fashion, the evolution of time, and fashion is the reflection of it **Have you ever been influenced or moved by the reaction to your designs?** You have to fight that...! **What's your definition of beauty?** Marlow said: there is no beauty without some strangeness in the proportions **What's your philosophy?** Every decision (also in fashion) is a refusal (Spinoza) **What is the most important lesson you've learned?** You can only learn what not to do – there are no lessons what to do...

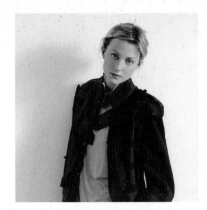

CHLOÉ

"I'm inspired by sunsets, sunrises, being with horses and love"

PHOEBE PHILO

It's hard to believe that a world-renowned brand like Chloé – currently headed up by British designer Phoebe Philo – should have its origins in six cotton poplin dresses. But from humble cotton acorns, big fashion oaks grow. Egyptian-born Gaby Aghion first arrived in Paris in 1945 and created Chloé in 1952, producing a small collection of dresses; Maria Callas and Grace Kelly were early fans. A young Karl Lagerfeld (with only a year's design experience at Jean Patou under his belt) was appointed house designer in 1966. During the late '60s and '70s, the label blossomed. Legend has it that heiress Christina Onassis bought 36 blouses in one visit to the boutique. The '80s were a time of upheaval for Chloé, with Lagerfeld decamping to Chanel (1983) and the luxury goods company Richemont Group buying out Aghion (1985). Following Lagerfeld's departure, Martine Sitbon took over, bringing her trademark graphic sensibilities to Chloé. Although Lagerfeld returned once again to the house in 1992, it was Stella McCartney in 1997 who next transformed the brand's fortunes. McCartney's fusion of a London rock'n'roll vibe with Chloé's chic Parisian heritage revived the brand for a new generation. When McCartney's celebrity friends – Kate Moss, Madonna, Cameron Diaz – began to wear the clothes, the label's status was further established. McCartney's friend Phoebe Philo, who had worked closely with Stella throughout her four-year reign, has further improved on the brand's youthful and feminine reputation – delicate, vintage-style camisole tops and sexy trousers are signatures – since taking over in 2001. Philo, who was born in Paris in 1973 and graduated from Central Saint Martins, also initiated a diffusion line, See. She picked up a British Designer of the Year prize in 2004 and is now at the helm of a bona fide success story.

Kaum zu glauben, dass eine weltbekannte Marke wie Chloé – derzeit unter der Führung der britischen Designerin Phoebe Philo – einmal mit sechs Kleidern aus Baumwollpopeline angefangen haben soll. Doch aus bescheidenen Baumwoll-Kapseln wachsen irgendwann große Mode-Eichen. Die in Ägypten geborene Gaby Aghion war 1945 nach Paris gekommen und hatte dort 1952 mit einer kleinen Kleiderkollektion Chloé gegründet. Maria Callas und Grace Kelly zählten zu den ersten Fans. Der junge Karl Lagerfeld (dessen Erfahrung damals nur aus einem Jahr als Designer bei Jean Patou bestand) wurde 1966 Chefdesigner des Hauses. In den späten 1960er und den 1970er Jahren boomte das Label. Gerüchten zufolge soll die Millionenerbin Christina Onassis bei einem einzigen Besuch der Boutique 36 Blusen gekauft haben. Die 1980er Jahre waren eine unruhige Zeit für Chloé, weil Lagerfeld zu Chanel abwanderte (1983) und der Luxusartikelkonzern Richemont Group Aghions Anteile erwarb (1985). Nach Lagerfelds Abgang übernahm Martine Sitbon dessen Funktion und brachte das grafische Gespür mit, für das sie bekannt ist. Und auch wenn Lagerfeld 1992 noch einmal in das Modehaus zurückkehrte, so war es doch erst Stella McCart-

ney, die das Schicksal der Firma als nächste wendete. Ihr Mix aus Londoner Rock 'n' Roll Feeling und Chloés traditionellem Pariser Chic machte das Label für eine neue Generation interessant. Als McCartneys prominente Freundinnen – Kate Moss, Madonna, Cameron Diaz – begannen, die Teile zu tragen, festigte das den Status der Marke. MacCartneys Freundin Phoebe Philo, die mit Stella während ihrer vierjährigen Tätigkeit eng zusammenarbeitete, unterstreicht, seit sie den Job 2001 übernommen hat, weiter den jugendlichen und femininen Ruf des Hauses – zarte Miederjäckchen im Vintage-Stil und sexy Hosen gelten als besonders typisch. Philo, die 1973 in Paris geboren wurde und am Central Saint Martins studiert hat, startete auch eine Nebenlinie namens See. 2004 wurde sie mit dem Preis British Designer of the Year ausgezeichnet und steuert jetzt bona fide auf eine Erfolgsstory zu.

Difficile d'imaginer qu'une marque aussi internationale que Chloé (actuellement dirigée par la créatrice britannique Phoebe Philo) ait vu le jour à partir de six robes en popeline de coton. Mais des humbles glands de coton poussent parfois de grands chênes de la mode. En 1945, l'Egyptienne Gaby Aghion débarque à Paris et lance la marque Chloé en 1952 avec une petite collection de robes ; Maria Callas et Grace Kelly comptent parmi ses premières fans. Le jeune Karl Lagerfeld (qui n'a alors qu'un an de métier en tant que styliste chez Jean Patou) est nommé couturier de la maison en 1966. A la fin des années 60 et dans les années 70, la griffe prospère. La légende dit même que l'héritière Christina Onassis aurait acheté 36 chemisiers en une seule visite à la boutique. Les années 80 marquent une période de perturbations chez Chloé, avec le départ de Lagerfeld pour Chanel (1983) et le rachat d'Aghion par le groupe de luxe Richemont (1985). Succédant à Lagerfeld, Martine Sitbon reprend la direction de la griffe et lui insuffle sa sensibilité graphique si caractéristique. Malgré le retour de Lagerfeld en 1992, c'est Stella McCartney qui, en 1997, réussit à remettre la marque sur les rails. Fusionnant une attitude rock'n'roll très londonienne avec l'héritage du chic parisien de Chloé, elle parvient à moderniser la marque à l'attention d'une nouvelle génération. Quand les amies célèbres de Stella McCartney (Kate Moss, Madonna, Cameron Diaz) commencent à porter ses créations, la réputation de la griffe est faite. Depuis qu'elle a pris sa succession en 2001, Phoebe Philo, l'amie avec laquelle Stella McCartney a étroitement collaboré pendant ses quatre années de règne, continue à rehausser l'image jeune et féminine de Chloé, avec de délicats caracos d'inspiration vintage et des pantalons sexy devenus les signatures de la maison. Phoebe Philo, née en 1973 à Paris et diplômée de Central Saint Martins, a également lancé une ligne secondaire baptisée See by Chloé. Après avoir reçu le prix de British Designer of the Year en 2004, elle tient désormais la barre d'une véritable success story.

LAUREN COCHRANE

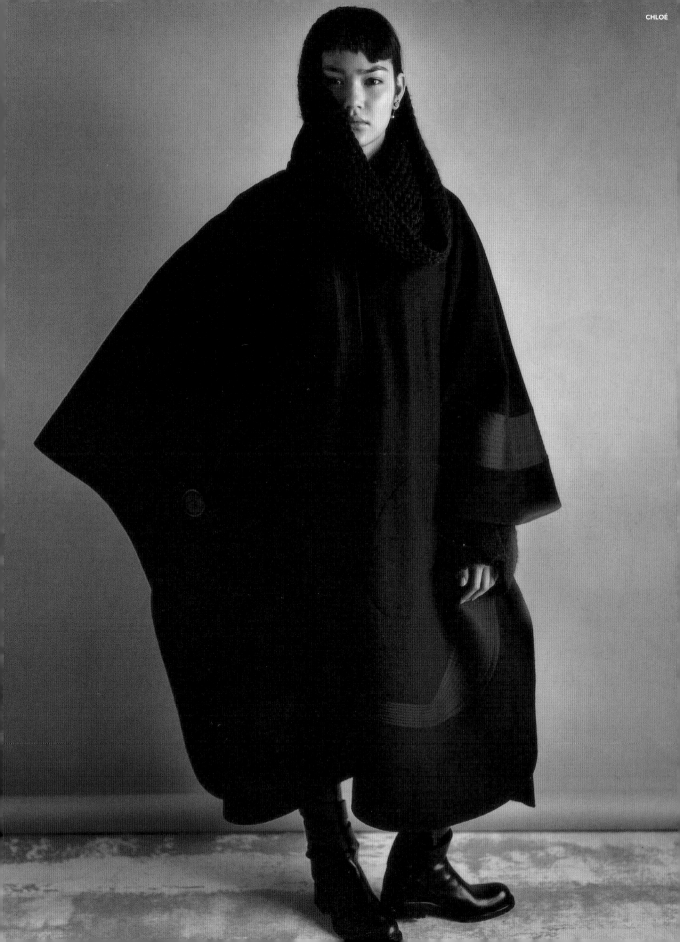

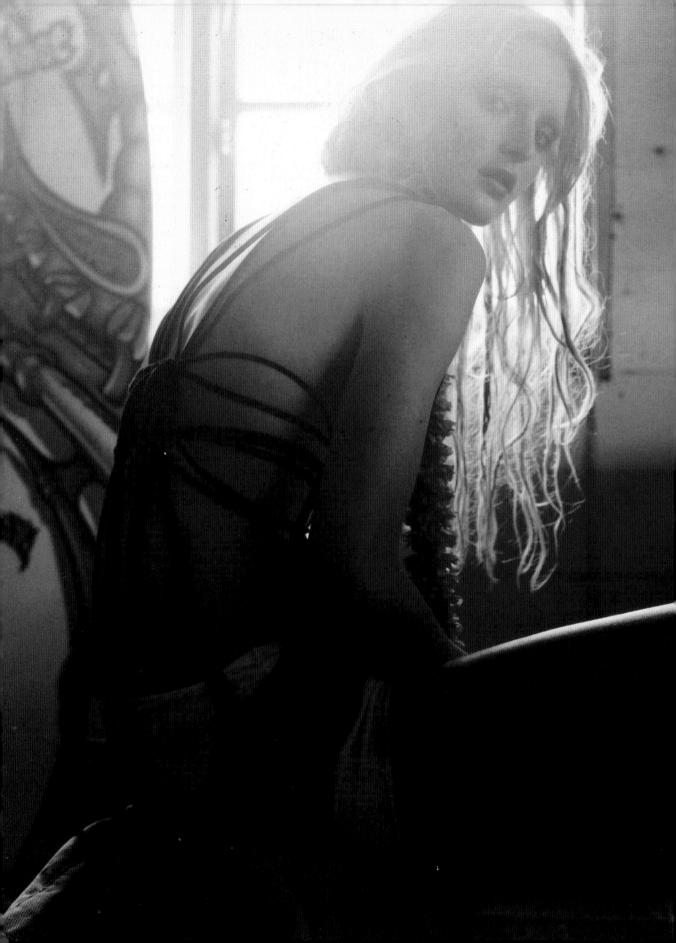

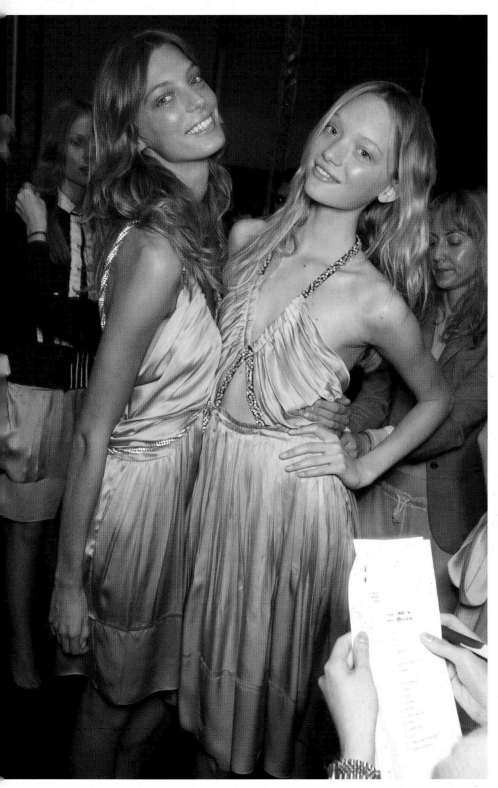

What are your signature designs? There's not one thing that sums it up. A bit of everything. Although the trousers do give a lovely bottom **What's your favourite piece from any of your collections?** Often the least commercial **How would you describe your work?** Work in progress **What's your ultimate goal?** To enjoy **What inspires you?** Sunsets, sunrises, being with horses and a lot of love **Can fashion still have a political ambition?** Tricky… **Who do you have in mind when you design?** People that inspire me **Is the idea of creative collaboration important to you?** I like the idea, although I haven't done much yet **What has been the greatest influence on your career?** Relationships probably with family, friends, people I have met in the street, life in Cuba and learning to bogle **How have your own experiences affected your work as a designer?** I try not to assess it too much. Things are just the way they are. My reactions to experiences in my life can't be divided between me and me as a designer **Is designing difficult for you and, if so, what drives you to continue?** Sometimes it is relentless but when it is good, it is great **Have you ever been influenced or moved by the reaction to your designs?** Seeing someone you really love or respect wearing something you created can drive and move you **What's your definition of beauty?** My friend Mel **What's your philosophy?** A bit of everything is good **What is the most important lesson you've learned?** Don't fuck with people.

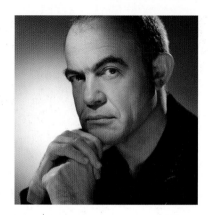

CHRISTIAN LACROIX

"My fashion is more a way of living life
with your roots, and finding your own true self,
than having a logo to put on your back"

Christian Lacroix made fashion history with his July 1987 debut couture collection backed by LVMH. His was the first Paris haute couture house to open since Courrèges in 1965. Lacroix took the bustles, bows, corsets and crinolines painted by 18th century artists Boucher, Fragonard and Nattier and mixed them up with ruffles, feathers and fringes of Toulouse-Lautrec's can-can dancers and the gypsies in his hometown Trinquetoulle, Provence. Lacroix's puffball skirt – a taffeta or satin balloon of fabric that gathered a crinoline at the hem – reinvented the ball gown for the late 20th century. "Personally I've always hovered between the purity of structures and the ecstasy of ornament," says the designer who brought Rococo back to couture. Born on 16 May 1956, Lacroix moved to Paris in 1971, where he studied at the Sorbonne and the Ecole du Louvre, where he planned a career as a museum curator. Instead, he began designing, first for Hermès (1978), then Guy Paulin (1980) and Patou (1981) before being offered the keys to his own couture house by Bernard Arnault of LVMH in 1987. Lacroix's inspiration was as broad as Arnault's plans for the label: Cecil Beaton's Ascot Scene in 'My Fair Lady'; Oliver Messel's neo-Rococo interiors; Velasquez Infantas; Lautrec soubrettes; Provencal gypsies and his dynamic wife Françoise. Christian Lacroix ready-to-wear followed the couture in 1998 and diffusion line Bazar arrived in 1994. Lacroix's sensibility translates superbly to theatre, opera and ballet. He designed landmark productions of 'Les Enfants du Paradis', 'La Gaiete Parisienne' and 'Sheherazade' as well as the jewelled corsets worn by Madonna for her 2004 Reinvention Tour. In 2002, Lacroix was appointed creative director of Florentine print house Pucci, and in 2005 a new chapter began for the designer when his fashion house was sold by LVMH to an American company, the Falic Group.

Christian Lacroix schrieb im Juli 1987 mit seiner Couture-Debüt-Kollektion, unterstützt von LVMH, Modegeschichte. Seit der Eröffnung von Courrèges 1965 war dies das erste neue Pariser Haute-Couture-Haus. Lacroix übernahm die Tournüren, Schleifen, Korsetts und Krinolinen aus den Gemälden von Künstlern des 18. Jahrhunderts wie Boucher, Fragonard und Nattier und kombinierte sie mit den Rüschen, Federn und Fransen von Toulouse-Lautrecs Cancan-Tänzerinnen sowie den traditionellen Kleidern der Zigeunerinnen in seiner provençalischen Heimatstadt Trinquetoulle. Sein Ballonrock – aus Taft oder Seide, am Saum von einer Krinoline zusammengehalten – war die neue Ballrobe für das ausgehende 20. Jahrhundert. „Ich habe immer zwischen klaren Strukturen und ekstatischen Ornamenten geschwankt", sagt der Designer, der das Rokoko in die Couture zurückbrachte, über sich selbst. Geboren wurde er am 16. Mai 1956. 1971 zog Lacroix nach Paris, um an der Sorbonne und der Ecole du Louvre zu studieren. Er hatte damals den festen Vorsatz, Museumskurator zu werden. Stattdessen begann er jedoch Mode zu entwerfen. Zunächst für Hermès (1978), dann für Guy Paulin (1980) und schließlich für Patou (1981). Im Jahr 1987 übergab ihm Bernard Arnault von LVMH die Schlüssel für sein eigenes Couture-Haus. Die Inspi-

rationen des Designers waren so weit gefasst wie Arnaults Pläne mit dem Label: von Cecil Beatons Ascot-Szene in „My Fair Lady" über Olivier Messels Einrichtungen im Neo-Rokoko-Stil, die Infantin von Velázquez, Lautrecs Soubretten, provençalische Zigeunerinnen bis hin zu seiner dynamischen Ehefrau Françoise. Seit 1998 entwirft Lacroix auch Prêt-à-porter. 1994 kam die Nebenlinie Bazaar hinzu. Die Empfindsamkeit und das Gespür des Designers passen perfekt zu Theater, Oper und Ballett, so dass er Meilensteine wie „Les Enfants du Paradis", „La Gaieté Parisienne" und „Sheherazade" ausstattete, aber auch Madonna für ihre Reinvention Tour 2004 mit juwelenverzierten Corsagen belieferte. 2002 wurde Christian Lacroix Creative Director des für seine grafischen Muster berühmten florentinischen Modehauses Pucci. Ein neues Kapitel begann 2005 für den Designer, als LVMH sein Modehaus an die amerikanische Falic Group verkaufte.

Christian Lacroix est entré dans l'histoire de la mode avec sa première collection de haute couture présentée en juillet 1987 grâce au soutien financier de LVMH. Depuis Courrèges en 1965, personne n'avait ouvert de maison de haute couture à Paris. Lacroix emprunte les tournures, les nœuds, les corsets et les crinolines présentés dans les tableaux de peintres du XVIIIᵉ siècle, tels que Boucher, Fragonard et Nattier, et les mélange avec les volants, les plumes et les franges des danseuses de cancan de Toulouse-Lautrec et des gitans de sa ville natale de Trinquetoulle en Provence. La jupe « boule » de Lacroix, sorte de ballon en taffetas ou en satin froncé en crinoline à l'ourlet, réinvente la robe de bal de la fin du XXᵉ siècle. « Personnellement, j'ai toujours oscillé entre la pureté structurale et l'extase ornementale », déclare ce créateur qui a remis le rococo au goût du jour. Né le 16 mai 1956, Lacroix s'installe à Paris en 1971 pour étudier à la Sorbonne et à l'Ecole du Louvre, envisageant alors de devenir conservateur de musée. Il se lance finalement dans la mode, d'abord chez Hermès (1978), puis pour Guy Paulin (1980) et Jean Patou (1981), avant de se voir remettre les clés de sa propre maison de haute couture en 1987 par Bernard Arnault, P-DG de LVMH. Les inspirations de Lacroix sont aussi diverses que les projets d'Arnault pour la griffe : le décor créé par Cecil Beaton pour la scène d'Ascot dans « My Fair Lady », les intérieurs néo-rococo d'Oliver Messel, les infantes de Velasquez, les soubrettes de Lautrec, les gitans de Provence, ou encore sa dynamique épouse Françoise. Une collection de prêt-à-porter Christian Lacroix est lancée en 1998, après la ligne secondaire Bazar en 1994. La sensibilité de Lacroix s'applique magnifiquement bien au théâtre, à l'opéra et au ballet : il a réalisé les costumes de grosses productions telles que « Les Enfants du Paradis », « La Gaieté Parisienne » et « Shéhérazade », ainsi que les corsets ornés de bijoux portés par Madonna lors de sa tournée Reinvention Tour de 2004. En 2002, Lacroix est nommé directeur de la création de la maison florentine Pucci, connue pour ses imprimés. En 2005, un nouveau chapitre de l'histoire du créateur s'est ouvert quand LVMH a vendu sa griffe à une entreprise américaine, le Falic Group.

JAMES SHERWOOD

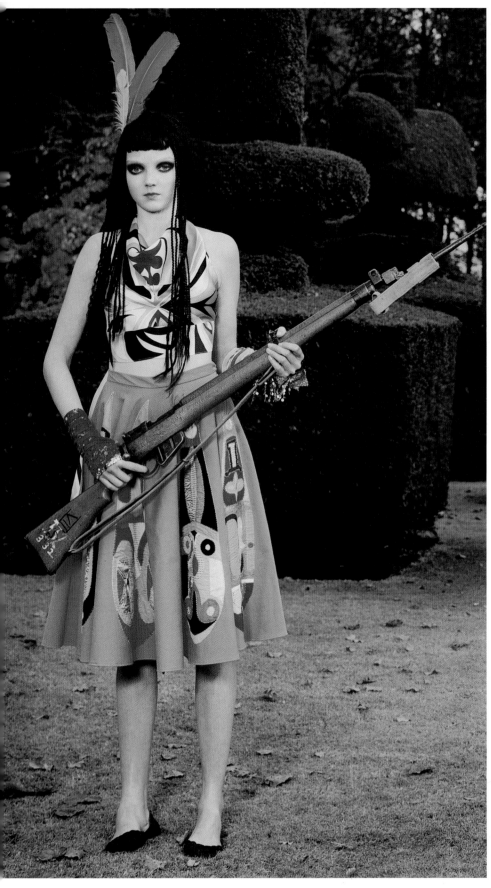

What are your signature designs? Let's say – red. Something crazy! **How would you describe your work?** It's based on individuality and self-expression. It's not exactly anti-fashion, but it's contrary to the way that fashion is. My fashion is much more a way of living life with your roots, and finding your own true self, than having a logo put on your back **Can fashion still have a political ambition?** I would like to express much more violence in my work. I'm very, very angry when I see all this globalisation. If we want the most sensual things in life, we have to fight for them. My house is based on an ethnic art and on gypsies, and I hope that through it I will succeed in expressing their heritage, something that is stronger than the poor everyday life that globalisation would like us to have **Who do you have in mind when you design?** A kind of gypsy. Everybody who is free enough to express this way of life **Who has been the greatest influence on your career?** My wife: if I had not met her, I would be in the South of France, eating goat's cheese. I was lazy, I was shy and she gave me a spine **What's your definition of beauty?** Beauty is not a very well-balanced thing; it has to be disturbing and uncomfortable. It's about the period and art rather than anything physical **What's your philosophy?** I'm totally despairing and totally joyful at the same time.

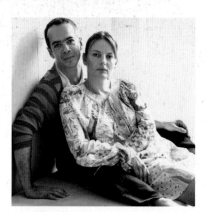

CLEMENTS RIBEIRO

"It is hard to imagine what kind of designers
we would be without each other"

Superior and slightly eccentric dressing-up clothes, frivolous essentials and the most divine colourful cashmere jumpers you'll find on the planet are what Clements Ribeiro habitually deliver. British-born Suzanne Clements and Brazilian Inacio Ribeiro are the husband-and-wife team who have made the luxe end of the clothes market a fun place to shop. After both graduating with first-class honours from Central Saint Martins (1991), they showed their first collection in October 1993 and rapidly became known for their quirky, elegant knitwear. By 1995 they were on schedule at London Fashion Week with a catwalk show and a full-sized collection of traditional womenswear pieces, each one enhanced by a classic Clements Ribeiro twist. Glamorous, witty clothing craftily echoing the conservative and combining it with high-style detail is the fashion game they play. And it's become a fruitful industry as today the couple design everything from lingerie to bags, shoes (in collaboration with Manolo Blahnik), menswear (launched in full in summer 2000) and a children's collection. In May 2000 they were appointed creative directors at Cacharel, where they commissioned print designer Celia Birtwell to contribute whimsical patterns, and also collaborated with British fashion illustrator Julie Verhoeven. After decamping to Paris for three seasons (October 2001 to October 2002) they returned to show their mainline collection in London in February 2003, where they remain one of its highlights. Ever ready to challenge the expected, 2004 saw the first Clements Ribeiro-Peter Saville menswear collection.

Erlesene und leicht exzentrische Edel-Outfits, frivole Basics und die göttlichsten bunten Kaschmirpullover der Welt bilden das Standardsortiment von Clements Ribeiro. Die Britin Suzanne Clements und der Brasilianer Inacio Ribeiro sind privat wie beruflich ein Team und haben dafür gesorgt, dass Shopping auch am luxuriösen Ende der Skala wieder Spaß macht. Nachdem beide 1991 ein erstklassiges Examen am Central Saint Martins abgelegt hatten, präsentierten sie ihre erste Kollektion im Oktober 1993 und wurden mit ihren witzig-eleganten Stricksachen rasch bekannt. Ab 1995 gehörten sie zum offiziellen Programm der London Fashion Week, und zwar mit einer Catwalk-Show und einer kompletten Kollektion traditioneller Damenmode, bei der jedes Stück den typischen Clements-Ribeiro-Kick aufwies. Glamourös, intelligent, handwerklich konservativ gearbeitet und mit anspruchsvollen Details versehen – das ist ihr Stil. Aus die-

sen Grundsätzen ist ein florierendes Unternehmen geworden, denn inzwischen entwirft das Designerehepaar praktisch alles, von Dessous bis zu Taschen, von Schuhen (in Zusammenarbeit mit Manolo Blahnik) über Herrenmode (erstmals im Sommer 2000 lanciert) bis hin zu einer Kinderkollektion. Im Mai 2000 wurden die beiden Creative Directors bei Cacharel, wo sie u.a. die Stoffdesignerin Celia Birtwell verpflichteten und mit der britischen Modezeichnerin Julie Verhoeven zusammenarbeiteten. Nach drei Saisons in Paris (von Oktober 2001 bis Oktober 2002) kehrten sie mit der Schau ihrer Hauptkollektion im Februar 2003 nach London zurück, wo diese nach wie vor als eines der Highlights gilt. Stets auf der Suche nach neuen Herausforderungen, zeigten sie 2004 die erste Herrenkollektion unter dem Namen Clements Ribeiro-Peter Saville.

Tenues de soirée luxueuses et légèrement excentriques, basiques frivoles et pulls en cachemire colorés les plus divins de la planète sont ce que Clements Ribeiro produit habituellement. Le couple marié formé par la Britannique Suzanne Clements et le Brésilien Inacio Ribeiro est venu apporter une petite touche d'humour sur le marché des vêtements de luxe. Tous deux diplômés de Central Saint Martins avec les félicitations du jury (1991), ils présentent leur première collection en octobre 1993 et se forgent rapidement une réputation grâce à leur maille étrange et élégante. En 1995, ils défilent à la London Fashion Week avec une collection complète de pièces féminines classiques, toutes rehaussées du décalage si typique de Clements Ribeiro. Leur jeu préféré consiste à créer des vêtements glamour de facture artisanale, pleins d'esprit et de références à la mode classique pour la combiner avec des détails très stylés : une entreprise fructueuse puisque le couple dessine aujourd'hui de la lingerie, des sacs, des chaussures (en collaboration avec Manolo Blahnik), une ligne pour homme (lancée à l'été 2000) et une collection pour enfant. En mai 2000, ils sont nommés directeurs artistiques chez Cacharel, où ils commandent des imprimés fantaisie à la créatrice Celia Birtwell et collaborent avec l'illustratrice britannique Julie Verhoeven. Après avoir défilé à Paris pendant trois saisons (d'octobre 2001 à octobre 2002), le duo revient à Londres en février 2003 pour présenter sa collection principale, qui reste l'un des moments forts de la Fashion Week. Toujours prêts à relever le défi de l'inattendu, ils lancent en 2004 la première collection pour homme Clements Ribeiro/Peter Saville.

TERRY NEWMAN

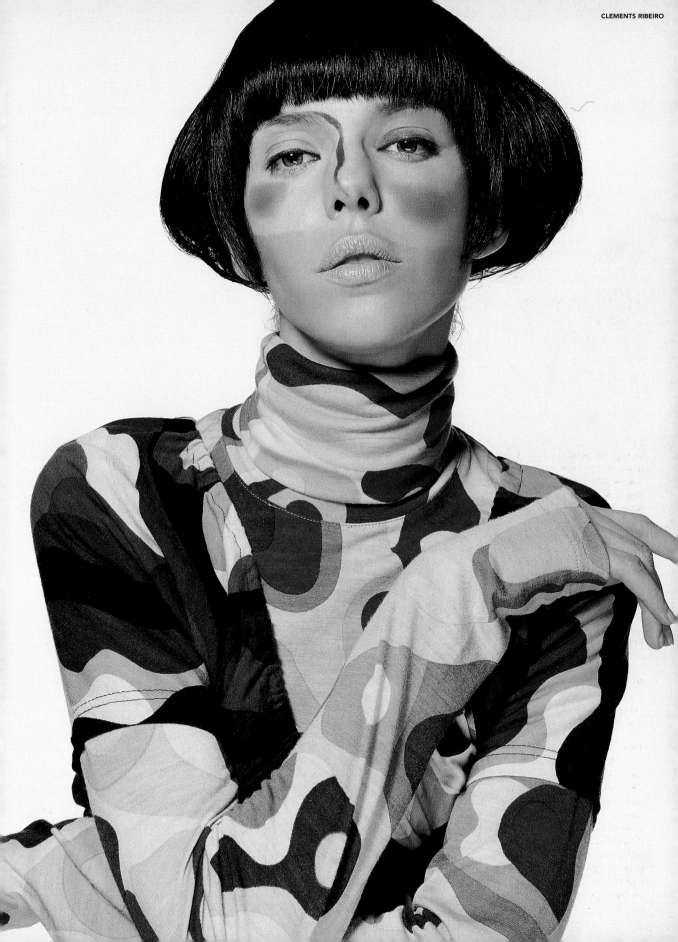

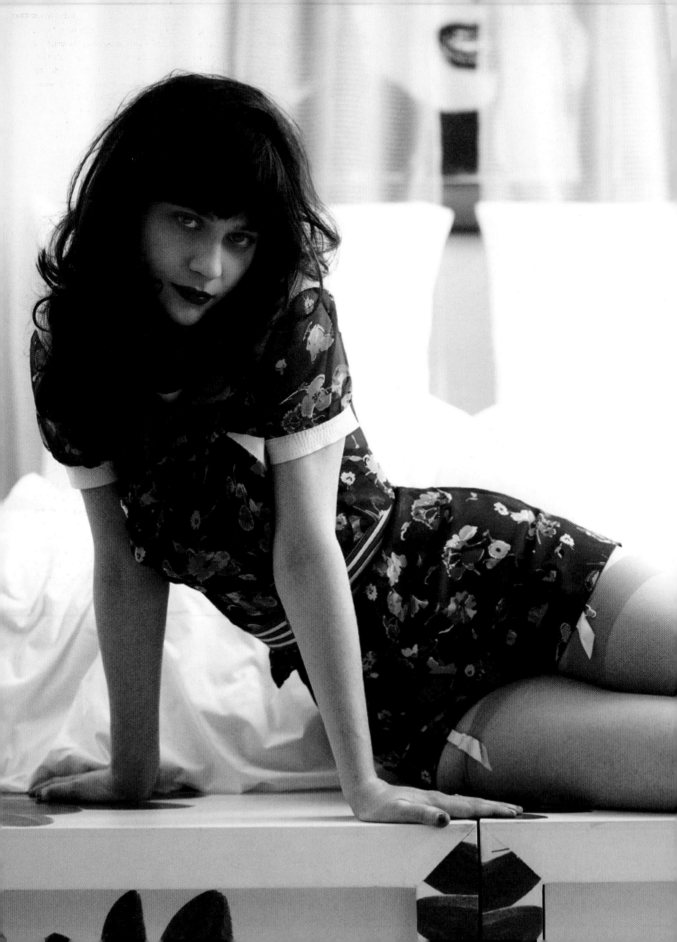

PHOTOGRAPHY BY KEHRON O'CONNOR. STYLING BY ELISA NALIN. MODEL: ZOOEY DESCHANEL. MAY 2005.

What are your signature designs? Eclectic mixes, often bohemian, always eccentric **What is your favourite piece from any of your collections?** Probably a dress called Alice. A loose dress, in hand marbled silk, embroidered with multi-coloured flowers and graphic lines **How would you describe your work?** The work is inevitably organic, each season bringing its own pace depending on our level of harmony! The rich layers of themes, details and colours often stem from the accumulation of our different whims. More often than not though, it is the choice of prints and colours that trigger the whole process, with the knits being the graphic leveller **What's your ultimate goal?** To build a solid brand and be able to concentrate solely on our collections **What inspires you?** We thrive on the adrenaline of each collection and its show. It always provides the seeds for the next collection **Can fashion still have a political ambition?** It is increasingly difficult to create and maintain a political stance as fashion is now such a big cultural/ entertainment scene. We don't believe the catwalk is a great space for political statements in our times, but outside of it, fashion can be a very cunning tool **Who do you have in mind when you design?** We have a fantasy personage, without whom we find it difficult to navigate the many elements we use every season. This character will be dressed up during the season and carry all our contradictions. Halfway through, as we are actually doing fittings and making many important practical decisions, we think about our customer and give it a good reality check. Throughout it though, we need to feel confident we are going our own way **Is the idea of creative collaboration important to you?** It is essential. Over the years we have created a Clements Ribeiro creative team, our very own think tank. We often work with other designers to 'dynamize' the process (Peter Saville, Julie Verhoeven, Shona Heath, Simon Costin...) **Who has been the greatest influence on your career?** Each other, predictably. Living and working together is pretty intense and after so long, it has transformed us. It is hard to imagine what kind of designers we would be without each other **How have your own experiences affected your work as designer?** Life runs parallel to the collections and, as designers, they work as a sort of diary and they outline our ups and downs. Losing a friend, a relative, having our son, 09/11, travels – it is all imprinted in our work in ways only Suzanne and I can read **Which is more important in your work: the process or the product?** The process is everything, the result a kind of reward **Is designing difficult for you, if so, what drives you to continue?** Design is a great joy. Sorting out our ideas and going through the motions in order to realise them is a thrill. It is the relentlessness of the fashion cycle that is a bitch **Have you ever been influenced or moved by the reaction to your designs?** All the time. Fashion is interactive, is a dialogue, and a dialogue with lots of different people. Praise or criticism can be enlightening and seeing 'real people' reacting to your designs is quite an eye-opener **What's your definition of beauty?** There is so much beauty around – natural or not – and so much art. Character is what makes a difference for us. Something odd, something subversive, something bizarre, some bad taste, irony, something ridiculous: such elements make a difference, make beauty irresistible **What's your philosophy?** Two three standing strong **What is the most important lesson you've learned?** There's always next season.

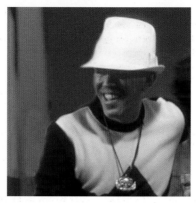

COLLECTION PRIVÉE?

"My first sketch uses a pencil that is 100 kilos heavy, then straight afterwards gets less heavy and becomes a feather that needs to be stopped" MASSIMO BIZZI

Massimo Bizzi, designer of Collection Privée?, was born in Bologna on 26 July 1961. Bizzi initially attended Liceo Scientifico, but a passion for fashion and craftsmanship was in his blood – his father has worked as a shoemaker since the '50s. Bizzi began designing under his own name in 1980, and started his Collection Privée? label in 1988, initially as a collection of footwear and bags. Bizzi says that he made a gamble in starting the enterprise, and for this reason a question mark appears in the name of his brand. Menswear was introduced to the Collection Privée? range in 1991 and womenswear followed soon after, in 1994. Bizzi spent two years working for trainer company, Superga, followed by three at leather goods label Henry Beguelin. Currently, in addition to Collection Privée?, Bizzi also designs for shoemakers Duccio del Duca, a fur company, and for an Italian leather laboratory where he also develops new materials which he then incorporates into his own collections. Bizzi's work for Collection Privée? focuses on the idiosyncrasies of different materials, and he is best known for his pioneering leather work, in particular his development and use of washed leathers. Bizzi will take iconic garments – for instance, a classic trenchcoat – and re-work them using his trademark washed leathers, updating the proportions, cut and details in the process. October 2004 saw the first Collection Privée? women's catwalk show, in Milan. A new Collection Privée? showroom and studio in Milan's Corso Concordia was opened in February 2005, a joint design project between Bizzi and his long-term collaborator, the architect Marco Costanzi. With the established support of retailers as influential as Luisa Via Roma in Italy and Barney's in America, Bizzi is planning expansion for Collection Privée? into Japan.

Der Designer von Collection Privée?, Massimo Bizzi, wurde am 26. Juli 1961 in Bologna geboren. Zunächst besuchte er das Liceo Scientifico, doch lag ihm die Leidenschaft für Mode und Handwerk im Blut – schließlich war seit Vater seit den 1950er Jahren als Schuster tätig. Also begann Bizzi 1980 unter eigenem Namen zu entwerfen und gründete 1988 sein Label Collection Privée?, das sich anfänglich auf Schuhe und Taschen beschränkte. Heute sagt Bizzi, die Firmengründung sei ein Hasardspiel gewesen, weshalb er den Schriftzug der Marke auch mit einem Fragezeichen versehen habe. 1991 kam Herrenmode zur Produktpalette der Collection Privée?, bald darauf, 1994, folgte die Damenmode. Zwei Jahre lang arbeitete Bizzi für den Sportschuhhersteller Superga, danach folgten drei Jahre bei der Lederwarenfirma Henry Beguelin. Außer für Collection Privée? designt Bizzi gegenwärtig auch für die Schuhmarke Duccio del Duca, eine Pelzfirma und für eine italienische Lederwerkstatt, wo er auch neue Materialien entwickelt, die dann in seine eigenen Kollektionen integriert wer-

den. Bizzis Entwürfe für Collection Privée? basieren auf seinen Vorlieben für bestimmte Materialien. Er ist berühmt für seine Pionierarbeit im Bereich Leder, insbesondere für die Entwicklung und Verwendung von Waschleder. Bizzi sucht sich Modeklassiker, etwa einen Trenchcoat, und kreiert ihn aus Waschleder neu, modernisiert Proportionen, Schnitt und Details während des Designprozesses. Im Oktober 2004 war die erste Collection Privée?-Catwalk-Show für Damen in Mailand zu sehen. Ein neuer Showroom und ein Atelier am Mailänder Corso Concordia wurden im Februar 2005 eröffnet, und zwar als gemeinsames Design-Projekt von Bizzi und dem Architekten Marco Costanzi, mit dem Bizzi schon lange zusammenarbeitet. Angespornt durch die tatkräftige Unterstützung einflussreicher Einzelhändler wie Luisa Via Roma in Italien und Barney's in den USA, plant Bizzi nun die Expansion von Collection Privée? nach Japan.

Massimo Bizzi, styliste de Collection Privée?, est né le 26 juillet 1961 à Bologne. Il entame d'abord des études au Liceo Scientifico, mais découvre vite que la passion de la mode et de l'artisanat coule dans ses veines (son père crée des chaussures depuis les années 50). Bizzi se lance dans la mode sous son propre nom dès 1980 et présente sa griffe Collection Privée? en 1988, qui inclut au départ uniquement des chaussures et des sacs. Considérant la création de son entreprise comme un véritable pari, il ajoute un point d'interrogation derrière le nom de sa marque. Collection Privée? s'enrichit d'une ligne pour homme en 1991, puis d'une ligne pour femme en 1994. Bizzi travaille pendant deux ans pour le fabricant de chaussures de sport Superga, puis trois ans pour le maroquinier Henry Beguelin. Outre Collection Privée?, Bizzi dessine actuellement des chaussures pour le fourreur Duccio del Duca et pour un laboratoire italien spécialisé dans le cuir où il développe de nouveaux matériaux qu'il intègre ensuite à ses propres collections. La démarche de Bizzi pour Collection Privée? se concentre sur les idiosyncrasies de matières particulières, mais on le connaît surtout pour son travail visionnaire du cuir, notamment pour le développement et l'utilisation des cuirs délavés. Bizzi excelle à transformer les classiques de la mode, par exemple le trench-coat, en utilisant ses cuirs délavés signature pour moderniser les proportions, la coupe et les détails. En octobre 2004, il présente le premier défilé pour femme de Collection Privée? à Milan. Un nouveau showroom et un nouvel atelier Collection Privée? ouvrent sur le Corso Concordia de Milan en février 2005, projet de design développé par Bizzi et l'architecte Marco Costanzi, son collaborateur de longue date. Fort du soutien de distributeurs aussi influents que Luisa Via Roma en Italie et Barney's aux Etats-Unis, Bizzi prévoit prochainement d'exporter Collection Privée? au Japon. DAVID LAMB

What are your signature designs? My first collection is Collection Privée? with a question mark because it was created as a game What is your favourite piece from any of your collections? The accessories, leather goods, the coats – but the 'discovery' above all How would you describe your work? It's a job that, the way it is, seems horrible, but when there is passion, it is unparalleled What's your ultimate goal? My last show during Milan's catwalk shows What inspires you? Everything and nothing. My head goes crazy researching and then at a certain point stops. And that's okay Can fashion still have a political ambition? No, and it does not have to Who do you have in mind when you design?

Everything that does not have to be taken for granted Is the idea of creative collaboration important to you? I have had, and I have very pleasurable working experiences. I have worked as a fashion designer for Superga, three years for Henry Beguelin and I am now following the creation of new leather materials for a famous Italian leather factory. I am also the art director for the shoes collection Duccio Del Duca Who has been the greatest influence on your career? To make my father happy How have your own experiences affected your work as a designer? I was born in a fashion family, my father manufactures shoes, and together with my brother they have opened another clothing

one. I was in charge of the commercial part, and was not very satisfied with my position so I decided to create Collection Privee? First the shoes, then menswear, then further childrenswear and the womenswear 8 years ago Which is more important in your work: the process or the product? Both. I am both fortunate and not, working for my own company, and when I am working for other companies I bring my double experience Is designing difficult for you, if so, what drives you to continue? No. Not yet, fortunately. But in any case my first sketch uses a pencil that is 100 kilos heavy, then straight afterwards gets less heavy and becomes a feather that needs to be stopped Have you ever been

influenced or moved by the reaction to your designs? I don't mind too much, sometimes incredibly beautiful things are not taken in, then after a few seasons become a 'cult'. This is our work (craft) What's your definition of beauty? It's everything that is both beautiful or ugly, but that we like at the right moment What's your philosophy? To try and try again is useless. Things should work immediately, otherwise it's better to leave it there. Therefore promptness and casualness are my best skills What is the most important lesson you've learned? Learning how to accept joy and aches and pains, but unfortunately pain is much more heavy than happiness.

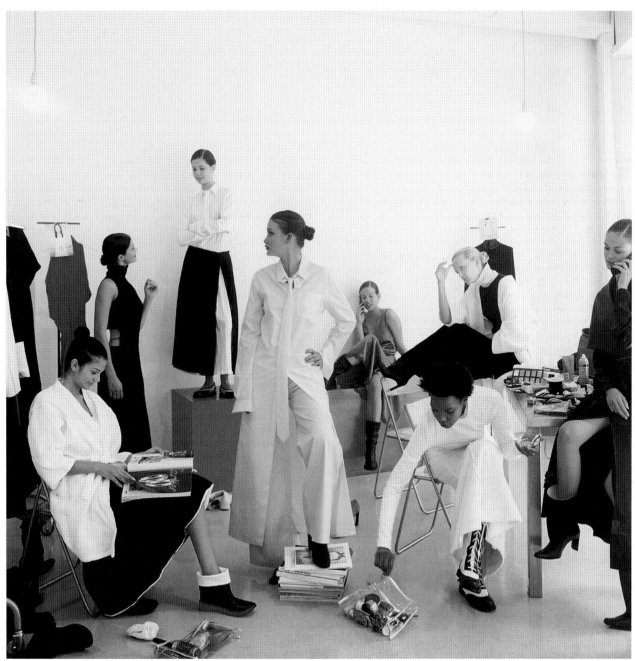

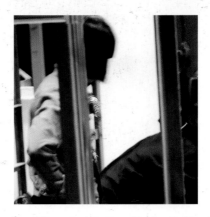

COMME DES GARÇONS

"The same spirit runs through everything I do" REI KAWAKUBO

Rei Kawakubo may be better known to many under the name of the label she established in Tokyo in 1973, and for which she showed her first collection two years later: Comme des Garçons, a moniker chosen, the designer has said, simply because she liked the sound of it. Certainly it is a name readily on the lips of the many other designers who invariably cite Kawakubo as an inspiration. A designer who has dispensed with the rule book, who cuts and constructs in such a way that her clothes have skirted art, Kawakubo's readiness to challenge conventions – to produce uniform-like clothes that are neither obviously for men nor women, that distort rather than enhance the female form, that use atypical fabrics and deconstruct them sometimes to the point of destruction – has nevertheless created a global concern. She launched Comme to the West in 1981, when she showed her first collection in Paris and was among the avant-garde Japanese to introduce black as an everyday fashion staple – unthinkingly dubbed 'Hiroshima Chic' by some critics. Then as now, it bewildered as much as it excited. The self-taught, multiple award-winning Kawakubo (born in Tokyo in 1942) did not, however, follow the standard route into the fashion industry. She began her career by reading literature at Tokyo's Keio University and, on graduation in 1964, joined the Ashai Kasei chemical and textiles company, working in its advertising department. Unable to find the garments she wanted for herself, she started to design them. She launched menswear in 1978, and a furniture line in 1982. Comme remains progressive: the label's fragrances, for instance, have played with tar, rubber and nail polish odours. Recent retail projects have included short-term 'guerrilla' stores in the backwater areas of, for the fashion world, unexpected cities, through to London's monolithic Dover Street Market, in which the company, which she co-runs with British husband Adrian Joffe, also rents space to other like-minded designers.

Rei Kawakubo ist vielen vermutlich eher unter der Bezeichnung des 1973 von ihr in Tokio gegründeten und zwei Jahre später erstmals mit einer Kollektion präsentierten Labels bekannt. Für die Bezeichnung Comme des Garçons entschied sich die Designerin nach eigener Aussage nur deshalb, weil ihr der Klang gefiel. Einen guten Klang hat der Name auch in den Ohren der vielen Kollegen, die Kawakubo als Inspirationsquelle anführen. Sie ist eine Designerin, die alle Regeln bricht und so zuschneidet und konstruiert, dass ihre Kleider geschneiderte Kunstwerke sind. Weltweite Beachtung erfuhr sie durch ihre Bereitschaft, Konventionen in Frage zu stellen, indem sie uniformähnliche Teile produzierte, die weder eindeutig als Herren- noch als Damenmode identifizierbar waren, die weibliche Formen eher verzerrten als unterstrichen und die aus ungewöhnlichen, oft bis zur Zerstörung dekonstruierten Materialien gefertigt waren. Im Westen wurde Comme des Garçons erstmals 1981 lanciert, als Kawakubo ihre erste Kollektion in Paris zeigte. Damals gehörte sie zu den avantgardistischen Japanern, die Schwarz in der Alltagsmode etablierten – was einige Kritiker gedankenlos als „Hiroshima Chic" geißelten. Damals wie heute ruft diese Mode ebenso viel Verwirrung wie Interesse hervor. Die 1942 in Tokio geborene und mit zahlreichen Auszeichnungen überhäufte Autodidaktin kam übri-

gens nicht auf dem klassischen Pfad in die Modeindustrie. Vielmehr begann sie ihre Berufslaufbahn mit einem Literaturstudium an der Keio Universität von Tokio. Nach ihrem Abschluss 1964 trat sie in die Werbeabteilung des Chemie- und Textilunternehmens Ashai Kasei ein. Weil sie keine Kleidung fand, die ihr gefiel, begann sie, eben diese selbst zu entwerfen. Ihre erste Herrenkollektion präsentierte sie dann 1978, eine Möbellinie kam 1982 hinzu. Das Label bleibt progressiv: So experimentierte man etwa bei den Comme des Garçons Düften mit Teer, Gummi und dem Geruch von Nagellack. Jüngste Projekte im Verkauf waren u. a. die zeitlich begrenzten Guerilla-Stores in rückständigen Gegenden von – zumindest für die Modewelt – unbedeutenden Städten. Nicht zu vergessen der gigantische Dover Street Market in London, wo das Unternehmen, das Kawakubo gemeinsam mit ihrem britischen Ehemann Adrian Joffe führt, auch anderen gleichgesinnten Designern Raum bietet.

Nombreux sont ceux qui connaissent Rei Kawakubo sous le nom de la griffe qu'elle a créée à Tokyo en 1973 et dont elle a présenté la première collection deux ans plus tard : Comme des Garçons, un nom choisi, dit-elle, simplement parce qu'elle trouvait qu'il sonnait bien. Un nom que l'on peut aujourd'hui lire sur toutes les lèvres des nombreux créateurs qui citent invariablement Rei Kawakubo parmi leurs principales sources d'inspiration. Tournant le dos aux règles établies, Rei Kawakubo taille et construit des vêtements qui ressemblent plus à des œuvres d'art qu'à des créations de mode. Son enthousiasme à défier les conventions attire l'attention du monde entier avec des vêtements confinant à l'uniforme – dont on n'arrive pas vraiment à savoir s'ils ont été conçus pour les hommes ou les femmes, qui déplacent la forme du corps féminin plutôt que de la souligner, qui utilisent des tissus atypiques et les déconstruisent parfois jusqu'au point de non retour. En 1981, elle lance Comme des Garçons en Occident lors de son premier défilé parisien et s'impose alors à l'avant-garde de la mode japonaise, qui introduit le noir comme un basique de la mode : un style que certains critiques peu inspirés surnommeront le « Hiroshima Chic ». A l'époque comme aujourd'hui, sa mode déroute autant qu'elle ravit. Autodidacte maintes fois primée, Rei Kawakubo (née en 1942 à Tokyo) est arrivée dans l'univers de la mode par des chemins détournés. Elle étudie d'abord la littérature à l'université Keio de Tokyo. En 1964, après l'obtention de son diplôme, elle travaille pour le département publicité d'Ashai Kasei, un fabricant de produits chimiques et textiles. Comme elle n'arrive pas à trouver dans le commerce les vêtements qu'elle a envie de porter, elle apprend à les confectionner elle-même. Elle lance une ligne pour homme en 1978, puis une collection de meubles en 1982. Comme des Garçons reste une griffe progressiste : par exemple, les parfums Comme des Garçons jouent sur d'étonnantes notes de goudron, de caoutchouc ou de vernis à ongles. Parmi ses projets les plus récents, elle a installé des boutiques-concepts éphémères dans des quartiers peu fréquentés de villes inattendues pour l'univers de la mode. Et dans le monolithique Dover Street Market de Londres, l'entreprise qu'elle dirige avec son mari anglais Adrian Joffe loue également des ateliers d'autres créateurs partageant le même état d'esprit.

JOSH SIMS

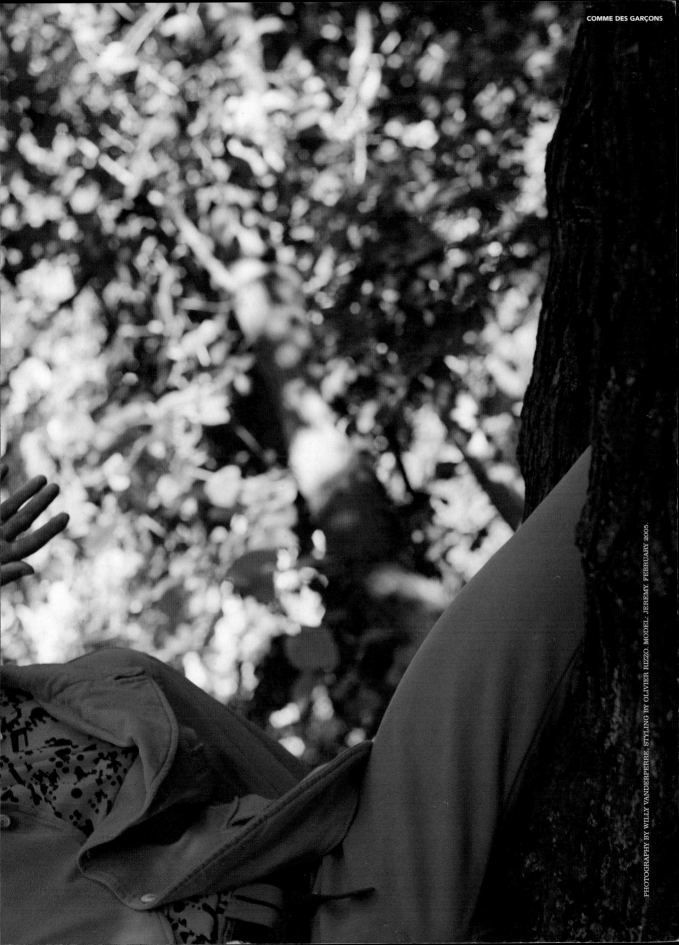

PHOTOGRAPHY BY WILLY VANDERPERRE. STYLING BY OLIVIER RIZZO. MODEL: JEREMY. FEBRUARY 2005.

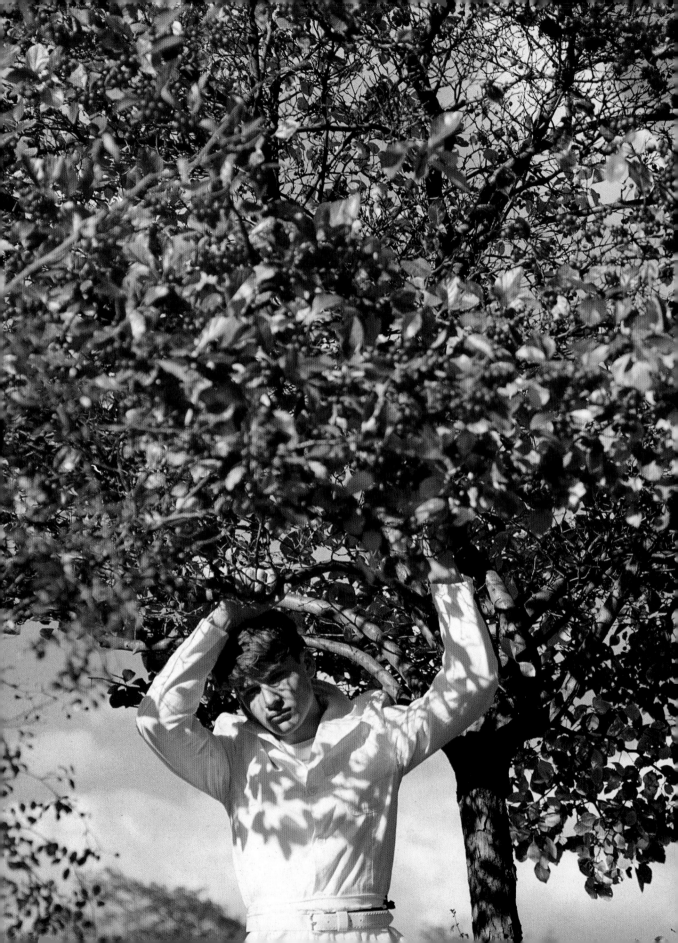

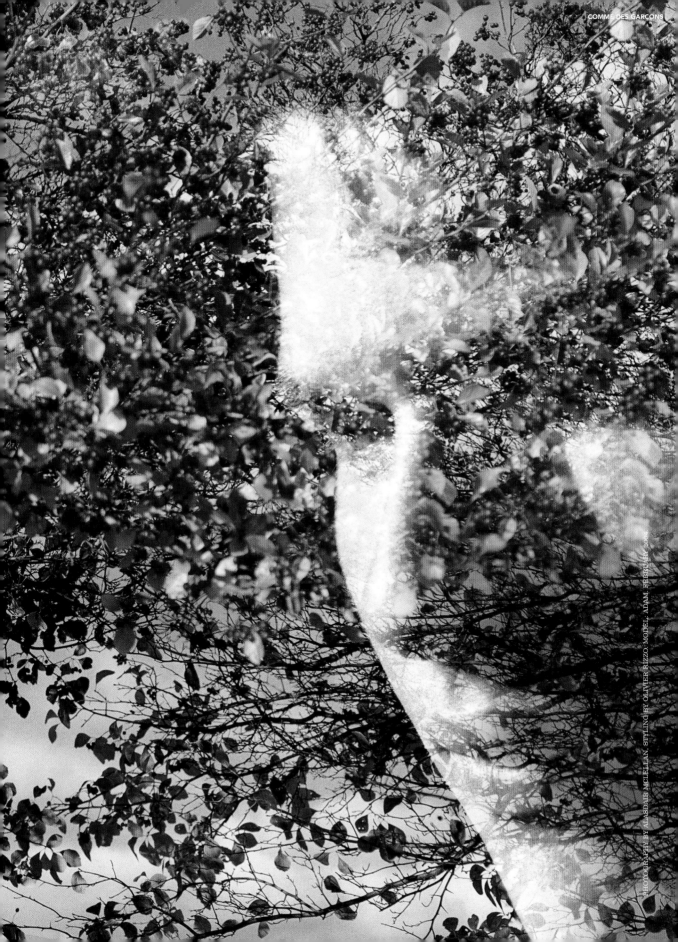

PHOTOGRAPHY BY ALASDAIR MCLELLAN. STYLING BY OLIVIER RIZZO. MODEL: ADAM. FEBRUARY 2004.

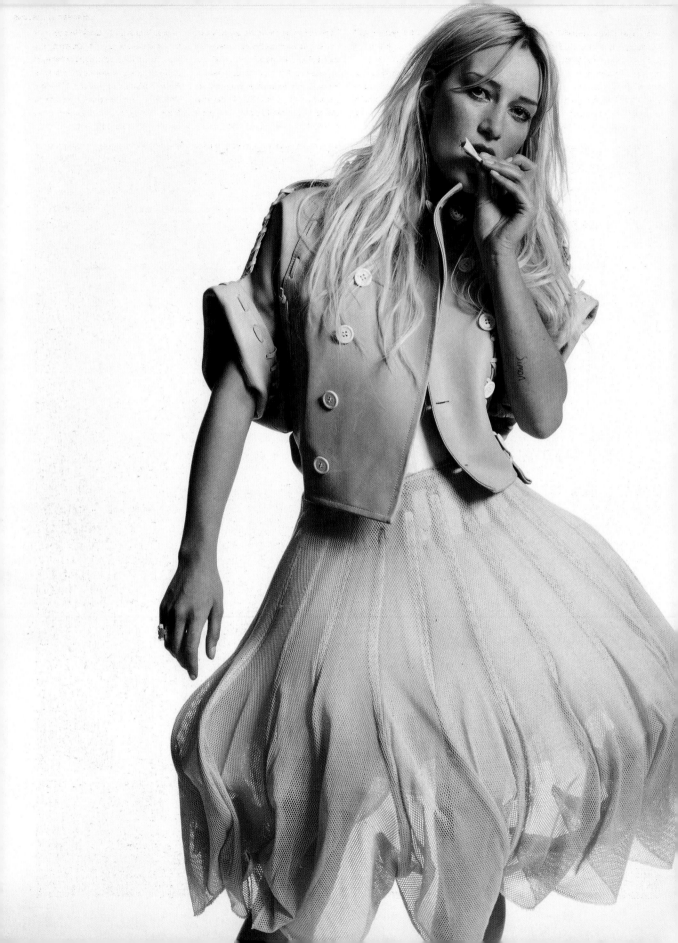

What are your signature designs? There are no signature designs, as such. But the same spirit runs through everything I do **What is your favourite piece from any of your collections?** I have none **How would you describe your work?** My job, my responsibility, it's what I do **What's your ultimate goal?** I have none. I want to carry on having a free and independent company **What inspires you?** Many, many things. Strength and beauty **Can fashion still have a political ambition?** Not for me **Who do you have in mind when you design?** Depends on each collection. Every time it is different **Is the idea of creative collaboration important to you?** I find it interesting **Who has been the greatest influence on your career?** No one **How have your own experiences affected your work as a designer?** No one is not affected by their own experiences. My experiences made me **Which is more important in your work: the process or the product?** Both **Is designing difficult for you, and if so, what drives you to continue?** It is very difficult, but I have a responsibility to my company **Have you ever been influenced or moved by the reaction to your designs?** Never **What's your definition of beauty?** Beauty is whatever anyone thinks is beautiful **What's your philosophy?** Freedom **What is the most important lesson you've learned?** Every lesson is important. I don't believe in a hit parade of lessons.

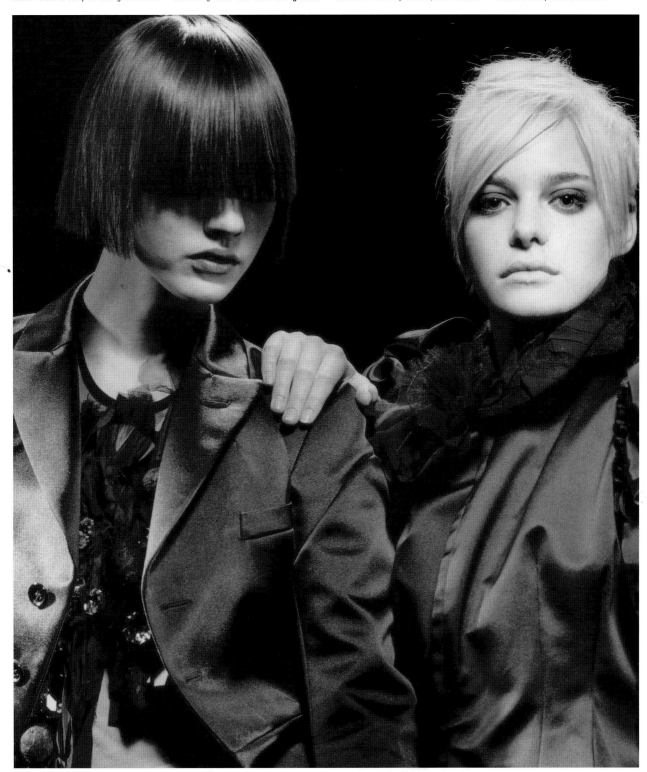

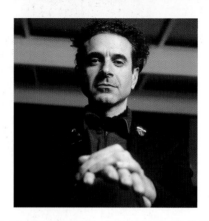

COSTUME NATIONAL

"There is no distinction between who I am and what I do"

ENNIO CAPASA

Born in Puglia, Lecce in 1960, Ennio Capasa was influenced by oriental culture from an early age, and travelled around Japan when he was 18 before being accepted into the sculpture course at Milan's Academia di Belle Arti di Brera. On graduation, Capasa was invited to return to Japan to train under Yohji Yamamoto, who had been sent some of Capasa's illustrations by a friend. He stayed for three years (1982-1985), before setting up the label Costume National in Milan in 1986 with his brother Carlo (who had himself worked with Romeo Gigli and as consultant to Dawn Mello at Gucci). Combining Japanese purism with a more streetwear-influenced silhouette, the first Costume National women's ready-to-wear collection appeared in 1987, along with a shoe collection. However, reaction to Capasa's sensual, minimalist vision was muted in Milan (where the fashion federation had refused requests by Japanese designers to show in the early '80s), so in 1991 they decided to follow Yamamoto and Rei Kawakubo to Paris. It was in France that they found the respect of critics and peers alike and in 1993 they added a men's footwear range and a ready-to-wear menswear collection (partly because Ennio, a self-confessed "vintage addict", was unable to find pieces to wear himself). In 2000, bags, lingerie and leather accessories were added, together with Costume National Luxe, featuring a limited series of garments made from particularly precious and unusual materials. Footwear now comprises around a third of the business, and the company owns its own shoe factory in Padua, an apparel plant near Vicenza and a leather treatment company near Lecce – not to mention flagship stores in Milan, Rome, Paris, New York, Los Angeles, Tokyo, Osaka and Hong Kong. In 2002, a fragrance line (the typically minimalist 'Scent') was launched, followed by eyewear a year later.

Der 1960 im apulischen Lecce geborene Ennio Capasa war schon in jungen Jahren von der orientalischen Kultur fasziniert. Mit 18 Jahren reiste er kreuz und quer durch Japan und wurde an der Mailänder Academia di Belle Arti di Brera für das Studium der Bildhauerei zugelassen. Nach seinem Abschluss erhielt Capasa eine Einladung zur Rückkehr nach Japan, um dort bei Yohji Yamamoto weiter zu lernen. Ein Freund hatte dem Stardesigner einige Illustrationen Capasas geschickt. Von 1982 bis 1985 blieb er in Japan und gründete 1986 in Mailand zusammen mit seinem Bruder Carlo (der schon mit Romeo Gigli sowie als Berater von Dawn Mello bei Gucci gearbeitet hatte) das Label Costume National. Als eine Kombination aus japanischem Purismus und einer eher in Richtung Streetwear orientierten Silhouette kam 1987 die erste Prêt-à-porter-Damenkollektion sowie eine Schuhkollektion heraus. Die Reaktionen auf Capasas sinnlich-minimalistische Vision waren in Mailand (wo der Modeverband Anfang der 1980er Jahre Präsentationsanfragen japanischer Designer abgelehnt hatte) eher gedämpft. Deshalb beschlossen die Brüder 1991, Yamamoto und Rei Kawakubo nach Paris zu folgen. Dort ernteten sie den Respekt sowohl der Kritiker als auch der Kollegen. 1993 wurde die Palette des Labels um eine Schuhkollektion sowie eine Prêt-à-porter-Kollektion für Herren erweitert (das lag nicht zuletzt daran, dass Ennio als bekennender Vintage-Addict selbst nichts zum Anziehen fand). Taschen, Dessous und Accessoires aus Leder kamen im Jahr 2000 hinzu, außerdem Costume National Luxe mit limitierten Stückzahlen von Kleidungsstücken aus besonders kostbaren und ungewöhnlichen Materialien. Der Bereich Schuhe umfasst inzwischen etwa ein Drittel des Geschäfts. So ist es nur zu verständlich, dass das Unternehmen eine eigene Schuhfabrik in Padua, eine Näherei bei Vicenza und einen Lederverarbeitungsbetrieb nahe Lecce besitzt. Nicht zu vergessen die Flagship Stores in Mailand, Rom, Paris, New York, Los Angeles, Tokio, Osaka und Hongkong. 2002 wurde die typisch minimalistische Duftlinie Scent vorgestellt, im Jahr darauf eine eigene Brillenkollektion.

Né en 1960 à Lecce dans les Pouilles, Ennio Capasa démontre un intérêt précoce pour la culture orientale et part à la découverte du Japon à peine âgé de 18 ans, avant d'être accepté au cours de sculpture de l'Academia di Belle Arti di Brera de Milan. Une fois diplômé, Capasa est invité à revenir au Japon pour être formé par Yohji Yamamoto, qui avait reçu certaines illustrations de Capasa par le biais d'un ami commun. Il y passe trois ans (de 1982 à 1985) avant de fonder la griffe Costume National à Milan en 1986 avec son frère Carlo (qui avait travaillé avec Romeo Gigli et comme consultant de Dawn Mello chez Gucci). Mêlant purisme japonais et silhouette plus streetwear, Costume National lance sa première collection de prêt-à-porter pour femme en 1987, accompagnée d'une ligne de chaussures. Cependant, la vision sensuelle et minimaliste de Capasa ne séduit pas Milan (où la fédération de la mode avait rejeté les demandes des créateurs japonais qui voulaient venir y présenter leurs collections au début des années 80). En 1991, les frères Capasa décident donc de suivre Yohji Yamamoto et Rei Kawakubo à Paris. C'est en France qu'ils gagnent finalement le respect de la presse comme celui de leurs pairs. En 1993, ils lancent également une ligne de chaussures et une collection de prêt-à-porter pour homme (en partie parce qu'Ennio, qui avoue être «accro au vintage», ne parvient pas à trouver les pièces qu'il a envie de porter). En l'an 2000, la griffe lance des collections de sacs, de lingerie et de maroquinerie, ainsi que Costume National Luxe : une série limitée de vêtements taillés dans des étoffes rares et particulièrement précieuses. Aujourd'hui, les ventes de chaussures représentent près d'un tiers du chiffre d'affaires de l'entreprise, qui possède sa propre usine de chaussures à Padoue, une autre qui produit des vêtements près de Vicenza, ainsi qu'une société de tannage près de Lecce, sans oublier des boutiques à Milan, Rome, Paris, New York, Los Angeles, Tokyo, Osaka et Hong Kong. En 2002, Costume National lance «Scent», un parfum résolument minimaliste, suivi d'une collection de lunettes dès l'année suivante.

MARK HOOPER

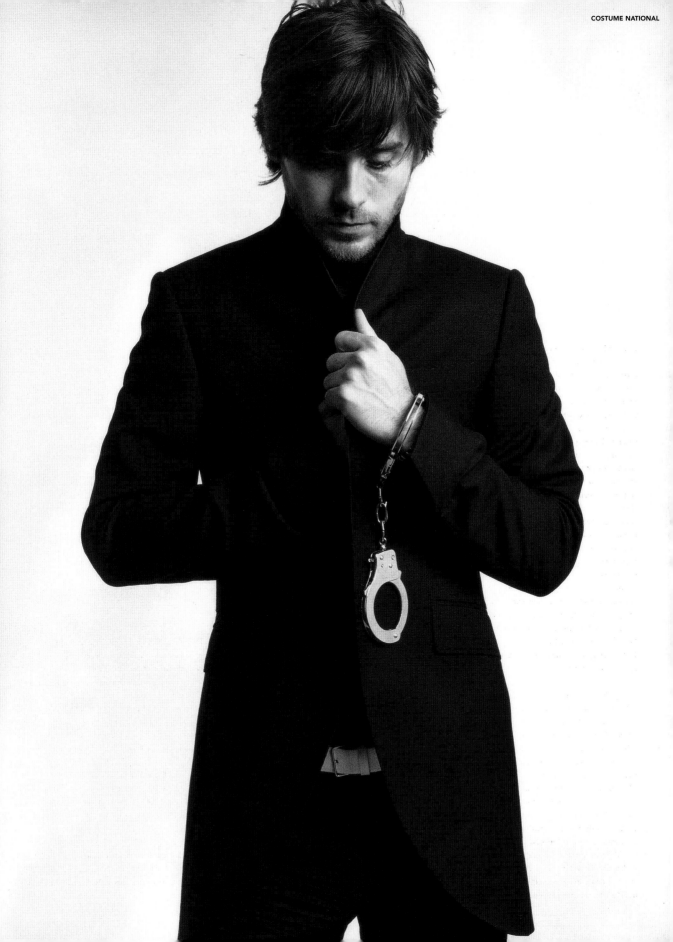

What do you consider your signature designs? My lean, sharp, sensual silhouette **What is your favourite piece or pieces from any of your collections?** I like my jackets and trousers **How would you describe your work?** Positive **What is your ultimate goal?** Pleasure **What inspires you?** Bodies and rhythms **Can fashion still have a political ambition?** Any action is political **Who do you have in mind when you design?** My personal icons **Is the idea of creative collaboration important to you?** Only if I think I will fully recognize myself in the result **Who or what has been the greatest influence on your career?** Women, myself, and perseverance **How have your own experiences affected your work as a designer?** To such an extent that there is no distinction between who I am and what I do **Which is more important to you in your work: the process or the product?** The product **Is designing difficult for you and, if so, what drives you to continue?** If it wasn't difficult I wouldn't enjoy it **Have you ever been influenced or moved by the reaction to your designs?** I like to see people wearing my clothes **What's your definition of beauty?** It is what makes you feel totally good **What's your philosophy?** Forget your brain and stay true to your emotions **What is the most important lesson you've learned?** Always trust your first impression.

PHOTOGRAPHY BY ELLEN VON UNWERTH. STYLING BY MARK MORRISON. MODEL: NAOMI CAMPBELL. DECEMBER 2003

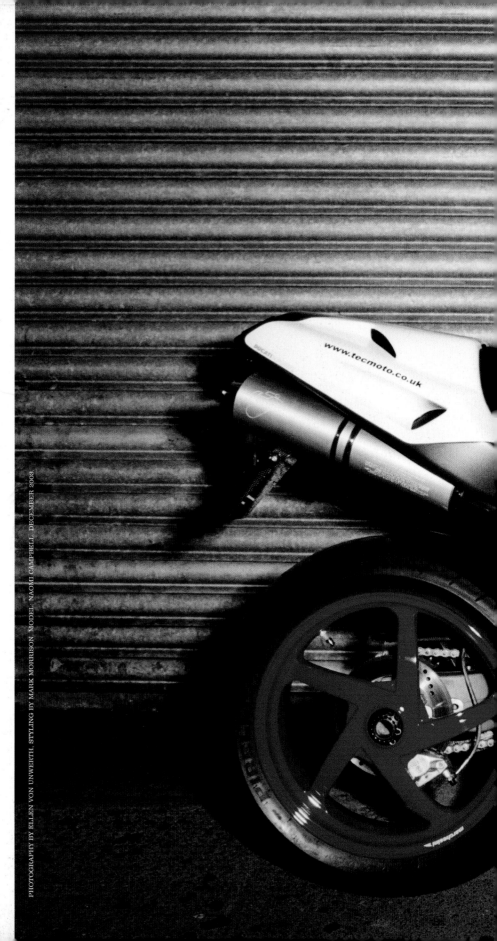

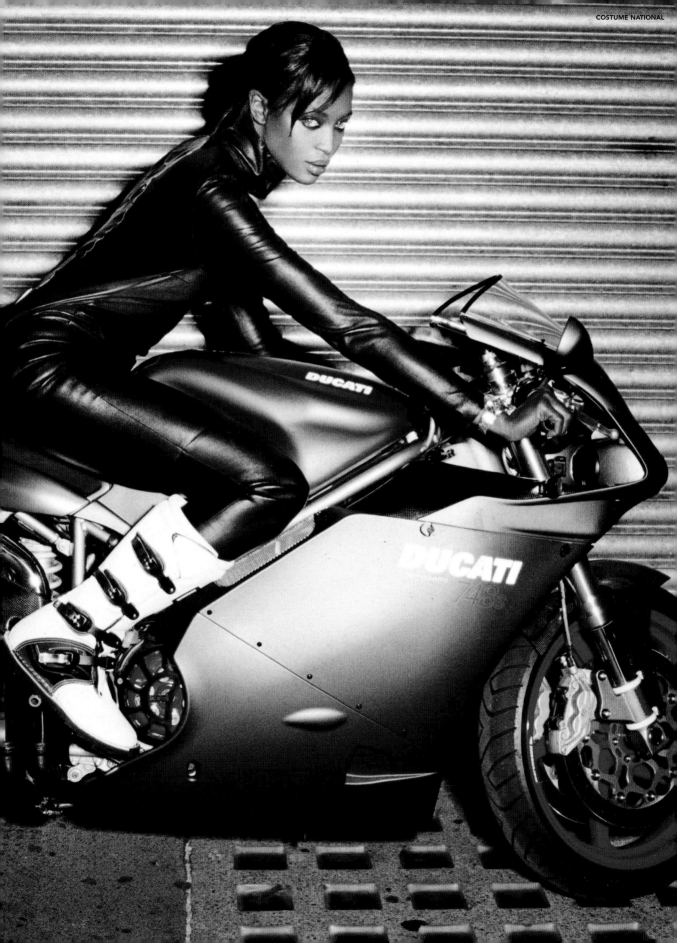

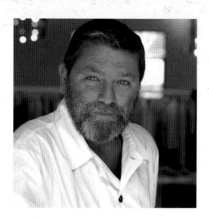

C. P. COMPANY & STONE ISLAND

"Textiles are living, fascinating materials. Our job is to carry on evolving them, to carry on experimenting" CARLO RIVETTI

Carlo Rivetti may keep a low profile, but the brands that his Sportswear Company fronts are among the most influential in modern menswear: Stone Island and C. P. Company. Rivetti in fact did not launch either label – Massimo Osti, Bolognese graphic designer and owner of the one of the world's largest collections of military clothing, created them in 1974 and 1982 respectively through his Chester Perry company. In the UK they quickly became totems of laddish style. Elsewhere, though, they have been recognised as pioneering lines in which not fashion but everyday functionality, fabric innovation and groundbreaking dyeing techniques have been driving forces. It was Osti, for instance, who first 'stonewashed' garments. But it has been under Rivetti, together with his wife and colleague Sabina, that both labels have flourished to become global concerns. Rivetti (born 1956) became a major partner and shareholder in Osti's company in 1983 through GFT, the Turin-based clothing manufacturing giant (for the likes of Armani, Ungaro, Valentino) founded by Rivetti's father Silvio in the late '50s. Ten years later, with Osti choosing to leave to pursue other projects, Rivetti decided to break away from GFT, becoming sole owner of C. P. Company and Stone Island. Since then, Rivetti – an economics graduate and lecturer in Industrial Design Marketing – kept Osti's much-imitated design philosophy alive. Since taking the helm, Rivetti has encouraged Stone Island to become ever more creative under designer Paul Harvey and its labs push the boundaries of practical clothing design, with an archive of over 60,000 colour formulae and thousands of fabric prototypes and techniques. The latest innovations include the creation of cotton felt, and cutting double-sided fabrics on the loom to create seamless garments. Rivetti has also hired designer Alessandro Pungetti to refresh the C. P. Company brand.

Carlo Rivetti selbst mag weniger bekannt sein, doch die Marken, die zu seiner Sportswear Company gehören, zählen zu den einflussreichsten in der modernen Herrenmode: Stone Island und C. P. Company. Allerdings hat Rivetti keines der beiden Label lanciert. Das tat der Grafikdesigner Massimo Osti aus Bologna, der eine der größten Uniformsammlungen der Welt besitzt, 1974 bzw. 1982 im Rahmen seiner Firma Chester Perry. In Großbritannien wurden die Marken rasch zum Inbegriff des „Laddish Style". Andernorts anerkannte man den Pionier-charakter der beiden Linien, bei denen nicht modische Qualitäten, sondern Funktionalität im Alltag, innovative Materialien und neuartige Färbetechniken im Vordergrund stehen. So war es beispielsweise Osti, der Kleider als erster dem „Stonewash"-Verfahren unterzog. Es gelang allerdings erst Rivetti, zusammen mit seiner Frau und Kollegin Sabina beiden Labels zu internationalem Erfolg zu verhelfen. Rivetti, Jahrgang 1956, wurde 1983 Mehrheitsaktionär in Ostis Unternehmen. Und zwar über die riesige Kleiderfabrikation GFT, die für Marken wie Armani, Ungaro und Valentino produziert und schon Ende der 1950er Jahre von Carlo Rivettis Vater Silvio gegründet worden war. 1993 verließ Osti die Firma, um sich neuen Projekten zuzuwenden, während Rivetti sich von der GFT löste und Alleineigentümer von C. P. Company und Stone Island wurde. Seit damals erhält Rivetti – der übrigens einen Abschluss in Wirtschaftswissenschaften besitzt und als Dozent Industriedesign-Marketing lehrt – Ostis oft kopierte Designphilosophie am Leben. Seit er die Unternehmensleitung übernommen hat, treibt er Stone Island sogar zu noch größerer Kreativität an. Designer Paul Harvey und sein Labor erweitern ständig die Grenzen funktionaler Klei-dung, wofür ihnen ein Archiv mit über 60 000 Farbformeln sowie Tausende von Stoffprototypen und Techniken zur Verfügung stehen. Zu den jüngsten Innova-tionen gehören Baumwollfilz und das Schneiden von doppellagigen Stoffen noch am Webstuhl, um daraus nahtlose Kleidung zu kreieren. Um die Marke C. P. Company neu zu beleben, verpflichtete Rivetti außerdem den Designer Alessandro Pungetti.

Carlo Rivetti a beau se faire discret, Stone Island et C. P. Company, les marques lancées par son entreprise de sportswear, exercent une influence considérable sur la mode masculine d'aujourd'hui. En fait, Carlo Rivetti n'a personnellement lancé aucune de ces griffes: c'est Massimo Osti, graphiste de Bologne également propriétaire de l'une des plus vastes collections de vêtements militaires au monde, qui les a créées respectivement en 1974 et 1982 par le biais de sa société Chester Perry. Au Royaume-Uni, ces griffes s'imposent rapidement comme l'uni-forme des jeunes Anglais. Ailleurs, elles se distinguent surtout comme des lignes pionnières motivées non par la tendance, mais par une fonctionnalité quoti-dienne, utilisant des tissus innovants et des techniques de teinture révolution-naires. Par exemple, Massimo Osti est le premier à avoir utilisé le « stonewash » pour délaver les vêtements. Mais c'est sous l'impulsion de Carlo Rivetti, de sa femme et de leur collaboratrice Sabina que les deux griffes prospèrent jusqu'à devenir de véritables multinationales. Carlo Rivetti (né en 1956) devient parte-naire et actionnaire majoritaire de l'entreprise d'Osti en 1983 par le biais de GFT, géant turinois de l'habillement (également fabricant pour Armani, Ungaro et Valentino) fondé à la fin des années 50 par Silvio Rivetti, le père de Carlo. Dix ans plus tard, Osti quitte l'entreprise pour se consacrer à d'autres projets et Rivetti décide de se séparer de GFT pour devenir l'unique propriétaire de C. P. Company et de Stone Island. Depuis, ce diplômé en économie, également confé-rencier en marketing du design industriel, continue de faire vivre la philosophie créative d'Osti, très souvent imitée. Depuis qu'il a repris le flambeau, Rivetti sti-mule la créativité de Stone Island grâce au styliste Paul Harvey, et ses labora-toires repoussent les frontières de la mode pratique avec des archives réperto-riant plus de 60 000 formules de teinture et des milliers de prototypes de tissus et techniques de production. Les dernières innovations de l'entreprise incluent la création du coton feutré, ainsi que la découpe de tissus double face directe-ment sur le métier à tisser pour créer des vêtements sans couture. Carlo Rivetti a également recruté le styliste Alessandro Pungetti pour moderniser la marque C. P. Company.

JOSH SIMS

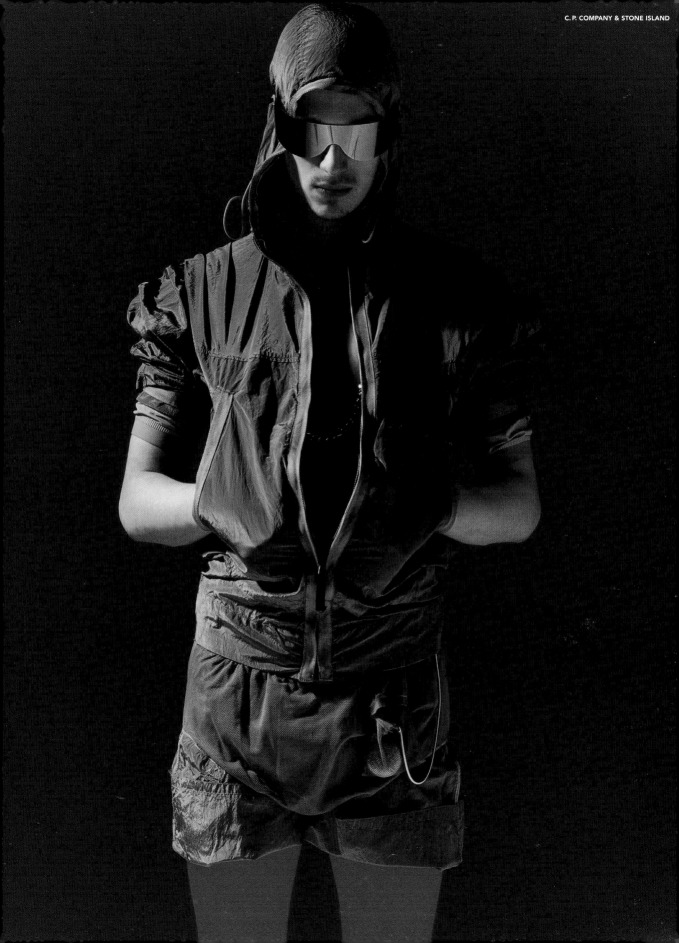

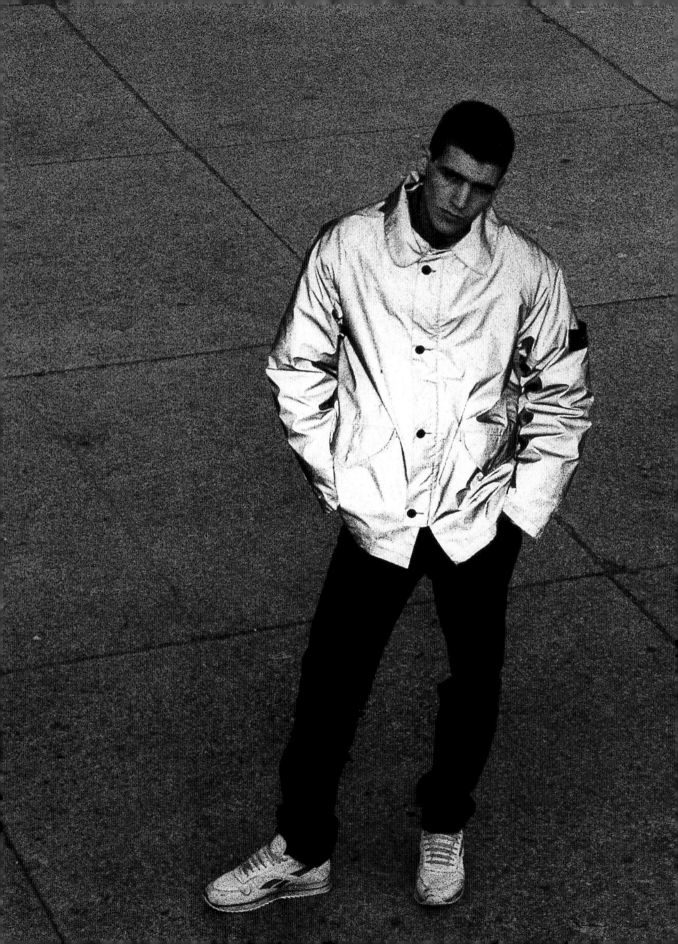

What are your signature designs? Timeless and refined elegance in an informal context **How would you describe your work?** The real fascination of this job is fabrics. Textiles are living, fascinating materials. Our job is to carry on evolving them, to carry on experimenting. Starting from the same canvas, every six months you can interpret and reinterpret, evolve, refine and blend forms, materials and colours, keeping an eye on the street and society. This is a job that continues 24 hours a day because everything can be used to stimulate research. My company is a machine dedicated to translating research into something that can reach the market **What is your ultimate goal?** We were asked to display a C.P. Company transformable item and a Stone Island stainless steel parka at the Beaubourg Museum in Paris. Some of our pieces are travelling the world in design exhibitions. I would like to see one of our pieces displayed alongside the Olivetti Lettera 22 at MoMA in New York **Can fashion still have a political ambition?** I really hope so. I will always defend respect, ethics and mutual understanding. Fashion has to respect the individual and has to be ethical at every step of the supply chain **What do you have in mind when you work on your collections?** We really are product-more than marketing-driven. I don't entirely agree that the consumer is central to the whole process. He doesn't often know what he wants. Or that what he wants is already 'old'. Ideas and innovations must always be in line with the brand philosophy and its historic heritage – so that we can offer innovative solutions that are also reassuring **Is design difficult for you, and if so, what drives you to continue?** I am not a designer but over two-thirds of the people in the company work on all aspects of research and prototyping. Today's market is driven by increasingly tight schedules that are counterproductive for pure creativity. We are one of the few companies that can afford to finish projects without being slaves to collections or seasons. When we feel that an innovative product for C.P. Company or Stone Island is ready – and it can take years – we include it in the collection. We do not follow the logic of what the market wants, but strangely, in the long term, it is just what the market 'wanted' **What is your definition of beauty?** A harmonious balance in everything **What is your philosophy?** Ethics. Teamwork. Consistency **What is the most important lesson you've learned?** Everything can be lost in a trice. Don't get attached to things, but to individuals, to the heart and mind of people.

PHOTOGRAPHY BY ALASDAIR MCLELLAN. STYLING BY SIMON FOXTON. MODEL LUKE. DECEMBER 2008

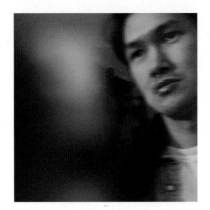

DAVID SZETO

"When I've designed something I love,
I usually can't believe I made it"

Little-known though David Szeto (born 1967) may be, he has provoked lavish praise from an exclusive list of private clients since 2004. This was the year that savvy international womenswear buyers snapped up his first, French-made, wholesale collections. Along with Yves Saint Laurent, it is Madeleine Vionnet who is his inspiration – she was the designer who, during the '20s and '30s, freed women from corsetry and developed the bias cut. Szeto, who is Chinese-Canadian, is a master technician. His haute couture-style skill lies in his innovative cutting on the bias or half-bias. This allows his fabric – often hard-wearing but easily-manipulated men's suiting cloth – to flow with its grain. Rather than sketching and then creating a pattern, Szeto designs by hand-draping cloth on a mannequin before folding, twisting and bunching it into the desired voluminous form. The resulting smocking – hand sewn before the final garment is pieced together – is architectural without losing any softness or wearability. The style is conceptual and masculine without being difficult or unfeminine, and is flattering to women of all shapes and sizes. Signature details include a fabric-roll style of puff sleeve referred to by Szeto as a 'sushi'. Szeto grew up in Vancouver but studied at New York's Fashion Institute of Technology, where a Comme des Garçons exhibition first inspired him to break traditional dressmaking rules. He applies this approach as much to his business as to his design, rejecting the global brand mentality of many luxury conglomerate labels, and preferring, for the time being at least, to remain small and focused. After graduation, Szeto worked for himself in London for five years, before moving to Paris in 1992 where he remains today. He has also professed a desire to try designing menswear.

So wenig bekannt der 1967 geborene Szeto auch sein mag, seit 2004 ist ihm das überschwängliche Lob einer exklusiven Liste von Privatkunden gewiss. Im selben Jahr sicherten sich nämlich kluge Einkäufer auf dem internationalen Markt für Damenmode seine ersten, in Frankreich produzierten Großhandelskollektionen. Neben Yves Saint Laurent wurde der Designer von Madeleine Vionnet inspiriert. Die Modeschöpferin befreite in den 1920er und 1930er Jahren die Frauen aus den Korsetts und entwickelte den Diagonalschnitt. Szeto ist chinesisch-kanadischer Abstammung und beherrscht sein Handwerk meisterhaft. Seine größte Begabung im Haute-Couture-Stil ist sein innovativer Diagonal- und Halbdiagonalschnitt. Das lässt seine Stoffe – oft schweres, aber durch entsprechende Manipulation leicht gemachtes Tuch für die Herrenkonfektion – fließen. Anstatt zu zeichnen und anschließend ein Schnittmuster anzufertigen, entwirft Szeto, indem er von Hand Stoff an einem Mannequin drapiert, bevor er diesen durch Falten, Verdrehen und Bauschen in die gewünschte voluminöse Form bringt. Der so gesmokte Stoff – von Hand genäht, bevor das Kleidungsstück zusammengefügt wird – wirkt geradezu architektonisch, ohne dadurch an Weichheit oder

Tragbarkeit zu verlieren. Der Stil ist konzeptual und maskulin, allerdings ohne dadurch verkopft und unweiblich zu wirken – und er schmeichelt Frauen aller Größen mit jeglicher Figur. Zu den charakteristischen Details zählen Puffärmel aus auf besondere Weise hochgerolltem Stoff, die Szeto selbst als „Sushi" bezeichnet. Der Designer wuchs in Vancouver auf und studierte am New Yorker Fashion Institute of Technology, wo ihn eine Ausstellung mit Kreationen von Comme des Garçons erstmals auf die Idee brachte, mit den traditionellen Gesetzen der Schneiderei zu brechen. Diesen Ansatz verfolgt er in geschäftlicher wie in kreativer Hinsicht, indem er sich der globalen Markenmentalität der zahlreichen Luxuslabel-Konzerne verweigert und es – zumindest im Moment – vorzieht, klein und unabhängig zu bleiben. Nach seinem Studienabschluss arbeitete Szeto zunächst fünf Jahre lang selbstständig in London, bevor er 1992 nach Paris ging, wo er noch heute lebt. Irgendwann möchte er auch Herrenmode entwerfen.

David Szeto (né en 1967) n'est peut-être pas très connu, mais depuis 2004 il suscite les éloges d'une liste exclusive de clients privés. Cette année-là, les acheteurs internationaux spécialisés en mode féminine ont tous sauté sur ses premières collections fabriquées en France. Aux côtés d'Yves Saint Laurent, Madeleine Vionnet figure parmi ses principales sources d'inspiration : c'est la styliste qui, pendant les années 20 et 30, a libéré les femmes du corset et inventé la coupe en biais. D'origine sino-canadienne, David Szeto maîtrise parfaitement la technique. Son style haute couture repose sur une méthode innovante de coupe dans le biais ou le demi-biais qui confère au tissu (souvent du tissu de costume pour homme très résistant mais facile à manipuler) un tombé extrêmement fluide. Plutôt que de tracer et de découper des patrons, Szeto travaille en drapant le tissu sur un mannequin, puis le plie, l'enroule et le fronce en fonction de la forme et du volume qu'il recherche. Les smocks ainsi obtenus, cousus main avant l'assemblage du vêtement final, affichent un aspect architectural, sans perdre ni douceur ni résistance à l'usure. Conceptuel et masculin, le style Szeto est pourtant féminin et facile à porter, flattant toutes les femmes, quel que soit leur physique. Ses détails signature incluent notamment une sorte de manche bouffante en tissu roulotté que Szeto appelle « sushi ». Après avoir grandi à Vancouver, Szeto étudie au Fashion Institute of Technology de New York, où une exposition consacrée à Comme des Garçons lui inspire pour la première fois le désir de briser les règles traditionnelles de la couture. Une approche qu'il applique à son entreprise comme à son travail de création, rejetant la mentalité de marque mondiale adoptée par les grands groupes de luxe et préférant, du moins pour l'instant, rester petit et spécialisé. Après l'obtention de son diplôme, David Szeto travaille à son compte à Londres pendant cinq ans avant de venir s'installer à Paris en 1992, où il vit encore aujourd'hui. Il dit aussi avoir très envie de s'essayer à la mode pour homme.

JOSH SIMS

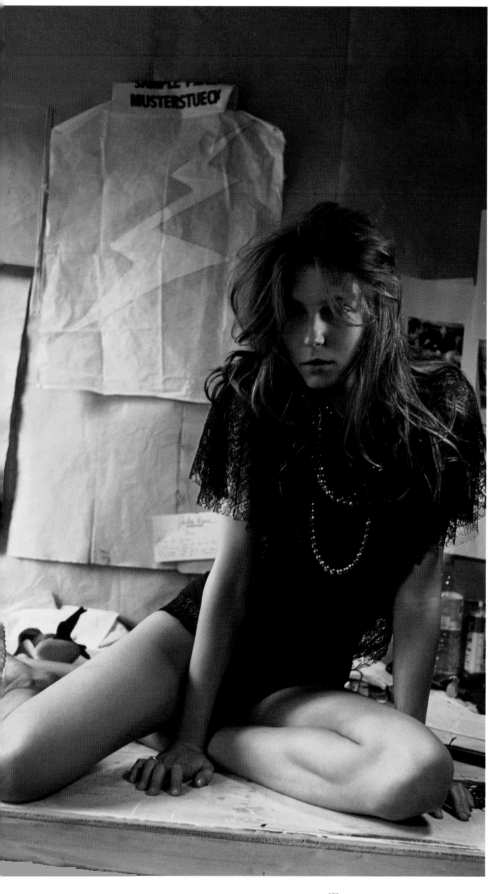

What are your signature designs? Signature designs are a sort of origami bias-cutting technique that results in a feminine silhouette without being obvious **What is your favourite piece from any of your collections?** I have two; a dress called guillemette that took about 20 fittings. This dress is for me incredibly flattering on so many shapes, it looks appealing on the hanger and the pattern work is a complex pattern; and I was very impressed that I could get it manufactured without too many problems or costing a fortune. The second is the simplest pattern, a jacket with almost no seams at all, the fit happens in about 159 little hand-stitched tucks around the neck **How would you describe your work?** Complex patternmaking but easy comfortable pieces that respect the woman's form **What's your ultimate goal?** To see my clothes being worn on the street, to make the wearer feel great, to give the client a desire to buy something special and eventually design the ultimate store **What inspires you?** Everything inspires me, but people I meet can give me the most inspiration **Can fashion still have a political ambition?** For me, no, but for others maybe **Who do you have in mind when you design?** The wearer **Is the idea of creative collaboration important to you?** This is always an interesting way of working. I find that one can create wonderful unexpected results when one collaborates with someone of another aesthetic. I personally love to work with people who have a completely different vision than me **Who has been the greatest influence on your career?** Calvin Klein, for his approach to business and his simplistic vision, especially in the early '80s. Vionnet for her increadible cutting techniques, Comme des Garçons for her abstract way of looking at clothes, and Yves Saint Laurent because it's so damn chic! **How have your own experiences affected your work as a designer?** My design is a reflection of my life, always trying to keep it balanced **What is more important in your work: the process or the product?** Both **Is designing difficult for you? If so, what drives you to continue?** Designing is second nature to me, it is the best part of my work **Have you ever been influenced or moved by the reaction to you designs?** When I've designed something I love, I usually can't believe I made it **What's your definition of beauty?** Believe that there is beauty in everything **What's your philosophy?** Try and do the best that you can. Keep a balanced life and be happy **What is the most important lesson you've learned?** In business: if you do a show, it helps to have a PR person.

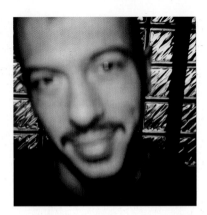

DENIS SIMACHEV

"Strive for the impossible"

Born in Moscow in 1974, Denis Simachev is extremely well-educated in many areas of creativity, having studied painting, advertising, hairstyling and gained a degree in footwear design. Fashion design is his true calling, however. Simachev set up his menswear label at Moscow fashion week in the spring of 2001. His womenswear label was launched the following season. From the start, it was clear Simachev had no intention of producing poor imitations of Western fashion. His label is proudly Russian. The designer uses his friends to present the clothes. An original soundtrack is written for each season by Simachev and Russian electronic genius Igor Vdovin. The clothes, like the music, explore Russia's rich cultural heritage. They reference constructivism, communist iconography, peasant detailing and military uniforms. Simachev mixes these historical references with unapologetically modern materials. His spring/summer 2005 collection included a high-tech fabric only previously used by NASA, and a disposable jacket that was intended to be worn for only one season. This was combined with the colours of the Russian flag and a belt buckle based on one worn by the Odessa Navy. Simachev has received praise from the international media and retailers throughout his short career, becoming the first home-grown designer to be stocked in high-class St Petersburg boutique, Day and Night. Meanwhile, his global prominence has grown since 2002, when he began staging shows in Paris and Milan.

Der 1974 in Moskau geborene Denis Simachev ist in vielen kreativen Bereichen hervorragend bewandert, nachdem er Malerei und Werbung studiert, eine Friseurausbildung absolviert und einen Abschluss in Schuhdesign erworben hat. Modedesign ist jedoch seine wahre Berufung. Sein Herrenmodelabel präsentierte Simachev erstmals im Frühjahr 2001 im Rahmen der Moskauer Modewoche. Das Damenmodelabel kam in der darauf folgenden Saison dazu. Von Beginn an war deutlich erkennbar, dass Simachev nicht vorhatte, ärmliche Imitationen westlicher Mode zu produzieren. Seine Marke ist russisch und stolz darauf. Freunde des Designers präsentieren seine Entwürfe, und für jede Saison wird von Simachev und dem russischen Elektronikgenie Igor Vdovin ein Original-soundtrack geschrieben. Kleider wie Musik schöpfen aus dem reichen kulturellen Erbe Russlands und stellen Bezüge zum Konstruktivismus, zur kommunistischen Ikonografie, zu bäuerlichen Mustern und Soldatenuniformen her.

Simachev kombiniert diese historischen Zitate mit eindeutig modernen Materialien. So fand in seiner Kollektion Frühjahr/Sommer 2005 ein High-Tech-Stoff Verwendung, den bis dato nur die NASA benutzt hatte. Außerdem war da eine Wegwerf-Jacke, die zum Tragen in einer einzigen Saison bestimmt war. Das Ganze präsentierte sich in den Farben der russischen Flagge und mit Gürtel-schnallen, die denen der Odessa-Marine nachempfunden waren. In seiner noch relativ kurzen Karriere erhielt Simachev bereits Lob von Medien und Einzel-händlern aus aller Welt. Er ist auch der einzige einheimische Designer, den die St. Petersburger Nobelboutique Day and Night führt. Seine internationale Bekanntheit wurde nicht zuletzt dadurch gesteigert, dass er seit 2002 bei den Schauen in Paris und Mailand vertreten ist.

Né en 1974 à Moscou, Denis Simachev revendique une excellente formation dans de nombreux domaines créatifs, puisqu'il a étudié la peinture, la publicité et la coiffure et qu'il est diplômé en création de chaussures. La mode reste toutefois sa véritable vocation. Simachev lance sa griffe pour homme au printemps 2001 lors de la semaine de la mode de Moscou, et présente sa ligne pour femme la saison suivante. Dès ses débuts, il semble évident que Simachev n'a aucune intention de produire de piètres imitations de la mode occidentale. Sa griffe affiche avec fierté ses origines russes. Le créateur fait appel à ses amis pour présenter ses vêtements. En collaboration avec le génie russe de l'électro Igor Vdovin, il compose une bande-son originale pour chaque collection. Les vêtements comme la musique explorent le riche héritage culturel de la Russie, avec des références au constructivisme, à l'iconographie communiste, aux détails des habits de paysans et aux uniformes militaires. Simachev n'a pas peur de mêler ces clins d'œil historiques à des matières résolument modernes. Sa collection printemps/été 2005 présente un tissu high-tech jusqu'alors uniquement réservé à la NASA, ainsi qu'une veste recyclable, censée n'être portée qu'une saison. Le tout combiné aux couleurs du drapeau russe, avec une ceinture inspirée de celles de la marine d'Odessa. Au cours de sa courte carrière, Denis Simachev a reçu les éloges de la presse et des acheteurs internationaux, devenant le premier créateur du cru à vendre ses créations dans la boutique de luxe « Day and Night » de Saint-Pétersbourg. Par ailleurs, sa notoriété mondiale ne cesse de croître depuis qu'il a commencé à présenter ses défilés à Paris et Milan en 2002. LAUREN COCHRANE

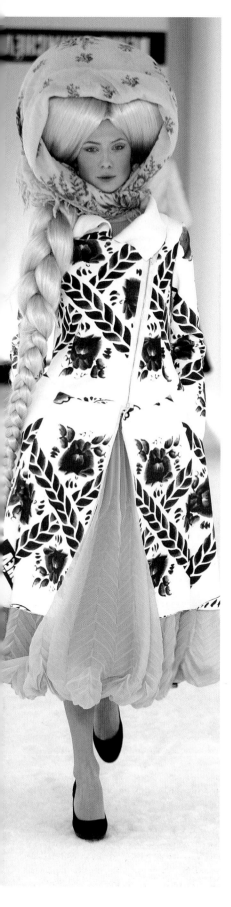

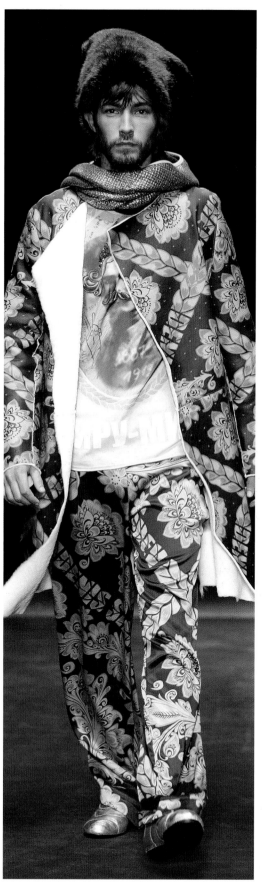

What are your signature designs? Russian style, sarcasm, irony, to strive for the impossible **What is your favourite piece from any of your collections?** Olympic sports-jacket **How would you describe your work?** To achieve success, thanks to other people **What's your ultimate goal?** Big love **What inspires you?** Everything ugly **Can fashion still have a political ambition?** Yes, fashion can achieve some political goal **Who do you have in mind when you design?** Crowds of people **Is the idea of creative collaboration important to you?** Yes, it is important **Who has been the greatest influence on your career?** My parents **Which is more important in your work: the process or the product?** The process **Is designing difficult for you, if so, what drives you to continue?** Designing is not difficult **Have you ever been influenced or moved by the reaction to your designs?** Criticism proves my assumptions **What's your definition of beauty?** Nature and harmony **What is the most important lesson you've learned?** I've had no lessons to remember.

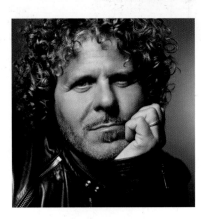

DIESEL

> "I think that Diesel is special because we have always had our own views on styles and trends" RENZO ROSSO

Renzo Rosso (born 1955) is the force behind iconic Italian company Diesel. Renowned for its jeans, the brand is as equally acclaimed for its advertising campaigns. The brand's multi-award-winning catch line – 'Diesel: For Successful Living' – parodies advertising's dictum that products will make you happy, and encapsulates Rosso's confrontational, ironic fashion ethos. The son of a peasant farmer, Rosso studied industrial textile manufacturing in his native Padua, followed by economics at university in Venice. Something of a master entrepreneur, in 1978, before his degree was completed, he co-founded the influential Genius Group to develop new fashion brands, among them Replay and Diesel. In 1985 Rosso acquired Diesel and by 1991 had unified its first global marketing strategy. In 2000 the company acquired Staff International, holding agent for Dsquared, Martin Margiela and Vivienne Westwood Red Label. New brands have also been launched, among them Diesel Kids, 55 DSL and the experimental Diesel Style Lab. Diesel has an annual turnover in excess of € 750 m and even has its own hotel, the Art Déco Pelican on South Beach, Miami, and a farm in the Maristoca hills that produces wine and olive oil. Still true to its core product, Diesel recently launched the Diesel Denim Gallery, offering specially-treated jeans billed as one-of-a-kind denim art pieces. While the brand is sold in over 80 countries, Diesel denim jeans remains 100 per cent made in Italy.

Der 1955 geborene Renzo Rosso ist die treibende Kraft hinter der italienischen Kultfirma Diesel. Die für ihre Jeans berühmte Marke für ihre Werbekampagnen ist auch bekannt. Der vielfach ausgezeichnete Slogan der Marke – „Diesel: For Successful Living" – parodiert das Versprechen der Werbung, dass bestimmte Produkte glücklich machen, und bringt Rossos kampflustiges, ironisches Verständnis von Mode auf den Punkt. Der Kleinbauernsohn studierte zunächst Textilingenieurwesen in seiner Heimatstadt Padua und anschließend Betriebswirtschaft in Venedig. Noch bevor er seinen Abschluss hatte, beteiligte er sich 1978, sozusagen als sein Gesellenstück, an der Gründung der einflussreichen Genius Group, um mit ihr neue Modemarken wie Replay und Diesel zu entwickeln. 1985 kaufte Rosso Diesel; 1991 konnte er seine erste globale Marketingstrategie vorweisen. Im Jahr 2000 kaufte das Unternehmen mit Staff International einen Hersteller von Lizenzprodukten für Dsquared, Martin Margiela und Vivienne

Westwood Red Label. Neue Marken in Form von autonomen Spin-Offs wurden ebenfalls lanciert, darunter Diesel Kids, 55 DSL sowie die experimentierfreudige Marke Diesel Style Lab. Der geschätzte Umsatz des Konzerns liegt bei über 750 Millionen Euro, dazu kommen noch das Art-Déco-Hotel Pelican in South Beach, Miami, und ein Landgut in den Maristoca-Hügeln, das Wein und Olivenöl produziert. Trotzdem bleibt Diesel auch seinem Kernprodukt treu, etwa mit der kürzlich präsentierten Diesel Denim Gallery aus spezialbehandelten Jeans, die als einzigartige Kunstwerke aus Denim vermarktet wurden. Auch wenn die Marke in mehr als 80 Ländern verkauft wird, befindet sich die Produktion der Diesel-Denim-Jeans nach wie vor zu 100 Prozent in Italien.

Renzo Rosso (né en 1955) est le véritable moteur de la célèbre marque italienne Diesel. Réputée pour ses créations en denim, la griffe Diesel est tout aussi plébiscitée pour ses campagnes publicitaires. Tout en exprimant l'éthique ironique et offensive de Rosso en matière de mode, le slogan maintes fois primé « Diesel : For Successful Living » parodie le diktat de la publicité qui cherche à faire croire aux gens que les produits peuvent les rendre heureux. Fils d'agriculteur, il étudie la production textile industrielle dans sa ville natale de Padoue avant de suivre un cursus en économie à l'université de Venise. Alors qu'il n'est pas encore diplômé, ce futur homme d'affaires avisé est cofondateur de l'influent groupe Genius en 1978 pour développer de nouvelles griffes de mode, parmi lesquelles Replay et Diesel. Rosso rachète Diesel en 1985 et unifie sa première stratégie marketing mondiale en 1991. En l'an 2000, l'entreprise acquiert Staff International, fabricant de produits sous licence pour Dsquared, Martin Margiela et Vivienne Westwood Red Label. Diesel se diversifie à travers de nouvelles marques secondaires autonomes telles que Diesel Kids, 55 DSL et l'expérimental Diesel Style Lab. Diesel enregistre aujourd'hui un chiffre d'affaires annuel de plus de 750 millions d'euros et possède même son propre hôtel à South Beach Miami, l'Art Déco Pelican, ainsi qu'une ferme dans les montagnes Maristoca qui produit du vin et de l'huile d'olive. Toujours fidèle au produit qui a fait sa gloire, Diesel a récemment lancé la collection Diesel Denim Gallery, qui propose des jeans ayant subi des traitements spéciaux et tarifés comme des œuvres d'art à part entière. Bien que l'entreprise soit présente dans plus de 80 pays, la production des jeans Diesel reste 100 % « made in Italy ».

SKYE SHERWIN

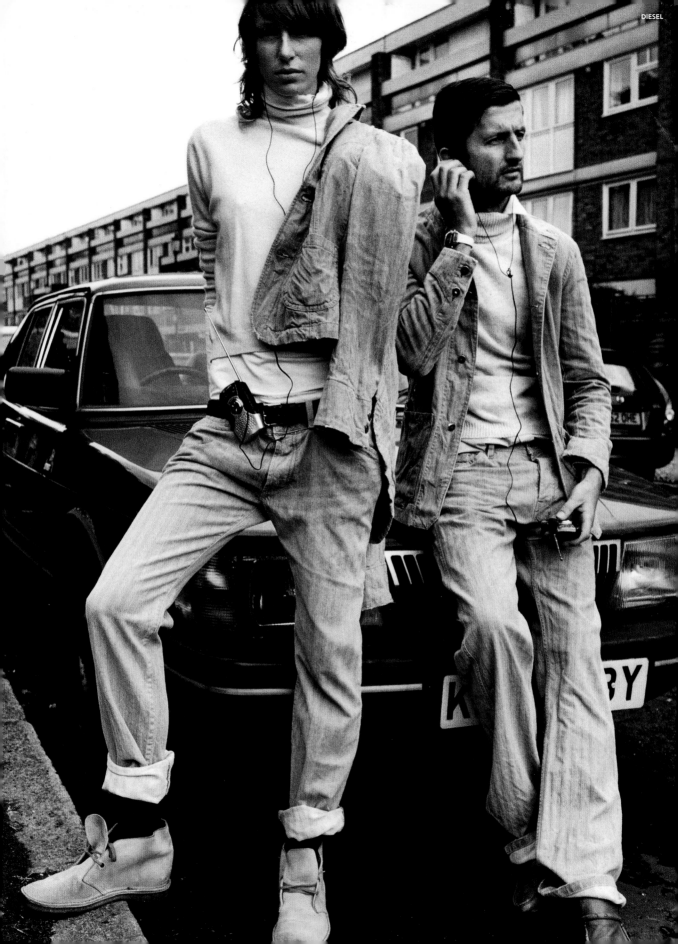

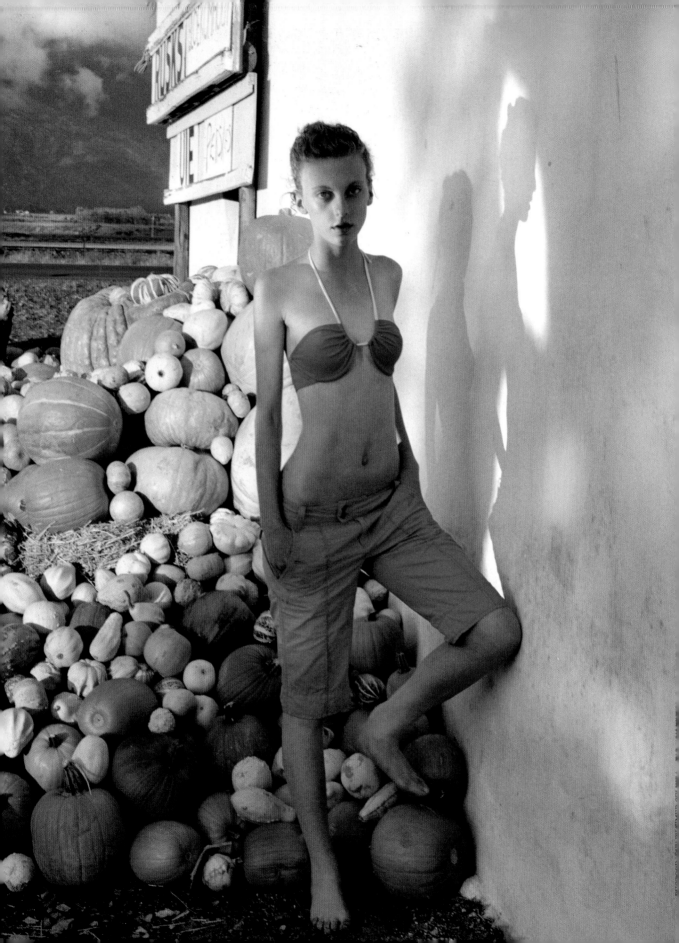

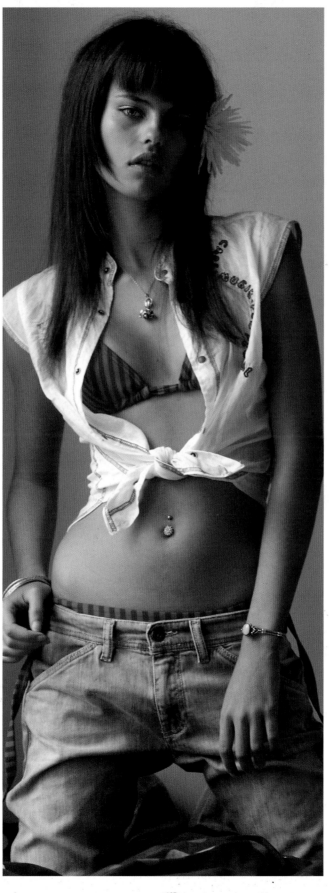

What are your signature designs? Every season I have my 'favourite' pieces in each collection, be it clothing or accessories. Clearly, among them I think we are internationally recognized for our denim, so yes, you may call that our signature piece **What is your favourite piece from any of your collections?** The next one! **How would you describe your work?** A heap of passion, creativity, energy and positive attitude that constantly pushes me to do something different, better and before the others **What's your ultimate goal?** At this precise moment I want to further increase the quality of our products, from clothing to licences, from the stores to our advertising – I want Diesel to always be a worldwide benchmark in all we do! **What inspires you?** Inspiration has no boundaries and can come from anywhere: a picture, a painting, a face, a street, a sound… **Can fashion still have a political ambition?** Fashion has the power to send out positive messages to the people, to make them feel special and different. It helps them dream – and God only knows how much this is needed in today's world **Who do you have in mind when you design?** An independent mind and spirit **Is the idea of creative collaboration important to you?** It's fundamental. Diesel's success comes from the passionate work of a creative team which constantly exchange views and ideas **Who has been the greatest influence on your career?** Many different people inspired me over the years. I couldn't name only one **How have your own experiences affected your work as a designer?** Every single life experience, every single thing you do in your life – positive or negative – affects you and your actions **Which is more important in your work: the process or the product?** The product and style are key. The process follows **Is designing difficult for you, if so, what drives you to continue?** I am not a designer myself but my positive approach to life helps me turn bad things into good ones. And this is the spirit I try to pass on to my team **Have you ever been influenced or moved by the reaction to your designs?** I care about people's reactions to our collections because there's always something interesting to acknowledge. However I do think that Diesel is special also because we have always had our own views on styles and trends – this is what differentiates us from many others and what the true aficionados love **What's your definition of beauty?** 90-60-90?!? **What's your philosophy?** Be true to yourself and your ideas, always work with passion and enthusiasm, enjoy your life **What is the most important lesson you've learned?** To listen to people.

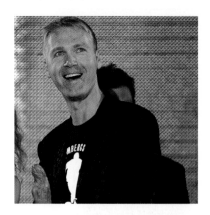

DIRK BIKKEMBERGS

"I'm inspired by youth, health, sport, raw energy"

The work of Dirk Bikkembergs is pure muscle. Part of the original 'Antwerp Six' he transfers the codes and nuances of sportswear to a sharp signature style that lies somewhere between the ideas of strength, health and durability. The German-born designer (born 1959) graduated from Antwerp's Royal Academy in 1982 before working for a variety of Belgian fashion companies, picking up the prestigious Golden Spindle Award for Best Young Designer in 1985. The son of army parents, Bikkembergs often makes references to the military in his work with tightly structured pieces and the odd fetish-like leather detail. Launching his first collection of men's shoes in 1986, the designer set out a strict design formula that included his trademark double stitch (his clothing not only appears robust but is actually physically strong). In 1987 he introduced his menswear line, with the focus on knitwear, and the following year presented his first full collection menswear in Paris. By 1993 his reputation had strengthened further and he adapted his perfectly masculine aesthetic for the first Dirk Bikkembergs womenswear line, which proposed tailored capes and reefer jackets. In the years since, numerous additional lines and projects have been introduced, including the White Labels for men and women and the Red Label Bikkembergs Jeans collection in 2000. In the same year the designer also picked up the Moet et Chandon Esprit du Siècle award. In 2003, Bikkembergs became the official designer to Italian football giants Internationale, tightly trussing thighs with his unique translation of sportswear. Bikkembergs continues to infuse a physical energy into his clothes, a comforting muscle-bound heaviness, sharp detail, durability and a hard-nosed eroticism.

Die Arbeiten von Dirk Bikkembergs, einem der echten „Antwerp Six", sind die pure Muskelkraft. Er überträgt die Codes und Nuancen der Sportmode in einen absolut unverwechselbaren Stil, der irgendwo zwischen den Idealen von Stärke, Gesundheit und Dauerhaftigkeit liegt. 1959 in Deutschland geboren, machte der Designer 1982 seinen Abschluss an der Königlichen Akademie in Antwerpen und arbeitete danach für eine Vielzahl belgischer Modefirmen. 1985 erhielt er den angesehenen Golden Spindle Award als Best Young Designer. Der Sohn von Armeeangehörigen lässt in seinen Entwürfen von streng strukturierten Stücken und an Fetische erinnernden Lederdetails oft Bezüge zum Militär erkennen. Als er 1986 seine erste Herrenschuhkollektion lancierte, legte sich der Designer auf eine strikte Formel fest, zu der auch sein Markenzeichen – die Doppelnaht – gehört (seine Kleidung wirkt nicht nur robust, sondern ist tatsächlich extrem widerstandsfähig). 1987 präsentierte er seine Herrenmodelinie mit dem Schwerpunkt Strickwaren, ein Jahr später die erste komplette Herrenkollektion in

Paris. In den folgenden Jahren stieg sein Bekanntheitsgrad kontinuierlich, so dass er 1993 seine absolut männlich geprägte Ästhetik für die erste Dirk Bikkembergs Damenlinie adaptierte, die er mit streng geschnittenen Capes und Matrosenjacken vorstellte. Seither sind viele zusätzliche Linien und Projekte hinzu gekommen, darunter je ein White Label für Damen und Herren sowie die Red Label Bikkembergs Jeans Collection im Jahr 2000. Im selben Jahr wurde der Designer übrigens mit dem Preis Esprit du Siècle von Moët & Chandon ausgezeichnet. 2003 wurde Bikkembergs offizieller Designer eines italienischen Fußballclubs und kleidete stramme Fußballerbeine in seine unverwechselbare Interpretation von Sportswear. Nach wie vor transportiert Bikkembergs' physische Kraft in seine Kleidung, eine angenehme, muskelbepackte Schwere, exakte Details, Langlebigkeit und eine hartnäckige Erotik.

Membre des premiers «Antwerp Six», Dirk Bikkembergs présente un travail pour le moins musclé. Il traduit les codes et les nuances du sportswear en un style signature sévère qui réside quelque part entre les idées de force, de bonne santé et de longévité. Le créateur allemand (né en 1959) sort diplômé de l'Académie Royale d'Anvers en 1982, avant de travailler pour diverses maisons belges et de recevoir le prestigieux Golden Spindle du meilleur jeune créateur en 1985. Fils de parents militaires, Bikkembergs fait souvent référence à l'armée dans son travail, à travers des pièces très structurées et d'étranges détails en cuir au style légèrement fétichiste. En lançant sa première collection de chaussures pour homme en 1986, le styliste met au point une formule créative stricte qui inclut sa double piqûre caractéristique (ses vêtements ne se contentent pas de paraître robustes, ils le sont vraiment). En 1987, il présente une ligne pour homme articulée autour de la maille, puis lance dès l'année suivante sa première collection masculine complète à Paris. En 1993, sa réputation ne cesse de croître et il transpose son esthétique purement masculine dans la première ligne pour femme Dirk Bikkembergs, qui propose des capes et des cabans aux coupes sévères. Depuis, il a lancé de nombreuses lignes complémentaires et différents projets, notamment White Labels pour homme et pour femme, ainsi que la ligne de jeans Red Label Bikkembergs en l'an 2000. La même année, il remporte le prix Esprit du Siècle de Moët et Chandon. En 2003, Bikkembergs devient le couturier officiel de l'équipe nationale de football d'Italie, moulant les cuisses des joueurs de la Squadra Azzura avec sa traduction unique du sportswear. Bikkembergs continue à proposer des vêtements empreints d'énergie physique, d'une solidité musclée rassurante, de détails incisifs, d'une grande robustesse et d'un érotisme sans détour.

DAN JONES

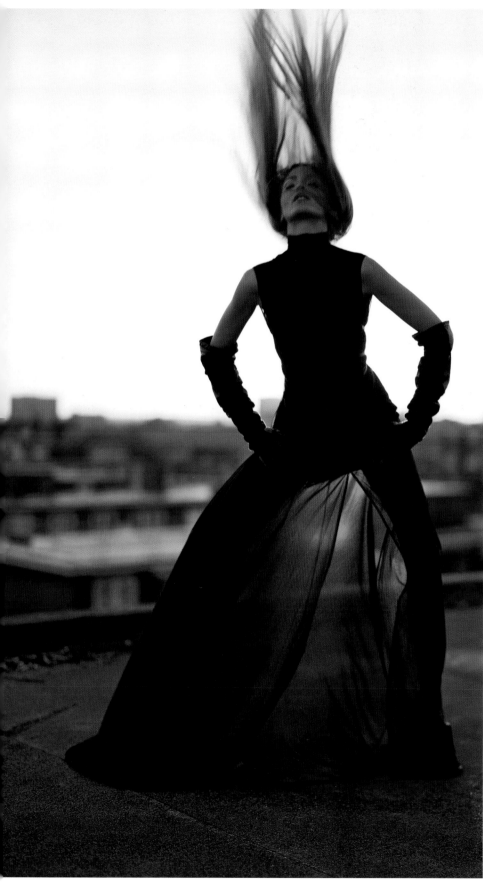

What are your signature designs? Rather than say a particular design I would say there is a common element running through all my work. My clothes express power, health, energy and sexiness **What is your favourite piece from any of our collections?** The project I am currently working on is a pair of real performance football boots. It will be the culmination of the marriage between fashion and sport. My football logo is also something that I am proud of because it distils the essence of what I want to express in my work: the energy and movement **How would you describe your work?** Very intense, very sexy, very healthy, very modern, very sporty. I feel I have been able to translate this energy in clothes and shoes that cover all aspects of modern life: from the smell of the football stadium over the hectic and cosmopolitan city life to sophisticated and exclusive nightlife **What's your ultimate goal?** To see a stunning goal in a World Cup final scored in a pair of Dirk Bikkembergs football boots **What inspires you?** Youth, health, sport, raw energy. The individual who pulls that all together for me is a football player. He is an expression of our times. He is an icon of the 21st century **Who do you have in mind when you design?** Ordinary men and women who share the same values I express in my work: health in mind and body **Who or what has been the greatest influence on your career?** Football… A few years ago I began to work with a young football player, for my fittings. He was an athlete without any particular interest in the fashion world. Yet he was so genuine in his reactions to how my clothes went on his body, that I could take it as a barometer as to how other young sporty guys would respond. Here I had in front of me a person who embodied the people I wanted to dress. **Which is more important in your work: the process or the product?** PROCESS. Because it is my life, and it is an expression of my philosophy **Is designing difficult for you, if so what drives you to continue?** No. Designing is not a job for me. It is a translation of the world I see around me, the means by which I re-interpret things. I could never stop **Have you ever been influenced or moved by the reaction to your designs?** No **What's your definition of beauty?** For me beauty is not a cold aesthetic value. I see beauty in persons whose way of being and physicality express: energy, vibrancy and health **What's the most important lesson you've learned?** Respect your instincts and follow your gut. Remain faithful to yourself.

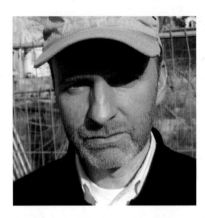

DIRK VAN SAENE

`"Beautify life!"`

The work of Dirk Van Saene (born 1959) defies definition. His unshakeable enthusiasm is applied to a constantly shifting signature style. Altering his approach to fashion with each collection, the designer disregards prevailing trends and submerges himself in one leftfield idea after another. After graduation from Antwerp's Royal Academy in 1981, Van Saene opened a small shop, Beauties And Heroes, selling his own homemade clothes; a bold move that won him the gold award at Belgium's Golden Spindle contest two years later. His professional life has been dominated by a close working relationship with Walter Van Beirendonck, the two often collaborating on projects and sharing shop space. In 1987 both designers were part of the 'Antwerp Six' presentation in London and, three years later, Van Saene staged his first show in Paris. Ever since, the designer has twisted and tweaked clever concepts for his runway presentations. For instance, he has allowed his audience a view of the fraught backstage area, with its hairdressers' chairs, make-up tables and weepy models (spring/summer 1998), or has handed out portable stereos to his models, each blaring out a different crackly song (spring/summer 2000). His designs switch from deconstruction to sharp refinement and back again. Van Saene has also drawn inspiration from the fine arts, citing the sculptor Louise Bourgeois and the work of Diane Arbus as starting points for collections. A fan of classic couture, Van Saene accepted the invitation to curate a Coco Chanel exhibition in Antwerp in 2001, part of the fashion project 'Mode 2001 Landed/Geland'.

Die Arbeiten des 1959 geborenen Dirk van Saene entziehen sich eigentlich jeglicher Definition. Nur sein unerschütterlicher Enthusiasmus ist an seinem sich ständig ändernden Stil abzulesen. Der Designer, der sich der Mode mit jeder seiner Kollektionen auf andere Weise nähert, ignoriert aktuelle Trends und widmet sich einer abseitigen Idee nach der anderen. Im Anschluss an sein Studium an der Königlichen Akademie von Antwerpen eröffnete er 1981 einen kleinen Laden namens Beauties and Heroes, wo er seine selbst genähten Kleidungsstücke verkaufte. Dieses gewagte Unternehmen brachte ihm zwei Jahre später den ersten Preis beim belgischen Wettbewerb Golden Spindle ein. Seine Karriere ist stark von der Zusammenarbeit mit Walter van Beirendonck geprägt; die beiden realisierten mehrere gemeinsame Projekte und teilten sich auch schon Verkaufsfläche. 1987 nahmen sie an der Präsentation der „Antwerp Six" in London teil, drei Jahre später stellte van Saene seine erste Schau in Paris auf die Beine.

Schon immer hat sich der Designer kluge Konzepte für seine Laufsteg-Präsentationen ausgedacht. So gewährte er beispielsweise einmal dem Publikum freie Sicht hinter die Kulissen – mit Friseurstühlen, Schminktischen und zickigen Models (Frühjahr/Sommer 1998). Oder er drückte seinen Models tragbare Stereoanlagen in die Hand, die alle verschiedene Songs quäkten (Frühjahr/Sommer 2000). Seine Entwürfe oszillieren zwischen Dekonstruktion und höchster Raffinesse. Van Saene holte sich auch schon Anregungen bei der bildenden Kunst, etwa als er die Bildhauerin Louise Bourgeois oder das Werk von Diane Arbus zitierte und zum Ausgangspunkt seiner Kollektionen machte. Als Verehrer der klassischen Couture nahm van Saene das Angebot, 2001 in Antwerpen eine Ausstellung über Coco Chanel als Kurator zu betreuen, gerne an. Die Veranstaltung war Teil des Modeprojekts „Mode 2001 Landed/Geland".

Le travail de Dirk Van Saene (né en 1959) défie toute définition. Il applique son indéfectible enthousiasme à un style signature sans cesse changeant. Modifiant son approche de la mode à chaque nouvelle collection, le créateur ignore les tendances dominantes et préfère toujours aller à contre-courant. Diplômé de l'Académie Royale d'Anvers en 1981, Van Saene ouvre une petite boutique, Beauties And Heroes, dans laquelle il vend les vêtements qu'il confectionne chez lui : une initiative audacieuse qui lui vaudra le premier prix du concours belge des Golden Spindle deux ans plus tard. Sa carrière professionnelle est marquée par son étroite relation avec Walter Van Beirendonck, avec lequel il partage un espace de vente et collabore à divers projets. En 1987, les deux stylistes participent à la présentation londonienne des « Antwerp Six » et trois ans plus tard, Van Saene organise son premier défilé à Paris. Depuis, il épice tous ses défilés d'idées astucieuses : par exemple, il présente à son public les coulisses du podium, avec leur atmosphère tendue, leurs fauteuils de coiffeur, leurs tables de maquillage et leurs mannequins éplorés (printemps/été 1998), ou distribue des postes de radio grésillants à ses mannequins, chacun diffusant une chanson différente (printemps/été 2000). Ses créations ne cessent de faire l'aller-retour entre déconstruction et raffinement haute couture. Van Saene s'inspire également des beaux-arts, citant notamment le sculpteur Louise Bourgeois et le travail de Diane Arbus comme les points de départ de certaines collections. Grand fan de la haute couture classique, Van Saene a été invité à organiser une exposition Coco Chanel à Anvers en 2001 dans le cadre du projet « Mode 2001 Landed/Geland ». PETER DE POTTER

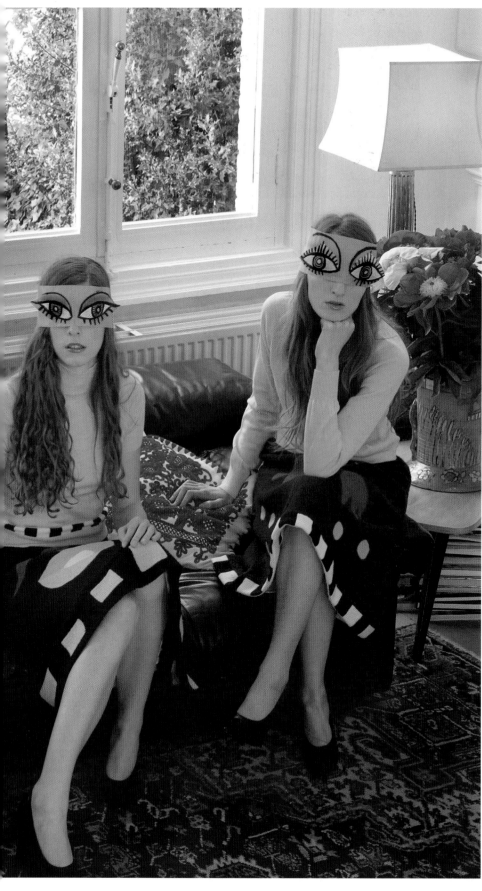

What are your signature designs? The whole collection of spring/summer 2005! Check it out! **How would you describe your work?** Always stronger and better! **What's your ultimate goal?** Forget the hype! Now I want to be famous for my looks! **What inspires you?** A documentary from 1972 about a mother and her daughter Edie, living in what used to be a very chic house but is now completely run down. They are members of the Bouvier family. Edie is everything that inspires me: eccentric, always wearing scarves very tight around her head and fastened with expensive jewellery, dancing like a ballerina between the garbage. Always complaining she had to give up her ballet career in order to take care of her tyrannical mother! And singing with a voice that is incomparable! **Can fashion still have a political ambition?** I am always sceptical about designers (ab)using political statements in order to promote their product **Is the idea of creative collaboration important to you?** Every collaboration is important, as long as it is creative **Who has been the greatest influence on your career?** I have the feeling my career has not started yet! **How have your own experiences affected your work as a designer?** All experiences, good and bad, influence my way of thinking. It's obvious this reflects also in my work **Is designing difficult for you, if so, what drives you to continue?** The designing part is the easiest. Everything else is difficult **Have you ever been influenced or moved by the reaction to your designs?** I am always moved by reactions, positive or negative, to my designs **What's your definition of beauty?** Beauty equals originality, honesty, intelligence **What's your philosophy?** Beautify life! **What is the most important lesson you've learned?** We're all equal.

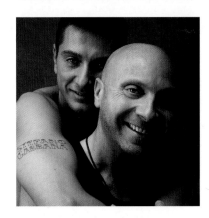

DOLCE & GABBANA

"We are both creative, both in a different way.
We complete each other"

Dolce & Gabbana are fashion's answer to Viagra: the full throbbing force of Italian style. The winning combination of Dolce's tailoring perfectionism and Gabbana's stylistic theatrics has made the label a powerhouse in today's celebrity-obsessed age and just as influential as the ambassadors of sport, music and film that they dress. Domenico Dolce was born in 1958 to a Sicilian family, his father a tailor from Palermo who taught him to make a jacket by the age of seven. Stefano Gabbana was born in 1962, the son of a Milanese print worker. But it was Sicily, Dolce's birthplace and Gabbana's favourite childhood holiday destination, that sealed a bond between them when they first met, and which has provided a reference for their aesthetic signatures ever since: the traditional Sicilian girl (opaque black stockings, black lace, peasant skirts, shawl fringing), the Latin sex temptress (corsetry, high heels, underwear as outerwear), and the Sicilian gangster (pinstripe suits, slick tailoring, fedoras). And it is the friction between these polar opposites – masculine/feminine, soft/hard and innocence/corruption – that makes Dolce & Gabbana so exciting. Established in 1985, the label continues to pay homage to such Italian film legends as Fellini, Visconti, Rossellini, Anna Magnani and Sophia Loren; in glossy art books, Dolce & Gabbana documents its own contribution to today's legends of film ('Hollywood'), music ('Music') and football ('Calcio'). With an empire that includes the younger D&G line, childrenswear, swimwear, underwear, eyewear, fragrance (eight in total), watches, accessories and a global distribution through their own boutiques, Dolce & Gabbana are, quite simply, fashion's Italian stallions.

Dolce & Gabbana sind quasi die Antwort der Mode auf Viagra: die ganze pulsierende Kraft italienischer Eleganz. Die gewinnbringende Kombination aus Dolces Schneiderkunst in Perfektion und Gabbanas stilvoller Theatralik verliehen dem Label in unserer promibesessenen Zeit denselben Einfluss wie den Vertretern aus Sport, Musik und Film, die sich in D&G kleiden. Domenico Dolce wurde 1958 auf Sizilien geboren. Schon im Alter von sieben Jahren lehrte ihn sein Vater, ein Schneider aus Palermo, ein Jackett zu nähen. Der 1962 geborene Stefano Gabbana ist der Sohn eines Mailänder Setzers. Es war jedoch Sizilien, wo Dolce geboren wurde und Gabbana als Kind seine schönsten Ferien verbrachte, das die beiden von Anfang an verband. Die ästhetischen Markenzeichen der beiden haben seit jeher hier ihre Ursprünge: bei den traditionell streng erzogenen sizilianischen Mädchen (mit blickdichten schwarzen Strümpfen, schwarzer Spitze, Bauernröcken und Fransentüchern), beim Latino-Vamp (in Corsage, High Heels und gut sichtbar getragenen Dessous) und dem sizilianischen Gang-

ster (in schick geschnittenem Nadelstreifenanzug und weichem Filzhut). Es sind die Brüche zwischen diesen extremen Gegensätzen – maskulin/feminin, weich/hart, unschuldig/korrupt –, die Dolce & Gabbana so aufregend machen. Das 1985 gegründete Label zollt zum einen italienischen Filmlegenden wie Fellini, Visconti, Rossellini, Anna Magnani und Sophia Loren Tribut und dokumentiert zum anderen in Hochglanz-Kunstbänden seinen eigenen Beitrag zu Legenden des Films („Hollywood"), der Musik („Music") und des Fußballs („Calcio"). Mit ihrem Firmenimperium, das inzwischen die jugendlichere D&G-Linie, Kindermode, Bademode, Dessous, Brillen, Düfte (bislang acht), Uhren, Accessoires und ein globales Vertriebsnetz über eigene Läden umfasst, sind Dolce & Gabbana schlichtweg die typischen italienischen Machos der Modebranche.

Cœur palpitant du style italien, Dolce & Gabbana sont la réponse de la mode au Viagra. La combinaison gagnante formée par le perfectionnisme de Dolce et le cabotinage de Gabbana a imposé la griffe comme un incontournable de notre époque obsédée par la célébrité, comme une marque aussi influente que les ambassadeurs du sport, de la musique et du cinéma qu'elle habille. Domenico Dolce est né en 1958 dans une famille sicilienne ; son père, tailleur à Palerme, lui apprend à faire une veste alors qu'il n'a que sept ans. Stefano Gabbana est né en 1962, fils d'un ouvrier d'imprimerie milanais. Patrie de Dolce et destination de vacances favorite de Gabbana lorsqu'il était enfant, c'est la Sicile qui scelle leur relation dès la première rencontre, une référence qui transparaît continuellement dans leur esthétique : la fille sicilienne traditionnelle (bas noirs opaques, dentelle noire, jupes de paysanne, franges « châle »), la séductrice latine (corseterie, talons hauts, sous-vêtements portés en vêtements du dessus) et le gangster sicilien (costumes mille-raies, coupes élégantes, chapeaux mous). Ce sont ces oppositions de masculin et de féminin, de douceur et de dureté, d'innocence et de corruption qui rendent les créations de Dolce & Gabbana si fascinantes. Créée en 1985, la griffe continue de rendre hommage aux légendes du cinéma italien telles que Fellini, Visconti, Rossellini, Anna Magnani et Sophia Loren ; dans de superbes livres d'art, elle documente aussi sa propre contribution aux mondes du cinéma (« Hollywood »), de la musique (« Music ») et du football (« Calcio »). Avec un empire incluant la ligne plus jeune D&G, une collection pour enfant, des maillots de bain, de la lingerie, des lunettes, des parfums (huit en tout), des montres et des accessoires, mais aussi un réseau de distribution mondial composé de nombreuses boutiques indépendantes, Dolce & Gabbana restent, tout simplement, de vrais machos italiens.

JAMIE HUCKBODY

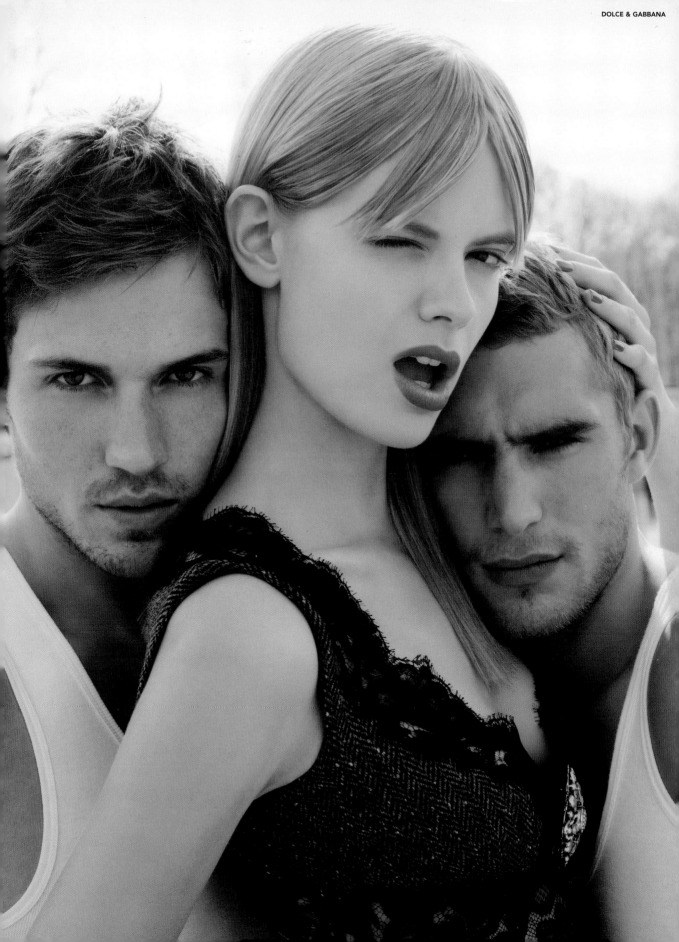

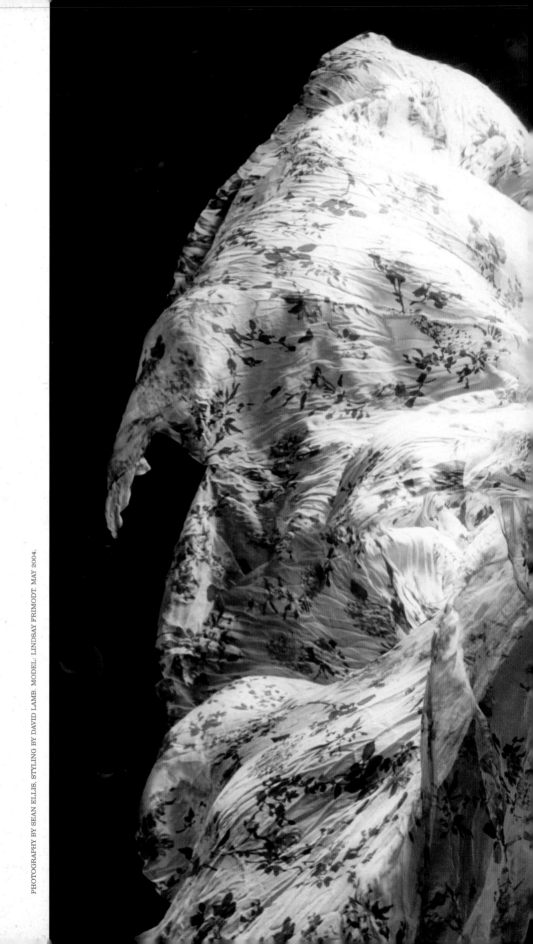

PHOTOGRAPHY BY SEAN ELLIS. STYLING BY DAVID LAMB. MODEL: LINDSAY FRIMODT. MAY 2004.

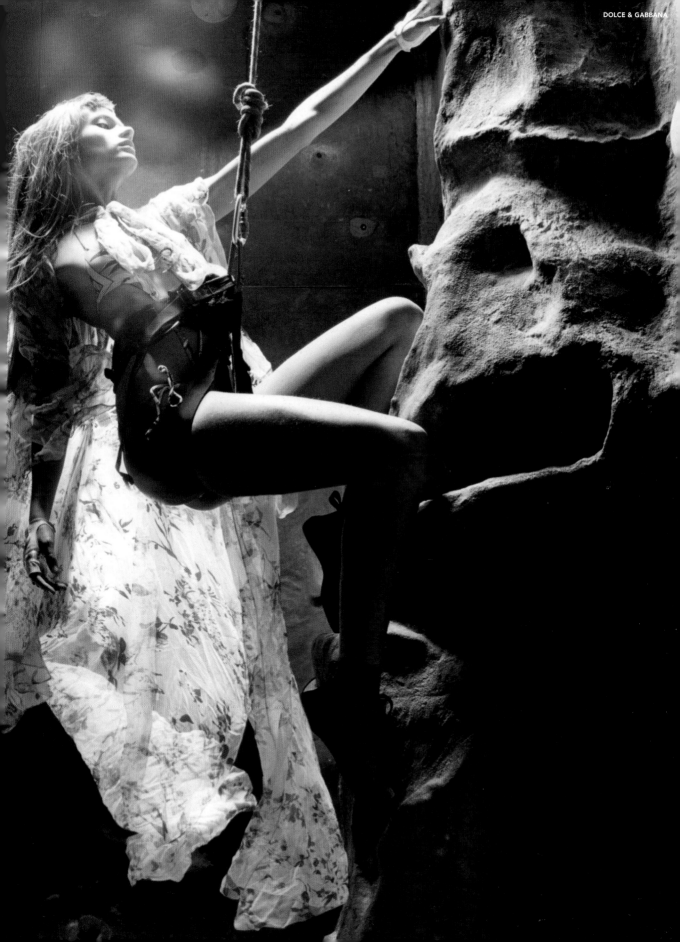

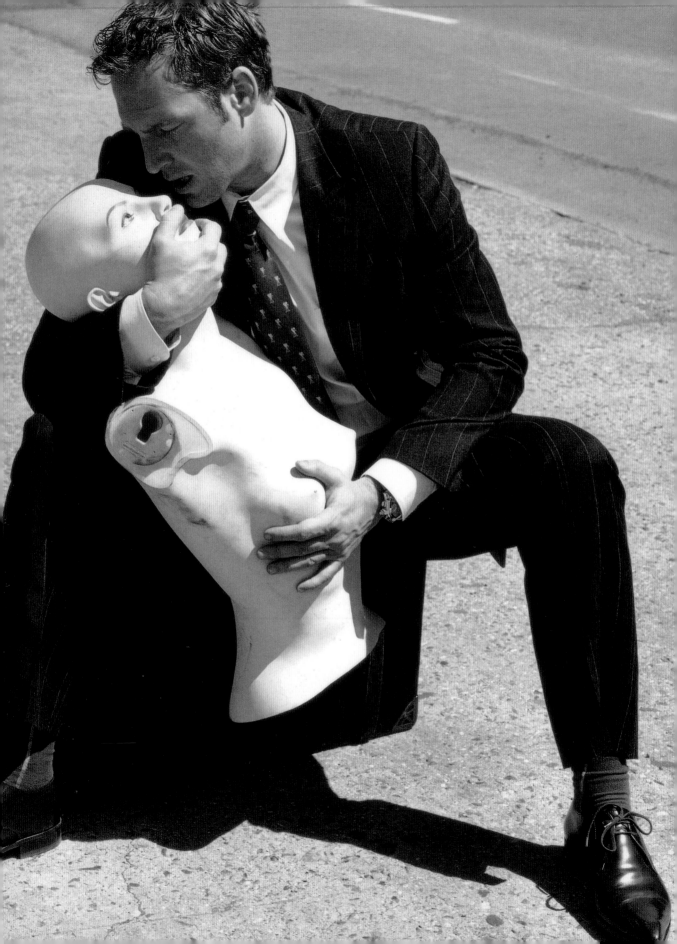

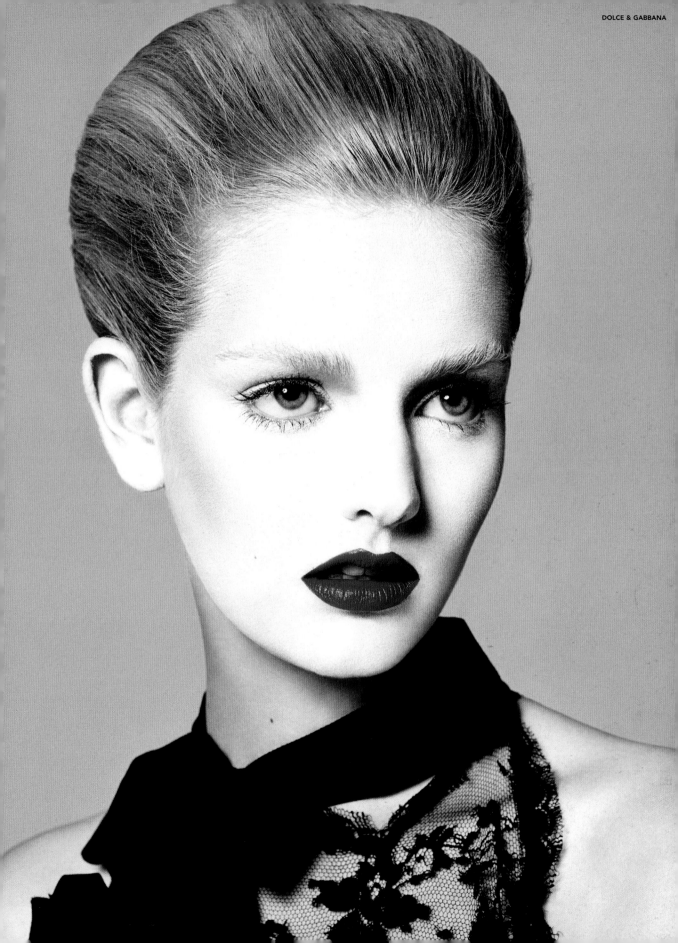

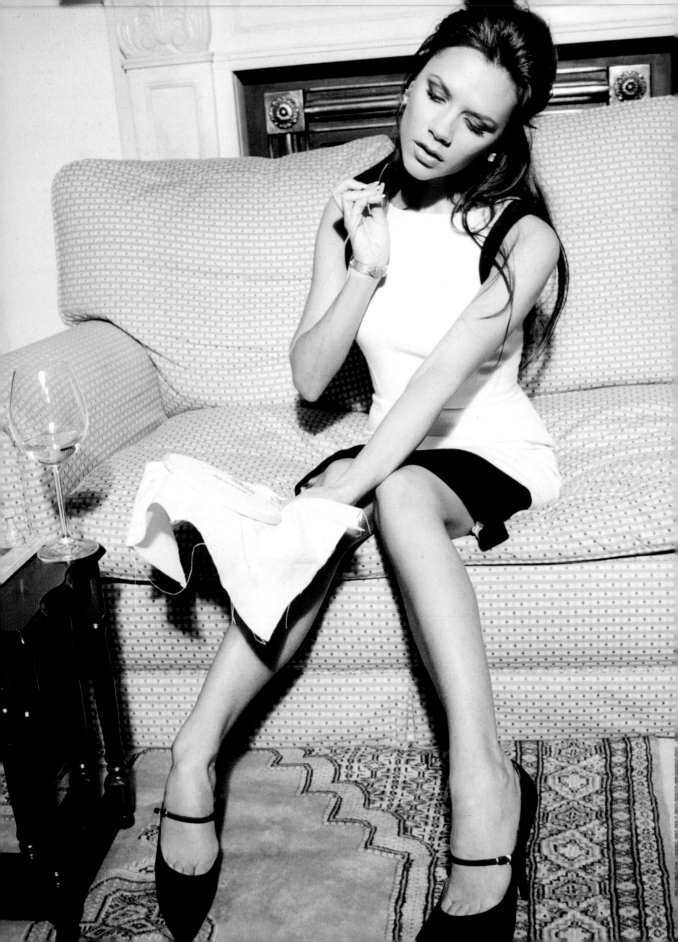

What are your signature designs? Guépière dresses, pinstripe suits, Sicilian caps, tank tops **What are your favourite pieces from any of your collections?** The above-mentioned because they are classic, signature pieces that we love and that we like to show again and again, reinterpreting them according to the spirit of each collection **How would you describe your work?** Our job is the most beautiful one in the world! It is very exciting, never boring, and allows us to express our creativity and experiment **What's your ultimate goal?** As far as our private life is concerned, our goal is happiness, always and everywhere! As far as our work, to create a style that will remain throughout the years and that will be remembered **What inspires you?** We are inspired by everyday life, by the world and by the people that surround us. Besides that, there are key elements that are our constant and continuous sources of inspiration (and that represent our identity and our roots); that is to say, the Mediterranean, Sicily, black and white, and the films of Italian neo-realism. But we are also inspired by opposites that attract each other, by contrasts, by music and cinema **Can fashion still have a political ambition?** Fashion is one of the expressions of the time we live in and of all changes that happen. It can have a specific position and make statements, but for us it is essentially a way of expressing creativity **What do you have in mind when you design?** When we sketch an outfit, we are at the end of an elaborate process because the sketch is the result of many conversations between the two of us, of many deep thoughts, of many notes that we have taken, of many different experiences that we have put together. When we design we think about all these different things and about all that has led us to achieve that specific outfit **Is the idea of creative collaboration important to you?** For us it is the essence of our work. We are both creative, both in a different way because we complete each other. To have different opinions is important because it is a challenge **Who has been the greatest influence on your career?** For sure Madonna, who has been our muse and icon because of her strong personality **How have your own experiences affected your work as designers?** Our work is part of ourselves – our life. We reflect in the clothes we design all of our personal feelings **Which is more important in your work: the process or the product?** They are both important. However, the final product gives more satisfaction because when you see it, you forget all the efforts you've made to achieve it! **Is designing difficult for you?** We love our work – it is our passion, our life. To design clothes is a joy for us, it is a continuous challenge but, at the same time, it allows us to express ourselves. We are lucky to be in a privileged position; that is to say, our creations have a worldwide exposure and our message is accessible to a lot of people. This is a great support and it pushes us to go on, always and in the best possible way **Have you ever been influenced or moved by the reaction to your designs?** Of course we have, be these reactions positive or negative. If you listen to people's reactions you are challenged and led to think **What's your definition of beauty?** Beauty is something you have inside. Beauty is life. Beauty is love **What's your philosophy?** To always be ourselves and consistent **What is the most important lesson you've learned?** That you always have to be yourself, without betraying your personality and without losing your identity.

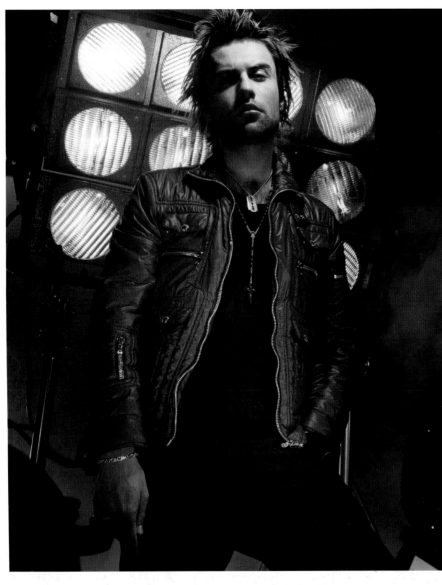

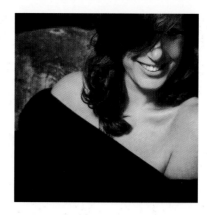

DONNA KARAN

*"I never see one woman when I design,
it's always a universe of women"*

While she was still a student at the Parsons School of Design in New York, Long Island native Donna Karan was offered a summer job assisting Anne Klein. After three years as associate designer, Karan was named as Klein's successor and, following her mentor's death in 1974, Karan became head of the company. After a decade at Anne Klein, where she established a reputation for practical luxury sportswear separates, typically in stretch fabrics and dark hues, Karan founded her own company in 1984 with her late husband, Stephan Weiss. A year later, her highly acclaimed Donna Karan New York Collection, based around the concept of 'seven easy pieces', unveiled the bodysuit that was to become her trademark. Karan's emphasis on simple yet sophisticated designs, including everything from wrap skirts to corseted eveningwear, captured the popular mood of 'body consciousness' that swept Hollywood in the '80s. By 1989, she had expanded this philosophy to the street-smart diffusion line DKNY. In 1992, inspired by the desire to dress her husband, a menswear line was launched. Since then, Donna Karan International has continued to diversify and expand to cover every age and lifestyle, including a children's range, eyewear, fragrances and home furnishings. She has been honoured with an unprecedented seven CFDA awards, including 2004's Lifetime Achievement Award to coincide with her 20th anniversary. The company became a publicly-traded enterprise in 1996 and was acquired by French luxury conglomerate LVMH in 2001 for a reported 643 million US-$. Karan remains the chief designer.

Noch während ihres Studiums an der New Yorker Parsons School of Design bekam die aus Long Island stammenden Donna Karan ein Ferienjob als Assistentin von Anne Klein angeboten. Nach drei Jahren als Associate Designer wurde sie schließlich Kleins Nachfolgerin und übernahm nach dem Tod ihrer Mentorin 1974 die Firmenleitung. Nach einem Jahrzehnt bei Anne Klein, in dem sie den Ruf des Modehauses als erste Adresse für praktische, aber zugleich luxuriöse Sportswear-Separates – üblicherweise aus Stretchmaterialien und in dunklen Farbtönen – etabliert hatte, erfolgte 1984 die Gründung der eigenen Firma, zusammen mit Stephan Weiss, ihrem späteren Ehemann. Ein Jahr später wurde die viel gelobte Donna Karan New York Collection präsentiert, die auf dem Konzept von „sieben einfachen Teilen" basierte. Dazu zählte auch der schwarze Body, der ihr Markenzeichen werden sollte. Karans Faible für schlichte und doch raffinierte Entwürfe, egal ob Wickelröcke oder Abendkleider mit Corsage, entsprach ganz dem Trend zu mehr Körperbewusstsein, der im Hollywood

der 1980er Jahre so verbreitet war. 1989 wandte Karan diese Philosophie auch auf die street-smarte Nebenlinie DKNY an. Inspiriert von dem Wunsch, den eigenen Mann einzukleiden, entstand 1992 eine Linie für Herrenmode. Seit damals diversifiziert und expandiert Donna Karan International weiter und bedient inzwischen jedes Alter und diverse Lebensstile, u. a. mit Kindermode, Brillen, Düften und Wohnaccessoires. Bislang unerreicht sind ihre sieben Auszeichnungen durch die CFDA, darunter 2004 ein Lifetime Achievement Award, der mit ihrem zwanzigjährigen Berufsjubiläum zusammenfiel. Zum börsennotierten Unternehmen wurde die Firma 1996. Im Jahr 2001 kaufte sie schließlich der französische Luxuswarenkonzern LVMH für angeblich 643 Millionen Dollar auf. Karan blieb allerdings Chefdesignerin.

Alors qu'elle est encore étudiante à la Parsons School of Design de New York, la jeune Donna Karan originaire de Long Island se voit proposer un job d'été comme assistante d'Anne Klein. Après trois années au poste de styliste associée, elle est nommée à la succession d'Anne Klein et, à la mort de son mentor en 1974, reprend la direction de l'entreprise. Après une décennie passée chez Anne Klein, où elle se forge une solide réputation en créant des séparés sportswear luxueux et faciles à porter généralement coupés dans des tissus stretch aux couleurs sombres, Donna Karan fonde sa propre griffe en 1984 avec son mari Stephan Weiss, aujourd'hui décédé. Un an plus tard, sa collection à succès Donna Karan New York articulée autour du concept des « seven easy pieces » dévoile le bodysuit qui devait devenir sa signature. Sa prédilection pour les pièces simples mais sophistiquées, de la jupe portefeuille aux tenues de soirée corsetées, capture tout l'esprit de la tendance au « body consciousness » qui déferle sur Hollywood dans les années 80. En 1989, elle étend cette philosophie à sa ligne de diffusion DKNY. Inspirée par l'envie d'habiller son mari, elle lance une ligne pour homme en 1992. Depuis, la société Donna Karan International ne cesse de se diversifier et de se développer pour couvrir toutes les tranches d'âge et différents modes de vie, notamment avec une gamme pour enfant, des lunettes, des parfums et des meubles. Elle a reçu sept prix du CFDA, un record sans précédent, notamment un Lifetime Achievement Award couronnant sa carrière en 2004, une année où elle célèbre également le 20ᵉ anniversaire de sa société. Bien que Donna Karan reste à la direction de la création, son entreprise, introduite en bourse en 1996, a été rachetée par le groupe de luxe français LVMH en 2001 pour un montant estimé à 643 millions de dollars.

MARK HOOPER

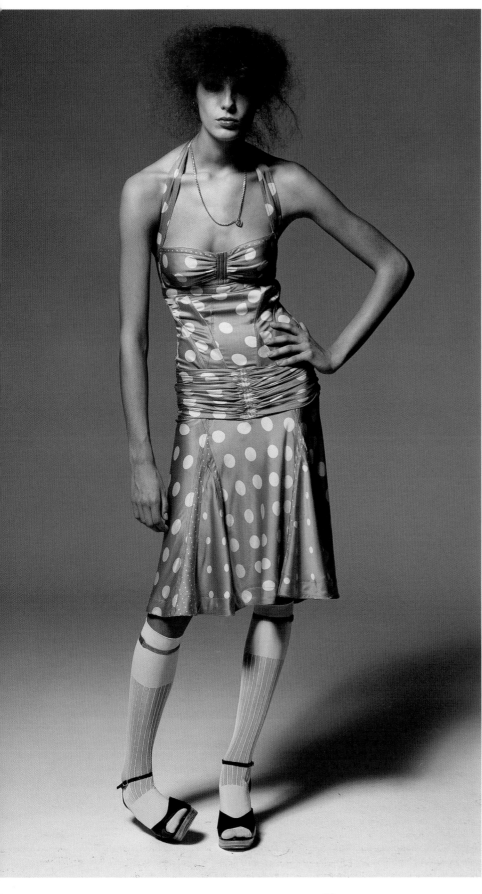

What are your signature pieces? My seven easy pieces wardrobe. It's a simple, sophisticated system of dressing that takes a woman from day into evening, weekday to weekend **How would you describe your work?** Sensual, urban and body conscious **What's your ultimate goal?** Professionally, it's always what I haven't done that excites me. But my ultimate goal in life is to find peace and happiness **What inspires you?** Any and everything. Passion. Sensuality. Nature – the textures of the beach, the melding colours of water, the electricity of the night. **Can fashion still have a political ambition?** Absolutely. When you're creating something, you must be sensitive to what people want and the times they live in. However innovative it is, what you create must be relevant and reflect the here and now **Who do you have in mind when you design?** I never see one woman when I design, it's always a universe of women. Strong passionate women, women who are true to themselves and their visions. I see clothes as a canvas to their individuality. The woman is the first thing you see, not the clothes **Is the idea of creative collaboration important to you?** You are only as good as the people behind you. It can't be done alone. **Who has been the greatest influence on your career?** Anne Klein – her passing pushed me into becoming a designer. It wasn't something I was sure I wanted to do **How have your own experiences affected your work as a designer?** My own personal needs – what works and doesn't work – affect my work. The fact that I'm a woman and, like all women, want to be taller, thinner and look sophisticated without a lot of effort. Everything I create works to that end **Which is more important in your work: the process or the product?** When all becomes one. When the product fulfils the dream of inspiration **Is designing difficult for you and, if so, what drives you to continue?** The challenge of creation. I try to stay open to new things. To live is to move forward, to discover new means of expression **Have you ever been influenced or moved by the reaction to your designs?** Yes – I have to think twice about the way people react. People's reactions can motivate me to another level. **What's your definition of beauty?** Beauty is about individuality. There is nothing more attractive than a woman who values her uniqueness. She has the confidence to express herself, to say something new, to create from within **What's your philosophy?** Never stop challenging yourself. When I design, I'm always looking for a balance between purpose and expression **What is the most important lesson you've learned?** No matter how bad or good it is, it will always change. Everything is in constant motion.

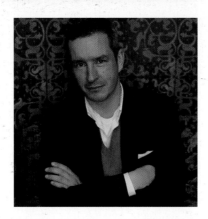

DRIES VAN NOTEN

"I aim to create fashion that is neutral in such a way
that each person can add his or her own personality to it"

Dries Van Noten's culturally diverse style has made him one of the most successful of the 'Antwerp Six' designers who arrived at the London collections back in March 1986. His signature full skirts, soft jackets and scarves are embroidered or beaded using the traditional folkloric techniques of India, Morocco or Eastern Europe – whichever far-flung culture has caught his attention that season. Born in Antwerp, Belgium, in 1958 to a family of fashion retailers and tailors, Van Noten enrolled at the city's Royal Academy in 1975; to support his studies, he worked both as a freelance designer for various commercial fashion companies and as a buyer for his father's boutiques. Following the legendary group show in London, Van Noten sold a small selection of men's shirts to Barneys in New York and Whistles in London; these stores then requested that he make smaller sizes, for women. In the same year, Van Noten opened his own tiny shop in Antwerp, subsequently replaced by the larger Het Modepaleis in 1989. In 1991, he showed his menswear collection in Paris for the first time; a womenswear line followed in 1993. Van Noten is perhaps the most accessible of the Belgian designers, but his theory of fashion is far from conventional. He prefers to design collections 'item by item', offering his clients a sense of individuality, rather than slavishly creating a collection around one silhouette or a single theme. In 2004 he celebrated his fiftieth fashion show with a dinner in Paris where models walked along dining tables wearing his spring/summer 2005 collection; the anniversary was also marked with the publication of a book, Dries Van Noten 01-50. He now has three stores and around 500 outlets worldwide, and continues to live and work in his hometown of Antwerp.

Dries van Notens multikultureller Stil hat ihn zu einem der erfolgreichsten Designer der „Antwerp Six" gemacht, die erstmals bei den Londoner Kollektionen 1986 in Erscheinung traten. Seine Markenzeichen sind lange Röcke, weiche Jacken und Schals, oft bestickt oder perlenverziert mit den traditionellen volkstümlichen Techniken Indiens, Marokkos oder Osteuropas – je nachdem, welches Land in der jeweiligen Saison seine Aufmerksamkeit besonders gefesselt hat. 1958 wurde van Noten im belgischen Antwerpen in eine Familie geboren, die vom Einzelhandel mit Mode und von der Schneiderei lebte. Die Ausbildung an der Königlichen Akademie seiner Heimatstadt begann er 1975. Um sich sein Studium zu finanzieren, arbeitete er zum einen als selbstständiger Designer für verschiedene kommerziell ausgerichtete Modefirmen, zum anderen als Einkäufer für die Läden seines Vaters. Nach der legendären gemeinsamen Modenschau in London verkaufte van Noten eine kleine Auswahl von Herrenhemden an Barneys, New York, und Whistles, London. Genau diese Läden verlangten bald Hemden in kleineren Größen – für Damen. Noch im selben Jahr eröffnete van Noten auch ein winziges eigenes Geschäft in Antwerpen, aus dem er dann 1989 in Het

Modepaleis – bis heute der Dries van Noten Flagship Store – umzog. 1991 präsentierte er erstmals eine Herrenkollektion in Paris; die Damenlinie folgte 1993. Obwohl sein Verständnis von Mode alles andere als konventionell ist, gelten van Notens Kreationen als die tragbarsten aller belgischen Designer. Er zieht es vor, seine Kollektionen „Stück für Stück" zu kreieren, was seinen Kunden mehr Raum für Individualität lässt, anstatt sklavisch um eine Silhouette oder ein einziges Thema herum zu entwerfen. Im Jahr 2004 feierte der Designer seine fünfzigste Modenschau mit einem Diner in Paris, bei dem die Models in seiner Kollektion Frühjahr/Sommer 2005 über die Tische flanierten. Aus Anlass dieses Jubiläums kam auch das Buch „Dries Van Noten 01–50" heraus. Inzwischen besitzt der Modeschöpfer drei Läden und etwa 500 Outlets in aller Welt. Er lebt und arbeitet jedoch weiterhin in seiner Heimatstadt Antwerpen.

Parmi les jeunes créateurs du «Antwerp Six» qui ont débarqué aux collections de Londres en mars 1986, Dries Van Noten, grâce à son style culturellement éclectique, est l'un de ceux qui ont rencontré le plus de succès. Selon la culture lointaine qui l'inspire pour la saison, il brode et perle ses jupes amples, ses vestes souples et ses écharpes inimitables à l'aide de techniques folkloriques traditionnelles venues d'Inde, du Maroc ou d'Europe de l'Est. Né en 1958 à Anvers dans une famille de tailleurs et de commerçants spécialisés dans l'habillement, Van Noten entre à l'Académie Royale de la ville en 1975; pour financer ses études, il travaille à la fois comme créateur free-lance pour diverses griffes commerciales et comme acheteur pour les boutiques de son père. A l'issue du défilé londonien légendaire des Six d'Anvers, Van Noten vend une petite collection de chemises pour homme au grand magasin Barneys de New York et à Whistles à Londres; les deux lui demanderont ensuite de fabriquer des tailles plus petites, pour les femmes. La même année, Van Noten ouvre une minuscule boutique à Anvers, remplacée en 1989 par le plus important Het Modepaleis, qui reste aujourd'hui sa boutique phare. En 1991, il présente pour la première fois sa collection pour homme à Paris, suivie d'une ligne pour femme en 1993. Van Noten est sans doute le plus accessible des créateurs belges, mais sa théorie de la mode n'a pourtant rien de conventionnel. Pour offrir à ses clients un certain sens de l'individualité, il préfère dessiner ses collections «pièce par pièce» plutôt que de concevoir servilement ses lignes autour d'une seule silhouette ou d'un même thème. En 2004, il célèbre son cinquantième défilé lors d'un dîner parisien où les mannequins paradent sur les tables, vêtues de sa collection printemps/été 2005; cet anniversaire est également marqué par la sortie d'un livre, «Dries Van Noten 01–50». Bien qu'il possède aujourd'hui trois boutiques et compte près de 500 points de vente à travers le monde, Van Noten vit et travaille toujours dans sa villé natale d'Anvers.

SUSIE RUSHTON

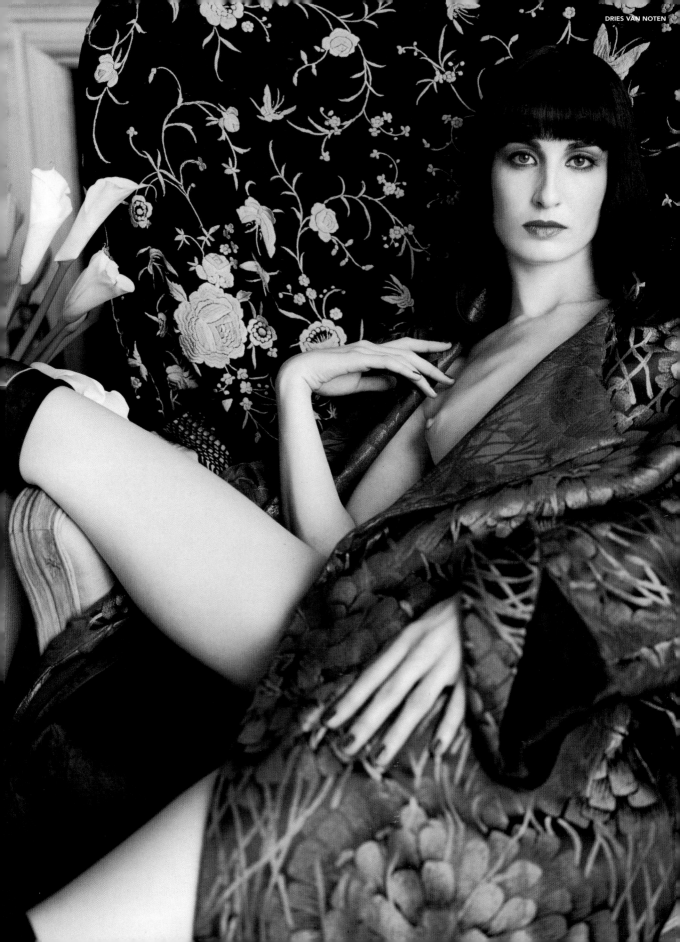

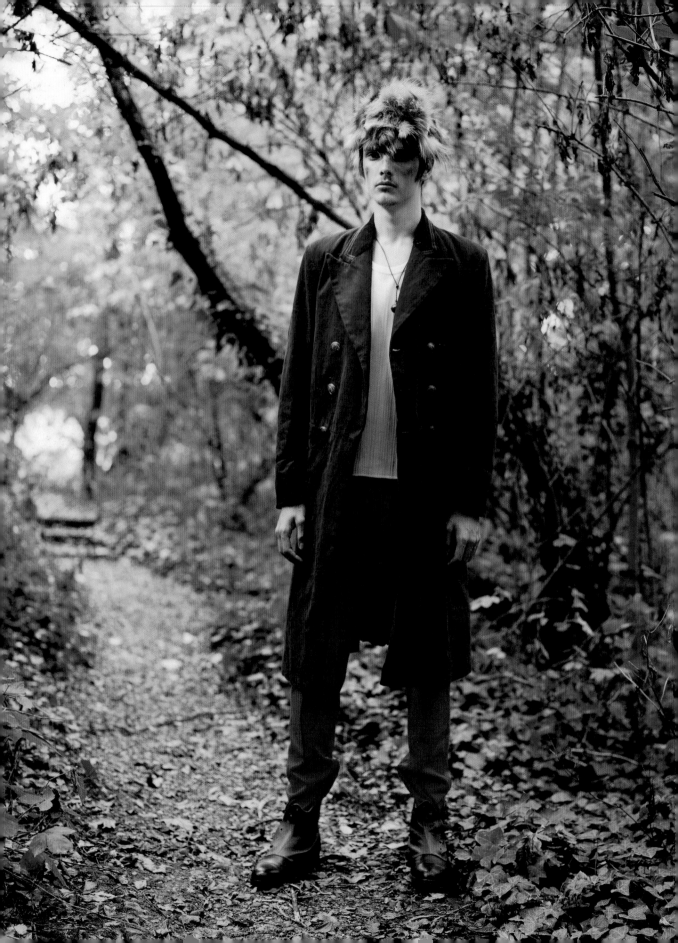

What are your signature designs? Prints, colours and fabrics converging in good designs **What is your favourite piece from any of your collections?** My favourite pieces are those that I can associate with personal memories or people, ranging from a simple T-shirt to a very elaborate piece **How would you describe your work?** I start from the fabrics and I aim to create fashion that is neutral in such a way that each person can add his or her own personality to it. It's about fashion that doesn't overwhelm your own personality **What's your ultimate goal?** To create beautiful things **What inspires you?** Everything that surrounds me. This can be a flower, a painting or a human being **Can fashion still have a political ambition?** The atmosphere of a collection often reflects what's going on around you. I believe you can manifest yourself and express your ideas through the way you dress, but after all, it remains just clothes **Who do you have in mind when you design?** I don't have some mental image of a Dries Van Noten man or woman. What's in my mind is the individual garment I'm working on, but I also wonder how people are going to wear it or combine it with other garments. Because finally, you create fashion not for the catwalk, but to be worn **Is the idea of creative collaboration important to you?** Creativity is at its best when it's an interaction between different people **Who has been the greatest influence on your career?** All that I do now is a result of my education and of people sharing with me the things they love **How have your own experiences affected your work as a designer?** It's difficult, if not impossible, to separate my private and professional lives. My work is obviously influenced and inspired by the constant interplay between both **Which is more important in your work: the process or the product?** The product, that's what people get to see. But I enjoy the process more **Is designing difficult for you, if so, what drives you to continue?** It's not difficult, as long as it's not limited to working on the collections only. It's the mixture of different elements that drives me, ranging from the business aspect to the design process and the artistic input **Have you ever been influenced or moved by the reaction to your designs?** You have to take into account the reactions to your work. Sometimes, I have been stimulated more by negative reactions. Paradoxically enough, these can give you a hint that you're moving on in the right direction **What's your definition of beauty?** Beauty is a most personal thing **What's you philosophy?** Enjoy your life, fashion is not that important **What's the most important lesson you've learned?** Fashion is not so important.

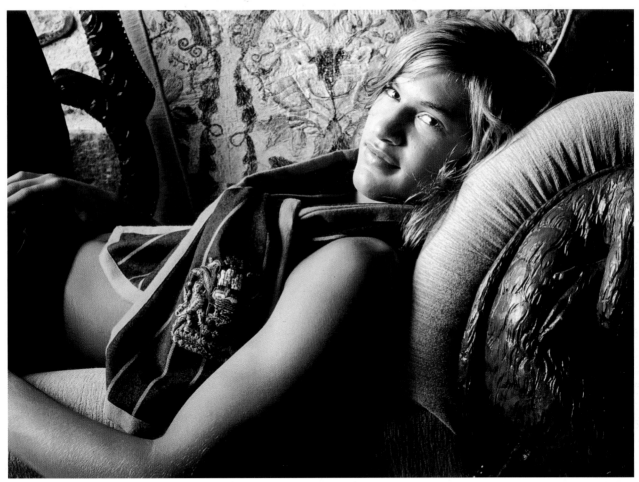

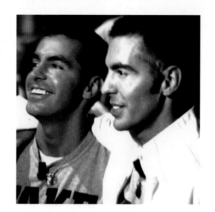

DSQUARED

"We're inspired by things that are normally not fashionable"

DEAN & DAN CATEN

Dean and Dan Caten of Dsquared know a thing or two about mixing and matching. Not only did the 40-year-old identical twins leave their native Canada in 1991 for Italy, the homeland of their paternal grandmother (Caten is short for Catenacci, while the maternal side is English), they've managed to turn the fashion world on its head with a ballsy blend of American pop culture and superior Italian tailoring. The Milan debut of their men's line in 1994 garnered fans such as Lenny Kravitz, Justin Timberlake and Ricky Martin for its cheeky, MTV-ready ebullience paired with precision craftsmanship. Soon thereafter, the duo further solidified their fashion credibility by creating the costumes for Madonna's 'Don't Tell Me' video and the cowboy segment of her 2002 Drowned World tour, as well as the outfits for Christina Aguilera's 2003 Stripped tour (the diminutive diva was later recruited to walk the catwalk for the spring/summer 2005 men's collection). The launch of a women's line in 2003 saw supermodels Naomi Campbell, Eva Herzigova, Karolina Kurkova and Fernanda Tavares saunter out of a pink private jet in unapologetically sex-charged regalia. For autumn/winter 2005, the brothers, who spent their childhoods as born-again Christians, looked to a higher power with skinny ties stitched with 'John 3:16', caps and T-shirts printed with the word 'Angel' and sweaters emblazoned with 'Jesus Loves Me' or, on one notable cardigan, 'Jesus Loves Even Me'. Apparently, even fashion designers know God is in the details, a well-worn principle that, along with recent backing from the Italian conglomerate Diesel, has shot sales for the erstwhile party boys into the heavens. It seems the Caten twins have finally found their square roots.

Dean und Dan Caten von Dsquared verstehen einiges von Mixing und Matching. 1991 verließen die beiden 40-jährigen eineiigen Zwillinge ihr kanadisches Zuhause, um nach Italien zu ziehen, in die Heimat ihrer Großmutter väterlicherseits (Caten ist die Abkürzung von Catenacci; die Familie mütterlicherseits hat englische Wurzeln). Mit einer gewagten Mixtur aus amerikanischer Popkultur und anspruchsvoller italienischer Schneiderkunst ist es ihnen gelungen, die Modewelt auf den Kopf zu stellen. Nach ihrem Mailänder Debüt der Herrenlinie 1994 zählten dank des frechen, mit handwerklicher Präzision gepaarten Überschwangs Lenny Kravitz, Justin Timberlake und Ricky Martin zu ihren Fans. Bald danach untermauerte das Duo seine modische Glaubwürdigkeit durch Madonnas Kostüme für das Video zu „Don't Tell Me" und die Cowboy-Outfits ihrer Drowned World Tour 2002. Es folgte die Ausstattung von Christina Aguilera bei ihrer Tour Stripped 2003 (die kleine Diva wurde später anlässlich der Herrenkollektion Frühjahr/Sommer 2005 für den Catwalk verpflichtet). Bei der Präsentation der Damenlinie im Jahr 2003 sah man die Supermodels Naomi Campbell, Eva Herzigova,

Karolina Kurkova und Fernanda Tavares mit eindeutig zweideutigen Insignien einem pinkfarbenen Privatjet entsteigen. Für die Kollektion Herbst/Winter 2005 orientierten sich die Brüder, die ihre Kindheit in einer Gemeinde wiedergeborener Christen verbrachten, an einer höheren Macht und bestickten schmale Krawatten mit „Johannes 3.16", bedruckten Baseballcaps und T-Shirts mit dem Wort „Angel" und verzierten Pullover mit „Jesus Loves Me" sowie eine Strickjacke mit dem bemerkenswerten „Jesus Loves Even Me". Offenbar wissen selbst Modedesigner, dass Gott sich im Detail verbirgt. Dieses kluge Prinzip sorgte neben der kürzlich erfolgten Unterstützung durch den italienischen Diesel-Konzern dafür, dass die Verkaufszahlen der einstigen Partyboys in himmlische Höhen schossen. Es scheint, als hätten die Caten-Zwillinge schließlich und endlich ihre Wurzeln gefunden.

On peut dire que Dean et Dan Caten de Dsquared s'y connaissent en métissage des styles. Ces vrais jumeaux âgés de 40 ans quittent leur Canada natal en 1991 pour l'Italie, patrie de leur grand-mère paternelle (Caten est une abréviation de Catenacci tandis qu'ils sont d'origine anglaise du côté de leur mère), et réussissent à bouleverser l'univers de la mode avec leur fusion osée entre pop culture américaine et coupe virtuose à l'italienne. En 1994, les débuts milanais de leur ligne pour homme ravissent des fans tels que Lenny Kravitz, Justin Timberlake et Ricky Martin grâce à leur exubérante insolence formatée pour MTV mais conjuguée à un savoir-faire de précision. Peu de temps après, le duo assoie sa crédibilité en créant les costumes du clip «Don't Tell Me» de Madonna et les tenues de cow-boy de sa tournée mondiale Drowned en 2002, sans oublier les costumes de la tournée Stripped de Christina Aguilera en 2003 (la mini-diva sera plus tard recrutée pour défiler lors de leur collection pour homme printemps/été 2005). Le lancement d'une ligne pour femme en 2003 voit les top models Naomi Campbell, Eva Herzigova, Karolina Kurkova et Fernanda Tavares sortir d'un jet privé rose avec nonchalance et arrogance, vêtues d'attributs royaux sexuellement très chargés. Pour l'automne/hiver 2005, les frères jumeaux élevés dans la doctrine évangélique des « Born-Again Christians » semblent retrouver la foi avec des cravates étroites cousues de l'inscription « Jean 3.16 », de casquettes et de T-shirts imprimés du mot « Angel » et de pulls proclamant « Jesus Loves Me » ou, sur un certain cardigan, « Jesus Loves Even Me ». Apparemment, même les créateurs de mode savent que Dieu se trouve dans les petits détails, un principe éprouvé qui, allié au récent soutien financier du conglomérat italien Diesel, propulse les ventes de ces anciens fêtards au firmament. On dirait bien que les jumeaux Caten ont fini par trouver leurs racines carrées.

LEE CARTER

PORTRAIT BY ALEX GIACOMÉ · PHOTOGRAPHY BY LAETITIA NEGRE, JEAN-LUC & PHILIPPE MEISSIRE...

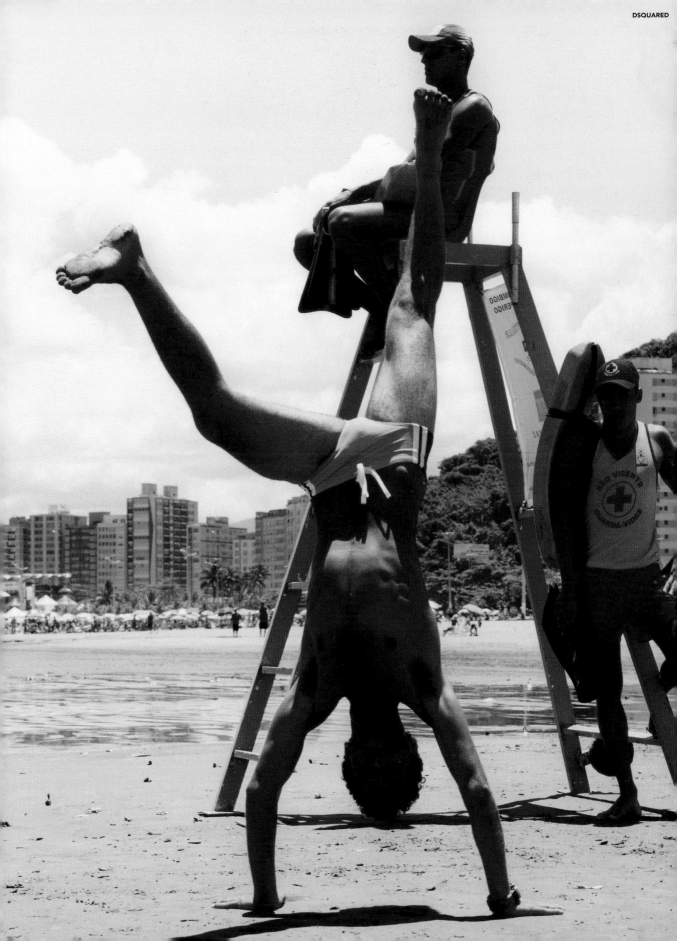

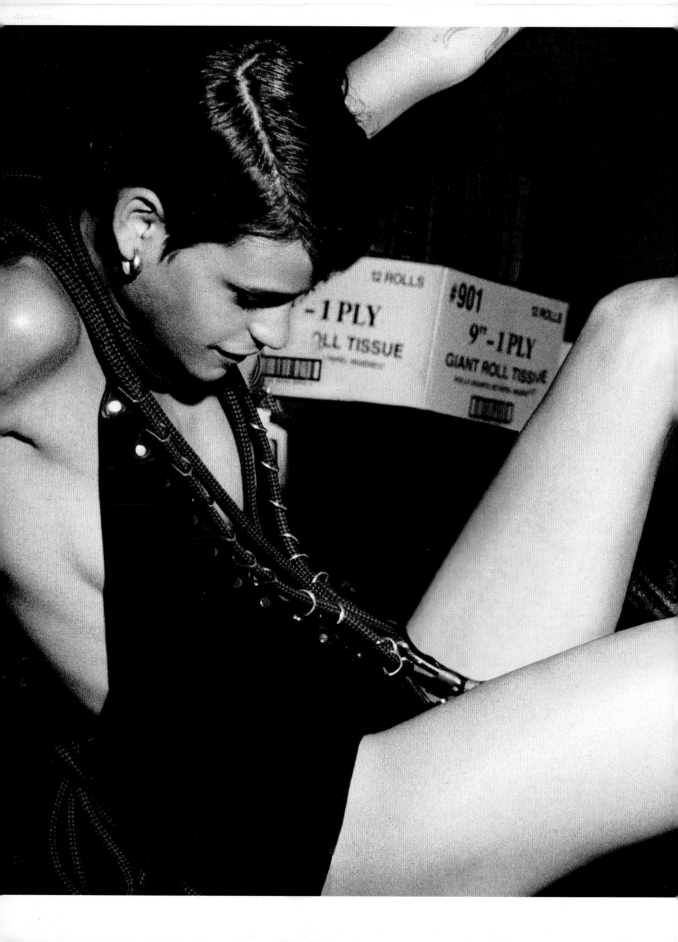

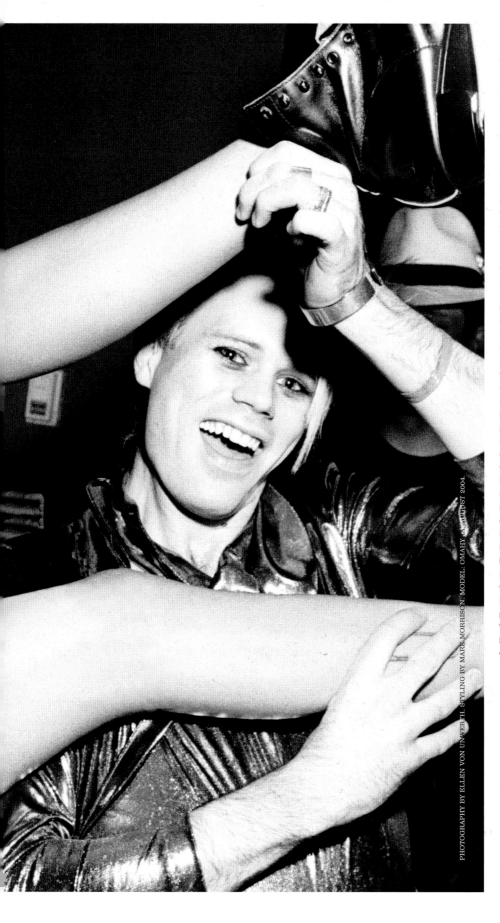

PHOTOGRAPHY BY ELLEN VON UNWERTH. STYLING BY MARK MORRISON. MODEL: OMAHY. A, AUGUST 2004.

What are your signature designs? Super sexy, super low cut trousers **What is your favorite piece from any of your collections?** Our brown leather "chiodo" pant with quilted knees and gold snaps **How would you describe your work?** Honest and real **What's your ultimate goal?** To contribute to the fashion industry with something real and be respected for it… **What inspires you?** Our lives, our pasts, things we've done and things we haven't! We're inspired by things that are normally not fashionable, making a negative into a positive, everyday people **Can fashion still have a political ambition?** We don't get political in anything! **Who do you have in mind when you design?** Ourselves be it men or women… we can get into anything! **Is the idea of creative collaboration important to you?** We're a design team, "per forza" collaboration is second nature to us! **Who has been the greatest influence on your career?** The man who gave us the chance at 19 to design, Mr Luke Tanabe, our maestro who taught us discipline and sensibility and fine-tuned our eye **How have your own experiences affected your work as a designer?** In every sense our work is a product of our lives and the experiences that surround us **Which is more important in your work: the process or the product?** They go hand in hand, the product is the consequence of the procedure **Is designing difficult for you, if so, what drives you to continue?** Difficult or not, it's the challenge to come up with new ideas that drives us to continue **Have you ever been influenced or moved by the reaction to your designs?** We are moved by the incredible loyal following we have. It stimulates us to kept them smiling **What's your definition of beauty?** Something that can evoke a personal positive reaction, you absorb it, it warms you and makes you feel good. Beauty is soo subjective… **What's your philosophy?** Free to be and do as you please **What is the most important lesson you've learned?** Go with your gut and stay true to your heart and always believe in yourself.

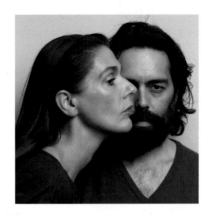

E2

"Each piece is a new story" MICHÈLE & OLIVIER CHATENET

Michèle (born 1956) and Olivier (1960) Chatenet are the husband-and-wife design team behind the Parisian vintage-recycling label, E2. Before founding the company in 1999, their pre-E2 careers included design stints at Azzedine Alaïa, Thierry Mugler, Comme des Garçons and Chanel. They began designing together in 1987, first as Mariot Chanet before developing E2, a concept-label based on their obsession with making old clothes new. Using superior flea market finds by the likes of Madame Grès, Chanel and YSL, they amalgamate and alter antique garments to produce one-off creations that play with the original design. Their reworking could involve anything from subtle changes (new buttons, added sequins) to fashioning old fabrics into entirely new pieces. The one-off allure of their creations has attracted stars like Gwyneth Paltrow and Madonna, who are secure in the knowledge that their E2 item will never be worn by anyone else. They also have a history of revitalising French labels. Before E2, they styled for Hermès for three years, and from 2001 to 2003 the duo took their ideas to print house Léonard, bringing new life to the label known for its hothouse flower motifs. From 2003, rubber mac brand Ramosport made use of their magic touch when the pair created a one-off collection for Paris boutique Colette and a line for French mail order company, La Redoute. E2 itself tends to shun the conventions of fashion: although they present their clothes on the fashion calendar, they prefer to use the medium of the exhibition rather than the catwalk. And because of the unique nature of their designs, clients don't have the usual six-month wait until clothes are in the shops – delighted devotees can buy what they like there and then.

Das Ehepaar Michèle (Jahrgang 1956) und Olivier (Jahrgang 1960) Chatenet bildet das Designteam des Pariser Labels E2, dessen Spezialität das Recyceln von Vintage-Mode ist. Vor der Firmengründung 1999 waren die beiden bei Azzedine Alaïa, Thierry Mugler, Comme des Garçons und Chanel kreativ. Ihre gemeinsame Arbeit begann 1987 unter dem Namen Mariot Chanet, bevor sie das Konzept von E2 entwickelten. Dabei lautet das Motto: Aus alt mach neu. Sie verwenden Flohmarktfunde der gehobenen Kategorie, etwa von Madame Grès, Chanel oder YSL. Diese Teile werden miteinander verschmolzen und umgearbeitet und ergeben so einzigartige Kreationen, die mit dem Originaldesign spielen. Der Arbeitsprozess reicht von subtilen Veränderungen (neue Knöpfe, zusätzliche Pailletten) bis zur Herstellung völlig neuer Stücke aus alten Stoffen. Die so erzielte Einzigartigkeit rief Stars wie Gwyneth Paltrow und Madonna auf den Plan, die sich bei E2-Kreationen sicher sein können, dass keine andere das gleiche Stück trägt. Das Designerpaar ist auch bekannt für seine erfolgreiche Wiederbelebung französischer Traditionsmarken. Vor E2 entwarfen sie drei Jahre

lang für Hermès, von 2001 bis 2003 hauchte das Duo mit seinen Ideen dem für seine tropischen Blumenmotive bekannten Haus Léonard neues Leben ein. 2003 profitierte die Gummiregenmantel-Marke Ramosport von den Chatenets, die eine einmalige Kollektion für die Pariser Boutique Colette und eine Linie für das französische Versandhaus La Redoute kreierten. E2 selbst schert sich nicht viel um die Konventionen der Modebranche: Sie präsentierten ihre Kollektion zwar während der großen Schauen, bevorzugen aber als Medium eher Ausstellungen als die üblichen Catwalk-Shows. Dank der Einzigartigkeit der Entwürfe müssen die Kunden auch nicht die üblichen sechs Monate warten, bis die Sachen in die Läden kommen – begeisterte Fans erstehen an Ort und Stelle, was ihnen gefällt.

La griffe parisienne E2 de recyclage vintage a été formée par les créateurs Michèle (née en 1956) et Olivier (né en 1960) Chatenet, partenaires en affaires comme dans la vie. Avant de fonder leur entreprise en 1999, ils avaient travaillé dans les équipes de création d'Azzedine Alaïa, Thierry Mugler, Comme des Garçons et Chanel. Ils commencent à collaborer dès 1987, d'abord sous la marque Mariot Chanet, puis développent E2, une griffe-concept où ce duo passionné redonne une nouvelle vie aux vieux vêtements. A partir des trouvailles griffées Grès, Chanel et YSL qu'ils dénichent sur les marchés aux puces, ils amalgament et transforment des pièces anciennes pour produire des vêtements uniques inspirés de leur modèle d'origine. Leur travail de customisation couvre toutes sortes de transformations, des changements subtils (nouveaux boutons, ajout de paillettes) au remontage d'anciens tissus en nouvelles pièces entièrement inédites. Ce côté unique attire des stars telles que Gwyneth Paltrow et Madonna, rassurées à l'idée qu'elles ne retrouveront jamais leurs vêtements E2 sur qui que ce soit d'autre. Le duo a également ressuscité certaines griffes françaises. Avant E2, les Chatenet ont été stylistes pour la maison Hermès pendant trois ans, puis de 2001 à 2003, ils ont occupé la direction de la création chez Léonard, apportant un souffle nouveau à cette maison révérée pour ses flamboyants motifs et imprimés floraux. En 2003, Ramosport, la marque de l'imperméable, fait appel à leur magie et demande au duo de créer une collection unique pour la boutique parisienne Colette, ainsi qu'une autre pour La Redoute. Pour E2, les Chatenet ont tendance à fuir les conventions de l'industrie : bien qu'ils participent aux semaines de la mode, ils préfèrent présenter leur travail par le biais d'expositions plutôt que sur les podiums des défilés. Et grâce au côté unique de leurs créations, leurs clients n'ont pas besoin d'attendre six mois pour trouver les vêtements en boutique : les fans les plus enthousiastes peuvent immédiatement acquérir les créations de leur choix.

LAUREN COCHRANE

What are your signature designs ? New spirit to antique clothing is always the goal. Then, it depends on the garment. Each piece is a new story **What is your favorite piece from any collection?** Embroidered kilts, tops & dresses made reversible, lingerie as eveningwear **How would you describe your work?** Art & craft **What's your ultimate goal?** Redefining luxury **What inspires you?** Each piece in itself **Can fashion still have a political ambition?** Fashion is more a social message than political **Who do you have in mind when you design?** The women that know and can afford everything **Is the idea of creative collaboration important to you?** Idem **Who has been the greatest influence on your career?** Idem + conceptual '70s women designers as Jean Muir, Sonia Rykiel **How have your experiences affected your work as a designer?** Idem **Which is more important in your work the process or the product?** The final product is the goal, but the process is changing from one piece to another **Is designing difficult for you. If so, what drives you to continue?** Idem **Have you ever been influenced or moved by the reaction to your designs?** Of course! We need to feel that our clients fall in love with E2 **What's your definition of beauty?** Beauty makes you forget your human condition **What's your philosophy?** Idem **What's the most important lesson you've learned?** Learn every day.

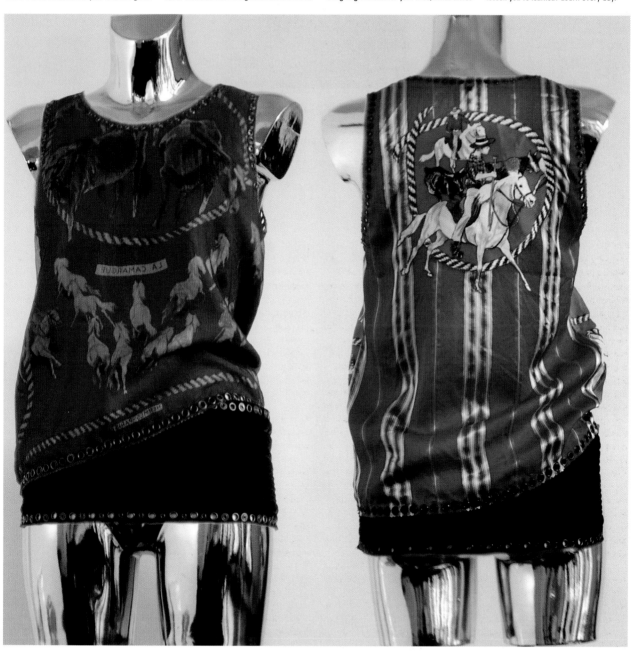

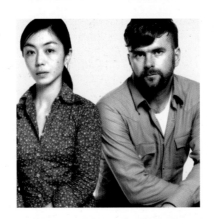

ELEY KISHIMOTO

"Our work is our life, so our daily activities, whether work or play, are intrinsically involved with our creative output"

Eley Kishimoto are British fashion's favourite double act. Best known for their boldly innovative prints, husband-and-wife design team Mark Eley and Wakako Kishimoto are recognised foremost as womenswear designers, but also work their magic on furniture, wallpaper, ceramics and glass, plus a tidy range of see-them-want-them accessories that includes sunglasses, hats, bags, shoes and hosiery. Eley was born in Wales and graduated from Brighton Polytechnic in 1990 with a degree in fashion and weave. Kishimoto (born in Sapporo, Japan, in 1965) finished her fashion and print degree at Central Saint Martins in 1992 at which time the pair founded their own label, designing prints for the likes of Joe Casely-Hayford, Hussein Chalayan and Alexander McQueen. In 1995 their debut fashion collection, 'Rainwear', hit town – cheerfully prim printed fabric umbrellas, coats and gloves. Since then, wave after wave of imaginative and stylish products has kept coming from the Eley Kishimoto studio and from 2001 they have shown at London Fashion Week. EK have gained a reputation for their own designs as well as securing print commissions from international labels such as Marc Jacobs, Jil Sander and Yves Saint Laurent. They also work as consultants for textile producers in Italy and Japan, and in 2002 the V&A Museum presented a retrospective exhibition of the duo's work. In 2003 they opened a shop in Bermondsey, south London, and signed a manufacturing deal with CIT Spa in Milan, enabling further expansion. Spring 2005 heralded the first Eley Kishimoto-Ellesse collection – part of a three-season deal – and also a new collaboration with luggage brand Globetrotter who utilised the classic EK print 'flash' on their classic cases. Here's to the queen and king of prints charming!

Eley Kishimoto ist die Lieblingsmarke vieler Trendsetter. Am bekanntesten ist das Ehepaar und Designerteam Mark Eley und Wakako Kishimoto für seine innovativen Muster in kräftigen Farben. Die beiden entwerfen zwar in erster Linie Damenmode, lassen ihren Zauber aber auch in den Bereichen Möbel, Tapeten, Keramik und Glas wirken. Dazu kommt noch eine beträchtliche Auswahl an Accessoires, die man auf den ersten Blick sofort haben möchte: Sonnenbrillen, Hüte, Taschen, Schuhe und Strumpfwaren. Eley stammt aus Wales und machte 1990 einen Abschluss in Mode und Weberei am Polytechnikum in Brighton. Die 1965 im japanischen Sapporo geborene Kishimoto schloss das Central Saint Martins 1992 in den Fächern Mode und Textildruck ab. Im selben Jahr gründeten die beiden ihr eigenes Label und begannen Stoffmuster für Joe Casely-Hayford, Hussein Chalayan und Alexander McQueen zu entwerfen. 1995 gaben sie ihr Debüt mit der Modekollektion „Rainwear" – mit Schirmen, Mänteln und Handschuhen aus quietschvergnügt gemusterten Stoffen. Seit damals kommen mit schöner Regelmäßigkeit Wellen von phantasievollen und eleganten Produkten aus dem Atelier Eley Kishimoto, die seit 2001 bei der London Fashion Week

gezeigt werden. EK hat sich einen Ruf nicht nur für die eigenen Kreationen erworben, sondern auch als regelmäßiger Musterlieferant für internationale Labels wie Marc Jacobs, Jil Sander und Yves Saint Laurent. Das Team berät darüber hinaus Webereien in Italien und Japan. Im Victoria & Albert Museum war 2002 eine Retrospektive ihrer Arbeiten zu sehen. Seit 2003 gibt es einen eigenen Laden in Bermondsey, im Süden Londons, und eine Kooperation mit CIT Spa in Mailand, was weitere Expansionsmöglichkeiten eröffnet. Im Frühjahr 2005 kam die erste Eley Kishimoto-Ellesse-Kollektion heraus – als Beginn einer auf drei Saisons angelegten Zusammenarbeit. Ebenfalls neu ist die Kooperation mit dem Reisegepäck-Hersteller Globetrotter, der das klassische EK-Muster „Flash" für seine traditionellen Koffer verwendet. Ein Hoch auf die Königin und den König der bezaubernden Muster!

Eley Kishimoto est le duo préféré de plus d'un lanceur de tendances. Réputé pour leurs imprimés audacieux et novateurs, le couple marié formé par les créateurs Mark Eley et Wakako Kishimoto est surtout connu pour ses créations pour femme, bien qu'il applique aussi sa magie aux domaines du mobilier, du papier peint, de la céramique et du verre, sans oublier une gamme soignée d'accessoires irrésistibles qui inclut des lunettes de soleil, des chapeaux, des sacs, des chaussures et des collants. Né au pays de Galles, Mark Eley obtient un diplôme en mode et tissage de l'école polytechnique de Brighton en 1990. Eley Kishimoto (née en 1965 à Sapporo au Japon) sort diplômée en mode et en impression de Central Saint Martins en 1992, date à laquelle le duo fonde sa propre griffe, dessinant des imprimés pour Joe Casely-Hayford, Hussein Chalayan et Alexander McQueen. En 1995, ils présentent une première collection de mode baptisée « Rainwear » : parapluies, manteaux et gants taillés dans un tissu aux imprimés à la fois sages et réjouissants. Depuis, l'atelier Eley Kishimoto ne cesse de présenter des produits stylés et pleins d'imagination. Ils défilent à la London Fashion Week depuis 2001. EK doit sa réputation à ses propres créations, mais aussi aux nombreuses commandes d'imprimés passées par de grandes maisons internationales telles que Marc Jacobs, Jil Sander et Yves Saint Laurent. Le couple travaille également comme consultants pour des fabricants textiles en Italie et au Japon. En 2002, le Victoria & Albert Museum leur a même consacré toute une rétrospective. En 2003, ils ont ouvert une boutique à Bermondsey dans le sud de Londres et signé un contrat de fabrication avec CIT Spa à Milan afin de poursuivre leur expansion. Le printemps 2005 a vu naître la première collection Eley Kishimoto-Ellesse (dans le cadre d'un contrat portant sur trois saisons), ainsi qu'une nouvelle collaboration avec la marque de bagages Globetrotter qui reprend le célèbre imprimé « flash » d'EK sur ses valises classiques. Alors longue vie au roi et à la reine des imprimés!

TERRY NEWMAN

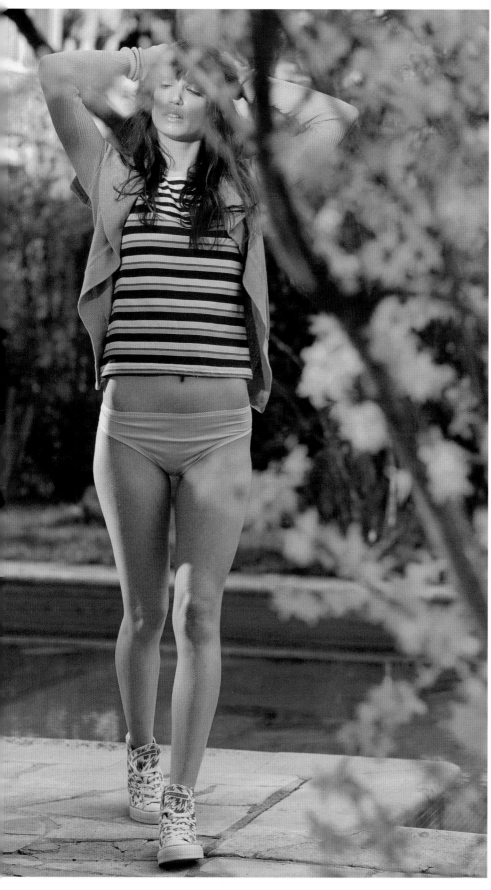

What are your signature designs? Our company is known for its prolific output of print which manifests itself in many varying categories **What is your favourite piece from any of your collections?** This is a difficult one to answer because on reflection there are different notions and identities attached to archive pieces that were not provoked when they first existed. So the favourites then are maybe not the favourites today **How would you describe your work?** Honest and a show of motivated creative experimentations that hold as much integrity as possible **What's your ultimate goal?** To survive **What inspires you?** Everything that happens on everyday basis **Can fashion still have a political ambition?** Fashion deals with many issues in today's world and I think it's important not to close boundaries to any one who wishes to have a voice whether it be political or purely superfluous **Who do you have in mind when you design?** A woman who knows a thing or two **Is the idea of creative collaboration important to you?** Yes, it enables us to touch or be party to creations that would otherwise be impossible for us to create **Who has been the greatest influence on your career?** Each other **How have your own experiences affected your work as a designer?** Our work is our life, so our daily activities, whether work or play, are intrinsically involved with our creative output **Which is more important in your work: the process or the product?** I like to think these two are balanced along with the communication **Is designing difficult for you, if so, what drives you to continue?** It is a responsibility that we are happy to live with **Have you ever been influenced or moved by the reaction to your designs?** Every time we witness someone who has made a commitment to our work in whatever way, it always provokes a personal reaction; sometimes happiness and sometimes embarrassment.

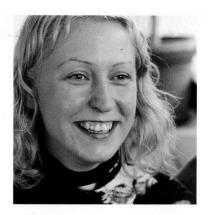

EMMA COOK

"I suppose I just make clothes that I and
my friends like to wear"

Emma Cook (born 1975) turns fashion into a game. Since graduating from a womenswear MA at Central Saint Martins in 1999, Manchester-born Cook's nine collections have all featured her very own fashion imaginary friend, Susan. To add another challenge, the said Susan dips into the wardrobe – and art – of various eras for each collection. So far, Susan has played dress-up as a surrealist goddess, a '60s space age siren and a Rodchenko-inspired '20s avant-gardist. Now flying high on the London scene, Cook was hotly tipped for success following her graduation show. She has won many awards during her career, including the second-ever VS Vidal Sassoon Award for emerging talent and for three years Topshop's New Generation sponsorship. However, Cook's is not a story of the new kid on the block forever. Unlike other hyped graduates of her generation, Cook has matured into a designer with the depth and complexity required for longevity. Following her autumn/winter 2003 monochrome collection, critical praise now comes in thick and fast. Devotees are seduced by Cook's ability to create new garments with vintage spirit; hand-drawn prints are always key. As with a one-off vintage find, Cook's creations seem unique and irreplaceable. Always very graphic with strong construction techniques, Cook is obsessed with finding the story behind the clothes. A skirt is not just a skirt in her world – each line, colour, shape has a narrative behind it. All her collections feature signature motifs that symbolise the story, from baby deer to bicycle wheels and the birds of her recent spring/summer 2005 collection; her esoteric, narrative-driven inspirations create charming and commercially viable pieces. She launched an accessory line in 2005.

Die 1975 geborene Emma Cook verwandelt Mode in ein Spiel. Seit ihrem 1999 erworbenen Master in Damenmode am Central Saint Martins hat die aus Manchester stammende Designerin neun Kollektionen für ihre imaginäre Freundin Susan präsentiert. Als zusätzlicher Reiz schlüpft diese Susan für jede Kollektion nicht nur in das Gewand, sondern umgibt sich auch mit der Kunst der jeweiligen Ära. Bislang zeigte sie sich als surreale Göttin, als spacige Sixties-Sirene und als eine von Rodtschenko inspirierte Avantgardistin der 1920er Jahre. Die in der Londoner Szene inzwischen hoch gehandelte Cook galt schon nach ihrer Abschluss-Show als heißer Tipp. Seither hat sie viele Preise gewonnen, darunter den zweiten ausgelobten VS Vidal Sassoon Award für junge Talente und das dreijährige Stipendium Topshop's New Generation. Ihre Karriere ist jedoch nicht die eines ewigen Wunderkinds. Im Gegensatz zu anderen hochgepushten Absolventen ihrer Generation ist Cooks Erfolg von Dauer. Nach ihrer monochromen Kollektion für Herbst/Winter 2003 fließt das Lob der Kritiker nun konstant und reichlich. Ihre Fans lieben Cooks Fähigkeit, neue Dinge mit Vintage-Flair zu

kreieren; von Hand gezeichnete Muster gehören immer dazu. Wie echte Vintage-Fundstücke wirken auch Cooks Entwürfe einmalig und unersetzlich. Neben der starken grafischen Wirkung legt Cook Wert auf deutlich sichtbare Konstruktionsdetails und versucht, die Geschichte hinter jedem Kleidungsstück zu entdecken. In ihren Augen ist ein Rock eben nicht nur ein Rock: Jede Linie , seine Farbe und Form haben etwas zu erzählen. In allen Kollektionen gibt es charakteristische Motive, die eine Geschichte symbolisieren – vom Rehkitz über Fahrradreifen bis zu den Vögeln ihrer jüngsten Kollektion für Frühjahr/Sommer 2005. Die esoterischen und erzählerischen Inspirationen bringen bezaubernde und zugleich verkäufliche Teile hervor. 2005 präsentierte die Designerin erstmals eine Linie mit Accessoires.

Pour Emma Cook (née en 1975), la mode doit d'abord être un jeu. Depuis l'obtention de son Master en mode féminine à Central Saint Martins en 1999, les neuf collections de l'enfant de Manchester tournent toutes autour de son amie imaginaire : Susan. Pour compliquer un peu les choses, à chaque collection ladite Susan plonge dans la mode et l'art de différentes périodes historiques. Jusqu'à présent, Susan s'est déguisée en déesse surréaliste, en sirène Space Age tout droit sortie des années 60, ou encore en avant-gardiste des années 20 inspirée de Rodchenko. Désormais incontournable sur la scène londonienne, la presse britannique prédisait déjà un grand succès à Emma Cook à l'issue de sa collection de fin d'études. Elle a reçu de nombreux prix au cours de sa carrière, notamment le second prix Jeune Talent de Vidal Sassoon et la bourse de soutien Nouvelle Génération de Topshop pendant trois ans. Pourtant, Emma Cook ne pourra pas éternellement jouer les nouvelles venues. Contrairement à d'autres diplômés remarqués de sa génération, elle a gagné en maturité, s'imposant comme une créatrice qui dure. Depuis sa collection monochrome automne/hiver 2003, les critiques sont prompts à chanter ses louanges. Ses fans sont séduits par sa capacité à créer de nouveaux vêtements à l'esprit vintage, où les imprimés dessinés à la main ont toujours la part belle. A l'instar d'une trouvaille vintage, les créations d'Emma Cook semblent uniques et irremplaçables. Se distinguant par une esthétique très graphique et de solides techniques de construction, Emma Cook est obsédée par l'histoire cachée des vêtements. Dans son univers, une jupe n'est pas qu'une jupe : chaque ligne, chaque couleur, chaque forme a une histoire à raconter. Toutes ses collections présentent des motifs signature qui symbolisent l'histoire, du bébé faon aux roues de vélo en passant par les oiseaux de sa récente collection printemps/été 2005 ; ses inspirations ésotériques et narratives produisent des pièces charmantes et viables sur le plan commercial. La créatrice a lancé une ligne d'accessoires en 2005.

LAUREN COCHRANE

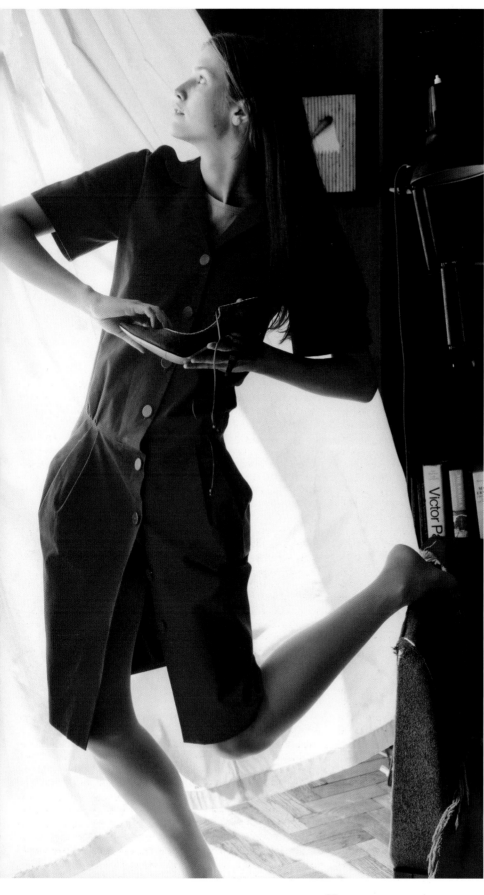

What are your signature designs? I think that they are girlie pieces that have a sense of humour **What is your favourite piece from any of your collections?** My favourite pieces are always the "showpieces" from each season. I usually make 2-3 pieces for each season that are not selling items but more a way of punctuating what the collection is about. I always hand-make these pieces myself and it is the most enjoyable part as I get to do whatever I like and get it all out of my system **How would you describe your work?** I had always found that question really hard – I suppose I just make clothes that me and my friends like to wear. I love the way I can say, Oh imagine if you had a jacket that looked like a Dada collage with whippets running all over it? And then I can go away and make one. That's really good! **What's your ultimate goal?** To do more of what I like and less of what I don't like **What inspires you?** Everything. I think as a designer you are always looking for inspiration in everything and you build a library in your mind of these things that you reference when its relevant **Can fashion still have a political ambition?** Depends, not sure about that **Who do you have in mind when you design?** Lots of people, me and my friends. I try things out on them so you end up with lots of different things that work on different types and shapes of girls **Is the idea of creative collaboration important to you?** Yes, definitely, I am lucky as I always work with my friends Cathy Edwards and Shona Heath and their input is vital. It's good to work through ideas with people who you respect, and it makes it much more fun **Who has been the greatest influence on your career?** Cathy Edwards. We have worked together really since the very beginning. She is one of my best friends and also the best stylist **How have your own experiences affected your work as a designer?** Trust your instincts **Which is more important in your work: the process or the product?** The process is what it's all about. **Is designing difficult for you, if so, what drives you to continue?** Designing is the easy bit, it's all the other stuff that is difficult, and unfortunately as a small designer you have a lot of other stuff to do **Have you ever been influenced or moved by the reaction to your designs?** It's really exiting when you see someone in the street wearing them. And of course it's always nice when your friends want to wear them **What's your definition of beauty?** Clutter and chaos **What's your philosophy?** Don't take yourself too seriously **What is the most important lesson you've learned?** My dad always told me it says Persil on a bus but they don't do washing.

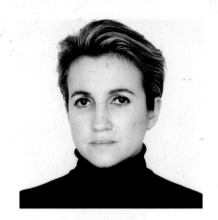

FENDI

"When I design, sometimes I have sensations
which I could call 'visionary'" MARIA SILVIA VENTURINI FENDI

Fendi is a house of extremes: big furs and little handbags, a family business with a worldwide reputation, a chic past and a street-cool future. Established in 1925, the Fendi empire was founded by Adele Fendi from a small leather-goods shop and workroom in Rome, where she and her husband Eduardo worked with private clients. The family business expanded with the opening of a larger shop in 1946, but it wasn't until the death of Eduardo, eight years later, that the modern Fendi image emerged, when the family's five daughters injected the little company with some youthful glamour. After the death of Adele in 1978, each sister adopted a corner of the empire to look after. Paola (born 1931) worked with the furs, Anna (born 1933) the leather goods, Franca (born 1935) the customer relations, Carla (born 1937) the business co-ordination, and Alda (born 1940) the sales. By the end of the '80s, the name of Fendi had become shorthand for jet-set elitist luxury, thanks to its signature furs and instantly recognisable double F logo (designed by Karl Lagerfeld). The politically correct '90s saw the company re-focus on Adele Fendi's traditional leather goods, and so the Baguette bag was re-born and Fendi's star was in the ascendant yet again. Amid the late-'90s' appetite for baroque excess, LVMH and Prada bought a 51 per cent stake in the label, with LVMH eventually becoming the sole partner in 2001. But Fendi is still very much a family business. The future lies with Maria Silvia Venturini Fendi (born 1960, the daughter of Anna Fendi), who created the Fendissime line in 1987 and is now designer of accessories and menswear. Karl Lagerfeld, as chief designer, continues to work with the sisters – as he has done since 1965 – and Maria Silvia.

Fendi ist ein Modehaus der Extreme: mit opulenten Pelzen und winzigen Handtaschen, ein Familienbetrieb mit Weltruf, einer eleganten Vergangenheit und zeitgemäß cooler Zukunft. Das Fendi-Imperium wurde 1925 von Adele Fendi gegründet, in einem kleinen römischen Laden für Lederwaren mit angeschlossener Werkstatt. Dort arbeiteten sie und ihr Mann für einen kleinen Kreis von Privatkunden. 1946 expandierte das Familienunternehmen mit der Eröffnung eines größeren Geschäfts. Das moderne Image von Fendi begann sich jedoch erst acht Jahre später nach dem Tod von Eduardo Fendi herauszukristallisieren, als die fünf Töchter jugendlichen Charme in die Firma brachten. Nachdem 1978 auch Adele gestorben war, übernahm jede der Schwestern einen eigenen Bereich: die 1931 geborene Paola die Pelzabteilung, die 1933 geborene Anna die Lederwaren, die 1935 geborene Franca Werbung und PR, die 1937 geborene Carla die Finanzen und die 1940 geborene Alda den Verkauf. Ende der 1980er Jahre war der Name Fendi dank der typischen Pelze und dem unverwechselba-

ren Logo aus zwei Fs (eine Idee von Karl Lagerfeld) zum Synonym für elitären Luxus des Jet-Set avanciert. In den 1990er Jahren mit ihrer Political Correctness besann man sich wieder verstärkt auf Adele Fendis traditionelle Lederwaren, entdeckte die Baguette-Tasche neu, und Fendis Stern stieg erneut. Angesichts der Lust an barocker Üppigkeit Ende der 1990er Jahre kauften zunächst LVMH und Prada 51 Prozent des Unternehmens; seit 2001 ist LVMH einziger Partner. Trotzdem hat Fendi noch viel von einem Familienbetrieb. Die Zukunft liegt in den Händen von Maria Silvia Venturini Fendi (der 1960 geborenen Tochter von Anna Fendi). Sie gründete 1987 die Linie Fendissime und ist heute die Designerin von Accessoires und Herrenmode. Chefdesigner Karl Lagerfeld arbeitet – wie seit 1965 – weiterhin mit den Schwestern und inzwischen auch mit Maria Silvia.

Fendi est la marque des extrêmes: grosses fourrures et petits sacs à main, affaire familiale et réputation internationale, passé chic et avenir «street-cool». L'empire Fendi a été fondé en 1925 par Adele Fendi à partir du petit atelier de maroquinerie de Rome où elle travaillait pour une clientèle privée avec son mari Eduardo. La petite affaire familiale se développe grâce à l'ouverture d'une plus grande boutique en 1946, mais ce n'est que huit ans plus tard, à la mort d'Eduardo, que naît l'image moderne de Fendi, lorsque leurs cinq filles commencent à insuffler tout leur glamour et leur jeunesse à l'entreprise. Quand Adele meurt en 1978, chaque sœur hérite d'un morceau de l'empire: Paola (née en 1931) s'occupe des fourrures, Anna (née en 1933) de la maroquinerie, Franca (née en 1935) des relations avec les clients, Carla (née en 1937) de la coordination et Alda (née en 1940) des ventes. A la fin des années 80, le nom Fendi est devenu synonyme de luxe élitiste et jet-set grâce à ses fourrures signature et à son logo en double F immédiatement identifiable (dessiné par Karl Lagerfeld). Pendant les années 90 du politiquement correct, l'entreprise ressort les sacs d'Adele Fendi: la Baguette est ressuscitée et l'étoile de Fendi remonte au firmament. L'appétit pour les excès baroques de la fin des années 90 voit LVMH et Prada racheter 51% de la griffe, mais c'est LVMH qui finit par en devenir l'unique partenaire en 2001. Toutefois, Fendi reste encore une affaire très familiale: son avenir repose sur les épaules de Maria Silvia Venturini Fendi (née en 1960, fille d'Anna Fendi), à l'origine de la ligne Fendissime en 1987 et qui occupe aujourd'hui la direction des départements Accessoires et Mode pour homme. Karl Lagerfeld, directeur de la création, continue à travailler pour les sœurs et pour Maria Silvia, comme il l'a toujours fait depuis 1965.

JAMIE HUCKBODY

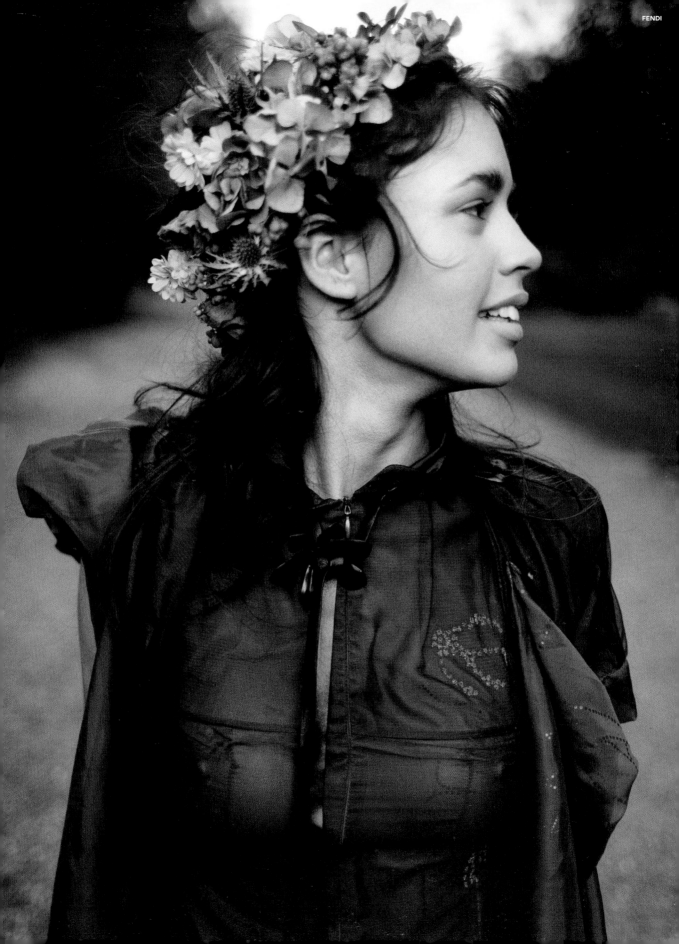

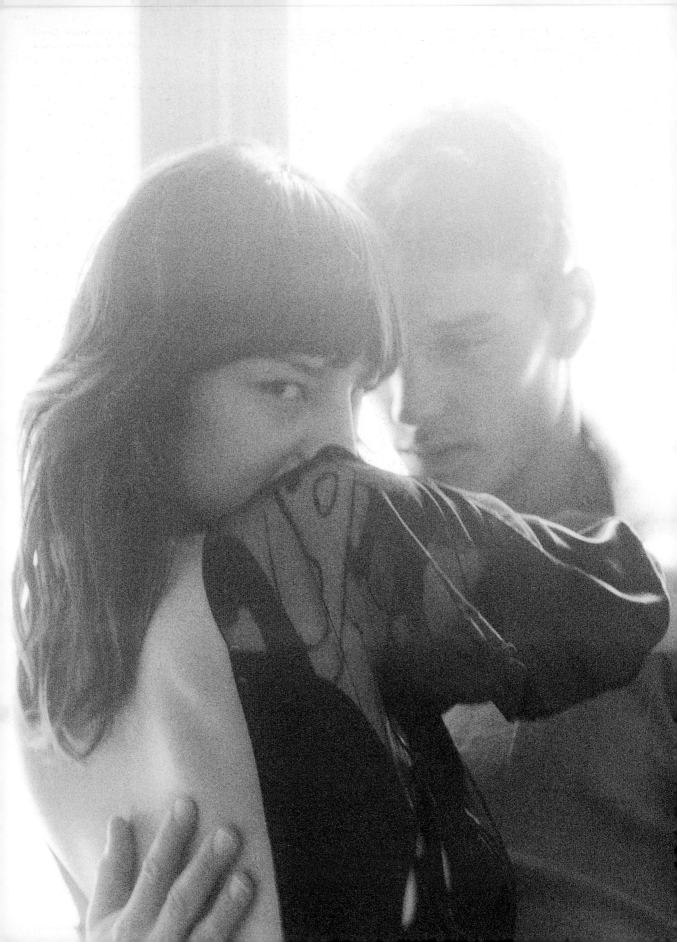

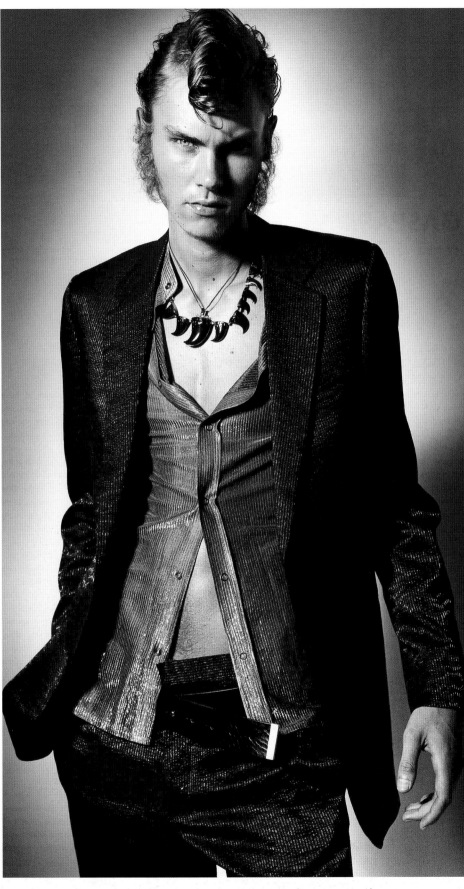

What are your signature designs? Manual ability and technique **What's your favourite piece from any of your collections?** The Baguette **How would you describe your work?** Dreaming and realising **What's your ultimate goal?** The Ostrik bag **What inspires you?** Anything, but above all, the challenges **Can fashion still have a political ambition?** It should not – but it can because fashion has great power when it influences costume and society **What do you have in mind when you design?** It depends. Sometimes I have images in mind, sometimes I have only sensations which I would call 'visionary' **Is the idea of creative collaboration important to you?** Creativity grows when it is shared **Who has been the greatest influence on your career?** My mother **How have your own experiences affected your work as a designer?** Irony, which I have acquired through my life experiences, allows me to have a sort of detachment and to dampen the creative obsession **Which is more important in your work: the process or the product?** It is impossible to separate one from the other. However, the process is the longer and more fascinating phase, which culminates in the realisation of the product **Is designing difficult for you and, if so, what drives you to continue?** It is not easy, but always challenging **Have you ever been influenced or moved by the reaction to your designs?** Yes, because creativity is neither blind nor deaf **What's your definition of beauty?** Energy **What's your philosophy?** To be afraid of convictions and to have the courage to change ideas **What is the most important lesson you have learned?** To be ready to reverse the norms that up to that moment seemed to be absolute.

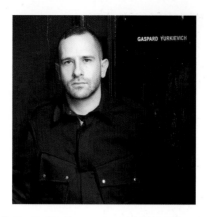

GASPARD YURKIEVICH

"I fight conservatism and conformity"

Born in 1972 in Paris, Gaspard Yurkievich is of French and Argentine origin. Brought up in an artistic family, his father was a poet and art critic, his sister a painter and his brother a writer; the latter now manages his business. His decision, then, to become a fashion designer did not come as a revelation to his family. Yurkievich studied at the Studio Berçot from 1991 to 1993. During that time, he juggled his studies with an internship at Thierry Mugler (1992). The following year, he moved to Jean Paul Gaultier. In 1994 he went on to assist Jean Colonna. This experience proved to be invaluable. By working at an independent label, Yurkievich learned how to run a fashion business, absorbing every facet of fashion design and production. In 1997 he started his own womenswear label; that same year he was awarded the prestigious womenswear prize at the Hyères Festival. In 1998 he received funding from ANDAM, an organisation set up by the French Ministry of Culture to support young designers, and showed his first collection in Paris. Constantly exploring female sexuality, a Yurkievich design always possesses a modern elegance, or in Yurkievich's words, "an urban flavour with a touch of femininity". His first menswear collection, entitled 'Pornographie', showed in June 2003 and was performed by four professional dancers at the Centre Georges Pompidou. In March 2004, his shoe collection was launched. His fashion shows – which combine performance art, live music and design elements – reveal Yurkievich's passions to be broad and varied. His foray into the art world led to his creation of Aurore Overnight, a girl band, for Fondation Cartier in July 2003.

Der 1972 in Paris geborene Gaspard Yurkievich ist französisch-argentinischer Abstammung und wuchs in einer echten Künstlerfamilie auf: der Vater Dichter und Kunstkritiker, die Schwester Malerin, der Bruder Schriftsteller und heute sein Manager. Daher stellte Gaspards Entscheidung, Modedesigner zu werden, für seine Familie keine Überraschung dar. Von 1991 bis 1993 studierte er am Studio Berçot. Noch in dieser Zeit polierte er seinen Lebenslauf mit einem Praktikum bei Thierry Mugler (1992) auf. Ein Jahr später ging er zu Jean Paul Gaultier und 1994 schließlich als Assistent zu Jean Colonna. Diese Erfahrung sollte sich als unschätzbar wertvoll und prägend erweisen, denn bei der Arbeit für das unabhängige Label lernte Yurkievich, wie man ein Modebusiness führt. Er nahm dabei jede Facette des Design- und Produktionsprozesses in sich auf. 1997 startete er sein eigenes Damenmode-Label und erhielt noch im gleichen Jahr den angesehenen Preis für Damenmode beim Festival von Hyères. ANDAM, eine vom französischen Kultusministerium gegründete Organisation zur Förderung jun-

ger Designer, sponserte ihn 1998, so dass er seine erste Kollektion in Paris präsentieren konnte. Yurkievichs Entwürfe erkunden permanent die weibliche Sexualität, besitzen aber zugleich immer eine moderne Eleganz. Oder, wie der Designer es selbst ausdrückt: „Urbanes Flair mit einem Touch Weiblichkeit." Seine erste Herrenkollektion mit dem Titel Pornographie wurde im Juni 2003 von vier Profitänzern im Centre Georges Pompidou vorgestellt. Im März 2004 lancierte Yurkievich seine Schuhkollektion. Diesen Rundumschlag vollendete der Designer schließlich mit der Eröffnung seines ersten Ladens in der Rue Charlot. Die Modenschauen – eine Kombination aus Performance-Kunst, Live-Musik und Designelementen – zeugen von Yurkievichs vielfältigen Passionen. So führte sein Ausflug in die Welt der Kunst im Juli 2003 für die Fondation Cartier zur Gründung der Girl Band Aurore Overnight.

Né en 1972 à Paris, le franco-argentin Gaspard Yurkievich grandit dans une famille d'artistes : son père était poète et critique d'art, sa sœur est peintre et son frère écrivain gère désormais sa griffe. Sa décision de devenir créateur de mode n'a donc rien d'une révélation aux yeux de sa famille. Yurkievich prend des cours au studio Berçot de 1991 à 1993, une période pendant laquelle il jongle entre ses études et un stage chez Thierry Mugler (1992). L'année suivante, il part travailler chez Jean Paul Gaultier, puis devient assistant de Jean Colonna en 1994. Cette expérience au sein d'une griffe indépendante s'avère cruciale et précieuse dans la mesure où elle lui permet d'intégrer chaque aspect de la création et de la production de mode. En 1997, il lance sa propre griffe pour femme, qui lui vaut la même année le prestigieux prix de meilleur styliste pour femme au Festival de Hyères. En 1998, il présente à Paris une première collection financée par l'AN-DAM, organisation de soutien aux jeunes créateurs fondée par le ministère de la Culture. Explorant inlassablement la sexualité féminine, les créations Yurkievich possèdent toujours une élégance moderne, ou selon les propres mots du créateur, « un parfum urbain avec une touche de féminité ». En juin 2003, il présente au Centre Georges Pompidou une première collection pour homme, « Pornographie », sur quatre danseurs professionnels. En mars 2004, il lance sa collection de chaussures. Après une incursion dans la mode pour homme et la chaussure, Gaspard Yurkievich complète le tableau avec l'ouverture de sa première boutique dans la rue Charlot. Combinant art de la performance, musique live et éléments design, ses défilés révèlent sa passion pour l'ouverture et la polyvalence. Son expérience du monde de l'art le conduit à former Aurore Overnight, un groupe féminin, pour la Fondation Cartier en juillet 2003.

KAREN LEONG

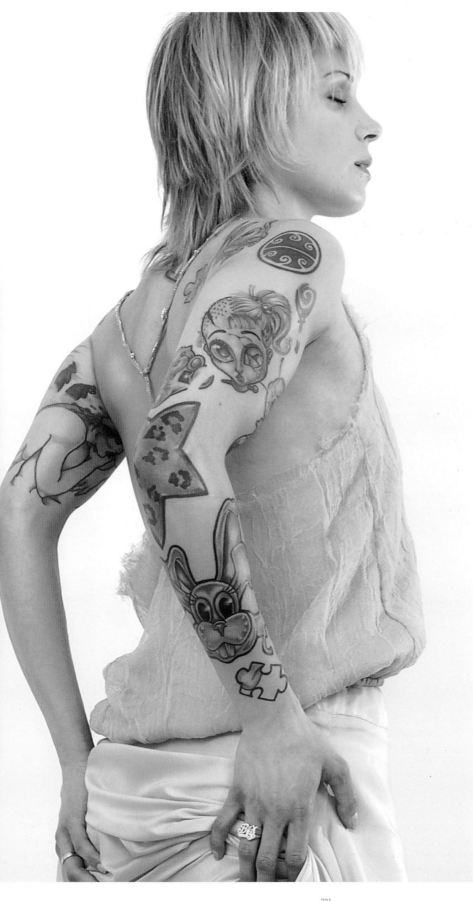

What are your signature designs? Casual glamour **What is your favourite piece from any of your collections?** It's like choosing between your kids. Love grows with your production. The more I produce, the more I approach what I love **How would you describe your work?** Personal and distressed **What's your ultimate goal?** My business independence is the key to my freedom **What inspires you?** Free, creative and individual people **Can fashion still have a political ambition?** Fashion is a proposition of a way of life, so yes, it can be political. For my own work, I fight conservatism and conformity **Who do you have in mind when you design?** Nobody except the following two reactions, "I want it now" and "I always dreamed of wearing something like that." **Is the idea of creative collaboration important to you?** It's the only way to make real an idea which is deep in your mind and it's inspiring to share your vision with people you admire **Who has been the greatest influence on your career?** My older sister using fashion to confront my parents and society with her rebellion and vision of life. Hey! It was the '80s **How have your own experiences affected your work as a designer?** I don't know how. It's all about optimism and energy maybe **Which is more important in your work: the process or the product?** The process is fascinating and very confidential and the product is a satisfaction. I see this with the opening of my first boutique. It makes my purpose and vision even more global **Is designing difficult for you, if so, what drives you to continue?** Designing can sometimes be very confusing and deeply introspective because everything is in your mind and you have to express it to your team to make it concrete… but then it makes me happy **What's your definition of beauty?** You can't materialise it, it's a supernatural phenomenon **What's your philosophy?** Join the body to the spirit **What is the most important lesson you've learned?** "Travail et le temps nous le dira" and there are no fairy tales.

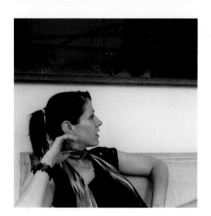

GEORGINA GOODMAN

"I believe in simplicity, timeless elegance, the perfection of imperfection and the mark of the hand"

Georgina Goodman, the shoe and accessory designer, was a rebellious teen. Born in Brighton in 1965, she grew up in London and would sneak, underage, into Taboo to hang out with avant-garde '80s label Bodymap and dreamily plan out her creative future. What followed was the perfect fashion education: a history of incongruous, yet successful, career choices that ranged from writing books and plays to TV research and styling. Finally she focused on shoes, graduating from London's Cordwainers College in 1999 and then taking the Footwear MA at the Royal College of Art. It was here that her work attracted the attention of Manolo Blahnik. Goodman works primarily in leather and wood. Her shoes are hand-painted and constructed with her signature visible stitching. Couture pieces are created from single pieces of leather and 'wet moulded' in a process more commonly used in saddlery. This technique results in subtle imperfections that Goodman manipulates and encourages. Her ultimate strength is her instinctive re-thinking of the shoe – her designs are strongly contemporary but display a dedication to craft and tradition. Goodman opened her first shop in Mayfair in 2002 and went on to show her first couture collection of footwear and accessories at London Fashion Week in 2003. That same year the British chain store New Look commissioned Goodman to create a capsule collection, and her own first ready-to-wear range was introduced internationally in 2004. Alongside a bespoke service for men, jewellery, bags and belts, Goodman is also a consultant for the Italian distribution company Aeffe, through which she has created an exclusive shoe collection for Rifat Ozbek. She also collaborates with boutique Oki-ni, has exhibited at London's Design Museum, the 'Fashion at Belsay' project, and in 2004 created a film, 'Love & Shoes', with photographer and filmmaker Mark Lebon. The scale of her enterprise is growing, but Goodman's agenda is simple. Her overwhelming desire is to create beautiful things.

Die Schuh- und Accessoire-Designerin war ein rebellischer Teenager. 1965 in Brighton geboren, wuchs sie in London auf und stahl sich noch minderjährig ins Taboo, um in den 1980ern mit den damals avantgardistischen Leuten vom Label Bodymap herumzuhängen und sich ihre kreative Zukunft auszumalen. Was folgte, war die perfekte Modeausbildung: Eine Reihe von ungereimten, aber erfolgreichen Karrieremöglichkeiten, angefangen beim Bücher- und Stücke-schreiben über Fernsehforschung bis hin zum Styling. Schließlich konzentrierte sie sich auf Schuhe, schloss 1999 das Londoner Cordwainers College ab und machte anschließend ihren Master im Bereich Schuhwerk am Royal College of Art. Dort fiel sie Manolo Blahnik auf. Goodman arbeitet vornehmlich mit Leder und Holz, von Hand bemalt und mit ihrem Markenzeichen – den sichtbaren Näh-ten. Couture-Exemplare werden aus einem einzigen Stück Leder gefertigt und „nass geformt". Diese Technik ist sonst eher in der Sattlerei verbreitet. Daraus resultieren kleine Fehler, die Goodmann bearbeitet und betont. Ihre größte Stärke ist die instinktive Neuinterpretation von Schuhen – ihre Entwürfe sind zum einen sehr modern, zeigen aber zugleich ihre tiefe Verbundenheit mit Hand-werk und Tradition. Ihren ersten Laden eröffnete Goodman 2002 in Mayfair. Die

erste Couture-Kollektion mit Schuhen und Accessoires zeigte sie bei der London Fashion Week 2003. Im selben Jahr erteilte die britische Kette New Look Good-man den Auftrag zu einer Mini-Kollektion. 2004 wurde ihre erste eigene Prêt-à-porter-Linie international präsentiert. Neben der Maß-Schuhanfertigung für Herren, Schmuck, Taschen und Gürteln berät Goodman auch die italienische Vertriebsfirma Aeffe, durch deren Vermittlung sie den Auftrag für eine exklusive Schuhkollektion bei Rifat Ozbek bekam. Die Designerin arbeitet außerdem mit der Boutique Oki-ni zusammen, stellte im Londoner Design Museum und beim Projekt „Fashion at Belsay" aus und realisierte 2004 zusammen mit dem Foto-grafen und Filmemacher Mark Lebon den Film „Love & Shoes". Der Umfang ihrer Aktivitäten wächst, Goodmans Richtung bleibt jedoch simpel: Das über-wältigende Verlangen, schöne Dinge zu kreieren.

La créatrice de chaussures et d'accessoires Georgina Goodman a vécu une ado-lescence rebelle. Née en 1965 à Brighton, elle grandit à Londres où, bien qu'en-core mineure, elle s'incruste au Taboo pour traîner avec les créateurs avant-gar-distes de Bodymap dans les années 80, rêvant d'une carrière artistique. Elle entame ensuite une formation idéale pour travailler dans la mode : une histoire de choix de carrière incongrus mais avisés qui vont de l'écriture de livres et de pièces de théâtre à un job de documentaliste et de styliste pour la télévision. Finalement, elle se consacre à la chaussure et sort diplômée du Cordwainers Col-lege de Londres en 1999 avant de suivre un Master spécialisé au Royal College of Art. C'est là que son travail attire l'attention de Manolo Blahnik. Georgina Goodman travaille principalement le cuir et le bois, qu'elle peint à la main et signe d'une couture apparente désormais incontournable. Elle crée des modèles très luxueux à partir d'une seule et même pièce de cuir « moulée en phase humide » grâce à un procédé plus couramment utilisé en sellerie. Cette tech-nique produit de subtiles imperfections que la créatrice manipule et encourage. Sa grande force réside dans sa capacité instinctive à réinterpréter la chaussure : hautement contemporaines, ses créations trahissent néanmoins sa passion pour l'artisanat et la tradition. Georgina Goodman ouvre sa première boutique à May-fair en 2002 et présente sa première collection de chaussures et d'accessoires haute couture à la London Fashion Week de 2003. La même année, la chaîne bri-tannique New Look lui commande une mini-collection. L'année 2004 est mar-quée par le lancement international de sa première gamme de prêt-à-porter. Outre un service sur mesure pour homme, des bijoux, des sacs et des ceintures, Georgina Goodman est également consultante auprès du distributeur italien Aeffe, par le biais duquel elle a créé une collection de chaussures exclusive pour Rifat Ozbek. Elle collabore également avec la boutique Oki-ni, a été exposée au Design Museum de Londres et a participé au projet « Fashion at Belsay ». En 2004, elle a réalisé un film, « Love & Shoes », avec le photographe-cinéaste Mark Lebon. Elle n'arrête jamais de travailler, toujours à plus grande échelle, mais ses exigences restent pourtant très simples : ce qu'elle désire avant tout, c'est créer de belles choses.

DAN JONES

What are your signature designs? Hand-painted natural leather in loose stripes and sculptural lines. I believe in simplicity, time-less elegance, the perfection of imper-fection and the mark of the hand What is your favourite piece from any of your collections? My Almond Lip shoe from my Couture collection How would you describe your work? An expression of how I feel. I approach work and my life from the inside out, not the outside in What's your ultimate goal? To be independent and not to have to answer to anybody while I do what I love and be who I really am What inspires you? My inspiration comes mainly from the feelings I get which are tuned by the people I meet and the places I find myself in. In particular I would say my daughter, my husband and my friends Can fashion still have a political ambition? Sure. Fashion can have whatever it wants; I think that's part of

the point Who do you have in mind when you design? My customer. I know her and get to know her better every day. She isn't an age or an income bracket. She is of an attitude and I design for her spirit, her sense of self Is the idea of creative collaboration important to you? Absolutely. Collaboration is my psychology. I know how important it is to me in my creativity and I love the energy that is released when it comes together Who has been the greatest influence on your career? Probably my husband who has supported me and believed in me from the day I decided to go back to college to study shoe design all the way through to setting up our business together How have your own experiences affected your work as a designer? My experience makes me who I am, it shapes the way I look at the world, it is my past and as such a constant part of my future Which is more important in your work:

the process or the product? For me it is the process. For BJ (my husband and partner) it is the product Is designing difficult for you, if so, what drives you to continue? Getting started is difficult for me. Such anxiety. Once I'm off I'm gone and it's like flying. When I'm in the process it's like being in a delicious dream state, I get tingling in my fingers and time stands still and everything flows. I can produce loads of work in a few hours. It's that feeling that drives me forward Have you ever been influenced or moved by the reaction to your designs? I've been very upset by people who react negatively and people who react positively constantly surprise me. I take it all very personally. I'm trying to learn to let go. There is a great mantra I try to live up to which says "altim bras malti"; it means "I am fearless, immune to criticism, above nor beneath no one and detached from the

outcome." How fabulous is that? That's what I'd like to answer, one day What's your definition of beauty? Love What's your philosophy? A principal that motivates me is All is One. This principle removes the illusion of separation. The illusion says that up is separate from down, right separate from wrong, male separate from female, joy separate from sadness. The more I consider this idea, the more I realise that all separa-tions are points of measurement on the same line, they are of the same energy. By this I mean joy and sadness are actually of the same energy, they just describe the energy resonating at different frequencies. Yes, I recognise and honour difference but not division. And I find this thought gives me freedom. All is One inspires my couture collection; it means One pattern, considering each piece of design as a whole What is the most important lesson you've learned? I can.

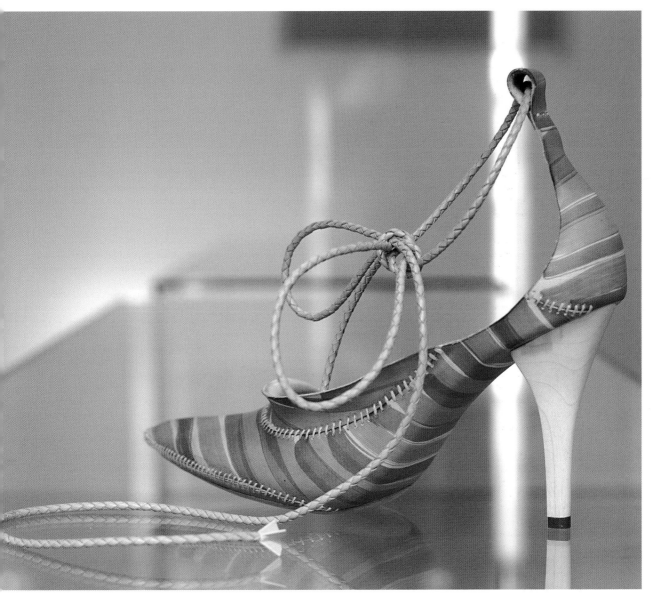

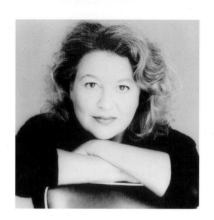

GHOST

"I have all women in mind when I design" TANYA SARNE

Now that it is celebrating its 20th anniversary, it's hard to imagine that Ghost was set up, as the brainchild of ex-model Tanya Sarne, with just £ 11,000. Today the west London-based company has a multi-million pound turnover, hundreds of stockists, four of its own boutiques scattered on both sides of the Atlantic, plus homewear, eyewear and several fragrances. Sarne has received much recognition from the British fashion establishment for the achievements of her company, which has been nominated for, and won, numerous industry awards. Ghost has also designed successful capsule collections for the British retail giant Marks & Spencer. The key to the company's success is practicality. The label specialises in clothing made from a textile that, despite having the appearance of vintage crepe, can be flung into a washing machine and worn without ironing. At Ghost's inception, sole owner and creative director Sarne adopted an ingenious new fashion fabric – a viscose, initially stiff and grey that, when dyed, shrinks and takes on a delicate antique appearance. To allow for the huge shrinkage, garments have to be cut to outsized patterns. The process is time-consuming and not always predictable. Finished Ghost pieces are unstructured, soft, feminine and gently bohemian; perennial Ghost looks, such as bias-cut dresses, narrow or floppy trousers and embroidered vests or tunics are cut to flatter curvaceous or boyish bodies alike. After a brief decampment to New York, Tanya Sarne continues to show the Ghost collections during London Fashion Week. Not content to rest as one of the UK's most commercially successful labels, a new specialist knitwear collection, a first men's fragrance, and a jeans range are taking the label forward into the next 20 years.

Nun, wo schon der 20. Geburtstag der Marke gefeiert wird, kann man sich kaum vorstellen, dass Ghost als Erfindung des Ex-Models Tanya Sarne einst mit nur 11 000 Pfund Kapital startete. Heute macht das Unternehmen mit Sitz im Westen Londons mehrere Millionen Pfund Umsatz im Jahr, beliefert Hunderte von Einzelhändlern und besitzt vier eigene Läden dies- und jenseits des Atlantiks. Dazu kommen noch eine Homewear-Kollektion, Brillenmode und diverse Düfte. Sarne erhielt vom britischen Mode-Establishment große Anerkennung für die Verdienste ihrer Firma, die ihr viele Preise und noch mehr Nominierungen eingebracht hat. Ghost produzierte auch schon gelungene Mini-Kollektionen für den britischen Einzelhandelsriesen Marks & Spencer. Der Schlüssel zum Erfolg des Unternehmens sind seine praktischen Kreationen. Das Label hat sich auf Kleidung aus einem Material spezialisiert, das wie klassischer Crêpe aussieht, aber maschinenwaschbar und bügelfrei ist. In der Anfangsphase entdeckte Sarne, Alleineigentümerin und Chefdesignerin in einer Person, einen genialen neuen Stoff: eine ursprünglich graue, steife Viskose, die beim Färben einläuft und ein leicht antikes Aussehen annimmt. Um das starke Schrumpfen zu berück-

sichtigen, müssen die Sachen extrem großzügig geschnitten sein. Der Produktionsvorgang ist zeitaufwändig und nie ganz vorhersehbar. Die fertigen Kreationen von Ghost sind jedoch allesamt fließend, weich, feminin und ein bisschen bohèmehaft. Über Jahre tragbare Looks wie Kleider im Diagonalschnitt, schmale oder weite Hosen, bestickte Westen oder Tuniken sind so geschnitten, dass sie kurvenreichen wie knabenhaften Figuren gleichermaßen schmeicheln. Nach einem kurzen Intermezzo in New York präsentiert Tanya Sarne die Ghost-Kollektionen nun wieder im Rahmen der Londoner Modewoche. Sie gibt sich allerdings nicht damit zufrieden, eines der kommerziell erfolgreichsten Labels Großbritanniens zu sein. Stattdessen sollen eine neue Strickwarenkollektion, ein erster Herrenduft sowie eine Jeanslinie das Label gut über die nächsten zwanzig Jahre bringen.

Alors que Ghost s'apprête à fêter son XXᵉ anniversaire, difficile d'imaginer que cette marque a été créée par l'ex-mannequin Tanya Sarne avec seulement 11 000 livres en poche. Aujourd'hui, l'entreprise du West London enregistre un chiffre d'affaires de plusieurs millions de livres, compte des centaines de stockistes, quatre boutiques réparties des deux côtés de l'Atlantique, sans oublier une ligne d'articles pour la maison, une gamme de lunettes et plusieurs parfums. Tanya Sarne a été largement adoptée par l'establishment de la mode britannique, qui a nominé et récompensé son travail à de nombreuses reprises. Ghost a également conçu plusieurs mini-collections à succès pour le géant britannique de la distribution Marks & Spencer. La clé de la réussite de Ghost réside dans son sens pratique. La griffe se spécialise dans les vêtements taillés à partir d'un textile qui, bien qu'il ressemble à du crêpe ancien, peut être lavé en machine et porté sans repassage. Dès la fondation de Ghost, l'unique propriétaire et directrice de la création Tanya Sarne découvre un nouveau tissu très mode et ingénieux : une viscose initialement rigide et grise qui, une fois teinte, rétrécit et prend un aspect ancien raffiné. Pour prévoir leur rétrécissement, les vêtements doivent être coupés sur des patrons surdimensionnés, un procédé qui prend beaucoup de temps et ne donne pas toujours les résultats escomptés. Les pièces finies de Ghost sont déstructurées, douces, féminines et légèrement bohèmes ; ses indémodables tels que les robes asymétriques, les pantalons étroits ou souples et les gilets et tuniques brodés sont coupés de façon à flatter les corps voluptueux comme les physiques androgynes. Après un bref passage à New York, Tanya Sarne continue de présenter les collections Ghost à la London Fashion Week. Mais Ghost ne se repose pas sur ses lauriers de griffe la plus rentable d'Angleterre : la marque reste plus que jamais tournée vers l'avenir et propose aujourd'hui une nouvelle collection de pièces en maille, un tout premier parfum pour homme et une ligne de jeans.

LAUREN COCHRANE

What are your signature designs? I have developed a unique group of fabrics which enables Ghost clothing to have a signature style. If I had to pick one piece I would say our spaghetti strap dress What is your favourite piece from any of your collections? I have created over 80 collections since I started so to say one piece is my favourite is impossible! Mind you, I love my long satin spaghetti strap slip which I've been wearing for years How would you describe your work? My work is very much aimed at understanding the female shape What's your ultimate goal? For Ghost to be successful for another 20 years and to dress as many women in the world as possible! What inspires you? I get inspired by anything from different ethnic origins, nature, old movies to people in the street who have their own eclectic style Can fashion still have a political ambition? Personally one can but not through design. Fashion design is always influenced by social and economic factors but in a more subtle way Who do you have in mind when you design? I have all women in mind when I design, all shapes, all sizes, all ages Who has been the greatest influence on your career? Many different designers in different eras; Susan Small in the '50s, Biba in the '60s, Ossie Clark in the '70s, Vivienne Westwood in the '80s and Comme des Garçons in the '90s How have your own experiences affected your work as a designer? I started Ghost when I was a single mother with two small children. I realised there was a severe lack of designer clothes that were stylish whilst still catering for a hectic lifestyle. I needed functional feminine affordable designer clothing and no-one else seemed to be creating it Which is more important in your work: the process or the product? Since we incorporate textile conversion into our designs, we cannot separate the process from the product Is designing difficult for you, if so, what drives you to continue? Designing is my life, it is what I do and will continue to do Have you ever been influenced or moved by the reaction to your designs? I have been very moved by women who tell me their lives have been changed by Ghost What's your definition of beauty? It ultimately comes from within. What one wears on the outside can only enhance that What's your philosophy? Feeling confident in whatever one does in life is always important. Confidence comes from being comfortable and from expressing ones femininity and individuality, and I hope that my clothes help women do this What is the most important lesson you've learned? To be steady and consistent in my work – you just have to get on with things and ignore what is going on around you.

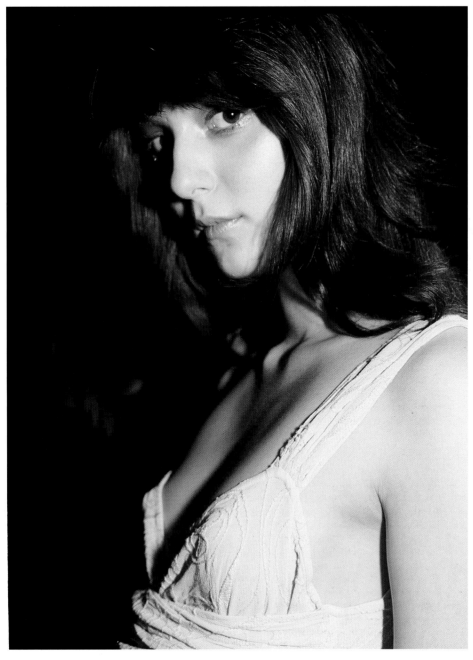

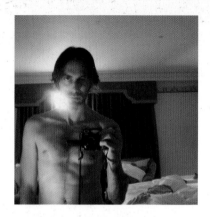

GIAMBATTISTA VALLI

`"I cannot live without design. I am design-addicted"`

In March 2005 Giambattista Valli showed his first eponymous collection in Paris. His debut emphasised polished pieces such as curvy tuxedos or tiny cocktail frocks in scarlet chiffon or black tulle. The Italian designer (born in Rome, 1966) already had an impressive CV by that time however, with a role as artistic director of Emanuel Ungaro's ready-to-wear collections as his most high profile appointment to date. Valli, who grew up in Rome, cites quintessential glamorous movie icons such as Claudia Cardinale, Marilyn Monroe and Rita Hayworth as early influences. His formal studies focused more squarely on fashion from 1980 when he studied at Rome's School of Art, followed by fashion training at the European Design Institute (1986) and an Illustration degree at Central Saint Martins in London (1987). In 1988 Valli worked for seminal Roman designer Roberto Capucci, moving to Fendi as a senior designer of the Fendissime line in 1990; in 1995 he was appointed senior designer at Krizia. The following year, through a mutual friend, Valli met Emanuel Ungaro. The master couturier named Valli head designer of his ready-to-wear collections in 1997, eventually promoting him to the position of creative director of Ungaro ready-to-wear two years later. At Ungaro, Valli translated the established house codes of tumbling ruffles, tropical-flower colours and elegantly draped, ultra-feminine gowns for a younger generation of jet-setting glamour girls. Besides glitzier idols such as Halston and Marie-Hélène de Rothschild, Valli also cites Francis Bacon, Kurt Cobain and Nan Goldin as continual sources of inspiration.

Im März 2005 präsentierte Giambattista Valli in Paris seine erste Kollektion unter eigenem Namen. Im Mittelpunkt standen Hingucker wie figurbetonte Smokings oder winzige Cocktailkleidchen aus dunkelrotem Chiffon oder schwarzem Tüll. Der 1966 in Rom geborene und aufgewachsene Designer hatte zu diesem Zeitpunkt bereits eine eindrucksvolle Vita vorzuweisen. Die höchste Position, die er bisher innehatte, war die des künstlerischen Direktors der Prêt-à-porter-Kollektionen bei Emanuel Ungaro. Als früheste Einflüsse gibt der Designer glamourösen Filmdiven wie Claudia Cardinale, Marilyn Monroe und Rita Hayworth an. Seine offizielle Ausbildung konzentrierte sich jedoch eher auf die Mode der 1980er Jahre, während er an der Kunsthochschule in Rom studierte, dann am European Design Institute (1986) und schließlich noch einen Abschluss im Fach Illustration am Central Saint Martins in London (1987) machte. 1988 begann Valli für den aufstrebenden römischen Designer Roberto

Capucci zu arbeiten, bis er 1990 als Senior Designer der Linie Fendissime zu Fendi wechselte. 1995 wurde er Senior Designer im Hause Krizia. Schon im folgenden Jahr lernte er über einen gemeinsamen Freund Emanuel Ungaro kennen. 1997 machte der Meister-Couturier Valli zunächst zum Chefdesigner seiner Prêt-à-porter-Kollektionen und zwei Jahre später zum Creative Director desselben Bereichs. Bei Ungaro übersetzte der Designer den etablierten Stil des Hauses mit seinen Rüschenkaskaden, Farben tropischer Blumen und elegant drapierten, ultra-femininen Roben für eine jüngere Generation von Glamour-Girls des Jetset. Neben schillernden Vorbildern wie Halston und Marie-Hélène de Rothschild zählt Valli Francis Bacon, Kurt Cobain und Nan Goldin zu den beständigen Quellen seiner Inspiration.

En mars 2005, Giambattista Valli présente sa première collection éponyme à Paris. Ses débuts mettent en scène des pièces telles que des smokings aux lignes arrondies et de minuscules robes de cocktail en mousseline écarlate ou en tulle noir. A ce stade, le créateur italien (né en 1966 à Rome) affiche déjà un CV impressionnant, dont la plus prestigieuse référence reste son poste de directeur artistique des collections de prêt-à-porter d'Emanuel Ungaro. Giambattista Valli, qui a grandi à Rome, dit avoir été largement influencé par les stars les plus glamour du grand écran comme Claudia Cardinale, Marilyn Monroe et Rita Hayworth. Il oriente plus sérieusement sa formation vers la mode dès 1980 en s'inscrivant d'abord à l'école d'art de sa ville, puis en suivant des études de mode à l'European Design Institute (1986) avant de sortir diplômé en illustration de Central Saint Martins à Londres (1987). En 1988, Valli travaille pour l'influent créateur romain Roberto Capucci, puis pour Fendi en tant que styliste senior de la ligne Fendissime en 1990; en 1995, il est nommé styliste senior chez Krizia. L'année suivante, Valli rencontre Emanuel Ungaro par le biais d'un ami commun. Le maître couturier le nomme styliste principal de ses collections de prêt-à-porter en 1997, puis le promeut au poste de directeur de la création du prêt-à-porter Ungaro deux ans plus tard. Chez Ungaro, Valli traduit les codes bien établis de la maison – cascades de volants, couleurs de fleurs tropicales et robes très féminines aux drapés élégants – à l'intention d'une plus jeune génération de filles chic et branchées. Outre des idoles un peu paillettes telles que Halston et Marie-Hélène de Rothschild, Valli cite également Francis Bacon, Kurt Cobain et Nan Goldin comme d'inépuisables sources d'inspiration.

SUSIE RUSHTON

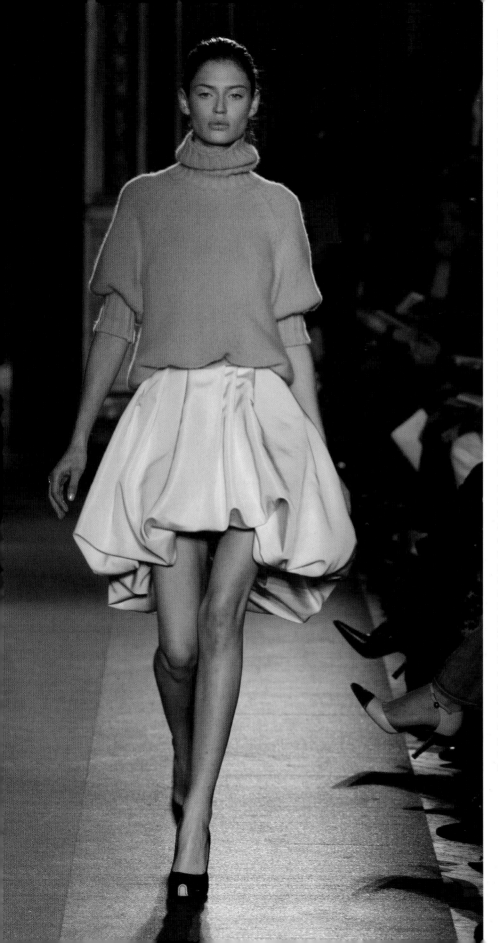

What are your signature designs? Eclectic **What is your favourite piece from any of your collections?** Dresses, comfortable as a T-shirt but glamorous and for the red carpet **How would you describe your work?** I put fragments together to create an ageless image. It is not seasonal or trend driven. You can wear the dresses over and over again **What's your ultimate goal?** To find and interpret 100% myself and invest it in my own work **What inspires you?** 1. Opposites, 2. Flashes of my personal life, 3. Art **Can fashion still have a political ambition?** Street fashion can have a political ambition, when it becomes a designer one, it is a moment after. **Who do you have in mind when you design?** People I have come across who gave me an emotion. For example in the way they walk or smoke or their style of life. It is the opposite of a dream **Is the idea of creative collaboration important to you?** Yes – very important. Something interesting always comes out. I like working with assistants and artists like Marcus Tomlinson **Who has been the greatest influence on your career?** Vionnet, Halston, YSL, Loulou de la Falaise, Antonio Lopez, Andy Warhol and Studio 54, and disco music **How have your own experiences affected your work as a designer?** Growing up in Rome gave me eclecticism: the mix-up of style from Roman to Renaissance, to Baroque, to Fascist architecture all living in harmony… **Which is more important in your work: the process or the product?** The process: project and style. Millions of women interpreting my style **Is designing difficult for you, if so, what drives you to continue?** I cannot live without design. I am design addicted. Sometimes it would be nice to detox **Have you ever been influenced or moved by the reaction to your designs?** Friends and press people make critiques. I always listen to their suggestions. Sometimes a negative critique can confirm I was right or a good critique can encourage discussion. Critiques are very important because it means your style is still alive and it is always important to evolve **What's your definition of beauty?** Something hidden, not obvious, an unconscious beauty **What's your philosophy?** To share **What is the most important lesson you've learned?** To be open to the unexpected in life so that it is always surprising.

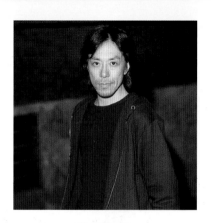

GIBO

"Fashion, craftsmanship, comfort" ICHIRO SETA

A new chapter of the Gibo story began in September 2001 when Japanese designer Ichiro Seta became the second designer of the company's signature line, presenting his debut collection in Milan. Gibo, which was founded by Franco Pene in the '60s, has played a vital part in the contemporary fashion world. As any designer will testify, the manufacture and distribution of fashion collections are crucial to the establishment of a brand and, over the years, Gibo has succeeded in developing this infrastructure for a dazzling array of household names: Alexander McQueen, Helmut Lang, Paul Smith, Viktor & Rolf, to name but a few. In 2002 Gibo's very own label was launched in London with the British illustrator-designer Julie Verhoeven as its creative director. Inevitably, with such an industry heritage behind it, the first Gibo collection was an immediate success and the brand quickly opened two flagship stores to showcase its wares in London and Milan. Verhoeven made the label famous for quirkily illustrative prints and streetwise chic shapes with an off-centre, outsider vibe. Verhoeven's successor at Gibo, the 39-year-old Seta, studied at the Mode Gakuen Institute of Tokyo. Following graduation he worked first with Jean Paul Gaultier and then with Yohji Yamamoto before launching an eponymous collection in 1998. His work for Gibo combines avant-garde experimentation with subtly feminine prints and appealing accessories, such as wide-brimmed summer hats.

Als der Japaner Ichiro Seta im September 2001 zweiter Designer für die Hauptlinie des Hauses wurde und seine Debütkollektion in Mailand präsentierte, begann ein neues Kapitel der Gibo-Story. Die in den 1960er Jahren von Franco Pene gegründete Marke Gibo spielte in der jüngeren Modegeschichte eine entscheidende Rolle. Wie jeder Designer bezeugen kann, sind Herstellung und Vertrieb von Modekollektionen der springende Punkt für die Etablierung einer Marke, und über die Jahre ist es Gibo gelungen, diese Infrastruktur zur Verfügung zu stellen. Und zwar für eine glanzvolle Sammlung klingender Namen: Alexander McQueen, Helmut Lang, Paul Smith, Viktor & Rolf, um nur einige zu nennen. 2002 wurde Gibos eigenes Label mit der britischen Illustratorin und Designerin Julie Verhoeven als Creative Director in London vorgestellt. Die erste Kollektion wurde, was bei einem solchen Hintergrund ja fast unvermeid-

lich ist, ein durchschlagender Erfolg. So eröffnete man bald je einen Flagship Store in London und Mailand. Verhoeven machte die Marke bekannt für eigenwillige illustrative Stoffmuster und aus dem Alltag abgeschaute schicke Silhouetten mit exzentrischem Außenseitercharme. Verhoevens Nachfolger bei Gibo, der 39-jährige Seta, hat am Gakuen Institute in Tokio Mode studiert. Nach dem Ende seiner Ausbildung arbeitete er zunächst mit Jean Paul Gaultier und anschließend mit Yohji Yamamoto, bevor er 1998 eine Kollektion unter eigenem Namen lancierte. Seine Entwürfe für Gibo kombinieren avantgardistische Experimentierfreude mit dezenten, femininen Mustern und ansprechenden Accessoires wie breitkrempigen Sommerhüten.

Le nouveau chapitre de l'histoire de Gibo a commencé en septembre 2001, quand le créateur japonais Ichiro Seta, second styliste de la ligne signature de l'entreprise, a présenté sa première collection à Milan. Fondée par Franco Pene dans les années 60, la maison Gibo joue un rôle vital dans l'univers de la mode contemporaine. Comme n'importe quel créateur pourrait en témoigner, la fabrication et la distribution des collections sont absolument cruciales pour établir une marque. Au fil des années, Gibo a réussi à développer cette infrastructure pour une impressionnante palette de stars de la mode : Alexander McQueen, Helmut Lang, Paul Smith et Viktor & Rolf, pour n'en citer que quelques-uns. En 2002, Gibo lance sa propre griffe à Londres, avec l'illustratrice anglaise Julie Verhoeven à la direction de la création. Forte d'une telle expérience de l'industrie, la première collection Gibo remporte un succès immédiat et la marque ouvre rapidement deux boutiques pour présenter ses créations à Londres et à Milan. Julie Verhoeven a rendu la griffe célèbre pour ses imprimés originaux et ses vêtements chic inspirés du streetwear, avec leur côté d'outsider décalé. Le successeur de Julie Verhoeven chez Gibo, Ichiro Seta, 39 ans, a fait ses études au Mode Gakuen Institute de Tokyo. Une fois diplômé, il a d'abord travaillé avec Jean Paul Gaultier, puis avec Yohji Yamamoto avant de lancer sa collection éponyme en 1998. Son travail pour Gibo combine une expérimentation d'avant-garde avec des imprimés subtilement féminins et des accessoires irrésistibles, comme ses chapeaux d'été à large bord.

TERRY NEWMAN

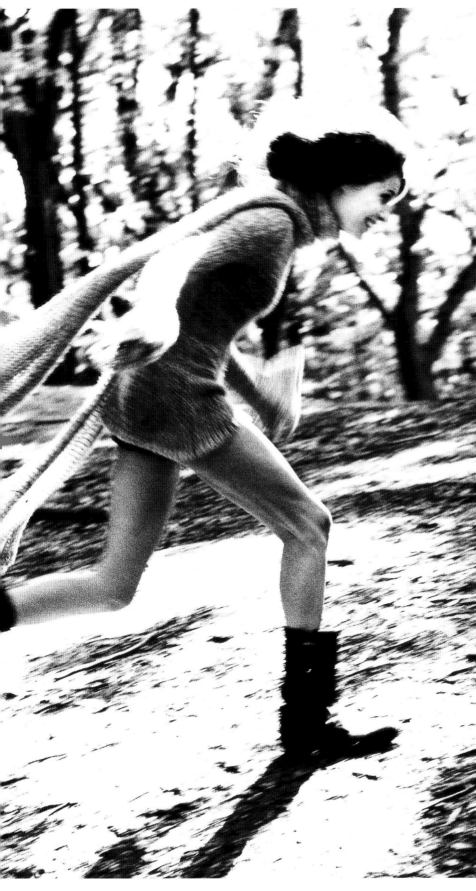

What are your signature designs? Asymmetric flared skirt with volume **What is your favourite piece from any of your collections?** The knit dress **How would you describe your work?** Fashion, craftsmanship, comfort **What's your ultimate goal?** To establish my own brand **What inspires you?** My life, every single day **Can fashion still have a political ambition?** I think yes **Who do you have in mind when you design?** No-one specific but every one **Is the idea of creative collaboration important to you?** I'm very interested in the collaboration between the skilled and the skilled **Who has been the greatest influence on your career?** Mr. Yohji Yamamoto **Which is more important in your work: the process or the product?** I think, both **Is designing difficult for you, and if so, what drives you to continue?** I think it's very difficult, but I love it **Have you ever been influenced or moved by the reaction to your designs?** Yes **What's your definition of beauty?** Everything that impresses me. Like sport, literature, etc. **What's your philosophy?** I am valued or formed by another person **What is the most important lesson you've learned?** Human warmth.

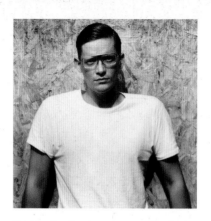

GILES DEACON

"I am always happy if people give my designs the time of day"

From one-time fashion illustrator to the British Fashion Awards 2004's Best New Designer, Giles Deacon's star is certainly in the ascendant. Following an art foundation course in Harrogate, England, he graduated in fashion design from London's Central Saint Martins in 1992 – a course selected, he has said, purely for novelty value. From here, Yorkshire-born Deacon worked with Jean-Charles de Castelbajac in Paris for two years before being appointed in 1998 to a dream job: he was selected by Tom Ford, then of the Gucci Group, as head designer for the luxury accessories brand Bottega Veneta. As it turned out, the experience was a salutary one that eventually persuaded Deacon to go it alone. In 2004 he launched his first full solo collection, which he titled 'Disco Jacobean Fairytale'. Sophisticated, feminine womenswear such as calf-length skirts, pussycat bow blouses, and '40s-style nipped-in jackets featured in his debut, which was shown during London Fashion Week, and modelled by world-famous super-models. Deacon (born 1969) has been particularly quick to establish a glamorous signature look, one from which, he professes, there will be little deviation over the coming years. With his designs also showing an obvious leaning towards the hand-crafted, Deacon is fast winning a reputation for working closely with many smaller British specialist companies – experts in their field of embroidery or beading, for instance. His prints are often inspired by Art Nouveau, which is perhaps a reflection of his ongoing interest in illustration; an exhibition of this area of his work was recently staged in Rome. Deacon has also created a collection for the lingerie company Agent Provocateur.

Nachdem er es vom Modezeichner zum Best New Designer 2004 bei den British Fashion Awards gebracht hat, kann man wohl mit Fug und Recht behaupten, dass Giles Deacons Stern im Steigen begriffen ist. Nach dem Grundstudium im englischen Harrogate machte er 1992 seinen Abschluss am Londoner Central Saint Martins. Laut eigener Aussage war für ihn allein der Reiz des Neuen ausschlaggebend für die Studienwahl. Später arbeitete der aus Yorkshire stammende Deacon zwei Jahre lang mit Jean-Charles de Castelbajac in Paris, bevor er 1998 das Angebot für einen Traumjob bekam: Tom Ford, damals noch bei Gucci, bestimmte ihn zum Chefdesigner der luxuriösen Accessoire-Marke Bottega Veneta. Diese Erfahrung war ein echter Segen, denn sie bewog Deacon, es schließlich allein zu versuchen. So lancierte er 2004 seine erste komplette Solo-kollektion unter dem Namen Disco Jacobean Fairytale. Raffiniert feminine Damenmode wie wadenlange Röcke, Blusen mit weichen Schleifen und Schlupf-jacken im Stil der 1940er Jahre prägten sein Debüt, das auf der Londoner Mode-woche von weltberühmten Supermodels präsentiert wurde und für phänomenale

Kritiken sorgte. Der 1969 geborene Deacon schaffte es in unglaublich kurzer Zeit, einen glamourösen eigenständigen Look zu entwickeln, von dem er nach eigener Aussage in den nächsten Jahren auch nicht stark abzuweichen gedenkt. Seine Entwürfe zeigen auch sein Faible für handwerklich Anspruchsvolles. So erwarb er sich rasch den Ruf, jemand mit engen Kontakten zu vielen kleinen britischen Spezialbetrieben zu sein – Experten in den Bereichen Stickerei oder Pailletten etwa. Seine Muster sind oft vom Jugendstil inspiriert, was mit sei-nem nach wie vor regen Interesse an Illustrationen zusammenhängen mag. Eine Ausstellung seiner Arbeiten in diesem Bereich war kürzlich in Rom zu sehen. Zuletzt entwarf Deacon für das Label Agent Provocateur eine Dessous-Kol-lektion. Im Übrigen gilt er heute als einer der vielversprechendsten Designer Großbritanniens.

D'une expérience d'illustrateur de mode au prix de Best New Designer des Bri-tish Fashion Awards 2004, on ne prend pas trop de risque en affirmant que Giles Deacon est une étoile en pleine ascension. Après avoir suivi des cours à l'école d'art de Harrogate en Angleterre, il sort diplômé en mode de Central Saint Mar-tins en 1992 : un cursus choisi, avoue-t-il, surtout pour l'attrait de la nouveauté. Ensuite, le jeune créateur du Yorkshire travaille pendant deux ans avec Jean-Charles de Castelbajac à Paris avant d'obtenir un job de rêve en 1998 : repéré par Tom Ford, qui travaille alors pour le Groupe Gucci, il est nommé styliste princi-pal de la marque d'accessoires de luxe Bottega Veneta. Cette expérience s'avère salutaire pour Deacon, qui finit par trouver le courage de lancer sa propre griffe. En 2004, il présente une première collection complète baptisée « Disco Jacobean Fairytale » : les vêtements féminins et sophistiqués de ses débuts, tels que les jupes au mollet, les chemisiers à lavallière et les vestes cintrées très années 40, sont présentés lors de la London Fashion Week sur des top models mondiale-ment célèbres et suscitent les louanges de la critique. Giles Deacon (né en 1969) a été particulièrement prompt à établir son glamour signature, dont il pense ne pas trop s'éloigner au cours de ces prochaines années. Avec des créations qui rendent un hommage évident au savoir-faire à l'ancienne, Deacon s'est aussi fait connaître pour ses étroites collaborations avec de petits artisans anglais, par exemple des experts spécialisés dans la broderie ou les perles. Ses imprimés pui-sent souvent leur inspiration dans l'Art Nouveau, peut-être en référence à son intérêt de longue date pour l'illustration ; une exposition de son œuvre illustra-tive a d'ailleurs été récemment organisée à Rome. Figurant aujourd'hui parmi les chouchous de la mode britannique, Giles Deacon a aussi créé une collection pour la griffe de lingerie Agent Provocateur.

JOSH SIMS

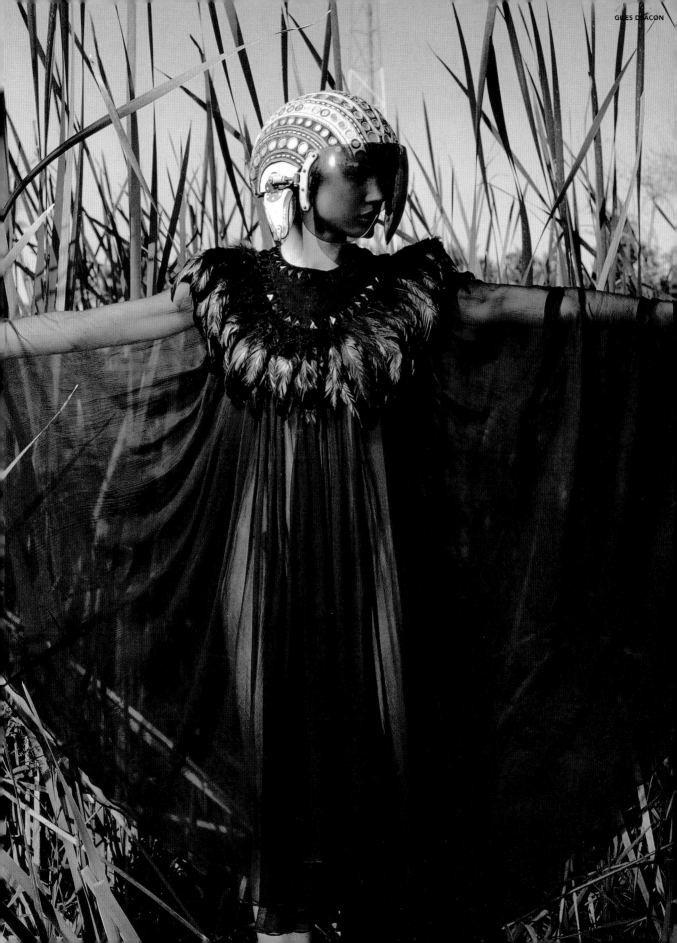

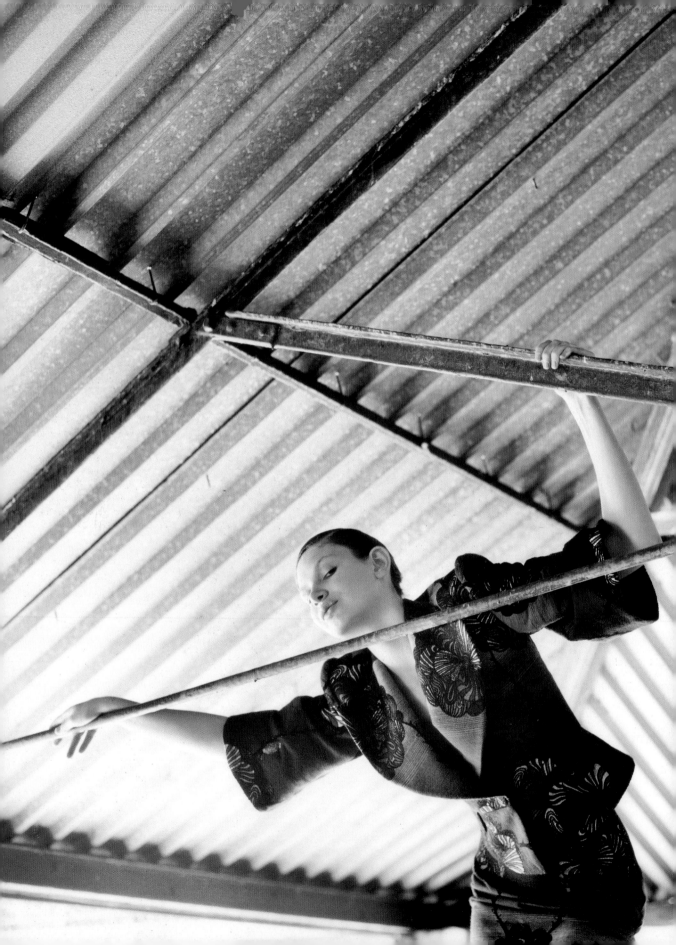

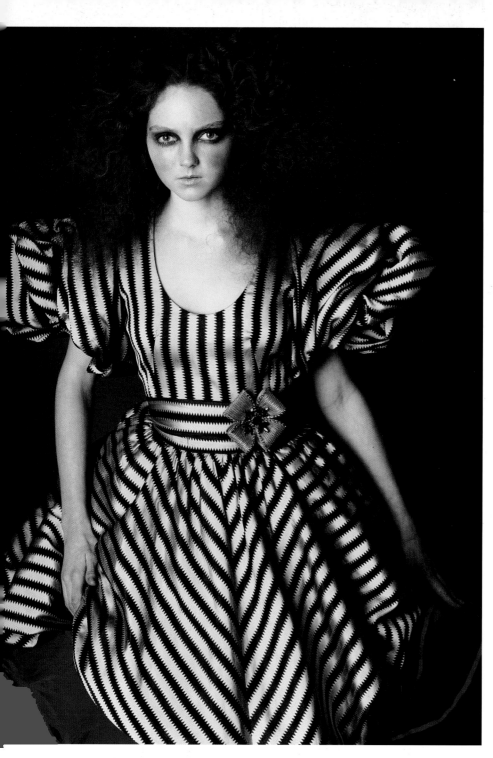

What are your signature designs? Specialist-designed fabrics, sharp suits and cult leader dresses **What is your favourite piece from any of your collections?** From the first collection the glitter prints and rose jacquard suits, from spring/summer 2005 meteor print dresses and the 'dazzle' skirts/suits **How would you describe your work?** Hopefully an interesting emotive thing **What's your ultimate goal?** Just to be happy working in an interesting environment keeps me going **What inspires you?** Nature, spontaneity and eccentricity **Can fashion still have a political ambition?** Only in an environmental way **Who do you have in mind when you design?** A mix of a whole host of various people's attributes **Is the idea of creative collaboration important to you?** I love it **Who has been the greatest influence on your career?** Keith Haring **How have your own experiences affected your work as a designer?** All the time and hopefully always will **Which is more important in your work: the process or the product?** Both are of equal importance, although the process is more fun **Is designing difficult for you, if so, what drives you to continue?** No, not difficult though things do not always go to plan which can also be interesting **Have you ever been influenced or moved by the reaction to your designs?** I am always happy that people give the designs the time of day to think about them **What's your definition of beauty?** Wit and a nice pair of legs **What's your philosophy?** The grass is always greener underneath you **What is the most important lesson you've learned?** Keep on working and have some fun.

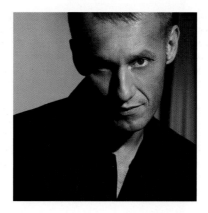

GILLES ROSIER

"I would love to be designing clothes that reveal personality"

Known for sculpting fabric around the human form with his complex constructions, Gilles Rosier is that rare thing in modern Parisian fashion – a native Frenchman. Born in Paris in 1961 to a French father and German mother, Rosier had an itinerant childhood, travelling through Algiers, Port-Gentil and Kinshasa with his family. On his return to Paris, Rosier had acquired both a talent for drawing and the ability to adapt to changing circumstances, skills that have served him well over his career. He studied at the Ecole de la Chambre Syndicale de la Couture, graduating in 1982. Apprenticeships right at the heart of haute couture – with Pierre Balmain and Christian Dior – were followed by a position at Guy Paulin. In 1987, he became assistant to Jean Paul Gaultier and five years later finally went solo, with a single season designing menswear for print house Léonard. In the same year, Rosier launched his own label entitled GR816, while simultaneously taking up the role of creative director at Lacoste, where he remained for seven years. But it was at Kenzo that Rosier made perhaps his greatest impact so far when he was chosen by Kenzo Takada himself to succeed him as artistic director at the LVMH-owned label. From 1998 to 2003, the younger designer managed to evolve the house's exuberant history with the introduction of a sophisticated new image that harnessed his own fascination with colour and contrast. In February 2004, yet another new location beckoned: Milan, where Rosier re-launched his eponymous label with romantic black tailoring for women, produced by Italian group Miroglio. For spring/summer 2005, he extended his repertoire to include menswear. Gilles Rosier also occasionally finds time to act in theatrical productions of plays by Shakespeare and Chekhov.

Er ist bekannt dafür, wie er Stoff geradezu bildhauerisch um den menschlichen Körper drapiert. Außerdem ist Gilles Rosier etwas ganz Seltenes in der modernen Pariser Modeszene – ein Franzose. Geboren wurde er 1961 in Paris als Kind eines französischen Vaters und einer deutschen Mutter. Seine Kindheit verbrachte er zwischen Algier, Port-Gentil und Kinshasa. Bei seiner Rückkehr nach Paris hatte Rosier sowohl zeichnerisches Talent mitgebracht als auch die Fähigkeit, sich an veränderte Umstände anzupassen – zwei Eigenschaften, die ihm im Laufe seiner Karriere noch von großem Nutzen sein sollten. Er studierte an der Ecole de la Chambre Syndicale de la Couture, die er 1982 abschloss. Auf Praktika quasi im Herzen der Haute Couture – bei Pierre Balmain und Christian Dior – folgte ein Intermezzo bei Guy Paulin. 1987 wurde Rosier Assistent von Jean Paul Gaultier. Fünf Jahre später versuchte er sich schließlich allein in Herrenmode, und zwar in einer einzigen Saison für das Haus Léonard. Noch im selben Jahr lancierte der Designer sein eigenes Label unter dem Namen GR816, während er gleichzeitig die Funktion des Creative Director bei Lacoste übernahm, die er sieben Jahre lang ausüben sollte. Es war jedoch bei Kenzo, wo Rosier sein bislang größter Coup gelang, als ihn Kenzo Takada höchstpersönlich zu seinem Nachfolger als Artistic Director des Labels im Besitz von LVMH bestimmte. Zwischen 1998 und 2003 gelang es ihm, aus der reichen Geschichte des Labels ein raffiniertes neues Image zu formen, bei dem ihm sein Faible für Farben und Kontraste zugute kam. Im Februar 2004 lockte Rosier eine neue Location: Mailand. Dort kümmerte er sich mit romantischer Schneiderkunst in Schwarz und unterstützt von der italienischen Miroglio-Gruppe um den Relaunch des nach ihm benannten Labels. Für Frühjahr/Sommer 2005 erweiterte er sein Spektrum um Herrenmode. Gelegentlich findet Gilles Rosier sogar noch Zeit, um in Theaterstücken von Shakespeare und Tschechow mitzuspielen.

Réputé pour son art de sculpter le tissu autour du corps humain Gilles Rosier fait figure de véritable rareté dans la mode parisienne d'aujourd'hui : c'est un créateur français. Né en 1961 à Paris d'un père français et d'une mère allemande, Rosier passe son enfance à déménager, suivant sa famille entre Alger, Port-Gentil ou Kinshasa. Lorsqu'il revient à Paris, il a acquis le talent du dessin et la capacité de s'adapter aux changements, des compétences qui lui seront fort utiles au cours de sa carrière. Il étudie à l'Ecole de la Chambre Syndicale de la Couture, dont il sort diplômé en 1982. Après des stages d'apprentissage au cœur même de la haute couture (chez Pierre Balmain et Christian Dior), il collabore avec Guy Paulin. En 1987, il devient assistant de Jean Paul Gaultier et finit par se lancer en solo cinq ans plus tard, après une seule saison en tant que styliste de la collection pour homme du roi des imprimés Léonard. La même année, Rosier lance sa propre griffe baptisée GR816, tout en assumant son poste de directeur de la création de Lacoste, où il passera sept ans. Mais c'est sans doute chez Kenzo que Rosier se fait le plus remarquer, quand Kenzo Takada en personne le choisit comme son successeur au poste de directeur artistique de sa maison, qui appartient désormais à LVMH. De 1998 à 2003, le jeune créateur réussit à faire évoluer les archives exubérantes de Kenzo vers une nouvelle image plus sophistiquée qui révèle sa propre fascination pour la couleur et le contraste. En février 2004, il délaisse Paris pour Milan, où il relance sa ligne éponyme avec des tailleurs noirs romantiques produits grâce au soutien du groupe italien Miroglio. Pour le printemps/été 2005, il étend son répertoire pour inclure une collection masculine. Par ailleurs, Rosier trouve parfois le temps de jouer dans des pièces de théâtre de Shakespeare et de Tchekhov.

SUSIE RUSHTON

What are your signature designs? Construction of the garment that reveals the body, and the balance between purity, construction and a certain humility of the clothes that, by this humility, the body of the person is revealed What is your favourite piece from any of your collections? I love the pieces that are never stable, that you can play with, it's like a work in progress, that you can make it evolve every time. For instance you take off sleeves, you take off collars, according to your mood, according to where you are, it's like work in progress What inspires you? Grace. Movement inspires me. Human gesture inspires me. Distortion inspires me a lot – that is why I love to go to see ballet because distortion of the body inspires clothes and attitudes and silhouettes How would you describe your work? My work is not only focusing on fashion, it's focusing on the architecture of clothes What's your ultimate goal? I would love to be designing clothes that reveal personality What is more important in your work: the process or the product? I think it's the process Is your idea of creative collaboration important to you? It is really important. It's super-important. The more you collaborate the more you know about your own creation Can fashion still have a political ambition? Yes. To me, there is a social purpose What's your philosophy? I love to create things that have no past. I mean, they can have a flavour of past, but they have to inscribe themselves into the future and I love to create things that people discover step by step What's your definition of beauty? Beauty is when something or someone is really being itself. It's about purity, it's about being honest with oneself, and I think everyone can be beautiful. It's just a matter of accepting oneself How have your own experiences affected your work as a designer? They affect it a lot Have you ever been influenced by or moved by the reactions to your designs? Sometimes, yes I am. I've been moved because I'm not even conscious about the strength of what I propose Who has been the biggest influence on your career? I think that it's really both my mother and my grandmother, because they really cared about clothes What is the most important lesson you've learned? The most important lesson I've learned is never to be really satisfied with what you do. And to persevere.

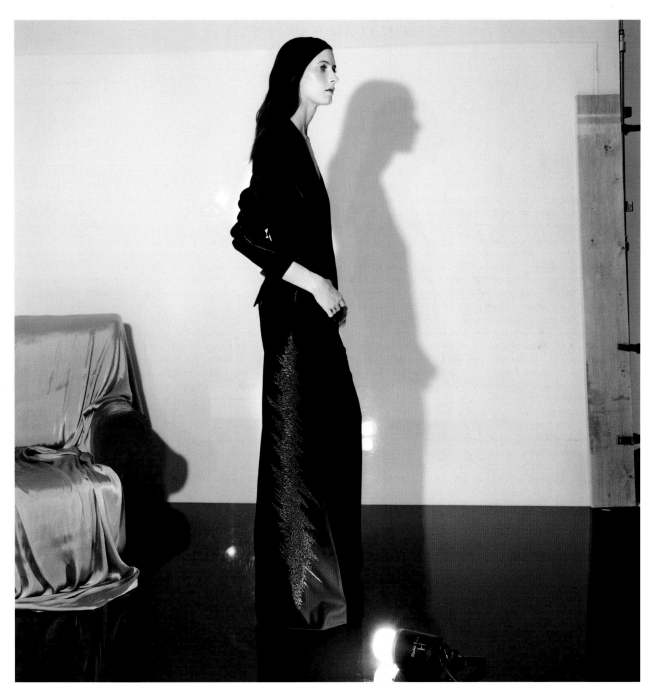

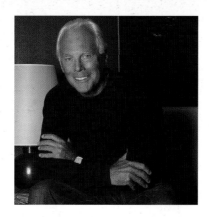

GIORGIO ARMANI

"I have realised over time that I have to take responsibility for my actions and beliefs"

Now in his fifth decade working in fashion, Giorgio Armani is more than just a designer – he's an institution, an icon and a multinational, billion-dollar brand. Armani the man was born in 1934 in Piacenza, northern Italy. He spent his formative years not in fashion but studying medicine at university and completing his national service. After working as a buyer for Milanese department store La Rinascente, he scored his first break in 1964, when he was hired by Nino Cerruti to design a menswear line, Hitman. Several years as a successful freelance designer followed, but it was in 1975 that the Giorgio Armani label was set up, with the help of his then business partner Sergio Galeotti. Armani's signature 'unstructured' jackets for both men and women (a womenswear line was established in 1976), knocked the stuffing out of traditional tailoring and from the late '70s, his clothes became a uniform for the upwardly mobile. Men loved his relaxed suits and muted colour palette of neutral beiges and greys. His designs for women, meanwhile, were admired for an androgynous and modern elegance. Richard Gere's suits in 'American Gigolo' (1980) were a landmark for the designer, as was the cover of Time magazine in 1982. The brand now encompasses six major fashion lines and has diversified into bedlinen, chocolates and even hotels. Armani has won countless awards, including an Honorary Doctorate from the RCA in 1991; from 2000 his designs have been exhibited in a major retrospective show that has travelled worldwide. Armani has also picked up a dedicated Hollywood following, and January 2005 saw the launch in Paris of 'Giorgio Armani Privé', an haute couture-like collection.

Er arbeitet inzwischen seit über vierzig Jahren in der Modebranche und ist viel mehr als „nur" ein Designer. Giorgio Armani ist eine Institution, eine Ikone und ein internationales, millionendollarschweres Markenzeichen. Geboren wurde er 1934 im norditalienischen Piacenza. Die ersten Jahre als Erwachsener verbrachte Armani jedoch nicht in der Modeszene, sondern beim Medizinstudium an der Universität und beim Militär. Nach einer Anstellung als Einkäufer für das Mailänder Kaufhaus La Rinascente landete er 1964 seinen ersten Coup, nachdem Nino Cerruti ihn mit dem Entwurf einer Herrenlinie namens Hitman beauftragt hatte. Es folgten einige Jahre als gefragter freischaffender Designer, bis 1975 mit der Gründung des Labels Giorgio Armani die Weichen für die Zukunft der Mode neu gestellt wurden. Daran beteiligt war damals auch Armanis Geschäftspartner Sergio Galeotti. Markenzeichen waren die „unstrukturierten" Jacketts für Männer wie Frauen (eine Damenlinie wurde 1976 gegründet), die im Unterschied zu traditionell geschneiderten Modellen ganz ohne Polster auskamen. Ab Ende der 1970er galt seine Mode als eine Art Uniform für Leute, die Karriere machten. Männer liebten seine legeren Anzüge und gedämpften Beige- und Grautöne.

Dagegen fanden die Entwürfe für Frauen wegen ihrer Androgynität und modernen Eleganz großen Zuspruch. Richard Geres Anzüge in „American Gigolo" (1980) waren ein Meilenstein für den Modemacher, ebenso das Time Cover von 1982. Heute umfasst die Marke Armani sechs große Modelinien, aber auch Bereiche wie Bettwäsche, Schokolade und sogar Hotels. Neben zahllosen Auszeichnungen erhielt der Designer 1991 die Ehrendoktorwürde des Royal College of Art. 2000 wurden seine Entwürfe im Rahmen einer großen Retrospektive weltweit gezeigt. Armani hat sich aber auch eine treue Anhängerschaft in Hollywood aufgebaut. Vielleicht eines seiner ambitioniertesten Projekte war die Präsentation von „Giorgio Armani Privé" im Januar 2005 in Paris, eine Kollektion im Stil der Haute Couture.

Avec cinquante ans de métier derrière lui, Giorgio Armani est bien plus qu'un couturier : c'est une véritable institution, une icône et une multinationale qui pèse plusieurs milliards de dollars. Armani est né en 1934 à Piacenza dans le nord de l'Italie. Il suit d'abord des études de médecine à l'université avant de faire son service militaire. Après avoir travaillé comme acheteur pour La Rinascente, le grand magasin milanais, il se lance dans la mode en 1964 quand Nino Cerruti le recrute pour dessiner une ligne pour homme, Hitman. Les années suivantes, il rencontre un grand succès en tant que styliste free-lance mais il faut attendre 1975 pour voir l'avenir de la mode se transformer grâce à la création de la griffe Giorgio Armani, qu'il fonde avec l'aide de Sergio Galeotti, son partenaire en affaires de l'époque. Les vestes « déstructurées » pour homme et pour femme devenues la signature d'Armani (une ligne pour femme sera lancée en 1976) bouleversent les codes et dès la fin des années 70, ses créations s'imposent comme l'uniforme des ambitieux aux dents longues. Les hommes adorent ses costumes décontractés et sa palette de beiges et de gris neutres, tandis que ses vêtements pour femme séduisent grâce à leur élégance androgyne et moderne. Les costumes dessinés pour le personnage de Richard Gere dans « American Gigolo » (1980) marquent un tournant dans la carrière du créateur, qui connaît la consécration en 1982 en faisant la couverture du magazine Time. La marque, qui regroupe aujourd'hui six grandes lignes de mode, s'est aussi diversifiée dans des domaines tels que la literie, les chocolats et même les hôtels. Armani s'est vu décerner d'innombrables distinctions, notamment un Doctorat Honorifique du Royal College of Art en 1991 ; en l'an 2000, son travail a fait l'objet d'une grande rétrospective qui a voyagé dans les musées du monde entier. Armani revendique aussi des fans parmi l'élite d'Hollywood. Son projet le plus ambitieux à ce jour a été révélé en janvier 2005 à Paris, théâtre du lancement de « Giorgio Armani Privé », collection de haute couture de coupe traditionnelle. LAUREN COCHRANE

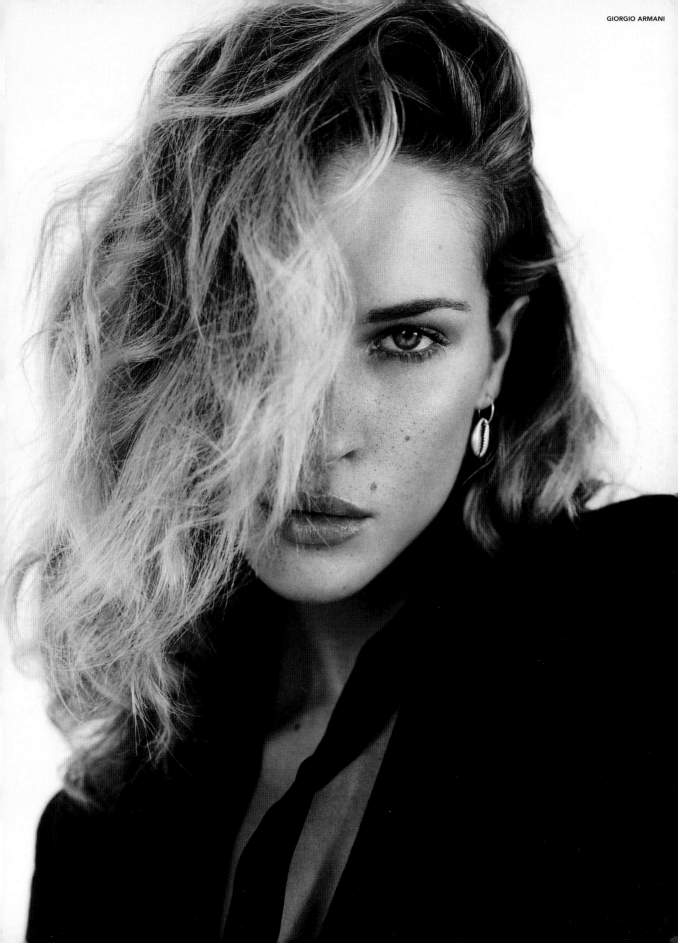

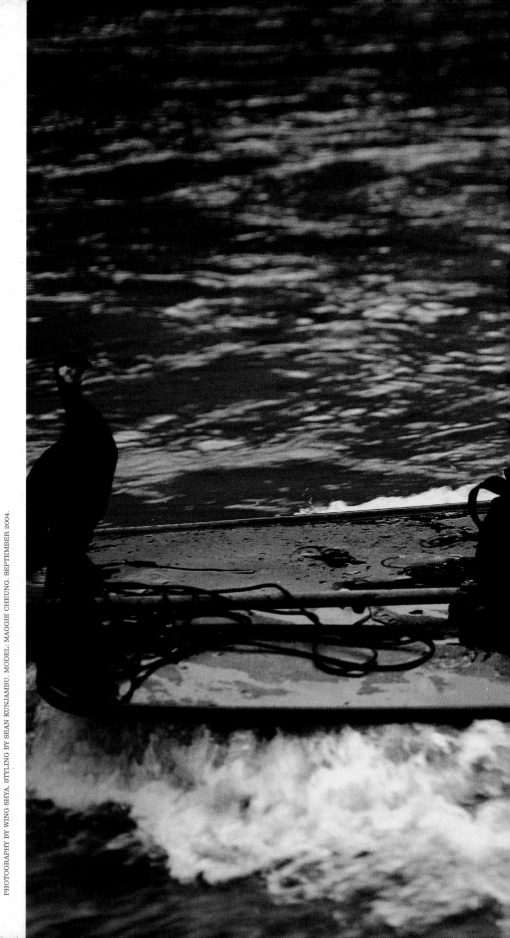

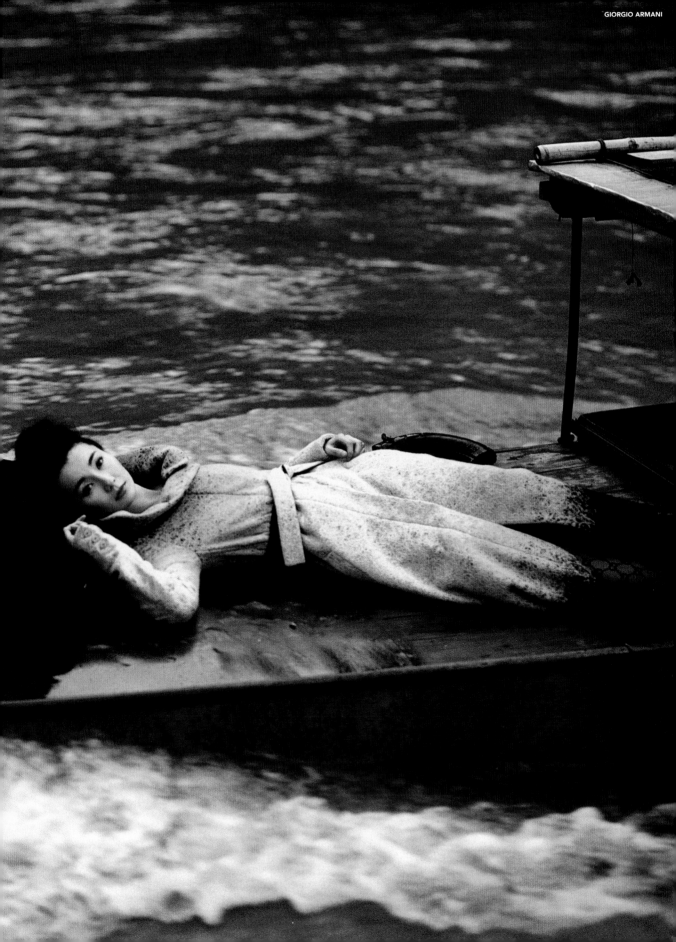

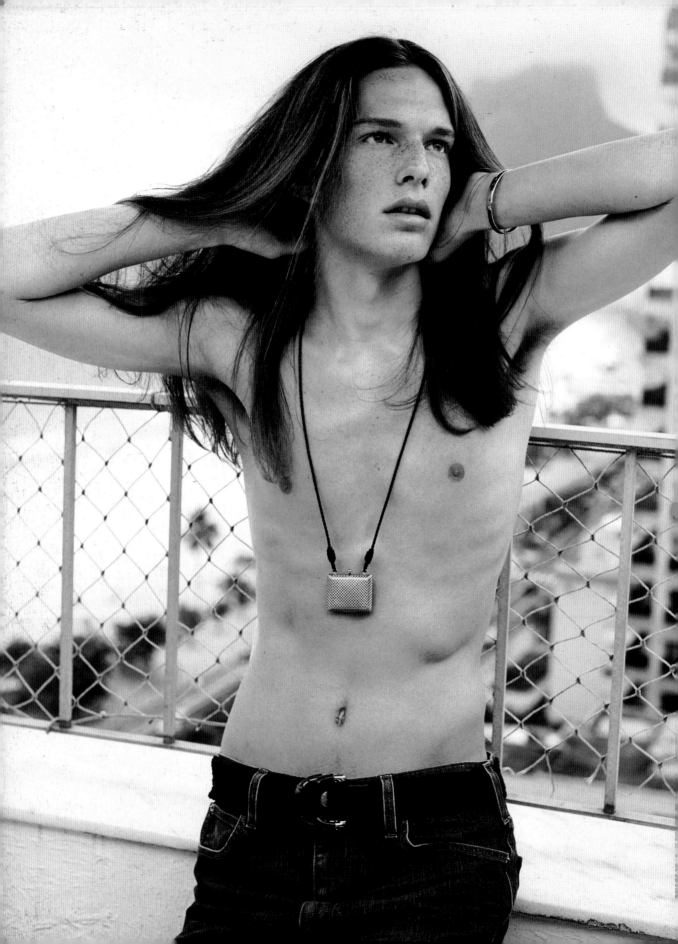

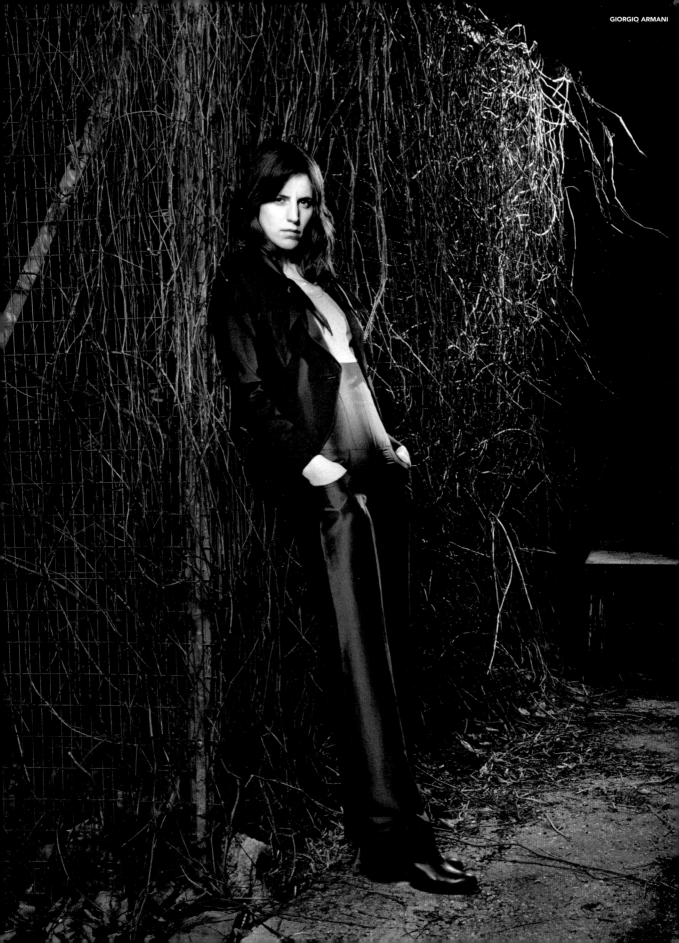

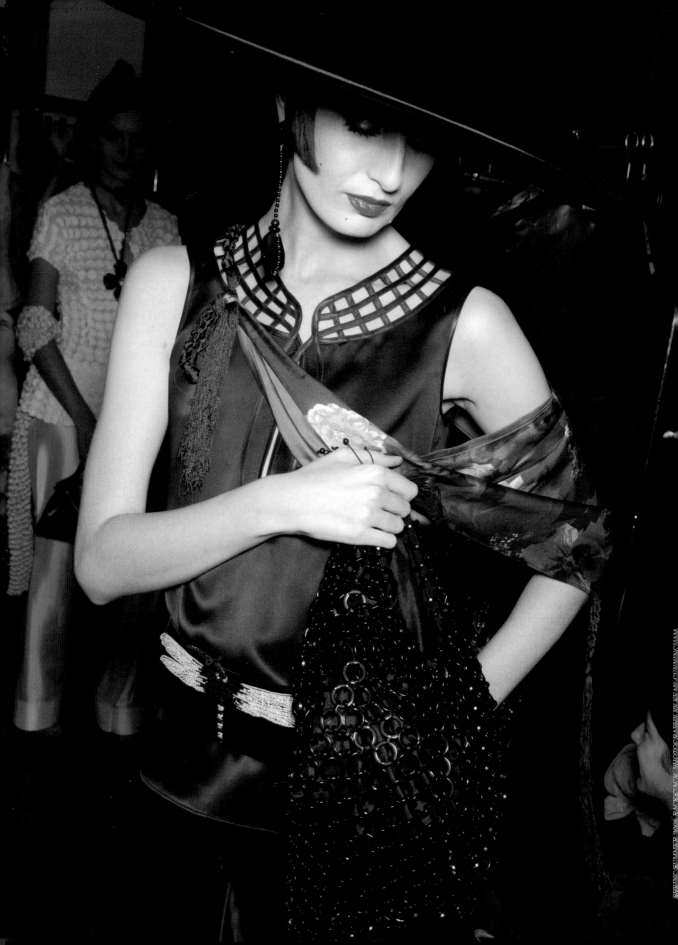

What are your signature designs? I would say that I am best known for my deconstructed jackets, for men and for women **What is your favourite piece from any of your collections?** I would have to say "the Jacket." In early years, it was the deconstructed style, and most recently the close-fitting cardigan style 'Beckham' jacket **How would you describe your work?** Maybe that I strive to keep the world of fashion personal **What's your ultimate goal?** I like to think that I can introduce people to the idea of simplicity and elegance **What inspires you?** I am a great people-watcher, and I suppose they are my greatest inspiration – the way people behave, move, dress – this is what really interests me **Can fashion still have a political ambition?** Yes, of course. My notions of deconstruction were political in as much as I was advocating a change to the status quo – and I still believe that people should be allowed to be themselves where their clothes are concerned **Who do you have in mind when you design?** I sometimes might base a design on a specific person. But mostly I design without actual people in mind – more a notion of a certain type of person who will understand and appreciate my aesthetic **Is the idea of creative collaboration important to you?** Absolutely. I have found my experience working in film, for example, extremely stimulating. I find that any creative dialogue you enter into with another person or another medium (furniture, for example) is bound to push you and make you grow. If you are the kind of fashion designer who looks no further than the runway, you will never really progress **Who has been the greatest influence on your career?** There have been several influential people in my working life, but perhaps the greatest was my first business partner, Sergio Galeotti. It was Sergio who saw what I was capable of and encouraged me to start a label that bore my name. It was Sergio who through his irrepressible flair got me to believe that anything was possible **How have your own experiences affected your work as a designer?** All experiences can have an influence on your work – both major and minor. When I was a kid I was severely burnt during the Second World War when an unexploded shell I was playing with went off. It killed my friend and I spent weeks in hospital in a vat of alcohol recovering. I lost my sight for about ten days – I thought I was blind. Something like that doesn't leave you, but if you come through it, the chances are you will be a survivor. Then there's the less serious stuff, like when I bought a boat a couple of years ago. I decided to design the interior myself and I also looked at the way I could make the hull more suited to my tastes. The experience clearly had an influence on my next collection, which contained the colours of the ocean and naval details and fastenings **Which is more important in your work: the process or the product?** I think for many designers the process is the important thing, and they consider the product more important for the customer than for themselves. But without customers you have nothing, so for me both process and product are critical **Is designing difficult for you, if so, what drives you to continue?** No, I am lucky in that I find designing relatively easy. It is running the business that is difficult **Have you ever been influenced or moved by the reaction to your designs?** I used to take great interest in what the press had to say, which to begin with was a real problem as my first collections were regarded by many as a type of heresy **What's your definition of beauty?** A natural, clean, effortless quality. Beautiful people are not necessarily the best looking – more the ones with poise, and self-confidence **What's your philosophy?** Be true to what you believe in and follow your passions **What is the most important lesson you've learned?** To trust my own instincts. I have realised over time that I have to take responsibility for my actions and beliefs. In terms of fashion, this means that I stand by what I do. If others don't like it, then that's fair enough. But I have to be consistent, and create what I believe in. Otherwise I have nothing.

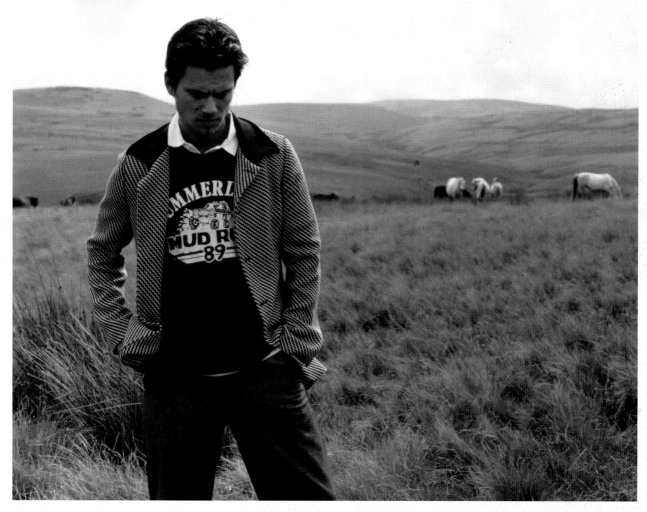

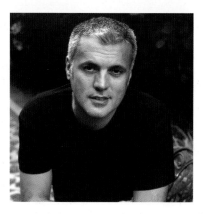

GIUSEPPE ZANOTTI

"When I design, I think of women's charm, and their feet"

Born in San Mauro Pascoli, Italy (1958), Giuseppe Zanotti designs high fashion, ultra-glamorous shoes for a dazzlingly eclectic range of tastes. As he stresses, 'Does only one type of woman exist?' Starting out as a design apprentice, Zanotti forged his reputation as a footwear designer for Italian and international companies before trying his hand at his own label, in 1994. And hasn't looked back. Having created luxury footwear for women for over 20 years, Zanotti has perfected the blend of quality and design, finding his inspiration in music videos, art and design. His embellished, extravagant creations range from point-toed pumps to sandals smothered with baroque-style jewellery and outrageous stiletto boots. "Informal or ultra chic, it makes no difference," says Zanotti. "What matters is the way it's worn." However, a certain type of Italian high glitz is a common factor in his designs and for this exuberance (and his craftsmanship) Zanotti has attracted a cult following. With the help of his wife Cinzia – who is the driving force behind his advertising campaigns, special events and VIP endorsements – Zanotti remains entirely in step with the times.

Der 1958 im italienischen San Mauro Pascoli geborene Giuseppe Zanotti entwirft nobelste, ultraglamouröse Schuhkreationen für jeden nur erdenklichen Geschmack. „Gibt es vielleicht nur einen einzigen Typ Frau?" rechtfertigt er seine fast schon verwirrende Vielseitigkeit. Nach einem Beginn als Lehrling erwarb sich Zanotti als Schuhdesigner für italienische und internationale Hersteller einen Namen, bevor er sich 1994 an einem eigenen Label versuchte. Von da an ging es nur noch steil bergauf. Seit mehr als zwanzig Jahren kreiert er nun luxuriöses Schuhwerk für Damen und hat die Verbindung von Qualität und Design perfektioniert. Seine Inspirationen holt er sich aus Musikvideos, Kunst und Design. Seine verzierten, extravaganten Kreationen reichen von spitzen Pumps über barocke, reich mit Schmuck besetzte Sandalen bis hin zu unglaublichen Stiletto-Stiefeln. „Lässig oder ultra-chic, das spielt keine Rolle", sagt Zanotti. „Was zählt ist die Art, wie man Schuhe trägt." Eine bestimmte Form italienischen Glamours findet sich allerdings oft in seinen Arbeiten, und um seiner Üppigkeit (und seiner Kunstfertigkeit) willen wird er von einer Fangemeinde verehrt. Nicht zuletzt dank seiner Frau Cinzia – der treibenden Kraft hinter Werbekampagnen, Special Events und VIP-Support – hält Zanotti mit den sich wandelnden Zeiten mühelos Schritt.

Né en 1958 à San Mauro Pascoli en Italie, Giuseppe Zanotti crée des chaussures de luxe très glamour qui répondent aux goûts les plus éclectiques. Car comme il le dit lui-même : « N'existerait-il donc qu'un seul type de femme ? ». Débutant comme apprenti, Zanotti forge sa réputation de créateur de chaussures auprès de maisons italiennes et internationales avant de lancer sa propre griffe en 1994. Il ne fera plus machine arrière. Créant des modèles féminins luxueux depuis plus de vingt ans, Zanotti a perfectionné le mélange entre qualité et créativité, puisant son inspiration dans les clips vidéo, l'art et le design. Ses créations extravagantes et chargées vont des escarpins à bouts pointus aux sandales ornées de bijoux baroques, sans oublier de scandaleuses bottes à talons aiguille. « Style informel ou ultra chic, ça ne fait aucune différence », explique Zanotti. « Ce qui compte, c'est la façon dont les chaussures sont portées ». Néanmoins, un certain style paillettes et strass à l'italienne reste le dénominateur commun de ses créations, et grâce à cette exubérance (et à son savoir-faire artisanal), Zanotti a été hissé au rang de créateur culte par ses fans. Avec le soutien de sa femme Cinzia, qui supervise les campagnes publicitaires et les manifestations spéciales à qui il doit sa clientèle VIP, Zanotti reste un créateur très à l'aise avec son temps. HOLLY SHACKLETON

What are your signature designs? The jewelled sandals. To design a jewelled sandal, for me, is to "raise" it from a shoe to a decorated accessory **What is your favourite piece from any of your collections?** It's the one that has a story to tell because it's born from a particular inspiration, for example the flat sandal from the spring/summer 2005 collection. For this shoe, I took inspiration from a Jimi Hendrix' cover from the '70s **How would you describe your work?** My work is based on watching the things that I like, for example movements in music, architecture, design, nature, and to transform the emotions that they give me into objects, into shoes that are going be able to give emotions to the women who'll wear them **What is your ultimate goal?** To be able to reach to 'my woman', the one who understands and appreciates my product, wherever she is in the world **What inspires you?** My study room is full of pictures, magazines, fabrics and colours, from the past and from present, and every day, I can see in this chaos a new combination or a new element that can be included in a new product **Can fashion still have a political ambition?** For sure, fashion and art are instruments of communication and they throw out messages that can make a noise **Who do you have in mind when you design?** I think of women's charm and their feet. Shoes, sandals, mules or boots can cover or uncover the foot, but all this needs a sense of proportion and lightness. The woman has to feel like stroked by a sandal. So when I draw, I think how can I manage these balances, proportions, colours... **Is the idea of creative collaboration important to you?** Absolutely! My creative staff are fundamental to the final goal **Who has been the greatest influence on your career?** First of all my mum, she was a tailor and she taught me the difference between fabrics and cuts, but also the village where I lived had a very important role, because it has a tradition of shoemaking **How have your own experiences affected your work as a designer?** My previous experiences, especially during the '70s, condition my work **Which is more important in your work: the process or the product?** In the beginning, I thought they were two incompatible things, nowadays I think they're both fundamental **Is designing difficult for you, if so, what drives you to continue?** It's not hard at all to draw, but the hard thing is to draw and to have a structured company, with press offices, show rooms, franchise stores, 300 employees, a product that that can be competitive and visibility in stores all over the word - this is the difficult part **Have you ever been influenced or moved by the reaction to your designs?** It's very important to listen to the market, but it's not enough just to observe the commercial results because the numbers by themselves don't let you see where the challenges might lie in the future. So we to listen to the market reactions, but we also have to interpret them **What's your definition of beauty?** A flower **What is the most important lesson you've learned?** From this job I've learned a big lesson, which is that things are not always as they seem to be. That means, behind everything we say, for example, "Oh, I like that", there are so many efforts, dreams, bitterness, passions, emotions, positive and negative feelings.

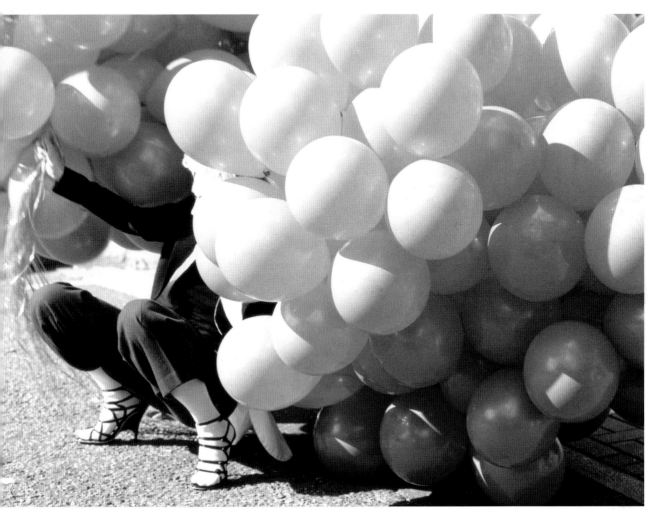

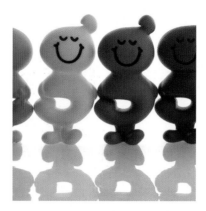

GOODENOUGH

"I don't have anybody in mind when I work.
My design is all about design" HIT

Mouthed breathlessly through hallowed halls, the words 'Hiroshi Fujiwara' commands a respect normally reserved for mythical sorcerers, kings from a forgotten realm or dragon slaying warriors. A one-time member of the Massive Attack-influenced band Major Force West, Hiroshi left the band to concentrate on his solo efforts, both in music and in design. In 1990 Fujiwara started streetwear label Goodenough and, live and direct, two years later it was popping up on the backs of people in London town before going global in 2000, where it was soon stocked in LA and Italy. Slap-bang right in the heart of Shibuya-ku, Tokyo's most lively shopping district, Fujiwara is the area's biggest-paying taxpayer, with Headporter, Goodenough and Nike as projects he dedicates his valuable time to. Goodenough doesn't stand in line with the regimented seasons, providing goods when and where deemed necessary, normally at intervals of six weeks. Neither is theirs an aesthetic that dictates new shapes. Instead, the strength of Goodenough clothing lies in heightening what is already there. Fabrics are integral, features embellished, designs tweaked to within an inch of their lives and covetable limited-edition classics are produced. Although Fujiwara still contributes to the brand, the mantle has been passed to London-based designer HIT who continues the Goodenough legacy, producing famous items like their flight pants, canvas pea coats, This Machine Kills Fascists collection, and the MA1 with insert sleeves.

In heiligen Hallen geflüstert, erzeugt der Name Hiroshi Fujiwara einen Respekt, der normalerweise mythischen Zauberern, Königen eines vergessenen Reiches oder Drachentötern vorbehalten ist. Fujiwara verließ die von Massive Attack beeinflusste Band Major Force West, um sich auf Soloprojekte in der Musik wie in der Mode zu konzentrieren. 1990 gründete er das Streetwear-Label Goodenough, das bereits zwei Jahre später am Leib mancher Londoner zu sehen war, bevor es ab dem Jahr 2000 den internationalen Markt eroberte. Bald führte man die Marke in LA und Italien. Mitten im Herzen von Shibuya-ku, dem quirligsten Einkaufsviertel Tokios, ist Fujiwara der größte Steuerzahler weit und breit. Die Projekte, denen er seine wertvolle Zeit widmet, heißen Headporter, Goodenough und Nike. Goodenough kümmert sich nicht um die offiziellen Saisons der Modebranche. Vielmehr liefert man dann und dort aus, wann und wo man es für nötig erachtet, meist in einem Rhythmus von sechs Wochen. Es gibt auch keine festge-

legte Ästhetik, die neue Formen bestimmt. Die Stärke von Goodenough liegt eher darin, bereits Vorhandenes bis zum absoluten Geht-nicht-mehr zu überhöhen. Dabei spielen die Materialien eine entscheidende Rolle. Besonderheiten werden unterstrichen, Entwürfe bis ins kleinste Detail optimiert und begehrte Klassiker in limitierten Auflagen produziert. Und obwohl Fujiwara nach wie vor für das Label tätig ist, wurde die Stafette an den in London lebenden Designer HIT weitergereicht. Er bewahrt das Vermächtnis von Goodenough, indem er berühmte Teile wie die Fliegerhosen, Kurzmäntel aus Segeltuch, die Kollektion ‚This Machine Kills Fascists' und die MA1 mit den eingesetzten Ärmeln produziert.

Discrètement murmurés dans les lieux sacrés de la mode, les mots « Hiroshi Fujiwara » imposent un respect habituellement réservé aux sorciers mythiques, aux rois de royaumes oubliés ou aux chevaliers pourfendeurs de dragons. Autrefois membre du groupe Major Force West inspiré par Massive Attack, Hiroshi Fujiwara quitte le groupe pour se concentrer sur sa propre carrière, tant dans la musique que dans la création. En 1990, il lance la griffe de streetwear Goodenough et deux ans plus tard, on la retrouve déjà sur le dos des Londoniens, avant d'être commercialisée mondialement en l'an 2000 et rapidement distribuée à Los Angeles et en Italie. Installé au cœur même de Shibuya-ku, Fujiwara est le plus gros contribuable du quartier de shopping le plus vivant de Tokyo, consacrant son temps précieux à des projets tels que Headporter, Goodenough et Nike. Goodenough n'entre pas dans les rangs des saisons biannuelles. Au contraire, la griffe propose des produits quand et où cela s'avère nécessaire, généralement à des intervalles de six semaines. Son esthétique ne cherche pas à dicter de nouvelles formes. En fait, la force des vêtements Goodenough réside dans la mise en valeur de ce qui existe déjà, élevé à des hauteurs si vertigineuses que faire mieux serait presque mission impossible. Les tissus jouent un rôle essentiel, les lignes sont embellies et les créations travaillées parfois jusqu'au point de destruction ; les classiques produits en édition limitée sont très recherchés. Bien que Fujiwara travaille encore pour la marque, il a passé le flambeau au créateur londonien HIT qui poursuit la tradition Goodenough en produisant de célèbres articles tels que les pantalons d'aviateur, les cabans en toile, la collection This Machine Kills Fascists et le modèle MA1 à manches amovibles.

BEN REARDON

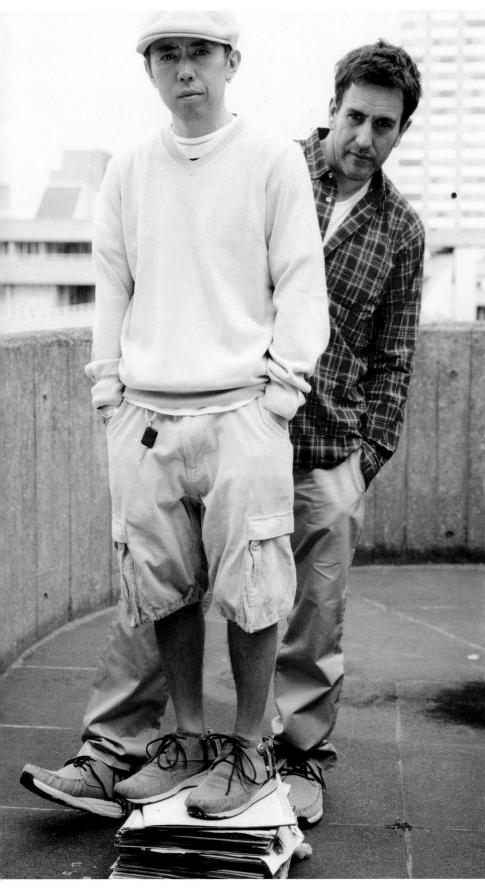

What are your signature designs? 'All over print' T-shirt (where the T-shirt colour is left to show through the ink) **What is your favourite piece from any of your collections?** The next one I have in my brain **How would you describe your work?** Graphic design **What's your ultimate goal?** To see my daughter Ivy in the the Olympic gymnastics in 2016 **What inspires you?** My partner and my daughter **Can fashion still have a political ambition?** It's important to stand up for your beliefs **Who do you have in mind when you design?** Nobody: the design is all about design **Is the idea of creative collaboration important to you?** I don't know if it's important, but sometimes two brains are better than one **Who has been the greatest influence on your career?** My friend Jun (Undercover). He always does exciting things; I respect him a lot. Also James Lebon: he is my hero **How have your own experiences affected your work as a designer?** My culture has coloured my work **Which is more important in your work: the process or the product?** Both **Is designing difficult for you, if so, what drives you to continue?** No, I enjoy design **Have you ever been influenced or moved by the reaction to your designs?** I'm happy when my friends send pictures of my new gear **What's your definition of beauty?** A happy feeling **What's your philosophy?** Have a good and happy life **What is the most important lesson you've learned?** I can see my bad points coming back to me through my daughter. I think it can be like a mirror: I'm learning a lot from her.

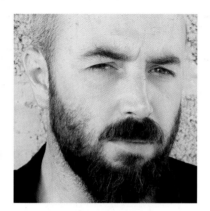

GRIFFIN

"It's about survival and yourself"

Best known for his interpretations of classic military designs for men and his innovative utilitarian twists on everyday garments (his self-explanatory sleeping bag jacket being a good example), Jeff Griffin's designs are as conceptual as they are functional. Born in 1967 in Petersfield, Portsmouth, he graduated from Central Saint Martins with an MA in Fashion Design in 1990. Subsequently moving to Italy to work for the Gian Marco Venturi design team, Griffin was headhunted by Little Italy Family design studio, working across an array of houses including Valentino, Ferré and Fiorucci. Eventually, in 1993, he set up his own label, Griffin Laundry (now known as Griffin). After four successful catwalk shows, Griffin decided to move away from the traditional show concept, choosing instead to produce a technological installation for the British Design Council. Later presentations have included launching his collection on the internet in 1998, followed by a joint cinematic venture with Channel 4 for the showing of his collection in 1999. Collaboration is also important to Griffin: past projects include work with Sony, Mandarina Duck, Kenzo Ki and Hugo Boss, plus his long-time friend, photographer Donald Christie. February 2001 saw the opening of the Griffin concept store in West London, while in May of the same year he jointly established the Parka Rock surf and streetwear label. A second concept store was opened in Tokyo in August 2003. Jeff Griffin is now based in rural Wiltshire with his wife and children, where he has his design studio.

Am bekanntesten ist Jeff Griffin für seine Interpretationen klassischer Militäruniformen für Männer sowie für seine zweckmäßigen Neuerungen von Alltagskleidung (bestes Beispiel: die für sich selbst sprechende Schlafsack-Jacke). Die Entwürfe sind ebenso künstlerisch wie funktional. 1967 in Petersfield (Portsmouth) geboren, schloss Griffin das Central Saint Martins 1990 mit einem Master in Modedesign ab. Danach zog es ihn nach Italien, wo er für das Design-Team Gian Marco Venturi arbeitete, von einem Headhunter für das Atelier Little Italy Family angeworben wurde und noch für diverse andere Modehäuser, unter anderem Valentino, Ferré und Fiorucci, tätig war. 1993 gründete er schließlich mit Griffin Laundry (das heute nur noch unter dem Namen Griffin firmiert) sein eigenes Label. Nach vier erfolgreichen Schauen auf dem Laufsteg entschied sich Griffin gegen das traditionelle Modenschaukonzept und produzierte stattdessen

eine hoch technisierte Installation für das British Design Council. 1998 verlegte er die Präsentation seiner Kollektion ins Internet; 1999 zeigte er seine Modelle im Rahmen einer Koproduktion mit dem Sender Channel 4. Grundsätzlich hält Griffin viel von Synergien: so realisierte er in der Vergangenheit bereits gemeinsame Projekte mit Sony, Mandarina Duck, Kenzo Ki, Hugo Boss und – nicht zu vergessen – mit seinem langjährigen Freund, dem Fotografen Donald Christie. Im Februar 2001 stand die Eröffnung des Griffin Concept Stores im Westen Londons an. Im Mai desselben Jahres wurde das Gemeinschaftslabel Parka Rock für Surf- und Streetwear gegründet. Inzwischen lebt Griffin mit Frau und Kindern im ländlichen Wiltshire, wo sich auch sein Atelier befindet.

Surtout connu pour son interprétation des uniformes militaires classiques pour homme et son détournement innovant et utilitaire des vêtements de tous les jours (dont la veste-sac de couchage offre un bon exemple), Jeff Griffin crée une mode tout aussi conceptuelle que fonctionnelle. Né en 1967 à Petersfield près de Portsmouth, il obtient un Master en mode de Central Saint Martins en 1990. Il part ensuite pour l'Italie, où il travaille avec l'équipe de création de Gian Marco Venturi. Repéré par le studio de création Little Italy Family, il travaille ensuite pour de nombreuses maisons, notamment Valentino, Ferré et Fiorucci. Il finit par fonder sa propre griffe en 1993, Griffin Laundry (aujourd'hui rebaptisée Griffin). Après quatre présentations très remarquées, Griffin décide de s'éloigner du concept traditionnel des défilés, préférant produire une installation technologique pour le British Design Council. En 1998, il lance une collection sur Internet, suivie d'un partenariat cinéma avec Channel Four pour la présentation de sa collection en 1999. Griffin aime travailler avec les autres : parmi ses projets passés figurent des collaborations avec Sony, Mandarina Duck, Kenzo Ki et Hugo Boss, ainsi qu'avec le photographe Donald Christie, son ami de longue date. En février 2001, il ouvre une boutique-concept à Londres-Ouest, tandis qu'en mai de la même année il participe à la création de la griffe surf et streetwear Parka Rock. Une seconde boutique-concept ouvre ses portes à Tokyo en août 2003. Jeff Griffin vit actuellement avec sa femme et ses enfants à la campagne dans le Wiltshire, où il a également installé son atelier de création.

DAVID LAMB

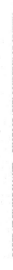

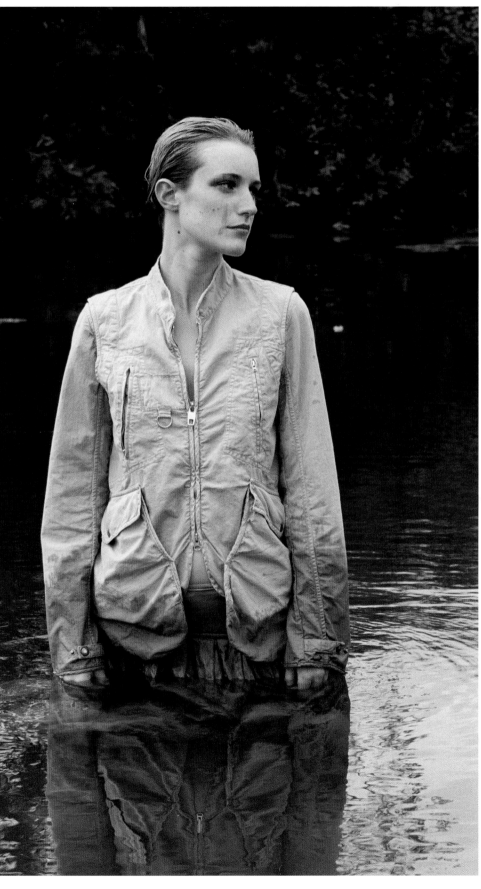

What are your signature designs? The look, the spirit, the heart and a lot of bloody work **What is your favourite piece from any of your collections?** Every season you have a favourite piece and it's always your latest. It was the upside down coat in the beginning, the sleeping bag coat in the middle and more recently the bladecut **How would you describe your work?** We are a diverse team of like-minded people and we are all aspiring to fulfil a dream of producing quality ideas **What's your ultimate goal?** I would love to cultivate an organic forest that would provide produce for a sophisticated alternative to this rat race we live in. The ultimate goal would be to create a near completely self-sustained ecological system that promoted natural methods of self-sufficiency as a thoroughly modern issue... I'm not a hippy **What inspires you?** 'Knowledge' is great. Seeing through the black and white trash the media feed us **Can fashion still have a political ambition?** Fashion has political ambition only if it sells product, except for individuals who do it for love **Who do you have in mind when you design?** It's not who I have in mind but what's in my mind **Is the idea of creative collaboration important to you?** Collaborations are great. The unpredictability involved when working with an artist who has little respect for commercial and financial restraints is inspiring and that makes it refreshing **Who has been the greatest influence on your career?** I could write many things, but it's bollocks. It's about survival and yourself **How have your own experiences affected your work as a designer?** Your experiences are you, which means they are your designs **Which is more important in your work: the process or the product?** The process is great... but people talk too much bullshit so the product is King **Is designing difficult for you, if so, what drives you to continue?** Designing is easy if you're in the mood, but life isn't that simple. Stop thinking so black and white **Have you ever been influenced or moved by the reaction to your designs?** A guy called Dik23 has been continuously mailing me on our website message board to use Ventile (a military fabric from World War 2). So now it's in the collection; this is people power, well done Dik23 **What's your definition of beauty?** Beauty? I'm sorry but it has to be women... **What's your philosophy?** My personal philosophy has changed as time has moved on. Hate fashion crap as usual, but you must believe more and more in what you do. Life is short **What is the most important lesson you've learned?** Eat everything on your plate as you never know when your next meal is...

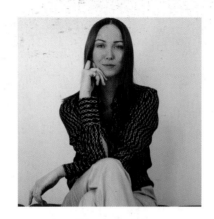

GUCCI

"I think of a mood, a way of living, of certain needs"

FRIDA GIANNINI

In March 2005 Frida Giannini was charged with pushing Gucci, one of the most recognisable status labels of the late 20th century, into a new era. She is responsible for its high-profile accessories and womenswear collections, which has become synonymous with figure-hugging pencil skirts, glamorous sportswear and vixen-ish eveningwear, a look established by Gucci's former designer, Tom Ford, during the '90s. Established in 1921 by Guccio Gucci as a saddlery shop in Florence, the company had been a traditional family-run Italian business until Guccio's grandson Maurizio sold his final share of the brand in 1993. It was Guccio who first intertwined his initials to create the iconic logo. Yet until Tom Ford came along in the mid-'90s, the brand's image was lacklustre; from autumn/winter 1995, Ford designed full womenswear collections for Gucci, supported by slick advertising campaigns often shot by Mario Testino and a die-hard following among celebrities. In 2004, Ford exited Gucci and its parent company, the Gucci Group (which also controls brands such as Stella McCartney, Yves Saint Laurent Rive Gauche, Balenciaga and Alexander McQueen), and new management filled Ford's position not with a single designer but with a team of three, all of whom were promoted internally: John Ray, for menswear, Alessandra Facchinetti for womenswear and Frida Giannini for accessories. In March 2005 Facchinetti also departed Gucci, and Giannini, who lives in a 15th century apartment in Florence and owns 7000 vinyl records, is now also responsible for women's clothing collections. Born in Rome in 1972, Giannini studied at the city's Fashion Academy; in 1997 she landed a job as ready-to-wear designer at Fendi, before first joining Gucci in 2002. Her 'Flora' collection of flowery-printed accessories was the commercial hit of 2004, and, at the time of writing, her first ready-to-wear collection was scheduled for autumn/winter 2005.

Im März 2005 erhielt Frida Giannini den Auftrag, eines der bekanntesten Statuslabels des ausgehenden 20. Jahrhunderts in eine neue Ära zu führen. Sie ist zuständig für Guccis viel beachtete Accessoires sowie für die Damenkollektionen, die für ihre figurbetonten Bleistiftröcke, glamouröse Sportswear und aggressive Abendmode bekannt ist. Diesen Look hatte der frühere Gucci-Designer Tom Ford etabliert. 1921 hatte Guccio Gucci die Firma in Florenz als Sattlerei gegründet. Und sie blieb auch ein traditioneller italienischer Familienbetrieb, bis Guccios Enkel Maurizio seine letzten Anteile an der Marke 1993 verkaufte. Doch war es bereits Guccio gewesen, der seine Initialen zum berühmten Logo zusammenfügte. Bis Tom Ford Mitte der Neunziger auf den Plan trat, war das Markenimage jedoch ziemlich glanzlos. Ab Herbst/Winter 1995 entwarf er alle Damenkollektionen des Hauses unterstützt von schicken, oft von Mario Testino fotografierten Werbekampagnen unterstützt sowie von einer eingeschworenen Fangemeinde. 2004 verließ Ford Gucci und auch den Mutterkonzern Gucci Group (der zudem Firmen wie Stella McCartney, Yves Saint Laurent Rive Gau-

che, Balenciaga und Alexander McQueen besitzt). Das neue Management entschied sich bei der Nachfolge nicht für einen einzigen Designer, sondern für ein Dreierteam, dessen Mitglieder alle aus dem eigenen Haus stammten: John Ray für die Herrenmode, Alessandra Facchinetti für die Damenmode und Frida Giannini für die Accessoires. Als Facchinetti im März 2005 das Unternehmen verließ, übernahm Giannini, die in einem florentinischen Palazzo aus dem 15. Jahrhundert lebt und eine Sammlung von 7000 Schallplatten besitzt, die Damenmode noch mit. Giannini wurde 1971 in Rom geboren und studierte an der dortigen Modeakademie. 1997 ergatterte sie bei Fendi den Job der Designerin für Prêt-à-porter. 2002 fing sie dann bei Gucci an. Dort landete sie mit ihrer blumenbedruckten Kollektion Flora den kommerziellen Hit des Jahres 2004. Zurzeit ist ihre erste Prêt-à-porter-Kollektion für Herbst/Winter 2005 angesetzt.

En mars 2005, Frida Giannini se voit confier la mission de faire entrer Gucci, l'une des griffes les plus incontournables de la fin du XXe siècle, dans une nouvelle ère. Elle y est responsable des collections pour femme et des lignes d'accessoires de luxe, qui est surtout connue pour ses jupes droites moulantes, son sportswear glamour et ses tenues de soirée archi-sexy, un look établi par Tom Ford, anciennement styliste de Gucci. La petite boutique de sellier fondée en 1921 à Florence par Guccio Gucci reste une affaire familiale traditionnelle à l'italienne jusqu'à ce que Maurizio, petit-fils de Guccio, revende sa dernière part de l'entreprise en 1993. C'est Guccio le premier qui a entrecroisé ses initiales pour produire le logo signature. Mais jusqu'à l'arrivée de Tom Ford au milieu des années 90, l'image de la marque manquait sérieusement de lustre; dès l'automne/hiver 1995, Ford commence à créer des collections féminines complètes pour Gucci, accompagné de sublimes campagnes publicitaires souvent photographiées par Mario Testino, et d'une foule de clientes célèbres et intransigeantes. En 2004, Tom Ford quitte Gucci et sa société mère, le Groupe Gucci (qui contrôle également les marques Stella McCartney, Yves Saint Laurent Rive Gauche, Balenciaga et Alexander McQueen). La nouvelle équipe de direction le remplace non pas par un nouveau créateur, mais par une écurie de trois stylistes, tous promus en interne: John Ray à la mode masculine, Alessandra Facchinetti à la collection pour femme et Frida Giannini aux accessoires. En mars 2005, Alessandra Facchinetti quitte également Gucci et c'est désormais Frida Giannini, qui habite un appartement du XVe siècle à Florence et possède une collection de 7000 vinyles, qui dirige les collections pour femme. Née en 1972 à Rome, Frida Giannini étudie à la Fashion Academy de la ville; en 1997, elle décroche un poste de styliste en prêt-à-porter chez Fendi, puis rejoint Gucci en 2002. Sa collection «Flora» aux imprimés floraux s'impose comme le grand succès commercial de l'année 2004. Aux dernières nouvelles, sa première collection de prêt-à-porter est prévue pour l'automne/hiver 2005.

SUSIE RUSHTON

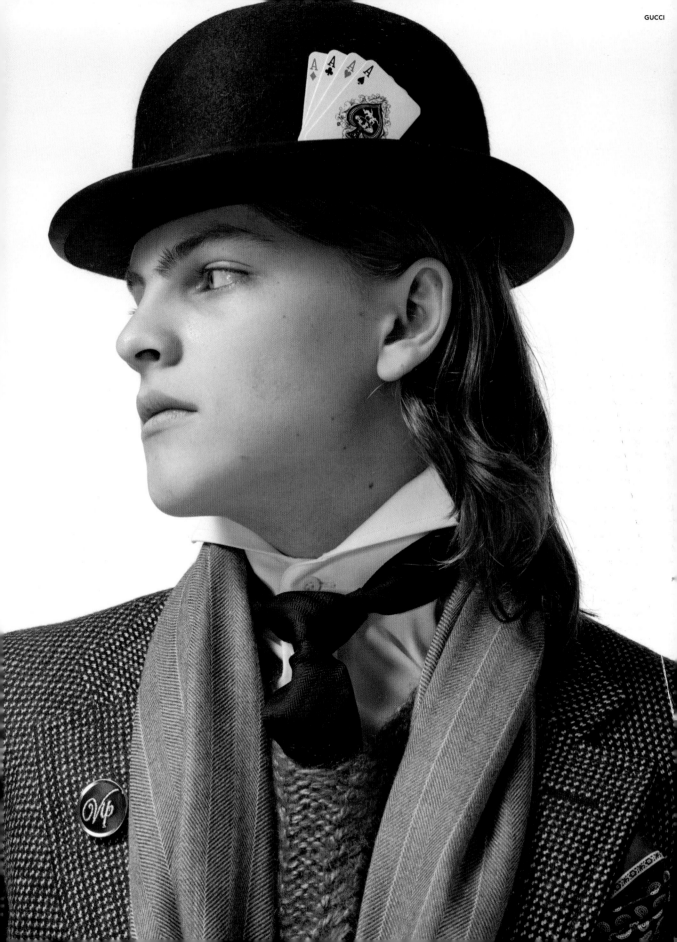

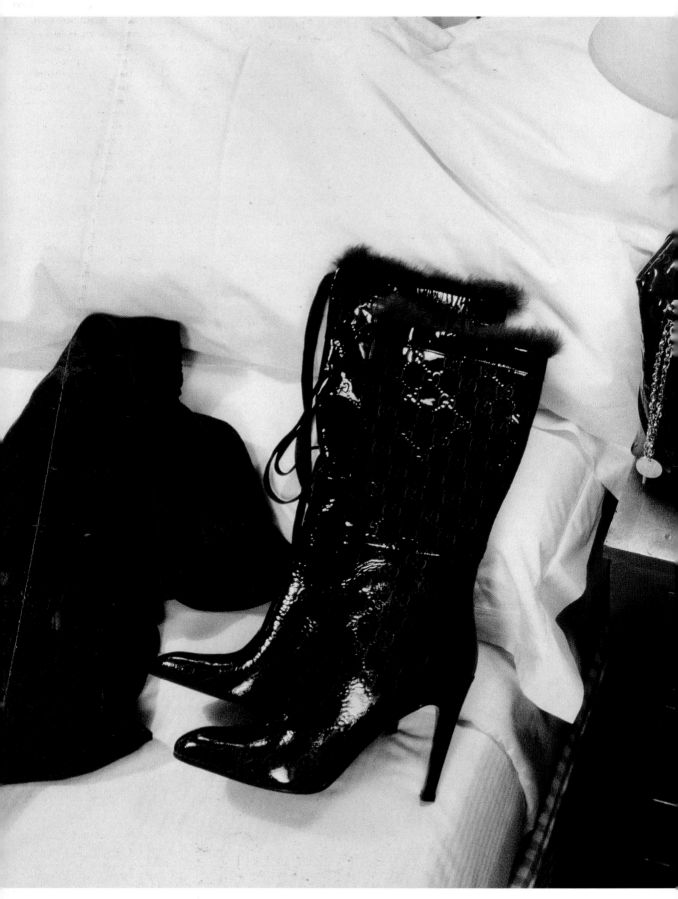

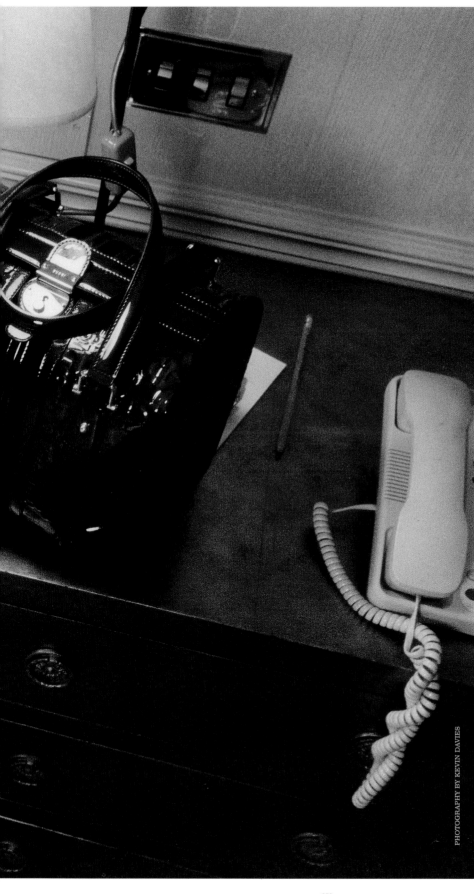

How would you describe your work? Great research. Necessary adaptation. Fabulous team work. Very hard work. Reflection. Attention to what is happening in the world. Great results **Can fashion still have political ambition?** Fashion and politics do not go hand in hand, but generally speaking, I believe that fashion can reflect the sociological mood of the moment **What is your ultimate goal?** I have many. One of the most important is to live in harmony with myself and with others **What inspires you?** Jackie Kennedy Onassis, who, to me, is the ultimate in elegance **What do you have in mind when you design?** I think of a mood, a way of living, of certain needs for women and men. The possibility to link the history of the Gucci brand, of Gucci's iconic pieces, with contemporary design and styles **Who has been the greatest influence in your career?** My passion. My family. My drive. Music. The world of vintage **Have you ever been influenced or moved by reactions to your design?** All reactions from the 'public', whether positive or negative, can only be productive and open 'new roads' for the next direction **How have your own experiences affected your work as a designer?** Through my experience, I have learnt to become a leader, and have learnt how important communicating, expressing, and listening is within your own team. I am not afraid to say the final "yes" or to say the final "no" **Which is more important in your work: the process or the product?** Definitely both. And the harmony that exists between the two. Always with the utmost respect for the brand **What is your definition of beauty?** Beauty is very subjective and personal, and I believe that when something gives pleasure to your eyes and to your soul... well, that's beautiful.

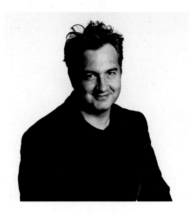

GUCCI

"I am always attracted by the unknown and inspired by the undiscovered" JOHN RAY

In March 2004, John Ray, then aged 42, was named as successor to Tom Ford as Gucci's creative director of menswear. Ray, who was born in Scotland, had already worked under Ford in the Gucci menswear studio for eight years. Gucci menswear had become known for its blatantly sexual and flamboyant style: figure-hugging trousers, flashy double-G logo belt buckles, velvet smoking jackets with wide '70s-style lapels and shiny satin shirts, worn unbuttoned to the (perfectly tanned) navel. Under Ray's direction – spring/summer 2005 was his first solo collection – Gucci menswear acknowledges that opulent template, with a softer and subtler edge. Ray also places a special emphasis on tailoring. His debut was based on an idea of exotic travel, and featured Moroccan-style kurtas embellished with coins, beads and embroidery; long caftans; paisley smoking suits; tiny swimming trunks. Ray, who describes himself as an extremely private person, grew up in Scotland and first worked as a graphic designer. At the age of 23 he realised fashion was his true calling, and enrolled on the menswear course at Central Saint Martins (1986), followed by an MA at the Royal College of Art (1989); while at fashion college, Ray used a Savile Row tailor to execute his student designs. In 1992 Ray joined Katharine Hamnett, where he eventually became head of menswear. In 1996 his career at Gucci began when Tom Ford hired him as a menswear consultant. By 1998 Ray was appointed senior menswear designer and in 2001 named vice president of menswear, overseeing all product categories. Ray, then, is as familiar with the evolution of the Gucci man as any designer could be. Like his counterpart in womenswear, Frida Giannini, Ray shows his collections in Milan. He lives and works in London.

Im März 2004 wurde der damals 42-jährige John Ray Nachfolger von Tom Ford als Creative Director der Herrenmode bei Gucci. Der aus Schottland stammende Ray hatte damals bereits acht Jahre unter Ford im Herrenatelier von Gucci gearbeitet. Der Stil der Kollektionen ist offenkundig sexy und extravagant: figurbetonte Hosen, auffällige Gürtel mit dem Doppel-G-Logo als Schnalle, Smokings aus Samt mit breiten Revers im Stil der 1970er Jahre und glänzende Satinhemden, die man bis zum (perfekt gebräunten) Bauchnabel offen trägt. Unter Rays Leitung – seine erste Solokollektion sah man Frühjahr/Sommer 2005 – blieb die Herrenmode von Gucci diesem opulenten Vorbild treu, wenn auch vielleicht mit etwas weicheren, subtileren Zügen. Außerdem legt Ray besonderes Gewicht auf die handwerklichen Details. Sein Debüt spielte mit dem Thema exotische Reisen und zeigte Kurtas im marokkanischen Stil mit Münzen, Perlen und Stickereien verziert, lange Kaftane, Smokings mit Paisleymuster und winzige Badehosen. Ray, der sich selbst als extrem öffentlichkeitsscheu beschreibt, wuchs in Schottland auf und arbeitete zunächst als Grafikdesigner. Im Alter von 23 erkannte er

seine Berufung für Mode und schrieb sich 1986 am Central Saint Martins im Fach Herrenmode ein. 1989 machte er noch einen Master am Royal College of Art. Während der Studienzeit ließ Ray seine Entwürfe von einem Schneider aus der Savile Row realisieren. 1992 fing er bei Katharine Hamnett an, wo er schließlich Chef der Herrenmode wurde. Seine Karriere bei Gucci begann 1996, als Tom Ford ihn als Consultant für die Herrenmode engagierte. 1998 wurde er Senior Menswear Designer, 2001 Vice President der Herrenmode, was die Leitung aller Produktkategorien umfasste. Schon zu jenem Zeitpunkt war Ray mit der Entwicklung von Gucci Man vertrauter als jeder andere Designer. Wie seine Kollegin in der Damenmode, Frida Giannini, präsentiert Ray seine Kollektionen in Mailand, während er in London lebt und arbeitet.

En mars 2004, John Ray, alors âgé de 42 ans, est nommé directeur de la création des collections masculines de Gucci à la succession de Tom Ford. Né en Ecosse, Ray avait déjà travaillé pour Ford pendant huit ans dans l'atelier pour homme de Gucci. La mode masculine de Gucci est synonyme de flamboyance ouvertement sexuelle : pantalons moulants, logo double G flashy ornant les boucles de ceintures, vestons en velours à larges revers très années 70 et chemises en satin brillant portées déboutonnées jusqu'au nombril (sur un bronzage parfait, cela va sans dire). Sous l'impulsion de John Ray, qui présente sa première collection en solo pour le printemps/été 2005, la mode masculine de Gucci reste fidèle à ce modèle opulent, quoique avec légèrement plus de douceur et de subtilité. Le créateur fait également la part belle aux costumes. Pour ses débuts, il s'inspire de l'idée d'un voyage exotique et présente des kurtas marocaines ornées de pièces de monnaie, de perles et de broderies, mais aussi de longs caftans, des vestes en velours à motifs cachemire et de minuscules maillots de bain. John Ray, qui se considère comme quelqu'un de très secret, grandit en Ecosse et travaille d'abord comme graphiste. A 23 ans, il comprend que la mode est sa véritable vocation et s'inscrit au cours en mode pour homme de Central Saint Martins (1986), avant de suivre un MA au Royal College of Art (1989), période pendant laquelle il demande à un tailleur de Savile Row d'exécuter ses créations d'étudiant. En 1992, il rejoint Katharine Hamnett, chez qui il se hisse au poste de directeur de la collection masculine. En 1996, il entame sa carrière chez Gucci quand Tom Ford l'embauche en tant que consultant. En 1998, il est nommé styliste senior pour homme, puis vice-président de la mode masculine en 2001, supervisant toutes les catégories de produits. A ce stade, John Ray est aussi familiarisé avec l'évolution de l'homme Gucci que tout autre créateur digne de ce nom. A l'instar de Frida Giannini, son homologue à la direction des lignes féminines, John Ray présente ses collections à Milan. Il vit et travaille à Londres.

SUSIE RUSHTON

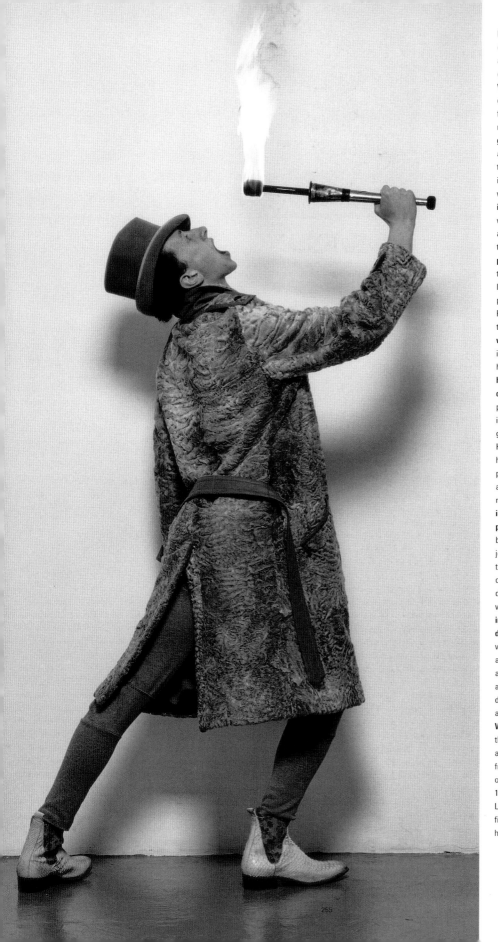

How would you describe your work? It's chemical. I have surrounded myself with a small but strong team of honest, creative individuals with diverse ideas. We stimulate each other, make each other think. This pushes the product further and makes the whole process more interesting **What's your ultimate goal?** I have never had any goals or made any great plans in my life. I have always truly followed my instincts. From choosing a career in fashion to what I am working on today for tomorrow **What inspires you?** What I have to do next and where that might lead me, I am always attracted by the unknown and inspired by the undiscovered **Can fashion still have a political ambition?** Fashion reflects the times and how we choose to live our lives. The reflection of which can be political, i.e. good times v hard times. Fashion can be at its most creative when times are hard **Who do you have in mind when you design?** The Gucci man. Who he is and what clothes mean to him now in his life and what he actually needs **Who has been the greatest influence on your career?** It is very difficult to separate my private life from work, they both merge into one. I am lucky to have had two great professional influences, Katharine Hamnett and Tom Ford. In my private life I have been influenced by two other people who have shown me how to approach life differently and this is reflected in my work **Which is more important in your work: the process or the product?** The product – fashion is a business. The process is the fascinating journey full of dreams that takes you there. Ultimately the product has to work off the runway and fulfil other people's dreams; otherwise I am not sure there would be any point. **Have you ever been influenced or moved by the reaction to your designs?** Criticism – I love honesty and when someone says something negative about your work, you have probably already felt the same. So I use criticism in a very positive way. I do believe that most designers are their own biggest critics anyway, constantly striving for perfection **What's your definition of beauty?** Beauty or the concepts or ideas of it are manifold and ever-changing. From a simple smile from a stranger in the street, two people obviously in love, a great piece of Louis 16th furniture or a big cloudy sky over London. It is all around us, it is easy to find, and it is up to the individual where he looks.

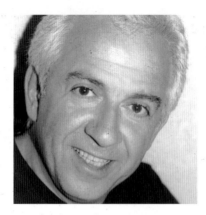

GUESS?

"Our products and our advertising images are both sexy and adventurous" PAUL MARCIANO

Guess? is known for its sexy jeans – and its equally sexy advertising campaigns. Established in 1980, Guess? is a family business headed up by Paul and Maurice Marciano, who share titles as joint Chairmen and CEOs of the company. Paul is the brains behind the company's iconic advertising, which takes its stylistic cues from the archetypal '50s sex-kitten actresses including Brigitte Bardot. He's picked up Clio and Design and Art Directors awards for his campaigns – which are often shot by Ellen Von Unwerth – and has established the Guess Girl as a symbol of American pop culture. Iconic models, actresses and all-round sex-bombs, including Claudia Schiffer, Eva Herzigova, Laetitia Casta, Drew Barrymore, Anna Nicole Smith and, in 2005, Paris Hilton, have pouted and preened on Californian beaches for Guess? Meanwhile Paul's brother Maurice has overseen design direction and has also led the company's commercial expansion since 1982. In 2003 Guess? registered a net revenue of about $636.6 million and sells in 36 countries worldwide.

Guess? kennt man für seine sexy Jeans und seine ebenso ansprechenden Werbe-kampagnen. Die 1980 gegründete Marke ist ein Familienunternehmen unter der Leitung von Paul und Maurice Marciano, die sich die Titel Präsident und CEO brüderlich teilen. Paul steckt hinter der kultigen Werbung, die stilistische Anlei-hen beim Schauspielerinnen-Archetyp der Fünfzigerjahre-Häschen wie Brigitte Bardot nimmt. Für seine Kampagnen, oft Ellen von Unwerth fotografiert, hat er schon diverse Preise – Clio, Design und Art Directors – kassiert. Außerdem eta-blierte er das Guess-Girl als ein Symbol der amerikanischen Popkultur. Super-models, Schauspielerinnen und vielseitige Sexbomben wie Claudia Schiffer, Eva Herzigova, Laetitia Casta, Drew Barrymore, Anna Nicole Smith und 2005 Paris Hilton haben schon für Guess? an kalifornischen Stränden Schmollmünder gezogen. Pauls Bruder Maurice kümmert sich um die Leitung der Designabtei-lung und um die kommerzielle Expansion seit 1982. Im Jahr 2003 verzeichnete Guess? Nettoeinnahmen in Höhe von ca. 636,6 Millionen Dollar durch Verkäufe in weltweit 36 Ländern.

La marque Guess? est connue pour ses jeans sexy et ses campagnes publi-citaires tout aussi troublantes. Fondée en 1980, Guess? est une entreprise fami-liale dirigée par Paul et Maurice Marciano, qui se partagent les fonctions de président et de directeur général. C'est au cerveau de Paul que l'on doit les publicités cultes de la griffe, dont la stylistique s'inspire des sulfureuses actrices typiques des années 50 comme Brigitte Bardot. Souvent réalisées par Ellen von Unwerth, ses campagnes ont été couronnées par plusieurs récom-penses de l'industrie publicitaire (comme les Clio Awards ou le Club des Di-recteurs Artistiques) et ont hissé la Guess Girl au rang de symbole de la culture pop américaine. Des top models, des actrices et autres bombes sex-sym-bols tels que Claudia Schiffer, Eva Herzigova, Laetitia Casta, Drew Barrymore, Anna Nicole Smith et Paris Hilton en 2005, se componnent et font la moue sur les plages californiennes pour Guess?, tandis que Maurice, le frère de Paul qui supervise la création, encourage l'expansion commerciale de l'entreprise depuis 1982. En 2003, Guess? a enregistré un chiffre d'affaires net d'envi-ron 636,6 millions de dollars, fort d'une présence dans 36 pays à travers le monde. SUSIE RUSHTON

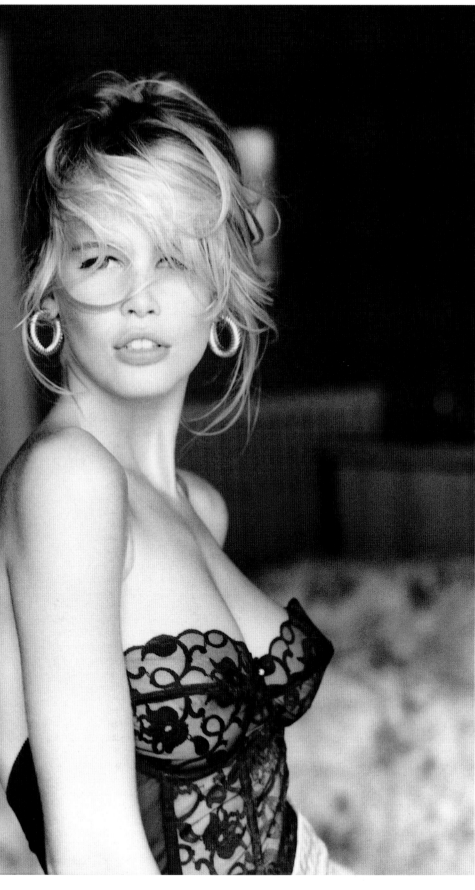

What are your signature designs? Though Guess? is now a global lifestyle brand, it started as a small California jeansmaker in 1981. Denim is Guess signature fabric, and we continually push the envelope of denim design with innovative washes, distressing techniques and great fits **What is your favourite piece from any of your collections?** My favourite piece is the three-zip Marilyn jeans. It's a slim-fitting cropped jeans with zips at each hem and the signature Guess? triangle on the back pocket. This is the jeans that started it all – initially retailers greeted denim with skepticism, but Bloomingdale's agreed to sell two dozen pairs of the Marilyn jeans as a favour to my brothers and me. The entire stock sold out within hours and the rest is history! **How would you describe your work?** Guess? is sensuous, strong and chic. Our products and our advertising images are sexy and adventurous. If I had to express the essence of the Guess? brand in three words they would be wonder, passion and freedom **What inspires you?** My inspiration comes from many places, but I truly love American and Italian movies from the '50s. There's something about people like Brigitte Bardot that is so charmingly seductive and sexy. The '50s were an amazing time of such fresh-faced optimism and energy, and this energy drives both our products and our advertising images **Is the idea of creative collaboration important to you?** Creative collaboration is a true founding principle of Guess? From the very beginning Guess? has been a family affair. My brother Maurice and I still run the business, and we learn from each other every day. Each of us possesses something the other doesn't; we have worked together every step of the way to make the brand what it is today. You have to surround yourself with bright, energetic people with a strong creative vision **What's your philosophy?** My philosophy has always been to create an identifiable, strong image for the Guess? brand. With a strong image comes strong customer loyalty, and that is the basis for success in this industry.

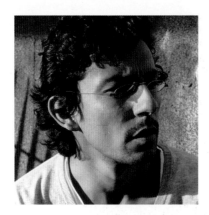

HAIDER ACKERMANN

"You can only design what you know"

One of Antwerp's brightest young stars, Haider Ackermann has seen many more ports than the one fronting the town in which he now lives and works. Born in Santa Fe de Bogotá, Colombia, in 1971, he was adopted by a French family. Due to his father's business obligations, he spent his childhood moving around the globe. After living in Ethiopia, Chad, France, Algeria and the Netherlands, he decided fashion was his vocation. High school finished, he left home in 1994 and headed for Belgium to study at the fashion department of Antwerp's Royal Academy. During his three-year stay (he left the four-year course prematurely because of financial difficulties) he also worked as an intern at John Galliano's Paris office. Taking a job as an assistant to his former academy teacher Wim Neels in 1998, he worked on both the men's and womenswear collections of the Belgian designer. After saving money and taking encouragement from his friends and acquaintances – among them Raf Simons – Ackermann finally took the plunge and presented his first, self-financed women's collection in Paris for autumn/winter 2002. His subtle, dignified and sensuous clothes immediately struck a chord with buyers and editors, as they did with Italian leather manufacturer Ruffo. Just two weeks after his debut show, Ackermann was hired as the head designer for Ruffo Research and commissioned to create two collections (spring/summer and autumn/winter 2003), while continuing to produce his own line. Ackermann is now receiving even wider acclaim, not least in the form of the prestigious Swiss Textiles Award at the 2004 Grand Fashion Festival.

Haider Ackermann gilt als einer der viel versprechenden Jungstars von Antwerpen und hat schon einiges mehr von der Welt gesehen als nur die Stadt, in der er jetzt lebt und arbeitet. Geboren wurde er 1971 im kolumbianischen Santa Fe de Bogotá und kurz darauf von einer französischen Familie adoptiert. Aufgrund der geschäftlichen Verpflichtungen seines Vaters kam er schon als Kind in der ganzen Welt herum. Nachdem er in Äthiopien, dem Tschad, Frankreich, Algerien und den Niederlanden gelebt hatte, erkannte er in der Mode seine Berufung. Als er 1994 die Schule abgeschlossen hatte, machte er sich auf den Weg nach Belgien, um an der Königlichen Akademie in Antwerpen zu studieren. Während seines dreijährigen Aufenthalts (er musste die an sich vierjährige Ausbildung wegen finanzieller Schwierigkeiten vorzeitig abbrechen) jobbte Ackermann bereits als Praktikant im Pariser Atelier von John Galliano. Nachdem er 1998 eine Assistentenstelle bei seinem ehemaligen Dozenten Wim Neels bekommen hatte, arbeitete er sowohl an Herren- wie an Damenkollektionen des belgischen Designers mit.

Als er etwas Geld gespart hatte, wagte er mit Unterstützung seiner Freunde und Bekannten – darunter Leute wie Raf Simons – schließlich den Sprung ins kalte Wasser. In Paris präsentierte Ackermann seine erste selbst finanzierte Damenkollektion, und zwar für Herbst/Winter 2002. Seine raffinierten, würdevollen und sinnlichen Kreationen kamen bei Einkäufern und Journalisten wie auch beim italienischen Lederwarenhersteller Ruffo auf Anhieb gut an. So wurde Ackermann nur zwei Wochen nach seinem Debüt Chefdesigner von Ruffo Research und erhielt den Auftrag für zwei Kollektionen (Frühjahr/Sommer und Herbst/Winter 2003). Nebenbei entwarf der Designer noch für seine eigene Linie. Heute erhält er mehr Zuspruch denn je, nicht zuletzt 2004 mit dem angesehenen Swiss Textiles Award im Rahmen des Grand Fashion Festival.

Célébré comme l'une des étoiles montantes d'Anvers, Haider Ackermann a fait étape dans bien d'autres ports que celui qui borde la ville dans laquelle il travaille et vit aujourd'hui. Adopté par une famille française, il est en fait né en 1971 à Santa Fe de Bogota en Colombie. En raison des obligations professionnelles de son père, il passe son enfance à parcourir le monde. Après avoir vécu en Ethiopie, au Tchad, en France, en Algérie et aux Pays-Bas, il se rend compte que la mode est sa véritable vocation. En 1994, il termine le lycée et part pour la Belgique afin d'étudier la mode à l'Académie Royale d'Anvers. Pendant son cursus de trois ans (il abandonnera prématurément la quatrième année en raison de problèmes financiers), il fait un stage dans les bureaux parisiens de John Galliano. En 1998, il devient l'assistant de son ancien professeur à l'Académie, le styliste belge Wim Neels, travaillant sur les collections pour homme et pour femme. Il réussit sagement à mettre de l'argent de côté et, encouragé par ses amis et relations, parmi lesquels Raf Simons, Ackermann fait finalement le grand plongeon et présente une première collection féminine autofinancée aux défilés parisiens automne-hiver 2002. Grâce à leur style subtil et voluptueux néanmoins empreint de dignité, ses vêtements séduisent immédiatement les acheteurs et les rédacteurs de mode, ainsi que le maroquinier italien Ruffo qui, deux semaines après son premier défilé, nomme Ackermann styliste principal de Ruffo Research et lui demande de créer deux collections (printemps-eté et automne-hiver 2003) tout en lui permettant de continuer à travailler sur sa propre griffe. Aujourd'hui, la réputation d'Ackermann n'est plus à faire. Il a notamment reçu le prestigieux Swiss Textiles Award décerné au Grand Fashion Festival en 2004.

PETER DE POTTER

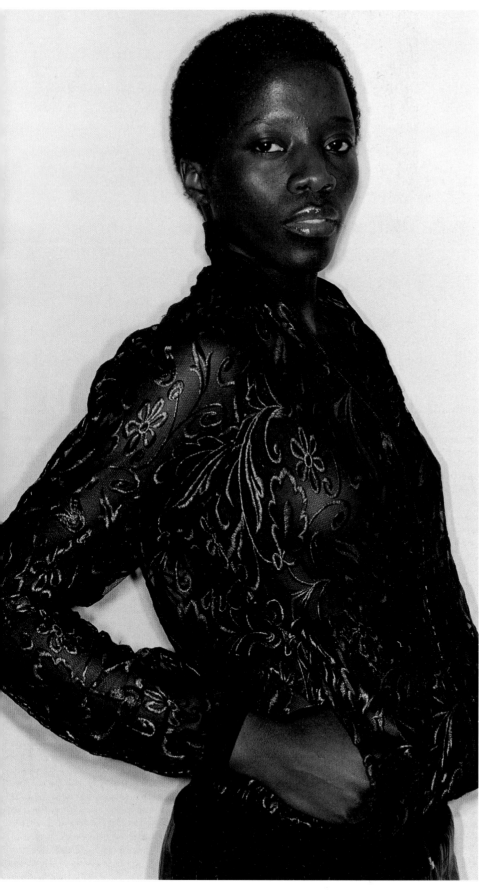

What are your signature designs? I can't define that, it would be up to others, but beside that, I guess it is still too early to talk about a certain signature. There are elements, there is a constant search. There are muted non-colours, the smock, the timelessness, the masculinity… **What is your favourite piece from any of your collections?** I am still waiting for that feeling of a favourite. Still chasing that moment… **What's your ultimate goal?** To find the right balance **What inspires you?** The contrast. **Can fashion still have a political ambition?** It somehow always reflects the time and all aspect of life we are living in **Who do you have in mind when you design?** It is getting more abstract with time. A gesture, a mood, an attitude, a passerby **Is the idea of creative collaboration important to you?** Yes it is, though the difficulty is allowing yourself to be lost in the trust of the other. **Who has been the greatest influence on your career?** My friends for their encouragment and support! **How have your own experiences affected your work as a designer?** You can only design what you know… there is no distinction between you and your memories, your experiences and your daily life. And that all is attached to my work **Is designing difficult for you, if so, what drives you to continue?** Yes …it puts me in doubt, in a situation where you are not confident with yourself, but it challenges me and driven by the unknown, the dissatisfaction **Have you ever been influenced or moved by the reaction to your designs?** Impossible not to be **What's your definition of beauty?** The intriguing thing that makes your heart beat **What's your philosophy?** Never stop challenging yourself! Never loose enthousiasm! **What is the most important lesson you've learned?** The richness of friendship.

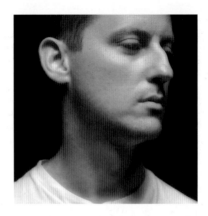

HAMISH MORROW

"I'm inspired by ideas, their evolution and the future"

Hamish Morrow was born in South Africa in 1968, eventually moving to London in 1989 to study fashion at Central Saint Martins. Due to financial problems, however, he was forced to quit the course, thereafter undertaking freelance design and pattern cutting work until 1996, when he began further studies at the Royal College of Art. From here he obtained an MA in menswear, which subsequently helped secure him employment. This included designing for Byblos in Milan and stints at other design houses in Paris and New York. In 2000 Morrow returned to London and began working on the launch of his eponymous line. By 2001, his collection for autumn/winter of the same year, 'The Life Cycle of An Idea', was shown off-schedule (the presentation also featured flowers in various stages of decay) and earned him rave reviews. Continuing to uphold an intelligent, conceptual approach to his designs – far removed from more flashy, celebrity-endorsed forms, of which he has expressed his dislike – Morrow has since become a force to be reckoned with. His eponymous collections are infused with sensibilities that might be culled from high art or cutting-edge music, always with an eye for exquisite fabrics and adventurous cutting. Morrow has collaborated with various internationally-renowned design houses, including Fendi, Krizia and Louis Féraud. He has also produced capsule collections for British mass market chain Topshop over the past two years and, for autumn/winter 2004, created a collection of denim and metallic textiles for online retailer Yoox.com. Morrow's experience-rich CV, quiet determination and undeniable talents would seem to ensure his future success.

Hamish Morrow wurde 1968 in Südafrika geboren und ging 1989 nach London, um am Central Saint Martins Mode zu studieren. Wegen finanzieller Probleme war er jedoch gezwungen, die Ausbildung abzubrechen. Er arbeitete in der Folge als freischaffender Designer und Musterschneider, bis er 1996 sein Studium am Royal College of Art wieder aufnahm. Mit dem dort erlangten Master in Herrenmode fand er anschließend rasch einen Job. Er designte für Byblos in Mailand und hatte kurze Engagements bei anderen Modehäusern in Paris und New York. Im Jahr 2000 kehrte Morrow nach London zurück und begann an der Präsentation seines nach ihm benannten Labels zu arbeiten. 2001 wurde seine Herbst/Winter-Kollektion für das gleiche Jahr, The Life Cycle of An Idea, außerhalb des offiziellen Modekalenders gezeigt (bei der Präsentation waren auch Blumen in verschiedenen Stadien des Verwelkens zu sehen) und brachte ihm phantastische Kritiken ein. Seither hält Morrow bei seinen Entwürfen kontinuierlich an die-

sem intelligenten, konzeptionellen Ansatz fest und hat sich zu einer Figur in der Branche entwickelt, mit der man rechnen muss. Protzigere, auf den Beifall von Prominenten ausgerichtete Bekleidung ist ihm dagegen ein Graus. Die nach ihm benannten Kollektionen sind durchdrungen von einer Empfindsamkeit, die auch aus der anspruchsvollen Kunst oder Musik stammen könnte. Dazu kommt der richtige Blick für exquisite Stoffe und gewagte Schnitte. Neben der Zusammenarbeit mit verschiedenen international bekannten Designhäusern wie Fendi, Krizia und Louis Féraud produzierte er in den vergangenen zwei Jahren Minikollektionen für die britische Kette Topshop sowie für Herbst/Winter 2004 eine Kollektion aus Jeans- und Metallic-Kleidung für den Internet-Einzelhändler Yoox.com. Morrows reicher Erfahrungsschatz, seine stille Entschlossenheit und seine unleugbare Begabung werden seinen Erfolg auch in Zukunft sichern.

Né en 1968 en Afrique du Sud, Hamish Morrow s'installe à Londres en 1989 pour étudier la mode à Central Saint Martins. En raison de problèmes d'argent, il est toutefois contraint d'abandonner son cursus et se met à travailler comme créateur free-lance et traceur de patrons. En 1996, il reprend ses études au Royal College of Art et décroche un MA en mode masculine, un diplôme qui lui garantit une bonne place sur le marché de l'emploi. Il travaillera notamment pour Byblos à Milan et pour d'autres maisons de mode à Paris et New York. En l'an 2000, Morrow revient à Londres et se consacre au lancement de sa ligne éponyme. En 2001, il présente sa collection automne/hiver intitulée «The Life Cycle of An Idea» (mettant en scène des fleurs à différents stades de décomposition) dans le cadre des défilés «off» et suscite les éloges de la critique. Respectant une approche intelligente et conceptuelle de la création, bien loin des formes plus flashy dont raffolent les stars et dont il a clairement exprimé son dégoût, Morrow s'est imposé comme une force créative absolument incontournable. Ses collections éponymes expriment diverses sensibilités inspirées de l'art contemporain ou de la musique d'avant-garde, toujours avec un œil aiguisé pour les tissus précieux et les coupes insolites. Après avoir collaboré avec de grandes maisons mondialement célèbres comme Fendi, Krizia et Louis Féraud, il produit depuis deux ans des mini-collections pour la chaîne britannique Topshop. Pour l'automne/hiver 2004, il crée une collection en denim et en textiles métalliques pour le détaillant en ligne Yoox.com. L'impressionnant CV de Morrow, sa détermination tranquille et son indéniable talent devraient continuer à assurer son succès pour longtemps.

JAMES ANDERSON

What are your signature designs? A fusion of glamour with industrial process, technology with luxury and sport with couture What is your favourite piece from any of your collections? The gathered Prince of Wales check wool dresses that incorporated draped industrial web tape and were layered with Swarovski crystal harnesses How would you describe your work? Very controlled, analytical and technical What's your ultimate goal? To lose control What inspires you? Ideas, their evolution and the future Can fashion still have a political ambition? Yes, but it would be unwise Who do you have in mind when you design? No-one specifically. My work is entirely ideas based. Through the process of resolving those ideas I relate them to the body – anybody, not somebody Is the idea of creative collaboration important to you? Paramount, it is the very core of my creative process Who has been the greatest influence on your career? All the incredible people I have ever collaborated with How have your own experiences affected your work as a designer? They have taught me to take risks and be fearless in my creative pursuit Which is more important in your work: the process or the product? I love the process but the product is the final affirmation of that – it lives on and its success or failure is the final test of that process Is designing difficult for you, if so, what drives you to continue? No, it is the constant dissatisfaction with everything that I do that drives me Have you ever been influenced or moved by the reaction to your designs? Once your work goes out into the world it no longer belongs to you – the reaction can either be distressing or elating What's your definition of beauty? Beauty is neither pretty nor young What's your philosophy? Life is short What is the most important lesson you've learned? You reap what you sew.

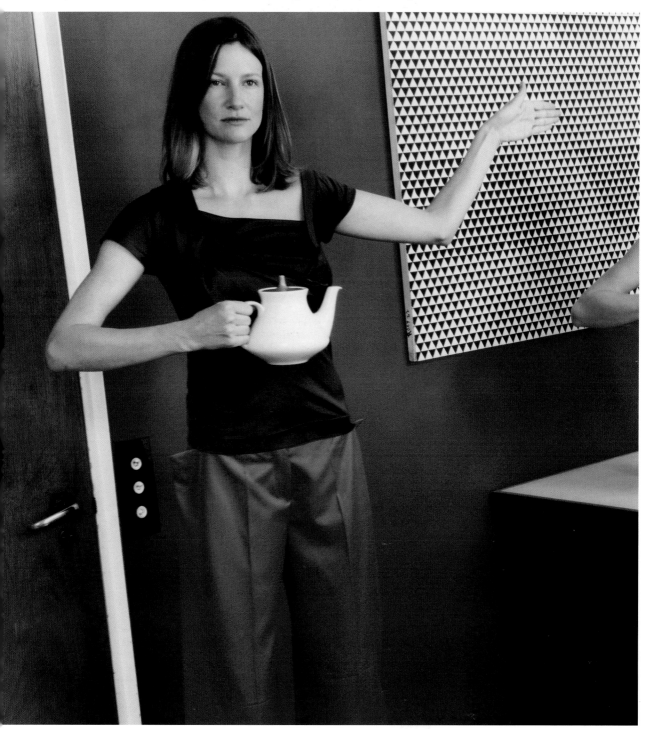

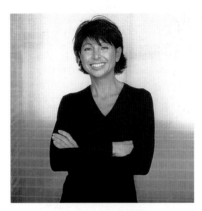

HERMÈS

"I try to balance the values of innovation and tradition"
VÉRONIQUE NICHANIAN

Hermès is one of the grandest houses in the lexicon of luxury goods. Established in 1837 by Thierry Hermès as a fine harness-making business and today world-renowned for its handcrafted, exceptionally desirable (and expensive) leather goods, most notably its Kelly and Birkin handbags, in recent years Hermès has also become a major player in ready-to-wear fashion. Since 2004, Jean Paul Gaultier has designed the brand's womenswear collections (he succeeded Martin Margiela, who was appointed in 1998) while Hermès' menswear designer Véronique Nichanian has designed sophisticated 'clothing objects' for the company since 1988. The company first created clothing in the '20s: sportswear that was intended to complement the accessories. However it wasn't until the '50s that Hermès won a wider male audience for its clothes, when it first launched its printed silk ties. Nichanian, who is based in a studio on rue du Faubourg Saint-Honoré in Paris, has made Hermès synonymous with menswear pieces so luxurious that they quickly attain an iconic status among men of a certain income. Formal tailoring is always exquisite; casual clothing is no less luxurious, yet often offered in luscious colour combinations and given subtly ironic details. Nichanian has impeccable credentials, graduating from the Ecole de la Chambre Syndicale de la Couture Parisienne, followed by a period working for Cerruti. Her very first collection for Hermès won her the City of Paris Grand Prix of Creative Art prize. "I am lucky to have been able to use the most exceptional materials for Hermès," says Nichanian, who has maintained a discreet personal profile during her time at the house, "It is essential for me to work with the know-how of traditional craftsmanship, combined with the latest technological advances." [Also see Jean Paul Gaultier.]

Hermès ist eine der nobelsten Adressen für Luxusgüter. 1837 gründete der Sattlermeister Thierry Hermès ein Geschäft für edles Zaumzeug. Heute ist die Marke berühmt für ihre handgefertigten, extrem begehrten (und kostspieligen) Lederwaren. Am berühmtesten sind die Kelly Bag und die Birkin Bag. In den letzten Jahren hat sich Hermès aber auch zu einem wichtigen Player im Bereich Prêt-à-porter entwickelt. Seit 2004 entwirft Jean Paul Gaultier die Damenkollektionen der Marke (er folgte auf den 1998 verpflichteten Martin Margiela), während die Designerin der Herrenmode bei Hermès, Véronique Nichanian, schon seit 1988 raffinierte „Bekleidungs-Objekte" für das Unternehmen kreiert. Erstmals versuchte sich Hermès in den 1920er Jahren an Kleidung: zunächst mit Sportsachen, die zu den angebotenen Accessoires passten. Erst in den 1950er Jahren gelang es jedoch, eine größere männliche Klientel zu gewinnen, als man die bekannten gemusterten Seidenkrawatten lancierte. Die in einem Atelier in der Pariser Rue du Faubourg Saint-Honoré arbeitende Nichanian machte Hermès zum Synonym für luxuriöse Herrenmode, die unter Männern mit gewissem Ein-

kommen rasch Kultstatus erlangte. Die klassische Herrenschneiderei ist immer exquisit, die Freizeitkleidung aber auch nicht weniger luxuriös, allerdings oft in prächtigen Farbkombinationen gehalten und mit leicht ironischen Details versehen. Nichanian hat übrigens tadellose Referenzen vorzuweisen – nach ihrem Abschluss an der Ecole de la Chambre Syndicale de la Couture Parisienne arbeitete sie für Cerruti. Mit ihrer ersten Kollektion für Hermès gewann sie den Großen Preis für Kreative Kunst der Stadt Paris. „Ich hatte das Glück, für Hermès mit den außergewöhnlichsten Materialien arbeiten zu können", sagt Nichanian selbst, die ihre Karriere im Hause Hermès ansonsten ziemlich nüchtern betrachtet. „Für mich ist es entscheidend, mit den Kenntnissen der traditionellen Handwerkskunst zu arbeiten und diese mit den neuesten technologischen Errungenschaften zu kombinieren." [Siehe auch Jean Paul Gaultier.]

Hermès est l'une des plus grandes maisons de l'industrie du luxe. Cette entreprise de sellerie haut de gamme fondée en 1837 par Thierry Hermès est aujourd'hui mondialement connue pour sa maroquinerie artisanale extrêmement recherchée (et onéreuse), en particulier ses fameux sacs à main Kelly et Birkin. Ces dernières années, la maison Hermès s'est également imposée comme un acteur incontournable du prêt-à-porter de luxe. Depuis 2004, Jean Paul Gaultier dessine les collections féminines de la marque (succédant à Martin Margiela, nommé à ce poste en 1998) tandis que Véronique Nichanian, styliste des lignes pour homme d'Hermès, crée des «objets d'habillement» sophistiqués depuis 1988. La griffe s'était déjà lancée dans le vêtement dans les années 20, avec un sportswear destiné à compléter les accessoires. Mais Hermès doit attendre les années 50 pour élargir sa clientèle masculine grâce au lancement de ses cravates en soie imprimées. Entre les mains de Véronique Nichanian, qui travaille dans un atelier de la rue du Faubourg-Saint-Honoré, Hermès devient synonyme de pièces masculines si luxueuses qu'elles se transforment rapidement en signes extérieurs de réussite sociale parmi les hommes aisés. Ses costumes classiques sont toujours magnifiquement coupés ; la mode décontractée n'est pas moins luxueuse, quoique souvent proposée dans des combinaisons de couleurs plus vives avec des détails subtilement ironiques. Nichanian affiche un CV idéal : diplômée de l'Ecole de la Chambre Syndicale de la Couture Parisienne, elle a travaillé pour Cerruti avant de rejoindre Hermès, où sa toute première collection lui vaut le Grand Prix Artistique de la Ville de Paris. «J'ai beaucoup de chance car Hermès me permet de travailler les matières les plus exceptionnelles », explique Véronique Nichanian, restée discrète tout au long de sa carrière dans la maison. «Pour moi, il est essentiel de respecter le savoir-faire artisanal traditionnel tout en le combinant aux derniers progrès de la technologie ». [Voir aussi Jean Paul Gaultier.]

SUSIE RUSHTON

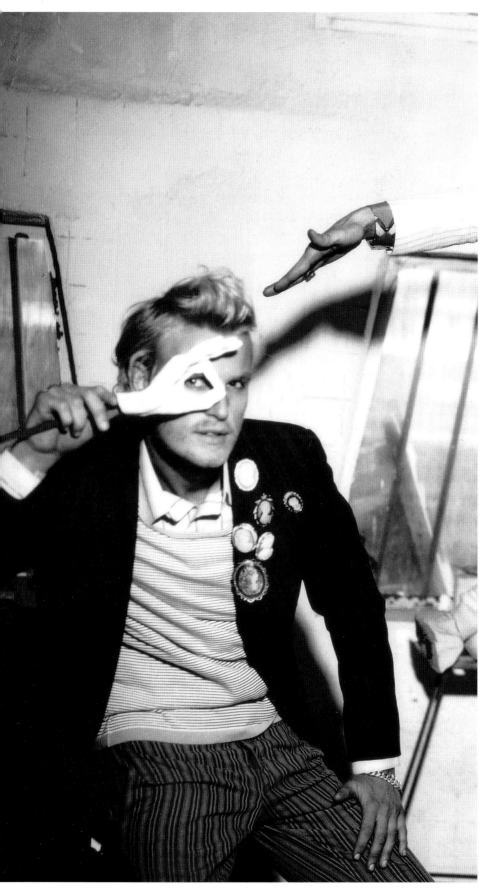

What are your signature designs? The research into new fabrics and the mix of materials, the refining of the details, the strictness of the form. I create clothes as 'vêtements-objets' **What's your favourite piece from any of your collections?** I have a lot of them. I am very attached to the work I am doing on knitwear, leather and the idea of a more informal evening look **How would you describe your work?** I try to develop a timeless style within this exceptional house, one which balances the values of innovation and tradition **What's your ultimate goal?** To allow men to become attractive, but at the same time respecting their personality and their individuality. I like the idea that men cultivate their differences. I also like the fact that the clothes come into their lives and that they then appropriate them. Finally, I love to see my designs being worn in the street **What inspires you?** People and interactions and the energy of big cities **Can fashion still have a political ambition?** I don't think so, I'd rather say an emotional ambition **Who do you have in mind when you design?** I don't have a particular type of man in mind **Is the idea of creative collaboration important to you?** Yes, with the team in my studio and the technicians in the ateliers with whom I work. Dialogue is essential **Who has been the greatest influence on your career?** Meeting Jean-Louis Dumas-Hermès **How have your own experiences affected your work as a designer?** I'm an emotional person… **Which is more important in your work: the process or the product?** Both, the process is for me a source of energy and the clothes a source of emotion **Is designing difficult for you, if so, what drives you to continue?** The concept for some collections comes quite quickly – others have been more hesitant – but it's at the moment of constructing the catwalk show that the magic happens. Each collection has a life of it's own **Have you ever been influenced or moved by the reaction to your designs?** I listen to the people that I like and admire. I am attentive to criticism when it's constructive – it's very stimulating **What's your definition of beauty?** Harmony **What's your philosophy?** Enjoy **What is the most important lesson you've learned?** Modesty, it's only clothes!

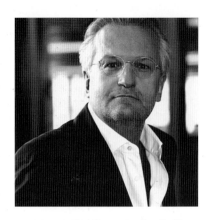

HUGO BOSS

"Our aim is not to be avant-garde, but to make customers feel comfortable and confident in our clothes" LOTHAR REIFF

Next to Armani, global giant Hugo Boss is arguably the most recognisable suiting label in the world. In the forty-five years since the house began making suits, the label has been a dominant force in the market, with six hundred stores worldwide and a presence in 108 countries. With collections for every demographic, from urban sport to demi-bespoke, Hugo Boss continues to expand its global reach. Founded in 1923 by the eponymous Austrian tailor, Hugo Boss began life as a manufacturer of workwear, shifting gear in the '60s to produce men's suiting and again in 1970 with the launch of fashion brand Boss. Listed on the German stock exchange in 1985, the majority shareholding of Hugo Boss GmbH was acquired by Italian fashion group Marzotto SpA in 1991. Under Marzotto, Boss diversified with the younger, directional Hugo label (which is designed by Volker Kaechele) and more sophisticated Baldessarini brand. Boss – which is led by designer Lothar Reiff, photographed above – is now split into Boss Selection (demi-bespoke suiting), Boss Black (mainline), Boss Orange (urban sportswear) and Boss Green (active sportswear) with Hugo womenswear launched in 1998 and Boss Black womenswear in 2000. In 2004 Marzotto reported that Boss menswear turned over € 1,000 million and Boss womenswear a further € 69 million. Hugo Boss was early in adopting the policy of linking the brand to glamorous men's sports, such as their pioneering sponsorship deals with Porsche (1971), the Davis Cup (1988), Seve Ballesteros (1988), AC Milan (1995) and Chelsea FC (2004). Like Prada Group CEO Patrizio Bertelli, the house has become affiliated to sailing and sponsored Hugo Boss Farr 65 in the Fastnet Race in 2003. In 1996 Hugo Boss established the biannual Hugo Boss Art Prize in conjunction with the Solomon R. Guggenheim Museum in New York.

Neben Armani ist der internationale Großkonzern Hugo Boss wohl der weltweit bekannteste Hersteller von Anzügen. Seit man vor 45 Jahren damit begann, hat das Label mit seinen 600 Läden und der Präsenz in 108 Ländern echte Marktdominanz entwickelt. Mit Kollektionen für alle Bevölkerungsschichten, von urban-sportlich bis teilweise maßgeschneidert, baut Hugo Boss seine globale Reichweite ständig aus. Die 1923 von einem österreichischen Schneider dieses Namens gegründete Firma war zunächst eine Manufaktur für Arbeitskleidung. In den 1960er Jahren stellte man die Produktion auf Herrenanzüge um, und seit den 1970er Jahren firmiert man unter dem Markennamen Boss. 1985 ging die Firma an die Börse. 1991 erwarb dann der italienische Modekonzern Marzotto SpA die Aktienmehrheit der Hugo Boss GmbH. Unter Marzotto erfolgte die Diversifizierung in das jüngere, geradlinige Label Hugo (für das Volker Kaechele design) und die elegantere Marke Baldessarini. Die Linie Boss selbst – unter der Leitung des Designers Lothar Reiff – ist gesplittet in Boss Selection (teilweise Maßanfertigung von Anzügen), Boss Black (die Hauptkollektion), Boss Orange (urbane Sportswear) und Boss Green (active sportswear – sprich: echte Sport-

kleidung). Bei Hugo gibt es Damenmode seit 1998, bei Boss Black seit 2000. Im Jahr 2004 gab Marzotto die Umsätze mit der Herrenmode von Boss mit über 1000 Millionen Euro an, die mit der Damenmode mit weiteren 69 Millionen Euro. Hugo Boss entdeckte früh den Vorteil, die Marke mit glamourösen Männersportarten zu verknüpfen. In diese Kategorie fallen der pionierhafte Sponsor-Deal mit Porsche (1971), der Davis Cup (1988), Seve Ballesteros (1988), AC Mailand (1995) und Chelsea FC (2004). Wie Patrizio Bertelli, der CEO des Pradakonzerns, hat auch Boss ein Faible fürs Segeln entwickelt und sponserte im Fastnet Race 2003 Hugo Boss Farr 65. 1996 stiftete Hugo Boss in Kooperation mit dem New Yorker Solomon R. Guggenheim Museum den alle zwei Jahre vergebenen Hugo Boss Art Prize.

Aux côtés d'Armani, le géant mondial Hugo Boss est sans conteste la marque de costumes pour homme la plus connue au monde. Depuis qu'elle a commencé à produire des costumes il y a de cela quarante-cinq ans, elle s'est imposée comme une force dominante du marché, avec six cents boutiques dans le monde et une présence dans 108 pays. Proposant des collections pour toutes les tranches d'âge, du style sport urbain aux costumes « demi-bespoke » (où le client choisit lui-même le tissu de son costume), Hugo Boss continue à étendre sa notoriété mondiale. Créé en 1923 par le tailleur autrichien éponyme, Hugo Boss produit d'abord des vêtements utilitaires, puis se reconvertit dans le costume pour homme au cours des années 60, puis de nouveau dans les années 70 avec le lancement de la griffe Boss. Coté à la Bourse allemande en 1985, Hugo Boss GmbH vend une part majoritaire de son entreprise au groupe de mode italien Marzotto SpA en 1991. Sous l'impulsion de Marzotto, Boss se diversifie avec la griffe Hugo, plus jeune et plus innovante (dessinée par Volker Kaechele), et la marque plus sophistiquée Baldessarini. La maison Boss, dirigée par le styliste Lothar Reiff, se divise désormais entre Boss Selection (costumes « demi-bespoke »), Boss Black (ligne principale), Boss Orange (sportswear urbain) et Boss Green (sportswear actif), sans oublier les collections pour femme Hugo et Boss Black, respectivement lancées en 1998 et en l'an 2000. En 2004, Marzotto annonce un chiffre d'affaires de plus d'un milliard d'euros pour les collections masculines, et de 69 millions d'euros pour les lignes féminines. Hugo Boss est l'une des premières marques à avoir saisi l'intérêt de lier son image à celle des sports masculins élitistes, notamment par le biais d'accords de partenariat visionnaires avec Porsche (1971), la Coupe Davis (1988), le golfeur Seve Ballesteros (1988), le Milan AC (1995) et le Chelsea FC (2004). Comme Patrizio Bertelli, P-DG du groupe Prada, la maison s'est aussi associée au monde de la voile et sponsorise le Farr 65 Hugo Boss lors de la course nautique Fastnet en 2003. En 1996, la marque fonde le prix artistique biennal Hugo Boss en collaboration avec le musée Guggenheim de New York.

JAMES SHERWOOD

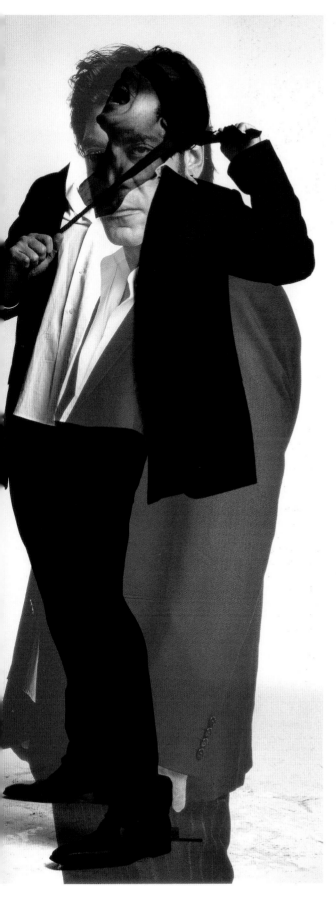

Lothar Reiff

What are your signature designs? Every line has its own signature. In the case of Hugo Boss with its various brands, we cannot really talk about a certain signature design. What definitely unifies all our brands is the general appreciation of design and quality **What is your favourite piece from any of your collections?** There are too many styles that I personally enjoy. But actually, what I really like a lot about all our collections is the fact that we pay a lot of attention to detail, which makes our products special **How would you describe your work?** As a creative director I need to be very sensitive to new ideas. We want to find a balance between creativity and the needs of the market. We have to be fashionable but at the same time remain market-oriented **What's your ultimate goal?** In my job, the launch of a collection is always exciting and a great challenge. The ultimate goal is definitely to continue the Hugo Boss success story and to see the company grow **What inspires you?** I keep a close eye on cultural developments in art, music, etc., and these have a strong influence on my work. It's also inspiring for me to travel and encounter different people, characters and cultures **Can fashion still have a political ambition?** Fashion is always a reflection of our times, but we realise that people feel an intense need for optimism and therefore it's important to present optimistic fashion **Who do you have in mind when you design?** A self-confident person who wants to underline his or her own personality. Who is aware of quality and interested in fashion **Is the idea of creative collaboration important to you?** Yes, definitely – our work at Hugo Boss is always team-oriented **Who has been the greatest influence on your career?** There is no single person – there have been different people in different phases **Which is more important in your work: the process or the product?** Both are important – at the start, developing a new collection and at the end, the final products. A professional process leads to a professional product **Is designing difficult for you, if so, what drives you to continue?** No, it's a great passion and always a new challenge for me **What's your definition of beauty?** Beauty is not just endowed by nature, but is also a state of mind **What's your philosophy?** Our aim is not to be avant-garde, but to make customers feel comfortable and confident in our clothes **What is the most important lesson you've learned?** Being grateful for everything that happens in my everyday life and listening to my own inner voice.

Volker Kächele

What are your signature designs? In each collection there are great, sexy, slim fitting tailored pieces for men that usually have a bold contrast lining or a quirky detail for a young, fun look **What is your favourite piece from any of your collections?** It is a brown leather coat, which is from one of the first Hugo collections. I still love it **How would you describe your work?** Classic tailoring meets contemporary sportswear **What's your ultimate goal?** Being successful with the brand Hugo **What inspires you?** Travelling, people, cities, music and music videos, books, movies **Can fashion still have a political ambition?** Generally, I think fashion can be used to make a political statement, but only to a point **Who do you have in mind when you design?** Our clothing is tailored for young, hip people who love fashion and care about what they wear to work and also in their private life **Is the idea of creative collaboration important to you?** Yes, it is very important because it is inspiring and brings you to reflect your own work **Who has been the greatest influence on your career?** There are several people I have met in my life and who I have worked with that have influenced my career and helped in different ways to make me who I am today **How have your own experiences affected your work as a designer?** Designing is always a process, which lives almost exclusively from own experiences and personal feelings. My work is very much influenced from what I see, from discussions with people I work with, from my feelings **Which is more important in your work: the process or the product?** The product is "only" the final result of the complex design process and the process is what it is all about **Is designing difficult for you, if so, what drives you to continue?** No, I would not say designing is difficult for me. The excitement about the challenge and the feeling you get after a successful season is the force which motivates me again and again **Have you ever been influenced or moved by the reaction to your designs?** As a matter of course I am influenced by the reaction to my designs. I believe this is the only way for further advancement **What's your definition of beauty?** For me, "beauty" related to a person is not only the look of the face and the shape of a body. Sometimes you meet somebody, who does not conform to the beauty norm of the season but has an overwhelming charisma **What's your philosophy?** Treat everybody in the same way as you would expect to be treated by them **What is the most important lesson you've learned?** To be aware that nothing is forever and everything is subject to permanent change.

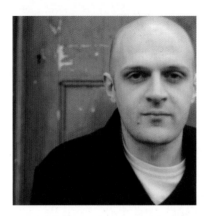

HUSSEIN CHALAYAN

"My inspiration comes from anthropology, genetic anthropology, migration, history, social prejudice, politics, displacement, science fiction and, I guess, my own cultural background"

Hussein Chalayan (born 1970) takes a conceptual approach to fashion, pushing clothing across generic boundaries into sculpture, furniture, performance art and beyond. Since his graduate collection at Central Saint Martins in 1993 where clothes were buried in the ground for several weeks, he has confirmed his reputation as one of the most original designers working anywhere in the world today. Chalayan is famed for his spectacular shows in which anything could happen, from coffee tables turning into dresses to the use of confessional boxes and trampolines as catwalk props. At the same time, the designer's attention to technical detail, structure and stitching is exceptional. His collections have often focused on cultural displacement, something which Chalayan himself has experienced; his spring/summer 2003 collection 'Kinship Journey', for example, was inspired by Viking, Byzantine, Georgian and Armenian cultures following a DNA test taken by the designer. Born in Nicosia to Turkish-Cypriot parents, at the age of 12 Chalayan left Cyprus to attend school in England. Aside from his eponymous label, Chalayan has during his career worked for cashmere brand TSE and was appointed creative director of Asprey in 2001, departing the company in 2004. His creative touchstones are science and new technology. He is a twice-crowned British Designer of the Year, having picked up the prize in 1999 and 2000. Chalayan now shows in Paris although his studio remains in London, and his work is as likely to be seen in international art spaces as on the catwalk. Recent awards include the Tribe Art Commission, from which he made the short film 'Place to Passage' (2003). 2004 saw Chalayan open his first store in Tokyo; to complement his existing womenswear and menswear collections, in 2005 he also launched a younger line, 'Chalayan'. In the same year, the Netherlands' Groningen Museum mounted a full-scale retrospective exhibition of the designer's work.

Der 1970 geborene Hussein Chalayan beschäftigt sich auf konzeptionelle Weise mit Mode und überwindet mit seiner Kleidung die Grenzen zu Bildhauerei, Möbelherstellung, Performancekunst und weiteren Bereichen. Seit seiner Abschlusskollektion am Central Saint Martins im Jahr 1993, für die er seine Entwürfe mehrere Wochen lang in der Erde vergraben hatte, ist es ihm gelungen, seinen Ruf als einer der weltweit originellsten Designer der Gegenwart weiter zu festigen. Chalayan ist berühmt für seine spektakulären Modenschauen, bei denen alles Mögliche passieren kann, von Kaffeetischen, die sich in Kleider verwandeln, bis zu Beichtstühlen und Trampolinen als Requisiten auf dem Laufsteg. Dazu kommt die außergewöhnliche Sorgfalt des Designers hinsichtlich technischer Details, Strukturen und Nähte. Oft stehen kulturelle Verschiebungen, die Chalayan auch selbst erfahren hat, im Mittelpunkt seiner Kollektionen. So war etwa seine Kollektion Frühjahr/Sommer 2003 von den Kulturen der Wikinger, Byzantiner, Georgier und Armenier inspiriert, nachdem der Designer sich einem DNA-Test unterzogen hatte. Als Kind türkisch-zyprischer Eltern in Nicosia geboren, verließ Chalayan die Insel im Alter von 12 Jahren, um in Eng-

land zur Schule zu gehen. Außer für das nach ihm benannte Label hat er im Laufe seiner Karriere für die Kaschmirmarke TSE sowie von 2001 bis 2004 als Creative Director für Asprey entworfen. Seine kreativen Prüfsteine sind Wissenschaft und neue Technologien. 1999 und 2000 wurde er mit dem Titel British Designer of the Year ausgezeichnet. Inzwischen präsentiert Chalayan seine Kollektionen in Paris, auch wenn sich sein Atelier nach wie vor in London befindet und man seine Arbeiten eher in Ausstellungsräumen rund um die Welt als auf einem Catwalk findet. Zu seinen jüngsten Preisen gehört die Tribe Art Commission, aus der er den Kurzfilm „Place to Passage" (2003) gemacht hat. 2004 eröffnete Chalayan seinen ersten Laden in Tokio. Und als Ergänzung der Damen- und Herrenkollektion lancierte er 2005 mit ‚Chalayan' eine noch jüngere Linie. Im selben Jahr stellte das holländische Groningen Museum eine umfassende Retrospektive seines bisherigen Werkes zusammen.

Hussein Chalayan (né en 1970) approche la mode de façon conceptuelle, repoussant ses frontières génériques aux confins de la sculpture, du mobilier, du théâtre et même au-delà. Depuis sa collection de fin d'études à Central Saint Martins en 1993, où ses vêtements sont restés enterrés sous le sol pendant plusieurs semaines, il a confirmé sa réputation de créateur parmi les plus originaux actuellement en exercice dans le monde. Chalayan est connu pour ses défilés spectaculaires où tout peut arriver, des tables basses transformées en robes aux confessionnaux et trampolines utilisés en guise de podiums. Parallèlement, le créateur fait preuve d'une attention exceptionnelle aux détails techniques, à la structure et aux coutures. Ses collections parlent souvent du « déplacement culturel », une expérience vécue par Chalayan en personne ; par exemple, pour sa collection printemps/été 2003 « Kinship Journey », il s'est inspiré des cultures viking, byzantine, géorgienne et arménienne après avoir obtenu les résultats de son test ADN. Né à Nicosie de parents turcs-chypriotes, Chalayan quitte Chypre à l'âge de 12 ans pour aller étudier en Angleterre. Outre sa griffe éponyme, Chalayan a travaillé pour la marque de cachemire TSE. En 2001, il a été nommé styliste d'Asprey, une maison qu'il quittera en 2004. Les pierres d'angle de sa démarche créative sont les sciences et les nouvelles technologies. Il a été couronné deux fois British Designer of the Year, en 1999 et en l'an 2000. Chalayan présente désormais ses collections à Paris, bien que son atelier soit toujours à Londres. On a autant de chances d'admirer son travail dans les galeries d'art internationales que sur le podium des défilés. Récemment, il a reçu la Tribe Art Commission, ce qui lui a permis de réaliser le court-métrage « Place to Passage » (2003). En 2004, Chalayan a ouvert sa première boutique à Tokyo. Afin de compléter ses collections pour homme et pour femme, il a également lancé en 2005 une ligne plus jeune baptisée « Chalayan ». La même année, le Groningen Museum des Pays-Bas a organisé une grande rétrospective de l'œuvre du couturier.

SKYE SHERWIN

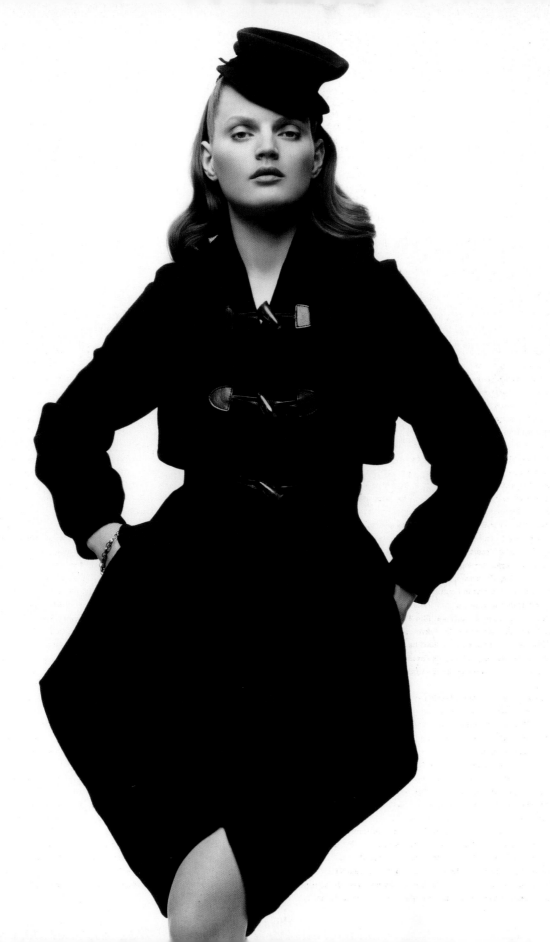

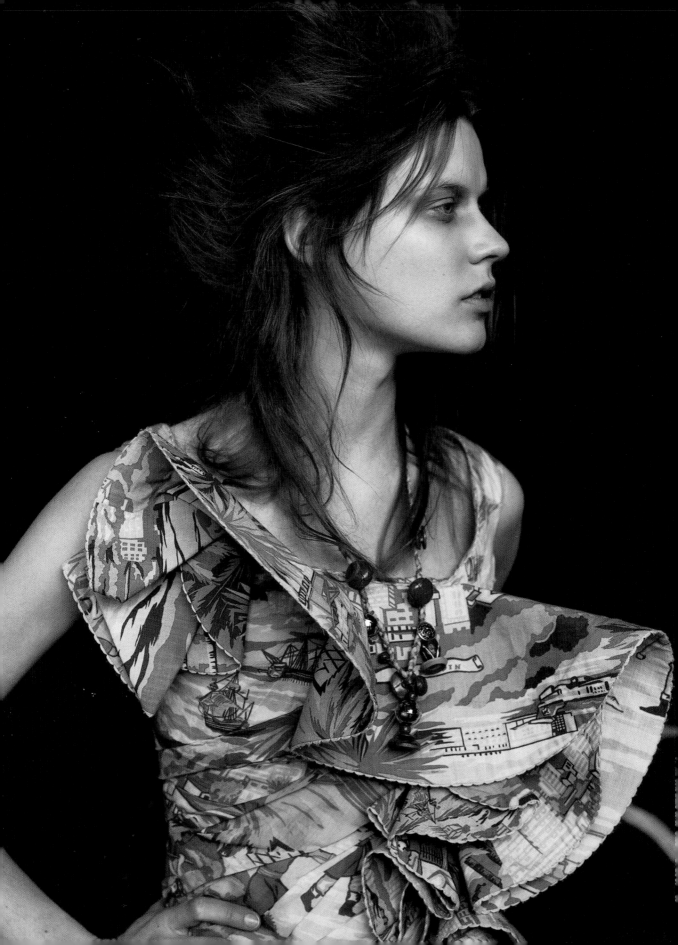

What are your signature designs? It's hard to define the signature designs as each project for me has different monuments, but roughly speaking I would say they are: the buried dresses, the paper floral suits, airmail clothing, the shaved tulle dresses, all the mechanical dresses, all the low-armholed loop dresses, the historically layered collection etc. However, ultimately the sequential way in which we work creates the basis of the signature **What is your favourite piece from any of your collections?** My favourite pieces to date are the printed dresses based on the Cyprus border, spring/summer 2004 **How would you describe your work?** I feel that my work somehow lies in a gap between reality and fantasy **What's your ultimate goal?** My ultimate goal is to have a stable life, where I don't have to travel to fit a seam, and to have the opportunity to build up my vision without too much conflict. But ultimately to live in an environment where prejudice does not eat me up **What inspires you?** My inspiration comes from anthropology, genetic anthropology, migration, history, social prejudice, politics, displacement, science fiction and, I guess, my own cultural background **Can fashion still have a political ambition?** Fashion can be informed and inspired by political aspirations but to actually make it literally carry it is in my view often contrived **Who do you have in mind when you design?** Mostly Jane How (my long-term stylist and consultant), partly an architect woman and partly for a girl who is more boy-like but who can dress in a surprisingly feminine way for a special occasion **Is the idea of creative collaboration important to you?** Creative and practical collaboration is what makes things actually happen even if the project and the approach are the vision of one person. You can have the vision, but I think it's also important to recognise what other people can add to it **Who has been the greatest influence on your career?** My driving influence is not one person... **How have your own experiences affected your work as a designer?** My experience has made me feel that being independent is what I value the most **Which is more important in your work: the process or the product?** The product, ultimately, is the most important thing but it can be said that the final product is for the buyer, and the process, which other people don't always need to know about, is the part that is for your personal satisfaction and, at times, growth **Is designing difficult for you, if so, what drives you to continue?** Designing is not difficult. Doing it under strict deadlines when there is no time makes it difficult. What drives me to continue is the feeling that I still have new things to learn **Have you ever been influenced or moved by the reaction to your designs?** If people are moved by what you do, who wouldn't be affected... however, to base your self-confidence on fickle remarks and inconsistent journalists who don't know your history is disastrous **What's your definition of beauty?** My definition of beauty is a kind of 'truth' that may not always be aesthetically beautiful (Patti Smith... one minute the childlike smile on stage... one minute the hard-core spitting of gob on the floor whilst performing... what a beauty she is...) **What's your philosophy?** My philosophy (not as a part of any dogmatic belief) is based on the idea that whatever you do comes back to you **What is the most important lesson you've learned?** The most important lesson has been the realisation that you should live ultimately for yourself and less for others. And that people in the world are not really that different when it comes down to the basic facts.

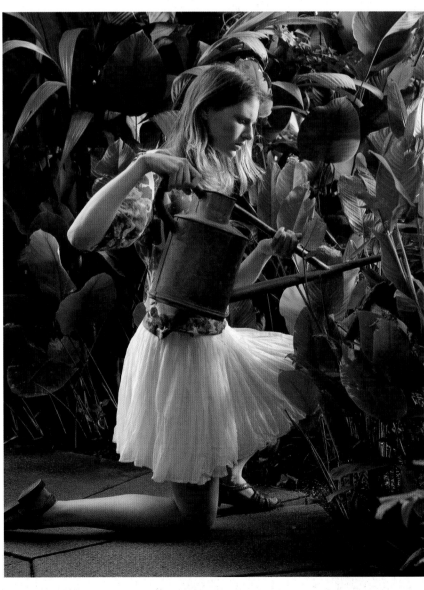

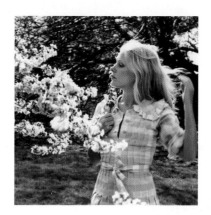

IMITATION OF CHRIST

"I am just an actress posing as a designer"

TARA SUBKOFF

The genesis of the New York-based label Imitation of Christ in 2000 was anything but holy. Reacting to what they believed was the over-commodification of fashion, the label's co-founders and art-school drop-outs Tara Subkoff and Matt Damhave defiantly resurrected thrift-store finds by slashing them into pieces, removing the label, incorporating subversive text and slapping on a cross insignia. As a result, their rise to darling status was swift. At one point, thanks in part to the modelling/consulting efforts of long-time friend and disciple Chloë Sevigny, herself a thrift-store devotee, the duo showed a collection in a funeral parlour, watched on by Vogue's Anna Wintour and Andre Leon Talley. But good things don't last forever – not even for a divinely-christened label – and now only Subkoff (born 1974) remains. She works tirelessly to keep the faith alive with a team of equally politically-motivated colleagues who regard themselves more as social engineers than designers. Examples are many. In 2001, Subkoff – also a part-time indie film actress – and the IOC team produced a short film starring Reese Witherspoon which was intended to illustrate the prevalence of sweatshops and child labour. In a following collection, a mock auction was staged at Sotheby's where models were presented as items for sale by an auctioneer. In 2002, IOC trekked to Paris to hold a renegade show outside the Christian Dior venue, to which the models arrived in ambulances and made their appearances on stretchers in a presumed statement about the death of fashion. In a role-reversing show later that year, models were seated, with pen and paper in hand, waiting to critique guests who were escorted down the catwalk, in a poignant critique of the critical process itself. Is nothing sacred?

Die Genese des in New York ansässigen Labels Imitation of Christ im Jahr 2000 hat so gar nichts Heiliges. Als Reaktion auf die in ihren Augen völlig übersteigerte Kommerzialisierung von Mode belebten die beiden Firmengründer und Studienabbrecher Tara Subkoff und Matt Damhave trotzig Fundstücke aus Second-Hand-Läden neu, indem sie sie zerschnitten, die Etiketten entfernten, sie mit subversiven Texten versahen und ein Kreuzzeichen darauf befestigten. Das Ergebnis war ihr rascher Aufstieg zur Lieblingsmarke. Irgendwann zeigte das Duo, nicht zuletzt dank der Model- und Consulting-Hilfe der langjährigen Freundin und Schülerin Chloë Sevigny, die selbst ein großer Fan von Second-Hand-Läden ist, eine Kollektion in den Geschäftsräumen eines Bestattungsunternehmens. Damals waren Andre Leon Talley und Anna Wintour von Vogue zugegen. Aber selbst die besten Dinge halten nicht ewig – nicht einmal bei einem göttlich getauften Label. Deshalb ist inzwischen nur noch die 1974 geborene Tara Subkoff übrig. Sie arbeitet unermüdlich, um das Unternehmen am Leben zu halten, zusammen mit einem Team von ebenso politisch motivierten Kollegen, die sich selbst nicht so sehr als Designer, sondern eher als Sozialingenieure sehen. Beispiele für ihr Engagement gibt es viele. 2001 etwa produzierten Sub-

koff, die selbst als Teilzeit-Darstellerin in Independent-Filmen mitspielt, und ihr Team von IOC einen Kurzfilm mit Reese Witherspoon über die Zunahme von Sweatshops und Kinderarbeit. Im Zuge einer späteren Kollektion fand eine fingierte Auktion bei Sotheby's statt, wo Models wie Verkaufsobjekte von einem Auktionator präsentiert wurden. 2002 zog IOC nach Paris, um vor dem Sitz von Christian Dior eine hintergründige Schau zu veranstalten. Die Models kamen in Rettungsfahrzeugen und wurden auf Krankenbahren präsentiert – als Sinnbild für das Sterben der Mode. Ein Jahr später saßen bei einer Schau mit vertauschten Rollen die Models ausgerüstet mit Stift und Papier auf den Zuschauerstühlen, um die Gäste zu beurteilen, die über den Catwalk geleitet wurden. Sozusagen als scharfe Kritik am Vorgang der Kritik selbst. Ist denen denn gar nichts heilig?

La genèse de la griffe new-yorkaise Imitation of Christ en l'an 2000 n'avait vraiment rien de sacré. En réaction à ce qu'ils estiment être la surmarchandisation de la mode, les cofondateurs de la marque et diplômés en art Tara Subkoff et Matt Damhave ressuscitent d'un air de défi les vêtements dénichés dans les magasins d'occasion en les tailladant, en arrachant leurs étiquettes, en intégrant des textes subversifs et en les parant de leur croix signature. Leur ascension au rang de chouchous de l'underground se fait donc rapidement. Grâce aux efforts de mannequinat et de consulting de leur disciple et amie de longue date Chloë Sevigny, elle-même fan de vieux vêtements, le duo présentera même une collection dans un salon funéraire, sous les yeux des journalistes de Vogue Anna Wintour et Andre Leon Talley. Mais toutes les bonnes choses ont une fin, même pour une griffe si divinement baptisée: aujourd'hui, il ne reste plus que Tara Subkoff (née en 1974). Elle fait tout son possible pour garder la foi, soutenue par une équipe de collaborateurs tout aussi motivés politiquement et qui se considèrent davantage comme des ingénieurs sociaux que comme des créateurs de mode, une approche illustrée par de nombreux exemples. En 2001, Tara Subkoff, également actrice à temps partiel pour le cinéma indépendant, et l'équipe d'IOC produisent un court-métrage avec Reese Witherspoon destiné à réveiller les consciences sur le problème des ateliers clandestins et du travail des enfants. Dans une autre collection, ils organisent de fausses enchères chez Sotheby's, où un commissaire-priseur présente les mannequins comme des articles à vendre. En 2002, IOC se rend à Paris pour donner un défilé dissident juste devant le siège de Christian Dior, avec des mannequins qui débarquent en ambulance sur des brancards comme pour déclarer la mort de la mode. Plus tard la même année, ils présentent un défilé où les rôles sont inversés: les mannequins restent assises armées de stylos et de bloc-notes et regardent défiler les journalistes escortés le long du podium, dans une critique poignante du processus de critique en soi. Mais n'y aurait-il donc plus rien de sacré ?

LEE CARTER

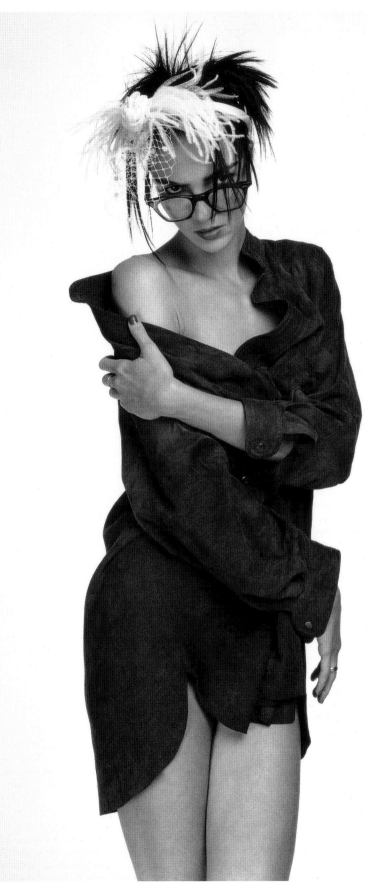

What are your signature designs? Something with a hood **What is your favourite piece from any of your collections?** Same as above **How would you describe your work?** Best described by other people **What's your ultimate goal?** World domination and take over **What inspires you?** "The Collection is T Rex meets Gertrude Stein if they lived together in Madagascar" **Can fashion still have a political ambition?** It's difficult to say: I've tried in the past and it has not worked very well **Is the idea of creative collaboration important to you?** Yes **Who has been the greatest influence on your career?** Gore Vidal **How have your own experiences affected your work as a designer?** My own experiences have driven me to be a designer. I am just an actress posing as a designer **What's your definition of beauty?** The spark in someone's eyes; that special something when someone truly gets your joke **What's your philosophy?** Changes daily **What is the most obvious lesson you've learned?** Obviously I have not learned it yet.

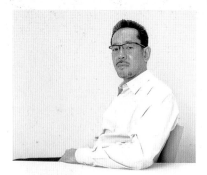

ISSEY MIYAKE BY NAOKI TAKIZAWA

"Creations from a fresh and innovative vision, which are free from the existing theories of making clothes"

Few titans of 20th century fashion have had the inclination to crown a successor. In 1993 when Issey Miyake launched his 'Pleats Please' line, the designer handed over his menswear collection to Naoki Takizawa, a member of the Miyake Design Studio. In 1999, when Miyake began his A-POC (A Piece of Cloth) concept, he chose Takizawa to take over the womenswear too. Born in Tokyo in 1960, Takizawa entered the Miyake Design Studio in 1982 immediately after graduating from the Kuwasawa Design Institute. Initially he worked as designer of the newly formed Plantation line, a range that used natural fibres and focused primarily on comfort and affordability. He was a relative unknown outside Tokyo's fashion industry when Miyake entrusted Takizawa with the task of moving his label forward into the next century. Takizawa has been clever to work with the experimental vocabulary Miyake introduced – bouncing pleats, oil-soaked paper, heat-pressed metallic paper-backed jersey, twisted synthetics – but uses Miyake Design Studio technology to move the label on to the next chapter. His exuberant use of clashing colours, in particular, has helped develop his distinctive identity. The Miyake Design Studio has always collaborated with artists, musicians and illustrators, and Takizawa has continued this tradition. "For me, collaboration with artists is a fascinating and essential part of my work", he says. For autumn/winter 2004, Takizawa invited sci-fi cartoonist Aya Takano to create Manga-meets-NASA prints for the womenswear 'Journey to the Moon' collection. Issey Miyake shows are performances and Takizawa has invited DJ Tsuyoshi, Pierre Bastien, Silent Poets and Nobukazu Takemura to sculpt sound that complements his clothing. Art photographers Warren du Preez and Nick Thornton Jones, Miwa Yanagi, Mika Ninagawa and Daido Moriyama have all been inspired by Takizawa's collections and in 2004 Kanazawa's 21st Century Museum of Contemporary Art invited Takizawa to design the institution's uniforms.

Nur wenige Titanen der Mode des 20. Jahrhunderts waren geneigt, einen Nachfolger zu inthronisieren. Issey Miyake jedoch übergab seine Herrenkollektion, als er 1993 seine neue Linie 'Pleats Please' herausbrachte, an Naoki Takizawa, ein Mitglied des Miyake Design Studios. Nachdem er 1999 mit seinem Konzept A-POC (A Piece of Cloth) begonnen hatte, überließ Miyake Takizawa auch die Damenmode. Der 1960 in Tokio geborene Takizawa wurde 1982 ins Miyake Design Studio aufgenommen, unmittelbar nach seinem Abschluss am Kuwasawa Design Institute. Anfänglich arbeitete er als Designer der neu gegründeten Linie 'Plantation', für die man Naturfasern verwendete und die vornehmlich auf Bequemlichkeit und Erschwinglichkeit ausgerichtet war. Außerhalb der Tokioter Modeszene war Takizawa noch ein relativ unbeschriebenes Blatt, als Miyake ihm auftrug, sein Label ins nächste Jahrhundert zu führen. Klugerweise bediente er sich des experimentellen Vokabulars, das Miyake eingeführt hatte – elastische Plisseefalten, ölgetränktes Papier, gebügelter metallischer Jersey mit Papierrückseite, geknäuelte Synthetikmaterialien. Er nutzte aber auch die Technologie des Miyake Design Studios, um das Label voranzubringen. Insbesondere seine reichliche Verwendung sich beißender Farben half bei der Entwicklung

einer eigenständigen Identität. Schon immer kooperierte das Miyake Design Studio mit bildenden Künstlern, Musikern und Illustratoren. Takizawa setzt diese Tradition fort. „Für mich ist die Zusammenarbeit mit Künstlern ein faszinierender und grundlegender Teil meiner Arbeit", meint er. Für Herbst/Winter 2004 lud er Aya Takano, einen Zeichner von Science-Fiction-Comics, ein, Muster im Stil von Manga-meets-NASA für die Damenkollektion 'Journey to the Moon' zu kreieren. Die Issey-Miyake-Schauen sind Performances, zu denen Takizawa schon DJ Tsuyoshi, Pierre Bastien, Silent Poets und Nobukazu Takemura bat, einen Sound zu kreieren, der seinen Entwürfen schmeichelt. Kunstfotografen wie Warren du Preez und Nick Thornton Jones, Miwa Yanagi, Mika Ninagawa und Daido Moriyama ließen sich alle schon von Takizawas Kollektionen inspirieren. 2004 wurde Takizawa damit beauftragt, die Uniformen der Angestellten des 21st Century Museum of Contemporary Art in Kanazawa zu entwerfen.

Les titans de la mode du XXᵉ siècle sont rarement enclins à couronner leur successeur. Pourtant, quand Issey Miyake lance sa ligne «Pleats Please» en 1993, il confie sa collection pour homme à Naoki Takizawa, membre du Miyake Design Studio. En 1999, quand Miyake décide de se consacrer entièrement à son concept A-POC (A Piece of Cloth), il choisit aussi Takizawa pour reprendre la création de sa ligne pour femme. Né en 1960 à Tokyo, Takizawa entre au Miyake Design Studio en 1982, fraîchement diplômé du Kuwasawa Design Institute. Il y travaille d'abord comme styliste de Plantation, une nouvelle ligne en fibres naturelles principalement axée sur le confort et l'accessibilité. Il fait encore figure de quasi-inconnu en dehors de l'industrie de la mode japonaise quand Miyake lui confie la mission de propulser sa griffe dans le XXIᵉ siècle. Takizawa réussit sans difficulté à travailler avec le vocabulaire expérimental inventé par Miyake (plis élastiques, papier huilé, jersey métallique renforcé et pressé à chaud, synthétiques tordus), mais utilise la technologie du Miyake Design Studio pour écrire le nouveau chapitre de l'histoire de la griffe. En particulier, son utilisation exubérante des contrastes de couleurs contribue à développer sa propre identité. Le Miyake Design Studio a toujours collaboré avec des artistes, des musiciens et des illustrateurs et Takizawa reste fidèle à cette tradition. «Pour moi, la collaboration avec les artistes constitue une part fascinante et essentielle de mon travail», dit-il. Pour l'automne/hiver 2004, Takizawa invite Aya Takano, dessinateur de BD de science-fiction, à créer des imprimés mêlant univers Manga et imagerie de la conquête spatiale destinés à une collection pour femme intitulée «Voyage sur la Lune». Les défilés Issey Miyake sont de véritables performances : Takizawa a fait appel à DJ Tsuyoshi, Pierre Bastien, aux Silent Poets et à Nobukazu Takemura pour sculpter des bandes-son mettant ses vêtements en valeur. Les photographes d'art Warren du Preez, Nick Thornton Jones, Miwa Yanagi, Mika Ninagawa et Daido Moriyama ont tous été inspirés par ses collections. En 2004, Takizawa a créé les nouveaux uniformes des employés du 21st Century Museum of Contemporary Art de Kanazawa.   JAMES SHERWOOD

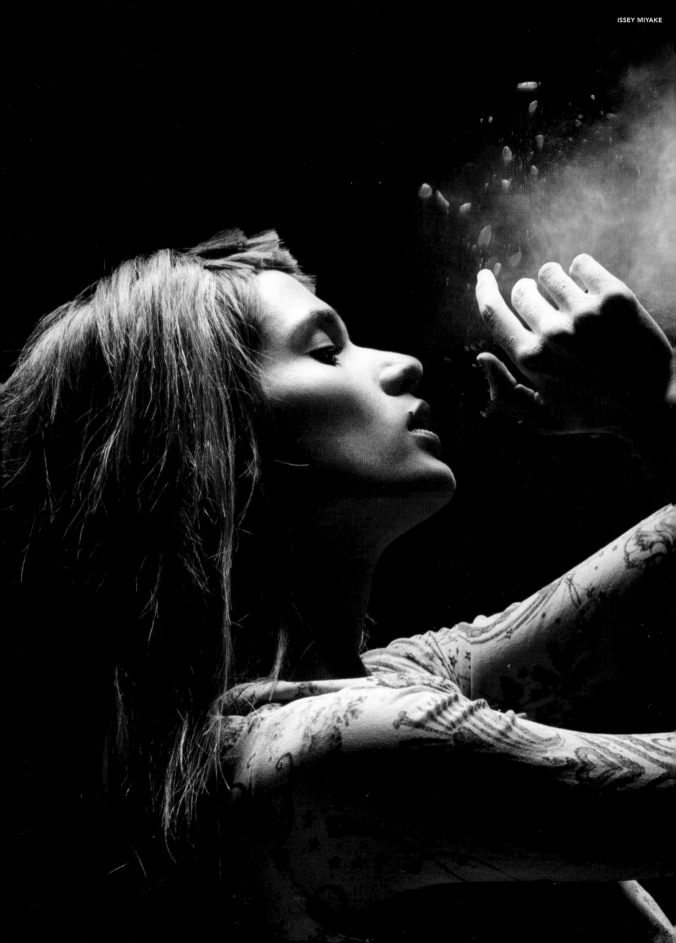

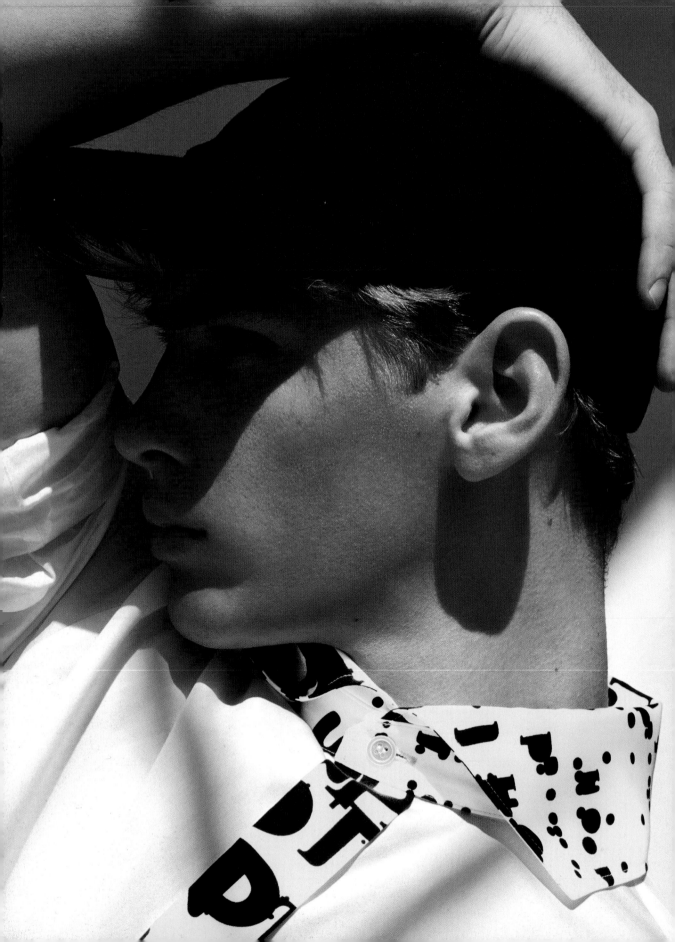

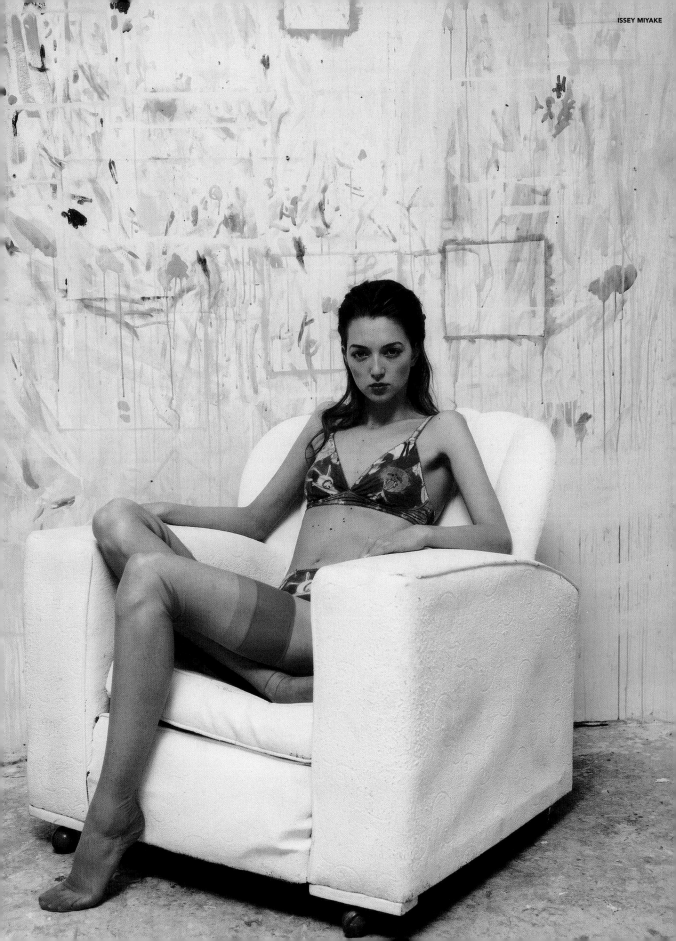

What are your signature designs? Creations from a fresh and innovative vision, which are free from the existing theories of making clothes **What is your favourite piece from any of your collections?** Autumn/winter 2004 collection – a dress made from just a circle of fabric and a piece of rope **How would you describe your work?** A mirror that reminds me of a part of myself that I have never been conscious of **What's your ultimate goal?** To be accepted by as many people as possible **What inspires you?** Something amusing and joyful **Can fashion still have a political ambition?** It can probably be said that fashion has a political ambition as a system. However in my opinion, fashion should be a personal expression – no more and no less **Who do you have in mind when you design?** Sometimes it is an imaginary person, and other times it is someone who is close to me **Is the idea of creative collaboration important to you?** "Friction" arising from the encounter of two different creators transforms into "communication" ultimately. I believe that this "friction" has the power to create a new way of communicating with the people who actually wear and enjoy the final result **Who has been the greatest influence on your career?** Issey Miyake **How have your own experiences affected your work as a designer?** For me, the word "experience" is pronoun of "the time spent". Ongoing present exists only on top of experience. Obviously, it influences my technique, aesthetic, and judgments – everything about me **Which is more important in your work: the process or the product?** Both are important. Sometimes I envisage the product first, and explore the process to lead to the result. Other times, I accidentally extract ideas from the process, which result in the unexpected. For me, these two things are connected to each other, and exist in the same line **Is designing difficult for you, if so, what drives you to continue?** The more I gain experience, the more I find it difficult to design. However, the strong will to continue designing becomes associated with the need for social change. This creates new energy for me **Have you ever been influenced or moved by the reaction to your designs?** Yes. I think that the reaction is an objectively valuable judgment. Sometimes it gives me a new direction and opens my eyes to new possibilities. I believe that I can change this reaction into energy, and can explore the future **What's your definition of beauty?** Harmony with people **What's your philosophy?** I am still on my journey to finding it. If I could tell you, I would not be here designing! **What is the most important lesson you've learned?** Teamwork.

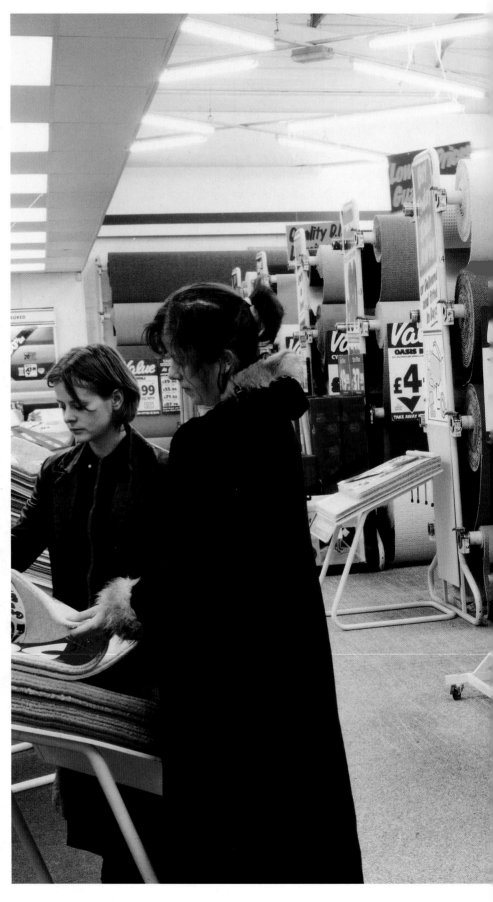

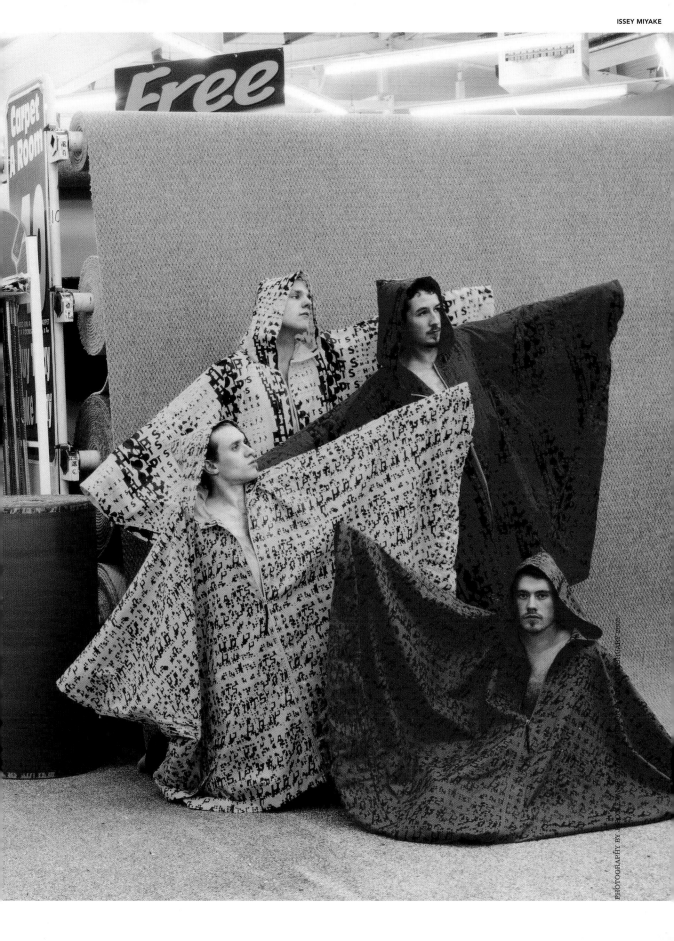

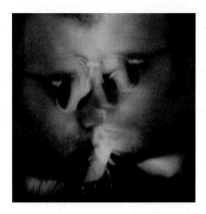

JEAN COLONNA

"Fashion, which is drowned in rules, could have a
revolutionary ambition"

Jean Colonna brought the dark side of Paris's Pigalle nightclubs, left-bank sex clubs and S&M shops onto the catwalk. He championed deconstruction in the early '90s, making clothes in deliberately cheap fabrics and shoddy finishes. Yet Colonna wanted to make his clothing accessible for all, not just fashion victims who thought his 'pauvre chic' was an amusing joke. Truly an 'enfant terrible', Colonna had a surprisingly conventional training. Born in Algeria in 1955, Colonna was raised in Aix-en-Provence and moved to Paris in 1975, where he studied at the Ecole de la Chambre Syndicale de la Couture Parisienne. After graduating, Colonna assisted couturier Pierre Balmain. In 1985 he presented his first collection, eschewing the catwalk in favour of catalogues shot by friends Bettina Rheims and Stéphane Sednaoui. He also designed jewellery and accessories for contemporaries Claude Montana, Thierry Mugler and Jean Paul Gaultier. 1990 saw Colonna take his collections to the runway and pioneer the use of monolithic warehouse spaces and gawky androgynous models. Colonna was at the vanguard of deconstruction, and his all-black collections were reminiscent of '70s 'slash and burn' punk. His use of cheap sex-shop cloths such as lamé, leatherette and PVC, and hems unceremoniously over-locked or left raw were a deliberate slap in the face for bourgeois Parisian fashion. During this period, Colonna collaborated with photographer David Sims on a 1993 window for French department store Le Printemps. Deconstruction soon lost its charm and between 1993 and 1994 Colonna was designing capsule collections for French mail-order company La Redoute. Overlooked by those who don't support Colonna's message (real clothes for real people), the designer remains a maverick talent in French fashion with a cult following in Japan.

Jean Colonna brachte die dunkle Seite der Nachtclubs des Pariser Viertels Pigalle, der Sexclubs und S/M-Läden am linken Seineufer auf den Laufsteg. Weitaus gefährlicher wurde seinen Kollegen aus der High Fashion jedoch sein Hang zur Dekonstruktion Anfang der Neunzigerjahre, als er Kleider aus bewusst billigen Stoffen mit schundigem Finish ablieferte. Colonna wollte seine Mode für jedermann zugänglich machen, nicht nur für Fashion Victims, die seinen „Pauvre Chic" für einen amüsanten Gag hielten. Das Enfant terrible Colonna besitzt eine erstaunlich konventionelle Ausbildung. 1955 in Algerien geboren, wuchs der Designer in Aix-en-Provence auf und zog 1975 nach Paris, um an der Ecole de la Chambre Syndicale de la Couture Parisienne zu studieren. Nach seinem Examen assistierte Colonna dem Couturier Pierre Balmain. 1985 präsentierte er seine erste Kollektion, wobei er zugunsten von Katalogfotos seiner Freunde Bettina Rheims und Stéphane Sednaoui auf eine Laufstegschau verzichtete. Nebenbei entwarf er Schmuck und Accessoires für Altersgenossen wie Claude Montana, Thierry Mugler und Jean Paul Gaultier. 1990 bediente sich Colonna dann erstmals des Laufstegs, wobei er als einer der Ersten monotone Lagerhallen und ausdruckslose, androgyne Models einsetzte. Er zählte zu den Vorreitern der Dekonstruktion, jener Bewegung Anfang der Neunziger, die das

Innenleben der Kleider nach außen kehrte; seine rein schwarzen Kollektionen erinnerten an den „Slash and burn"-Punk der 1970er Jahre. Die Verwendung von billigen Materialien, die man aus Sexshops kennt – Lamé, Kunstleder und PVC –, nachlässig genähte oder offen gelassene Säume waren ein gezielter Schlag ins Gesicht der bürgerlichen Pariser Modeszene. Während dieser Zeit gestaltete Colonna auch gemeinsam mit dem Fotografen David Sims die Schaufenster der französischen Kaufhauskette Le Printemps. Irgendwann zwischen 1993 und 1994 verlor die Dekonstruktion ihren Reiz, und Colonna widmete sich dem Entwerfen von Mini-Kollektionen für das französische Versandhaus La Redoute. Ignoriert von Leuten, die sein Anliegen – echte Kleider für echte Menschen – nicht gutheißen, ist der Designer in der französischen Mode nach wie vor ein talentierter Einzelgänger. In Japan genießt er dagegen Kultstatus.

Jean Colonna a amené la face sombre des night-clubs parisiens de Pigalle, des clubs d'échangisme de la Rive Gauche et des boutiques sado-maso sur les podiums des défilés. Bien plus dangereux pour ses pairs de la haute couture, Colonna défend la déconstruction au début des années 90 en taillant délibérément ses vêtements dans des tissus bon marché et sans réel travail de finition. Colonna voulait que ses créations soient accessibles à tous, et pas seulement aux fashion victims qui considéraient son « chic pauvre » comme une bonne blague. Véritable enfant terrible, Colonna a néanmoins suivi une formation très classique. Né en 1955 en Algérie, il grandit à Aix-en-Provence avant de s'installer à Paris en 1975 pour suivre des cours à l'Ecole de la Chambre Syndicale de la Couture Parisienne. Une fois diplômé, il devient assistant de Pierre Balmain. En 1985, il présente sa première collection par le biais de catalogues dont il confie la photographie à ses amis Bettina Rheims et Stéphane Sednaoui. Il crée également des bijoux et des accessoires pour ses contemporains, notamment Claude Montana, Thierry Mugler et Jean Paul Gaultier. En 1990, Colonna finit par organiser son premier défilé et fait figure de précurseur en s'installant dans de grands entrepôts dépouillés et en utilisant des mannequins androgynes dégingandés. Colonna occupe alors l'avant-garde de la tendance déconstructionniste, mouvement qui au début des années 90 prônait le retrait des doublures, avec des collections entièrement noires rappelant l'esprit punk « slash and burn » des années 70. L'utilisation de tissus bon marché trouvés dans les sex shops, tels que le lamé, le simili cuir et le PVC, et des ourlets surjetés sans cérémonie, ou même pas finis, représentent une véritable claque à la figure de la mode bourgeoise de Paris. En 1993, Colonna collabore avec le photographe David Sims à la création d'une vitrine pour Le Printemps. La tendance à la déconstruction perd rapidement de son charme, et entre 1993 et 1994, Colonna dessine plusieurs mini-collections pour La Redoute. Dédaigné par ceux qui ne cautionnent pas son message (de vrais vêtements pour de vrais gens), le talentueux créateur reste aujourd'hui un franc-tireur de la mode française et compte de très nombreux fans japonais, qui l'ont hissé au rang de couturier culte.

JAMES SHERWOOD

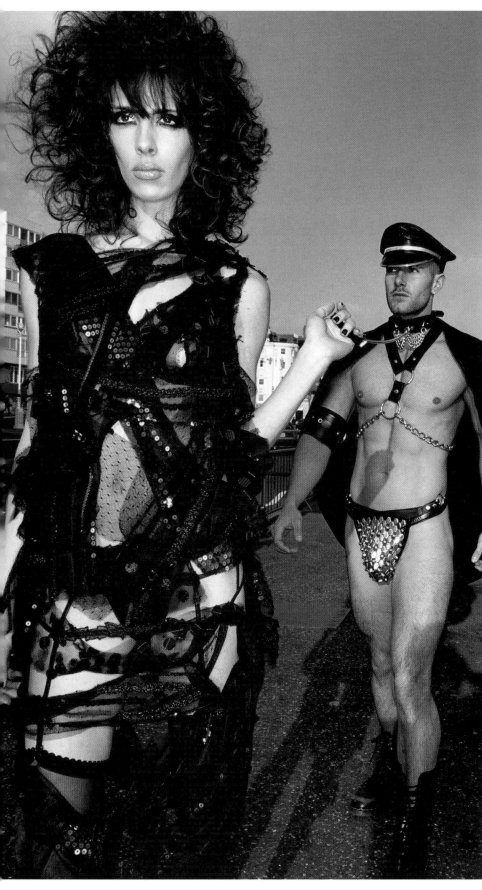

What are your signature designs? Like a scar, something that belongs to you What is your favourite piece from any of your collections? The black sheep, the intruder, the one that will carry me elsewhere How would you describe your work? It will always be the same: a tribute to the modern female consciousness What's your ultimate goal? Pleasure What inspires you? The ashes of the Fashion System Can fashion still have a political ambition? Yes. Fashion, which is drowned in rules, could have a revolutionary ambition, I guess… Who do you have in mind when you design? Souls Is the idea of creative collaboration important to you? Can we live without breathing? Who has been the greatest influence on your career? Anyone who gives a little something to make things go forward How have your own experiences affected your work as a designer? The work is part of the experience, I don't make the difference Which is more important in your work: the process or the product? Time out on the process, the process is ultimate Is designing difficult for you, if so, what drives you to continue? Less and less difficult … Are Doctor Jekyll and Mister Hyde getting divorced? Have you ever been influenced or moved by the reaction to your designs? I generously helped myself to both, the good and the bad feedback from encounters in my life What's your definition of beauty? Once more, beauty is this trail of light, indefinable, volatile, eternal What's your philosophy? To be alive What is the most important lesson you've learned? Life is ugly, but I still love it. It's a daily training.

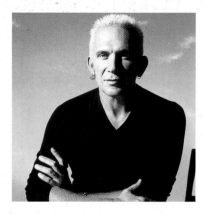

JEAN PAUL GAULTIER

"I didn't want to be famous"

The former 'enfant terrible' of French fashion is one of the most significant designers working today, his appeal bridging the elite and mass markets. On one hand, Jean Paul Gaultier is hailed as the saviour of haute couture (Gaultier Paris was launched 1997) and since 2004 has designed refined womenswear for Hermès, alongside his own well-established ready-to-wear label. On the other, he is one of the world's most famous living Frenchmen, partly due to a presenting job on the TV show Eurotrash in the early '90s (not to mention his personal fondness for striped Breton shirts and other Gallic clichés). Born in 1952, he was beguiled by fashion from a young age and would sketch showgirls from the Folies Bergère to impress his classmates. In the early '70s he trained under Pierre Cardin and Jean Patou, eventually launching his own ready-to-wear collection in 1976. He soon became known for iconoclastic designs such as the male skirt, corsetry worn as outerwear, and tattoo-printed body stockings. The classics of Parisian fashion are also central to his repertoire, particularly the trench coat and le smoking. In 1998 he launched a diffusion line, Junior Gaultier (since replaced by JPG), followed by excursions into perfumes (1993), and film costume (notably for Luc Besson's 'The Fifth Element' and Peter Greenaway's 'The Cook, The Thief, His Wife and Her Lover'). But it was his wardrobe for Madonna's Blonde Ambition tour of 1990 that made him world-famous, in particular for a certain salmon-pink corset with conical bra cups. A celebrity and a genius possessed of both a piquant sense of humour and a deadly serious talent, in 2004 Gaultier staged an unique exhibition at the Fondation Cartier in Paris, entitled 'Pain Couture', that showcased clothing constructed entirely from bread. [See also Hermès]

Das frühere Enfant terrible der französischen Mode ist einer der bedeutendsten Designer der Gegenwart, dem es gelingt, Eliteklientel und breite Masse gleichermaßen anzusprechen. Einerseits wurde Jean Paul Gaultier als Retter der Haute Couture gepriesen (Gaultier Paris existiert seit 1997) und entwirft seit 2004 neben seinem eigenen bestens eingeführten Prêt-à-porter-Label elegante Damenmode für Hermès. Andererseits ist er einer der berühmtesten Franzosen weltweit, nicht zuletzt dank seiner Moderation der Fernsehshow Eurotrash Anfang der 1990er Jahre (von seiner Vorliebe für gestreifte bretonische Fischerhemden und andere gallische Klischees ganz zu schweigen). 1952 geboren, war er schon früh von Mode fasziniert und beeindruckte seine Klassenkameraden mit Zeichnungen der Tänzerinnen der Folies Bergère. In den frühen 1970er Jahren lernte er bei Pierre Cardin und Jean Patou, bis er schließlich 1976 seine eigene Prêt-à-porter-Kollektion herausbrachte. Er erlangte bald Berühmtheit für ikonoklastische Entwürfe wie Männerröcke, Korsetts als Oberbekleidung und Bodystockings mit Tatoo-Muster. Aber auch die Klassiker der Pariser Mode sind aus seinem Repertoire nicht wegzudenken, insbesondere der Trenchcoat und der Smoking. 1998 gründete er die Nebenlinie Junior Gaultier (inzwischen ersetzt durch JPG), unternahm Ausflüge zu den Parfumeuren (1993) und in die Kostümbildnerei beim Film (für Luc Bessons „Das Fünfte Element" und für Peter Greenaways „Der Koch, der Dieb, seine Frau und ihr Liebhaber"). Weltberühmt machten ihn jedoch erst die Kostüme für Madonnas „Blonde Ambition"-Tour 1990, insbesondere das lachsrosa Korsett mit den konischen Körbchen. Inzwischen ist er selbst Promi und Genie, besessen von einem pikanten Sinn für Humor und todernstem Talent. 2004 präsentierte er in der Pariser Fondation Cartier eine einzigartige Ausstellung unter dem Titel „Pain Couture" mit Kleidungsstücken, die ausschließlich aus Brot gefertigt waren. [Siehe auch Hermès]

L'ancien «enfant terrible» de la mode française reste l'un des plus importants couturiers actuellement en exercice, capable de bâtir un pont entre le marché du luxe et celui de la grande consommation. D'une part, Jean Paul Gaultier est acclamé comme le sauveur de la haute couture (la collection Gaultier Paris a été lancée en 1997) et depuis 2004, il dessine également une ligne pour femme très raffinée chez Hermès, en plus de sa propre griffe de prêt-à-porter déjà bien établie. D'autre part, c'est aussi l'un des Français vivants les plus connus au monde, en grande partie grâce à son job de présentateur dans l'émission de télé Eurotrash au début des années 90 (sans parler de sa passion pour les pulls rayés bretons et autres clichés gaulois). Né en 1952, il s'intéresse très tôt à la mode et dessine des danseuses des Folies Bergère pour impressionner ses petits camarades de classe. Au début des années 70, il entame sa formation auprès de Pierre Cardin et de Jean Patou, avant de lancer sa propre collection de prêt-à-porter en 1976. Il se fait rapidement remarquer pour ses créations iconoclastes comme la jupe pour homme, le corset porté en vêtement de dessus et les collants de corps imprimés de tatouages. Les classiques de la mode parisienne occupent aussi un rôle central dans son répertoire, en particulier le trench-coat et le smoking. En 1998, il crée Junior Gaultier, une ligne de diffusion (remplacée depuis par JPG) suivie par le lancement de plusieurs parfums (1993), puis par la création de costumes pour le cinéma (pour «Le Cinquième Elément» de Luc Besson et «Le Cuisinier, le Voleur, sa Femme et son Amant» de Peter Greenaway, entre autres). Mais ce sont les costumes dessinés en 1990 pour la tournée Blonde Ambition de Madonna qui lui valent sa notoriété mondiale, notamment un certain corset rose saumon à bonnets coniques. Star et génie doté d'un sens de l'humour piquant et d'un talent incontestable, Gaultier a organisé en 2004 une exposition exclusive à la Fondation Cartier de Paris : baptisée «Pain Couture», elle présentait des vêtements entièrement faits de pain. [Voir aussi Hermès]

SUSIE RUSHTON

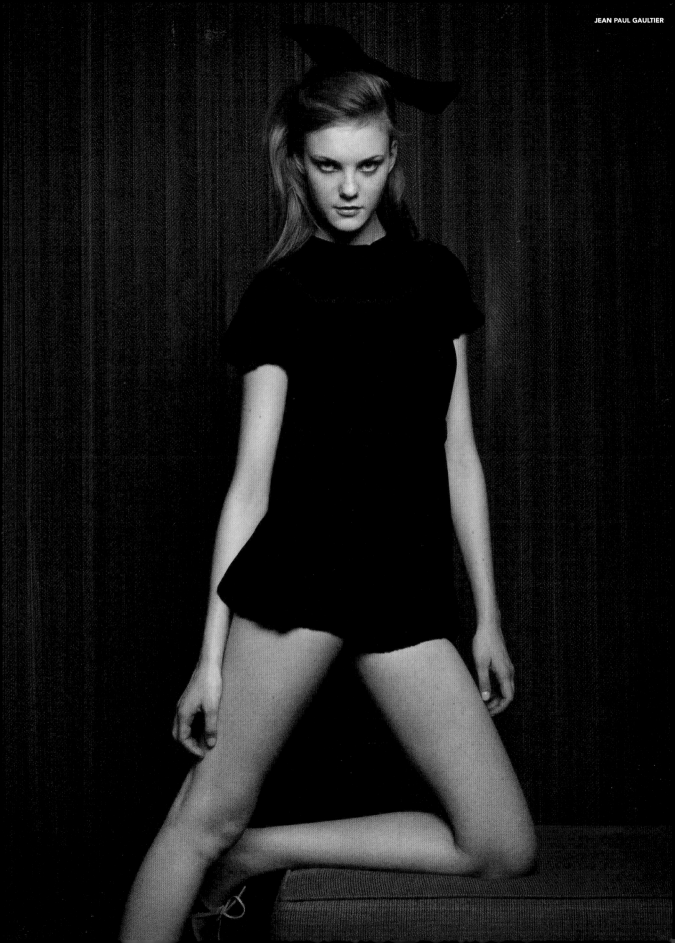

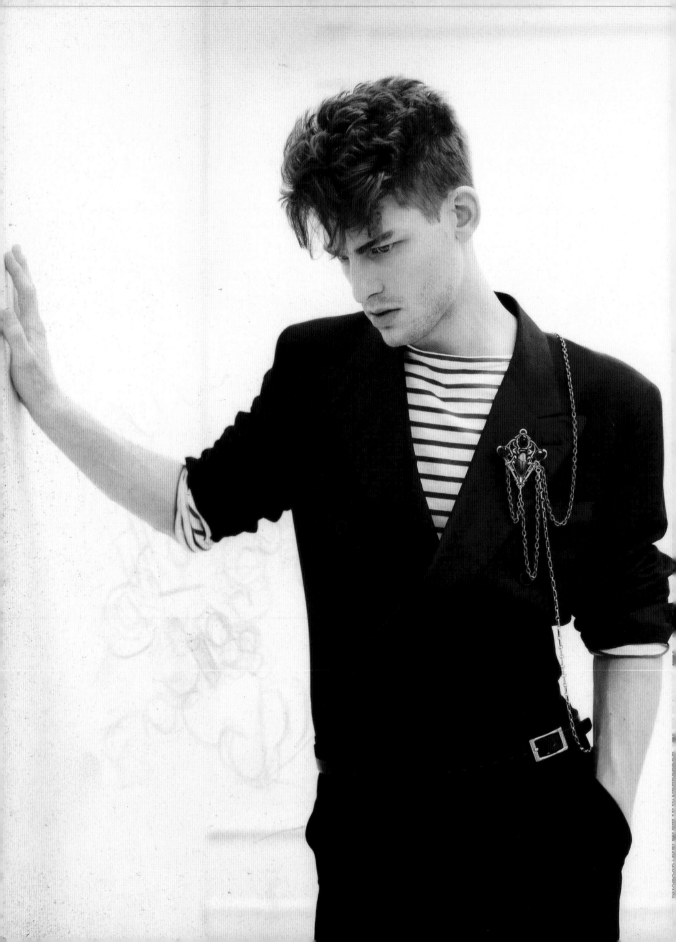

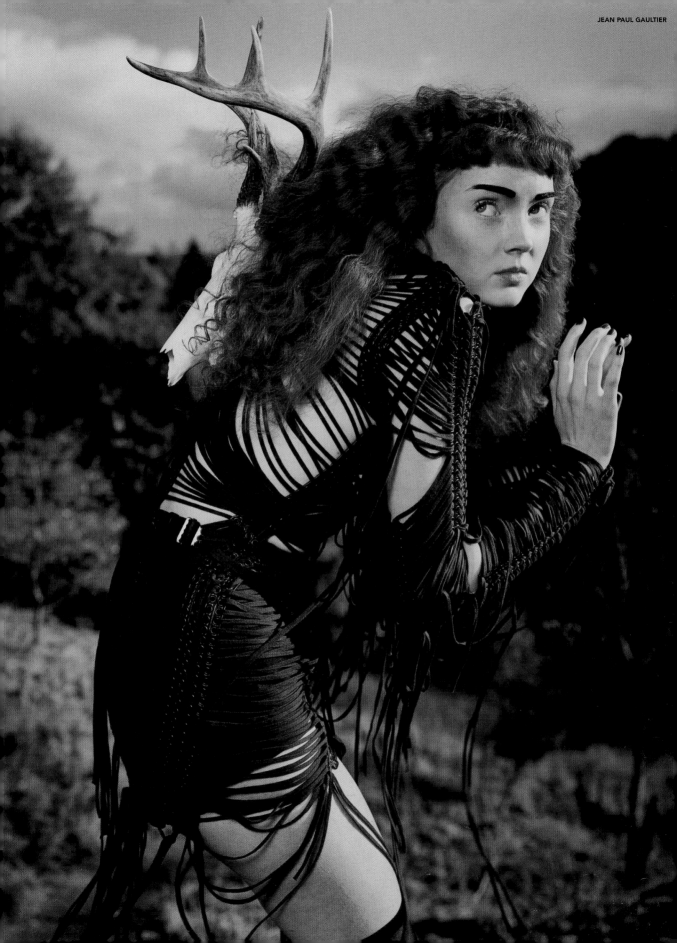

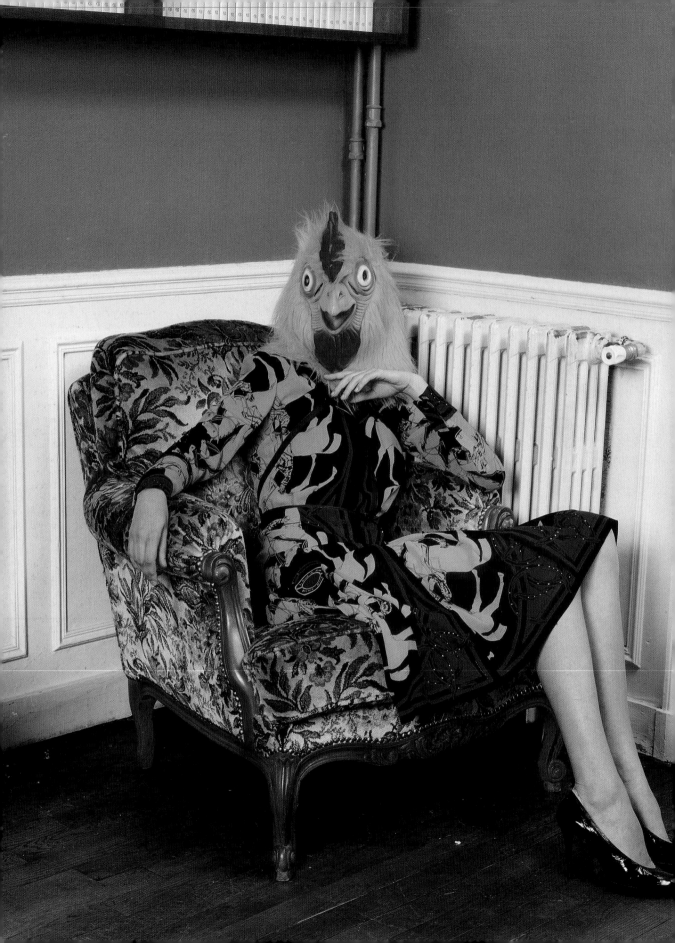

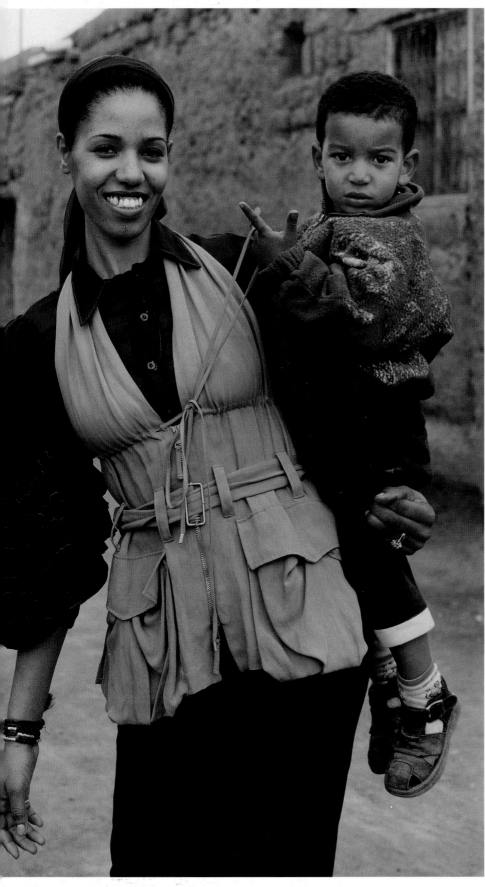

What are your signature designs? The corset is probably the thing I am known for **What are your favourite pieces from any of your collections?** Probably the ones that other people have liked most, because I do the collections for people to like. And through that, to like me. So I love the clothes which they love, because it makes me loved **What inspires you?** I think that to look is my biggest pleasure. Once I was in Ibiza, in a very, very bad club, and there was a live parrot in a cage. And I just looked at him for three hours. I wanted to absorb all the colours. And that inspired a dress in my first couture show. I had no photo, nothing but my memory. I truly love that **Who do you have in mind when you design?** Not one person, because I want to be open to difference. That would be too restrictive. I like very different types of people, different types of beauty, different types of living. **Is the idea of creative collaboration important to you?** I enjoy collaboration… **Exactly what kind of collaboration do you mean? What has been the greatest influence on your career?** Seeing the scandal Yves Saint Laurent caused in the '70s was important, because he captured everything that I love – glamour and sexual aggressiveness and even political shock. It was all the things that ever made me dream about being a part of the world of fashion. What he did definitely influenced me later and also made me realise the point in fashion: that if you are too much in advance, it appears as a provocation **How have your own experiences affected your work as a designer?** I was quite rejected at school because, let's say, I was more effeminate. So I was always on my own, sketching. One time, when I was about seven, I saw the Folies-Bergère on TV – the feathers, the fishnets – and I drew it at school the next day. The teacher, wanting to punish me, pinned it to my back and made me walk from class to class. But everyone was smiling. So I thought, well, people like you when you do your sketches. It comforted me and gave me a lot of confidence. After that I drew a lot of fishnets and feathers **Is designing difficult for you and, if so, what drives you to continue?** I love fashion and I love making fashion. But to deal with problems of organisation is not exactly my cup of coffee **What's your definition of beauty?** I don't have one. You can find beauty everywhere **What's your philosophy?** In fashion you are supposed to hate what you have loved before. I cannot do that. And I do not appreciate that part of the industry. It's a kind of snobbery. You feel like you have to hate something to show that you are a part of the new trend. **What is the most important lesson you've learned?** To be yourself. I am still very shy; I suppose you'd say I have a complex that people only like me because of what I do.

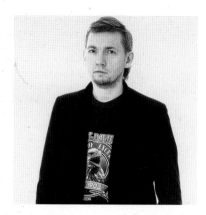

JENS LAUGESEN

"If you can touch one person profoundly,
you can touch the whole world"

Born in Denmark in 1967, Jens Laugesen moved to Paris in 1987 to study haute couture at the Chambre Syndicale de la Couture Parisienne. Following his graduation in 1991, he worked for the Scandinavian press as a freelance fashion journalist, before venturing back to Paris to undertake a Master's degree in Fashion Management at the Institut Français de la Mode. By 2000, Laugesen had worked for a variety of esteemed design fashion houses in Paris for over half a decade, across both haute couture and ready-to-wear disciplines. That year, he moved to London and embarked on the MA fashion course at Central Saint Martins, specialising in womenswear. His final collection, in 2002, earned him a distinction, was duly snapped up by Paris boutique Maria Luisa and was exhibited in the store's windows throughout haute couture week. By September 2002, Laugesen presented his first, highly accomplished catwalk show as part of London's Fashion East event. Here, the pure white clothing – including beautifully-cut utility pants, bibbed dungarees and vests – marked him out as a designer little concerned with shock tactics or wilful obscurity, but instead confident enough in his abilities to allow his ideas to speak for themselves. Sure enough, in February of the following year he was awarded the prestigious Topshop New Generation Award – the funds from which meant he could up his ante and unveil his 'Ground Zero 02' autumn/winter 2003 collection on the official schedule of London Fashion Week. For spring/summer 2005, Laugesen presented a collection of coolly minimalist tailoring at his show held at the Danish Embassy, further sealing his reputation as a designer who understands when less can mean more.

Der 1967 in Dänemark geborene Jens Laugesen kam 1987 nach Paris, um am Chambre Syndicale de la Couture Parisienne zu studieren. Nach seinem Abschluss im Jahr 1991 arbeitete er zunächst als freier Moderedakteur für skandinavische Blätter, bis er zurück in Paris noch einen Master-Studiengang im Fach Mode-Management am Institut Français de la Mode absolvierte. Bis 2000 war er dann gute fünf Jahre für eine Vielzahl geschätzter Pariser Modehäuser sowohl im Bereich Haute Couture als auch Prêt-à-porter tätig. Dann entschloss er sich zum Umzug nach London, wo er das Modestudium (spezialisiert auf Damenmode) am Central Saint Martins aufnahm. Seine Abschlusskollektion im Jahr 2002 wurde ausgezeichnet und noch rechtzeitig von der Pariser Boutique Maria Luisa aufgekauft, um während der Haute-Couture-Woche deren Schaufenster zu schmücken. Im September desselben Jahres schließlich präsentierte Laugesen

seine erste, höchst anspruchsvolle Catwalk-Show im Rahmen des Londoner Events Fashion East. Dort zeichneten ihn seine schlichten weißen Entwürfe – darunter wunderbar geschnittene Freizeithosen, Arbeitshosen mit Latz und Westen – als einen Designer aus, der mit Schocktaktik oder absichtlicher Unverständlichkeit nichts am Hut hat. Stattdessen zeigte er genügend Vertrauen in die eigenen Fähigkeiten, um seine Ideen einfach für sich sprechen zu lassen. Kein Wunder, dass er im Februar des darauf folgenden Jahres den angesehenen Topshop New Generation Award erhielt. Das Preisgeld wusste er gut zu nutzen und zeigte seine Kollektion „Ground Zero 02" für Herbst/Winter 2003 im offiziellen Programm der London Fashion Week. Für Frühjahr/Sommer 2005 präsentierte Laugesen bei seiner Schau in der dänischen Botschaft eine Kollektion kühl-minimalistischer Schneiderkunst. Dies festigte seinen Ruf als Designer, der genau weiß, wann weniger mehr ist.

Né au Danemark en 1967, Jens Laugesen s'installe à Paris en 1987 pour étudier la haute couture à la Chambre Syndicale de la Couture Parisienne. Après l'obtention de son diplôme en 1991, il travaille pour la presse scandinave en tant que journaliste de mode free-lance, mais revient à Paris pour suivre le cursus du Master's en Fashion Management de l'Institut Français de la Mode. En l'an 2000, Laugesen travaille déjà pour toute une palette de grandes maisons parisiennes depuis plus de cinq ans, tant en haute couture qu'en prêt-à-porter. Cette année-là, il part pour Londres et suit le MA en mode de Central Saint Martins, se spécialisant en mode féminine. En 2002, sa collection de fin d'études lui vaut un prix et est achetée par la boutique parisienne Maria Luisa, qui l'expose en vitrine tout au long de la semaine de la haute couture. En septembre 2002, Laugesen présente un premier défilé parfaitement maîtrisé dans le cadre de l'événement londonien Fashion East : les vêtements d'un blanc immaculé tels que ses pantalons utilitaires, le distinguent comme un créateur peu concerné par la stratégie du choc ou de l'obscurité obstinée, mais assez sûr de lui pour que ses idées parlent d'elles-mêmes. Logiquement, il remporte en février 2003 le prestigieux prix New Generation de Topshop, dont le financement lui permet de viser plus haut et de présenter sa collection « Ground Zero 02 » de l'automne/hiver 2003 lors des défilés officiels de la London Fashion Week. Pour le printemps/été 2005, Laugesen propose une collection de tailleurs minimalistes aux lignes épurées dans le cadre d'un défilé donné à l'ambassade du Danemark, scellant ainsi sa réputation de styliste de l'épure.

JAMES ANDERSON

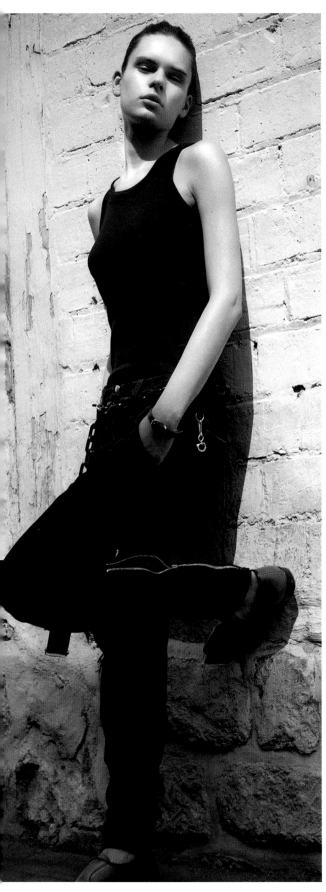

What are your signature designs? Hybrid and reconstructed garments that morph ideas into a new utilitarian and tailored vocabulary, which aims to redescribe, redefine or redesign generic garments into a new form that will push the boundaries of humanity **What is your favourite piece from any of your collections?** There are actually three pieces which you always find in my collections. The boiler suit, because it is a transversally functional piece that has no gender. The rib vest, since it is a unisex generic garment, which is adapted to different occasions. The tuxedo jacket, since it is a garment where form and usage transcend traditional function and utility **How would you describe your work?** Both conceptual and wearable at the same time **What's your ultimate goal?** A global design led brand that unites people transversally by the ideology, the ethos and the honesty that are linked to and communicated through the final design outcome **What inspires you?** Everyday generic objects, that define the moment, the present, that correspond to an idea of 'normality' **Can fashion still have a political ambition?** Yes, if fashion aims to relate to and reflect the world it evolves in and arrives from **Who do you have in mind when you design?** Always the person, either boy or girl, who is able to intelligently make their own decisions for both rational and/or emotional reasons and who chooses to wear the garment. The question we ask ourselves is why would someone want to wear the garment we are designing **Who is it for?** If you can touch one person profoundly, you can touch the whole world **Is the idea of creative collaboration important to you?** Yes, for me a brand is not about the vision of just one person, but rather the result of all the creative forces that unite in the collective effort of telling one story. The more sincere contributors there are who adhere to the design ethos, the richer the story becomes **Who has been the greatest influence on your career?** Three different people, who in their own way have helped me to define the creative person I am today: first there was Gunnar Larson,

a Danish photographer whom I assisted as a stylist in Paris in the late '80s. Secondly, Monsieur Marco, my draping teacher at the Chambre Syndicale de la Couture in Paris who in the past had worked with Cristobal Balenciaga. He taught me how to drape and to create three dimensional shapes out of two dimensional fabrics. Thirdly, Louise Wilson, the MA course director at Central Saint Martins, who pushed and helped me to re-define myself as a designer **How have your own experiences affected your work as a designer?** I realise that the more intensely you work, the more autobiographical your work becomes **Which is more important in your work: the process or the product?** As a creative person, it is normal that the process seems more interesting than the final outcome. But I also think the designed object only makes sense when it reflects the process, when it expresses the individuality and integrity of the creative minds that are behind its origin **Is designing difficult for you, if so, what drives you to continue?** Yes, the more personal the design becomes, the more difficult it becomes to start the creative process **Have you ever been influenced or moved by the reaction to your designs?** Yes, I am always very moved when I see the respect I receive from the Japanese buyers, who are really into designed objects with soul that reflect the normality, but that conceptually are based on intellectual ideas **What's your definition of beauty?** Something effortlessly put together in a non-linear design process, something that seems both done and undone at the same time, that reflects the multi-dimensional hybrid and linear society we live in **What's your philosophy?** Hybrid Reconstruction: a personally-developed design philosophy morphing different generic garments into one hybrid object in a seamless process of reconstruction, where the possibilities are endless **What is the most important lesson you've learned?** To work hard, to believe in your inner self, and to always push new ideas forward.

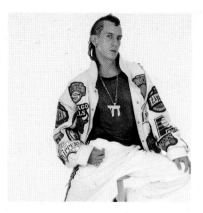

JEREMY SCOTT

`"I love creating and I hate the empty feeling when it's done"`

Jeremy Scott's story is the stuff of fairy-tales and syndicated game shows. Born in 1974 and raised in Kansas City, Missouri, Scott was the boy who read Italian Vogue between classes and wrote about fashion in French essays. After graduating from New York's Pratt Institute, the 21-year-old made a pilgrimage to Paris where his collection, made out of paper hospital gowns and inspired by the body-modifying artist Orlan, went down in fashion folklore. His first formal runway presentation in October 1997, 'Rich White Women', presenting asymmetrically cut trousers and multifunctional T-shirts, established Scott as a substantial Parisian presence. But controversy clings to the designer like a Pierre Cardin teddy bear brooch. Later collections, such as March 1998's infamous 'Contrapied' show, have met with a mixture of incredulity and derision, all the while establishing key details of the Scott aesthetic: attention to volume, obsession with logos (including best-selling back-to-front Paris print), a hard-edged Mugler-esque glamour and a wicked way with fur. In autumn 2001, Scott relocated to Los Angeles, a city that has welcomed his über-trash style with open arms to such an extent that in January 2002 he achieved one of his long-term ambitions, appearing as a celebrity contestant on 'Wheel of Fortune'. Scott continues to show in New York and LA, with recent projects including a short feature film starring celebrity clients and friends such as Asia Argento and Lisa Marie. As Scott himself might say, vive l'avant-garde!

Jeremy Scotts Biografie klingt wie der Stoff, aus dem Märchen sind. Oder Fernsehshows. Der 1974 geborene und in Kansas City, Missouri, aufgewachsene Scott las tatsächlich schon als Schüler in der Pause die italienische Vogue und schrieb in Französisch Aufsätze über Mode. Nach einem Abschluss am New Yorker Pratt Institute pilgerte der damals 21-jährige nach Paris, wo seine Kollektion aus papierenen Krankenhaushemden in die Modegeschichte einging. Dazu inspiriert hatte ihn die Künstlerin Orlan, die ihren Körper u.a. durch Schönheitsoperationen zum Kunstobjekt gemacht hat. Scotts erste offizielle Laufsteg-Schau präsentierte im Oktober 1997 unter dem Titel „Rich White Women" asymmetrisch geschnittene Hosen und multifunktionale T-shirts, mit denen der Designer sich in der Pariser Szene etablierte. Doch haftet ihm Widersprüchlichkeit wie eine Teddybär-Brosche von Pierre Cardin an. So wurden spätere Kollektionen, etwa die berüchtigte Show „Contrapied" vom März 1998, zwar mit einer Mischung aus Skepsis und Spott aufgenommen, setzten aber dennoch Maßstäbe für die Markenzeichen von Scotts Ästhetik: Volumen, eine Passion für Logos (inklusive des Bestsellers in Gestalt eines umlaufenden Parisdrucks), kantiger, an Mugler erinnernder Glamour und ein verrücktes Faible für Pelz. Im Herbst 2001 verlegte Scott seinen Wohnsitz nach Los Angeles – in die Stadt, die seinen extrem kitschigen Stil mit solcher Begeisterung aufgenommen hatte. Die Resonanz war so groß, dass im Januar 2002 ein lang gehegter Wunsch Scotts in Erfüllung ging: Er war Stargast in der TV-Show Wheel of Fortune. Seine Kollektionen zeigt Scott weiterhin in New York und LA. Zu den neueren Projekten zählt ein kurzes Feature über prominente Kunden und Freunde wie Asia Argento und Lisa Marie Presley. Getreu Scotts Motto: Vive l'avant-garde!

L'histoire de Jeremy Scott est une affaire de contes de fées et de jeux télévisés. Né en 1974, il grandit à Kansas City dans le Missouri, où il est bien le seul à lire le Vogue italien entre les cours et à disserter sur la mode dans ses rédactions de français. Une fois diplômé du Pratt Institute de New York à 21 ans, Scott part en pèlerinage à Paris. La collection qu'il y présente marque un véritable tournant dans l'histoire de la mode, avec ses robes d'hôpitaux en papier inspirées par l'œuvre de l'artiste plasticien Orlan. En octobre 1997, lors de son premier défilé officiel intitulé « Rich White Women », il présente des pantalons asymétriques et des T-shirts multifonctions qui assoient définitivement sa présence sur la scène parisienne. Mais la controverse s'accroche à lui comme une broche-nounours de Pierre Cardin. Les collections suivantes, par exemple le terrible défilé « Contrepied » de mars 1998, sont accueillies dans un mélange d'incrédulité et de dérision, bien que certains détails – clés parviennent à imposer l'esthétique de Scott : l'attention portée au volume, l'obsession des logos (notamment l'imprimé intégral « Paris » qui s'est très bien vendu), un glamour « mugleresque » aux lignes acérées et une utilisation scandaleuse de la fourrure. A l'automne 2001, Scott s'installe à Los Angeles, une ville qui accueille son style ultra-trash à bras ouverts. A tel point qu'en janvier 2002, il réalise l'un de ses plus vieux rêves : il participe à « La Roue de la Fortune » en tant que candidat de marque Scott continue à présenter ses collections à New York et L. A. et s'est récemment investi dans des projets annexes, notamment un court métrage où il a fait jouer ses amies et clientes célèbres telles qu'Asia Argento et Lisa Marie Presley. Comme le dirait Scott lui-même, « vive l'avant-garde » !

GLENN WALDRON

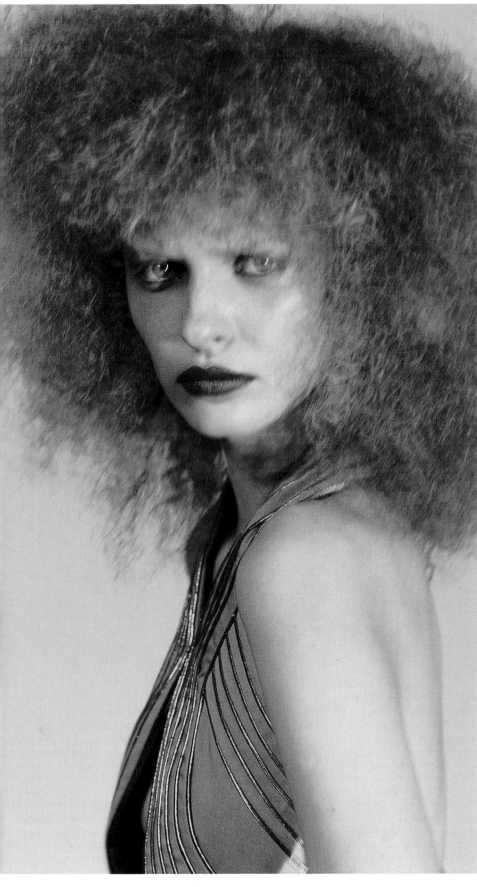

What are your signature designs? Avant-garde high fashion streetwear with a touch of humour **What is your favourite piece from any of your collections?** They are all like li'l children to me, it would be a sin to pick a favourite! **How would you describe your work?** Thought provoking and defining of the times **What's your ultimate goal?** I want to touch people's lives **What inspires you?** Looking back at where I've come from, and thinking about where I want to go **Can fashion still have a political ambition?** You bet! The slippery side to all this is that fashion can play both sides of the fence **Who do you have in mind when you design?** Myself, my friends, the kids in Harajuku **Is the idea of creative collaboration important to you?** No, not really – after working in film, which is reliant upon collaboration medium, I realised how spoilt I am to do what I want and how I want – not having to be accountable to anyone else **Who has been the greatest influence on your career?** Myself, as I'm a self-made man **How have your own experiences affected your work as a designer?** I can't separate the two – what's my own and what's my work? There is no differentiation **Which is more important in your work: the process or the product?** More and more it's the process – I love creating and I hate the empty feeling when it's done **Is designing difficult for you, if so, what drives you to continue?** Easy breezy – I do this stuff in my sleep now **Have you ever been influenced or moved by the reaction to your designs?** Of course, I've felt many emotions linked to people's reaction to my work. I've been flattered, touched and mind-blown by what my work has meant to others **What's your definition of beauty?** Ever-changing **What's your philosophy?** Leap first, look later **What is the most important lesson you've learned?** Get while the getting's good!

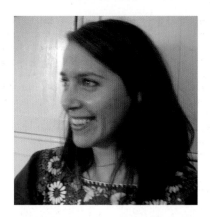

JESSICA OGDEN

"My ultimate goal is to continue creative work
and build a studio that produces work of integrity"

Jessica Ogden (born 1970) is an exceptional figure in fashion for many reasons. She makes her samples in a size 12. She has often shown her collections on 'real' women rather than models. She is completely self-taught. And she is a true original. The daughter of a commercials director and a model-turned-curator, the Jamaican-born Ogden had global potential from birth. She studied as a teenager at the Rhode Island School of Design in the US before moving to London in 1989 to study sculpture at Byam Shaw School of Art. It was while in London that her fashion career blossomed under somewhat unconventional circumstances. Working as a volunteer for Oxfam's NoLogo project, Ogden re-worked other people's cast-offs into new, original and desirable garments. Realising she was onto something, Ogden set up her own label in 1993. Revitalising vintage textiles has occupied her ever since, often in the form of patchwork, which is a recurring theme. Fittingly for an ex-sculptor, texture is also important in Ogden's work. By manipulating the structure of a garment's fabrics, she makes clothes that also function as new, abstract forms. Such experimentation has endeared her to legions of Japanese fans, celebrities like Sofia Coppola and institutions including the Crafts Council and the Design Museum in London. Her work has also been exhibited in Antwerp, Tokyo and Prague. Besides hand-me-downs, her inspirations include her Jamaican roots. Spring/summer 2005's collection dipped into the colours, music and atmosphere of island life after a visit home to take part in Caribbean Fashion Week. Ogden has also collaborated with French label APC since 2001, creating a children's collection and, more recently, a resort line inspired by Indian textiles named 'Madras'.

Die 1970 geborene Jessica Ogden ist aus vielerlei Gründen eine außergewöhnliche Gestalt in der Modeszene: Sie fertig ihre Modelle in Größe 42; ihre Kollektionen werden oft von „normalen" Frauen statt von Models präsentiert; sie ist absolute Autodidaktin und ein richtiges Original. Als Tochter eines Werbefilm-Regisseurs und eines ehemaligen Bounty-Models, das inzwischen als Kuratorin arbeitet, wurde der auf Jamaika geborenen Ogden ihr kosmopolitisches Potential quasi in die Wiege gelegt. Als Teenager besuchte sie die Rhode Island School of Design, bevor sie 1989 nach London zog, um an der Byam Shaw School of Art Bildhauerei zu studieren. Während der Zeit in London nahm unter ziemlich unkonventionellen Umständen ihre Karriere in der Modebranche ihren Anfang. Als Praktikantin bei Oxfams Projekt NoLogo verwandelte Ogden die abgelegten Kleider anderer Leute in neue, einzigartige und begehrte Kleidungsstücke. Nachdem sie hier Feuer gefangen hatte, gründete sie 1993 ihr eigenes Label. Das Umarbeiten von Vintage-Sachen hat sie seit damals nicht mehr losgelassen und ist bei ihr, oft in Form von Patchwork, ein immer wiederkehrendes Thema. Wie es sich für eine ehemalige Bildhauerin gehört, spielen auch Texturen eine wichtige Rolle in Ogdens Arbeit. Indem sie die Strukturen von Stoffen manipuliert, kreiert sie Kleidungsstücke, die man auch als neue, abstrakte Formen betrachten kann. Dieses Experimentieren

hat ihr die Zuneigung von Scharen japanischer Fans, von Prominenten wie Sofia Coppola, aber auch von Institutionen wie dem Crafts Council und dem Design Museum in London beschert. Ausstellungen ihrer Arbeiten gab es bereits in Antwerpen, Tokio und Prag. Außer von abgelegter Kleidung bezieht Ogden Inspiration auch aus ihren jamaikanischen Wurzeln. Nach einem Besuch in der Heimat, um an der Jamaican Fashion Week teilzunehmen, war ihre Kollektion Frühjahr/Sommer 2005 in die Farben, die Musik und die Atmosphäre des Insellebens getaucht. Seit 2001 arbeitet Ogden auch mit dem französischen Label APC zusammen, für das sie eine Kinderkollektion sowie erst kürzlich eine von indischen Stoffen inspirierte Urlaubskollektion namens ‚Madras' entwarf.

Dans l'univers de la mode, Jessica Ogden (née en 1970) fait figure d'exception à plus d'un titre. Elle conçoit ses prototypes en taille 40. Pour présenter ses collections, elle préfère souvent faire défiler de « vraies » femmes plutôt que des mannequins. Elle est entièrement autodidacte. Et c'est une véritable originale. Née en Jamaïque d'un père réalisateur de spots publicitaires et d'une mère mannequin pour les barres Bounty devenue depuis conservatrice, Jessica Ogden est destinée à un parcours international depuis sa plus tendre enfance. Adolescente, elle suit des cours à la Rhode Island School of Design aux Etats-Unis, puis s'installe à Londres en 1989 pour étudier la sculpture à la Byam Shaw School of Art. C'est pendant cette période que sa carrière décolle, et ce, dans des circonstances pour le moins inattendues. Travaillant comme bénévole sur le projet NoLogo d'Oxfam, elle transforme les vieilles frusques dont personne ne veut plus en nouveaux vêtements originaux et hautement désirables. Consciente qu'elle vient de mettre la main sur un bon filon, elle crée sa propre griffe en 1993. Depuis, elle ne cesse de redonner vie aux tissus vintage, souvent sous la forme du patchwork, thème récurrent dans son travail. En tant qu'ex-sculpteur, rien d'étonnant à ce que la texture occupe une place aussi importante dans ses créations. En manipulant la structure des tissus d'un vêtement, elle parvient à produire d'autres créations qui fonctionnent aussi comme de nouvelles formes abstraites. Cette expérimentation lui vaut des légions de fans au Japon, des clientes célèbres telles que Sofia Coppola et la reconnaissance des institutions, notamment du Crafts Council et du Design Museum de Londres. Son travail a aussi été exposé à Anvers, Tokyo et Prague. Outre les vieilles nippes dont se débarrassent les gens, elle puise également son inspiration dans ses racines jamaïcaines. Après avoir participé à la semaine de la mode de Jamaïque, elle plonge dans les couleurs, la musique et l'atmosphère de son île natale pour concevoir sa collection printemps/été 2005. Depuis 2001, Jessica Ogden collabore aussi avec la griffe française APC, pour laquelle elle dessine une collection pour enfant, et dernièrement une ligne de maillots de bain baptisée « Madras », inspirée des textiles indiens.

LAUREN COCHRANE

What are your signature designs? Patchwork pieces, antique fabric re-worked, handwork details looking towards craft What is your favourite piece from any of your collections? A patchwork dress from found fabrics spring/summer 2000. It says it all to me How would you describe your work? Instinctive, naïve, romantic, storytelling What's your ultimate goal? To continue creative work, to build a workshop studio that produces work of integrity What inspires you? Found objects, found cloth, fleeting moments, memories, half asleep dreams Can fashion still have a political ambition? I think so. It can make a change without thinking Who do you have in mind when you design? Real and make-believe friends; what do I want to wear tomorrow Is the idea of creative collaboration important to you? The exchange of thought is always interesting. It's learning Who has been the greatest influence on your career? Not just one…my mum…the first encouragers… many How have your own experiences affected your work as a designer? I cannot separate the two Which is more important in your work: the process or the product? Process dominates, but the product must live on its own Is designing difficult for you, if so, what drives you to continue? The difficult moment is sometimes if you forget to dream. So then it's making space for dreaming Have you ever been influenced or moved by the reaction to your designs? Yes, I am always. It gets weirder as the work becomes more known What's your definition of beauty? Right now… daring, cheeky, playful What's your philosophy? In a few words… to create What is the most important lesson you've learned? There is openness and to create is relevant.

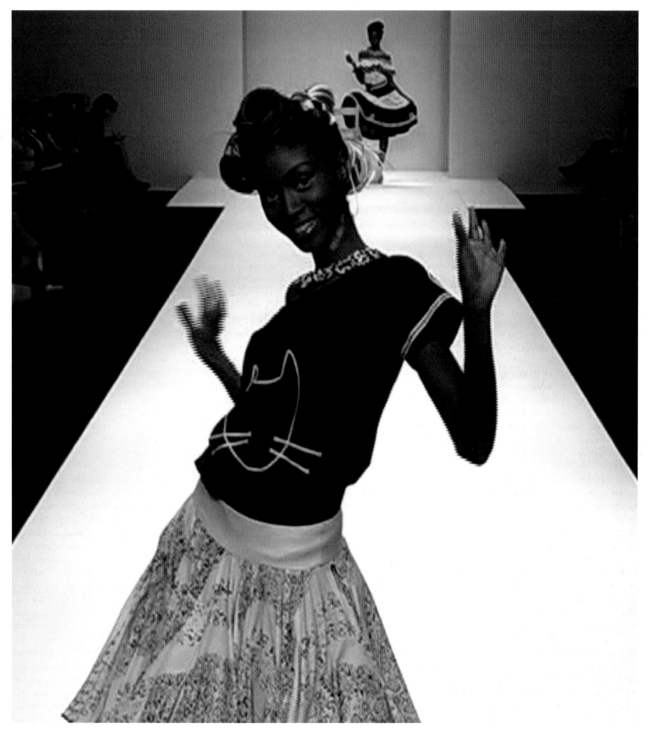

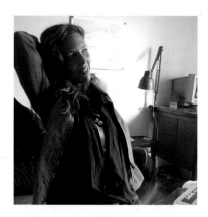

JESSICA TROSMAN

"It is good to know how and when to combine inspiration with common sense"

Jessica Trosman (born 1966, Buenos Aires) has brought avant-garde fashion to Argentina – and a peculiarly South American brand of inventiveness to the rest of the world. Combining unexpected materials such as feathers, plants, beads and photographs with paint, canvas and vintage jewellery in her unique clothing designs, Trosman and her team have an experimental approach that is rich with surprises yet avoids fussiness. Trosman lived in Buenos Aires until the age of twelve when she moved to Miami, a city where she eventually studied fashion design, at the University of Miami. However, after completing her formal training, Trosman returned to her native country where she worked as a freelance consultant for Buenos Aires-based fashion companies such as Ona Saez and Kosiuko. In 2002, she launched her eponymous label, building on a reputation she had built during five years of co-creating another brand, Trosmanchurbia, with fellow Argentinian Martin Churbia. In April 2000 the pair won the Silver Scissors Award, a prize for the best designer in Argentina, and their collections were shown in New York Fashion Week as part of the Gen Art platform for young designers. Meanwhile for her solo brand, Trosman struck a deal with Onward Kashiyama to manufacture and distribute her handcrafted garments. While she has invented various craft techniques such as fusing plastic beads onto fabric, she is also known for her understated tailoring in muted shades. Trosman is now sold in prestigious stores in London, Paris, Tokyo and New York, among other cities. Although she presents her collection twice a year in Paris, Trosman remains based in Buenos Aires, the city which supplies her with endless inspiration.

Die 1966 in Buenos Aires geborene Jessica Trosman brachte die Avantgarde-Mode nach Argentinien – und dem Rest der Welt ein besonderes, von Erfindergeist geprägtes südamerikanisches Label. In ihren einzigartigen Designs kombiniert sie unvermutete Materialien wie Federn, Pflanzen, Perlen und Fotografien mit Farbe, Segeltuch und altem Schmuck. Der experimentelle Ansatz von Trosman und ihrem Team ist reich an Überraschungen, aber unaufgeregt. Trosman lebte bis zu ihrem zwölften Lebensjahr in Buenos Aires, dann zog sie nach Miami, wo sie später an der University of Miami ihr Modestudium absolvierte. Nachdem sie die formale Ausbildung abgeschlossen hatte, kehrte sie jedoch in ihr Heimatland zurück und arbeitete als freie Beraterin für Modefirmen wie Ona Saez und Kosiuko in Buenos Aires. 2002 gründete sie ein Label unter eigenem Namen, das sie auf dem Ruf aufbauen konnte, den sie sich in den fünf Jahren erworben hatte, als sie mit ihrem argentinischen Kollegen Martin Churbia die Marke Trosman-

churbia entwickelt hatte. Im April 2000 gewann das Paar die Silberne Schere, den Preis als beste Designerin Argentiniens. Ihre Kollektionen waren im Rahmen der New Yorker Modewoche bei Gen Art, einer Plattform für Jungdesigner, zu sehen. Für ihr Solo-Label traf Trosman eine Abmachung mit Onward Kashiyama hinsichtlich Herstellung und Vertrieb ihrer handgefertigten Kleidungsstücke. Zum einen hat sie diverse handwerkliche Methoden entwickelt, etwa wie man Plastikperlen zum Zweck innovativer ornamentaler Effekte auf Stoff befestigt, sie ist aber zugleich bekannt für ihre dezenten Schnitte in gedämpften Schattierungen. Trosman wird heute in Nobelboutiquen in London, Paris, Tokio, New York und anderen Großstädten verkauft. Auch wenn sie ihre Kollektionen zweimal jährlich in Paris präsentiert, bleibt Buenos Aires ihre Basis, denn diese Stadt versorgt sie mit unendlicher Inspiration.

Jessica Trosman (née en 1966 à Buenos Aires) a fait connaître la mode d'avant-garde en Argentine et une marque douée d'une inventivité typiquement sud-américaine au reste du monde. Combinant des matières inattendues dans ses créations uniques, où plumes, plantes, perles et photos côtoient la peinture, la toile et les bijoux vintage, Jessica Trosman et son équipe adoptent une approche expérimentale riche en surprises, mais toujours justifiée. A l'âge de 12 ans, Jessica Trosman quitte Buenos Aires pour Miami, où elle finit par étudier la mode à l'université de la ville. Une fois sa formation terminée, elle décide toutefois de revenir dans son pays natal et travaille comme consultante free-lance pour différentes griffes de Buenos Aires telles qu'Ona Saez et Kosiuko. En 2002, elle lance sa griffe éponyme, forte de la réputation qu'elle s'est forgée pendant cinq ans en tant que cofondatrice de Trosmanchurbia, une autre marque créée avec l'Argentin Martin Churbia. En avril 2000, le duo remporte le Silver Scissors Award, un prix remis aux meilleurs créateurs d'Argentine, et leurs collections sont présentées à la New York Fashion Week dans le cadre de la plate-forme Gen Art dédiée aux jeunes talents. Parallèlement, pour sa griffe en solo, Jessica Trosman conclut un accord avec Onward Kashiyama pour produire et distribuer ses vêtements faits à la main. Bien qu'elle ait inventé diverses techniques artisanales, par exemple en fondant des perles en plastique sur du tissu pour créer un effet ornemental inédit, elle est également connue pour ses coupes discrètes et ses couleurs neutres. La griffe Jessica Trosman est aujourd'hui en vente dans de prestigieuses boutiques à Londres, Paris, Tokyo et New York, entre autres. Elle présente sa collection deux fois par an à Paris mais reste fermement ancrée à Buenos Aires, une ville qui ne cessera jamais de l'inspirer.   SUSIE RUSHTON

What are your signature designs? It just does not feel right for me to describe my work as something already proved. If I were capable of defining my "signature design" it would put me in a position of no return. As if there was no further need to continue **What is your favourite piece from any of your collections?** I am never attracted to any specific piece. I am always interested in the general idea. I work quite a lot on the relation between the parts. I try to see how a certain thing would be helpful for another **How would you describe your work?** Hard, Late, Annoying, Fascinating **What's your ultimate goal?** Get my work appreciated and followed **What inspires you?** I am mostly inspired by the actual process of my work. I put things together, see how they work, turn them around and look at them again.

I am always guided by abstract shapes and volumes that I later combine with some other more conservative or simple structure. Also I do not think that inspiration leads the whole thing. It is good to know how and when to combine inspiration with common sense **Can fashion still have a political ambition?** I hope not **Who do you have in mind when you design?** I do not think of anyone in particular. I guess the one who chooses what I do may share some of my points of view, at least aesthetically **Is the idea of creative collaboration important to you?** I believe in collaboration in general, even if it happens to be creative or not **Who has been the greatest influence on your career?** My greatest influence has always been the experience of working everyday and there are many people involved to

make that possible **How have your own experiences affected your work as a designer?** There is a very intimate relationship and I could say that in fact my whole challenge is about trying to translate what I see and what happens to me into my designs **Which is more important in your work: the process or the product?** It is impossible for me to see them separated. I just think that process and product are two different stages of the same "virtuous circle". Process leads you to products and those products often lead you to new processes **Is designing difficult for you, if so, what drives you to continue?** It is very difficult because it involves not only the technical part which takes so much effort, but also it demands of you a lot of decisions that often may question the way you have been thinking on some basic

issues, such as what is modern, what is beauty, or what makes sense **Have you ever been influenced or moved by the reaction to your designs?** Until now, I must say that the reaction to my designs is very similar to my original intention, so I think that reactions most often confirm my vision **What's your definition of beauty?** I think that beauty is a very dynamic concept. I would never say that something is absolutely beautiful or not. It's always very related to the context and to the purpose. I like to think that beauty could be described as something that you need and has a purpose **What's your philosophy?** Get along with myself **What is the most important lesson you've learned?** You never know.

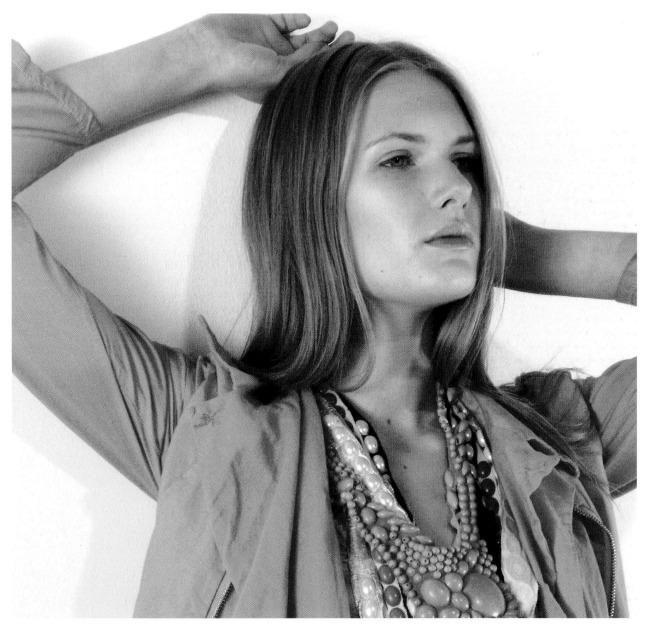

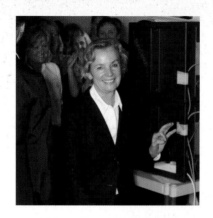

JIL SANDER

"We need to learn to decipher and translate the symbols, signals and hieroglyphs that tell us about the future. Even if only to find them in ourselves"

Jil Sander is a name synonymous with a particularly pure and understated type of fashion. The German-born designer, who launched her first women's collection back in 1973, is closely associated with '90s minimalism, yet her philosophy of fashion is far from simplistic. On opening her first shop, in Hamburg, at the age of 24, Sander used fabrics traditionally associated with menswear for her women's clothing, demonstrating an androgynous aesthetic that would endure throughout her career; a long-time signature design is the perfectly-cut white shirt, as is the trouser suit. Jil Sander is also renowned for the development and use of high-tech, yet extremely luxurious, fabrics. The rigorously-considered proportions of her clothing gained Sander a faithful following among sophisticated working women who valued graceful, clean lines over obvious sex appeal or froth. In 1979 Jil Sander Cosmetics was launched, followed by a leather collection in 1984. The company became a publicly-traded concern in 1989 and a period of rapid expansion followed, with flagship stores opening in Paris, Milan and New York in the early '90s. In 1997, the first menswear collection was shown in Milan. The serenity of Jil Sander clothing is in marked contrast to the corporate history of the company. In 1999 the Prada Group acquired a majority holding in Jil Sander AG and the following year Sander exited her own company; in November 2000 Milan Vukmirovic was named creative director of both men's and women's collections. However, to the surprise of industry observers, in 2003 Sander returned to the company she founded and for three seasons wowed press and customers with a subtly feminine aesthetic. But in November 2004 she split from her brand and the Prada Group once again. A team of studio designers, many of whom had trained directly under Sander, took over the reigns at the house for a period, until it was announced in May 2005 that Raf Simons was to be the new artistic director of the brand.

Jil Sander gilt als Synonym für besonders puristische und auf Understatement abzielende Mode. Die in Deutschland geborene Designerin, die ihre erste Damenkollektion 1973 präsentierte, wird oft mit dem Minimalismus der 1990er Jahre assoziiert, wobei ihre Philosophie von Mode alles andere als simpel ist. Als sie mit 24 Jahren in Hamburg ihren ersten Laden eröffnete, benutzte Sander für ihre Damenmode Stoffe, die traditionell in der Herrenschneiderei Verwendung finden, und erzeugte damit eine androgyne Coolness, die sie ihre ganze Karriere hindurch begleiten sollte. Die perfekt geschnittene weiße Bluse und der Hosenanzug galten lange Zeit als ihre Markenzeichen. Jil Sander ist aber auch bekannt für die Entwicklung und Verarbeitung von extrem luxuriösen High-Tech-Materialien. Die wohl überlegten Proportionen ihrer Entwürfe brachten Sander eine treue Gefolgschaft unter den berufstätigen Frauen ein. 1979 kamen die Jil Sander Cosmetics auf den Markt, gefolgt von einer Lederkollektion 1984. 1989 ging das Unternehmen an die Börse, und es folgte eine Phase der raschen Expansion, mit neuen Flagship Stores in Paris, Mailand und New York Anfang der 1990er

Jahre. 1997 wurde dann die erste Herrenkollektion in Mailand präsentiert. Die Klarheit von Jil Sanders Mode steht in deutlichem Kontrast zur Entwicklung des gleichnamigen Unternehmens. 1999 erwarb der Prada-Konzern die Aktienmehrheit der Jil Sander AG, ein Jahr später verließ die Namensgeberin die Firma. Im November 2000 ernannte man Milan Vukmirovic zum Creative Director der Herren- und Damenkollektionen. Zur Überraschung aller Beobachter kehrte Sander jedoch 2003 in das Unternehmen, das sie einst gegründet hatte, zurück und sorgte drei Saisons lang mit einer dezent femininen Ästhetik bei Presse und Kunden für Begeisterung. Im November 2004 trennte sie sich abermals von der Prada-Gruppe. Seither arbeitet ein Team aus Atelierdesignern, von denen viele direkt unter Sander gelernt haben, daran, ihre puristische und unbeirrbare Vision weiter zu interpretieren. Im Mai 2005 gab das Haus Jil Sander bekannt, dass Raf Simons die Position des Creative Director übernehmen wird.

Le nom de Jil Sander est devenu synonyme d'une mode particulièrement épurée et discrète. La créatrice allemande, qui a lancé sa première collection pour femme en 1973, est étroitement associée au minimalisme des années 90, bien que sa philosophie de la mode soit loin d'être simpliste. Lorsqu'elle ouvre sa première boutique à Hambourg à l'âge de 24 ans, Jil Sander utilise dans ses créations féminines des tissus traditionnellement associés à la mode pour homme, produisant un style cool et androgyne qui devait perdurer tout au long de sa carrière : parmi ses signatures de l'époque, on peut citer la chemise blanche parfaitement coupée et le tailleur-pantalon. Jil Sander est également connue pour avoir développé et utilisé des tissus high-tech extrêmement luxueux. Les proportions rigoureuses de ses vêtements lui ont valu des clientes fidèles parmi les femmes actives. En 1979, la créatrice lance la gamme Jil Sander Cosmetics, suivie d'une collection en cuir en 1984. Après la cotation en bourse de son entreprise en 1989 s'ensuit une période d'expansion rapide qui voit l'ouverture de boutiques à Paris, Milan et New York au début des années 90. En 1997, Jil Sander présente sa première collection pour homme à Milan. La sérénité de ses vêtements tranche de façon très contrastée avec l'histoire de son entreprise. En 1999, le Groupe Prada rachète une part majoritaire de Jil Sander AG et, l'année suivante, Jil Sander quitte la société qu'elle a fondée ; en novembre 2000, Milan Vukmirovic est nommé directeur de la création des collections pour homme et pour femme. Mais à la plus grande surprise des observateurs de l'industrie, Jil Sander revient dans son entreprise en 2003 et, pendant trois saisons, elle impressionne la presse comme ses clientes grâce à une esthétique subtilement féminine. En novembre 2004, elle se sépare à nouveau de sa marque et du groupe Prada. Depuis, une équipe de créateurs, dont la plupart des membres a été directement formée par Jil Sander, continue d'interpréter sa vision pure et sans concession. En mai 2005, la maison Jil Sander annonce le recrutement de Raf Simons au poste de directeur de la création. SUSIE RUSHTON

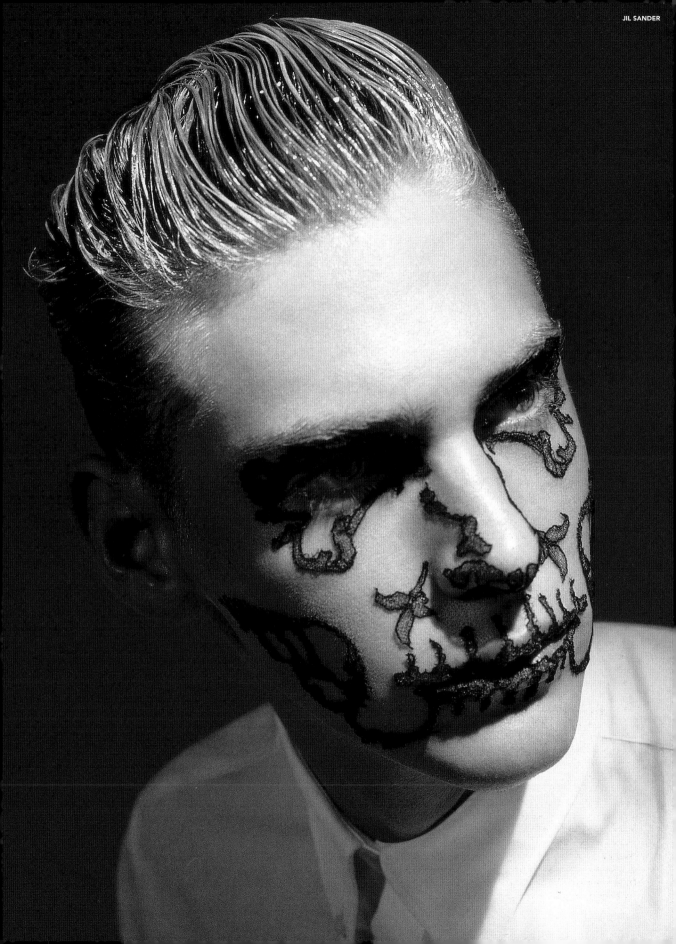

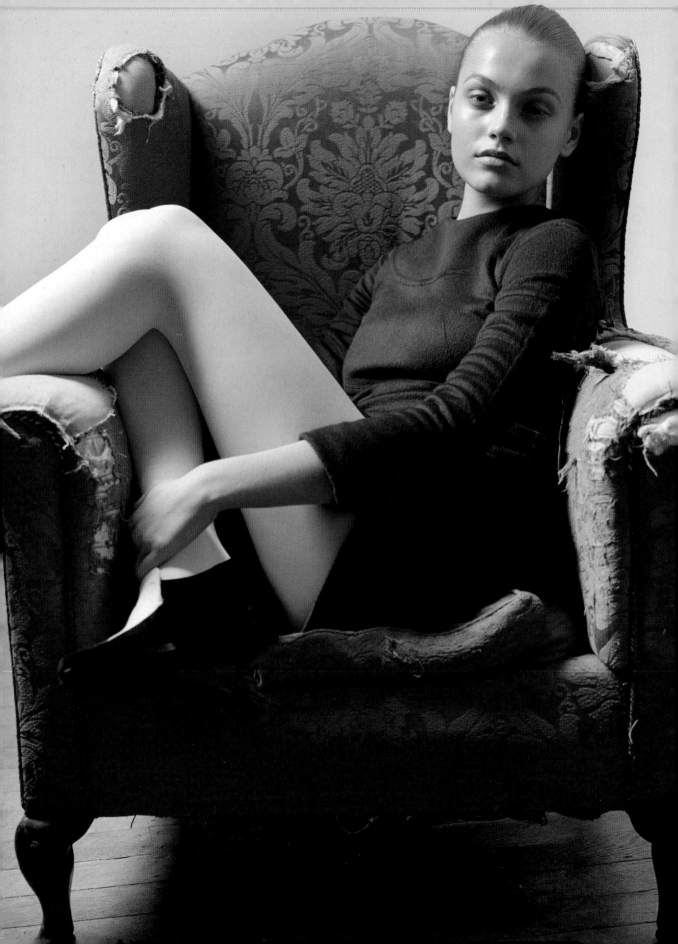

What are your signature designs? My ideas are transported through the strict aesthetic proportional relationship of form, material and colour **What is your favourite piece from any of your collections?** The one that was the most difficult and looks the most at ease **How would you describe your work?** To bring traces of ideas, inspirations, notions and interests into my aesthetics. This has proved to be a very dynamic source over the years. Of course, every aesthetic is subject to a continual creative process. This is a silent process, but a very effective one **What's your ultimate goal?** I think that an "ultimate goal" in fashion is always somewhat vague, somehow hard to pin down. If this was not the case, then you would have your final ultimate collection and that would be the end of it. However, what actually happens is more like this: with each step the "ultimate goal" changes a little. It flits about. This is an interesting phenomenon that fashion has in common with art. It is also a

drive to continue. Or has the goal already been achieved and you just don't believe it? I really don't know **What inspires you?** Firstly, I am inspired by something, and I don't know where it comes from. Secondly, by something that lies behind me. And thirdly, by everything that could shape the future. We need to learn to decipher and translate the symbols, signals and hieroglyphs that tell us about the future. Even if only to find them in ourselves **Can fashion still have a political ambition?** I see fashion as part of an ethic of the personal, which has to do with all the decisions, actions and behaviour of a person **Who do you have in mind when you design?** I work for everyone who likes my fashion and for those who might like it **Is the idea of creative collaboration important to you?** Yes and no. A reciprocal relationship is important. Especially if you are doing several things at once and sometimes things just go all over the place. On the other hand, the basic idea

must not be destroyed and that can happen very quickly **Who has been the greatest influence on your career?** The greatest influence? For me it is a combination of many larger and smaller influences **How have your own experiences affected your work as a designer?** I assume that my own experiences have a great deal to do with my design. But I could not really say how that works exactly. It makes me think of that famous iceberg; we only ever see its tip **Which is more important in your work: the process or the product?** There may well be designers who find a half-finished jacket really chic; I prefer a finished one. Therefore, it is the product, indeed, the finished product, that is more important to me. The fact that the process that leads to the finished product is interesting is another matter entirely **Is designing difficult for you, if so, what drives you to continue?** The difficulties that you have as designer are important for design. Resolved difficulties

open up new ideas, create tensions from which something unexpected can evolve. So there is no real reason to give up if you are able to work creatively with difficulty **Have you ever been influenced or moved by the reaction to your designs?** Of course, but I never loose sight of my goal **What's your definition of beauty?** You cannot produce beauty just for itself. Beauty is created when all of the parts are in a relationship to each other and "sit". Beauty in design is also connected with the dignity of the wearer. Ethics and aesthetics are both equally important for beauty **What's your philosophy?** My "philosophy" is complex because it is simple: I work on a modernity that is directed towards the future. Modernity is not a playground for moodiness or hysterical outbursts **What is the most important lesson you've learned?** That it is a good thing to stay true to your original impulse.

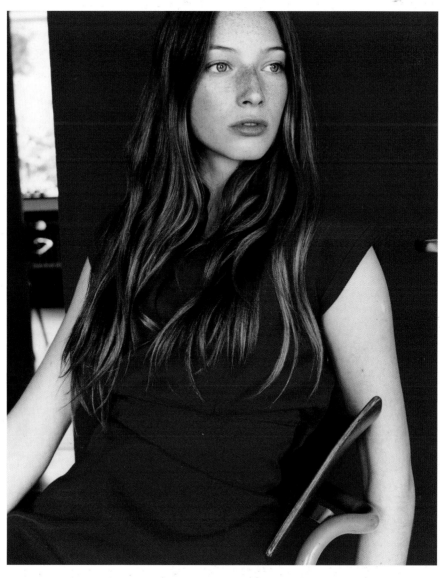

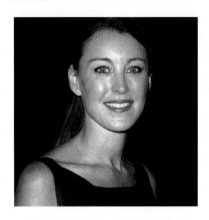

JIMMY CHOO

"Every time I see someone wearing Jimmy Choo
I still feel overwhelmed with excitement" TAMARA MELLON

Jimmy Choo's shoes were coveted long before the designer signed a partnership deal with Tamara Mellon, a former accessories editor at Vogue. A graduate of Cordwainers College, Choo had been creating handmade footwear in London's East End for some time when Mellon approached him with a big idea and together, they launched the company Jimmy Choo in 1996. The Malaysian-born shoemaker had made his first pair at the tender age of 12; his designs are noted for their exquisite craftsmanship and dreamy colourways. Today they are to be seen on the tiptoes of the international jet set, socialite A-list and red carpet Hollywood megastars. Mellon's game plan involved sourcing Italian manufacturers who could produce Jimmy's fabulous shoes on a large scale. The first Choo boutique opened in London's Knightsbridge in 1996. In 2001 the company's ambition took off big-time when Equinox Luxury Holdings Ltd acquired Mr Choo's share of the ready-to-wear business. The next three years saw a heady expansion, as the company opened a further 26 stores and introduced handbags to the brand. And this was by no means as good as it got. In November 2004 Hicks Muse Europe announced the takeover of a majority shareholding that valued Jimmy Choo at a whopping £101 million. The ethos and design of the product, however, are likely to remain the same. Tamara, along with creative director Sandra Choi, oversees three collections each year and by 2008 the company plans to have 50 shops in which to showcase its very fancy footwork.

Schuhe von Jimmy Choo waren schon heiß begehrt, lange bevor der Designer eine Kooperation mit der ehemaligen Vogue-Journalistin Tamara Mellon einging. Der Absolvent des Cordwainers College produzierte bereits einige Zeit handgemachtes Schuhwerk im Londoner East End, als Mellon ihm das entscheidende Angebot machte und die beiden 1996 gemeinsam die Firma Jimmy Choo gründeten. Der in Malaysia geborene Schuhmacher hatte sein erstes Paar im zarten Alter von 12 Jahren gefertigt. Inzwischen sind seine Entwürfe für ihre exquisite handwerkliche Verarbeitung und die traumhaften Farbzusammenstellungen berühmt. Man sieht sie heute an den Füßen des internationalen Jetsets, der Superreichen und der Megastars von Hollywood. Zu Mellons Konzept gehörte das Ausfindigmachen italienischer Manufakturen, die Jimmys märchenhafte Schuhe in großen Stückzahlen produzieren können. Der erste Choo-Laden wurde 1996 im Londoner Viertel Knightsbridge eröffnet. Ab 2001 ließen sich die Ambitionen der Firma im großen Stil realisieren, nachdem die Equinox Luxury Holding Ltd Choos Anteile am Prêt-à-porter-Geschäft übernommen hatte. In den drei darauf folgenden Jahren expandierte man kräftig: Es wurden 26 neue Filialen eröffnet und außerdem Handtaschen ins Programm des Labels genommen. Aber das sollte noch nicht alles sein. Im November 2004 kündete Hicks Muse Europe die Übernahme der Aktienmehrheit an und bewertete Jimmy Choo mit sagenhaften 101 Millionen Pfund. Charakter und Design der Produkte blieben jedoch unverändert. Zusammen mit ihrer Chefdesignerin Sandra Choi entwirft Tamara alljährlich drei Kollektionen und plant, bis 2008 das kunstvolle Schuhwerk in insgesamt 50 Läden zu präsentieren.

Les chaussures de Jimmy Choo étaient déjà très recherchées bien avant que le créateur ne signe un accord de partenariat avec Tamara Mellon, ancienne journaliste de Vogue spécialisée dans les accessoires. Diplômé du Cordwainers College, Choo fabrique des chaussures faites main dans l'East End de Londres depuis un certain temps, quand Tamara Mellon lui soumet l'idée géniale de lancer ensemble la maison Jimmy Choo en 1996. Né en Malaisie, ce chausseur a créé sa première paire dès l'âge de 12 ans. Ses créations sont prisées pour leur côté artisanal exquis et leurs ravissants coloris. Aujourd'hui, on les retrouve aux pieds de la jet-set internationale, des membres du gotha et des superstars hollywoodiennes. Le plan d'action de Tamara Mellon consistait à faire appel à des fabricants italiens capables de produire les fabuleuses chaussures de Jimmy à grande échelle. La première boutique Choo ouvre ses portes à Londres en 1996, sur Knightsbridge. En 2001, les ambitions de la griffe décollent enfin quand Equinox Luxury Holdings Ltd rachète la part de Jimmy Choo dans l'activité de prêt-à-porter. Les trois années suivantes, l'entreprise se développe à une vitesse vertigineuse en ouvrant 26 nouvelles boutiques et en lançant une ligne de sacs à main. Et les choses ne devaient pas s'arrêter en si bon chemin. En novembre 2004, alors que Hicks Muse Europe annonce le rachat d'une part majoritaire dans l'entreprise, la griffe Jimmy Choo est évaluée à 101 millions de livres. Toutefois, son éthique et sa démarche créative resteront probablement les mêmes. Tamara Mellon, aux côtés de la directrice artistique Sandra Choi, collabore à la création de trois collections par an. D'ici 2008, l'entreprise prévoit de posséder 50 points de vente où présenter son travail plein de fantaisie. TERRY NEWMAN

What are your signature designs? Very strappy stiletto knee high boots, courts and jewelled shoes. Our Tulita hobo bag has also become increasingly recognisable as a Jimmy Choo signature design What is your favourite piece from any of your collections? My all-time favourite shoe is called "Smooth". We introduced it in autumn/winter 2002 and it was so popular that we have made it a house style for every season designed in a variety of satins, leathers and exotic skins for day and evening How would you describe your work? Taking a brand forward and maintaining a global business whilst collaborating on the creative in the process.

The product is very important to me and I like to be involved with every aspect of the design process What's your ultimate goal? Health & happiness What inspires you? Travelling to exotic countries and observing different cultures Can fashion still have a political ambition? Personally, I don't think fashion should hold a political statement. It can evoke a trend or a general mood but not a political message as such Who do you have in mind when you design? A sophisticated & stylish woman – feminine yet determined Is the idea of creative collaboration important to you? It can be fun and inspiring to get creative minds together Who has been the

greatest influence on your career? My father has been the greatest influence in my life. He had amazing strength of character and was a continuous guiding light in my personal and professional life How have your own experiences affected your work as a designer? The way I live my life certainly influences the product. If I see a gap in our line for example, weekend boots I will ensure we introduce them into the collection Which is more important in your work: the process or the product? Both are important but at the end the product is what really matters. Seeing the end result is what makes the process so interesting Is designing

difficult for you, if so, what drives you to continue? No, it's the part I enjoy the most. I am constantly inspired by things around me Have you ever been influenced or moved by the reaction to your designs? Every time I see someone wearing Jimmy Choo I still feel overwhelmed with excitement What's your definition of beauty? I find beauty in so many places – it's all around us and more to the point how you look at something What's your philosophy? To always live with a clear conscience What is the most important lesson you've learned? Always follow your intuition.

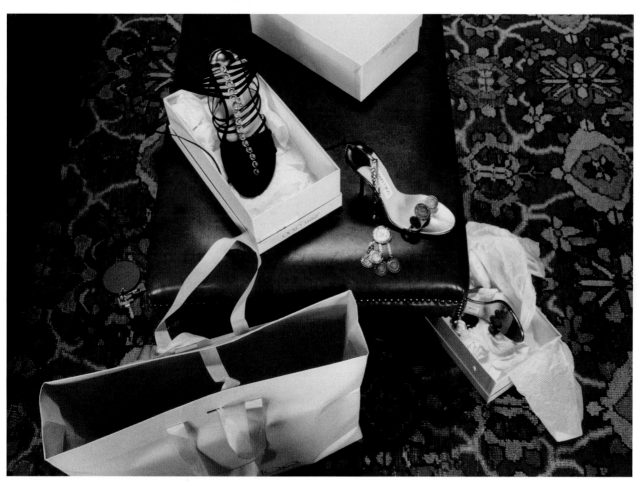

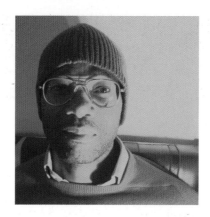

JOE CASELY-HAYFORD

"I am interested in the explosion caused
when disparate cultural fragments collide"

Joe Casely-Hayford has remained true to the aims he established at the outset of his career thirty years ago – to create clothing that simultaneously subverts tradition, yet is always infused with principles of sound craftsmanship. His signature – classic English fabrics and ingenious darting, pleating and layering – might be defined as 'deconstructed tailoring'. Born in Kent in 1956, Casely-Hayford commenced his design journey in 1974, first by training in London's Savile Row, then attending the Tailor and Cutter Academy. In 1975 he enrolled at Central Saint Martins college, graduating in 1979, followed by a one-year history of art course at London's Institute of Contemporary Art (ICA). His design for men and women combines this knowledge of fashion, tailoring, art and social history with an appreciation of youth culture. Although it was not until 1991 that Casely-Hayford made his London Fashion Week debut, he had already enjoyed considerable related success – working as a styling consultant for Island Records, creating clothing for The Clash in 1984, and being nominated for the Designer of The Year Award in 1989. Throughout the '90s his reputation was further enhanced when he dressed the likes of Lou Reed, Bobby Gillespie, Suede and U2. Casely-Hayford was also one of the first designers to co-operate with high street fashion chains such as Topshop, for whom he designed a sell-out womenswear range in 1993. His work has consistently ventured beyond the catwalk to be featured in prestigious exhibitions such as the 'Rock Style' show at the Metropolitan Museum in New York in 1999 and the V&A's 'Black British Style' in 2004. Casely-Hayford has also written a number of articles on fashion and associated social issues for i-D, True and Arena Homme Plus.

Joe Casely-Hayford ist bis heute den Grundsätzen treu geblieben, die er am Beginn seiner Karriere vor dreißig Jahren für sich aufgestellt hat: Kleidung zu entwerfen, die mit Traditionen bricht, zugleich aber immer von den Prinzipien solider Handwerkskunst geprägt ist. Sein Markenzeichen – klassische englische Stoffe und geniale Abnäher, Falten und Lagen – könnte man in dem Begriff dekonstruierte Schneiderei zusammenfassen. 1956 in Kent geboren, begann Casely-Hayford seine Designerlaufbahn 1974 mit einer Ausbildung in der Londoner Savile Row. Danach besuchte er die Tailor and Cutter Academy und schrieb sich 1975 im Central Saint Martins ein, wo er 1979 seinen Abschluss machte. Anschließend belegte er noch einen einjährigen Kurs in Kunstgeschichte am Institute of Contemporary Art (ICA) in London. In seinen Entwürfen für Männer und Frauen spiegelt sich dieses Wissen über Mode, Schneiderei, Kunst und Sozialgeschichte sowie sein Interesse an Jugendkultur. Auch wenn er sein Debüt bei der London Fashion Week erst 1991 gab, konnte er vorher bereits vergleichbare Erfolge feiern – etwa bei seiner Tätigkeit als Styling-Berater von

Island Records, wo er 1984 die Garderobe für The Clash entwarf. 1989 gehörte er zu den Nominierten für den Designer of The Year Award. In den 1990er Jahren stieg sein Ansehen, als er Leute vom Kaliber eines Lou Reed, Bobby Gillespie oder die Mitglieder von Suede und U2 einkleidete. Casely-Hayford war auch einer der ersten Designer, die mit Nobelketten wie Topshop kooperierten. Für sie entwarf er 1993 eine rasch ausverkaufte Damenlinie. Seine Arbeit reichte schon immer über den Catwalk hinaus und wurde in angesehenen Ausstellungen wie „Rock Style" im New Yorker Metropolitan Museum (1999) und „Black British Style" im Victoria & Albert Museum (2004) präsentiert. Casely-Hayford hat auch bereits einige Artikel über Mode und verwandte gesellschaftlich relevante Themen in i-D, True und Arena Homme Plus veröffentlicht.

Joe Casely-Hayford a su rester fidèle aux objectifs qu'il s'était fixés en débutant sa carrière il y a trente ans : créer des vêtements qui bouleversent les traditions tout en affichant les principes du savoir-faire artisanal. Son style signature (vieux tissus anglais et utilisation ingénieuse des fronces, des plis et des superpositions) peut être apparenté au déconstructionnisme. Né en 1956 dans le Kent, Casely-Hayford a débuté son voyage dans la mode en 1974, d'abord en se formant chez les tailleurs londoniens de Savile Row, puis à la Tailor and Cutter Academy. En 1975, il entame un cursus à Central Saint Martins dont il sort diplômé en 1979, avant de suivre un cours d'histoire de l'art pendant un an à l'Institute of Contemporary Art de Londres. Dans ses créations pour homme et pour femme, il combine ses connaissances en mode, en histoire de l'art et de la société à son savoir-faire de tailleur pour homme, tout en gardant un œil sur la culture jeune. Bien que Casely-Hayford n'ait fait ses débuts à la London Fashion Week qu'en 1991, il avait déjà remporté de grands succès, notamment en tant que styliste-consultant pour Island Records, créateur des vêtements des Clash en 1984, sans oublier une nomination au titre de Designer of the Year en 1989. Au cours des années 90, il étoffe sa réputation en habillant Lou Reed, Bobby Gillespie, Suede et U2. Casely-Hayford est également l'un des premiers créateurs à avoir collaboré avec de grandes chaînes de mode telles que Topshop, pour laquelle il a dessiné une ligne pour femme qui s'est très bien vendue en 1993. Il a toujours cherché à faire sortir son travail du circuit officiel des défilés pour le présenter dans le cadre d'expositions prestigieuses telles que le show « Rock Style » du Metropolitan Museum de New York en 1999 et l'exposition « Black British Style » du Victoria & Albert Museum en 2004. Casely-Hayford a également écrit de nombreux articles sur la mode et les questions de société qu'elle soulève pour des magazines tels que i-D, True et Arena Homme Plus.

JAMES ANDERSON

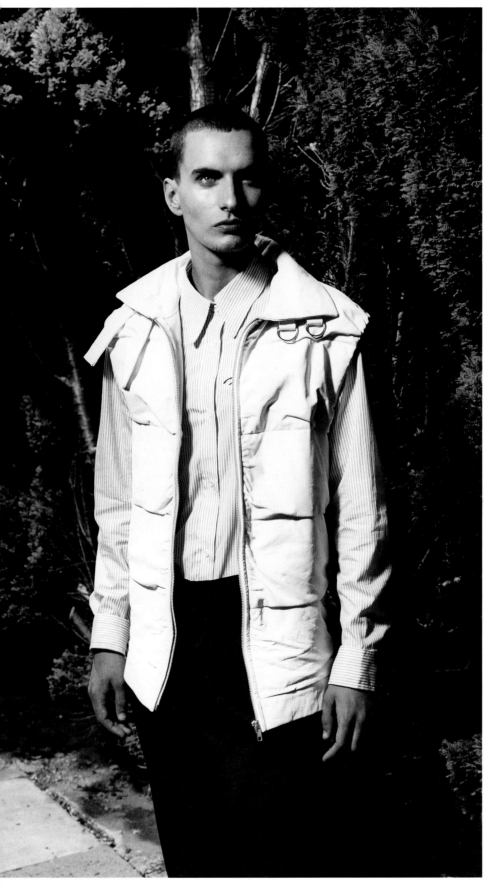

What are your signature designs? Deconstructed tailoring has been a recurring theme **What is your favourite piece from any of your collections?** My favourite piece is always from my current collection. I have been working on a Black Rock – Afro Punk theme. I love the slim brightly coloured button jeans worn with a JCH wax print hoodie **How would you describe your work?** Multi-layered, metaphorically speaking **What's your ultimate goal?** I am living my ultimate goal by enjoying a career based on original design ethics – to create clothes without boundaries **What inspires you?** The madness and sanity of London, the future. I am interested in the explosion caused when disparate cultural fragments collide **Can fashion still have a political ambition?** The only thing we can accurately predict in fashion is change. Things have become so apolitical and commercially driven, I would say that a new, more politically inspired agenda is a distinct possibility **Who do you have in mind when you design?** Through the effects of globalisation, much of today's fashion is homogenised and lacks personal identity. Too many draw from the same reference points, and as a result, the human element and craftsmanship are in decline. Now is the time to reclaim your identity **Is the idea of creative collaboration important to you?** Yes, only when it's real, not just for association **Who has been the greatest influence on your career?** My wife, Maria, has influenced every aspect of my work **How have your own experiences affected your work as a designer?** Very much, I am a black man, living and working in London and my work reflects this **Which is more important in your work: the process or the product?** If an idea is developed through a solid creative process, aesthetically, ethically, and fulfils its function, the end product is likely to reflect this – which is why I believe the process and the product are of equal value **Is designing difficult for you, if so, what drives you to continue?** Designing isn't difficult for me, but some seasons flow more easily than others. This is because fashion doesn't evolve in neat six monthly cycles **Have you ever been influenced or moved by the reaction to your designs?** There have been times when I have seen my designs in other people's collections **What's your definition of beauty?** Truth. Purity **What's your philosophy?** Truth and integrity **What is the most important lesson you've learned?** That logic or reason in this industry is down to coincidence.

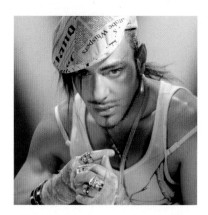

JOHN GALLIANO

"I am here to make people dream, to seduce them into buying beautiful clothes and to strive to make amazing clothing to the best of my ability. That is my duty"

John Galliano is one of Britain's fashion heroes. Born in 1960 to a working class Gibraltan family, Galliano lived on the island until leaving at the age of six for south London. But it was the young Juan Carlos Antonio's early life, with its religious ceremonies and sun-drenched culture, which has proved a constant inspiration for Galliano; stylistic eclecticism wedded to the Latin tradition of 'dressing-up' has become his signature. Having attended Wilson's Grammar School for boys, Galliano won a place at Saint Martins college, graduating in 1984. And it was that graduation collection – inspired by the French Revolution and titled 'Les Incroyables' – that was bought by Joan Burstein of Browns, catapulting the young designer into the spotlight. In 1990 – after suffering a period notorious for problems with backers and collections deemed uncommercial because they dared to dream beyond the conventional – Galliano started to show in Paris, moving to the city in 1992. A champion of the romantic bias-cut dress and the dramatic tailoring of '50s couture at a time when minimalism and grunge dominated fashion, it was announced in 1995 that Galliano would succeed Hubert de Givenchy at the dusty maison de couture. Two seasons later, and with an unprecedented four British Designer of the Year awards under his belt, Galliano became creative director at Christian Dior, presenting his first collection for the spring/summer 1997 haute couture show. Since then, Galliano has financially and creatively revitalised the house, while continuing to design his own collections for men and women in Paris, a city where he is accorded the status of fashion royalty.

John Galliano ist eine Ikone der britischen Mode. Er wurde 1960 als Arbeiterkind auf Gibraltar geboren und verbrachte die ersten sechs Lebensjahre auf der Insel. Dann zog er mit seiner Familie in den Süden Londons. Es waren jedoch die frühen Jahre des Juan Carlos Antonio mit ihren religiösen Zeremonien und der sonnendurchfluteten Umgebung, die Galliano bis heute inspirieren. Eklektizismus in Verbindung mit der südländisch-katholischen Tradition des „Sichschön-Anziehens" wurde zu seinem Markenzeichen. Nach dem Besuch von Wilson's Grammar School for Boys ergatterte Galliano einen Studienplatz am Central Saint Martins, das er 1984 abschloss. Seine von der Französischen Revolution inspirierte Schlusskollektion mit dem Namen „Les Incroyables", die Joan Burstein für Browns aufkaufte, katapultierte den Jungdesigner ins Rampenlicht. Nach einer schwierigen Phase – geprägt von Problemen mit Geldgebern und Kollektionen, die als nicht kommerziell genug abgeschmettert wurden, weil er darin Unkonventionelles wagte – begann Galliano 1990, seine

Kreationen in Paris zu präsentieren. Zwei Jahre später verlegte er auch seinen Wohnsitz hierher. Als Verfechter des romantischen Diagonalschnitts und der dramatischen Effekte der Couture der 1950er Jahre in einer Zeit, als Minimalismus und Grunge die Mode dominierten, wurde Galliano 1995 als Nachfolger von Hubert de Givenchy in dessen leicht verstaubtes Couture-Haus gerufen. Zwei Saisons später und mit noch nie da gewesenen vier Titeln als British Designer of the Year in der Tasche wurde Galliano schließlich Creative Director bei Christian Dior, wo er als erste Kollektion die Haute Couture für Frühjahr/ Sommer 1997 präsentierte. Seit damals ist es dem Designer gelungen, das Haus sowohl in finanzieller wie in kreativer Hinsicht zu revitalisieren. Gleichzeitig entwirft er noch eigene Kollektionen für Herren wie für Damen und genießt in Paris königliches Ansehen als Modeschöpfer.

John Galliano est un héros de la mode britannique. Né en 1960 à Gibraltar dans une famille d'ouvriers, il quitte son île natale pour le sud de Londres à l'âge de six ans. La tendre enfance du jeune Juan Carlos Antonio, avec ses cérémonies religieuses et sa culture du soleil, représente une source d'inspiration constante pour Galliano ; l'éclectisme stylistique et la tradition du « chic latin » sont devenus sa signature. En sortant du lycée pour garçons Wilson's Grammar School, Galliano réussit à entrer à Central Saint Martins, dont il sort diplômé en 1984. Inspirée par la Révolution française et baptisée « Les Incroyables », sa collection de fin d'études est achetée par Joan Burstein de chez Browns, ce qui le catapulte directement sur le devant de la scène. En 1990, après de célèbres déboires avec ses financiers et des collections vouées à l'échec commercial parce qu'elles osaient défier les conventions, Galliano commence à présenter ses défilés à Paris, où il s'installe en 1992. Fervent défenseur des coupes asymétriques romantiques et de la haute couture théâtrale des années 50 au sein d'une mode alors dominée par le minimalisme et le grunge, sa nomination à la succession d'Hubert de Givenchy dans l'antique maison éponyme est annoncée en 1995. Deux saisons plus tard et couronné de quatre British Designer of the Year Awards, un exploit sans précédent, Galliano devient directeur de la création chez Christian Dior et présente sa première collection aux défilés haute couture printemps/été 1997. Depuis, Galliano a redonné vie à la maison Dior tant sur le plan financier que créatif, tout en continuant à dessiner ses propres collections pour homme et pour femme à Paris, qui le considère désormais comme un membre de la famille royale de la mode.

JAMIE HUCKBODY

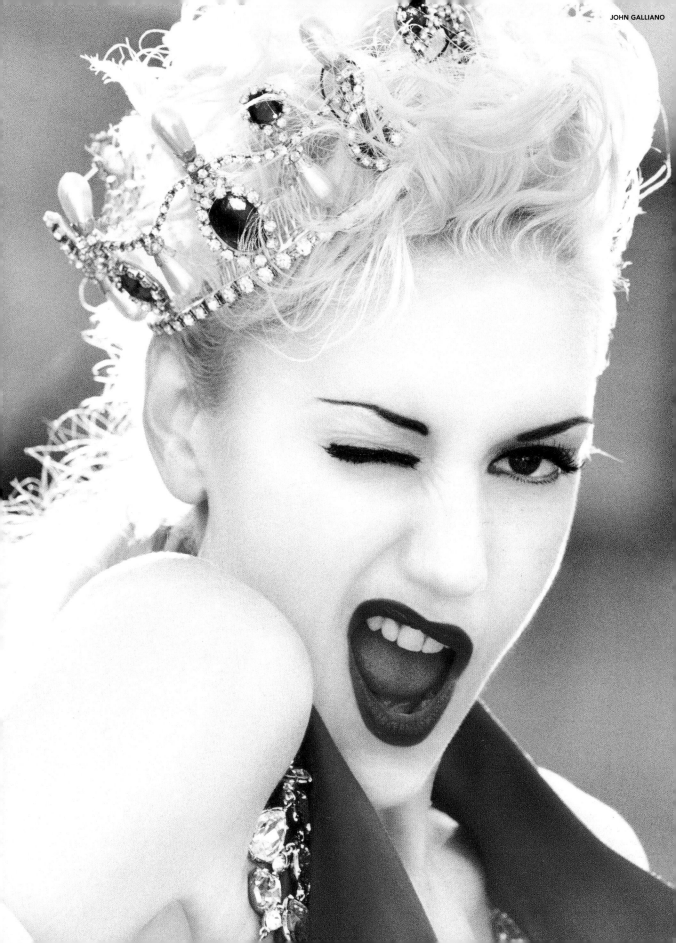

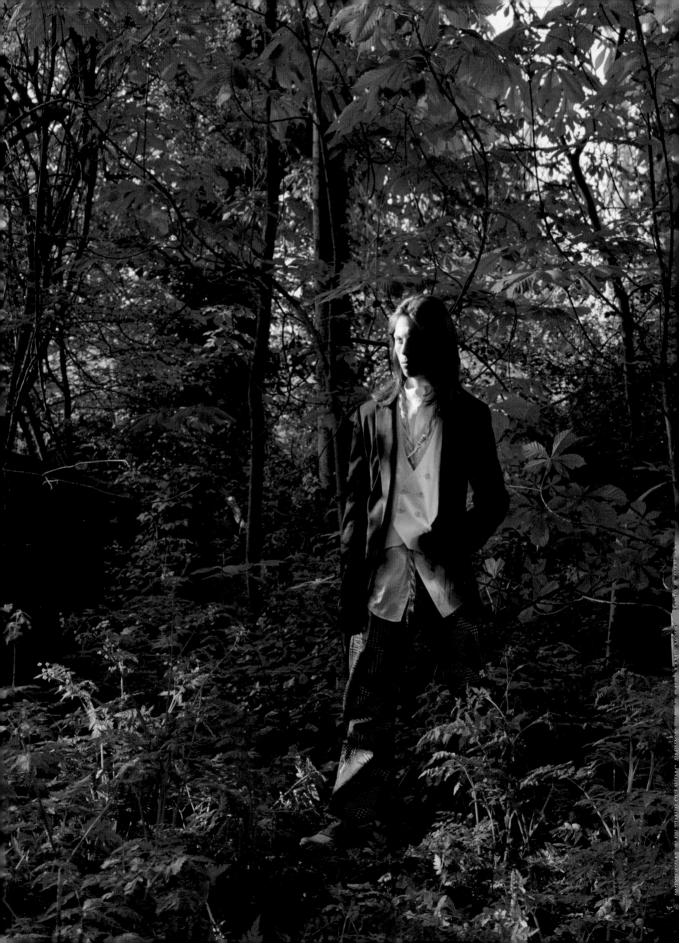

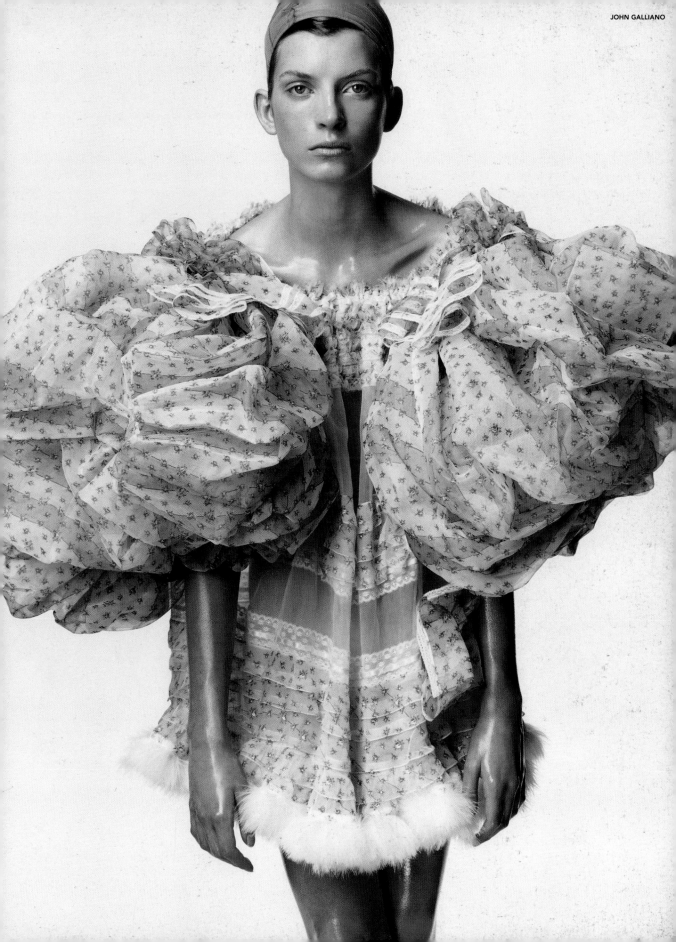

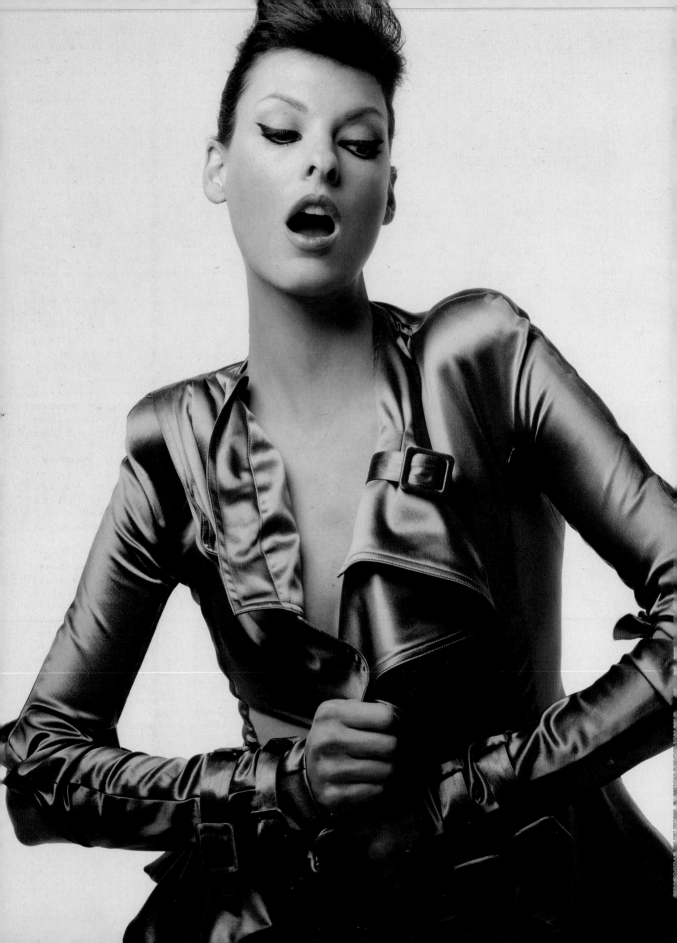

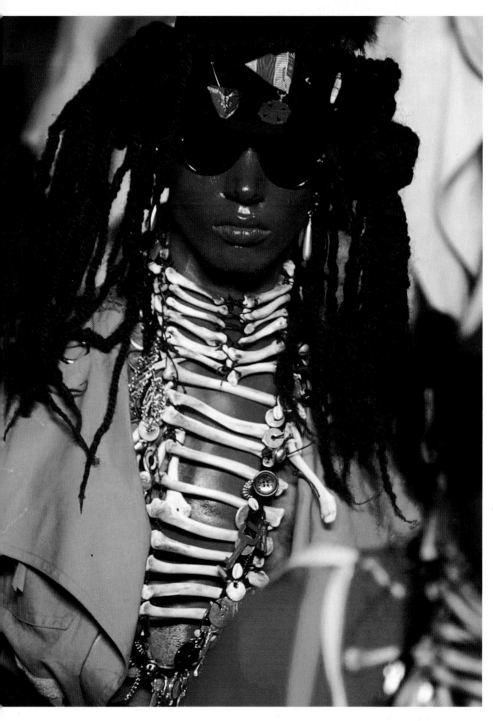

clothing to the best of my ability. That is my duty **Who do you have in mind when you design?** In the course of my career I have discovered that having a specific muse (either a historical figure or a living person) can be inhibiting rather than inspiring. Now I would say that I think of a more abstract notion of a modern-day woman, someone who is assertive and controls her own destiny **Is the idea of creative collaboration important to you?** I share my passion and my love of clothing with my creative team, the Studio, the Ateliers at both Dior and Galliano, with the fantastic French artisans and embroiderers like Lesage... **Who has been the greatest influence on your career?** My mother and my grandmother and their love for life and their sense of occasion for dress have been the first and lasting influence on me. When I lived in Gibraltar, to go to school in Spain I had to go through Tangiers. The souks, the markets, the fabrics, the carpets, the smells, the herbs, the Mediterranean colour is where my love of textiles comes from. Later, when I started my studies at Saint Martins I was greatly influenced by the fantastic teachers I had and by the theatre **How have your own experiences affected your work as a designer?** My experiences are a vital part of my work... **Which is more important in your work: the process or the product?** One is nothing without the other **Is designing difficult for you, if so, what drives you to continue?** I have always seen work as a positive challenge. I love what I am doing, I love the very act of creating. Even in my darkest moments I would continue working – I had no choice. Then and now, it was all I could and can do **Have you ever been influenced or moved by the reaction to your designs?** A few weeks before the showing of the autumn/winter 2002 collection I received a letter with some drawings from a ten year old boy. It turns out that he had seen the Dior show on the telly. He did not want to go to sleep and stayed up until two in the morning drawing the clothes. His mother was first exasperated but then moved by his enthusiasm and she sent us the drawings. The drawings were so lovely I was very touched. I invited the boy to the Dior show and met him afterwards. Something like this makes it all worth while **What's your definition of beauty?** A woman in charge of her own destiny **What is the most important lesson you've learned?** Mr Arnault once told me, "John, you have to learn to live with your critics." That was a very good lesson.

What are your signature designs? The bias cut for women and now for men as well **What is your favourite piece from any of your collections?** It is too difficult to give an answer. It would be like choosing which of your children you like best **How would you describe your work?** My work is about femininity and romance, about pushing the boundaries of creation. It is a constant search for new creative solutions **What's your ultimate goal?** To live life to the fullest, to hold on to every minute as if it were my last **What inspires you?** Everything that surrounds me can be an inspiration. I am inspired by music, film, art, street culture, my girlfriends... **Can fashion still have a political ambition?** I am a fashion designer, not a politician. I am here to make people dream, to seduce them into buying beautiful clothes and to strive to make amazing

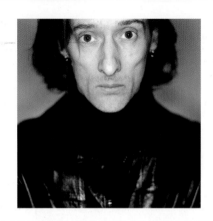

JOHN RICHMOND

"I never get bored! I often think how lucky I am just for being able to do all the things I wanted to do"

'Destroy, Disorientate, Disorder' and Debenhams, the British department store: John Richmond is equal parts raring-to-rock and ready-to-wear. The music-loving Mancunian has a singular talent for reconciling anarchic punk aesthetics with elegant tailoring. Born in 1961, Richmond graduated from Kingston Polytechnic in 1982 and worked as a freelance designer for Emporio Armani, Fiorucci and Joseph Tricot before forming his first label, Richmond-Cornejo, a collaboration with designer Maria Cornejo, in 1984. In 1987 he struck out on his own. During his career Richmond has dressed pop icons such as Bryan Adams, David Bowie, Madonna and Mick Jagger; George Michael wore Richmond's Destroy jacket in the video for 'Faith'. John Richmond designs are synonymous with the spirit of rock and the smell of leather. Today, his label comprises three clothing lines: John Richmond, Richmond X, and Richmond Denim, with eyewear and underwear collections also recently launched. A business partnership with Saverio Moschillo has provided Richmond with a worldwide network of showrooms, from Naples, Rome and Paris to Munich, Düsseldorf and New York. They house his leather biker jackets, oil-printed T-shirts, acid-orange pleated skirts and long-line sweaters. Richmond's newest flagship store in London's Conduit Street joins two Italian shops in Milan and Bari. Then there's the Designers At Debenhams collection, the John Richmond Smart Roadster car – needless to say, a John Richmond fragrance and a childrenswear collection are also both in the pipeline.

„Destroy, Disorientate, Disorder" und das britische Kaufhaus Debenhams: John Richmond ist zu gleichen Teilen „ready-to-rock" und Prêt-à-porter. Der Musikliebhaber aus Manchester besitzt ein einzigartiges Talent für die Versöhnung von anarchischer Punk-Ästhetik mit eleganter Schneiderkunst. 1961 geboren, beendete Richmond 1982 das Kingston Polytechnikum und designte danach zunächst als Freelancer für Emporio Armani, Fiorucci und Joseph Tricot, bevor er 1984 mit Richmond-Cornejo in Kooperation mit der Designerin Maria Cornejo sein erstes Label gründete. Ab 1987 versuchte er sein Glück dann wieder allein. Im bisherigen Verlauf seiner Karriere kleidete er Popikonen wie Bryan Adams, David Bowie, Madonna und Mick Jagger ein. George Michael trug in seinem Video zu „Faith" die Destroy-Jacke von Richmond. Seine Entwürfe sind Synonyme für den Spirit of Rock und den Geruch von Leder. Heute umfasst sein Label drei verschiedene Linien: John Richmond, Richmond X und Richmond

Denim; kürzlich kamen noch Brillen- und Dessouskollektionen dazu. Die geschäftliche Verbindung mit Saverio Moschillo ermöglicht Richmond den Zugang zu einem weltweiten Netz von Showrooms, sei es in Neapel oder Rom, in Paris oder München, Düsseldorf oder New York. Dort führt man seine Biker-Jacken, ölbedruckte T-Shirts, seine Faltenröcke in Neonorange und die lang geschnittenen Sweater. Richmonds neuester Flagship Store in der Londoner Conduit Street steht in Verbindung mit zwei Läden in Italien – genauer gesagt: in Mailand und Bari. Außerdem wären da noch die Kollektion At Debenhams und das Auto namens John Richmond Smart Roadster. Dass ein eigener Duft und eine Kinderkollektion bereits in Planung sind, versteht sich da fast von selbst.

Entre son slogan « Destroy, Disorientate, Disorder » et le grand magasin anglais Debenhams, on peut dire que John Richmond est à la fois rock'n'roll et prêt-à-porter. Originaire de Manchester, ce fan de musique possède un talent unique pour réconcilier esthétique anarchique du punk et coupes élégantes. Né en 1961, Richmond sort diplômé de l'école polytechnique de Kingston en 1982 et travaille comme créateur free-lance pour Emporio Armani, Fiorucci et Joseph Tricot. En 1984, il fonde sa première griffe, Richmond-Cornejo, en collaboration avec la créatrice Maria Cornejo, mais décide de se lancer en solo dès 1987. Au cours de sa carrière, Richmond a habillé des icônes pop telles que Bryan Adams, David Bowie, Madonna et Mick Jagger ; George Michael a même porté son blouson Destroy dans son clip « Faith ». Les créations de John Richmond fusionnent l'esprit du rock et l'odeur du cuir. Aujourd'hui, sa griffe comprend trois lignes de mode : John Richmond, Richmond X et Richmond Denim, sans oublier le récent lancement de collections de lunettes et de sous-vêtements. Grâce à son partenariat commercial avec Saverio Moschillo, Richmond dispose d'un réseau mondial de showrooms installés à Naples, Rome, Paris, Munich, Düsseldorf et New York. Tous accueillent ses blousons de motard en cuir, ses T-shirts imprimés à l'huile, ses jupes plissées orange fluo et ses pulls aux lignes allongées. La boutique londonienne flambant neuve de Richmond dans Conduit Street vient s'ajouter aux deux boutiques italiennes de Milan et de Bari. Sans compter la collection Designers At Debenhams et la voiture John Richmond Smart Roadster. Logiquement, un parfum et une ligne pour enfant John Richmond ne devraient plus tarder à voir le jour.

NANCY WATERS

What are your signature designs? Observers decide what your signature is. Yes, I'm well known for leather jackets or 'RICH' jeans – in my head I change radically every season. Others see the signature of my work with a slight seasonal change **What are your favourite pieces from any of your collections?** I do not have a favourite piece. I just see the mistakes and changes that I want to make. I am never satisfied – I just enjoy creating the next piece **How would you describe your work?** 'Eclectic'. It draws upon the past, present and future **What's your ultimate goal?** With a career of 20 years, including two children, one's goals change. I wake up everyday and do something different from the day before. One day menswear, the next women's; maybe a meeting with the sunglasses or childrenswear licensee or to Como to do the underwear or to the shoe factory! Is it men's or women's shoes today or childrenswear? I never get bored! I often think how lucky I am just to be able to do all the things I wanted to do **What inspires you?** Waking up thinking what am I going to do today? Another blank sheet of paper and I can do what I want **Can fashion still have a political ambition?** No. In its very nature it can't be taken seriously. Tomorrow we are going to change our mind **What do you have in mind when you design?** I get many images in my head of different people. Musicians, personalities, people I've seen on the street, the people around me **Is the idea of creative collaboration important to you?** Yeah. It's fun working with other people, but sometimes it's difficult to be democratic **Who has been the greatest influence on your career?** Different periods have seen different people and circumstances. All have been important; it possibly started with David Bowie and Mick Ronson on Top of the Pops singing Starman around '72 **Which is more important in your work: the process or the product?** The process is much more enjoyable. The product is for other people's enjoyment **Is designing difficult for you?** Designing is fun and easy. There are days when you are on top of the world and others where you can't even draw a straight line **Have you ever been influenced or moved by the reaction to your designs?** Of course. If you get a positive reaction it's great for your confidence; and when it's negative you feel shit – but it makes me want to prove them wrong, and to work harder. But that is probably the Capricorn in me **What's your definition of beauty?** I hate this question, maybe because I can't articulate the answer. When it is in front of us, it's a bit like trying to put into words what a hiccup is. We all know, but we cannot write it down in a satisfying way **What's your philosophy?** You only get out what you put in **What is the most important lesson you've learned?** Try and be honest to others, but especially yourself. Only you can be you, what's the the point in trying to be something else?

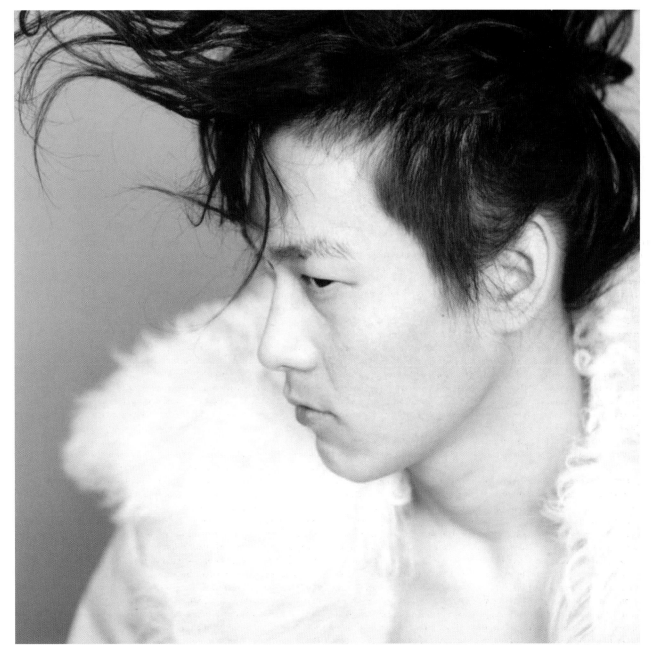

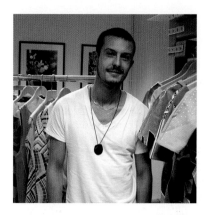

JONATHAN SAUNDERS

"I'm inspired by movements in design and fine art that challenged what was perceived as beautiful"

Is Jonathan Saunders (born 1977) the future of British fashion? A Printed Textiles graduate of the Glasgow School of Art, the Scottish-born creative has helped make prints relevant to 21st century fashion. Inspired by anything from the strict lines of Bauhaus to the eccentricity of Milan's Memphis Furniture, Saunders' prints are angular and abstract, often presented on the blank canvas of skin-tight silhouettes. Any severity is softened by a colour palette that seems to invent shades unknown even to Pantone. After graduating with a distinction from Central Saint Martins' MA fashion course in 2002, his arresting aesthetic won him the Lancôme Colour Award. It also caught the attention of Alexander McQueen, who hired Saunders just two days after his graduation. Chloé and Pucci are other high profile fashion houses who have hired him as a consultant. Although kept more than busy working for such major names, solo stardom beckoned in February 2003, when he launched the Jonathan Saunders label. Instantly admired for its refreshing colour and graphic inventiveness, fashion editors rushed backstage after the show, and celebrities like Samantha Morton and Kylie Minogue were immediately on the phone. In January 2004, his 'Ziggy' dress (from a collection inspired by Bowie) graced the cover of British Vogue on model-of-the-moment Natalia Vodianova. However Saunders has not let success go to his head, and he continues to consult for other labels, including Roland Mouret. Standing by traditional silkscreen printing techniques, he has used these to develop a more couture-style product and process. Each piece is printed by hand. His team are also integral to his label, particularly business partner Sam Logan who styles each show. Still at the beginning of his career, Saunders is deliciously precocious, and his future looks as bright as his vivacious prints.

Ist Jonathan Saunders (Jahrgang 1977) die Zukunft der britischen Mode? Als Absolvent der Glasgow School of Art im Fach Textildruck trug der in Schottland geborene Kreative dazu bei, Mustern in der Mode des 21. Jahrhunderts die angemessene Relevanz zu verleihen. Inspiriert durch alles mögliche, von den strengen Linien des Bauhauses bis zur Exzentrik der Mailänder Memphis-Möbel sind Saunders' Muster eckig und abstrakt und präsentieren sich oft auf der bloßen Leinwand hautenger Silhouetten. Daraus möglicherweise resultierende Strenge wird von Farbschattierungen gemildert, die selbst Pantone noch nicht kennen dürfte. Nach seinem 2002 mit Auszeichnung abgeschlossenen Magisterstudium am Central Saint Martins gewann er mit seiner fesselnden Ästhetik den Lancôme Colour Award. Gleichzeitig erregte er die Aufmerksamkeit von Alexander McQueen, der Saunders bereits zwei Tage nach Studienende anheuerte. Chloé und Pucci sind weitere Nobelmarken, die ihn schon als Consultant engagierten. Obwohl er damit mehr als ausgelastet war, reizte Saunders doch auch der Starruhm des Solisten, so dass er im Februar 2003 das Label Jonathan Saun-

ders lancierte. Seine erfrischenden Farben und sein grafischer Erfindungsreichtum fanden auf Anhieb Anklang. Moderedakteure drängelten sich nach der Show hinter der Bühne, und Prominente wie Samantha Morton oder Kylie Minogue hingen sofort am Telefon. Im Januar 2004 zierte das damals gefragteste Model Natalia Vodianova in Saunders' Ziggy-Kleid (aus einer von Bowie inspirierten Kollektion) den Titel der britischen Vogue. Trotz allem ist dem Designer der Erfolg nicht zu Kopfe gestiegen. Er berät weiterhin auch andere Labels, darunter Roland Mouret. Und er hält an traditionellen Seidendrucktechniken fest, um in der Couture angemessene Ergebnisse zu erzielen. Hier wird jedes Stück von Hand gedruckt. Integraler Bestandteil von Saunders' Labels ist sein Team, insbesondere die Geschäftspartnerin Sam Logan, die jede Show stylt. Und auch wenn er gerade erst am Beginn seiner Karriere steht, ist Saunders entzückend frühreif und seine Zukunft erscheint so strahlend wie seine lebendigen Muster.

Jonathan Saunders (né en 1977) incarne-t-il l'avenir de la mode anglaise? Diplômé en impression textile de l'école d'art de Glasgow, cet Ecossais créatif a fait entrer les imprimés dans la mode du XXIe siècle. Inspiré par toutes sortes de choses, des lignes rigoureuses du Bauhaus à l'excentricité des meubles Memphis milanais, Saunders présente souvent ses imprimés angulaires et abstraits sur la toile vierge de silhouettes moulantes. Ce style sévère est adouci par une palette de couleurs qui semble inventer des nuances jusqu'alors inconnues, même à Pantone. Décrochant son MA avec les honneurs de Central Saint Martins en 2002, son esthétique saisissante lui vaut le Colour Award de Lancôme. Son travail attire également l'attention d'Alexander McQueen, qui embauche Saunders seulement deux jours après l'obtention de son diplôme. Chloé et Pucci comptent aussi parmi les grandes maisons de mode qui le sollicitent en tant que consultant. Bien qu'il soit très occupé par ces noms si prestigieux, il connaît la gloire en solo en février 2003 en lançant la griffe Jonathan Saunders. Les journalistes de mode, éblouis d'emblée par ses couleurs rafraîchissantes et son inventivité graphique, se précipitent dans les coulisses de son défilé, tandis que des stars telles que Samantha Morton et Kylie Minogue se ruent sur leurs téléphones pour le féliciter. En janvier 2004, sa robe « Ziggy » (issue d'une collection inspirée par Bowie) fait la couverture du Vogue anglais, portée par Natalia Vodianova, le mannequin du moment. Pourtant, Saunders n'a pas laissé le succès lui monter à la tête et continue à travailler comme consultant pour d'autres marques, dont Roland Mouret. S'en tenant aux techniques de sérigraphie traditionnelles, il a développé un produit et un procédé mieux adapté à la mode, où chaque pièce est imprimée à la main. Son équipe joue également un rôle essentiel dans le succès de sa griffe, en particulier son associé Sam Logan qui met en style chaque défilé. Alors que sa carrière ne fait que commencer, le délicieusement précoce Jonathan Saunders semble promis à un avenir aussi brillant que ses imprimés.

LAUREN COCHRANE

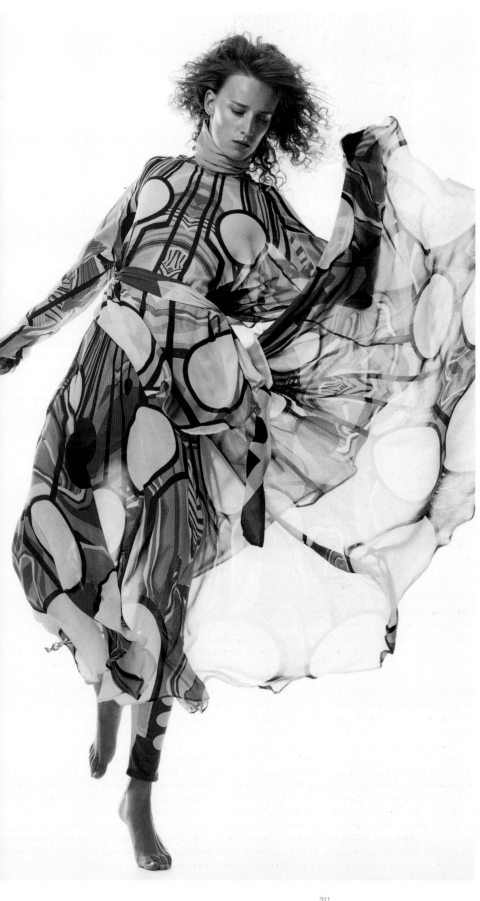

What are your signature designs? Garments with engineered prints that are designed specifically for each individual piece, with emphasis on colour and proportion **What is your favourite piece from any of your collections?** K.I.T Waistcoat and K.I.T Skirt – the last look from the spring/summer 2005 show, and Ruched dress – the first look from the spring/summer 2005 show **What's your ultimate goal?** To master a technique, to maintain a successful business that doesn't require the compromising of an idea. To learn new ways of using textiles and print design and to make sure there is enough time to learn about and collaborate with other areas of design **What inspires you?** Movements in design and fine art that presented a change in thinking and aesthetic, that challenged what was perceived as beautiful. Bauhaus or Pop Art. Also artists' use of colour and the proportion of that colour, for example Richard Hamilton and Mapplethorpe. And those who mastered a craft in order to produce their work, like Brancusi or Victor Vasarely **Who do you have in mind when you design?** I don't have a muse. I never think of an individual, more of a type of woman. **Can fashion still have a political ambition?** Maybe – not with me though. Like any form of design, I suppose it can be used as an indicator of social climate. **Is the idea of creative collaboration important to you?** I think it is vital to any design process whether it is working on a joint project or merely listening to someone's opinion. I really enjoy working on consultancy projects as this gives you insight to another mindset. **Who has been the greatest influence on your career?** Sam Logan. She styles the show and researches the collection with me but is also my business partner and above all has been a friend to me since the beginning **How have your own experiences affected your work as a designer?** Working as a print consultant straight after college gave me a crash course in the practicalities of producing a collection by seeing how to translate an idea into a producible product. Also, coming from a textile background makes you approach fashion design from another perspective **Which is more important in your work: the process or the product?** Both are as vital as each other **Is designing difficult for you, if so, what drives you to continue?** I sometimes have doubts about my ability because I had no formal training in pattern cutting and have had to learn very quickly (and am still learning!). However I'm driven by the fact I am doing something that I love every day, it's following a concept to its completion – from the research to the textile to the finished garment, I work with a great bunch of people who take the piss out of me on a daily basis, and I still get to go in the print room and get my hands dirty.

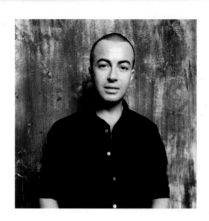

JULIEN MACDONALD

"Ultra-sexy, ultra-glamourous, sparkly and short:
that sums up what I do"

"I don't want to be avant-garde," says Julien Macdonald of his upfront brand of showgirl glamour: "I like beautiful clothes. I don't care what people think about me." Macdonald's love for fashion was inspired by the knitting circles his mother held at home in the Welsh village of Merthyr Tydfil. Studying fashion textiles at Brighton University, his sophisticated knitwear went on to win him a scholarship at London's Royal College of Art. By the time he graduated in 1996, with a spectacular collection styled by Isabella Blow, he had already designed for Koji Tatsuno, Alexander McQueen and Karl Lagerfeld. Lagerfeld spotted Macdonald's knits in the pages of i-D and appointed him head knitwear designer for Chanel collections in 1997. Utterly devoted to the female form, Macdonald reinvigorated knitwear with his glitzy red-carpet creations. His barely-there crochet slips of cobwebs and crystals, shocking frocks and furs guarantee headlines for a devoted throng of starlets and celebrities. Macdonald's catwalk antics – including appearances from the Spice Girls and a Michael Jackson lookalike, plus an autumn/winter 2001 presentation held at the Millennium Dome and directed by hip-hop video supremo Hype Williams – have earned him a reputation as a showmaster. After being crowned the British Glamour Designer of the Year for the first time in 2001 (an award he picked up again in 2003) Macdonald went on to take his high-octane street-style to couture house Givenchy, where he succeeded Alexander McQueen as creative director. Under his direction, sales for the luxury label increased despite some mixed reviews from fashion critics, and with three years under his belt he produced an acclaimed farewell show for autumn/winter 2004. For now, Macdonald continues to present his flamboyant collections in London, where he also oversees his homeware, fragrance and high street lines.

„Ich möchte nicht Avantgarde sein", sagt Julien Macdonald über seine freizügige Revuegirl-Mode. „Ich mag schöne Kleider. Und es ist mir egal, was die Leute von mir denken." Macdonalds Interesse an Mode wurde von den Strickkränzchen seiner Mutter zu Hause in dem walisischen Dorf Merthyr Tydfil geweckt. Nach dem Modestudium an der Universität Brighton brachten ihm seine raffinierten Stricksachen ein Stipendium am Londoner Royal College of Art ein. Als er 1996 mit einer spektakulären, von Isabella Blow gestylten Kollektion seinen Abschluss machte, hatte er bereits für Koji Tatsuno, Alexander McQueen und Karl Lagerfeld entworfen. Lagerfeld entdeckte Macdonalds Strickkreationen in i-D und machte ihn 1997 zum Chefdesigner der Strickwaren für die Chanel-Kollektion. Als absolutem Verehrer weiblicher Formen gelang es Macdonald mit seinen schillernden Kreationen, die für den roten Teppich prädestiniert sind, die Strickmode neu zu beleben. Seine klitzekleinen Häkelslips aus Spinnwebmustern und Kristallen, die schockierenden Kleider und Pelze garantieren der treuen Anhängerschaft aus Starlets und Prominenten Schlagzeilen. Macdonalds Mätzchen auf dem Laufsteg, wie Auftritte der Spice Girls und eines Michael-Jackson-Doubles

oder die Präsentation der Kollektion Herbst/Winter 2001 im Millennium Dome unter der Regie des Hip-Hop-Videostars Hype Williams, haben ihm den Ruf eines Showmasters eingebracht und seinen Status als König der Londoner Glitzerwelt gefestigt. Nach der ersten Auszeichnung als British Glamour Designer of the Year 2001 (ein Preis, der ihm auch 2003 verliehen wurde) machte Macdonald sich daran, seinen hochklassigen Street Style auf die Couture bei Givenchy zu übertragen, wo er als Creative Director die Nachfolge von Alexander McQueen antrat. Unter seiner Leitung stiegen die Verkaufszahlen des Luxuslabels, auch wenn einige Journalisten ihn kritisierten. Nach drei Jahren lieferte er mit der Kollektion für Herbst/Winter 2004 eine hochgelobte Abschiedsshow. Gegenwärtig präsentiert Macdonald seine extravaganten Kollektionen weiterhin in London, wo er auch über seine Wohnkollektion, seine Düfte und hochwertigen Street-Labels wacht.

« Je ne cherche pas à être avant-garde », dit Julien Macdonald de son glamour sans détour digne des showgirls de Las Vegas : « J'aime les beaux vêtements. Je me fiche pas mal de ce que les gens pensent de moi ». La passion de Macdonald pour la mode est née dans les cercles de tricot que sa mère organisait chez eux dans le village gallois de Merthyr Tydfil. Après avoir étudié le textile à l'Université de Brighton, sa maille sophistiquée lui vaut une bourse d'études pour le Royal College of Art de Londres. Lorsqu'il en sort diplômé en 1996 avec une collection spectaculaire mise en style par Isabella Blow, il a déjà collaboré avec Koji Tatsuno, Alexander McQueen et Karl Lagerfeld. Ce dernier, qui avait repéré les créations de Macdonald dans les pages du magazine i-D, l'embauche comme responsable de la maille des collections Chanel en 1997. Entièrement dévoué aux formes du corps féminin, Macdonald a ressuscité la maille à travers ses créations brillantes et ultra-glamour. Ses combinaisons très osées réalisées au crochet en toile d'araignée et ornées de cristaux, ses robes choquantes et ses fourrures garantissent la une des journaux à une foule dévouée de starlettes et autres célébrités. Grâce à l'extravagance de ses défilés, avec des apparitions des Spice Girls et d'un sosie de Michael Jackson, sans oublier la présentation de sa collection automne/hiver 2001 au Millennium Dome sous la direction du parrain de la vidéo hip-hop Hype Williams, Macdonald s'est forgé une réputation de maître du spectacle. Couronné British Glamour Designer of the Year pour la première fois en 2001 (un prix qu'il raflera de nouveau en 2003), Macdonald traduit son streetwear explosif pour la maison Givenchy, où il succède à Alexander McQueen en tant que directeur de la création. Sous son impulsion, la griffe de luxe voit ses ventes décoller en dépit de critiques mitigées, mais après trois années à ce poste, Macdonald fait ses adieux à Givenchy avec une collection automne/hiver 2004 cette fois largement plébiscitée. Aujourd'hui, il continue de présenter ses flamboyantes collections à Londres, d'où il supervise également ses lignes de mobilier, de parfums et de grande diffusion.

JAMIE HUCKBODY

What are your signature designs? Ultra-sexy, ultra-glamorous, sparkly and short: that sums up what I do **What's your favourite piece from any of your collections?** The hand crocheted or cobweb knits are my favourites. There's nothing of them, so they look best on people with gorgeous bodies who just want to squeeze into something small **How would you describe your work?** It's dangerous, exciting, high-octane glamour but, most of all, it's fun. I create clothes people would notice when you walk into a room **What's your ultimate goal?** To build up both my brand name and my label – I've got a goal in both fashion and power **What inspires you?** Life itself **Can fashion still have a political ambition?** I think fashion is basically a service provider, it's as simple as that **Who do you have in mind when you design?** I suppose I design for a kind of Amazonian woman; someone who's not afraid of her body and wants to go out and show it **Is the idea of creative collaboration important to you?** As a designer you basically work on your own. You have an idea for a collection and then you just bring in different people to help you achieve it. The designer is the person it stems from – without them, there's nothing **Who has been the greatest influence on your career?** I spent two years working with Karl Lagerfeld at Chanel and he educated me in the way a woman with culture and status dresses **How have your own experiences affected your work as a designer?** I think that the older you get, the more interesting you become as a person and the more interesting you become as a designer. **Which is more important in your work: the process or the product?** People don't pay attention to the process – they just want the product **Is designing difficult for you and, if so, what drives you to continue?** I don't think designing is difficult. What is difficult is managing and running a business **Have you ever been influenced or moved by the reaction to your designs?** There's nothing more satisfying than seeing a woman looking fantastic in one of your outfits. My aim is to make women feel comfortable, happy and glamorous **What's your definition of beauty?** Beauty is in the eye of the beholder, as they say. Beauty can be very cruel or very pretty. It's a difficult one **What's your philosophy?** I don't really have one. I just want to design clothes and be happy and enjoy what I do – if you don't enjoy it, give up **What is the most important lesson you've learned?** Always be nice.

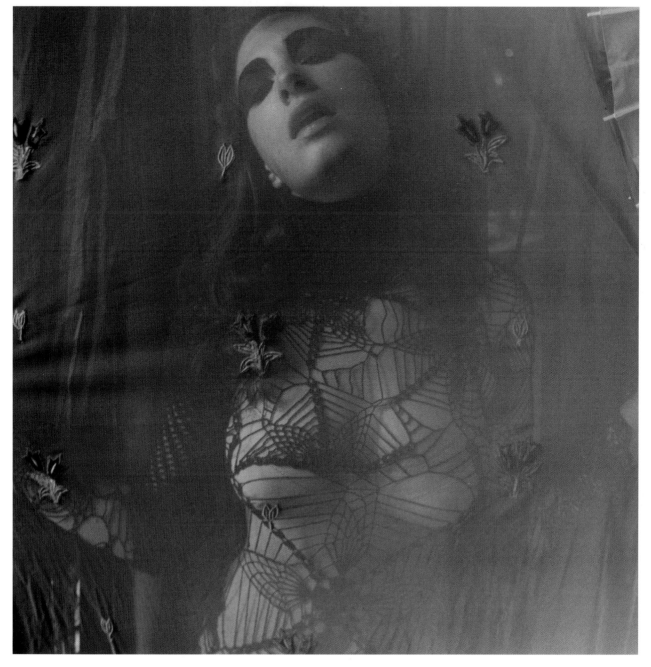

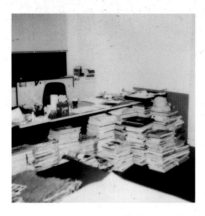

JUNYA WATANABE

"I do what I do and those who sympathise with my work will wear it"

Junya Watanabe (born Tokyo, 1961) is the much-fêted protégé of Rei Kawakubo. Graduating from Bunka Fashion College in 1984, he immediately joined Comme des Garçons as a pattern-cutter. By 1987 he was designing their Tricot line. He presented his first solo collection in 1992 at the Tokyo collections; a year later, he showed at Paris Fashion Week. (Although designing under his own name, he is still employed by Comme des Garçons, who fund and produce the collections.) Despite an obvious debt to Rei Kawakubo in his work, Watanabe still stands apart from his mentor and friend with a vision that is indisputably his own. He has often used technical or functional fabrics, creating clothes that still retain a sense of calm and femininity. This was displayed most explicitly at his autumn/winter 1999 show, where the catwalk was under a constant shower of water: rain seemed to splash off the outfits, which were created in fabric by the Japanese company Toray, who develop materials for extreme conditions. Despite the wealth of creativity on display, Watanabe's clothes were a response to more fundamental issues: a practical answer to conditions and lifestyles. In contrast to this, Watanabe's designs are also an exercise in sensitivity and, through his remarkably complex pattern-cutting, his sculptural clothing presents a virtually unrivalled delicacy. In 2001, Watanabe presented his first menswear collection in Paris. Today, he is one of the most celebrated designers in Paris fashion.

Der 1961 in Tokio geborene Junya Watanabe ist der viel gefeierte Protegé von Rei Kawakubo. Unmittelbar nach seinem Abschluss am Bunka Fashion College 1984 fing er als Zuschneider bei Comme des Garçons an. 1987 entwarf er bereits die Nebenlinie Tricot des japanischen Modehauses. Die erste Solokollektion präsentierte Watanabe dann 1992 in Tokio, ein Jahr später war er auf der Pariser Modewoche vertreten. (Auch wenn er inzwischen unter eigenem Namen entwirft, ist der Japaner noch Angestellter des Unternehmens Comme des Garçons, das seine Kollektionen auch finanziert und produziert.) Obwohl er in seiner Arbeit von Rei Kawakubo entscheidend beeinflusst wurde, unterscheidet sich Watanabe doch mit einer zweifellos eigenständigen Vision von seiner Mentorin und Freundin. Oft benutzt er Mikrofasern und andere funktionale Stoffe für seine Kreationen, die dennoch eine Aura von Gelassenheit und Weiblichkeit besitzen. Am deutlichsten wurde dies bisher bei seiner Schau für Herbst/Winter 1999, als er den Catwalk ununterbrochen beregnen ließ. Das Wasser schien von den Outfits abzuperlen, die aus einem Material der japanischen Firma Toray gefertigt waren. Dieses Unternehmen ist auf die Herstellung von Geweben für Extrembedingungen spezialisiert. Doch trotz dieser originellen Präsentation waren die Kreationen von Watanabe die Reaktion auf fundamentalere Herausforderungen, nämlich eine praktische Antwort auf verschiedene Lebensumstände und -stile. Zugleich ist die Mode des Japaners aber auch eine Art Sensitivitäts-

training, und dank seiner bemerkenswert komplexen Schnitte sind die skulpturalen Entwürfe auch von einer unvergleichlichen Zartheit. 2001 präsentierte Watanabe seine erste Herrenkollektion in Paris. Hier verzichtete der Designer auf den großen handwerklichen Aufwand, den er für seine Damenmode betreibt, und verfremdete eher schlichte Männerkleidung. Für seine Debütshow – einer Kooperation mit Levi's – schien er Americana im Hinterkopf zu haben, denn man sah jede Menge Jeanshosen und -jacken. Bei der zweiten Schau kümmerte er sich dagegen nicht um eine akademische Ikonografie und setzte vor allem auf optische Effekte von Materialien und Farben. Wie es aussieht, wird Watanabe irgendwann so einflussreich sein wie seine berühmten japanischen Vorgänger.

Junya Watanabe (né en 1961 à Tokyo) est le célèbre protégé de Rei Kawakubo. Une fois diplômé du Bunka Fashion College en 1984, il commence immédiatement à travailler chez Comme des Garçons en tant que traceur de patrons. En 1987, il dessine déjà pour la ligne Tricot. Il présente sa première collection « en solo » aux défilés de Tokyo ; un an plus tard, il est invité à la Semaine de la Mode de Paris (bien qu'il dessine sous son propre nom, Watanabe est toujours employé par Comme des Garçons, qui finance et produit ses collections). Très marqué par l'influence de Rei Kawakubo, le travail de Watanabe se distingue toutefois de celui de son amie et mentor grâce à une approche indiscutablement personnelle. Les vêtements qu'il taille souvent dans des tissus techno et fonctionnels n'en sont pas moins empreints de calme et de féminité. Son talent apparaît de façon explicite à l'occasion de son défilé automne/hiver 1999, où les mannequins défilent sur un podium constamment aspergé d'eau : les gouttes de pluie rebondissent sur les vêtements coupés dans un tissu produit par Toray, une entreprise japonaise qui développe des matériaux résistant aux conditions extrêmes. Bien qu'ils démontrent l'immense créativité de Watanabe, ses vêtements apportent avant tout une réponse à des problèmes plus fondamentaux, une solution pratique aux divers climats et modes de vie. Ils témoignent également de la grande sensibilité du créateur qui, grâce à des coupes d'une complexité remarquable, confère à ses pièces sculpturales une délicatesse presque incomparable. En 2001, Watanabe présente sa première collection pour homme à Paris. Renonçant au savoir-faire artisanal qui caractérise sa ligne pour femme, il préfère proposer sa vision décalée des basiques masculins. Inspiré en partie par un style américain des plus « country », son premier défilé, en collaboration avec Levi's, fait la part belle aux jeans et aux vestes en denim. Son second défilé met en avant l'iconographie des uniformes universitaires, où tissus et couleurs se fondent pour créer des effets visuels détonants. Issu de la nouvelle génération de créateurs japonais, Watanabe semble aujourd'hui bien parti pour devenir aussi influent que ses prestigieux prédécesseurs.

MARCUS ROSS

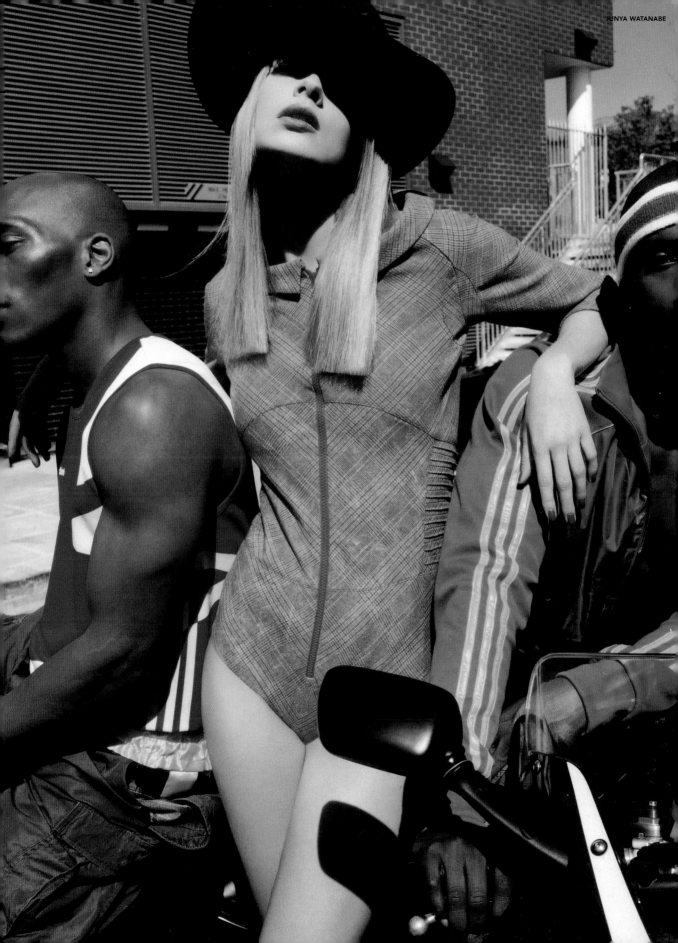

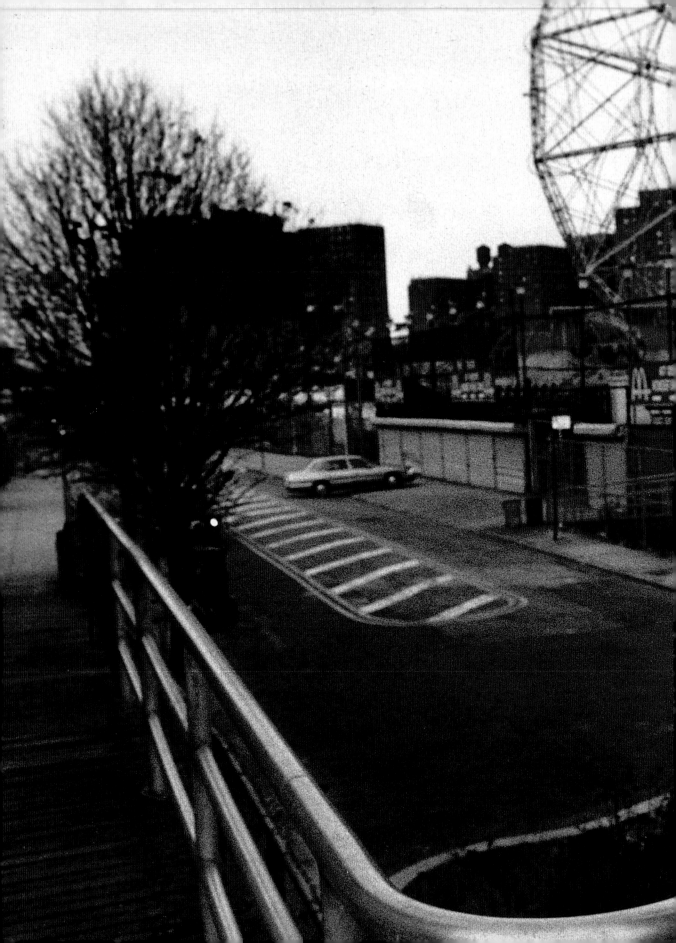

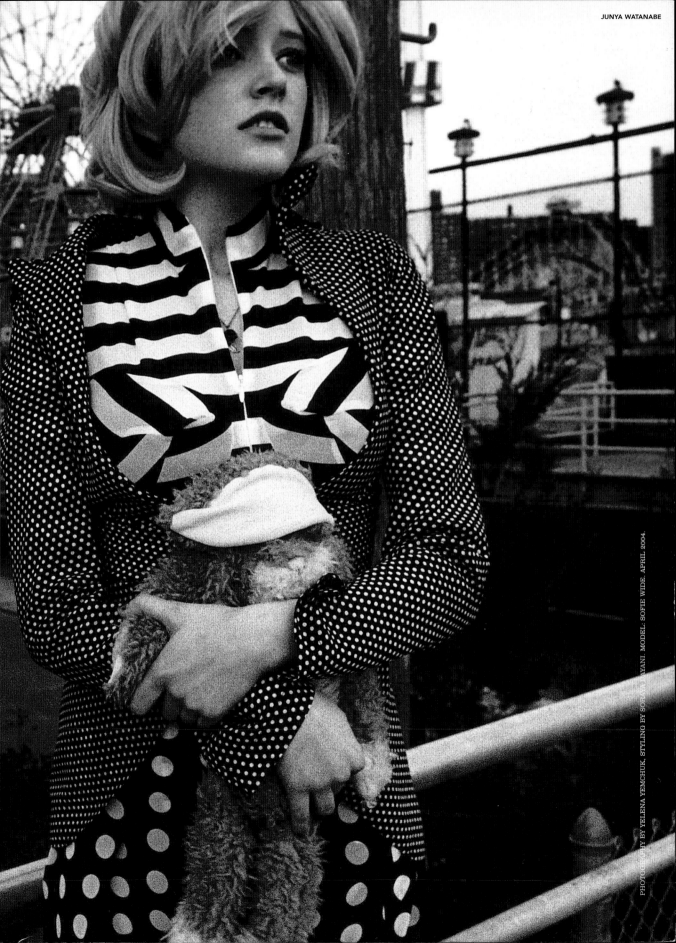

PHOTOGRAPHY BY YELENA YEMCHUK. STYLING BY SORAYA DAYANI. MODEL: SOFIE WIDE. APRIL, 2004.

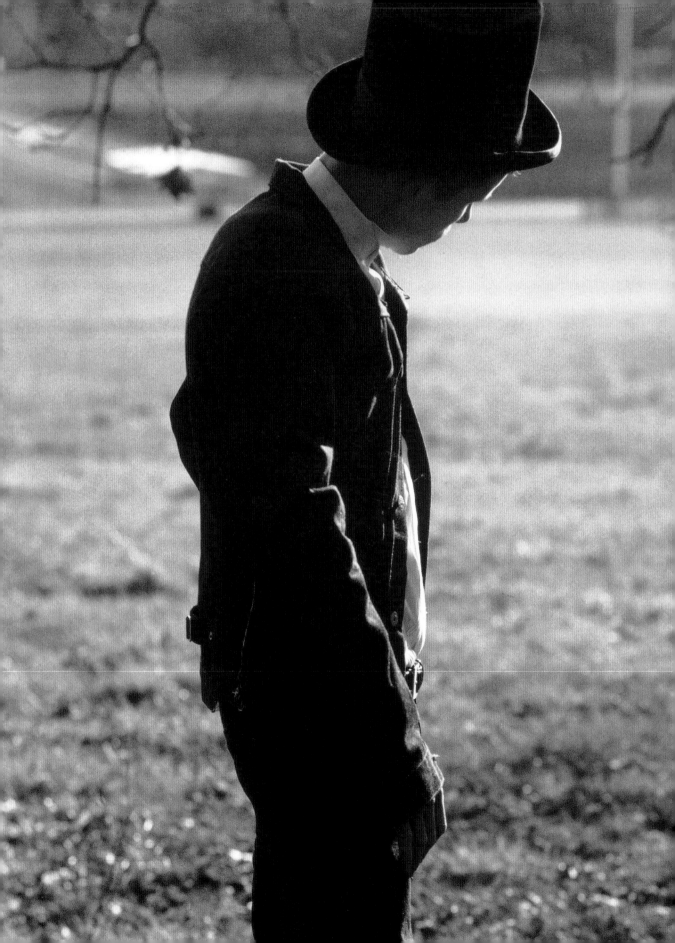

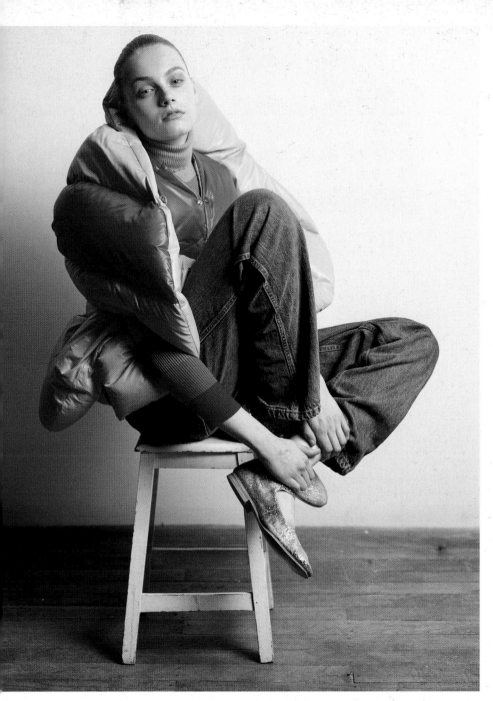

How would you describe your work? Strength and tenderness that I try my best every time to express in the clothes, in a straightforward way **What's your ultimate goal?** I have the same attitude towards work and creativity that Rei Kawakubo and all of us at Comme des Garçons have **What inspires you?** To make strong clothes **Can fashion still have a political ambition?** While I respect the viewpoint that fashion reflects social and political issues, that is not the basis of my designs **Who do you have in mind when you design?** The ideal customer – that is, I do what I do, and those who sympathise with my work will wear it **Is the idea of creative collaboration important to you?** It is an inestimable experience and enrichment to work with companies such as Levi's, to come into contact with the depth of their technique and expertise and the weight of history **Who has been the greatest influence on your career?** I learned everything about creation at Comme des Garçons **Which is more important in your work: the process or the product?** Both. In my women's collection, each time I put all my energy into new challenges, searching for new patterns and innovative fabrics. But I'm also conscious that groping for new forms is not everything in clothes-making **Have you ever been influenced or moved by the reaction to your designs?** I have never thought about whether or not I am successful. My aim is only to create a good collection.

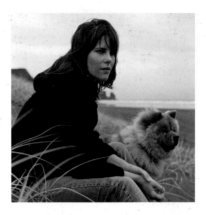

KAREN WALKER

"I think that playing in the global fashion game
while living in the forest in New Zealand
brings a certain casualness to my work"

Teenage runaways, misfit schoolgirls and daydreams of roguish monsters: Karen Walker is fascinated with the outsider. Born in Auckland, New Zealand, in 1969, Walker left high school at 18, bypassed fashion college and set about learning to pattern-cut. With her mother's sewing machine and $100, Walker created her first piece, a man's shirt in a clash of oversized Liberty prints. She sold it, made another and within three years, had her first Auckland store. After her first show in London in 1999, her look was instantly adopted by dressed-down individualists. There is nothing pretentious or cumbersome about her work. Simplicity is matched with accomplished tailoring; luxury ingredients are edited against quirky, hand-drawn prints. Walker constructs characters for her collections, outsiders each playing out a dark fiction: '30s aviator Amelia Earhart crash-landing on an island of cannibals is one playful inspiration. Besides her three New Zealand stores, Walker has a strong international presence. She began to design an exclusive Karen Walker for New Look label for the British mass-market store in 2002. In 2004 she launched Karen Walker Runaway, a capsule collection of affordable classics, alongside a major jewellery collection, and has produced leftfield projects involving sunglasses, exclusive household paints and a brand of vodka. There is a feel of genuine exuberance in her collections with strong graphics and prints resulting in a colourful sense of whimsy. Yet, for all the perceived cuteness of Walker's work, she designs for a self-confident, creative woman. Karen Walker's outsider is bold, tough and focused, yet embodies a clash of opposites.

Jugendliche Ausreißer, Mauerblümchen und Tagträume von schalkhaften Monstern – Karen Walker ist fasziniert vom Außenseiter schlechthin. Geboren wurde sie 1969 in Auckland, Neuseeland. Mit 18 Jahren verließ sie die Highschool, überging das Mode-College und machte sich daran, das Musterschneiden zu lernen. Mit der Nähmaschine ihrer Mutter und 100 Dollar in der Tasche schneiderte sie ihr erstes Stück, ein Herrenhemd mit überdimensionalem, knalligem Liberty-Muster. Sie verkaufte es, nähte ein weiteres, und innerhalb von drei Jahren hatte sie ihren ersten Laden in Auckland. Nach ihrer ersten Schau in London 1999 wurde ihr Look sofort von zurückhaltend gekleideten Individualisten angenommen. An ihren Arbeiten ist nichts Prätentiöses oder Schwerfälliges. Schlichtheit wird mit meisterhafter Schneiderei kombiniert; luxuriöse Ingredienzien treffen auf eigenwillige, handgezeichnete Muster. Walker sucht sich Persönlichkeiten für ihre Kollektionen, Außenseiter in düsteren Fantasiegeschichten: Die Fliegerin Amelia Earhart, die in den 1930er Jahren auf einer von Kannibalen bewohnten Insel notlandete, ist eine dieser verspielten Inspiratio-

nen. Neben ihren drei Läden in Neuseeland ist Walker auch international stark vertreten. So begann sie 2002 eine exklusive Linie namens Karen Walker für das Label New Look einer britischen Kette zu entwerfen. 2004 präsentierte sie Karen Walker Runaway, eine Minikollektion erschwinglicher Klassiker, dazu eine umfangreiche Schmuckkollektion. Zu den etwas ungewöhnlicheren Produkten ihrer Palette zählen Sonnenbrillen, exklusive Wandfarben und eine eigene Wodkamarke. Ihre Kollektionen vermitteln den Eindruck von authentischer Opulenz. Kräftige grafische Muster sorgen für gute Laune. So süß man Walkers Arbeit aber auch finden mag, sie designt für die selbstbewusste, kreative Frau. Ihre Außenseiterinnen sind stark, tough und zielbewusst, verkörpern aber auch das Aufeinanderprallen von Gegensätzen.

Adolescents fugueurs, écolières inadaptées et rêves de monstres charmants : Karen Walker est fascinée par les outsiders. Née en 1969 à Auckland en Nouvelle-Zélande, elle quitte le lycée à 18 ans. Peu séduite par les écoles de mode, elle préfère se former à la coupe de patrons. Avec la machine à coudre de sa mère et 100 dollars en poche, Karen Walker crée son tout premier vêtement sous la forme d'une chemise pour homme aux imprimés Liberty surdimensionnés et aux contrastes choquants. Elle réussit à la vendre, en crée une autre et en l'espace de trois ans, ouvre sa première boutique à Auckland. Dès son premier défilé londonien en 1999, son look est immédiatement adopté par les individualistes fans de simplicité. Son travail n'a rien de prétentieux ni de pesant. La simplicité s'allie à des coupes maîtrisées, où les ingrédients du luxe se transforment au contact d'imprimés étranges dessinés à la main. Pour ses collections, Karen Walker invente des personnages, des rebelles tout droit sortis d'une sombre fiction : par exemple, elle s'inspire non sans humour de l'histoire de l'aviatrice des années 30, Amelia Earhart, dont l'avion s'était écrasé sur une île habitée par des cannibales. Outre ses trois boutiques de Nouvelle-Zélande, Karen Walker bénéficie d'une solide présence internationale. En 2002, elle crée une griffe exclusive baptisée Karen Walker for New Look pour le grand détaillant britannique. En 2004, elle lance Karen Walker Runaway, une mini-collection de classiques abordables, ainsi qu'une vaste collection de bijoux, et produit d'autres projets annexes dans les domaines des lunettes de soleil, de la peinture de luxe et même une vodka à son nom. Ses collections dégagent une impression d'authentique exubérance, avec des graphiques et des imprimés voyants qui expriment sa vision colorée de la fantaisie. Bien que son travail puisse être perçu comme joli et mignon, elle s'adresse néanmoins à une femme créative et sûre d'elle. L'outsider audacieux, fort et déterminé que chérit Karen Walker incarne donc le choc des contraires. DAN JONES

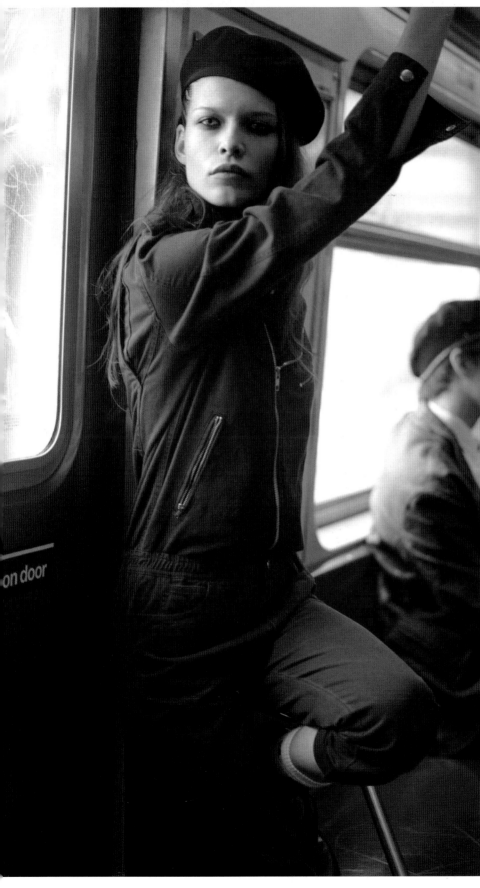

on door

What are your signature designs? Everyday clothes – we cut a good pant, we do a good tailored jacket, our T-shirt graphics and fabric graphics have a following and we do a nice party dress that's glam without being too red carpet **What is your favourite piece from any of your collections?** I really love the poppy print cotton sundress from our spring/summer 2005 collection. It captures the essence of what we stand for – effortless and fun **How would you describe your work?** High casual. Effortless and unpretentious **What's your ultimate goal?** To make clothes that become favourite pieces **What inspires you?** I'm inspired by outsiders and imperfection, by characters who don't fit in, characters like Ally Sheedy in 'The Breakfast Club', 'Annie Hall' or 'Amelia Earhart' **Can fashion still have a political ambition?** Sure, but at the end of the day if the pants don't make your bum look smaller no one's going to wear them **Who do you have in mind when you design?** Me and my friends **Is the idea of creative collaboration important to you?** Yes, I love collaborating with other people. We've worked with Heathermary Jackson for many seasons now and it's great every season. I also like working with other people on various projects **Who has been the greatest influence on your career?** My husband Mikhail **How have your own experiences affected your work as a designer?** I think that playing in the global fashion game while living in the forest in New Zealand brings a certain casualness to my work and also the isolation gives me an empathy with the outsider character I love so much **Which is more important in your work: the process or the product?** The product, it doesn't really matter how you get there as long as you get there **Is designing difficult for you?** It's a mixture of torture and ecstasy **Have you ever been influenced or moved by the reaction to your designs?** It's always a thrill to get a nod from people I respect **What's your definition of beauty?** Effortlessness **What's your philosophy?** Don't overcook it **What is the most important lesson you've learned?** Do it cause it feels good.

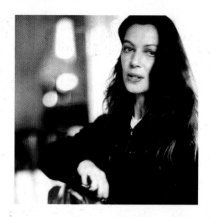

KATHARINE HAMNETT

"Thank God I always wore dark glasses in
the '80s. Nobody recognises me now"

For many fans, Katharine Hamnett defines '80s style. Her trademark use of functional fabrics such as parachute silk and cotton jersey has continued to inspire many in the industry since. She spearheaded a number of style directions including the military look, utility fashion, and casual day-to-evening sportswear, all of which still resonate today. And 21 years after her logo T-shirts first became front-page news (in 1984 she famously met Mrs Thatcher and wore one that read: '58% Don't Want Pershing') Hamnett can still make the fashion world sit up and pay attention to her ideas. Born in 1948, she graduated from Saint Martins college in 1969 and freelanced for 10 years before setting up her own label, Katharine Hamnett London. This was followed in 1981 by menswear and a denim diffusion range in 1982. She became the BFC's Designer of The Year in 1984 and her ad campaigns helped to launch the careers of photographers including Juergen Teller, Terry Richardson and Ellen Von Unwerth. Projects such as her flagship stores in London's Brompton Cross and Sloane Street, designed by Norman Foster, Nigel Coates and David Chipperfield, were famous for their forward-thinking retail design. A political conscience has always been key to the Katharine Hamnett ethos. She created anti-war T-shirts ('Life is Sacred') in 2003 that were widely worn by peace protesters marching in London; Naomi Campbell modelled a 'Use a Condom' design for Hamnett's spring/summer 2004 catwalk show in order to highlight the designer's concern over the Aids epidemic in Africa. She decided to relaunch as Katharine E Hamnett for autumn/winter 2005 and often voices her concerns about unethical and non-environmental manufacturing processes.

Für viele Fans verkörpert Katharine Hamnett den Stil der 1980er Jahre. Ihr Markenzeichen ist die Verwendung funktionaler Materialien wie Fallschirmseide und Baumwolljersey, womit sie seither viele in der Modeindustrie inspiriert hat. Sie war Vorkämpferin für viele Stilrichtungen wie etwa den Military Look, Utility Fashion und lässige Sportswear für tagsüber und abends. All diese Trends wirken bis heute fort. Und selbst 21 Jahre, nachdem sie mit ihren „Slogan"-T-Shirts erstmals Schlagzeilen machte (unvergessen, wie sie 1984 bei einem Treffen mit Margaret Thatcher ein T-Shirt mit dem Aufdruck „58% Don't Want Pershing" trug), gelingt es Hamnett immer noch, in der Modewelt für Aufmerksamkeit zu sorgen. Die 1948 geborene Designerin machte 1969 ihren Abschluss am Central Saint Martins. Danach war sie zehn Jahre lang freischaffend tätig, bevor sie ihr eigenes Label – Katharine Hamnett London – gründete. 1981 kam Herrenmode dazu, 1982 eine Nebenlinie für Jeans. Den Titel BFC's Designer of The Year erhielt Hamnett 1984. Nebenbei beflügelten ihre Werbekampagnen auch die Karrieren von Fotografen wie Jürgen Teller, Terry Richardson und Ellen von Unwerth. Projekte wie ihre Londoner

Flagship Stores in der Brompton Cross und der Sloane Street nach Entwürfen von Norman Foster, Nigel Coates und David Chipperfield erregten durch ihr innovatives Ladenkonzept Aufsehen. Katharine Hamnetts Ethos war schon immer von poltischem Bewusstsein geprägt. So kreierte sie T-Shirts gegen den Krieg („Life is Sacred"), die 2003 unter den Londoner Friedensdemonstranten sehr verbreitet waren. In Hamnetts Catwalk Show für Frühjahr/Sommer 2004 präsentierte Naomi Campbell den Schriftzug „Use a Condom", um die Betroffenheit der Designerin angesichts der Ausmaße der Aids-Epidemie in Afrika zum Ausdruck zu bringen. Für die Kollektion Herbst/Winter 2005 entschloss sie sich zu einem Relaunch ihres Labels unter dem Namen Katharine E Hamnett und kritisiert nach wie vor unmoralische und umweltschädliche Produktionsbedingungen.

Aux yeux de ses nombreux fans, Katharine Hamnett est « la » créatrice des années 80. Son utilisation caractéristique des tissus utilitaires tels que les soies de parachute et le jersey de coton continue depuis à inspirer bon nombre de stylistes. Elle a lancé de nombreuses tendances, notamment le look militaire, la mode utilitaire et un sportswear décontracté à porter le jour comme le soir, autant d'innovations qui résonnent encore de nos jours. 21 ans après que ses T-shirts à slogan aient fait la une des journaux (en 1984, elle a rencontré Margaret Thatcher vêtue d'un T-shirt proclamant : « 58% Don't Want Pershing »), Katharine Hamnett peut encore étonner l'univers de la mode et attirer l'attention sur ses idées. Née en 1948, elle sort diplômée de Central Saint Martins en 1969 et travaille en free-lance pendant 10 ans avant de fonder sa propre griffe, Katharine Hamnett London, qui sera suivie d'une ligne pour homme en 1981 et d'une autre collection en denim en 1982. Elle est nommée British Designer of the Year en 1984, et ses campagnes publicitaires donnent un coup de pouce aux carrières des photographes Juergen Teller, Terry Richardson et Ellen Von Unwerth. Des projets tels que ses boutiques de Brompton Cross et Sloane Street à Londres, conçues par Norman Foster, Nigel Coates et David Chipperfield, deviennent célèbres pour leur conception visionnaire en matière d'espace de vente. Une certaine conscience politique occupe toujours une place centrale dans l'éthique de Katharine Hamnett. En 2003, elle a créé des T-shirts anti-guerre (« La vie est sacrée ») largement portés par les défenseurs de la paix qui manifestaient à Londres ; lors de son défilé printemps/été 2004, Naomi Campbell arborait un T-shirt proclamant « Mettez des capotes » afin d'exprimer les inquiétudes de la créatrice quant à l'épidémie de sida en Afrique. Pour la saison automne/hiver 2005, elle décide de relancer sa griffe sous le nom de « Katharine E Hamnett » et continue à clamer son inquiétude face aux procédés de fabrication non équitables et nuisibles à l'environnement.

TERRY NEWMAN

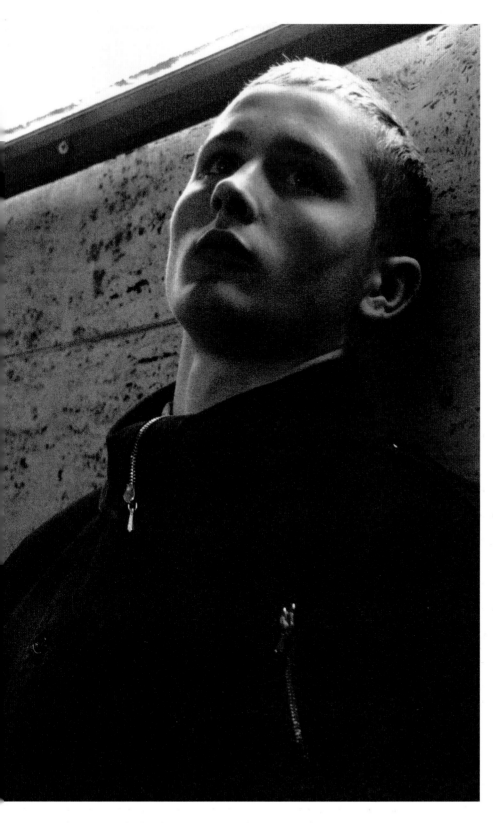

What are your signature designs? Nice clothes you don't throw away **What is your favourite piece from any of your collections?** I am not interested in what I have done before **How would you describe your work?** Creating a fresh persona **What's your ultimate goal?** Reforesting the desert **What inspires you?** Banishing ugliness, not having anything to wear. Being horrified by the clothes your date is wearing **Can fashion still have a political ambition?** Yes, industry runs the planet and the fashion industry is the fourth largest. How we design and consume fashion to an extent decides our future **Who do you have in mind when you design?** Myself, my friends, beautiful strangers **Is the idea of creative collaboration important to you?** No, I'm a loner with occasional exceptions, design by committee is death **Who has been the greatest influence on your career?** My parents, movies and everybody I've ever met or read **How have your own experiences affected your work as a designer?** Every experience permanently alters the way you perceive beauty **Which is more important in your work: the process or the product?** The idea **Is designing difficult for you, if so, what drives you to continue?** It's easy when you're happy. Bills and the fact that every thousand pair of organic cotton trousers we sell means another African farmer can convert from pesticide intensive farming to growing cotton organically which has the potential to deliver a fifty percent increase in income as well as huge health benefits **Have you ever been influenced or moved by the reaction to your designs?** I am really touched by people who keep on contacting us and say that I made the best pair of trousers they ever had or Andy Birkin at the Stop the War Coalition telling me that the marches they organised all over the world against the invasion of Iraq, came from the T-shirts we did straight after September 11th after Bush declared 'The War on Terror': STOP AND THINK, NO WAR, LIFE IS SACRED **What's your definition of beauty?** The outward appearance of an inner quality **What's your philosophy?** If you take on something you have to do it with a passion, to the best of your ability or not at all **What is the most important lesson you've learned?** Fame is a mistake, thank God I always wore dark glasses in the '80s so nobody recognises me.

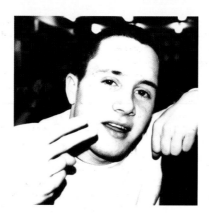

KIM JONES

"I find it very easy to get inspired"

When Kim Jones' models walked casually down the catwalk for his MA menswear at Central Saint Martins in 2001, it was like a toke on a bong for a sober Snoop Dogg. The relief and easiness was captivating. Kim Jones, who had studied illustration in Brighton and Camberwell before Saint Martins, came along at the perfect time: a time when boys who buy clothes know reference points like the back of their hand. On his graduation runway Jones styled the models in limited edition Vans and Vision Streetwear trainers (he's an avid collector) and old faded Levi's. Printed T-shirts were inspired by underground Chicago house club Edge Of The Looking Glass (also the name of his newly opened Tokyo store); Disney prints merged with classic Stüssy prints, the repeat logo replaced with the heads of the Seven Dwarves. Post-show, a symbiotic relationship blossomed between Jones and stylist Nicola Formichetti, a collaboration still going strong to this day. Each season saw the Kim Jones collection grow in design, popularity and concept, whilst maintaining a sense of silliness expertly matched with commercial viability. Collaborations with Louis Vuitton, Topman, Mulberry, Absolut and Umbro all followed. Although based in London, after he showed for the first time in the UK capital in 2003, Jones moved his catwalk presentations to Paris. From Disney-style doodles and cartoon Pacman prints to long-forgotten club flyers, Jones elevates the mundane and champions the throwaway, all with a tireless sense of fun. "I try to see 'The Simpsons' every day and any horror films that are any good. I'm also listening to DJ Pierre tapes and music for the next show," he explains. But he's not just a laugh-a-minute type of guy. Kim Jones is a talent that, like a big old tough yukka plant, continues to grow stronger each season.

Als Kim Jones' Models bei seiner Abschlusskollektion in Männermode am Central Saint Martins im Jahr 2001 lässig den Catwalk entlangschlenderten, da war das wie ein Zug aus der Wasserpfeife für einen nüchternen Snoop Dogg. Die Abwechslung und Leichtigkeit waren faszinierend. Kim Jones hatte vor seiner Zeit am Saint Martins in Brighton und Camberwell Illustration studiert und erwischte damals den perfekten Zeitpunkt: Jungs, die sich etwas zum Anziehen kaufen wollten, kannten entsprechende Bezugspunkte wie ihre Westentasche. Bei seiner Abschluss-Schau steckte Jones die Models in Turnschuhe von Vans und Vision Streetwear aus limitierten Auflagen (er ist ein leidenschaftlicher Sammler) sowie in alte, ausgeblichene Levi's. Die bedruckten T-Shirts waren inspiriert vom Chicagoer Underground House Club Edge of the Looking Glas (übrigens auch der Name seines neu eröffneten Ladens in Tokio). Disney-Motive verschwammen mit klassischen Stüssy-Prints, anstelle des Logos waren die Köpfe der Sieben Zwerge zu sehen. Nach dieser Show entwickelte sich eine symbiotische Beziehung zwischen Jones und der visionären Stylistin Nicola Formichetti. Bis heute arbeiten die beiden eng zusammen. Die Kollektionen nahmen Saison für Saison an Kreativität, Popularität und Konzeptionalität zu, bewahr-

ten sich aber zugleich eine gewisse Albernheit, die gekonnt mit kommerzieller Lebensfähigkeit gepaart war. Es kam zu Kooperationen mit Louis Vuitton, Topman, Mulberry, Absolut und Umbro. Und obwohl er seinen Stützpunkt in London behielt, nachdem er die erste Schau in der britischen Metropole absolviert hatte, verlegte Jones seine Laufsteg-Präsentationen nach Paris. Von Disneyfiguren und Pacman-Comics bis zu längst verjährten Programmzetteln für Clubs – Kim überhöht Alltägliches und tritt für Wegwerfartikel ein, und das alles mit einem unerschöpflichen Sinn für Humor. „Ich versuche, jeden Tag die Simpsons zu sehen und dazu alle Horrorfilme, die irgendwie nützlich sein könnten. Ich höre mir auch Tapes von DJ Pierre und Musik für die nächste Show an", erklärt er. Dabei ist Jones trotzdem keine Lachnummer für einen Auftritt. Vielmehr ähnelt sein Talent einer großen alten Yuccapalme, die mit jeder Saison noch ein bisschen kräftiger wird.

En 2001, quand les mannequins de Kim Jones défilent nonchalamment le long du podium pour son MA en mode masculine à Central Saint Martins, l'effet produit revient à laisser un Snoop Dogg encore à jeun tirer une taf sur son bong. En effet, cette collection dégage un sens du soulagement et de la facilité absolument captivant. Kim Jones, qui avait étudié l'illustration à Brighton et à Camberwell avant de s'inscrire à Saint Martins, est arrivé à point nommé dans une époque où les garçons qui achètent des vêtements connaissent les dernières tendances comme leur poche. Pour son défilé de fin d'études, il habille ses mannequins de survêtements Vans et Vision Streetwear en édition limitée (qu'il collectionne avidement) et de vieux jeans Levi's délavés. Ses T-shirts imprimés s'inspirent d'Edge Of The Looking Glass, célèbre club de house music de Chicago (un nom dont il baptise sa toute nouvelle boutique de Tokyo) ; les imprimés Disney fusionnent avec les graphiques Stüssy classiques, où le double logo est remplacé par les têtes des Sept Nains. Après ce défilé, une relation symbiotique se noue entre Jones et le styliste visionnaire Nicola Formichetti, une collaboration encore d'actualité à ce jour. Au fil des saisons, la collection Kim Jones gagne en maturité, en popularité et en concept, tout en conservant un côté idiot intelligemment conjugué à la viabilité commerciale. S'ensuivent des collaborations avec Louis Vuitton, Topman, Mulberry, Absolut et Umbro. Bien qu'il soit installé à Londres, Jones délaisse les podiums londoniens pour Paris après sa première présentation dans la capitale britannique. Des griffonnages à la Disney et des imprimés Pacman aux flyers de clubs sombrés dans l'oubli, Kim Jones ennoblit le banal et se fait défenseur du jetable, le tout avec un inlassable sens de l'humour. « J'essaie de regarder les Simpson tous les jours ainsi que tous les films d'horreur pas trop mauvais. J'écoute les bandes et la musique de DJ Pierre pour mon prochain défilé », explique-t-il. Mais Jones n'est pas qu'un petit rigolo. C'est un vrai talent qui, comme un bon vieux yucca, pousse de plus en plus haut chaque saison.

BEN REARDON

What are your signature designs? Well, I like to use cotton cheesecloth and overdye it and have used it in every collection. It's also great to print onto and I've used it for all-in-one-suits, jackets, trousers and T-shirts What is your favourite piece from any of your collections? Well, I would say the paneled trousers from spring/summer 2004 and the cropped pinstripe jacket from autumn/winter 2004. Also, the oversized schoolboy blazer from my graduate collection How would you describe your work? High-end casual wear which is wearable What's your ultimate goal? To be happy and keep on working on projects I enjoy and keep working with the people I work with What inspires you? Everything is inspirational, from a movie to a song to a piece of clothing to a person. I find it very easy to get inspired Can fashion still have a political ambition? I'm not really a political person Who do you have in mind when you design? At the moment Andres, whom I work with a lot Is the idea of creative collaboration important to you? Yes. You can learn so much working with other people and it's also more fun. I have such a great team of people I work with and I wouldn't want it any other way Who has been the greatest influence on your career? Well, I suppose Louise Wilson from the MA course at Saint Martins, who really just made me believe in myself and she was the one who made me brave enough to take risks to get to where I am today, whether they are personal or financial risks How have your own experiences affected your work as a designer? Of course. I grew up all over the world so this will affect anything I do Which is more important in your work: the process or the product? For me it's the overall image so I would say it's the process I like, the general overview Is designing difficult for you, if so, what drives you to continue? Well, I find the design part easy and now I have a team behind me so that takes the pressure off. I'm driven because I know they all need to get paid at the end of the day and we are all very close, so I have to make sure they are looked after Have you ever been influenced or moved by the reaction to your designs? Well, the reaction to my first Paris show made me feel very emotional. All these editors and stylists whom I admire came back to congratulate me and say hello: so it was quite overwhelming What's your definition of beauty? If you're talking in the context of my work, I like to use guys who aren't super unrealistic in terms of looks. They're just healthy-looking and really nice people, so I like to stick with them. I have the seasonal change in models – sure, you have to change a few as some give up or move away – but I usually have 10 or so that I always use and they are my friends too. So I guess it's a case of both inside and outside count What's your philosophy? I don't have one: just be true to yourself and those around you What is the most important lesson you've learned? Believe in yourself and be loyal to friends.

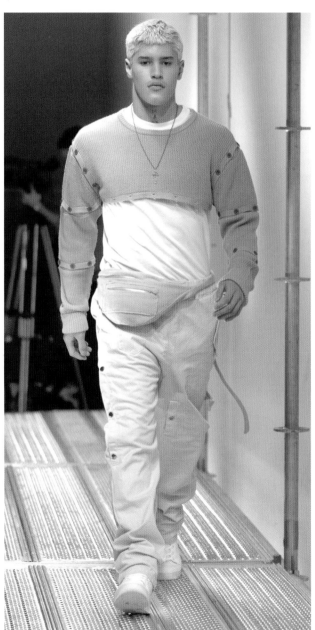
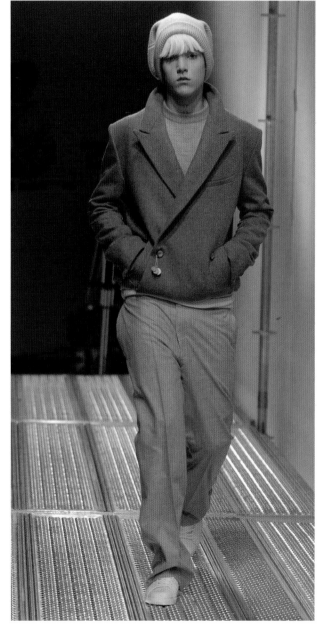

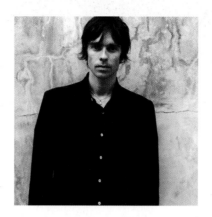

LACOSTE

"I find designing actually quite natural and exciting"

CHRISTOPHE LEMAIRE

Recognised for his fresh, flawless cuts and elegant tailoring, Christophe Lemaire of Lacoste is concerned more with the quality of his lines than with slavishly following trends. With a style he describes as "graphic, pure, relaxed and precise", he captures the balance between fashion and function, creating classic, wearable clothing season after season. Born in Besançon, France, in April 1965, Lemaire initially assisted at the Yves Saint Laurent design studio before going on to work for Thierry Mugler and Jean Patou. Through the Jean Patou house he met Christian Lacroix who was so impressed with the young designer that he appointed him head of his own woman's ready-to-wear line in 1987. Lemaire went solo with his eponymous womenswear label in 1990. His functional designs, with their understated elegance, ensured the label's success and a menswear label followed in 1994. In May 2001 Lemaire became creative director of heritage sportswear brand Lacoste, where he has re-established the company's position on the fashion map. Infusing his own contemporary, sharp style into classics such as the tennis skirt, polo shirt or preppy college jumper, he has attracted new customers while retaining enough of the brand's 70-year-old tradition so as not to lose the old. In June 2001, under his direction, Lacoste staged its first catwalk show. A true fashion DJ, for his own collections Lemaire mixes Western classics with one-of-a-kind ethnic pieces. The result is resolutely modern yet always wearable. "I don't create in a rush," he explains. "I always take time so I can distance myself from things that are too fashionable. As a designer I aim for an accessible balance between beauty and function to create a vision of contemporary 'easy wearing'".

Der für seine frischen, tadellosen Schnitte und die elegante Verarbeitung bekannte Christophe Lemaire kümmert sich mehr um die Qualität seiner Linien als um die sklavische Befolgung von Trends. Sein Stil, den er selbst „grafisch, puristisch, entspannt und präzise" nennt, trifft exakt den richtigen Ton zwischen Fashion und Function und bringt Saison für Saison klassische, tragbare Kreationen hervor. Lemaire wurde im April 1965 im französischen Besançon geboren. Bevor er für Thierry Mugler und Jean Patou arbeitete, war er zunächst Assistent im Atelier von Yves Saint Laurent. Über Jean Patou lernte er Christian Lacroix kennen, der von dem jungen Designer so begeistert war, dass er ihn 1987 zum Chef seiner Prêt-à-porter-Linie für Damen machte. Sein eigenes, nach ihm benanntes Damenmode-Label brachte Lemaire 1990 auf den Markt. Die funktionalen Entwürfe mit ihrer zurückhaltenden Eleganz sorgten für unmittelbaren Erfolg. Ein entsprechendes Männerlabel folgte 1994. Im Mai 2001 wurde Lemaire Creative Director der traditionellen Sportswear-Marke Lacoste und brachte das Unternehmen zurück in die modische Erste Liga. Er ließ seinen eigenen zeitgemäß klaren Stil in Klassiker wie Tennisröcke, Polohemden und College-Pullover einfließen und sprach damit eine neue Klientel an. Zugleich bewahrte er aber auch genug von der 70-jährigen Tradition der Marke, um die Stammkundschaft nicht zu verprellen. Im Juni 2001 veranstaltete Lacoste unter Lemaires Leitung seine erste Catwalk-Show. Als wahrer Fashion-DJ mixt Lemaire für seine eigenen Kollektionen abendländische Klassiker mit Ethno-Unikaten. Das Ergebnis ist entschieden modern, aber immer tragbar. „Meine Entwürfe folgen nie einem spontanen Impuls", erläutert er seine Arbeitsweise. „Ich lasse mir immer Zeit, um Abstand zu Dingen zu gewinnen, die mir zu modisch sind. Als Designer suche ich einen gangbaren Weg zwischen Schönheit und Funktionalität, um eine Vision von zeitgemäßem ‚Easy Wearing' zu kreieren."

Reconnaissable à ses coupes inédites et parfaites comme à ses tailleurs élégants, Christophe Lemaire s'intéresse plus à la qualité de ses lignes qu'aux tendances servilement suivies. Dans un style qu'il décrit comme «graphique, pur, décontracté et précis», il saisit l'équilibre entre mode et fonction en créant saison après saison des classiques faciles à porter. Né en avril 1965 à Besançon, Lemaire commence sa carrière comme assistant dans l'atelier d'Yves Saint Laurent avant de travailler pour Thierry Mugler et Jean Patou. Par l'intermédiaire de la maison Jean Patou, il rencontre Christian Lacroix, qu'il impressionne à tel point que ce dernier le nomme directeur de sa propre ligne de prêt-à-porter en 1987. Lemaire lance sa griffe éponyme pour femme en 1990. Ses créations fonctionnelles douées d'une élégance discrète assurent le succès de la griffe et une collection pour homme suit en 1994. En mai 2001, Lemaire devient directeur de la création de la respectable marque de sportswear Lacoste, où il redore le blason de l'entreprise. Insufflant son style contemporain et précis à des classiques tels que la jupe tennis, le polo ou le pull BCBG à l'américaine, il attire une nouvelle clientèle tout en respectant suffisamment les 70 ans d'histoire de Lacoste pour ne pas perdre ses clients d'origine. Sous son impulsion, Lacoste donne son tout premier défilé en juin 2001. Véritable DJ de la mode, pour ses propres collections, Lemaire mélange les classiques occidentaux à des pièces ethniques absolument uniques en leur genre. Le résultat est résolument moderne mais toujours portable. «Je n'aime pas créer dans l'urgence», explique-t-il. «J'ai toujours pris mon temps afin d'avoir suffisamment de recul par rapport aux choses trop à la mode. En tant que créateur de mode, je cherche à trouver un équilibre accessible entre beauté et fonction pour proposer une vision contemporaine de ‹l'easy wearing›».

HOLLY SHACKLETON

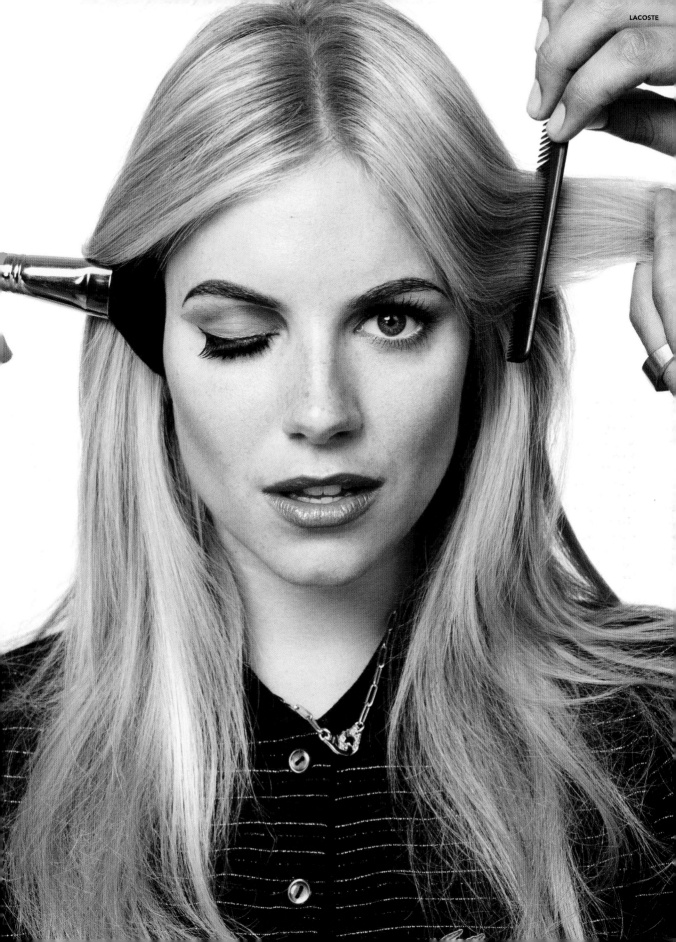

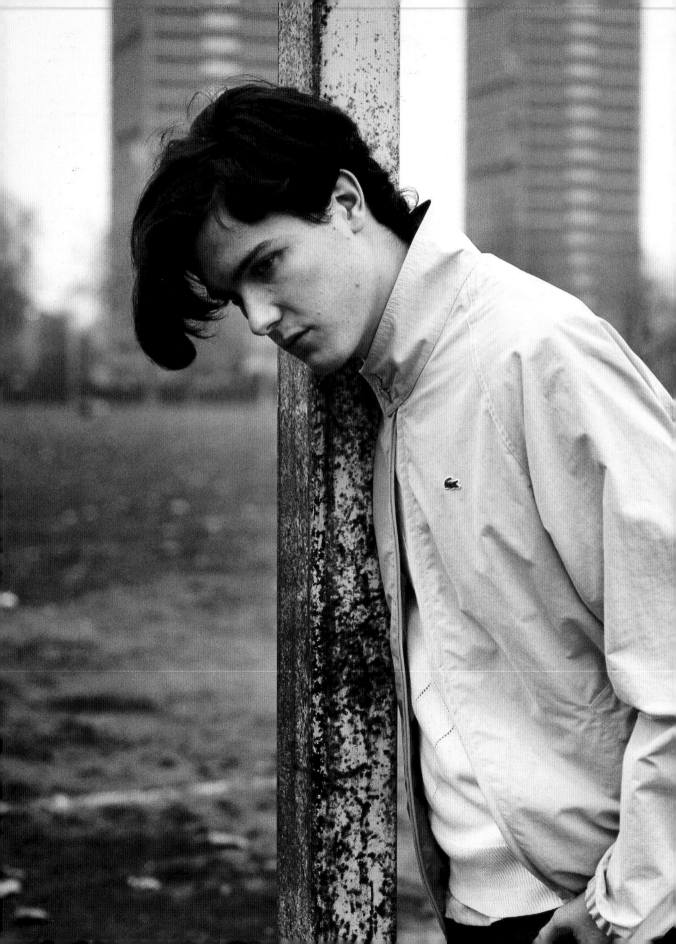

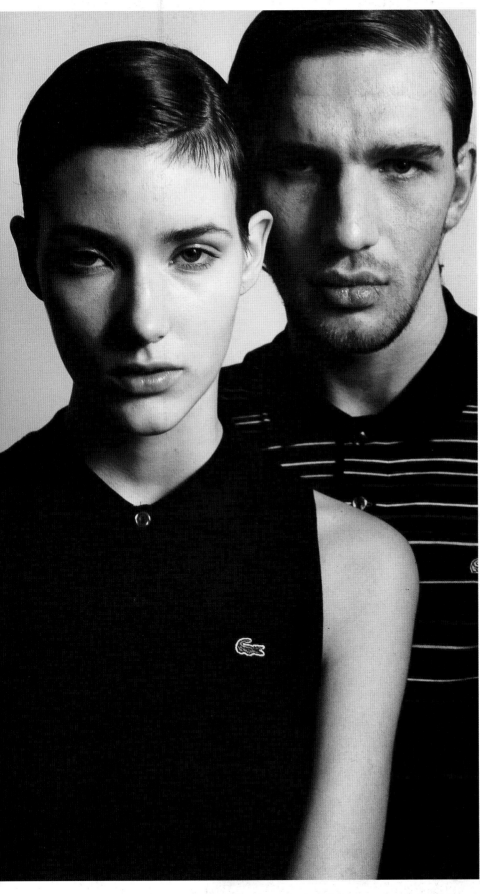

What are your signature designs? The essential wardrobe, mixing modern classics with pop elements in subtle, twisted ways **How would you describe your work?** I always look for "good sense" in style, a certain "evidence", simplicity and function with allure, taste, and precision **What inspires you?** Everything… life… **Can fashion still have a political ambition?** Fashion really is about aesthetics… Of course if we think about fashion as an expression of individuality, as style, as attitude towards others, then yes, style can have a political meaning. I would rather say that fashion must have a cultural meaning **Who do you have in mind when you design?** I am generally inspired by people from the music scene, like Nick Cave, Serge Gainsbourg, PJ Harvey, Deborah Harry… I have always found that people connected to music are more stylish, free-minded and expressive than the majority of the fashion crowd **Is the idea of creative collaboration important to you?** Fundamental. That's what everyday life should be about – sharing ideas. My work as a designer would mean nothing without the team around me **Who has been the greatest influence of your career?** Japanese culture, rock'n'roll (Stooges, The Who, Bo Diddley), my training with Christian Lacroix, Yves Saint Laurent and Street "Free-Style" (the second hand culture) **How have your own experiences affected your work as a designer?** Too complex, unconscious, to answer precisely! **Which is more important in your work: the process or the product?** As a designer, what really matters at the end of the day is the product: is it good or is it bad? But through the years, I have also learned how essential the process was. A better process – creative, focused, positive – makes a better product **Is designing difficult for you. If so, what drives you to continue?** I find designing actually quite natural and exciting. What's more difficult for me and demands more discipline and concentration (I am rather impulsive and impatient) is all the process to make the design happen, become real and faithful to my first intuition. That's why the process is as important as the product **Have you ever been influenced or moved by the reaction to your designs?** I am probably too sensitive to the opinions of others and I try to free myself from that dependence. I can easily lose my confidence if I don't feel good reactions to my work **What's your definition of beauty?** Grace **What's you philosophy?** Stay faithful to my dreams. Listen to my heart as much as my brain, fight against laziness, conformism, mediocrity (starting with my own) and look for quality in everything. Show respect to others **What is the most important lesson you've learned?** Patience.

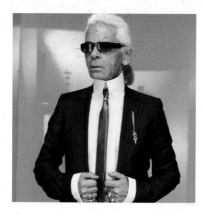

LAGERFELD GALLERY

"I love fashion and the evolution of times"

Karl Lagerfeld is perhaps the ultimate fashion designer. Prolific and driven by change, he is certainly one of the industry's most successful 'mercenary' designers. Yet he is far from a behind-the-scenes figure. Lagerfeld's ever-present pony-tail, fan and sunglasses are iconic; his personal preference for bespoke white shirts by Hilditch & Key, Chrome Hearts jewellery and Dior Homme suits is well documented. In addition to his work for both Chanel and Fendi, since 1998 Lagerfeld has designed his own label Lagerfeld Gallery. Born in Hamburg in 1938, Lagerfeld moved to Paris at the age of 14. At just 17 he landed his first job, at Pierre Balmain, moving to Jean Patou three years later. Despite this traditional start, Lagerfeld chose not to establish his own house but instead to pursue a career as a freelance designer. From 1963–83 and 1992–97 Lagerfeld designed Chloé. In 1965 he also began to design for Fendi, a role that he retains to this day; in 1983 he was appointed artistic director of Chanel. 1984 saw the first incarnation of his own label, Karl Lagerfeld, which was later superseded by Lagerfeld Gallery, an art/retail venture. It is the latter that expresses the remarkable range of this genuine polymath. In addition to ready-to-wear collections, Lagerfeld Gallery is a platform for his myriad passions, including photography (he often shoots his own ad campaigns, along with editorial for numerous magazines), books (he has his own imprint, 7L, and a personal library of 230,000 volumes), perfume, art and magazines. In December 2004 it was announced that Tommy Hilfiger had purchased Lagerfeld Gallery. This followed a phenomenally successful link-up with mass market retailer H&M in autumn 2004, when shoppers clamoured for a garment designed by an acknowledged maestro of fashion. [Also see Chanel]

Man könnte Karl Lagerfeld als den Inbegriff des Modedesigners bezeichnen. Produktiv und inspiriert von Veränderungen aller Art, ist er zweifellos der erfolgreichste „gedungene" Designer der Modeindustrie. Er ist jedoch keiner, der nur hinter der Bühne die Fäden zieht. Lagerfelds Pferdeschwanz, sein Fächer und seine Sonnenbrille sind legendär, seine persönlichen Vorlieben für weiße Maßhemden von Hilditch & Key, Schmuck von Chrome Hearts und Anzüge von Dior Homme bestens dokumentiert. Neben seiner Tätigkeit für Chanel und Fendi entwirft Lagerfeld seit 1988 auch für sein eigenes Label Lagerfeld Gallery. Geboren wurde der Modeschöpfer 1938 in Hamburg. Mit 14 Jahren kam er nach Paris, und mit 17 Jahren hatte er bereits seinen ersten Job, und zwar bei Pierre Balmain. Drei Jahre später wechselte er zu Jean Patou. Trotz dieses traditionellen Karrierestarts entschied Lagerfeld sich gegen die Gründung eines eigenen Modehauses und schlug stattdessen die Laufbahn eines unabhängigen Designers ein. Von 1963 bis 1983 sowie von 1992 bis 1997 entwarf er für Chloé. 1965 begann er außerdem mit seiner Tätigkeit für Fendi, die bis heute andauert. 1983 berief man ihn schließlich zum künstlerischen Leiter von Chanel. 1984 machte er dann erstmals mit einem eigenen Label, Karl Lagerfeld, von sich reden, das später von dem Kunst- und Einzelhandelsprojekt Lagerfeld Gallery abgelöst wurde. Dieses Unternehmen wird der bemerkenswerten Bandbreite des Universalgenies am besten gerecht. Neben den Prêt-à-porter-Kollektionen ist Lagerfeld Gallery auch Bühne für die unzähligen Passionen des Designers, darunter Fotografie (oft fotografiert er außer Fotostrecken für zahlreiche Magazine auch seine Kampagnen selbst), Bücher (sein eigenes Imprint heißt 7L, die Privatbibliothek umfasst 230000 Bände), Parfüm, Kunst und Zeitschriften. Im Dezember 2004 wurde bekannt, dass Tommy Hilfiger Lagerfeld Gallery gekauft hatte. Dem war eine ungeheuer erfolgreiche Kooperation mit der Kette H&M im Herbst desselben Jahres vorausgegangen. Damals rissen sich die Kunden um die Entwürfe des berühmten Modezaren. [Siehe auch Chanel]

Karl Lagerfeld est peut-être l'incarnation même du créateur de mode. Prolifique et motivé par le changement, c'est sans conteste l'un des couturiers «mercenaires» qui remporte le plus de succès. Pourtant, il n'est pas du genre à rester dans l'ombre. La queue de cheval, l'éventail et les lunettes noires qu'il porte en permanence sont devenus culte; son goût personnel pour les chemises blanches taillées sur mesure par Hilditch & Key, les bijoux Chrome Hearts et les costumes Dior Homme a été largement documenté. Outre son travail chez Chanel et Fendi, Lagerfeld dessine sa propre griffe depuis 1998 sous le nom de Lagerfeld Gallery. Né en 1938 à Hambourg, Lagerfeld s'installe à Paris dès l'âge de 14 ans. A 17 ans seulement, il décroche son premier emploi chez Pierre Balmain, puis part chez Jean Patou trois ans plus tard. En dépit de ces débuts très classiques, Lagerfeld décide toutefois de ne pas ouvrir sa propre maison, préférant poursuivre sa carrière en tant que créateur free-lance. De 1963 à 1983 et de 1992 à 1997, il dessine les collections de Chloé. En 1965, il commence également à travailler pour Fendi, poste qu'il occupe encore aujourd'hui; en 1983, il est nommé directeur artistique de Chanel. 1984 voit la naissance de sa propre griffe, Karl Lagerfeld, plus tard remplacée par Lagerfeld Gallery, un projet mêlant art et mode. Lagerfeld Gallery, avec sa boutique rue de Seine à Paris et une autre à Monaco, exprime toute la palette des talents de ce grand érudit. Outre les collections de prêt-à-porter, Lagerfeld Gallery représente une belle plate-forme d'expression pour sa myriade de passions, notamment la photographie (il réalise souvent ses propres campagnes publicitaires ainsi que des shootings photo pour de nombreux magazines), les livres (il possède sa propre maison d'édition, 7L, ainsi qu'une bibliothèque personnelle de 230000 volumes), le parfum, l'art et les magazines. En décembre 2004, Tommy Hilfiger annonce le rachat de Lagerfeld Gallery, peu de temps après une collaboration couronnée de succès avec la chaîne commerciale H&M à l'automne 2004: la mise en vente de la petite collection dessinée par Lagerfeld a provoqué de véritables scènes d'empoigne, avec des clients tous impatients de s'offrir des vêtements signés par un maestro reconnu de la mode. [Voir aussi Chanel]

SUSIE RUSHTON

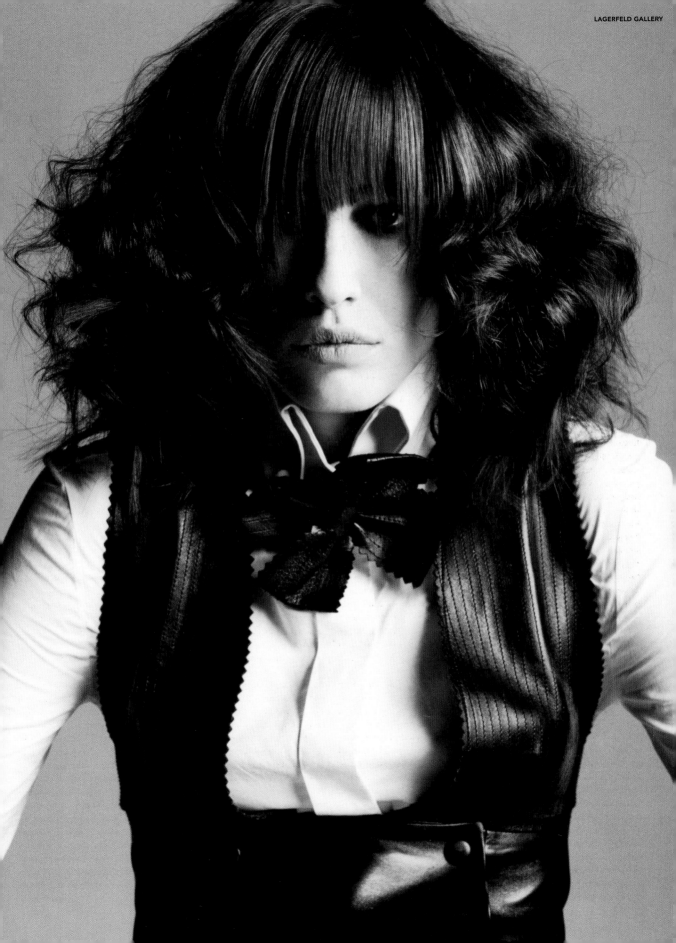

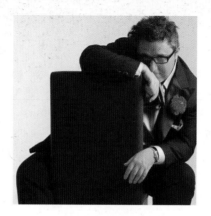

LANVIN

"I guess it's the search for perfection
from season to season that moves me forward" ALBER ELBAZ

Alber Elbaz is the modern romantic who found his perfect match in Lanvin, the Parisian house where he has been artistic director since 2001. His signature designs for the label – pleated silk dresses, satin ribbon details and costume jewellery – are now among the most sought-after in fashion, making his switch-back route to success all the more surprising. Elbaz was born in Casablanca, Morocco, and raised in the suburbs of Tel Aviv by his mother, a Spanish artist. His father, an Israeli barber, died when he was young. He studied at the Shenkar College of Textile Technology and Fashion, Tel Aviv, but received some of his most valuable training in New York, where for seven years he was right hand man to the late Geoffrey Beene, couturier to East Coast high society. In 1996, Elbaz was appointed head of ready-to-wear for Guy Laroche in Paris, where he remained for almost three years. In November 1998 he was appointed artistic director for Yves Saint Laurent Rive Gauche, effectively taking over design duties from Saint Laurent himself. In his tenure at YSL, Elbaz attracted a younger clientele – Chloë Sevigny wore one of his dresses to the Oscars. However, at the start of 2000 big business intervened when the Gucci Group took control of YSL Rive Gauche and Tom Ford stepped into Elbaz's position. Following a short but successful spell at Milanese brand Krizia and time out travelling the world, in October 2001 Elbaz returned to French fashion via Lanvin, the couture house founded by Jeanne Lanvin in the 1880s. Under his direction, Lanvin has developed jewellery, shoe and handbag collections. His most outstanding talent however is for the creation of ultra-feminine cocktail dresses that are the epitome of Parisian chic. In 2005, he won the CFDA's International Award. Fashion's favourite comeback kid, Elbaz also wears bow ties very well.

Alber Elbaz ist ein moderner Romantiker, der bei Lanvin seine ideale Heimat gefunden hat. Seit 2001 ist er künstlerischer Direktor des Pariser Modehauses. Seine Markenzeichen bei diesem Label – plissierte Seidenkleider, Verzierungen aus Satinband und Modeschmuck – gehören inzwischen zum Gefragtesten in der Modewelt und lassen seinen Zickzackkurs zum Erfolg umso erstaunlicher erscheinen. Geboren wurde Elbaz im marokkanischen Casablanca. Seine Mutter, eine spanische Künstlerin, zog ihn in der Vorstadt von Tel Aviv allein groß, nachdem sein Vater, ein israelischer Friseur, früh gestorben war. Am Shenkar College of Textile Technology and Fashion in Tel Aviv absolvierte Elbaz sein Studium, seine wertvollsten Erfahrungen erwarb er jedoch in den sieben Jahren in New York. Dort war er die rechte Hand des heute verstorbenen Geoffrey Beene, des legendären Couturiers der Ostküsten-High-Society. 1996 wurde Elbaz für knapp drei Jahre Chef des Prêt-à-porter-Bereichs bei Guy Laroche in Paris. Im November 1998 übernahm er praktisch von Monsieur Saint Laurent höchstpersönlich die Designerpflichten, als er zum Artistic Director von Yves Saint Laurent Rive Gauche berufen wurde. In seiner Zeit bei YSL zog er eine deutlich jüngere Klientel an – so trug etwa Chloë Sevigny bei einer Oscar-Verleihung eines seiner Kleider. Anfang 2000 machte ihm jedoch das Big Business zu schaffen, als der Gucci-Konzern die Kontrolle über YSL Rive Gauche erwarb und Tom Ford seine Position einnahm. Es folgten ein kurzes, aber erfolgreiches Intermezzo beim Mailänder Label Krizia und eine Auszeit, in der er durch die Welt reiste. Im Oktober 2001 kehrte Elbaz über das in den 1880er Jahren gegründete Modehaus Lanvin in die französische Couture zurück. Unter seiner Ägide brachte Lanvin erstmals Schmuck-, Schuh- und Handtaschenkollektionen heraus. Sein überragendes Talent liegt jedoch im Kreieren höchst femininer Cocktailkleider – dem Inbegriff des Pariser Chics. 2005 erhielt er den CFDA International Award. Dem liebsten Comeback-Kid der Modebranche gelingen aber auch Frackschleifen ganz ausgezeichnet.

Le romantique moderne Alber Elbaz a fini par trouver le job idéal chez Lanvin, maison parisienne dont il occupe la direction artistique depuis 2001. Ses créations signature pour la griffe (robes plissées en soie, détails en rubans de satin et bijoux fantaisie) comptent aujourd'hui parmi les pièces de mode les plus recherchées, ce qui rend son retour au succès d'autant plus surprenant. Né à Casablanca au Maroc, Alber Elbaz grandit auprès de sa mère, une artiste espagnole, dans la banlieue de Tel Aviv. Son père, un Israélien coiffeur pour homme, meurt quand Alber est encore jeune. Il étudie au Shenkar College of Textile Technology and Fashion de Tel Aviv, mais c'est New York qui lui offre sa formation la plus précieuse : pendant sept ans, Elbaz sera le bras droit de feu Geoffrey Beene, le couturier de l'élite de la côte est. En 1996, il est nommé directeur de la création du prêt-à-porter chez Guy Laroche à Paris, où il passe près de trois ans. En novembre 1998, il devient directeur artistique d'Yves Saint Laurent Rive Gauche, succédant avec efficacité à monsieur Saint Laurent en personne. Pendant cette période, Elbaz réussit à attirer une clientèle plus jeune : Chloë Sevigny portera l'une de ses robes pour la nuit des oscars. Mais au début de l'an 2000, le groupe Gucci prend le contrôle d'YSL Rive Gauche et remplace Elbaz par Tom Ford. Après avoir travaillé avec succès pour la maison milanaise Krizia pendant quelques mois et pris un congé sabbatique pour voyager à travers le monde, Elbaz fait son retour dans la mode parisienne en octobre 2001 via Lanvin, maison de haute couture fondée par Jeanne Lanvin dans les années 1880. Sous sa direction, Lanvin développe des collections de bijoux, de chaussures et de sacs à main. Son talent le plus remarquable réside avant tout dans la création de robes de cocktail archi-féminines qui symbolisent tout le chic parisien. En 2005, il remporte le CFDA International award. Fils prodigue de la mode, Elbaz porte également très bien le nœud papillon.

SUSIE RUSHTON

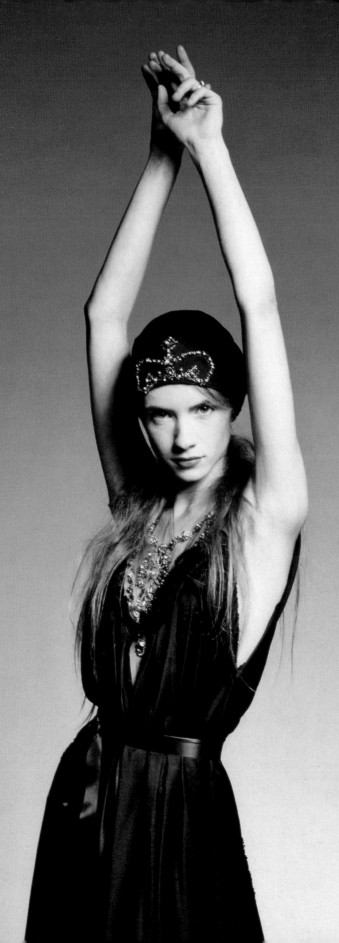

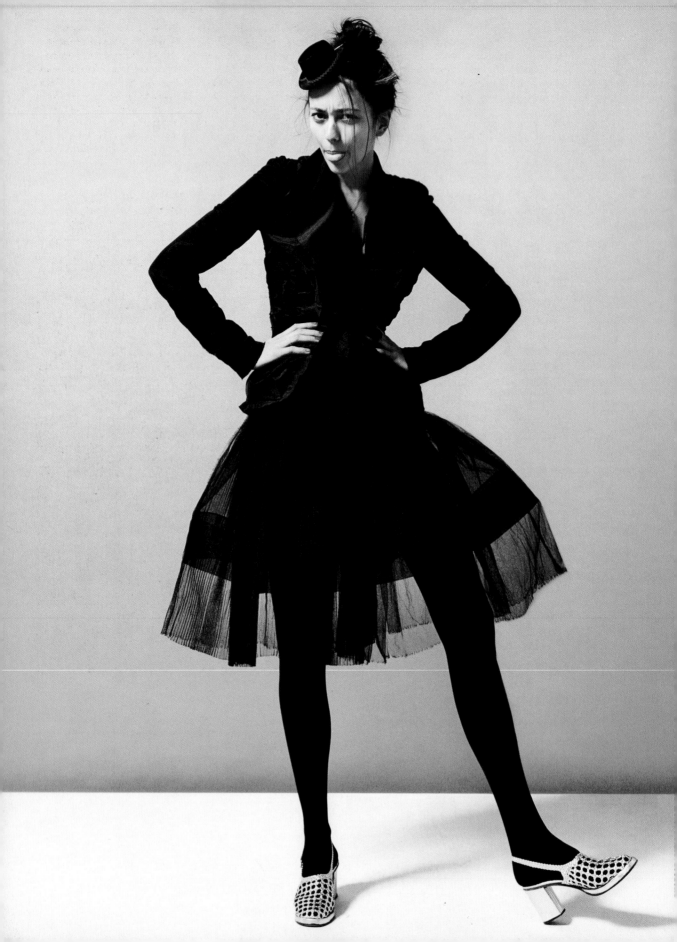

What are your signature designs? A mix of two worlds, the old and the new. Old technique with new proportions What is your favourite piece from any of your collections? It's like asking a mother who is her favourite kid! I can't! I love them all How would you describe your work? Passioning, passioning, passioning! What's your ultimate goal? To make women beautiful What inspires you? Everything, everybody, anywhere and all the time Can fashion still have a political ambition? Politics was never my thing, therefore I moved to Paris rather than Washington Who do you have in mind when you design? Women that I know, women that I want to know, women that I love Is the idea of creative collaboration important to you? Very much. The best of fashion was in the '20s and in the '60s when everybody collaborated: artists, fashion designers, musicians… all working together, inspired each other and gave to each other. I believe that working with others can only give Who has been the greatest influence on your career? Geoffrey Beene How have your own experiences affected your work as a designer? My work is a voyage of my life. A voyage between Morocco, Tel Aviv, New York and Paris. Each city, each country, gave me different colours, different senses, different feelings Which is more important in your work: the process or the product? Both. The process leads to the product Is designing difficult for you, if so, what drives you to continue? In theory, designing should not be difficult. In reality unfortunately, it is. So, it's not easy being me. My drive is to perfect the last collection, which I never find perfect. I guess it's the search for perfection from season to season that moves me forward. The moment I find perfection I guess I'll retire Have you ever been influenced or moved by the reaction to your designs? All the time What's your definition of beauty? Individuality What's your philosophy? Being me.

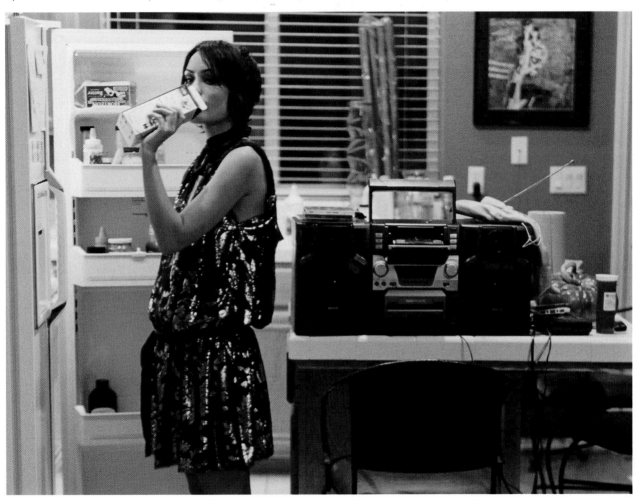

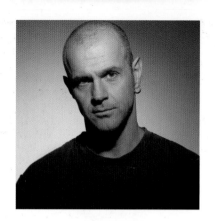

LEVI'S

"Clothing is a subliminal language that communicates how you want to be perceived." GARY HARVEY

"I'd much rather be forever in blue jeans," sang Neil Diamond in 1978. Almost 30 years later, Diamond's words echo the thoughts of a jeans-obsessed world. 2003 saw the 130th anniversary of the birth of blue jeans and 150 years since the founding of Levi Strauss & Co. As American as apple pie and Dolly Parton, Levi Strauss was created by San Francisco trader Strauss and a Reno tailor called Jacob Davis who bought his denim from Strauss. Davis riveted trousers for a client who complained that his tore too easily, and when other customers asked for the same service he decided to patent the idea with the financial backing of Levi Strauss. In 1873 the first 'patented riveted overall' was produced, featuring the still-famous double arc pockets. Fast forward over 100 years and Levi's iconic TV advert starring Nick Kamen taking off his Levi's in a launderette (1985) helped to revive the flagging reputation of denim, increasing sales of the 501 jeans by 820 per cent. Other memorable Levi's ads include mermaids in 1997, Flat Eric in 1999 and a bunch of kids with mouse heads in 2004. In the late '90s and into the new millennium, denim continued in popularity and the number of companies competing for the jeans-buying customer's attention is no longer restricted to heavyweights like Levi's, Lee and Wrangler. Levi's response to this has been to introduce various new iconic jeans shapes. The Levi's Red range introduced the successful twisted leg in 1999, while 2003 saw the launch of the Type 1, and in 2004, the Anti-Fit 501. 150 years after their creation, Levi's jeans are a powerful symbol of popular dress culture in the 20th century and beyond. Gary Harvey is creative consultant for Levi's Europe, having previously been creative director of the brand for five years.

„I'd much rather be forever in blue jeans", sang Neil Diamond 1978. Knapp drei-ßig Jahre später geben Diamonds Worte noch immer wie ein Echo die Gedanken einer jeansbesessenen Welt wieder. 2003 feierte man den 130. Geburtstag der Bluejeans und das 150-jährige Gründungsjubiläum der Firma Levi Strauss & Co. Die Marke, die so amerikanisch ist wie Apple-Pie und Dolly Parton, wurde von einem Kaufmann namens Levi Strauss aus San Francisco und einem Schneider aus Reno namens Jacob Davis, der bei Strauss Denim kaufte, gegründet. Davis nietete Hosen für einen Kunden zusammen, der sich beschwert hatte, dass sie zu leicht zerreißen würden. Als dann andere Kunden den gleichen Service verlangten, entschloss sich der Schneider, seine Idee patentieren zu lassen. Was er schließlich mit finanzieller Unterstützung von Levi Strauss auch tat. 1873 wurde der erste genietete Overall produziert und an den Taschen mit dem bis heute berühmten doppelten Bogen bestickt. Spulen wir jetzt gut hundert Jahre nach vorn, landen wir bei Levi's kultigem TV-Werbespot, in dem Nick Kamen seine Jeans in einem Waschsalon auszieht (1985). Das gab dem etwas angeschla-

genen Ruf von Levi's neuen Glanz und trieb den Absatz der 501 um unglaubli-che 820 Prozent in die Höhe. Andere denkwürdige Levi's-Spots waren die Meer-jungfrauen (1997), Flat Eric (1999) und eine Horde Kids mit Mäuseköpfen (2004). Ende der 1990er und zu Beginn des neuen Jahrtausends blieb Denim weiterhin gefragt, nur beschränkte sich die Zahl der Unternehmen, die um die Aufmerksamkeit der Jeanskäufer buhlen, nicht mehr auf große Marken wie Levi's, Lee oder Wrangler. Levi's Antwort darauf war die Einführung diverser neuer Schnitte mit Kultcharakter. Die Levi's Red hatte ab 1999 großen Erfolg mit dem „twisted leg". 2003 kam Type 1 und 2004 die Anti-Fit 501 dazu. So sind Levi's Jeans auch 150 Jahre nach ihrer Erfindung noch ein starkes Symbol populärer Modekultur im 20. Jahrhundert und darüber hinaus. Gary Harvey ist Kreativberater für Levi's Europa, nachdem er zuvor fünf Jahre lang Creative Director der Marke war.

«I'd much rather be forever in blue jeans», chantait Neil Diamond en 1978. Presque 30 ans plus tard, ses mots se font l'écho des pensées d'un monde obsédé par le denim. En 2003, le blue jean fête son 130e anniversaire, et Levi Strauss & Co ses 150 ans d'histoire. Aussi américaine que l'apple pie et Dolly Parton, la marque Levi Strauss est créée par Strauss, négociant à San Francisco, et Jacob Davis, un tailleur de Reno qui achetait son denim chez Strauss. Un jour, Davis pose des rivets sur des pantalons pour satisfaire un client qui se plaignait de voir les siens se déchirer trop facilement. Quand d'autres clients commencent à exi-ger le même service, il décide de breveter l'idée, fort du soutien financier de Levi Strauss. En 1873, le duo produit le premier «jean à rivets breveté», dont les poches surpiquées d'un arc doublé restent toujours aussi célèbres aujourd'hui. Plus d'un siècle plus tard, le spot publicitaire phare de Levi's, où Nick Kamen retire son jean dans une laverie (1985), redore la réputation du denim et les ventes de 501 enregistrent une incroyable hausse de 820%. Parmi les autres campagnes publicitaires les plus mémorables de Levi's, on peut citer le spot des sirènes en 1997, celui avec Flat Eric en 1999 et la pub avec des ados à tête de sou-ris en 2004. Entre la fin des années 90 et le début du nouveau millénaire, la cote du denim continue à grimper et le nombre d'entreprises en concurrence pour atti-rer l'attention des acheteurs de jeans ne se limite plus aux poids lourds tels que Levi's, Lee et Wrangler. En réaction à ce phénomène, Levi's réussit à imposer plu-sieurs nouveaux modèles sur le marché. La gamme Levi's Red présente avec suc-cès son jean Twisted en 1999, tandis que 2003 voit le lancement du Type 1, suivi du 501 Anti-Fit en 2004. 150 ans après la création de Levi's, ses jeans demeurent un puissant symbole de la mode populaire du XXe siècle, et ce pour longtemps encore Après avoir été directeur de la marque pendant cinq ans, Gary Harvey tra-vaille désormais en tant que consultant pour Levi's Europe. STEVE COOK

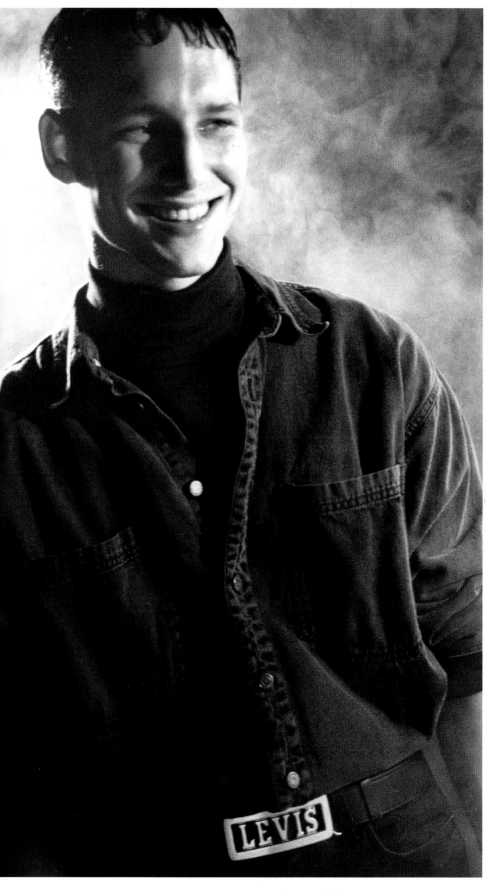

What are your signatu[...]
501 jeans with anti-fi[...]
Engineered Jeans **W[...]**
from any of your coll[...]
'Rigid'. A balancin[...]
Levi's brand imag[...]
history (over 130 years), whilst defining
the new direction and future relevance
What's your ultimate goal? To inspire a new
generation to re-appropriate denim and
jeanswear as a means of self-expression
What inspires you? An urge to create and
continually move forward, redefining 'our
culture' in reaction to the blandness and
conformity of 'their culture' **Can fashion still
have a political ambition?** Absolutely, fashion
should be political. Clothing is a subliminal
language that communicates how you want
to be perceived, your personal identity is
a political statement chosen each morning,
be it 'boring conformity' or 'aggressive
reactionary' **Who do you have in mind when
you design?** I usually design with an attitude
or feeling, something I want the wearer to
relate to, it's usually sexual, tough and fuck
you **Is the idea of creative collaboration
important to you?** Yes, some of our best ideas
come from collaborations, we have some of
the best denim designers in the world and
currently we are collaborating on projects
with Comme des Garçons, Common Threads,
Oki-Ni and the stylist Glen McEvoy **Who has
been the greatest influence on your career?**
Every person I've met has influenced my life
in some way, yet no one person has specifically influenced my career **How have your
own experiences affected your work as a
designer?** I have a very straightforward, no
nonsense approach to problem solving and
clothing **Which is more important in your
work: the process or the product?** The
product is king, the process should be
designed so it never compromises the
product **Is designing difficult for you, if so,
what drives you to continue?** Designing
happens very naturally, any design process
involves a challenge and this is ultimately
what stimulates me, getting the product
made is when it can become difficult **Have
you ever been influenced or moved by the
reaction to your designs?** Yeah, it's the
ultimate high seeing people wearing the stuff
on the streets, what really stimulates me
creatively is when people wear something
differently and exert their own style **What's
your definition of beauty?** It's in the eye of the
beholder, if it moves you or excites you then
it's beautiful **What's your philosophy?** Enjoy
stuff, relax and laugh about it, things could
always be so much worse **What is the most
important lesson you've learned?** You have a
choice in everything you do and there are
always consequences.

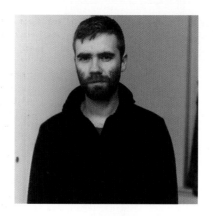

LUTZ

"I take things that are basic, integral parts of everyday life, and mix and meld them together so that they stay familiar but at the same time become something completely different"

Before anyone knew he was actually a fashion designer, German-born Lutz became a familiar face (and body) after appearing in Wolfgang Tillmans' now infamous fashion story 'Like Sister Like Brother', published in i-D's Sexuality Issue of November 1992. He kept popping up in his friend's pictures, but in retrospect it's now clear that Lutz was not gearing up to be a model. After making the move from his native village near Cologne to London, Lutz – whose full name is Lutz Huelle – studied fashion at Central Saint Martins. Graduating in 1995, he got an internship at Martin Margiela's Paris atelier, becoming Margiela's assistant and focusing on knitwear and the production of the Belgian designer's 'artisanale' line (garments based on vintage and found pieces). With three years of professional training under his belt, he returned to London to accept a teaching job at his former school, a position he holds to this day. In 2000, he set up his own company, presenting his first women's collection in Paris for autumn/winter 2000. Taking the garment and its emotional versatility as a starting point, Lutz makes the unconventional wearable and beautiful by cutting up and subsequently assembling different pieces, as well as giving them a new identity through transformation. Sweaters become sleek dresses with the aid of smartly placed zips, bomber jackets are decorated with smoking lapels: in order to make sense (and innovative fashion), Lutz above all throws the unexpected and fragmented into the equation. In 2004 Lutz staged a retrospective exhibition in Reims called Reims/Encens, supported by the local contemporary art fund of the Champagne region. In October of the same year, Lutz opened a new showroom in Paris, where he now lives.

Bevor irgendjemand wusste, dass er eigentlich Designer ist, machte sich der in Deutschland geborene Lutz einen Namen als Fotomodell: Sein Gesicht und sein Körper waren in Wolfgang Tillmans' legendärer Modegeschichte „Like Sister Like Brother" in der Sex-Nummer von i-D 1992 zu sehen. Danach tauchte er immer mal wieder in den Bildern seines Freundes auf, aus heutiger Sicht ist jedoch klar, dass er keine Karriere als Model anstrebte. Nach dem Umzug aus seinem Heimatdorf bei Köln nach London studierte Lutz, der mit vollem Namen Lutz Huelle heißt, Mode am Central Saint Martins. Nachdem er 1995 seinen Abschluss gemacht hatte, ergatterte er einen Praktikumsplatz im Pariser Atelier von Martin Margiela, wurde anschließend Assistent des belgischen Designers und konzentrierte sich auf Strickwaren sowie die Linie „artisanale" (auf der Basis von Vintage-Mode und Fundstücken). Nach diesen drei Jahren zusätzlicher Ausbildung kehrte Lutz nach London zurück und begann an seinem ehemaligen College zu unterrichten, was er bis heute tut. Im Jahr 2000 gründete er

eine eigene Firma und präsentierte in Paris seine erste Herbst/Winter-Kollektion für Damen. Ausgehend von der emotionalen Vielseitigkeit jedes Kleidungsstücks, macht der junge Designer das Unkonventionelle tragbar. Die Schönheit seiner Mode entsteht, indem er verschiedene Stücke auftrennt, sie anders zusammenfügt und ihnen durch diese Transformation eine neue Identität verleiht. So verwandeln sich Pullover mit Hilfe klug platzierter Reißverschlüsse in schmal geschnittene Kleider, Bomberjacken werden mit Smokingrevers aufgeputzt. Um innovative Mode mit Verstand zu kreieren, bringt Lutz vor allem Unerwartetes und Fragmente ins Spiel. 2004 präsentierte er mit Unterstützung der lokalen Stiftung für moderne Kunst in der Champagne in Reims eine Retrospektive unter dem Titel „Reims/Encens". Im Oktober des gleichen Jahres eröffnete Lutz an seinem Wohnort Paris einen Showroom.

Avant d'être connu comme créateur de mode, l'Allemand Lutz s'est fait surtout remarquer pour son visage (et son corps), apparu dans le célèbre article de Wolfgang Tillmans « Like Sister Like Brother » publié dans le numéro Sexualité du magazine i-D en novembre 1992. Il continue pendant quelque temps à poser pour ses amis photographes, mais avec le recul, il semble aujourd'hui évident que Lutz n'était pas destiné à une carrière de mannequin. Après avoir quitté son village natal près de Cologne pour venir à Londres, Lutz – qui s'appelle en réalité Lutz Huelle – étudie la mode à Central Saint Martins. Une fois diplômé en 1995, il décroche un stage dans l'atelier parisien de Martin Margiela et devient son assistant. Il travaille principalement sur la maille, ainsi qu'à la production de la ligne artisanale du créateur belge (composée de pièces vintage et de vêtements dénichés à droite à gauche). Fort de trois années d'expérience professionnelle, il revient à Londres pour accepter un poste d'enseignant dans son ancienne école, une position qu'il occupe encore aujourd'hui. En l'an 2000, il monte sa propre entreprise et présente sa première collection pour femme à Paris aux défilés automne/hiver 2000. Avec le vêtement et sa flexibilité émotionnelle comme points de départ, Lutz rend la mode anti-conformiste à la fois belle et portable, découpant et assemblant différentes pièces pour qu'elles trouvent une nouvelle identité à travers la transformation. Les pulls se métamorphosent en de sublimes robes grâce à des zips astucieusement placés et les blousons d'aviateur se parent de revers de veston d'intérieur : pour que tout cela ait un sens (et pour innover dans la mode), Lutz s'attache avant tout à réunir l'inattendu et le fragmenté. En 2004, il organise une rétrospective à Reims intitulée « Reims/Encens », avec le soutien du fonds pour l'art contemporain de la région Champagne. En octobre 2004, il ouvre un nouveau showroom à Paris, où il vit désormais. PETER DE POTTER

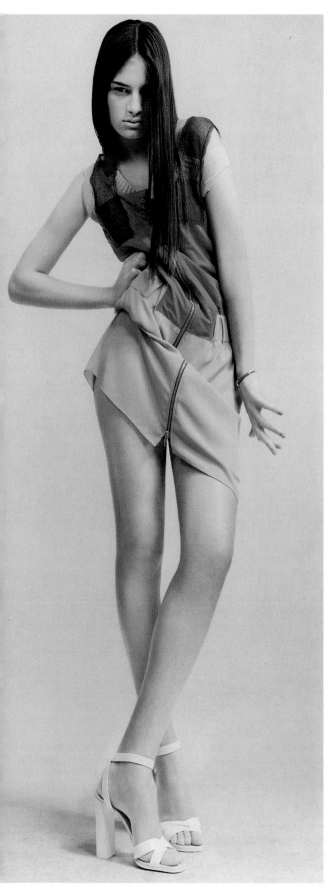

What are your signature designs? The bomber jacket finished with a tuxedo-lapel, the skirt cut in the shape of a trouser, the dresses with double-openings changing shape and volume according to how they are being worn, the trench-sweater hybrid, the corkscrew-skirt **What is your favourite piece from any of your collections?** My favourite has to be the men's jacket in English wool with long red fringing, a mixture between a men's jacket and a flapper cocktail dress, because it's purely Lutz, and it sums up perfectly the collection **How would you describe your work?** I would call it 're-structuration'. I take things that are basic, integral parts of everyday life, and mix and meld them together, so they stay familiar but at the same time become something completely different **What's your ultimate goal?** To keep an open mind and heart **What inspires you?** I always look at how people wear their clothes. And then I wonder what it says about them. I've never been interested in fashion as a product, but as something which defines identity **Can fashion still have a political ambition?** I think it should have. If it doesn't have a political or human dimension that goes further than just product, it doesn't mean anything **Who do you have in mind when you design?** Friends and people around me **Is the idea of creative collaboration important to you?** The most exciting things are always done through creative collaboration **Who has been the greatest influence on your career?** Studying at Central Saint Martins was the best thing that happened to me. When you come from Germany, there is no chaos. Everything is very much thought-through and planned. To come to a college that is completely based on chaos, to just do whatever you like... It was a complete culture shock. It really changed my life **How have your own experiences affected your work as a designer?** I would say that they're the reason why I find myself in this business – I have always felt that my physical aspect conveys very little about me as a person, but as we all form opinions about people at first sight, this first impression always sticks, whether in the end it is true or not. My collection has always used this fact as a starting point – what I would like to do is make that first impression impossible to judge by creating clothes that confuse with multiple meanings, and in the process create space **Is designing difficult for you, if so, what drives you to continue?** It is not the designing, it is the huge corporate machine we're up against. The space in which small designers exist is constantly diminishing. What keeps me going is that I am extremely passionate about my work, and because we have acquired such a loyal following **Have you ever been influenced or moved by the reaction to your designs?** The thing that touches me most right now is when I see people wearing my clothes. That's incredible. It's one thing to sit and design, but in the end it doesn't matter if it doesn't touch anybody outside, somebody who is willing to pay for something I've thought of **What's your definition of beauty?** Dignity **What's your philosophy?** See all the above... **What is the most important lesson you've learned?** That love is all we need.

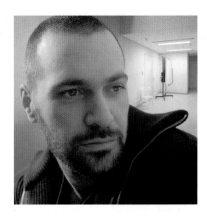

MAHARISHI

"I am inspired by figures who encourage radical rethinking"

HARDY BLECHMAN

Since establishing the label in 1994 Hardy Blechman has cultivated Maharishi beyond a stock streetwear label and into a thriving creative empire. From importing surplus clothing into the UK to gaining international notoriety for the 'Snopant' trousers in 1995, Blechman (born in Bournemouth in 1963) has bypassed the traditional methods of formal design and has maintained Maharishi as a privately-owned company with a unique ethos and environmental concerns at the heart of its business. Specialising in the use of hemp and natural fibres and drawing on the creative input of artists such as graffiti legend Futura 2000, Maharishi has created consistently innovative collections for men, women and children. 2001 saw the opening of the conceptual flagship store in Covent Garden, London. The space was developed to house each strand of the business from the Mhi clothing range to non-violent toys (in particular figurines of Warhol and Basquiat). The space mirrors the thinking behind the clothes – a combination of technical structuralism and the freedom of nature. Sticking to his roots Hardy has acknowledged the influence of camouflage with the recent publication of DPM (Disruptive Pattern Material), an encyclopaedic book charting the history of camouflage. In fact, camouflage has been a central trademark of Blechman's design. The military-issue textile is reinterpreted to create designs beautiful in their own right, taking influence from nature and art with tiger stripes and Warhol-inspired bright coloured prints. With such a strong foundation it is hard to imagine that Maharishi will continue to be anything other than one of the most innovative brands around.

Seit der Gründung von Maharishi im Jahr 1994 hat Hardy Blechman aus dem einstigen Lagerverkauf-Label für Streetwear ein florierendes Kreativimperium gemacht. Begonnen hatte er als Importeur von überschüssiger Kleidung nach Großbritannien, 1995 erlangte er dann internationale Berühmtheit mit der Erfindung der Snopant-Hose. Der 1963 in Bournemouth geborene Blechman ignorierte die traditionellen Methoden des Designs und behielt Maharishi als Firma mit einzigartigem Ethos und ökologischen Geschäftsgrundsätzen in Privatbesitz. Als Spezialist für die Verwendung von Hanf und anderer Naturfasern und durch kreativen Input von Künstlern wie der Graffitilegende Futura 2000 gelingen Maharishi immer wieder innovative Kollektionen für Männer, Frauen und Kinder. 2001 wurde der als Flagship Store geltende Laden im Londoner Stadtteil Covent Garden eröffnet. Der dort verfügbare Raum ist so aufgeteilt, dass jeder Geschäftszweig seinen Platz hat, von der Kleiderlinie Mhi bis zum gewaltfreien Spielzeug (vor allem Figuren nach Vorlagen von Warhol und Bas-

quiat). Das Ganze spiegelt die Denkweise, die hinter der Mode steckt, wider – eine Kombination aus technischem Strukturalismus und der Freiheit der Natur. Getreu seinen Wurzeln, hat Hardy in einer kürzlich erschienenen Veröffentlichung von DPM (Disruptive Pattern Material), einer Enzyklopädie über die Geschichte der Camouflage, die Bedeutung der Tarnmuster bestätigt. Schließlich war Camouflage eines der wichtigsten Markenzeichen von Blechmans Entwürfen. Er interpretierte den militärisch vorbelasteten Stoff neu und kreierte daraus Kleidung ganz eigener Schönheit. Dazu nutzte er Anregungen aus der Natur und der Kunst, wie Tigerstreifen oder von Warhol inspirierte leuchtend bunte grafische Muster. Angesichts eines so stabilen Fundaments kann man sich kaum vorstellen, dass Maharishi irgendwann einmal nicht mehr zu den innovativsten Marken schlechthin zählen sollte.

Depuis qu'il a lancé Maharishi en 1994, Hardy Blechman a transformé son business de stockiste streetwear en un prospère empire de la mode. De l'importation de vêtements de surplus au Royaume-Uni à la notoriété internationale que lui vaut son pantalon «Snopant» en 1995, Blechman (né en 1963 à Bournemouth) ignore les méthodes formelles de la création de mode et réussit à préserver l'indépendance de Maharishi, entreprise privée sensible aux problèmes d'environnement et dont le cœur palpite d'une éthique unique. Spécialisé dans la production de vêtements en chanvre et en fibres naturelles, Maharishi fait appel au talent de différents artistes, par exemple la légende du graffiti Futura 2000, ce qui permet à la griffe de proposer des collections toujours innovantes, que ce soit pour l'homme, la femme ou l'enfant. En 2001, Hardy Blechman ouvre une boutique-concept à Covent Garden. Conçu pour accueillir chaque ligne de Maharishi, de la gamme de vêtements Mhi aux jouets non violents (comme les figurines de Warhol et de Basquiat), cet espace reflète la pensée qui sous-tend sa démarche créative: une combinaison entre le structuralisme de la technique et la liberté de la nature. Fidèle à ses racines, Hardy Blechman célèbre l'impact de l'imprimé camouflage à travers la récente publication de DPM (Disruptive Pattern Material), un ouvrage encyclopédique qui retrace l'histoire de ce motif. En fait, le camouflage a toujours occupé un rôle central dans le travail de Blechman. Il revisite ce tissu militaire pour y couper de superbes créations, s'inspirant de la nature et des arts, par exemple avec des rayures de tigre ou des imprimés aux couleurs vives très Andy Warhol. Avec des fondations aussi solides, difficile d'imaginer que Maharishi puisse devenir autre chose que l'une des griffes les plus novatrices de notre époque.

WILL FAIRMAN

What are your signature designs? Performance hemp fabrics, Snopants, Dragon embroidery. The consistent use of camouflage in a non-military context in order to emphasise its natural and artistic roots What is your favourite piece from any of your collections? The Barbouta Hood, a kind of balaclava with a strong Italian medieval knight influence, or the Tour Jacket with interpretations of Playmospace characters (the original Playmo toys were clearly inspired by Stanley Kubrick's 2001: Space Odyssey) How would you describe your work? A mix of East/West, nature/technology, military/peace, utility/beauty What's your ultimate goal? To become at ease with my work and to relax into being What inspires you? Using Maharishi as a vehicle for a positive message and positive influence on fashion. I am also inspired, in general, by figures who encourage radical rethinking and ask people to consider life from different points of view, whether it be Mahatma Gandhi, Abbott Thayer (19th century American artist who pointed out how camouflage works in nature) or Stanley Kubrick Can fashion still have a political ambition? Yes. The media coverage it attracts means it can be an effective channel for expressing political messages. Politically charged clothing can also help people assume their chosen political identity (for example, an environmentalist might wear hemp clothing and an anti-war protester might wear recycled military surplus) Who do you have in mind when you design? Stylish people who appreciate the design influences of the natural world and global (often mystical) cultures, as well as technical innovations and up-to-date fabrics. I often create something I want to wear myself Is the idea of creative collaboration important to you? Collaboration has always been a crucial aspect for me, as the creation of Maharishi clothing is dependent on a team of people who are experts in their particular fields. I have also found that collaborating with various external guest artists has injected new ideas into the company Who has been the greatest influence on your career? Brendan Backmann, Alf Martin and Polly King How have your own experiences affected your work as a designer? Experience in the professional world constantly adds new facets. Personal experiences often influence themes for seasonal collections, and Maharishi would likely not exist if I hadn't travelled extensively in Asia in my late teens Which is more important in your work: the process or the product? I realise that the journey is the destination and strive to enjoy it as such but I'll still endure hardship and pain for the final product! Is designing difficult for you, if so, what drives you to continue? Sometimes it flows whereas at times it is just hard work. Rather than being driven to continue, I would need something to drive me to consider stopping Have you ever been influenced or moved by the reaction to your designs? Positive feedback about my designs has pushed me to seek out more and more engaging themes for my collections. Seeing my designs ripped off by other companies also encourages me to make Maharishi products more unique than the run-of-the-mill copies that proliferate in the market What's your definition of beauty? My idea of beauty is rooted in the natural world that surrounds us. I like to strive to translate the diversity and complexity of natural forms into my designs to encourage wider respect and admiration for them. It is important to remind humans of their relationship with nature, especially in these times of increasing urbanisation What's your philosophy? Planting seeds that inspire positive change in the wider high-street market What is the most important lesson you've learned? Life is temporary and full of illusion.

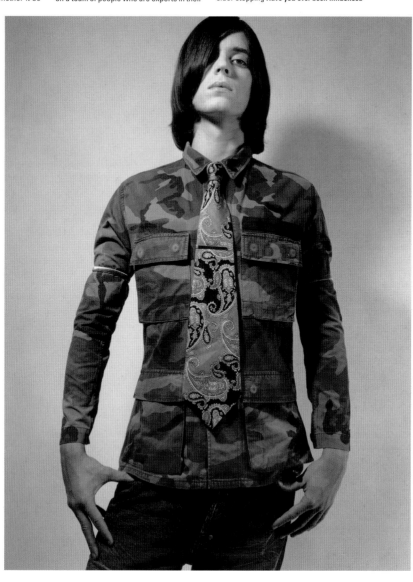

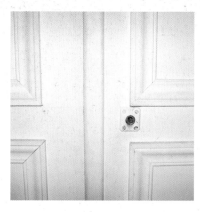

MAISON MARTIN MARGIELA

"To evolve is to continue to breathe creatively"

Martin Margiela is the fashion designer's fashion designer. Normally this comment could be read as a casual cliché, but in the case of Margiela it is justified. For unlike any other designer, he produces work which could be seen as a distinct form of 'metafashion': his clothes are essentially about clothes. With his own peculiar yet precise vision, he is one of the most influential and iconoclastic designers to have emerged over the past fifteen years. Born in 1959 in Limbourg, Belgium, he studied at Antwerp's Royal Academy and was part of the first wave of talent which would emerge from the city. Between 1984 and 1987 he assisted Jean Paul Gaultier; in 1988, Maison Martin Margiela was founded in Paris and his first womenswear collection, for spring/summer 1989, was shown the same year. Struggling to come to terms with a definition of Margiela's fashion, with its exposure of and mania for the process and craft of making clothes, the press labelled this new mood 'deconstruction'. Eschewing the cult of personality that attends many designers, Martin Margiela has instead fostered a cult of impersonality. Never photographed, never interviewed in person or as an individual ('Maison Margiela' answers faxed questions), even the label in his clothing remains blank (as in the main womenswear line) or simply has a number circled ('6' for women's basics and '10' for menswear). In 2000, the first Margiela shop opened in Tokyo, followed by stores in Brussels, Paris and London, and three further shops in Japan. From 1997 to 2003, in addition to his own collections, Margiela designed womenswear for Hermès, and in July 2002, Renzo Rosso, owner and president of the Diesel Group, became the major shareholder in Margiela's operating group, Neuf SA, allowing the company further expansion. Margiela has also participated in numerous exhibitions and in 2004 curated 'A' Magazine.

Martin Margiela ist der Modedesigner der Modedesigner. Diese Aussage könnte wie ein unbedachtes Klischee klingen, doch im Fall von Margiela hat sie tatsächlich ihre Berechtigung. Im Unterschied zu allen anderen Modeschöpfern erschafft er etwas, das man als besondere Form von „Meta-Mode" bezeichnen könnte: Seine Kleider sind die Quintessenz ihrer selbst. Dank seiner eigenwilligen, aber präzisen Vorstellungen ist er einer der einflussreichsten und umstürzlerischsten Designer, der in den vergangenen 15 Jahren von sich reden gemacht hat. Geboren wurde Margiela 1959 im belgischen Limbourg. Nach seinem Studium an der Königlichen Akademie in Antwerpen gehörte er zur ersten Welle neuer Talente aus dieser Stadt. Von 1984 bis 1987 arbeitete Margiela als Assistent für Jean Paul Gaultier, 1988 gründete er dann in Paris sein Label Maison Martin Margiela und präsentierte noch im selben Jahr seine erste Damenkollektion für Frühjahr/Sommer 1989. Die Presse taufte diese neue Strömung Dekonstruktivismus, weil es ihr schwer fiel, den Stil des Designers mit seiner Passion für die Entstehung von Mode und die Offenlegung dieses Prozesses genau zu

umreißen. Margiela lehnte den Personenkult ab, den so viele Designer pflegen, und machte stattdessen eher Unpersönlichkeit zum Kult. Der Designer lässt sich weder fotografieren noch als Person oder als Individuum interviewen – Maison Margiela beantwortet lediglich gefaxte Anfragen. Und selbst die Etiketten in den Kleidern bleiben leer (wie in der Hauptkollektion für Damen) oder tragen nur einen Kreis mit einer Ziffer darin (eine 6 für Damen-Basics, eine 10 für Herrenmode). Im Jahr 2000 wurde der erste Margiela-Laden in Tokio eröffnet, gefolgt von Filialen in Brüssel, Paris und London sowie drei weiteren Dependancen in Japan. Zwischen 1997 und 2003 entwarf Margiela zusätzlich zu seinen eigenen Kollektionen auch Damenmode für Hermès. Im Juli 2002 wurde der Eigentümer und Präsident der Diesel-Gruppe, Renzo Rosso, Mehrheitsaktionär von Margielas Betreibergesellschaft Neuf SA, was dem Unternehmen die weitere Expansion ermöglichte. Margiela hat bereits an zahlreichen Ausstellungen teilgenommen und kuratierte 2004 das „A"-Magazin.

Martin Margiela est le créateur de mode par excellence et en l'occurrence, ce banal cliché est tout à fait justifié. Contrairement à tout autre créateur, il produit un travail qui s'apparente à une forme distincte de « métamode » : en effet, ses vêtements parlent avant tout de vêtements. Sa vision particulière et bien définie l'a imposé comme l'un des stylistes les plus influents et les plus iconoclastes qui ont émergé ces quinze dernières années. Né en 1959 à Limbourg en Belgique, Martin Margiela étudie à l'Académie Royale d'Anvers et fait partie de la première vague de nouveaux talents de la ville. Entre 1984 et 1987, il est assistant de Jean Paul Gaultier ; en 1988, il fonde Maison Martin Margiela à Paris et présente sa première collection pour femme printemps/été 1989 la même année. Cherchant désespérément à définir la mode de Margiela, avec sa franchise et sa manie du procédé artisanal, la presse baptise ce nouveau style « déconstruction ». Evitant le culte de la personnalité qui guette de nombreux designers, Martin Margiela cherche au contraire à développer un culte de l'impersonnalité. Jamais pris en photo, jamais interviewé en personne (c'est Maison Margiela qui répond aux questions envoyées par fax), même la griffe de ses vêtements reste vierge (comme c'est le cas de la ligne principale pour femme) ou comporte simplement un numéro dans un cercle (« 6 » pour les basiques féminins et « 10 » pour les hommes). En l'an 2000, la première boutique Margiela ouvre ses portes à Tokyo, suivie par Bruxelles, Paris et Londres, puis par trois autres boutiques au Japon. Entre 1997 et 2003, outre ses propres collections, Margiela travaille comme styliste des lignes pour femme chez Hermès. En juillet 2002, Renzo Rosso, propriétaire et président du groupe Diesel, devient actionnaire majoritaire de Neuf SA, le groupe d'exploitation de Margiela, ce qui permet à l'entreprise de poursuivre son expansion. Margiela a également participé à de nombreuses expositions et présidé le comité de rédaction du magazine « A » en 2004. JO-ANN FURNISS

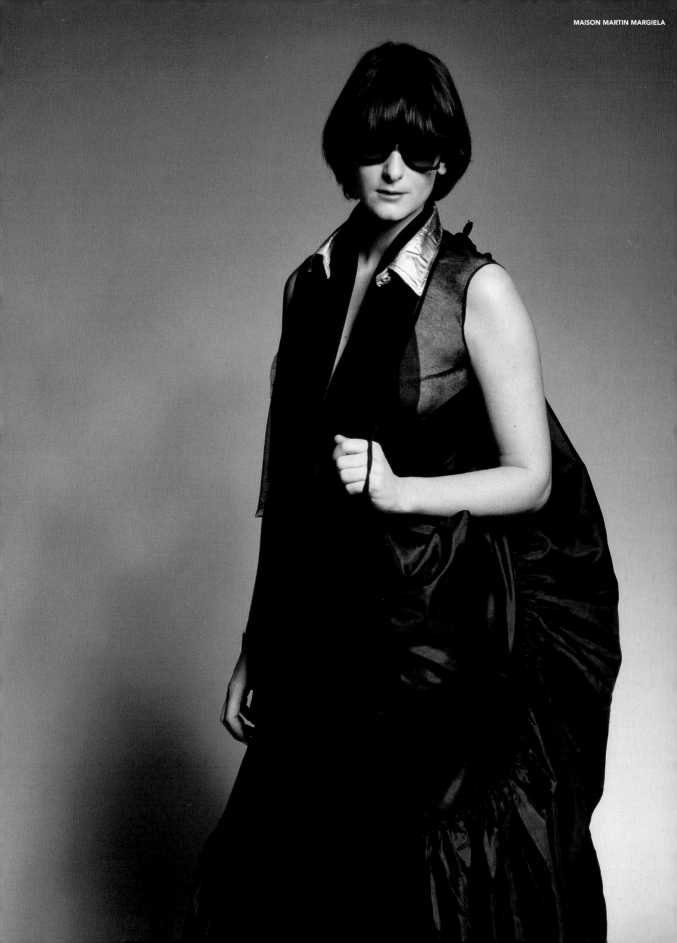

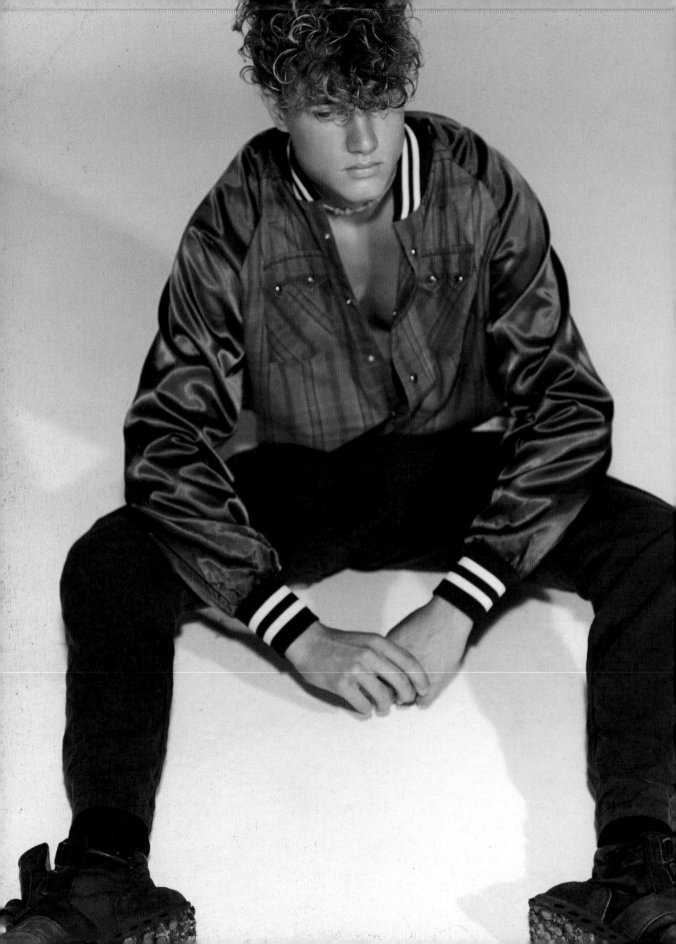

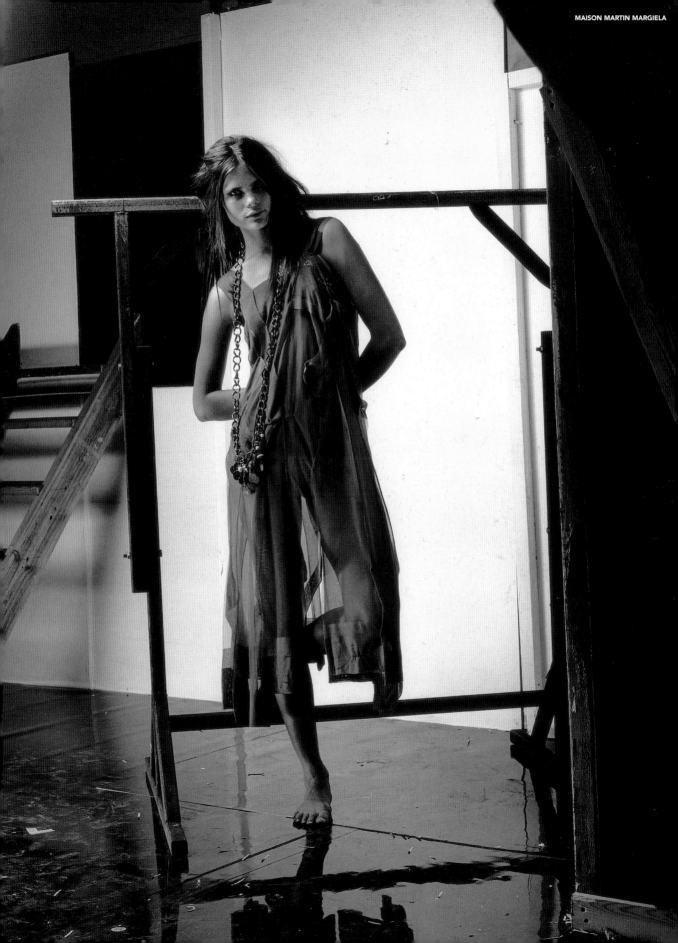

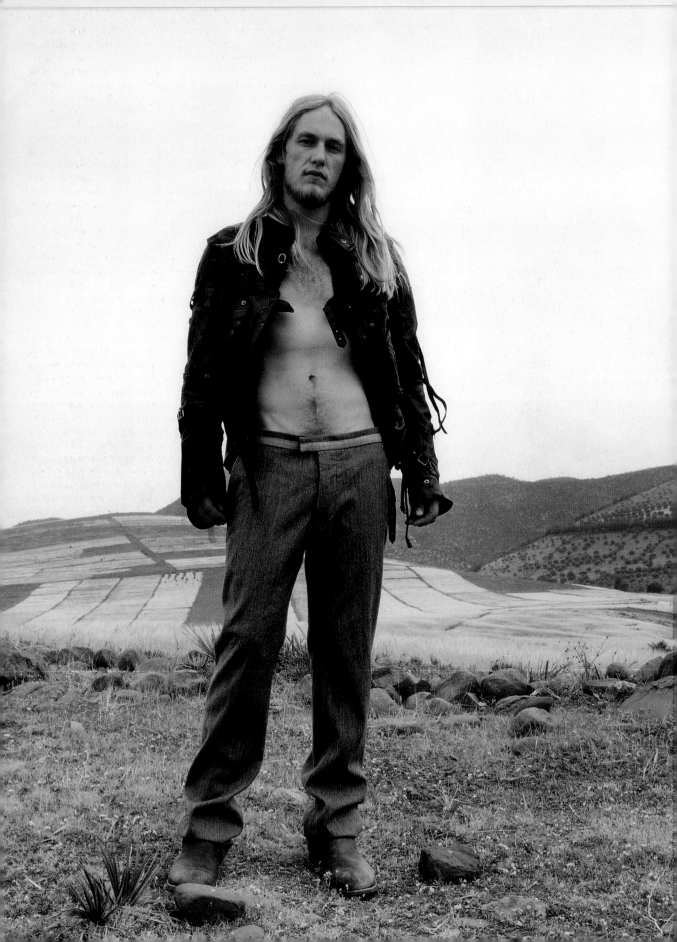

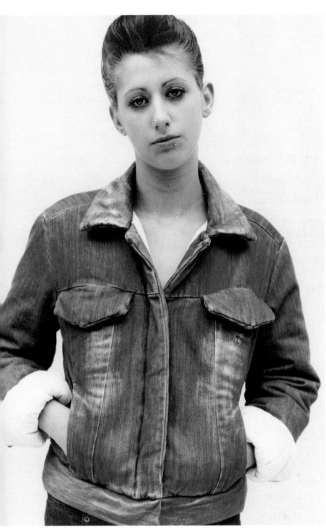

What are your signature designs? This is always a very tricky thing for a team in our position to answer. Others – especially those who follow our work and wear our clothes – will always have a totally different view on this. We will however venture to suggest some individual garments, as well as a few overriding themes of our collections, that might be worthy of being remembered after we are long gone! Among these might be... Our work for every collection since our first on what we refer to as our 'Artisanal Production' – the reworking of men's and women's vintage garments, fabrics and accessories. The silhouette that dominated our first ten collections – the 'cigarette' shoulder for which a roll of fabric was placed above the shoulder leaving the wearer's natural shoulder line define the garment. These were usually worn with long apron skirts in washed men's suiting fabric or men's jeans and suit trousers that were opened and reworked as skirts. The Martin Margiela

'Tabi' boot 6 spring/summer 1989 to the present day – based on a Japanese 'Tabi' sock these have been present in all of our collections and first commercialised in 1995. They were made up in leather, suede and canvas and mounted on a wooden heel of the diameter of the average human heel. Since 1991 – Vintage jeans and jeans jackets painted by hand. Winter 1991 – A sweater made entirely from opened and assembled military socks. The heels of the original socks helped form the shoulders, elbows and bust of the sweater. Autumn/winter 1994 – Elements of a doll's wardrobe were enlarged 5.2 times to a human scale. The disproportions and structures of the dolls pieces were maintained in the up-scaled reproductions – often rendering oversized, knit, collars, buttons and zips etc. Summer 1996 – A wardrobe for summer of photographed elements of a man's and woman's winter wardrobe. The photographs were printed on light fluid summer fabrics. Summer 1997 & winter 1997 – garments evoke the trial and development of prototype garments as worked on with a 'Tailor's Dummy'. A jacket of each of these seasons was in the shape of a 'Tailor's Dummy'. Spring/summer 2000 – autumn/winter 2001: A work on scale. The creation of a fictive Italian size 78. Elements of a man's and woman's wardrobe – dress jackets, suit jackets, bombers, pants and jeans are proposed in this one size and over the seasons the ways of treating these up-scaled garments varied. Trousers are fitted to size by folding them over and stitching them. The final version was for spring/spring 2002 when these garments were raw cut to the waistline of the wearer. Spring/summer 2002 – garments constructed entirely as circles. When laid flat they seem as an object and when worn they take the form of the body offering a draping effect. Vintage men's perfecto leather flight jackets are reworked into a circular shape making them seem cropped when worn. Autumn/winter 2003 – The gesture of lifting the hem of a garment incorporated into their structure. Hemlines of shirts and dress are lifted and attached onto the garment – at the waistline or even the shoulder – creating a draping effect and often making their lining visible. Spring/summer 2005 – Garments inspired by vintage dresses, skirts, men shirts etc. constructed to be worn shifted horizontally on the body. Evening dresses in bright colours seem as short skirts with necklines and arms draped to one side of the skirt and the original skirt hanging to the opposite side. The neckline of a man's shirt becomes an armhole with the line of central buttons worn horizontally

across the chest **What is your favourite piece from any of your collections?** Impossible to say – so many have their own place, importance and significance for us in our memory of our work and development **How would you describe your work?** A continuation and deepening of our creativity, technical experience, collaboration and craft **What's your ultimate goal?** Evolving while seeking out those new challenges that continue to stimulate us **What inspires you?** Integrity, attentiveness, conviction, individuality, patience, respect and courage **Can fashion still have a political ambition?** Garments, creativity, tradition and style, rather than fashion, will always touch on the human politic **Who do you have in mind when you design?** Not one person, male or female, in particular and more an overall, yet sometimes, specific attitude **Is the idea of creative collaboration important to you?** Yes, it is a lifeblood albeit not often easy! An individual creative point of view has often little to do with the democracy of a group in its collective expression! It is for this reason that individual conviction within a team often demands extra effort and the unremitting respect of which it is so, so worthy **Who has been the greatest influence on your career?** Those who support us and above all those who encourage us by taking what we produce into their lives, wardrobes and style **How have your own experiences affected your work as a designer?** We all here have another approach to this – yet, in the main – a constant questioning of our 'purpose' and our creative point of view. Our recognition that we have a constant responsibility to reassess and challenge ourselves in our work and lives together. That to evolve is to continue to breathe creatively **Which is more important in your work: the process or the product?** The process of course and the result! – As it hangs on the hanger and more so, on the body **Is designing difficult for you and, if so, what drives you to continue?** Yes! The great liberty and stimulation which the expression of our creativity brings us. The fact that our creative expression touches and encourages others **Have you ever been influenced or moved by the reaction to your designs?** Constantly, thankfully **What's your definition of beauty?** The courage of honesty. Subjectivity. Integrity. Reality. Nature **What's your philosophy?** That the heart should and can always rule the head **What is the most important lesson you've learned?** That talent, in others and one's self, is to be cherished and nurtured. That a team is only as fast as its slowest member.

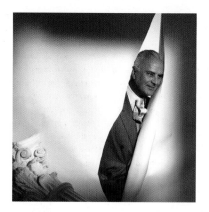

MANOLO BLAHNIK

"I have a passion for work"

Manolo Blahnik was wrong when he said "shoes help transform a woman". He should have said "my shoes transform a woman." Born on the Canary Islands in 1942 to a Spanish mother and a Czech father, Blahnik studied law and literature in Geneva, moving onto art in Paris in the mid-'60s, and set design in London soon after. Always in the right place at the right time, he met Diana Vreeland on a visit to New York in 1970. Seeing his sketches of shoes, the influential American Vogue editor advised him to pursue a career in footwear. To the delight of women ever since – and in particular one Carrie Bradshaw, who made him a household name 30 years later – Blahnik did so. Back in London, he learnt his craft by visiting shoe factories and studying each stage of footwear alchemy (he is still very much hands-on, and makes shoe himself). Within a year, Blahnik was making the delicate, resolutely feminine shoes he has become famous for. In 1968 he opened his first boutique in London's Chelsea. It attracted such fans as Bianca Jagger, Jerry Hall and Marie Helvin. Very much part of this glamorous set, in 1974 Blahnik was the first man featured on the cover of British Vogue. He started collaborating with young designers in the '70s – first, with Ossie Clark in 1972. Names as diverse as Calvin Klein, John Galliano and Proenza Schouler have all had their footwear created by him. Blahnik has won countless awards, including an Honorary Doctorate from the RCA in 2001 and the first ever Silver Slipper Award given to a shoe designer in 1999. To add to his design icon status, London's Design Museum staged the first Blahnik retrospective in 2003.

Manolo Blahnik irrte, als er konstatierte: „Schuhe können eine Frau verwandeln." Er hätte sagen sollen: „Meine Schuhe können eine Frau verwandeln." Der 1942 auf den Kanaren geborene Sohn einer spanischen Mutter und eines tschechischen Vaters studierte in Genf Jura und Literatur, dann im Paris der 1960er Jahre Kunst, um schließlich in London Bühnenbildner zu werden. Immer zur rechten Zeit am rechten Ort, lernte er bei einem New-York-Aufenthalt 1970 Diana Vreeland kennen. Nachdem er ihr seine Entwürfe für Schuhe gezeigt hatte, riet ihm die einflussreiche Journalistin von der amerikanischen Vogue zu einer Karriere in der Schuhbranche. Zur Freude der Frauen im allgemeinen und zu der von Carrie Bradshaw im besonderen, die seinen Namen dreißig Jahre später in aller Munde brachte, befolgte Blahnik diesen Rat. Zurück in London lernte er sein Handwerk, indem er Schuhfabriken besuchte und jedes Stadium der Schuh-Alchemie studierte (er ist nach wie vor sehr praxisverbunden und fertigt auch noch selbst Schuhe). Innerhalb eines Jahres war Blahnik damals so weit, dass er die feinen, dezidiert femininen Schuhe schuf, mit denen er berühmt werden sollte. Seinen ersten Laden eröffnete er 1968 im Londoner Viertel Chelsea.

Dort fanden sich bald Fans wie Bianca Jagger, Jerry Hall und Marie Helvin ein. Da er rasch selbst ein Teil dieser glamourösen Gesellschaft wurde, konnte man ihn 1974 als ersten Mann auf dem Cover der britischen Vogue sehen. Seine Zusammenarbeit mit jungen Designern begann ebenfalls in den 1970er Jahren – zunächst 1972 mit Ossie Clark. So ließen Designer wie Calvin Klein, John Galliano und Proenza Schouler ihre Schuhe von ihm kreieren. Blahnik selbst wurde mit zahllosen Auszeichnungen dekoriert, darunter die Ehrendoktorwürde des Royal College of Art und 1999 der erste Silver Slipper Award, der je an einen Schuhdesigner verliehen wurde. Seinen Status als Design-Ikone festigte 2003 das Londoner Design Museum mit der ersten Blahnik-Retrospektive.

Manolo Blahnik s'est mal exprimé quand il a déclaré que les chaussures aidaient à transformer les femmes. Il aurait dû dire : « Mes chaussures transforment les femmes ». Né en 1942 aux îles Canaries d'une mère espagnole et d'un père tchèque le jeune Blahnik suit des études de droit et de littérature à Genève, puis part à Paris pour étudier l'art au milieu des années 60 avant de s'installer à Londres, peu de temps après, pour se consacrer à la décoration. Toujours au bon endroit au bon moment, il rencontre Diana Vreeland en 1970 lors d'un séjour à New York. Après avoir vu ses croquis de chaussures, l'influente rédactrice en chef du Vogue américain lui conseille de se lancer dans la chaussure, et ce, pour le plus grand bonheur des femmes, notamment de Carrie Bradshaw qui le rendra célèbre trente ans plus tard. Blahnik décide de suivre ce conseil avisé. De retour à Londres, il se forme en visitant des fabriques de chaussures et en étudiant chaque étape du processus de production (il adopte encore une approche très pratique de son art et fabrique lui-même les formes de ses modèles). En moins d'un an, Blahnik réussit à créer les chaussures délicates et résolument féminines qui feront sa gloire. En 1968, il ouvre une première boutique à Chelsea (Londres) qui attire des fans tels que Bianca Jagger, Jerry Hall et Marie Helvin. Membre à part entière de cette scène glamour, Blahnik devient en 1974 le premier homme à faire la couverture du Vogue anglais. Il commence à collaborer avec de jeunes créateurs des années 70, d'abord avec Ossie Clark en 1972. Des noms aussi divers que Calvin Klein, John Galliano et Proenza Schouler lui ont tous commandé des modèles de chaussures. Blahnik s'est vu décerner d'innombrables distinctions, dont un doctorat honorifique du Royal College of Art en 2001, ainsi que le tout premier Silver Slipper Award jamais remis à un créateur de chaussures, en 1999. Et pour compléter le tableau de cette icône de la mode, le Design Museum de Londres a organisé la première rétrospective Manolo Blahnik en 2003.

LAUREN COCHRANE

What are your signature designs? High, sexy but always elegant **What is your favourite piece from any of your collections?** There are so many. Although the beaded up the leg sandals I did for John Galliano for his Dior couture 'Masai Warrior' collection are a particular favourite. And I still adore my futuristic collection from 1986 **How would you describe your work?** It is one of the most satisfying parts of my life **What's your ultimate goal?** To always be a challenge to myself **What inspires you?** The changes from day to day. It even surprises me… movies, books, painting, architecture, landscapes and certain women I see sometimes in the streets **Can fashion still have a political ambition?** I know nothing about ambition and even less about politics, but fashion often reflects the times **Who do you have in mind when you design?** So many things of totally different natures **Is the idea of creative collaboration important to you?** Sometimes **Who or what has been the greatest influence on your career?** Mr Luciano Visconti comes to mind right away and great fashion icons like Diana Vreeland, and of course Balenciaga, and my homeland Spain **How have your own experiences affected your work as a designer?** Don't you think all our experiences influence our lives and our work? At least for me I can say yes **Which is more important in your work: the process or the product?** Both envelop us, but I love the process because I know that little by little it will determine the product **Is designing difficult for you, if so, what drives you to continue?** I have a passion for work and all passions can have their difficulties **Have you ever been influenced or moved by the reaction to your designs?** Always **What's your definition of beauty?** Beauty is captured in fleeting moments and reflected in one's eyes **What's your philosophy?** Work hard **What is the most important lesson you've learned?** Whatever you do… always do your best.

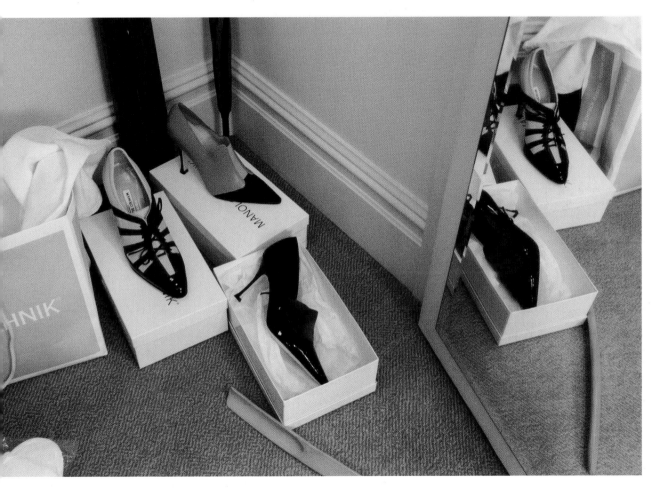

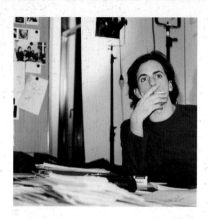

MARC JACOBS

"It's important for me that my clothes are not just an exercise in runway high jinks"

Season after season, Marc Jacobs (born New York, 1963), manages to predict exactly what women all over the world want to wear, whether that be his super-flat 'mouse' pumps, Sergeant Pepper-style denim jackets or 'Venetia' handbags fitted with outsized silver buckles. Born in New York's Upper West Side to parents who both worked for the William Morris Agency, Jacobs was raised by his fashion-conscious grandmother. As a teenager, Jacobs immersed himself in club culture, observing the beautiful people at the Mudd Club, Studio 54 and Hurrah. Today, Jacobs' most fruitful source of inspiration is still the crowd of cool girls that surround him (including the stylist Venetia Scott, director Sofia Coppola and numerous art-house actresses). After high school, Jacobs completed a fashion degree at Parsons School of Design; his graduation collection (1984), which featured brightly-coloured knits, caught the eye of Robert Duffy, an executive who remains Jacobs' business partner to this day. Together they launched the first Marc Jacobs collection (1986), winning a CFDA award (the first of six, to date) the following year. In 1989 Jacobs was named head designer at Perry Ellis. His experience there was tempestuous and his infamous 'grunge' collection of 1992 – featuring satin Birkenstocks and silk plaid shirts – marked his exit from the company. By 1997 Jacobs' star was in the ascendant once again, when LVMH appointed him artistic director at Louis Vuitton. Jacobs has enhanced the luggage company's image – not least through his collaborations with artists Takashi Murakami and Stephen Sprouse on seasonal handbag designs – and re-positioned it as a ready-to-wear fashion brand. Meanwhile LVMH have supported Jacobs' own company, which has since launched Marc by Marc Jacobs (2001), his first perfume (2001) and a homeware collection (2003).

Saison für Saison gelingt es dem 1963 in New York geborenen Marc Jacobs, exakt vorherzusagen, was die Frauen überall auf der Welt tragen wollen – seien es superflache Mouse-Pumps, Jeansjacken im Sergeant-Pepper-Stil oder Venetia-Handtaschen mit überdimensionalen Silberschnallen. Der an der Upper West Side als Kind von Eltern, die beide für die William Morris Agency tätig waren, geborene Jacobs wurde von einer modebewussten Großmutter aufgezogen. Als Teenager vertiefte er sich in die Clubkultur und studierte die Beautiful People der 1970er Jahre im Mudd Club, im Studio 54 sowie im Hurrah. Noch heute ist Jacobs' fruchtbarste Inspirationsquelle die Truppe von coolen Girls, die ihn umgeben (darunter die Stylistin Venetia Scott, die Regisseurin Sofia Coppola und zahlreiche Art-House-Schauspielerinnen). Nach der Highschool machte Jacobs sein Modeexamen an der Parsons School of Design. 1984 erregte seine Abschlusskollektion mit leuchtend bunten Stricksachen die Aufmerksamkeit des Managers Robert Duffy, der bis heute sein Geschäftspartner ist. Gemeinsam brachten sie 1986 die erste Marc-Jacobs-Kollektion heraus und gewannen damit

ein Jahr später den ersten von mittlerweile sechs CFDA-Preisen. 1989 wurde Jacobs Chefdesigner bei Perry Ellis. Dort erlebte er ziemlich stürmische Zeiten und verabschiedete sich mit seiner berüchtigten Grunge-Kollektion von 1992, zu der Birkenstocks aus Satin und Karohemden aus Seide gehörten. Ab 1997 war Jacobs' Stern wieder im Steigen begriffen, als ihn der LVMH-Konzern zum künstlerischen Direktor von Louis Vuitton ernannte. Jacobs verbesserte das Image des traditionellen Reisegepäck-Labels, nicht zuletzt durch seine Zusammenarbeit mit den Künstlern Takashi Murakami und Stephen Sprouse im saisonalen Handtaschendesign. Außerdem hat er die Prêt-à-porter-Mode des Hauses neu positioniert. Inzwischen unterstützt LVMH auch Jacobs' eigenes Unternehmen, das die Linien Marc by Marc Jacobs (2001), einen ersten Duft (2001) und eine Homeware-Kollektion (2003) umfasst.

Saison après saison, Marc Jacobs (né en 1963 à New York) réussit à prédire exactement ce que les femmes du monde entier auront envie de porter, qu'il s'agisse de ses ballerines « souris » ultraplates, de ses vestes en denim à la Sergeant Pepper ou des sacs à main Venetia ornés d'énormes boucles en argent. Né à New York dans l'Upper West Side de parents travaillant tous deux pour la William Morris Agency, Jacobs est élevé par sa grand-mère passionnée de mode. Adolescent, il s'immerge dans la culture club du milieu des années 70 et aime à observer les beautiful people qui se retrouvent au Mudd Club, au Studio 54 et au Hurrah. Aujourd'hui, la source d'inspiration la plus fructueuse de Jacobs réside dans la foule de filles branchées qui l'entoure (incluant la styliste Venetia Scott, la réalisatrice Sofia Coppola et de nombreuses actrices du cinéma indépendant). Après le lycée, Jacobs obtient un diplôme en mode de la Parsons School of Design ; sa collection de fin d'études (1984), avec sa maille aux couleurs vives, attire l'attention de l'homme d'affaires Robert Duffy, qui reste son partenaire commercial à ce jour. Ensemble, ils lancent la première collection Marc Jacobs (1986), couronnée l'année suivante par un prix du CFDA (le premier d'une série de six). En 1989, Jacobs est nommé styliste principal de Perry Ellis. Son expérience chez Perry Ellis est orageuse et sa scandaleuse collection « grunge » de 1992, avec ses Birkenstocks en satin et ses chemises en soie à carreaux écossais, signe ses adieux à la maison. En 1997, l'étoile de Marc Jacobs remonte au firmament quand LVMH le nomme directeur artistique de Louis Vuitton. Jacobs révolutionne l'image du fabricant de bagages, notamment grâce à des collaborations artistiques avec Takashi Murakami et Stephen Sprouse sur la création de sacs à main de saison, et repositionne la griffe comme une marque de prêt-à-porter. Parallèlement, LVMH finance la griffe éponyme de Jacobs, qui depuis a lancé Marc by Marc Jacobs (2001), son premier parfum (2001) et une collection d'articles pour la maison (2003).

SUSIE RUSHTON

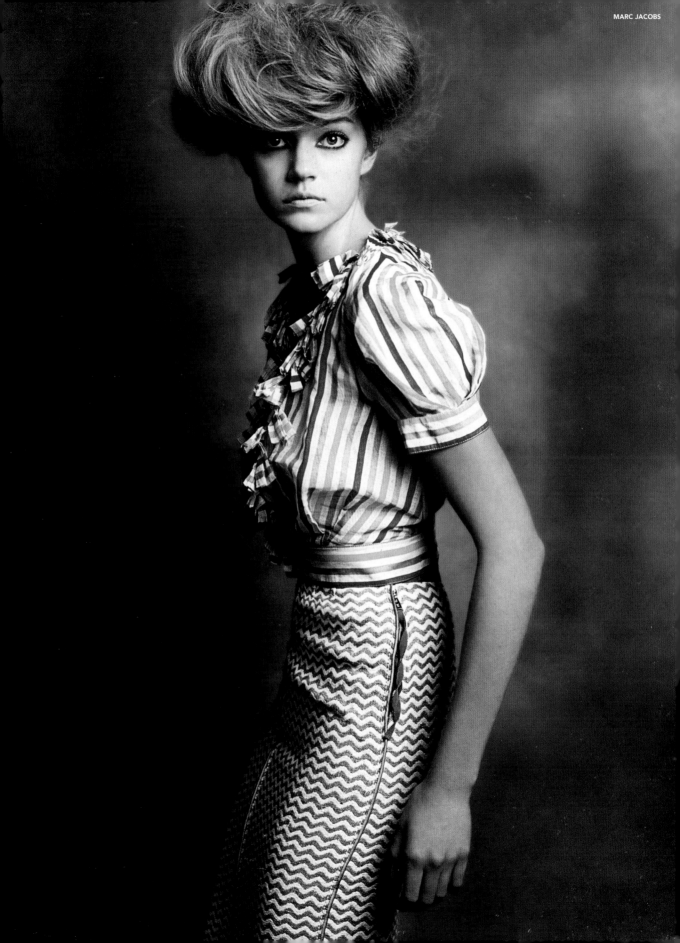

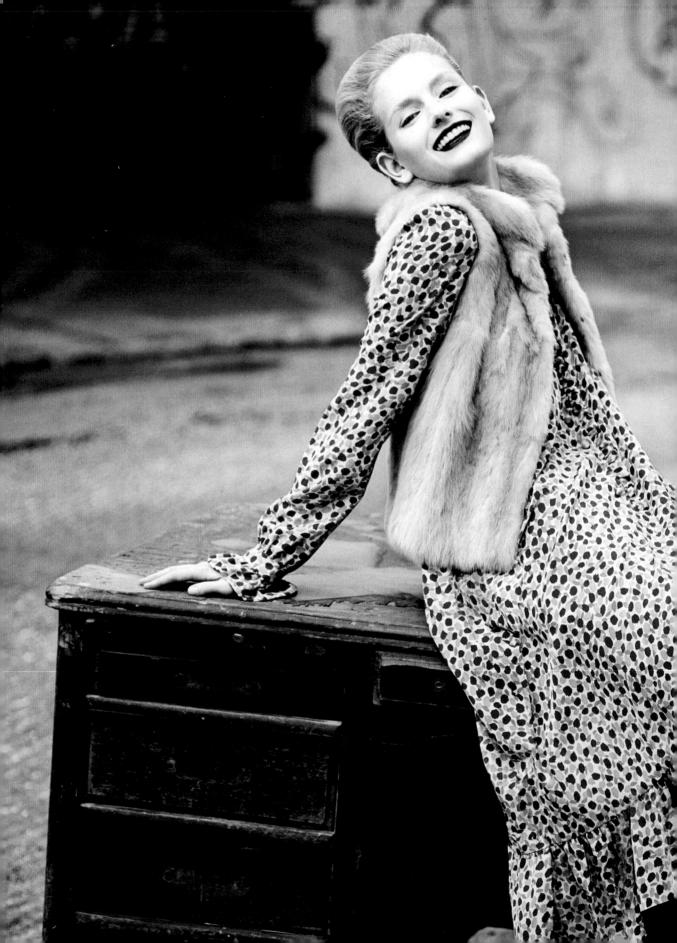

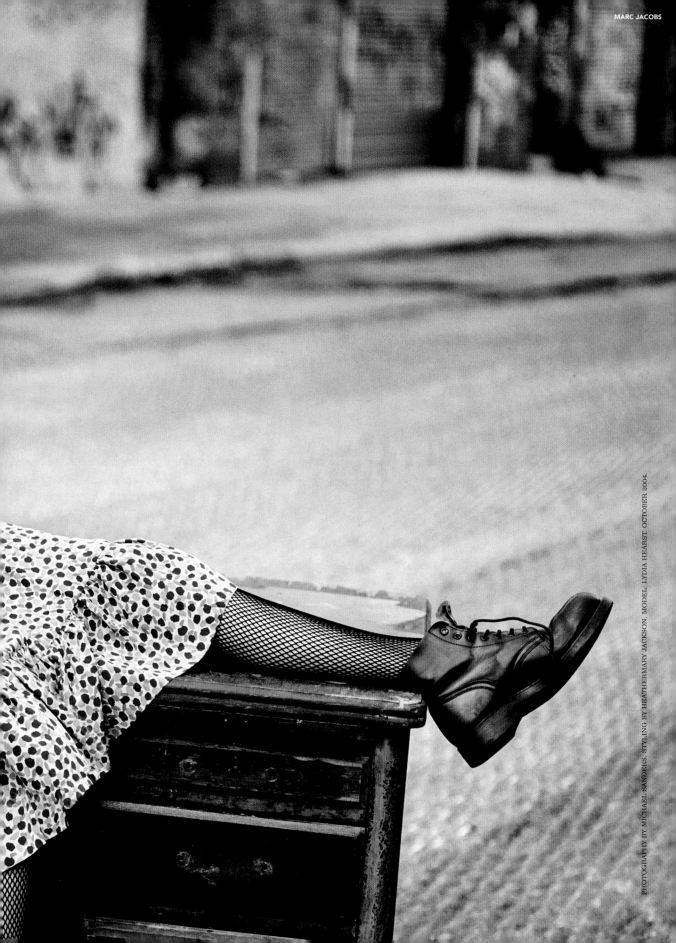

PHOTOGRAPHY BY MICHAEL SANDERS. STYLING BY HEATHERMARY JACKSON. MODEL: LYDIA HEARST. OCTOBER 2004.

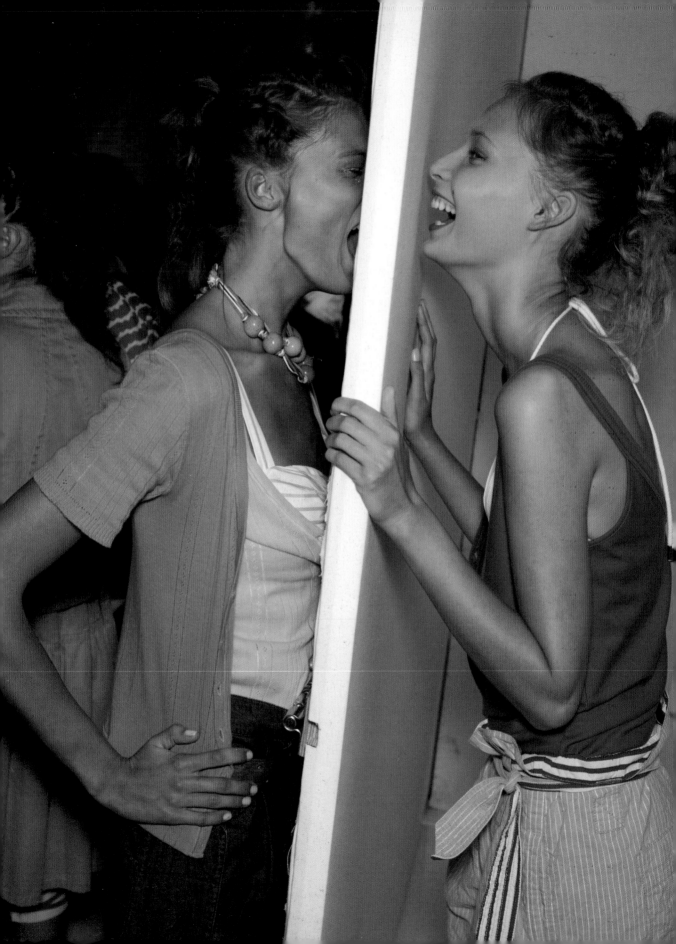

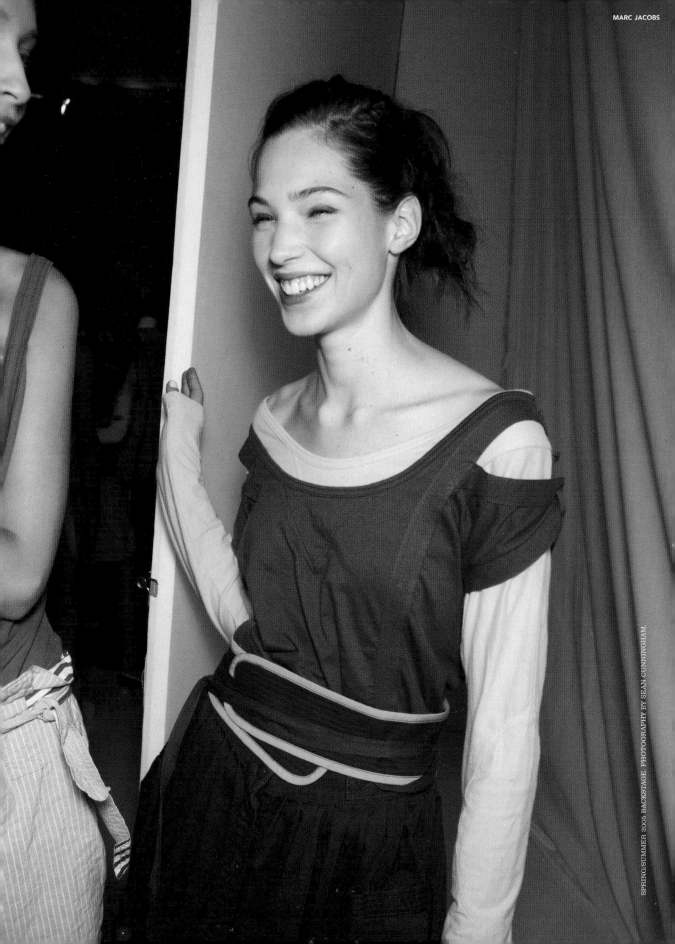

SPRING/SUMMER 2005 BACKSTAGE. PHOTOGRAPHY BY SEAN CUNNINGHAM.

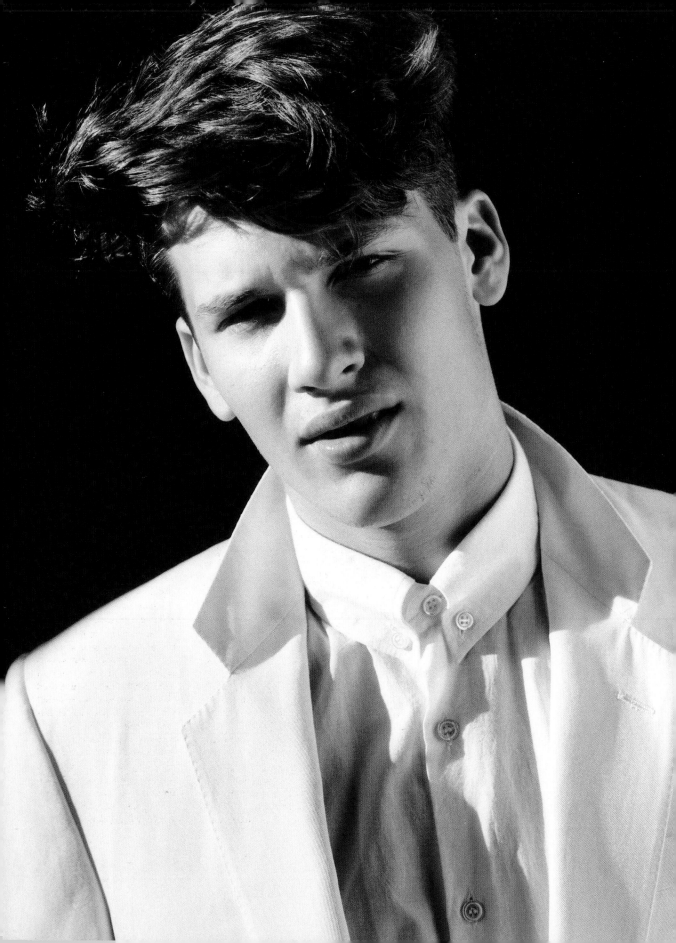

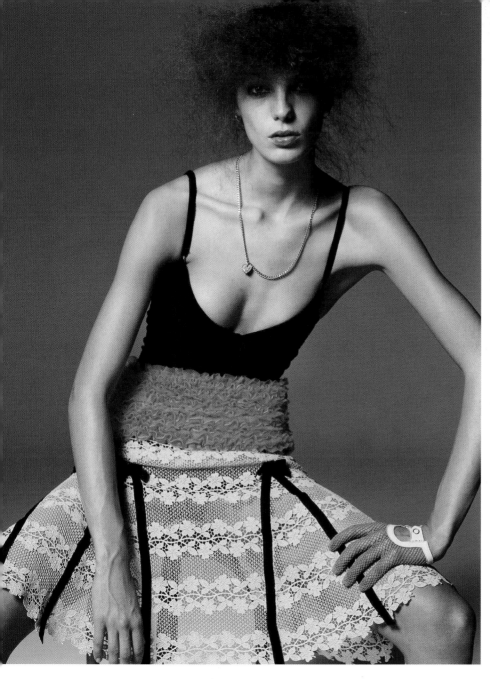

important, because everything we make is some kind of fantasy; even if it's quite practical, it's still a heightened reality. But I like the believability factor in clothes, so I like to think that a person I know, or some person I don't know who has an eclectic sense of style, could actually be walking down a street in one of those looks. It's important for me to think that it's not just an exercise in runway high jinks **Is the idea of creative collaboration important to you?** I love working with people. Everybody brings something to the party **Who has been the greatest influence on your career?** I've always been very influenced by the mystique of the house of Saint Laurent. That's my fashion fantasy. But I guess I'm just influenced by people who are really, really passionate about their work. That could be musicians or artists or fashion designers, whoever, just somebody being so committed, and so truly connected, always inspires me **How have your own experiences affected your work as a designer?** I can imagine there were seasons when certain designers did such a good collection they must have felt like they were 'it' for the season. But I've never felt like 'it' and I don't think I ever will. I feel very outside. I'm comfortable acting within the fashion system. But I think I'm quite separate in a way **Which is more important in your work: the process or the product?** You can't have one without the other **Is designing difficult for you and, if so, what drives you to continue?** I define design as a series of creative choices. And there are so many choices that one can make. I don't know how it is with other people, but for me it is a very painful process because I feel like there has to be integrity and meaning in the choices. And I doubt myself a lot, I don't really have a lot of self-confidence. But I really, really enjoy being a part of this process and, even though it's painful for me sometimes, there's nothing else I'd rather be doing. I guess it's a gift to feel so passionate about something. What got us to this point is doing what we believe in our hearts is right **Have you ever been influenced or moved by the reaction to your designs?** Yeah, I have. I love it when I see strangers wearing my clothes, because there is such a vast amount of choice out there, and somebody choosing the work that we've done over somebody else's is a big thing **What is the most important lesson you've learned?** It has very little to do with fashion. The most important lesson I've learned is to just be present. Enjoy life today.

What's your favourite piece from any of your collections? Although there are pieces that I love, it's not only about the piece, but the piece on the right girl. What I really, truly love is the whole image **How would you describe your work?** I find it easy, perhaps too easy, to make things seem naughty or too – I hate this word – edgy. I find that all too easy. I quite like the idea of doing something more intelligent **What's your ultimate goal?** People say, 'Well, what's left?

All I want to do is what I'm doing today. And I would like to be able to do it tomorrow **What inspires you?** I do love rock 'n' roll music, I do love going out, I do love partying and having a good time. When it comes to fashion I'm inspired by those things, but I try not to hold a mirror up to them and present a sort of clichéd, surface poseur version **What do you have in mind when you design?** I like to think that the clothes could have a life after the show is over. And that's

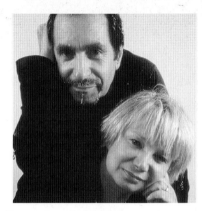

MARITHÉ + FRANÇOIS GIRBAUD

"We have always favoured the collaboration
between a man and a woman who are very different"

Inspired by the America of the European imagination, the Girbaud brand brings the work garment of the cowboy, blue jeans, to those raised on a diet of American music and cinema. Steering their work away from the edicts of fashion, Marithé and François Girbaud strive to create garments that complement the realities of life and style. Laser-cut, Lycra-fused, distressed and ripped denims are used to create clothing that is both striking and wearable. Comfort and functionality are placed on an equal footing. Despite their innovative approach to design, the couple stress that their work is governed more by attitude than by trend. Both born during the '40s, Marithé and François met in 1960 and by 1964 had begun to import cowboy clothing for Western House, the first Parisian boutique of its kind. Over the next few years they began to tamper with the classic blue jeans template, employing harsh cleaning and abrasive techniques to soften and fade denim, creating the stonewashed look that now dominates the marketplace. In 1969 they signed their first licensing agreement for the brand CA, and in 1972 they opened their first shop, Boutique, in Les Halles, Paris. The Girbauds continued to experiment, and in 1986 they made their first appearance at Paris Fashion Week, finally designing under their own name. Since then the brand has grown exponentially, and now claims stores and franchises in several countries throughout the world. Building on the foundations laid by jeans design, the Girbaud brand has expanded into other areas, including footwear and accessories, sportswear and glasses. Although jeans and denim detail remain a recurring theme throughout their work, the Girbauds' collections now include a variety of fabrics and print designs that range from leather and tartan to pinstripe and floral cotton.

Inspiriert von der europäischen Vorstellung von Amerika, bringt die Marke Girbaud mit der Bluejeans die Arbeitskleidung der Cowboys zu Leuten, die mit amerikanischer Musik und amerikanischen Filmen groß geworden sind. Fern von den Zwängen der Mode bemühen sich Marithé und François Girbaud, Kleider zu kreieren, die den Realitäten von Alltag und Lebensstil gerecht werden. Lasergeschnittene, mit Lycra gemischte, abgenutzte und zerschlissene Denimstoffe werden zu Kleidung verarbeitet, die verblüfft, aber zugleich tragbar ist. Komfort und Funktionalität stehen hier auf einer Stufe. Trotz seines innovativen Designansatzes legt das Paar Wert darauf, eher von seiner Einstellung als von irgendwelchen Trends beeinflusst zu sein. Beide sind Mitte der 1940er Jahre geboren und lernten sich 1960 kennen. Ab 1964 importierten sie Cowboykleidung für Western House, die erste Pariser Boutique dieser Art. Im Laufe der nächsten Jahre fingen sie an, mit dem klassischen Bluejeans-Modell zu experimentieren. Sie nutzten radikale Wasch- und Schleifmethoden, um das Material weicher und heller zu machen, und kreierten auf diese Weise den inzwischen marktbeherr-schenden Stonewashed-Look. 1969 unterzeichneten sie den ersten Lizenzvertrag für die Marke CA, 1972 wurde ihr erster Laden namens Boutique im Pariser Viertel Les Halles eröffnet. Die Girbauds setzten ihre Experimente fort und gaben 1986 ihr Debüt bei der Pariser Modewoche. Erst ab diesem Zeitpunkt entwarfen sie unter eigenem Namen. Seit damals ist die Marke exponentiell gewachsen und beliefert inzwischen eigene Läden und Franchise Stores in mehreren Ländern auf der ganzen Welt. Ausgehend vom Jeansdesign, hat das Label Girbaud zwischenzeitlich auch in andere Bereiche expandiert, darunter Schuhe und Accessoires, Sportswear und Brillen. Auch wenn Jeanshosen und Denim ein Dauerthema ihrer Arbeit sind, umfassen die Kollektionen der Girbauds heute eine Vielzahl von Stoffen und Mustern, die von Leder und Schottentuch bis hin zu Nadelstreifen und floral gemusterter Baumwolle reichen.

Inspirée par l'image que les Européens se font de l'Amérique, la marque Girbaud propose l'uniforme du cow-boy, le « blue jeans », à tous ceux qui ont grandi bercés par la musique et le cinéma américains. Ignorant les diktats de la mode, Marithé et François Girbaud s'efforcent de créer des vêtements capables d'accompagner les réalités de la vie. Les denims coupés au laser, thermocollés de Lycra, vieillis et déchirés leur permettent de créer des pièces très originales et néanmoins portables. Ils placent le confort et la fonctionnalité sur un pied d'égalité. Malgré son approche innovante de la mode, le couple insiste sur le fait que son travail reste davantage gouverné par l'attitude que par la tendance. Tous deux nés dans les années 40, Marithé et François se rencontrent en 1960 et commencent à importer les uniformes des cow-boys américains dès 1964 pour Western House, première boutique parisienne du genre. Les années suivantes, ils s'attaquent au blue jean classique en employant des techniques agressives de lavage et d'abrasion pour assouplir et délaver le denim, et inventent le « stonewash », procédé industriel aujourd'hui incontournable. En 1969, ils signent leur premier accord de licence pour la marque CA, puis en 1972, ils ouvrent un premier espace de vente simplement baptisé « Boutique » dans le quartier des Halles à Paris. Les Girbaud poursuivent leurs expérimentations et présentent finalement en 1986 une collection sous leur propre nom lors de la Semaine de la Mode de Paris. Depuis, la marque se développe à un rythme exponentiel et revendique aujourd'hui plusieurs boutiques et franchisés dans divers pays du monde. A partir de son cœur de métier, la marque Girbaud s'est diversifiée dans d'autres domaines tels que les chaussures, les accessoires, le sportswear et les lunettes. Bien que les jeans et les pièces en denim restent le thème récurrent de leur travail, les collections des Girbaud incluent désormais toute une variété de tissus et d'imprimés, du cuir aux carreaux écossais en passant par le coton mille-raies et les motifs floraux.

DAVID VASCOTT

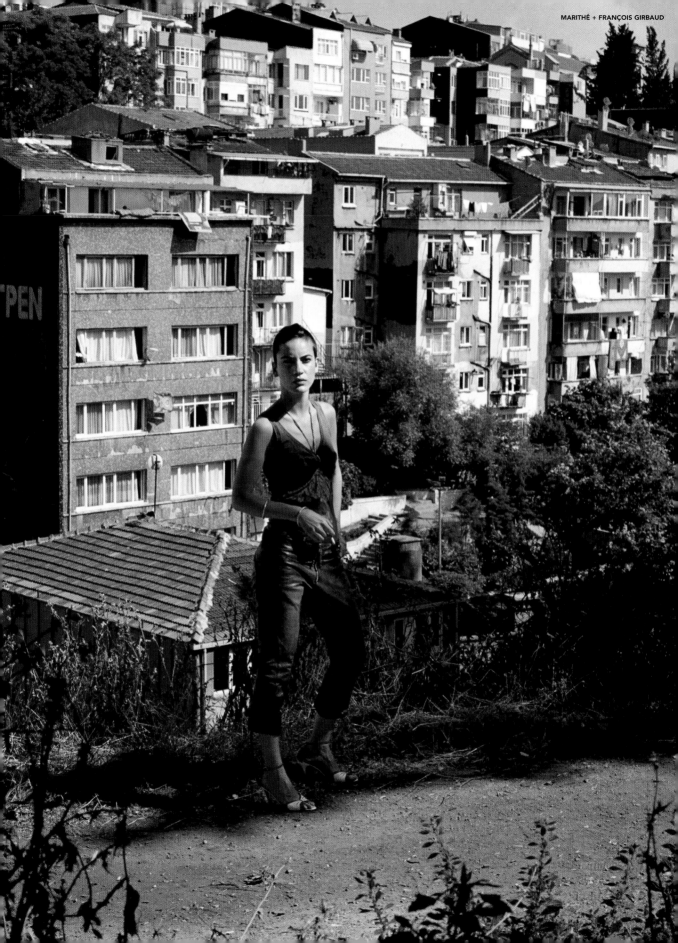

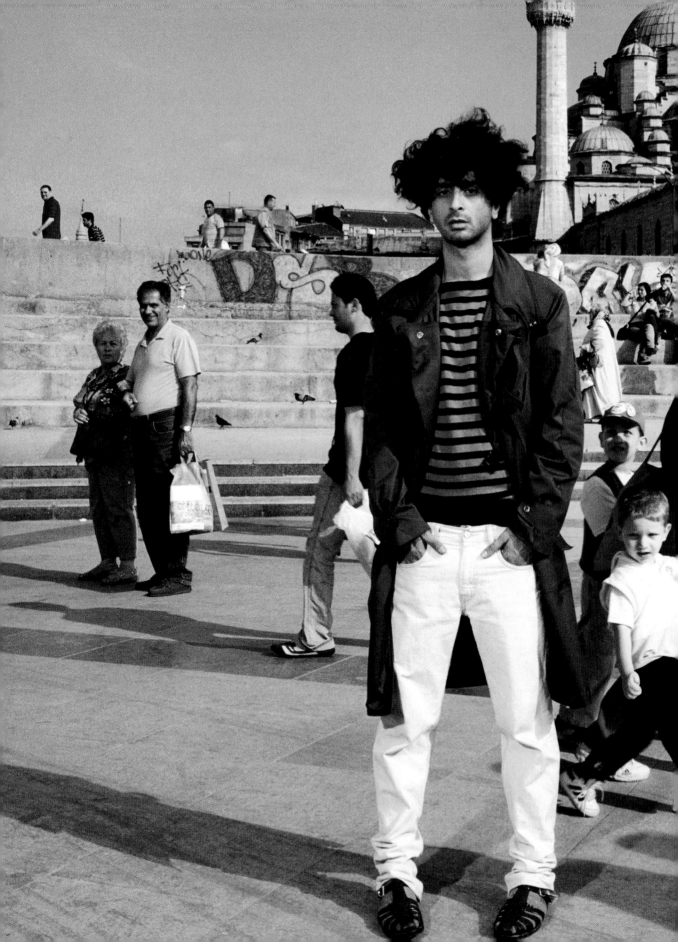

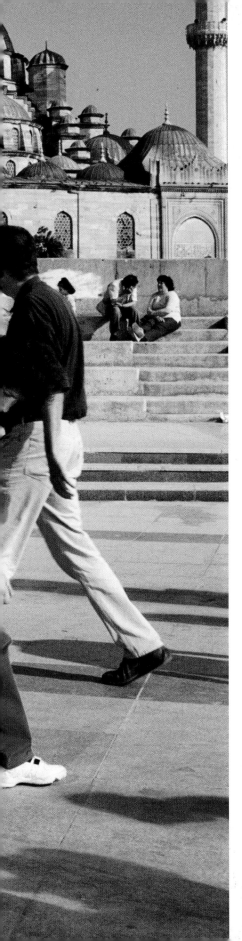

What are your signature designs? We have redesigned the way jeans are worn since 1964. Design it, treat it, capture the prevalent attitude in the moment and introduce our inventions in its vocabulary. We invented a new "jeans' language": Marithé + François Girbaud = the other jeans **What is your favourite piece from any of your collections?** The jeans. From the very beginning, we have worked with leather and denim as a foundation for our treatments and fits. Despite the fact that they're not garments per se, those materials are the canvas of our creations. Our clay to mould shapes **How would you describe your work?** As a work in progress. Every season comes in addition to the previous one and recreates a particular universe that has become ours. This translates into our own style, which works for millions of people **What's your ultimate goal?** That our work serves as a bridge for the next generations. After designing 5000 pairs of trousers, we have looked at trousers from many possible angles. Was that the point? If it can energise and inspire someone, our work will have achieved a lot **What inspires you?** Everything that surrounds us **Can fashion still have political ambition?** Perhaps not 'fashion' per se but the textile industry reaches everyone. Buying and consuming are political acts. It's easy to condemn Third World countries which produce at very low prices while we are the ones shaping that situation with our conquest or economic wars with napalm and our guerrillas **Who do you have in mind when you design?** Ourselves **Is the idea of creative collaboration important to you?** Since the beginning of our duo, we have always favoured the collaboration between a man and a woman who are very different. This is obviously difficult at times. But we reach beyond crisis. The collaboration is obvious and is an important factor of our success

Who has been the greatest influence on your career? Elvis, rock'n'roll and cowboys for me. Brigitte Bardot for Marithé. The entire trade for "dynamique des copies" **How have your own experiences affected your work as a designer?** They're related to raw materials on which we worked at the very beginning. The initial difficulties encountered have cemented our partnership and success made it evolve **Which is more important in your work: the process or the product?** Product first **Is designing for you difficult? If so, what drives you to continue?** Drawing can be a very important part of the process and can be very, very violent and difficult. It is used to communicate with a technician, a specialist. But drawing is not always essential: osmosis and understanding of the subject induce progress and the will to carry on after 40 years **Have you ever been influenced or moved by the reactions to your designs?** Constantly. The idea goes to the Street, but we have been influenced by others. The way a garment is received and appropriated allows for dynamic observations which could not take place at the initial stages of design. We constantly bounce back on previous ideas whether it's immediately or a decade later. When the idea is understood or accepted by others, it becomes an additional source of perpetual inspiration **What's your definition of beauty?** To succeed in designing a jeans that is so hideous and far from what we've done in the past: accomplish the thesis and antithesis once more **What's your philosophy?** The voice of the brand is inside. "Clothes as a means, well-being as an end" **What's the most important lesson you've learned?** It is hard to be recognised in your country of origin… France. Also, after 10 years spent in England, we are still complete unknowns. Famous elsewhere…

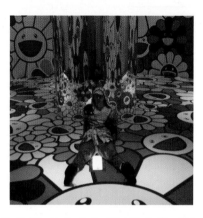

MARJAN PEJOSKI

"No matter what else I do, the swan dress is definitely something that will stay as a signature piece"

To step into the world of Marjan Pejoski (born 1968) is to tumble, Alice In Wonderland-style, down a rabbit hole. It was immediately clear that the Macedonian-born designer had a colourful future when a model for his Central Saint Martins graduation show (1999) appeared on the catwalk wearing a water-filled dress full of live tropical fish. Since then, equally unconventional and technically brilliant collections have earned him a dedicated band of celebrity patrons, including Courtney Love, Kate Moss and Björk, the latter infamously sporting Pejoski's 'swan' dress at the 2001 Academy Awards. Operating under his eponymous label since 2001, Pejoski has also gained commercial success with prêt-à-porter lines that are humorously eccentric. Tour outfits designed for Japanese pop princess Misia have made him famous in Japan, and his highly-conceptual 'biomorphic' designs command critical praise. Human chess pieces, padded Mickey Mouse heels and tops constructed out of toy rabbits' ears have all been spotted at a Pejoski show in Paris. In addition to his fashion designs, Pejoski founded the Kokon To Zai record-stores-cum-fashion-boutiques, with outlets in London and Paris. They sell his own line as well as the collections of budding new designers. Under the pink-and-blue graffiti ceiling of the London store, giant polka dot sweatshirts vie for attention with oversized ladybird prints and cute gingham suits. A standout piece from his 2005 collection was a watermelon green balloon dress, alive with sequins. With a 'more is more' colour palette and a penchant for the unexpected, Pejoski continues to evolve and innovate his bold aesthetic.

Wenn man in die Welt des 1968 geborenen Marjan Pejoski eindringt, ist das, als falle man wie bei „Alice im Wunderland" in einen Kaninchenbau. Dass dem aus Mazedonien stammenden Designer eine farbenprächtige Zukunft bevorstand, war bereits klar, als ein Model bei seiner Abschluss-Show am Central Saint Martins (1999) mit einem wassergefüllten Kleid voller lebender tropischer Fische auf den Laufsteg trat. Seit damals haben ihm seine ebenso unkonventionellen wie technisch brillanten Kollektionen eine treue Gemeinde prominenter Gönner eingebracht. Darunter Courtney Love, Kate Moss und Björk, die bei der Oscar-Verleihung 2001 Pejoskis berühmtes Schwanenkleid trug. Mit dem im selben Jahr unter eigenem Namen gegründeten Label erzielt Pejoski auch bei den humorvoll-exzentrischen Prêt-à-porter-Linien kommerzielle Erfolge. Die Tour-Outfits, die er für die japanische Pop-Prinzessin Misia entwarf, machten ihn auch in Japan berühmt, und seine extrem konzeptuellen „biomorphen" Kreationen sorgten für das Lob der Kritiker. Menschen als Schachfiguren, angeklebte Mickey-Mouse-Füße und Tops aus den Ohren von Spielzeughasen – all das war schon auf Pejoskis Schauen in Paris zu sehen. Zu seiner Arbeit als Designer kommt noch die Gründung von Kokon to Zai, einem Platten- und Modeladen, von dem es Filialen in London und Paris gibt. Dort werden neben den eigenen auch Kollektionen von Newcomern verkauft. Unter dem rosa-blauen Grafittihimmel der Londoner Filiale buhlen Sweatshirts mit fetten Tupfen, Riesenmarienkäfer und süße Gingham-Anzüge um Aufmerksamkeit. Ein Blickfang aus seiner Kollektion für 2005 war ein wassermelonengrünes Ballonkleid, das durch die vielen Pailletten geradezu lebendig erschien. Mit einer Farbpalette nach dem Motto „mehr ist mehr" und einer ausgeprägten Vorliebe für das Unerwartete arbeitet Pejoski weiter an der Entwicklung und Erneuerung seiner kraftvollen Ästhetik.

Pénétrer dans l'univers de Marjan Pejoski (né en 1968) revient à tomber dans le trou du lapin d'Alice aux pays des merveilles. Quand un mannequin de son défilé de fin d'études à Central Saint Martins (1999) apparaît sur le podium vêtue d'une robe transparente remplie d'eau et de vrais poissons tropicaux, il semble évident qu'un avenir coloré attend le jeune créateur d'origine macédonienne. Depuis, ses collections à la fois originales et techniquement brillantes lui gagnent les faveurs d'une clientèle de fans célèbres, dont Courtney Love, Kate Moss et Björk, cette dernière ayant fait sensation en portant la robe « cygne » de Pejoski, lors de la nuit des oscars, en 2001. Travaillant sous sa griffe éponyme depuis 2001, Pejoski rencontre également le succès commercial avec des lignes de prêt-à-porter excentriques et pleines d'humour. Les costumes de scène qu'il dessine pour la tournée de Misia, princesse de la pop japonaise, le font connaître au pays du Soleil levant, où ses créations «biomorphiques» hautement conceptuelles suscitent les éloges de la presse. Pièces de jeu d'échecs humain, talons compensés à l'effigie de Mickey Mouse et petits hauts composés d'oreilles de lapins en peluche ne passent pas inaperçus lors de l'un de ses défilés parisiens. A côté de la création de mode, Pejoski lance les boutiques de vêtements et de disques Kokon to Zai, avec des points de vente à Londres et à Paris. Il y vend ses propres lignes, ainsi que les collections de jeunes créateurs émergents. Sous le plafond aux graffitis roses et bleus de la boutique londonienne, des pulls à gros pois rivalisent à côté d'imprimés de coccinelles géantes et de ravissants tailleurs vichy. L'une des pièces les plus exceptionnelles de sa collection 2005 était une robe-ballon couleur pastèque illuminée de paillettes. Avec une palette de couleurs très osée et un penchant pour l'inattendu, Pejoski ne cesse d'innover et de faire évoluer son audacieuse esthétique.

NANCY WATERS

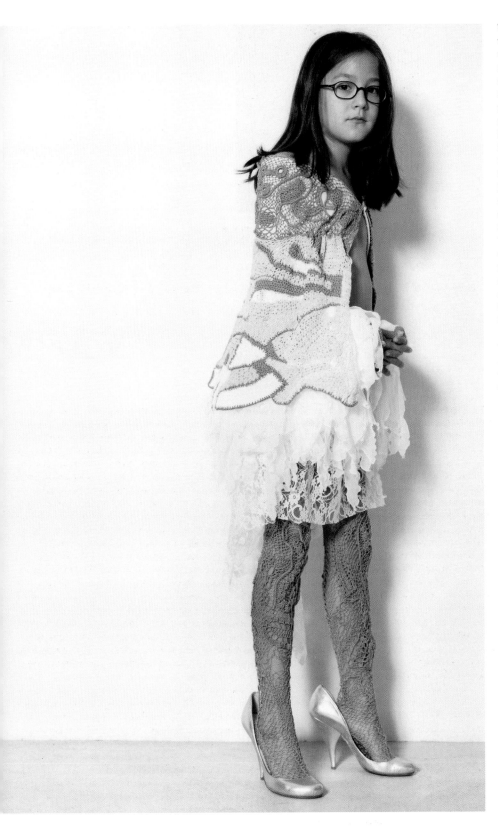

What are your signature designs? No matter what else I do, the swan dress is definitely something that will stay as a signature piece **What is your favourite piece from any of your collections?** The three-dimensional crochet hanging skeleton dress **How would you describe your work?** Pure fantasy **What's your ultimate goal?** To have a beautiful old house by the beach full of my children and friends **What inspires you?** Many things … like life itself… the courage of some people in doing things that they don't need to do, jeopardising their own comfort to help others **Can fashion still have a political ambition?** Political ambition? I really don't now how that is possible, aren't we talking "Fashion"! **Who do you have in mind when you design?** She is an imaginative character, usually with a split personality. Basically she is a combination of few different characters **Is the idea of creative collaboration important to you?** Definitely **Who has been the greatest influence on your career?** My cousin; and she even is not aware of that. She is the one through whom I first smelled the perfume "Opium", touched the first fox… **How have your own experiences affected your work as a designer?** They do in a very spontaneous way and they do take a part in my work and designs, although I cannot pinpoint an example, as there are so many things happening to me **Which is more important in your work: the process or the product?** I am trying to get the balance between those two **Is designing difficult for you, if so, what drives you to continue?** Designing is probably the easiest part of creating a collection, and the drive is a mix of masochisms and will power for success in life **Have you ever been influenced or moved by the reaction to your designs?** No **What's your definition of beauty?** Beauty is in the eye of the beholder (cliché but true) **What's your philosophy?** Learn something new every day **What is the most important lesson you've learned?** I am still in the process of learning, so I will tell you some other time.

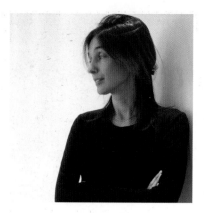

MARNI

"In every collection
there are pieces with which I literally fall in love"
CONSUELO CASTIGLIONI

In little more than a decade, Consuelo Castiglioni's label Marni has become a byword for innovative Italian design, charming its way into fashion folklore with an eclectic vision of femininity. What began as a stint of fashion consulting for her husband's fur and leather company, Ciwi Furs, has developed into a business that has produced some of the most cultish items of the last few years – ponyskin clogs, corsages, charm-embellished bags, the cropped jacket – and a look that has helped define contemporary notions of prettiness. Marni was launched in 1994 with an experimental collection produced through Ciwi Furs (supplier to Prada and Moschino). Treating fur like a fabric, Castiglioni removed the lining, and with it the bulkiness, of the usual rich-bitch fur coat. With each collection she gradually introduced new fabrics, mixing fur with perfectly-cut leathers and suedes, and by 1999 Marni had become an established line independent from its furrier origins. The arts and crafts richness of the Marni look comes from a considered mismatching of print, cut and texture. Marni girl wears a veritable haberdashery of luxurious and love-worn fabrics which are layered across the body and nipped in at the waist with a decorative belt. The Marni print – from faded florals and mattress ticking stripes to '50s retro and block prints – may have become an influential motif, but one that can distract from the slick couture finish that adds to the creatively haphazard look. Since 2000 Marni has undergone giddying retail expansion, opening 10 boutiques around the world, all designed by architecture firm Future Systems, and selling menswear (introduced 2001), childrenswear and homeware alongside a successful line of accessories.

In wenig mehr als einem Jahrzehnt ist Consuelo Castiglionis Label Marni zum Synonym für innovatives italienisches Design geworden. Mit einer eklektischen Vision von Weiblichkeit hat sich die Marke ihren Weg in die folkloristisch angehauchte Mode gebahnt. Begonnen hat es mit einem Job als Fashion Consultant für den Kürschnerbetrieb Ciwi Furs, der ihrem Mann gehört. Doch bald entwickelte sich das Ganze zu einem eigenständigen Geschäft, das einige der kultigsten Produkte der letzten Jahre hervorbrachte – Ponyfell-Clogs, Bandschleifen-Corsagen, mit Glücksbringern verzierte Taschen, Boleros. Der Marni-Look hat das gegenwärtige Verständnis von Schönheit mitbestimmt. Gegründet wurde Marni 1994 mit einer Versuchskollektion, die bei Ciwi Furs (u. a. Zulieferer von Prada und Moschino) produziert wurde. Castiglioni verarbeitete Pelz wie Stoff, verzichtete auf das Futter und reduzierte so das Volumen des traditionellen protzigen Pelzmantels. Mit jeder Kollektion führte sie neue Materialien ein, mixte Pelz mit perfekt geschnittenem Leder und Wildleder, so dass Marni sich etwa ab 1999 als eine von ihren pelzigen Ursprüngen unabhängige eigenständige Marke etabliert hatte. Der bohemienhafte Marni-Look verdankt sich den absichtlichen Gegensätzen von Muster, Schnitt und Textur. So trägt das typische Marni-Girl

einen veritablen Mischmasch aus luxuriösen und abgetragenen Stoffen, die sich schichtweise um ihren Körper legen, in der Taille von einem dekorativen Gürtel zusammengehalten werden und eine organische Silhouette erzeugen. Das Marni-Muster – ob verblichen-floral, gestreift wie Matratzendrillich, 50er-Jahre-Retro oder Blockstreifen – mag ein wichtiges Motiv sein, kann jedoch nicht vom raffinierten Couture-Finish ablenken, das unverzichtbar für den bewusst kreierten, aber zufällig wirkenden Look ist. Seit dem Jahr 2000 hat Marni im Einzelhandel auf geradezu Schwindel erregende Weise expandiert und zehn Boutiquen rund um den Globus eröffnet. Alle sind vom Architekturbüro Future Systems entworfen. Außer Damenmode wird dort die 2001 eingeführte Herrenlinie verkauft, daneben Kinderkleidung, Wohnbedarf sowie ein erfolgreiches Sortiment diverser Accessoires.

En un peu moins de dix ans, la griffe Marni de Consuelo Castiglioni est devenue synonyme d'innovation à l'italienne, se frayant un chemin dans le folklore de la mode grâce à sa vision éclectique de la féminité. Ce qui a commencé par un job de consultante pour Ciwi Furs, fabricant de cuirs et de fourrures dirigé par son mari, s'est transformé en une grande entreprise qui produit certaines des pièces les plus culte de ces dernières années : sabots en vachette, corsages, sacs ornés de grigris porte-bonheur, vestes tondues… pour un look qui a contribué à définir les canons contemporains de la beauté. Consuelo Castiglioni lance sa griffe Marni en 1994 avec une collection expérimentale produite par le biais de Ciwi Furs (fournisseur de Prada et Moschino). Travaillant la fourrure comme du tissu, elle en retire la doublure, et avec elle la lourdeur généralement associée au manteau de fourrure tape-à-l'œil. Au fil des collections, elle introduit progressivement de nouvelles matières, coordonnant la fourrure à des cuirs et des daims parfaitement coupés ; en 1999, la griffe devient entièrement indépendante de ses origines de fourreur. La richesse artistique et artisanale du style Marni naît d'un assortiment d'imprimés, de coupes et de textures volontairement dépareillé. La fille Marni arbore donc avec amour tout un arsenal de tissus luxueux superposés sur le corps et pincés à la taille à l'aide d'une ceinture décorative pour produire une silhouette organique. Des floraux passés aux rayures matelas, des motifs rétro années 50 aux impressions à la planche, les imprimés Marni exercent certes beaucoup d'influence sur la mode, mais ils réussissent toujours à détourner l'attention du fini haute couture irréprochable qui caractérise ce look assez aléatoire sur le plan créatif. Depuis l'an 2000, les ventes de Marni connaissent une ascension vertigineuse : la marque a ouvert 10 boutiques à travers le monde, toutes conçues par le cabinet d'architecture Future Systems. Elles proposent notamment des vêtements pour homme (depuis 2001), une ligne pour enfant et des meubles, ainsi qu'une ligne d'accessoires à succès.

AIMEE FARRELL

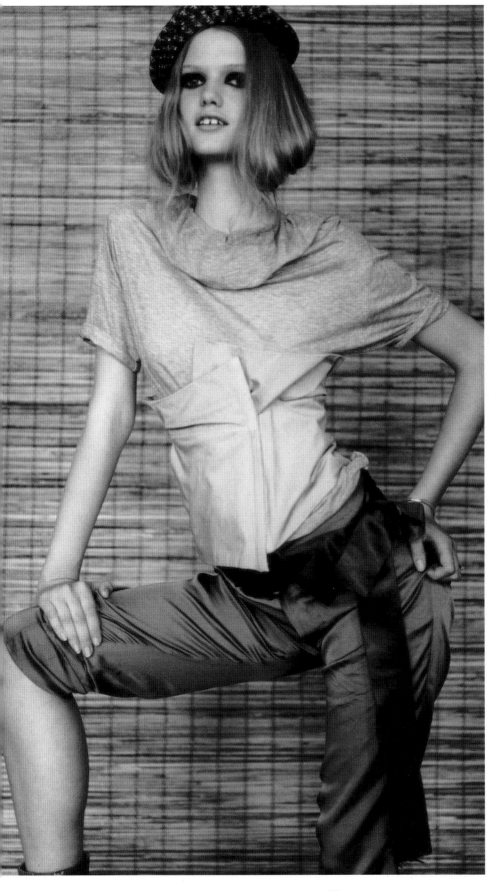

What do you consider your signature designs? My signature characteristics are: prints, combinations of fabrics, colours and lengths, details, luxury and ease **What is your favourite piece from any of your collections?** In every collection there are pieces with which **How would you describe your work?** Free from formal constraints. It's dressing with patchworks of fragments, shreds, tinkers of style **What is your ultimate goal?** The fashion world is now becoming extremely competitive. Our ultimate goal as a company is to control all the value chain from design up to retail and distribution. My personal objective is to continue to design and produce collections in which every item receives a special attention. This has always been for me a focus and a privilege **What inspires you?** Memories and passions, fashions and costumes, arts and techniques **Can fashion still have a political ambition?** In a strict sense, I do not feel it ever had **Who do you have in mind when you design?** When I design I do not have a particular woman in mind, I merge different elements which I like. My inspiration comes from a combination of emotions **Is the idea of creative collaboration important to you?** "Creative collaboration" means to me the people who surround me in my daily work. At Marni the family approach is important. I do not only work for myself, I work for them and they for me **Who or what has been the greatest influence on your career?** Every single person who has believed in the Marni project giving us the chance to develop it, from the fabric companies to the editors worldwide **How have your own experiences affected your work as a designer?** My personal experiences, feelings and moods constantly affect my design **Which is more important to you in your work: the process or the product?** In my work the product really depends on the process: at the beginning it's always a fabric or a print which stimulates my creativity. Then I start mixing and matching **Is designing difficult to you and if so what drives you to continue?** For the moment designing is still a pleasure for me and the mere fact that I enjoy it so much drives me to continue **Have you ever been influenced or moved by the reaction to your designs?** Obviously a positive response encourages you to put increasing effort in your work **What's your definition of beauty?** Beauty does not have age or sex, I see it as a combination of qualities from within, which are projected to the exterior **What's your philosophy?** Creating timeless pieces **What is the most important lesson you've learned?** I feel that I am constantly learning, I strongly believe it is important to keep an open mind towards different stimulations.

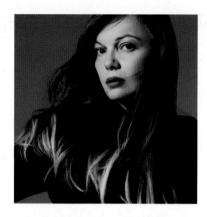

MARTINE SITBON

"The perpetual 'restart' of fashion is very interesting and this permanent evolution is what pushes me to stay in this profession"

Martine Sitbon is a designer whose eye roves the globe for inspiration, referencing and subverting an eclectic mix of cultures while never exploiting her exotic upbringing. The child of an Italian mother and French father, Sitbon was born in Casablanca in 1951. At the age of ten she moved to Paris, where she experienced first-hand the social transformations the city went through in the late '60s. She studied at the famed Studio Berçot, graduating in 1974 before going travelling – adding a multicultural edge and love of lush textiles to the technical fashion skills she had acquired. After spending seven years rummaging through Hong Kong, Mexico, India, New York and Milan, she later fed this blend of the exotic and urban into her designs. In 1985 Sitbon launched her own label and presented her first show in Paris with a collection that famously gathered together monks' hoods, pastel colours, bloomers and a Velvet Underground soundtrack. Black may be key to the palette of the artistic intelligentsia, but Sitbon has enticed them with combinations of sober shades that threaten to clash head-on, but swerve just at the last minute. Her coolly dishevelled clothing often uses elements of leather and masculine tailoring to juxtapose the flea-market femininity of velvets, silks and satins. These contrasting combinations saw her recruited by Chloé in 1988 to design the label's womenswear line, a collaboration that lasted for nine seasons. In 1996 Sitbon opened her first boutique in Paris, and in 1999 she launched a menswear collection into which she introduced her unapologetically androgynous aesthetic. From 2001 to 2002 Sitbon was head designer for womenswear at Byblos. Now concentrating on her own-label menswear and womenswear, Sitbon remains the choice for those who love fashion's more eclectic side.

Martine Sitbon ist eine Designerin, die rund um den Globus nach Inspiration, Bezugspunkten und Subversion für einen eklektischen Mix der Kulturen sucht, ohne dafür ihre exotische Herkunft auszuschlachten. Sie wurde 1951 als Kind einer italienischen Mutter und eines französischen Vaters in Casablanca geboren. Als sie zehn Jahre alt war, zog sie mit ihrer Familie nach Paris, wo sie die gesellschaftlichen Umwälzungen Ende der 1960er aus unmittelbarer Nähe miterlebte. Sie studierte am berühmten Studio Berçot, das sie 1974 abschloss, um danach auf Reisen zu gehen. So ergänzte sie ihre technischen Fähigkeiten um den multikulturellen Aspekt und die Leidenschaft für prachtvolle Stoffe. Nach sieben Jahren, die sie in Hongkong, Mexiko, Indien, New York und Mailand verbracht hatte, ließ sie diese Melange aus exotischen und urbanen Eindrücken in ihre Kreationen einfließen. 1985 präsentierte Sitbon ihr eigenes Label und ihre erste Schau in Paris mit einer denkwürdigen Kollektion aus Mönchskutten, Pastellfarben, Pumphosen und einem Soundtrack von Velvet Underground. Schwarz mag die dominierende Farbe der Künstler-Intelligenzia sein, doch Sit-

bon lockte sie mit Kombinationen sachlicher Farbtöne, die sich zu beißen scheinen, im letzten Augenblick aber doch noch harmonieren. Für ihre auf eine coole Art wirren Kleider benutzt sie oft Elemente aus der Leder- und Herrenschneiderei, die sie mit der Weiblichkeit von Flohmarktfunden aus Samt, Seide und Satin konfrontiert. Diese gegensätzlichen Kombinationen brachten sie 1988 zu Chloé, wo sie die Damenlinie des Labels entwarf. Eine Partnerschaft, die neun Saisons lang hielt. 1996 eröffnete Sitbon ihre erste Pariser Boutique, 1999 stellte sie eine eigene Herrenkollektion mit dezidiert androgyner Ästhetik vor. Als Chefdesignerin der Damenmode war sie von 2001 bis 2002 für Byblos tätig. Heute konzentriert sich Sitbon ausschließlich auf die Damen- und Herrenmode ihres eigenen Labels und empfiehlt sich damit allen, die die eklektische Seite der Mode lieben.

La créatrice Martine Sitbon parcoure le monde en quête d'inspiration, faisant référence de façon subversive à un mélange éclectique de cultures sans jamais exploiter ses propres origines exotiques. Martine Sitbon naît en 1951 à Casablanca d'une mère italienne et d'un père français. Elle arrive à Paris à l'âge de dix ans, où elle assiste aux premières loges aux transformations sociales que subit la capitale française jusqu'à la fin des années 60. Elle sort diplômée du célèbre Studio Berçot en 1974, puis part en voyage pour enrichir les compétences techniques qu'elle a déjà acquises d'un aspect multiculturel et de sa passion des tissus luxueux. Après sept années de découvertes entre Hong Kong, le Mexique, l'Inde, New York et Milan, elle insufflera plus tard ce mix exotique et urbain à ses créations. En 1985, Martine Sitbon lance sa propre griffe et présente son premier défilé à Paris avec une collection restée dans les annales qui mêle capuches monastiques, couleurs pastel, salopettes et musique du Velvet Underground. Le noir a beau être essentiel aux yeux de l'intelligentsia artistique, Martin Sitbon la convertit à d'autres couleurs sobres dans des combinaisons pas nécessairement harmonieuses, mais qui évitent toutefois le chaos chromatique. Ses vêtements tranquillement désordonnés conjuguent souvent des éléments du cuir et des costumes pour homme avec la féminité vintage des velours, des soies et des satins. Ces combinaisons contrastées attire l'attention de la maison Chloé, qui embauche Martine Sitbon en 1988 pour dessiner sa ligne pour femme, une collaboration qui durera neuf saisons. En 1996, la créatrice ouvre sa première boutique à Paris, puis lance en 1999 une collection pour homme où elle introduit son esthétique androgyne sans concession. En 2001 et 2002, elle travaille comme styliste principale de la collection pour femme de Byblos. Aujourd'hui, Martine Sitbon se consacre à sa propre griffe pour homme et pour femme. Elle reste une créatrice de choix pour tous ceux qui privilégient le côté plus éclectique de la mode. LIZ HANCOCK

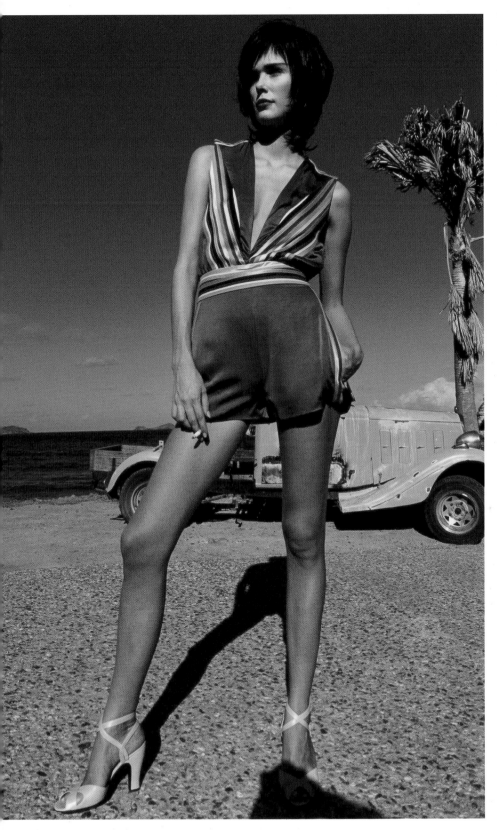

What are your signature designs? The mix of opposites – femininity and androgyny, fragility and rock, reality and dream – defines my style. I work with contrasts; I try in each collection to distance myself from obvious references. Mix up. Confuse **What is your favourite piece from any of your collections?** This question is difficult for me to answer… In a way my favourite piece is always the next to come! **How would you describe your work?** Always a dichotomy between old clothes from the military and tailoring to flowing bias and draping. A mix of ordinary clothes with extraordinary pieces, respecting reality **What inspires you?** I accumulate extremely diverse emotions that may come from films, rock concerts, ballet, exhibitions **Can fashion still have a political ambition?** I hope so, everything shouldn't come down solely to commercialism **Who do you have in mind when you design?** A girl who is lively, off-beat, original… **Is the idea of creative collaboration important to you?** Definitely. I love to work as a team; there is a synergetic effect, stimulation and an exchange of ideas invaluable in creative work **Who has been the greatest influence on your career?** When I was young, David Bowie, the Rolling Stones and Syd Barrett gave me the desire to do fashion **How have your own experiences affected your work as a designer?** Music has brought a lot to me and going to second-hand markets has been a fundamental starting-point of my research. Later, contemporary dance and art have left an impression on me. I have the impression that everything I have experienced has affected my work **Which is more important in your work: the process or the product?** With the product, history becomes real, but the most interesting part is the process. Evolution is what pushes me to stay in this profession **Is designing difficult for you, if so, what drives you to continue?** The perpetual 'restart' of fashion is very interesting and this permanent evolution is what pushes me to stay in this profession. We can never sleep, we cannot count on anything and there is a real idea of a game **Have you ever been influenced or moved by the reaction to your designs?** Success, like failure, pushes you to do your work better **What's your philosophy?** Keep your feet on the ground and your head in the clouds.

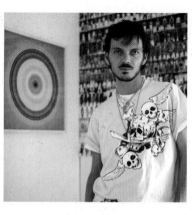

MATTHEW WILLIAMSON

"Colour is the thing I'm best known for. If people pigeonhole me, so what? Long live the pink dress!"

Matthew Williamson uses colour in a way very few designers dare match. He routinely splashes ultra pinks, fluorescent yellows and acid greens with an energising flourish onto women's day and evening wear. This has become his signature style since the debut of his first collection, 'Electric Angels', in 1997 – a combination of kaleidoscopic bias-cut dresses and separates, sometimes embroidered and fused with a bohemian edge. Modelled by friends Jade Jagger, Kate Moss and Helena Christensen, it was a presentation that affirmed the London-based designer's influences: fame, glamour and India (Williamson's garments often read like a travel diary, tracing his love of exotic destinations). Celebrity was the all-important catalyst which made the fashion world sit up and pay attention to his work, but since that first collection, it's been the intricate detail, contemporary styling and sexy silhouettes that have kept the applause coming. Born in Chorlton, Manchester, in 1971, Matthew Williamson graduated from Central Saint Martins in 1994 and set up his own label in 1996 after spending two years as consultant at UK mass market chain Monsoon. 2002 saw the launch of a homewear range and a move to show his womenswear collections at New York Fashion Week. A first foray into perfume and home fragrance – a collaboration with perfumer and friend Lyn Harris – saw the creation of a limited edition perfume 'Incense'. Now selling to over 80 stores worldwide, the first Matthew Williamson flagship store opened in 2004 on London's Bruton Street, and there are plans for a New York store.

Matthew Williamson kombiniert Farben mit einem Wagemut, den nur sehr wenige Designer aufbringen. Mit kräftigem Schwung verteilt er knallige Pinktöne, Neongelb und -grün auf Alltags- und Abendmode für Damen. Das ist sein Markenzeichen seit dem Debüt 1997 mit seiner ersten Kollektion „Electric Angels" – einer Kombination von diagonal geschnittenen kaleidoskopischen Kleidern und Einzelteilen, die teilweise bestickt oder mit einem Touch Bohème versehen waren. Die Models damals waren seine Freundinnen Jade Jagger, Kate Moss und Helena Christensen, und die Schau bestätigte die Einflüsse auf den in London lebenden Designer: Prominenz, Glamour und Indien (so lesen sich Williamsons Kleider oft wie ein Reisetagebuch, das seine Vorliebe für exotische Ziele dokumentiert). Prominenz war der wichtigste Katalysator, der die Branche aufhorchen ließ und für die Beachtung seiner Arbeit sorgte. Nach jener ersten Kollektion waren jedoch raffinierte Details, zeitgemäßes Styling und sexy Silhouetten für den anhaltenden Applaus verantwortlich. Der 1971 in Manchester geborene

Williamson machte 1994 seinen Abschluss am Central Saint Martins und gründete 1996 sein eigenes Label, nachdem er zwei Jahre lang als Berater für die britische Modekette Monsoon gearbeitet hatte. 2002 kam noch eine Homewear-Kollektion dazu. Außerdem zog der Designer nach New York, wo er im Rahmen der Modewoche seine Damenkollektionen präsentierte. Ein erstes Hineinschnuppern in den Markt der Düfte und Home Fragrances war die Zusammenarbeit mit der Parfümeurin und Freundin Lyn Harris bei der Kreation des in limitierter Auflage auf den Markt gebrachten Parfums „Incense". Nachdem er seine Kreationen schon in mehr als 80 Läden weltweit verkaufte, eröffnete Williamson 2004 in der Londoner Bruton Street den ersten nach ihm benannten Flagship Store. Eine Filiale in New York befindet sich gerade im Planungsstadium.

Matthew Williamson utilise la couleur comme peu d'autres créateurs oseraient le faire. Régulièrement, il éclabousse avec panache et énergie ses tenues féminines de jour et de soir à l'aide de roses flashy, de jaunes fluorescents et de verts acidulés. Depuis sa première collection « Electric Angels » en 1997, ce style s'est imposé comme sa signature : une combinaison de robes et de séparés kaléidoscopiques coupés en biais, parfois brodés et au look un peu bohème. Grâce à ses amies mannequins Jade Jagger, Kate Moss et Helena Christensen, ce défilé confirme les influences du créateur londonien : la gloire, le glamour et l'Inde (les vêtements de Williamson se lisent souvent comme des carnets de voyage qui témoignent de sa passion pour les destinations exotiques). Ce sont d'abord les célébrités qui attirent l'attention du monde de la mode sur son travail, mais depuis cette première collection, il remporte un succès croissant grâce aux détails complexes, au style contemporain et à la silhouette sexy de ses vêtements. Né en 1971 dans le quartier Chorlton de Manchester, Matthew Williamson sort diplômé de Central Saint Martins en 1994. Après avoir travaillé pendant deux ans comme consultant pour la chaîne de distribution britannique Monsoon, il crée sa propre griffe en 1996. En 2002, il lance une gamme d'articles pour la maison et décide de présenter ses collections pour femme à la New York Fashion Week. Une première incursion dans les domaines du parfum et du parfum d'intérieur, fruit d'une collaboration avec son amie parfumeuse Lyn Harris, voit la création d'une fragrance en édition limitée, « Incense ». A ce jour, ses créations sont vendues dans plus de 80 boutiques à travers le monde. La première boutique indépendante Matthew Williamson a ouvert ses portes en 2004 dans Bruton Street à Londres et la marque prévoit également d'ouvrir un espace de vente à New York.

TERRY NEWMAN

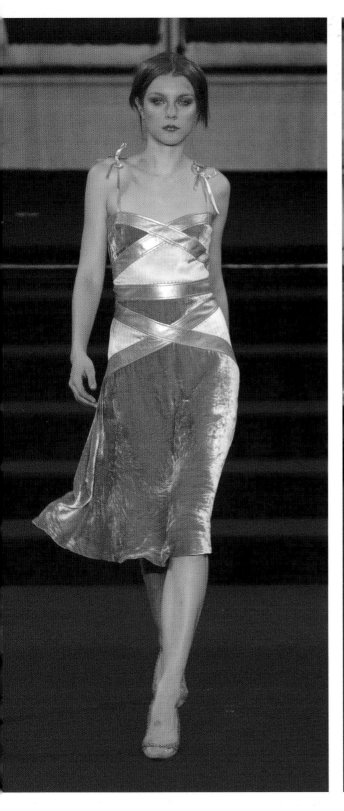
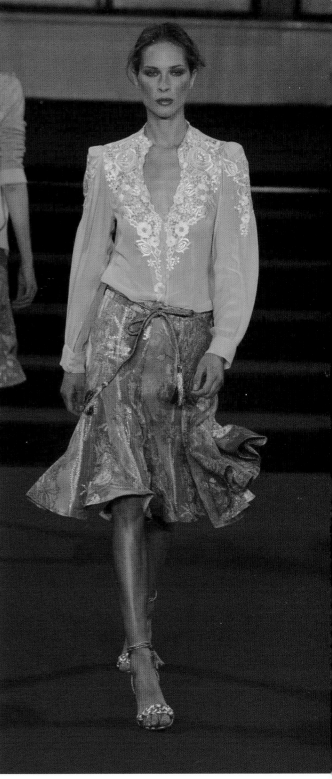

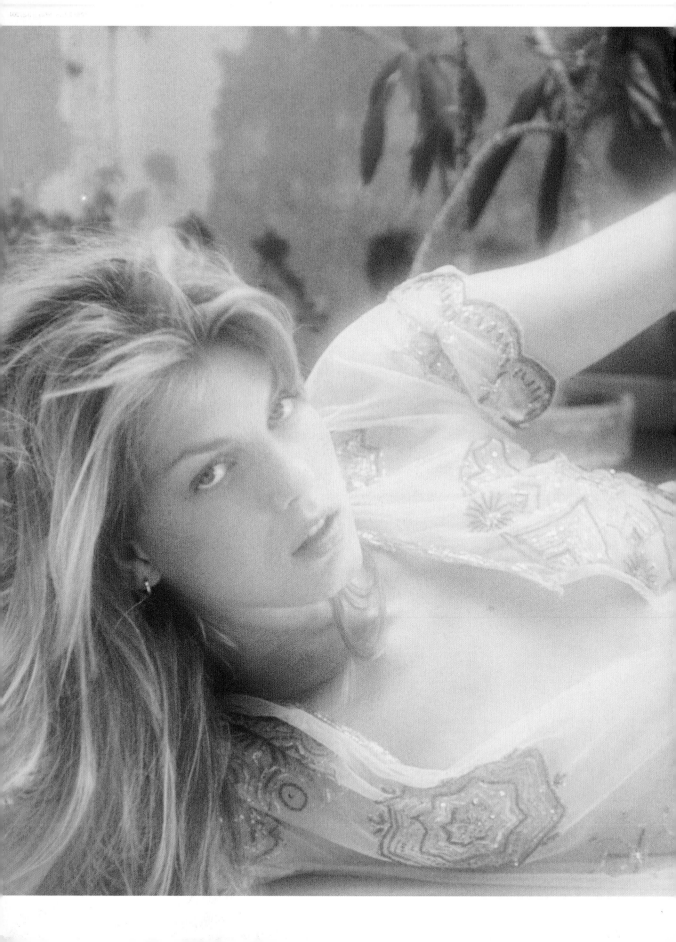

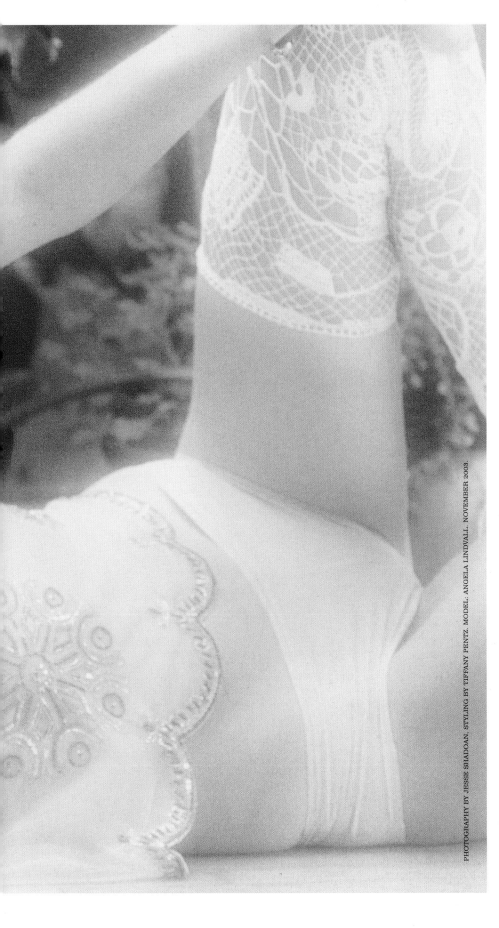

PHOTOGRAPHY BY JESSE SHADOAN. STYLING BY TIFFANY PENTZ. MODEL. ANGELA LINDVALL. NOVEMBER 2003.

What are your signature designs? My style is all about creating very feminine, sexy clothes that women really desire **What's your favourite piece from any of your collections?** I love the first dress that I ever did. It's pink with a turquoise cowl at the neck, so simple. But I love it most because of what it did for my career **What's your ultimate goal?** To be bought by an Italian or French house very quickly. You start out in London and it's great in the beginning because everyone is so hungry for new designers. But when you get to my stage, you're not new anymore. It's very difficult in this country because we don't take fashion seriously as a business **What inspires you?** Ultimately I'm most inspired by travel, by the places that I visit. I try to fuse Western style with a very Eastern, exotic feel. I pick up all of the colour and texture when I'm abroad, particularly in India, Thailand and Bali **Who do you have in mind when you design?** It's a combination of women **Is designing difficult for you and, if so, what drives you to continue?** If it was easy, it wouldn't be interesting **What's your definition of beauty?** I think people are most attractive when they appear confident and happy in themselves **What's your philosophy?** Everything in moderation **What is the most important lesson you've learned?** How to work for myself and be responsible. If shit goes wrong, I'm much more comfortable blaming myself.

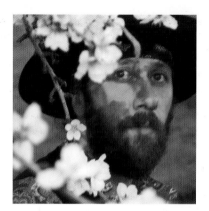

MIGUEL ADROVER

"I use clothing as a venue
to exhibit my interpretations and expressions"

Miguel Adrover's themed collections, which are often inspired by the people and cultures he sees in New York and when travelling, are unique for their authentic interpretation of everyday dress. Born in a small village in Majorca in 1965, Adrover moved to New York in 1991 and began producing a line of customised T-shirts with his friend Douglas Hobbs and in 1995, the pair opened a boutique, Horn. Adrover is entirely self-taught; friends and supporters, not tutors and examinations, have shaped his career. In 1999 the first Miguel Adrover collection, 'Manaus-Chiapas-NYC' was shown at New York Fashion Week. His debut, which showed deconstructed thrift-store clothes alongside virtuoso tailoring, was met with equal amounts of bemusement and praise. Adrover's recycled pieces have always impressed, and for spring/summer 2001, he fashioned a sharp town coat from mattress ticking that had been thrown out on the street by Quentin Crisp – it is now part of the Metropolitan Museum of Arts' fashion collection. In June 2000 he won the CFDA award for Best New Designer and the Pegasus Apparel Group began financing his label, a partnership that lasted until autumn 2001, when the post-September 11 mood worked against his multicultural themes and political assertions. After splitting from Pegasus, Adrover re-built his reputation and studio and returned to the catwalk for spring/summer 2003 with a beautifully-tailored collection entitled 'Citizen of the World'. Again, it paid tribute to the cosmopolitan mix of nationalities found in New York; the show climaxed with a pale blue dress fashioned from a United Nations flag. In 2005, Adrover moved his studio back to Spain. Always diverse in its inspiration, challenging and immaculately stitched, Adrover's clothing has paved the way for a new generation of young and experimental designers who have adopted New York as their home.

Miguel Adrovers themenbezogene Kollektionen sind oft von den Menschen und ihren unterschiedlichen Kulturen geprägt, die ihm in New York und auf seinen Reisen begegnen. Seine authentischen Interpretationen von Alltagskleidung sind einzigartig. Geboren wurde Adrover 1965 in einem kleinen Dorf auf Mallorca. 1991 zog er nach New York, wo er zusammen mit seinem Freund Douglas Hobbs T-Shirts zu produzieren begann und vier Jahre später eine Boutique namens Horn eröffnete. Adrover ist der totale Autodidakt. Nicht Lehrer und Dozenten, sondern Freunde und Mentoren haben seine Karriere bestimmt. Im Jahr 1999 war seine erste Kollektion, „Manaus-Chiapas-NYV", bei der New Yorker Fashion Week zu sehen. Dieses Debüt, bei dem der Designer umgearbeitete Second-Hand-Stücke, aber auch virtuose Schneiderkunst zeigte, sorgte für viel Erstaunen und Lob. Mit seinen recycelten Kreationen erregt er immer viel Aufmerksamkeit. So entwarf er etwa für seine Kollektion Frühjahr/Sommer 2001 einen originellen Kurzmantel aus einer Matratze, die Quentin Crisp ausgemustert hatte. Heute ist dieses Stück Teil der Modesammlung des Metropolitan Museum of Arts. Im Juni 2000 wurde Adrover von der CFDA als bester neuer Designer ausgezeichnet. Daraufhin begann die Pegasus-Apparel-Gruppe, sein

Label zu finanzieren. Diese Partnerschaft hielt allerdings nur bis zum Herbst 2001. Denn in Folge der Anschläge vom 11. September passten Adrovers multikulturelle Themen und sein politischer Anspruch nicht mehr so recht zur herrschenden Stimmung. Nach der Trennung von Pegasus baute der Designer seinen Ruf und sein Atelier neu auf und kehrte für Frühjahr/Sommer 2003 mit einer wunderschönen Kollektion namens „Citizens of the World" auf den Laufsteg zurück. Wieder zollte er damit dem kosmopolitischen Mix der Nationen, den er aus New York kannte, Tribut. Höhepunkt der Show war ein hellblaues Kleid, geschneidert aus einer Fahne der Vereinten Nationen. 2005 verlegte Adrover sein Atelier zurück nach Spanien. Dennoch wirkte er mit seiner so vielfältig inspirierten, herausfordernden und handwerklich perfekten Mode als Wegbereiter einer neuen Generation von jungen, experimentierfreudigen Designern, die sich New York als Heimat gewählt haben.

Les collections à thèmes de Miguel Adrover, souvent inspirées par les gens et les cultures qu'il observe à New York et lors de ses voyages, sont uniques en ceci qu'elles réinterprètent avec authenticité l'habillement du quotidien. Né dans un petit village de Majorque en 1965, Adrover s'installe à New York en 1991 et commence à produire une gamme de T-shirts customisés avec son ami Douglas Hobbs. En 1995, le duo ouvre une boutique baptisée Horn. Entièrement autodidacte, Adrover ne doit sa carrière ni aux professeurs ni aux examens, mais à ses amis et à ses fans. En 1999, la première collection Miguel Adrover, « Manaus-Chiapas-NYC », est présentée à la New York Fashion Week. Avec des vêtements d'occasion déconstruits côtoyant des pièces à la coupe virtuose, ses débuts suscitent autant de stupéfaction que de louanges. Les vêtements recyclés d'Adrover ne cessent d'impressionner : pour le printemps/été 2001, il façonne un manteau de ville aux lignes sévères à partir d'un vieux matelas jeté sur le trottoir par Quentin Crisp, une pièce qui fait désormais partie de la collection de mode du Metropolitan Museum of Arts. En juin 2000, le CFDA le consacre Best New Designer. Le groupe Pegasus Apparel commence alors à financer sa griffe, un partenariat qui ne tient que jusqu'à l'automne 2001, période peu propice à ses thématiques multiculturelles et à ses opinions politiques en raison du traumatisme consécutif an 11 septembre. Après s'être séparé de Pegasus, Adrover reconstruit sa réputation comme atelier et revient sur les podiums au printemps/été 2003 avec une collection aux coupes superbes intitulée « Citizen of the World ». De nouveau, elle rend hommage au melting-pot si caractéristique de New York, dans un défilé qui culmine avec une robe bleu pâle taillée dans le drapeau des Nations unies. En 2005, Adrover installe son atelier en Espagne. Toujours variés dans leurs inspirations, défiant les conventions et cousus à la perfection, les vêtements de Miguel Adrover ont « essuyé les plâtres » pour une nouvelle génération de créateurs expérimentaux qui a choisi New York comme ville d'adoption.

SUSIE RUSHTON

PORTRAIT BY VALÉRIE ELOGNY · PHOTOGRAPHY BY JEROME ALBERTINI STYLING BY MIGUEL ADROVER. JUNE 2003

What are your signature designs? The Mirror of Society **What is your favourite piece from any of your collections?** I don't have a favourite piece because I always do collections in a different way; it's more like characters, where everybody has their role that's important to my work **How would you describe your work?** My work is a learning process, what I've learnt in life up until now, and I express that with clothing. I try and take things from around the world and present them. My work is my expression, my observation of what I experience and what I feel about the world around me at a particular time. I use clothing as a venue to exhibit my interpretations and expressions **What's your ultimate goal?** My ultimate goal is living one day after the other. For my work, I guess just to continue doing it and expressing myself **What inspires you?** Life. What happens in the world: that's how I really inspire myself **Can fashion still have a political ambition?** I won't do fashion if it doesn't have political vision. Because for

me, it's very important how you see society and the world and the problems that there are, rather than it just being about fashionable clothes **Who do you have in mind when you design?** A lot of people. It's not about one person and you just design clothes for that person – most of the time I don't see sex when I design clothing. I don't mind if it's a character who's a man and then I make clothes for a woman, I just put the characters and their clothes where they look the most simple and elegant, depending on the person. I challenge myself with how best I can express the story or idea, while at the same time creating a wearable item for a customer. I'm not a fanatical designer and I don't create characterised outfits only meant for the dream world of the catwalk **Is the idea of creative collaboration important to you?** Collaboration with other creators has been a very important part that I think gave us an opportunity to share our views and build a message more complex **What has been the greatest**

influence on your career? Life. My life **How have your own experiences affected your work as a designer?** My life is attached to my work, I'm inspired by everyday life and so that's my work, too. This is the inspiration: the situation of the planet, everyday living **Which is more important in your work: the process or the product?** In my work each thing needs to have a connection with each other. When we are in the process we always need to work for that to became a product. In my work each thing needs to have a connection with each other. When we are in the process we always need to work for that to became a product **Is designing difficult for you, if so, what drives you to continue?** Designing has not been difficult, what has been difficult and drives us to continue is to have the responsibility to communicate or report in an industry that is normally repressed by the truth of the times we are living in **Have you ever been influenced or moved by the reaction to your designs?** I have been moved by the

reaction and support of so many people and the press. The recognition for our work represents the voices and hopes of a lot of people and that it is supposed to draw attention to a particular situation or moment… that moved us **What's your definition of beauty?** I don't think there should be a definition of beauty because when you define you exclude the rest – so what are the others meant to be? **What's your philosophy?** My philosophy combines several things, particularly designing clothes based on observations in the present. My expression is directly affected by today, what I see now. My representation makes no distinction between poor and rich. I aim to put everyone on the same level. My philosophy also includes a constant interest in representing different cultures. This is important to me as it pushes me to learn about other places and people so that I can in turn present to others what I've seen **What is the most important lesson you've learned?** That it is very hard to walk with the truth.

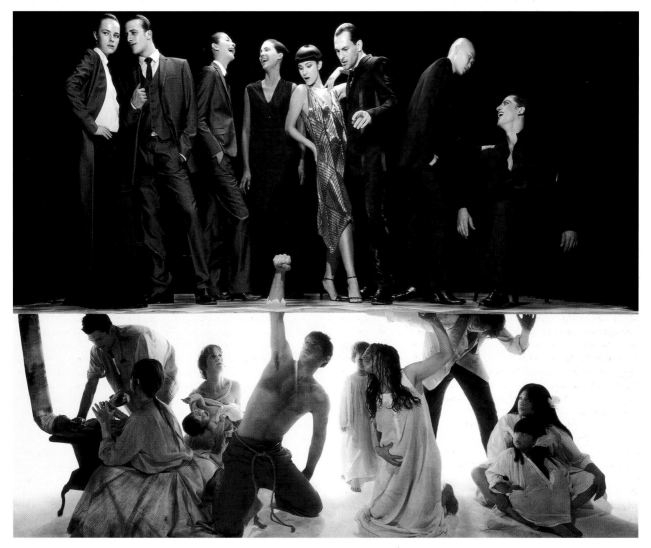

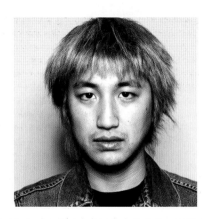

MIHARA YASUHIRO

"The important thing for me before or when I
design is to change myself mentally"

For a designer so young, Mihara Yasuhiro has achieved a phenomenal amount of success: and all without really stepping into the spotlight. Born in 1972, Mihara Yasuhiro was raised with his older brother in Fukuoka, Japan. The son of an abstract painter mother and a research scientist father, Yasuhiro graduated from the Tama Art University with a Major in Textile Design in 1997. Whilst at college he taught himself the traditional ways of shoe making, culminating in the launch of his shoe label Archi Doom in 1996. This evolved into the Mihara Yasuhiro label in 1997, and 1998 saw Mihara open his first store in Tokyo's Aoyama district. Mihara Yasuhiro's work is concerned with breaking down visual boundaries and quietly subverting the normal. Yasuhiro showed his first official on-schedule collection in Milan (January 2005), following a typically leftfield unofficial street-presentation, also in Milan in June 2004. Mihara Yasuhiro's design studio (SOSU) is currently in Tokyo, where he now employs 31 staff. Whilst his designs combine good humour, visual trickery and streetwear influences with technical expertise, he manages to sidestep the realms of novelty fashion or costume. Present in almost all his work are intricate, colourful trompe l'oeil prints, a design signature which is extended into Yasuhiro's trademark leather pieces (shoes and boots with embossed laces and detailing). Since 2000, he has also collaborated with Puma, designing both footwear and apparel collections under the name Puma by Mihara Yasuhiro.

Als relativ junger Designer hat Mihara Yasuhiro bereits ungeheuren Erfolg – und das, ohne wirklich ins Rampenlicht zu treten. Er wurde 1972 geboren und wuchs zusammen mit einem älteren Bruder im japanischen Fukuoka auf. Als Sohn einer abstrakten Malerin und eines Wissenschaftlers machte Yasuhiro 1997 seinen Abschluss im Hauptfach Textildesign an der Kunsthochschule Tama. Am College hatte er sich das Schuhmacherhandwerk selbst beigebracht, was in der Präsentation seines Schuh-Labels Archi Doom im Jahr 1996 gipfelte. Daraus entwickelte sich im darauf folgenden Jahr die nach ihm benannte Marke Mihara Yasuhiro, und bereits 1998 eröffnete Mihara seinen ersten eigenen Laden im Tokioter Stadtteil Aoyama. Dem Designer geht es in seiner Arbeit um die Überwindung visueller Grenzen und um das stille Untergraben des Norma-len. Seine erste Kollektion im Rahmen des offiziellen Show-Kalenders zeigte er in Mailand (Januar 2005), nach einer typischerweise inoffiziellen Straßenprä-sentation ebenfalls in Mailand im Juni 2004. Mihara Yasuhiros Designatelier (SOSU) befindet sich in Tokio und beschäftigt derzeit 31 Mitarbeiter. Während seine Entwürfe Sinn für Humor, optische Täuschungen und Einflüsse aus dem Alltag verbinden, gelingen dem Designer außerdem Ausflüge ins Reich von Novelty Fashion und Kostümbildnerei. Fast in allen seinen Arbeiten stößt man auf komplizierte farbige Trompe-l'œil-Muster – ein Markenzeichen, das selbst auf Miharas typischen Lederwaren zu finden ist (Schuhe und Stiefel mit Spitzen-mustern und geprägten Verzierungen). Yasuhiro arbeitete auch schon mit der Firma Puma zusammen: Seit 2000 entwirft er Schuh- und Kleiderkollektionen unter dem Label Puma by Mihara Yasuhiro.

En dépit de son très jeune âge, Mihara Yasuhiro rencontre déjà un succès phé-noménal, et ce, sans avoir jamais vraiment occupé le devant de la scène. Né en 1972, Mihara Yasuhiro grandit auprès de son frère aîné à Fukuoka au Japon. Fils d'une mère peintre abstrait et d'un père scientifique, il sort diplômé de la Tama Art University en 1997 avec une spécialisation en création textile. Encore étu-diant, il se forme aux techniques traditionnelles de la fabrication de chaussures et lance sa griffe de chaussures Archi Doom en 1996, qu'il rebaptise Yasuhiro Yasuhiro en 1997 avant d'ouvrir sa première boutique dans le quartier Aoyama de Tokyo en 1998. Le travail de Mihara Yasuhiro cherche à briser les frontières visuelles et propose tranquillement sa version subversive de la normalité. Après une présentation non officielle et typiquement anti-conformiste dans les rues milanaises en juin 2004, Yasuhiro finit par présenter sa première collection offi-cielle lors de la semaine de la mode de Milan (janvier 2005). Situé à Tokyo, l'ate-lier de Mihara Yasuhiro (SOSU) emploie aujourd'hui 31 personnes. Combinant bonne humeur, effets visuels et influences streetwear avec une grande expertise technique, Yasuhiro se débrouille toujours pour voir au-delà des modes fantaisie et du costume. Presque toutes ses créations présentent des imprimés en trompe-l'œil colorés et complexes, une signature que l'on retrouve dans ses pièces en cuir caractéristiques (chaussures et bottes gaufrées de dentelles et autres détails). Yasuhiro collabore également avec Puma, dessinant des collections de chaussures et de vêtements sous le nom Puma by Mihara Yasuhiro. DAVID LAMB

What are your signature designs? If I had to choose, it would be leather shoes with different types of techniques as I began my career as a shoe designer. For example, I like using leathers with a wrinkled effect (which are wrung by hands). That means people can feel and see the different materials and textures of each shoes. Since last year, I have been putting the idea of trompe l'œil into shoes as well as my clothes (embossed leather series) and accessories **What is your favourite piece from any of your collections?** It's really difficult for me to choose as I have special feelings for each item in my collection. It's all precious to me, even if a particular piece is not the exact way I had envisioned it to be **How would you describe your work?** I would describe my work as 'underground industry' **What's your ultimate goal?** I don't start off by having any specific goals in mind. I aim to push myself beyond my limits whenever I design for my collections and continue challenging myself **What inspires you?** I'm inspired by everything that I have experienced in my life to date – people I meet, things I've seen, places I've been to, they all inspire me a lot **Can fashion still have a political ambition?** I think so. Fashion is one way of expressing political beliefs and interests. Everyone pays attention to fashion so it's easy to convey anything to people. It's one of the privilege in fashion, I guess. However I think fashion today is more concerned with business and a label is rated against it's sales figures. I think it's such a shame **Who do you have in mind when you design?** It depends really, so I can't actually specify what comes up in my mind. I'm very conservative so when I design I try to be objective at first. Meaning, before I design I tell myself to be objective in order to understand what other people think and want. Being objective is not one of my characteristics therefore the important thing for me before or when I design is to change myself mentally **Is the idea of creative collaboration important to you?** Definitely all types of creative collaborations are important. For example, I have been concentrating on making leather shoes for a long time. Much as I enjoy it, I wanted to extend my scope and hence looked into pursuing another category of shoes. I then started working with sneakers. There is so much technology involved with making sneakers and it has opened up new design possibilities for me. I have been making sneakers for my PUMA by MIHARAYASU-HIRO label, and I very much enjoy designing them **Who has been the greatest influence on your career?** People around me **How have your own experiences affected your work as a designer?** As I mentioned above, I have been conservative since I was young. On the other hand, as time goes by, I feel that I have become more and more courageous to express myself **Which is more important in your work: the process or the product?** They are both very important to me. The right process will ensure the best possible product. In addition, my creation is completely finished when people include our products their wardrobe and wear them **Is designing difficult for you, if so, what drives you to continue?** In any work, there is always some difficulty involved. However, I like what I do and this includes the highs and the lows of designing. Sometimes overcoming the difficulties is the most important part, but I am encouraged by the final product and that drives me **Have you ever been influenced or moved by the reaction to your designs?** I honestly did not expect such a positive reaction to my designs and the way it has influenced me is that I am now able to pay for my own food and meals! **What's your definition of beauty?** Beauty is 'ambiguous' **What's your philosophy?** Sublime meets ridiculous **What is the most important lesson you've learned?** Think deeply.

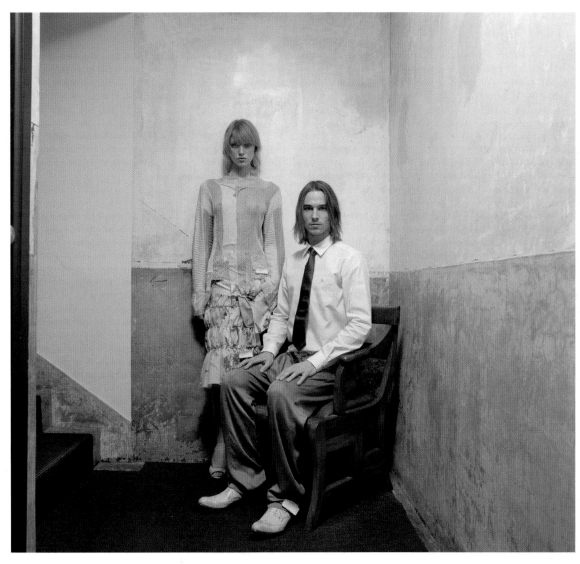

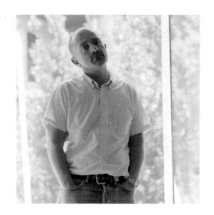

MISS SIXTY

"I believe designing to be the world's most beautiful work"

WICHY HASSAN

Miss Sixty is a teenager, just like most of the girls that wear its clothes. Established in 1991 as the sister line to Italian streetwear label Energie, the label has experienced accelerated growth in its short lifetime. The first UK store opened on Neal Street, London, in 1991. By 2004, there were 122 outlets internationally, with eight in Britain. Their popularity is largely due to the label's body-conscious silhouette and a copious array of denim. Head Designer Wichy Hassan is the man to thank for that. Born in Libya in 1955, Hassan studied languages and art in Milan before settling on fashion. Although never formally trained, he had designed and co-founded Energie. The first Miss Sixty jeans were made in 1989 with the help of a local tailor, after Wichy became frustrated with women wearing unflattering unisex jeans. He persuaded his Energie business partner Renato Rossi to join the crusade and Miss Sixty was born. The 'Tommy' jean – with its curve-hugging cut – was the first really popular style. Despite adding cute girly separates to its range, the label's obsession with denim-with-sex-appeal continues to this day. There are now 35 styles available each season, each in a variety of washes. 2004 even saw the label introduce a demarcated 'Denim Area' to each store. While not a grown-up status denim brand like Earl or Seven for All Mankind, Miss Sixty nevertheless has a huge street following, staying true to trademark quality and fit without compromising on price. The slick brand image, meanwhile, owes a lot to advertising that has come courtesy of fashion leaders including photographers Mario Testino and Ellen Von Unwerth and stylist Katie Grand.

Miss Sixty ist ein Teenager, genau wie die meisten jungen Mädchen, die ihre Sachen tragen. Die 1991 als Nebenlinie des italienischen Streetwear-Labels Energie gegründete Marke hat rasch an Ansehen gewonnen. Die erste englische Filiale wurde 1991 in der Londoner Neal Street eröffnet. 2004 waren es schon 122 Outlets weltweit, davon acht in Großbritannien. Seine Popularität verdankt das Label vor allem seiner figurbetonten Silhouette und der reichlichen Verwendung von Denim. Dafür zeichnet der Chefdesigner Wichy Hassan verantwortlich. Der 1955 in Libyen geborene Hassan studierte in Mailand Sprachen und Kunst, bevor er sich der Mode zuwandte. Obwohl er keine formale Ausbildung in diesem Bereich besitzt, war er Designer und Mitbegründer von Energie. Die erste Miss-Sixty-Jeans entstand 1989 mit Hilfe eines ortsansässigen Schneiders, weil es Wichy frustrierte mit anzusehen, dass Frauen wenig vorteilhafte Unisex-Jeans trugen. Er überzeugte seinen Geschäftspartner bei Energie, Renato Rossi, sich an diesem Feldzug zu beteiligen, und damit war Miss Sixty geboren. Die Tommy-Jeans mit ihrem die weiblichen Kurven umschmeichelnden Schnitt

war das erste, ungeheuer beliebte Modell. Die Passion des Labels für Jeans mit Sexappeal ist bis heute ungebrochen. Heute gibt es pro Saison 35 verschiedene Modelle – alle in einer Vielzahl von Farbnuancen. 2004 führte man sogar in jeder Filiale eine deutlich abgegrenzte „Denim Area" ein. Miss Sixty ist zwar keine Jeansmarke mit Erwachsenen-Status wie Earl oder Seven for All Mankind, besitzt jedoch eine riesige Anhängerschaft, weil man Markenqualität und -sitz bietet, ohne Kompromisse beim Preis einzugehen. Das schicke Image verdankt die Marke nicht zuletzt ihrer Werbung, in der sich führende Köpfe der Modeszene engagiert haben, etwa die Fotografen Mario Testino und Ellen von Unwerth und die Stylistin Katie Grand.

Miss Sixty est une adolescente, comme la plupart des filles qui portent ses vêtements. Fondée en 1991 comme la petite sœur de la marque de streetwear italienne Energie, la toute jeune griffe bénéficie d'une croissance impressionnante qui ne va qu'en s'accélérant. La première boutique Miss Sixty ouvre ses portes en 1991 sur Neal Street à Londres. En 2004, on compte déjà 122 points de vente à l'international, dont huit en Grande-Bretagne. Leur succès repose en grande partie sur la silhouette moulante proposée par la griffe et sur un copieux choix de denims, une réussite que l'on doit au styliste principal Wichy Hassan. Né en 1955 en Libye, Hassan étudie les langues et les arts à Milan avant de se lancer dans la mode. Sans formation préalable, il devient créateur et cofondateur d'Energie. Frustré de voir les femmes porter des jeans unisexe peu flatteurs, Wichy Hassan commence à produire les premiers jeans Miss Sixty en 1989 avec le soutien d'un tailleur local. Il persuade Renato Rossi, son associé dans Energie, de rejoindre sa croisade : Miss Sixty est née. Le modèle Tommy, coupé pour embrasser les courbes féminines, est le premier à remporter un véritable succès. Malgré l'ajout d'adorables petits séparés dans la gamme, l'obsession de la griffe pour la combinaison denim et sex-appeal est encore tout à fait d'actualité à ce jour. Miss Sixty propose désormais 35 modèles de jean chaque saison, tous déclinés dans un large choix de délavages. En 2004, la griffe introduit même une Zone Denim bien démarquée dans chacune de ses boutiques. Bien qu'elle ne revendique pas le statut adulte d'autres marques de denim telles qu'Earl Jean ou Seven for All Mankind, Miss Sixty remporte toutefois un énorme succès commercial, restant fidèle à sa qualité supérieure et à sa coupe signature sans augmenter les prix. Par ailleurs, l'image brillante de la marque doit beaucoup à ses campagnes publicitaires, réalisées par de grands noms de la mode comme les photographes Mario Testino et Ellen Von Unwerth, ou encore la styliste Katie Grand.

LAUREN COCHRANE

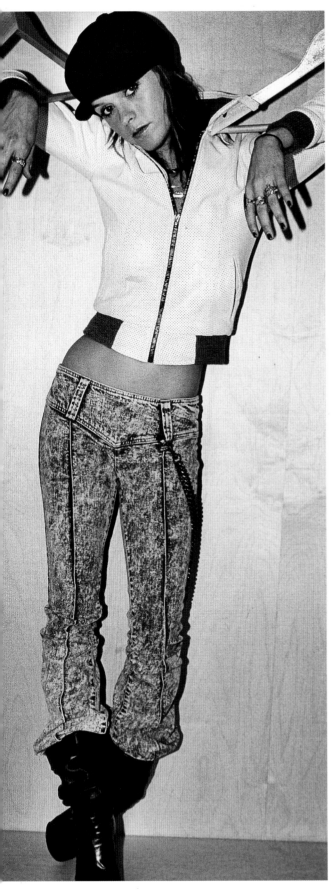

What are your signature designs? I don't like to categorise the Miss Sixty label into one style as my approach to fashion design is to completely re-invent the collection every season **What is your favourite piece from any of your collections?** It's a bit like asking a father which son he likes more! Each collection is made up of so many different pieces that it's impossible to choose one. Certainly there are always key pieces that I love; they're the most fashionable ones – more creative, experimental, and less commercial, but sometimes a simple T-shirt with the right graphic, or an unusual detail, is amazing **How would you describe your work?** I believe designing to be the world's most beautiful work. The only thing I can compare it to is a "cross-pollinating" process. I look at shapes, materials, or different ideas from whatever I see, then translate them into a clothing design, using original elements of my inspiration and inputting them to create the styles. Through the process, I start with something existing to arrive at something that did not exist before **What's your ultimate goal?** To open a Miss Sixty Restaurant **What inspires you?** I find the unexpected pleasures and unpredictability of every day life a real inspiration to me. Sometimes, I also find even ugly things are really inspirational **Can fashion still have a political ambition?** I would like to think so, but actually I don't, especially in Italy. It's up to people to give to fashion political ambitions or meanings, not to a fashion designer. **Who do you have in mind when you design?** I do not design with a particular sort of person in mind, but rather ask myself, 'Does this garment have a personality? Or is it just a pretty clothing?' **Is the idea of creative collaboration important to you?** I could not work on eight collections without collaborations. I'm lucky because

I have always found very good collaborators, who were and are able to push their ideas even if I didn't agree with them. Creative collaborations are means to an exchange of ideas **Who has been the greatest influence on your career?** Pop artists like Andy Warhol and Keith Haring **How have your own experiences affected your work as a designer?** Massively: I was a shop assistant, then a shop owner and now a designer. The first two steps gave me the possibility to have direct contact with the public, and that's really helpful to understand how it all works. To meet real women and men can allow you to gain feedback, which no catwalk show can do **Which is more important in your work: the process or the product?** Both. The process is a great part of my everyday life; the product is the result of my hard work **Is designing difficult for you, if so, what drives you to continue?** I don't find it difficult, it's fun actually **Have you ever been influenced or moved by the reaction to your designs?** I strongly believe in what I do so the reactions to my work affect me personally. I met a girl from Denmark wearing Miss Sixty jeans many years ago. It was unexpected, but she said they were the only jeans she could wear to make herself feel sexy. I thought it was great. The girl's perception of the jeans was perfect, exactly the one we wanted to have. The product was talking for itself **What's your definition of beauty?** I don't know how to define it. I believe beauty means to feel good within yourself. If you like how you are, you are beautiful **What's your philosophy?** I'm not a philosopher, I design clothes, but I basically have an aesthetic approach to life in general. **What is the most important lesson you've learned?** I'm still trying to learn: how to stop learning? It's impossible!

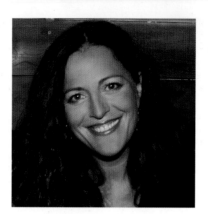

MISSONI

"I grew up with my parents' work" ANGELA MISSONI

With a history that spans over 50 years, the house of Missoni is that rare phenomenon in fashion, an enduring force to be reckoned with. Established in 1953 by Rosita and Ottavio Missoni, what began as a small knitwear factory following the traditional Italian handicraft techniques has evolved into a world – famous luxury label whose technical innovation and free-thinking approach have redefined notions of knitwear. A fateful meeting with Emmanuelle Khanh in Paris resulted in an important early collaboration and the first Missoni catwalk show took place in Florence, in 1967. By 1970, the Missoni, fusion of organic fabrics, a mastery of colour and instantly recognisable motifs – stripes, zig-zags, Greek keys and space-dyed weaves – saw the house become the last word in laid-back luxury. The layered mismatching of pattern and colour, mainly in the form of slinky knits, has become synonymous with Missoni inspiring the American press to describe the look as "put-together". Since taking over design duties in 1997, Angela Missoni has imaginatively updated the brand, introducing florals and even denim without losing the essence of classic Missoni. After working alongside her mother Rosita for 20 years, in 1993 Angela produced her own collection, becoming Missoni's overall creative director when her parents retired a few years later. Angela has subtly transformed the beguiling feminine looks of the Missoni archive with tailored lines and sassy slim-line silhouettes. Missoni has stood the test of time by attracting a new generation of devotees whilst maintaining the kudos of cool it established during its '70s heyday. Constantly referenced by the mass market, the Missoni style sits as happily on the red carpet as it does in the wardrobe of modern day bohemians.

Mit seiner über 50-jährigen Geschichte ist das Modehaus Missoni eines der seltenen Phänomene der Branche: eine beständige Kraft, mit der man rechnen muss. Aus der 1953 von Rosita und Ottavio Missoni gemäß der italienischen Handwerkstradition gegründeten kleinen Strickwarenfabrik entwickelte sich ein weltberühmtes Luxuslabel, dessen technische Innovationen und freimütiger Ansatz die Wahrnehmung von Strickwaren neu definierte. Ein schicksalhaftes Treffen mit Emmanuelle Kahn in Paris führte zu einer wichtigen frühen Zusammenarbeit. Die erste Missoni-Kollektion wurde dann 1966 präsentiert. 1970 war Missoni dank der Verbindung von Naturmaterialien, dem meisterhaften Umgang mit Farbe und unverwechselbaren Motiven – Streifen, Zickzack, griechische Mäander zum Inbegriff des legeren Luxus avanciert. Die Lagen aus eigentlich nicht zusammenpassenden Mustern und Farben, vornehmlich aus hautengem Strick, wurden zum Synonym für Missoni und von der amerikanischen Presse als „put-together" tituliert. Seit sie das Familienunternehmen 1997 von ihren Eltern übernahm, hat Angela Missoni die Marke phantasievoll aktualisiert, etwa durch die Einführung von floralen Mustern und sogar Denim, ohne darüber den klassischen Missoni-Stil zu vernachlässigen. Nachdem sie zwanzig Jahre lang an der Seite ihrer Mutter Rosita gearbeitet hatte, produzierte Angela 1993 ihre erste eigene, auch nach ihr benannte Kollektion. Damit war der Weg zum Creative Director der Firma vorgezeichnet, als ihre Eltern sich einige Jahre später aus dem Geschäft zurückzogen. Mit Hilfe ihrer Tochter und Muse Margherita änderte Angela auf subtile Weise die betörend femininen Looks aus dem Missoni-Archiv durch tadellos gearbeitete Linien und schicke, schmale Silhouetten. Missoni hat den Wandel der Zeiten bestens überstanden, indem man eine neue Generation von Fans anzog und zugleich den Ruhm der 1970er Jahre bewahrte. Und während der Stil der Marke permanent vom Massenmarkt kopiert wird, tummelt sich Missoni zufrieden auf dem roten Teppich und in den Schränken der Bohemiens unserer Tage.

Avec plus d'un demi-siècle d'histoire, la maison Missoni est un phénomène rare dans la mode, une force endurante absolument incontournable. Créée en 1953 par Rosita et Ottavio Missoni, ce qui a commencé avec une petite manufacture de tricot respectant les techniques artisanales italiennes traditionnelles s'est transformée en une griffe de luxe mondialement connue et dont l'innovation technique et la libre pensée ont redéfini la notion même de maille. Le destin de la petite maison est scellé lors d'une réunion fatidique avec Emmanuelle Kahn à Paris, première collaboration importante qui voit naître la première collection Missoni en 1966. En 1970, la fusion typique de Missoni entre tissus naturels, maîtrise de la couleur et motifs immédiatement identifiables (rayures, zigzags, motifs grecs et tissus à fils teints par zone) voit la griffe occuper l'avant-garde du luxe décontracté. A travers l'utilisation de tricots moulants, les superpositions de motifs et de couleurs dépareillés sont devenues synonymes de Missoni, incitant la presse américaine à qualifier ce look de «put-together». Depuis qu'elle a repris l'affaire familiale de ses parents en 1997, Angela Missoni modernise la marque avec imagination, introduisant les motifs floraux et même le denim sans pourtant perdre de vue le style Missoni des origines. Après avoir travaillé pendant 20 ans aux côtés de sa mère Rosita, Angela produit en 1993 sa propre collection éponyme, une expérience bienvenue pour devenir directrice de la création de Missoni, ce qu'elle fera quand ses parents prendront leur retraite quelques années plus tard. Avec l'aide de sa fille et muse Margherita, Angela transforme avec subtilité les looks étonnamment féminins des archives Missoni à travers de nouvelles coupes et des silhouettes élancées plutôt branchées. Missoni a su résister à l'épreuve du temps en attirant une nouvelle génération de fans tout en préservant le côté cool qui a fait l'âge d'or de la marque dans les années 70. Constamment copié par les grandes enseignes commerciales, le style Missoni est aussi à l'aise sur les tapis rouges de Hollywood que dans la garde-robe des bohémiennes d'aujourd'hui.

AIMEE FARRELL

What are your signature designs? Knit design: with fringes, bias-cuts, applications, inserts **What is your favourite piece from any of your collections?** My favourite changes all the time. I don't look back. In the spring/summer 2005 collection I like the bouquet print lace dress with cream background, tulle inserts with raspberry knit ribbon edging **How would you describe your work?** It needs a 360° attention. I see it as a never ending commitment **What's your ultimate goal?** I always look for perfection. So, until my last day at work, perfection will be my ultimate goal. Which is also why I dream to step out from the fashion business in five-six years... at that point I would finally have time for myself **What inspires you?** Many different things, nothing especially. It can be a trip, a walk in town, a work of contemporary art, a classic or recent movie, the way one of my friends or one of my daughters put some pieces, shapes, colours together when they dress up. What mostly inspires me is the way they interpret and reinterpret the clothes I design. How they mix them with clothes they already have in their wardrobe, vintage pieces and other designers' clothes. How they express their personality. I guess I am trying to always have a type of natural attitude in mind when I think of a collection. A certain fresh, spontaneous way of being elegant... **Can fashion still have a political ambition?** Fashion is mirroring women's condition, it talks of the freedom most women have on this planet. It is a medium of expression and a channel of communication: the authority of fashion brands can be used to bring to the public attention crucial problems of our culture and society, to raise funds and to increase public participation **Who do you have in mind when you design?** My daughter Margherita is not my muse, but I often have a type like her in mind when I design. I look for a fresh, natural concept of elegance **Is the idea of creative collaboration important to you?** Absolutely, I don't like to be by myself. Talking, sharing and discussing ideas is quite necessary to me: I always work together with other people, the crew of my collaborators and assistants and occasionally some friends.. **Who has been the greatest influence on your career?** My mother especially. I have learnt my work by watching and then assisting her for years **How have your own experiences affected your work as a designer?** I grew up together with my parents' work: my personal experiences are therefore definitely, strictly connected with fashion design. That creative mood, that meeting interesting people, that watching and listening to what my parents were doing, has certainly shaped me **Which is more important in your work: the process or the product?** They are strictly connected. I find both aspects very important and creative. I like to follow and control the all process **Have you ever been influenced or moved by the reaction to your designs?** The public's positive reaction is always important and flattering. But I don't think it ever influences my next decisions in terms of design. I like to move forward **What's your definition of beauty?** The autumn sunsets' range of reds, oranges and pinks I can see in the landscape out of my window **What's your philosophy?** Practice. Improvement **What is the most important lesson you've learned?** I always feel I haven't learnt enough.

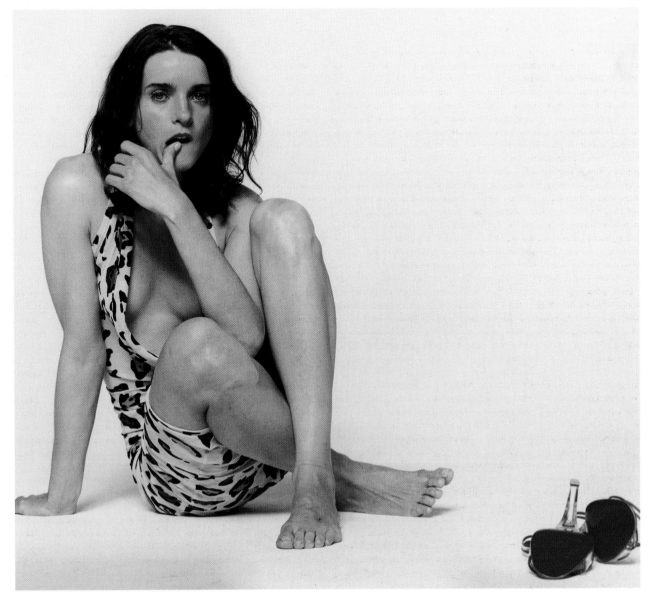

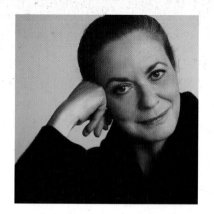

MOSCHINO

"My ultimate goal is always to improve on the last collection"

ROSSELLA JARDINI

The Italian fashion house Moschino owes much to Rossella Jardini who, since the untimely death of its founder Franco Moschino in 1994, has successfully held the reins of a brand which today still puts the kook into kooky. Moschino, having burst onto the scene in 1983, has grown up since its logo-mania '80s heyday (remember phrases like 'Ready To Where?' or 'This Is A Very Expensive Shirt' splashed onto garments?). But Jardini, as creative director of all Moschino product lines (sold through 22 shops worldwide), has steered this label in a contemporary direction while retaining its traditional wit. Since the millennium we have seen Jardini and her team continue to tease the market through parody and stereotype, both of which are central to the original philosophy of the house. Rompish catwalk parades featuring housewives in curlers and sleeping masks, demure '50s ladies à la Chanel (one of Jardini's most important personal influences), over-the-top prints, trompe l'oeil and swishy petticoats have all provided gleeful style moments. Born in Bergamo in 1952, Jardini began her career selling clothes rather than designing them. Then, in 1976, she met Nicola Trussardi and began assisting with the development of that company's clothing and leather goods. Creating her own line in 1978 with two model friends, she soon made the acquaintance of Franco Moschino and in 1981 began assisting him. A stint designing accessories for Bottega Veneta followed, but by 1984 she had settled into a permanent role at Moschino. Ten years later, before his tragically early death, Franco Moschino made it quite clear he wished Jardini to take over the helm. She has been there ever since.

Das italienische Modehaus Moschino verdankt Rossella Jardini viel. Seit dem frühen Tod des Firmengründers Franco Moschino im Jahr 1994 steuert sie eine Marke, die man bis heute als verrückt im besten Sinne des Wortes bezeichnen kann. Moschino hatte 1983 sein Debüt in der Modeszene und ist erwachsen geworden, wenn man an die Logo-Manie im Boom der 1980er Jahre denkt (wer erinnert sich nicht an auf Kleidungsstücken prangenden Sätze wie „Ready To Where?" oder „This Is A Very Expensive Shirt"?). Als Chefdesignerin aller Produktlinien des Hauses (die weltweit in 22 Läden verkauft werden) hat Jardini das Label in eine moderne Richtung gesteuert und dabei seinen traditionellen Witz bewahrt. Seit der Jahrtausendwende kann man wieder verstärkt beobachten, wie Jardini und ihr Team den Markt mit Parodien und Klischees necken, die beide von zentraler Bedeutung für die ursprüngliche Unternehmensphilosophie sind. So präsentierte man auf dem Catwalk schon Paraden von Hausfrauen mit Lockenwicklern und Schlafmasken, prüden Damen im 50er Jahre-Stil von Chanel (einer der wichtigsten Einflüsse für Jardini), völlig verrückten Mustern,

Trompe l'œil und raschelnden Petticoats – was für jede Menge Ausgelassenheit sorgte. Die 1952 in Bergamo geborene Jardini begann ihre Karriere übrigens nicht mit dem Design, sondern mit dem Verkauf von Textilien. 1976 lernte sie Nicola Trussardi kennen und begann, ihm bei der Entwicklung des Textil- und Lederwarengeschäfts seiner Firma zu assistieren. Gemeinsam mit zwei befreundeten Models kreierte sie 1978 ihr eigenes Label und lernte bald darauf Franco Moschino kennen, dessen Assistentin sie ab 1981 war. Es gab noch ein kurzes Intermezzo als Designerin für Accessoires bei Bottega Veneta, bis sie 1984 ihre Dauerstellung bei Moschino einnahm. Zehn Jahre danach und kurz vor seinem tragischen frühen Tod ließ Franco Moschino keinen Zweifel an seinem Wunsch, Jardini das Ruder zu überlassen. Seither hat sie es nicht mehr aus der Hand gegeben.

La maison italienne Moschino doit beaucoup à Rossella Jardini, car depuis le décès prématuré de son fondateur Franco Moschino en 1994, elle tient avec succès les rênes d'une marque qui reste aujourd'hui fidèle à son côté fou et décalé. Apparue sur la scène de la mode en 1983, la griffe Moschino s'est depuis départie de la logomania qui a marqué son âge d'or dans les années 80 (qui aurait pu oublier les slogans «Ready To Where?» ou «Cette chemise coûte très cher»?). Mais Rossella Jardini, directrice de la création de toutes les lignes de produits Moschino (vendues dans 22 boutiques à travers le monde), a orienté la griffe vers un style plus contemporain tout en respectant l'état d'esprit qui a fait son succès. Depuis l'an 2000, Rossella Jardini et son équipe continuent à séduire le marché à travers la parodie et le stéréotype, deux piliers de la philosophie originelle de la maison. Défilés tapageurs où paradent des ménagères portant bigoudis et masques de nuit, discrètes dames années 50 à la Chanel (l'une des plus importantes contributions personnelles de Rossella Jardini), imprimés surchargés, effets trompe-l'œil et jupons précieux nous ont tous offert des moments de mode jubilatoires. Née en 1952 à Bergame, Rossella Jardini débute dans le métier par la vente et non par la création. En 1976, elle rencontre Nicola Trussardi et commence à l'assister dans le développement des vêtements et des articles de maroquinerie de sa marque. Elle crée sa propre ligne en 1978 avec deux amis mannequins, mais peu de temps après, elle fait la connaissance de Franco Moschino, dont elle devient l'assistante en 1981. Après un bref détour par Bottega Veneta pour qui elle crée des accessoires, elle revient définitivement chez Moschino en 1984. Dix ans plus tard, avant sa mort tragique et précoce, Franco Moschino exprimera clairement son désir de voir Rossella Jardini reprendre le flambeau. Elle n'a plus jamais quitté la maison.

SIMON CHILVERS

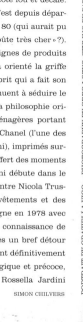

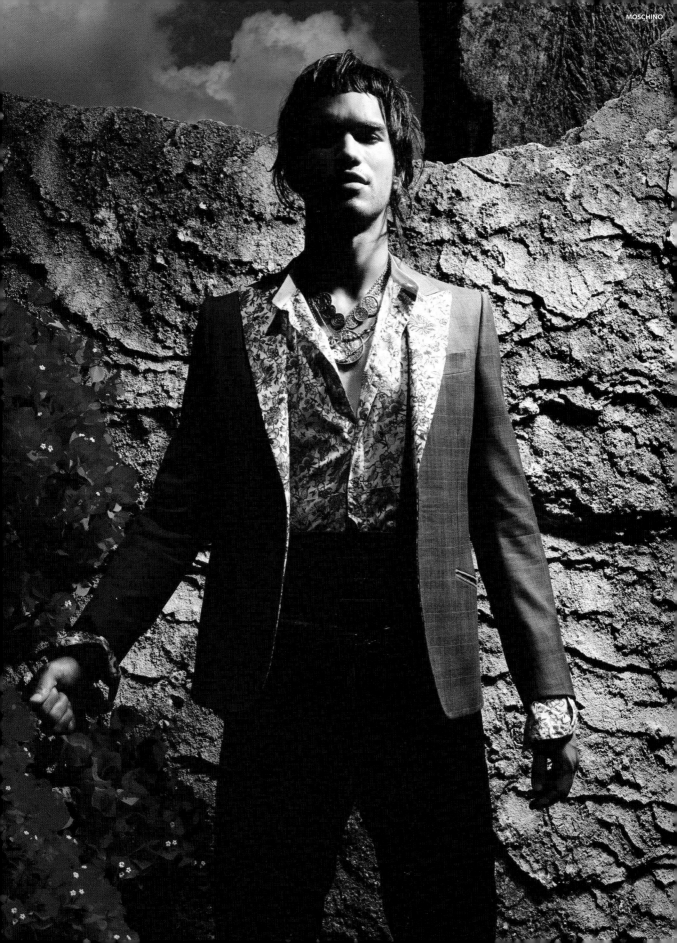

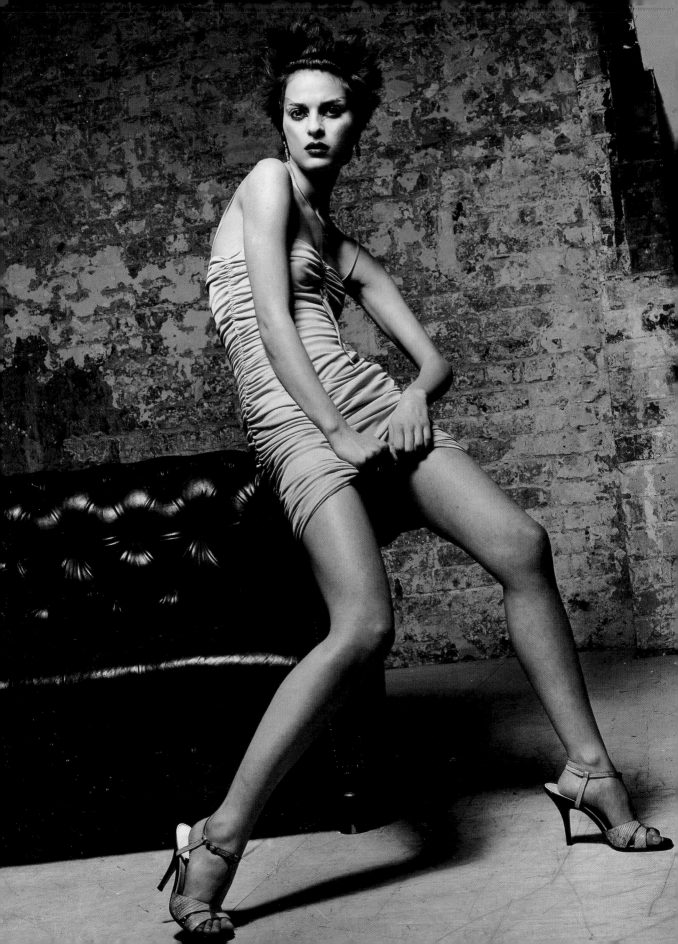

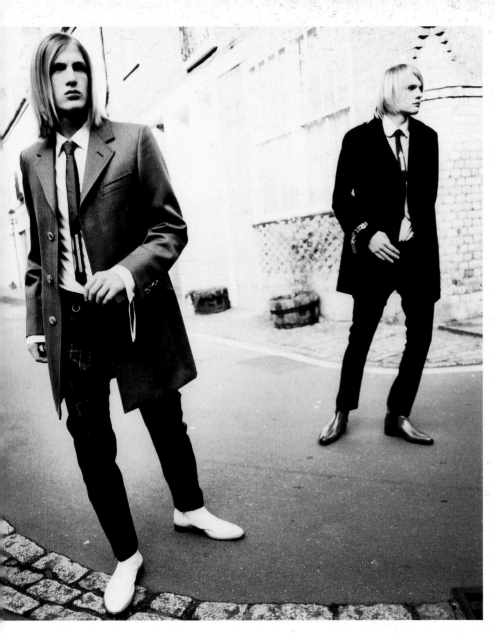

What is your favourite piece from any of your collections? The lurex bouclé overcoat with mink coat collar from the Moschino autumn/winter 2004 collection **How would you describe your work?** My work is constant, at times it can be tiring and challenging, but always very satisfactory; anyway, a work that allows you to bet on yourself and try always to do your best **What's your ultimate goal?** To always improve upon the last collection **What inspires you?** I always start my work from the fabrics, from the fashion icons Claire McCardell, Diana Vreeland, Cecil Beaton. I also get my inspiration from clothes I see on passers-by on the streets **Can fashion still have a political ambition?** In such difficult times, it seems unlikely to think of fashion as something "political" **Who do you have in mind when you design?** Franco Moschino **Is the idea of creative collaboration important to you?** Definitely **Who has been the greatest influence on your career?** Franco Moschino **How have your own experiences affected your work as a designer?** My career and my private life have always been deeply entangled, so that it seems difficult for me to think about an influence **Which is more important in your work: the process or the product?** I think the product, now **Is designing difficult for you, if so, what drives you to continue?** At the beginning of every season it seems to be very difficult, but as the work goes on, a kind of mechanism starts and continues by itself **Have you ever been influenced or moved by the reaction to your designs?** I am influenced by those clothes I love most **What's your definition of beauty?** All that is good becomes beautiful **What's your philosophy?** To work honestly, respecting the members of my staff **What is the most important lesson you've learned?** Humility.

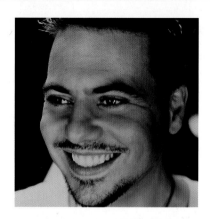

NARCISO RODRIGUEZ

"As hard and painful as designing can be, it is the thing
I have always been most passionate about"

Narciso Rodriguez designs clothes that are sliced, cut and put together with apparently effortless finesse. They are fluid and simple, architectural and modern, easy to wear but not casual, dressed-up but not too over-the-top. Rodriguez has an impeccable list of credentials. He graduated from Parsons School of Design in 1982, and after a brief period freelancing, joined Donna Karan at Anne Klein in 1985. He worked there for six years before moving to Calvin Klein as womenswear designer. In 1995 he relocated to Paris where he stayed for two years with Cerruti, first as women's and men's design director, and then as creative director for the entire womenswear division. Never one to slow down the pace, in 1997 Rodriguez not only showed his debut signature line in Milan, but also became the womenswear design director at leather goods brand Loewe, a position he retained until 2001. In 2003 he received the CFDA's womenswear Designer of the Year Award and in 2004 was the recipient of the Hispanic Heritage 'Vision Award'. Since 2001 he has concentrated on his eponymous line, which is produced and distributed by Aeffe SpA and shown at New York Fashion Week. Rodriguez's Latin roots (he was born in 1961 in New Jersey to Cuban-American parents) inspire the slick, glamorous side of his work while his experience in Europe has honed his fashion craftsmanship and tailoring expertise. This perfectly stylish balance has seduced some of the world's loveliest ladies, including Salma Hayek, Julianna Margulies and the late Carolyn Bessette, who married John F. Kennedy Jnr. in a Rodriguez creation. His autumn/winter 2005 collection was, as ever, perfect and precise fashion design, aimed at uptown sophisticates: black dresses were cut to reveal a sliver of décolletage and mannish suits had a lean, body-conscious line.

Narciso Rodriguez entwirft Kleider, die mit scheinbar müheloser Finesse zugeschnitten und zusammengefügt sind. Sie sind fließend und schlicht, skulptural und modern, tragbar, aber nicht alltäglich, schick, jedoch nicht überkandidelt. Die Referenzen, die der Designer vorzuweisen hat, sind tadellos. 1982 machte er seinen Abschluss an der Parsons School of Design, darauf folgte eine kurze Phase als freischaffender Designer. 1985 fing er unter Donna Karan beim Label Anne Klein an. Nach sechs Jahren wechselte er als Damenmodedesigner zu Calvin Klein. Im Jahr 1995 zog er nach Paris, wo er zwei Jahre für Cerruti tätig war. Zunächst als Design Director für Damen wie für Herren und schließlich als Creative Director der gesamten Damenmode. In diesem Tempo ging es weiter – 1997 präsentierte Rodriguez nicht nur in Mailand die erste Kollektion seiner eigenen Linie, sondern wurde auch Design Director der Damenmode beim Lederwarenhersteller Loewe, was er bis 2001 bleiben sollte. 2003 wurde er von der CFDA zum Designer of the Year für den Bereich Damenmode gewählt; 2004 zeichnete man ihn mit dem Hispanic Heritage „Vision Award" aus. Seit 2001 konzentriert sich der Designer ausschließlich auf seine eigene Linie, die von Aeffe SpA produziert und vertrieben und bei der New Yorker Modewoche vorgestellt wird. Seine Wurzeln (er wurde 1961 als Kind kubanisch-amerikanischer Eltern in New Jersey geboren) inspirieren Rodriguez zu den schicken glamourösen Aspekten seiner Arbeit, während die in Europa gesammelten Erfahrungen ihm im handwerklich-technischen Bereich zugute kommen. Wie perfekt sich beides ergänzt, konnte man schon an einigen der schönsten Frauen der Welt bewundern, etwa an Salma Hayek, Julianna Margulies und der inzwischen verstorbenen Carolyn Bessette, die John F. Kennedy Junior in einer Rodriguez-Kreation geheiratet hat. Seine Kollektion für Herbst/Winter 2005 war – wie immer – perfektes und präzises Modedesign für die elegante bessere Gesellschaft: schwarze Kleider, die einen Blick aufs Dekolleté gewährten, sowie sehr maskuline Anzüge mit schmalem, figurbetonendem Schnitt.

Narciso Rodriguez dessine des vêtements taillés, coupés et assemblés avec une grande finesse et une apparente facilité. Ses créations sont simples et fluides, architecturales et modernes, faciles à porter mais pas trop informelles, chic mais jamais surchergées. Rodriguez revendique une liste de références idéales : diplômé de la Parsons School of Design en 1982, il travaille en free-lance pendant une brève période avant de rejoindre Donna Karan chez Anne Klein en 1985. Il y reste six ans, puis part travailler chez Calvin Klein en tant que styliste pour femme. En 1995, il s'installe à Paris où il passe deux ans chez Cerruti, d'abord comme directeur des lignes pour femme et pour homme, puis comme directeur de la création de toutes les collections féminines. N'étant pas du genre à ralentir le rythme, en 1997 Rodriguez présente non seulement sa première collection signature à Milan, mais devient également directeur de la création féminine du maroquinier Loewe, un poste qu'il occupe jusqu'en 2001. En 2003, le CFDA le couronne Womenswear Designer of the Year, puis il reçoit en 2004 le Vision Award de la fondation Hispanic Heritage. Depuis 2001, il se consacre à sa ligne éponyme, produite et distribuée par Aeffe SpA et présentée à la New York Fashion Week. Ses racines latines (il est né en 1961 dans le New Jersey de parents d'origine cubaine) inspirent le côté brillant et glamour de son travail, tandis que son expérience européenne aiguise son savoir-faire et son expertise de la coupe : un savant équilibre stylistique qui séduit certaines des plus belles femmes du monde telles que Salma Hayek, Julianna Margulies et feue Carolyn Bessette, qui avait épousé John F. Kennedy Junior dans une robe dessinée par Rodriguez. Comme toujours, sa collection automne/hiver 2005 propose une mode parfaite et précise destinée aux snobs des beaux quartiers : la coupe de ses robes noires laisse apparaître un peu de décolleté et ses tailleurs d'inspiration masculine affichent des lignes épurées et près du corps.

TERRY NEWMAN

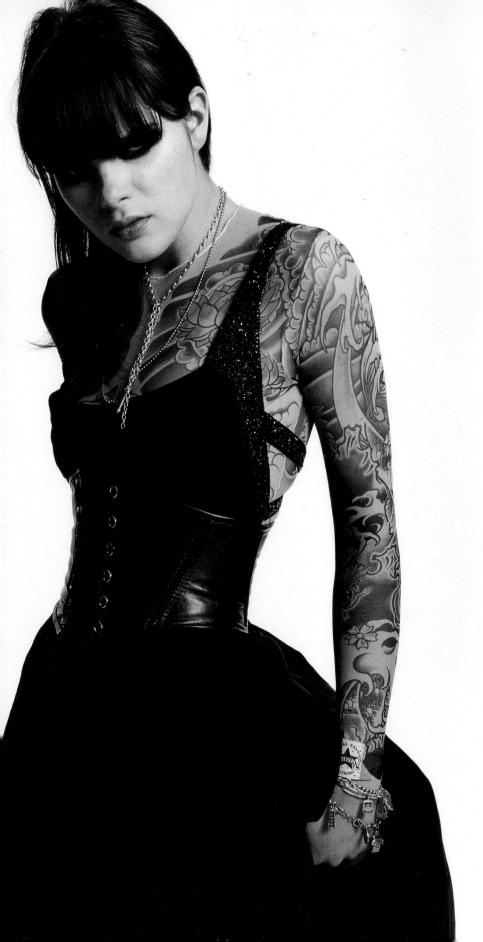

What are your signature designs? A dress **What's your favourite piece from any of your collections?** Autumn/winter 2000 black look on Carmen Kass opening the show **How would you describe your work?** Clean, tailored, feminine **What inspires you?** Life on the streets **Can fashion still have a political ambition?** Anything is possible **Who do you have in mind when you design?** A modern woman **Who has been the greatest influence on your career?** Cristobal Balenciaga **Which is more important in your work: the process or the product?** Both **Is designing difficult for you and, if so, what drives you to continue?** As hard and painful as it can be, it is the thing I have always been most passionate about **Have you ever been influenced or moved by a reaction to your designs?** Whether you're slammed or applauded, you're always moved **What's your definition of beauty?** Grace **What's your philosophy?** Keep it simple! **What is the most important lesson you've learned?** To appreciate every day what life has to offer.

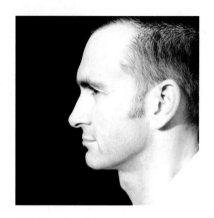

NEIL BARRETT

"It's good to listen, to discuss, but it has to be your own conviction that makes each decision"

With his own Milan-based label, a host of celebrity clients and a stint as an MTV presenter, Neil Barrett has come a long way from his Devonshire roots. Known for clothes that focus on detail and cut, Barrett's is an approach underpinned by an extensive knowledge of fabric production, which he employs to rejuvenate classic designs. With subdued colours and restrained tailoring, Barrett's menswear range is avowedly masculine – a factor that has contributed to its widespread appeal. Born in 1965, Barrett graduated in 1986 from Central Saint Martins, and received an MA from the Royal College of Art in 1989. Within a year he was made senior menswear designer at Gucci in Florence, where he worked until 1994 – a period in which the brand underwent an important revival, both creatively and financially. Success at Gucci enabled Barrett to approach Prada with a proposal for a menswear line. Prada accepted his offer and he began work as the company's menswear design director. He remained at Prada until 1998, when he launched his first self-named menswear collection. This was an immediate success that was snapped up by over 100 designer stores across the world. The following year Barrett set up White, his own Prada-produced label, which was invited to open the Pitti Immagine Uomo Fair in 2000 where he also introduced his first womenswear collection. The next few years saw Barrett sign a footwear deal with Puma and in 2004 he redesigned the Italian national football team's strip for the European Championship – an honour for a non-Italian and a testament to the worldwide success of his label.

Ein eigenes Label mit Sitz in Mailand, eine Schar prominenter Kunden und ein Job als Moderator bei MTV – Neil Barrett, dessen Wurzeln in Devonshire liegen, hat es zweifellos weit gebracht. Er ist bekannt für den Detailreichtum und Schnitt seiner Kleider, dazu kommt noch sein umfangreiches Wissen über die Stoffproduktion, das er nutzt, um klassische Designs zu verjüngen. Mit gedämpften Farben und schlichten Schnitten ist Barretts Herrenlinie dezidiert maskulin – was zu seiner großen Beliebtheit sicher beigetragen hat. Der 1965 geborene Designer machte 1986 seinen Abschluss am Central Saint Martins und 1989 seinen Master am Royal College of Art. Innerhalb eines Jahres brachte er es dann zum Chefdesigner der Herrenmode bei Gucci in Florenz, wo er bis 1994 tätig war – in dieser Zeit erfuhr die Marke eine wichtige Renaissance, sowohl im kreativen wie im wirtschaftlichen Sinne. Der Erfolg bei Gucci versetzte Barrett in die Lage, Prada eine eigene Herrenlinie anzubieten. Dort ging man auf sein Angebot ein, und Barrett fing als Design Director der Herrenmode an. Bis 1998 blieb er bei Prada und präsentierte dann seine erste Herrenkollektion unter eigenem Namen. Der Erfolg stellte sich unmittelbar ein – über hundert Designläden in aller Welt sicherten sich seine Entwürfe. Ein Jahr später gründete Barrett White, sein eigenes, bei Prada produziertes Label. 2000 wurde er eingeladen, die Messe Pitti Immagine Uomo zu eröffnen. Dort lancierte Barrett dann seine erste Damenkollektion. In den folgenden Jahren unterzeichnete Barrett u.a. einen Kooperationsvertrag mit Puma über eine Schuhkollektion und entwarf 2004 anlässlich der Europameisterschaft ein neues Dress für die italienische Fußballnationalmannschaft. Das war zum einen eine Auszeichnung für den Nicht-Italiener, zum anderen ein Beleg für den weltweiten Erfolg seines Labels.

Avec sa propre griffe à Milan, une profusion de clients célèbres et un job de présentateur sur MTV, on peut dire que Neil Barrett a fait du chemin depuis son Devon natal. Réputé pour des vêtements qui font la part belle aux détails et à la coupe, Barrett adopte une approche étayée par sa grande connaissance de la production de tissus, qu'il exploite pour rajeunir les classiques. Marquée par des couleurs sobres et des coupes maîtrisées, la mode pour homme de Barrett est, de son propre aveu, très masculine : un aspect qui contribuera à son immense succès. Né en 1965, Neil Barrett sort diplômé de Central Saint Martins en 1986 avant d'obtenir un MA du Royal College of Art en 1989. Un an plus tard, il devient styliste senior de la ligne masculine de Gucci à Florence, où il travaille jusqu'en 1994 : pendant cette période, la marque connaît un véritable renouveau, tant sur le plan créatif que financier. Son succès chez Gucci lui permet d'approcher Prada en proposant la création d'une ligne pour homme. Prada accepte son offre et le nomme directeur de la création pour homme. Il quittera Prada en 1998 pour lancer sa première collection éponyme de vêtements masculins. Il remporte un succès immédiat et ses créations sont achetées par plus de 100 boutiques de créateurs à travers le monde. L'année suivante, Barrett crée White, sa propre griffe produite par Prada, et il est invité à faire l'ouverture du salon professionnel Pitti Immagine Uomo en l'an 2000, à l'occasion duquel il lance également sa première collection pour femme. Les années suivantes, Puma lui commande une collection de chaussures, puis en 2004 il redessine la tenue officielle de l'équipe nationale de football d'Italie pour l'Euro 2004 : un véritable honneur pour un « étranger » et une reconnaissance du succès mondial de sa griffe.

DAVID VASCOTT

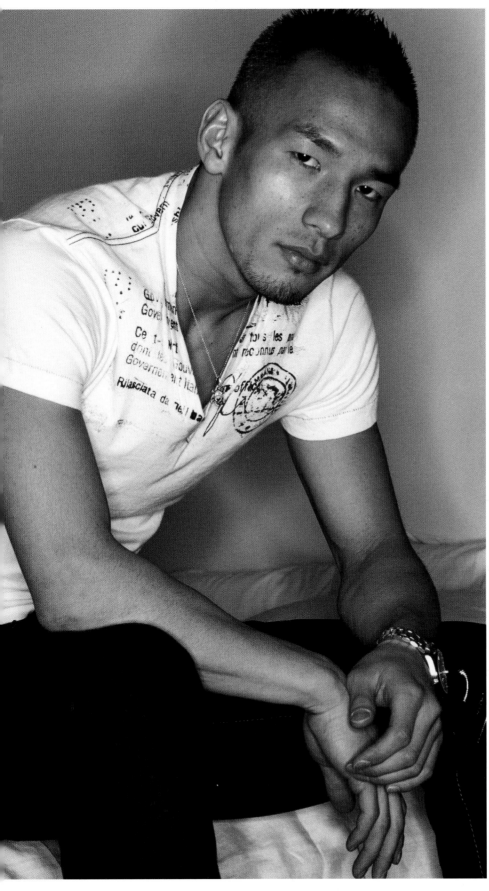

What are your signature designs? Hybrids of (reworked) "iconic" menswear **What is your favourite piece from any of your collections?** Spring/summer 2005, the hand-polished fine pinstripe jacket – autumn/winter 2004, the waxed denim jeans – spring/summer 2004, the worn-in shrunken cotton blue blazer – autumn/winter 2003, the hob-nail, Dickensian boots, etc… all of these I continue to wear today… together **Who do you have in mind when you design?** Me in the body of different people **Is the idea of creative collaboration important to you?** Yes, it's good to listen, to discuss, but it has to be your own conviction that makes each decision **Who has been the greatest influence on your career?** For personal inspiration, it's definitely my mother. For creative influence, it's seeing my clothes on clients and in stores worldwide and wanting to do more **How have your own experiences affected your work as a designer?** All personal experiences, good or bad, contribute to your work, both driving you and inspiring you **Which is more important in your work: the process or the product?** The product of course, the final garment on the body: this is my goal, the process just happens to be the enjoyable (or not!) means to this end **Is designing difficult for you, if so, what drives you to continue?** No, it's straightforward, your instinct dictates what is right or wrong **Have you ever been influenced or moved by the reaction to your designs?** Of course, it's when the final customer understands and gets your design, that the satisfaction is greatest **What's your definition of beauty?** When the inner goodness is visible **What's your philosophy?** Follow your instinct **What is the most important lesson you've learned?** Never take anything for granted and no matter what you do, learn from the past, live for the present and dream of your future.

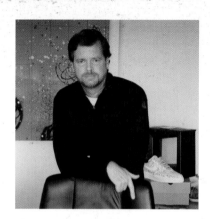

NIKE

"A passion for sports is something shared by nearly all cultures throughout the world, so we're fortunate to be a part of something that connects people and is healthy" MARK PARKER

The story of Nike, the biggest sports brand in the world, is the quintessential case study of how globalism has changed the production and politics of fashion over the past three decades. Set up by business graduate Phil Knight and his former running coach Bill Bowerman, the company began by importing Japanese training shoes during the '60s. They established the firm officially under the title of the Greek goddess of victory – and the $35 'swoosh' logo that was to become so central to their identity – in 1972. Success was almost immediate, but it wasn't until the early '80s that Nike began to pose a serious threat to its main competitor, Adidas. The signing of Chicago Bulls basketball player Michael Jordan to promote his own range of shoes, coupled with an aggressive marketing campaign based around his 'jumpman' silhouette, catapulted Nike into what became known as the 'trainer wars' in 1986. Though its market-leader status was briefly challenged by Reebok's shrewd exploitation of the female market via its 'Freedom' aerobics shoe, the cross-gender appeal of Nike's 'Just Do It' advertising campaign in 1988 secured them a position at the forefront of international sales for footwear, clothing and equipment, where they have remained ever since. During the '90s, Nike cultivated the burgeoning collectors markets by issuing select footwear in limited numbers whilst maintaining their ongoing commitment to the development of products designed to enhance athletes' performance. The company experienced the flipside of commercial success at the end of the decade, when it was one of the brands demonised by a range of anti-capitalist polemics including Naomi Klein's 'No Logo' (2000). Mark Parker is responsible for all products and brand management. He joined the company in 1979 as a footwear designer and over the past 26 years has held numerous influential roles within the company before becoming Nike's brand president. Parker is widely recognised as the creative driving force behind Nike.

Die Geschichte von Nike, der größten Sportmarke der Welt, ist ein Paradebeispiel dafür, wie die globalisierte Wirtschaft die Modeproduktion und -politik in den letzten drei Jahrzehnten verändert hat. Die von dem frischgebackenen Betriebswirtschaftler Phil Knight und seinem früheren Lauftrainer Bill Bowerman gegründete Firma begann in den 1960er Jahren mit dem Import japanischer Turnschuhe. 1972 benannten die beiden das Unternehmen offiziell nach der griechischen Siegesgöttin und legten sich für 35 Dollar das „Swoosh"-Logo zu, aus dem noch große Bedeutung für ihre Identität erwachsen sollte. Der Erfolg stellte sich fast sofort ein, doch erst ab den frühen 1980er Jahren begann Nike eine ernsthafte Bedrohung für seinen Hauptkonkurrenten Adidas zu werden. Der Vertrag mit dem Basketballer Michael Jordan von den Chicago Bulls über die Promotion seiner eigenen Schuhlinie katapultierte Nike zusammen mit einer aggressiven Marketingkampagne rund um die Silhouette des „Jumpman" 1986 in den so genannten Turnschuh-Krieg. Die Rolle des Marktführers wurde dann zwar kurz von Reebok in Frage gestellt, als die Firma mit ihrem Aerobic-

schuh Freedom die weibliche Kundschaft klug abschöpfte. Doch der Unisex-Appeal der Kampagne „Just do it" sicherte Nike 1988 wieder den Platz an der Spitze der internationalen Verkäufe bei Schuhen, Kleidung und Sportausrüstung. In den 1990er Jahre stellte sich Nike auf die wachsende Zahl der Sammler und die Wünsche der Modemärkte ein, indem man ausgewählte Schuhe in limitierten Auflagen herausbrachte. Die Kehrseite des kommerziellen Erfolgs lernte das Unternehmen am Ende jenes Jahrzehnts kennen, als es zu den Marken gehörte, die von zahlreichen kapitalismuskritischen Publikationen wie Naomi Kleins „No Logo" (2000) dämonisiert wurden. Mark Parker ist verantwortlich für das Produkt- und Markenmanagement. Er kam 1979 als Schuhdesigner zur Firma und hatte seitdem zahlreiche einflussreiche Positionen inne, bevor er Nikes Brand President wurde. Parker gilt als kreativer Motor der Firma Nike.

L'histoire de Nike, la plus grande marque de sportswear du monde, symbolise par excellence la façon dont la mondialisation a transformé la production et la politique de la mode au cours de ces trente dernières années. Créée par le diplômé en business Phil Knight et son ancien coach sportif Bill Bowerman, l'entreprise commence à importer des chaussures de sport japonaises dans les années 60. En 1972, ils baptisent officiellement leur société du nom de la déesse grecque de la victoire et achètent pour 35 dollars le fameux logo « swoosh » qui devait devenir synonyme de l'identité Nike. La marque remporte un succès quasi-immédiat, mais doit attendre le début des années 80 pour commencer à menacer sérieusement Adidas, son principal concurrent. En 1986, le contrat signé avec Michael Jordan pour promouvoir la ligne de baskets du joueur des Chicago Bulls, associé à une campagne marketing offensive autour de sa silhouette « jumpman », catapulte Nike dans une guerre sans merci avec ses concurrents. Bien que sa position dominante sur le marché soit brièvement remise en question par Reebok, qui exploite judicieusement le filon féminin avec ses modèles d'aérobic « Freedom », l'attrait unisexe de la campagne publicitaire « Just Do It » de Nike en 1988 sécurise sa place au top des ventes internationales de chaussures, de vêtements et d'accessoires de sport, que la marque n'a plus quittée depuis. Au cours des années 90, Nike s'adresse au marché bourgeonnant des collectionneurs en sortant une sélection de modèles en édition limitée. L'entreprise connaît la rançon de la gloire commerciale à la fin des années 90, diabolisée entre autres marques par une série de polémiques anti-capitalistes, dont la controverse suscitée par le livre « No Logo » de Naomi Klein (2000). Mark Parker est responsable de tous les produits et de la direction de la marque. Il a rejoint l'entreprise en 1970 en tant que designer de chaussures, et au cours de ces 26 dernières années, il a occupé de nombreux postes d'influence au sein de la maison avant de devenir Président de la marque Nike. Aujourd'hui, Parker est largement reconnu comme la véritable force créative de Nike.

PENNY MARTIN

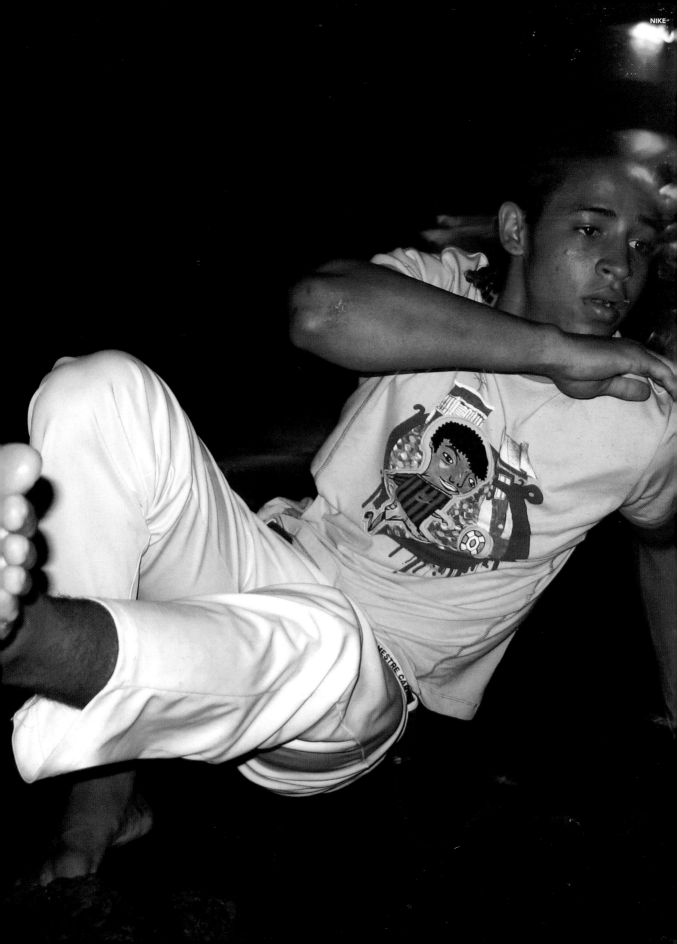

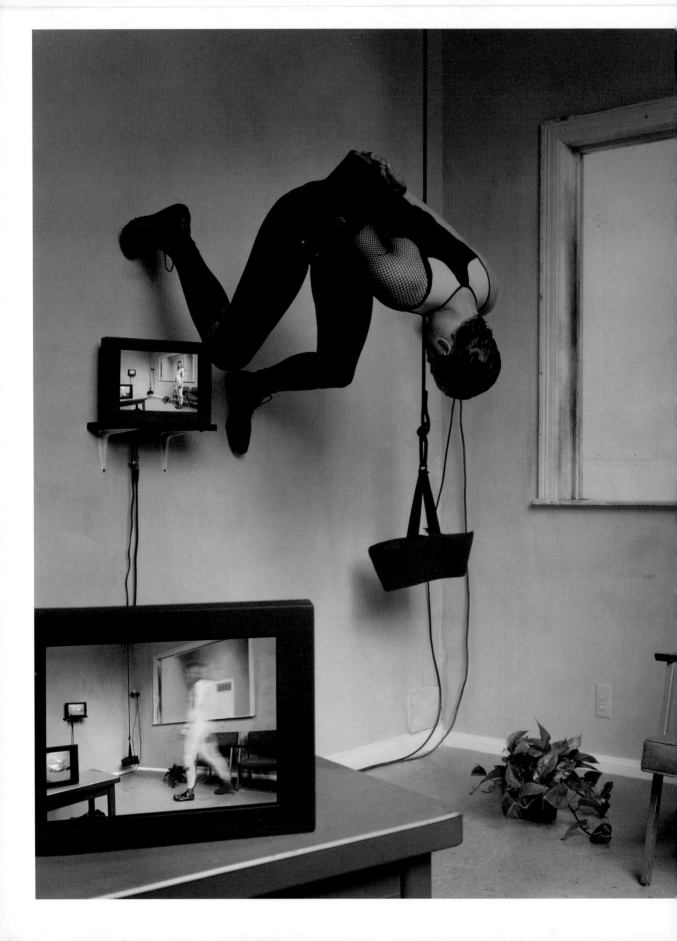

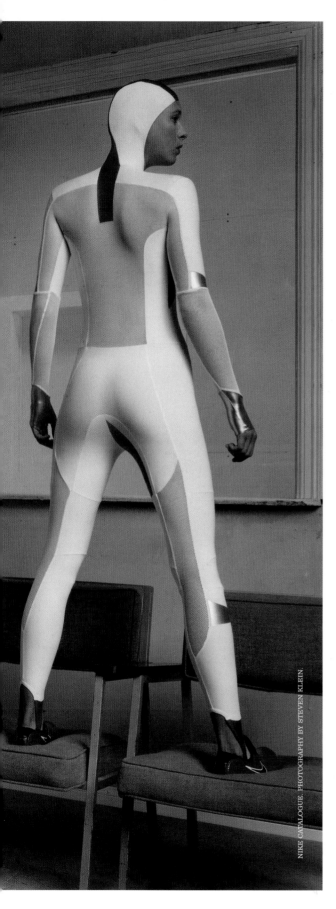

NIKE CATALOGUE. PHOTOGRAPHY BY STEVEN KLEIN

What are your signature designs? Designs that work with the body in movement, from the ultimate in athletic performance to everyday active life. Design that reflects and helps define sports culture. The Air Force 1, the Dunk, the Swift Suit, the AIR MAX, the Dri-Fit shirt, NIKE Sphere, Jordan's 1-20 Designs that transform perceptions of performance and style, inspiring new generations of product **What is your favourite piece from any of your collections?** Simple, uncluttered, wearable design that performs at a high level like the Dri-Fit Shirt and Presto shoe **How would you describe your work?** Grounded in sport, fixated on performance, innovate with purpose **What's your ultimate goal?** Serve the athlete in all of us **What inspires you?** Ultimately, just about everything: failure, success, nature, the body, physics, architecture, sports, music, art, sustainability, solving problems, simple solutions **Can fashion still have a political ambition?** Certainly, if that's the motivation. As a sports brand, our position is different. A passion for sports is something shared by nearly all cultures throughout the world, so we're fortunate to be a part of something that connects people and is healthy **Who do you have in mind when you design?** Athletes and their needs. We listen to them, study them and focus on solving their problems, which is how we are able to continually evolve new ways of thinking and fuel our creativity **Is the idea of creative collaboration important to you?** Absolutely, we have always collaborated.

We have a constant dialogue with athletes, coaches, trainers, to gain the insights needed to drive innovation. And with a diverse and eclectic group of artists and other designers for their cultural insights and perspectives. We do this to stimulate and inform our own design process, constantly seeking new sources of inspiration and insight **Who has been the greatest influence on your career?** The many who have challenged and inspired **How have your own experiences affected your work as a designer?** Having the insights as an athlete to understand the critical relationship of design and performance. How they inspire and feed each other and how this relationship can create a unique and beautiful aesthetic born of purpose **Which is more important in your work: the process or the product?** Product people don't wear process **Is designing difficult for you, if so, what drives you to continue?** Great design is a challenge we love, ultimately the most important thing we do, our source of strength and passion, our origins and our future **Have you ever been influenced or moved by the reaction to your designs?** Always. The feedback is essential to validate real performance. It works or it doesn't! **What's your philosophy?** Dig deep, open your mind, don't avoid conflict, seek diversity, trust your instincts, create with courage, work hard, be yourself, be honest, keep moving, laugh a lot! **What is the most important lesson you've learned?** That there's so much more to learn and unlearn.

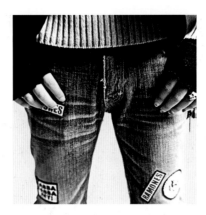

NUMBER (N)INE

"I just really like fashion and clothes" TAKAHIRO MIYASHITA

A certain type of man wears Number (N)ine. Self-taught Takahiro Miyashita established the brand in Tokyo in November 1996, taking his influences from street culture and music. The result is a label as edgy and raw as his aspirations. There's something tough yet resolutely elegant, something avant-garde yet nostalgic, about his collections, which have included both corduroy underpants and fur sandals. In a more wearable mode, bold red-and-black checks, bondage trousers, and large hoodies are all signatures for Miyashita's cult label. Fabrics are always juxtaposed and clothes are often layered; his models trail the catwalks with heads hung low, eyes to the floor. Miyashita's inspirations include '90s grunge and rock music, and the names of his collections often reflect these influences: 'Beat Generation (Beat Nick)' or 'Touch Me I'm Sick' are just two examples – the latter, a reference to American grunge outfit Mudhoney. Miyashita's clothes are designed to resonate one's 'spiritual state', and allude to something beneath the surface, something moody, angst-ridden, and Gothic. In short, Number (N)ine has the kudos of a secret club. The brand has boutiques in New York and Tokyo.

Ein bestimmter Typ Mann trägt Number (N)ine. Gegründet wurde die Marke im November 1996 von dem Autodidakten Takahiro Miyashita. Er ließ sich von Alltagskultur und Musik beeinflussen, was in einem Label resultierte, das mit seinen Ecken und Kanten genau den Bestrebungen des Designers entsprach. Seine Kollektionen haben so etwas Toughes, aber zugleich entschieden Elegantes, etwas Avantgardistisches und auch Nostalgisches. Sowohl Cordunterhosen als auch Pelzsandalen fanden darin bereits Platz. Bei den leichter tragbaren Sachen sind kräftig rot-schwarz karierte Hemden, Bondage-Hosen und große Kapuzenpullis Markenzeichen des Kultlabels. Verschiedene Stoffe prallen aufeinander, und die Kleider bestehen oft aus mehreren Lagen. Die Models schleichen stets mit hängenden Köpfen und gesenkten Blickes über den Catwalk. Miyashitas

Inspirationen sind u. a. die Grunge-Bewegung der 1990er Jahre und Rockmusik, was sich auch oft in den Namen seiner Kollektionen niederschlägt: Beat Generation (Beat Nick) oder Touch Me I'm Sick sind da nur Beispiele – letzteres bezieht sich auf das amerikanische Grunge-Outfit Mudhoney. Miyashitas Entwürfe wollen das „spirituelle Befinden" ihrer Träger widerspiegeln und spielen auf etwas an, das sich unter der Oberfläche befindet, etwas Trübsinniges, Angstbesetztes und Gruseliges. Kurz gesagt: Number (N)ine pflegt den Ruf eines Geheimbunds. Die Marke betreibt eigene Läden in New York und Tokio.

Seul un certain type d'homme porte du Number (N)ine, la griffe créée par l'autodidacte Takahiro Miyashita à Tokyo en novembre 1996. Il puise son inspiration dans la musique et la culture de la rue pour donner vie à une marque aussi pointue et brutale que ses aspirations. Entre caleçons en velours côtelé et sandales en fourrure, ses collections dégagent un mélange de dureté et d'élégance résolue, un avant-gardisme teinté de nostalgie. Les pièces plus portables incluent d'audacieux carreaux rouges et noirs, des pantalons à l'esprit bondage et des sweats à capuche extra-larges, autant de signatures de cette griffe culte. Les tissus sont toujours juxtaposés et les vêtements souvent superposés ; Miyashita fait défiler ses mannequins tête baissée, les yeux au plancher. Il s'inspire, entre autres, de la musique grunge et du rock des années 90, des influences qui se reflètent souvent dans les titres de ses collections : par exemple « Beat Generation (Beat Nick) » ou « Touch Me I'm Sick », ce dernier en référence au look grunge du groupe américain Mudhoney. Les vêtements de Miyashita sont conçus pour entrer en résonance avec l'état d'esprit de ceux qui les portent et font allusion à ce qui se cache sous le vernis extérieur, un côté maussade et gothique motivé par l'angoisse. Autrement dit, Number (N)ine semble aussi difficile d'accès qu'un club privé. La marque a ouvert des boutiques à New York et Tokyo.

HOLLY SHACKLETON

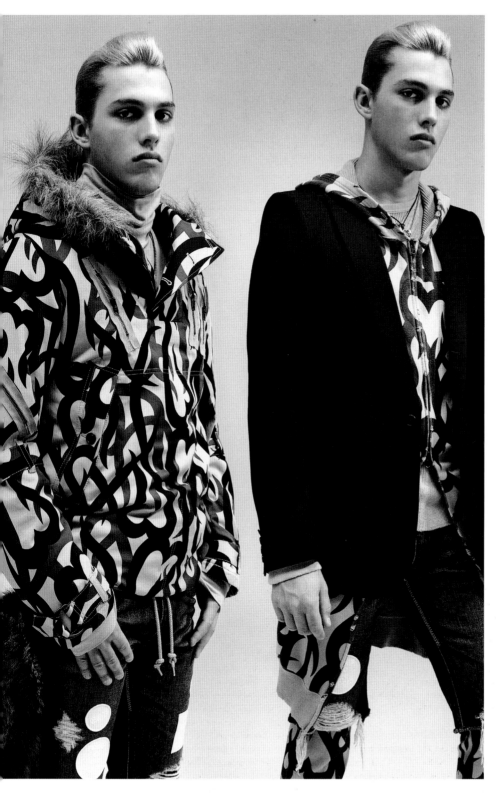

What are your signature designs? The Rock 'n' Roll spirit **What is your favourite piece from any of your collections?** At the moment it's the sleeveless leather jackets in the new spring/summer 2005 collection **How would you describe your work?** Fashion design **What's your ultimate goal?** Conquering big maisons as an independent brand **What inspires you?** Music, rock and punk, a few movies, photos and books **Can fashion still have a political ambition?** No. Therefore we have to do it. I'm doing it **Who do you have in mind when you design?** Another me, the other side of me, the dark side **Is the idea of creative collaboration important to you?** For me working and collaborating with talented people is really important and very interesting **Who has been the greatest influence on your career?** John Lennon **How have your own experiences affected your work as a designer?** It's not exactly my experiences, I just really like fashion and clothes **Which is more important in your work: the process or the product?** The end result, the product **Is designing difficult for you, if so, what drives you to continue?** I've never thought designing is difficult, I always feel I must reduce my thoughts and my ideas for a collection **Have you ever been influenced or moved by the reaction to your designs?** No, never **What's your definition of beauty?** Living the Rock life, living the Punk life and being anti-establishment **What's your philosophy?** Never flattering the mass and of course living the rock and punk life, and continuing that **What is the most important lesson you've learned?** It's a secret.

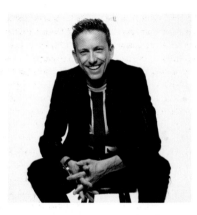

PATRICK COX

"I like to think everything I do is fun and
has a sense of humour, reflecting my personality"

For almost 20 years Patrick Cox has epitomised everything sexy, adventurous and ironic about the shoe business. Having been at the forefront of men's and women's shoe design for the past two decades, Cox has become, in many ways, the father of avant-garde design in his field. Born in 1963 in Edmonton, Canada, Cox moved to London at the age of 20 as a shoe design student at Cordwainers College. Enticed by the world of fashion, it wasn't long before Vivienne Westwood's World's End gang adopted the cobbler as one of their own, eventually commissioning Cox to design a collection of shoes for one of Westwood's earliest shows. Since then, he has designed for and collaborated with such names as Anna Sui, John Galliano and Katharine Hamnett. In 1993 Cox launched what was to become known as the shoe brand of the mid-'90s – Patrick Cox Wannabe. The diffusion line has been described by the designer as having an 'edge', with distinctive trademark features such as the square toe and soft sole. Cox's success was recognized by the British Fashion Council in 1994 and 1995 when he picked up back-to-back Accessory Designer of the Year awards. His work went on to be featured in galleries around the world, including the V&A in London, the Australian National Gallery in Canberra and the FIT Museum in New York. Cox is now busy infusing a jolt of his trademark sex and glamour into the definitively French footwear brand Charles Jourdan after being appointed head of design in early 2003. It seems fitting that a boy who lusted after a pair of 30 cm platform boots worn by Kiss frontman Gene Simmons would turn out to be one of the most successful shoe designers of all time.

Seit fast zwanzig Jahren verkörpert Patrick Cox in der Schuhbranche Sex, Abenteuerlust und Ironie schlechthin. In den letzten beiden Jahrzehnten war er Vorreiter im Herren- und Damenschuhdesign und avancierte in vielerlei Hinsicht zum Vater der Avantgarde. Er wurde 1963 im kanadischen Edmonton geboren und kam im Alter von zwanzig Jahren als Student für Schuhdesign am Cordwainers College nach London. Angelockt von der Welt der Mode, dauerte es nicht lange, bis die World's-End-Gang von Vivienne Westwood den Schuster als einen der ihren aufnahm und Cox schließlich den Auftrag zu einer Schuhkollektion für eine von Westwoods ersten Modenschauen erhielt. Seit damals hat er für so bekannte Leute wie Anna Sui, John Galliano und Katharine Hamnett entworfen bzw. mit ihnen zusammengearbeitet. 1993 lancierte Cox etwas, das zur Schuhmarke der späten 1990er Jahre werden sollte – Patrick Cox Wannabe. Der Designer selbst attestiert dieser Nebenlinie ein gewisses Etwas, dazu gehören Markenzeichen wie die eckige Spitze und die weiche Sohle. Cox' Erfolg fand auch Anerkennung beim British Fashion Council, das ihn 1994 und 1995 als Accessory Designer of the Year auszeichnete. In Museen auf der ganzen Welt kann man Cox' Werke bewundern, etwa im Victoria & Albert Museum in London, in der Australian National Gallery in Canberra oder im FIT Museum in New York. In seiner Funktion als Chefdesigner versucht Cox seit Anfang 2003 der so typisch französischen Schuhmarke Charles Jourdan einen Schuss Sex und Glamour zu verleihen, wofür er ja bekannt ist. Irgendwie passt es, dass gerade der Bursche, den es einst nach einem Paar der 30 Zentimeter hohen Plateauschuhe des Kiss-Sängers Gene Simmons verlangte, zu einem der erfolgreichsten Schuhdesigner aller Zeiten avancierte.

Depuis près de 20 ans, Patrick Cox symbolise tout ce qui est sexy, osé et ironique dans l'univers de la chaussure. Comme il ne cesse d'innover pour les hommes et les femmes depuis deux décennies, Cox s'est imposé à de nombreux titres comme le père de l'avant-garde de son domaine. Né en 1963 à Edmonton au Canada, Patrick Cox s'installe à Londres à l'âge de 20 ans pour étudier l'art de la chaussure au Cordwainers College. Attiré par le monde de la mode, il est vite adopté par le gang du World's End de Vivienne Westwood, qui finit par lui commander une collection de chaussures pour l'un de ses premiers défilés. Depuis, il collabore avec de grands noms tels qu'Anna Sui, John Galliano et Katharine Hamnett. En 1993, Cox lance ce qui devait devenir «la» marque de chaussures du milieu des années 90 : Patrick Cox Wannabe. Il la décrit comme une ligne décalée reconnaissable à ses caractéristiques distinctives telles que le bout carré et la semelle souple. Le succès de Cox est couronné par le British Fashion Council qui lui décerne le prix d'Accessory Designer of the Year en 1994 et en 1995. Son travail a été exposé dans plusieurs musées à travers le monde, notamment au Victoria & Albert Museum de Londres, à l'Australian National Gallery de Canberra et au FIT Museum de New York. Aujourd'hui, Cox insuffle son célèbre style sexy et glamour à Charles Jourdan, une marque très française dont il est directeur de la création depuis début 2003. Rien d'étonnant donc à ce que ce garçon, autrefois fasciné par les bottes à talons compensés de 30 cm de Gene Simmons, le chanteur du groupe Kiss, soit devenu l'un des plus grands créateurs de chaussures de tous les temps.

STEVEN TAYLOR

What are your signature designs? Obviously loafers are pretty key! A signature material would be python and I also do wearable 'killer heels'; square toes are very important to me What is your favourite piece from any of your collections? Something glamorous, sexy and ready to rock the dance floor like the disco ball clogs (spring/summer 2004) or my fibre-optic light boots (spring/summer 2001) How would you describe your work? Yes, we have our chic moments but I like to think everything I do is fun, has a sense of humour, reflecting my personality. My favourite reaction when people come into my showroom is to smile What's your ultimate goal? I've done so much in the past 20 years, I just wish to continue being known for my contribution to innovative design and keep enjoying it What inspires you? Anything and everything, but the most important thing is being in London Can fashion still have a political ambition? Next! Who do you have in mind when you design? I don't have any one person in mind when I design the women's collection, it's more about attitude, the Cox girl is confident and independent with a fun loving, hard edged attitude – men's is purely personal, as I am the sample size, everything is fitted on my foot. If I would wear it, it's in, if not it's out! Who has been the greatest influence on your career? Vivienne Westwood, I suppose, as she inspired me to move to London 21 years ago How have your own experiences affected your work as a designer? Working at Charles Jourdan has been a great learning experience for me as it has made me more structured in the way I work, with deadlines being met and many, many people to motivate all the time, these are all things which are already benefiting my own business today Which is more important in your work: the process or the product? The product, the product, always the product! Is designing difficult for you, if so, what drives you to continue? I don't believe in the tortured artist, designing should be fun and I hope that comes across in my work Have you ever been influenced or moved by the reaction to your designs? I am moved by the fact that so many influential people's first real pair of shoes were Patrick Cox Wannabe, it's amazing and sometimes embarrassing hearing how my shoes have played such a role in some of my friends' sex lives What's your definition of beauty? Beauty = fuckable! What's your philosophy? Whatever... What is the most important lesson you've learned? Always be true to yourself.

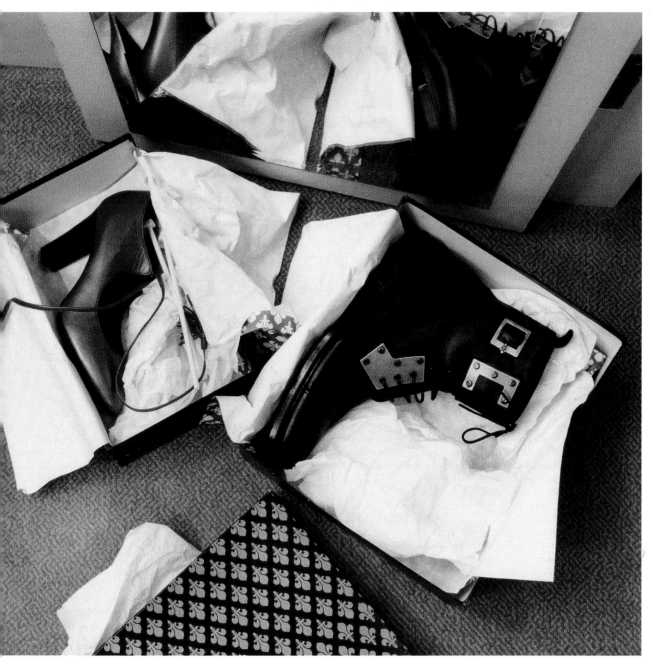

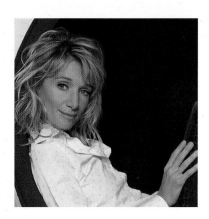

PAUL & JOE

"The collection would not grow
if I didn't have the customers' thoughts in mind" SOPHIE ALBOU

Created by Sophie Albou and named after her two sons, Paul & Joe has found a comfortable and profitable niche within the fashion system. After graduating from the Institut Français de la Mode in Paris, Albou designed for Le Garage, a French shirt company, before presenting her first menswear collection in 1995. The colourful and retro look was well received. Her clients then demanded a womenswear collection, which Albou delivered the following year. From that point on, the Paul & Joe label has evolved into a well-rounded fashion and lifestyle brand. The clothes Albou designs are an extension of her life. They represent freedom, youth and individuality, all tied up in a bow. The same applies to any one of her thirty flagship stores dotted around the globe. Rather than simply displaying her designs among the sterile straight edges of a conventional shop, she has created spaces that act as a natural habitat to the clothes. Each shop is adorned with antiques and feminine touches that reflect the informal yet classic tone of each collection. 2001 saw the launch of the Paul & Joe beauty line at the Takashimaya department store Tokyo; a fragrance and lingerie line followed soon after. Albou has ensured the success of Paul & Joe through the application of simple, strong and timely design that also conveys what might, after all, be the most important aspects of fashion: fun and frivolity.

Das von Sophie Albou gegründete und nach ihren beiden Söhnen benannte Label füllt eine komfortable und zugleich profitable Nische im Modebusiness aus. Nach ihrem Abschluss am Institut Français de la Mode in Paris entwarf Albou zunächst für die französische Hemdenfirma Le Garage, bevor sie 1995 ihre erste Herrenkollektion präsentierte. Der farbenfrohe Retrolook kam sehr gut an. Ihre Klientel verlangte nach einer Damenkollektion, die Albou im darauf folgenden Jahr vorlegte. Von da an entwickelte sich Paul & Joe zu einer vielseitigen Mode- und Lifestyle-Marke. Die Teile, die Albou designt, sind Ausdruck ihrer eigenen Lebensweise. Sie stehen für Freiheit, Jugend und Individualität – allesamt perfekt zusammengefügt. Das gleiche gilt für jeden ihrer dreißig Flagship Stores rund um den Globus. Anstatt ihre Kreationen in den sterilen Ecken eines konventionellen Ladens einfach auszustellen, hat sie Räume geschaffen, die quasi als natürlicher Lebensraum ihrer Kleider fungieren. Jeder Store ist mit Antiquitäten und der weiblichen Note eingerichtet, die auch den informellen, aber zugleich klassischen Stil ihrer Kollektionen prägt. 2001 wurde die Kosmetiklinie von Paul & Joe im Kaufhaus Takashimaya in Tokio präsentiert. Ein eigener Duft und eine Dessous-Linie folgten. Den Erfolg von Paul & Joe sichert Albou durch schlichtes, kraftvolles und zeitgemäßes Design, das die vielleicht wichtigsten Aspekte von Mode zum Ausdruck bringt: Spaß und Leichtigkeit.

Créée par Sophie Albou et baptisée du nom de ses deux fils, la griffe Paul & Joe s'est trouvé une niche confortable et rentable dans le système de la mode. Une fois diplômée de l'Institut Français de la Mode de Paris, Sophie Albou travaille pour Le Garage, une marque française de chemises, avant de présenter en 1995 une première collection pour homme au look coloré et rétro bien accueilli par la critique. Ses clients lui réclament ensuite une collection pour femme, que Sophie Albou lance l'année suivante. Depuis, la griffe Paul & Joe s'est transformée en une élégante marque de mode et de lifestyle. Sophie Albou dessine ses vêtements comme une extension de sa propre vie. Ils incarnent brillamment la liberté, la jeunesse et l'individualité. La créatrice applique la même approche à chacune de ses trente boutiques réparties à travers le monde. Plutôt que de présenter simplement ses créations sur les portants stériles d'une boutique standard, elle crée des espaces qui agissent comme un habitat naturel pour les vêtements. Toutes les boutiques sont décorées d'antiquités et de touches féminines qui reflètent le ton informel mais classique de chaque collection. En 2001, la marque lance la ligne de beauté Paul & Joe au grand magasin Takashimaya de Tokyo; un parfum et une gamme de lingerie suivent peu de temps après. Sophie Albou assure le succès de Paul & Joe grâce à sa démarche créative simple, forte et opportune qui véhicule également ce qui constitue finalement deux aspects parmi les plus importants de la mode : l'humour et la frivolité.

WILL FAIRMAN

What are your signature designs? Freshness, bright colours and prints. The 'joie de vivre' is always present in my designs **What is your favourite piece from any of your collections?** The lingerie silk printed tops to wear with a pair of jeans and a cashmere pullover, I design them season after season as they are such a key piece for every wardrobe **How would you describe your work?** I don't take it as work, it's such an exciting job, it's a part of my life, like my family **What's your ultimate goal?** Have fun in what I'm doing and being surrounded by my friends and family and make them all as happy as I can **What inspires you?** Every-thing can be a source of inspiration you just have to be aware of what's going on around you **Can fashion still have a political ambition?** Absolutely not, fashion is a dream and politics is shit! **Who do you have in mind when you design?** Me, my family, my friends, people I've met… my life **Is the idea of creative collaboration important to you?** You must be open-minded and share different feelings with people you work with. I need to work with people who complete me and understand me **Who has been the greatest influence on your career?** My parents, they have really supported me throughout and made me feel confident and strong **How have your own experiences affected your work as a designer?** Having my children. My sons Paul & Joe influenced me with their youth and playfulness **Which is more important in your work: the process or the product?** Both, one cannot work without the other. I love the idea that nothing is impossible so I try to get things very close to my initial ideas, the final product has to be like the one I dreamed of. It's like a little girl who dreams of a special present, if she gets something different she will be very disappointed **Is designing difficult for you, if so, what drives you to continue?** Passion and challenges drives me to continue **Have you ever been influenced or moved by the reaction to your designs?** I always like to hear what people think of my designs, the collection would not grow if I didn't have the customers' thoughts in mind **What's your definition of beauty?** Beauty is elegance, class, self-confidence and it's also the feeling of being loved **What's your philosophy?** Be yourself, trust your instincts **What is the most important lesson you've learned?** To never give up, as I already said nothing is impossible if you really believe in it.

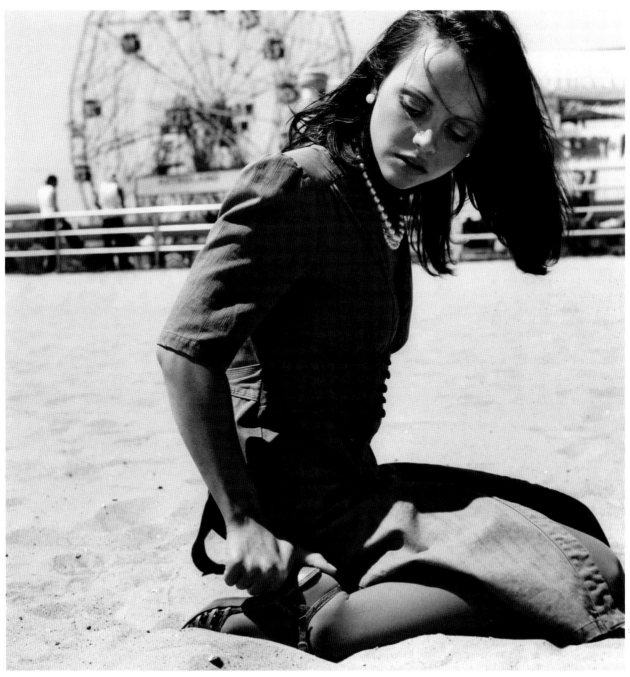

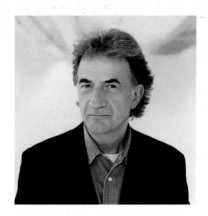

PAUL SMITH

"The thing I'm most interested in is continuity. I've always worked hard at not being today's flavour"

A serious accident while riding his bike put paid to Paul Smith's dream of becoming a professional racing cyclist. However, this mishap propelled him to pursue a career involving his other passion: fashion. In 1970, Smith (born Nottingham, 1946) opened a store in his native city, selling his own early designs that reflected the types of clothing he loved but was unable to buy anywhere else. Studying fashion design at evening classes, and working closely with his wife, Pauline Denyer, a graduate of the Royal College of Art, by 1976 he was showing a full range of menswear in Paris. Carving out a distinctive look that combined the best of traditional English attire often with unusual or witty prints, Smith blazed a trail throughout the late '70s. His progress continued into the '80s – when he put boxer shorts back on the fashion map – and beyond, with stores opened in New York (1987), and Paris (1993). The designer now has a staggering 200 shops in Japan, and also offers a range of womenswear (launched in 1994) and clothing for kids, in addition to accessories, books, jewellery, fragrances, pens, rugs and china. In 2001 Smith was knighted, and despite the success and breadth of his company – wholesaling to thirty-five countries around the globe – his hands-on involvement remains integral to its success. Commercial accomplishments aside, Smith's aesthetic has retained its idiosyncrasies. His autumn/winter 2005 womenswear collection, with its tartan tailoring and trilbies, was a sideways glance at the '60s; for his menswear, in the same season, Smith gave a lesson in clash and contrast, putting python trousers with checked jackets and floral shirts.

Ein schwerer Unfall zerstörte Paul Smiths Traum von einer Karriere als Radrennfahrer. Allerdings veranlasste ihn dieses Missgeschick, aus seiner zweiten Passion – der Mode – eine Karriere zu machen. Der 1946 in Nottingham geborene Smith eröffnete 1970 in seiner Heimatstadt einen Laden, wo er seine frühen eigenen Entwürfe verkaufte – lauter Dinge, die er selbst gern getragen hätte, aber nirgends auftreiben konnte. In Abendkursen studierte er Modedesign und arbeitete außerdem eng mit seiner Frau Pauline Denyer, einer Absolventin des Royal College of Art, zusammen. 1976 konnte Smith eine komplette Herrenkollektion in Paris präsentieren. Sein ausgeprägt individueller Look vereinte die Vorzüge der traditionellen englischen Schneiderkunst mit oft ungewöhnlichen oder witzigen Mustern und hinterließ in den 1970er Jahren deutliche Spuren. Die positive Entwicklung hielt bis in die 1980er Jahre an – als er die Boxershorts wieder ins allgemeine Modebewusstsein zurück brachte – und darüber hinaus, mit Neueröffnungen von Läden in New York (1987) und Paris (1993). Inzwischen besitzt der Designer unglaubliche 200 Shops in Japan, wo er auch eine Damenkollektion (seit 1994), Kindersachen sowie Accessoires, Bücher, Schmuck, Düfte, Schreibgeräte, Teppiche und Porzellan führt. Im Jahr 2001 wurde Smith zum Ritter geschlagen, und trotz des Erfolges und der großen Produktpalette seines Unternehmens – man beliefert Großhändler in 35 Ländern rund um den Globus – ist nach wie vor sein ganz persönliches Engagement integraler Bestandteil des Gelingens. Abgesehen von seinen kommerziellen Talenten hat sich Smith in seiner Ästhetik auch Eigenheiten bewahrt, die zum Teil auf Ablehnung stoßen. So war etwa die Damenkollektion Herbst/Winter 2005 mit ihren Schottenkaros und weichen Filzhüten ein scheeler Blick zurück auf die 1960er Jahre. Den Männern erteilte Smith in derselben Saison eine Lektion zum Thema Kollision und Kontraste, indem er beispielsweise Hosen mit Pythonmuster, karierte Jacken und Hemden mit floralem Muster kombinierte.

Un grave accident de vélo met un terme aux premières ambitions du jeune Paul Smith, qui rêvait de devenir cycliste professionnel, mais cette mésaventure le conduit à se consacrer à son autre passion : la mode. En 1970, Smith (né en 1946) ouvre une boutique dans sa ville natale de Nottingham où il vend ses premières créations, qui reflètent le type de vêtements qu'il adore mais qu'il n'arrive à trouver nulle part. Etudiant la mode en cours du soir tout en travaillant en étroite collaboration avec Pauline Denyer, son épouse diplômée du Royal College of Art, il développe si bien son entreprise qu'il finit par présenter une collection pour homme complète à Paris dès 1976. Forgeant un look original qui combine le meilleur du style anglais traditionnel à des imprimés souvent insolites ou pleins d'esprit, Paul Smith reste sur cette lancée jusqu'à la fin des années 70. Il poursuit son ascension pendant les années 80 et au-delà, époque à laquelle il remet les boxer shorts au goût du jour, avec l'ouverture de nouvelles boutiques à New York (1987) et à Paris (1993). Aujourd'hui, le créateur ne compte pas moins de 200 points de vente au Japon et propose également une ligne pour femme (lancée en 1994) ainsi qu'une collection pour enfant, sans mentionner les accessoires, les livres, les bijoux, les parfums, les stylos, les tapis et la porcelaine Paul Smith. En 2001, Paul Smith est fait Chevalier de Sa Majesté, et malgré l'immense succès et la diversification de son entreprise, qui vend dans trente-cinq pays à travers le monde, son approche pratique reste un facteur essentiel de sa réussite. Outre ces exploits commerciaux, l'esthétique de Smith conserve ses traits distinctifs. Sa collection pour femme automne/hiver 2005, avec ses tailleurs et ses chapeaux mous en tartan, lorgne du côté des années 60, tandis que dans sa ligne masculine de la même saison, Smith nous donne une vraie leçon de choc et de contraste, juxtaposant pantalons en python, vestes à carreaux et chemises à fleurs.

JAMES ANDERSON

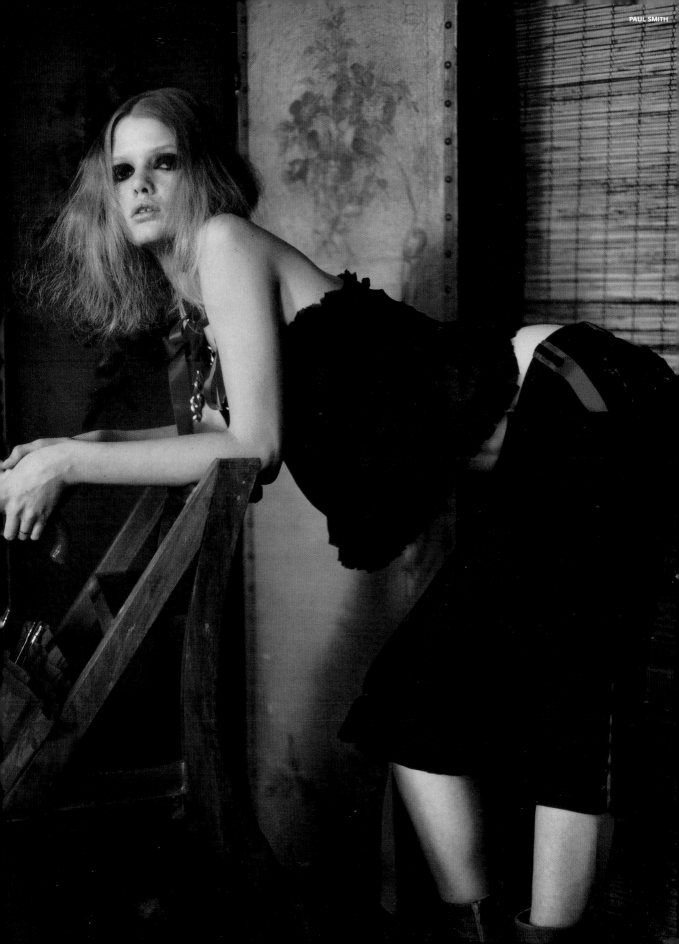

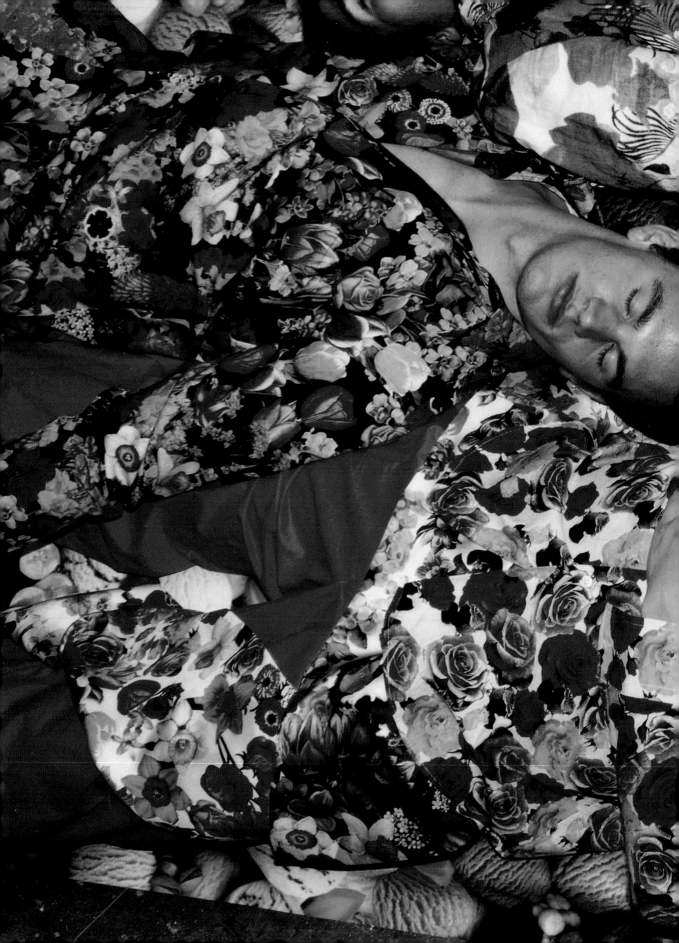

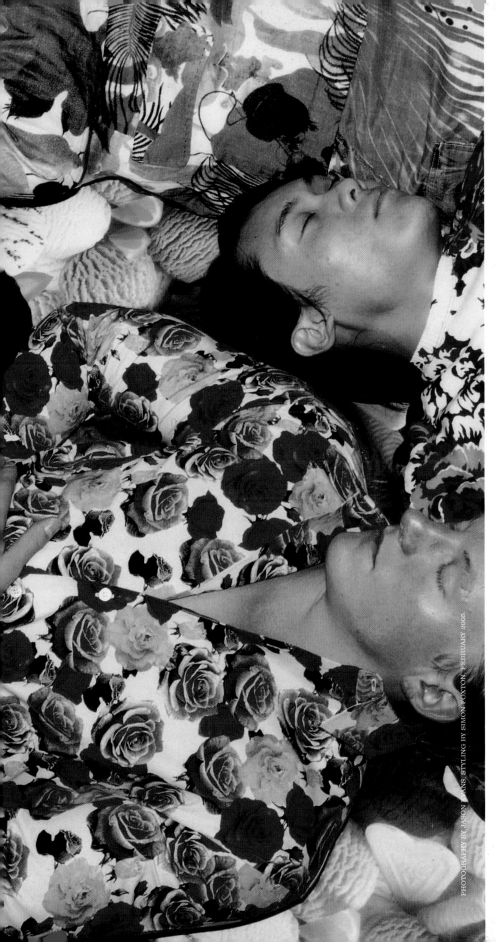

What are your signature designs? Tradition mixed with the unexpected **What's your favourite piece from any of your collections?** I have no favourite piece, but the simplicity of my suits mixed with the eccentricity of special linings I like very much **How would you describe your work?** Curious **What's your ultimate goal?** Keeping things simple and having a business with a heart **What inspires you?** Observation and thinking **Can fashion still have a political ambition?** In my case, no **Who do you have in mind when you design?** People who want to show their own character **Is the idea of creative collaboration important to you?** A creative collaboration should be inspiring – if it is, then it is important **Who has been the greatest influence on your career?** My father and my wife **How have your own experiences affected your work as a designer?** They go hand in hand **Which is more important in your work: the process or the product?** Personally, the process, but the product pays my wages **Is designing difficult for you and, if so, what drives you to continue?** I never think about design, the ideas seem to come naturally **Have you ever been influenced or moved by the reaction to your designs?** As my designs are not radical, this has never come to mind **What's your definition of beauty?** Something that is natural and not forced **What's your philosophy?** Making clothes for people from everyday walks of life **What is the most important lesson you've learned?** Always give yourself time to answer important requests.

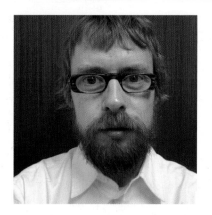

PETER JENSEN

"I like anti-heroines"

Fruit-and-veg printed dresses, sweaters emblazoned with cockerels, hand-knitted balaclavas: Peter Jensen expertly combines humour with simplicity in his distinctive collections. Jensen was born in Løgstør, Denmark, in 1970 and underwent a rigorous technical education, including studies in embroidery, graphic design and tailoring. He studied for a BA in fashion at the Denmark Design School, graduating in 1997. Moving to London the same year, he studied for an MA in fashion at Central Saint Martins; today, he teaches at the college, as Head of menswear. On graduating in 1999, Jensen immediately began to create his own menswear line, which sold to the London boutique The Library in its first season; his third menswear collection was shown on the official Paris schedule. For autumn/winter 2001, Jensen introduced womenswear, which for the past nine seasons has been presented during London Fashion Week. For spring/summer 2005, Jensen commandeered an ice rink in west London for a spectacular fashion-show-on-ice, modelled entirely by teenaged figure-skating champions. Jensen says that his Danish background provides much inspiration for his designs. The dresses that belonged to his grandmothers, in particular, are always reference points for his designs. Each womenswear collection is named after a famous woman who fascinates him: autumn/winter 2005 was christened 'Fanny' after Ingmar Bergman's 'Fanny and Alexander'. Other show titles have included 'Gertrude' (after Gertrude Stein), 'Nancy' (Mitford), 'Allison' (Steadman) and 'Tonya', a tribute to disgraced ice skater Tonya Harding. In 2005 Jensen introduced a bag collection and a full range of both shoes and men's underwear are planned for the near future.

Peter Jensen kombiniert in seinen Kollektionen, die zu den ausgefallensten in ganz London zählen, auf gekonnte Weise Humor und Schlichtheit. Er ist sowohl für seine mädchenhafte, oft eigenwillig bedruckte Damenmode als auch für die gut geschnittene Sportswear für Herren bekannt. Jensen wurde 1970 im dänischen Løgstør geboren und absolvierte eine harte technische Ausbildung, die Stickerei, Grafikdesign und Schneiderei umfasste. Anschließend erwarb er einen Bachelor in Mode an der Denmark Design School (1997), zog noch im selben Jahr nach London und hängte dort ein Master-Studium am Central Saint Martins an. Heute unterrichtet er selbst an dieser Hochschule, als Leiter des Bereichs Herrenmode. Unmittelbar nach Studienende begann Jensen 1999 an seiner ersten Herrenlinie zu arbeiten, die er bereits in der ersten Saison an die Londoner Boutique The Library verkaufte. Schon seine dritte Herrenkollektion wurde im offiziellen Programm der Pariser Modewoche gezeigt. Ab Herbst/Winter 2001 präsentierte Jensen auch Damenmode, die er in den letzten neun Saisons immer im Rahmen der London Fashion Week vorstellte. Für die Kollektion

Frühjahr/Sommer 2005 organisierte er sich ein Eisstadion im Westen Londons für eine spektakuläre Show-on-Ice, bei der ausschließlich jugendliche Eislauf-champions modelten. Jensen meint, seine dänische Herkunft liefere ihm eine Menge Inspirationen für seine Entwürfe. Insbesondere die Kleider seiner Großmutter sind immer wieder Bezugspunkte seiner Kreationen. Jede Damenkollektion wird nach einer Frauenfigur, die den Designer fasziniert hat, benannt: So wurde Herbst/Winter 2005 nach Ingmar Bergmans Heldin aus „Fanny und Alexander" Fanny getauft. Andere hießen „Gertrude" (nach Gertrude Stein), „Nancy" (Mitford), „Allison" (Steadman) und „Tonya" (nach der geächteten Eiskunstläuferin Tonya Harding). 2005 zeigte Jensen erstmals eine Taschenkollektion. Weitere Projekte für die nahe Zukunft sind eine komplette Schuhkollektion sowie Herrenunterwäsche.

Peter Jensen combine de façon experte humour et simplicité dans ses collections, qui comptent parmi les plus originales de Londres. Il est connu pour sa mode féminine très « jeune fille » aux imprimés souvent étranges et pour le sportswear bien coupé de sa mode masculine. Né en 1970 à Løgstør au Danemark, Peter Jensen suit une formation technique rigoureuse, étudiant la broderie, le graphisme et la coupe. Il suit ensuite un BA en mode à la Denmark Design School, dont il sort diplômé en 1997. Il s'installe à Londres la même année et s'inscrit à un MA en mode à Central Saint Martins ; aujourd'hui, il enseigne dans ce college en tant que directeur de la mode pour homme. Après l'obtention de son diplôme en 1999, Jensen crée immédiatement sa propre ligne pour homme, vendue à la boutique londonienne The Library dès sa première saison ; il présente sa troisième collection pour homme lors des défilés officiels de Paris. Pour l'automne/hiver 2001, Jensen lance une collection pour femme, qui depuis neuf saisons défile à la London Fashion Week. Pour le printemps/été 2005, il réquisitionne une patinoire du West London pour un spectaculaire défilé sur glace, entièrement présenté par de jeunes champions de patinage artistique. D'après Jensen, ses origines danoises lui offrent d'inépuisables sources d'inspiration. Les robes de ses grands-mères, en particulier, sont autant de références que l'on retrouve toujours dans ses créations. Il baptise chacune de ses collections féminines du nom d'une femme célèbre qui le fascine : il intitule sa collection automne/hiver 2005 « Fanny » en clin d'œil au film « Fanny et Alexandre » d'Ingmar Bergman et baptise d'autres défilés du nom de « Gertrude » (d'après Gertrude Stein), « Nancy » (Mitford), « Allison » (Steadman) et « Tonya », en hommage à la patineuse Tonya Harding tombée en disgrâce. En 2005, Jensen introduit une collection de sacs. Une gamme complète de chaussures et de sous-vêtements pour homme devrait sortir très prochainement.

SUSIE RUSHTON

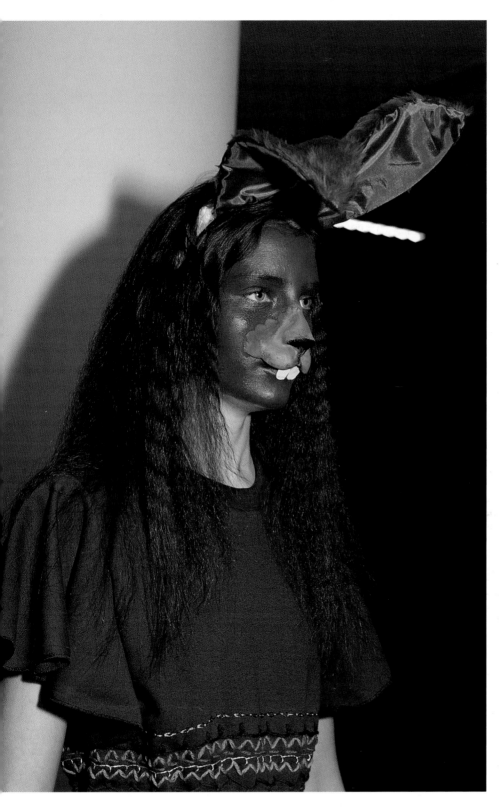

What are your signature designs? Simple clothes with a sense of humour, details, conversational prints **What is your favourite piece from any of your collections?** The jersey 'cardigan dress' from autumn/winter 2003. It's a jersey dress that looks like you have a cardigan tied around your waist **How would you describe your work?** Nice to wear **What's your ultimate goal?** To make a decent living **What inspires you?** I'm particularly interested in personalities, the idea of the muse. I like to pick people who are not necessarily obvious fashion icons to research. I like anti-heroines particularly – Tonya Harding and Olga Korbut have been past muses. But then a lot of the inspiration comes from the process **Can fashion still have a political ambition?** No **Who do you have in mind when you design?** The people who are around me. For menswear I always think about whether I would like to wear something myself – it's very important to me that people would want to wear the clothes **Is the idea of creative collaboration important to you?** It's essential. There is so much collaboration in what we do and I'm really lucky that I can collaborate with people I like. People that I have worked with for a long time, like Lucy Ewing and Åbäke have become inseparable from my work **Who has been the greatest influence on your career?** Johanne Andersen, my grandmother. She was always very supportive of what I wanted to do and she helped me pay for my education. And she was funny **Which is more important in your work: the process or the product?** The product. I think the process is important, but if you don't end up with a good product then what is the point? No one cares how you got there **Is designing difficult for you, if so, what drives you to continue?** It's everything else that's difficult, not really the designing. I have no idea what I would do if it weren't this though **Have you ever been influenced or moved by the reaction to your designs?** Last season, lots of people told me they had a tear in their eye at our show, which I thought moving **What's your definition of beauty?** I can't define beauty. It can be lots of different things **What's your philosophy?** Recycle **What is the most important lesson you've learned?** It's harder than you think to run a business.

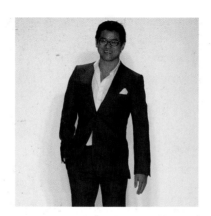

PETER SOM

"It's all about effortlessness and romance"

Peter Som shines brightest among America's next generation of star designers. His well-heeled aesthetic is marked by a studied but carefree sophistication and a skilful use of sumptuous fabrics. He is as daring with brooches, fur and floral prints as other nascent designers might be with deconstruction. Using a colour scale of greys, Som is quietly emerging as America's next great champion of women's sportswear. A native of San Francisco, the upwardly mobile créateur studied at Connecticut College before graduating from Parsons School of Design in New York, later plucked by not one, but two of the most successful American designers to date. Apprenticing at Calvin Klein and Michael Kors, and later for the legendary Bill Blass, Som gained the kind of experience and industry connections others can only hope for, and laid the foundations for a successful company of his own. Soon after launching his eponymous line in 1997, Som was recognised by the Council of Fashion Designers (CFDA) as a rising talent in its first Scholarship Competition, and was later nominated for the prestigious CFDA Perry Ellis Award for Emerging Talent. In 2004, Som was among the ten finalists in the CFDA/Vogue fashion fund initiative, the same year he was identified by Cathy Horyn, fashion editor of the New York Times, as "one of the best young designers working today." With regular mentions in such magazines as Vogue, W, Town and Country, Harpers & Queen and InStyle he is patronised by a following that includes style arbiters Plum Sykes, Princess Olga of Greece and Marina Rust. Som now has the capacity to create a classic apparel brand that reflects nothing less than the American dream itself.

Peter Soms Stern strahlt unter Amerikas neuer Generation von Stardesignern am hellsten. Seine kostspielige Ästhetik ist geprägt von einer wohl überlegten, aber zugleich lässigen Raffinesse und der gekonnten Verwendung edler Stoffe. Er spielt so mutig mit Broschen, Pelzen und floralen Mustern wie andere aufstrebende Designer vielleicht mit den Elementen der Dekonstruktion. Mit einer Palette von Grauschattierungen avanciert Som heimlich, still und leise zu Amerikas nächstem großen Star der Damen-Sportswear. Der in San Francisco geborene ambitionierte Modeschöpfer studierte am Connecticut College, bevor er seinen Abschluss an der New Yorker Parsons School of Design machte. Danach riss sich nicht einer, sondern gleich zwei der namhaftesten Designer der USA um ihn. In seiner Lehrzeit bei Calvin Klein und Michael Kors und später beim legendären Bill Blass erwarb Som Erfahrungen und Verbindungen zur Modeindustrie, von denen andere nur träumen können. Damit legte er den Grundstein für ein erfolgreiches eigenes Unternehmen. Bald nachdem er 1997 seine nach ihm benannte Linie herausgebracht hatte, erkannte das Council of Fashion Desig-

ners (CFDA) bei dem ersten Stipendiums-Wettbewerb sein Potential. Etwas später wurde er für den angesehenen Perry Ellis Award for Emerging Talents des CFDA nominiert. 2004 zählte Som zu den zehn Finalisten bei der Fashion Fund Initiative von CFDA und Vogue. Im selben Jahr bezeichnete ihn die Modekritikerin der New York Times, Cathy Horyn, als „einen der besten jungen Designer der Gegenwart". Dank regelmäßiger Erwähnungen in Zeitschriften wie Vogue, W, Town and Country, Harpers & Queen und InStyle fördert ihn eine Fangemeinde, zu der modische Autoritäten wie Plum Sykes, Prinzessin Olga von Griechenland und Marina Rust gehören. Som befindet sich heute in der Position, eine klassische Kleidermarke kreieren zu können, die nichts weniger widerspiegelt als den American Dream höchstselbst.

Parmi la nouvelle constellation d'étoiles de la mode américaine, Peter Som brille de mille feux. Son esthétique opulente est marquée par une sophistication à la fois étudiée et informelle, comme par une utilisation experte des tissus somptueux. Il est aussi audacieux avec les broches, la fourrure et les imprimés floraux que les autres créateurs émergents le sont avec la déconstruction. Privilégiant les dégradés de gris, Peter Som est en train de devenir tranquillement le prochain champion américain du sportwear féminin. Né à San Francisco, ce créateur socialement ambitieux étudie au Connecticut College, puis obtient un diplôme de la Parsons School of Design de New York avant d'être cueilli non par un, mais par deux des plus grands créateurs américains du moment. Grâce à son apprentissage chez Calvin Klein et Michael Kors, puis pour le légendaire Bill Blass, Peter Som acquiert le genre d'expérience et le réseau de relations dont les autres se contentent généralement de rêver, et pose les bases du succès de sa propre entreprise. Peu de temps après avoir lancé sa ligne éponyme en 1997, il est reconnu comme un nouveau talent qui compte lorsqu'il essaie pour la première fois de décrocher une bourse du CFDA (Council of Fashion Designers), avant d'être nominé pour le prestigieux prix Perry Ellis décerné aux jeunes talents. En 2004, Peter Som figure parmi les dix finalistes candidats à la bourse CFDA/Vogue, alors que Cathy Horyn, journaliste de mode au New York Times, l'étiquette comme «l'un des meilleurs jeunes créateurs actuellement en exercice». Avec des apparitions régulières dans les pages de magazines tels que Vogue, W, Town and Country, Harpers & Queen et InStyle, il bénéficie également du soutien de ses fans, parmi lesquelles la déesse du style Plum Sykes, la princesse Olga de Grèce et Marina Rust. Peter Som a désormais toutes les cartes en main pour créer une griffe classique à l'image même du rêve américain.

LEE CARTER

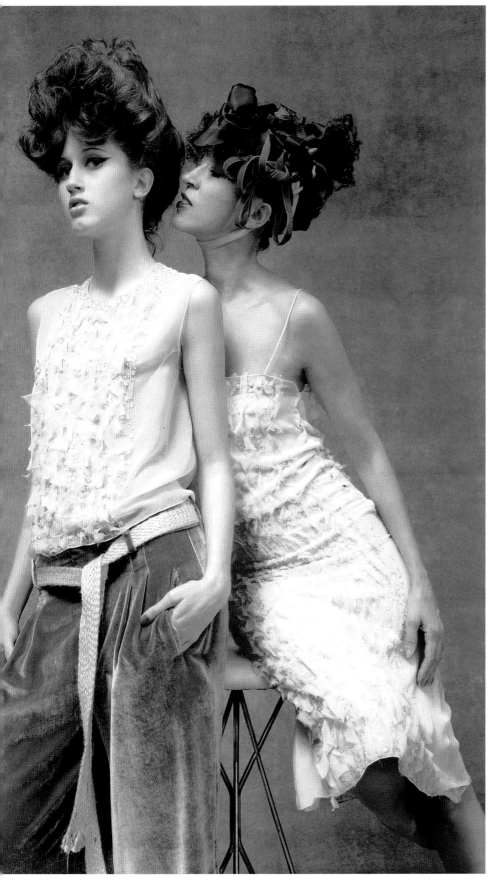

What are your signature designs? No matter what I'm designing – it's all about effortlessness and romance with a healthy dash of refined and relaxed elegance. Lots of cocktail dresses, floral prints with a graphic edge. It's always about contrast – masculine/feminine, hard/soft, day/evening **What is your favourite piece from any of your collections?** Very hard. That's like picking a favourite child. Currently I am happy with a series of cotton voile gowns with bias ruffles **How would you describe your work?** A delicate but bold balance of romantic, practical and sleek. Say that ten times very fast **What's your ultimate goal?** To enjoy life to fullest in all parts of my life. A house in the country would be nice too **What inspires you?** Everything. Especially real people. NYC. Paris **Can fashion still have a political ambition?** Fashion is a reflection of our times – it can be a statement – a means to an end. Fashion is also a language in itself – how you choose to articulate yourself through it is up to you **Who do you have in mind when you design?** It's an amalgamation of all the amazing and inspiring women in my life. As I sketch, there's always a voice in the back of my head saying – Would Christine wear this? Would Roopal wear this? **Is the idea of creative collaboration important to you?** Yes. It's all about the exchange of ideas. I can't design in a bubble. But of course one has to go into a creative dialogue knowing what one stands for **Who has been the greatest influence on your career?** There's not one single person who has influenced my career. There are a handful of amazing and inspirational people I always seem to turn to **How have your own experiences affected your work as a designer?** Designing is a bit like therapy – it can reflect my mood or create a new one. The creative process is always very personal. My head is like a constant slideshow – an archive of images, places and people **Which is more important in your work: the process or the product?** Both – they're totally intertwined **Is designing difficult for you, if so, what drives you to continue?** The designing part is the easy part. It's everything else that is difficult **Have you ever been influenced or moved by the reaction to your designs?** Yes, when I see a woman on the street wearing my clothes – it's both thrilling and humbling to see something I designed being a part of a total stranger's life **What's your definition of beauty?** Individuality **What's your philosophy?** Soak it up, take time to enjoy it **What is the most important lesson you've learned?** Do what comes naturally.

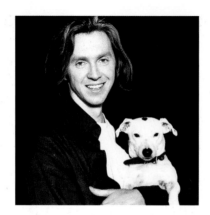

PHILIP TREACY

"Making a hat is like throwing a party!"

Philip Treacy's feathered, fur-trimmed or velvety creations have little in common with conventional headwear. In fact, Treacy's glamorous and fantastical hat designs have completely re-defined modern millinery. Fashion leaders such as Franca Sozzani, Amanda Harlech and Isabella Blow (the latter has worn Treacy hats from the beginning of his career) covet his work. Oversized orchids, fans of pheasant feathers, model ships and Andy Warhol-style motifs have all decorated his deftly-sculpted hats. Treacy was born in Ahascragh, western Ireland, in 1967. By the age of five, he was making clothes for his sister's dolls. His fashion education began in 1985 at Dublin's National College of Art and Design where he started to make hats as a hobby. Following a work experience placement at Stephen Jones, Treacy began an MA womenswear course at London's Royal College of Art in 1988. However, he decided to ditch clothing design and take a place on the college's first-ever millinery course. In 1991, at the age of 23, he started making hats for Chanel and, in the same year, won the Accessory Designer prize at the British Fashion Awards for the first time; to date he has won three such accolades. In 1993 he staged his debut fashion show during London Fashion Week, where Naomi Campbell and Christy Turlington walked his catwalk in return for free hats. In 1994 he opened his first boutique, in London's Belgravia, and in 2000 Treacy became the first accessories designer to be invited by the Chambre Syndicale de la Haute Couture to show his work during Paris couture week. Treacy collaborates with some of the world's finest artists and designers, including Alexander McQueen and Vanessa Beecroft, and his work is displayed in museums such as the V&A and the Design Museum in London and the Irish Museum of Modern Art. In 2004 he won the Chinese International Designer of the Year Award; 2005 sees the completion of his first interior design project, at The G, a five-star hotel in Galway, Ireland.

Philip Treacys gefiederte, pelzbesetzte oder samtige Kreationen haben mit konventionellen Kopfbedeckungen wenig gemein. Seine glamourösen und phantastischen Hutgebilde haben das moderne Modistenhandwerk völlig neu definiert. Führende Vertreter der Modebranche wie Franca Sozzani, Amanda Harlech oder Isabella Blow (sie trug von Beginn an Hüte von Treacy) lechzen nach seinen Arbeiten. Überdimensionale Orchideen, Fächer aus Fasanenfedern, Schiffsmodelle und Motive im Stil Andy Warhols haben seine gekonnt konstruierten Hüte bereits geziert. Geboren wurde Treacy 1967 im westirischen Ahascragh. Bereits im Alter von fünf Jahren machte er Kleider für die Puppen seiner Schwester. Seine Modeausbildung begann 1985 am Dublin's National College of Art and Design, wo er die Hutmacherei als Hobby begann. Nach einem Praktikum bei Stephen Jones nahm Treacy 1988 den Magister-Studiengang für Damenmode am Londoner Royal College of Art auf. Bald entschied er jedoch, das Designen von Kleidung zugunsten des ersten Hutmacher-Studiengangs aufzugeben. 1991 begann er im Alter von 23 Jahren Hüte für Chanel zu kreieren. Noch im gleichen Jahr gewann er erstmals den Preis als Accessory Designer bei den British

Fashion Awards. Bis heute hat er diese Auszeichnung bereits dreimal erhalten. Sein Debüt bei der Londoner Modewoche gab er 1993 mit einer Schau, bei der Naomi Campbell und Christy Turlington seine Kreationen auf dem Catwalk präsentierten (Als Honorar verlangten sie Gratis-Hüte). 1994 eröffnete Treacy seine erste Boutique im Londoner Stadtteil Belgravia; im Jahr 2000 wurde er als erster Designer von Accessoires vom Chambre Syndicale de la Haute Couture eingeladen, seine Arbeiten im Rahmen der Pariser Couture-Woche zu zeigen. Der Hutschöpfer kooperiert mit einigen der besten Künstler und Designern der Welt, etwa Alexander McQueen oder Vanessa Beecroft. Seine Kreationen sind u. a. im Victoria & Albert Museum und dem Design Museum in London oder dem Irish Museum of Modern Art zu bewundern. 2004 gewann er den Chinese International Designer of the Year Award. 2005 vollendete er sein erstes Inneneinrichtungsprojekt im The G, einem Fünf-Sterne-Hotel im irischen Galway.

Parées de plumes, de fourrure ou de velours, les créations de Philip Treacy n'ont pas grand-chose à voir avec ce que produisent habituellement les modistes. En fait, les chapeaux glamour et fantasques de Treacy ont entièrement révolutionné la chapellerie moderne. Les lanceurs de tendances tels que Franca Sozzani, Amanda Harlech et Isabella Blow (cette dernière porte les chapeaux de Treacy depuis le début de sa carrière) suivent son travail de très près. Orchidées géantes, éventails en plumes de faisan, maquettes de bateau et motifs à la Andy Warhol viennent tous décorer ses chapeaux savamment sculptés. Né en 1967 à Ahascragh dans l'ouest de l'Irlande, Treacy n'a que cinq ans quand il commence à confectionner des vêtements pour les poupées de sa sœur. En 1985, il entame sa formation au National College of Art and Design de Dublin, où il s'essaie à un nouveau hobby : la création de chapeaux. Après un stage chez Stephen Jones, Philip Treacy décide de suivre un cursus en mode féminine au Royal College of Art de Londres en 1988, mais laisse rapidement tomber la création de vêtements pour s'inscrire au tout premier cours de chapellerie du College. En 1991, à l'âge de 23 ans, il commence à dessiner des chapeaux pour Chanel et remporte la même année le prix de British Accessory Designer pour la première fois, une récompense qu'il a déjà reçu trois fois à ce jour. En 1993, il présente son premier défilé lors de la London Fashion Week, soutenu par Naomi Campbell et Christy Turlington qui défilent pour lui en échange de chapeaux gratuits. En 1994, il ouvre sa première boutique à Londres dans le quartier de Belgravia, puis devient en l'an 2000 le premier créateur d'accessoires jamais invité par la Chambre Syndicale de la Haute Couture à présenter son travail pendant la Semaine de la Mode de Paris. Treacy collabore avec certains des plus grands artistes et créateurs tels qu'Alexander McQueen et Vanessa Beecroft, et son travail est exposé dans plusieurs musées, notamment au Victoria & Albert Museum et au Design Museum de Londres, ainsi qu'à l'Irish Museum of Modern Art. En 2004, il remporte le prix de Chinese International Designer of the Year ; en 2005, il finalise son premier projet de design d'intérieur pour The G, un hôtel cinq étoiles situé à Galway en Irlande.

TERRY NEWMAN

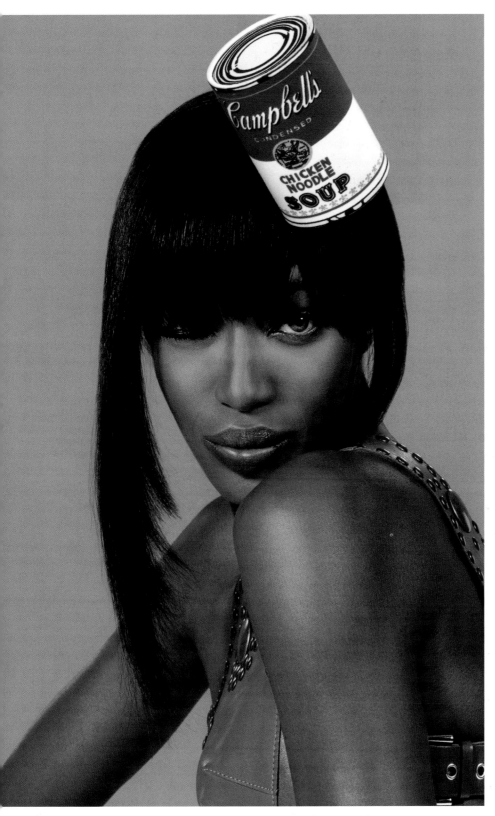

What are your signature designs? Sculptural shape What's your favourite piece from any of your collections? My Ship hat How would you describe your work? An illusion What's your ultimate goal? To challenge people's perception of hats in the 21st century Who inspires you? Isabella Blow Can fashion still have a political ambition? Politics and fashion are a ridiculous mix Who do you have in mind when you design? Everybody Is the idea of creative collaboration important to you? Yes – when it's truly a collaboration Who has been the greatest influence on your career? My sister How have your own experiences affected your work as a designer? This is what creativity is all about Which is more important in your work: the process or the product? Both Is designing difficult for you? No Have you ever been influenced or moved by the reaction to your designs? Every day What's your definition of beauty? A hat What's your philosophy? The pursuit of perfection What is the most important lesson you've learned? Craftsmanship.

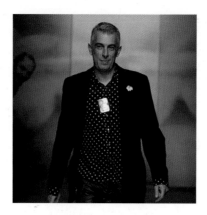

POLLINI

"Creativity makes me carry on" RIFAT OZBEK

Rifat Ozbek, designer of Pollini since 2004, has a magical talent for picking and mixing alluring shapes and ethnic fabrics and translating them into cool, contemporary fashion collections. He was born in Istanbul in 1953 and first moved to England in 1970 in order to study architecture, a field that, along with interiors, has consistently influenced his work. However by 1974 he had entered Central Saint Martins to study fashion, graduating in 1977 to join Trell in Milan where he worked with Walter Albini, a pioneer of luxury leisurewear. 1980 saw his return to London where he worked for Monsoon, an English chain store known for its use of Indian fabrics. In 1984 Ozbek launched his own line, which was inspired by his passion for London streetwear and club life. He collaborated with Leigh Bowery on tailored pieces and was part of the post-New Romantic underground scene in London. Ozbek made a definitive statement of the times in 1990 when his love of sporty silhouettes gave rise to an all-white collection that the fashion press dubbed as 'New Age'. His autumn/winter 1990 and spring/summer 1991 collections were presented in video form (directed by John Maybury) as a pioneering alternative to catwalk shows. In 2001 Rifat decided to slow down the pace and opt out of the fashion system. Instead, he elected to work on rebuilding and renovating a summerhouse in Bodrum, on the Turkish coast. But in January 2004 he returned to the international fashion circuit with a new post as consultant creative director at Pollini. Bought by the Aeffe group in 2001, Pollini is a classic Italian shoe and leather accessories brand which has branched out into womenswear. His autumn/winter 2005 collection for the house, his third to date, was an eclectic blend of golden lace, brocade dresses, hippie patchworks and long, tiered skirts.

Rifat Ozbek ist seit 2004 Designer von Pollini und besitzt eine magische Begabung für die Auswahl und Zusammenstellung verführerischer Formen und Ethno-Materialien, die er dann in coole, zeitgemäße Kollektionen transponiert. Geboren wurde er 1953 in Istanbul. 1970 kam er erstmals nach England um Architektur zu studieren. Ein Fach, das neben der Innenarchitektur seine Arbeit nachhaltig beeinflusst hat. 1974 begann er sein Modestudium am Central Saint Martins, das er 1977 abschloss, um bei Trell in Mailand anzufangen, wo er mit Walter Albini, einem Pionier der luxuriösen Freizeitkleidung, arbeitete. Im Jahr 1980 kehrte er nach London zurück, um für die englische Kette Monsoon zu arbeiten, die für die Verwendung indischer Stoffe bekannt ist. Seine eigene Linie lancierte Ozbek 1984. Er hatte sich dazu vom Londoner Streetwear und der Atmosphäre in den Clubs inspirieren lassen. Zusammen mit Leigh Bowery arbeitete er an maßgefertigten Stücken und war Teil der post-neoromantischen Underground-Szene Londons. Ein definitives Statement zu jener Zeit gelang Ozbek 1990, als er aus seiner Vorliebe für sportliche Silhouetten eine schneeweiße Kollektion aus Trainingsanzügen entwarf, die die Modepresse mit dem

Etikett „New Age" versah. Die Kollektionen Herbst/Winter 1990 sowie Frühjahr/Sommer 1991 wurden in Form von Videos (unter der Regie von John Maybury) und als progressive Alternative zu Catwalk-Shows präsentiert. 2001 beschloss Rifat, das Tempo etwas zu drosseln und sich vorläufig aus dem Modebusiness zurückzuziehen. Stattdessen arbeitete er am Umbau und der Renovierung seines Sommerhauses in Bodrum an der türkischen Küste. Im Januar 2004 kehrte er in den internationalen Modezirkus zurück, und zwar als Consultant Creative Director von Pollini. Die klassisch italienische Marke für Schuhe und Lederaccessoires wurde 2001 vom Aeffe-Konzern gekauft und hat ihre Produktpalette inzwischen auch um Damenmode erweitert. Ozbeks Kollektion für Herbst/Winter 2005 ist seine dritte im Hause Pollini und zeigt sich als eklektischer Mix von Goldspitze, Brokatkleidern, Hippie-Patchwork und langen, mehrlagigen Röcken.

Styliste de Pollini depuis 2004, Rifat Ozbek possède un talent magique pour choisir et mélanger formes séduisantes et tissus ethniques et les traduire en une mode cool et contemporaine. Né en 1953 à Istanbul, il s'installe d'abord à Londres en 1970 pour étudier l'architecture, une discipline qui, à côté du design d'intérieur, influence constamment son travail. Pourtant, il entre à Central Saint Martins en 1974 pour étudier la mode. Il en sort diplômé en 1977 avant de rejoindre Trell à Milan, où il travaille avec Walter Albini, pionnier du leisurewear de luxe. En 1980, il revient à Londres et travaille pour Monsoon, une grande chaîne britannique réputée pour ses vêtements en tissus indiens. En 1984, Rifat Ozbek lance sa propre ligne inspirée par sa passion du streetwear et des boîtes de nuit londoniennes. Il collabore avec Leigh Bowery à la création de tailleurs et compte parmi les membres de la scène underground post-néoromantique de la capitale britannique. En 1990, Ozbek finit par frapper un grand coup quand son amour des silhouettes sportives donne naissance à une collection entièrement blanche composée de survêtements que la presse spécialisée qualifie de « New Age ». Il présente ses collections automne/hiver 1990 et printemps/été 1991 sous la forme de vidéos (réalisées par John Maybury), une alternative novatrice aux défilés. En 2001, Rifat Ozbek décide de ralentir le rythme et de sortir du système de la mode pour se consacrer à la reconstruction et à la rénovation d'une résidence secondaire à Bodrum, station balnéaire de la côte turque. Mais en janvier 2004, il revient dans le circuit international de la mode avec un nouveau poste de consultant à la direction de la création chez Pollini. Rachetée par le groupe Aeffe en 2001, Pollini est une marque italienne classique de chaussures et d'accessoires en cuir qui s'est diversifiée dans la mode féminine. La collection automne/hiver 2005 qu'il signe pour la maison, la troisième à ce jour, se distingue par son mélange éclectique de dentelle dorée, de robes en brocart, de patchworks hippie et de longs jupons superposés.

TERRY NEWMAN

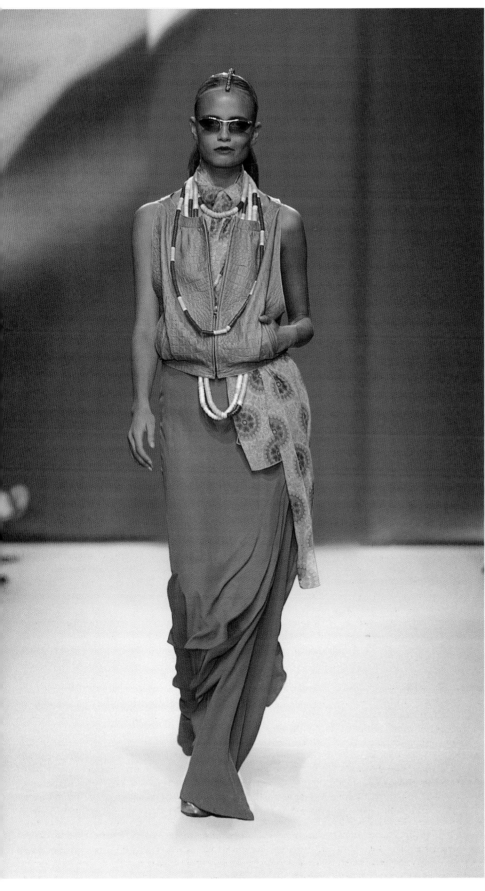

What are your signature designs? My white New Age collection **What is your favourite piece from any of your collections?** My native American confederate jacket **How would you describe your work?** Clean lines and opulence **What's your ultimate goal?** To reach Nirvana **What inspires you?** Anything in my perimetric vision **Can fashion still have a political ambition?** For someone maybe **Who do you have in mind when you design?** A fabulous woman **Is the idea of creative collaboration important to you?** Yes, very much **Who has been the greatest influence on your career?** My friends **How have your own experiences affected your work as a designer?** Where and how I live **Which is more important in your work: the process or the product?** The process **Is designing difficult for you, if so, what drives you to continue?** It's difficult, but the creativity makes me carry on **Have you ever been influenced or moved by the reaction to your designs?** Always **What's your definition of beauty?** A great smile **What's your philosophy?** Live and let live **What is the most important lesson you've learned?** To be true to myself.

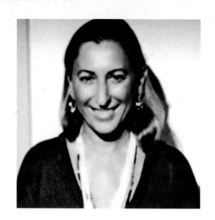

PRADA

"When people think of fashion, they always prefer to see the crazy side, the clichéd side of it. But I think that's wrong. Fashion is an important part of a woman's life"

In 1971 Miuccia Prada entered the family business. Twenty years later, the highly traditional leather goods company had changed beyond all recognition. The innovation of something as simple as a nylon bag meant there was no looking back: Prada was on the way to redefining luxury, subtlety and desirability in fashion. Prada the company – led by the designer and her husband, Patrizio Bertelli, who started work with Prada in 1977 and is now CEO of the Prada Group – seem to have an uncanny ability to capture the cultural climate in fashion. This sensitivity has been unashamedly teamed with commercial savvy, which has made the brand's influence over the past decade vast and its growth enormous. From bags and shoes to the first womenswear collection (1988), the Miu Miu line for the younger customer (1993), menswear (1994), Prada Sport (1997) and Prada Beauty (2000), all are directly overseen by Miuccia Prada herself. Yet, unlike many other Leviathan brands, there is something both unconventional and idiosyncratic in Miuccia Prada's aesthetic. Much of this may be down to her contradictory character. Born in Milan in 1950, Miuccia Prada studied political science at the city's university and was a member of Italy's Communist Party, yet is said to have worn Yves Saint Laurent on the barricades. The designer, who has made the Wall Street Journal's '30 Most Powerful Women In Europe' list, also spent a period studying to be a mime artist. These dualities have led to her expert ability in balancing the contrary forces of art and commerce within the super-brand, sometimes quite literally: Prada has its own art foundation and has collaborated with the architect Rem Koolhaas on stores in New York (2001) and Los Angeles (2004). From the late '90s, the Prada Group embarked upon a policy of rapid expansion, purchasing brands including Azzedine Alaïa, Helmut Lang and Church & Co.

1971 trat Miuccia Prada in das Familienunternehmen ein. Zwanzig Jahre danach hat sich die bis dahin eher traditionelle Lederwarenfabrik bis zur Unkenntlichkeit verändert. Etwas so Simples wie eine Nylonhandtasche markierte den Neuanfang. Prada gab den Begriffen Luxus, Raffinesse und Begehrlichkeit in Sachen Mode eine neue Bedeutung. Unter der Leitung der Designerin und ihres Mannes Patrizio Bertelli, der 1977 in das Unternehmen eintrat und heute CEO des Konzerns ist, beweist Prada einen untrüglichen Instinkt, wenn es darum geht, aktuelle Modeströmungen aufzunehmen. Dieses Gespür sorgte, gepaart mit dem nötigen Geschäftssinn, in den letzten zehn Jahren für das ungeheure Wachstum und den enormen Einfluss der Marke. Von den Taschen und Schuhen, der ersten Damenkollektion, dem Label Miu Miu für jüngere Kundinnen (1993) über Männermode (1994) und die Linie Prada Sport (1997) bis hin zu Prada Beauty (2000) unterstehen alle Bereiche nach wie vor Miuccia Prada. Doch im Unterschied zu anderen großen Marken ist Miuccia Pradas Ästhetik höchst unkonventionell und individuell. Vieles davon mag auf ihren ungewöhnlichen

Werdegang zurückzuführen sein. 1950 in Mailand geboren, studierte Miuccia Prada in ihrer Heimatstadt Politikwissenschaft und war Mitglied der Kommunistischen Partei. Doch angeblich trug sie selbst auf den Barrikaden Yves Saint Laurent. Die vom Wall Street Journal zu einer der „30 mächtigsten Frauen Europas" gekürte Geschäftsfrau absolvierte auch eine Schauspielausbildung. Ihre Vielseitigkeit mag dazu beitragen, dass es ihr immer wieder hervorragend gelingt, Kunst und Kommerz unter dem Dach der Supermarke miteinander zu versöhnen. Und das ist gelegentlich durchaus wörtlich zu verstehen: So betreibt Prada eine eigene Kunststiftung und ließ die Läden in New York (2001) und Los Angeles (2004) vom Stararchitekten Rem Koolhaas gestalten. Seit Ende der 1990er Jahre setzt der Prada-Konzern auf rasche Expansion und kaufte in diesem Zuge Marken wie Azzedine Alaïa, Helmut Lang oder Church & Co. auf.

Miuccia Prada rejoint l'entreprise familiale en 1971. Vingt ans plus tard, ce maroquinier ultra-classique a subi une transformation si radicale qu'il en est devenu méconnaissable. Une innovation telle que le sac en nylon prouvait bien que la maison ne regardait plus en arrière : Prada était sur le point de redéfinir le luxe, la subtilité et les avantages de la mode. Patrizio Bertelli, mari de Miuccia mais également directeur de l'entreprise, designer et actuel P-DG du groupe Prada, avait commencé à travailler pour la maison en 1977. La société semble douée d'une étrange facilité à capter le climat culturel de la mode. Cette intuition se mêle sans complexe à un esprit de conquête commerciale qui n'a fait qu'augmenter l'influence de la marque ces dix dernières années et lui a permis d'enregistrer une croissance vertigineuse. Des chaussures aux sacs en passant par la première collection de vêtements pour femme (1988), la ligne Miu Miu pour les jeunes (1993), la ligne masculine (1994), Prada Sport (1997) et Prada Beauty (2000), tout est directement supervisé par Miuccia Prada en personne. Contrairement à la plupart des géants de la mode, l'esthétique de Miuccia Prada se distingue par son anti-conformisme très caractéristique. Cette ambivalence repose en grande partie sur l'esprit de contradiction de Miuccia. Née en 1950 à Milan, elle étudie les sciences politiques à l'université de la ville et s'inscrit au Parti Communiste Italien, n'hésitant pas à monter sur les barricades habillée en Yves Saint Laurent. La créatrice, incluse dans la liste des « 30 femmes les plus puissantes d'Europe » du Wall Street Journal, a également suivi une formation pour devenir mime. Ces dualités lui ont permis de réconcilier les forces contradictoires de l'art et du commerce au sein de la « supermarque », parfois même au pied de la lettre : Prada possède sa propre fondation artistique et a collaboré avec l'architecte Rem Koolhaas à la création des boutiques de New York (2001) et de Los Angeles (2004). Dès la fin des années 90, le Groupe Prada a adopté une politique d'expansion rapide, rachetant des marques telles qu'Azzedine Alaïa, Helmut Lang et Church & Co.

JO-ANN FURNISS

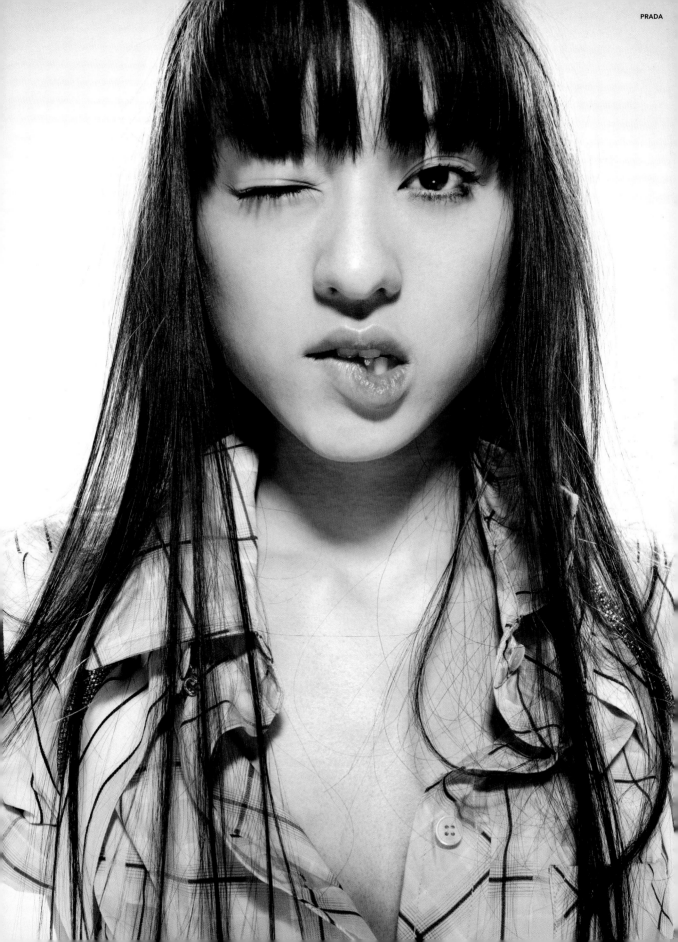

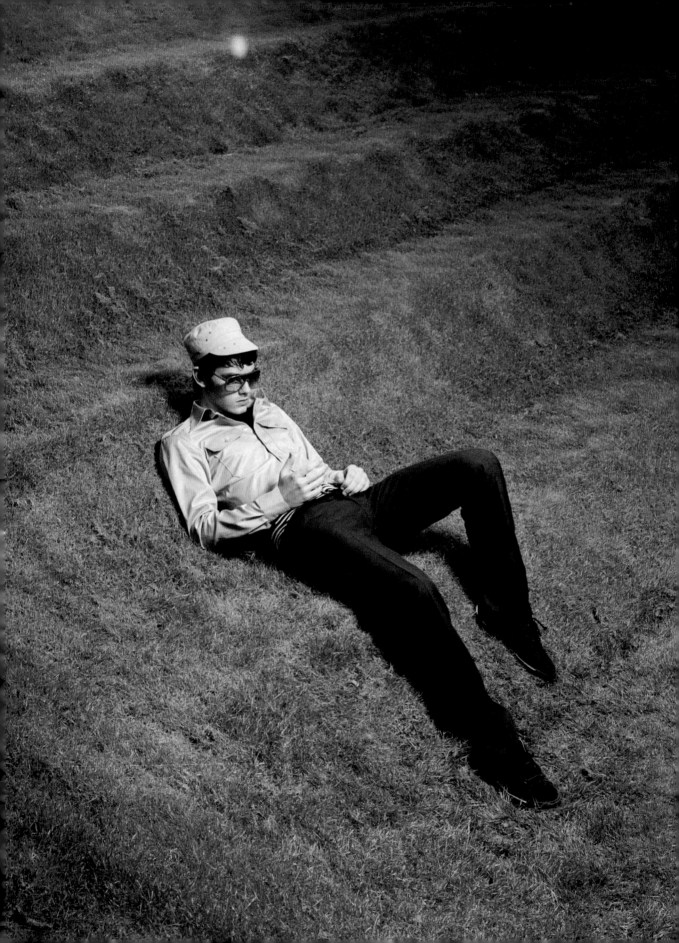

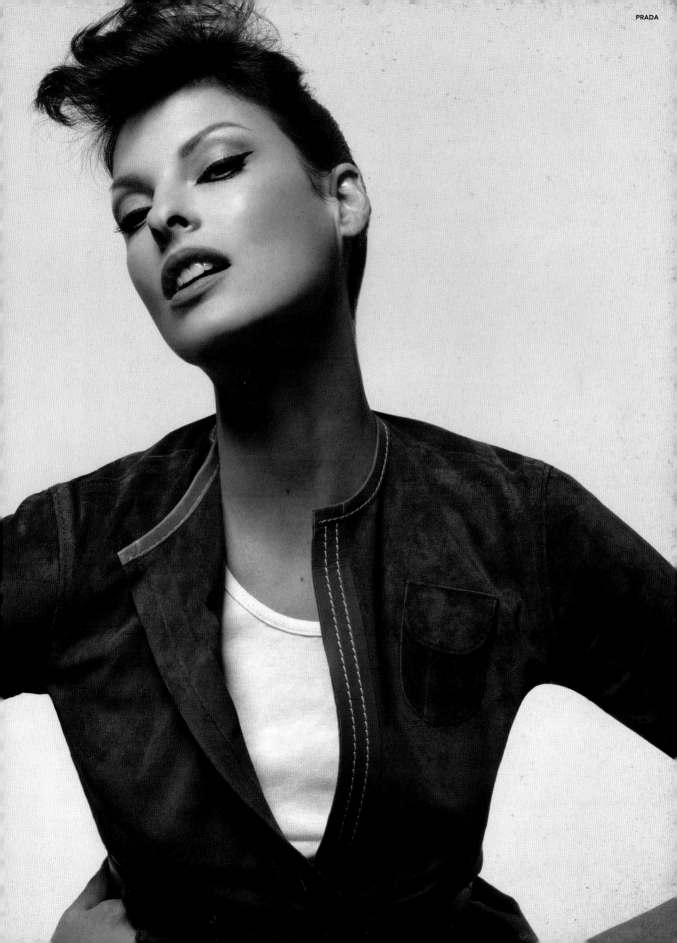

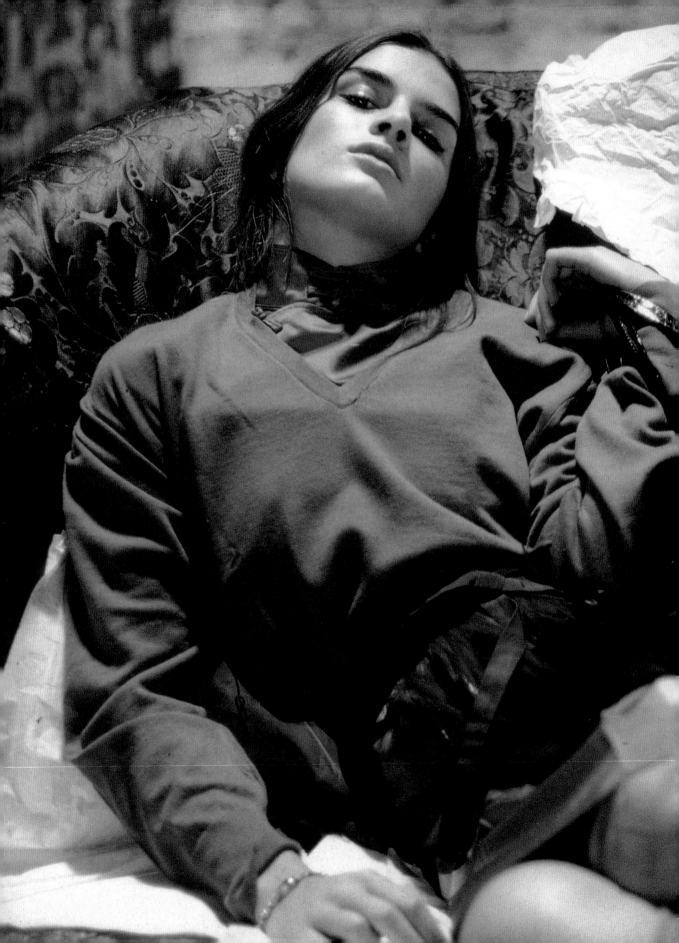

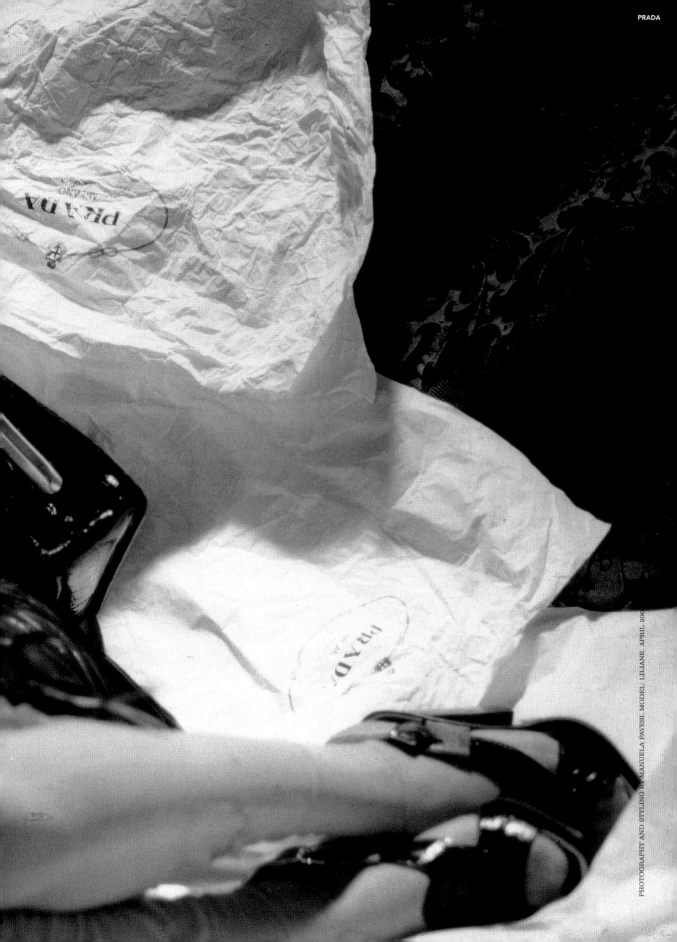

PHOTOGRAPHY AND STYLING BY MANUELA PAVESI. MODEL: LILIANE. APRIL 200

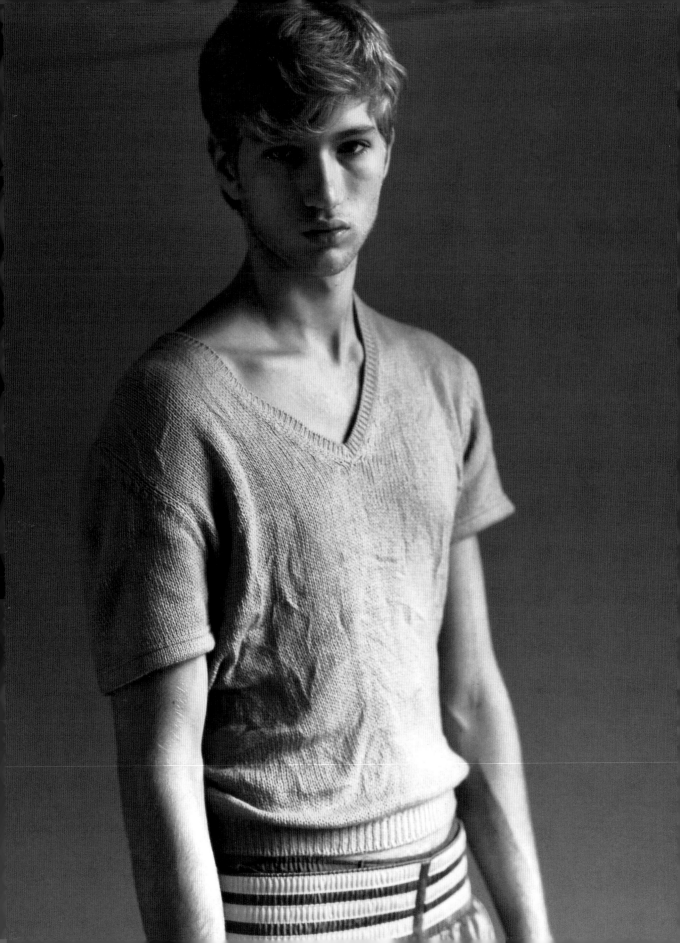

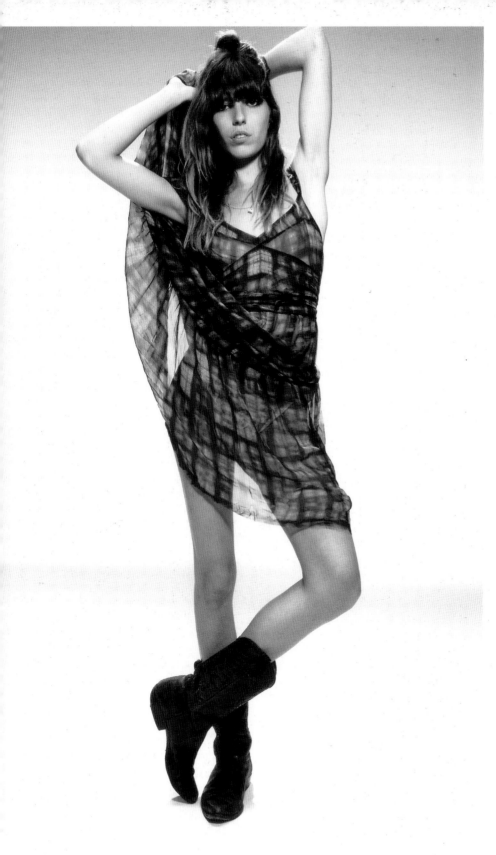

How would you describe your work? To have to express in a simple, banal object, a great complexity about women, aesthetics and current times **What's your ultimate goal?** To do my work as well as I can **What inspires you?** At the moment, I am intrigued by the increasingly ambiguous boundary between what is real and what is unreal, or what is beauty and what is fake, which we can no longer tell **Can fashion still have a political ambition?** I try to express the contemporary woman and do it through fashion because that's my instrument. When people think of fashion, they always prefer to see the crazy side, the clichéd side of it. But I think that's wrong. Fashion is an important part of a woman's life **Who do you have in mind when you design?** I do not have anyone in mind, there isn't just one. I am a complicated person: I am different people at different times. So I do not have one woman in mind. Prada and Miu Miu are the opposite of that idea because it's just not one thing **Is the idea of creative collaboration important to you?** Working as a designer allows me to have a lot of connections and relationships that can turn into important collaborations. Working on projects with artists, architects, directors, philosophers and creative people in general feeds my interests and my need of better understanding the complexity of the world we live in **How have your own experiences affected your work as a designer?** Of course I am what I feel, see, listen, read and meet. My fashion is a reflection of myself **Which is more important in your work: the process or the product?** It is difficult to say because the two things cannot be separated. The product is the process itself. Depending on the kind of product I have in mind, I use a different process: a couture process when I want to refer to that; more schizophrenic when I want to express something naïf…. My research for the new pushes me to invent every time a different process, and that is one of the things I like more **Is designing difficult for you, if so, what drives you to continue?** Designing, if you want to push boundaries, is not easy. I like to embrace the complexity and choose one theme through which I try to express it **Have you ever been influenced or moved by the reaction to your designs?** Not by the reaction, but by the reason for the reaction. You have to balance creativity with an understanding of what happens around you and the reality is that selling is the only way to prove that what you are doing makes sense to people.

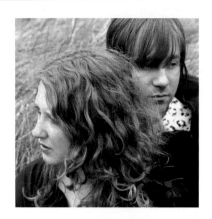

PREEN

"The starting point for each new collection
is the previous collection" JUSTIN THORNTON & THEA BREGAZZI

Preen is Justin Thornton (born 1969) and Thea Bregazzi (born 1969). The pair grew up on the Isle of Man, meeting at the age of just eighteen while both were studying for an art foundation course. However, the duo – and couple – did not start designing together until their island upbringing was in the past. Both attended fashion college on the mainland before setting out on their own after graduating. Thornton designed for Helen Storey's innovative 'Second Life' collection and Bregazzi started styling. It was Storey who brought them back together, asking them to jointly consult on her autumn/winter 1996 collection. The formation of Preen was the next logical step. The duo launched their first stand-alone collection in 1997, creating a buzz around individually crafted, deconstructed pieces that fused Victoriana with streetwear elements in a sharp tailored silhouette. Issues of construction and deconstruction have fascinated the couple ever since. Darlings of the style press during their formative years, Preen have developed their deconstruction tendencies, consistently providing alternatives to classic tailoring. Inspirations include circus performers, Pearly Kings and Queens and ballgowns. Such eccentricity had somewhat mystified fashion critics until recently. Since their spring/summer 2003 collection, which was shown at London Fashion Week, the duo have begun to soften their gritty, streetwear look for gentler shapes inspired by seminal fashion movie 'Belle de Jour' and even '70s rag doll Holly Hobby. They have also gained celebrity fans including American Vogue's Anna Wintour, Claudia Schiffer and Gwyneth Paltrow, while Alexander McQueen recently nominated them as one of his top ten young design companies. They also have mass-market presence with a range for Topshop, and their menswear line, launched in 2003, has been well received. Ewan McGregor and David Bowie are fans.

Preen, das sind Justin Thornton und Thea Bregazzi, beide Jahrgang 1969. Das Paar wuchs auf der Isle of Man auf und lernte sich mit gerade mal 18 Jahren als Teilnehmer an einem Kunstseminar kennen. Mit den gemeinsamen Entwürfen begann das berufliche wie private Team jedoch erst, nachdem es die Insel verlassen hatte. Beide besuchten eine Modeschule auf dem Festland und gingen nach dem Abschluss erst einmal getrennte Wege. Thornton entwarf für Helen Storeys innovative Kollektion „Second Life", während Bregazzi zunächst als Stylistin arbeitete. Es war Storey, die die beiden wieder zusammenbrachte, als sie sie als Berater für ihre Kollektion Herbst/Winter 1996 engagierte. Die Gründung von Preen war dann nur noch der nächste logische Schritt. Die erste eigene Kollektion lancierte das Duo 1997. Ihre individuell gearbeiteten, dekonstruktiven Kreationen vereinten Aspekte viktorianischer Mode mit Streetwear-Elementen in klar umrissenen Silhouetten. Das Thema Konstruktion und Dekonstruktion fasziniert die beiden Designer seit jeher. Als Liebling der Modepresse in den Anfangsjahren hat Preen die Neigung zur Dekonstruktion inzwischen weiter ausgebaut und bietet konsequent Alternati-

ven zu klassisch geschneiderter Kleidung. Als Inspiration dienen dabei Zirkuskünstler, Pearly Kings and Queens sowie Ballroben. Diese Exzentrik bezauberte bis vor kurzen alle Kritiker. Seit seiner Kollektion für Frühjahr/Sommer 2003 hat das Designerpaar jedoch begonnen, den gewagten Streetwear-Look im Stil von „Belle de Jour" und der Lumpenpuppe Holly Hobby aus den 1970er Jahren etwas abzuschwächen. Zu den prominenten Anhängern des Labels gehören Anna Wintour von der amerikanischen Vogue, Claudia Schiffer und Gwyneth Paltrow. Alexander McQueen zählt Preen zur Top Ten seiner Lieblingsfirmen unter den Jungdesignern. Mit einer Kollektion für Topshop ist die Marke auch im Massenmarkt vertreten. Die 2003 vorgestellte Herrenlinie wurde ebenfalls wohlwollend aufgenommen. Hier zählen Ewan McGregor und David Bowie zu den Fans.

Preen, c'est Justin Thornton (né en 1969) et Thea Bregazzi (née en 1969). Bien qu'ils aient tous deux grandi sur l'île de Man, ils se rencontrent seulement à l'âge de dix-huit ans dans une école d'art. Néanmoins, ce duo qui forme aussi un vrai couple dans la vie ne collaborera pas avant d'avoir laissé derrière lui son enfance passée sur l'île. Ils suivent des études de mode sur le continent et se lancent après l'obtention de leurs diplômes. Justin Thornton dessine pour la collection innovante Second Life de Helen Storey tandis que Thea Bregazzi travaille dans le stylisme. C'est justement Helen Storey qui les réunit lorsqu'elle leur demande de travailler ensemble en tant que consultants sur sa collection automne/hiver 1996. Logiquement, l'étape suivante voit la création de leur griffe Preen. Le duo lance sa première collection en 1997 et tout le monde ne parle plus que de leurs pièces déconstruites de production artisanale qui fusionnent l'époque victorienne à des éléments streetwear au sein d'une silhouette bien définie. Depuis, le couple reste fasciné par les questions de construction et de déconstruction. Chouchous de la presse spécialisée pendant leurs années formatrices, ils développent à travers Preen leur tendance déconstructionniste et ne cessent de proposer des alternatives aux coupes classiques. Entre autres, ils s'inspirent des artistes de cirque, des « Pearly Kings and Queens » et des robes de bal, une excentricité qui encore récemment laissait les critiques de mode dubitatifs. Depuis leur collection printemps/été 2003 présentée à la London Fashion Week, ils commencent à adoucir leur look streetwear dérangeant avec des formes plus faciles inspirées de « Belle de Jour » et même de la poupée en chiffon Holly Hobby des années 70. Ils séduisent également des clientes célèbres telles qu'Anna Wintour du Vogue américain, Claudia Schiffer et Gwyneth Paltrow, tandis qu'Alexander McQueen a récemment classé Preen dans son top ten des meilleures jeunes griffes de mode. La marque bénéficie également d'une présence sur le marché plus commercial avec une collection conçue pour Topshop. Leur ligne pour homme lancée en 2003 a été bien accueillie : Ewan McGregor et David Bowie en sont fans. LAUREN COCHRANE

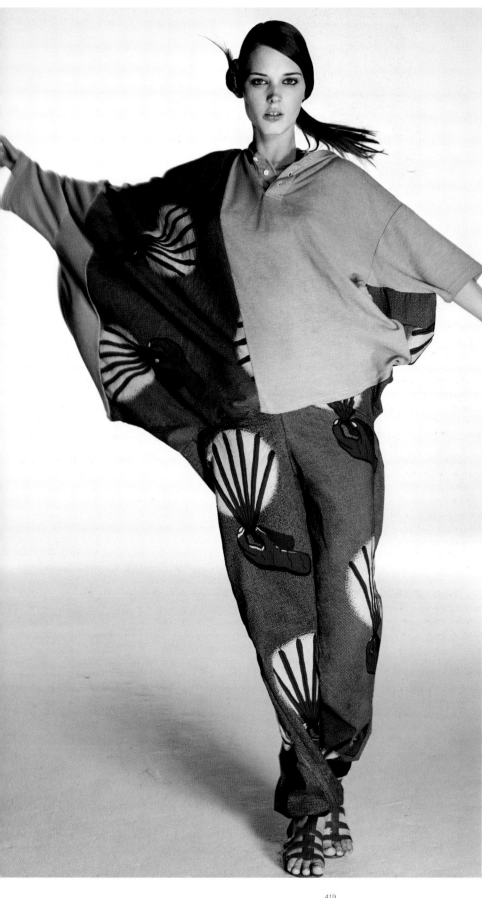

What are your signature designs? A Preen signature design would be a garment which is craft-worked mixing opposing fabrics that would have an overall urban feel What is your favourite piece from any collection? Each season we have new favourites but it's nice when we rediscover an old favourite in the back of our wardrobe How would you describe your work? We describe our work as an extension of how we are feeling at the time when we design a collection. The starting point for each new collection is the previous collection What's your ultimate goal? Independence and security in both work and life What inspires you? People and life experiences Can fashion still have a political ambition? No Who do you have in mind when you design? Not one particular person, each season is an amalgamation of attitudes and feelings Is the idea of creative collaboration important to you? Yes, collaboration encourages the development of ideas Who has been the greatest influence on your career? No one person has been a major influence How have your own experiences affected your work as a designer? It's difficult to say, as every experience affects us in a new and different way Which is more important in your work: the process or the product? Both are important but the product is what matters in the end Is designing difficult for you? If so what dries you to continue? No, designing is not difficult, it is the fashion timetable and the pressure of business that are testing Have you ever been influenced or moved by the reaction to your designs? When people love what we do it makes us very happy What's your definition of beauty? Individuality What's your philosophy? We don't have a philosophy as such, as long as we are true to our own ideas and thoughts and it doesn't matter what others think. What's the most important lesson you've learned? To always trust our instincts.

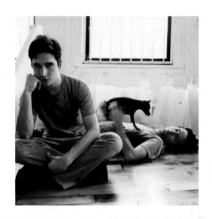

PROENZA SCHOULER

"The collection has so many different components. But that's how we design and how people dress — with intellect, with spirit, and an eye for the mix" LAZARO HERNANDEZ & JACK MCCOLLOUGH

Lazaro Hernandez and Jack McCollough are the American duo behind Proenza Schouler. The label has secured accounts with the world's most exclusive stores, won a Council of Fashion Designers of America (CFDA) award for new talent and, for many, has put the New York collections back on the must-see fashion map. Its fans include American Vogue's editrix Anna Wintour and her super-chic French counterpart Carine Roitfeld. All this has been achieved within the space of a few seasons. Both born in 1978, Hernandez, who was born in Miami of Spanish Cuban heritage, and McCollough, who was born in Tokyo and raised in New Jersey, first met at Parson's College in NYC. After Hernandez completed an internship at Michael Kors (on Anna Wintour's recommendation) and McCollough at Marc Jacobs, they made the unusual decision of working together on their senior collection. Winning the Designer of the Year award at Parson's student show and with their whole graduation collection snapped up by Barneys, Hernandez and McCollough quickly had to find a name. They came up with the nom de plume Proenza Schouler, combining each of their mothers' maiden names. Since then, Proenza Schouler have become part of a new breed of American designers who are choosing polish and sincere sophistication over grunge and thrift store irony, quickly perfecting a style that is particular to New York: a blend of tailored uptown glamour with sporty downtown nonchalance. Inspired by '50s couture – Christian Dior, Cristobal Balenciaga and Coco Chanel – and pictures by Avedon and Penn, Proenza Schouler's signatures include their play with proportion, bolero jackets, bustiers and heavily worked detailing – a fusion of old-world luxury and new-world lifestyle. In 2004 the duo scooped the first-ever Vogue/CFDA Fashion Fund award, winning a $200,000 cash prize and business mentoring.

Lazaro Hernandez und Jack McCollough sind das amerikanische Duo hinter Proenza Schouler. Das Label hat sich seinen Platz in den exklusivsten Läden der Welt gesichert, einen Preis des Council of Fashion Designers of America (CFDA) für neue Talente gewonnen und in den Augen vieler den New Yorker Kollektionen zu neuem Ansehen in der Modebranche verholfen. Zu den Fans gehören die Herausgeberin der amerikanischen Vogue, Anna Wintour, und deren französischer super-schicker Widerpart Carine Roitfeld. All das erreichte man innerhalb weniger Saisons. Hernandez, 1978 als Kind spanisch-kubanischer Eltern in Miami geboren, und der im selben Jahr in Tokio geborene, in New Jersey aufgewachsene McCollough lernten sich am Parson's College in New York kennen. Nachdem Hernandez (auf Empfehlung von Anna Wintour) ein Praktikum bei Michael Kors und McCollough eines bei Marc Jacobs absolviert hatte, fällten die beiden die ungewöhnliche Entscheidung, sich für ihre Abschlusskollektion zusammenzutun. Nachdem sie damit den Preis Designer of the Year bei der Studentenschau am Parson's gewonnen hatten und Barneys sich ihre komplette Kollektion gesichert hatte, mussten sich Hernandez und McCollough rasch

einen Namen einfallen lassen. Sie kamen auf den Kunstnamen Proenza Schouler, für den sie die Mädchennamen ihrer Mütter kombinierten. Seit damals ist Proenza Schouler Teil einer neuen Generation amerikanischer Designer, die strahlender echter Eleganz den Vorzug vor Grunge und Second-Hand-Ironie geben. Daraus entwickelte sich rasch ein Stil, der eng mit New York verbunden ist: ein Mix aus maßgeschneidertem Uptown-Glamour und sportlicher Downtown-Lässigkeit. Inspiriert von den Couturiers der 1950er – Christian Dior, Cristobal Balenciaga und Coco Chanel – sowie den Bildern von Avedon und Penn, gehören das Spiel mit Proportionen, Bolerojäckchen, Bustiers und arbeitsaufwändige Details zu den Markenzeichen von Proenza Schouler. Kurz gesagt: eine Melange aus dem Luxus der Alten und dem Lifestyle der Neuen Welt. Im Jahr 2004 sicherte sich das Designerduo den erstmals ausgelobten Vogue/CFDA Fashion Fund, der 200 000 Dollar in bar und Business Mentoring umfasste.

Proenza Schouler est l'œuvre du duo américain formé par Lazaro Hernandez et Jack McCollough. Cette griffe vendue dans les boutiques les plus sélectives du monde leur a valu le prix du CFDA (Council of Fashion Designers of America) décerné aux nouveaux talents et beaucoup estiment qu'elle a contribué à remettre les collections new-yorkaises sur le devant de la scène. Proenza Schouler compte des fans tels que la rédactrice du Vogue américain Anna Wintour et son homologue française ultra-chic Carine Roitfeld, un exploit accompli en l'espace de quelques saisons seulement. Tous deux nés en 1978, Hernandez grandit à Miami dans une famille d'origine hispano-cubaine tandis que McCollough, né à Tokyo, grandit dans le New Jersey. Ils se rencontrent au Parson's College de New York et effectuent des stages pendant leurs études, Hernandez chez Michael Kors (sur les recommandations d'Anna Wintour) et McCollough chez Marc Jacobs. Contrairement aux habitudes, ils décident de travailler ensemble sur leur collection de fin d'études, avec un défilé couronné par le prix de Parson's Designer of the Year et une collection complète achetée par Barneys. Hernandez et McCollough doivent alors rapidement se trouver un nom de plume : ils optent pour Proenza Schouler, une combinaison des noms de jeune fille de leurs mères. Depuis, Proenza Schouler fait partie de la nouvelle génération de griffes américaines qui préfèrent la sophistication classe et sincère à l'ironie du grunge et du vintage, perfectionnant rapidement un style typiquement new-yorkais : coupes sophistiquées et glamour alliées à une nonchalance sport. Inspirées par la haute couture des années 50 (Christian Dior, Cristobal Balenciaga et Coco Chanel) comme par les photos d'Avedon et de Penn, les signatures de Proenza Schouler se distinguent par un jeu sur les proportions qui se décline dans des boléros, des bustiers et des détails très travaillés : une fusion entre luxe à l'ancienne et lifestyle du nouveau monde. En 2004, le duo remporte la toute première bourse de mode décernée par Vogue et le CFDA, qui correspond à un prix de 200 000 dollars et un soutien en gestion d'entreprise.

JAMIE HUCKBODY

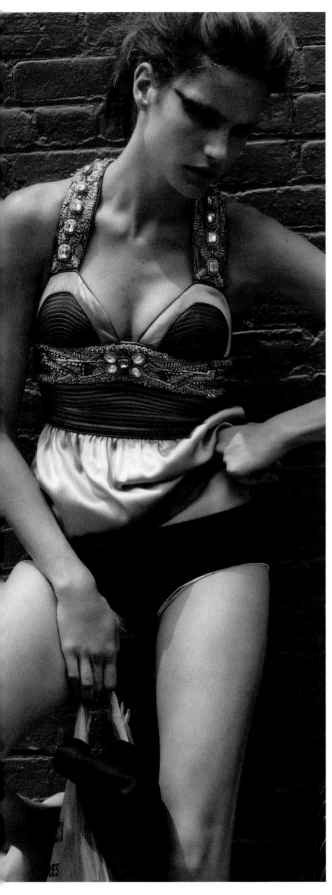

What are your signature designs? Many would say the Bustier and the Trapunto stitching that we have visited in several of our collections, and we always show jackets, which we like because of their versatility. But we like to think of our clothes in terms of a signature theme instead, which is that they are both luxurious and comfortable. We hope they are pieces that have an easy dialogue with all parts of a woman's wardrobe and her life **What is your favourite piece from any of your collections?** It would be impossible to isolate a favourite because we have attachments to things for different reasons – you can love one thing because it was the first, or most successful, or the easiest – or the most challenging **What's your ultimate goal?** Right now it's not to have an "ultimate" goal – for things to constantly evolve without a particular destination in mind **What inspires you?** The visual arts, especially photography and painting. The work of master couturiers. Travel. But there is never one specific reference – inspiration comes from everything, even if you don't recognise it at the time **Who do you have in mind when you design?** It's not one person. There is not one woman who is quint-essentially Proenza Schouler. One of the most interesting things we have learned from doing this is that we have teenagers who wear our clothes and grandmothers who do too – which we love. The collection has so many different components, and all of the components can have many different lives, depending on the point of view. But that's what we want because that's how we design and how people dress – with intellect, with spirit, and an eye for the mix **Is the idea of creative collaboration important to you?** Is this a trick question? Naturally creative collaboration is our process and we share work and credit equally. But people do often wonder about the division of work and labour, which is not really how we work. We work separately for a period, then come together – and the results are often remarkably similar. We agree far more often than we argue, and we refine silhou-ettes and ideas as a team always **Which is more important in your work: the process or the product?** One can't be more important than the other because of how closely they are linked: the process drives the product, and the product enables the process to begin all over again **Is designing difficult for you: if so, what drives you to continue?** Like any job there are periods, or projects that are more challenging than others – but that doesn't force you to quit; you just get through it. This is what we do and enjoy and are trained for. So that, if nothing else, is what keeps us going **Have you ever been influenced or moved by the reaction to your designs?** One of the greatest compliments you can receive as a designer is to see a complete stranger wearing things you designed. Critical praise, awards and accolades, commercial success – those are a certain kind of award, but there is something so personal and immediate about seeing someone you have never seen before walking down the street wearing just one piece that you created with other things that she loves and expresses who she is. To know that someone has a reaction to this thing – encountered and pursued it and wanted to own it. It really affects you **What's your definition of beauty?** Beauty is not only hard to define but it's impossible to prescribe. One of the most arresting things about beauty is often that it's a surprise – it's some-thing that takes you off guard. If you tried to define it, you might restrict it, or run the risk of diluting it **What is the most important lesson you've learned?** That the most important lesson is probably yet to be learned.

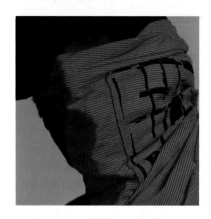

RAF SIMONS

"The collections have been part of the process of growing up"

Although he is now one of the indisputable kings of menswear, Raf Simons (born 1968) never took a single fashion course. Instead, he studied industrial design in Genk, Belgium, close to his hometown Neerpelt. Nevertheless he took an internship at the Walter Van Beirendonck Antwerp office while still at school, citing fashion as a major point of interest. Afterwards Simons started working as a furniture designer, but gradually grew unhappy with this direction. In 1995, after moving to Antwerp and meeting up with Linda Loppa, head of the fashion department at the city's Royal Academy, he decided to switch career. Obsessed both by traditional, formal menswear and the rebellious dress codes of present and past youth cultures, Simons distilled a groundbreaking new style from these inspirations. From his first collection for autumn/winter 1995 on, he drew a tight, linear silhouette executed in classical materials that encapsulated references like English schoolboys, gothic music, punk, Kraftwerk and Bauhaus architecture. Despite international acclaim, Raf Simons surprisingly shut down his company after presenting his autumn/winter 1999 collection, in order to take a sabbatical and re-arrange the internal structure of his business. After sealing a close cooperation with Belgian manufacturer CIG, Simons returned for autumn/winter 2000 with a new, multi-layered and radical look, worn as ever by non-professional models scouted on the streets of Antwerp. These teenage boys were the subject of a collaboration with David Sims, resulting in photographs compiled in a book ('Isolated Heroes', 1999). Raf Simons designed the Ruffo Research men's collections for two seasons in 1999. Since October 2000, he has taught fashion at the University of Applied Arts in Vienna, and in February 2001 he guest edited an issue of i-D. In 2003 Simons curated two exhibitions ('The Fourth Sex' at Pitti Immagine, Florence, and 'Guided By Heroes' in Hasselt, Belgium) and collaborated with Peter Saville on his autumn/winter 2003 collection, 'Closer'. In May 2005 it was announced that Simons would take over as creative director at Jil Sander.

Auch wenn er heute zu den unumstrittenen Königen der Herrenmode zählt, hat der 1968 geborene Raf Simons nie auch nur ein einziges Seminar zum Thema Mode besucht. Stattdessen studierte er im belgischen Genk nahe seiner Heimatstadt Neerpelt Industriedesign. Allerdings absolvierte er noch als Schüler ein Praktikum im Antwerpener Atelier von Walter van Beirendonck und interessierte sich bereits damals sehr für Mode. Zunächst arbeitete Simons als Möbeldesigner. Nachdem er nach Antwerpen gezogen war und dort Linda Loppa, die Leiterin der Modefakultät an der Königlichen Akademie, kennen gelernt hatte, beschloss er 1995 umzusatteln. Fasziniert sowohl von der traditionellen klassischen Herrenmode wie auch von den rebellischen Dresscodes der Jugendlichen verschiedenster Generationen, destillierte Simons aus diesen Inspirationen einen bahnbrechenden neuen Stil. Schon in seiner ersten Kollektion, Herbst/Winter 1995, entschied er sich für eine schmale, lineare Silhouette aus klassischen Materialien. Dazu kamen Bezüge zu englischen Schuluniformen, Gothic Music, Punk, Kraftwerk und Bauhausarchitektur. Trotz internationaler Anerkennung schloss Simons seine Firma überraschenderweise nach der Präsentation seiner Kollektion für Herbst/Winter 1999, um sich eine Auszeit zu gönnen und sein Geschäft international neu zu strukturieren. Nachdem die enge Zusammenarbeit mit dem belgischen Hersteller CIG besiegelt war, kehrte Simons für die Saison Herbst/Winter 2000 mit einem neuen, radikalen Look aus vielen Lagen zurück. Den präsentierten wie immer Amateur-Models, die man auf den Straßen von Antwerpen angeworben hatte. Um eben diese Teenager-Jungs ging es auch bei einem Projekt mit David Sims, das in dem Fotoband „Isolated Heroes" (1999) dokumentiert ist. Im Jahr 1999 entwarf Simons bei Ruffo Research die Herrenkollektionen für zwei Saisons. Seit Oktober 2000 lehrt er Mode an der Universität für Angewandte Kunst in Wien. Als Gastredakteur wirkte er im Februar 2001 an einer Ausgabe von i-D mit. 2003 war Simons Kurator von zwei Ausstellungen („The Fourth Sex" in der Fondazione Pitti Immagine in Florenz und „Guided By Heroes" im belgischen Hasselt) und erarbeitete zusammen mit Peter Saville seine Kollektion „Closer" für Herbst/Winter 2003. Im Mai 2005 gab Jil Sander bekannt, dass Raf Simons Creative Director wird.

Bien qu'il soit sans conteste devenu l'un des rois de la mode pour homme, Raf Simons (né en 1968) n'a jamais suivi la moindre formation en mode. En fait, il a étudié le design industriel à Genk, près de sa ville natale de Neerpelt en Belgique. Pendant ses études, il fait toutefois un stage au bureau anversois de Walter van Beirendonck, car la mode figure parmi ses principaux centres d'intérêt. Ensuite, Simons commence à travailler comme designer de meubles. En 1995, après avoir emménagé à Anvers et rencontré Linda Loppa, directrice du département mode de l'Académie Royale de la ville, il décide de changer de carrière. Obsédé à la fois par la mode masculine classique et les codes vestimentaires de la jeunesse rebelle d'hier et d'aujourd'hui, Simons puise dans ces inspirations et invente un nouveau style révolutionnaire. Dès sa première collection à l'automne/hiver 1995, il définit une silhouette étroite et linéaire, façonnée dans des matières classiques pleines de références aux collégiens anglais, à la musique gothique, au punk, à Kraftwerk ou encore à l'architecture Bauhaus. Malgré un succès international, contre toute attente, Raf Simons ferme sa maison après avoir présenté sa collection automne/hiver 1999, décidant de prendre un congé sabbatique et de revoir la structure interne de son entreprise. Il signe ensuite un accord d'étroite coopération avec le fabricant belge CIG, puis revient à l'automne/hiver 2000 avec un nouveau look radical aux multiples facettes, présenté comme toujours sur des mannequins non professionnels recrutés dans les rues d'Anvers. Ces adolescents font d'ailleurs l'objet d'une collaboration avec David Sims, qui sort un livre de photographies (« Isolated Heroes », 1999). Par ailleurs, Raf Simons a conçu deux collections masculines pour Ruffo Research en 1999. Depuis octobre 2000, il enseigne la mode à l'Université des Arts Appliqués de Vienne et a été invité au comité de rédaction du numéro de février 2001 du magazine i-D. En 2003, il a organisé deux expositions (« The Fourth Sex » au Pitti Immagine de Florence et « Guided By Heroes » à Hasselt en Belgique) et collaboré avec Peter Saville sur « Closer », sa collection automne/hiver 2003. En mai 2005, la maison Jil Sander annonce le recrutement de Raf Simons au poste de directeur de la création.

PETER DE POTTER

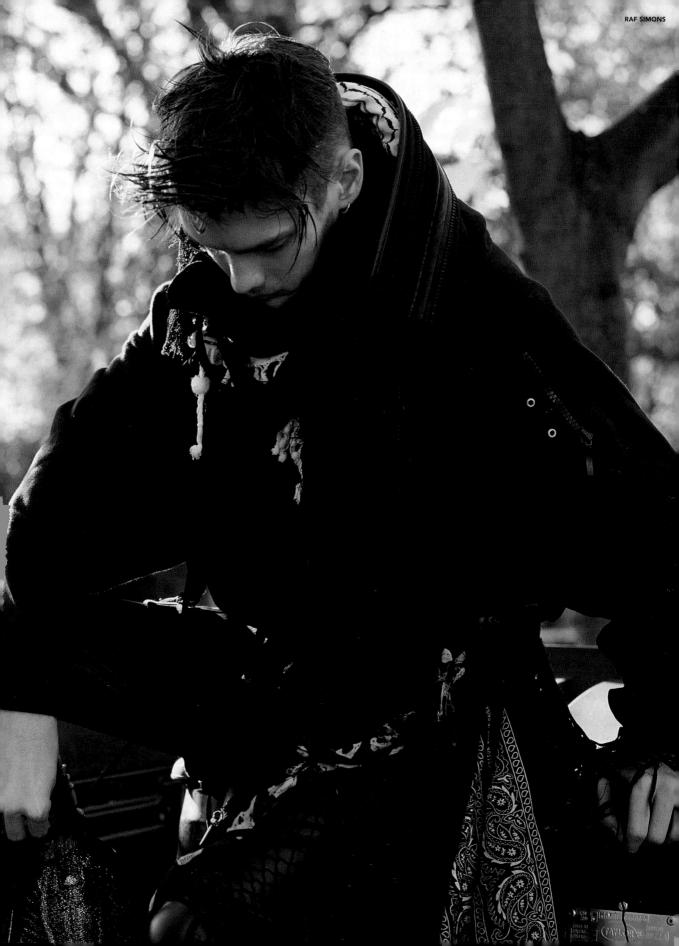

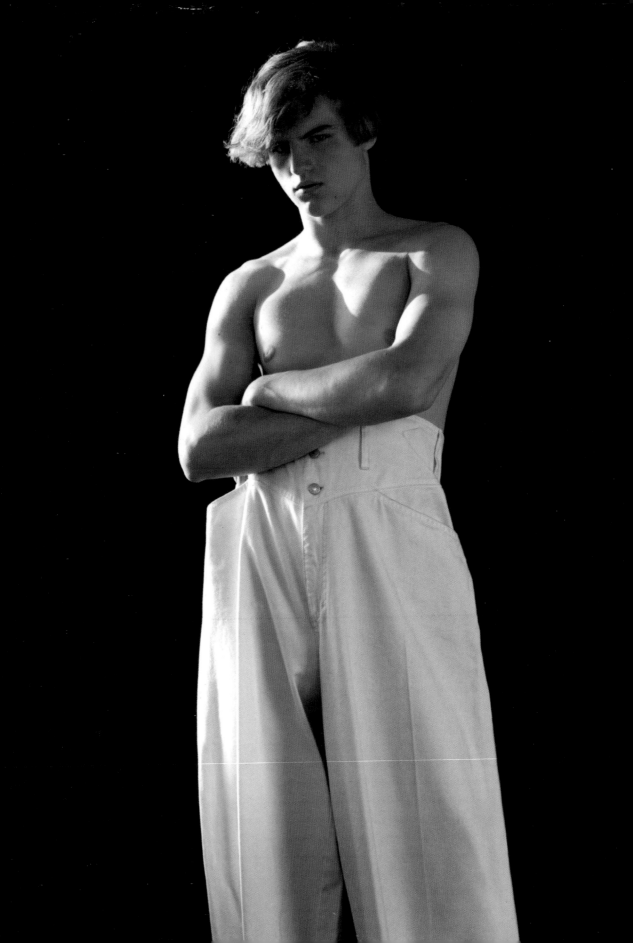

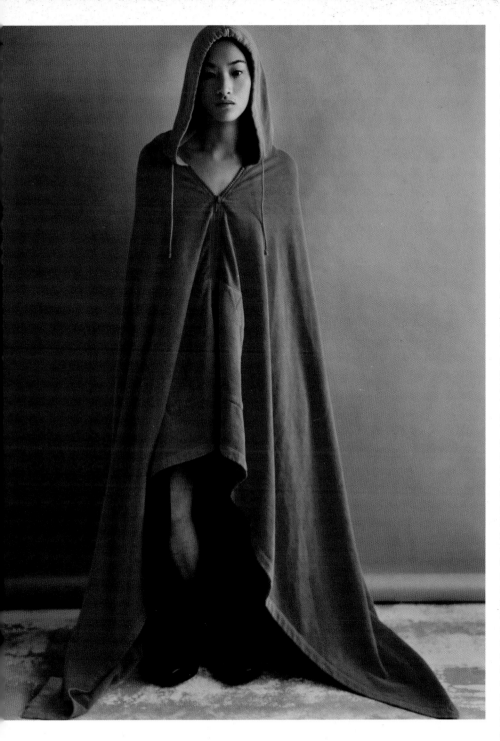

What is your favourite piece from any of your collections? I really like the work for the hippy summer collection. I think that more than ever it was the moment that we concentrated on what we believed in. We moved away from all the other things that you think about, like the industry and everything. Of course it was a very uncommercial collection; it was a very difficult collection. It was a very special procedure to work on it. It was very unindustrial. For example, there were about 50 people involved in the hand painting for it **How would you describe your work?** I think that more and more, all the collections have been part of the process of growing up. It is connected with casting. In the show, I used all the boys that I was using eight years ago, that are now all 30 years old. Alexander, who was doing the last show, just became a father. You know, five or six years ago all they were interested in is a T-shirt with a print and baggy pants. But now they have graduated and are starting to find jobs. They go out looking for jobs and they come back to me, and you know it's that suit from five years ago. So that makes me think, and look at the form that I am bringing out now. The second thing is that in fashion in general people will look to the piece itself. They concentrate on, 'How can I make this seam look special?' or 'What am I going to do with that button so it looks interesting?' I am not interested in that. At the moment, I am more interested in the shape and the form. I have a big desire to make clothes without defining them, because we don't know what it means, to make it right for the 21st century, to make it for the future **Who do you have in mind when you design?** I think there was a certain period when the show was an instrument to stay young. I was making these young, teenage collections, while I myself was already 30. And now I don't feel like that. Now, I am interested in making clothes for all audiences **Which is more important in your work: the process or the product?** In the past the process was more important than the result. Now I am also focusing on the product **What is the most important lesson you've learned?** To protect your 'baby'. I know that my business is not big. My business and my image are very out of balance with each other. I know that the business could have been bigger, but I would have had to make sacrifices and compromises. But now it is time to concentrate on the product – that's for sure. I am happy to do that. I used to have a real love-hate relationship with fashion, but at the moment I love it. I really love it. I love the fashion, I love the product, and I love people who are really interested in buying clothes. It is not a new reaction; I have been feeling like this for a couple of years now.

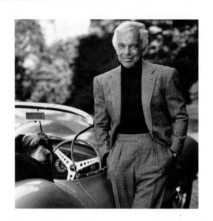

RALPH LAUREN

"I believe in style, not fashion"

Ralph Lauren (born 1939) is a household name. Jamaica has even issued a commemorative stamp (in 2004) featuring Lauren. The man and his brand's logo of a polo player riding a horse is recognised by all. From a $50,000 loan in 1968, Polo Ralph Lauren's humble beginnings grew into the internationally famous lifestyle brand which everyone knows today. Lauren was one of the first designers to extend his production of clothing lines to houseware and furniture. He was also the first of the megabrand American designers to set up shop in Europe, in 1981; the Polo Ralph Lauren Corporation now has 280 stores in operation globally and its collections are divided into myriad different labels. In October 2004 in Boston the company opened its first Rugby store, a lifestyle collection for the 18-to-25 year-old men and women. The Rugby line joins Lauren's other collections, Purple Label (1994), Blue Label (2002) and Black Label (2005). Underpinning Lauren's designs is an unmistakable preference for old-world gentility. In fact, he has made the Ivy League, preppy style his own. "I don't want to be in fashion – I want to be a fashion," he once told Vogue magazine. And indeed, the Ralph Lauren look is distinctive, nowhere more purely expressed than in his advertising campaigns that always feature a cast thoroughbred models, often posed as if holidaying in the Hamptons. Lauren's entrance into fashion can be traced back to 1964 with Brooks Brothers, and then Beau Brummell Neckwear in 1967, where he designed wide ties. In the following year, the beginnings of what was to become a billion dollar brand took root. The Polo menswear line was launched and in 1970 he won the Coty Menswear Award; Lauren added womenswear to the brand in 1971. He has been awarded the CFDA's Lifetime Achievement Award (1992) along with its menswear designer (1995) and Womenswear designer (1996) prizes. Lauren is also involved in philanthropic activities. The Polo Ralph Foundation organises campaigns such as Pink Pony (2000), which supports cancer care and medically underserved communities.

Ralph Lauren (Jahrgang 1939) ist ein allgemein bekannter Name. Jamaika brachte 2004 sogar eine Lauren-Gedenkbriefmarke heraus. Polo Ralph Laurens bescheidene Anfänge mit einem Kredit über 50 000 Dollar im Jahr 1968 haben sich zu einem international berühmten Lifestyle-Label, das heute jeder kennt, entwickelt. Lauren dehnte als einer der ersten Modedesigner seine Produktpalette auf Wohnaccessoires und Möbel aus. Er war auch einer der ersten Designer amerikanischer Megamarken, die Läden in Europa eröffneten (1981). Heute betreibt die Polo Ralph Lauren Corporation 280 Läden rund um den Globus und hat ihre Kollektionen auf unzählige verschiedene Labels verteilt. Im Oktober 2004 eröffnete das Unternehmen in Boston den ersten Laden namens Rugby, der eine Lifestyle-Kollektion für 18- bis 25-jährige Männer und Frauen führt. Rugby ergänzt die Linien Purple Label (1994), Blue Label (2002) und Black Label (2005). Allen Entwürfen Laurens liegt eine unzweifelhafte Vorliebe für das Elitedenken der Alten Welt zugrunde. Genau genommen hat sich der Designer den Ivy-League- und Preppy-Stil zu eigen gemacht. „Ich möchte nicht in Mode sein – ich möchte eine Mode sein", hat er der Vogue einmal gesagt. Und tatsächlich ist sein

Look unverwechselbar und springt nirgendwo klarer ins Auge als in seinen Werbekampagnen, die immer eine kultivierte Schar von Models zeigen, die wirken, als machten sie gerade Ferien in den Hamptons. Laurens Anfänge in der Modebranche lassen sich bis ins Jahr 1964 und zu Brooks Brothers zurückverfolgen. 1967 entwarf er bei Beau Brummell Neckwear breite Krawatten, und bereits im folgenden Jahr nahm das, was einmal eine Milliarden-Dollar-Marke werden sollte, seinen Anfang. Alles begann mit der Herrenlinie Polo, für die Lauren 1970 den Coty Menswear Award erhielt. 1971 kam Damenmode ins Sortiment des Labels. Von der CFDA wurde er mit dem Lifetime Achievement Award (1992) ausgezeichnet, bevor er den Designerpreis sowohl für Menswear (1995) als auch für Womenswear (1996) erhielt. Lauren ist aber auch gemeinnützig tätig. Die Polo Ralph Lauren Foundation organisiert Kampagnen wie Pink Pony (2000), die Krebspatienten und medizinisch unterversorgten Gemeinden in den USA zugute kommen.

Ralph Lauren (né en 1939) est connu dans le monde entier. En 2004, la Jamaïque a même édité un timbre commémoratif à son effigie. Tout le monde connaît l'homme, comme son logo de joueur de polo. A partir d'un prêt de 50 000 dollars obtenu en 1968, les débuts modestes de Polo Ralph Lauren se sont transformés en une marque de lifestyle incontournable et mondialement connue. Ralph Lauren est l'un des premiers créateurs de mode à s'être diversifié dans le meuble et les articles pour la maison. Sa mégamarque américaine est également la première à ouvrir une boutique en Europe dès 1981 ; Polo Ralph Lauren Corporation possède aujourd'hui 280 boutiques à travers le monde et ses collections sont divisées en une myriade de griffes différentes. En octobre 2004, l'entreprise ouvre sa première boutique Rugby à Boston, une collection complète destinée aux 18–25 ans, hommes et femmes. La ligne Rugby vient s'ajouter à Purple Label (1994), Blue Label (2002) et Black Label (2005). Une indubitable prédilection pour la distinction à l'ancienne étaye les créations de Lauren, qui s'est en fait approprié le chic BCBG de l'Ivy League. « Je ne veux pas être à la mode : je veux être une mode », déclare-t-il un jour au magazine Vogue. En effet, le look distingué de Ralph Lauren s'exprime de façon plus qu'évidente dans ses campagnes publicitaires qui présentent toujours un casting de mannequins racés, souvent mis en situation dans un décor de vacances rappelant les Hamptons. Les débuts de Lauren dans la mode remontent à 1964 chez Brooks Brothers, puis chez Beau Brummell Neckwear en 1967, où il commence à dessiner des cravates larges. L'année suivante voit la naissance de ce qui devait devenir un énorme groupe évalué à un milliard de dollars. Après avoir lancé la ligne masculine Polo, Ralph Lauren remporte le Coty Menswear Award en 1970, puis crée une collection pour femme en 1971. Le créateur a été couronné du Lifetime Achievement Award du CFDA (1992), avant d'obtenir des prix dans les catégories masculines (1995) et féminines (1996). Ralph Lauren s'implique également dans des activités caritatives : la fondation Polo Ralph organise des campagnes telles que Pink Pony (2000) en faveur du traitement contre le cancer et des communautés mal desservies sur le plan médical.

KAREN LEONG

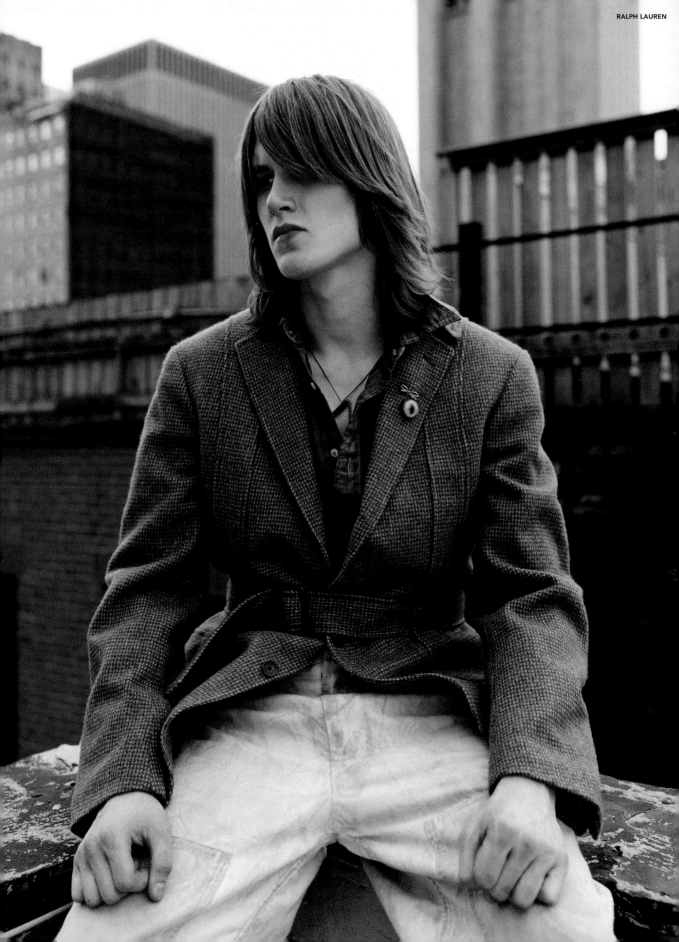

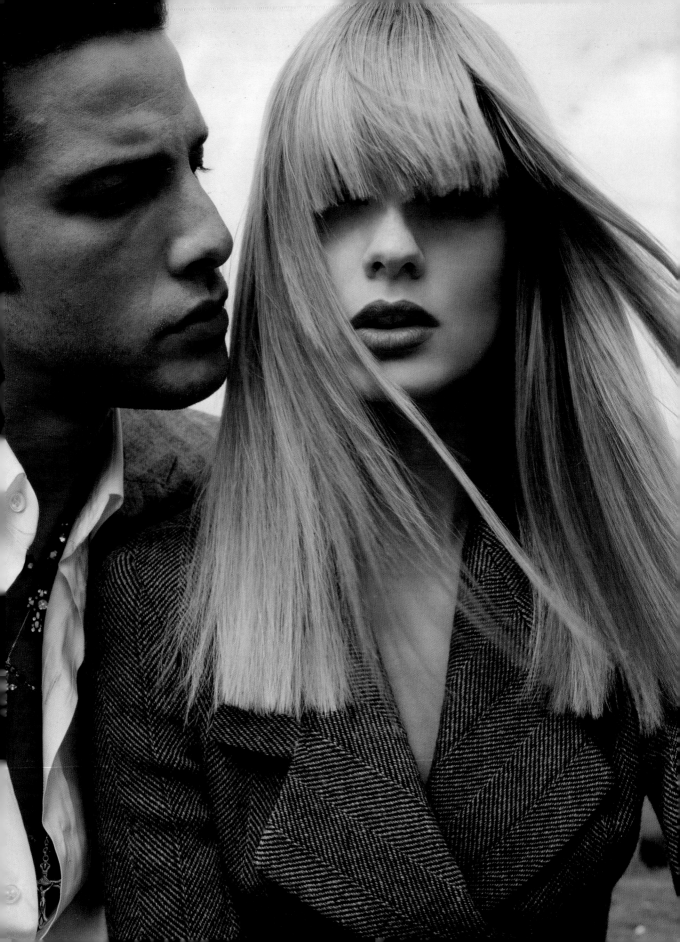

What is your favorite piece or pieces from any of your collections? I don't really think in terms of pieces... Each piece is a complement to the bigger picture **What is your ultimate goal?** I am satisfied with my life and feel fortunate to be doing what I love **What inspires you?** I'm constantly drawing inspiration from everything I see – places I travel to, people I know, films, photographs, classic cars... I'm always inspired by authenticity **Is the idea of creative collaboration important to you?** It's very stimulating to go from designing menswear to womenswear to a home collection; to meet about a new store concept or ad campaign. I enjoy being connected with all that I do **Who or what has been the greatest influence on your career?** My family – everything I do is a reflection of my life **Which is more important to you in your work: the process or the product?** For me, designing is not merely about an idea for a suit or a dress. I also see each detail as a complement to the bigger picture – whether the collar is turned, the proportions of a jacket, the colour and size of the buttons. For me, it's about building a concept and nurturing an idea. I'm not just creating products; I'm creating a whole world **Is designing difficult for you and, if so, what drives you to continue?** I like the excitement of the challenge. The question I ask myself is: What can we do next? How much further can we go? **What's your philosophy?** Fashion is transient, trends come and go. I believe in style, not fashion **What is the most important lesson you've learned?** Business is about taking risks, but it's also about being consistent with your vision.

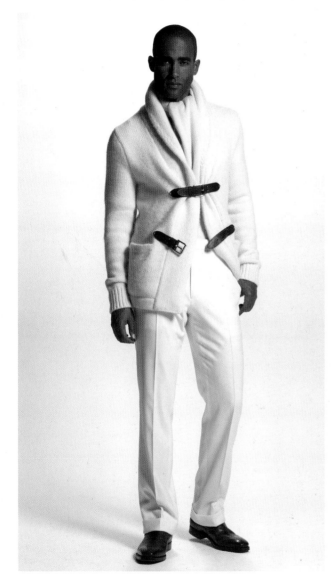

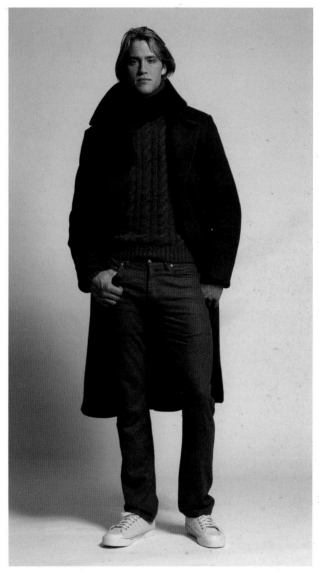

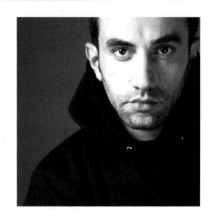

RICCARDO TISCI

"My definition of beauty is something between
extremely ugly and extremely fantastic"

In September 2004, Riccardo Tisci presented a show unconventional for high-gloss Milan Fashion Week: supermodels wearing intricately ruched and tiered black gowns moving around a smoky, atmospheric set littered with disused car parts and large black balls. Born in Italy (1975), Tisci moved to London at the age of 18 and graduated from Central Saint Martins in 1999. The following year, he moved back to Italy where he developed a small collection of dresses and T-shirts for the London boutique Kokon To Zai. British Vogue photographed them and Björk bought some, but production was a low-key affair with everything handmade by the designer's mother and eight sisters. In 2002 Tisci was appointed creative director of the Italian fashion house Coccapani, where he designed four well-received collections. During the same period, he designed the first Puma Rudolf Dassler Schuhfabrik collection, injecting his sense of playful volume into women's sports pieces. 2004 was set to be his big breakthrough year – the designer won a contract with Ruffo Research, but after a few months the company behind the brand put the project on hold, forcing Tisci to reconsider his plans. It was then that he launched his own label. The 12 outfits presented in September 2004 and modelled by the likes of Karen Elson and Maria Carla Boscono – the latter, his muse and best friend – were just a taste of things to come. In March 2005 Tisci was presented with his greatest challenge to date when he was named the new chief designer of womenswear at Givenchy. The Italian has since shelved his eponymous line in favour of concentrating all his energy on the grand Parisian couture house. Tisci is the fourth designer to head up the LVMH-owned brand since founder Hubert de Givenchy retired from fashion in 1995.

Im September 2004 präsentierte Riccardo Tisci eine für die ansonsten auf Hochglanz abonnierte Mailänder Modewoche reichlich ungewohnte Show: Supermodels in kompliziert gerüschten, aus mehreren Lagen bestehenden schwarzen Roben bewegten sich auf einem rauchigen, atmosphärisch dichten Set, auf dem alte Autoteile und große schwarze Bälle herumlagen. Der 1975 in Italien geborene Tisci zog mit 18 nach London und machte 1999 seinen Abschluss am Central Saint Martins. Im darauf folgenden Jahr ging er zurück nach Italien, wo er eine kleine Kollektion aus Kleidern und T-Shirts für die Londoner Boutique Kokon To Zai entwarf. Die britische Vogue fotografierte diese, und Björk kaufte ein paar Teile. Das Ganze war jedoch ein Low-Budget-Projekt – alles handgenäht von der Mutter des Designers und seinen acht Schwestern. 2002 ernannte das italienische Modehaus Coccapani Tisci zu seinem Chefdesigner. Er entwarf dort vier Kollektionen, die sehr gut aufgenommen wurden. Im selben Zeitraum designte Tisci auch die erste Kollektion für Rudolf Dasslers Schuhfabrik Puma, bei der sein Gespür für verspielte Fülle sich in Sportmode für Damen nieder-

schlug. 2004 war dann das Jahr des großen Durchbruchs – der Designer ergatterte zunächst einen Vertrag mit Ruffo Research. Nach ein paar Monaten setzte das Unternehmen hinter der Marke das Projekt jedoch aus, was Tisci dazu zwang, seine Pläne zu überdenken. So kam es, dass er sein eigenes Label lancierte. Die zwölf Outfits, die im September 2004 von Models wie Karen Elson und Maria Carla Boscono – letztere ist die Muse und beste Freundin des Designers – präsentiert wurden, waren nur ein Vorgeschmack dessen, was noch kommen sollte. Denn im März 2005 stellte sich Tisci seiner bisher größten Herausforderung, als er zum neuen Chefdesigner der Damenmode bei Givenchy ernannt wurde. Die nach ihm benannte Linie lässt der Italiener im Moment ruhen, um all seine Energie für das große Pariser Modehaus aufzuwenden. Tisci ist der vierte Designer an der Spitze der Couture-Marke im Besitz von LVMH, seit sich ihr Gründer Hubert de Givenchy 1995 aus dem Modegeschäft zurückzog.

En septembre 2004, Riccardo Tisci présente un défilé tout à fait inattendu pour la très glamour Milan Fashion Week : des top models vêtues de robes noires décorées de volants et de ruchés complexes défilent autour d'un décor atmosphérique et enfumé, jonché de vieilles pièces détachées automobiles et de grands ballons noirs. Né en Italie (1975), Riccardo Tisci débarque à Londres à l'âge de 18 ans et sort diplômé de Central Saint Martins en 1999. L'année suivante, il revient en Italie pour développer une petite collection de robes et de T-shirts commandée par la boutique londonienne Kokon To Zai. Le Vogue anglais les photographie et Björk achète quelques pièces, mais la production reste modeste puisque tout est fait à la main par la mère et les huit sœurs du créateur. En 2002, Tisci est nommé directeur de la création de la maison italienne Coccapani, où il conçoit quatre collections plutôt bien accueillies. Au cours de cette période, il dessine également la première collection Puma Rudolf Dassler Schuhfabrik, à laquelle il insuffle son sens ludique du volume dans des créations sport pour femme. C'est en 2004 qu'il perce enfin pour de bon : il remporte un contrat avec Ruffo Research mais au bout de quelques mois, l'entreprise qui possède la marque suspend le projet et contraint Tisci à revoir ses plans ; il décide alors de lancer sa propre griffe. Les douze tenues présentées en septembre 2004 sur des mannequins telles que Karen Elson et Maria Carla Boscono, sa muse et meilleure amie, n'offrent qu'un avant-goût des collections à venir. En mars 2005, Riccardo Tisci doit relever son plus grand défi à ce jour lorsqu'il est nommé styliste principal des lignes pour femme de Givenchy. L'Italien met sa griffe éponyme en sommeil afin de consacrer toute son énergie à cette grande maison parisienne de haute couture. Depuis que son fondateur Hubert de Givenchy a pris sa retraite en 1995, Tisci est le quatrième créateur à superviser la marque de LVMH. SIMON CHILVERS

What are your signature designs? The treatment of tulle by distorting it, by embroidering it. I love tulle because it is romantic but sexy. Also experimental jersey that's rawcut and draped. Leather that's double layered and burnt to expose Swarovski crystals **What is your favourite piece from any of your collections?** The skirt with the leg holes with side drapes. That and the giant leather bomber with gathering on the shoulders that I featured in my most recent collection **How would you describe your work?** Conceptual, sensual and romantic raw **What's your ultimate goal?** Doing my own collection **What inspires you?** A lot of things: my eight sisters and my mum, Maria Carla, art, cinematography especially old, cultural cinematography, music (going out to clubs) and the darkness when you go deep under the water **Can fashion still have a political ambition?** Yes it can, but it's not about taking sides, it's about giving emotion to the people who wear the clothes **Who do you have in mind when you design?** A woman that's confident in personality and body and she understands my sexiness **Is the idea of creative collaboration important to you?** Yes, because a designer is the heart of a collection and of his own world but without a good pattern cutter, good production in the factory and a good presentation team he cannot express 100% of himself **Who has been the greatest influence on your career?** The people who really believed in me right from the beginning, Central Saint Martins, Maria Carla, Diane Koutsis Hemmi, Seiko Matsuda and my family **How have your own experiences affected your work as a designer?** Yes, because I come from a very poor family and I had to fight with life to get here without changing who I am and am always having to search for ways to express myself **Which is more important in your work: the process or the product?** Process is more important because I'm always trying to find something new and experimental. And it's more fun basically **Is designing difficult for you, if so, what drives you to continue?** No, it's not difficult. I am very shy. Designing is my way of communicating **Have you ever been influenced or moved by the reaction to your designs?** If it's well-thought criticism it makes me happy, because I know it will make me grow. And when the criticism is good, it makes me emotional and drives me to give more **What's your definition of beauty?** Something between extremely ugly and extremely fantastic. I think skulls are beautiful, but most people find them horrifying **What's your philosophy?** Do good things and forget them, do bad things and remember them. That's the way my mamma taught me **What is the most important lesson you've learned?** The most important thing I learnt in life is that if someone does something bad to you, you must sit on the riverbank and watch the corpse float by. Which means never repay bad with bad, but wait for destiny to take care of it.

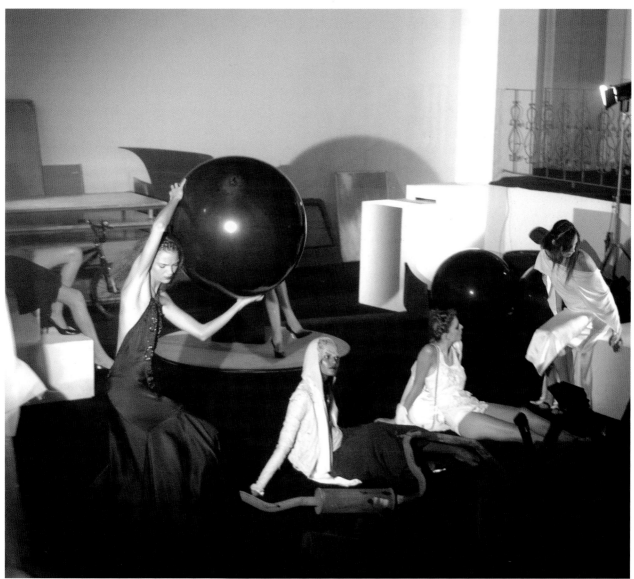

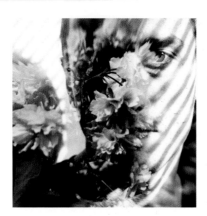

RICHARD NICOLL

"Both the process and the product are important. In a way, the process forms the product's soul"

Richard Nicoll was born in London in 1977 to New Zealander parents. From the age of three, Nicoll grew up in the Australian city of Perth where his ophthalmologist father raised him and his older sister. On leaving school, Nicoll returned to London and enrolled at Central Saint Martins where he completed a BA in Menswear. A brief period of hectic creativity ensued with Nicoll selling his own T-shirts through Paris store Colette and assisting the stylist Camille Bidault-Waddington. It was at this time that he first began collaborating on projects with i-D photographer Jason Evans, a partnership that remains intact to this day. (Evans produced a photographic slide show for Nicoll's spring/summer 2005 collection as part of London Fashion Week's Fashion East group show for new talent). In 2002, he completed and gained an MA in womenswear, back at Saint Martins; Italian design duo Dolce & Gabbana bought Nicoll's final collection and, following graduation, the young designer was awarded a bursary that enabled him to establish his own label. To date, Nicoll has shown twice as part of Fashion East (October 2004 and February 2005) and also during Osaka Fashion Week in Japan. Nicoll seems equally adept at fine drapery – as in his Madame Grès-inspired spring/summer 2005 collection – as he is at sophisticated tailoring, using Perspex and wood for unusual details. Print, too, is emerging as a bold design signature for this promising designer, lending his work an energetic Pop Art slant.

Richard Nicoll wurde 1977 als Kind neuseeländischer Eltern in London geboren. Ab seinem dritten Lebensjahr wuchs er mit seiner älteren Schwester bei seinem Vater, einem Augenarzt, im australischen Perth auf. Nachdem er die Schule beendet hatte, zog Nicoll zurück nach London und immatrikulierte sich am Central Saint Martins, wo er einen Bachelor im Fach Herrenmode erwarb. Darauf folgte eine kurze Phase hektischer Kreativität, in der Nicoll seine eigenen T-Shirts über das Pariser Kaufhaus Colette vertrieb und der Stylistin Camille Bidault-Waddington assistierte. Zu jener Zeit begann auch die projektbezogene Zusammenarbeit mit dem i-D-Fotografen Jason Evans, die bis heute andauert. (Evans produzierte eine Diaschau für Nicolls Kollektion Frühjahr/Sommer 2005, die bei der Londoner Modewoche im Rahmen von Fashion East, der Gruppenschau für neue Talente, gezeigt wurde.) 2002 machte Nicoll – wiederum am Cen-

tral Saint Martins – noch seinen Master in Damenmode. Das italienische Designerduo Dolce & Gabbana kaufte seine Abschlusskollektion. Nach bestandenem Studium erhielt der Jungdesigner ein Stipendium, das es ihm ermöglichte, sein eigenes Label zu gründen. Inzwischen hat Nicoll bereits zweimal im Rahmen von Fashion East präsentiert (im Oktober 2004 und im Februar 2005) sowie bei der Osaka Fashion Week in Japan. Er scheint in der feinen Draperie – zu sehen in seiner von Madame Grès inspirierten Kollektion Frühjahr/Sommer 2005 – ebenso bewandert wie in der raffinierten Maßschneiderei, wo er Perspex und Holz für außergewöhnliche Details benutzt. Ein weiteres Markenzeichen dieses viel versprechenden Designers sind kräftige Muster, die seinen Arbeiten einen kräftigen Touch Pop-Art verleihen.

Richard Nicoll est né en 1977 à Londres de parents néo-zélandais. Dès l'âge de trois ans, il grandit dans la ville australienne de Perth auprès de son père ophtalmologiste et de sa grande sœur. Après le lycée, Nicoll revient à Londres pour étudier à Central Saint Martins, où il obtient un BA en mode masculine. S'ensuit une brève période de créativité mouvementée pendant laquelle Richard Nicoll vend ses T-shirts via la boutique parisienne Colette et assiste la styliste Camille Bidault-Waddington. C'est à cette époque qu'il commence à collaborer avec le photographe d'i-D Jason Evans, un partenariat encore d'actualité à ce jour (Evans a produit un diaporama photographique pour la collection printemps/été 2005 de Nicoll dans le cadre du groupe Fashion East dédié aux nouveaux talents de la London Fashion Week). En 2002, il décroche un MA en mode féminine de Central Saint Martins avec une collection de fin d'études achetée par le duo italien Dolce & Gabbana. Après l'obtention de son diplôme, le jeune créateur se voit remettre une bourse qui lui permet de fonder sa propre griffe. A ce jour, Richard Nicoll a effectué deux présentations dans le cadre de Fashion East (octobre 2004 et février 2005) et participé à la Semaine de la Mode d'Osaka au Japon. Il semble tout aussi adepte des beaux drapés, comme en témoigne sa collection printemps/été 2005 inspirée par Madame Grès, que des coupes sophistiquées, utilisant du Perspex et du bois pour créer des détails insolites. Les imprimés émergent également comme l'une des signatures audacieuses de ce couturier prometteur et confèrent à son travail un côté Pop Art plein d'énergie.

DAVID LAMB

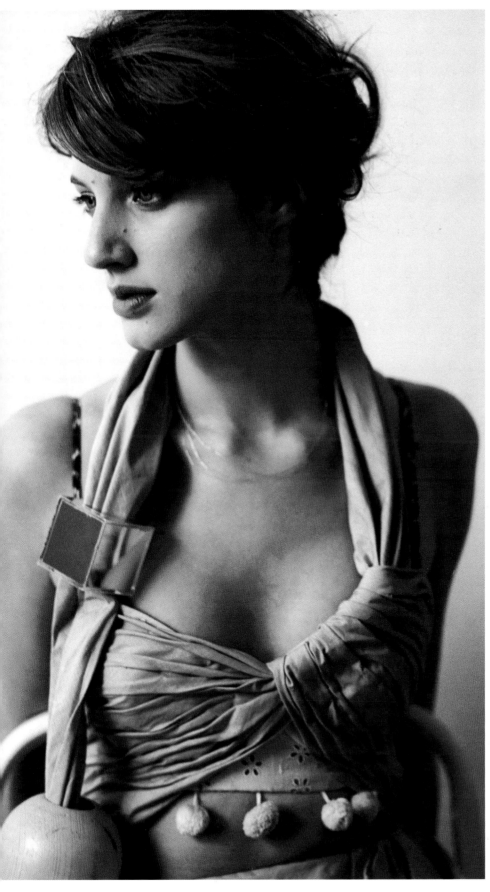

What are your signature designs? I think it is too early for me to have formed any signatures, but I have been exploring a technique of twisting and knotting fabric around the body, most recently with the addition of outsized beads **What is your favourite piece from any of your collections?** It is a dress from my MA collection that was used by my friend Thom Murphy in a Dizzie Rascal video. It was pretty weird but oddly attractive and sexy. It's a salmon-coloured wool jersey stretch dress with engineered cut outs and a stretch chiffon lining in tangerine with grey chiffon bloomers attached **How would you describe your work?** It is a bit like my best friend and my worst enemy at the same time **What's your ultimate goal?** Continued happiness **What inspires you?** My friends and an ideal of obtainable Utopia **Can fashion still have a political ambition?** Of course, but I think it falls on deaf ears. Maybe to have a social conscience is not really in harmony with the essence of the fashion industry **Who do you have in mind when you design?** I always start with a mood that reflects the way that I'm feeling at the time and apply it to my ideal subject, which is basically a hybrid of three of my friends **Is the idea of creative collaboration important to you?** Yeah, I love collaborating because it keeps the work fresh and it's always more fun. You learn a lot about the essence of creativity from collaborating **Who has been the greatest influence on your career?** Well I'm pretty inspired by anyone who has the courage to make original work with conviction and can retain a strong sense of humility and consideration for other people (I like Issey Miyake's and Jil Sander's approach) **How have your own experiences affected your work as a designer?** It's impossible to say **Which is more important in your work: the process or the product?** They are both important but at the end of the day, the life of the product only really begins when the process is finished. In a way the process forms the product's soul **Is designing difficult for you, if so, what drives you to continue?** Sometimes it is really difficult and sometimes it is easy, but I think that if you are a designer you don't have a choice, it is fundamentally part of you **Have you ever been influenced or moved by the reaction to your designs?** Well it's obviously encouraging if people like what you do **What's your definition of beauty?** Happiness **What's your philosophy?** To deal with the fundamental elements of life and to try to instil those into a product that reflects a purity of design **What is the most important lesson you've learned?** Not to take life too seriously and to treat other people well.

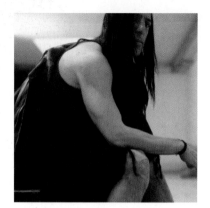

RICK OWENS

"I'd describe my work as Frankenstein and Garbo, falling in love in a leather bar"

Rick Owens (born 1961) stands alone in the international fashion industry. He is that rare thing: an LA designer. Owens' draped, dark, and perfectly-cut aesthetic is the antithesis of the sunshine-saturated, bleached-teeth image of LA. Born in the city, Owens grew up in Porterville, a small town in California. Moving back to LA in 1984 after high school, he studied painting at the Otis Parsons Art Institute, but dropped out after two years and began to pursue his career in fashion. However he rejected fashion college and instead studied pattern cutting at a trade school. In 1988 he took a job in LA's garment district, where he earned his keep as a pattern cutter for six years. In 1994, Owens set up his own label and began selling his small collections through Charles Gallay, an up-and-coming boutique. Nineties pop culture and Hollywood's red carpet influenced his designs, resulting in bias-cut gowns and trailer park vests. Owens playfully describes his darkly chic clothes as 'glunge' – a mix of glamour and grunge. Rather than show on a catwalk, he instead travelled the world throughout the '90s presenting his clothes to fashion buyers and developing an impressive client list that includes Madonna and Courtney Love. His reputation continued to grow by word of mouth and in 2002, American Vogue offered to sponsor his autumn/winter collection, his first on a runway. In the same year, Owens won the Perry Ellis Emerging Talent Award from the Council of Fashion Designers of America (CFDA). Moving to Paris in 2003 after scoring an artistic director contract with fur house Revillon, Owens – and his dark designs – have now found a home in his adopted city.

Der 1961 geborene Rick Owens ist eine Ausnahme in der internationalen Mode-industrie, denn er gehört einer seltenen Spezies ein: Er ist ein Designer aus Los Angeles. Seine verhüllende, düstere und perfekt geschnittene Ästhetik ist das Gegenteil des gängigen Images von LA mit Sonne bis zum Abwinken und gebleichten Zähnen. In Los Angeles geboren, wuchs Owens in der kalifornischen Kleinstadt Porterville auf. 1984 zog er nach dem High-School-Abschluss zurück in die Großstadt und studierte am Otis Parsons Art Institute Malerei. Zwei Jahre später brach er diese Ausbildung ab und begann an seiner Karriere als Mode-designer zu arbeiten. Er tat dies jedoch nicht an einer Modeschule, sondern ent-schied sich für das Musterschneiden an einer Handelsschule. 1988 suchte er sich einen Job als Musterschneider im Garment District von LA, womit er sechs Jahre lang seinen Lebensunterhalt bestritt. Dann gründete er 1994 sein eigenes Label und begann seine kleinen Kollektionen über die angesagte Boutique Charles Gallay zu verkaufen. Die Popkultur der 1990er Jahre und Hollywoods roter Teppich beeinflussten seine Entwürfe und sorgten für diagonal geschnit-tene Roben und Trailer-Park-Westen. Owens nennt seine Kleider mit dem düste-ren Chic ironisch „glunge" – eine Mixtur aus Glamour und Grunge. Anstatt sie auf dem Catwalk zu zeigen, reiste der Designer in den 1990er Jahren lieber kreuz und quer durch die Welt und präsentierte seine Mode den Käufern direkt, was ihm eine respektable Kundenliste mit Namen wie Madonna und Courtney Love einbrachte. Seine Reputation wuchs vornehmlich durch Mundpropaganda, bis 2002 die amerikanische Vogue anbot, seine Herbst/Winterkollektion – die erste auf dem Catwalk – zu sponsern. Im gleichen Jahr verlieh das Council of Fashion Designers of America (CFDA) Owens den Perry Ellis Emerging Talent Award. Als ihn das Pelzhaus Revillon als künstlerischen Leiter unter Vertrag nahm, zog Owens 2003 nach Paris. Dort haben er und seine dunklen Kreationen nun eine zweite Heimat gefunden.

Rick Owens (né en 1961) apparaît comme un franc-tireur dans l'industrie de la mode internationale car il fait figure de véritable rareté : c'est un créateur de Los Angeles. L'esthétique drapée, sombre et parfaitement coupée d'Owens se trouve à l'antithèse de l'image saturée de soleil et de dents blanches si typique de Los Angeles. Né à L. A., Owens grandit à Porterville, une petite ville de Californie. Après le lycée, il revient à Los Angeles en 1984 pour étudier la peinture à l'Otis Parsons Art Institute, qu'il quitte au bout de deux ans pour se lancer dans la mode. Toutefois, il rejette les formations en mode proposées par les universités, préférant étudier la coupe de patrons dans un collège technique. En 1988, il décroche un job dans le quartier des fabricants de vêtements bas de gamme de L. A., où il gagne sa vie en tant que traceur de patrons pendant six ans. En 1994, Owens crée sa propre griffe et commence à vendre ses petites collections par le biais de Charles Gallay, la boutique montante de l'époque. La culture pop et le glamour hollywoodien des années 90 influencent ses créations et s'expriment à travers des robes coupées en biais et des débardeurs d'inspiration white trash. Owens qualifie avec humour ses vêtements chic et sombres de « glunge », mélange de glamour et de grunge. Au lieu de présenter son travail de façon for-melle, il voyage dans le monde entier tout au long des années 90 pour présenter ses vêtements aux acheteurs et se constituer ainsi une impressionnante liste de clientes, parmi lesquelles Madonna et Courtney Love. Le bouche-à-oreille contri-bue à asseoir sa réputation et en 2002, le Vogue américain lui propose de spon-soriser sa collection automne/hiver, la première qu'il présente sur un vrai podium de défilé. La même année, Owens remporte le prix Perry Ellis remis aux jeunes talents par le CFDA (Council of Fashion Designers of America). En 2003, il s'installe à Paris après avoir été nommé directeur artistique du fourreur Revil-lon. Depuis, Owens et ses obscures créations ont élu domicile dans leur ville d'adoption.

LAUREN COCHRANE

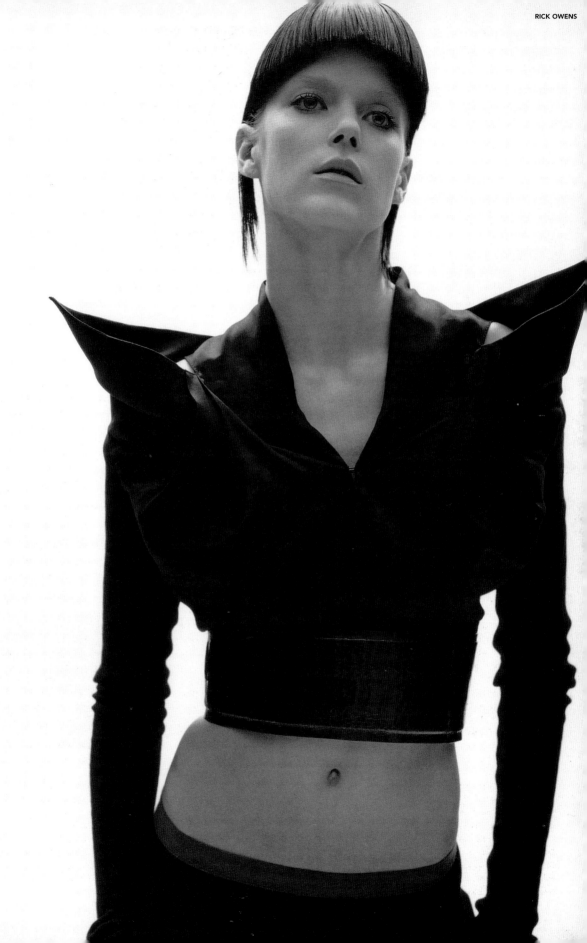

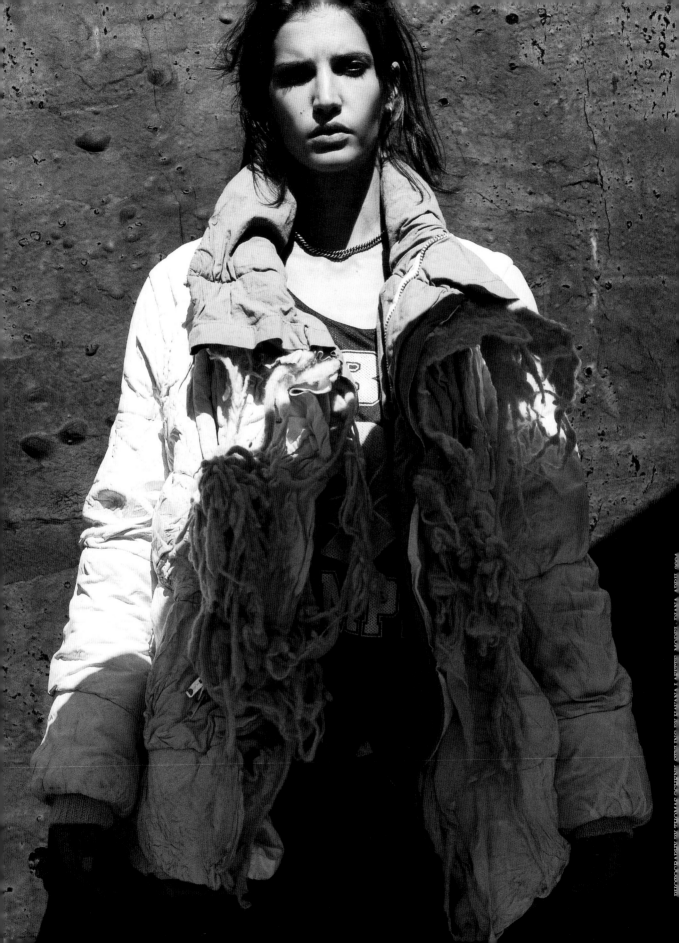

What are your signature designs? I suppose I'm best known for narrow jackets with small shoulders and long narrow sleeves, worn over draped jerseys in grey and beige, washed and aged leathers and cashmeres **What is your favourite piece from any of your collections?** I once had Lemarie, the famous French feather house, turn pearl-grey vulture feathers into a coat that was like wearing a fog... **How would you describe your work?** Frankenstein and Garbo falling in love in a leather bar... **What's your ultimate goal?** Frankly, I try to appreciate where I am; I have a lot to learn and a lot to improve but being in a position where I'm able to create is more than my fair share **What inspires you?** I recharge my batteries by looking at architecture and furniture designers: Oscar Niemeyer, Piero Portaluppi, Le Corbusier, Carlo Mollino, Jo Columbo, Jean Michel Frank, are always soothing favourites **Can fashion still have a political ambition?** I've always seen fashion as a response, reaction or protest to social conditions. I'd have a hard time considering it more... **Who do you have in mind when you design?** Someone with a practical attitude; who's experienced the joy and damage that life has to offer and found a good humoured balance there **Is the idea of creative collaboration important to you?** I sincerely wish I could collaborate, but I was always such a loner, I'm afraid I'm more comfortable being a cruel dictator **Who has been the greatest influence on your career?** I had great mentors in legendary retailing pioneers who helped me out at the beginning – Charles Gallay and Maxfield in LA, Linda Dresner in New York and Maria Luisa in Paris... people with an adventurous eye who really support this business. **How have your own experiences affected your work as a designer?** Everything I do is completely autobiographical; wreckage and stillness **Which is more important in your work: the process or the product?** Without the product, it's just self-indulgence **Is designing difficult for you, if so, what drives you to continue?** I'm lucky I know what I want to do and have a place to do it. I have no patience with sensitive torture artists **Have you ever been influenced or moved by the reaction to your designs?** I remember a shy woman, uncomfortable with her body, blossoming in front of her husband while trying some things on **What's your definition of beauty?** Anyone, anyone, anyone can be wildly attractive. Fitness, grooming and an open heart can do way more than any designer dress **What's your philosophy?** A million years from now no-one will care so get over yourself **What is the most important lesson you've learned?** We're all freaks.

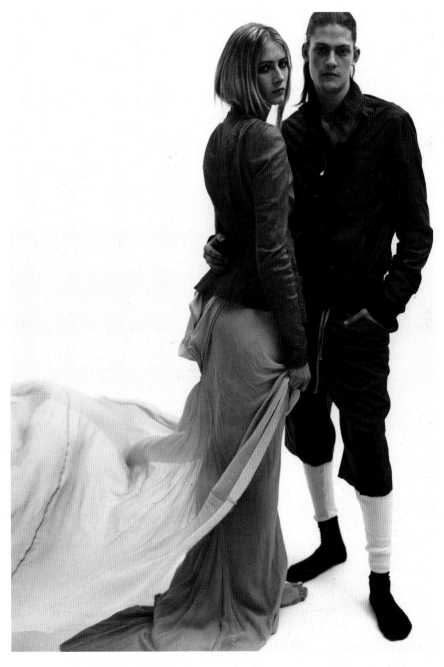

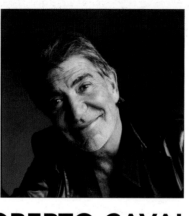

ROBERTO CAVALLI

"Nature is my main source of inspiration — I will never stop taking hints from what I call 'the greatest artist'"

Roberto Cavalli (born 1940, Florence) designs some of the most glamorous clothes in fashion: baroque combinations of exotic feathers, overblown florals, animal prints and incredibly lightweight leathers comprise the signature Cavalli look for day or night, which is always shown on his Milan runway atop the highest heels and with the biggest, blow-dried hair in the city. In winter collections, fur – the more extravagant the better – is dominant. And to think it all started on a ping-pong table. This is where, as a student at Florence's Academy of Art, Cavalli first began to experiment with printing on leather, later patenting a similar technique. The son of a tailor and the grandson of a revered painter (of the Macchiaioli movement), Cavalli is an expert embellisher and decorator of textiles. After founding his own fashion company in the early '60s, Cavalli was one of the first to put leather on a catwalk, patchworking it together for his debut show in 1972, which was staged at the Palazzo Pitti in Florence. Cavalli was an outsider to high fashion during the '80s, but staged a remarkable comeback in the '90s. In this renaissance period, Cavalli has become the label of choice among the R&B aristocracy, not to mention any starlet with both the bravado and the body to carry off one of his attention-seeking frocks. Assisted by his second wife Eva Düringer, a former Miss Universe, Cavalli brought his distinctive look – a unique combination of thrusting sex appeal, artisanal prints and frankly eccentric themes and catwalk shows – to the Milan collections, where press and clients alike received him with open arms. The collections bearing his name now include Just Cavalli, a menswear line, a childrenswear line and perfume licences, among others. In 2003 his company scored a turnover of € 289 million and its collections are distributed in over 30 countries. Cavalli also owns one of Italy's best racehorse stud farms.

Der 1940 in Florenz geborene Roberto Cavalli entwirft einige der glamourösesten Modekreationen überhaupt: Barocke Kombinationen aus exotischen Federn, schwülstigen Blumenmustern, Raubtier-Prints und unglaublich leichten Ledersorten ergeben zusammen den typischen Cavalli-Look für den Tag und den Abend. Präsentiert wird dieser ausschließlich auf dem Mailänder Catwalk des Designers, mit allerhöchsten Absätzen und den voluminösesten Fönfrisuren der ganzen Stadt. In den Winterkollektionen dominiert Pelz – je extravaganter desto besser. Kaum zu glauben, dass das alles auf einer Tischtennisplatte angefangen hat. Doch genau dort begann Cavalli als Student der florentinischen Kunstakademie mit dem Bedrucken von Leder zu experimentieren. Später ließ er sich diese Technik sogar patentieren. Als Sohn eines Schneiders und Enkel eines geachteten Malers (aus der Macchiaioli-Schule) ist Cavalli ein begnadeter Verschönerer und Dekorateur von Textilien. Nachdem er in den frühen 1960er Jahren seine eigene Modefirma gegründet hatte, war er einer der Ersten, der Leder auf den Laufsteg brachte. Für seine Debütschau von 1972 im Palazzo Pitti in Florenz nähte er es im Patchworkstil zusammen. Die 1980er Jahre erlebte er als

Außenseiter der Haute Couture, in den 1990er Jahren gelang ihm jedoch ein beachtliches Comeback. Im Zuge dieser Renaissance avancierte Cavalli zum Lieblingslabel der R&B-Stars, gar nicht zu reden von den zahlreichen Starlets, die die Courage und den Körper besaßen, eines von seinen Aufsehen erregenden Kleidern zu tragen. Unterstützt von seiner zweiten Frau, der ehemaligen Miss Universum, Eva Düringer, brachte Cavalli seinen unverwechselbaren Look – eine Kombination aus offensivem Sexappeal, künstlerischen Mustern sowie exzentrischen Themen – in Mailand heraus, wo ihn Presse und Publikum mit offenen Armen empfingen. Zu den Labels unter seinem Namen zählen inzwischen u. a. Just Cavalli, eine Herrenlinie, eine Kinderkollektion und eine Parfümlizenz. 2003 machte das Unternehmen 289 Millionen Euro Umsatz mit dem Vertrieb der Kollektionen in mehr als 30 Ländern. Cavalli besitzt übrigens auch eines der besten italienischen Gestüte für Rennpferde.

Roberto Cavalli (né en 1940 à Florence) dessine certains des vêtements les plus glamour de la mode : combinaisons baroques de plumes exotiques, motifs de fleurs géantes, imprimés d'animaux et cuirs incroyablement légers composent son look signature pour le jour ou le soir, toujours présenté sur les podiums milanais par des mannequins haut perchées sur leurs talons et coiffées des brushings les plus flamboyants de la ville. Ses collections d'hiver font la part belle à la fourrure, toujours plus extravagante. Tout a commencé sur la table de ping-pong où l'étudiant de l'Académie des Beaux-Arts de Florence s'essayait à l'impression sur cuir, une technique qu'il finira par faire breveter. Fils de tailleur et petit-fils d'un illustre peintre (du mouvement Macchiaioli), Roberto Cavalli excelle dans l'embellissement et la décoration des textiles. Après la création de sa propre griffe au début des années 60, Cavalli fait figure de précurseur en proposant du cuir travaillé sous forme de patchworks pour son premier défilé donné au Palazzo Pitti de Florence en 1972. Pendant les années 80, Cavalli se marginalise un peu par rapport à la mode haut de gamme, mais fait un retour remarqué dans les années 90. Pendant cette période de renaissance, Cavalli devient la griffe de prédilection des stars du R&B, sans oublier toutes les starlettes assez courageuses et bien roulées pour oser porter ses robes scandaleuses. Epaulé par sa seconde épouse Eva Düringer, une ex-Miss Univers, Cavalli présente son look original (une combinaison unique entre sex-appeal explosif, imprimés artisanaux, thématiques et défilés franchement excentriques) aux collections milanaises, où la presse comme les acheteurs l'accueillent à bras ouverts. Les collections qu'il signe de son nom incluent désormais Just Cavalli, une ligne pour homme, une ligne pour enfant et des licences de parfums, entre autres. En 2003, son entreprise a réalisé un chiffre d'affaires de 289 millions d'euros, avec des collections distribuées dans plus de 30 pays à travers le monde. Cavalli possède également l'un des plus beaux haras de chevaux de course d'Italie.

SUSIE RUSHTON

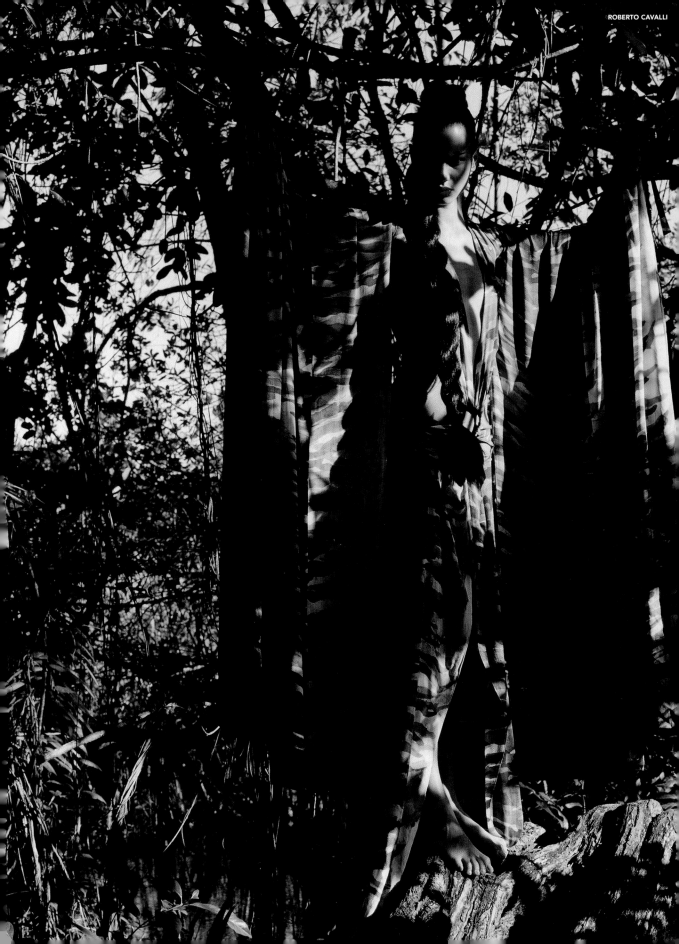

ROBERTO CAVALLI

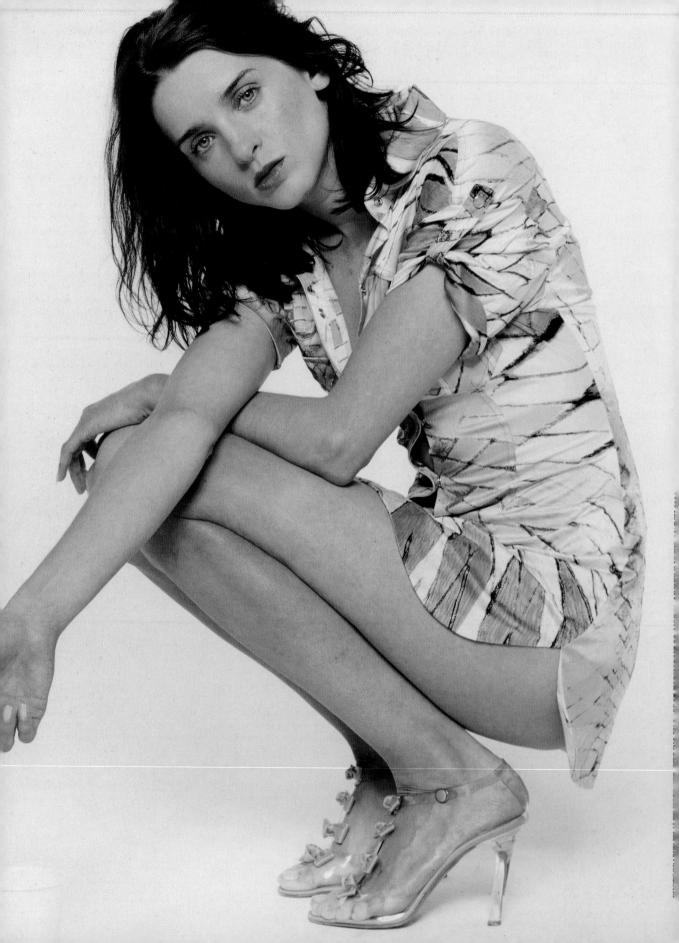

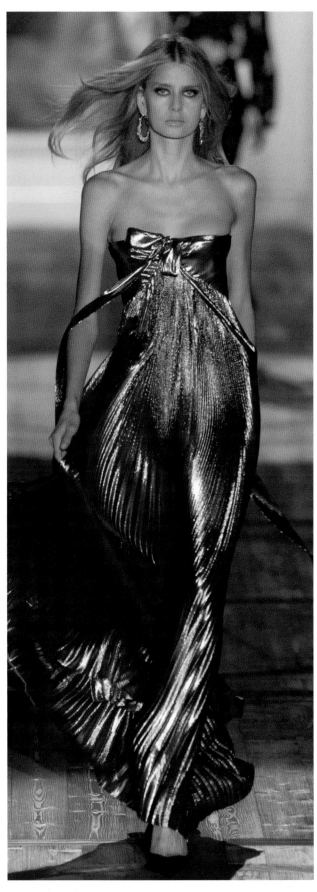

What are your signature designs? It is a skilful mixture of innovation, technology, cheerful fantasies and well-fitted cuts. My experiments on prints together with Eva's ability in setting them off with the right cut made Roberto Cavalli well known for its feminine, elegant, unique fashion **What is your favourite piece from any of your collections?** It is really difficult to choose. If I have to select I am particularly attached to the first patchwork jeans I designed, an experiment that led to a big success. As I started matching denim with leather, I could say I will always consider them my favourite materials **How would you describe your work?** Highly creative, elaborate, innovative, only one of its kind **What's your ultimate goal?** I will keep on expanding my commercial network following the openings of recent months… an early 18th century edifice at the corner of rue Cambon and St Honoré in Paris, dedicated to innovative fashion: a Roberto Cavalli Palazzo in the heart of haute couture! I will also produce, together with Dino De Laurentiis, a film. An ambitious venture based on a Italian literature's masterpiece: Giovanni Boccaccio's 'Decamerone' **What inspires you?** Nature is the main source of inspiration with its multicoloured animal coats, flowers, landscapes… I will never stop taking hints from what I call "the greatest artist". Also Eva is my muse. She is my wife, the mother of my children and she is the only person able to interpret my dream and my ideas **Can fashion still have a political ambition?** I believe that fashion has partially lost its political ambition. Just think about the difference between the folk fashion in the '70s and the ethnic trend of the last period: while in the past it meant a radical rebellion against the institution, nowadays it represents a charming journey towards unexplored territories in search of new vibes **Who do you have in mind when you design?** When I design I have in mind sunny people: that love life, nature and love; women or men who like to express their strong personality through my colours and my print **Is the idea of creative collaboration important to you?** Yes, it is very important but at the same time very difficult to reach. I thank my lucky stars that I met my wife Eva: we have a wonderful mutual understanding in both, our private and professional life **Who has been the greatest** influence on your career? Painting has been one of the greatest influences in my career. Following in my grandfather's path, I attended the Academy of Art… in a sense my way was already marked out **How have your own experiences affected your work as a designer?** In fact, my devotion to my job was from a personal defeat: my first girlfriend's parents rejected me because I was neither rich nor attending university. I was really in love with her and this hurt me deeply. Therefore I decided I would demonstrate to them what a big mistake they have made! **Which is more important in your work: the process or the product?** It is very difficult to choose. While creating I am completely absorbed by the process: testing new prints, designing original cuts, searching for fabrics. But I don't leave the final product out of consideration: if I am not satisfied with it, even though I have experimented with new fabulous techniques, I step back and start again **Is designing difficult for you, if so, what drives you to continue?** Fortunately not: it comes spontaneously **Have you ever been influenced or moved by the reaction to your designs?** No, I have never been influenced by the reaction to my designs. Fashion is my way of translating art: I cannot think of market rules directing my creative process **What's your definition of beauty?** Beauty is something coming from the inside; it is a reflection of the personality. This is the reason why, unlike the good looks, it does not grow old **What's your philosophy?** My philosophy is to live day by day **What is the most important lesson you've learned?** I have learned that somehow you have to adapt yourself to the circumstances. I am a Scorpio: if I had not been so stubborn, probably I would have been successful 20 years ago. At that time I did not feel like being a personality and attending parties all the time: maybe because I refused to wear a tuxedo… or maybe because I was too shy. Afterwards I have realised that people expect a designer to be recognisable: his face, the story of his life, his opinions are as much important as his creations. I have started to organise beautiful parties and I have taken a liking to it: I really enjoy the idea that people have a good time! But you know what? Now I am criticised because my parties are "too much". Sometimes life is funny!

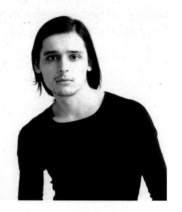

ROCHAS

"My favourite pieces from any of my collections are the ones closest to perfection" OLIVIER THEYSKENS

Olivier Theyskens remains one of fashion's most enigmatic characters. Since arriving on the scene in 1998, swathed in an air of dark mystery, he has produced nine collections to date – most recently for the prestigious French house Rochas – and attracted high profile fans, including Madonna, Nicole Kidman and Melissa Auf der Maur. Born in Brussels in 1977, Theyskens dropped out of the city's Ecole Nationale Supérieure des Arts Visuels de la Cambre in 1997 before presenting his debut collection, 'Gloomy Trips', later that year. Living in a 19th-century brothel and collecting stuffed animal heads at the time, his decidedly Gothic reputation was established from the start; the first collection included clothes embroidered with human hair and voluminous Victorian governess-style dresses (including one worn by Madonna in her 'Frozen' video). The following few seasons saw the Belgian adding a lighter, more romantic tone to his vision and also taking a creative break to restructure his studio. After much speculation over his future (the designer famously turned down the role of creative director at Givenchy), Theyskens was appointed artistic director of Rochas and, in March 2003, presented his first show for the esteemed house. Playing on the unique themes and signature styles of Marcel Rochas – chantilly lace, the colour pink, an emphasis on tailoring and evening gowns – the collection also pursued his own attention to volume. With a further three collections to date, Theyskens continues to respectfully move the house forward. Whilst remaining true to Maison Rochas' original couture spirit, the 27-year-old is nonetheless attempting to develop new representations of femininity and elegance. In March 2004, Theyskens was also appointed artistic director of Rochas Fragrances. His work has also been exhibited in various international exhibitions, including 'Belgian Fashion Designers' at the Fashion Institute of Technology museum in New York.

Olivier Theyskens ist nach wie vor einer der rätselhaftesten Charaktere der Modebranche. Seit er 1998 erstmals auf den Plan trat, umgeben von einer düster-geheimnisvollen Aura, hat der kamerascheue Designer neun Kollektionen produziert – zuletzt für das angesehene französische Modehaus Rochas – und damit höchst prominente Fans wie Madonna, Nicole Kidman und Melissa Auf der Maur angezogen. 1977 in Brüssel geboren, verließ Theyskens die dortige Ecole Nationale Supérieure des Arts Visuels de la Cambre 1997 ohne Abschluss. Allerdings präsentierte er noch im selben Jahr seine Debütkollektion „Gloomy Trips". Da er in einem ehemaligen Bordell aus dem 19. Jahrhundert lebte und ausgestopfte Tierköpfe sammelte, brauchte er sich von Beginn an um sein Gothic-Image nicht zu sorgen. Zur ersten Kollektion gehörten Stücke, die mit Menschenhaar bestickt waren, sowie voluminöse Kleider im Stil viktorianischer Gouvernanten (Madonna trug eines davon in ihrem Video „Frozen"). In den folgenden Saisons schlug der Belgier etwas hellere, romantischere Töne an und nahm sich auch eine kreative Auszeit, um sein Atelier neu zu strukturieren. Nach vielen Spekulationen über seine Zukunft (Aufsehen erregte seine Ableh-

nung des Chefdesigner-Postens bei Givenchy) wurde Theyskens künstlerischer Direktor des angesehenen Hauses Rochas, für das er im März 2003 seine erste Schau präsentierte. Darin waren die typischen Themen und Stilelemente von Marcel Rochas zu sehen – Chantilly-Spitze, die Farbe Rosa, großes Augenmerk auf Maßschneiderei und Abendroben –, es kam aber auch Theyskens' Vorliebe für Volumen zum Tragen. In den bislang drei weiteren Kollektionen bringt der Designer die Traditionsmarke respektvoll nach vorn. Während er dem echten Couture-Geist von Maison Rochas treu bleibt, versucht der 27-Jährige zugleich, neue Ausdrucksformen von Weiblichkeit und Eleganz zu entwickeln. Im März 2004 wurde Theyskens zusätzlich künstlerischer Direktor von Rochas Fragrances. Seine Arbeiten waren schon bei verschiedenen internationalen Ausstellungen zu sehen, unter anderem im Rahmen von „Belgian Fashion Designers" im Museum des Fashion Institute of Technology in New York.

Olivier Theyskens reste l'un des personnages les plus énigmatiques de la mode. Depuis ses débuts en 1998, ce créateur qui fuit les caméras d'un air mystérieux a produit neuf collections, dont récemment pour la prestigieuse maison française Rochas, et suscité l'admiration de célèbres fans tels que Madonna, Nicole Kidman et Melissa Auf der Maur. Né en 1977 à Bruxelles, Olivier Theyskens sort diplômé de l'Ecole Nationale Supérieure des Arts Visuels de la Cambre en 1997 avant de présenter sa première collection, « Gloomy Trips », un peu plus tard la même année. A l'époque, comme il vit dans un bordel du XIX{e} siècle et collectionne les têtes d'animaux empaillés, sa réputation résolument gothique est vite forgée ; sa première collection présente des vêtements brodés de vrais poils et des robes volumineuses dignes des gouvernantes de l'ère victorienne (dont une sera portée par Madonna dans son clip « Frozen »). Les saisons suivantes, le créateur belge atténue sa vision d'un ton plus léger et romantique et interrompt temporairement ses activités créatives pour se consacrer à la restructuration de son atelier. Après moult spéculations au sujet de son avenir (personne n'a oublié son célèbre refus de travailler pour Givenchy), Olivier Theyskens est nommé directeur artistique de Rochas et signe son premier défilé pour la grande maison en mars 2003. Jouant sur les thèmes uniques et les styles signature de Marcel Rochas (la dentelle chantilly, la couleur rose, la part belle accordée aux tailleurs et aux robes du soir), la collection témoigne également de son attention caractéristique aux volumes. Avec trois autres collections à ce jour, Olivier Theyskens continue à propulser la marque dans le futur tout en respectant son héritage. Bien qu'il reste fidèle à l'esprit haute couture original de la Maison Rochas, le jeune créateur de 27 ans essaie néanmoins de développer de nouvelles représentations de la féminité et de l'élégance. En mars 2004, Olivier Theyskens est également nommé directeur artistique des Parfums Rochas. Son travail a été présenté dans plusieurs expositions internationales, notamment lors de l'expo « Belgian Fashion Designers » organisée au musée du Fashion Institute of Technology de New York.

GLENN WALDRON

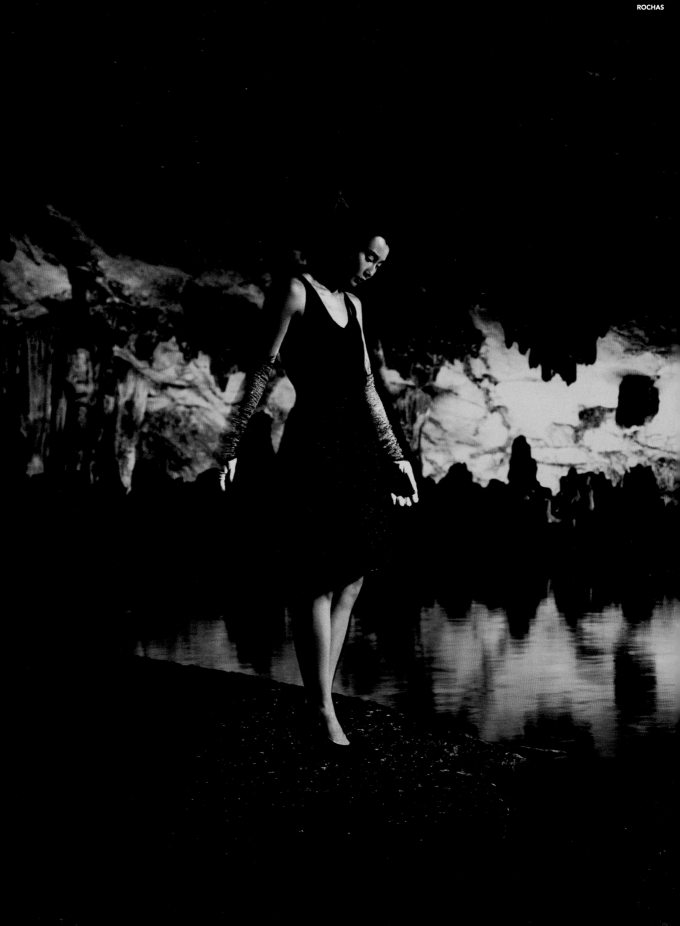

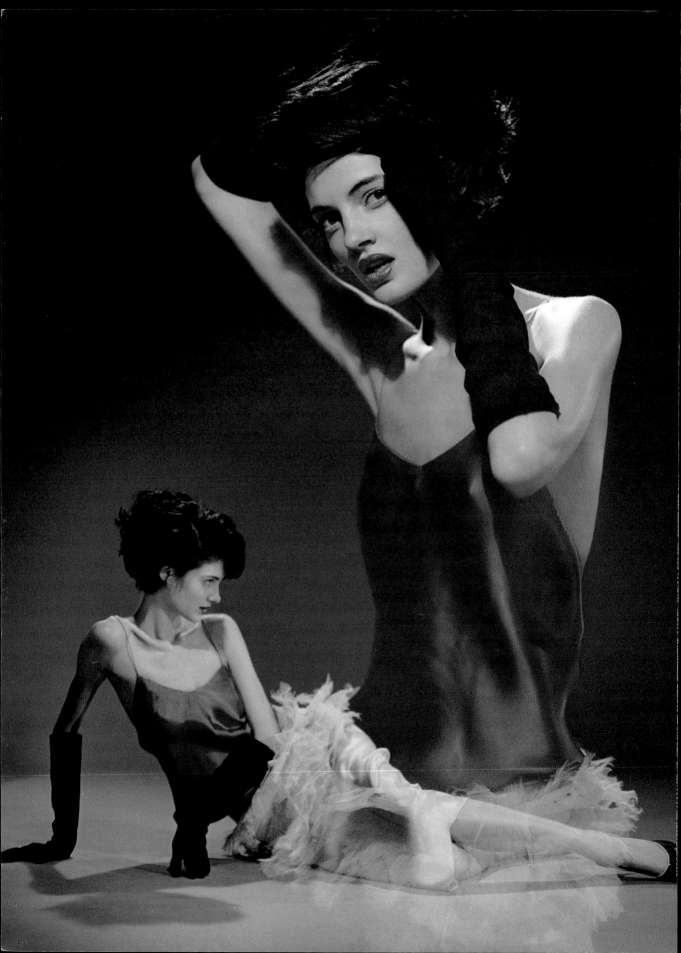

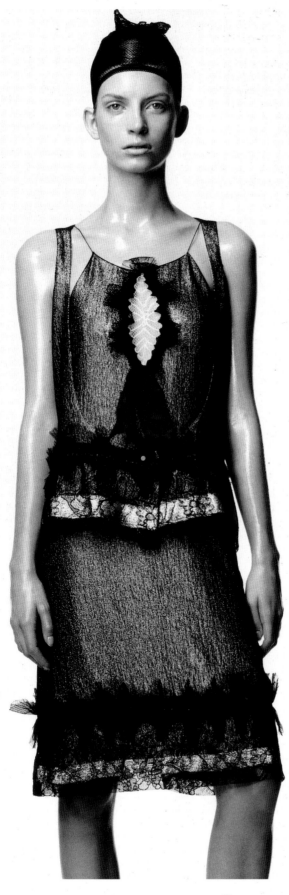

What are your signature designs? I love super-achieved garments, from simple to ultra-sophisticated. They all should match and have a sort of "Theyskenian" attitude **What is your favourite piece from any of your collection?** My favourite pieces are the ones closest to perfection **How would you describe your work?** My work is to design Fashion and to create Style. I particularly focus on the interaction between my aesthetics and an attitude that is presented at the right moment **What's your ultimate goal?** Bringing something strong and ultra-positive **What inspires you?** My childhood has a great influence. Everything I have seen at that time, I have it now inside of me. I am also stimulated by any sort of media and by the women around me. **Can fashion still have a political ambition?** As fashion designers, we're obviously reacting to our environment (even if you're denying it by escaping reality). Then we're expressing a certain point of view which can be considered as social and political **Who do you have in mind when you design?** I rarely have a particular person in mind but sometimes it could happen **Is the idea of creative collaboration important to you?** Not necessarily **Who has been the greatest influence on your career?** More a vision of women but it evolves all the time! **How have your own experiences affected your work as a designer?** My daily life and what happens all around move my approach of design in general **Which is the more important in your work: the process or the products?** The product and the process are one for me because you have to to deal with the little differences between what you think, what you draw and what you have in your hands and put on the body **Is designing difficult for you if so, what drives you to continue?** It is difficult when you are really demanding with yourself. I don't accept mediocrity and I don't hesitate to walk on the exigent way of work **Have you ever been influenced or moved by the reaction to your designs?** I have been disturbed sometimes **What's your definition of beauty?** When I see something really beautiful, I may cry about it. It doesn't happen really often. I am still critical and cynical about what I see **What's your philosophy?** My philosophy is to learn and to leave bad things behind. You learn and forget. What's interesting is to have a lot of experiences, things that press you on to a higher level in your own humanity and in your own thinking. But things have to be good, not bad. And people also **What is most important lesson you've learned?** Not to trust good-looking people… and also bad-looking people because, in life, you may grow by yourself but you cannot underestimate the importance of the people that are around you. This is so important, to have good people around you.

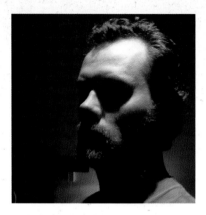

ROGAN

"Why not choose to buy clothes made of responsible materials?"

ROGAN GREGORY

The brainchild of sculptor and furniture-maker Rogan Gregory, New York-based design company Rogan prides itself on creating easy, intelligent clothing for individuals with a distinct, modern style. With an emphasis on form, function and wearability, Rogan is the kind of company that gives its customers exactly what they need – essential clothing that borrows the most innovative ideas from the past and melds them with contemporary advancements in design and a thoroughly avant-garde minimalism. Heavily inspired by Americana, Rogan takes the staples of classic workwear such as denim, T-shirts, canvas trousers and work shirts, and rethinks them for today's market. A tailored suit is recreated in workwear fabrics to emphasise Rogan's progressive approach to traditional items and the company's intention to reassess the core items of American apparel. Rogan Gregory's background in art and furniture design is an obvious influence on the design and finish of the company's clothing. Gregory often gives his fabrics added surface interest by using abrasion techniques to expose the yarn in materials – a technique he also uses in his sculptures to expose the grain of the wood. The effects of everyday wear and tear are integral to the company's finished pieces. Rogan eschews branding, preferring to provide subtle labelling inside the garments, and also produces a range of exclusive furniture and sculpture.

Die Erfindung des Bildhauers und Möbelbauers Rogan Gregory, das Design-unternehmen Rogan mit Sitz in New York, ist stolz auf ihre lässige, intelligente Mode für Individualisten mit einer speziellen, modernen Eleganz. Mit ihren Schwerpunkten Form, Funktion und Tragbarkeit ist Rogan die Art von Marke, die ihren Kunden exakt das liefert, was sie brauchen – Basics, deren innovative Ideen größtenteils aus der Vergangenheit stammen, sich aber mit den aktuellen Fortschritten beim Design und einem absolut avantgardistischen Minimalismus verbinden. Stark inspiriert von Amerikana, nimmt sich Rogan stapelweise klassische Arbeitskleidung wie Jeans, T-Shirts, Segeltuchhosen und Arbeitshemden vor und erfindet sie für den gegenwärtigen Markt neu. Da unterstreicht ein aus Arbeitskleidungsstoff genähter klassischer Anzug Rogans progressive Einstel-

lung zu klassischen Kleidungsstücken und die Zielsetzung der Firma, amerika-nische Modeklassiker neu zu bewerten. Rogan Gregorys beruflicher Hintergrund in der Kunst und im Möbeldesign hat deutlichen Einfluss auf Schnitt und Finish der Kleider seines Unternehmens. Oft betont der Designer die Oberflächen seiner Stoffe durch Abschleifmethoden, die das Garn des jeweiligen Materials sichtbar machen – diese Technik verwendet er auch bei seinen Skulpturen, etwa damit die Struktur des Holzes erkennbar wird. Der Effekt der alltäglichen Abnutzung spielt in der Vollendung der Entwürfe eine entscheidende Rolle. Rogan scheut den Markenkult und bevorzugt dezente Hinweise auf das Label in den Kleidungsstücken. Gregory produziert außerdem eine exklusive Möbelkollektion sowie Skulpturen.

Créée par le sculpteur et designer de meubles Rogan Gregory, la griffe new-yor-kaise Rogan se targue de créer des vêtements faciles et intelligents pour les indivi-dus au style de vie original et moderne. Avant tout axée sur la forme, la fonc-tion et la portabilité, Rogan est le genre d'entreprise qui offre à ses clients exactement ce dont ils ont besoin : des basiques qui reprennent les plus grandes innovations du passé pour les fusionner aux derniers développements de la mode et à un minimalisme résolument avant-gardiste. Largement inspiré par le style country, Rogan réinvente les bases de la mode utilitaire classique tels que le denim, les T-shirts, les pantalons en toile et les chemises de travail à l'atten-tion du marché d'aujourd'hui. Un tailleur sera reproduit dans des tissus utili-taires pour souligner l'approche progressiste de Rogan envers les articles tradi-tionnels et son intention de revisiter les basiques de la garde-robe américaine. La carrière de Rogan Gregory dans l'art et le design influence de façon évidente la conception et la finition des créations de sa griffe. Il attire souvent l'attention sur la texture apparente de ses tissus à l'aide de techniques d'abrasion qui révè-lent le fil des matières : une méthode qu'il utilise également dans ses sculptures pour exposer le grain du bois. Les effets quotidiens de l'usure jouent un rôle cru-cial dans les créations de la griffe. Rogan n'aime pas les logos et préfère griffer ses vêtements d'une discrète étiquette intérieure. La marque produit également une gamme de meubles luxueux et une collection de sculptures. STEVE COOK

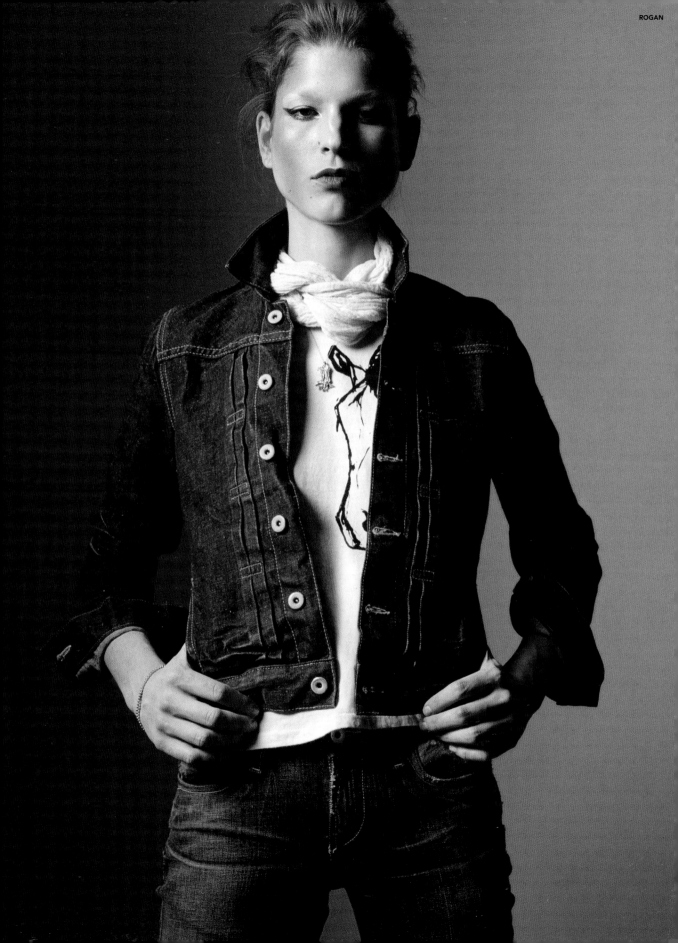

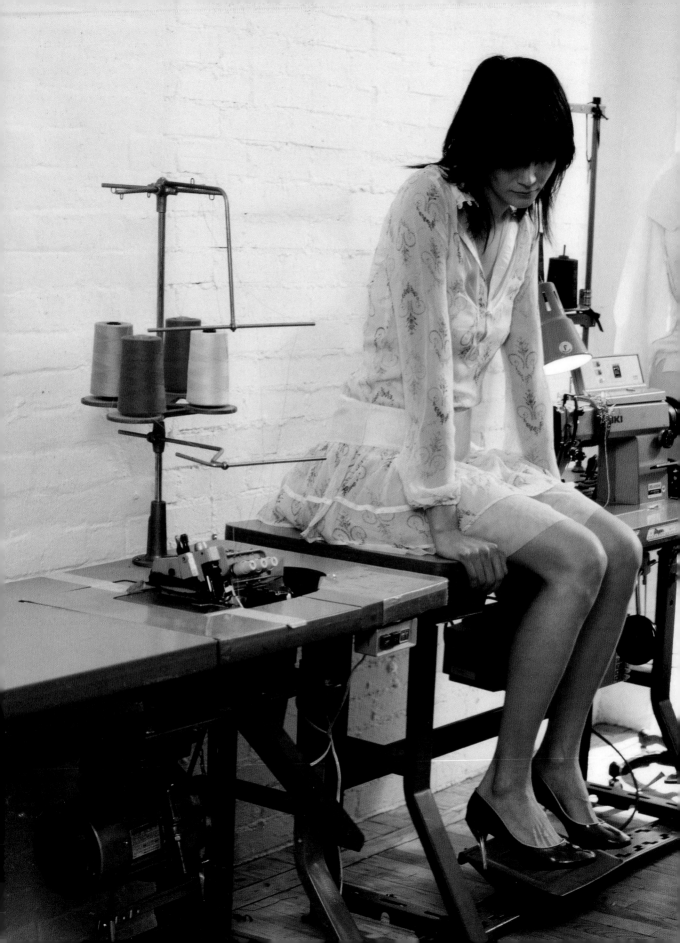

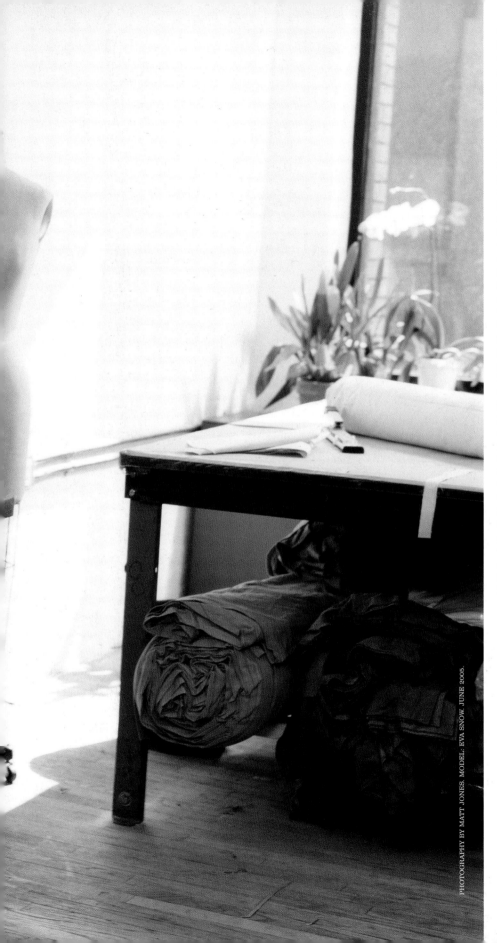

What are your signature designs? Best known for denim-related workwear I think **How would you describe your work?** Uncompromising **What's your ultimate goal?** Create an environment where people I respect can create good shit and have a laugh **What inspires you?** Trees, dogs, ocean, individuals, ladies, garbage, fabric, evolution, metamorphosis, erosion **Can fashion still have a political ambition?** Oh yeah, there has to be more to life than the daily rat race. It's time to pay attention to what is happening around us. The health of the planet and the people living on it is in jeopardy. You can make a difference by what you choose to purchase and the lifestyle you choose to lead. Why not choose to buy clothes made of responsible materials and manufactured by responsible people. We have a responsibility to future generations to take care of the planet one step at a time **Who do you have in mind when you design?** Various acquaintances of mine **Is the idea of creative collaboration important to you?** Yes. I enjoy working with smart people **Who has been the greatest influence on your career?** My father… he does not follow a conventional thought process, which rubbed off on me **Which is more important in your work: the process or the product?** Some day I will have enough time to enjoy the process – until then, the product is paramount **Is designing difficult for you, if so, what drives you to continue?** Designing is the easy part. I'll never get bored of designing. Getting it produced is the difficult part **Have you ever been influenced or moved by the reaction to your designs?** Some people notice the barely detectable little details. I always seem to get along with those types **What's your definition of beauty?** Beauty is hard to define in words. I see it everywhere **What is the most important lesson you've learned?** Keep your eye on the ball.

PHOTOGRAPHY BY MATT JONES. MODEL: EVA SNOW. JUNE 2005.

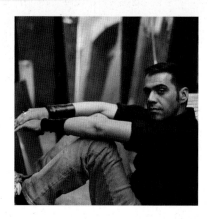

ROLAND MOURET

"My ultimate goal is to build a fashion house that outlives me"

When Roland Mouret (born 1961) set up his label in 1998, he was no newcomer to fashion. Then aged 36, the butcher's son from Lourdes had previous experience as a model, art director and stylist in Paris and London. While Jean Paul Gaultier, Paris Glamour and i-D are namechecked on his stylist CV, he had little experience of making clothes, with only two years at fledgling label People Corporation under his belt. His first collection of fifteen one-off pieces threw the need for patterns out of the window. Instead, the critically acclaimed garments were put together using skilful draping and strategically placed hatpins. While his method may have become more refined with subsequent collections, Mouret's motto remains the same: "It all starts from a square of fabric". Inspired by folds, Mouret makes staggeringly beautiful clothes with the minimum of fuss. This formula has been hugely successful. His label is stocked all over the world in high profile stores including Harrods and Bergdorf Goodman. As well as the clothing line, it now includes rough diamond jewellery line RM Rough and the recently introduced cruise collection. Since 2003, the London-based designer has chosen to show in New York and such a move has seen more Mouret on the red carpet. The fashion world is just as devoted as his celebrity clientele. Mouret's work has been acknowledged with a Vidal Sassoon Cutting Edge award and the Elle Style Awards named him British Designer of the Year in 2002.

Als der 1961 geborene Roland Mouret 1998 sein Label gründete, war er in der Mode längst kein Newcomer mehr. Der damals 36-jährige Metzgerssohn aus Lourdes hatte bereits Erfahrungen als Model, Art Director und Stylist in Paris und London gesammelt. Während Jean Paul Gaultier, Paris Glamour und i-D in seiner Stylisten-Vita auftauchten, hatte er mit lediglich zwei Jahren beim Anfänger-Label People Corporation wenig Erfahrung in der Produktion von Kleidern. Bei seiner ersten Kollektion, die aus 15 Unikaten bestand, scherte er sich überhaupt nicht um Schnittmuster. Stattdessen wurden die von der Kritik hoch gelobten Kleider durch kunstvolle Drapierungen und strategisch platzierte Hutnadeln zusammengehalten. Und auch wenn sich seine Methoden in den folgenden Kollektionen etwas verfeinert haben, bleibt Mourets Motto doch unverändert: „Alles beginnt mit einem quadratischen Stück Stoff." Von der Faltkunst animiert, erzeugt der Designer mit minimalem Aufwand umwerfend schöne Kleider. Diese

Formel erwies sich als überaus erfolgreich. Sein Label ist überall auf der Welt in Nobelkaufhäusern wie Harrods und Bergdorf Goodman vertreten. Zur Kleiderlinie kommt inzwischen noch Schmuck aus Rohdiamanten unter dem Namen RM Rough hinzu sowie die kürzlich präsentierte Cruise Collection. Seit 2003 präsentiert der in London lebende Designer seine Kreationen in New York und ist dadurch auch öfter auf den roten Teppichen dieser Welt vertreten. Die Modewelt verehrt ihn ebenso wie seine prominente Klientel. Seine Arbeit wurde bereits mit dem Vidal Sassoon Cutting Edge ausgezeichnet. Bei den Elle Style Awards war er 2002 British Designer of the Year.

Quand Roland Mouret (né en 1961) lance sa griffe en 1998, ce n'est déjà plus un débutant. Alors âgé de 36 ans, ce fils de boucher venu de Lourdes a déjà travaillé comme mannequin, directeur artistique et styliste à Paris et à Londres. Bien que Jean Paul Gaultier, le Glamour français et le magazine i-D figurent sur son CV de styliste, il ne possède pratiquement aucune expérience de la création de mode, avec seulement deux années de travail pour la bébé griffe People Corporation à son actif. Composée de quinze pièces uniques, sa première collection prouve qu'on peut créer des vêtements sans utiliser de patrons. En fait, ces pièces saluées par la critique sont assemblées à l'aide de drapés experts et d'épingles à chapeau stratégiquement placées. Bien qu'il ait affiné sa méthode au fil des collections, la devise de Mouret reste la même : « Tout commence à partir d'un carré de tissu. » Inspiré par les plis, Mouret propose des vêtements d'une beauté renversante et pourtant extrêmement simples, une formule qui s'avère largement gagnante. Sa griffe est vendue dans le monde entier par des magasins haut de gamme tels que Harrods et Bergdorf Goodman. Outre sa ligne de vêtements, Mouret propose aujourd'hui la gamme de bijoux en diamants bruts RM Rough, ainsi qu'une collection d'inspiration marine lancée récemment. Depuis 2003, le créateur désormais basé à Londres préfère défiler à New York, ce qui explique pourquoi on peut admirer de plus en plus de créations signées Mouret sur les tapis rouges de Hollywood. Et l'univers de la mode lui est tout aussi dévoué que ses célèbres clientes : son travail a été honoré d'un prix Vidal Sassoon Cutting Edge et les Elle Style Awards l'ont couronné British Designer of the Year en 2002.

LAUREN COCHRANE

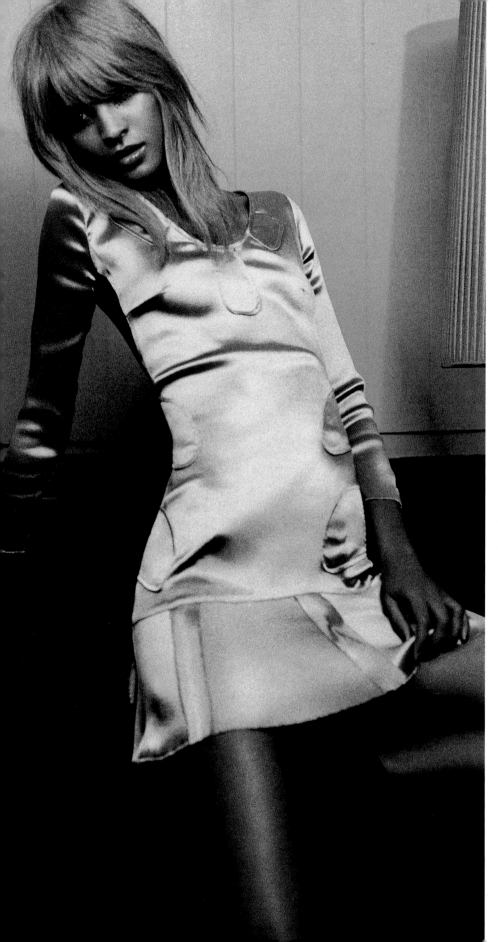

What are your signature designs? Draping, folding and the sensual relationship between fabric and the skin **How would you describe your work?** It is a necessity for me **What's your ultimate goal?** To build a fashion house that outlives me **What inspires you?** People's strengths and weaknesses **Can fashion still have a political ambition?** For me fashion is more about social politics than a political ambition **Who do you have in mind when you design?** Skin, movement and memories **Is the idea of creative collaboration important to you?** Yes, because it challenges my own perceptions **Who has been the greatest influence on your career?** Many women and few men – from my grandmother, who first placed a needle in my hand, to my business partner who allowed me to not just be a dressmaker **How have your own experiences affected your work as a designer?** My work allows me to provide without words the answers to my childhood questions **Which is more important in your work: the process or the product?** It is a bitter sweet relationship – you can't love without the reality of pain **Is designing difficult for you, if so, what drives you to continue?** Ask the same question to an athlete – yes, of course it is, but you have to continue, the way you have to keep breathing **Have you ever been influenced or moved by the reaction to your designs?** It's always emotional when my vision becomes part of the public domain **What's your definition of beauty?** Imperfect, unique, a raw diamond **What's your philosophy?** You are a good master when you are a good slave **What is the most important lesson you've learned?** Time needs time.

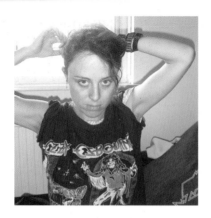

SILAS

"Our designs are very simple and understated; an important part of our philosophy is to be as unrecognisable as possible"

SOFIA PRANTERA

Adored by Japanese fashion obsessives but often ignored by the wider fashion fraternity, the Silas label is the stuff of cult legend. Taking inspiration everywhere from skate culture to high fashion, the London-based brand is best known for its simple men's knitwear and cool, understated women's styles, combining a quirky, offbeat spirit with an immediate wearability. "There's an underlying vintage feel in what we do, a bit of '70s hippie, a bit of '80s sportswear and a touch of Amerikana," explains designer Russell Waterman, who, alongside Sofia Prantera, created the label back in 1998. Initially hooking up through infamous London store Slam City Skates, the pair worked together on cult skate brand Holmes before launching out on their own. "I've never met anyone who has as deep a passion for clothes, whereas I like all the kinds of ridiculous ideas and art stuff that we use in our graphics," Waterman explains of their creative relationship. Over the past six years they have attracted a dedicated customer base for their highly covetable designs whilst also cultivating a creative stable of fellow artists, designers and collaborators, such as James Jarvis, PAM and Tonite. Achievements to date include three stand alone stores in Tokyo, Nagoya and Osaka, several touring exhibitions, an upmarket womenswear brand, Babette, and a recently launched homeware collection. Nonetheless the brand remains true to its DIY roots, refusing to sell to department stores, advertise in fashion magazines or even provide conventional catalogues for their collections. This is not, they are quick to state, a brand for children's television presenters. "If celebrities want to wear Silas they're in more of a position than most to pay for it." Colourful and quixotic, it's this fierce commitment to independence that ensures Silas's continued success.

Das Label Silas wird von vielen japanischen Fashion-Victims verehrt, von der größeren Modegemeinde jedoch meist noch ignoriert. Dabei hat es das Zeug zum Kult. Die Marke mit Sitz in London holt sich ihre Anregungen von überall her, sei es aus der Skaterszene oder der Haute Couture. Am bekanntesten sind die schlichten Stricksachen für Herren und die coole, auf Understatement ausgerichtete Damenmode, die Extravaganz und Eigenwilligkeit mit absoluter Tragbarkeit kombiniert. „Dem, was wir tun, liegt ein Vintage-Feeling zugrunde, ein bisschen Hippie der Siebziger, ein bisschen Sportswear der Achtziger und ein Touch Amerikana", erklärt der Designer Russell Waterman, der das Label gemeinsam mit Sofia Prantera 1998 gegründet hat. Kennen gelernt haben sich die beiden über den berüchtigten Londoner Laden Slam City Skates. Zusammen arbeitete das Paar vor der Selbstständigkeit für Holmes, die Kultmarke der Skater. „Ich kenne niemanden mit einer größeren Leidenschaft für Kleidung. Mir dagegen liegen vor allem die witzigen Ideen und das Kunstzeug, das wir für unsere grafischen Sachen verwenden", beschreibt Waterman ihre kreative Beziehung. Im Verlauf der letzten sechs Jahre haben die beiden einen treuen Kundenstamm für ihre heiß begehrten Entwürfe aufgebaut und auch die Zusammenar-

beit mit Künstler- und Designerkollegen wie James Jarvis, PAM und Tonite kultiviert. Zu den bisherigen Errungenschaften gehören drei unabhängige Läden in Tokio, Nagoya und Osaka, mehrere Wanderausstellungen, eine gehobene Damenkollektion namens Babette und eine kürzlich präsentierte Homeware-Kollektion. Dennoch ist man den Do-it-yourself-Wurzeln der Marke treu geblieben und verkauft nicht an Kaufhäuser, wirbt nicht in Modemagazinen und erstellt schon gar keinen konventionellen Katalog für die Kollektionen. Sie sind, wie die Macher gerne klarstellen, keine Marke für Kinder-TV-Moderatoren. „Wenn Prominente Silas tragen wollen, dann können sie es sich leichter als jeder andere leisten, dafür auch zu bezahlen." Farbenfroh und donquichotisch bekennt sich Silas energisch zu seiner Unabhängigkeit und sichert so seinen anhaltenden Erfolg.

Révérée par les fashion victims japonaises mais souvent ignorée par la grande communauté de la mode, la déjà culte griffe Silas promet d'entrer dans la légende. Puisant son inspiration partout, de la culture skate à la haute couture, la marque londonienne est surtout connue pour sa maille simple pour homme et ses vêtements cool et discrets pour femme, mêlant son étrange excentricité à un look immédiatement portable. « Il y a un côté vintage sous-jacent dans tout ce que nous faisons, un peu de hippie seventies, un peu de sportswear années 80 et même une petite touche country », explique le créateur Russell Waterman, co-fondateur de la griffe avec Sofia Prantera en 1998. Après s'être rencontrés dans la célèbre boutique londonienne Slam City Skates, ils travaillent tous deux pour la marque culte du skate, Holmes, avant de lancer leur propre griffe. « Je n'ai jamais rencontré quelqu'un qui vouait une telle passion aux vêtements, tandis que moi, j'aime toutes les idées ridicules et arty que nous utilisons dans nos graphiques », affirme Waterman à propos de leur collaboration créative. Grâce à une écurie d'artistes, de créateurs et de collaborateurs tels que James Jarvis, PAM et Tonite, leurs créations hautement désirables ont acquis à leur cause une clientèle dévouée au cours de ces six dernières années. A ce jour, la marque revendique trois boutiques indépendantes à Tokyo, Nagoya et Osaka, plusieurs expositions itinérantes, une marque de vêtements haut de gamme pour femme baptisée Babette, ainsi qu'une collection récente d'articles pour la maison. La griffe reste pourtant fidèle au « système D » de ses origines, refusant d'être vendue dans les grands magasins, de faire de la pub dans les magazines de mode et même de produire les catalogues qui accompagnent habituellement les collections. Comme ses fondateurs sont prompts à le dire, Silas n'est pas une marque qui s'adresse aux animateurs d'émissions TV pour enfants : « Si les célébrités veulent porter du Silas, elles n'ont qu'à payer. Après tout, elles en ont les moyens ». Coloré et plein d'imagination, c'est ce féroce engagement à l'indépendance qui garantit le succès continu de Silas. GLENN WALDRON

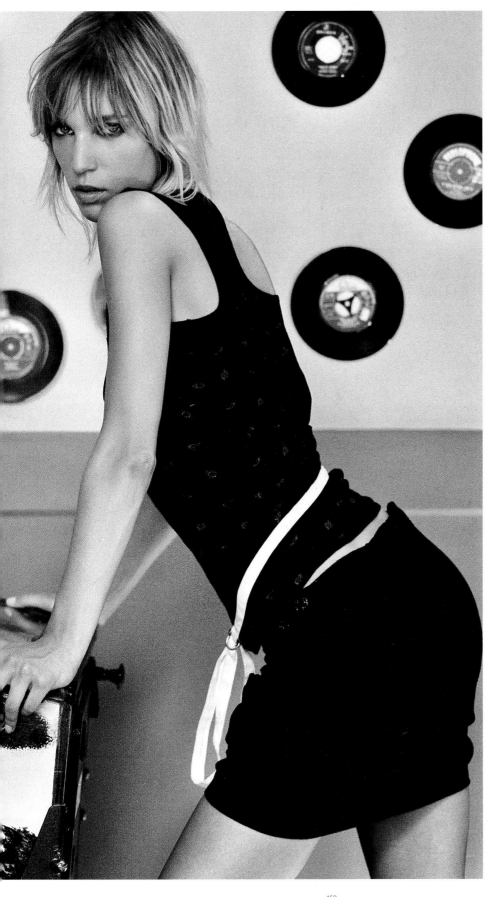

What are your signature designs? Our line is very simple and understated and an important part of the Silas philosophy is to be as unrecognisable as possible. We want our clothes to be tools for individuals to style themselves. We are probably best known for traditional British knitwear in our menswear and quirky narrow shouldered pretty puff-sleeved tops in our womenswear **What is your favourite piece from any of your collections?** Right now I love the handcrafted leather skull bag we have just produced for summer 2005, but it changes all the time as I very quickly get bored of stuff **How would you describe your work?** With great difficulty, I am afraid **What's your ultimate goal?** To have a great life **What inspires you?** Other people and their different outlook on things **Can fashion still have a political ambition?** I feel it is impossible to still make a political statement with clothes. But you can make it with the way you run your business and portray yourself, if that counts **Who do you have in mind when you design?** Someone that possibly does not exist **Is the idea of creative collaboration important to you?** Our best work comes along when Russell and I have time to sit and work together... but collaborating with new people is really important to keep moving forward, otherwise it can be very easy to become self-indulgent and sterile **Who has been the greatest influence on your career?** Probably Russell, I would not have had one without him... my mother? **How have your own experiences affected your work as a designer?** Everything I do influences my work as a designer, it is impossible to narrow it down **Which is more important in your work: the process or the product?** When you are running a business it is the product that has to be the most important. The process is important to myself and it is very personal, hard to talk about and very incoherent **Is designing difficult for you, if so, what drives you to continue?** Yes it can be, especially having to produce a new line every six months. But I need to design, as when I am not working I can become deflated and uninspired by life **Have you ever been influenced or moved by the reaction to your designs?** I am often influenced by the way people wear our clothes, when they wear them in a way I had not thought of **What's your definition of beauty?** Beauty is a fine balance between all the parts that compose an object for a person. Often the smallest detail can make something beautiful or ugly **What's your philosophy?** To be as free as possible from having to conform. We created Silas as an entity that would be independent, yet profitable, and a vehicle for any of our ideas, as weird and incoherent as they might have been **What is the most important lesson you've learned?** Don't dance with The Man.

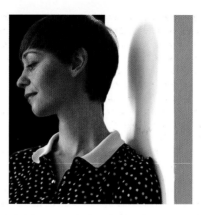

SIV STØLDAL

"I would describe my work as research into how and why people form relationships with their clothes"

Norwegian-born, London-based menswear designer Siv Støldal is part of a special crew. When she enrolled on the MA course at Central Saint Martins in 1997, she holed up in a flat with designers and buddies Peter Jensen and Michelle Lowe-Holder in London's Bethnal Green. She still shares her studio with Lowe-Holder, whilst Ann-Sofie Back and Wolfgang Tillmans do their thing within spitting distance of their East London creative commune. From disparate corners of the global spectrum, this exciting batch of designers have turned the locality into something of a talking point. For Støldal, who was born in 1973, growing up on an island with less than 40 inhabitants has shaped everything she believes in. From her bowl haircut to her hand-drawn doodle prints, she reflects her background and references her upbringing quite openly, with each trip home adding extra layers to her wealth of historical knowledge. Long-forgotten treasure chests unopened in dusty attics, closets stocked full of clothes, family weddings and trips on rowing boats have all shaped her collections. Støldal has catalogued people and their attire, location and actions from day one, interpreting them as trompe l'œil screen prints, on her jackets, tops and look books. She mashes together unusual colourways with traditional crafts (multicoloured chunky cardigans, re-imagined mint green Berghaus jackets) forging an indie aesthetic totally her own, totally now and totally wearable. Støldal's look is a bit Kurt Cobain, a touch terrace culture and a big splash of Scandinavian skill. In her own words: "I've always been interested in clothes that are outside their setting. You know how with second-hand clothing there is a romantic idea about the past? It has a wearer and it has a life. You know it's coming from somewhere and someone's 'everyday'. It's not a picture of a celebrity; it's a picture of a normal person."

Die in Norwegen geborene, aber in London lebende Herrenmode-Designerin Siv Støldal gehört zu einer besonderen Truppe. Als sie sich zum Studium am Central Saint Martins immatrikulierte, zog sie mit ihren Freunden und Designerkollegen Peter Jensen und Michelle Lowe-Holder in eine WG im Londoner Bethnal Green. Das Atelier teilt sie nach wie vor mit Michelle, aber auch Ann-Sofie Back und Wolfgang Tillmans arbeiten nur einen Steinwurf von dort entfernt in dieser kreativen Kommune von East London. Aus entlegenen Winkeln der Erde ist diese spannende Schar Designer zusammengekommen und hat den Ort zu etwas gemacht, worüber man spricht. Die 1973 geborene Støldal wurde in jeder Hinsicht von ihrer Kindheit geprägt, die sie auf einer Insel mit weniger als 40 Einwohnern verbrachte. Von ihrem Topfhaarschnitt bis zu den handgezeichneten Kritzelmustern spiegelt alles ihre Herkunft wider, worauf sie sich auch ganz offen bezieht, denn mit jeder Fahrt nach Hause wächst ihr Reichtum an historischem Wissen. Lange vergessene, ungeöffnete Schatztruhen auf staubigen Dachböden, mit Kleidern vollgestopfte Schränke, Familienhochzeiten und Ausflüge mit Ruderbooten – all das prägt ihre Kollektionen. Von Tag eins an hat Støldal

Menschen, ihre Kleidung, ihren Aufenthaltsort und ihr Verhalten katalogisiert. Sie interpretiert sie als Trompe-l'œil-Szenen auf ihren Jacken, Oberteilen und in ihren Lookbooks. Siv vermengt ungewöhnliche Farbgebungen mit traditionellen Handwerkstechniken (zu bunten dicken Strickjacken oder neu erfundenen mintgrünen Berghaus-Jacken) und erkämpft sich dadurch eine ganz eigene Independent-Ästhetik, die absolut zeitgemäß und tragbar ist. Ihr Look ist ein bisschen Kurt Cobain, eine Spur Terrace Culture und eine große Portion skandinavisches Talent. Sie selbst drückt es so aus: „Ich interessiere mich schon immer für Kleider außerhalb ihrer ‚natürlichen' Umgebung. Sie wissen schon, wie das mit Second-Hand-Sachen so ist, man hat eine romantische Vorstellung von ihrer Vergangenheit. Sie hatten schon einen Besitzer, ein Leben. Man weiß, dass sie von irgendwoher kommen, aus jemandes Alltag. Da hat man nicht die Vorstellung von einem Prominenten, sondern von einem ganz normalen Menschen."

Née en Norvège et installée à Londres, la créatrice pour homme Siv Støldal fait partie d'une équipe très spéciale. Pendant ses études à Central Saint Martins, elle se terre dans un appartement du quartier londonien de Bethnal Green avec ses amis créateurs Peter Jensen et Michelle Lowe-Holder. Elle partage encore son atelier avec Michelle, tandis qu'Ann-Sofie Back et Wolfgang Tillmans travaillent à un jet de pierre de leur communauté créative de l'East London. Venus des quatre coins du globe, cette bande de créateurs passionnants a fait du quartier le dernier endroit à la mode. Selon Siv Støldal (née en 1973), avoir grandi sur une île de moins de 40 habitants a formé tout ce en quoi elle croit. De sa coupe au bol à ses imprimés griffonnés à la main, elle affiche ses origines et fait référence à son enfance avec une certaine franchise, chaque retour au pays ne faisant qu'enrichir ses connaissances historiques. Coffres à trésors depuis longtemps oubliés dans des greniers poussiéreux, armoires remplies de vêtements, fêtes de famille et promenades en barque sont autant de souvenirs qui transparaissent dans ses collections. Depuis le premier jour, Siv Støldal répertorie les gens, leurs vêtements, leurs lieux de vie et leurs actes, et réinterprète ce catalogue dans des imprimés sérigraphiés en trompe-l'œil sur des vestes, des petits hauts et dans ses lookbooks. Siv fusionne couleurs insolites et artisanat traditionnel (gros cardigans multicolores, vestes Berghaus vert menthe revisitées), proposant une esthétique indépendante bien à elle, totalement actuelle et absolument portable. Le look Siv Støldal semble influencé par Kurt Cobain, une touche de culture footballistique et une haute dose de savoir-faire scandinave. Comme elle le dit elle-même : « J'ai toujours été intéressée par les vêtements sortis de leur contexte. Dans les vêtements d'occasion, n'y a-t-il pas une idée romantique liée au passé ? Le vêtement a été porté par quelqu'un, il a eu une vie. Il raconte le quotidien d'un endroit ou d'une personne. Ce n'est pas l'image d'une célébrité ; c'est l'image d'une personne normale ».

BEN REARDON

What is your favourite piece from any of your collections? With each collection I find myself attracted to the classic, tailor-made, suit jacket. Somehow it is like returning to the point where my journey began. I love to explore and question the restrictions and strictness of its shape and challenge what a suit jacket represents. The last suit jacket I made was white cotton eyelet jersey with a white Aertex lining – elements of outerwear and underwear meeting in a new way! **How would you describe your work?** I research how and why people form relationships with their clothes and what role they play in our lives. I am interested in how we group clothes together, for example as 'underwear' or 'outerwear', and how a garment's detailing decides where it belongs. I am interested in the symbolic importance of a zip, a fabric or a shape, that tells us in which group the garment belongs. I am also fascinated by a garment's history. I'm excited when I discover old clothing worn by my ancestors, something that still holds onto their character. These things help me unlock the past and I try to honour their history and translate them into the present **What's your ultimate goal?** My goal is always to express these ideas more clearly in each new collection.

I want a greater understanding of what clothes can represent, how they can affect us, and what their hidden purpose is in our everyday lives **What inspires you?** Accidental discoveries of clothing; trips, events or assignments that come my way; but mostly people around me. When I talk to people about clothes it often leads to them telling stories from their life **Can fashion still have a political ambition?** Clothes are a very powerful way to communicate. A designer's work ends up being worn on somebody else's skin and taking part in somebody else's life. So political ideas can definitely be communicated through fashion by designers prepared to address them **Who do you have in mind when you design?** I think of the people and relics that are the case-studies for the collection. They might be young or old; family, friends or strangers; living remotely or in the city. I think about how people choose their clothes, not only what they wear, but when they wear them, what is thrown away, why some garments are never worn? Why do some garments end up stored in the attic and others are used as rags to wash the floor? **Is the idea of creative collaboration important to you?** Since the starting point for each collection often is

wrapped up in the found objects from someone else's history, I feel each collection is a slight collaboration. I am simply extending and translating parts of people's lives into contemporary and wearable clothes. It's not retro since these starting points are not grounded in fashion but rather how people live. The people involved in the projects are so important that I find it hard to completely divide the collection from where it stemmed from – so in this sense I am always collaborating. I also enjoy collaborating with other designers or more commercial labels – it can be fun and very inspirational **Who has been the greatest influence on your career?** Probably moving to London and meeting the tutors and fellow students at the Saint Martins MA **How have your own experiences affected your work as a designer?** The life and history of myself and the people around me are my main source of inspiration. Different experiences lead to different collections. The Entropy collection was about how things decay over time. I was studying how clothes hung outside on scarecrows changed during one year. Whilst researching this project I happened to find 36 ancient shoes discarded in the wall of a 250 year old house. Water and clay had

been running over them for 150 years and they looked like twisted, stone sculptures. The experience of uncovering them became a large part of the collection **Which is more important in your work: the process or the product?** A good starting point and process are vital to the integrity of the end product. The scarecrow collection could not have happened unless I visited seven houses on an island in Norway and collected unwanted clothing they gave me to dress a scarecrow. My father and I built the scarecrows, one for each house, and put them out in nature. I did the scarecrow collection based on this selection and display of the clothes. One year later I returned to them for inspiration for the Entropy collection **Is designing difficult for you, if so, what drives you to continue?** I am privileged to be able to use my curiosity to ask questions and comment on what I find out through my work – it can be hard but I wouldn't want to do anything else **Have you ever been influenced or moved by the reaction to your designs?** I am moved when my clothes end up as someone's favourite garment **What's your definition of beauty?** Honesty.

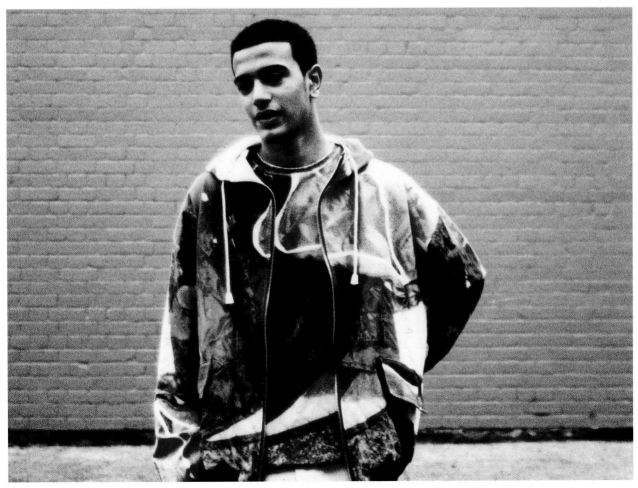

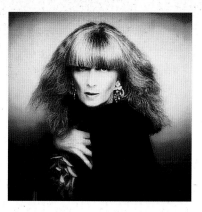

SONIA RYKIEL

"I hope that my creations can give a little bit of joy"

The so-called 'Queen of Knits', Sonia Rykiel is synonymous with Paris. Born in the city in 1930, she went on to encapsulate Parisian style with her chic fashion line. As an expectant mother, she had discovered that there were no sweaters available that were soft and flexible enough for her to wear through her pregnancy, so, in 1962, she created her own line of knitwear. This was so successful that she opened her first boutique in that momentous Parisian year, 1968. And, in their own way, Rykiel's designs were revolutionary. Her flattering knits – often in what was to become her trademark stripes – symbolised liberation for women's bodies from the stiff silhouette of the previous decade. She also increased the sex appeal of knits: freed from linings and hems, her dresses and sweaters were like second skins for the women who wore them. Rykiel has continued to build her very own French Empire since the '70s. She recognised the wisdom of establishing a beauty line early on, launching a perfume in 1978 and cosmetics in 1987. Completely independent, Rykiel's business is very much a family affair. Husband Simon Bernstein is her business partner and daughter Nathalie Rykiel has been involved in the company since 1975. With such support, Sonia has the freedom to do other things. Today, Madame Rykiel is something of a French institution. She has written novels, decorated hotels, sung a duet with Malcolm McLaren and even had a rose named after her. And the accolades keep on coming. Rykiel has been awarded an Oscar by Fashion Group International and in December 2001, the French government named her Commandeur de l'Ordre National du Mérite. Now in her seventies, the grande dame of French fashion shows no signs of giving up. She has an army of sweater-loving women depending on her, after all.

Die so genannte „Königin des Strick", Sonia Rykiel, gilt inzwischen als Synonym für Paris. Dort wurde sie auch 1930 geboren, und später gelang es ihr, die Pariser Eleganz in ihrer schicken Modelinie auf den Punkt zu bringen. Als werdende Mutter hatte sie 1962 feststellen müssen, dass es keine Pullover gab, die für eine Schwangerschaft weich und elastisch genug waren, also entwarf sie kurzerhand ihre eigene Strickkollektion. Der Erfolg war so groß, dass Rykiel im für Paris so bedeutsamen Jahr 1968 ihre erste Boutique in der Stadt eröffnete. Und auf ihre Weise waren auch die damaligen Kreationen von Sonia Rykiel revolutionär. Ihre schmeichelnden Stricksachen – oft mit Streifen, die ihr Markenzeichen werden sollten – symbolisierten die Befreiung des weiblichen Körpers von der starren Silhouette des vorangegangenen Jahrzehnts. Sie steigerte auch den Sexappeal von Strick: frei von Futter und Säumen, wirkten ihre Kleider und Pullover wie eine zweite Haut ihrer Trägerin. Seit den 1970er Jahren baut Rykiel kontinuierlich an ihrem ganz privaten französischen Imperium. Früh erkannte sie den Wert eigener Beautyprodukte und brachte 1978 ihren ersten Duft, 1987 die ersten Kosmetika unter ihrem Namen heraus. Das völlig autarke Unternehmen ist im Prinzip ein Familienbetrieb. Ehemann Simon Bernstein ist ihr Geschäftspartner, Tochter Nathalie Rykiel seit 1975 in die Firma integriert. Dieser Rückhalt gibt Rykiel die Freiheit, auch andere Dinge als Mode zu machen. Inzwischen gilt Madame Rykiel als eine Art Institution. Sie hat Romane veröffentlicht, Hotels eingerichtet, ein Duett mit Malcolm McLaren gesungen, ja sogar eine Rose ist nach ihr benannt. Und die Reihe der Auszeichnungen reißt nicht ab: So erhielt Rykiel von der Fashion Group International einen Oscar; im Dezember 2001 ehrte die französische Regierung sie mit dem Titel Commandeur de l'Ordre National du Mérite. Auch wenn sie inzwischen in den Siebzigern ist, macht die Grande Dame der französischen Mode keine Anstalten, sich zur Ruhe zu setzen. Und das ist auch gut so, denn schließlich ist ein Heer von Frauen, die Pullover lieben, von ihr abhängig.

La « reine du tricot » Sonia Rykiel est devenue synonyme de Paris. Née en 1930 dans la capitale française, elle saisit la quintessence du style parisien dans ses collections de mode très chic. Pendant sa grossesse, elle n'arrive pas à trouver de pulls assez souples pour son ventre de femme enceinte, ce qui l'incite à créer sa propre ligne de maille en 1962. Elle remporte un tel succès qu'elle ouvre sa première boutique dès 1968, une année de bouleversement pour les Parisiens. A leur façon, les créations Rykiel sont tout aussi révolutionnaires : ses tricots flatteurs, souvent déclinés dans ce qui deviendra ses rayures signature, symbolisent alors l'émancipation des femmes, libérant leurs corps de la silhouette rigide imposée par la décennie précédente. Elle rehausse également le sex-appeal de la maille ; dépourvus de doublures et d'ourlets, ses robes et ses pulls enveloppent celles qui les portent comme une seconde peau. Depuis les années 70, Sonia Rykiel ne cesse de développer son propre empire français. Elle comprend très tôt l'intérêt de créer une ligne de beauté et lance un parfum en 1978, puis une gamme de maquillage en 1987. Entièrement indépendante, l'entreprise de Sonia Rykiel reste avant tout familiale. Son mari Simon Bernstein y est associé et sa fille Nathalie Rykiel y travaille depuis 1975. Forte d'un tel soutien, Sonia trouve le temps de se consacrer à d'autres passions. Aujourd'hui, Madame Rykiel est devenue une sorte d'institution française. Elle a écrit des romans, décoré des hôtels, chanté un duo avec Malcolm McLaren et revendique même une rose à son nom. Et les distinctions ne cessent de pleuvoir. Sonia Rykiel a reçu un oscar de Fashion Group International, et le gouvernement français l'a adoubée commandeur de l'Ordre national du Mérite en décembre 2001. A soixante-dix ans passés, la grande dame de la mode française n'a aucune envie d'abandonner. Après tout, elle a toute une armée de fans du tricot à habiller.

LAUREN COCHRANE

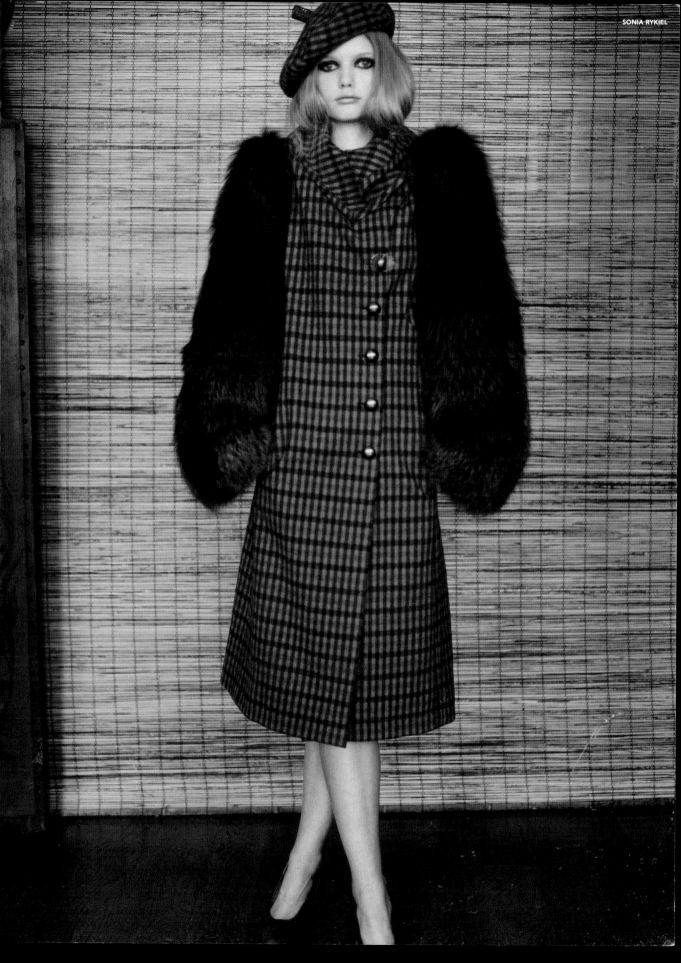

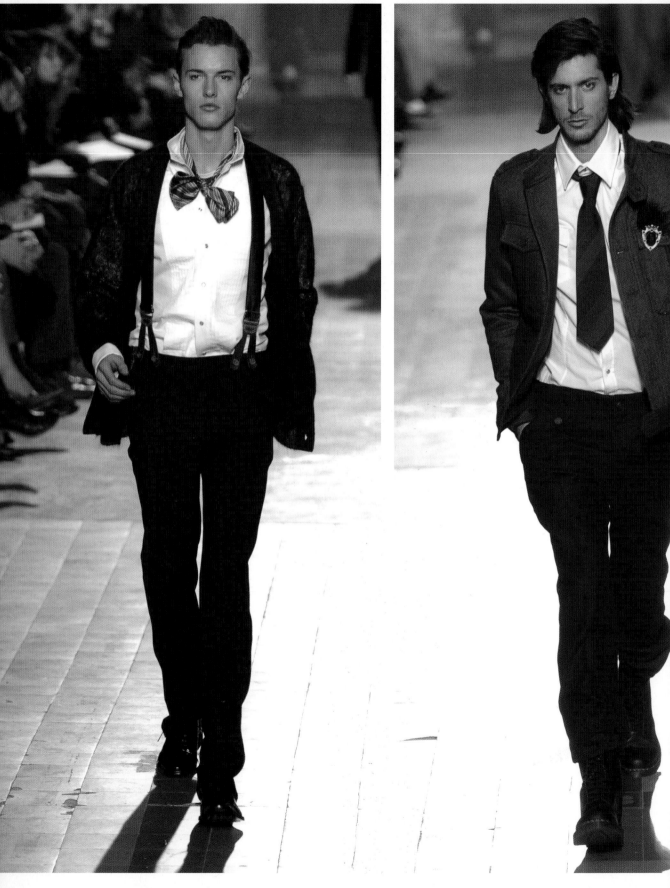

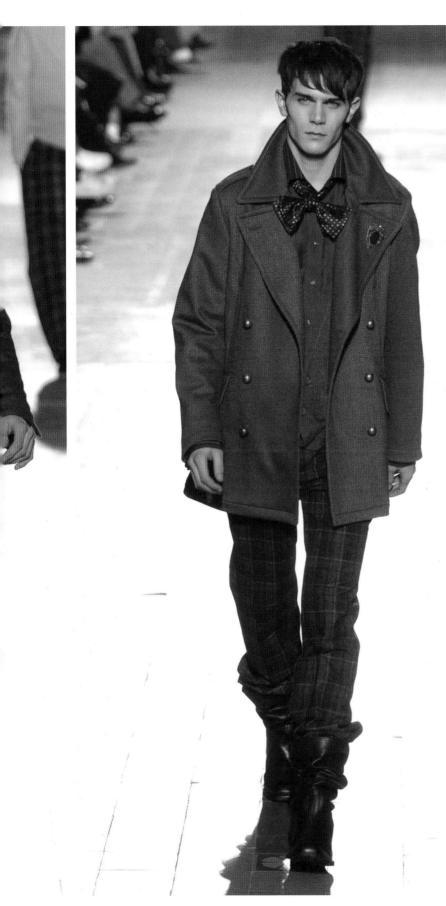

RYKIEL HOMME AUTUMN/WINTER 2005–2006. PHOTOGRAPHY BY MITCHELL SAMS.

What are your signature designs? I took away hems, discovered inside-out steams, abolished lining **What is your favourite piece from any of your collections?** A pullover. Very tight, sensuous. Black. My famous Poor Boy sweater **How would you describe your work?** It's a philosophy of fashion. I have called it the "Demode". Which means that every women must consider what's beautiful and also not perfect in her figure. **What's your ultimate goal?** To be happy. To create. To be a happy creator! I designed clothes, I write and I am involved in all sorts of creations **What inspires you?** My daughter Nathalie, my three granddaughters, women in the street. I am also influenced by the books I read, the movies and every arts. I am a sort of "thief": my eyes and ears are always open **Can fashion still have a political ambition?** Everything that happens in the world matters to me. I am often scared. I hope that my creations can give a little bit of joy and happiness **Who do you have in mind when you design?** Most of the time, nobody in particular and all the women I can meet in the same time **Is the idea of creative collaboration important to you?** My team is very important to me. A creator is, in a certain way, always alone, but I need to be surrounded **Who has been the greatest influence on your career?** My daughter, Nathalie **How have your own experiences affected your work as a designer?** Joy and pain are linked to my work. My creations are an expression of my feelings **Which is more important in your work: the process or the product?** Both are very important. The process is exciting, full of work and passion, full of doubts and tiredness too. The product is like a gift, a smile, something concrete and gratifying **Is designing difficult for you, if so, what drives you to continue?** It's the reason of my life **Have you ever been influenced or moved by the reaction to your designs?** Yes, of course! I am always open to reactions. It is necessary to be open-minded **What's your definition of beauty?** There isn't one definition of beauty. Beauty can be inside and outside. Beauty can be classical, eccentric, unusual, unexpected, intellectual… **What's your philosophy?** To love and to be loved **What is the most important lesson you've learned?** Every-thing that can hurt you can also make you stronger and learn something about yourself.

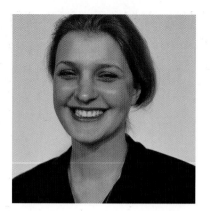

SOPHIA KOKOSALAKI

"My aim is always to hit a chord"

Sophia Kokosalaki has never gone about things the usual way. Instead, she relies on single-minded individualism. Born in Athens in 1972, Kokosalaki's first love was literature, studying Greek and English at the University of Athens. She came to London in 1996 and completed a womenswear MA at Central Saint Martins. For her graduation show she worked with Abigail Lane to produce the video installation 'Never Never Mind' and her graduate collection was snapped up by the (now defunct) London boutique Pellicano. Kokosalaki set up her own label in 1999 and quickly established a trademark style, dipping into the rich heritage of Ancient Greek drapery, a '70s folk aesthetic and complex leatherwork. It wasn't long before others wanted a piece of the action. In June 1999, Kokosalaki worked on a knitwear line for Joseph. By 2000, after just three solo collections, she was invited to work as a guest designer for Italian leather goods label Ruffo Research. She also entertained the more accessible end of the fashion market, producing two capsule collections for Topshop's TS label. In 2004, she was chosen to design the costumes for the Athens Olympic Games, the highlight of which was a vast marine-blue dress worn by Björk. Despite such demanding extracurricular activities, her day job has flourished. A menswear line was set up in 2000 and a shoe collection was added in 2003. The recipient of many awards, Kokosalaki's notable gongs include the first ever Art Foundation Award given to a fashion designer. Kokosalaki constantly develops her themes, and dedicated fans return every season as she evolves – rather than rethinks – her signatures. Spring/summer 2005 saw ruched pastels for a delicate seaside feel and a somewhat strategic move to the Paris schedule. Both cerebral and fun-loving, Kokosalaki is never complacent.

Sophia Kokosalaki ist die Dinge noch nie auf herkömmliche Weise angegangen. Stattdessen setzt sie auf zielstrebigen Individualismus. Die erste Liebe der 1972 in Athen geborenen Designerin galt der Literatur, weshalb sie zunächst Griechisch und Englisch an der Universität ihrer Heimatstadt studierte. 1996 ging sie nach London, wo sie einen Master in Damenmode am Central Saint Martins erwarb. Für ihre Abschlusskollektion tat sie sich mit Abigail Lane zusammen und produzierte die Videoinstallation „Never Never Mind". Die Kollektion selbst sicherte sich die inzwischen nicht mehr existierende Londoner Boutique Pellicano. 1999 gründete Kokosalaki ihr eigenes Label und etablierte schnell einen unverwechselbaren Stil. Dazu nahm sie Anleihen bei den im antiken Griechenland üblichen Drapierungen sowie der Folk-Ästhetik der 1970er Jahre und kombinierte beides mit aufwändigen Lederarbeiten. Schon bald waren ihre Entwürfe extrem begehrt. Kokosalaki kreierte im Juni 1999 eine Strickkollektion für Joseph. Und bereits im Jahr 2000, nach nur drei Solokollektionen, wurde sie als Gastdesignerin vom italienischen Lederwarenhersteller Ruffo Research eingeladen. Sie bediente aber auch das erschwinglichere Ende des Modemarktes mit

zwei Minikollektionen für das Label TS bei Topshop. 2004 bekam sie den Auftrag für die Kostüme zu den Olympischen Spielen von Athen. Das Highlight dieser Kollektion war das aufwändige marineblaue Kleid für die Sängerin Björk. Trotz solch anspruchsvoller Nebentätigkeiten ist die Designerin auch in ihrem Hauptberuf produktiv. Im Jahr 2000 wurde eine Herrenlinie ins Leben gerufen, eine Schuhkollektion kam 2003 hinzu. Unter ihren zahlreichen Auszeichnungen verdient der erste je für Modedesign verliehene Art Foundation Award besondere Beachtung. Kokosalaki entwickelt ihre Themen ständig weiter, und so kehren pflichtbewusste Fans in jeder Saison zu ihr zurück, um zu sehen, wie sie ihre Charakteristika mehr aus- als umarbeitet. Für Frühjahr/Sommer 2005 erzeugten pastellfarbene Rüschen ein Flair von Ferien am Meer, und die Designerin passte sich vermutlich aus strategischen Gründen dem Pariser Show-Kalender an. Kokosalaki ist rational und lustvoll zugleich, aber niemals selbstgerecht.

Privilégiant son farouche individualisme, Sophia Kokosalaki ne fait jamais rien comme tout le monde. Née en 1972 à Athènes, Sophia Kokosalaki se passionne d'abord pour la littérature et étudie le grec et l'anglais à l'université d'Athènes. Elle s'installe à Londres en 1996, où elle décroche un Master en mode féminine à Central Saint Martins. Pour sa collection de fin d'études, elle collabore avec Abigail Lane sur l'installation vidéo «Never Never Mind», une collection sur laquelle se jette la boutique londonienne Pellicano (fermée depuis). Sophia Kokosalaki crée sa propre griffe en 1999 et impose rapidement son style caractéristique inspiré par le riche héritage des drapés grecs antiques, une esthétique folk très années 70 et un travail élaboré du cuir. Son travail ne tarde pas à attirer l'attention d'autres créateurs. En juin 1999, Sophia Kokosalaki conçoit une ligne en maille pour Joseph. En l'an 2000, après seulement trois collections en solo, le maroquinier italien Ruffo Research lui commande également des collections. Elle a aussi travaillé pour le marché plus accessible de la grande consommation en produisant deux mini-collections pour la griffe TS de Topshop. En 2004, on lui confie la création des costumes des Jeux olympiques d'Athènes, dont personne n'oubliera jamais la volumineuse robe bleu marine portée par Björk. En dépit de ses nombreuses activités annexes, sa propre griffe prospère. Elle a lancé une ligne pour homme en l'an 2000 et une collection de chaussures en 2003. Couronnée de nombreux prix, elle a notamment reçu le premier Art Foundation Award jamais remis à un couturier. Sophia Kokosalaki n'a de cesse de développer ses propres thématiques et ses fans lui restent fidèles chaque saison, quand elle propose une évolution plutôt qu'une réinterprétation de ses looks signature. Pour la saison printemps/été 2005, elle présente des couleurs pastel et des ruchés au style balnéaire délicat, et défile désormais à Paris, une décision quelque peu stratégique. A la fois cérébrale et insouciante, Sophia Kokosalaki ne fait jamais dans la complaisance.

LAUREN COCHRANE

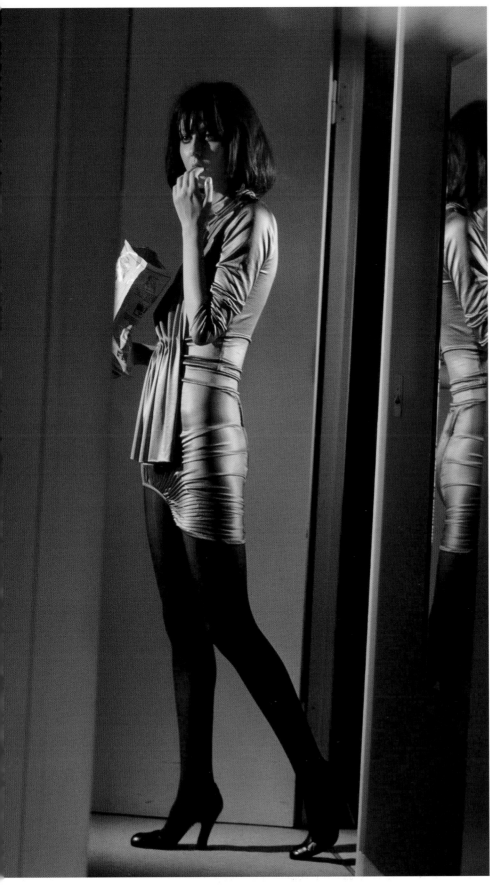

What are your signature designs? A signature design would have to involve elaborate handwork, traditional or military elements and an alternative or Teutonic silhouette **What's your favourite piece from any of your collections?** A draped patchwork leather and jersey dress from my spring/summer 2000 collection, as it was one of my first experiments **How would you describe your work?** Complex and labour intensive, but also light and contemporary **What's your ultimate goal?** Achieving perfect balance between life and work **What inspires you?** It is usually a combination of elements and situations **Can fashion still have a political ambition?** No, but it can have an emotional feel **Who do you have in mind when you design?** Nobody specific **Is the idea of creative collaboration important to you?** Yes, dialogue with people that share a similar aesthetic can be unexpectedly conclusive and productive **What has been the greatest influence on your career?** The need to be independent was the one thing that controlled my career **How have your own experiences affected your work as a designer?** In a decisive way because experiences define your personality and my personality interferes with my work a lot **Which is more important in your work: the process or the product?** Both **Is designing difficult for you and, if so, what drives you to continue?** Designing is never difficult but the technical complexities can be a challenge **Have you ever been influenced or moved by the reaction to your designs?** Of course, because with my work my aim is always to hit a chord **What's your definition of beauty?** It changes constantly, but a slight imperfection always adds more allure **What's your philosophy?** It's never as hard as it seems **What is the most important lesson you've learned?** You can never start working early enough.

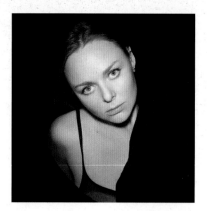

STELLA MCCARTNEY

"I represent something for women.
I've built up trust with them and that's important"

Stella McCartney's stratospheric success story has only a little to do with her fabulous connections. Born in 1971, she graduated from Central Saint Martins in 1995. Her final year collection was snapped up by the biggest names in retail (including Browns and Bergdorf Goodman) and a mere two years later her sharp-tailoring talents landed her the top job as creative director at Chloé. Trouser suits, vintage-inspired dresses and jet-setting holidaywear are trademark Stella-style. Her designs are often also possessed of that rarity in the fashion world, an exuberant sense of humour (folk went bananas over her fruity vests and knickers). In 2001 McCartney left Chloé and re-launched her own eponymous line, this time backed by the Gucci Group. The first Stella McCartney store opened in New York's meatpacking district in 2002, followed a year later by additional shops in London and Los Angeles. 2004 saw the girl with the golden touch honoured with a Designer of the Year award in London. Like her late mother Linda, she is serious about animal rights and refuses to use leather or fur in any of her designs. She also received a Women of Courage Award for her work with cancer charities. Whether working on experimental projects (such as the collaboration with artist Gary Hume in 2002 to produce handmade T-shirts and dresses), designing costumes for Gwyneth Paltrow's action movie 'Sky Captain' (2004) or enjoying the mainstream success of her perfume, McCartney is forever working a new angle. Summer 2005 saw her latest project unveiled, a new collection of keep-fit wear designed in conjunction with Adidas, with a special collection for H&M launched later the same year.

Stella McCartneys kometenhafter Aufstieg hat nur wenig mit ihren fabelhaften Connections zu tun. Die 1971 geborene Designerin machte 1995 ihren Abschluss am Central Saint Martins. Bereits die Kollektion ihres letzten Studienjahres wurde von einigen der größten Einzelhändler (u. a. Browns und Bergdorf Goodman) ins Sortiment genommen. Nur zwei Jahre später ergatterte sie dank ihrer verführerischen und perfekt geschneiderten Kreationen den Spitzenjob Creative Director bei Chloé. Hosenanzüge, vom Vintage-Look inspirierte Kleider und Ferienkleidung für Jet-Setter sind Markenzeichen des Stella-Style. Ihre Entwürfe besitzen oft auch etwas, das in der Modewelt ganz selten ist – einen ausgelassenen Sinn für Humor (so waren die Kunden beispielsweise verrückt nach ihren „fruchtigen" Hemdchen und Höschen). 2001 verließ McCartney Chloé und unternahm einen Relaunch des nach ihr benannten Labels, diesmal allerdings mit Unterstützung des Gucci-Konzerns. Der erste „Stella McCartney"-Laden eröffnete 2002 im New Yorker Meatpacking District, ein Jahr später folgten weitere Geschäfte in London und Los Angeles. 2004 wurde das Mädchen mit dem

goldenen Händchen in London mit einem Designer of The Year Award ausgezeichnet. Wie ihre verstorbene Mutter Linda engagiert sie sich sehr für den Tierschutz und weigert sich, Leder oder Pelz in ihren Entwürfen zu verwenden. Für die Unterstützung von Initiativen zum Schutz vor Krebs erhielt sie einen Women of Courage Award. Gleichgültig, ob es sich um eher experimentelle Projekte handelt (wie 2002 die Zusammenarbeit mit dem Künstler Gary Hume, wo es um die Produktion handgefertigter T-Shirts und Kleider ging), um Gwyneth Paltrows Kostüme in dem Actionfilm „Sky Captain" (2004) oder um die Freude am breiten Erfolg ihres Parfüms – McCartney tut immer alles aus einer neuen Perspektive. Im Sommer 2005 stellte sie ihr jüngstes Projekt vor: eine Kollektion von Fitnesskleidung in Zusammenarbeit mit Adidas sowie eine Sonderkollektion für H & M.

Contrairement à ce que l'on pourrait penser, la success story interplanétaire de Stella McCartney n'a pas grand chose à voir avec son fabuleux réseau de relations. Née en 1971, elle sort diplômée de Central Saint Martins en 1995. Sa collection de fin d'études est immédiatement raflée par les plus grands noms de la vente (tels que Browns et Bergdorf Goodman). A peine deux ans plus tard, sa mode sexy et ses coupes parfaites lui valent un poste important en tant que directrice de la création chez Chloé. Les tailleurs-pantalons, les robes d'inspiration vintage et les tenues de vacances spéciales jet-set représentent autant de signatures de Stella. De plus, ses créations possèdent souvent quelque chose de très rare dans l'univers de la mode : un sens de l'humour exubérant (les gens raffolent de ses gilets et de ses culottes à fruits). En 2001, Stella McCartney quitte Chloé pour relancer sa ligne éponyme, cette fois-ci avec le soutien du groupe Gucci. En 2002, la première boutique Stella McCartney ouvre ses portes à New York dans le quartier des anciens abattoirs, suivie un an plus tard par d'autres boutiques à Londres et Los Angeles. En 2004, celle qui transforme en or tout ce qu'elle touche remporte le Designer of The Year Award à Londres. Comme sa mère Linda aujourd'hui décédée, elle s'engage très sérieusement dans la défense des droits des animaux et se refuse à utiliser du cuir ou de la fourrure. Son travail auprès des associations de lutte contre le cancer lui a également valu un Women of Courage Award. Qu'elle travaille sur des projets expérimentaux (comme sa collaboration en 2002 avec l'artiste Gary Hume pour produire des T-shirts et des robes cousus main), qu'elle dessine les costumes du film d'action de Gwyneth Paltrow « Capitaine Sky et le monde de demain » (2004) ou qu'elle profite de l'immense succès de son parfum, Stella McCartney ne se lassera jamais d'explorer de nouvelles approches. Elle dévoile son tout dernier projet à l'été 2005, une nouvelle collection de sportswear conçue avec Adidas. TERRY NEWMAN

PORTRAIT BY MARY McCARTNEY DONALD · PHOTOGRAPHY BY PAUL WETHERELL, STYLING BY JO BARKER · MODEL · JOVITA · MARCH 2005

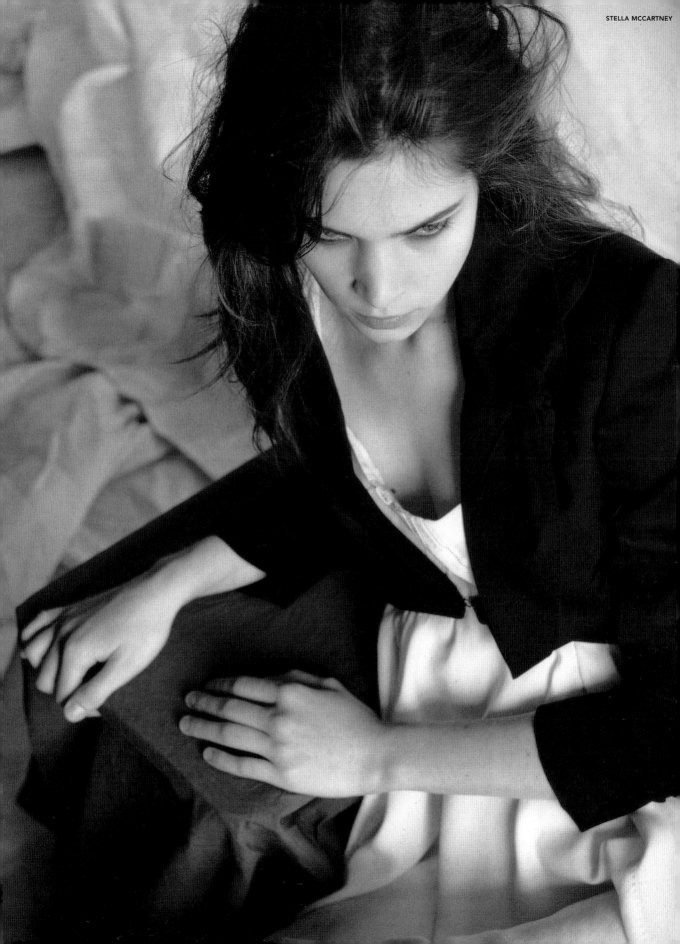

What are your signature designs? Sexy trousers! What's your favourite piece from any of your collections? I don't have one. I love them all. Is that allowed? How would you describe your work? It hopefully covers all facets of a woman: sexy, feminine, humorous, confident and fucking cool What's your ultimate goal? I'm in the process, hopefully, of achieving it. My ultimate goal is to be happy. If my company succeeds and that means I'm happy, or if it doesn't but I'm still happy, it's all for the good What inspires you? My mum Who do you have in mind when you design? Me and my friends Can fashion still have a political ambition? Sure it can. You can take it as seriously as you want, but fashion on a daily basis is always political because it's people expressing themselves Is the idea of creative collaboration important to you? I think that collaborating with people, doing limited editions and one-off pieces, is really exciting. I'm increasingly interested in trying to make individual, special pieces rather than mass producing things Who has been the greatest influence on your career? Just the customer. The girls that I know who wear my clothes. Only the cool ones, of course Which is more important in your work: the process or the product? The product. Because if the process is brilliant but the product's shit… who cares? Is designing difficult for you and, if so, what drives you to continue? If I'd settled for being a cliché of myself and just making tons of money, it'd be fine. I've taken an option that's a bit more difficult and I'm pushing myself. But I love it. And I do it for the genuine reason that I think I have a place in the industry. I have a role; I represent something for women. I've built up trust with them and I think that's important. And I keep doing it because I'm totally a fucking glutton for punishment and am trying to prove myself, though to God knows who Have you ever been influenced or moved by the reaction to your designs? I had an event at a store to meet my clients. This woman came in who was about 75 years old and she was so stylish. And she said to me, "Your clothes make me so happy". And she really meant it. She wasn't a fashion person. She was a client. And I just thought, that's what it's all about, that is really what it's all about for me. I never would have thought a 75-year-old woman would wear my clothes. And she was fucking cool. And that definitely moved me What's your definition of beauty? Inner peace What's your philosophy? Be true to yourself, believe in yourself and shine on What is the most important lesson you've learned? Do unto others as you would have them do unto you.

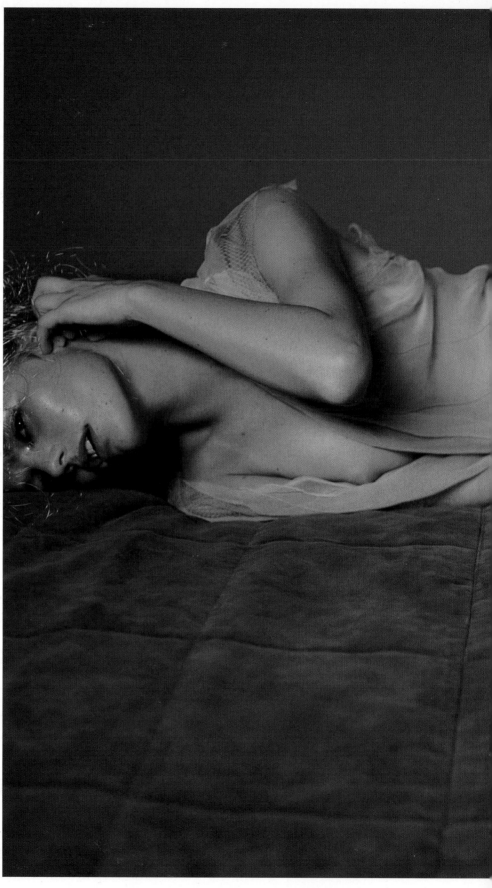

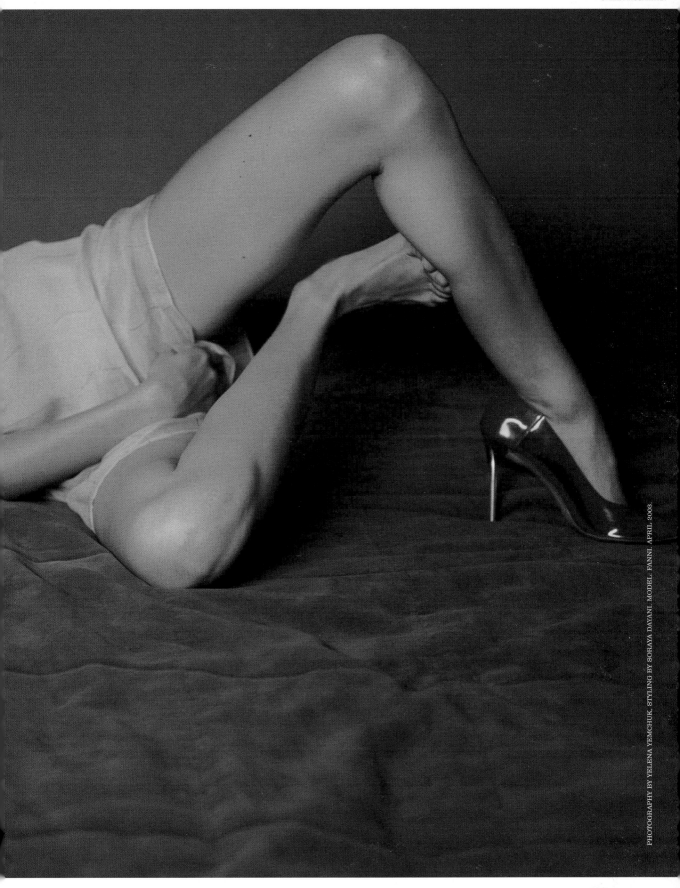

PHOTOGRAPHY BY YELENA YEMCHUK. STYLING BY SORAYA DAYANI. MODEL: FANNI. APRIL 2003.

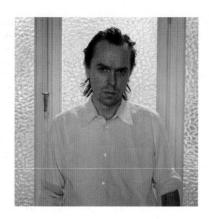

STEPHAN SCHNEIDER

"I draw my inspiration from reality. I get the best moments of inspiration when I'm bored"

Born in Duisburg, Germany in 1969, Stephan Schneider does not come from a family with a fashion background, he couldn't care less about celebrities or whether they wear his gear, and has a fairly simple ambition: "To stay independent and fresh". To say he doesn't pander to the glossier side of the fashion system is something of an understatement. Asked what sparked his interest in becoming a designer, he says, "Reading my first i-D with a mix of Sigue Sigue Sputnik, Paninari and Tokyo nightlife, which all fascinated me." The year was 1986. Eight years later he graduated from the Antwerp's Royal Academy with a collection deemed strong enough to earn the young designer a stand at Paris Fashion Week, where orders were placed and a business was born. During his studies he didn't seek work placements or training with other designers, preferring to keep as focused as possible on the development of his own aesthetic. Fascinated by what is considered banal or ordinary, Schneider produces fashion which often has something to say, without ever becoming overstated. A recent collection, therefore, mixed African influences with ideas based around the superficiality of consumerism, resulting in a print which appeared to be of African flavour but on closer inspection revealed itself to be a repeated image of a mobile phone. Such subtle comment is cleverly mixed with tailoring and sportswear resulting in designs for both sexes, all of which are cut by hand and produced in Belgian factories. With two stores in both Antwerp (opened within two years of his graduation) and Tokyo, and the label regularly showing during the men's Paris shows, Schneider's vision of crafting clothes which are 'merely extraordinarily ordinary' is now a very real success.

Der 1969 in Duisburg geborene Stephan Schneider stammt aus einer Familie, die mit Mode nicht das Geringste zu tun hat. Prominente, die eventuell seine Kleider tragen, sind ihm vollkommen gleichgültig, und auch seine Ambitionen klingen relativ bescheiden: „Frisch und unabhängig bleiben." Zu behaupten, er biedere sich nicht an die glamouröse Seite des Modebusiness an, wäre noch untertrieben. Fragt man nach, was dann überhaupt der Auslöser war, Modedesigner zu werden, lautet die Antwort: „Die Lektüre meiner ersten i-D mit einer Mischung aus Sigue Sigue Sputnik, Paninari und Tokioter Nachtleben. Das fand ich alles faszinierend." Das war im Jahr 1986. Acht Jahre später schloss Schneider die Königliche Akademie in Antwerpen mit einer Kollektion ab, die offenbar überzeugend genug war, um dem jungen Designer einen Stand auf der Pariser Modewoche zu ermöglichen. Dort erhielt er Orders, und sein Geschäft war gegründet. Während des Studiums hatte Schneider sich nicht um Praktika und Jobs bei anderen Designern bemüht, sondern konzentrierte sich lieber ganz auf die Entwicklung seiner eigenen Ästhetik. Fasziniert vom scheinbar Banalen oder Gewöhnlichen, produziert er Mode, die oft eine Botschaft hat, ohne je überzogen zu wirken. In einer seiner letzten Kollektionen kombinierte er afrikanische Einflüsse mit Überlegungen rund um die Oberflächlichkeit des Konsumdenkens. Eines der Stoffmuster daraus wirkte traditionell afrikanisch, entpuppte sich bei näherem Hinsehen jedoch als vervielfachte Abbildung eines Handys. Solche subtilen Kommentare sind Teil der intelligenten Mischung aus Schneiderkunst und Sportswear, die in Unisex-Entwürfen resultiert. Alle Teile werden von Hand zugeschnitten und in belgischen Fabriken produziert. Mit je einem Laden in Antwerpen (zwei Jahre nach Studienabschluss eröffnet) und Tokio sowie regelmäßigen Präsentationen seines Labels bei den Pariser Schauen für Herrenmode hat Schneider seine Vision von der Herstellung „einfach ungewöhnlich gewöhnlicher" Kleidung schon ziemlich erfolgreich umgesetzt.

Né en 1969 à Duisburg en Allemagne, Stephan Schneider n'a pas grandi dans une famille très portée sur la mode. Il se contrefiche de voir ses créations sur le dos des célébrités et entretient une ambition plutôt simple : « Rester indépendant et nouveau. » Dire qu'il ne se plie pas au côté strass et paillettes du système de la mode est un euphémisme. Interrogé sur la naissance de sa vocation, il répond : « Mon premier numéro d'i-D, les Sigue Sigue Sputnik, les Paninari et la vie nocturne à Tokyo, qui m'ont toujours fasciné.» C'était en 1986. Huit ans plus tard, il sort diplômé de l'Académie Royale d'Anvers avec une collection estimée assez accompli pour valoir au jeune créateur un stand d'exposition à la Semaine de la Mode de Paris, où il décroche ses premières commandes et crée son entreprise. Pendant ses études, il ne cherche aucun stage de formation auprès d'autres créateurs, préférant rester aussi concentré que possible sur le développement de sa propre esthétique. Passionné par le banal ou l'ordinaire, Schneider produit une mode qui a souvent quelque chose à dire, mais sans jamais sombrer dans l'exagération. Dans cet esprit, il a récemment présenté une collection fusionnant influences africaines et idées articulées autour de la superficialité du consumérisme, culminant dans un imprimé semblant africain de prime abord, mais qui, quand on y regarde de plus près, s'avère être l'image répétée d'un téléphone portable. Il conjugue astucieusement ce très subtil commentaire à des coupes et un sportswear déclinés pour les deux sexes, tous coupés à la main et produits dans des usines belges. Avec deux boutiques à Anvers (ouverte deux ans après l'obtention de son diplôme) et Tokyo, la griffe défile régulièrement pendant les collections pour homme de Paris. Les vêtements « simplement extraordinairement ordinaires », nés de la vision de Schneider, remportent aujourd'hui un succès bien réel.

SIMON CHILVERS

What are your signature designs? Let's describe it as contemporary tradition. My designs are neither 'anti' nor 'avant (-garde)'. Like my real signature they are not easy to read, never the same, still recognisable **What is your favourite piece from any of your collections?** My archive is like an old wine cellar to me. The older it gets the more precious it is to me. Once you have to consider, next to the design, the manufacturing and deliveries, the clothes get so much better. But I do appreciate some imperfection, the taste of cork **How would you describe your work?** Honestly, I want to make likeable clothes that make people aware of our reality. Likeable not in the sense of easy or wearable, but in the sense of pleasant and attractive. My work should be approached with basic human aspects like humour, curiosity and physical attraction. I don't want my work to become a status symbol or dress code. It would be easy for me to design some dramatic drapes for glossy pages and luxury clients **What's your ultimate goal?** Continuation with passion **What inspires you?** I draw all my inspiration from reality, my love-hate relationship with the mass-mess around us. To me it makes no sense to escape from it and fake a romantic, intact scenery of the past or future in my work. I get the best moments of inspiration when I'm bored **Can fashion still have a political ambition?** As all ideas in fashion are used by the mass industry to sell their products, the 'stop the war' T-shirts hang all over the high streets. The message became a commercial stunt. I guess every designer has the desire to reflect and influence our thoughts by his work. This means politics to me **Who do you have in mind when you design?** My own hunger, sometimes for a quicker speed of change, sometimes for more refinement **Is the idea of creative collaboration important to you?** My work is very personal and I wish I could do all by myself. Yet I love the work of the creative agency Nine Daughters and a Stereo, with whom I develop all my visual communication **Who has been the greatest influence on your career?** Luckily I am not considering having a career. A career shadows your whole life. I continue day by day and feel the luxury of being able to do something else at every moment. So far, nobody could influence me to do so **How have your own experiences affected your work as a designer?** The more you experience, the less you expect, the more you enjoy **Which is more important in your work: the process or the product?** As only my creative team can see the process it would be pretentious to say the process. As I want to communicate with my work, the product has become more important. Unfortunately **Is designing difficult for you, if so, what drives you to continue?** Yes it is. Perhaps my German background made me so disciplined and dedicated that I continue not to forget my total independence **Have you ever been influenced or moved by the reaction to your designs?** Designing is asking for dialogue and reaction. I don't design for myself. I live for those reactions and comments and I am moved and influenced by them **What's your definition of beauty?** Beauty has no pragmatic structure, no repeat. Like love, we cannot define it, which makes it so desirable **What's your philosophy?** Become stronger without becoming established **What is the most important lesson you've learned?** The more you hear, the more you have to select. Open your eyes but shut your ears.

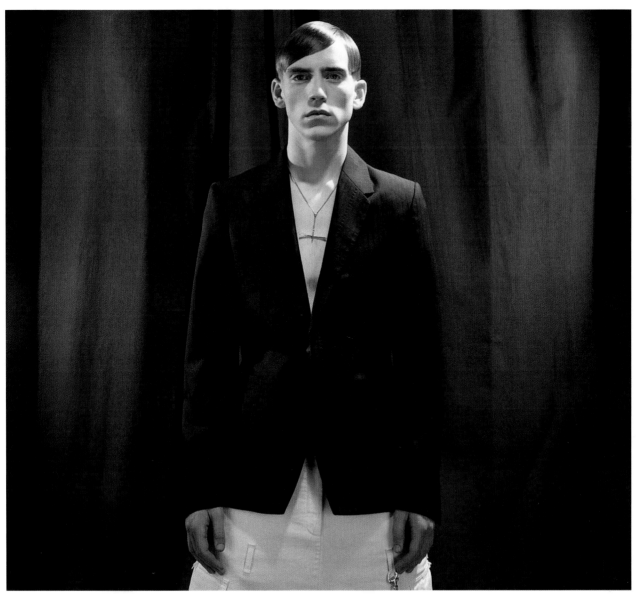

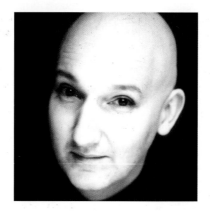

STEPHEN JONES

"For me designing is like breathing.
It's the editing that's difficult"

A Stephen Jones hat has the capacity to utterly transform its wearer. His groundbreaking collections are showcased in museums the world over, including the V&A in London, the Fashion Institute of Technology in New York and the Louvre in Paris. Traditional top hats, boaters, military caps, berets and bowlers are cheekily minaturised, unexpected details are added and Schiaparelli-esque twists are highlighted with delightful colour combinations. All of his work is sympathetically in tune with the current fashion climate. Jones (born in 1957) has always had guest-list cool. During the New Romantic era in '80s London he made headwear for friends Steve Strange and Boy George, clients for whom image was everything. In 1984 he conquered Paris when Jean Paul Gaultier and Thierry Mugler invited him to design hats for them. Since then, he has worked with fashion houses including Comme des Garçons, Balenciaga, Hermès and Vivienne Westwood. However his best-known association has been with John Galliano, with whom he celebrated 10 years of collaboration in 2004. Since graduating from Central Saint Martins in 1979 with a BA in fashion design, Jones's creative skills have worked their charm on shoes (he created a collection for Sergio Rossi), postage stamps (for the Royal Mail in England) and kimonos. However hats are his first love and he not only sells a mainline, Model Millinery, from his salon in London, but also produces two diffusion ranges, Miss Jones and Jonesboy, plus accessories including gloves, scarves, sunglasses and bags; in 2004 he created a new hat design for British Airways stewardesses.

Die Hüte von Stephen Jones können sogar ihren Träger verändern. Seine bahnbrechenden Kollektionen werden in Museen rund um die Welt gezeigt, so auch im Victoria & Albert Museum in London, im New Yorker Fashion Institute of Technology und im Pariser Louvre. Traditionelle Zylinder, Kreissägen, Militärkappen, Baskenmützen und Melonen werden augenzwinkernd miniaturisiert, mit überraschenden Details versehen und Effekte à la Schiaparelli mit entzückenden Farbkombinationen betont. Alle Arbeiten des Designers harmonieren auf angenehme Weise mit dem momentan in der Mode herrschenden Klima. Der 1957 geborene Jones war schon immer ein begehrter Partygast. Während der neoromantischen Ära im London der 1980er Jahre fertigte er Kopfbedeckungen für seine Freunde Steve Strange und Boy George, für Kundschaft also, der ihr Image über alles ging. 1984 eroberte er Paris, wo er auf Einladung von Jean Paul Gaultier und Thierry Mugler Hüte entwarf. Seit damals hat er unter anderem mit Comme des Garçons, Balenciaga, Hermès und Vivienne Westwood gearbeitet. Seine bekannteste Kooperation ist jedoch die mit John Galliano, deren zehnjähriges Jubiläum 2004 gefeiert wurde. Seit seinem Bachelor-Abschluss im Fach Modedesign am Central Saint Martins 1979 hat Jones seine kreativen Fähigkeiten auch in den Bereichen Schuhe (eine Kollektion für Sergio Rossi), Briefmarken (für die englische Royal Mail) und Kimonos unter Beweis gestellt. Hüte sind jedoch seine große Leidenschaft, und er verkauft sie nicht nur unter dem Hauptlabel Model Millinery von seinem Londoner Atelier aus, sondern betreibt auch zwei Nebenlinien, Miss Jones und Jonesboy. Dazu kommen noch Accessoires wie Handschuhe, Schals, Sonnenbrillen und Taschen. 2004 kreierte Jones eine neue Kopfbedeckung für die Stewardessen der British Airways.

Les chapeaux de Stephen Jones sont capables de transformer n'importe quelle tenue. Ses collections révolutionnaires sont exposées dans les musées du monde entier, notamment au Victoria & Albert Museum de Londres, au Fashion Institute of Technology de New York et au Louvre à Paris. Il miniaturise avec insolence les traditionnels chapeaux haut-de-forme, canotiers, casquettes militaires, bérets et autres chapeaux melon, y ajoute des détails inattendus et souligne leurs tournures « schiaparelliesques » à travers d'exquises combinaisons de couleurs. Son travail colle toujours aux dernières tendances avec bienveillance. Stephen Jones (né en 1957) possède ce côté cool des privilégiés dont le nom figure toujours sur la liste des invités. Pendant la période néo-romantique du Londres des années 80, il crée des chapeaux pour ses amis Steve Strange et Boy George, des clients qui accordent énormément d'importance à leur image. En 1984, il devient le premier modiste anglais à travailler à Paris quand Jean Paul Gaultier et Thierry Mugler l'invitent à venir leur dessiner des chapeaux. Depuis, il travaille avec de nombreuses maisons telles que Comme des Garçons, Balenciaga, Hermès et Vivienne Westwood. Mais son association la plus célèbre reste celle avec John Galliano, avec lequel il a célébré 10 ans de collaboration en 2004. Depuis qu'il a décroché son BA en mode à Central Saint Martins en 1979, le charme créatif de Jones a parfaitement opéré dans les domaines de la chaussure (il a créé une collection pour Sergio Rossi), des timbres-poste (pour la Royal Mail d'Angleterre) et du kimono. Cependant, les chapeaux restent son premier amour et il vend non seulement sa ligne principale, Model Millinery, dans sa boutique de Londres, mais produit également deux lignes secondaires, Miss Jones et Jonesboy, ainsi que des accessoires incluant des gants, des écharpes, des lunettes de soleil et des sacs ; en 2004, il a même créé un nouveau modèle de chapeau pour les hôtesses de l'air de British Airways.

TERRY NEWMAN

What are your signature designs? Anything that makes your heart beat faster **What is your favourite piece from any of your collections?** Autumn/winter 1996 Rose Royce. A rose shaped top hat in velvet and satin. Petulant & arch, romantic & lyrical **How would you describe your work?** It's not work, it's my life **What's your ultimate goal?** Total world domination! No, I don't have one **What inspires you?** Everything from broken garlands of fairy lights on a dark, rainy February afternoon on Brighton Pier to the Dior haute couture archives in Paris **Can fashion still have a political ambition?** Yes, but beware of pretension; it's only a frock

Who do you have in mind when you design? I channel Margaret Rutherford and Beyoncé at the same time **Is the idea of creative collaboration important to you?** Yes, not only with the greatest designers of our times such as John, Claude and Rei, but also with the fabulous milliners in my workrooms **Who has been the greatest influence on your career?** My reaction against my background. Knowing that I didn't fit in, and therefore having to create my own dream world, which I am still trying to describe, though hats. Stylist Kim Bowen who taught me spontaneity (left to my own devices I'm too anal). And recently John Galliano and his

team, my second family in Paris **How have your own experiences affected your work as a designer?** It's all about experiences and being able to re-interpret them with objects you put on your head **Which is more important in your work: the process or the product?** Neither, it's a non-stop negative-positive roller-coaster **Is designing difficult for you, if so, what drives you to continue?** For me designing is like breathing, it's the editing that's difficult **Have you ever been influenced or moved by the reaction to your designs?** In my first season in Paris 20 years ago, Jean Paul Gaultier was so pleased with the hats I made for him that half way through the

fashion show he pushed me out onto the runway and all the hatted models kissed me on top of my head. I received a standing ovation, burst into tears and more or less passed out **What's your definition of beauty?** Purity and honesty, complexity and lies; take your pick! **What's your philosophy?** Blue and green should never be seen without a colour in between **What is the most important lesson you've learned?** "Somewhere over the rainbow way up high, There's a land that I heard of once in a lullaby, Somewhere over the rainbow skies are blue, And the dreams that you dare to dream really do come true." Always a friend of Dorothy.

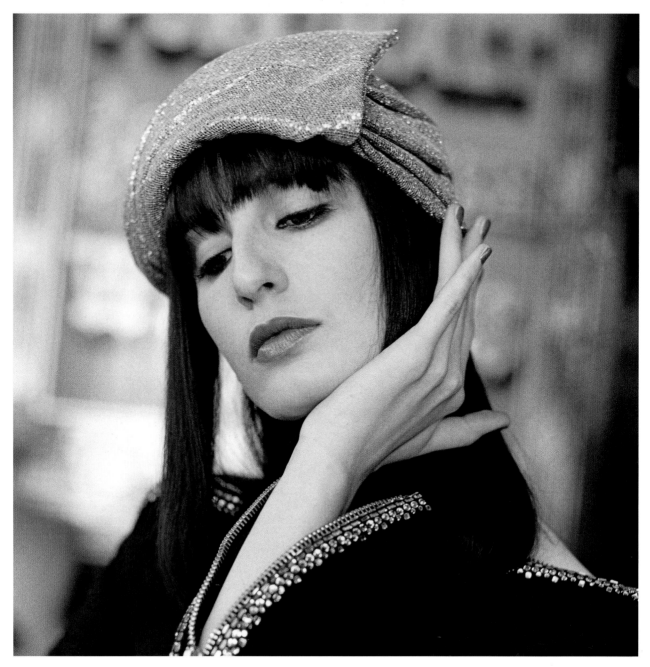

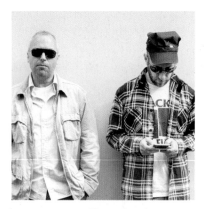

STÜSSY

"We describe our work as 'remixing'" SHAWN STÜSSY

Twenty-five years is a pretty long time in anyone's books. Most marriages fail at seven, cars conk out at ten, so to notch up a quarter-century anniversary is a feat in itself. Launched in Laguna Beach, California, back in the day, a certain Shawn Stüssy was so captivated by the lifestyle and apparel born on the beach that he decided to adopt the laconic uniform as his own, and morph his name – or, more accurately, his distinct signature – into one of the world's most recognised brands. Like a match to an unlit firecracker, things went fizzing sky-high in an instant, with like-minded surf rats empathising instantly with the graphic-based designs on boards, tees and sweats, all born of integrity and an unforced insider's knowledge. An instant cult hit, come the mid-'80s the brand effortlessly rode a tidal wave all the way to New York and London, and the coolest kids in the hottest clubs donned the label as an instant drag on the cigarette of cool. Limiting the global availability ensured the longevity of the brand, and come the '90s, Stüssy decided to fully realise their potential and opened flagship stores in London and New York. A stickler for perfection, Shawn ensured every product was executed to the highest standard, and kept local interest fixed up thanks to the ongoing collaborative site-specific projects with local designers and artists. Like a grand king happy to look down on his kingdom and reap the rewards he had sown, he decided to pass his heavyweight inscribed mantle onto a new team, and appointed Nicholas Bower and Paul Mittleman to lead and direct the creative direction for Stüssy. As integrated into popular culture as 'The Simpsons' or hip hop, Stüssy is populist, Stüssy is street culture. Long may it reign supreme.

25 Jahre sind in fast allen Bereichen eine ziemlich lange Zeit. Die meisten Ehen gehen im siebten Jahr in die Brüche, Autos geben oft nach zehn Jahren den Geist auf. Ein Vierteljahrhundert-Jubiläum feiern zu können, ist also schon eine Leistung an sich. Gegründet wurde das fragliche Unternehmen im kalifornischen Laguna Beach, und zwar an dem Tag, als ein gewisser Shawn Stüssy vom Lifestyle und den Klamotten am Strand so begeistert war, dass er beschloss, dem eine Extraportion Lifestyle hinzuzufügen. Nachdem er sich eine lakonische Uniform zu eigen gemacht hatte, verwandelte Stüssy seinen Namen – oder genauer gesagt: seine unverwechselbare Unterschrift – in eine der bekanntesten Modemarken weltweit. Als hätte man ein Streichholz an eine Feuerwerksrakete gehalten, stellte sich der Erfolg mit einem Schlag ein. Gleichgesinnte passionierte Surfer sympathisierten auf Anhieb mit den grafisch ausgerichteten Entwürfen auf Boards, T-Shirts und Sweatern, denn aus ihnen sprach die Integrität und das kein bisschen aufgesetzte Insider-Wissen ihres Designers. Aus dem Stand zum Kultschlager avanciert, ritt das Label Mitte der 1980er auf einer imposanten Welle bis nach New York und London. Die coolsten Kids in den heißesten Clubs

trugen das Label wie eine Auszeichnung in Sachen Coolness. Dass man die Verfügbarkeit auf der ganzen Welt limitierte, sicherte die Lebensdauer der Marke. Mit Beginn der Neunziger beschloss Stüssy, sein Potential voll auszuschöpfen und eröffnete Flagship Stores in London und New York. Als Perfektionist sorgte Stüssy dafür, dass jedes Stück höchsten Qualitätsansprüchen gerecht wurde. Dank fortgesetzter Kooperationsprojekte mit lokalen Designern und Künstlern hielt er auch das Interesse vor Ort aufrecht. Wie ein großer König, der glücklich auf sein Reich schaut und den Lohn seiner Anstrengungen erntet, beschloss Shawn Stüssy dann, seinen bedeutungsschweren, beschrifteten Königsmantel an ein neues Team weiterzugeben: Nicholas Bower und Paul Mittleman bestimmen seither die kreative Richtung, die Stüssy einschlägt. Als Teil der Popkultur wie die Simpsons oder Hiphop ist Stüssy bekennend populistisch, eben Street Culture. – Lang lebe der König!

25 ans, c'est long pour tout le monde. On divorce généralement après sept ans de mariage, on change de voiture tous les dix ans, alors fêter le vingt-cinquième anniversaire de son entreprise est un véritable événement en soi. Sur Laguna Beach en Californie, un certain Shawn Stüssy se passionne à tel point pour le style de vie et la mode de plage qu'il décide d'en rajouter une couche. S'appropriant cet uniforme laconique, Shawn transforme son nom, ou plus précisément sa signature distincte, en l'une des marques les plus célèbres du monde. Telle une traînée de poudre, la marque suscite un engouement immédiat et les surfeurs adoptent tout de suite ses motifs graphiques appliqués sur les planches, les T-shirts et les sweats, tous produits avec l'honnêteté et le savoir-faire d'un vrai membre de la culture skate. Devenant instantanément culte, la marée Stüssy déferle sans effort jusqu'à New York et Londres au milieu des années 80, et les branchés des derniers clubs à la mode arborent les créations de la griffe comme le summum du cool d'outre-Atlantique. Une distribution mondiale limitée garantit la longévité de la marque, mais au début des années 90, Stüssy décide d'exploiter tout son potentiel en ouvrant des boutiques à Londres et à New York. Maniaque de la perfection, Shawn respecte un cahier des charges très strict pour la fabrication de chaque produit. Il reste fidèle à ses origines à travers des projets de collaboration permanents spécifiquement californiens avec des créateurs et des artistes du cru. Tel un heureux roi contemplant son royaume et récoltant les fruits qu'il a semés, Shawn décide de passer son flambeau de champion poids lourd à une nouvelle équipe, nommant Nicholas Bower et Paul Mittleman à la direction de la création de Stüssy. Aussi intégré à la culture populaire que les Simpson ou le hip-hop, Stüssy est populiste, Stussy incarne la culture de la rue. Alors long règne à Stussy ! BEN REARDON

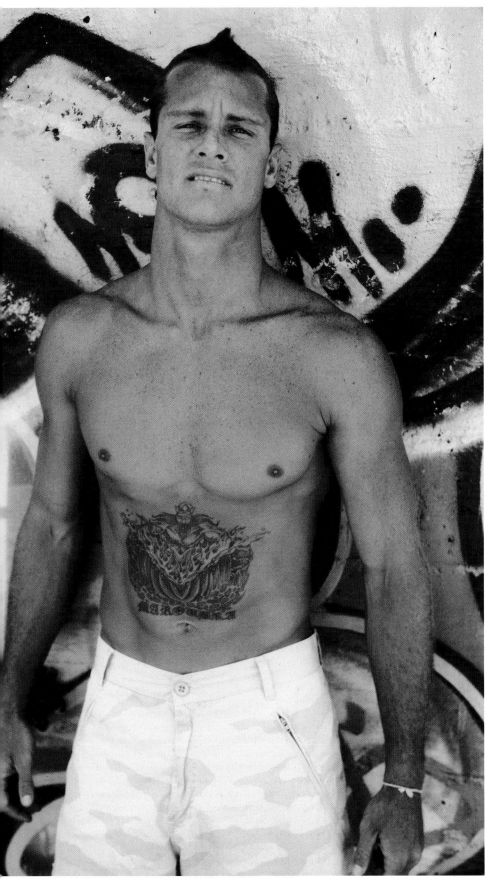

What are your signature designs? American classics i.e. varsity jackets/hooded sweats/ caps and tees **What is your favourite piece from any of your collections?** Classic California gramps walkshort **How would you describe your work?** Remixing **What's your ultimate goal?** Our ultimate goal is not related to clothing **What inspires you?** Popular culture **Can fashion still have a political ambition?** Possibly, but not at Stüssy **Who do you have in mind when you design?** Friends we know in streetwear culture **Is the idea of creative collaboration important to you?** Yes, collaboration has always been a big part of the Stüssy culture **Who has been the greatest influence on your career?** Many people have been influences… but what influences our career are people with style who continually redefine streetwear **How have your own experiences affected your work as a designer?** Our experiences have over the years kept us grounded as designers **Which is more important in your work: the process or the product?** Our work is the process and product is the result of our work **Is designing difficult for you, if so, what drives you to continue?** No, it is not difficult, but is always challenging **Have you ever been influenced or moved by the reaction to your designs?** Yes, definitely, we are in a commercial business **What's your definition of beauty?** Beauty is change **What's your philosophy?** On what… Sex , drugs and rock 'n' roll **What is the most important lesson you've learned?** a. You cannot fill a 40GB iPod with good music. b. The bus ride from Narita to the Park Hyatt is always longer than you think it will be. c. Harry Potter movies are getting steadily worse. d. Sneakers were more fun to collect before they became collectable.

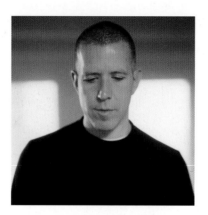

SUPREME

"It feels really nice when I go to Japan and I see a bunch of dope kids wearing our stuff" JAMES JEBBIA

Supreme (founded 1994) is a label that has pioneered skatewear styles for those outside the pro-skateboarding circuit. Initially only available in New York, Supreme has a sheen of exclusivity that has attracted and maintained a hardcore fan-base. Jeans, T-shirts and baseball caps are designed from a high fashion angle with top-end production values. The man behind the label is UK-born James Jebbia. Jebbia left London for New York in the mid-'80s, with no plans. He found himself in the midst of an inspiring and creative new scene, from hip-hop to clubs, fashion and art. After working at a couple of clothing stores, Jebbia along with his partner Mary Ann opened Union, a small SoHo boutique, through which they met Shawn Stüssy. Together they opened the Stüssy store from which Jebbia learned much, eventually going on to open his own Supreme store in the Little Italy neighbourhood of New York in 1994. Things really took off when they began their own clothing line in 1995. His concept was to present New York skateboarding style with an emphasis on high quality design while retaining a hardcore, rebellious edge. In 1997 Jebbia took Supreme to Japan, opening three stores, one each in Tokyo, Osaka and Fukuoka. A further shop followed in Los Angeles in 2004. At the LA store an above-ground skate bowl is the centrepiece of the 2,800 ft space and, true to the label's hippest, hottest status, it is a bowl like no other. Designed by Midwest art collective Simparch, and weighing nearly 5,000 lbs, it references minimalist sculptors Donald Judd and Carl Andre alongside LA's 'Dogtown And Z-Boys' days of skateboarding in drained swimming pools. Supreme lines are carried at a handful of stores throughout the world including The Hideout in London, Colette in Paris and Slam Jam in Milan.

Das 1994 gegründete Label Supreme war Pionier für Skatewear außerhalb professioneller Skateboarder-Kreise. Zunächst nur in New York erhältlich, besaß Supreme den Reiz der Exklusivität, die eine treue Fangemeinde anlockt und bei der Stange hält. Jeans, T-Shirts und Baseballcaps werden mit Couture-Anspruch entworfen und in Topqualität produziert. Der Mann hinter der Marke ist der in Großbritannien geborene James Jebbia. Er verließ London Mitte der 1980er Jahre ohne besondere Pläne in Richtung New York. Dort fand er sich inmitten einer inspirierenden und kreativen neuen Szene aus Hiphop, Clubs, Mode und Kunst wieder. Nachdem er in einer Reihe von Kleiderläden gejobbt hatte, eröffnete Jebbia zusammen mit seiner Partnerin Mary Ann in SoHo eine kleine Boutique namens Union, über die er mit Shawn Stüssy bekannt wurde. Gemeinsam starteten sie den Stüssy-Laden, wo Jebbia viel lernte, bis er schließlich 1994 in Little Italy seinen eigenen Supreme Store aufmachte. Richtig in Gang kam die Sache, als man 1995 mit der eigenen Kleiderlinie begann. Das Konzept lief darauf hinaus, New Yorker Skater-Mode zu präsentiert, die von

hoher designerischer Qualität, aber trotzdem noch authentisch und rebellisch war. 1997 brachte Jebbia Supreme nach Japan, wo er drei Läden eröffnete, je einen in Tokio, Osaka und Fukuoka. Eine weitere Filiale folgte 2004 in Los Angeles. In diesem Laden bildet eine oberirdische Skate-Bowl die Mitte der 850 m² großen Verkaufsfläche. Gemäß den Kriterien der Marke in Sachen Hipness ist diese Bowl einzigartig. Entworfen wurde sie vom Kunstkollektiv Simparch aus Midwest und wiegt knapp 2 300 Kilo. Es gibt erkennbare Bezüge zu den minimalistischen Bildhauern Donald Judd und Carl Andre sowie zu den Zeiten von „Dogtown And Z-Boys" in LA, als man in trockengelegten Swimmingpools skatete. Supreme-Mode findet man in einer Handvoll Läden rund um die Welt, darunter The Hideout in London, Colette in Paris und Slam Jam in Mailand.

La griffe Supreme (fondée en 1994) invente des looks de skateurs pour ceux qui n'appartiennent pas au circuit professionnel du skateboard. D'abord uniquement distribuées à New York, les créations Supreme dégagent un côté luxueux qui leur a valu l'intérêt et la fidélité d'une base de fans plutôt hardcore. Jeans, T-shirts et casquettes de baseball sont tous conçus sous l'angle de l'exclusivité avec des critères de production haut de gamme. L'homme derrière la marque est le Britannique James Jebbia. Sans projet particulier, ce dernier quitte Londres pour New York au milieu des années 80 et se retrouve au beau milieu d'une nouvelle scène créative et fort inspirante, du hip-hop à la culture club en passant par la mode et les arts. Après avoir travaillé pour deux magasins d'habillement, Jebbia et sa partenaire Mary Ann ouvrent Union, une petite boutique dans SoHo, par le biais de laquelle ils rencontrent Shawn Stüssy. Ensemble, ils ouvrent la boutique Stüssy, une expérience très enrichissante pour James Jebbia, qui finit par ouvrir la première boutique Supreme dans Little Italy à New York en 1994. Sa carrière décolle vraiment lorsqu'il commence à créer sa propre ligne en 1995. Son concept consiste à proposer des tenues de skate typiquement new-yorkaises en mettant l'accent sur une qualité supérieure mais en préservant un côté hardcore et rebelle. En 1997, Jebbia importe Supreme au Japon où il ouvre trois boutiques à Tokyo, Osaka et Fukuoka, avant d'inaugurer un autre espace de vente à Los Angeles en 2004 : ici, une rampe de skate surélevée constitue la pièce maîtresse d'un espace de 850 mètres carrés, et fidèle au statut ultra-branché de la griffe, cette rampe-là ne ressemble à aucune autre. Conçue par Simparch, un collectif artistique du Midwest, et pesant près de 2 300 kilos, elle évoque le travail des sculpteurs minimalistes Donald Judd et Carl Andre ainsi que la grande période du skateboard à L.A., pratiqué dans des piscines vides comme dans le film documentaire Dogtown And Z-Boys. Les collections de Supreme sont disponibles dans quelques boutiques internationales telles que The Hideout à Londres, Colette à Paris et Slam Jam à Milan.

SKYE SHERWIN

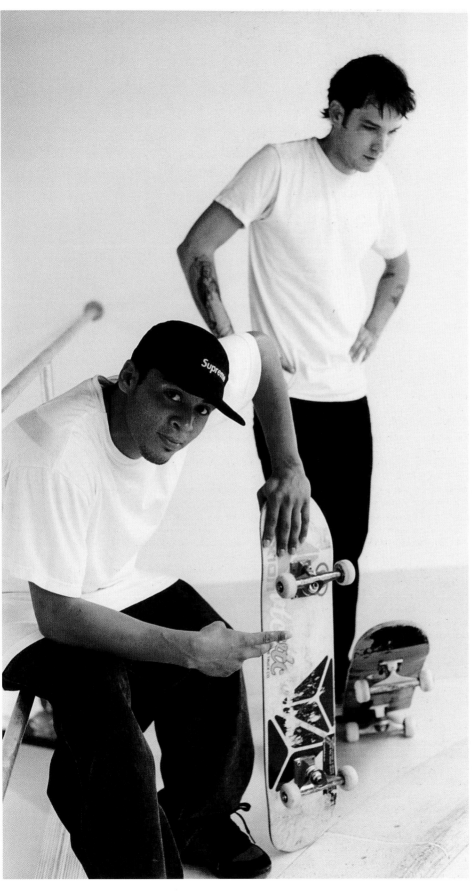

What are your signature designs? Hmmm… I think for us it's more about our overall look and what we stand for **What is your favourite piece from any of your collections?** Our "Fuck Bush" decks & stickers are my personal favourites **How would you describe your work?** We always strive for our stuff to be dope, hard and well-made **What's your ultimate goal?** To be at a level like APC but for a more bugged crowd **What inspires you?** When I see everyday people come together to protest, fight and risk arrest in order to shine some light on the evil shit that is going on in this fucked up world **Can fashion still have a political ambition?** I think that it can, whether the message actually resonates with the people that you're ultimately trying to reach is another story though, at least here in America where we are surrounded by dumb religious rednecks who have zero interest in differing views or opinions **Who do you have in mind when you design?** A good friend of ours named Aaron. He has his own great style and is often the first with new shit. He wouldn't be caught dead in anything slightly played out, but swears to God he doesn't give a fuck about clothing or brands or how he looks. For us if he likes it, so will a lot of other picky people **Is the idea of creative collaboration important to you?** Of course. I don't design anything myself, I work with a really talented young designer named Luke Meier. He and I will go over stuff many times a day, but I also collaborate with many people from graphics people, artists, photographers, my partner in LA to our production team **Who has been the greatest influence on your career?** Probably Shawn Stüssy & my old boss from Parachute named Morgan **How have your own experiences affected your work as a designer?** Subconsciously many important events and experiences end up shaping what we do, from the recent disastrous elections to a trip to Jamaica, to being in New York in the '80s **Which is more important in your work: the process or the product?** The product is most important but the process is where all of the hard work and determination comes into play **Is designing difficult for you, if so, what drives you to continue?** It certainly can be difficult to hold the whole thing together, make progress and stay on top of your game season after season. But I believe in what we are doing and this is how I make my living **Have you ever been influenced or moved by the reaction to your designs?** I have to say, it feels really nice when I go to Japan and I see a bunch of dope kids wearing our stuff **What's your definition of beauty?** Baby twins, boy and a girl **What is the most important lesson you've learned?** It's cool to work hard and do what you have to do so you can attain a certain level of success, but it doesn't mean shit if you don't have love and happiness in your life.

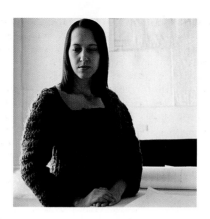

TESS GIBERSON

"The presence of the hand is a consistent element in my work"

New York-based designer Tess Giberson, winner in 2002 of the Ecco Domani sponsorship award, takes an unconventional approach to fashion. Raised by parents who moonlighted as artists, she grew up surrounded by creativity. Giberson has a folkloric aesthetic and her clothing is often noted for its hand-crafted details. A Rhode Island School of Design graduate (1996), Giberson's clothing has an intimate, playful quality. For example, special pieces are hand-sewn, knitted and knotted with macramé. For her show 'Assemblage' (autumn/winter 2004), each model removed one detail from her outfit before using these pieces to construct an entirely new outfit for the show's finale. For autumn/winter 2003, meanwhile, models undressed and draped their outfits over a bare frame-like structure, creating a communal living shelter. Giberson blends science, pretty fabrics, reconstruction and philosophy to bring her shows together, literally and figuratively, and her garments have been included in museum exhibits from New York to Milan. In 2004 she participated in a group show called "Invisible Birds" at the Taka Ishii Gallery in Tokyo that featured works on paper and fabric. Giberson's ethos is that creation is a never-ending process, allowing her to take us from point A to point B in a way that is earnest, ingenious and utterly charming.

Die in New York lebende Designerin Tess Giberson, die 2002 den Sponsor-Preis Ecco Domani gewann, vertritt in Sachen Mode einen ziemlich unkonventionellen Ansatz. Als Kind von Eltern, die nebenbei als Künstler arbeiteten, wuchs sie in einer von Kreativität geprägten Umgebung auf. Ihre Ästhetik ist folkloristisch, und oft fallen die handwerklichen Details ihrer Kleider ins Auge. Die Entwürfe der Absolventin der Rhode Island School of Design wirken vertraut und verspielt. So gibt es beispielsweise handgenähte, -gestrickte und mit Makramee versehene Einzelstücke. Bei ihrer Schau „Assemblage" (Herbst/Winter 2004) entfernte jedes Model ein Detail von seinem Outfit. Aus diesen wurde dann ein ganz neues Ensemble für das Finale gestaltet. Für die Kollektion Herbst/Winter 2003 dagegen zogen sich die Models aus und drapierten ihre Outfits auf eine kahle, rahmenartige Konstruktion, die so zu einer Art Gemeinschaftshöhle wurde. Giberson vermengt für ihre Shows Wissenschaft, hübsche Stoffe, Rekonstruktion und Philosophie im wörtlichen wie im übertragenen Sinn. Ihre Entwürfe waren schon bei Ausstellungen von New York bis Mailand zu bewundern. 2004 beteiligte sie sich an einer Gemeinschaftsschau unter dem Namen „Invisible Birds" in der Galerie Taka Ishii in Tokio. Dort waren Arbeiten auf Papier und Stoff zu sehen. Nach Gibersons Verständnis ist das Kreieren ein nie endender Prozess, der ihr erlaubt, uns auf gewissenhafte, raffinierte und überaus charmante Weise von A nach B zu bringen.

Lauréate de la bourse Ecco Domani en 2002, la créatrice new-yorkaise Tess Giberson approche la mode comme personne d'autre. Elevée par des parents artistes qui travaillaient au noir, elle grandit dans un environnement très créatif. Diplômée de la School of Design de Rhode Island (1996), Tess Giberson privilégie une esthétique folklorique, avec des vêtements qui se font souvent remarquer pour leurs détails artisanaux et leur côté à la fois intime et ludique. Par exemple, certaines pièces sont cousues, tricotés et nouées à la main au macramé. Lors de son défilé « Assemblage » (automne/hiver 2004), tous les mannequins ont retiré un détail de leurs tenues avant de les utiliser pour construire un tout nouveau vêtement destiné à clôturer le défilé. A l'automne/hiver 2003, les mannequins se sont déshabillées et ont drapé leurs vêtements sur une sorte de cage nue pour créer un abri communautaire. Tess Giberson mêle la science, les beaux tissus, la reconstruction et la philosophie pour construire ses présentations, tant au plan littéral que figuré. Ses créations ont été présentées dans plusieurs expositions, de New York à Milan. En 2004, elle participe à un défilé de groupe baptisé « Invisible Birds » à la galerie Taka Ishii de Tokyo, spécialisée dans les œuvres sur papier et sur tissu. Dans l'éthique de Tess Giberson, la création est un processus sans fin, ce qui lui permet de nous emmener d'un point A à un point B avec honnêteté et ingéniosité, et toujours avec une haute dose de charme.

LESLEY ARFIN

What are your signature designs? Intricate handwork details combined with tailoring and traditional sewing techniques are consistent elements throughout the clothing. These techniques are tools used within the pieces, yet the actual designs vary according to ideas I am working with at that particular time **What is your favourite piece from any of your collections?** I focus more on the whole of the collection so it's difficult to think of only one piece **How would you describe your work?** The collections are concept-driven, incorporating clothing that combines finished tailoring with intricate details of piecing, crochet and embroidery. The presence of the hand is a consistent element, resulting in pieces with a timeless and individual nature **What's your ultimate goal?** A long, independent career and the ability to continue to work with integrity on projects I remain interested in **What inspires you?** Conversations and experiences with family and friends **Can fashion still have a political ambition?** Depending on the context **Who do you have in mind when you design?** It's not so much a particular person but a combination of many I find attractive. They represent a wide age range but share a similar attitude and sensibility **Is the idea of creative collaboration important to you?** Definitely. Collaborations have produced the most interesting results in my experience especially with people who work outside of fashion. Through the process of collaboration the work is pushed in directions I may not have seen on my own **Who has been the greatest influence on your career?** My husband Jon has had the strongest influence on my work. Because he is an artist and works outside of fashion he is concerned mostly with ideas and the complete environment being created. He provides a point of view that isn't always practical but is essential as it challenges and balances my work **How have your own experiences affected your work as a designer?** My childhood and how my parents raised me created a foundation for my work today. My parents are both artists who moved to the country to raise our family in the late '60s. They placed a strong emphasis on freedom to express ourselves through working with our hands and thinking outside of convention **Which is more important in your work: the process or the product?** The process is most exciting but the product becomes most rewarding because it continues to exist after each collection **Is designing difficult for you, if so, what drives you to continue?** I begin a collection with ideas I am interested in developing. I think first about the actual show and how to build the idea through an environment and then how the clothing will be incorporated. Once I see the show in my mind and have worked through the details I can begin to focus on the actual clothing design and create a collection to fit into the overall concept. As long as I have an idea I am interested in developing, there is a reason to continue making clothing **What's your definition of beauty?** Creation in all forms.

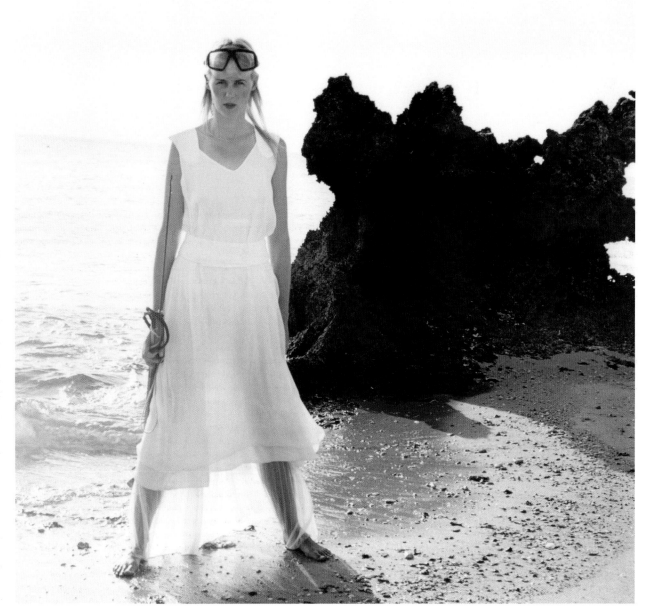

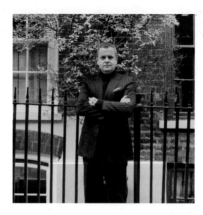

TIMOTHY EVEREST

"I'd like to be remembered as someone who made people take British clothing seriously"

Timothy Everest (born in Southampton in 1962) is at the forefront of the movement to revolutionise bespoke men's tailoring, producing an experimental and contemporary look while retaining a traditional conservative backbone and attention to detail. Such an approach should come as no surprise given that his mentor was Tommy Nutter, legendary tailor to The Beatles and The Rolling Stones. His headquarters are a restored Georgian house in Spitalfields, once home to Bloomsbury artist Mark Gertler, that has played host to a variety of well-dressed well-knowns including stars of parliament, the silver screen and the sports field. Away from his own label, Everest has been hired by Daks to help revive the quintessential British label and continues to work with Marks & Spencer on their Autograph line. More recently he has developed a premium bespoke range and diffusion line for Levi's at Oki-ni. His collaboration with Kim Jones for the younger designer's spring/summer 2005 collection was well received and led to a joint label for the autumn/winter 2005 season. The latest development to emerge from his own line is Timothy Everest's Made To Measure (MTM), a meeting point between the seasonal collection and the bespoke service. Reaching beyond 'the suit', the range comprises knitwear and outerwear and is aimed at both a male and female clientele. Since taking his first bespoke order in 1989, to the launch of his first ready-to-wear collection in 1999, Everest has continued to expand the accessibility of bespoke tailoring without compromising his meticulous attention to detail.

Der 1962 in Southampton geborene Timothy Everest steht an der Spitze einer Bewegung, die sich vorgenommen hat, die Herrenmaßschneiderei zu revolutionieren. Auf einer traditionell-konservativen Basis und mit Liebe zum Detail produziert er einen experimentellen und zeitgemäßen Look. Wenn man weiß, dass Tommy Nutter, der legendäre Schneider der Beatles und Rolling Stones, sein Mentor war, verwundert diese Einstellung nicht. Der Firmensitz befindet sich in einer restaurierten georgianischen Villa in Spitalfields, in der einst der Bloomsbury-Künstler Mark Gertler residierte. Eine Vielzahl gut gekleideter und gut bekannter Leute, darunter Stars aus Politik, Film und Sport, ist hier schon ein- und ausgegangen. Neben seinem eigenen Label war Everest auch schon an der Wiederbelebung von Daks, der britische Marke schlechthin, beteiligt. Und nach wie vor ist er für die Linie Autograph bei Marks & Spencer tätig. In jüngster Vergangenheit entwickelte er eine hochwertige Maßkollektion und Nebenlinie für

Levi's bei Oki-ni. Seine Zusammenarbeit mit Kim Jones für die Kollektion Frühjahr/Sommer 2005 des jüngeren Designers war so fruchtbar, dass sich daraus ein gemeinsames Label für die Kollektion Herbst/Winter 2005 ergab. Das neueste Projekt innerhalb seiner eigenen Linie ist Timothy Everest's Made To Measure (MTM) – hier kombiniert er die aktuelle Kollektion mit einem Maß-Service. Dabei reicht die Produktpalette weit über den klassischen Anzug hinaus und umfasst auch Strickwaren, Mäntel und Jacken. Die angepeilte Klientel sind Männer und Frauen. Seit seinem ersten Maßauftrag im Jahr 1989 und selbst nach der Präsentation seiner ersten Prêt-à-porter-Kollektion 1999 ist Everest seinem Vorsatz treu geblieben: der Maßschneiderei zu mehr Anerkennung zu verhelfen, ohne bei seiner Detailverliebtheit Kompromisse einzugehen.

Timothy Everest (né en 1962 à Southampton) occupe l'avant-garde du mouvement qui révolutionne la confection sur mesure pour homme: il produit en effet un look expérimental et contemporain tout en respectant le savoir-faire artisanal et en portant une grande attention aux détails. Une telle approche n'a rien de surprenant quand on sait qu'Everest a été formé par Tommy Nutter, tailleur légendaire des Beatles et des Rolling Stones. Il a installé ses bureaux dans une maison George V restaurée à Spitalfields, autrefois résidence de l'artiste de Bloomsbury Mark Gertler, qui accueille désormais toute une brochette de célébrités élégantes, notamment des stars de la politique, du grand écran et du sport. Outre sa propre griffe, Everest travaille aussi à moderniser Daks, marque typiquement anglaise, et continue à collaborer avec Marks & Spencer sur leur ligne Autograph. Récemment, il a développé une gamme tailleur de première qualité et une ligne de diffusion pour Levi's chez Oki-ni. Comme sa collaboration avec Kim Jones sur la collection printemps/été 2005 a été bien accueillie, ils ont décidé de créer une griffe commune pour la saison automne/hiver 2005. Le dernier projet de Timothy Everest pour sa ligne éponyme s'appelle Made To Measure (MTM), au carrefour de la collection saisonnière et du service sur mesure. Allant au-delà du simple costume, la gamme comprend de la maille et des vêtements d'extérieur destinés à une clientèle masculine et féminine. De la première commande qui lui a été passée en 1989 jusqu'au lancement de sa première collection de prêt-à-porter en 1999, Everest a toujours cherché à rendre le costume sur mesure plus accessible, sans pour autant compromettre son attention méticuleuse aux détails.

WILL FAIRMAN

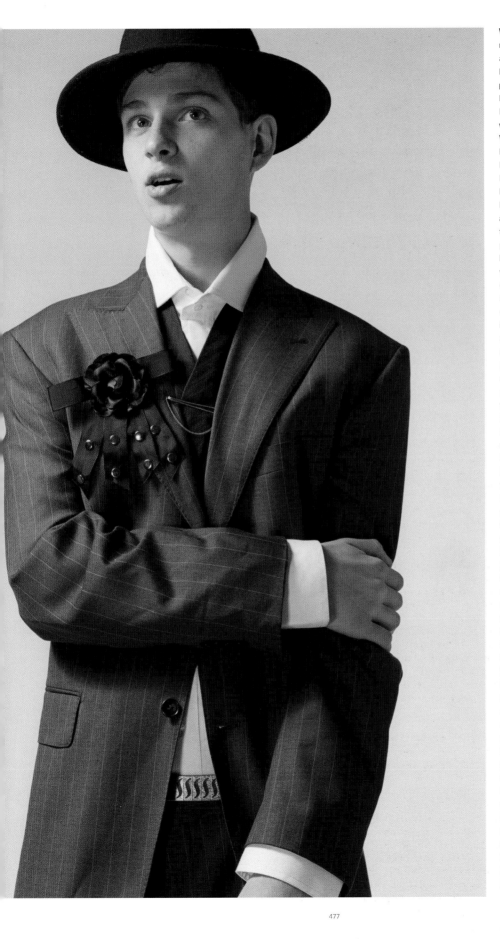

What are your signature designs? For me, it's not a particular style. It's about making sure a garment has the best fit, the best fabric, the best things for the job **What's your favourite piece from any of your collections?** An old blazer, which I've had for about eight years. It's very low key **How would you describe your work?** Individual styles for individual people **What's your ultimate goal?** To be remembered as someone who made people take British clothing seriously **What inspires you?** People, movies, travel, situations, challenges. I think visually so I get very inspired by aesthetics **Can fashion still have a political ambition?** Yes, I suppose so. To be yourself is the only way you can be modern. I just think people need depth and reason **Who do you have in mind when you design?** Somebody who is aware of their heritage, what the value of that is now and for the future, and who is sensitive to what's going on internationally on all levels **Is the idea of creative collaboration important to you?** Yes, it helps you grow and actually addresses reality. Smaller companies can bring a lot of nuances to bigger companies and bigger companies can help smaller companies. For us it's been very, very positive **Which is more important in your work: the process or the product?** All of it. It's no good having a concept without being able to make it work. The whole process, I love it. And the whole team makes it work, not just you **Who has been the greatest influence on your career?** Probably my uncle and his job in a dodgy old tailor's. I got a job there when I was about 17. It was really old-fashioned, but the best grounding I could have had. It was about old-fashioned retail and service, and proper standards. Tommy Nutter is also one of my biggest influences. He was a very modest person and able to articulate to his generation what tailoring was about **Is designing difficult for you and, if so, what drives you to continue?** I don't find it difficult to design in the sense of putting together what I think, the concept, the range and how it goes together. But sometimes it's difficult because I don't have the time to do much of anything because I am constantly running around **Have you ever been influenced or moved by the reaction to your designs?** I like the compliments which are not necessarily to your face – you just hear things and that is really, really nice **What's your philosophy?** Hard work is important and you must learn your trade. Be yourself and believe in yourself. Then everything is possible **What is your definition of beauty?** Depth and subtlety. I like those things you have to study **What is the most important lesson that you've learned?** To be patient with my impatience, that was what my old boss told me. What goes around comes around. Be very careful what you say about people, because you can go down as well as up, and believe in what you can do.

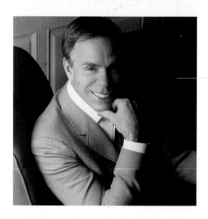

TOMMY HILFIGER

"People always want something unexpected and exciting.
That's what drives me"

Born one of nine children in 1951 in Elmira, New York, Tommy Hilfiger's eponymous brand is often viewed as epitomising the American Dream. His career famously began in 1969 with $150 and 20 pairs of jeans. When customers to his People's Palace store in upstate New York failed to find what they were after, he took to designing clothes himself, with no previous training. In 1984, having moved to New York City, Hilfiger launched his first collection under his own name. With his distinctive red, white and blue logo and collegiate/Ivy League influences, Hilfiger presented a preppy vision of Americana which, coupled with his looser sportswear aesthetic, found a surprising new audience in the burgeoning hip-hop scene of the early '90s. Hilfiger, a dedicated music fan himself, welcomed this re-interpretation of his work, but rumours that he was less than enamoured by his new audience led him to make an admirable response, lending his support to the Anti-Defamation League and the Washington DC Martin Luther King Jr National Memorial Project Foundation. By 1992 his company had gone public and Hilfiger was named the CFDA's Menswear Designer of the Year in 1995. A new 'semi-luxe' line of tailored separates, entitled simply 'H', was launched in 2004 as a higher-priced, more upmarket addition to the global brand, which now incorporates everything from denim and eyewear to fragrances, homeware, sporting apparel and children's lines. In keeping with his music and fashion influences, Hilfiger chose to market his new 'grown-up' range by asking David Bowie and Iman to appear in ad campaigns for H. In December 2004 Hilfiger looked set on further expansion when he announced an agreement made with Karl Lagerfeld to globally distribute the latter's own-label collections.

Die Marke des 1951 als eines von neun Kindern in Elmira, New York, geborenen Tommy Hilfiger gilt vielen als der Inbegriff des amerikanischen Traums. Seine Karriere begann, wie inzwischen allgemein bekannt ist, 1969 mit 150 Dollar und 20 Paar Jeans. Wenn die Kundschaft in seinem Laden People's Palace nicht fand, wonach sie suchte, stellte er die Stücke – ohne jegliche Vorkenntnisse – eben selbst her. Nach seinem Umzug nach New York City präsentierte Hilfiger 1984 seine erste Kollektion unter eigenem Namen. Mit seinem auffälligen Logo in Rot, Weiß und Blau sowie den Einflüssen des Ivy-League-Stils präsentierte Hilfiger eine Vision von Amerikana im Preppy-Look, die gepaart mit lässiger Sportswear-Ästhetik überraschenderweise eine neue Klientel in der gerade erblühenden Hip-Hop-Szene der frühen Neunziger fand. Als leidenschaftlicher Musikfan begrüßte Hilfiger diese Neuinterpretation seiner Arbeit. Dennoch brachten ihn Gerüchte, er sei von seiner neuen Anhängerschaft wenig angetan, zu dezidierten Reaktionen, etwa der Unterstützung der Anti-Defamation League und der Washington DC Martin Luther King Jr. National Memorial Project Foun-

dation. 1992 ging das Unternehmen an die Börse, 1995 wurde Hilfiger von der CFDA zum Menswear Designer of the Year gekürt. Unter dem schlichten Kürzel H kam 2004 eine neue, halb-luxuriöse Linie von aufwändiger geschneiderten Einzelstücken auf den Markt, quasi die höherpreisige, elitäre Ergänzung der internationalen Marke, die inzwischen von Jeans und Brillen über Düfte, Heimtextilien, Sportartikel bis hin zu Kinderkleidung praktisch alles umfasst. Passend zu seinen musikalischen und modischen Einflüssen entschloss sich Hilfiger, für seine neue „erwachsene" Linie bei David Bowie und Iman anzufragen, die anschließend in der Werbekampagne für H posierten. Im Dezember 2004 setzte Hilfiger weiter auf Expansion, als er eine Kooperation mit Karl Lagerfeld bekannt gab, die im weltweiten Vertrieb der Kollektionen von Lagerfeld bestand.

Né en 1951 dans une famille de neuf enfants à Elmira aux environs de New York, Tommy Hilfiger et sa marque éponyme sont souvent considérés comme l'incarnation du rêve américain. La légende dit qu'il a entamé sa carrière en 1969 avec 150 dollars en poche et 20 paires de jeans. Comme les clients de sa boutique People's Palace au nord de l'Etat de New York n'arrivent pas à trouver ce qu'ils cherchent, il décide de dessiner lui-même des vêtements, sans formation préalable. En 1984, une fois installé à New York, Hilfiger lance une première collection baptisée de son propre nom. Avec son célèbre logo rouge, blanc et bleu et influencé par le style des universités de l'Ivy League, Hilfiger présente une vision BCBG du style américain qui, associée à une esthétique sportwear plus décontractée, séduit une clientèle inattendue au sein de la jeune scène hip-hop du début des années 90. Lui-même passionné de musique, Hilfiger accepte cette interprétation de son travail, mais les rumeurs qui courent sur le fait qu'il ne soit pas particulièrement fan de son nouveau public le conduisent à réagir admirablement en offrant son soutien à la ligue anti-raciste américaine (Anti-Defamation League) et à la Fondation du projet de mémorial national de Martin Luther King Junior. En 1992, son entreprise est introduite en bourse et le CFDA le couronne Menswear Designer of the Year en 1995. Une nouvelle ligne « semi-luxe » de séparés baptisée tout simplement « H » est lancée en 2004 en guise de complément plus haut de gamme et plus onéreux pour cette marque mondiale qui intègre aujourd'hui toutes sortes de lignes, du denim aux lunettes en passant par les parfums, le mobilier, les articles de sport et la mode pour enfant. Fidèle à ses influences vestimentaires et musicales, Hilfiger décide de commercialiser sa nouvelle gamme « adulte » en demandant à David Bowie et Iman d'apparaître dans les campagnes publicitaires de H. En décembre 2004, Hilfiger poursuit son expansion en annonçant la conclusion d'un accord avec Karl Lagerfeld pour distribuer mondialement les collections Lagerfeld.

MARK HOOPER

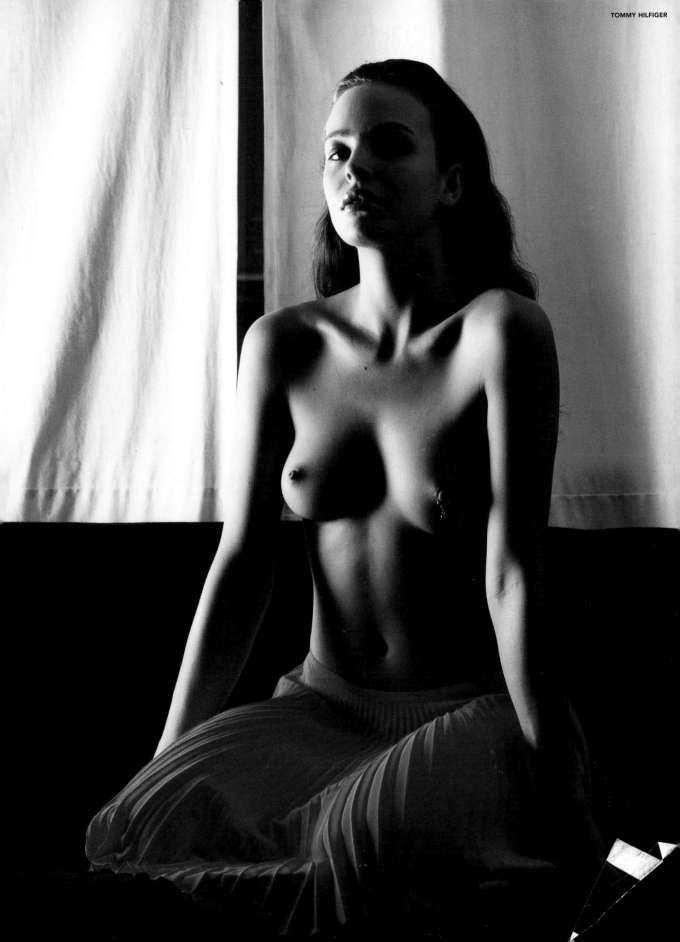

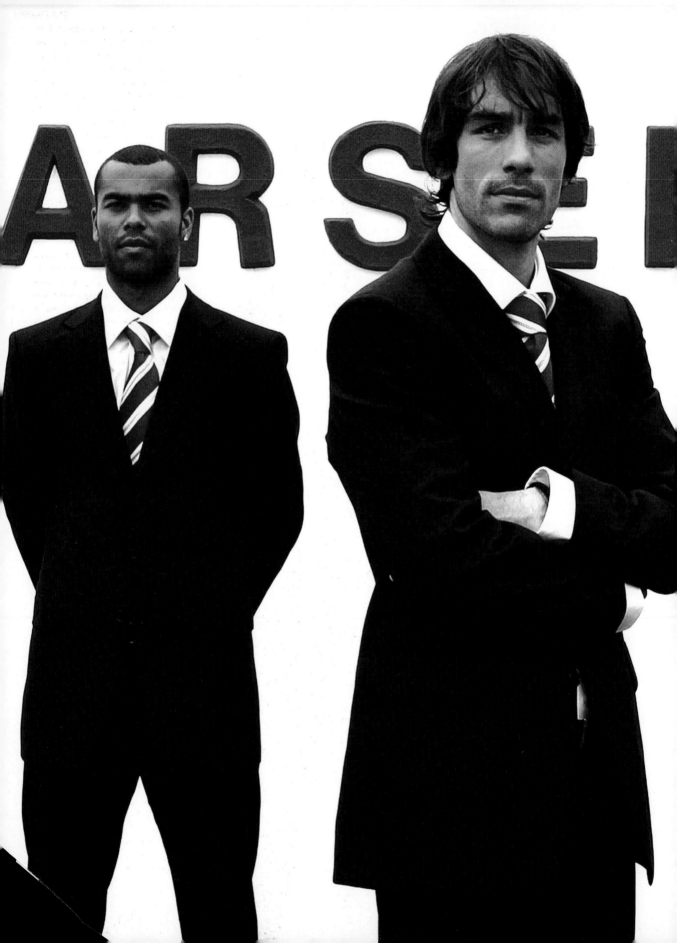

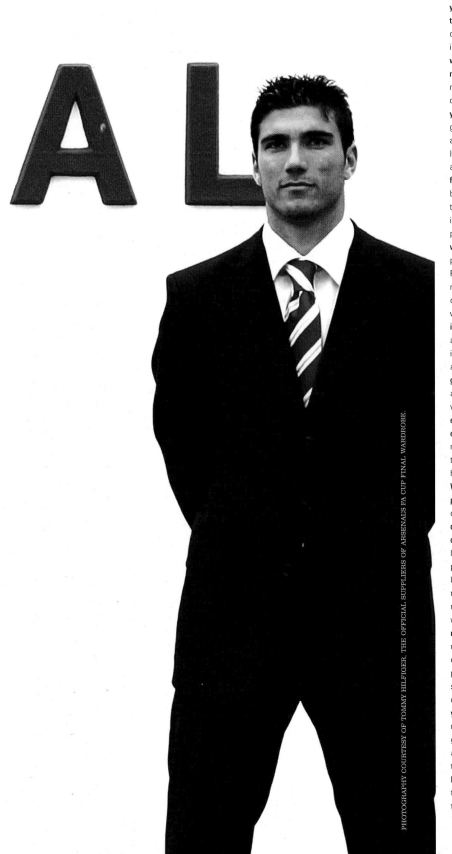

PHOTOGRAPHY COURTESY OF TOMMY HILFIGER, THE OFFICIAL SUPPLIERS OF ARSENAL'S FA CUP FINAL WARDROBE.

What are your signature designs? I am known best for "classics with a twist". For me it's about updating the classics. **What is your favourite piece from any of your collections?** A classic oxford shirt with a contrast collar. It is timeless and classic, and always in fashion **How would you describe your work?** In one word, classic **What's your ultimate goal?** I don't think in terms of one ultimate goal. For me, it's about seizing each opportunity as it reveals itself **What inspires you?** For me, pop culture has been my greatest inspiration. Pop culture to me is about being relevant and being very "now". I thrive on change, evolution and invention, and that's what pop culture is all about. **Can fashion still have a political ambition?** Yes, but for me it's more about self-expression than about politics. People are moved and influenced by different things and for some people, it's politics. **Who do you have in mind when you design?** I see everything through a pop culture lens. Andy Warhol, Jackson Pollock, The Stones, The Who. These guys really paved the way for pop culture and changed the way people think about the world **Is the idea of creative collaboration important to you?** Absolutely. In fact, I just acquired the Karl Lagerfeld trademark. Karl is a creative genius and I think we will learn a lot from each other **Who has been the greatest influence on your career?** My kids are an amazing influence. Their youth and vitality give me energy **How have your own experiences affected your work as a designer?** Every experience I have has affected me in some way. Life is really made up of thousands of different experiences. That is how we learn and grow as individuals. **Which is more important in your work: the process or the product?** Both. You can't do one successfully without the other. **Is designing difficult for you and, if so, what drives you to continue?** Design is my first love, my passion in life, and when you're passionate about something it never feels like hard work. It's a very organic and natural process for me. I love the challenge of reinterpreting things in new and different ways. **Have you ever been influenced or moved by the reaction to your designs?** The most rewarding thing about being a designer is you can see how your designs impact people. There's nothing I enjoy more than seeing someone on the street wearing my designs with their own personal flair **What's your definition of beauty?** There is nothing more beautiful than self-confidence. With a great attitude and an open mind, you can do anything in life **What's your philosophy?** Be true to yourself **What is the most important lesson you've learned?** The most important thing in life is to never let anyone tell you that your dreams are impossible.

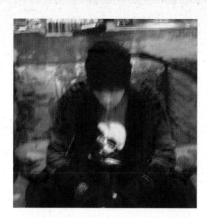

UNDERCOVER

"I cannot deny the difficulty involved in creating designs.
But I think I continue creating them because I enjoy it"

JUN TAKAHASHI

Founded by Japanese designer Jun Takahashi in 1994, the Undercover label now includes some seriously discerning types among its fan base, not least Rei Kawakubo, who in 2004 had the 34-year-old design a selection of blouses to sell in the Comme des Garçons store in Tokyo. Born in Kiryu, in 1969, and a graduate of the Bunka Academy, it was while studying at college that Takahashi began making clothes to wear himself, frustrated at not being able to find anything he liked in shops. His confidence and individuality sets him apart from many young Japanese designers, who are happy to rely on easily digestible, graphic-led T-shirts and slogans. Takahashi's approach is more complex and distinctive, and has been variously described as 'thrift-shop chic' or 'subversive couture'. Considering his belief that life is as much about pain as it is about beauty, it is not surprising that the resulting Undercover aesthetic makes for an anarchic collision of the violent (slashed, ripped and re-stitched fabrics) and the poetic (chiffon, lace and faded floral prints). Further clues to the designer's mindset are found in his fondness for defiant English punk bands – while still a student, he was a member of the Tokyo Sex Pistols, a tribute act, and is often spotted sporting a Crass T-shirt. Having won the Grand Prize in the prestigious Mainichi Fashion Grand Prize in 2001 and made his Paris catwalk debut with his spring/summer 2003 collection, Takahashi today continues to up the ante. Undercover is now split into five lines – Undercover, Undercoverism, Undakovit, Undakovrist and Undakovr, all of which are sold through a flagship store in Tokyo's fashionable Omotesando district. Further Undercover stores have opened in Paris and Milan, while global stockists continue to grow in tandem with appreciative converts to the label.

Das 1994 vom japanischen Designer Jun Takahashi gegründete Label Undercover kann einige wirklich scharfsichtige Leute zu seinen Fans zählen. Etwa Rei Kawakubo, die den 34-Jährigen im Jahr 2004 eine Auswahl von Blusen entwerfen und anschließend im Laden von Comme des Garçons in Tokio verkaufen ließ. Der 1969 in Kiryu geborene Absolvent der Bunka-Akademie begann schon im College-Alter, seine Kleidung selbst zu entwerfen – aus Ärger darüber, dass er in keinem Laden etwas fand, das ihm zusagte. Sein Selbstvertrauen und seine Individualität unterscheiden ihn von vielen japanischen Jungdesignern, die sich nur zu gern auf eine leichte Kost aus grafisch gestalteten T-Shirts und Slogans verlassen. Takahashis Zugang ist komplexer und unverwechselbar und wurde schon mit Begriffen wie „Thrift-shop Chic" oder „subversive Couture" versehen. Gemäß seiner Überzeugung, wonach Schmerz genauso Teil des Lebens ist wie Schönheit, kollidieren in der Ästhetik von Undercover folgerichtig gewalttätige Elemente (aufgeschlitzter, zerrissener und geflickter Stoff) mit poetischen (Chiffon, Spitze und verblichene Blumenmuster). Weiteren Aufschluss über die Denk-

weise des Designers gibt sein Faible für aufmüpfige englische Punkbands – in seiner Studentenzeit war er selbst Mitglied der Tokyo Sex Pistols. Außerdem sieht man Takahashi oft im Crass-T-Shirt. Nachdem er 2001 den Hauptpreis beim prestigeträchtigen Mainichi Fashion Grand Prize gewonnen und mit der Kollektion für Frühjahr/Sommer 2003 sein Debüt auf dem Pariser Catwalk gegeben hat, ist Takahashi heute dabei, seinen Marktwert weiter zu steigern. Undercover umfasst inzwischen fünf Linien – Undercover, Undercoverism, Undakovit, Undakovrist und Undakovr –, die allesamt im Flagship Store in Tokios In-Viertel Omotesando verkauft werden. Weitere Undercover-Läden wurden in Paris und Mailand eröffnet. Außerdem wächst parallel zur Zahl der dankbaren Anhänger des Labels auch die der interessierten Großhändler in aller Welt.

Fondée en 1994 par le créateur japonais Jun Takahashi, la griffe Undercover compte aujourd'hui parmi ses fans des personnages au goût très avisé, notamment Rei Kawakubo qui en 2004 a demandé au jeune styliste de 34 ans de lui dessiner une sélection de chemisiers pour les vendre dans la boutique Comme des Garçons de Tokyo. Né en 1969 à Kiryu et diplômé de la Bunka Academy, Jun Takahashi est encore étudiant quand il commence à confectionner ses propres vêtements, frustré de ne pas trouver ce qu'il aime dans les magasins. Son assurance et son individualité le distinguent de la plupart des autres jeunes créateurs japonais, qui se contentent souvent de proposer des T-shirts à l'esprit graphique et aux slogans facilement digestibles. L'approche de Takahashi est bien plus complexe et originale, souvent décrite comme du « chic d'occasion » ou de la « couture subversive ». Comme Takahashi croit que la vie est autant faite de douleur que de beauté, rien de surprenant à ce que l'esthétique d'Undercover propose une collision anarchique entre violence (tissus tailladés, déchirés et recousus) et poésie (mousseline, dentelle et imprimés floraux passés). On trouve d'autres indices de l'état d'esprit du créateur dans sa prédilection pour les groupes punk anglais les plus provocants : encore étudiant, il était membre des Tokyo Sex Pistols, formés en hommage au groupe britannique, et on le surprend souvent vêtu d'un T-shirt Crass. Après avoir remporté le prestigieux grand prix du Mainichi Fashion Grand Prize en 2001 et fait ses débuts à Paris avec sa collection printemps/été 2003, aujourd'hui Jun Takahashi ne cesse de faire monter les enjeux. Undercover se divise désormais en cinq lignes : Undercover, Undercoverism, Undakovit, Undakovrist et Undakovr, toutes vendues par sa boutique indépendante d'Omotesando, quartier branché de Tokyo. D'autres boutiques Undercover ont ouvert leurs portes à Paris et à Milan alors que les stockistes internationaux continuent à se développer, en tandem avec les admirateurs convertis à la griffe.

JAMES ANDERSON

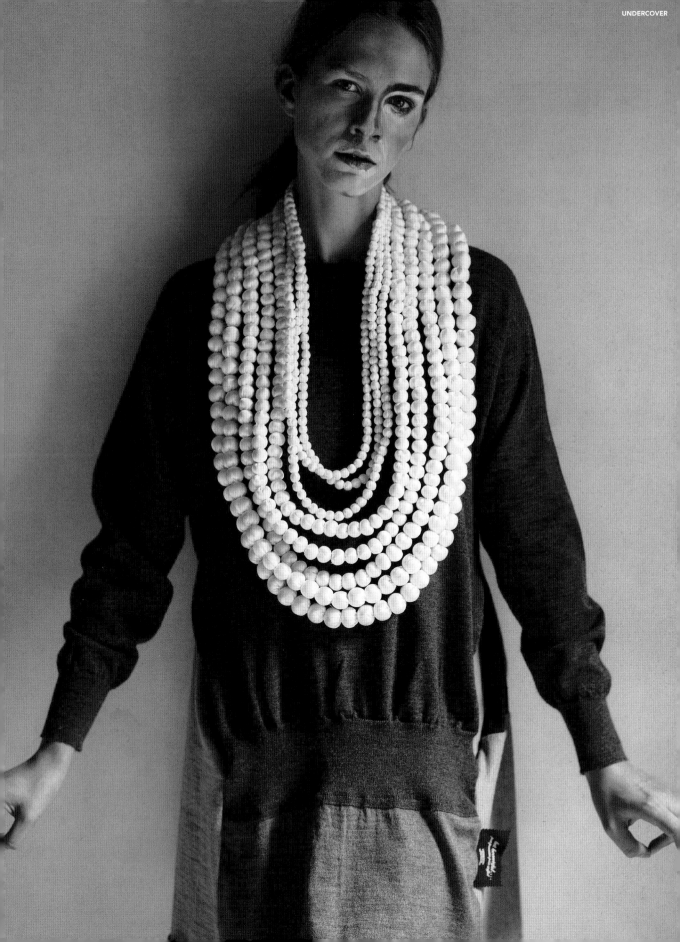

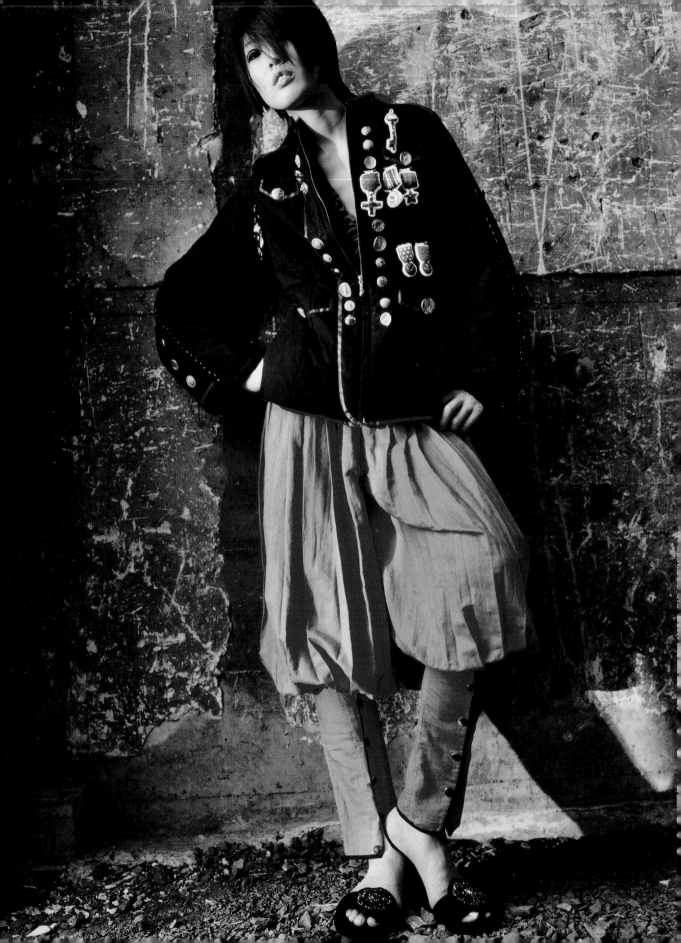

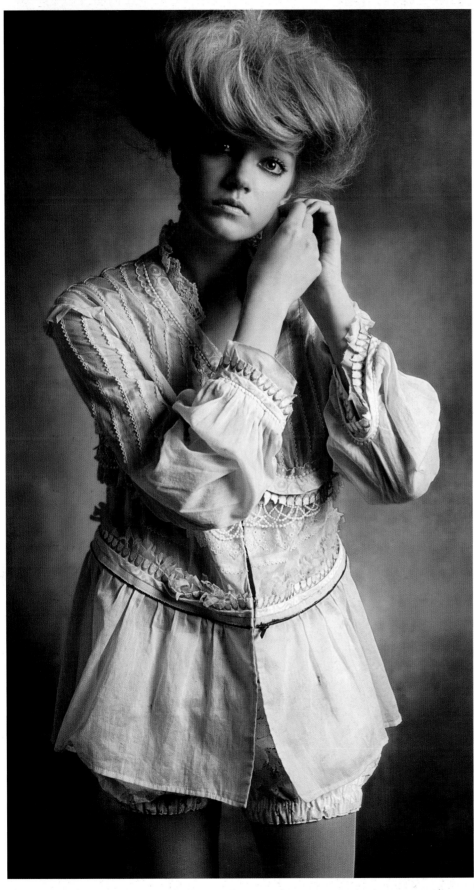

What is your favourite piece from any of your collections? The latest one (my collection for summer 2005) What's your ultimate goal? Peace What inspires you? All material things in the world, happenings, and emotions Can fashion still have a political ambition? Yes Who do you have in mind when you design? No one in particular. If I really need to give you a more specific answer, my wife Is the idea of creative collaboration important to you? Yes, once in a while Who has been the greatest influence on your career? Rei Kawakubo Which is more important in your work: the process or the product? Both Is designing difficult for you, if so, what drives you to continue? I cannot deny the difficulty involved in creating designs. But I think I continue creating them because I enjoy it Have you ever been influenced or moved by the reaction to your designs? Yes, just for two minutes What is the most important lesson you've learned? A defiant spirit and positive thinking.

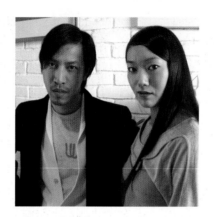

UNITED BAMBOO

"Our signatures are innovative cuts, sensible style"

MIHO AOKI & THUY PHAM

United Bamboo has made designers Miho Aoki and Thuy Pham the deans of downtown cool since the New York-based label was formed in 1998. Hailing from Japan and Vietnam respectively, the two have quietly set about re-imagining classic American sportswear through what they call "innovative cuts and sensible style". In other words, extreme layering, irregular cuts and experimental patterns merged with traditional silhouettes to create a near proper but ultimately risqué line of pieces. These include ruffled skirts emblazoned with a skull and crossbones, safari-meets-tuxedo suits, wrap-over pants, culottes and woven wedge shoes. By juxtaposing contrasting styles the two have carved out an identifiable niche, selling around the world in department stores and underground art shops alike. Aoki says: "We're inspired by all kinds of things all the time. Currently it's the sci-fi film 'Solaris', so we've made dresses that have tiny pleats along the stomach making a subtle bubble shape worn on top of bright and skin-tight body suits. And we made some pieces with diagonal zipper closures which are reminiscent of vintage astronaut suits." Ever adventurous, the two haven't lingered exclusively within fashion's confines for very long, recently seeking collaborations with artists and architects to expand their conceptual reach. A recent limited-edition T-shirt project featured the street-inspired vision of artists and curators James Fuentes, Spencer Sweeney, Hiroshi Sunairi and Daniel Reich, while other projects have included the music of avant-gardists like Hisham Bharoocha from the band Black Dice. After the success of their first freestanding store in Tokyo, with its stretchy PVC-covered interior designed by renowned architect Vito Acconci, there are plans to open a similar store in New York. United Bamboo's aim to bring the world a little closer together – a mission suggested by the company's name – seems altogether possible.

United Bamboo hat Miho Aoki und Thuy Pham seit der Gründung des New Yorker Labels im Jahr 1998 zu den Doyens der Downtown-Coolness gemacht. Die aus Japan bzw. Vietnam stammenden Designer haben sich heimlich, still und leise daran gemacht, die klassisch amerikanische Sportswear durch, wie sie es nennen, „innovative Schnitte und sensiblen Stil" neu zu erfinden. Das bedeutet: extremer Lagen-Look, asymmetrische Schnitte und experimentelle Muster kombiniert mit traditionellen Silhouetten, um eine nur annähernd ordnungsgemäße, aber absolut risikofreudige Linie aus Einzelstücken zu kreieren. Dazu gehören Röcke mit Rüschen und einem Dekor aus Totenkopf und gekreuzten Knochen, Smokings im Safaristil, Wickelhosen, Hosenröcke und gewebte Schuhe mit Keilabsatz. Indem sie gegensätzliche Stile nebeneinander stellen, haben die beiden sich eine erkennbare Nische geschaffen und verkaufen ihre Kreationen weltweit in Kaufhäusern wie in Kunstgalerien. Aoki berichtet: „Wir werden die ganze Zeit über von allem möglichen inspiriert. Zur Zeit ist es der Science-Fiction-Film ‚Solaris'. Deshalb haben wir Kleider mit kleinen Falten rund um den Bauch entworfen, die für eine dezente Bubble-Silhouette sorgen, wenn man sie über bunten, hautengen Bodys trägt. Außerdem haben wir einige Stücke mit diagonalen Reißverschlüssen kreiert, die an frühe Astronautenuniformen erinnern." Die beiden abenteuerlustigen Designer blieben nicht lange in den Grenzen der Mode, sondern suchten die Zusammenarbeit mit Künstlern und Architekten, um das Spektrum ihrer Möglichkeiten zu erweitern. Kürzlich präsentierten sie im Rahmen eines T-Shirt-Projekts in limitierter Auflage die vom Alltag auf der Straße inspirierte Vision der Künstler und Kuratoren James Fuentes, Spencer Sweeney, Hiroshi Sunairi und Daniel Reich. Andere Projekte umfassten Musik von Avantgardisten wie Hisham Bharoocha von der Band Black Dice. Nach dem Erfolg ihres ersten eigenständigen Ladens in Tokio, dessen flexible, PVC-überzogene Einrichtung von dem bekannten Architekten Vito Acconci stammt, gibt es Pläne für die Eröffnung einer ähnlichen Filiale in New York. Das Ziel von United Bamboo, alle Menschen einander ein wenig näher zu bringen – wie der Firmenname ja bereits vermuten lässt –, scheint immerhin im Bereich des Möglichen.

Depuis sa fondation à New York en 1998, la griffe United Bamboo a fait des créateurs Miho Aoki et Thuy Pham les doyens du cool urbain. Respectivement originaires du Japon et du Vietnam, le duo cherche tranquillement à revisiter le sportswear américain classique à travers ce qu'il appelle «des coupes innovantes et un style sensible». En d'autres termes, la superposition poussée à l'extrême, des coupes irrégulières et des motifs expérimentaux fusionnent avec des silhouettes traditionnelles pour créer une ligne de pièces presque «convenables», mais néanmoins très risquées: jupes à volants emblasonnées d'une tête de mort, tailleurs mêlant style safari et smoking, pantalons portefeuille, jupes-culottes et chaussures à semelles compensées en tissu. En juxtaposant des styles contrastés, le duo s'est forgé une niche bien identifiable qui lui permet de vendre ses créations dans le monde entier, que ce soit par le biais de grands magasins ou de galeries d'art underground. «Nous sommes constamment inspirés par toutes sortes de choses», explique Miho Aoki. «Actuellement, c'est le film de science-fiction Solaris: nous avons créé des robes avec de minuscules plis le long du ventre qui produisent une subtile forme de bulle une fois portées sur des body suits ultra-moulants aux couleurs vives. Nous avons aussi créé quelques pièces dotées de fermetures zippées en diagonale qui rappellent les anciennes combinaisons d'astronaute». Toujours aventureux, les deux créateurs ne sont pas restés très longtemps confinés aux frontières de la mode. Ils ont récemment collaboré avec des artistes et des architectes pour étendre la portée de leur concept. Dans une récente gamme de T-shirts en édition limitée, les artistes et conservateurs James Fuentes, Spencer Sweeney, Hiroshi Sunairi et Daniel Reich ont présenté leur propre vision du streetwear, tandis que d'autres projets ont vu la production d'une compilation musicale, avec la participation d'avant-gardistes tels que Hisham Bharoocha du groupe Black Dice. Face au succès rencontré par leur première boutique de Tokyo, avec son décor en PVC élastique conçu par le célèbre architecte Vito Acconci, United Bamboo prévoit d'ouvrir une boutique similaire à New York. Comme le suggère le nom de la griffe, United Bamboo s'est fixé une mission qui ne semble finalement pas si impossible: faire tomber les frontières qui séparent les gens.

LEE CARTER

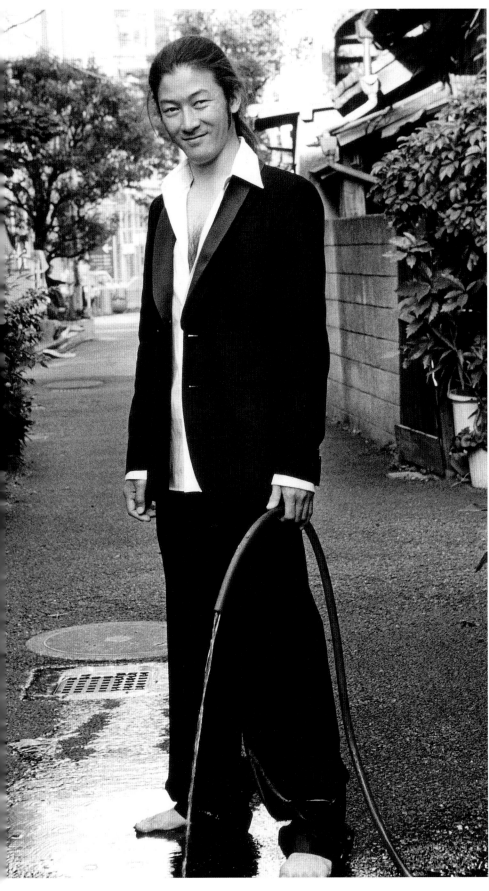

What are your signature designs? Innovative cuts. Sensible style **What is your favourite piece from any of your collections?** Side shifted dress **What's your ultimate goal?** To have a United Bamboo store designed by Vito Acconci in NY **What inspires you?** Movies, travel, outdoor sports **Can fashion still have a political ambition?** No, unless the politics in question addresses fashion directly **Who do you have in mind when you design?** Nobody particular **Is the idea of creative collaboration important to you?** Yes **Who has been the greatest influence on your career?** Too many people **How have your own experiences affected your work as a designer?** As you grow as a designer you can narrow your vision more specifically. You know what works and what doesn't **Which is more important in your work: the process or the product?** Both are important and mutually dependent on each other **Is designing difficult for you, if so, what drives you to continue?** Yes, it's very difficult. I don't want to give up **Have you ever been influenced or moved by the reaction to your designs?** Yes, sometimes **What's your definition of beauty?** Beauty is relative **What is the most important lesson you've learned?** Use lawyers.

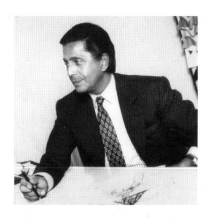

VALENTINO

"I design for romantic people"

Valentino Garavani – who, like all megastars, is known simply by his first name – is Italy's greatest couturier and one of the most respected designers showing in Paris. While wannabe glamour girls lust after his V-logo belts and bejewelled sandals, to his loyal following of moneyed couture clients Valentino is synonymous with showstopping evening dresses, which are immaculately cut in lean, feminine lines with dramatic flourishes such as ruffles, romantic embroideries and judicious use of his favourite shade of bright red. Born in Voghera, south of Milan, in 1932, Valentino travelled to Paris at just 17 and, following studies at the Chambre Syndicale de la Mode, was apprenticed to Jean Dessès and Guy Laroche. In 1959 he returned to Italy to establish his own atelier on Via Condotti in central Rome; Elizabeth Taylor, in town to film 'Spartacus', was one of Valentino's earliest clients. In 1962, he launched his first full collection, to universal acclaim, at the Palazzo Pitti in Florence, and by 1967 he had won the Neiman Marcus Award, the first of many accolades. Appearances on the covers of both Time and Life magazines followed, and in 1968 Valentino was chosen by Jackie Kennedy to design the dress for her wedding to Aristotle Onassis. At the end of the '60s, Valentino met Giancarlo Giametti, a former architecture student who would become the business brains behind the expanding fashion house and in 1970 ready-to-wear collections, for both men and women, were debuted. By 1998 the pair had decided to sell the house, to Italian conglomerate Holding di Partecipazioni Industriali, which in turn sold the brand to Marzotto, in 2002. In July 2005 Marzotto created Valentino Fashion Group, which operates as a separate, publicly-traded concern. Over the years the perfectly-groomed designer has dressed the most privileged women of the day, including Princess Margaret, Marella Agnelli and Begum Aga Khan. In 2002 his Hollywood credentials were re-affirmed when Julia Roberts wore an elegant black-and-white vintage Valentino dress to the Oscars. Valentino has been honoured by the governments of Italy, where he was awarded the Cavaliere di Gran Croce(1986) and France, which decorated him as a Chevalier de la Légion d'Honneur (2005).

Valentino Garavani – dem wie allen Megastars der Vorname genügt – ist Italiens größter Couturier und einer der renommiertesten Designer. Seine Gürtel mit V-Logo und seine Sandaletten mit Glitzersteinen sind Objekte der Begierde für ambitionierte Glamour Girls. Eine loyale Gefolgschaft von Couture-Kunden verbindet mit Valentino Abendkleider für sensationelle Auftritte, die schlanken, femininen Linien der makellosen Schnitte mit dramatischen Akzenten und dem strategisch geschickten Einsatz seiner Lieblingsfarbe, einem leuchtenden Rot. Valentino, Jahrgang 1932, geboren in Vorghera südlich von Mailand, zog es im zarten Alter von 17 Jahren nach Paris. Dort ging er im Anschluss an sein Studium an der Chambre Syndicale de la Mode bei Jean Dessès und Guy Laroche in die Lehre. 1959 kehrte er nach Italien zurück, um sein eigenes Atelier an der Via Condotti in Rom zu eröffnen. Elizabeth Taylor, die sich für die Filmarbeiten zu „Spartacus" in der Stadt aufhielt, war eine von Valentinos ersten Kundinnen. 1962 stellte Valentino im Palazzo Pitti in Florenz seine erste komplette Kollektion vor. 1967 gewann er den Neiman Marcus Award, die erste von zahllosen Auszeichnungen. Es folgten Titelbilder bei Time und Life, und 1968 ließ Jackie Kennedy ihr Kleid für die Hochzeit mit Aristoteles Onassis von Valentino entwerfen. Ende der 1960er Jahre begegnete Valentino Giancarlo Giametti, der sich fortan hinter den Kulissen des expandierenden Modehauses um die geschäftlichen Belange kümmerte. 1970 entstanden die ersten Prêt-à-porter-Kollektionen für Männer und Frauen. 1998 entschieden sich die beiden, das Haus an die italienische Holding di Partecipazioni Industriali zu verkaufen, die die Marke 2002 wiederum an Marzotto verkaufte. Im Juli 2005 bildete Marzotto die Valentino Fashion Group, die börsennotiert ist. Über die Jahre hat der stets sehr gepflegt auftretende Designer die privilegiertesten Frauen ihrer Zeit eingekleidet, darunter Prinzessin Margaret, Marella Agnelli und die Begum Aga Khan. 2002 brachte er sich auch Hollywood nachdrücklich in Erinnerung, als Julia Roberts in einem schwarz-weißen Vintage-Abendkleid von Valentino zur Oscarverleihung erschien. Valentino wurde in Italien zum Cavaliere di Gran Croce (1986) und in Frankreich zum Chevalier de la Légion d'Honneur (2005) ernannt.

Surtout connu par son prénom comme toutes les mégastars, Valentino Garavani est le plus grand couturier d'Italie et l'un des créateurs les plus respectés des défilés parisiens. Si les jeunes aspirantes au glamour s'arrachent ses ceintures à logo V et ses sandales ornées de bijoux, ses clientes fortunées restent fidèles aux signatures Valentino, à savoir ses renversantes robes du soir, toutes coupées à la perfection dans des lignes pures et féminines, avec de spectaculaires fioritures, sans oublier un usage judicieux du rouge vif, sa couleur préférée. Né en 1932 à Voghera au sud de Milan, Valentino s'installe à Paris dès l'âge de 17 ans. Après des études à la Chambre Syndicale de la Mode, il devient apprenti de Jean Dessès et de Guy Laroche. En 1959, il revient en Italie pour fonder son propre atelier dans la Via Condotti en plein cœur de Rome. Elizabeth Taylor, en ville pour le tournage de Spartacus, devient ainsi l'une de ses toutes premières clientes. En 1962, Valentino lance une première collection complète portée aux nues par la critique internationale lors d'un défilé au Palazzo Pitti de Florence. En 1967, il remporte le prix Neiman Marcus, le premier d'une longue liste de récompenses, avant de faire la couverture des magazines Time et Life. En 1968, Jackie Kennedy lui demande de dessiner la robe de son mariage avec Aristote Onassis. A la fin des années 60, Valentino rencontre Giancarlo Giametti, qui deviendra le cerveau commercial de l'entreprise, et lance des collections de prêt-à-porter pour homme et femme dès 1970. En 1998, le duo décide de vendre la maison au conglomérat italien Holding di Partecipazioni Industriali, qui la revendra à son tour à Marzotto en 2002. En juillet 2005, Marzotto crée Valentino Fashion Group, un groupe opérant de façon distincte et coté en bourse. Au fil des années, ce couturier, a habillé les femmes les plus privilégiées de son époque, de la Princesse Margaret à Marella Agnelli en passant par Begum Aga Khan. En 2002, son étoile remonte au firmament d'Hollywood quand Julia Roberts choisit de porter une élégante robe Valentino vintage noire et blanche aux Oscars. Valentino a été distingué par le gouvernement italien, qui l'a fait Cavaliere di Gran Croce (1986), mais aussi par la France, qui l'a décoré du titre de Chevalier de la Légion d'Honneur (2005).

SUSIE RUSHTON

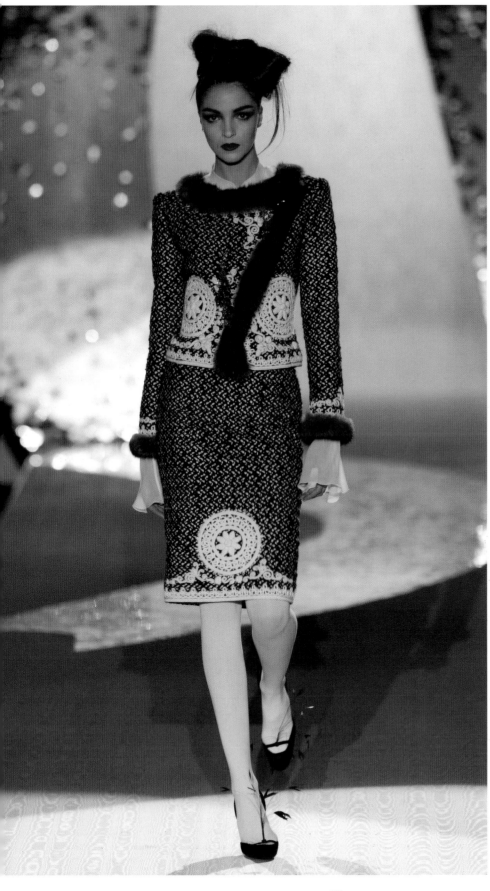

What are your signature designs? I always design for romantic people... indulgent maybe, glamorous, sometimes, but people who want classic design with an edge **What is your favourite piece from any of your collections?** Many, I cannot choose now... It's more about a style than about one dress **How would you describe your work?** Meticulous and fastidious... I don't take no for an answer **What's your ultimate goal?** Stay in power **What inspires you?** My drawing paper **Can fashion still have a political ambition?** Yes, because fashion gives work to so many people that it is a very important political power **Who do you have in mind when you design?** Many people and many artists. I like art and I think that in a way it did always inspire me **Is the idea of creative collaboration important to you?** I am difficult in this... I like to have the last word **Who has been the greatest influence on your career?** Challenge **How have your own experiences affected your work as a designer?** You cannot create without having your feelings of the moment influences your designs... I try to be cold and rational, but you can see when I am happy or sad in my work **Which is more important in your work: the process or the product?** The product and the commercial success of it... I don't design for the runway... I want my clothes to be alive, on the real people who wear them **Is designing difficult for you, if so, what drives you to continue?** I go to work like one goes to his office... I have eight hours in front of me, I have to produce X number of drawings... I do it... It's not very difficult **Have you ever been influenced or moved by the reaction to your designs?** No, if you want a life-long career you have to get accustomed to good or bad reactions and not be influenced by them... otherwise you will be paralysed **What's your definition of beauty?** What is nice to your eyes... I don't believe in tortured beauty, in hidden beauty. I know it exists but for my work I want a classic, real beauty **What's your philosophy?** Life must go on **What is the most important lesson you've learned?** Hear just what you want to hear.

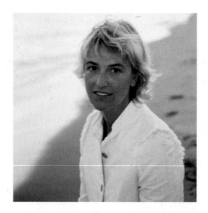

VANESSA BRUNO

"Easy clothes for difficult girls"

Vanessa Bruno is the ultimate purveyor of cool Parisian chic. Part of a renaissance of affordable independent designers that emerged in the '90s, Bruno's contemporary take on femininity has secured her a place at the heart of fashion. Her approach is twofold: she painstakingly refines the constants in every woman's wardrobe – the silhouette of the white shirt and the cut of the trouser – while at the same time staying on-trend. Taking inspiration from the refined beauty of vintage and handicrafts, Bruno adds bohemian touches to her easy, wearable clothes. Born in Paris to a Danish model mother and an Italian father (founder of knitwear house Emmanuelle Kahn), Bruno's fashion life began as a freelance stylist. After stints at a range of ateliers, the self-taught designer found she wasn't creating the kind of clothes she wanted to wear. So, aged just 24, she launched her eponymous label, followed shortly by her diffusion line Athé. Her first complete collection was presented at the Paris collections, but Bruno soon realised catwalk shows weren't for her, and concentrated on creating a boutique, what she calls "a universe around the brand." Her lo-fi strategy worked, and today Bruno sells internationally, with two stores in Paris and four in Tokyo. "I tried to focus on the personality of the women I wanted to touch," is how Bruno explains her success, "And be true to myself."

Vanessa Bruno ist eine zuverlässige Quelle coolen Pariser Chics. Als eine der bezahlbaren unabhängigen Designerinnen, die in den 1990er Jahren von sich reden machten, hat Bruno sich mit ihrem zeitgemäßen Verständnis von Weiblichkeit inzwischen ihren Platz im Zentrum des Modegeschehens gesichert. Ihr Ansatz ist ein zweifacher: Sie veredelt mit großer Sorgfalt die Basics in der Garderobe jeder Frau – die Silhouette der weißen Bluse und den Schnitt der Hose – und bleibt gleichzeitig im Trend. Indem sie sich Inspiration bei der kultivierten Schönheit von Vintage und Kunsthandwerk holt, versieht Bruno ihre leichten, tragbaren Kleider mit Bohème-Akzenten. Als Tochter eines dänischen Models und eines italienischen Vaters (der Gründer des Strickwarenherstellers Emmanuelle Kahn) wurde Bruno in Paris geboren. Ihre Modekarriere begann sie als freischaffende Stylistin. Nach Jobs in diversen Ateliers kam die Autodidaktin in Sachen Design zu dem Schluss, dass sie nie mit Kleidung zu tun hatte, die sie

selbst gerne tragen würde. Also gründete sie mit gerade mal 24 Jahren das nach ihr benannte Label, dem sie bald die Nebenlinie Athé folgen ließ. Ihre erste komplette Kollektion wurde bei den Pariser Schauen vorgestellt. Bruno erkannte jedoch schon bald, dass der Laufsteg nichts für sie war, und konzentrierte sich auf die Einrichtung einer Boutique, die sie „ein Universum rund um die Marke" nennt. Ihre kostengünstige Strategie funktionierte – heute verkaufen sich die Entwürfe weltweit, in zwei Läden in Paris und vier in Tokio. „Ich habe versucht, mich auf die Persönlichkeit der Frauen einzustellen, die ich erreichen wollte", erklärt Bruno ihren Erfolg. „Und ich habe versucht, mir treu zu bleiben."

En matière de chic parisien cool et branché, Vanessa Bruno est incontournable. Membre de la nouvelle génération de créateurs indépendants et abordables qui a émergé dans les années 90, sa vision contemporaine de la féminité lui garantit une place de choix au cœur de la mode. Son approche est double : elle revisite avec soin et élégance les basiques de la garde-robe féminine (la silhouette de la chemise blanche et la coupe du pantalon) tout en restant à la pointe des dernières tendances. Puisant son inspiration dans la beauté raffinée du vintage et de l'artisanat, Vanessa Bruno ajoute des touches bohème à ses vêtements très faciles à porter. Née à Paris d'une mère danoise mannequin et d'un père italien (fondateur d'Emmanuelle Kahn, la griffe de maille), Vanessa Bruno a commencé sa carrière dans la mode en tant que styliste free-lance. Après avoir travaillé dans divers ateliers, la créatrice autodidacte se rend compte qu'elle ne dessine pas le genre de vêtements qu'elle a envie de porter. A 24 ans seulement, elle lance donc sa griffe éponyme, rapidement suivie par sa ligne secondaire Athé. Elle présente sa première collection complète lors des défilés parisiens, mais comprend vite que ce type de présentation n'est pas fait pour elle. Elle décide alors de réorienter ses efforts sur la création d'une boutique qu'elle conçoit comme « l'univers autour de la marque ». Sa stratégie de discrétion fonctionne et aujourd'hui, Vanessa Bruno vend ses créations dans le monde entier, avec deux boutiques à Paris et quatre à Tokyo. « J'ai essayé de rester concentrée sur la personnalité des femmes que je souhaitais toucher », explique Vanessa Bruno à propos de son succès, « et de rester fidèle à moi-même ».

AIMEE FARRELL

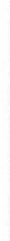

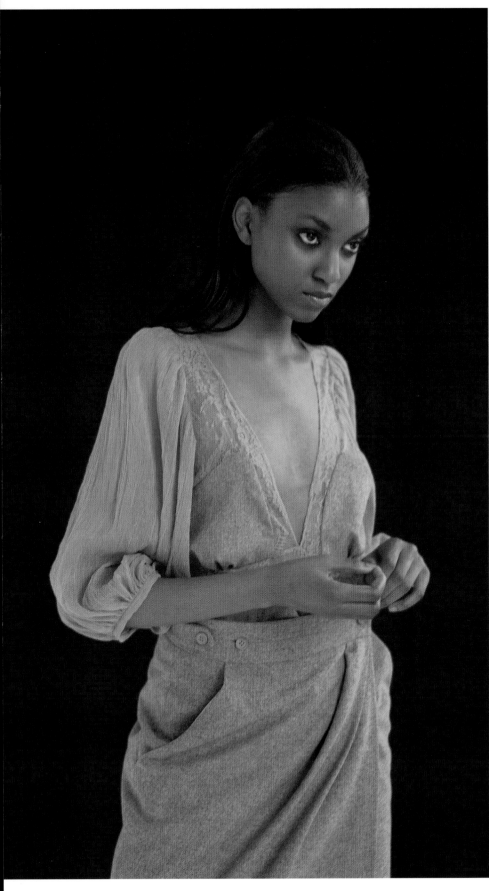

What are your signature designs? Easy clothes for difficult girls **What's your favourite piece from any of your collections?** Scottish cotton as a tank top **How would you describe your work?** My work is about freedom of movement and state of mind **What's your ultimate goal?** To enable women to creatively express their real nature **What inspires you?** Strong women with a voice such as artists, writers, singers or everyday women **Can fashion still have a political ambition?** Yes, I think there is a missing representation of women in the fashion world. "Doll models". Let's give them space to be real women **Who do you have in mind when you design?** My mother. She is my icon **Is the idea of creative collaboration important to you?** Creative tension **Who has been the greatest influence on your career?** Patti Smith, Virginia Woolf, Madeleine Vionnet, Cat Power **How have your own experiences affected your work as a designer?** All the travel I did with my mum gave me a broad and eclectic outlook which I still use today **Which is more important in your work: the process or the product?** Both **Is designing difficult for you, if so, what drives you to continue?** It is a challenge to find harmony in my clothing **Have you ever been influenced or moved by the reaction to your designs?** The biggest gift for me is to see real girls in the clothes! **What's your definition of beauty?** Natural and complicated **What's your philosophy?** I am not a philosopher. See above **What is the most important lesson you've learned?** To follow my gut instincts!

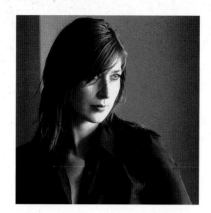

VÉRONIQUE BRANQUINHO

"I'm inspired by the inner complexity of a woman"

Véronique Branquinho doesn't design attention-seeking clothes. Instead, she prefers to create beautiful garments whose desirability is only enhanced by their functionality. Born in 1973 in the Belgian town of Vilvoorde, Branquinho first studied modern languages and then painting, switching to fashion in 1991 at Antwerp's Royal Academy. She graduated in 1995 and began working for some of Belgium's top commercial labels, but always maintained the desire to create her own line. In October 1997 she presented her first fashion collection at an art gallery in Paris. The show drew the attention of the international press and retailers, allowing her to launch, the following season, onto the official fashion calendar. With a discreet sexuality, her clothing uses a muted palette of colours, mannish tailoring and street references in order to temper the femininity of fabrics such as lace, satin and chiffon. Through her garments, she acknowledges the duality of female fashion identity – a constant seesaw between the masculine and feminine, the girl and the woman. For spring/summer 2005, she was inspired by '70s soft-core porn icon Emmanuelle; the long-line skirts and tailoring that actually appeared on Branquinho's runway however were as subtle as ever. Now central to Belgium's formidable fashion community, Branquinho has exhibited at Florence's Biennale Della Moda, Colette in Paris, New York's Fashion Institute of Technology and Walter Van Beirendonck's 2001 "Landed" exhibition in Antwerp. She received the 1998 VH1 Fashion Award for best new designer, the Moët Fashion Award in 2000, and was chosen by Ruffo Research to create their spring/summer and autumn/winter 1999 collections. In 2003, Branquinho launched her first men's collection in Paris, and opened her first flagship store in Antwerp.

Véronique Branquinho entwirft keine Aufsehen erregende Mode. Stattdessen kreiert sie lieber Kleidungsstücke, deren Reiz nur noch von ihrer Funktionalität übertroffen wird. Die 1973 im belgischen Vilvoorde geborene Branquinho studierte zunächst Philologie, dann Malerei und wechselte 1991 zur Mode an der Königliche Akademie von Antwerpen. Dort machte sie 1995 ihr Examen und war im Anschluss für einige der kommerziellen belgischen Spitzenlabels tätig. Schon damals hegte sie jedoch den Wunsch nach einer eigenen Linie. Im Oktober 1997 präsentierte sie schließlich ihre erste Kollektion in einer Pariser Galerie und erzielte damit bei der Presse und den Einkäufern aus aller Welt solchen Erfolg, dass sie bereits in der darauf folgenden Saison im offiziellen Kalender der Modeschauen erschien. Ihre diskrete Erotik verdanken ihre Kleider einer gedämpften Farbpalette, maskulinen Schnitten und Zitaten aus der Streetwear, die feminine Materialien wie Spitze, Satin und Chiffon ausgleichen. Die Designerin thematisiert in ihren Entwürfen den Dualismus weiblicher Identität in der Mode – das permanente Schwanken zwischen männlich und weiblich, zwischen dem Mäd-chenhaften und dem Fraulichen. Für die Kollektion Frühjahr/Sommer 2005 ließ sie sich von der Softporno-Ikone Emmanuelle aus den 1970er Jahren inspirieren. Die langen Röcke und Kostüme, die Branquinho dann letztlich bei ihrer Schau präsentierte, waren jedoch so raffiniert wie eh und je. Als wichtiges Mitglied der geachteten belgischen Fashion Community hat die Designerin bereits bei der Biennale Della Moda in Florenz, bei Colette in Paris, am New Yorker Fashion Institute of Technology sowie 2001 im Rahmen von Walter van Beirendoncks Projekt „Landed" in Antwerpen ausgestellt. 1998 erhielt sie den VH1 Fashion Award als beste neue Designerin, 2000 den Moët Fashion Award. Ruffo Research erteilte ihr den Auftrag, die Kollektionen für Frühjahr/Sommer und Herbst/Winter 1999 zu entwerfen. 2003 zeigte Branquinho ihre erste Herrenkollektion in Paris und eröffnete den ersten Flagship Store ihres Labels in Antwerpen.

Les vêtements dessinés par Véronique Branquinho ne cherchent pas à attirer l'attention. Au contraire, la créatrice préfère proposer de belles pièces qui seront d'autant plus désirables grâce à leur côté fonctionnel. Née en 1973 à Vilvoorde en Belgique, Véronique Branquinho étudie d'abord les langues modernes et la peinture avant d'entamer une formation en mode à l'Académie Royale d'Anvers en 1991. Diplômée en 1995, elle commence à travailler pour certaines des plus grandes marques commerciales de Belgique, mais envisage néanmoins de créer sa propre ligne. En octobre 1997, elle présente sa première collection de vête-ments dans une galerie d'art à Paris. L'exposition attire l'attention de la presse internationale et des acheteurs, lui permettant de se lancer dès la saison sui-vante dans le calendrier officiel des défilés de mode. Affichant une sensualité dis-crète, ses vêtements utilisent une palette de couleurs neutres, des coupes mas-culines et des références streetwear afin d'atténuer la féminité évidente des tissus tels que la dentelle, le satin et la mousseline de soie. A travers ses créa-tions, elle reconnaît la dualité de l'identité féminine dans la mode : une oscilla-tion constante entre le masculin et le féminin, la fille et la femme. Pour la saison printemps/été 2005, elle s'inspire d'Emmanuelle, l'icône érotique des années 70, mais ses jupes longues et ses tailleurs restent pourtant toujours aussi subtils. Membre désormais incontournable de la formidable scène fashion belge, Véro-nique Branquinho a exposé son travail à la Biennale Della Moda de Florence, à la boutique Colette de Paris, au Fashion Institute of Technology de New York, ainsi qu'à l'occasion de l'exposition «Landed» organisée par Walter Van Beiren-donck en 2001 à Anvers. En 1998, elle a reçu le prix de Best New Designer décerné par la chaîne VH1, puis le Moët Fashion Award en l'an 2000. On lui doit également les collections printemps/été et automne/hiver 1999 de Ruffo Research. En 2003, Véronique Branquinho a lancé sa première collection pour homme à Paris et ouvert sa toute première boutique à Anvers. LIZ HANCOCK

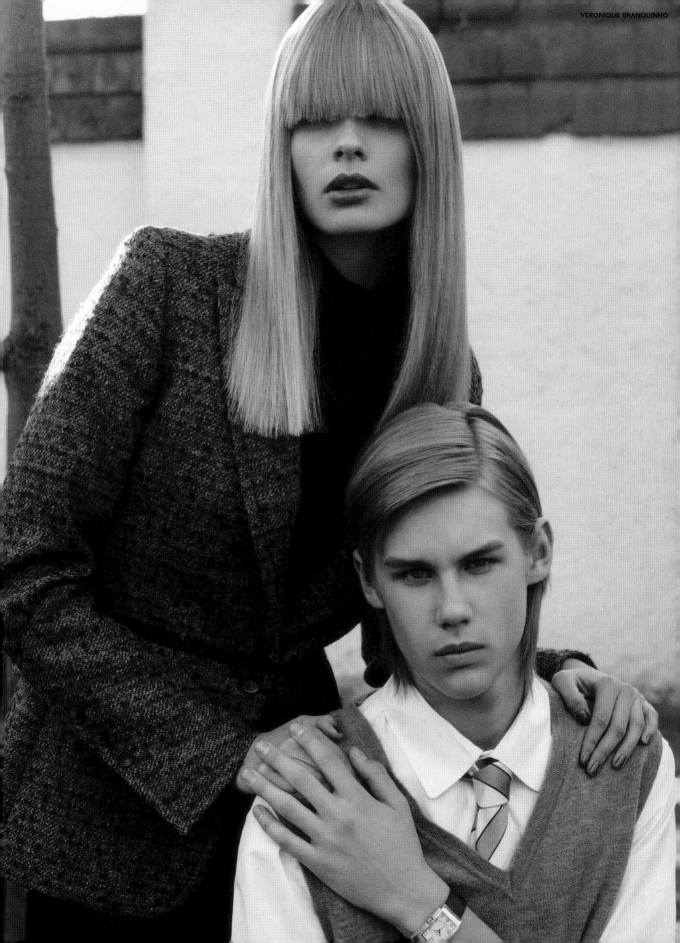

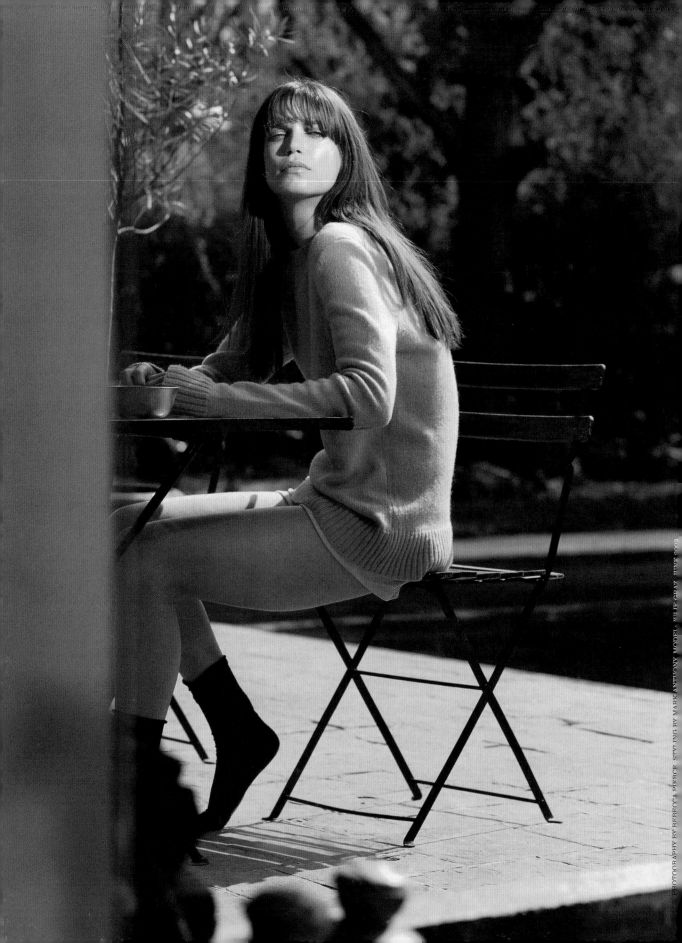

What are your signature designs? All my designs have my signature **What is your favourite piece from any of your collections?** The pants called 'Poison'. They have been in the collection since I started. And I don't see the point of changing them every six months just because there is a new fashion season **What's your ultimate goal?** To have the liberty to decide what I will be doing next **What inspires you?** People, their emotions as well what they can create **Who do you have in mind when you design?** I do not have a particular person in mind when I design. It's not about physique or features. It's more abstract. About a certain mood or state of mind. I'm inspired by the inner complexity of a woman. About the struggle she has with ambiguous feelings. About the attraction and rejection of those feelings, looking for harmony between them **Is the idea of creative collaboration important to you?** It is very rare, but if successful it really opens up new horizons **How have your own experiences affected your work as a designer?** I see my collections as a personal diary. They are very close to me. In a way, they reflect my feelings **Which is more important in your work: the process or the product?** I can not see process apart from product. It's about continuity. That makes them both equally important. It's a circle **Is designing difficult for you, if so, what drives you to continue?** I design very intuitively. It comes very naturally to express myself through my collections, so in a way it's not difficult **Have you ever been influenced or moved by the reaction to your designs?** More moved than influenced **What's your definition of beauty?** I don't want to define beauty. It's part of beauty that it can move you where you wouldn't expect it **What's your philosophy?** Freedom **What is the most important lesson you've learned?** That life and work become more interesting and satisfying when you have caring people around you.

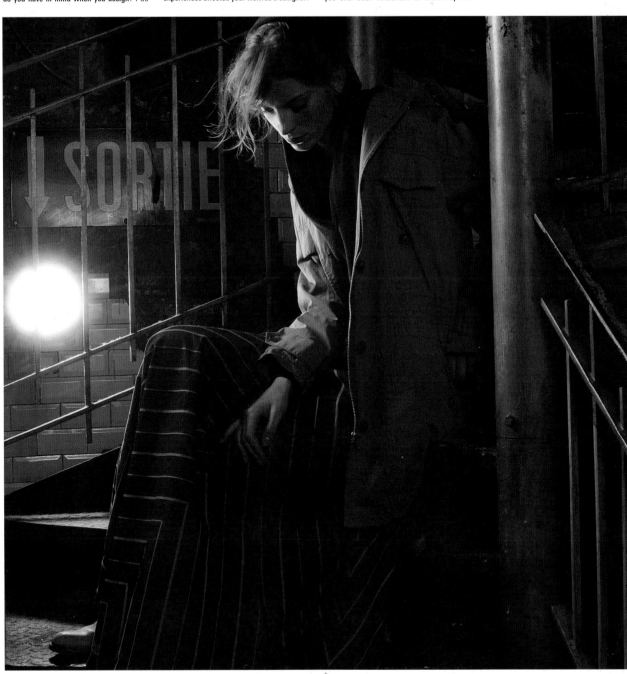

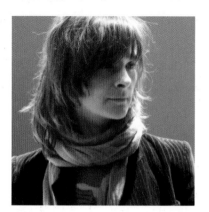

VÉRONIQUE LEROY

"Making clothes isn't exciting — but what is exciting is being able to give them soul"

Véronique Leroy (born 1965) has never toed the party line. Born and brought up in the industrial Belgian city of Liège, a 19-year-old Leroy decided to complete her training in Paris, at Studio Berçot, while most of her compatriots studied at Antwerp's Royal Academy. The designer has been at home in the French capital ever since. After assisting Parisian legends Azzedine Alaïa and Martine Sitbon, Leroy launched her solo line in 1991. From the beginning, it possessed what was to become her signature: juxtaposition – in this case, tailored high-waisted trousers and dandified satin shirts. Leroy creates clothes that women want to wear while also catching the eye of their partner; they are sexy and intelligent without becoming either trashy or scary. Devoted female fashion insiders now follow her every collection and she is laden with prizes for her work, winning the Vénus de la Mode prize for 'Le Futur Grand Créateur' no less than three times. Forever defying categorisation, Leroy continues to find her own way through the fashion jungle. Accompanying her on the expedition are her long-time collaborators and close friends, the photographic team Inez van Lamsweerde and Vinoodh Matadin, who have helped develop the look of the label. Each collection plays out an obsession with the female form. Structural distortion, subtle erogenous zones and layering of sensuous fabric have been used to celebrate women's bodies, while unlikely inspirations include wrestlers and 'Charlie's Angels'. Leroy has also been involved in fruitful collaborations. She recently produced a capsule denim collection for Levi's and her work with print maestro Léonard since 2001 has become an outlet for her distinctive graphic talents.

Véronique Leroy (Jahrgang 1965) war nie der Partytyp. In der belgischen Industriemetropole Liège geboren und aufgewachsen, entschloss sie sich im Alter von 19 Jahren, ihre Ausbildung in Paris, konkret im Studio Berçot, zu vervollständigen, während die meisten ihrer Landsleute an der Königlichen Akademie von Antwerpen studierten. Die Designerin fühlt sich jedoch schon von jeher in der französischen Hauptstadt zu Hause. Nach Assistenzen bei den Pariser Legenden Azzedine Alaïa und Martine Sitbon präsentierte Leroy 1991 ihre eigene Linie. Von Anfang an besaßen ihre Kleider etwas, das zu ihrem Markenzeichen werden sollte: Gegensätze. In diesem Fall waren das perfekt geschneiderte Hosen mit hoher Taille und Satinhemden im Dandy-Look. Nicht zu intellektuell, um Berührungsängste auszulösen, aber auch nicht so sexy, dass es trashig wirken würde. Leroy entwirft Kleider, die Frauen gerne tragen – für sich selbst und als Blickfang für ihren Partner. Treue Modeexpertinnen folgen ihr inzwischen von Kollektion zu Kollektion. Sie selbst wird mit Preisen überhäuft, darunter allein dreimal mit der Vénus de la Mode als Le Futur Grand Créateur. Beständig jeder

Einordnung trotzend, sucht sich Leroy nach wie vor ihren eigenen Weg durch den Fashion Jungle. Ihre Begleiter auf dieser Expedition sind langjährige Mitarbeiter und enge Freunde, wie das Fotografenteam Inez van Lamsweerde und Vinoodh Matadin, das geholfen hat, den Look ihres Labels zu entwickeln. Jede Kollektion zeugt von der Faszination weiblicher Formen. Strukturelle Verzerrungen, raffinierte erogene Zonen und Lagen sinnlicher Stoffe dienen Leroy dazu, den weiblichen Körper zu feiern. Dabei sind ihre Inspirationen ziemlich überraschend, wie z. B. ein Ringkampf oder „Drei Engel für Charlie". Leroy war auch an fruchtbaren Kooperationen beteiligt. Kürzlich entwarf sie für Levi's eine Minikollektion aus Denim. Ihre Zusammenarbeit mit Léonard, dem Meister der Stoffdrucke, ist seit 2001 Ausweis ihres ausgeprägten grafischen Talents.

Véronique Leroy (née en 1965 à Liège) n'a jamais renié ses convictions. A 19 ans, après avoir grandi dans la ville industrielle belge de Liège, elle décide de suivre une formation à Paris au Studio Berçot bien que la plupart de ses compatriotes étudient à l'Académie Royale d'Anvers. Depuis, la créatrice s'est toujours sentie chez elle dans la capitale française. Après avoir travaillé comme assistante pour différentes légendes parisiennes telles qu'Azzedine Alaïa et Martine Sitbon, Véronique Leroy lance sa propre griffe en 1991. Dès le départ, sa collection affiche ce qui deviendra son look signature : la juxtaposition. Dans sa première collection, ce style s'exprime à travers des pantalons à taille haute superbement coupés et des chemises en satin très dandy. Jamais trop intello pour éviter de faire peur ni trop sexy pour ne pas sombrer dans le trash, Véronique Leroy crée des vêtements que les femmes ont envie de porter et qui attirent l'attention de leurs partenaires. Les fashion victims les plus assidues ne ratent pas une seule de ses collections et le travail de la styliste a été couronné de nombreuses récompenses, notamment du prix Futur Grand Créateur des Vénus de la Mode qui lui a été décerné trois fois. Cherchant constamment à fuir toute catégorisation, Véronique Leroy continue à se frayer un chemin dans la jungle de la mode. Dans cette aventure, elle a bénéficié du soutien de ses collaborateurs et amis de longue date : les photographes Inez van Lamsweerde et Vinoodh Matadin l'aideront à développer l'image de sa griffe. Chaque collection exprime son obsession pour les formes féminines. Zones érogènes subtiles et superposition de tissus sensuels lui permettent tous de célébrer le corps de la femme, malgré des sources d'inspiration improbables telles que les lutteurs et les trois drôles de dames des « Charlie's Angels ». Véronique Leroy a aussi pris part à des collaborations très réussies : elle a récemment produit une mini-collection en denim pour Levi's et depuis 2001, son travail avec Léonard, maestro des imprimés, lui permet d'exprimer son talent original en matière de graphisme. LAUREN COCHRANE

PORTRAIT BY CHARLOTTE LOUPPE.   PHOTOGRAPHY BY MISCHA RICHTER, STYLING BY MARCUS ROSS. MAY 2003.

What are your signature designs? They have more to do with cut, shape and attitude than decoration. Therefore they are more about subtlety and self-expression than about designer branding **What is your favourite piece from any of your collections?** My favourite piece is often the 'black sheep' of the collection, which I usually spot after the show. It is this unconscious 'mistake' which forms the beginning of a new idea **How would you describe your work?** My work strives to translate ideas and envies into shape and attitude. Making clothes isn't exciting – what is exciting is being able to give them soul **What's your ultimate goal?** To keep focusing on the creative process. This state of mind is a total relief and a blessing **What inspires you?** I have always hated this question. I find it difficult to deconstruct the creative process, so perhaps inspiration is nothing more than an accumulative series of memories **Can fashion still have a political ambition?** Fashion is becoming more and more commercialised, but then again it's intertwined with politics, so perhaps there is a political element in it **Who do you have in mind when you design?** When I draw a collection I have no-one in particular in mind. A person appears when the collection is almost over. What I do have in mind is just the urge to complete the creative process. This process exists in the way in which my clothes, their cut in particular, allow women to express their sensuality through movement **Is the idea of creative collaboration important to you?** Yes it is. I always collaborate with my team and from time to time with people from the outside. I find it very enriching and challenging. It allows me to excel and to go further than I would have dared to imagine **Who has been the greatest influence on your career?** My previous answer was so stupid, but to be perfectly honest, I don't know **How have your experiences affected your work as a designer?** Although there is still no difference between Véronique Leroy the person and Véronique Leroy the designer, I'm becoming more selective in terms of how far I allow myself to be affected **Which is more important in your work, the process, or the product?** The process **Is designing difficult for you? If so, what drives you to continue?** Designing isn't difficult. The thing that is most difficult, is getting into it, looking for the rhythm. But when you feel that you have caught it, you get moments of grace, moments that are suspended in time. I think it's this feeling of pleasure which makes it vital to continue **Have you ever been influenced by or moved by the reaction to your designs?** Yes of course, indirectly, subconsciously and usually long after the reaction **What's your definition of beauty?** Beauty is fleeting, and it's furtive. It is something which evolves in time and space. It manifests itself both in abstract and concrete form **What's your philosophy?** I don't really have one. Perhaps I should **What is the most important lesson you've learned?** The less you say the better as nothing is ever certain.

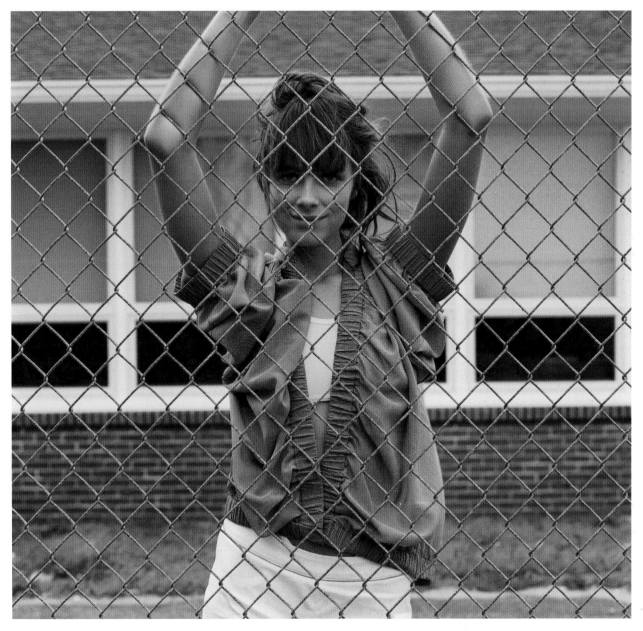

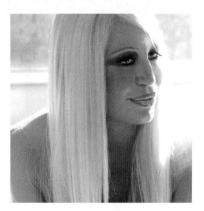

VERSACE

"I am always driven to push forward, searching for what is modern. That is what motivates me"

Donatella Versace (born 1959) is a goddess of fashion. The female figurehead of one of the few remaining family-run fashion houses, she presides over seven brands under the Versace name. Her flamboyant, party-girl image has become synonymous with Versace itself. Gianni (born 1946) and Donatella grew up in Reggio Calabria, southern Italy. While her much older brother moved to Milan to seek his fashion fortune, Donatella studied for a degree in languages at the University of Florence. While there, her brother's career took off. After working for Callaghan and Genny, he set up his solo label in 1978. Suggesting the family's love for bright colours, body-hugging shapes and a large dose of glamour, it was a great success. He called on his younger sister to help develop the brand. The two worked together for much of the '80s and '90s, with Donatella concentrating on the sumptuous advertising images for which Versace is known to this day. She also set up the children's line, Young Versace, in 1993 and worked as head designer on the diffusion label, Versus. When Gianni was tragically killed in 1996, his sister became chief designer and inherited a somewhat daunting legacy. She met the challenge. Versace was brought into the 21st century by fusing Gianni's very Italian glamour with Donatella's own rock'n'roll instincts. Versace is continually in the public eye, not least because of its – and Donatella's – famous friends. Jon Bon Jovi, Courtney Love and Elizabeth Hurley are all devoted Versace fans. Madonna even posed as a sexy secretary in Versace's spring/summer 2005 ad campaign. Donatella is also responsible for extending the brand's range, setting up both a cosmetics line and Palazzo Versace, the first six-star Versace hotel, which opened on the Gold Coast of Australia in 2000.

Die 1959 geborene Donatella Versace ist eine Modegöttin. Als weibliche Galionsfigur eines der wenigen noch in Familienbesitz befindlichen Modehäuser herrscht sie über sieben Marken mit dem Namen Versace. Ihr schillerndes Image als Party-Girl ist zum Synonym für Versace selbst geworden. Gianni (Jahrgang 1946) und Donatella wuchsen im süditalienischen Reggio Calabria auf. Während ihr deutlich älterer Bruder nach Mailand zog, um sein Glück in der Mode zu suchen, studierte Donatella an der Universität von Florenz Sprachen. In jener Zeit nahm die Karriere des Bruders ihren Anfang. Nachdem er zunächst für Callaghan und Genny gearbeitet hatte, gründete er 1978 sein eigenes Label. Gemäß der familiären Vorliebe für kräftige Farben, figurbetonte Schnitte und eine große Portion Glamour wurde es ein immenser Erfolg. So bat Gianni seine kleine Schwester bei der Weiterentwicklung der Marke um Hilfe. Die beiden arbeiteten in den 1980er und 1990er Jahren über weite Strecken zusammen, wobei Donatella sich stark auf die prachtvollen Werbeauftritte konzentrierte, für die Versace

bis heute bekannt ist. Sie gründete aber auch 1993 die Kinderlinie Young Versace und fungierte als Hauptdesignerin der Nebenlinie Versus. Nach Giannis tragischem Tod im Jahr 1996 wurde seine Schwester Chefdesignerin und übernahm ein in gewisser Hinsicht beängstigendes Erbe. Sie meisterte diese Herausforderung und führte Versace ins 21. Jahrhundert, indem sie Giannis sehr italienischen Glamour mit ihren eigenen Rock 'n' Roll-Instinkten verband. Das Haus Versace steht nach wie vor im Blickpunkt des öffentlichen Interesses, nicht zuletzt wegen seiner und ihrer prominenten Freunde. Jon Bon Jovi, Courtney Love und Elizabeth Hurley sind allesamt treue Versace-Fans. In der Werbekampagne für Frühjahr/Sommer 2005 spielt sogar Madonna eine sexy Sekretärin. Donatella verantwortet übrigens auch die Erweiterung des Spektrums von Versace, etwa mit eigenen Kosmetika und dem ersten Sechs-Sterne-Hotel der Marke, dem 2000 an der australischen Gold Coast eröffneten Palazzo Versace.

Donatella Versace (née en 1959) est une déesse de la mode. Figure féminine de l'une des rares entreprises encore familiales, elle supervise les sept marques de la griffe Versace. Sa flamboyante image de fêtarde est même devenue synonyme de Versace. Gianni (né en 1946) et Donatella ont grandi en Reggio Calabria, une région du sud de l'Italie. Quand son frère, de plus de vingt ans son aîné, s'installe à Milan pour faire carrière dans la mode, Donatella étudie les langues à l'université de Florence. C'est pendant cette période que la carrière de son frère décolle. Après avoir travaillé pour Callaghan et Genny, il crée sa propre griffe en 1978. Incarnant la passion de la famille pour les couleurs vives, les formes moulantes et une haute dose de glamour, il remporte un grand succès et demande à sa sœur de l'aider à développer la marque. Ils travaillent ensemble pendant la majeure partie des années 80 et 90, Donatella se concentrant sur les somptueuses images publicitaires qui feront la gloire de Versace. En 1993, elle lance également la ligne pour enfant Young Versace et travaille comme styliste principale sur la ligne Versus. Quand Gianni est tragiquement assassiné en 1996, sa sœur devient directrice de la création et hérite d'une mission quelque peu décourageante. Mais elle relève le défi. Versace entre dans le XXIe siècle en fusionnant le glamour très italien de Gianni avec les instincts rock'n'roll de Donatella. La marque Versace occupe constamment le devant de la scène, en partie grâce à ses amis célèbres : Jon Bon Jovi, Courtney Love et Elizabeth Hurley sont tous des fans dévoués de Versace. Madonna a même accepté de jouer le rôle d'une secrétaire sexy pour la campagne publicitaire printemps/été 2005. Donatella a également réussi à étendre l'offre de la marque, avec le lancement d'une ligne de maquillage et de Palazzo Versace, premier hôtel Versace six étoiles ouvert sur la Gold Coast australienne en l'an 2000.

LAUREN COCHRANE

PORTRAIT COURTESY OF VERSACE · PHOTOGRAPHY BY DESMOND MUCKIAN · STYLING BY CLAUDIA CARRETTI · MODEL: JENNY NILSEN · NOVEMBER 2003

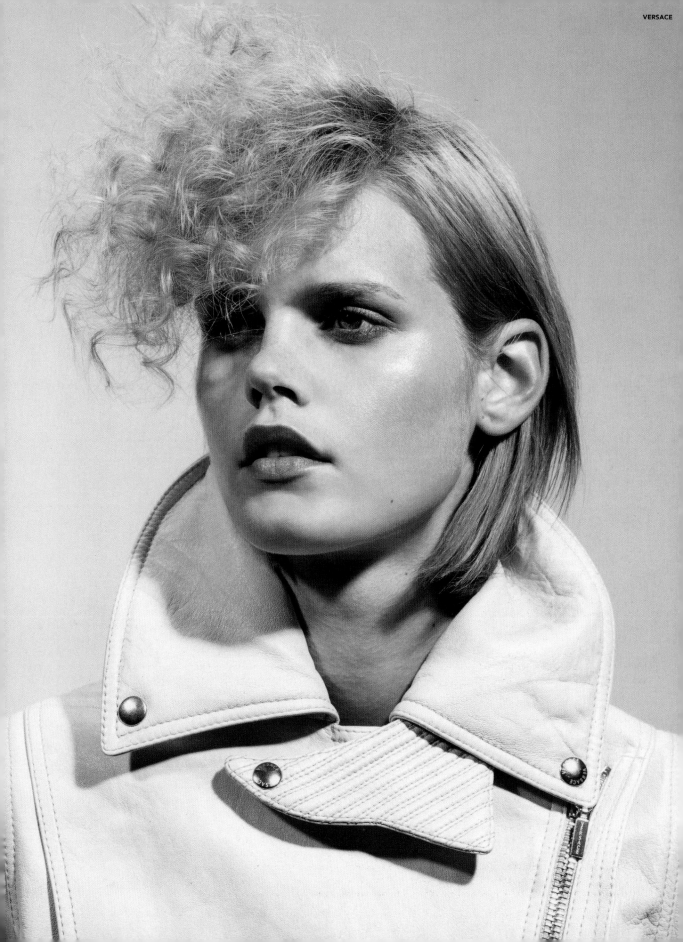

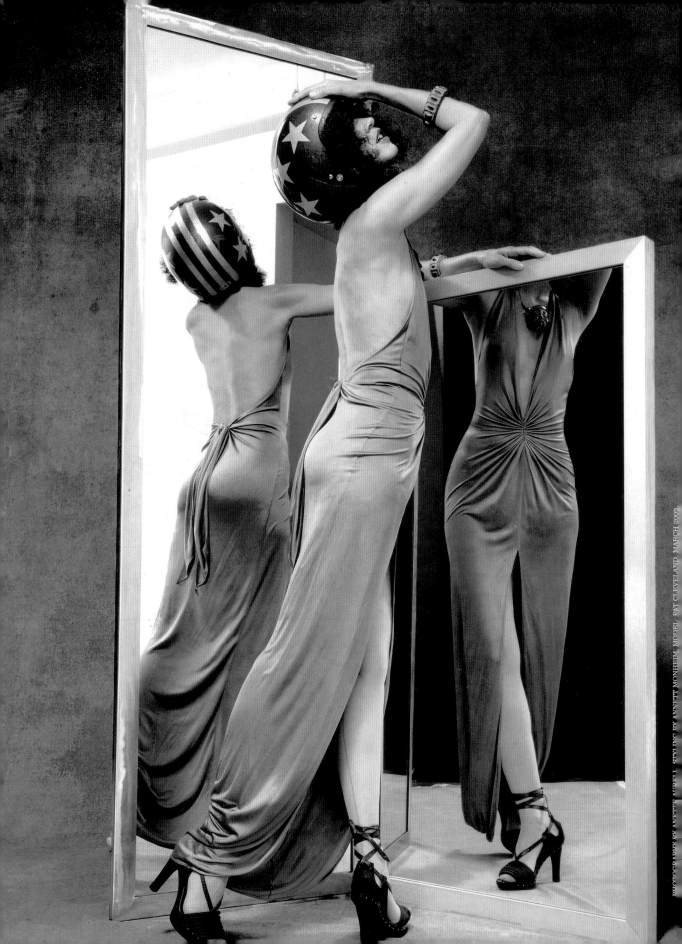

PHOTOGRAPHY BY ANDREW MONHEIM, STYLING BY ANDREW MONHEIM, MODEL: PAT CLEVELAND, MARCH 2005.

What are your signature designs? The jungle print, the evening dress that Catherine Zeta Jones wore to the Oscars in 2001, the silk fringe dress that Sharon Stone wore to the Oscars in 2002, the leather pant suit with lace-up details and fringes **How would you describe your work?** The style and ideas behind the collection always come from the same thought channel: Versace, myself and my team. Everything that goes on the runway and every Versace item is something that I 'feel for' **What inspires you?** I am a very curious person and therefore get my inspiration from music, photographs, films, from meeting people, discovering new places, attitudes and new trends around the world **Who do you have in mind when you design?** Someone who has individuality, intelligence, with an inner confidence which reflects on the outside **Is the idea of creative collaboration important to you?** My design team is composed of 30 people from all over the world who are like family to me. I believe fashion derives from group work and I have a very open-minded team. Not everyone agrees with me, which is the way I prefer it – I don't like to surround myself with 'yes' people. I am a great believer in the fact that creativity comes from a conflict of ideas **Who has been the greatest influence on your career?** My brother has been the best maestro I could ever have. Everything I know I have learned from him, and everything that I do, and will do, will always have a touch of Gianni **How have your own experiences affected your work as a designer?** New ideas come from having an open mind. I live intensely all the moments of my life and, in each one of those moments, I try to find an interesting and stimulating aspect **Is designing difficult for you?** I adore the world of fashion. It's a passion for me, so I don't think I will ever get tired of it **What's your definition of beauty?** I am convinced that looking good can only come from the inside. It is how you feel about yourself **What's your philosophy?** I am always driven to push forward, searching for what is modern. That is what motivates me **What is the most important lesson you've learned?** To live every day to the full, as if it were the last.

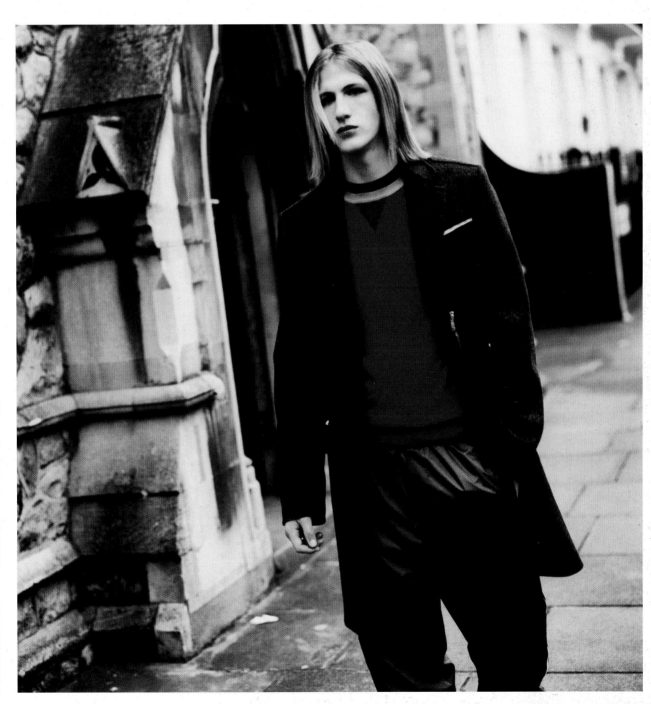

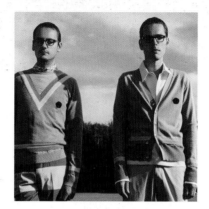

VIKTOR & ROLF

"The illusion that next time
it might be perfect keeps us going"

Inseparable since they met whilst studying at Arnhem's Fashion Academy, Dutch duo Viktor Horsting and Rolf Snoeren (both born 1969) decided to join forces after graduating in 1992. Their first feat was winning three awards at the 1993 Hyères Festival with a collection that already betrayed their preferences for sculptural, experimental clothes. Soon afterwards, they joined the ranks of Le Cri Néerlandais, a loose collective of like-minded young designers from Holland who organised two shows in Paris. However, once Le Cri disbanded, Viktor & Rolf continued to produce collections, including one in 1996 called 'Viktor & Rolf On Strike' that decried the lack of interest in their work from press and buyers. Refusing to give up, the duo created a toy-like miniature fashion show and a fake perfume bottle with an accompanying ad campaign. These artefacts, presented in the Amsterdam art gallery Torch in 1996, established them as upstart designers with an unconventional agenda. But what really launched their careers was their introduction to Paris couture in 1998, where Viktor & Rolf stunned ever-growing audiences with their highly innovative creations based on exaggerated volumes and shapes. To everyone's surprise and delight, the duo have managed to translate their earlier spectacular couture designs into wearable yet ground-breaking prêt-à-porter pieces, showing their first ready-to-wear collection for autumn/winter 2000. Clinging to a love of ribbons and perfectly-cut smoking suits, Viktor & Rolf shows have become a must-see on the Paris prêt-à-porter schedule, and in 2004 they launched their first fragrance, Flowerbomb. They continue to live and work in Amsterdam.

Seit sie sich als Studenten an der Modeakademie von Arnheim kennen lernten, sind die beiden Holländer Viktor Horsting und Rolf Snoeren (beide Jahrgang 1969) unzertrennlich. Nach ihrem Studienabschluss 1992 beschlossen sie folglich, ihre Kräfte zu bündeln. Ihre erste Meisterleistung waren drei Preise beim Hyères-Festival 1993, und zwar mit einer Kollektion, die ihre Vorliebe für skulpturale, experimentelle Kleidung zum Ausdruck brachte. Bald danach reihten sie sich bei Le Cri Néerlandais ein, einem losen Kollektiv von gleichgesinnten Jungdesignern aus Holland, die zwei Schauen in Paris organisierten. Nachdem Le Cri sich aufgelöst hatte, machten Viktor & Rolf jedoch mit der Produktion von Kollektionen weiter, darunter eine von 1996 mit dem Titel „Viktor & Rolf On Strike", die das geringe Interesse von Journalisten und Käufern beklagte. Das Designerduo gab jedoch nicht auf und schuf eine spielzeugartige Modenschau in miniature und einen falschen Parfümflakon mit dazugehöriger Werbekampagne. Diese Artefakte wurden 1996 in der Amsterdamer Kunstgalerie Torch präsentiert und etablierten die beiden als Newcomer mit unkonventionellem Programm.

Was ihrer Karriere jedoch den entscheidenden Schub gab, war ihre Einführung in die Pariser Couture 1998, wo Viktor & Rolf ein ständig wachsendes Publikum mit höchst innovativen Kreationen erstaunte, die auf extremem Volumen und überzeichneten Formen basierten. Zur allseitigen freudigen Überraschung gelang es dem Duo, seine frühere spektakuläre Couture in tragbare, aber dennoch völlig neuartige Prêt-à-porter zu transponieren, wovon man sich bei ihrer ersten Kollektion für Herbst/Winter 2000 überzeugen konnte. Mit ihrer Vorliebe für Bänder und perfekt geschnittene Smokings sind die Schauen von Viktor & Rolf Pflichtprogramm im Pariser Prêt-à-porter-Kalender. 2004 wurde mit Flowerbomb der erste Duft des Designerteams vorgestellt, das nach wie vor in Amsterdam lebt und arbeitet.

Inséparables depuis leur rencontre sur les bancs de l'académie de mode d'Arnhem, les Hollandais Viktor Horsting et Rolf Snoeren (tous deux nés en 1969) décident de travailler ensemble après l'obtention de leurs diplômes en 1992. Ils réalisent un premier exploit en remportant trois prix au Festival de Hyères en 1993 grâce à une collection qui trahit déjà leur prédilection pour une mode sculpturale et expérimentale. Peu de temps après, ils rejoignent les rangs du Cri Néerlandais, collectif libre de jeunes designers hollandais partageant tous le même état d'esprit et qui a présenté deux défilés à Paris. Après la dissolution du Cri, Viktor & Rolf continuent pourtant à travailler. En 1996, ils baptisent l'une de leurs collections « Viktor & Rolf On Strike » pour dénoncer le manque d'intérêt de la presse et des acheteurs à leur égard. Refusant d'abandonner, ils créent un mini-défilé jouet, un faux flacon de parfum et une campagne publicitaire pour l'accompagner : ces artefacts, présentés dans la galerie d'art Torch d'Amsterdam en 1996, les imposent comme de nouveaux rebelles à suivre de très près. Mais c'est lorsqu'ils débarquent dans la haute couture parisienne que leur carrière décolle enfin : depuis 1998, Viktor & Rolf éblouissent un public sans cesse croissant grâce à des créations très innovantes qui jouent sur l'exagération des volumes et des formes. A la surprise générale et pour le plus grand bonheur de tous, le duo parvient à traduire les créations haute couture de ses débuts spectaculaires sous forme de vêtements prêt-à-porter à la fois novateurs et portables, qu'ils présentent pour la première fois aux collections automne/hiver 2000. Revendiquant leur amour des rubans et des smokings aux coupes irréprochables, chaque défilé Viktor & Rolf est un événement absolument incontournable de la semaine du prêt-à-porter de Paris. En 2004, ils ont lancé leur premier parfum, Flowerbomb. Aujourd'hui, ils vivent et travaillent toujours à Amsterdam.

JAMIE HUCKBODY

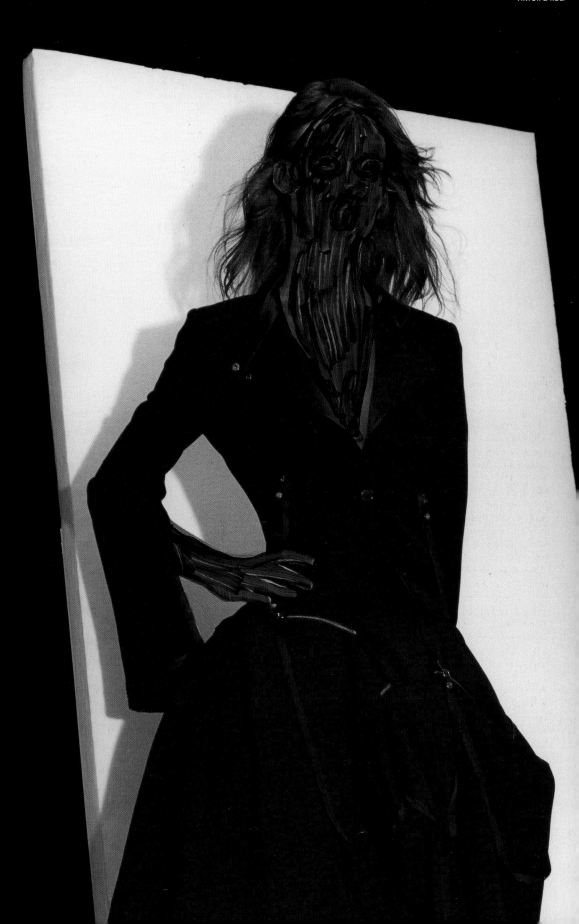

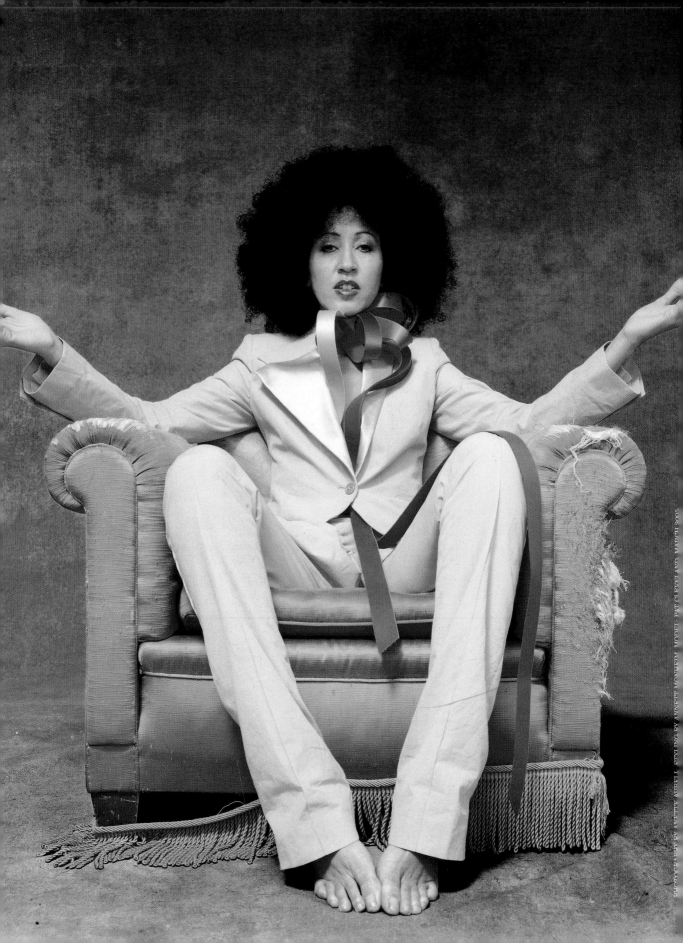

What are your signature designs? The ones that received the most attention. More important than the designs themselves is their capacity to communicate. Our signature designs are the designs that communicate best What is your favourite piece from any of your collections? The Babushka collection: the 'fashion dream' miniatures How would you describe your work? Difficult question What's your ultimate goal? 'Wanna be famous, wanna be rich, wanna be a star' What inspires you? Fashion itself Can fashion still have a political ambition? Yes, fashion is a reflection of all aspects of life Who do you have in mind when you design? We have never designed with a specific person in mind, but always regarded our collections as autonomous: once the designs are finished, they are for whoever appreciates them. Recently however, we are becoming more and more aware of the reality of the product we are creating. It was an inspiration to see our clothes worn by Tilda Swinton, who really brought them to life in a way we had imagined, but not yet seen in real life Is the idea of creative collaboration important to you? Collaborating is the essence of Viktor & Rolf. Working in tandem gives us an opportunity to go deeper. We have known each other for a long time and formed a very strong bond that is the basis of everything we do. Sometimes this can make it difficult to let other people in, but when they do succeed, it can feel like a breath of fresh air Who has been the greatest influence on your career? Inez van Lamsweerde and Vinoodh Matadin: they forced us to think in a more realistic way about fashion without being ashamed of it How have your own experiences affected your work as designers? Our work is always very personal. We try to translate our lives into our work. If we are down, we feel it is better to turn it into creative energy than to let it beat you. That is how the 'Black Hole' collection was born, for example Which is more important in your work: the process or the product? The result is the only thing that counts Is designing difficult for you and, if so, what drives you to continue? Being a fashion designer is a challenging profession because it requires a variety of skills that go far beyond designing. Designing itself is very difficult, but the illusion that next time it might be perfect keeps us going Have you ever been influenced or moved by the reaction to your designs? We never take candy from strangers, however, if it's enough candy from an important stranger etc What's your definition of beauty? Originality What's your philosophy? Viktor and Rolf first What's the most important lesson you've learned? There are others too.

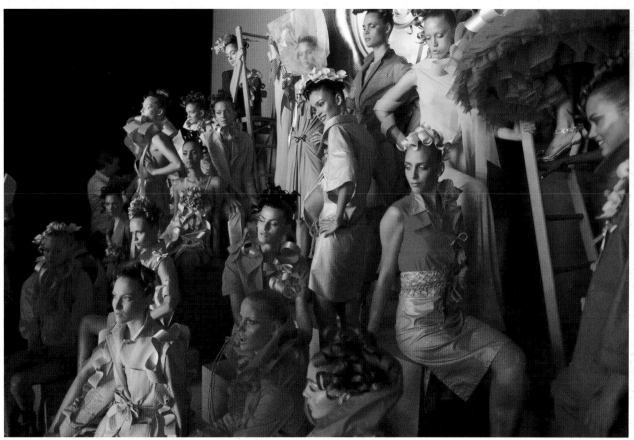

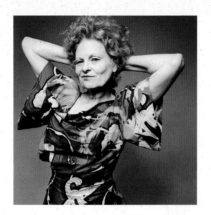

VIVIENNE WESTWOOD

"Power is sexy. I like the men and women
that I dress to look important"

Vivienne Westwood is a legend in her own lifetime, a designer who inspires many other designers and who makes clothes that delight her loyal customers. Born in Derbyshire in 1941, she first became a household name when, in partnership with Malcolm McLaren, she invented the punk uniform. Let It Rock, SEX, Seditionaries, Pirates, and Buffalo Girls were all early collections they created together at their shop in World's End, Chelsea. All became classics and served to challenge common preconceptions of what fashion could be. Since severing business ties with McLaren, Westwood has gone on to become one of the industry's most revered figures. She has achieved all this without any formal training. In the '80s she was hailed by Women's Wear Daily as one of the six most influential designers of all time, and in 2004 the Victoria & Albert Museum launched a travelling retrospective exhibition defining her iconic status – the tour will last 7 years and visit Australia, China and the USA. There is an intellectual method to the madness of her creative energy. Historical references, techniques and fabrics are intrinsic to her approach to design. The results are unconventional and alluring. Her subversive shapes and constructions have consistently proved to be ahead of their time. Awarded an OBE 15 years after being arrested on the night of the Queen's Silver Jubilee, she has now become a part of the establishment she continues to oppose. Myriad awards have been conferred on her, including British Designer of the Year, twice. Today she shows her ready-to-wear women's collection in Paris and a menswear collection, MAN, in Milan. While the interest in vintage Westwood has never been more intense, her diffusion line Anglomania regularly references pieces from her earlier collections. Westwood also has three best-selling perfumes – Libertine, Boudoir and Anglomania – and has shops in countries all over the world, including Hong Kong, Japan and Italy.

Vivienne Westwood ist schon zu Lebzeiten eine Legende – eine Designerin, die viele andere Modeschöpfer inspiriert und mit ihren Entwürfen eine treue Kundschaft entzückt. Geboren wurde sie 1941 in Derbyshire. Erstmals machte sie sich einen Namen, als sie gemeinsam mit Malcolm McLaren die Punk-Uniform erfand. Let It Rock, SEX, Seditionaries, Pirates und Buffalo Girls sind lauter frühe Kollektionen, die sie zusammen in ihrem Laden World's End in Chelsea entwarfen. Sie wurden allesamt zu Klassikern und stellten gängige Vorurteile darüber, was Mode sein könnte, in Frage. Nachdem sie die Geschäftsbeziehung mit McLaren beendet hatte, wurde Westwood zu einer der meistgeachteten Figuren der Branche. Erreicht hat sie all das ohne jegliche konventionelle Ausbildung. In den 1980er Jahren erkor Women's Wear Daily sie zu einem der sechs einflussreichsten Designer aller Zeiten. 2004 präsentierte das Victoria & Albert Museum eine Retrospektive rund um ihren Status als Mode-Ikone; die Wanderausstellung ist für sieben Jahre angesetzt und wird in dieser Zeit auch in Australien, China und den USA zu sehen sein. Westwoods kreative Arbeitswut hat intellektuelle Methode. So sind historische Bezüge, Techniken und Materialien

wesentliche Elemente ihres Designkonzepts. Die Ergebnisse sind so unkonventionell wie verführerisch. Ihre subversiven Silhouetten und Konstruktionen sind, wie man immer wieder feststellen kann, ihrer Zeit voraus. 15 Jahre nachdem sie in der Nacht des silbernen Thronjubiläums der Queen verhaftet worden war, zeichnete man sie als Officer of the Order of the British Empire aus. Inzwischen ist sie selbst Teil des Establishments, gegen das sie nach wie vor ankämpft. Myriaden von Auszeichnungen wurden ihr verliehen, darunter allein zweimal der Titel British Designer of the Year. Heute zeigt sie ihre Prêt-à-porter-Kollektion für Damen in Paris und eine Herrenkollektion namens MAN in Mailand. Während das Interesse an ihren Vintage-Teilen so groß ist wie noch nie, nimmt sie in ihrer Nebenlinie Anglomania selbst regelmäßig Bezug auf Entwürfe aus früheren Kollektionen. Westwood hat auch bereits drei Düfte auf den Markt gebracht, die sich als Bestseller erwiesen: Libertine, Boudoir und Anglomania. Ihre Läden findet man auf der ganzen Welt.

Vivienne Westwood est une légende vivante, une créatrice qui inspire de nombreux autres stylistes et dont les vêtements font le bonheur de ses fidèles clients. Née en 1941 dans le Derbyshire, elle devient d'abord célèbre dans toute l'Angleterre pour l'uniforme punk qu'elle invente avec Malcolm McLaren. Let It Rock, SEX, Seditionaries, Pirates et Buffalo Girls sont autant de collections qu'ils créent ensemble dans leur première boutique du World's End à Chelsea. Toutes sont devenues des classiques et ont servi à remettre en question les idées préconçues sur ce que la mode doit être. Depuis qu'elle a mis un terme à ses relations d'affaires avec McLaren, Vivienne Westwood est devenue l'un des personnages les plus révérés par le monde de la mode, et ce, sans la moindre formation. Dans les années 80, Women's Wear Daily la classe parmi les six créateurs les plus influents de l'époque. En 2004, le Victoria & Albert Museum lance une grande rétrospective itinérante qui assoie son statut d'icône : l'exposition durera 7 ans et voyagera jusqu'en Australie, en Chine et aux Etats-Unis. On distingue de la méthode et de l'intellect dans la folie de son énergie créative. Références, techniques et tissus historiques font partie intégrante de son approche de la mode pour produire des résultats insolites et renversants. Ses formes et ses constructions subversives se sont toujours avérées très en avance sur leur temps. Décorée officier de l'Empire britannique 15 ans après son arrestation, la nuit du jubilé d'argent de la reine, elle fait désormais partie de l'establishment auquel elle continue pourtant de s'opposer. Elle a reçu une myriade de distinctions, dont deux fois le prix de British Designer of the Year. Aujourd'hui, elle présente sa collection de prêt-à-porter pour femme à Paris et sa collection pour homme, MAN, à Milan. Alors que l'intérêt pour les pièces Westwood vintage n'a jamais été aussi intense, sa ligne secondaire Anglomania fait régulièrement référence aux vêtements de ses anciennes collections. Vivienne Westwood a également lancé trois parfums à succès, Libertine, Boudoir et Anglomania, et possède des boutiques dans le monde entier, notamment à Hong Kong, au Japon et en Italie.

TERRY NEWMAN

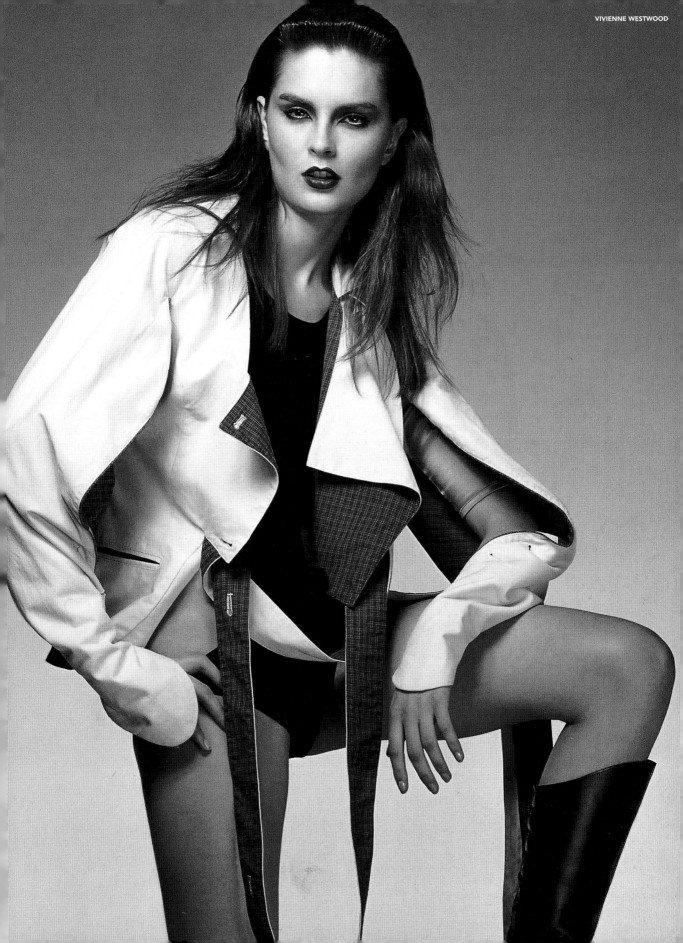

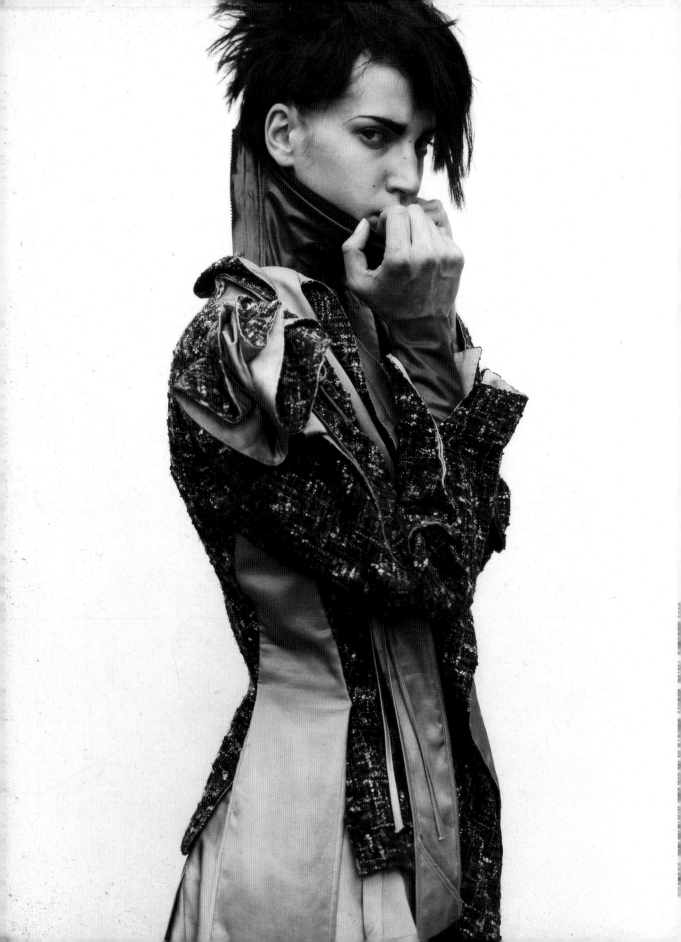

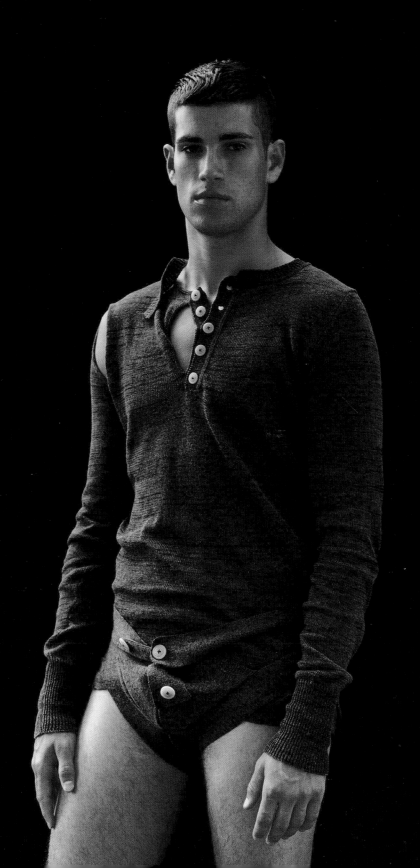

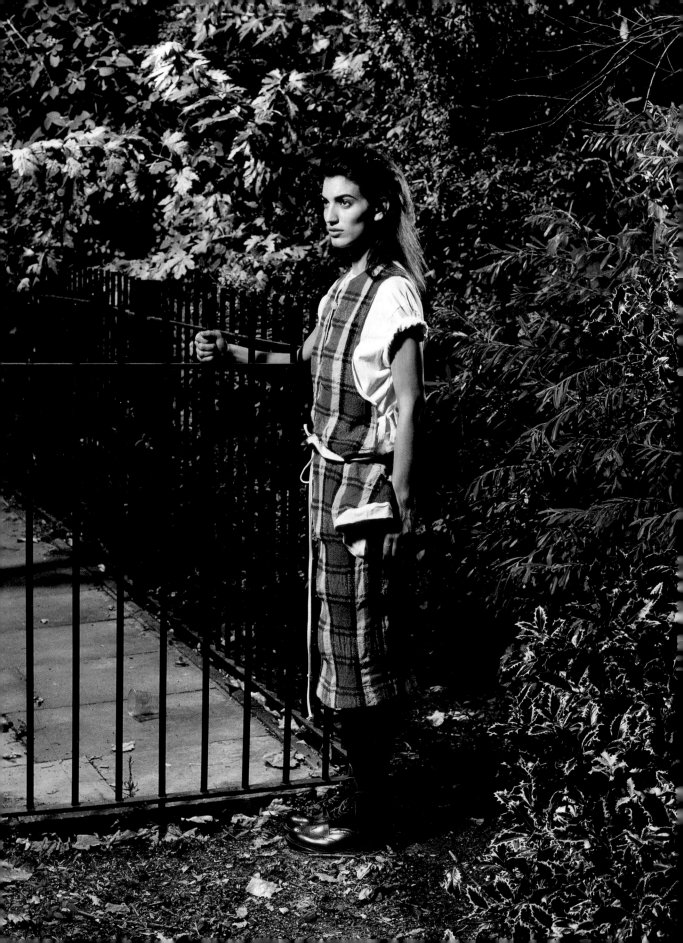

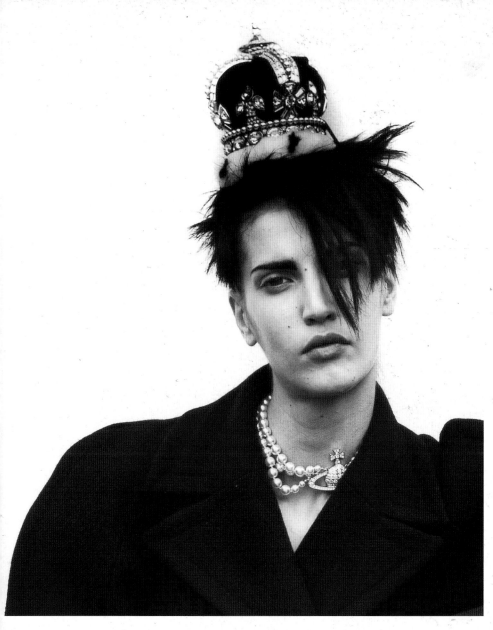

from the work itself. When you start to do something, then you find another way to do it. It's only by doing something one way that you have an idea of how it could be done another way. Of course, I also get inspired by things I see, but I do not get inspired by the street these days **Can fashion still have a political ambition?** I look upon government as a one-way corridor, to facilitate the interests of business. At the same time, the government tries to convince everybody else that this is good for them. And so people are being trained by the media to be perfect consumers of mass manufactured rubbish. The people who wear this stuff have bought the system, and their appearance demonstrates the fact that their brains have been removed. I think it's important to make great clothes so that people can look individual, and not a product of mass advertising **Who do you have in mind when you design?** The answer is nobody and everybody **What has been the greatest influence on your career?** I would say my World's End shop, which I've had since 1970. And that's because I was making clothes and selling them direct through the shop, so I always had access to the public and I always had customers. So I developed all my strengths without being frustrated in any way and I was always able to be the judge of my own work **How have your own experiences affected your work as a designer?** I had a cardinal change in my attitude after punk rock. I realised that my idea of attacking the establishment was naïve – if you try to attack the establishment, you actually feed the establishment. You give it all these ideas, it goes into mass manufacture and it has a big effect on the fashion world. So what I decided to do was go very fast and not care about attacking anything. Just to come up with the ideas and not be held back in any way. And since then, I've been miles down the road in front of anything **Is designing difficult for you and, if so, what drives you to continue?** When I view my catwalk show, my thought each season is the same: 'Six months ago that didn't exist; now it does exist. Nobody ever walked the planet wearing this before'. And that's what drives me on **What's your definition of beauty?** Everybody knows if a woman is beautiful or not. It's something that you can't deny. But I'm not terribly interested in beauty. What touches me is someone who understands herself **What's your philosophy?** Power is sexy. I like the men and women that I dress to look important. When I see that, I'm happy **What is the most important lesson you've learned?** Keep a smile on your face.

What are your signature designs? I think they're so well-known that you can fill this in yourself. One thing that people do forget is that I reintroduced the idea of fine knitwear into fashion. There's nothing more sexy than a twin set... more sexy still is the cardigan of the twin set, worn by itself with the buttons undone. You did not have this fine knitwear until I persevered, getting it from English companies when the machinery to make it didn't even exist in fashion knitwear companies. I'm just making the point that the things I do are very, very fundamental sometimes to what filters into the fashion world **What's your favourite piece from any of your collections?** My favourite garment of all time is my knitted dress, which I've been wearing for at least the last five years. You just look so stunning wearing this dress with very high heels. It uses the technique of hand-knitting to perfection. I will mention also that in my career I've done three special trousers, which I think are just the greatest: bondage trousers, pirate trousers, alien trousers. I always like my latest collections the best of all **How would you describe your work?** Very simply, avant-garde **What's your ultimate goal?** It's a question of organisation, to make the clothes more easily available in order to satisfy the demand. I just want people, once they've got their money together, to go and buy something, to be able to see my things straight away in order to choose them **What inspires you?** I get my ideas

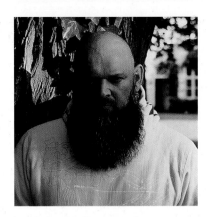

WALTER VAN BEIRENDONCK

"My goal is to change the boundaries of fashion"

If Walter Van Beirendonck were in a band, it would play a fusion of punk, folk, trash, pop, techno and chamber music. One of Belgium's most prolific fashion designers, Van Beirendonck places his sense of humour to the fore of his creations in an approach that humanises the sexuality which is often woven into his garments as patterns and graphics. Safe sex is a common thematic thread, as are literary, cinematic and folkloric references. Knitwear also plays a large part in Van Beirendonck's repertoire, but no prim twin sets or crewnecks for him – his jumpers are likely to come with matching balaclavas bearing garish cartoon faces, bold messages, or sexual motifs. Born in Belgium in 1957, Van Beirendonck studied at Antwerp's Royal Academy. Part of the legendary Antwerp Six who brought Belgian fashion to greater public consciousness with their 1987 London show, Van Beirendonck – along with Dirk Van Saene, Dries Van Noten, Dirk Bikkembergs, Marina Yee and Ann Demeulemeester – was responsible for moving fashion towards a new rationale. From 1993 to 1999 he created the cyberpunk label that was W&LT (Wild and Lethal Trash), after which he re-launched his eponymous line, Walter Van Beirendonck. A second line, Aestheticterrorists, was founded in 1999. He has taught at the Royal Academy since 1985 and has designed costumes for stage, film and for bands such as U2 and Avalanches. He has curated exhibitions in the world's top galleries and has also illustrated books, created his own comic and won numerous awards. In March 1998 the book 'Mutilate' was dedicated to Van Beirendonck's first 10 years in fashion, and in September 1998 he opened his own store, Walter, in Antwerp. Van Beirendonck could be described at the industry's blue-sky thinker, for both his visionary perspective, and his constantly optimistic outlook.

Wenn Walter van Beirendonck Mitglied einer Band wäre, würde die vermutlich eine Mischung aus Punk, Folk, Trash, Pop, Techno und Kammermusik spielen. Als einer der produktivsten Modedesigner Belgiens stellt er seinen Sinn für Humor in den Vordergrund seiner Kreationen. Das nimmt der Sexualität, die oft in Form von Mustern in seine Kleidung eingewoben ist, etwas von ihrer Schärfe. Safer Sex ist ein häufiges Thema, ebenso wie literarische, filmische und folkloristische Bezüge. Stricksachen spielen ebenfalls eine große Rolle in van Beirendoncks Repertoire, allerdings keine braven Twin Sets oder Matrosenkragen, seine Pullis kommen eher mit passenden wollenen Kopfschützern daher, auf denen grelle Comicgrimassen, forsche Botschaften oder sexuelle Motive zu sehen sind. Der 1957 in Belgien geborene van Beirendonck studierte an der Königlichen Akademie von Antwerpen und war einer der legendären Antwerp Six, die 1987 mit ihrer Schau in London der belgischen Mode die Aufmerksamkeit eines breiteren Publikums sicherten. Zusammen mit Dirk van Saene, Dries van Noten, Dirk Bikkembergs, Marina Yee und Ann Demeulemeester brachte er eine neue Form von Rationalität in die Mode. Zwischen 1993 und 1999 entwarf

er für das Cyberpunk-Label W&LT (Wild and Lethal Trash) und kümmerte sich anschließend um den Relaunch der nach ihm benannten Linie Walter van Beirendonck. Mit Aestheticterrorists wurde 1999 die zweite Linie gegründet. Seit 1985 lehrt der Designer an der Königlichen Akademie und entwirft außerdem Kostüme für Theater und Film sowie für Bands wie U2 und Avalanches. Er hat als Kurator Ausstellungen in den besten Galerien der Welt konzipiert, Bücher illustriert, einen eigenen Comic kreiert und zahlreiche Auszeichnungen gewonnen. Im März 1998 erschien das Buch „Mutilate", das sich van Beirendoncks ersten zehn Jahren in der Modebranche widmet. Im September desselben Jahres eröffnete der Modemacher mit Walter seinen ersten eigenen Laden in Antwerpen. Man könnte van Beirendonck mit seinen visionären Perspektiven einen unverbesserlichen Optimisten der Branche nennen.

Si Walter Van Beirendonck était membre d'un groupe, il jouerait une fusion de punk, de folk, de trash, de pop, de techno et de musique de chambre. Créateur parmi les plus prolifiques de Belgique, Van Beirendonck place son sens de l'humour au cœur de ses créations en adoptant une approche qui humanise la sexualité, souvent intégrée à ses vêtements sous forme de motifs et de graphiques. Le « safe sex » apparaît comme le fil rouge de son travail, à côté des références littéraires, cinématographiques et folkloriques. La maille joue également un grand rôle dans le répertoire de Van Beirendonck, mais point de twin-sets guindés, ni de convenables pulls à col rond chez lui : ses pulls s'accompagnent plutôt de passe-montagnes ornés de messages osés, de motifs sexuels ou de visages criards de bande dessinée. Né en 1957 en Belgique, Van Beirendonck étudie à l'Académie Royale d'Anvers. Membre des légendaires Antwerp Six qui ont fait connaître la mode belge lors de leur défilé londonien en 1987, Walter Van Beirendonck, aux côtés de Dirk Van Saene, Dries Van Noten, Dirk Bikkembergs, Marina Yee et Ann Demeulemeester, a contribué à faire avancer la mode vers une nouvelle logique. Entre 1993 et 1999, il crée une griffe cyberpunk baptisée W&LT (Wild and Lethal Trash) avant de relancer sa ligne éponyme, Walter Van Beirendonck, ainsi qu'une autre gamme, Aestheticterrorists, en 1999. Depuis 1985, il enseigne la mode à l'Académie Royale et dessine des costumes de théâtre, de cinéma et de scène, notamment pour les groupes U2 et Avalanches. Walter van Beirendonck a illustré des livres et organisé des expositions dans les plus grandes galeries d'art du monde, créé sa propre bande dessinée et remporté de nombreux prix. En mars 1998, le livre « Mutilate » retrace les 10 premières années de sa carrière et en septembre de la même année, il ouvre sa propre boutique, Walter, à Anvers. Van Beirendonck peut être considéré comme l'insouciant de la mode, tant pour sa perspective visionnaire que pour son indéfectible optimisme.

LIZ HANCOCK

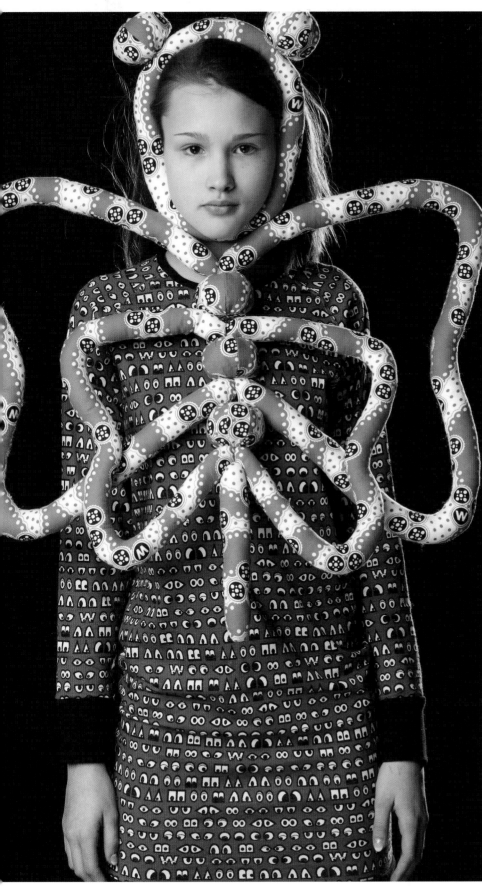

What are your signature designs? Experiments I did in every collection, designs to underline the silhouettes or statements of that particular collection **How would you describe your work?** A continuing challenge to create collections and clothes to reflect my personal vision and style independent of fashion trends and movements **What's your ultimate goal?** To change the boundaries of fashion and to achieve a personal satisfaction **What inspires you?** The world, my world, love... **Can fashion still have a political ambition?** Yes – fashion statements are still important, despite the fact that not many designers are thinking in that direction **Who do you have in mind when you design?** Nobody in particular. Gender, physique and age aren't important for my customers. It is more about being sensitive to my style, colours and forms **Is the idea of creative collaboration important to you?** Yes, very important. Most fascinating co-operations were with Stephen Jones, Bono, Mr Pearl, Mondino, Juergen Teller, Marc Newson, Paul Boudens **Who has been the greatest influence on your career?** My friend and colleague Dirk Van Saene **How have your own experiences affected your work as a designer?** I am still learning every day, but feel more mature than 20 years ago **Which is more important in your work: the process or the product?** Process and result are important. I do enjoy the process a lot **Is designing difficult for you and, if so, what drives you to continue?** I love it and despite the fact that it is a permanent (financial) struggle, I have never thought of giving it up **Have you ever been influenced or moved by the reaction to your designs?** Every reaction, good or bad, lets you think about what you are doing **What's your definition of beauty?** Rethink beauty! **What is your philosophy?** Think and dream **What is the most important lesson you've learned?** To stick to my own personality, style and ideas. A necessity in this fashion world.

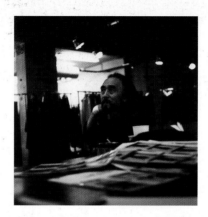

YOHJI YAMAMOTO

"You can say that designing is quite easy;
the difficulty lies in finding a new way to explore beauty"

Famed for his abstract silhouettes, flat shoes and unswerving loyalty to the colour black, Yohji Yamamoto is one of the most important and influential fashion designers working today. Uniquely, Yamamoto's clothing combines intellectual rigour with breathtaking romance; in his hands, stark and often extremely challenging modernity segues with references to Parisian haute couture. Born in Japan in 1943, Yamamoto was brought up by his seamstress mother, following his father's death in the Second World War. It was in an attempt to please his mother that he initially studied law at Tokyo's Keio University, later switching to fashion at the Bunka school, where he graduated in 1969. Following a trip to Paris and a period fitting customers at his mother's shop, Yamamoto established his own label in 1971, holding his first show in Tokyo in 1977. By the time he had made his Paris debut in 1981, along with his girlfriend at the time, Rei Kawakubo of Comme des Garçons, his label was already a commercial success back in Japan. Yamamoto sent out models wearing white make-up and asymmetric black clothing, and the establishment dubbed his look 'Hiroshima Chic'. However, a younger generation embraced Yamamoto, and both his womenswear and menswear – the latter shown in Paris for the first time in 1984 – became a status symbol for urban creative types. Despite his elite credentials, Yamamoto has expanded his business exponentially. He now has over 223 retail outlets worldwide, a groundbreaking collaboration with Adidas (Y-3), five fragrances, and casual collections, Y's For Women (established 1972) and Y's For Men (1971). He has been represented in numerous films, books and exhibitions; 'Juste des Vêtements, Yohji Yamamoto', his first major solo exhibition, was held in 2005 at the Musée de la Mode in Paris. Yamamoto is also a karate black belt and chief organiser of the Worldwide Karate Association.

Yohji Yamamoto ist berühmt für seine abstrakten Silhouetten, flachen Schuhe und die unverbrüchliche Treue zur Farbe Schwarz. Zudem ist er einer der wichtigsten und einflussreichsten Modedesigner der Gegenwart. Auf einzigartige Weise verbinden seine Kleider intellektuelle Schärfe mit atemberaubender Romantik. Unter seinen Meisterhänden verträgt sich absolute und oft extrem anspruchsvolle Modernität mit Bezügen zur Pariser Haute Couture. Yamamoto wurde 1943 in Japan geboren, und nachdem sein Vater im Zweiten Weltkrieg umgekommen war, sorgte seine Mutter als Näherin für den Lebensunterhalt. Auf Wunsch seiner Mutter studierte er zunächst Jura an der Tokioter Keio-Universität, wechselte dann aber zum Modestudium an die Bunka School, wo er 1969 seinen Abschluss machte. Nach einem Parisaufenthalt und einer kurzen Phase, in der er im Laden seiner Mutter den Kunden bei der Anprobe half, gründete Yamamoto 1971 sein eigenes Label. Die erste Schau fand 1977 in Tokio statt. Als er 1981 gemeinsam mit seiner damaligen Freundin Rei Kawakubo von Comme des Garçons sein Debüt in Paris gab, war seine Marke zu Hause in Japan bereits ein kommerzieller Erfolg. Yamamoto schickte die Models mit weißem Make-up und asymmetrischen schwarzen Kleidern auf den Laufsteg, woraufhin das Mode-

Establishment diesen Look mit dem Etikett „Hiroshima Chic" versah. Die jüngere Generation nahm den Designer jedoch mit offenen Armen auf, und bald waren sowohl seine Damen- wie seine Herrenmode – letztere wurde erstmal 1984 in Paris präsentiert – Statussymbole kreativer Stadtmenschen. Trotz der elitären Anerkennung expandierte Yamamotos Geschäft exponentiell. Inzwischen verfügt er über 223 Einzelhandelsgeschäfte weltweit, dazu kommen noch eine wegweisende Kooperation mit Adidas (Y-3), fünf verschiedene Parfüms, Casual-Kollektionen, Y's For Women (1972 gegründet) und Y's For Men (seit 1971). Der Designer war bereits Gegenstand zahlreicher Filme, Bücher und Ausstellungen. Seine erste große Einzelausstellung „Juste des Vêtements, Yohji Yamamoto" war 2005 im Pariser Musée de la Mode zu sehen. Yamamoto ist auch Träger des schwarzen Karategürtels und Chef-Organisator der Worldwide Karate Association.

Réputé pour ses silhouettes abstraites, ses chaussures plates et son inébranlable loyauté envers la couleur noire, Yohji Yamamoto est l'un des créateurs de mode les plus importants et les plus influents actuellement en exercice. De façon unique, la mode de Yamamoto combine rigueur intellectuelle et romantisme échevelé; dans ses mains expertes, une modernité austère et souvent extrêmement provocatrice s'adoucit de références à la haute couture parisienne. Né en 1943 au Japon, Yamamoto grandit seul auprès de sa mère couturière, son père étant mort pendant la Seconde Guerre mondiale. C'est en cherchant à faire plaisir à sa mère qu'il entre à l'université Keio de Tokyo pour étudier le droit, qu'il abandonnera plus tard au profit d'un cours de mode à l'école Bunka, dont il sort diplômé en 1969. De retour d'un séjour à Paris et après avoir habillé les clients de l'atelier de sa mère, Yamamoto fonde sa propre griffe en 1971 et présente son premier défilé à Tokyo en 1977. Lorsqu'il fait ses débuts parisiens en 1981 aux côtés de sa petite amie de l'époque, Rei Kawakubo de Comme des Garçons, sa griffe remporte déjà un grand succès commercial au Japon. Il fait défiler des mannequins au visage entièrement peint en blanc et portant d'étranges vêtements noirs asymétriques, ce qui incite l'establishment à qualifier son look de « Hiroshima Chic ». Mais la jeune génération adopte le style Yamamoto, et ses collections pour homme comme pour femme (sa ligne féminine étant présentée pour la première fois à Paris en 1984) deviennent un symbole de statut pour les jeunes urbains créatifs. Malgré ses références élitistes, Yamamoto a développé son entreprise à un rythme exponentiel. Il compte aujourd'hui à son actif plus de 223 points de vente à travers le monde, une collaboration révolutionnaire avec Adidas (Y-3), cinq parfums et deux collections plus faciles à porter, Y's For Women (créée en 1972) et Y's For Men (1971). Son travail a été présenté dans de nombreux films, ouvrages et expositions; « Juste des vêtements, Yohji Yamamoto », sa première grande expo en solo, a été organisée en 2005 au musée de la Mode de Paris. Yamamoto est également ceinture noire de karaté et organisateur de l'Association Mondiale de Karaté.

SUSIE RUSHTON

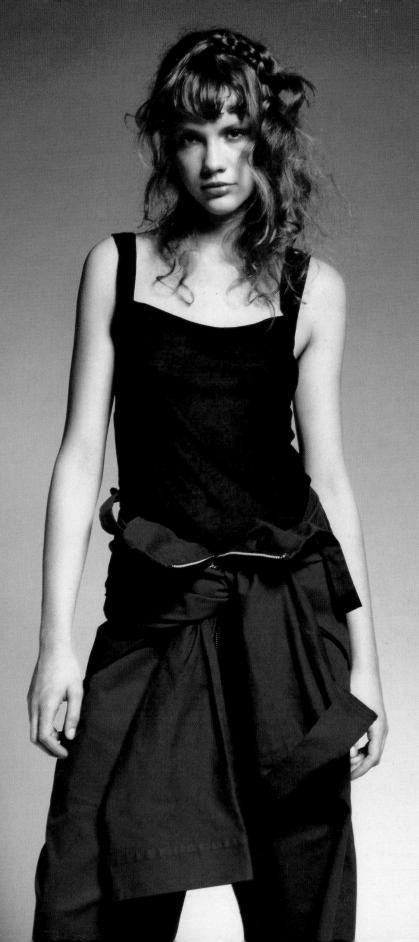

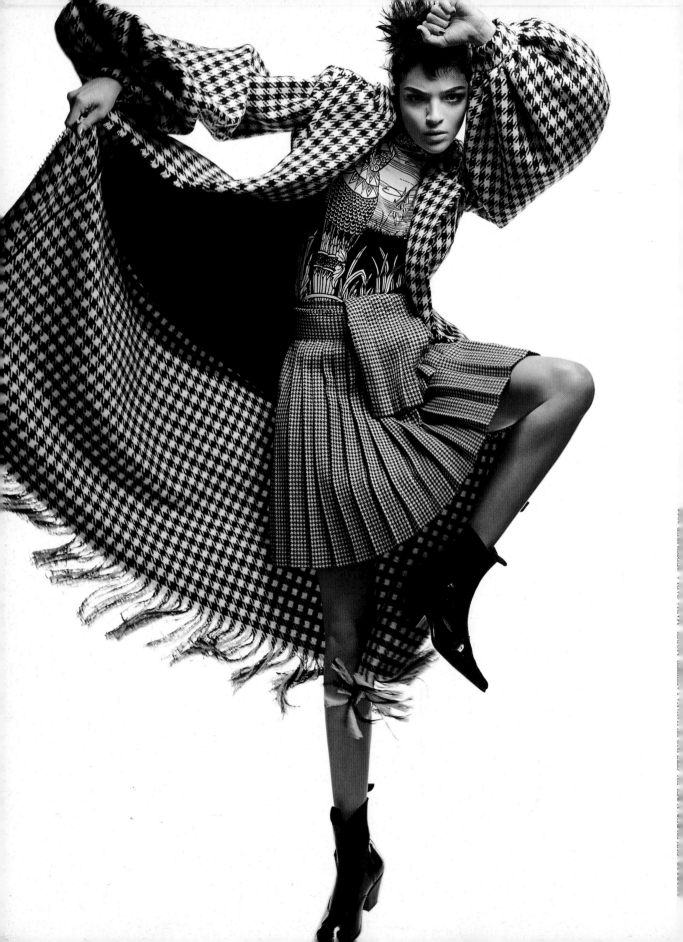

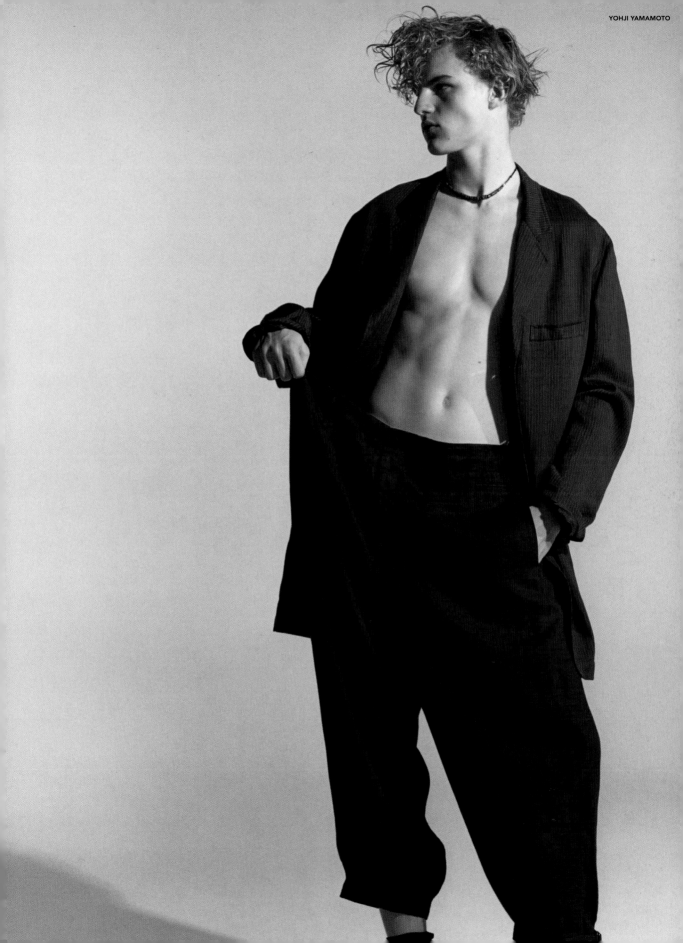

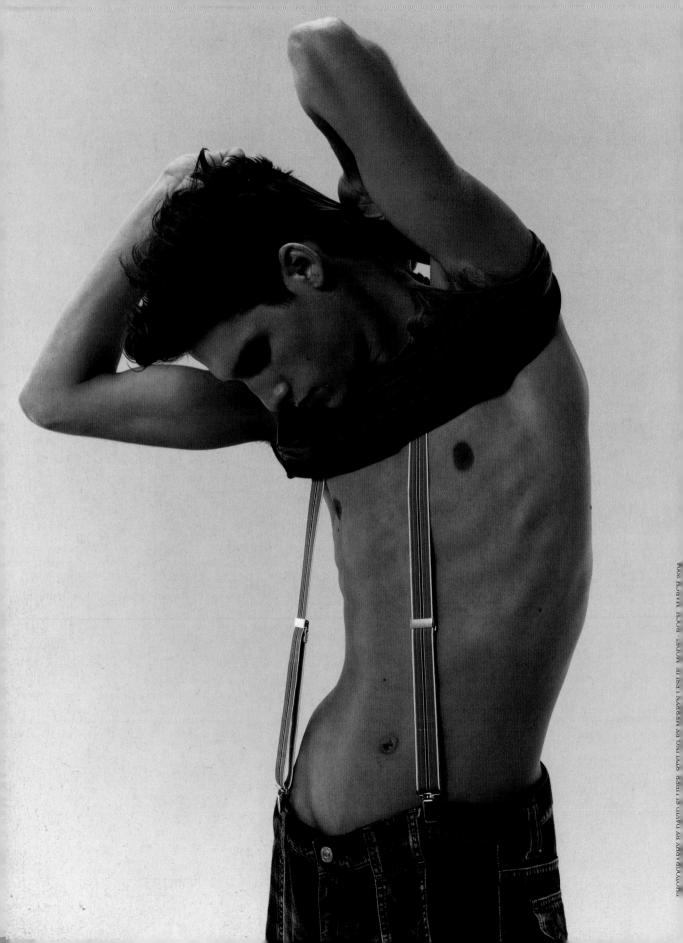

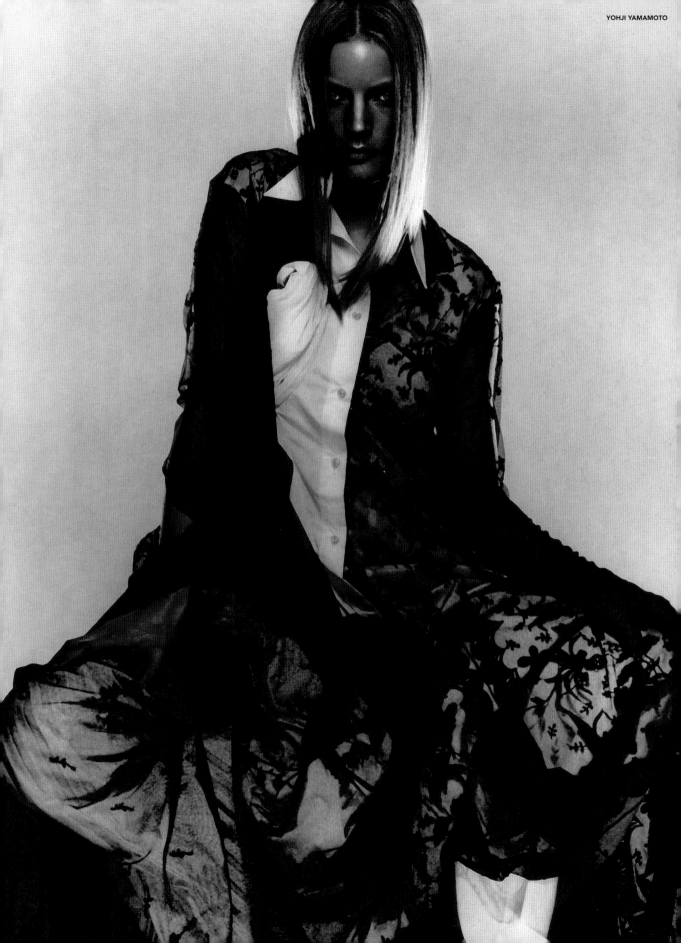

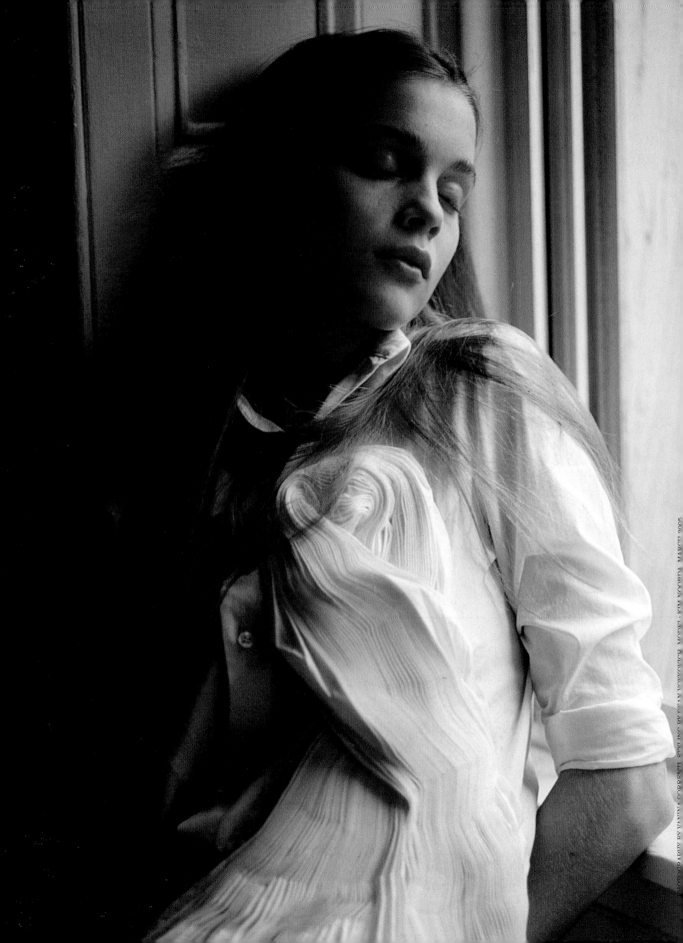

What are your signature designs? Over-sized coats, over-sized shirts, over-sized jackets… Anyway, anything over-sized **What's your favourite piece from any of your collections?** In terms of 'piece', I don't have the feeling of a favourite. Psychologically, to be human is to forget about sadness or bitterness, so I have few memories of those emotions. I've always thought that I want to forget about the things which have already passed. I always think that it might have been done in a better way. In terms of the show collections, some of them are still quite impressive in my opinion, I guess **How would you describe your work?** I've played all of my cards **What's your ultimate goal?** I've already reached a goal. I'm enjoying the rest of my life. Now it's time to enjoy time, time to spend time **What inspires you?** Inspire… the word which has been thrown at me a thousand times, and to which every time I've replied in a different way. I guess it's every phenomenon that inspires us every moment **Can fashion still have a political ambition?** If fashion has a role, it's to be immoral. A role to transfer the weak, humiliating and deplorable aspects of human nature into something charming. Art is always used or consumed by the authority of the time. Art co-operates by resistance. In this sense, fashion could have something to do with social ambition. But political ambition? I don't see it in fashion. But, if fashion does have such ambition, I would describe it as 'freedom'! **Who do you have in mind when you design?** The Sozzani sisters, Madonna, Jodie Foster. And Pina Bausch **Is the idea of creative collaboration important to you?** Important is not the right word. Creative collaboration can be used in a technological way; that is to combine technology with craftsmanship. But when we talk about creativity there must be ego, and when there are two egos we cannot help but compromise. So I don't find collaboration important in terms of creativity. I could find one collaboration in ten in which both sides influence each other in a good way. Conflict is expected from the beginning, so in a way you should go into collaboration with reason and intelligence **Who has been the greatest influence on your career?** Sigh-sigh-sigh. Mother… oh… Mother… again and forever. **How have your own experiences affected your work as a designer?** This is a matter which people should never speak about and which people never do speak about; this question is getting too close to it. It is trying to reach it. You could write a novel about it, I guess. Everyone has his own private stories, which he never speaks about, which he could never speak about, and it's a bit impertinent to ask. It's difficult, isn't it? **Which is more important in your work: the process or the product?** This is the best of all questions! I cannot be happier than being in the process. Then the product is a reality – and reality hits. In a season which has done well, I feel 'Ah, I've compromised…,' and in a season which did not work as much, I think 'It was the wrong time, I have not done enough.' I feel the responsibility as a result. My heart is beating whilst in the process… but daybreak always comes **Is designing difficult for you and, if so, what drives you to continue?** It should be said in this way: I can keep on designing just because of its difficulty. You can say that designing is quite easy; the difficulty lies in finding a new way to explore beauty **Have you ever been influenced or moved by the reaction to your designs?** I have opposite feelings: one is feeling a bit embarrassed and saying 'It's not such good work.' The other is such a strong feeling that it can't be expressed with the words 'influenced' or 'moved' but the words 'I'll kill everyone!' would fit better. Sometimes, I find a smart critic who analyses the unconscious phase which lies in my work. It gives me a lesson **What's your definition of beauty?** Condition; coincidence and by chance. A beautiful flower does not exist. There's only a moment when a flower looks beautiful **What's your philosophy?** Oh, come on **What is the most important lesson you've learned?** I am what I am due to four or five women. Please give me compensation!

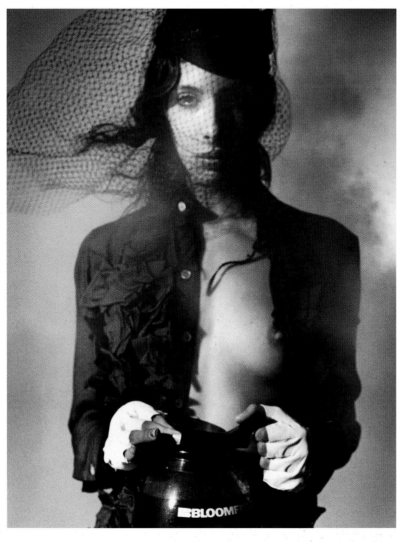

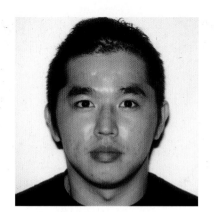

YONG FONG

"It is the cloth that makes women look beautiful"

Having Alexander McQueen describe your BA graduate collection as "very well executed and modern" before handing you the American Express Innovation Award must be among the favourite fantasies of most young designers. For Malaysian-born (1973), British-based design whippersnapper Yong Fong, it could hardly have been a better start to a career. On that very same evening in 2002, Fong was also crowned Graduate Designer of the Year. These prizes – the result of a winning six-piece collection featuring draped, twisted silk jersey that effortlessly fell into backless tops, ruffled skirts or harem pants – bagged him both a coveted work placement with McQueen and his own range for British chain store Topshop. With the stitching bug clearly in his family blood (his mother and aunt are both dressmakers), at 19 he studied pattern cutting and tailoring in Malaysia before heading to the UK in 1996. From the Edinburgh School of Art, where he completed his BA, Fong moved to London and the MA course at Central Saint Martins. It was here that he fine-tuned signature techniques: bias-cutting, draping and playing with volume. In 2004, he claimed the Harrods' Design Initiative Award and he continues to work for both Topshop and for British label Ghost.

Das muss eine der Lieblingsfantasien der meisten jungen Designer sein: Alexander McQueen nennt die Abschlusskollektion zum Bachelor „sehr gut ausgeführt und modern", bevor er einem den American Express Innovation Award überreicht. Der 1973 in Malaysia geborene, in Großbritannien lebende Designer-Frischling Yong Fong hätte kaum einen besseren Start in seine Karriere haben können. Am selben Abend im Jahr 2002 wurde Fong auch noch zum Graduate Designer of the Year gekürt. Diese Preise – als Ergebnis einer sechsteiligen Kollektion aus drapiertem, verschlungenem Seidenjersey, der sich mühelos zu rückenfreien Tops, gekräuselten Röcken und Pluderhosen formte – brachten ihm sowohl einen begehrten Job bei McQueen als auch eine eigene Linie bei der britischen Kette Topshop ein. Als jemand, dem das Nähen offensichtlich im Blut liegt (seine Mutter und seine Tante sind Schneiderinnen), lernte er in Malaysia Zuschneiden und Nähen, bevor er sich 1996 auf den Weg nach Großbritannien machte. Von der Edinburgh School of Art, wo er ein Bachelor-Studium absolvierte, zog er nach London, um am Central Saint Martins noch seinen Master zu machen. Hier perfektionierte er seine handwerklichen Markenzeichen: Diagonalschnitt, Drapieren und das Spiel mit Volumen. 2004 sicherte Fong sich den Harrods' Design Initiative Award. Im Moment ist er weiterhin für Topshop und das britische Label Ghost tätig.

Entendre Alexander McQueen décrire votre collection de fin d'études comme « moderne et très bien exécutée » avant qu'il vous remette le prix de l'innovation American Express doit certainement faire partie des fantasmes préférés de nombreux jeunes créateurs. Pour l'arrogant styliste Yong Fong, né en 1973 en Malaisie et désormais installé en Angleterre, on peut difficilement imaginer un plus beau début de carrière. Le même soir de 2002, le jeune diplômé est également couronné Graduate Designer of the Year. Justifiées par une superbe collection de six pièces taillées dans un jersey de soie drapé et travaillé pour tomber naturellement sur des hauts à dos nu, des jupes à volants et des pantalons de harem, ces récompenses lui valent à la fois un stage très convoité chez McQueen et la création de sa propre ligne pour la chaîne britannique Topshop. Le don de la couture coulant sans conteste dans les veines de sa famille (sa mère et sa tante sont toutes deux couturières), dès l'âge de 19 ans il étudie la coupe de patrons et la couture en Malaisie avant de s'installer en Angleterre en 1996. Après avoir décroché un BA à l'école des Beaux-Arts d'Edimbourg, Yong Fong part pour Londres et obtient un MA à Central Saint Martins. C'est là qu'il affine ses techniques caractéristiques : coupe en biais, drapé et jeu sur les volumes. En 2004, il remporte le Design Initiative Award de Harrods et continue à travailler à la fois pour Topshop et la griffe britannique Ghost.

SIMON CHILVERS

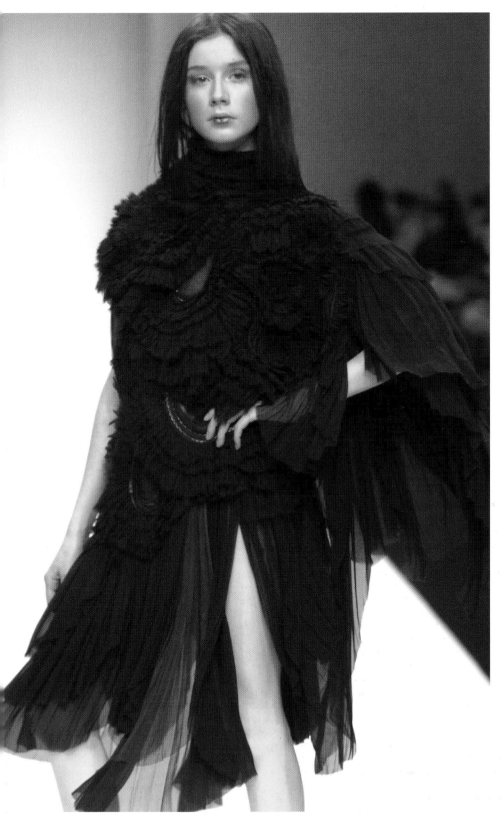

What are your signature designs? My signatures are detailed handwork, traditional couture elements, masculine and feminine, and asymmetric draped pieces. My favourite piece is from my MA collection – a beige coloured, hand-stitched dress **How would you describe your work?** I make technical clothing with strong feminine silhouettes. I am always interested in couture pieces and always want to find a way to surprise the audience **What's your ultimate goal?** My ultimate goal is the right balance between life and work **What inspires you?** Madeleine Vionnet. Memories and passions inspire me a lot **Can fashion still have a political ambition?** Yes, fashion can have a political ambition, but nobody takes fashion that seriously **Who do you have in mind when you design?** Nobody in particular. It is the cloth that makes women look beautiful, not the women. That is always in my mind when I design **Is the idea of creative collaboration important to you?** I have no idea. I am sure it is great to collaborate with someone creative. To have different ideas is important because it is a challenge **Who has been the greatest influence on your career?** My mum and my aunt, people and time are my greatest influences **How have your own experiences affected your work as a designer?** My work is part of me and my life, it has lots of feelings and emotion involved **Which is more important in your work: the process or the product?** The process and the product are both very important **Is designing difficult for you, if so, what drives you to continue?** I don't find it difficult to design, it is putting everything together and fitting that into the concept that's the hard part **Have you ever been influenced or moved by the reaction to your designs?** Yes, of course. They are made to be worn by someone who is appreciative of my work **What's your definition of beauty?** Beauty is from the inside of the person, not the outside **What's your philosophy?** Creating timeless pieces **What is the most important lesson you've learned?** Never give up what you do, be patient and believe in what you can do. And "It is not how good you are but it is how good you want to be".

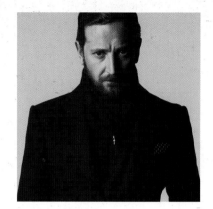

YVES SAINT LAURENT RIVE GAUCHE

"Because it's Saint Laurent, I think about silhouette, imagery and how I can refer to the past we have" STEFANO PILATI

In October 2004, Milanese designer Stefano Pilati presented his first collection for Yves Saint Laurent Rive Gauche. Featuring cute polka dot mini dresses with tulip hemlines and waists cinched with wide patent belts, Pilati's debut was both a clean break from the sexed-up vision Tom Ford had developed for Yves Saint Laurent, and something of a tribute to the '80s collections by Saint Laurent himself, who retired from fashion in 2002. Saint Laurent, who was born in Algeria in 1936, is one of the most important designers of the 20th century and takes the credit for numerous innovations in fashion, such as sheer clothing, le smoking, peasant-inspired designs, safari suits and pussy-bow blouses. He was also one of the first couturiers to embrace ready-to-wear fashion, launching his Rive Gauche shops in 1966. In 1998 Saint Laurent and his longtime business partner Pierre Bergé chose Alber Elbaz as the designer of Yves Saint Laurent Rive Gauche, but he was replaced by Ford a few years later following the Gucci Group's purchase of the YSL ready-to-wear business in 1999. When Ford exited the Gucci Group in 2004, Pilati succeeded him at YSL. Pilati grew up in Milan sketching outfits and stealing his sister's copies of Vogue magazine. In the early '80s, he abandoned a course in environmental design and landed an internship at Nino Cerruti. Over the following years, he immersed himself in the business of fashion until in 1993 he was hired as a menswear assistant at Giorgio Armani. Two years later, he joined Prada and began to work on research and development of textiles; by 1998 Pilati was assistant designer of Miu Miu menswear and womenswear, reporting directly to Miuccia Prada. In 2000 Tom Ford appointed Pilati as design director of Yves Saint Laurent Rive Gauche, where he quickly rose to a position overseeing all product categories. He now helms one of the most iconic brands in French fashion. "When I first fell in love with fashion, it was obvious that Mr. Saint Laurent was the master," Pilati has said.

Im Oktober 2004 präsentierte der Mailänder Designer Stefano Pilati seine erste Kollektion für Yves Saint Laurent Rive Gauche. Dazu gehörten süße Minikleidchen mit Tupfen, Tulpensaum und breiten Patentgürteln. Pilatis Debüt bedeutete sowohl einen klaren Bruch mit der sexuell aufgeladenen Vision, die Tom Ford für YSL entwickelt hatte, als auch eine Art Tribut an die 1980er-Jahre-Kollektionen von Saint Laurent selbst, der sich 2002 aus dem Geschäft zurückgezogen hatte. Der 1936 in Algerien geborene Designer Yves Saint Laurent gilt als einer der wichtigsten seines Faches im 20. Jahrhundert und zeichnet verantwortlich für zahlreiche modische Innovationen wie durchsichtige Kleidung, den Smoking, bäuerlich inspirierte Entwürfe, Safarianzüge und Blusen mit weichen Schleifen. Er war auch einer der ersten Couturiers, der sich mit Prêt-à-porter abgab, als er 1966 seine Rive-Gauche-Boutiquen eröffnete. 1998 bestimmten Saint Laurent und Pierre Bergé, sein langjähriger Geschäftspartner, Alber Elbaz zum neuen Designer von Yves Saint Laurent Rive Gauche. Nachdem der Gucci-Konzern 1999 das Prêt-à-porter-Geschäft von Yves Saint Laurent übernommen hatte, verpflichtete man ein paar Jahre später Tom Ford für diese Position. Als Ford sich 2004 von der Gucci-Gruppe trennte, wurde Pilati sein Nachfolger. Der Italiener wuchs in Mailand auf, wo er schon als Kind Outfits zeichnete und seiner Schwester die Vogue stibitzte. Als Mailand in den frühen 1980er Jahren zu einem Zentrum der Mode wurde, brach er sein Studium als Landschaftsarchitekt ab und begann ein Praktikum bei Nino Cerruti. In den folgenden Jahren stürzte er sich weiter ins Modegeschäft, bis man ihm 1993 die Assistentenstelle für Herrenmode bei Giorgio Armani anbot. 1995 heuerte er bei Prada an und begann, an der Erforschung und Entwicklung von Textilien zu arbeiten. 1998 wurde er Assistant Designer der Damen- und Herrenlinie von Miu Miu und unterstand direkt Miuccia Prada. Im Jahr 2000 schließlich holte ihn Tom Ford als Design Director zu Yves Saint Laurent Rive Gauche, wo er schnell zum Herrn über alle Produktkategorien avancierte. Jetzt lenkt er eine, wenn nicht die Ikone der französischen Mode. „Als ich mich das erste Mal in Mode verliebte, war klar, dass Yves Saint Laurent mein Vorbild war", meint Pilati.

En octobre 2004, le créateur milanais Stefano Pilati présente sa toute première collection pour Yves Saint Laurent Rive Gauche. Avec leurs adorables minirobes tulipe à pois cintrées par de larges ceintures en cuir verni, les débuts de Pilati tranchent avec la vision sexy développée par Tom Ford pour Yves Saint Laurent, tout en rendant un bel hommage aux collections des années 80 dessinées par Saint Laurent en personne, qui a pris sa retraite en 2002. Né en 1936 en Algérie, Yves Saint Laurent est l'un des plus importants couturiers du XXe siècle. On lui doit de nombreuses innovations dans le domaine de la mode, comme le chemisier transparent, le tailleur-pantalon, les créations d'inspiration folklorique, les ensembles safari et les cols lavallière. C'est également l'un des précurseurs du prêt-à-porter, ouvrant ses boutiques Rive Gauche dès 1966. En 1998, Saint Laurent et son associé de longue date Pierre Bergé choisissent Alber Elbaz comme styliste d'Yves Saint Laurent Rive Gauche, remplacé par Tom Ford quelques années plus tard après que le rachat de l'activité prêt-à-porter d'YSL par le groupe Gucci en 1999. Stefano Pilati succède à Tom Ford quand ce dernier quitte le groupe Gucci en 2004. Elevé à Milan, le jeune Pilati aimait déjà dessiner des vêtements et volait les exemplaires de Vogue de sa sœur. Quand Milan devient capitale de la mode au début des années 80, il abandonne ses études en design environnemental et décroche un stage chez Nino Cerruti. Les années suivantes, il s'immerge dans l'industrie de la mode avant d'être embauché comme assistant sur les collections masculines de Giorgio Armani en 1993. En 1995, il rejoint Prada où il commence à travailler dans la recherche et le développement de textiles ; en 1998, Pilati devient assistant-créateur des lignes pour homme et pour femme de Miu Miu, sous la responsabilité hiérarchique directe de Miuccia Prada. En l'an 2000, Tom Ford nomme Pilati directeur de la création d'Yves Saint Laurent Rive Gauche, où il gravit rapidement les échelons pour superviser finalement toutes les catégories de produits. Il tient désormais la barre de l'une des plus célèbres marques françaises : « Quand je suis tombé amoureux de la mode, il semblait évident que M. Saint Laurent était notre maître à tous », a déclaré Pilati. SUSIE RUSHTON

PORTRAIT BY MAX CARDELLI PHOTOGRAPHY BY MAX VADUKUL STYLING BY HAVANA LAFFITTE MODEL: LINDSAY ELIGSON MARCH 2005

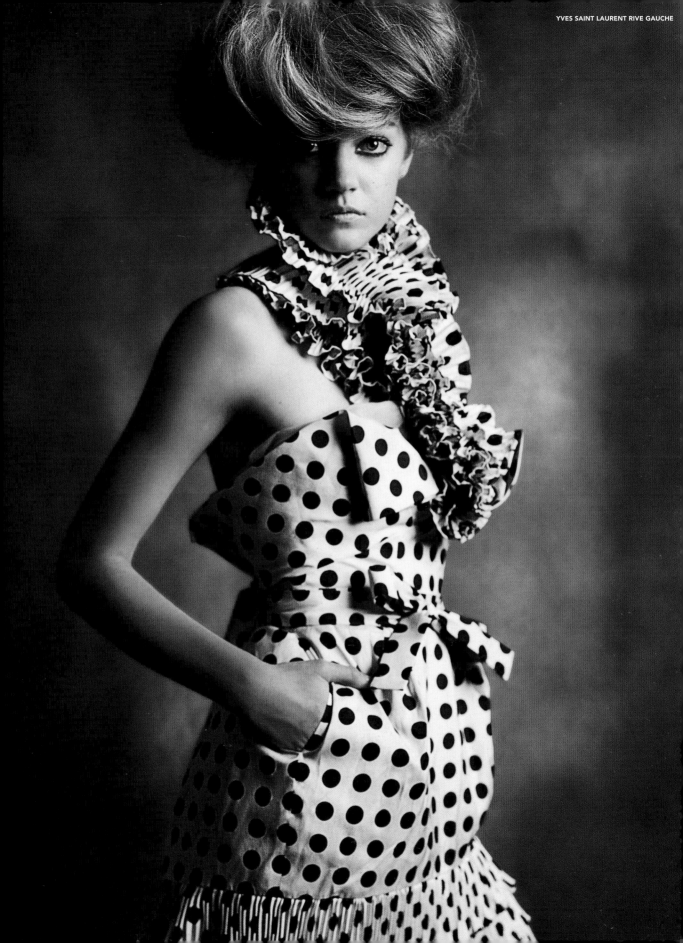

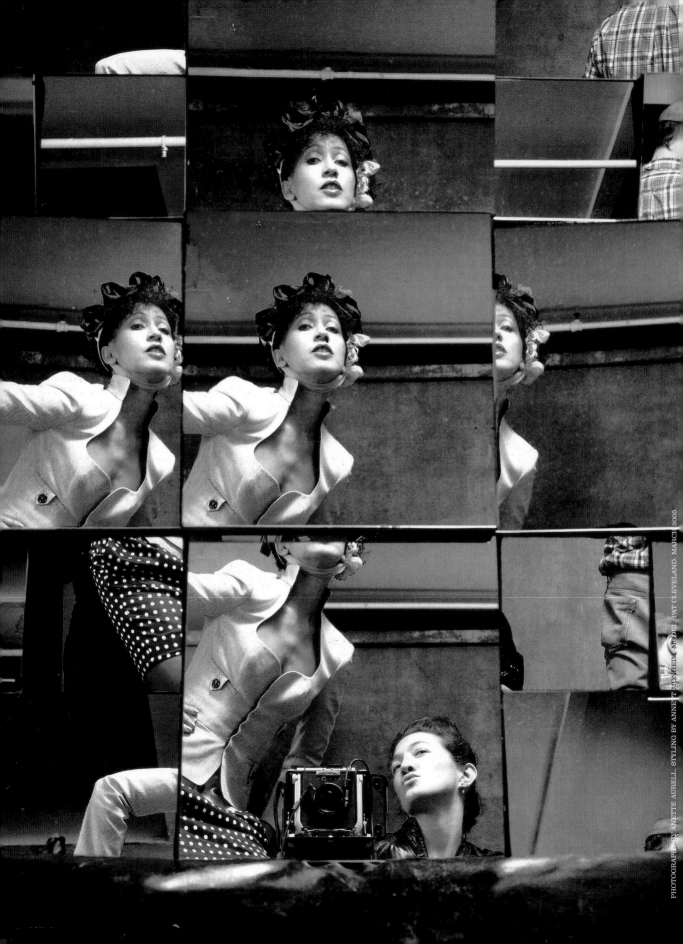

PHOTOGRAPHY BY ANETTE AURELL. STYLING BY ANNETT MONHEIM. MODEL PAT CLEVELAND. MARCH 2005.

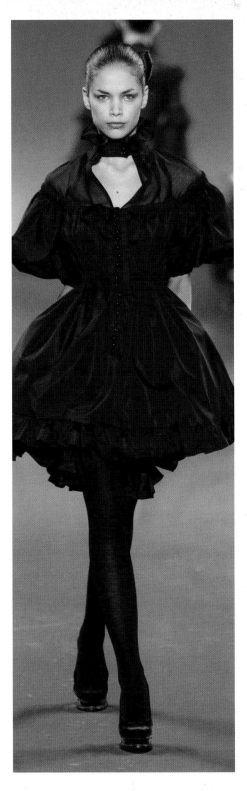

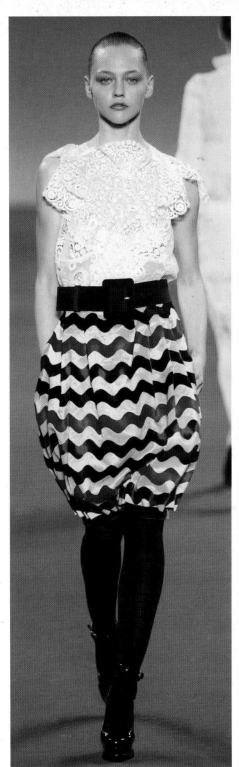

What are your signature designs? No matter what concept I have of fashion, the base I have to work from is an extreme sense of elegance, proportion, classicism and extravagance. Throughout Saint Laurent's work, he was spontaneous. He was perhaps the only one who could change each season, no matter where he wanted to take it. So the signature needs all of these elements **What is your favourite piece from any of your collections?** For me the most important thing was the monochrome aspect of how I treated outfits [in the autumn/winter 2005 collection]. Or, using colour in a way in which you don't have to think about it too much. For me, this is more important than a single favourite piece **What inspires you?** It's very personal. If I put something on and it gives me a certain sensation or it projects a mood that I'm looking for, then I start from that. Then, because I'm working at Saint Laurent, I think about things like the silhouette and the imagery and also how I can refer to the past we have. So out of that I start to draw up a full hand of notions and ideas. Then I build that around a theme **Can fashion still have a political ambition?** I think it would be genius if we achieved that. It would be a very mature step for fashion, to show that we can communicate something. Personally speaking, knowing how much I put into my work, such as a spiritual sense of making clothes, or a physical sense of making clothes, or the thoughts I have around women's evolution, men's roles, society and all of that; why not exchange it? Now could be a good moment to do that. Benetton was probably the only one who broke those barriers because it had that really huge machine behind it **Is the idea of creative collaboration important to you?** More and more. The difficulty that I have now is that ultimately, like it or not, being the most responsible one means that the pressure can't be shared with anybody. So sometimes it's difficult to balance yourself during the day or during a period when you have to stay cool. And also, in my situation – being at the beginning – I have to be in the shit by myself, without having someone to share it with me. It's a growing-up point for me **Who has been the greatest influence on your career?** I'm definitely influenced a lot by Saint Laurent – more than I would have expected, because I'm not French. From my background, the king for me has always been Armani. Working with Miuccia was also important, because she is a woman and her approach is inspiring. And then many other people: artists, icons. When I say 'inspired' I don't mean that I've tried to copy them, I mean that I am inspired by how they could talk to us for so long without getting bored, always finding something to say and always making sense.

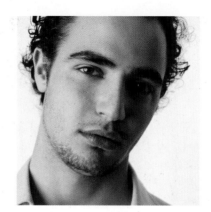

ZAC POSEN

"My work is about the female body, and ultimately, my clothes
are about making women feel and look beautiful"

Zac Posen, at only 25 years old, has already earned a place in fashion history. His leather dress, designed for the 'Curvaceous' exhibition at the Victoria & Albert Museum, was awarded the V&A Prize and acquired for the museum's permanent collection. This event marked the beginning of great things for the young New York native. Born in 1980, the son of a painter, Posen enrolled in the pre-college program at the Parsons School of Design, later joining Saint Ann's School for the Arts in Brooklyn. His fashion studies led him to Central Saint Martins in 1999 where he embarked on a BA in womenswear. However he soon packed in his studies in order to start his own label, which was an immediate success. His glamorous signatures include bias-cut gowns, fishtail hemlines and a passion for screen-siren style. His talent was swiftly recognised by the fashion industry: he was a finalist for the ENKA International Fashion Design Award in 2002 and a nominee for the CFDA award for new talent in both 2002 and 2003 before winning the Perry Ellis Award in 2004. That year proved to be a groundbreaking period for Posen. In April, Sean John, the fashion company backed by Sean 'Puff Daddy' Combs, announced it was making a long-term investment in Posen's label. However, it is Posen that continues to steer the label creatively, driving it forward with his vision of a strong, feminine silhouette. With Sean John's financial backing, the days when he was forced to fund his first catwalk show with the £14,000 prize from a fashion competition are a distant memory. Freed from monetary restraints, he is now able to concentrate on expanding his ready-to-wear collection and developing his accessories line.

Mit seinen gerade mal 25 Jahren hat Zac Posen seinen Platz in der Modegeschichte schon sicher. Das Lederkleid, das er für die Ausstellung „Curvaceous" im Victoria & Albert Museum entworfen hat, wurde mit dem V & A Prize ausgezeichnet und für die Dauerkollektion des Museums angekauft. Dieses Ereignis markierte für den gebürtigen New Yorker den Beginn einer großartigen Karriere. Geboren wurde er 1980 als Sohn eines Malers. An der Parsons School of Design nahm er am Pre-College-Programm teil, später schrieb er sich an der Saint Ann's School for the Arts in Brooklyn ein. Im Rahmen seines Modestudiums begann er 1999 den Bachelor-Studiengang Damenmode am Central Saint Martins in London. Bald schon brach er die Ausbildung jedoch ab, um sich voll auf die Gründung seines eigenen Labels zu konzentrieren, das sofort ein Erfolg war. Zu seinem typischen glamourösen Stil gehören diagonal geschnittene Roben, Schleppen und ganz allgemein die Liebe zum Stil der Leinwand-Diven. Sein Talent wurde innerhalb der

Branche rasch erkannt: Beim ENKA International Fashion Design Award 2002 gehörte Posen zu den Finalisten; beim CFDA-Preis für neue Talente war er 2002 und 2003 nominiert; 2004 gewann er schließlich den Perry Ellis Award. Jenes Jahr sollte ohnehin ein sehr bewegendes für Posen werden. Im April vermeldete Sean John, das Modeunternehmen von Sean „Puff Daddy" Combs, eine längerfristige Investition in Posens Label. Die kreative Richtung gibt allerdings weiterhin der Designer selbst vor und zwar mit seiner Vision von einer starken, femininen Silhouette. Mit der finanziellen Unterstützung von Sean John sind die Zeiten, als er seine erste Catwalk-Show mit den bei einem Modewettbewerb gewonnenen 14 000 Pfund bestreiten musste, nur noch Erinnerung. Finanzieller Beschränkungen enthoben, kann Posen sich nun auf den Ausbau seiner Prêt-à-porter-Kollektion und die Entwicklung einer Accessoire-Linie konzentrieren.

A 25 ans seulement, Zac Posen a déjà gagné sa place dans le panthéon de la mode. La robe en cuir qu'il a dessinée pour l'exposition « Curvaceous » du Victoria & Albert Museum lui a valu le V&A Prize et fait désormais partie de la collection permanente du musée. Cet événement marque le début d'une grande carrière pour ce jeune New-Yorkais. Né en 1980 d'un père peintre, Zac Posen s'inscrit à la prépa de la Parsons School of Design avant de partir pour la Saint Ann's School for the Arts de Brooklyn. En 1999, il débarque à Central Saint Martins où il entame un BA en mode féminine. Il interrompt ses études prématurément pour lancer sa propre griffe et rencontre un succès immédiat. Son style glamour et caractéristique se distingue par ses robes coupées en biais, ses ourlets en queue de poisson et une passion pour les sirènes du grand écran. Le monde de la mode ne tarde pas à reconnaître son talent : finaliste de l'ENKA International Fashion Design Award en 2002, nominé par le CFDA dans la catégorie nouveau talent en 2002 et 2003, il finit par remporter le prix Perry Ellis en 2004, une année révolutionnaire pour le jeune créateur. En avril, Sean John, la marque de Sean ‹ Puff Daddy › Combs, décide d'investir à long terme dans la griffe de Posen. Malgré toutes ces réussites, il continue à diriger sa griffe avec créativité et la fait évoluer grâce à sa vision d'une silhouette féminine prononcée. Fort du soutien de Sean John, la période où il était contraint de financer son premier défilé avec les 14 000 livres gagnées dans un concours de mode n'est plus qu'un lointain souvenir. Libéré de toute contrainte financière, il peut désormais se concentrer sur l'extension de sa collection de prêt-à-porter et sur le développement de sa ligne d'accessoires.

KAREN LEONG

PHOTOGRAPHY BY MATT JONES, STYLING BY HAVANA LAFFITTE. MODEL: SHANNYN SOSSAMON. JANUARY 2003.

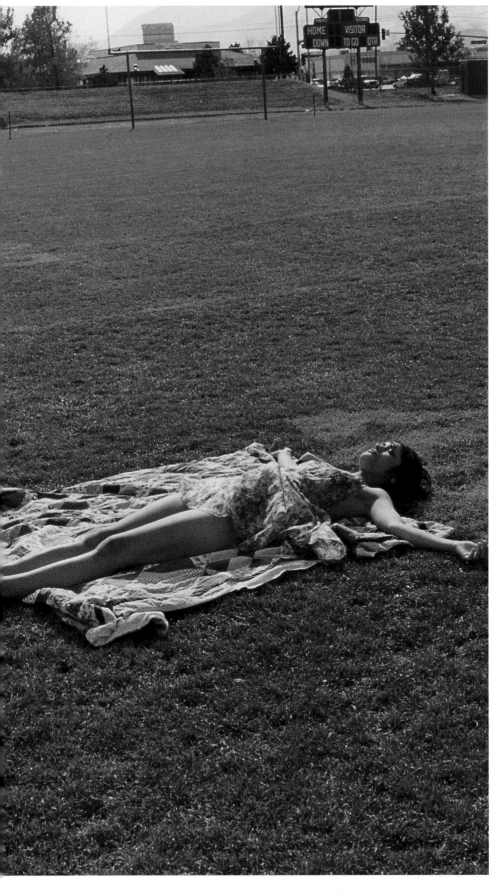

What are your signature designs? My signature designs are anatomical in their inspiration, and architectural in construction. They also incorporate movement and flair to accentuate a woman's personality **What is your favourite piece from any of your collections?** My favourites keep changing as my work evolves. The pieces that have really thrilled me have included: the cape skirt from Artemis, the snap gown and the papyrus dress from Circe, the Kaleidoscope dress from Leagues and Fathoms, the overall chic simplicity of the Sargasso collection, the Blixen gown and all of the knits from my resort and spring collections. Some of my ultimate favourites are the custom pieces I have designed for my private clients. There is nothing better than creating something special for an individual personality **How would you describe your work?** I make timeless clothing for feminine, strong, intelligent women. I pay enormous attention to design detail and artistry of construction in my clothing. I am drawn to textures and designs that are both ancient and futuristic. My work is about the female body and ultimately, my clothes are about making women feel and look beautiful. It's about creating a cool and glamorous lifestyle **What's your ultimate goal?** Wanting to make women feel strong, sexy, romantic and confident by creating the classics of the future **What inspires you?** Sensuality, life, craft and craftsmanship and most of all, the incredible women that surround me **Who do you have in mind when you design?** I love women of all ages, sizes and personalities – I am surrounded by them – and I keep them in mind when I design **Is the idea of creative collaboration important to you?** This is a collaborative business by nature. My work incorporates the genius of many experts, from the manufacturers of my materials, to my patternmakers and sewers. Within the creative studio, it is the variety of voices that lends depth and complexity to a collection **Who has been the greatest influence on your career?** My family **Is designing difficult for you?** The creative process is always tumultuous and intense but that's what keeps me going and keeps me fulfilled **Have you ever been influenced or moved by the reaction to your designs?** I love doing trunk shows and seeing women react to and inhabit my designs. I also love hearing stories from my clients of the experiences that they have had while wearing my clothes. For me, it's all about making women feel wonderful and expressive **What's your definition of beauty?** A woman who is intelligent, feminine, provocative, imaginative, playful and has a good sense of humour **What is the most important lesson you have learned?** Perseverance.

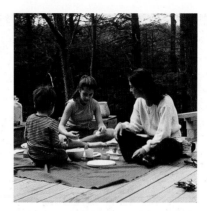

ZERO MARIA CORNEJO

"By questioning what you are doing, you evolve"

Chilean-born Maria Cornejo first arrived in the UK with her parents, having left their native country as political refugees. She later shot to prominence in the early half of the '80s, having graduated with flying colours from a fashion degree course at Ravensbourne College. Her subsequent designs, produced in conjunction with John Richmond, under the label Richmond-Cornejo, were championed by the style press and garnered the duo a strong cult following, helping to further establish her as a creative force – one able to see beyond mere seasonal modishness. Indeed, from the outset of her career Cornejo has been clear about her wish for longevity as a designer. By the late '80s, Cornejo had split from Richmond and was based in France, presenting her womenswear collections in Milan and Paris to much acclaim. She was also consulting and designing for British high street chain Jigsaw, in addition to overhauling the French ready-to-wear label, Tehen, as their creative director. Now based in New York under the label Zero, with her own store situated in the city's fashionable NoLita district, she continues to refine her design aesthetic, one which is wholly wearable yet frequently ever-so-slightly unconventional (Cornejo has been known to utilise her own hair as source material for prints). Her geometric constructions and pared-down approach to cutting attract a certain type of intelligent, open-minded woman – frequently those of a creative bent. High-profile advocates of Cornejo's clothing therefore include the likes of actresses Tilda Swinton, Sigourney Weaver and the artist Cindy Sherman. With global stockists currently ranging from stores such as Barneys in New York or Isetan in Japan, Cornejo clearly produces a style that can both cut though cultural difference and enhance the individuality of those who wear it.

Die in Chile geborene Maria Cornejo kam schon als Kind mit ihren Eltern nach Großbritannien, weil die Familie ihr Heimatland aus politischen Gründen verlassen musste. Anfang der 1980er Jahre wurde sie auf einen Schlag prominent, nachdem sie ihr Modestudium am Ravensbourne College mit Bravour absolviert hatte. Ihre nächsten Entwürfe, die sie zusammen mit John Richmond unter dem Namen Richmond-Cornejo realisierte, brachten den beiden viel Lob von Modejournalisten und eine treue Fangemeinde ein. Cornejo half dieser Erfolg, sich als kreative Größe zu etablieren – und zwar als eine, die über die modischen Trends der aktuellen Saison hinaus Bestand hat. Denn in der Tat war der Designerin vom Beginn ihrer Karriere an Langlebigkeit ganz wichtig. Ende der 1980er Jahre hatte Cornejo sich von Richmond getrennt und sich in Frankreich niedergelassen. Ihre Damenkollektionen präsentierte sie unter großem Beifall in Mailand und Paris. Außerdem war sie als Consultant und Designerin für die britische Nobel-Kaufhaus-Kette Jigsaw tätig und hatte beim französischen Prêt-à-

porter-Label Tehen die Funktion des Creative Director inne. Inzwischen arbeitet sie in New York für die Marke Zero und betreibt einen eigenen Laden im angesagten Viertel NoLita. Sie beschäftigt sich weiterhin mit der Verfeinerung ihrer Designästhetik, die absolut tragbare, aber sehr oft eine Spur unkonventionelle Stücke hervorbringt (berühmt wurde Cornejo mit der Verwendung ihrer eigenen Haare für Stoffmusterdrucke). Ihre geometrischen Konstruktionen und betont schlichten Schnitte sprechen einen bestimmten Typ intelligenter, aufgeschlossener Frauen – oft mit kreativem Background – an. Zu den angesehensten Fürsprecherinnen von Cornejos Mode zählen deshalb Schauspielerinnen wie Tilda Swinton, Sigourney Weaver und die Künstlerin Cindy Sherman. Gegenwärtig findet man ihre Entwürfe in Nobelkaufhäusern rund um die Welt, etwa bei Barneys in New York oder bei Isetan in Japan. Ihre Mode besitzt zweifellos die Fähigkeit, kulturelle Grenzen zu überwinden und gleichzeitig die Individualität der Trägerin zu unterstreichen.

La Chilienne Maria Cornejo est arrivée en Angleterre avec ses parents, qui fuyaient la répression politique exercée dans leur pays natal. Au début des années 80, elle se fait déjà remarquer en obtenant son diplôme de mode avec les félicitations du jury du Ravensbourne College. Elle s'associe ensuite avec John Richmond pour fonder la griffe Richmond-Cornejo. Encensées par la presse, les créations du duo remportent un énorme succès et deviennent rapidement culte, ce qui aide Maria à faire reconnaître son talent créatif : une force capable de voir au-delà des modes éphémères. Dès le début de sa carrière, Maria Cornejo déclarait déjà que son but était de durer dans le métier. A la fin des années 80, elle se sépare de John Richmond et s'installe en France, présentant avec grand succès ses collections pour femme à Milan et à Paris. Elle travaille également comme consultante et styliste pour la chaîne britannique des magasins Jigsaw, tout en assumant ses fonctions de directrice de la création du prêt-à-porter de Tehen. Aujourd'hui installée à New York sous la griffe Zero, avec sa propre boutique dans le quartier très tendance de NoLita (nord de Little Italy), elle continue à parfaire son esthétique de la mode à travers des créations très faciles à porter, mais toujours un peu surprenantes (elle est notamment connue pour avoir réalisé des imprimés à partir de ses propres cheveux). Ses constructions géométriques et son approche épurée de la coupe attirent un certain type de femmes, intelligentes et ouvertes d'esprit, souvent les plus créatives. Les étendards du style Cornejo incluent donc des actrices telles que Tilda Swinton et Sigourney Weaver, ou encore la comédienne Cindy Sherman. Distribuée dans le monde entier, de Barneys (à New York) à Isetan (au Japon), Maria Cornejo produit une mode qui fait clairement fi des différences culturelles tout en soulignant l'individualité de celles qui la portent.

JAMES ANDERSON

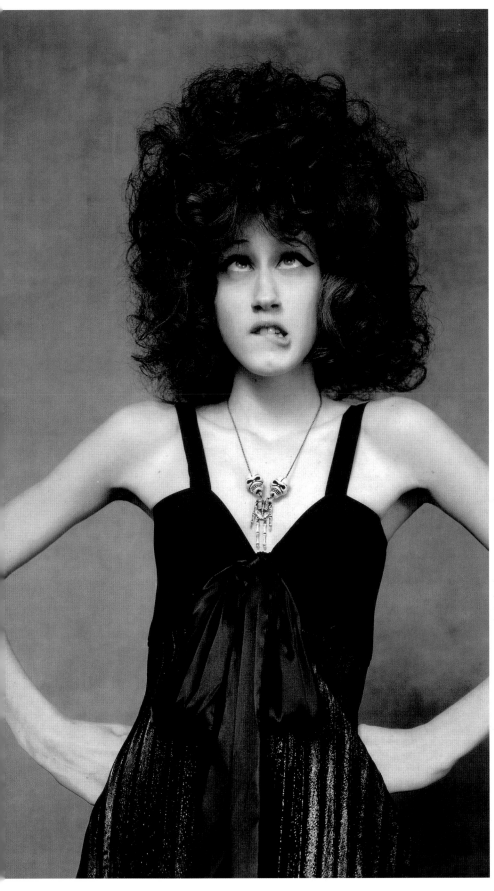

What are your signature designs? Circle top, drape front top, curve waistcoat, bike pants **What is your favourite piece from any of your collections?** The bubble dress, which was in the collection for the first time autumn/ winter 2001. It's a circular dress which is elasticated at the hem creating a bubble shape **How would you describe your work?** Organic Sculptural and three dimensional **What's your ultimate goal?** To be fulfilled and keep learning, to be successful and still have a life **What inspires you?** Architecture, people, all forms of organic life **Can fashion still have a political ambition?** Fashion can provoke thought and discussion, and through uniforms provoke fear and repression **Who do you have in mind when you design?** No particular person but shapes and forms **Is the idea of creative collaboration important to you?** Yes, collaborations are very important. They push you in different directions and by questioning what you are doing, you evolve **Who has been the greatest influence on your career?** My greatest influence in spirit is my husband Mark Borthwick. He has given me the confidence to find my identity as a designer **How have your own experiences affected your work as a designer?** I came from Chile with my parents as political refugees, so I am not sentimental about change **Which is more important in your work: the process or the product?** Both **Is designing difficult for you, if so, what drives you to continue?** Yes at times it is difficult, the challenges **Have you ever been influenced or moved by the reaction to your designs?** The different reactions always interest me as they can vary from a very intellectual point to a very amusing interpretation or a love of the way something fits **What's your definition of beauty?** Beauty in a person is a combination of the emotional and superficial **What's your philosophy?** Don't sweat the small stuff – look at the big picture **What is the most important lesson you've learned?** To trust my instincts.

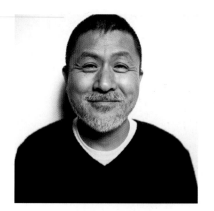

ZUCCA

"I need to design every day. It's like sport training" AKIRA ONOZUKA

Born in 1950, Akira Onozuka studied at Japan's first fashion school, Sugino college in Tokyo. A one-time assistant of Issey Miyake, Onozuka is the head designer of Zucca. This former Issey Miyake group label is now an international fashion house in its own right. Onozuka joined Miyake Design Studio in 1973, and established Huit Inc. as its subsidiary in 1988. In October of 1989, he introduced Zucca's first collection in Paris. It was met with much admiration from the French press. His designs are a study in movement and texture; drapery falls and folds to form edgy and modern silhouettes. Harbouring a wanderlust spirit, Onozuka's designs are also influenced by an ethnic sensibility. Zucca is both casual and artistic. The first Cabane de Zucca shop was opened in Tokyo, and in 1994 Onozuka launched Zucca Travail, a workwear-inspired collection produced by uniform factory S.A.Ets BERAHA in Bordeaux. In 1995, Onozuka launched Cabane de Zucca, a wristwatch series in collaboration with the Seiko Watch Corporation. The first model was a silicone ribbon watch, called "Chewing Gum", and a new model is launched every season. Zucca Design Office Inc. was established in 2003. Onozuka has likened the process of his work to that of a farmer tending to his vegetables, and in 2004 his work ethic paid off when he was awarded Le Trophée Elan by the Fédération du Prêt-à-porter Féminin, in recognition of Zucca Travail's contribution to the French manufacturing industry.

Der 1950 geborene Akira Onozuka hat an Japans erster Modeschule, dem Tokioter Sugino College, studiert. Der ehemalige Assistent von Issey Miyake ist Chefdesigner von Zucca. Dieses ehemalige Gruppenlabel Issey Miyakes präsentiert sich heute als eigenständiges internationales Modehaus. Onozuka trat 1973 ins Miyake Design Studio ein und etablierte 1988 Huit Inc. als Tochterunternehmen. Im Oktober des darauf folgenden Jahres stellte er Zuccas erste Kollektion in Paris vor und erntete damit große Bewunderung bei der französischen Presse. Seine Entwürfe sind Bewegungs- und Texturstudien; Drapierungen fallen und fälteln sich zu kantigen, modernen Silhouetten. Onozukas Entwürfe sprechen von Fernweh, zeigen aber auch folkloristische Neigungen. Zucca ist lässig und kunstvoll zugleich. Der erste Laden unter dem Namen Cabane de

Zucca wurde in Tokio eröffnet. 1994 lancierte Onozuka mit Zucca Travail eine von Arbeitskleidung inspirierte Kollektion, die die Uniformfabrik S.A.Ets BERAHA in Bordeaux produziert. Im folgenden Jahr kam in Zusammenarbeit mit dem Uhrenhersteller Seiko eine eigene Armbanduhr auf den Markt. Das erste Modell mit Silikonband hieß Chewing Gum. Seither wird pro Saison ein neuer Zeitmesser präsentiert. Die Firma Zucca Design Office Inc. wurde 2003 gegründet. So wie ein Bauer die Früchte seiner Arbeit erntet, machte sich auch für Onozuka sein Arbeitsethos 2004 bezahlt, als er mit Le Trophée Elan der Fédération du Prêt-à-Porter Féminin ausgezeichnet wurde. Dies geschah in Anerkennung seiner Verdienste um die französische Textilindustrie mit Zucca Travails.

Né en 1950, Akira Onozuka fait ses études au collège Sugino de Tokyo, la toute première école de mode du Japon. Cet ancien assistant d'Issey Miyake est aujourd'hui styliste principal de Zucca, ex-griffe du groupe Issey Miyake qui fait désormais figure de maison internationale à part entière. Onozuka rejoint le Miyake Design Studio en 1973 et fonde la filiale Huit Inc. en 1988. En octobre 1989, il présente la première collection Zucca à Paris et suscite l'admiration de la presse française. Ses créations impressionnent par leur étude du mouvement et de la texture ; il plie les drapés tombants de façon à former des silhouettes modernes et décalées. Marquées par l'esprit du voyage, les créations d'Onozuka subissent également l'influence de sa sensibilité ethnique, Zucca étant une griffe à la fois décontractée et artistique. La première boutique Cabane de Zucca ouvre ses portes à Tokyo. En 1994, Onozuka lance Zucca Travail, une collection inspirée par les vêtements utilitaires et produite par l'usine d'uniformes S.A.Ets BERAHA de Bordeaux. En 1995, Onozuka lance Cabane de Zucca, une série de montres développée en collaboration avec Seiko. La première montre présente un bracelet en silicone baptisé « Chewing Gum », avec un nouveau modèle lancé chaque saison. L'entreprise Zucca Design Office Inc. est fondée en 2003. Comparant sa méthode de travail à celle d'un paysan cultivant ses légumes, l'éthique professionnelle d'Onozuka finit par payer en 2004, quand la Fédération du Prêt-à-Porter Féminin lui remet le Trophée Elan en reconnaissance de la contribution de Zucca Travail à l'industrie de production française. KAREN LEONG

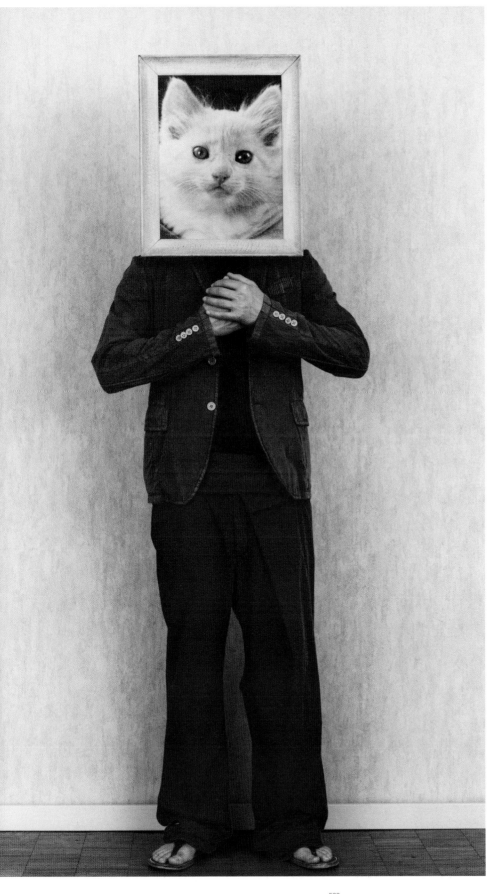

What are your signature designs? I think they are like modern ethnic costumes What is your favourite piece from any of your collections? The "Bhutanese" cotton velvet coat in black from my autumn/winter 2005–06 collection How would you describe your work? I think of it as something very similar to agricultural work. It takes a lot of patience and attention to detail What is your ultimate goal? I always pray for a bountiful harvest What inspires you? Travels Can fashion still have a political ambition? I cannot comment as to me it seems distant and far away Who do you have in mind when you design? I tend to imagine a free spirited individualistic person, like a person galloping across the steppes in Mongolia Is the idea of creative collaboration important to you? Yes, it is very important to me, especially the sewing factories and fabric manufacturers Who has been the greatest influence on your career? The viewpoints of Henri Cartier-Bresson How have your own experiences affected your work as a designer? It's similar to training or practising sports. I need to design everyday to come up with good ideas Which is more important in your work: the process or the product? They are equally important as they are linked Have you ever been influenced or moved by the reaction to your designs? Not really What is your definition of beauty? Something that disappears in the end What is your philosophy? The word "Ku" from Buddhism which covers the nuances of 'light' as in the sky, the heavens, and emptiness, as in everything starts from nothing and ends up nothing What is the most important lesson you've learned? The fashion world is like a vegetable field. To grow good vegetables, you have to water them just the right amount, make sure they get the right amount of sun, and sometimes you need to protect them so they don't get too much sun, and protect them if it gets too cold. The amount of attention and care one needs to give to growing vegetables is very similar to coming up with good designs.

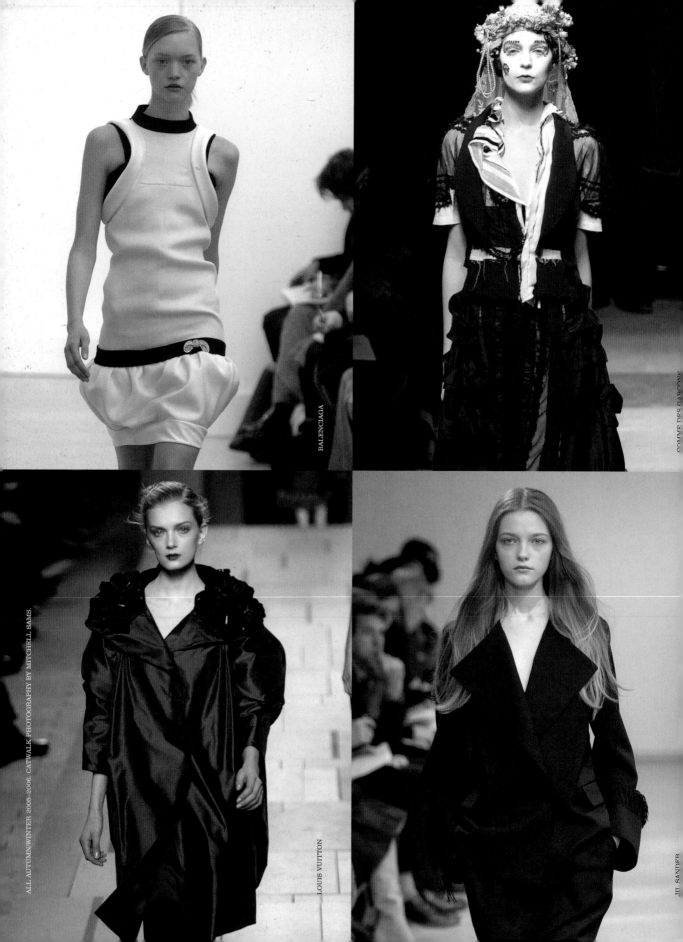

BALENCIAGA

COMME DES GARÇONS

ALL AUTUMN/WINTER 2005–2006. CATWALK PHOTOGRAPHY BY MITCHELL SAMS.

LOUIS VUITTON

JIL SANDER

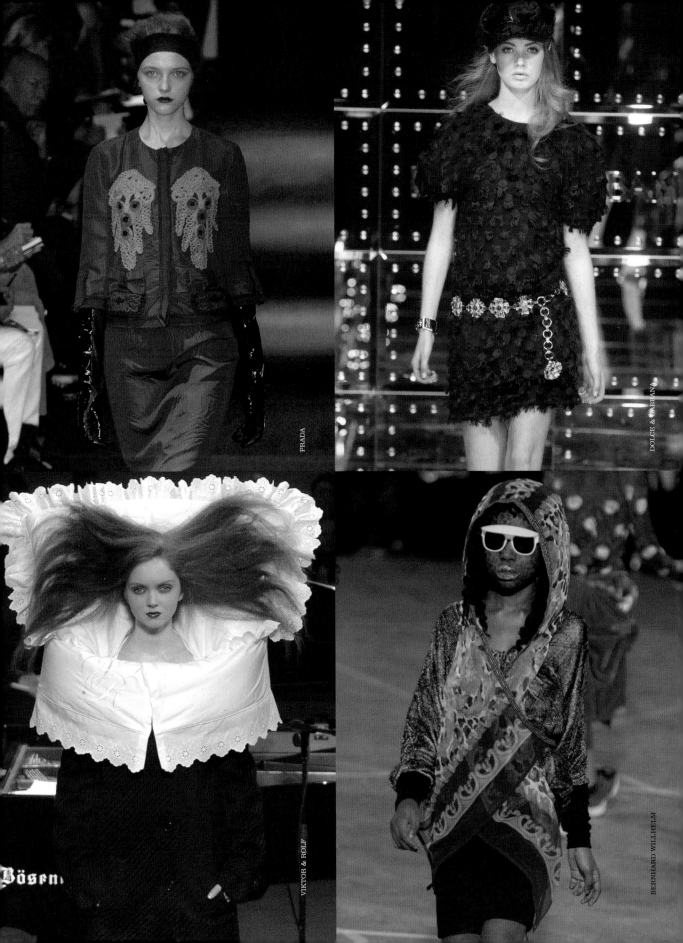

PRADA

DOLCE & GABBANA

Bösen

VIKTOR & ROLF

BERNHARD WILLHELM

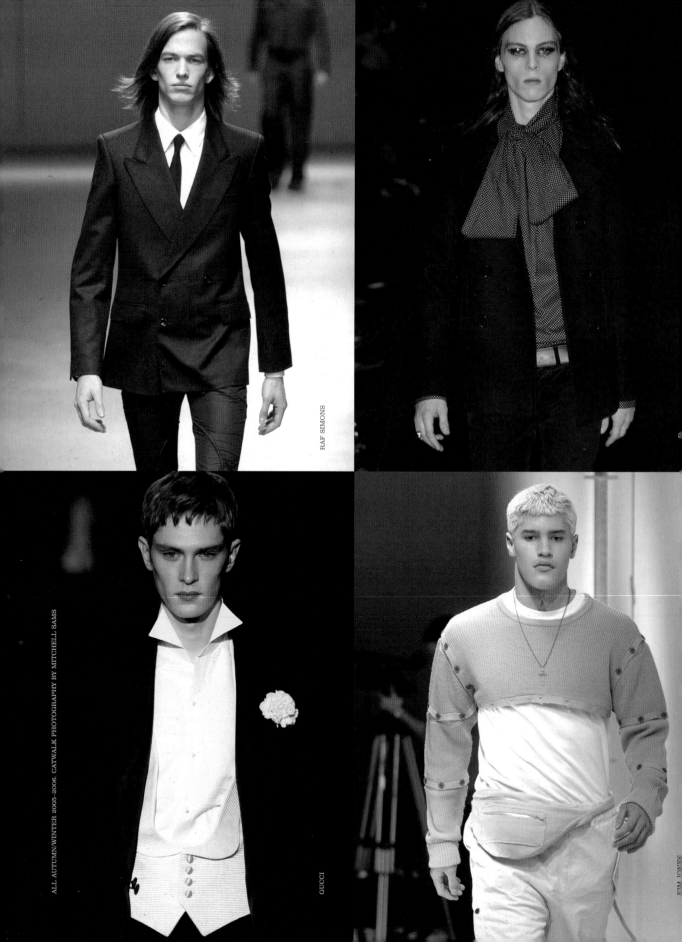

RAF SIMONS

ALL AUTUMN/WINTER 2005-2006. CATWALK PHOTOGRAPHY BY MITCHELL SAMS

GUCCI

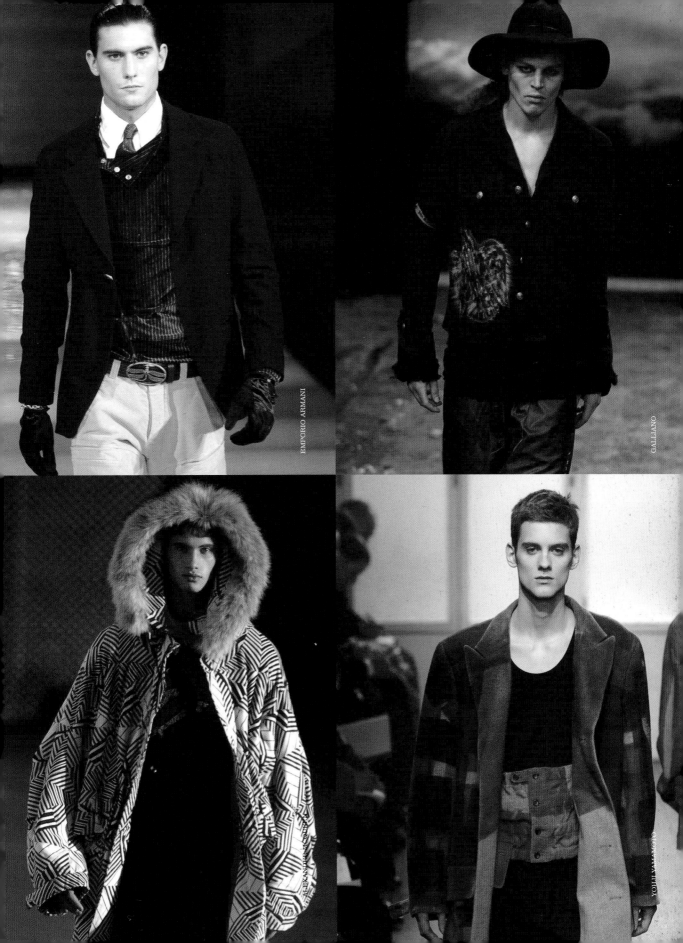

EMPORIO ARMANI

GALLIANO

ALEXANDER McQUEEN

YOHJI YAMAMOTO

FASHION SHOWS

The high-stepping models, the pristine white catwalk (protected with a clear plastic sheet until showtime), the ranks of carefully-dressed editors, department store buyers, stylists, writers and assistants perched along either side, the jostling media pit of photographers and TV cameramen, the throbbing music, the adrenalin and boredom of backstage, the bright white nuclear-dawn of the lights and the forty or so all-important outfits offered up for critique and interpretation: the 'show' is a ritual and an institution that has barely altered since the '50s. It is fashion's most mediagenic moment and, for all its predictability, its most glamorous. For certain designers, shows are central to their creative identity: the phenomenally imaginative defilés staged in Paris by Alexander McQueen, Hussein Chalayan, John Galliano and Viktor & Rolf have raised what is essentially a biannual marketing presentation to a form of performance art. At the other end of the scale, for young designers, a raw, hastily-organised and barely-financed show can be an invaluable way to draw attention to a budding label.

For many other designers, however, a fashion show is merely an unpleasant necessity, staged simply because custom requires it. Shows force a (sometimes unwelcome) early deadline on the design process. They're also very expensive – a large fashion house will have to foot a bill of € 200,000 upwards for each show. For a smaller designer, a comparable price tag of € 20,000 is no less prohibitive and usually requires the assistance of an outside sponsor.

It's not that the supremacy of this curiously rigid format hasn't over the years been challenged by some designers. Many have tried to find an alternative to the live, sashaying-back-and-forth fashion show: films have been shot, perfect-bound books of photographs published, installations staged. In April 1998 Helmut Lang became one of the first to harness the internet, by broadcasting a live presentation of his new collection to a worldwide audience; it turned out to be a one-off, but at the time, Lang's move felt like a revolution. Today of course internet images do play a crucial role in the system, but the live show also remains. Nothing, it seems, will usurp the catwalk.

According to Alex Betak of Bureau Betak – which stages shows for Christian Dior, Viktor & Rolf and Lanvin, among many others – the traditional format of a live defilé endures because it best fulfils the greatest number of industry requirements. "Fashion shows are the best format for the parameters we have to work within," he says, "We need to accommodate two hundred to three hundred lenses, trained on between thirty and sixty outfits. And then you have a maximum amount of time that the event can take – the show itself shouldn't exceed thirty minutes. And fashion isn't art, it needs to be shown as it is going to be used – on a body. This is the most telegenic way."

It's not simply a question of functionality and media compatibility however. A live show offers atmosphere, pressure, expectation, excitement, wonder, energy. It defines what is 'now'. Yohji

Yamamoto has said that the show – defined as moments when new designs are modelled, live, in front of an audience – in fact represents a crucial stage in his design process. Alex Betak meanwhile speaks of the "consensus reaction" of the large assembly of onlookers at a fashion show. A cynic might call it 'herd mentality'. However if the assembly's response is positive, Betak says, "it will ultimately serve the fashion house" and translate into good reviews, widespread coverage in fashion and mainstream media, an enhanced reputation and, finally, increased sales. And so fashion shows – old-fashioned and costly though they might be – persist.

MODESCHAUEN

Die tänzelnden Models, der schneeweiße Catwalk (bis zum Show-Beginn mit einer durchsichtigen Plastikfolie geschützt), die Reihen der sorgsam gekleideten Journalisten, der Einkäufer der Kaufhäuser, der Stylisten, Autoren und Assistente zu beiden Seiten, die drängelnde Medienmeute aus Fotografen und Kameraleuten vom Fernsehen, die hämmernde Musik, das Adrenalin und die Langeweile backstage, das grellweiße Licht und die rund vierzig alles entscheidenden Outfits, die man der Kritik und Interpretation preisgibt: Die Schau ist ein Ritual und eine altmodische Institution, an der sich seit den 1950er Jahren kaum etwas geändert hat. Es ist der telegenste Augenblick der Mode und bei aller Vorhersehbarkeit auch ihr glamourösester. Für einige Designer sind die Shows der zentrale Ausdruck ihrer kreativen Identität: Die ungeheuer phantasievollen Pariser Defilés von Alexander McQueen, Hussein Chalayan, John Galliano und Viktor & Rolf haben aus der halbjährlichen Marketingpräsentation Performance-Kunst gemacht. Am anderen Ende des Spektrums kann für junge Designer eine schlichte, schnell organisierte und knapp kalkulierte Schau eine unschätzbare Chance darstellen, Aufmerksamkeit auf ihr sprießendes Label zu lenken.

Vielen anderen Designern sind die Shows allerdings nicht mehr als eine unerfreuliche Notwendigkeit, etwas, das man auf die Beine stellt, weil die Kundschaft es verlangt. Die Schauen setzen dem Designprozess eine (manchmal unerwünschte) Deadline. Außerdem kosten sie eine Menge Geld – ein großes Modehaus muss pro Veranstaltung mit einem Betrag von 200 000 Euro aufwärts rechnen. Für Designer mit kleinerer Firma ist auch ein Preis von 20 000 Euro kaum erschwinglich und erfordert üblicherweise Hilfe von außen durch einen Sponsor.

Dabei haben Designer durchaus probiert, sich von dieser seltsam rigiden Präsentationsform zu lösen. Viele suchten nach Alternativen zur Live-Show mit ihrem Hin- und Hergetänzel: Man drehte Filme, publizierte aufwändige Fotobände oder brachte Installationen auf die Bühne. Im April 1998 war Helmut Lang einer der ersten, der sich des Internets bediente, indem er eine Live-Präsentation seiner neuen Kollektion für ein weltweites Publikum übertrug. Es blieb dann bei diesem einmaligen Versuch, doch damals hatte Langs Aktion revolutionären Charakter. Heute spielen die Bilder im Internet zwar eine wichtige Rolle, aber die Live-Präsentation ist geblieben. Nichts, so scheint es, kann den Catwalk ersetzen.

Nach Aussage von Alex Betak vom Bureau Betak – das u. a. Schauen für Christian Dior, Viktor & Rolf und Lanvin auf die Beine stellt – wird das traditionelle Live-Defilé überdauern, weil es dem Großteil der Anforderungen der Industrie gerecht wird. „Modenschauen sind das beste Format für die Parameter, mit denen wir zu arbeiten haben", meint er. „Wir müssen zwei- bis dreihundert Objektive unterbringen, auf dreißig bis sechzig Outfits gerichtet. Und dann gibt es noch die maximale Zeitspanne, die so ein Event in Anspruch nehmen darf – die Show selbst sollte nicht mehr als dreißig Minuten dauern. Und Mode ist nicht Kunst. Man muss sie so zeigen, wie sie getragen werden soll – am Körper. Das ist einfach die telegenste Form."

Das Ganze ist jedoch nicht allein eine Frage von Funktionalität und mediengerechter Darstellung. Eine Live-Schau erzeugt Atmosphäre, Druck, Erwartung, Spannung, Staunen und Energie. Sie definiert, was 'jetzt' ist. Yohji Yamamoto sagte einmal, dass die Show – also die Momente, in denen neue Entwürfe von Models getragen werden, live und vor Publikum – ein entscheidendes Stadium seines Schaffensprozesses ausmache. Alex Betak spricht von einer „Konsens-Reaktion" der versammelten Zuschauer bei einer Modenschau. Ein Zyniker würde vielleicht „Herden-Mentalität/Trieb" sagen. Fällt die Reaktion des Publikums jedoch positiv aus, so Betak, „dient sie letztlich dem Modehaus" und drückt sich in guten Kritiken, breitem Niederschlag in der Fach- und allgemeinen Presse, einem verbesserten Ruf und letztlich in steigenden Verkaufszahlen aus. Und so werden uns die Modeschauen – wie altmodisch und kostspielig sie auch sein mögen – erhalten bleiben.

DÉFILÉS DE MODE

Les mannequins au pas saccadé, le podium blanc immaculé (protégé par un film de plastique transparent jusqu'au moment du défilé), les rangées de rédacteurs soigneusement lookés, les acheteurs des grands magasins, les stylistes, les journalistes et les assistants penchés de chaque côté du podium, le carré des photographes et des cameramen qui jouent des coudes, la musique à fond, l'adrénaline et l'ennui des coulisses, l'éclairage blanc fluorescent digne de l'aube nucléaire et la quarantaine de tenues si importantes offertes à la critique et à l'interprétation : le défilé est un rituel et une vieille institution qui n'a subi que peu de changements depuis les années 50. C'est le moment le plus « médiagénique » et, malgré son aspect prévisible, le plus glamour de la mode. Pour certains créateurs, il représente la plate-forme d'expression centrale de leur identité créative : les défilés débordant d'imagination organisés à Paris par Alexander McQueen, Hussein Chalayan, John Galliano et Viktor & Rolf ont hissé ce qui n'est après tout qu'une présentation marketing biannuelle au rang d'art de la performance. En bas de l'échelle, pour les jeunes créateurs, un défilé tout simple, même organisé à la hâte sans beaucoup d'argent, peut s'avérer un moyen précieux pour attirer l'attention sur leur bébé griffe.

De nombreux autres créateurs considèrent le défilé comme un devoir désagréable dont il faut s'acquitter simplement parce que la coutume l'exige. Les défilés imposent un délai (parfois bienvenu) au processus de création. Ils coûtent également très cher : une grande maison devra investir plus de 200 000 euros dans chacune de ses présentations ; quant aux créateurs moins connus, une facture de 20 000 euros paraît tout aussi prohibitive et requiert généralement le soutien d'un sponsor extérieur.

Pourtant, certains créateurs ont remis en question la suprématie de ce format curieusement rigide. Ils sont nombreux à avoir trouvé une alternative au défilé en live et à ses allers-retours nonchalants : certains ont tourné des films, publié de superbes livres de photographies ou réalisé des installations. En avril 1998, Helmut Lang était le premier à tirer parti d'Internet en diffusant en direct et auprès d'un public mondial une présentation de sa nouvelle collection ; il n'a pas renouvelé l'expérience depuis, mais à l'époque sa démarche faisait figure de véritable petite révolution. Aujourd'hui, les images sur Internet jouent évidemment un rôle crucial dans le système, mais le défilé demeure. Il semble même que rien ne saurait le détrôner.

Selon Alex Betak du Bureau Betak, qui organise des défilés pour Christian Dior, Viktor & Rolf ou Lanvin, le format traditionnel du défilé en live perdure parce que c'est celui qui répond le mieux aux nombreuses exigences de l'industrie. «Les défilés de mode offrent le meilleur format pour les paramètres que nous devons respecter», dit-il. «Il faut faire en sorte que 200 à 300 appareils photo puissent immortaliser entre trente et soixante tenues. Il y a aussi une durée précise à respecter pour l'événement : le défilé en lui-même ne doit pas excéder trente minutes. Et la mode n'est pas de l'art, elle doit être présentée telle qu'elle sera utilisée, c'est-à-dire sur le corps. Ça reste le moyen le plus télégénique».

Toutefois, la pertinence du défilé ne relève pas que de la fonctionnalité ou de la compatibilité médiatique. Le défilé dégage une atmosphère, de la pression, il suscite des attentes, de l'enthousiasme, des surprises et donne de l'énergie. Il définit notre «aujourd'hui». Yohji Yamamoto a déclaré que le défilé, composé des moments où les nouvelles créations sont présentées en direct par des mannequins face à un public, représente en fait une étape cruciale dans son processus de création. Parallèlement, Alex Betak parle de la réaction de consensus de la grande assemblée des spectateurs, que les cyniques qualifieraient de «mentalité de troupeau». Néanmoins, si la réaction du public est positive, «au final c'est payant pour la griffe», comme le dit Betak. Cela se traduira sous forme de bonnes critiques, d'une large couverture dans la presse spécialisée et les médias, par une réputation rehaussée et finalement, une augmentation des ventes. Aussi démodés et onéreux qu'ils puissent être, voilà pourquoi les défilés de mode perdurent.

SUSIE RUSHTON
Editor, Fashion Now 2

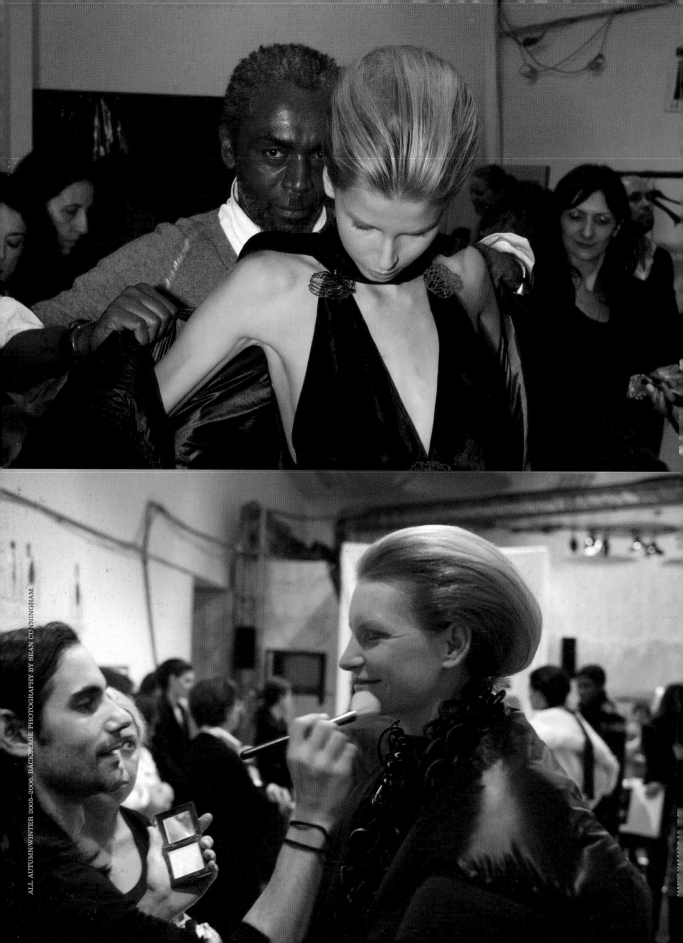

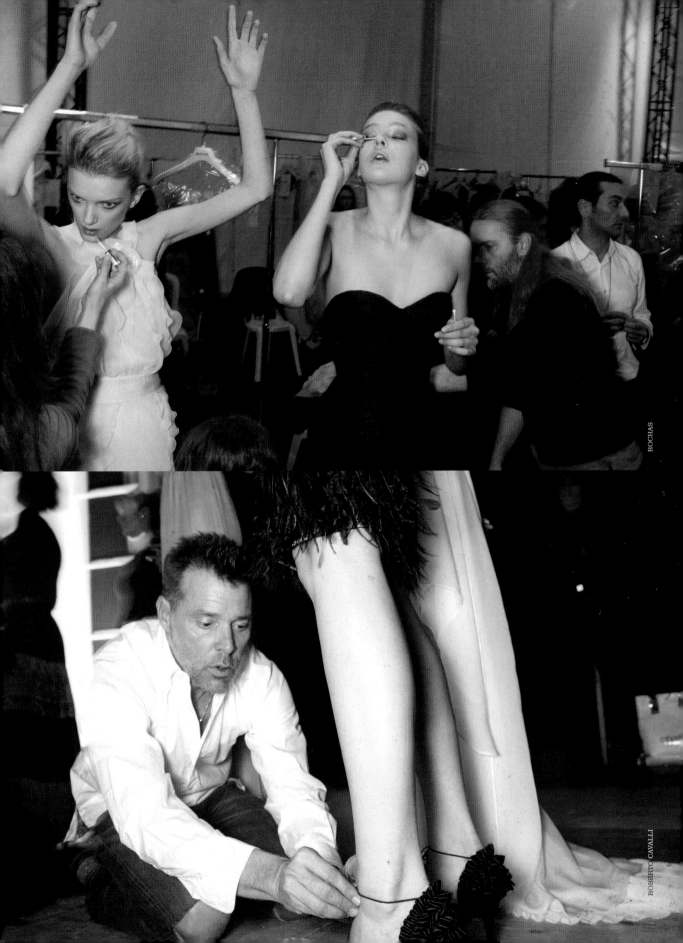

ROCHAS

ROBERTO CAVALLI

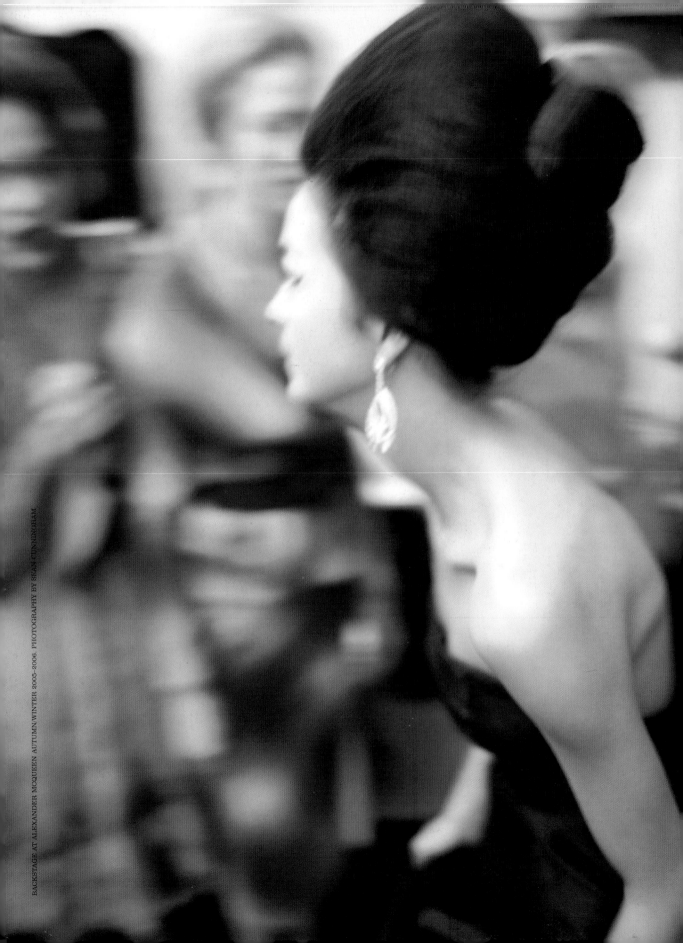

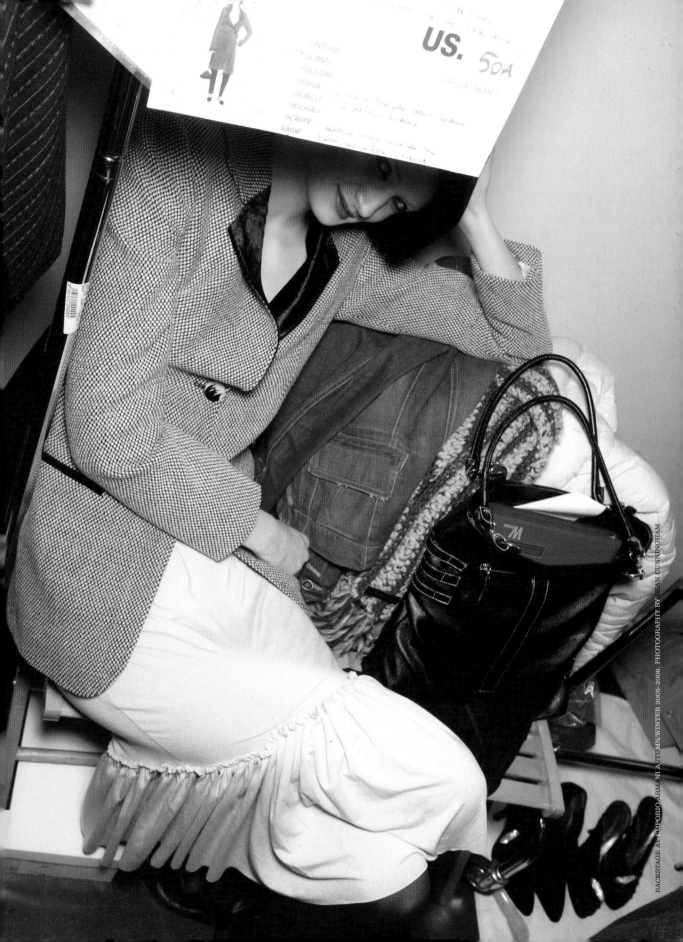

DESIGNER CONTACTS

A BATHING APE
"Busy work shop" London
4 Upper James Street
London WIF 90G, UK
T. +44 20 7494 4924

ADIDAS
Adidas-Salomon AG
Adi-Dassler-Str. 1–2
91074 Herzogenaurach, Germany
T. +49 9132 843830
www.adidas.com

A.F. VANDEVORST
Indienstraat 8
2000 Antwerp, Belgium
T. +33 1 49 23 79 79
F. +33 1 49 23 79 90
lamia@totemfashion.com
www.totemfashion.com

AGENT PROVOCATEUR
Europe: T. +44 20 7235 0229
America: T. +1 323 653 0229
enquiries@agentprovocateur.com
www.agentprovocateur.com

AGNÈS B.
35–36 Floral Street
Covent Garden
London WC2E 9DG, UK
Ami@agnesuk.co.uk
T. +44 20 7565 1188
www.agnesb.com

ALBERTA FERRETTI
Via Donizetti, 48
20122 Milan, Italy
London Press Office:
T. +44 20 7235 4113
Milan Press Office:
T. +39 02 760 591
Paris Press Office:
T. +33 1 42 61 34 36
New York Press Office:
T. +1 212 632 9300
Tokyo Press Office:
T. +81 33 2659067
www.aeffe.com
www.philosophy.it
www.albertaferretti.it

ALEXANDER MCQUEEN
4–5 Old Bond Street,
London W1S 4PD, UK
T. +44 20 7355 0088
oldbondstreet@alexandermcqueen.com

ALEXANDRE HERCHCOVITCH
Rua Haddock Lobo, 1151
São Paulo 01414–003, Brazil
T. +55 11 3063 2888

F. +55 11 3083 0798
herch@aol.com.br
www.herchcovitch.com

ANN DEMEULEMEESTER
184, rue Saint-Maur
75010 Paris, France
T. +33 1 42 03 1222
press@michelemontagne.com

ANN-SOFIE BACK
47 Lambers Conduit Street
London WC1 3MG, UK
T. +44 20 7739 7819
info@annsofieback.com
www.annsofieback.com

ANNA MOLINARI
Blufin
Via G. Ferraris, 13–15/a
42012 Carpi (MO), Italy
Europe:
Press office
T. +39 02 79 80 88
T. +39 02 48 51 98 97
America: T. +1 212 319 2222
info@blufin.it
www.blufin.it
ww.blufin.it

ANNA SUI
250 West 39th Street, 15th floor
New York, NY 10018, USA
T. +1 212 768 1951
F. +1 212 768 8824
contactus@annasui.com
www.annasui.com

ANNE VALÉRIE HASH
184, rue Saint-Maur
75010 Paris, France
T. +33 1 42 03 1222
press@michelemontagne.com

ANTONIO BERARDI
Karla Otto PR
35 Heddon Street
London W1B 4BP, UK
T. +44 20 7287 9890
mailuk@karlaotto.com

ANTONIO MARRAS
1, rue, du Pont-Neuf
75001 Paris, France
T. +33 1 73 04 20 00
F. +33 1 73 04 21 93

APC
France: T. +33 1 4222 1277
USA: T. +1 212 966 9685
Japan: T. +81 3 54 89 68 51
www.apc.fr (International Webside)
www.apcjp.com (Japanese website)

A-POC
11 Manresa Road
London SW3 6NB, UK
T. +44 20 7349 3300
press@issey.co.uk
www.isseymiyake.com

AS FOUR
86 Foursyth Street, 4th Floor
New York, NY 10002, USA
T. +1 212 343 9777
F. +1 212 343 9860
asfour@asfour.net
www.asfour.net
ww.asfour.net

ASHISH
Michael Oliveira-Salac
90 Berwick St
London W1F 0QB, UK
T. +44 20 7287 0041
F. +44 20 7287 5509
M. +44 7867 900 812
michael@blowpr.co.uk
mail@ashish.co.uk
www.blowpr.co.uk
www.ashish.co.uk

ATSURO TAYAMA,
81, rue des Saints-Peres
75006 Paris, France
T. +33 1 49 54 74 20

AZZEDINE ALAÏA SAS
7, rue de Moussy
75004 Paris, France
T. +33 1 40 27 8558
presse@alaia.fr

BALENCIAGA
40, rue du Cherche-Midi
75006 Paris, France
T. +33 1 5652 1717

BARBARA BUI
Paris:
43, rue des Francs-Bourgeois
75004 Paris, France
T. +33 1 44 59 94 06
F. +33 1 44 59 94 17
Milan:
Via Manzoni 45
20121 Milan, Italy
T. +39 02 29 06 13 80
F. +39 02 29 06 12 53
New York:
115–117 Wooster Street
New York, NY 10012, USA
T. +1 212 274 09 12
F. +1 212 625 19 39
info@barbarabui.fr
www.barbarabui.com

BENJAMIN CHO
Showroom Seven/Seven House PR
498 Seven Avenue, 24th Floor
New York, NY 10018, USA
T. +1 212 643 4810

BERNHARD WILLHELM
59, rue de Charonne
75001 Paris, France
T. +33 1 49 23 79 79
F. +33 1 49 23 79 90
sebastien@totemfashion.com
www.totemfashion.com

BLAAK
Mandi Lennard Publicity
2 Hoxton Street
London N1 6NG, UK
T. +44 20 77 29 27 70
F. +44 20 77 29 27 71
blaak@ml-pr.com
Pressing
99, rue du Faubourg du Temple
75010 Paris, France
T. +33 1 42 01 51 00
F. +33 1 42 01 50 99
info@pressingonline.com
Graphit Launch
T. +81 3 57 68 17 84
F. +81 3 57 68 17 88
k.kato@graphitlaunch.jp

BLESS
Bless Kaag/Heiss GBR
Rosa Luxemburg-Str. 17
10178 Berlin, Germany
T. +49 30 44010100
F. +49 30 44010101
blessberlin@csi.com
blessparis@wanadoo.fr
www.bless-service.de

BOSS BY HUGO BOSS
184–186 Regent Street
London W1 5DF, UK
T. +44 20 7534 2700
www.hugoboss.com

BOTTEGA VENETA
Viale Piceno 15/17
20129 Milan, Italy
T. +39 02 700 60 611

BOUDICCA
16d King's Yard, Carpenter's Road
London E15 2HD, UK
T. +44 20 8510 9868
F. +44 20 8533 5183
www.platform13.com

BURBERRY
18–22 Haymarket
London SW1Y 4SQ, UK
T. +44 20 7968 0000
T. 07000 785 676 (UK only)
www.burberry.com

CALVIN KLEIN
205 West 39th Street
New York, NY 10018, USA
Calvin Klein stores:
New York: T. +1 212 292 9000
Dallas: T. +1 214 520 9222
Paris: T. +33 1 56 88 12 12
Tokyo: T. +81 3 3470 3451
Seoul: T. +82 2 3444 3300
Singapore: T. +65 735 5790
Taipei: T. +88 62 2731 0020

CAROL CHRISTIAN POELL
Via G. Watt, 5
20143 Milan, Italy
T. +39 02 81 35 004
ccp@carolchristianpoell.com
www.carolchristianpoell.com

CÉLINE
23–25, rue du Pont-Neuf
75001 Paris, France
France: T. +33 1 55 80 12 12
UK: T. +44 20 7297 4999
www.celine.com

CHANEL
Chanel Boutique
26 Old Bond Street
London W1, UK
T. +44 20 7493 5040
www.chanel.com

CHLOÉ
54/56, rue du Faubourg-Saint-Honoré
75008 Paris, France
Europe: T. +33 1 44 94 33 33
America: T. +1 212 957 1100
Asia: T. +852 2532 7676
www.chloe.com

CHRISTIAN LACROIX
73, rue du Faubourg-Saint-Honoré
75008 Paris, France
Europe: T. +33 1 42 68 79 00
America: T. +1 212 931 2000
presse@christian-lacroix.com
www.christian-lacroix.com

CHRISTOPHE LEMAIRE
c/o Devanlay SA
92, rue Réaumur
75002 Paris, France
T. +33 1 44 82 69 36
whartmann@devanlay.fr

CLEMENTS RIBEIRO
413–419 Harrow Road
London W9 3QJ, UK
T. +44 20 8962 3060
F. +44 20 8962 3061
firstname@clementsribeiro.com

COLLECTION PRIVÉE
PR office:
Maximilian Linz
Via Arena 9
20123 Milan, Italy
T. +39 0289420673
F. +39 0289050660
0289420673@email.it

COMME DES GARÇONS
5–11–5 Minanmi Aoyama, Minato-ku
Tokyo 107, Japan
Europe: T. +33 1 47 03 60 90

America: T. +1 212 604 0013
Asia: T. +81 3 407 2684

COSTUME NATIONAL
Via Fusetti, 12
20143 Milan, Italy
T. +39 02 83 84 41
F. +39 02 83 84 42 51
www.costumenational.com

C.P. COMPANY & STONE ISLAND
SPW company
Via Savona, 54
20144 Milan, Italy
T. +39 02 42 20 141
F. +39 02 42 20 1420
www.cpcompany.com

DAVID SZETO
MO Communications
mesh@mocommunications.com

DENIS SIMACHEV
FBR PR Agency
Via S. Antonio 11
20122 Milan, Italy
T. +39 02 58 32 84 54
F. +39 02 58 32 84 47
www.denissimachev.com

DIESEL
Via Dell'Industria, 7
36060 Molvena (VI), Italy
Europe: T. +39 04 24 47 75 55
F. +39 04 24 41 19 55
America: T. +1 212 755 9200
info@diesel.com
www.diesel.com
ww.diesel.com

DIRK BIKKEMBERGS
59, rue de Turenne
75003 Paris, France
T. +33 1 402 70737
www.bikkembergs.com

DIRK VAN SAENE
Henri van Heurckstraat 3
2000 Antwerp, Belgium
T.+32 3 231 77 32

DOLCE & GABBANA
Via Goldoni 10
20129 Milan, Italy
T. +39 02 7742 71
www.dolcegabbana.it

DONNA KARAN
550 7th Avenue
New York, NY 10018, USA
T. +1 212 789 1500
www.donnakaran.com

DRIES VAN NOTEN
Godefriduskaai 36
2000 Antwerp, Belgium
T. +32 3221 9090
F. +32 3221 9091
info@driesvannoten.be

DSQUARED
Staff International
28–32 Britannia Street
London WC1X 9JF, UK
T. +44 20 7841 6000
www.dsquared2.com

E2
15, rue Martel
75010 Paris, France
T. +33 1 47 70 15 14
F. +33 1 48 01 03 88

ELEY KISHIMOTO
215 Lyham Road
London SW2 5PY, UK
T. +44 208 674 7411
F. +44 208 674 3516
info@eleykishimoto.com

EMMA COOK
18 Shacklewell Lane
London E8 2E2, UK
T. +44 20 7923 4840
www.emmacook.co.uk

FENDI
Via Flaminia 1068
00189 Rome, Italy
T. +39 06 334501
www.fendi.com

GASPARD YURKIEVICH
38 , rue Charlot
75003 Paris, France
T. +33 1 4277 4246
F. +33 4277 4247
info@gaspardyurkievich.com
www.gaspardyurkievich.com
Japan Hirao Press
T. +81 3 5744 1408
F. +81 3 5774 1409
info@hiraopress.com

GEORGINA GOODMAN
12–14 Shepherd Street,
London W1J 7JF, UK
T. +44 20 7499 8599
info@georginagoodman.com
www.georginagoodman.com

GHOST
The Chapel, 263 Kensal Road
London W10 5DB, UK
T. +44 20 8960 3121
info@ghost.co.uk
www.ghost.co.uk

GIAMBATTISTA VALLI
Giambattista Valli Studio
137, rue Vieille-du-Temple
75003 Paris, France

GIBO
Seta Ichiro
1–11–31, Minamiaoyama,
Minato-ku, Tokyo, 107–0062, Japan
T. +81 3 5414 3572
sidea@guitar.ocn.ne.jp

GILES DEACON
Studio: T. +44 20 7033 0552

GILLES ROSIER
Maison Gilles Rosier
4/6, rue de Braque
75003 Paris, France
T. +33 1 49 96 44 44
F. +33 1 49 96 44 39
www.gillesrosier.fr

GIORGIO ARMANI
Via Borgonuovo, 11
20121 Milan, Italy
Italy: T. +39 02 72 31 81
France: T. +33 1 42 86 64 90
UK: T. +44 20 7808 8100
Belgium: T. +32 2 51 38 115
Spain: T. +34 91 43 51 008
America: T. +1 212 366 9720
Japan: T. +81 3 32 63 30 89
Hong Kong: T. +85 2 25 06 20 18
www.giorgioarmani.com
www.armaniexchange.com (USA)

GOODENOUGH
Anyone@gimme5.com

GRIFFIN
Griffin Studio
Graceland, Edington Road,
Edington, Westbury, WILTS BA13
4NW UKI
UK: T. +44 1380 871133
F. +441380 871144
Griffin Store:
297 Portobello Road,
London W10 5TD, UK
UK: T +44 208 9609607
F. +44 208 9626333
Griffin Tokyo Store:
6–4-9, 1F Manami Aoyama, 107–0062,
T. +81 3 5464 6020

GUCCI
18 Sloane Street
London, UK
34 Old Bond Street
London, UK
www.gucci.com

GUESS? INC.
Executive offices
1444 South Alameda
Los Angeles, CA 90021, USA
T. +1 213 765 3100

HAIDER ACKERMANN
Stoofstraat 9
2000 Antwerp, Belgium
T. +32 3 2482486
F. +32 3 2482487
haider@haiderackermann.com

HAMISH MORROW
T. +44 20 7377 9444
F. +44 20 7377 5398
studio@hamishmorrow.com

HUSSEIN CHALAYAN
35 Heddon Street,
London W1B 4BD, UK
T. +44 20 72879 890
T. +33 1 42 61 34 36
(Rest of Europe/USA/Asia)

IMITATION OF CHRIST
498 Seventh Avenue, 24th floor
New York, NY 10018, USA
T. +1 212 643 4810 Ext.135
F. +1 212 971 6066
mandie@seventhhouse.com

ISSEY MIYAKE
1–12–20 Tomigaya, Shibuya-ku
Tokyo 151–8554, Japan
Europe: T. +33 1 44 54 56 00
America: T. +1 212 226 1334
Asia: T. +81 3 5454 1705
UK: T. +44 20 7349 3300
www.isseymiyake.com

JEAN COLONNA
jcolonnafr@yahoo.fr
www.jeancolonna.com

JEAN PAUL GAULTIER
325, rue Saint-Martin
75003 Paris, France
T. +33 1 72 75 83 96
F. +33 1 72 75 83 96
www.jeanpaulgaultier.com

JEREMY SCOTT
Jeremy Scott Studio
6996 La Presa Drive
Los Angeles CA 90068, USA
T. +1 310 927 6524
F. +1 323 651 3503

JESSICA OGDEN
2nd Floor, Unit 3
5–7 Anglers Lane
London NW5 5DG, UK
T. +44 20 72 84 08 81
F. +44 20 72 84 14 11
studio@jessicaogden.co.uk

JESSICA TROSMAN
Humboldt 291 Buenos Aires,
Argentina (1414)
T. +5411 4856 5288
F. +5411 858 0038
Trosman@trosman.com
Press@trosman.com
Cristine Mazza at MC2, Paris
T. +33 1 48040648
F. +33 1 48040649
mc2showroom@wanadoo.fr

JIL SANDER
Osterfeldstraße 32–34
22529 Hamburg, Germany
Europe: T. +49 40 55 30 20
F. +49 40 55 30 21 68
America: T. +1 212 447 9200
Asia: T. + 41 919 8660

JIMMY CHOO
Flagship store
32 Sloane Street,
London SW1, UK
Stockist number. +44 20 7823 1051
F. +44 20 7823 1052
www.jimmychoo.com

JOE CASELY-HAYFORD
Europe & USA:
T. +44 20 7739 3111
F. +44 20 7729 8700
Asia: T. +81 45 910 6360
Joecaselyhayford@btconnect.com

JOHN GALLIANO
60, rue d'Avron
75020 Paris, France
T. +33 1 55 25 11 11
F. +33 1 55 25 11 13
www.johngalliano.com

JOHN RICHMOND
54 Conduit Street
London W1S 2YY, UK
T: +44 20 7287 1860
londonshop@johnrichmond.com

JONATHAN SAUNDERS
191–205 Cambridge Heath Road,
London E2 0EL, UK
T. +44 20 7613 5959
F. +44 20 7613 4009

JULIEN MACDONALD
65 Golborne Road
London W10 5NP, UK
T. +44 20 8968 9955

JUNYA WATANABE
Comme des Garçons Co. Ltd
5–11–5 Minami Aoyama, Minato-ku
Tokyo 107, Japan
Europe: T. +33 1 47 03 60 80
America: T. +1 212 604 0013
Asia: T. +81 3 3407 2684

KAREN WALKER
Karen Walker International Ltd
Level 2, 14–16 Maidstone St,
Ponsonby, Auckland, New Zealand
T. +64 9 3610780
F. +64 9 3610790
karenwalker@ml-pr.com
karen@karenwalker.com

KATHARINE HAMNETT
Unit 3D, Aberdeen Studios
22–24 Highbury Grove
London N5 2EA, UK
T. +44 20 7354 2111
F: +44 20 7226 1929
M: +44 79 7721 3862
roxy@katharinehamnett.com

KIM JONES
KCD Paris
T. +31 49 96 44 77
kimjones@kcdworldwide.fr

LANVIN
15–22, rue du Faubourg-Saint-Honoré
75008 Paris, France
T. +33 1 55 90 52 92

LEVI'S
Levi's Plaza
1155 Battery Street
San Francisco, CA 94111, USA
Europe: T. +32 2 64 16 011
America: T. +1 415 501 6000
Asia: T. +65 6735 9303
www.levi.com

LUTZ
Polux Sarl
81, rue du Temple
75003 Paris, France
T. +33 1 4233 1803
F. +33 1 4233 1802
lutz.mail@wanadoo.fr

MAHARISHI
2–3 Great Pulteney Street, Soho
London W1F 9LY, UK
T. +44 870 888 0910
F. +44 870 888 0912
info@emaharishi.com
www.emaharishi.com
www.dpmhi.com
www.dpmpublishing.com

MAISON MARTIN MARGIELA
163, rue St-Maur
75011 Paris, France
T. +33 1 44 53 63 24
F. +33 1 44 53 63 36
roxanedanset@martinmargiela.net

MANOLO BLAHNIK
49/51 Old Church Street
London SW3 5EP, UK
Europe: T. +44 20 7352 8622
America: T. +1 212 582 1583
Asia: +85 2870 3436

MARC JACOBS
72 Spring Street
New York, NY 10012, USA
T. +1 212 343 0222

MARITHÉ + FRANÇOIS GIRBAUD
1 place Andre-Malraux
75001, Paris, France
T. +33 1 55 35 11 00
PR: MF Communication

MARJAN PEJOSKI
Design Studio:
12 Chippenham Mews
London W9 2AW, UK
T.+F. +44 20 7266 5994
info@Marjan Pejoski.com
www.marjan pejoski.com
Blow (PR)
15 Percy Street
London W1T 1DT
T. +44 20 7436 9449
F. +44 20 7436 7027

M. +44 7867 900 812
michael@blow.co.uk
www.blow.co.uk
ww.blow.co.uk

MARNI
Via Sismondi, 70/b
20133 Milan, Italy
T. +39 02 70 00 54 79
F. +39 02 70 10 19 77
verde@marni.it

MARTINE SITBON
6, rue de Braque
75003 Paris, France
T. +33 1 48 87 37 47
F. +33 1 48 87 11 32

MATTHEW WILLIAMSON
37 Percy Street
London W1T 2DJ, UK
T. +44 20 7637 4600
F. +44 20 7637 4681
joseph@matthewwilliamson.co.uk
www.matthewwilliamson.co.uk

MIGUEL ADROVER
12W 57th Street #904
New York, NY, USA
mgi@mginy.com

MIHARA YASUHIRO
Casapico #205
3–3–4 Sendagaya, Shibuya-Ku,
Tokyo, 151–0051, Japan
T. +81 3 5775 2681
www.sosu.co.jp

MISS SIXTY
T. +44 870 751 6040
www.misssixty.com

MISSONI
Via Luigi Rossi, 52
21040 Sumirago (VA), Italy
T. +39 03 31 98 80 00
F. +39 03 31 90 99 55
www.missoni.it

MOSCHINO
Via San Gregorio 28
20124 Milan, Italy
T. +39 026 787 731
F. +39 026 7877 301
America: T. +1 212 632 9300
info@moschino.it
www.moschino.it

NARCISO RODRIGUEZ
Via Donizetti 48
20122 Milan, Italy
Europe and Asia: T. +39 02 760 591
America: T. +1 212 632 9300

NEIL BARRETT
Press Office
Via Savona 97
20144 Milan, Italy
T. +39 02 42 41 11 211
F. +39 02 42 41 11 208
pressoffice@neilbarrett.com

NIKE USA
P.O. Box 4027
Beaverton, OR 97076–4027
www.nike.com

NUMBER (N)INE
Michèle Montagne
184, rue Saint-Maur
75010 Paris, France
T. +33 1 4203 9100
F. +33 1 4203 1222
press@michelemontagne.com

PATRICK COX
129 Sloane Street
London SW1X 9AT, UK
T. +44 20 7730 8886
www.patrickcox.co.uk

PAUL & JOE
Beverley Cable PR
11 St. Christopher's Place
London W1V 1NG, UK
T. +44 20 7935 1314
F. +44 20 7935 8314

PAUL SMITH
20 Kean Street,
London WC2B 4AS, UK
UK: T. +44 20 7836 7828
France: T. +33 1 53 63 13 19
Italy: T. +39 02 54 67 22 13
America: T. +1 212 229 2471
Asia: T. +81 3 3486 1500
www.paulsmith.co.uk

PETER JENSEN
18 Shacklewell Lane,
London E8 2EZ, UK
T. +44 20 7249 6894
mail@peterjensenltd.com

PETER SOM
215 West 40th Street, 11th Floor
New York, NY 10018, USA
T. +1 212 221 5991
F. + 1 212 221 1936
Risa Scobie PR
176 Grand Street, Room 602
New York, NY 10013, USA
T. +1 212 965 9155
F. +1 212 965 9353

PHILIP TREACY
1 Havelock Terrace,
London SW8 4AS, UK
www.philiptreacy.co.uk

POLLINI
Pollini spa
Via Bezzecca 5
20135 Milan, Italy
T. +39 02 54 11 66 77
F. +39 02 10 81 55
www.pollini.com

PRADA/MIU MIU
Communication and External
Relations
Via A. Fogazzaro, 28
20135 Milan, Italy
T. +39 02 541 921
F. +39 02 541 92933

PREEN
5 Portobello Road
281 Portobello Road
London W11 5TZ, UK
T. +44 20 8968 1542

PROENZA SCHOULER
www.proenzaschouler.com

RAF SIMONS
Detlef Rosier 32/34
2000 Antwerp, Belgium
T. +33 1 49 23 79 79
F. +33 1 49 23 79 90
sebastien@totemfashion.com
www.rafsimons.com

RALPH LAUREN
650 Madison Avenue
New York, NY 10022, USA
Europe: T. +44 20 7535 4600
America: T. +1 212 318 7000
www.polo.com

RICCARDO TISCI
Karla Otto PR
Via dell'Annunciata, 2
20121 Milan, Italy
T. +39 02 6556981
F. +39 02 29014510
mail@karlaotto.com

RICHARD NICOLL
T. +44 20 7242 5483
F. +44 20 7242 5454
rnicoll77@yahoo.co.uk
adi@cubecompany.com

ROBERTO CAVALLI
182–184 Sloane Street,
London SW1, UK
T. +44 20 7823 1879

ROCHAS
53, rue Nollet
75017 Paris, France
T. +33 1 53 11 20 60
F. +33 1 53 11 20 39
presse@rochas.com
www.rochas.com
ww.rochas.com

ROGAN
UK: Dean Ricketts
The Watch-Men Agency
44 Ossington Street
London W2 4LY, UK
T. +44 20 7243 0171
dean@thewatchmenagency.com
USA: Corinna Ellen Springer
Press Agent
91 Franklin Street
New York, NY 10013, USA
T. +1 212 680 1407 ext 1033
cs@rogannyc.com

ROLAND MOURET
Maddy Platt
Press Manager
The Courtyard, 250 King's Road
London SW3 5UE, UK
Europe:
T. +44 20 7376 5762
F. +44 20 7351 9935
New York, USA:
T. +1 212 242 9353
F. +1 212 367 9076
Los Angeles, USA:
T. +1 323 461 1100
F. +1 323 461 1874
maddy@rolandmouret.co.uk
www.net-a-porter.com

SILAS
Silas and Maria
Northgate House
2–8 Scrutton Street
London EC2, UK
T. +44 20 7375 1900
F. +44 20 7375 1868
info@silasandmaria.com
www.silasandmaria.com

SIV STØLDAL
B-Store
T. +44 20 7499 6628

SONIA RYKIEL
175, boulevard Saint-Germain
75006 Paris, France
France: T. +33 1 49 54 60 60
Italy: T. +39 02 33 13 179
USA: T. +1 212 223 2701
Asia: T. +81 3 3423 9434
www.soniarykiel.com

SOPHIA KOKOSALAKI
Unit 7, 47–49 Tudor Rd.
London E9 7SN, UK
T. +44 20 8986 6001
info@sophiakokosalaki.com

STELLA MCCARTNEY
30 Bruton Street
London W1J 6LG, UK
T. + 44 20 7518 3111
F. +44 20 7518 3112
sjaspar@stellamccartney.com
www.stellamccartney.com

STEPHAN SCHNEIDER
Reyndersstraat 53
2000 Antwerp, Belgium
T. +32 3 226 2614
F. +32 3 231 8443
info@stephanschneider.be

STEPHEN JONES
Stephen Jones Millinery
36 Great Queen Street
London WC2B 5AA, UK
Europe & America:
T. +44 20 7242 0770
F. +44 20 7242 0796
Asia: T. +81 3 3225 2471
www.shop@stephenjonesmillinery.com
www.stephenjonesmillinery.com

STÜSSY
17426 Daimler Street
Irvine, CA 92614, USA
www.stussystore.co.uk
www.stussy.com

SUPREME
Office
121 Wooster Street
New York, NY 10012, USA
T. +1 212 274–8855
Supreme Store New York:
274 Lafayette Street
New York, NY 10012, USA
T. +1 212 966–7799
Supreme Store Los Angeles, USA:
439 N. Fairfax
Los Angeles, CA 90036, USA
T. +1 323 655–6205
Supreme Stores Japan:
Supreme Tokyo
1–6 Daikanyama-Cho, Shibuya-Ku
Tokyo, Japan
T. +81 3–5456–0085
Supreme Osaka:
1–10–2 Minamihorie, Nishi-Ku
Osaka, Japan
T. +81 6 6533 0705
Supreme Fukuoka:
1–9–15–1 Daimyo, Chuo-Ku
Fukuoka, Japan
T. +81 92 732 5002

TESS GIBERSON
Kaleidoscope Consulting
601 W.26th Street, #M251
New York, NY 10001, USA
T. +1 212 414 8882
F. +1 212 414 8614
kaleidoscopeconsulting@earthlink.net

TIMOTHY EVEREST
32 Elder Street
London E1 6BT, UK
T. +44 20 7377 5770
F. +44 20 7377 5990
bespoke@timothyeverest.co.uk

TOMMY HILFIGER
11/F, Novel Industrial Building
850–870 Lai Chi Kok Road,
Cheung Sha Wan, Kowloon
Hong Kong, China
Europe: T. +31 20 58 99 888
America: T. +1 800 866 6922
Hong Kong & Taiwan:
T. +852 2721 2668
F. +852 2312 1368
Japan: T. +81 3 3407 6580
F. +81 3 3407 5392/90

UNDERCOVER
Unimat Bleu Cinq Point #C
5–3–18 Minami Aoyama, Minato-ku
Tokyo 107–0062, Japan
International: T. +33 1 42 03 91 00
Japan: T. +81 3 3407 1232

UNITED BAMBOO
270 Bowery No 2
New York, NY 10012, USA
T. +1 212 925 3311
F. +1 212 431 0283
daisuke@unitedbamboo.com
www.united bamboo.com

VALENTINO
22 Piazza Mignanelli
00187 Rome, Italy
T. +39 06 67391
F. +39 06 6796172
www.valentino.com

VANESSA BRUNO
8, rue de la Pierre-Levée
75011 Paris, France
Press, Commercial and Style Office:
T. +33 1 40 26 70 65
F. +33 1 40 26 70 67
press@vanessa bruno.fr

VÉRONIQUE BRANQUINHO
James nv Nationalstraat 123
2000 Antwerpen, Belgium
T. +33 1 49 23 79 79
F. +33 1 49 23 79 90
lamia@totemfashion.com
www.totemfashion.com

VÉRONIQUE LEROY
T. +33 1 44 87 90 90
F. +33 1 44 87 90 91
vleroy@veroniqueleroy.com

VERSACE
Via Manzoni, 38
20121 Milan, Italy
Europe: T. +39 02 76 09 31
America: T. +1 212 753 8595
Asia: T. +81 3 3261 3371
www.versace.com

VIKTOR & ROLF
Europe: T. +33 1 42 61 34 36
UK: T. +44 20 7287 9890
Asia: T. +81 3 3770 6911
F. +81 3 3770 6912
office@viktor-rolf.com
www.viktor-rolf.com

VIVIENNE WESTWOOD
44 Conduit Street
London W1S 2YL, UK
Europe: T. +44 20 7287 3188
F. +44 20 7734 6074
Paris: T. +33 1 49 27 05 09
Milan: T. +39 02 76 08 02 16
www.viviennewestwood.com

WALTER VAN BEIRENDONCK
Henri Van Heuckstraat 5
2000 Antwerp, Belgium
T. +32 3 231 7732
www.waltervanbeirendonck.com

YOHJI YAMAMOTO
T33 2–2–43 Higashi Shinagawa
Shinagawa-ku
Tokyo 140–0002, Japan
Europe: T. +33 1 42 78 94 11
T. +44 20 7491 4129
America: T. +1 212 966 9066
Asia: T. +81 3 5463 1500

YONG FONG
ayongfong@hotmail.com

**YVES SAINT LAURENT
RIVE GAUCHE**
5, avenue Marceau
75016 Paris, France
T. +33 1 4431 6417
F. +33 1 4723 6213
www.ysl.com

ZAC POSEN
13–17 Laight Street
New York, NY 10013, USA
T. +1 212 925 1263
F. +1 212 925 1264
info@zacposen.com
www.zacposen.com

ZERO MARIA CORNEJO
225 Mott Street
New York, NY 10012, USA
T. +1 212 925 3849
F. +1 212 343 0233
leila@mariacornejo.com
www.mariacornejo.com

ZUCCA
Cabane de Zucca
8, rue Saint-Roch
75001 Paris, France
T. +33 1 44 58 98 88
F. +33 1 42 86 88 78
zuccapress@anet-europe.com

PHOTOGRAPHER CONTACTS

ADRIAN WILSON
T. +44 7887 995 924
www.adrianwilson.com

ALASDAIR MCLELLAN
MAP
72 Rochester Place
London NW1 9JX, UK
T. +44 207 424 9144
F. +44 207 284 3274

ALEX HOERNER
T. +1 310 569 3639
alexhoerner@mac.com

ALEXIA SILVAGNI
Michele Filomeno (agent)
T. +33 1 55 35 35 00
www.mfilomeno.com

ALI MAHDAVI
www.alimahdavi.com

AMANDA DE CADENET
Steven Pranica
Creative Exchange Agnecy
T. +1 212 414 4100
amandadecadenet@mac.com
www.amandadecadenet.com

AMY TROOST
T. 347 267 9027
amy_troost@hotmail.com

ANETTE AURELL
MS Logan
T. +1 212 995 9079
info@mslogan.com

BEN HASSETT
Blunt London
T. +44 20 8960 2041
F. +44 20 8960 2039
www.bluntlondon.com

BEN KELWAY
+44 7881 656 409
benjamin.kelway@ntlworld.com

BIANCA PILET
contact@biancapilet.co

CARTER SMITH
Art + Commerce
755 Washington Street
New York, NY 10014, USA
T. +1 212 206 0737
F. +1 212 645 8724
www.artandcommerce.com

CELLINA VON MANSTEIN
M. +39 0335 709 49 34
F. +39 0473 448 476
cellirazzi@gmx.net

CHIDI ACHARA
M. +44 7880 506 756
chidiachara@hotmail.com

CHRISTIAN WITKIN
T. +1 212 463 0376
F. +1 212 463 8028

CHRISTOPHE CUFOS
Two P
Pascale Perez
9 rue de la Pierre Levée
75011 Paris, France
T. +33 1 43 14 09 12
F. +33 1 49 29 69 95
M. +33 6 09 20 86 89
p.perez@twop.fr
www.twop.fr

DAVID ARMSTRONG
Art + Commerce
755 Washington Street
New York, NY 10014, USA
T. +1 212 206 0737
F. +1 212 645 8724
www.artandcommerce.com

DAVID LACHAPELLE
David Lachapelle Studios
429 East 13th Street
New York, NY 10009, USA
T. +1 212 529 5385
F. +1 212 529 9571
studio@davidlachapelle.com

DAVID SLIJPER
CLM London
T. +44 20 7729 8001
david@davidslijper.com
www.clmuk.com

DELPHINE BEAUMONT
www.delphinebeaumont.com

DENNIS SCHOENBERG
One Photographic
T. +44 20 7287 2311
belinda@onephotographic.com
www.onephotographic.com

DEREK HENDERSON
derekhenderson_1@mac.com

DESMOND MUCKIAN
T. +44 777 179 1913
desmondmuckian@btinternet.com

DONALD CHRISTIE
dmac.christie@virgin.net

DONALD MILNE
donaldharrymilne@hotmail.com

DUC LIAO
www.ducliao.com

DUSAN RELJIN
Nice Producions
T. +1 212 431 0669

ED SYKES
T. +44 207 226 5329

ELFIE SEMOTAN
Walter Schupfer Management
413 West 14th, 4th floor
New York, NY 10014, USA
T. +1 212 366 4675
F. +1 212 255 9726

ELLEN NOLAN
T. +44 208 858 1128
M. +44 779534 0686
info@ellennolan.com
www.ellennolan.com

ELLEN VON UNWERTH
D+V Management
1 Lonsdale Road
London NW6 6RA, UK
T. +44 20 7372 2555
F. +44 20 7372 2123
www.dandvmanagement.com

GEMMA BOOTH
gem@gemmabooth.com
www.utan.co.uk

GERALD JENKINS
www.geraldjenkins.co.uk

GLEB KOSORUKOV
T. +33 6 64 25 36 29
glebk@aha.ru

GREG LOTUS
Artsphere
Carole Dardanne
T. +33 624 023 459
carole@artsphere.fr
www.artsphere.fr

GUSTAVO TEN HOEVER
T. +33 6 11 09 90 29
www.gustavotenhoever.com

HENRIQUE GENDRE
T. +1 212 671 0167
hvgendre@aol.com
www.henriquegendre.com

HIROSHI KUTOMI
Jonathan Tobin
T. +44 1273 242 330
M. +44 7956 609 872
jonathan.tobin1@ntlworld.com

HORST DIEKGERDES
T. +33 1 48000624
horst.diekgerdes@wanadoo.fr

IMMO KLINK
T. +44 207 226 5329

ISABEL ASHA PENZLIEN
T. +1 212 334 3383
Isabel@isabelashapenzlien.com

JAMES MOUNTFORD
info@jamesmountford.com
www.jamesmountford.com

JASON EVANS
MAP
72 Rochester Place
London NW1 9JX, UK
T. +44 207 424 9144
F. +44 207 284 3274
www.thedailynice.com

JENNIFER TZAR
T. +917 873 4503
tzarice@hotmail.com
www.jennifertzar.com

JEROME ALBERTINI
www.albertinistudio.net
Jesse Shadoan
Jesse Shadoan Studio
T. +1 212 414 4801
studio@jesseshadoan.com
www.jesseshadoan.com

JO METSON-SCOTT
M. +44 77795 92 709
jo@jometsonscott.co.uk
www.jometsonscott.co.uk

KARINA TAIRA
Moo Management
T. +1 718 218 8080
www.karinataira.com

KAYT JONES
Julian Meijer Associés
7, Rue Pasquier
Paris 75008, France
T. +33 1 4274 3035
F. +33 1 4274 3355

KEIRON O'CONNOR
Nathaniel Goldberg
Total Management
28 West 27 St #506
New York, NY 10001, USA
T. +1 212 481 9300

KERRY HALLIHAN
T. +1 917 754 4111
studio@kerryhallihan.com

KEVIN DAVIES
mr.kevin.davies@gmail.com

LAETICIA NEGRE
T. + 44 7960 932317
laetitia.negre@btinternet.com

LARRY DUNSTAN
mail@larrydunstan.com
www.larrydunstan.com

LENA MODIGH
T. +44 7779 726 622
post@lenamodigh.co.uk

MANUEL VASON
T. +44 7775 660 153
email@manuelvason.com
www.manuelvason.com

MANUELA PAVESI
T. +39 0376 222324
F. +39 0376 222183
manuelapavesi30@hotmail.com

MARIUS HANSEN
T. + 44 7712 776 964
 info@mariuswhansen.com

MARCUS TOMLINSON
marcus.tomlinson@btinternet.com

MARK LEBON
mark.lebon@btconnect.com

MARK SEGAL
Streeters London
2–4 Old Street
London EC1V 9AA, UK
T. +44 20 7253 3330

MATT BLACK
mattblacknyc@yahoo.com

MATT JONES
Moo Management
T. +1 718 218 8080
trish@moomanagement.com

MAX VADUKUL
T. +1 212 683 6160
studio@maxvadukul.com

MICHAEL ROBERTS
Maconochie Photography
4 Meard Street
London W1F 0EF, UK
T. +44 207 439 3159
F. +44 207 439 2552
info@macphoto.co.uk

MICHAEL SANDERS
msandersphoto@yahoo.com

MICHEL MOMY
NYC: Winston West
T. +1 212 691 67 88
London: ARM
T. 44 207 631 1114
Paris: Watchout
T. +33 1 422 510 35
michel.momy@wanadoo.fr

MIKAEL JANSSON
Wilson/Wenzel Inc.
149 Wooster Street
New York, NY 10012, USA
T. +1 212 614 9500
wilsonmurphy@wilsonwenzel.com

MISCHA RICHTER
mischarichter1@btinternet.com

MITCHELL SAMS
m@mitchell.sams.com

PATRICK DEMARCHELIER
T. +1 212 924 3561
studio@demarchelier.net

PAUL WETHERELL
MAP
72 Rochester Place
London NW1 9JX, UK
T. +44 207 424 9144
F. +44 207 284 3274
neil@mapltd.com
www.mapltd.com

PHILIP GAY
philipgay@hotmail.com

RANDALL MESDON
T. +1 631 742 8555
randallmesdon@hotmail.com

REBECCA LEWIS
T. +44 7957 287 818
www.rebecca-lewis.com
Skinny Dip(Agent)
T. +44 207 575 3222

REBECCA PIERCE
becpierce@hotmail.com

RICHARD BURBRIDGE
T. +1 212 206 0737
www.artandcom
merce.com

RICHARD BUSH
rachel@untitled.uk.com

RONALD STOOPS
ronaldstoops@hotmail.com

SATOSHI SAIKUSA
Management Artists
T. +1 212 931 9311
www.managementartists.com

SCHOHAJA STAFFLER
schohaja@yahoo.de
www.schohaja.com

SEAN CUNNINGHAM
T. +44 7768 890 395
fashionshowphotos@hotmail.com

SEAN ELLIS
T. +44 20 7336 6006
Kayte@theofficelondon.com

SHIRO KATAGIRI
shirokatagiri@hotmail.com

SOPHIE DELAPORTE
Michele Filomeno
T. +33 1 55 35 35 00
www.mfilomeno.com

STEVE SMITH
Era Management
T. +44 207 428 9277

TAKAY
Jed Root Inc
T. +1 212 226 6600 (New York)
T. +33 1 44 54 30 80 (Paris)
www.jedroot.com

TERRY TSIOLIS
T. +1 212 931 9311
F. +1 212 931 9312
nick@managementartists.com

TESH
Tony Jay Inc.
T. +1 2127271300
www.tonyjayinc.com

THOMAS SCHENK
Art Department
Jordan Shipenberg
jordans@art-dept.com
www.art-dept.com

TIMUR CELIKDAG
T. +44 7979 852209
timur@timur-celikdag.com

TIM MITCHELL
T. +44 7751 340902
timwmitchell@yahoo.co.uk

TODD COLE
T. +323 449 2521
tsputnik@pacbell.net

VANINA SORRENTI
MAP
72 Rochester Place
London NW1 9JX, UK
T. +44 207 424 9144
F. +44 207 284 3274
neil@mapltd.com
www.mapltd.com

VAVA RIBEIRO
contact@vavaribeiro.com
www.vavaribeiro.com

VIVIANE SASSEN
vivianesassen@hotmail.com

WILL SANDERS
T. + 44 7770 890077
www.willsbook.com

WILLY VANDERPERRE
Management Artists
T. +33 1 4271 6060
www.managementartists.com

WING SHYA
Room 1702, 111 Leighton Road
Causeway Bay, Hong Kong
T. +852 2575 3808
F. +852 2831 0069
info@shyalala.com
www.shyalala.com

XEVI
Xevi Muntane
NYC, Defacto (Agency)
T. +1 212 6274

YELENA YEMCHUK
Streeters New York
568 Broadway, Suite 504A
New York, NY 10012, USA
T. +1 212 219 9566
F. +1 121 219 9488

INDEX

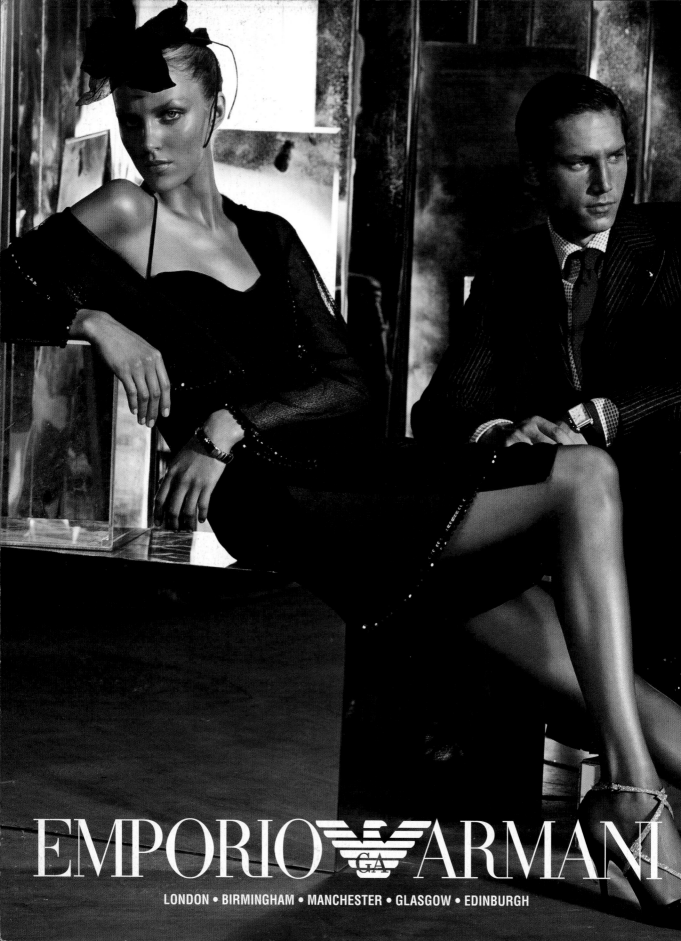

EMPORIO ARMANI

LONDON • BIRMINGHAM • MANCHESTER • GLASGOW • EDINBURGH

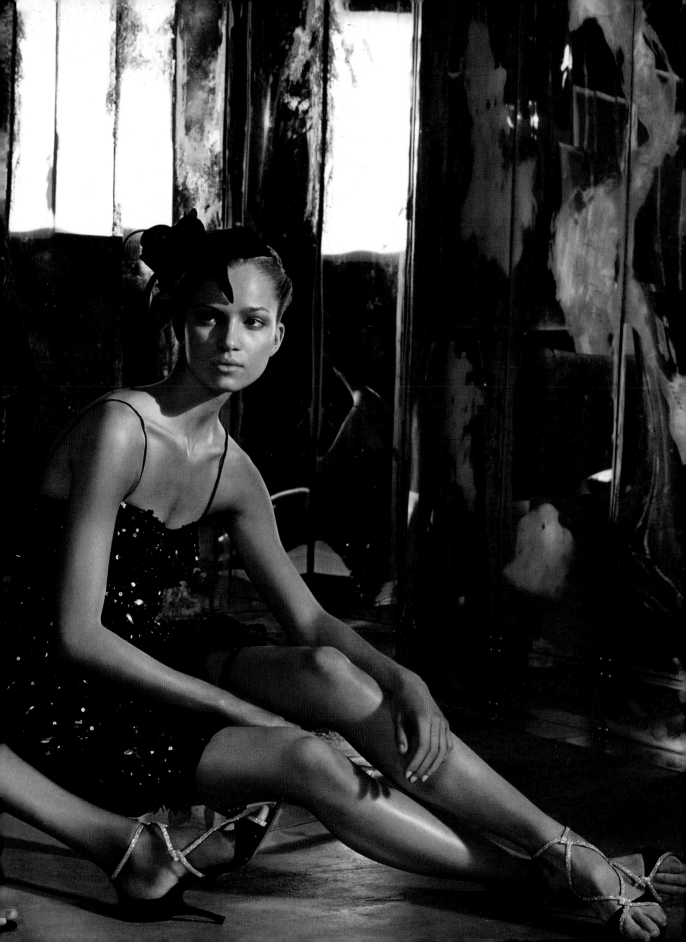

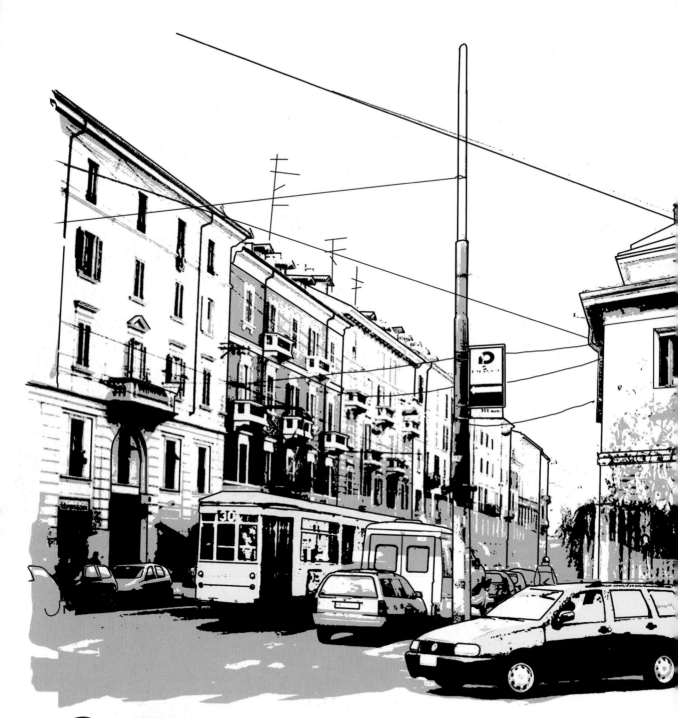

C.P.
COMPANY

www.cpcompany.com

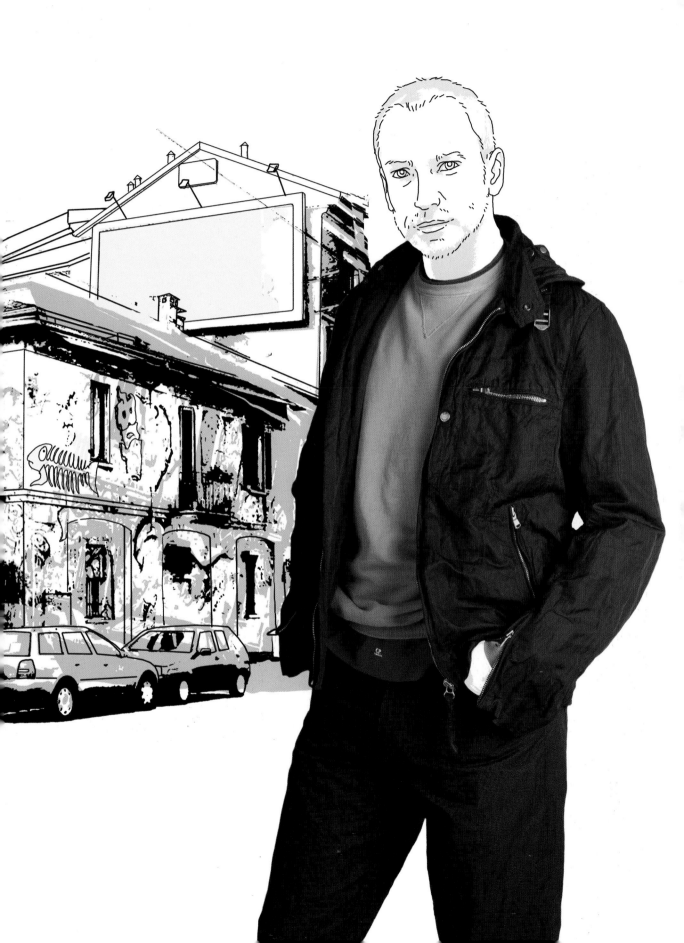

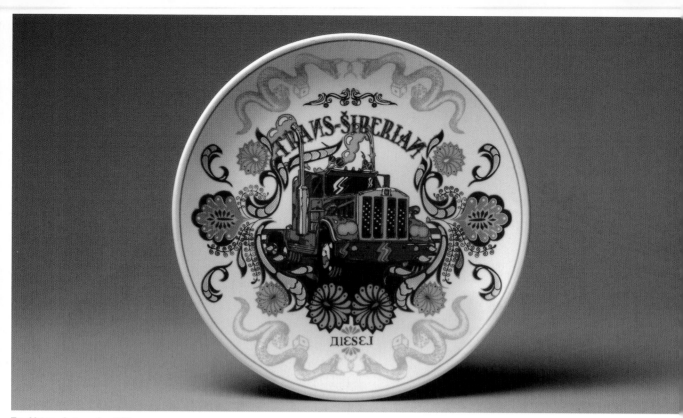

Truckistan - Lot number 101
This perfectly preserved dinner plate illustrates the great voyage from East to West. Many started the crossing, few completed it. The ones that succeeded, brought with them the fine art of crafty plate painting. Bidding starts from $15.000

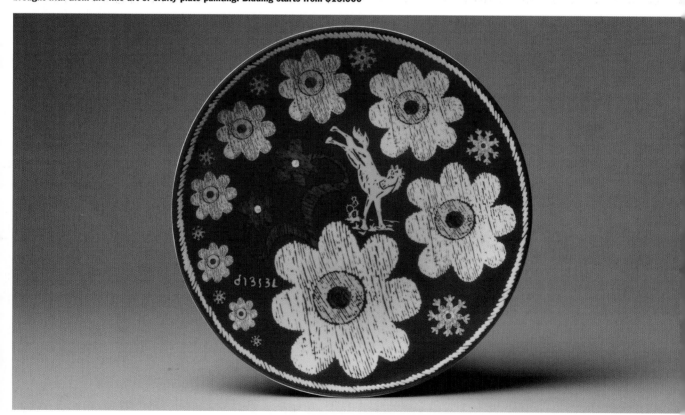

Silk Rush - Lot number 666
This ethnic-style plate was designed during the infamous silk rush by an unknown, but highly gifted artist. While many died in their quest for the silky stuff, some got rich and ate their borscht & burgers from lush plates like this. Rumor has it that this particular plate has a curse imbedded, evidence however has yet to be found. Bidding starts from $ 20.000

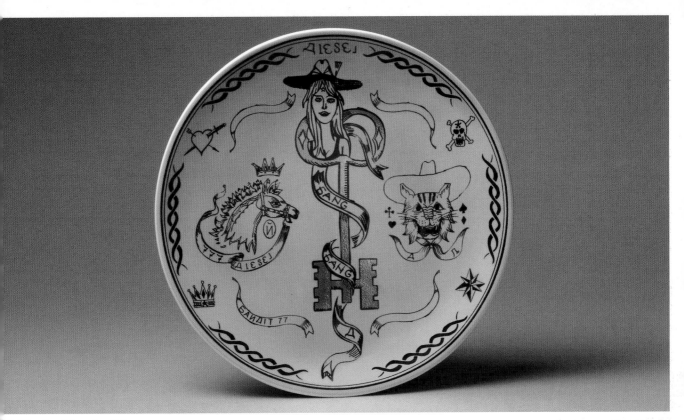

Bolshoi Bandits - Lot number 401

This sturdy plate was found in the best little whorehouse in Texas. It portrays the ritual tattoos only granted to members of the notorious Bolshoi Bandits. These gangster's roamed the newfound land in search of all things valuable… including loose women to put to work in brothels all over their new homeland. Bidding starts from $ 25.000

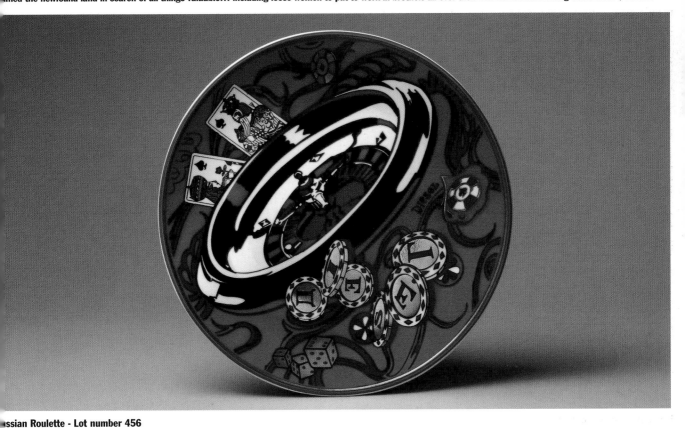

Russian Roulette - Lot number 456

Bidding for this extraordinary plate for sure is no gamble. All previous owners achieved great wealth & health during the period that Russian Roulette belonged to them. Even though it's uncertain the magic lives on in this century, it's worth the risk. Bidding starts from $ 50.000

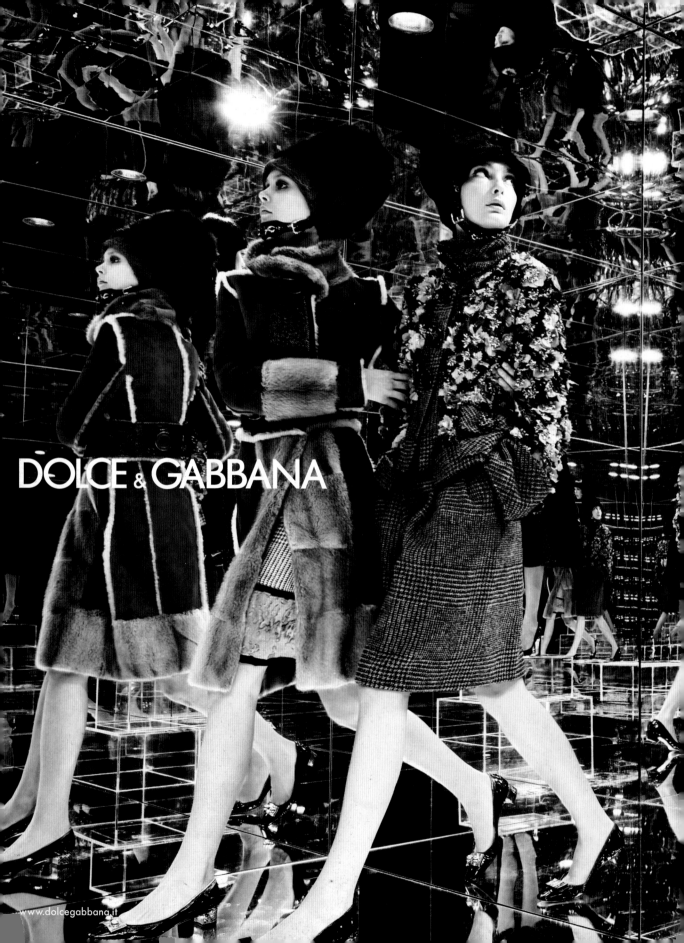

DOLCE & GABBANA

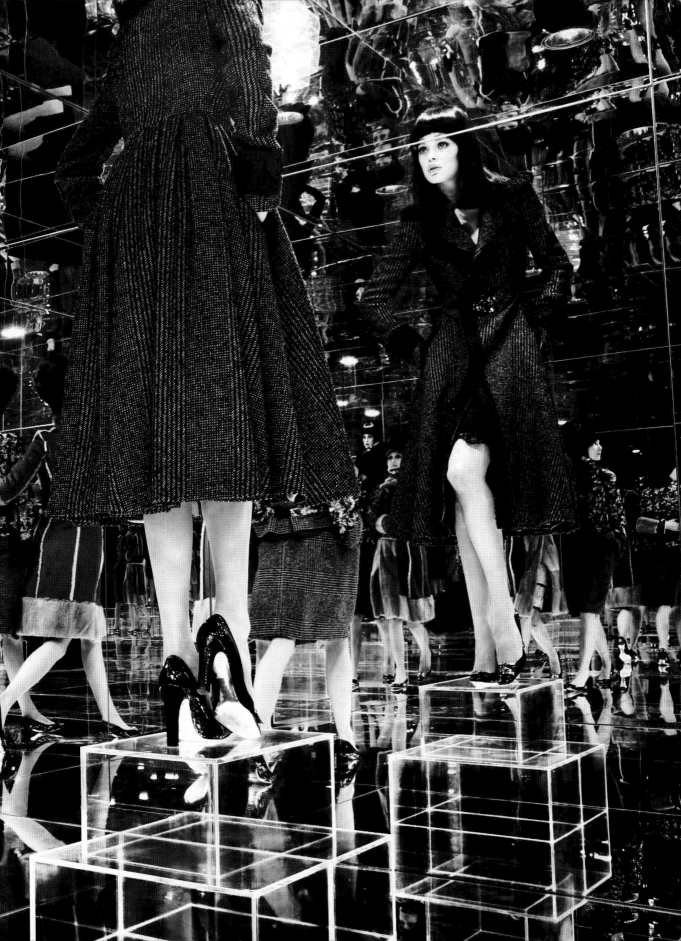

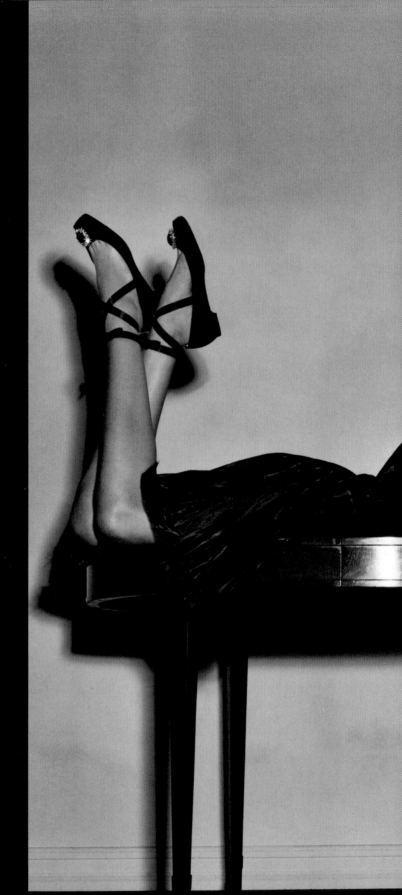

GIUSEPPE ZANOTTI DESIGN

MILAN - ROME - PARIS - NEW YORK
BAL HARBOUR - LAS VEGAS
MOSCOW - LISBON
WWW.GIUSEPPE-ZANOTTI-DESIGN.COM

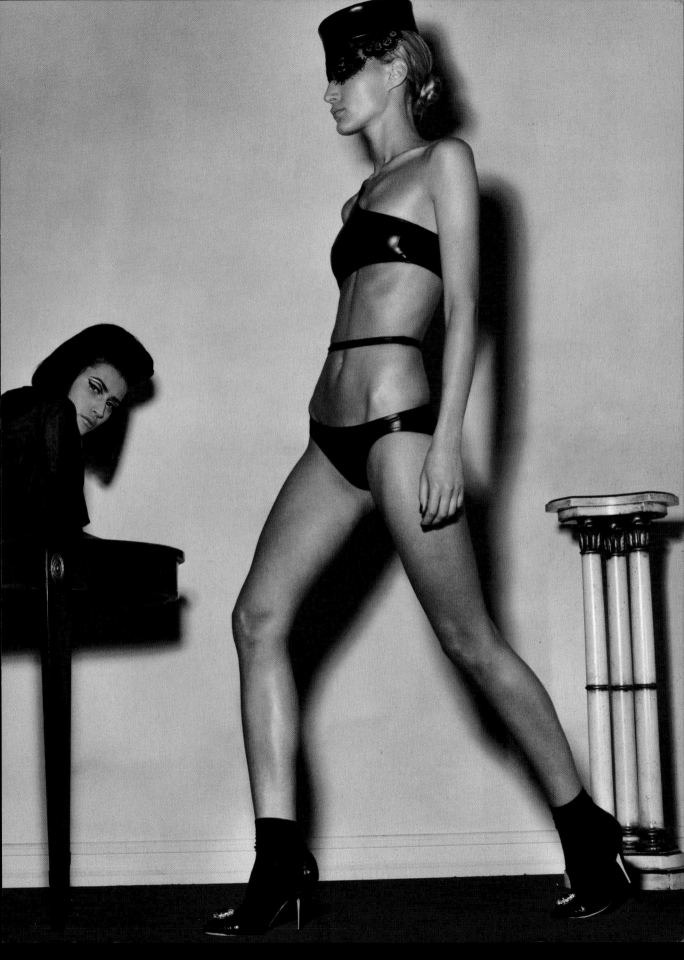

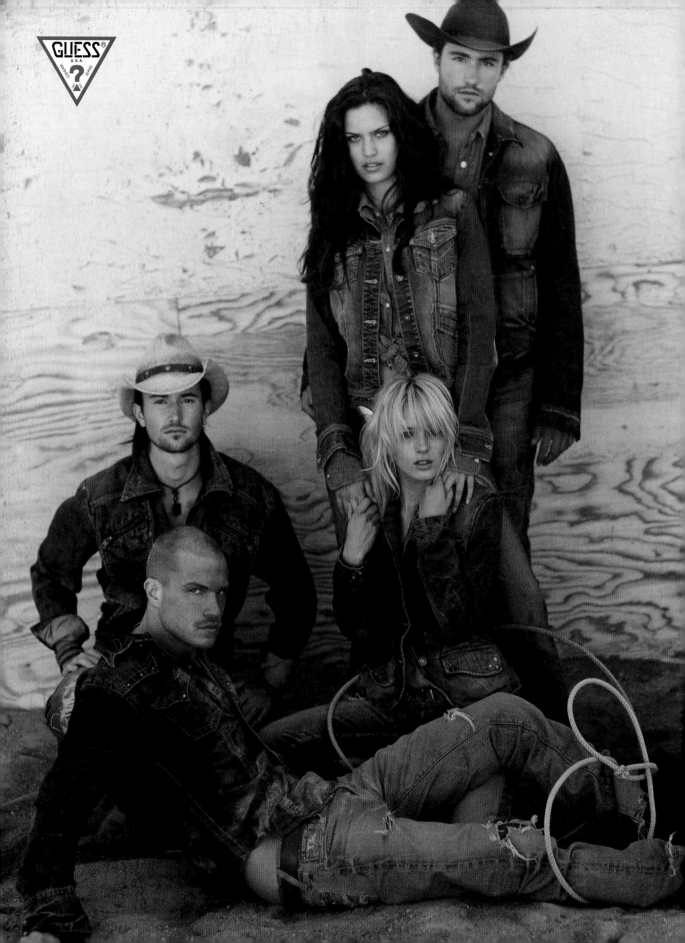

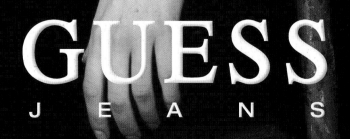

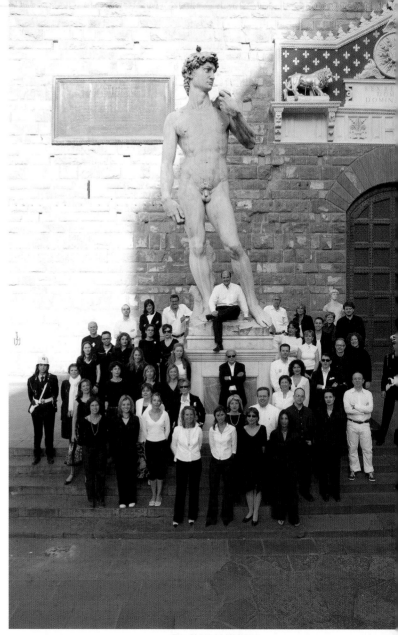

PH : OLIVIERO TOSCANI

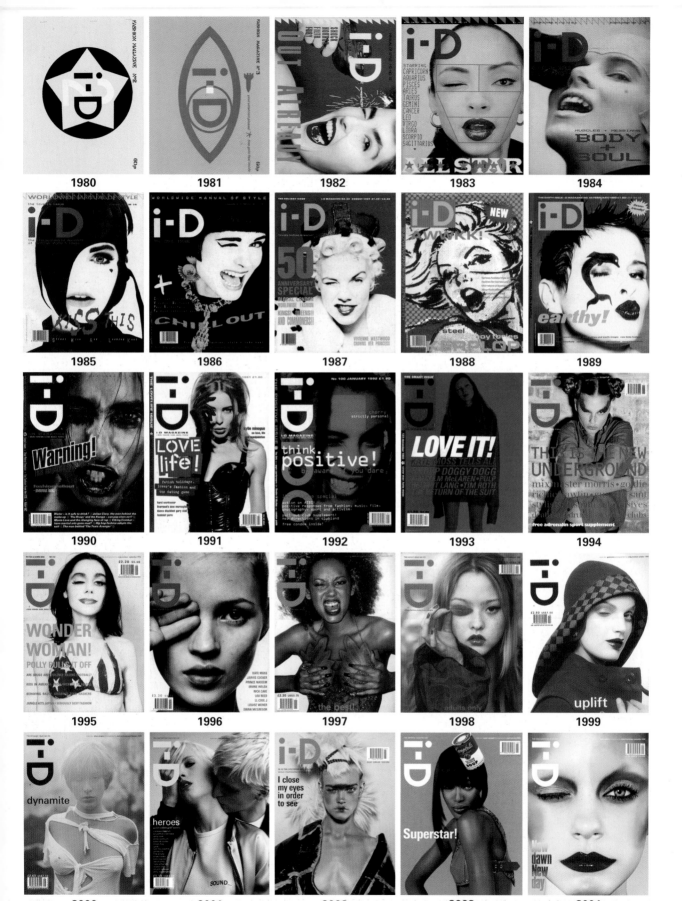

1980 **1981** **1982** **1983** **1984**

1985 **1986** **1987** **1988** **1989**

1990 **1991** **1992** **1993** **1994**

1995 **1996** **1997** **1998** **1999**

2000 **2001** **2002** **2003** **2004**

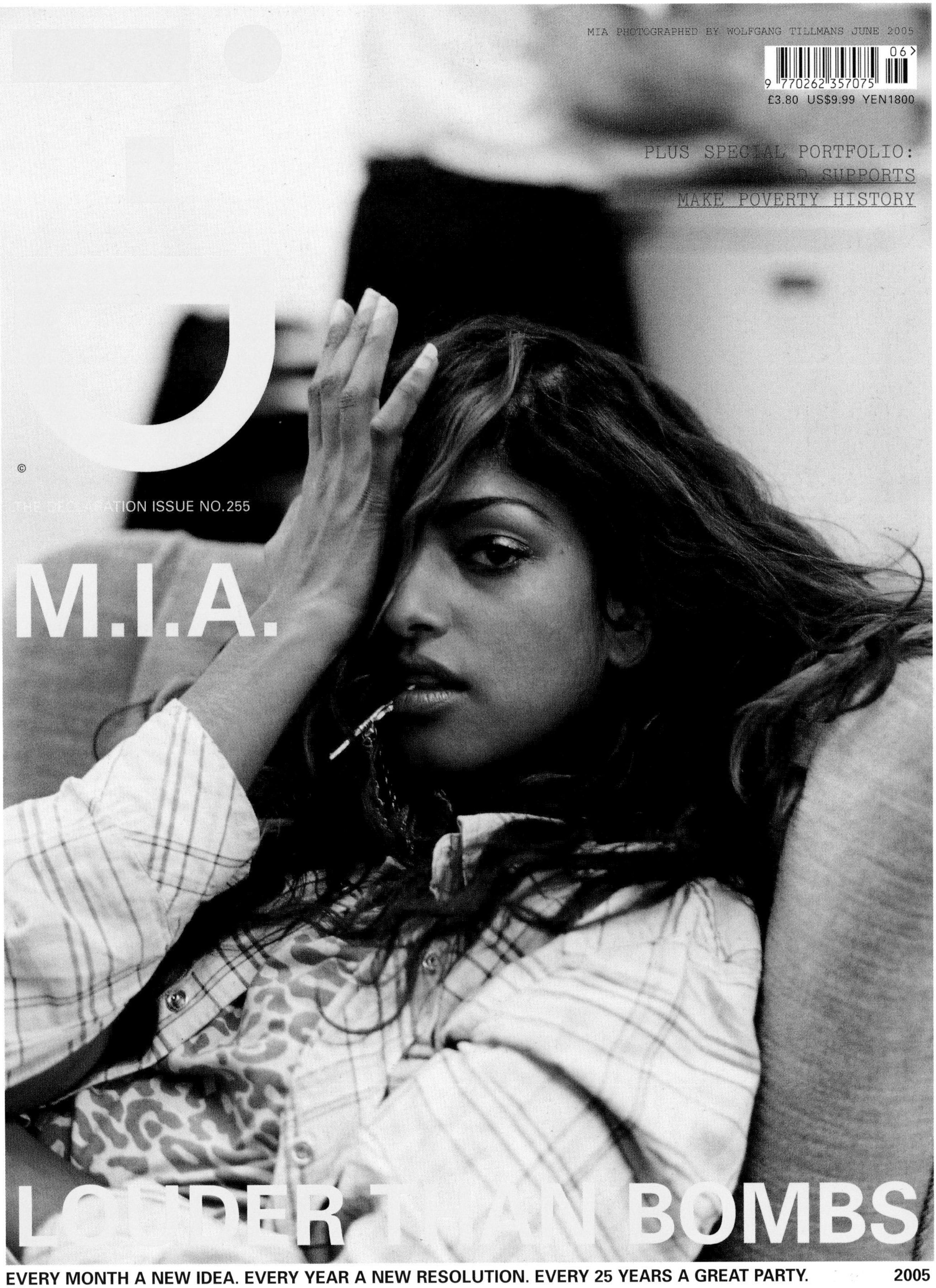

MIA PHOTOGRAPHED BY WOLFGANG TILLMANS JUNE 2005

9 770262 357075

06

£3.80 US$9.99 YEN1800

PLUS SPECIAL PORTFOLIO:
D SUPPORTS
MAKE POVERTY HISTORY

©

THE DECLARATION ISSUE NO.255

M.I.A.

LOUDER THAN BOMBS

EVERY MONTH A NEW IDEA. EVERY YEAR A NEW RESOLUTION. EVERY 25 YEARS A GREAT PARTY.   **2005**

Contemporary art, continued

Volume II of the indispensable guide to art in the world today

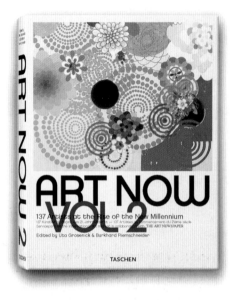

Featured artists—a selection:

FRANZ ACKERMANN
DARREN ALMOND
KAI ALTHOFF
GHADA AMER
ATLAS GROUP
MATTHEW BARNEY
VANESSA BEECROFT
CANDICE BREITZ
GLENN BROWN
ANDRÉ BUTZER
MERLIN CARPENTER
MAURIZIO CATTELAN
JAKE CHAPMAN
JOHN CURRIN
THOMAS DEMAND
RINEKE DIJKSTRA
PETER DOIG
MARLENE DUMAS

MARTIN EDER
TIM EITEL
OLAFUR ELIASSON
TRACEY EMIN
ELGER ESSER
YANG FUDONG
ELLEN GALLAGHER
ROBERT GOBER
ANTHONY GOICOLEA
DOUGLAS GORDON
ANDREAS GURSKY
JEPPE HEIN
THOMAS HIRSCHHORN
JIM HODGES
CANDIDA HÖFER
GARY HUME
PIERRE HUYGHE
MIKE KELLEY
JEFF KOONS
ULRICH LAMSFUSS

ZOE LEONARD
WON LIM
SHARON LOCKHART
SARAH LUCAS
VERA LUTTER
PAUL MCCARTHY
JONATHAN MEESE
BEATRIZ MILHAZES
MARIKO MORI
SARAH MORRIS
RON MUECK
VIC MUNIZ
TAKASHI MURAKAMI
YOSHITOMO NARA
SHIRIN NESHAT
ERNESTO NETO
FRANK NITSCHKE
TIM NOBLE/SUE WEBSTER
MOTOHIKO ODANI
ALBERT OEHLEN

CHRIS OFILI
GABRIEL OROZCO
JORGE PARDO
PHILIPPE PARRENO
MANFRED PERNICE
GREYSON PERRY
RAYMOND PETTIBON
ELIZABETH PEYTON
RICHARD PHILIPPS
RICHARD PRINCE
NEO RAUCH
TOBIAS REHBERGER
DANIEL RICHTER
PIPILOTTI RIST
MATTHEW RITCHIE
UGO RONDINONE
THOMAS RUFF
TOM SACHS
WILHELM SASNAL
JENNY SAVILLE

THOMAS SCHEIBITZ
GREGOR SCHNEIDER
RAQIB SHAW
CINDY SHERMAN
SANTIAGO SIERRA
SIMON STARLING
THOMAS STRUTH
CATHERINE SULLIVAN
WOLFGANG TILLMANS
RIRKRIT TIRAVANIJA
LUC TUYMANS
COSIMA VON BONIN
KARA WALKER
JEFF WALL
FRANZ WEST
PAE WHITE
JOHANNES WOHNSEIFER
CHRISTOPHER WOOL
ERWIN WURM

ART NOW. VOL. 2
Ed. Uta Grosenick / Flexi-cover, format: 19.6 x 24.9 cm
(7.7 x 9.8 in.), 640 pp.

ONLY € 29.99 / $ 39.99
£ 19.99 / 5.900

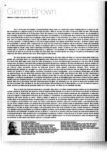
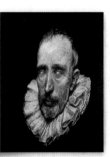
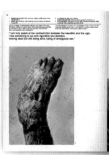

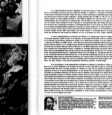
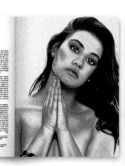

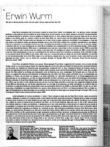
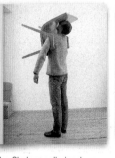
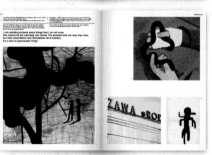
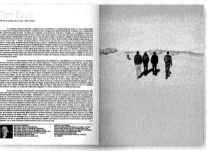

Unless you regularly trawl the Chelsea galleries, hang out at the Tate Modern, peruse the Pompidou, attend every Biennale, and religiously read *Artforum*, you could probably use a primer on the art scene in the world today. Fortunately we've created our second *Art Now* volume to keep art fans abreast of the latest trends and hottest names. Featuring over 130 artists in A-Z entries

with biographical information and exhibition history as well as images of important recent work—plus a bonus illustrated index of current auction prices—*Art Now II* is *the* guide to what's happening and who's who in contemporary art.

The editor: **Uta Grosenick** has worked at the Deichtorhallen in Hamburg and the Bundeskunsthalle in Bonn, and was curator at the Kunstmuseum Wolfsburg. Since 1996, she has been working as freelance editor and organizer of exhibitions. Her publications include TASCHEN's *Art at the Turn of the Millennium*, *Art Now*, and *Women Artists*.

The evolution of style

from antiquity to 1888

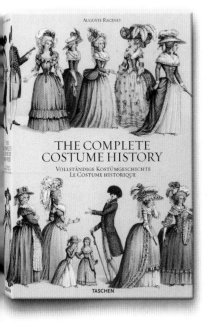

Contents:

Part I
The Ancient World
Egypt, Assyria, Israel, Persia
and Phrygia, Greece, Etruscan,
Greco-Roman, Rome, Barbarian
Europe, Celts and Gauls

Part II
**The 19th Century – Beyond
the Borders of Europe**
Oceania, Africa, Eskimos,
North American Indians, Mexican
Indians, South American Indians,
China,
Japan, India, Ceylon,
Middle East, Orient, Turkey

Part III
Europe 400 – 1800
Byzantium, France-Byzantine,
Poland, Italy, Spain, Germany,
France, England, Holland

Part IV
**Traditional Costume till the
Late 19th Century**
Scandinavia, Holland, Scotland,
England, Germany, Switzerland,
Russia, Poland, Hungary, Greece,
Italy, Spain, Portugal, France

Part V
Patterns and Templates

AUGUSTE RACINET, THE COMPLETE COSTUME HISTORY
Tétart-Vittu, Françoise, Hardcover,
290 x 440 mm (11.4 x 17.3 in.), 636 pages
ONLY € 150.00 / $ 200.00
£ 100.00 / ¥ 25000.00

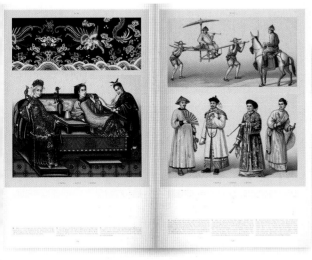

B Q

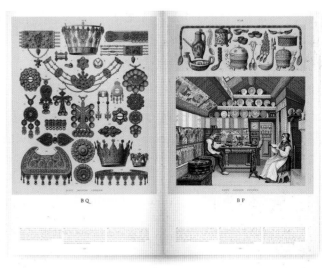

B F

Originally published in France between 1876 and 1888, Auguste Racinet's *Le Costume Historique* was the most wide-ranging and intelligent study of clothing ever published. Covering the world history of costume, dress, and style from antiquity through the end of the 19th century, the great work—"consolidated" in 1888 into 6 volumes containing nearly 500 plates—remains, to this day, completely unique in its scope and detail. Racinet's organization by culture and subject has been preserved in TASCHEN's magnificent and complete reprint, as have excerpts from his delightful descriptions and often witty comments. Perusing these beautifully detailed and exquisitely colored illustrations, you'll discover everything from the garb of ancient Etruscans to traditional Eskimo attire to 19th century French women's couture. Though Racinet's study spans the globe from ancient times through his own, his focus is on European clothing from the Middle Ages to the 1880s and this subject is treated with exceeding passion and attention to detail. The Complete Costume History is an absolutely invaluable reference for students, designers, artists, illustrators, and historians; it is also an immensely fascinating and inspirational book for anyone with an interest in clothing and style.

Françoise Tétart-Vittu, head of the graphic arts department at the Musée de la Mode et du Costume de la Ville de Paris. She studied art history at the Sorbonne and is specialized in costume history of the 18th and 19th centuries. Author of many books on costume history and curator of exhibits, she lives and works in Paris.

Couture: then and now

Three centuries of women's clothing

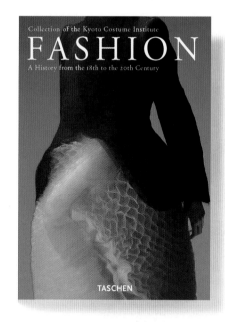

FASHION
The Collection of the Kyoto Costume Institute / Ed. The Kyoto Costume Institute / Flexi-cover, format: 19.6 x 27.3 cm (7.7 x 10.7 in.), 736 pp.

ONLY € 29.99 / $ 39.99
£ 19.99 / ¥ 5.900

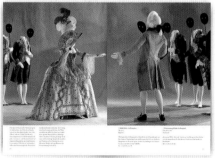

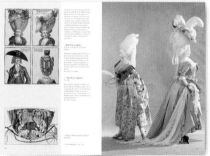

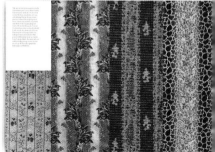

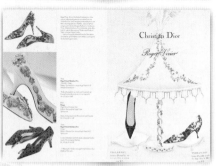

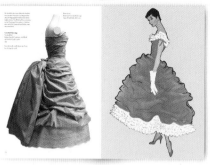

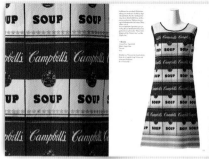

Clothes define people. A person's clothing, whether it's a sari, kimono, or business suit, is an essential key to his or her culture, class, personality, or even religion. The Kyoto Costume Institute recognizes the importance of understanding clothing sociologically, historically, and artistically. Founded in 1978, the KCI holds one of the world's most extensive clothing collections and has curated many exhibitions worldwide. With an emphasis on Western women's clothing, the KCI has amassed a wide range of historical garments, underwear, shoes,

and fashion accessories dating from the 18th century to the present day. Showcasing a vast selection from the Institute's archives of skilled photographs depicting the clothing expertly displayed and arranged on custom-made mannequins, *Fashion* is a fascinating excursion through the last three centuries of clothing trends. The KCI believes that "clothing is an essential manifestation of our very being" and their passion and dedication positively radiate from every page of this book.

The authors:
Akiko Fukai (Chief Curator of The Kyoto Costume Institute), **Tamami Suoh** (Curator of The Kyoto Costume Institute), **Miki Iwagami** (Lecturer of fashion history at Sugino Fashion College (Tokyo)), **Reiko Koga** (Professor of fashion history at Bunka Women's University), and **Rii Nie** (Assistant Curator of The Kyoto Costume Institute).

THE LEARNING CENTRE
CITY & ISLINGTON COLLEGE
444 CAMDEN ROAD

What makes Antwerp special to you? Memories... I call it the twilight zone <u>Where is the best place to stay in Antwerp?</u> My kitchen in my Antwerp flat <u>Where is your favourite place to shop in Antwerp?</u> Tif Tif for secondhand books and magazines, Walter in St Antoniusstraat for my clothes, Toys for Boys in Nosestraat for boys who like to play, and the Biological Café in Nationalestraat. But then again, Antwerp is so small you can do everything in one weekend — so don't mind my choices. BERNHARD WILLHELM

ANTWERP

TEXT BY PETER DE POTTER

Much to Brussels' dismay, foreign fashionistas often consider Antwerp to be the capital of Belgium. Of course it isn't – but the confusion surely has to do with the continuing flood of stellar fashion talent that comes from this Flanders city. Although Antwerp nurtured its own home-grown fashion stars in the '60s and '70s (most notably the eccentric doyenne of hippie chic Ann Saelens), it wasn't until the mid '80s that the city put itself firmly on the international fashion map with the Antwerp Six. This group of ex-graduates from the fashion department of the city's Royal Academy joined forces to get more attention from press and buyers abroad, staging fashion shows and events together. Due to their highly individual styles and unusual zeal, the attention-grabbing antics paid off – all of the original Six are now big players (Walter Van Beirendonck, Dries Van Noten, Ann Demeulemeester, Dirk Van Saene, Dirk Bikkembergs and Martin Margiela, although it must be noted that the latter only featured briefly in the gang and was swiftly replaced by Marina Yee). The first Belgian wave was followed by another, and yet another, mostly consisting of young men and women trained at the Royal Academy. To the amazement of fashion watchers from abroad, most of these designers still prefer Antwerp to New York or Paris as a working place, which surely has something to do with the relatively cheap estate rates and the solid infrastructure of Belgian clothing manufacturers. Practical reasons aside, Antwerp does have an undeniable charm: small, jovial and respectful to its historical heritage, but with an ambitious, international spirit. Being a harbour town, it's always on the outlook for the new – and can be quite critical in doing so (a characteristic many would-be entrepreneurs trying to conquer Antwerp can attest to). Quality is a word not used lightly here, which might explain why impeccable craftsmanship is the uniting factor for all Antwerp designers.

Zum großen Verdruss Brüssels halten Modefans aus dem Ausland Antwerpen oft für die Hauptstadt Belgiens. Das ist sie natürlich nicht, aber diese Annahme hängt sicherlich mit dem nicht abreißenden Strom von Modetalenten mit Starqualität aus der flandrischen Stadt zusammen. Obwohl Antwerpen auch in den 1960er und 1970er Jahren schon Designstars hervorbrachte (am bekanntesten ist wohl Ann Saelens, die exzentrische Doyenne des Hippie-Chic), wurde die Stadt erst Mitte der 1980er durch die Antwerp Six zum Fixpunkt auf der internationalen Landkarte der Mode. Diese Gruppe von Absolventen der Modefakultät der Königlichen Akademie tat sich zusammen, um bei Presse und Kunden im Ausland größere Aufmerksamkeit zu erregen; so gestaltete man gemeinsam Schauen und andere Events. Dank der höchst individuellen Stile und ihres ungewöhnlichen Engagements machte sich der gemeinschaftliche Auftritt bezahlt – heute sind alle sechs bedeutende Figuren in der Szene (Walter van Beirendonck, Dries van Noten, Ann Demeulemeester, Dirk van Saene, Dirk Bikkembergs und Martin Margiela, wobei Letzterer nur kurz zur Gruppe gehörte und rasch durch Marina Yee ersetzt wurde). Der ersten Belgienwelle folgte eine zweite und schließlich eine weitere, die allesamt größtenteils aus jungen Desig-

nerinnen und Designern bestanden, die ihre Ausbildung an der Königlichen Akademie von Antwerpen absolviert hatten. Zur Überraschung der Modeexperten aus dem Ausland ziehen die meisten dieser Modeschöpfer Antwerpen als Arbeitsplatz weiterhin Metropolen wie New York oder Paris vor. Das mag nicht zuletzt mit den relativ günstigen Mieten und der soliden Infrastruktur der belgischen Textilbranche zu tun haben. Abgesehen von diesen praktischen Gründen besitzt die Stadt unübersehbaren Charme: klein, gemütlich und voller Achtung vor ihrem historischen Vermächtnis, dennoch fehlt es nicht an einer ambitionierten, kosmopolitischen Atmosphäre. Als Hafenstadt ist Antwerpen immer offen für Neues – dabei aber durchaus auch kritisch (was viele aufstrebende Entrepreneurs, die versucht haben, sie zu erobern, sicher bestätigen können). Der Begriff Qualität wird hier nicht leichtfertig verwendet, und das mag eine Erklärung für die handwerkliche Perfektion sein, die alle Antwerpener Designer verbindet.

A la plus grande consternation des Bruxellois, les fashion victims du monde entier considèrent souvent Anvers comme la capitale de la Belgique. Evidemment ce n'est pas le cas, mais cette confusion vient probablement du flot croissant de jeunes créateurs talentueux issus de la cité des Flandres. Bien qu'Anvers ait couvé ses propres stars de la mode dans les années 1960 et 1970 (notamment la doyenne excentrique du hippie chic Ann Saelens), ce n'est qu'au milieu des années 1980 que la ville s'impose vraiment sur la carte de la mode internationale grâce aux Antwerp Six, un group de diplômés du département Mode de l'Académie Royale de la ville qui s'associent pour attirer l'attention de la presse et des acheteurs étrangers en organisant toutes sortes de défilés communs et d'autres événements. En raison de leurs styles hautement individuels et de leur zèle inhabituel, leur tapage médiatique porte ses fruits : tous les membres d'origine de l'Antwerp Six sont aujourd'hui des noms reconnus (Walter Van Beirendonck, Dries Van Noten, Ann Demeulemeester, Dirk Van Saene, Dirk Bikkembergs et Martin Margiela – il faut préciser que ce dernier n'a participé au groupe que peu de temps, rapidement remplacé par Marina Yee). La première vague belge fait suite à une autre, puis à une troisième principalement composée de jeunes diplômés, hommes et femmes, de l'Académie Royale. Au grand étonnement des observateurs étrangers, la plupart de ces créateurs continuent de travailler à Anvers plutôt qu'à New York ou Paris, ce qui a sans doute un rapport avec les prix de l'immobilier encore relativement accessibles et la solide infrastructure de l'industrie de l'habillement en Belgique. Outre ces raisons pratiques, Anvers possède un charme indéniable : de taille humaine, pleine de vie et respectueuse de son héritage historique, la ville n'en affiche pas moins une ambition internationale. En tant que ville portuaire, elle est toujours en quête de nouveauté – et peut s'avérer très critique dans ses choix (une caractéristique dont peuvent attester les nombreux entrepreneurs qui tentent de conquérir la ville). Ici, le mot qualité ne se prononce pas à la légère : en effet, le dénominateur commun à tous les stylistes anversois réside dans l'exécution impeccable de leurs créations.

FASHION SHOWS AND FAIRS

Since most Antwerp designers show their collections in Paris, the city has no fashion fairs. Still, the highlight of the year continues to be the graduation show of the fashion department of the Royal Academy, held mid-June. Pulling a crowd of international magazine editors, backers and other loyal supporters, this event has become a hunting ground for new talent.

Da die meisten Antwerpener Designer ihre Kollektionen in Paris präsentieren, gibt es in der Stadt keine Modemesse. Höhepunkt des Jahres ist jedoch nach wie vor die Abschluss-Schau der Modefakultät der Königlichen Akademie Mitte Juni. Sie lockt zahllose Moderedakteure aus aller Welt, Finanziers und andere Förderer an. Der Event gilt als wichtige Börse für neue Talente.

Etant donné que la plupart des créateurs anversois présentent leurs collections à Paris, la ville n'organise pas de salon de la mode. Néanmoins, le point fort de l'année restent les défilés de fin d'études du département Mode de l'Académie Royale, qui ont lieu à la mi-juin. Attirant la presse internationale, des sponsors venus de tous les pays et autres fidèles supporters, cet événement est devenu le terrain de chasse des nouveaux talents.

Vitrine

Each September, both young and established Antwerp designers are invited to present installations in various settings about town.

Jedes Jahr im September sind junge und etablierte Designer aus Antwerpen aufgefordert, Installationen an verschiedenen Schauplätzen in der ganzen Stadt zu präsentieren.

En septembre, les créateurs anversois, nouveaux venus ou noms bien établis, sont invités à présenter des installations dans différents lieux de la ville.

www.modenatie.com

FASHION SCHOOLS

Hogeschool Antwerpen

Now with a recently changed, official name, although more widely known as the Royal Academy of Antwerp, the school is incorporated into the Modenatie, the organisation that also houses MoMu.

Die weithin bekannte Königliche Akademie von Antwerpen hat seit kurzem einen neuen offiziellen Namen. Teil der Modenatie ist auch das MoMu.

Récemment rebaptisée d'un nom plus officiel bien qu'elle soit largement connue sous le nom d'Académie Royale d'Anvers, l'école est intégrée au Modenatie, l'organisation qui accueille également le MoMu.

Hogeschool Antwerpen
Fashion Department
Nationalestraat 28/3
2000 Antwerp
Tel. +32 (0)3206 0880
www.antwerp-fashion.be

FASHION MUSEUMS AND GALLERIES

MoMu

Belgium's premier and recently opened fashion museum houses a library, archive rooms and exhibition spaces.

Belgiens wichtigstes, erst kürzlich eröffnetes Modemuseum umfasst eine Bibliothek, Archive und Ausstellungsräume.

Ouvert récemment, le MoMu est le tout premier musée de la mode en Belgique. Il comprend une bibliothèque, des salles d'archives et des espaces d'exposition.

Nationalestraat 28
2000 Antwerp
Tel. +32 (0)3470 2770
www.momu.be

Fifty One

Gallery focusing on contemporary photography, also fashion photography.

Galerie mit den Schwerpunkten zeitgenössische Fotografie und Modefotografie.

Galerie d'art spécialisée en photographie contemporaine. Expose également des photos de mode.

Zirkstraat 20
2000 Antwerp
Tel. +32 (0)3289 8458
www.gallery51.com

Fotomuseum

A recent emphasis on fashion photography and new talent, both international and homegrown, makes this museum once again a haven for picture lovers.

Die jüngst gesetzten Schwerpunkte Modefotografie und neue einheimische wie internationale Talente machen dieses Museum wieder zu einem Anziehungspunkt für Kenner.

Récemment réarticulé autour de la photographie de mode et des nouveaux talents belges et internationaux, ce musée est redevenu le paradis des amateurs de photo.

Waalse Kaai 47
2000 Antwerp
Tel. +32 (0)3242 9300
www.fotomuseum.be

FASHION SHOPS

Ann Demeulemeester

Impeccable and spacious, Demeulemeester's shop perfectly reflects her sensuous, intelligent take on fashion. Here, the client rules: the changing rooms are actual salon-like spaces.

Makellos und geräumig, spiegelt Demeulemeesters Laden die sinnliche, intelligente Herangehensweise der Designerin an ihr Metier wider. Hier ist tatsächlich einmal der Kunde König: Die Umkleiden sind geräumige Salons.

Impeccable et spacieuse, la boutique d'Ann Demeulemeester reflète fidèlement sa vision intelligente et voluptueuse de la mode. Ici, le client est roi : les cabines d'essayage sont de véritables salons.

Verlatstraat 38
2000 Antwerp
Tel. +32 (0)3216 0133

Atelier 11

Well-known for their collaborations on Raf Simons jewellery, Atelier 11 have other hard-edged design treats to offer, all on show in their own jewellery shop.

Das Atelier ist bekannt für seine Mitarbeit an den Schmuckkollektionen von Raf Simons, hat aber auch anspruchsvolle Eigenkreationen zu bieten, die alle im Laden zu sehen sind.

Réputé pour avoir collaboré à la conception des bijoux de Raf Simons, Atelier 11 propose bien d'autres créations originales, toutes présentées dans sa propre bijouterie.

Scheldestraat 32
2000 Antwerp
Tel. +32 (0)3248 1164

Closing Date

Pivotal in turning Antwerp on to the more audacious fashion names, this cosy shop stocks Vivienne Westwood, Antwerp's bold and emerging Wouter Hoste and other labels that can make heads turn.

Eine der wichtigsten Adressen Antwerpens für gewagtere Marken. In dem gemütlichen Laden führt man Vivienne Westwood, das aufstrebende Antwerpener Label Wouter Hoste und andere Aufsehen erregende Designer.

Cette petite boutique a joué un rôle majeur dans l'accession d'Anvers au rang de capitale de la mode d'avant-garde. On y trouve du Vivienne Westwood, les créations audacieuses du jeune créateur anversois Wouter Hoste, ainsi que d'autres griffes dans la même veine excentrique.

Korte Gasthuisstraat 15
2000 Antwerp
Tel. +32 (0)3232 8722

Coccodrillo

Probably the most prestigious shoe shop in Antwerp, selling footwear by Ann Demeulemeester, Martin Margiela, Dries Van Noten, Véronique Branquinho, A. F. Vandevorst, Raf Simons, Balenciaga, Prada, Miu Miu and Rochas.

Im wahrscheinlich renommiertesten Schuhgeschäft ganz Belgiens verkauft man Schuhwerk von Ann Demeulemeester, Martin Margiela, Dries van Noten, Véronique Branquinho, A. F. Vandevorst, Raf Simons, Balenciaga, Prada, Miu Miu und Rochas.

Sans doute la boutique de chaussures la plus prestigieuse d'Anvers. On y trouve les créations d'Ann Demeulemeester, Martin Margiela, Dries Van Noten, Véronique Branquinho, A. F. Vandevorst, Raf Simons, Balenciaga, Prada, Miu Miu et Rochas.

Schuttershofstraat 9
2000 Antwerp
Tel. +32 (0)3233 2093

Het Modepaleis

Dries Van Noten's multi-floored shop, stocking his complete range of womenswear, menswear, shoes and accessories. The decor is a treat for the eye and the staff decidedly nonpushy.

Dries van Notens Laden präsentiert sein komplettes Sortiment an Damen- und Herrenmode, Schuhen und Accessoires auf mehreren Etagen. Die Dekoration ist ein Augenschmaus und das Personal angenehm zurückhaltend.

« Palais de la mode » de Dries Van Noten, avec plusieurs étages pour accueillir toutes ses collections pour femme, pour homme, ses chaussures et ses accessoires. Le décor est un vrai régal pour les yeux et le client n'est décidément pas harcelé par le personnel.

Nationalestraat 16
2000 Antwerp
Tel. +32 (0)3222 9210

Louis

The store that started selling Belgian designers in the days when most of them weren't even known to the Belgian public. Over the years, Louis has become an institution, stocking Martin Margiela, Raf Simons, Véronique Branquinho, A. F. Vandevorst, Haider Ackermann, Ann Demeulemeester, Véronique Leroy and some international designers like Balenciaga and Rick Owens.

In diesem Laden verkaufte man schon Arbeiten belgischer Designer, als die meisten von ihnen noch nicht einmal dem einheimischen Publikum ein Begriff waren. Im Laufe der Jahre hat sich Louis zu einer Institution entwickelt. Man findet hier Mode von Martin Margiela, Raf Simons, Véronique Branquinho, A. F. Vandevorst, Haider Ackermann, Ann Demeulemeester, Véronique Leroy und einigen internationalen Designern wie Balenciaga und Rick Owens.

La boutique a commencé par vendre les créations des stylistes belges à une époque où la plupart d'entre eux n'étaient même pas connus du public national. Au fil des années, Louis est devenu une véritable institution. On y trouve les créations de Martin Margiela, Raf Simons, Véronique Branquinho, A. F. Vandevorst, Haider Ackermann, Ann Demeulemeester et Véronique Leroy, ainsi que certaines griffes internationales telles que Balenciaga et Rick Owens.

Lombardenstraat 2
2000 Antwerp
Tel. +32 (0)3232 9872

Stephan Schneider

Small and humble, but well worth a visit, this German ex-Academy graduate sells pure and simple men's and womenswear.

Klein und bescheiden, aber auf jeden Fall einen Besuch wert. Hier verkauft der Akademieabsolvent aus Deutschland seine unverfälschte, schlichte Damen- und Herrenmode.

Petite boutique sans prétention qui vaut largement le détour. Ici, l'ancien diplômé allemand de l'Académie vend ses vêtements pour homme et pour femme à la coupe simple et épurée.

Reyndersstraat 53
2000 Antwerp
Tel. +32 (0)3226 2614

Véronique Branquinho

Quality meets mystery, fashion meets sensitivity: within her own shop, Véronique Branquinho creates the perfect backdrop for her womenswear, menswear and accessories.

Qualität trifft Geheimnis, Mode trifft Empfindsamkeit: In ihrem Laden erzeugt Véronique Branquinho den perfekten Hintergrund für ihre Damen- und Herrenmode und für ihre Accessoires.

La rencontre entre la qualité et le mystère, la mode et la sensibilité : dans sa propre boutique, Véronique Branquinho a créé le décor idéal pour ses collections féminines, masculines et ses accessoires.

Nationalestraat 73
2000 Antwerp
Tel. +32 (0)3233 6616

Verso

The size of an American department store (b-i-g), this superstore, with its salons, antique fireplaces and authentic historical arches and ceilings breathes luxury and the right kind of opulence. Dirk Bikkembergs, Dolce & Gabbana, Prada, Giorgio Armani, Dior Homme, Costume National and YSL (among many others) feel very much at home here.

Dieser Laden von der Größe eines amerikanischen Department Stores (b-i-g), mit seinen Salons, antiken Kaminen und echten historischen Bögen und Deckenverzierungen atmet Luxus und die rechte Form von Opulenz. Dirk Bikkembergs, Dolce & Gabbana, Prada, Giorgio Armani, Dior Homme, Costume National und YSL (um nur einige zu nennen) passen hier perfekt hin.

Aussi vaste qu'un grand magasin américain, ce mégastore respire le luxe et l'opulence de bon goût, avec ses salons, ses cheminées anciennes, ses voûtes historiques et ses plafonds d'époque. Les créations de Dirk Bikkembergs, Dolce & Gabbana, Prada, Giorgio Armani, Dior Homme, Costume National et YSL (entre autres) s'y sentent comme à la maison.

Lange Gasthuisstraat 9–11
2000 Antwerp
Tel. +32 (0)3226 9292

Walter

Walter Van Beirendoncks's shop, run with his partner Dirk Van Saene, sells their own labels alongside the likes of Bernhard Willhelm, Bruno Pieters and Christian Wijnants. Each designer or label has its own specific corner in this enormous space.

Walter van Beirendoncks Laden, den der Designer mit seinem Partner Dirk Van Saenen betreibt, verkauft neben den eigenen Labels auch Bernhard Willhelm, Bruno Pieters und Christian Wijnants. Jeder Designer hat in diesem ungemein geräumigen Laden eine eigene, speziell eingerichtete Ecke.

Boutique de Walter Van Beirendonck, gérée en partenariat avec Dirk Van Saene. On y trouve leurs propres griffes, aux côtés de celles de Bernhard Willhelm, Bruno Pieters et Christian Wijnants. Chaque styliste ou griffe bénéficie d'un carré dédié au sein de cet espace impressionnant.

St-Antoniusstraat 12
2000 Antwerp
Tel. +32 (0)3213 2644

VINTAGE FASHION SHOPS

Ave

Not vintage in the strict sense of the word, but recommended all the same. Customised fleamarket finds.

Keine Vintage-Mode im engeren Sinn, aber dennoch empfehlenswert. Individuell umgearbeitete Fundstücke von Flohmärkten.

Pas vraiment « vintage » au sens strict du terme, mais à voir absolument. Vêtements customisés à partir de pièces dénichées sur les marchés aux puces.

Lombardenstraat 18
2000 Antwerp
Tel. +32 (0)3227 4401

Francis

A shopping nirvana for both fashion-lovers and fashion professionals: top-notch vintage clothes from all decades as well as collectable furniture.

Ein Shopping-Nirvana für Modefans und -profis: Vintage-Kleidung der Spitzenklasse aus allen Epochen sowie Sammlermöbel.

Un nirvana du shopping, tant pour les fashion victims que pour les professionnels de la mode : vêtements vintage de grande qualité et de toutes les époques, mobilier de collection.

Steenhouwersvest 14
2000 Antwerp
Tel. +32 (0)3288 9433

Naughty I

Funky, sometimes zany, but always affordable.

Funkige, manchmal verrückte Mode zu stets erschwinglichen Preisen.

Des pièces funky, parfois importables mais toujours abordables.

Kammenstraat 65–67
2000 Antwerp
Tel. +32 (0)3213 3590

RESTAURANTS

Ciro's

Traditional brasserie, Antwerp-style. The best steaks to be found in the city, frequented by both elderly gents and ladies, and everyone who's involved in fashion, art or theatre.

Traditionelle Brasserie im typischen Antwerpener Stil. Die besten Steaks der Stadt. Gemischtes Publikum aus älteren Herrschaften und allen, die mit Mode, Kunst oder Theater zu tun haben.

Brasserie traditionnelle dans le plus pur style anversois. On y mange les meilleurs steaks de la ville. Une clientèle troisième âge s'y mêle au petit monde de la mode, de l'art ou du théâtre.

Amerikalei 6
2000 Antwerp
Tel. +32 (0)3238 1147

Dôme

Equally lauded for its interior and its food. Haute cuisine in the true sense of the term.

Lokal mit hoch gelobter Einrichtung und Küche. Haute Cuisine im wahrsten Sinne des Wortes.

Un restaurant plébiscité tant pour sa décoration que pour sa cuisine. On y déguste de la « haute cuisine », au sens littéral du terme.

Grote Hondstraat 2
2000 Antwerp
Tel. +32 (0)3239 9003

Euterpia

Expensive but worth every penny. The decor is intimate and chic, in an Art Nouveau neighbourhood.

Teuer, aber sein Geld wert. Die Einrichtung ist intim, chic und passt zu diesem Jugenstil-Viertel.

Prix élevés mais justifiés. Décor chic et intimiste dans un quartier Art Nouveau.

Generaal Capiaumontstraat 2
2000 Antwerp
Tel. +32 (0)3235 0202

Fair Food

Subtle fusion cuisine and impeccable service.

Feine Fusion-Küche und tadelloser Service.

Cuisine « fusion » subtile et service irréprochable.

Leopold de Waelplaats
2000 Antwerp
Tel. +32 (0)3238 9296

Hungry Henrietta

Simple but excellent cuisine, set in the shopping area of Antwerp.

Einfache, aber ausgezeichnete Küche im Antwerpener Einkaufsviertel.

Cuisine simple mais excellente, dans le quartier commerçant d'Anvers.

Lombardenvest 19
2000 Antwerp
Tel. +32 (0)3232 2928

Pizza Arte

Italian food. The restaurant's name wasn't chosen randomly: there's art everywhere you look.

Italienische Küche. Der Name des Restaurants ist nicht zufällig gewählt – Kunst, wohin man blickt.

Cuisine italienne. Le nom du restaurant n'a pas été choisi au hasard : de nombreuses œuvres d'art y sont exposées.

Suikerrui 24
2000 Antwerp
Tel. +32 (0)3226 2970

BARS

Berlin

Both laid-back bar and (rather fine) restaurant, this place has a modern, warm feel, reflected by its clientèle of young professionals and creative upstarts.

Legere Bar und (ziemlich nobles) Restaurant in einem. Ein Lokal mit moderner, aber gemütlicher Atmosphäre, was sich auch im Publikum aus Einsteigern ins Berufsleben und jungen Künstlern widerspiegelt.

A la fois bar lounge et restaurant (plutôt haut de gamme), le côté moderne et chaleureux de l'endroit se reflète dans sa clientèle de jeunes professionnels et d'artistes débutants.

Kleine Markt 2
2000 Antwerp
+32 (0)3227 1101

Witzli Poetzli
Small café near Antwerp Cathedral, serving fine coffee and playing jazz.

Kleines Café nahe der Kathedrale mit gutem Kaffee und Jazzmusik.

Petit café à deux pas de la cathédrale d'Anvers. Bon café et musique jazz.

Blauwmoezelstraat 8
2000 Antwerp

Zeezicht
Artistic café in a young, multicultural neighbourhood.

Künstlercafé in einem jungen, multi-kulturellen Stadtviertel.

Café artistique dans un quartier jeune et multiculturel.

Dageraadplaats 7
2000 Antwerp
Tel. +32 (0)3235 1065

HOTELS

De Witte Lelie
Pricey but very luscious hotel in a historical setting.

Kostspieliges, aber prachtvolles Hotel in historischer Umgebung.

Hôtel cher mais très luxueux, installé dans un immeuble d'époque.

Keizerstraat 16–18
2000 Antwerp
Tel. +32 (0)3226 1966
www.dewittelelie.be

Prinse Hotel
Nice and comfortable, with a no-non-sense design, in the old centre of Antwerp.

Nett und gemütlich mit schlichtem Design, mitten in der Antwerpener Altstadt.

Agréable, tout confort et design sans chichi. Au cœur de la Vieille Ville.

Keizerstraat 63
2000 Antwerp
Tel. +32 (0)3226 4050
www.hotelprinse.be

'T Sandt
Comfortable hotel near the border of the river Scheldt.

Gemütliches Hotel, nahe am Scheldt-ufer.

Hôtel tout confort près des rives de la Scheldt.

Zand 17–19
2000 Antwerp
Tel. +32 (0)3232 9390

AIRPORT

Antwerp International Airport
Luchthavenlei, Deurn
2000 Antwerp
Tel. +32 (0)3285 6500
www.antwerpairport.be

BERLIN

TEXT BY ZOË JACKSON; GUIDE BY ZOË JACKSON AND JÖRG KOCH

Berlin's streets are deceptively quiet. In New York or London, for example, pulsing pedestrian traffic is a dead giveaway of a stylish hot-spot; however, Berlin's most exciting areas, such as Mitte, Prenzlauer Berg and parts of Kreuzberg, are often strangely tranquil, as if everything goes on behind closed doors. Berlin has long been branded an essential place to visit, shop, and especially to live (cheaply), but visitors say it takes a few days for Berlin to show its true face. The tangled financial situation is partially responsible for this stillness; window shoppers are sure to be scarce with unemployment at nearly twenty percent. Despite this mysterious lull, you can be certain you are standing on very fertile, creative ground and once you peel back the neutral, uncertain exterior, you will find what you came looking for: a unique capital for fashion and culture. Like Berlin's political and social history, which has been marked by periods of transition, the fashion scene is also steadily changing with the times. In the new millennium, there is tremendous energy surrounding fashion, as opposed to the state of hibernation before the fall of the wall. Berlin has now also become a platform for fashion on a global level. Two tradeshows for international and Berlin-based designers – Bread & Butter and Premium – have made their homes in Berlin; for three days in January 2005, fifty percent of the 42,000 visitors to Bread & Butter were from outside of Germany. No doubt, this expanding audience has triggered many young designers to open their own shops, which have popped up at rapid speed of late. With all eyes on Berlin, let's hope it remains a place of never-ending possibilities – where all the magic lies just beneath the surface.

In den Straßen von Berlin herrscht eine trügerische Ruhe. In New York oder London etwa ist das pulsierende Treiben von Fußgängern ein todsicheres Zeichen für eine angesagte Gegend. Dagegen ist es in Berlins aufregendsten Vierteln wie Mitte, Prenzlauer Berg oder Teilen von Kreuzberg oft befremdlich still, so als würde alles hinter verschlossenen Türen passieren. Berlin gilt schon lange als einer der gefragtesten Orte zum Sightseeing, zum Shoppen und insbesondere auch zum (preiswerten) Leben, doch die meisten Besucher bestätigen, dass es ein paar Tage braucht, bis Berlin sein wahres Gesicht zeigt. Die kritische Finanzlage ist teilweise mitverantwortlich für diese Ruhe. Bei einer Arbeitslosenquote von fast zwanzig Prozent gibt es eben nicht so viele Menschen, die Lust auf einen Schaufensterbummel haben. Trotzdem befindet sich der Besucher auf zweifellos sehr fruchtbarem kreativem Boden, und wenn man erst einmal die neutrale, unscheinbare äußere Schicht entfernt hat, findet man das Gesuchte: eine einzigartige Hauptstadt der Mode und Kultur. Wie Berlins Geschichte, die von Zeiten des Umbruchs geprägt ist, befindet sich auch die Modeszene ständig im Wandel. Seit Beginn des neuen Jahrtausends gibt es ungeheuer viel Energie, im Gegensatz zu dem Winterschlaf-ähnlichen Zustand, der vor dem Mauerfall herrschte. Berlin ist inzwischen auch ein internationaler Laufsteg. Zwei Messen für internationale und einheimische Designer – Bread & Butter und Premium – sind in Berlin zu Hause. An drei Tagen im Januar 2005 kamen fünfzig Prozent der insgesamt 42 000 Besucher von Bread & Butter aus dem Ausland. Sicherlich hat dieses wachsende Publikum auch viele junge Modemacher ermutigt, eigene Läden zu eröffnen, die in letzter Zeit mit großem Tempo aus dem Boden schießen. Wo sich nun so viele Augen auf Berlin richten, bleibt zu hoffen, dass es ein Ort der unbegrenzten Möglichkeiten bleibt – wo sich der ganze Zauber unmittelbar unter der Oberfläche befindet.

Les rues de Berlin paraissent étrangement calmes. A New York ou à Londres, un intense trafic piéton témoigne de l'intérêt d'un quartier ; pourtant, les zones les plus intéressantes de Berlin telles que Mitte, Prenzlauer Berg et certains coins de Kreuzberg restent souvent étonnamment tranquilles, comme si tout se déroulait derrière des portes closes. Depuis longtemps, on nous vend Berlin comme une destination incontournable pour faire du tourisme, du shopping et surtout pour vivre (à bon marché), mais d'après ses visiteurs, il faut attendre plusieurs jours avant que la ville ne dévoile son véritable visage. Ce calme apparent est en partie dû à une situation économique confuse : avec un taux de chômage qui avoisine les 20 %, rien étonnant à ce que les lécheurs de vitrine ne courent pas les rues. Malgré cette mystérieuse tranquillité, la ville reste un terreau créatif très fertile. Une fois que vous aurez gratté son vernis neutre et incertain, vous découvrirez ce que vous êtes venu chercher : une capitale de la mode et de la culture absolument unique. A l'instar de l'histoire politique et sociale de Berlin, marquée par plusieurs périodes de transition, la scène de la mode berlinoise ne cesse d'évoluer avec son temps. A l'aube du nouveau millénaire, le monde de la mode vibre d'une énergie effervescente, du moins par rapport à l'état d'hibernation dans lequel il était plongé avant la chute du mur. La ville est aujourd'hui une plate-forme mondiale de la mode. Deux salons professionnels dédiés aux créateurs internationaux et berlinois, Bread & Butter et Premium, y ont même élu domicile ; la moitié des 42 000 visiteurs enregistrés en trois jours en janvier 2005 au salon Bread & Butter ne venait pas d'Allemagne. Evidemment, ce public croissant incite de nombreux jeunes créateurs à ouvrir leurs propres boutiques, qui qui commencent à pousser un peu partout comme des champignons. Alors que le monde entier garde les yeux rivés sur Berlin, espérons que cette ville restera celle de l'infini champ des possibles, où toute la magie se concentre juste sous la surface.

FASHION SHOWS AND FAIRS

Bread & Butter Berlin (BBB)
This twice-yearly fashion trade show has had great success in Berlin since January 2003.

Diese zweimal jährlich stattfindende Modemesse ist seit Januar 2003 ein riesiger Erfolg.

Depuis janvier 2003, ce salon bisannuel de la mode remporte un énorme succès à Berlin.

www.breadandbutter.com

Premium
Sharing the same dates with BBB, Premium's programming includes a trade show and runway presentations. As the name coyly decrees, this event promises only the best in new, national and international fashion design.

Zum gleichen Zeitpunkt wie BBB bietet Premium ein Programm aus Messe und Laufsteg-Präsentationen. Wie der Name schon sagt, verspricht dieses Event nur das Beste der neuen nationalen und internationalen Designerszene.

Organisé aux mêmes dates que BBB, le programme de Premium inclut un salon professionnel et des défilés de mode. Comme son nom l'indique avec coquetterie, cet événement ne réunit que le meilleur de la mode d'aujourd'hui, avec des créateurs allemands et internationaux.

www.premiumexhibitions.com

FASHION SCHOOLS

Universität der Künste Berlin
Vivienne Westwood was guest professor for fashion at the UDK Berlin, so it's all about technique, technique and, yes, technique.

Vivienne Westwood war an der UDK Berlin Gastprofessorin für Mode, entsprechend dreht sich hier alles um Technik, Technik und noch mal Technik.

Vivienne Westwood était professeur invité du département Mode de l'UDK Berlin, et donc on y parle de technique, de technique et encore de technique.

Joachim-Friedrich-Straße 37
10711 Berlin
Tel. +49 (0)30 318 50
www.udk-berlin.de

Kunsthochschule Weißensee
Bühringstraße 20
13086 Berlin
Tel. +49 (0)30 477050
www.kh-berlin.de

Lette-Verein, Berufsfachschule für Mode-Design
Viktoria-Luise-Platz 6
10777 Berlin
Tel. +49 (0)30 219940
www.lette-verein.de

FASHION MUSEUMS AND GALLERIES

Helmut Newton Foundation Museum
The great, late, Berlin-born lensman donated more than one thousand photographs to this new museum, which will present Newton's life work in alternating exhibitions.

Der große, bereits verstorbene, aber in Berlin geborene Fotokünstler schenkte diesem neuen Museum über 1000 Fotografien. In wechselnden Ausstellungen wird hier Newtons Lebenswerk präsentiert.

Le génial et très regretté photographe d'origine berlinoise Helmut Newton a légué plus d'un millier de photos à ce nouveau musée, qui compte présenter une rétrospective de son œuvre par le biais d'expositions temporaires.

Jebensstraße 2
10623 Berlin
Tel. +49 (0)30 2090 5566

FASHION SHOPS
All major fashion labels – including Gucci, Prada, Hermès, Jil Sander – are either located at Kurfürstendamm (Charlottenburg) or at Friedrichstraße (Mitte)

Alle wichtigen Label – unter anderem Gucci, Prada, Hermès, Jil Sander – findet man entweder am Kurfürstendamm (Charlottenburg) oder auf der Friedrichstraße (Mitte).

Toutes les grandes marques, dont Gucci, Prada, Hermès et Jil Sander, ont pignon sur rue soit sur le Kurfürstendamm (Charlottenburg), soit dans la Friedrichstraße (Mitte).

Quartier 206
Luxurious concept store with an extensive high-end beauty department, which tends to opt for the safer, more conservative pieces from designers' collections.

Luxuriöses Konzeptkaufhaus mit umfassender Beauty-Abteilung, das sich auf die dezenteren, konservativeren Stücke aus den Designerkollektionen konzentriert.

Luxueuse boutique-concept dotée d'un vaste espace beauté haut de gamme. Elle a tendance à privilégier les créations les plus portables et les plus conservatrices des collections de grands stylistes.

Friedrichstraße 71
10117 Berlin (Mitte)
Tel. +49 (0)30 2094 6240
www.quartier206.de

Van Ravenstein
Hailing from Amsterdam, this avant-garde fashion institution offers some of the best in Belgian fashion (Dries Van Noten, Martin Margiela, Véronique Branquinho, etc.)

Als Ableger eines Ladens in Amsterdam führt diese Institution der Avantgardemode einige der besten belgischen Designer (Dries van Noten, Martin Margiela, Véronique Branquinho, etc.).

Importée d'Amsterdam, cette institution de la mode d'avant-garde propose le meilleur des griffes belges (Dries Van Noten, Martin Margiela, Véronique Branquinho, etc.).

Leibnizstraße 49
10629 Berlin (Charlottenburg)
Tel. +49 (0)30 3100 4602
www.van-ravenstein.nl

Bless Shop
The minimalist-chic Bless aesthetic has become somewhat of a Berlin style institution. Their clothing, accessories, and furniture are regulars on the pages of countless international magazines including Vogue, Harper's Bazaar, 032c, Purple.

Der minimalistische Chic der Ästhetik von Bless ist zu einer Art Berliner Institution geworden. Kleidung, Accessoires und Möbel des Labels finden sich regelmäßig in zahllosen internationalen Magazinen wie Vogue, Harper's Bazaar, 032c und Purple.

L'esthétique du chic minimaliste de Bless est devenue une sorte d'institution berlinoise. Les vêtements, les accessoires et les meubles de la griffe apparaissent régulièrement dans les pages d'innombrables magazines internationaux tels que Vogue, Harper's Bazaar, 032c et Purple.

Mulackstrasse 38
10119 Berlin (Mitte)
Tel. +49 (0)30 2759 6566
www.bless-service.de

Comme des Garçons
Rei Kawakubo's second Berlin Guerilla Store graciously opened its doors in March 2005, taunting Berliners with another one-year-only stint. Be sure to check out the notoriously brilliant and unusual collections, and also take home one (or two) of their cult wallets.

Rei Kawakubos zweiter Guerilla Store in Berlin öffnete seine Türen gnädigerweise im März 2005, um die Berliner wieder mit einem einjährigen Intermezzo zu verspotten. Lassen Sie sich die berüchtigten brillanten und ungewöhnlichen Kollektionen nicht entgehen, und nehmen Sie unbedingt eine (oder zwei) der kultigen Geldbörsen mit nach Hause.

Le second Guerilla Store berlinois de Rei Kawakubo a ouvert ses élégantes portes en mars 2005, raillant les habitants de la capitale avec une nouvelle boutique-concept destinée à ne vivre qu'une année. Allez-y pour ses collections réputées brillantes et insolites, et n'oubliez pas de repartir avec un (ou deux) portefeuilles, ils sont culte.

Karl-Marx-Allee 78
10243 Berlin (Friedrichshain)
Tel. +49 (0)30 2804 5338
www.guerilla-store.com

Apartment
Those in-the-know head to a concept store hidden in a stylish basement, beneath a glass-box gallery just off Alexanderplatz. It carries designers from Bernhard Willhelm to Jeremy Scott, as well as limited-edition sneakers and accessories.

Eingeweihte besuchen diesen versteckten Konzeptladen in einem eleganten Untergeschoss unterhalb des Glaskastens einer Galerie ganz in der Nähe des Alexanderplatzes. Dort führt man Designer von Bernhard Willhelm bis Jeremy Scott sowie Sneakers in limitierter Auflage und Accessoires.

Les initiés passent régulièrement dans cette boutique-concept cachée dans un sous-sol élégant, sous une galerie d'art tout en verre derrière l'Alexanderplatz. On y trouve des créateurs tels que Bernhard Willhelm ou Jeremy Scott, ainsi que des baskets et des accessoires sortis en édition limitée.

Memhardstraße 8
10178 Berlin (Mitte)
Tel. +49 (0)30 2804 2253
www.apartmentberlin.de

Blush
A delicious, boudoir-like lingerie and swimwear boutique, carrying Chloé, La Perla, Missoni, and Princess Tam Tam. They also design an in-house line of jumpsuits, underwear, morning gowns, and matching sleeping masks.

Eine herrliche Boutique für Wäsche- und Bademoden im Stil eines Boudoirs. Hier findet man Chloé, La Perla, Missoni und Princess Tam Tam. Die hauseigene Marke bietet Overalls, Dessous, Morgenröcke und dazu passende Schlafmasken.

Ressemblant à un petit boudoir, cette adorable boutique de lingerie et de maillots de bain vend des marques telles que Chloé, La Perla, Missoni et Princesse Tam Tam. Elle propose également sa propre ligne de déshabillés, de sous-vêtements et de robes de chambre, avec masques de nuit coordonnés.

Rosa-Luxemburg-Straße 22
10178 Berlin (Mitte)
Tel. +49 (0)30 2809 3580
www.blush-berlin.com

The Best Shop
The Best Shop offers deconstructed daywear by Scandinavian and Berlin-based designers, and also creates highly collectible, custom-made, silk-screened sweat- and T-shirts in an hour. While you wait, soak up their hip magazine collection, records and accessories.

The Best Shop bietet dekonstruierte Alltagsmode von skandinavischen und Berliner Designern. Außerdem werden hier innerhalb einer Stunde nach Maß Siebdruck-T-Shirts und -Sweatshirts mit Sammlerwert gefertigt. Die Wartezeit können Sie sich beim Stöbern in der tollen Zeitschriftensammlung, in den Platten und Accessoires vertreiben.

Best Shop propose des vêtements originaux produits par des créateurs scandinaves et berlinois, mais crée également des sweats et des t-shirts sérigraphiés, personnalisés et hautement collectors en moins d'une heure. Pour patienter, plongez-vous dans leur sélection branchée de magazines, de disques et d'accessoires.

Alte Schönhauser Straße 6
10119 Berlin (Mitte)
Tel. +49 (0)30 2463 2522
www.bestshop-berlin.de

Mientus

The ultimate menswear department store with three nearby branches, stocking everything from Giorgio Armani to Paper Denim Cloth to Prada.

Der ultimative Herrenausstatter mit drei nebeneinander liegenden Filialen, in denen man von Giorgio Armani über Paper Denim bis hin zu Prada einfach alles findet.

Le meilleur grand magasin pour homme de la ville, avec trois succursales dans le quartier. Il propose tout, de Giorgio Armani à Paper Denim et Prada.

Wilmersdorfer Straße 73
10629 Berlin (Charlottenburg)
Tel. +49 (0)30 3239 077
www.mientus-berlin.de

VINTAGE FASHION SHOPS

Colours

Row upon row of vintage jeans, leather jackets and dresses in a huge factory loft.

Endlose Reihen von Vintage-Jeans, Lederjacken und Kleidern in einem riesigen Fabrikloft.

Des rangées et des rangées de jeans, blousons en cuir et robes vintage présentées dans un énorme loft industriel.

Bergmannstraße 102
10961 Berlin (Kreuzberg)
Tel. +49 (0)30 6943 348

Humana

This chain of charity shops offers the opportunity to do some fashion archaeology into Eastern Bloc chic with its acres of cheap secondhand clothing, fur and leather.

Diese Kette von Secondhand-Läden bietet die Möglichkeit zur Modearchäologie im Bereich Ostblock-Chic. Auf

vielen, vielen Quadratmetern preiswerte Kleidung, Pelze und Leder.

Cette chaîne de boutiques caritatives vous offre l'opportunité de pratiquer un peu d'archéologie de la mode, version pays de l'Est, avec ses hectares de vêtements, de fourrures et de cuirs d'occasion à bon marché.

Karl-Liebknecht-Straße 30
10178 Berlin (Mitte)
Tel. +49 (0)30 2423 000

Sterling Gold Moden

This shop primarily carries beautifully preserved vintage dresses. Arranged by colour, the rainbow spectrum of poufy frocks is akin to an irresistible candy store – and you might just walk out with a taste of everything.

Der Laden führt in erster Linie wunderbar erhaltene Vintage-Kleider. Dieser nach Farben sortierte Regenbogen verspielter Gewänder ähnelt einem unwiderstehlichen Süßigkeitengeschäft – vielleicht spazieren Sie mit dem Geschmack aller Farben wieder hinaus.

Cette boutique propose principalement des robes vintage en parfait état. Classé par couleur, l'arc-en-ciel des robes donne l'impression d'être dans une confiserie, dont vous ne manquerez pas de ressortir avec des friandises de toutes les couleurs.

Heckmann-Höfe
Oranienburgerstraße 32
10117 Berlin (Mitte)
Tel. +49 (0)30 2809 6500
www.sterling-gold.de

Ariane

There are four to five other second-hand shops along Mommsenstraße which, like Ariane, are happy to sell you Jil Sander or Chanel from the last few seasons, but this is the pick of them.

In derselben Straße befinden sich noch vier oder fünf weitere Läden, die ebenfalls Jil Sander und Chanel der letzten paar Saisons verkaufen, aber Ariane ist die erste Adresse.

Dans cette rue, quatre ou cinq autres boutiques d'occasion sont disposées à vous vendre du Jil Sander ou du Chanel des saisons précédentes, mais Ariane constitue le premier choix.

Mommsenstraße 4
10629 Berlin (Charlottenburg)
Tel. +49 (0)30 8817 436

TASCHEN Book Store

KÖNIG.TASCHEN Bookstore for photography

This photo book store in Berlin is TASCHEN's first joint bookstore. Sited in the Helmut Newton Foundation, TASCHEN presents their complete publishing program with

Europe's best art book dealer, Walther König. The store offers around 5.000 international photo titles from publishers throughout the world.

Dieser Fotobuchladen im Gebäude der Helmut Newton Foundation in Berlin ist TASCHENs erstes Joint Venture. Gemeinsam mit Europas bestem Kunstbuchhändler, Walther König, präsentiert TASCHEN sein gesamtes Verlagsprogramm und rund 5 000 internationale Fotografie-Titel von Verlagen aus aller Welt.

Cette librairie photo de Berlin située à la Fondation Helmut Newton est la première que TASCHEN ouvre dans le cadre d'un partenariat. TASCHEN y présente l'ensemble de ses collections aux côtés d'ouvrages sélectionnés par Walther König, le meilleur libraire de livres d'art en Europe. La librairie propose près de 5 000 ouvrages photographiques internationaux venus du monde entier.

Jebensstr. 2
10623 Berlin
Tel. +49-(0)30 3180 8558

FLEA MARKETS

Flohmarkt Straße des 17. Juni

The biggest flea market in Berlin – and consequently the most popular for tourists, making bargains harder to find.

Der größte Flohmarkt Berlins – und folglich ein Touristen-Magnet, was echte Schnäppchen selten macht.

Le plus vaste marché aux puces berlinois, et le plus prisé par les touristes. Traduction : il devient de plus en plus difficile d'y faire de bonnes affaires.

Straße des 17. Juni
10623 Berlin (Tiergarten)
Saturday/Sunday 11.00–17.00

Flohmarkt Arkonaplatz

Mitte hipsters hover at this leafy, pretty Platz on Sundays. This smaller market is excellent for vintage army gear, records, furniture and 1970s lamps.

An Sonntagen ist dieser hübsche, grüne Platz Mittes angesagtester Treffpunkt. Der kleine Flohmarkt ist perfekt für alte Armeeklamotten, Platten, Möbel und Lampen aus den 1970ern Jahren.

Chaque dimanche, tout Mitte se retrouve sur cette jolie place arborée. Ce petit marché est idéal pour dénicher de vieux vêtements militaires, des disques, des meubles vintage et des lampes années 70.

Arkonaplatz
10435 Berlin (Mitte)
Sunday 10.00–18.00

Flohmarkt Treptow

Great for everything from sleek, Easy Rider-era motorcycle jumpsuits, to old Céline bags, to totally kitsch Art Deco lamps. Bargaining is essential.

Ein toller Flohmarkt für alles mögliche, von engen Motorradoveralls aus der Easy-Rider-Zeit über alte Céline-Taschen bis hin zu total kitschigen Art-Deco-Lampen. Handeln ist hier Pflicht.

On y trouve de tout : des superbes combinaisons de motard à la Easy Rider aux vieux sacs Céline en passant par des lampes Art Déco totalement kitsch. Pas toujours évident de marchander les prix.

Eichenstraße 4
12435 Berlin (Treptow)
Saturday/Sunday 10.00–17.00

RESTAURANTS

Prater

Traditional, if slightly updated, German restaurant with a wonderful beer garden which also happens to be the oldest one in Berlin. Authentic and cool.

Dezent auf den Stand der Zeit gebrachte Traditionsgaststätte mit bezauberndem Biergarten, übrigens dem ältesten in Berlin. Authentisch und cool.

Un restaurant allemand traditionnel, bien que légèrement modernisé, et un merveilleux bar à bière en extérieur qui se trouve être le plus ancien de Berlin. Ambiance authentique et décontractée.

Kastanienallee 7–9
10435 Berlin (Prenzlauer Berg)
Tel. +49 (0)30 4485 688

Borchardt

If you want to have an intimate look at the German establishment – from politicians and actresses to the heads of industry – visit this restaurant, and delight yourself with the French cuisine while you're at it.

Wer das deutsche Establishment – von Politikern und Schauspielerinnen bis hin zu Wirtschaftsbossen – aus nächster Nähe betrachten möchte, ist in diesem Restaurant richtig. Und kann sich nebenbei noch mit französischer Küche verwöhnen lassen.

Si vous voulez vous faire une idée de l'establishment allemand, des hommes politiques aux actrices en passant par les hommes d'affaires, réservez une table dans ce restaurant, et profitez-en pour déguster sa délicieuse cuisine française.

Französische Straße 47
10117 Berlin (Mitte)
+49 (0)30 2038 7110

Sasaya

Reservations are recommended at this elegant and understated Japanese restaurant; the husband and wife owners serve the most delicate and irresistible sashimi in Berlin.

Reservierungen sind bei diesem eleganten, aber zugleich minimalistischen Japaner zu empfehlen. Die Besitzer servieren das köstlichste und unwiderstehlichste Sashimi Berlins.

Nous vous conseillons de réserver votre table si vous tenez à tester ce restaurant japonais élégant et discret géré par un couple; on y mange les sashimi les plus délicats et les plus fondants de Berlin.

Lychener Straße 50
10437 Berlin (Prenzlauer Berg)
Tel: +49 (0)30 4471 7721

Due Forni

This delicious and inexpensive pizzeria comes closest to welcoming Naples to Berlin. Its large outdoor terrace during the summer months is an irresistible destination. Also visit their sister restaurant along the canal in Kreuzberg, Casolare.

Mit dieser phantastischen und preiswerten Pizzeria kommen Sie Neapel so nahe, wie das in Berlin nur möglich ist. Die große Terrasse ist in den Sommermonaten ein unwiderstehlicher Anziehungspunkt. Besuchen Sie auch das Partnerlokal Casolare am Kanal in Kreuzberg.

Cette pizzeria délicieuse et pas chère, c'est un peu Naples qui débarque à Berlin. En été, sa grande terrasse extérieure est particulièrement prisée. Essayez également Casolare, leur autre restaurant situé le long du canal à Kreuzberg.

Schönhauser Allee 12
10119 Berlin (Mitte)
Tel. +49 (0)30 4401 7333

BARS

Schwarzsauer

A place to sit and enjoy the passing crowds of Mitte and Prenzlauer Berg hipsters from morning to night.

Hier sitzt man richtig, um von morgens früh bis tief in die Nacht das ständig wechselnde Publikum von Hipstern aus Mitte und Prenzlauer Berg an sich vorüberziehen zu lassen.

Un lieu idéal pour s'asseoir et regarder défiler du matin au soir la faune bigarrée des branchés de Mitte et de Prenzlauer Berg.

Kastanienallee 16
10435 Berlin (Prenzlauer Berg)
Tel. +49 (0)30 4485 633

Weekend

Recline on the black leather divans and take in the dancing and oh-so-fashionable bar scene. It is worth the visit for the panorama view of Alexanderplatz alone. Only open Thursdays, Fridays and Saturdays after 23:00.

Lehnen Sie sich auf den schwarzen Lederdiwanen zurück und lassen Sie die tanzenden ach-so-modischen Barbesucher auf sich wirken. Allein der Panoramablick auf den Alexanderplatz ist einen Besuch wert. Nur donnerstags, freitags und samstags ab 23 h geöffnet.

Relaxez-vous dans ses divans de cuir noir et observez les habitués de ce bar dansant on ne peut plus tendance. Il mérite le détour, ne serait-ce que pour sa vue panoramique sur l'Alexanderplatz. Ouvert uniquement le jeudi, le vendredi et le samedi à partir de 23h00.

Alexanderplatz 5, 12th floor
10178 Berlin (Mitte)
www.week-end-berlin.de

Paris Bar

A renowned hot-spot bar and restaurant for actors, artists, designers and powerbrokers in (West) Berlin for over 50 years. In recent years they have extended their space to a bar next door. A true institution, the likes of which are rare in Berlin.

Seit über 50 Jahren als Bar und Restaurant ein berühmter Treffpunkt für Schauspieler, Künstler, Designer und einflussreiche Leute aus Politik und Wirtschaft in (West-)Berlin. Vor ein paar Jahren hat man die Räumlichkeiten um eine Bar nebenan erweitert. Eine echte Institution, wie es sie in Berlin sonst nur selten gibt.

Ce bar-restaurant est réputé depuis plus de 50 ans comme le rendez-vous de prédilection des acteurs, des artistes, des créateurs et des puissants du jour de Berlin (Ouest). Récemment, les propriétaires ont racheté l'enseigne d'à côté pour agrandir le bar. Une institution comme il y en a peu à Berlin.

Kantstraße 152
10623 Berlin (Charlottenburg)
Tel. +49 (0)30 3138 052
www.parisbar.de

Münzsalon

This membership-only, super-hip spot for the fashion and art scene (with a very democratic € 4 entry for non-members) inhabits a beautiful, enormous Mitte apartment. Go for an intimate cocktail, or call ahead for a list of the weeks' parties and events.

Dieser superhippe Treff der Mode- und Kunstszene (eigentlich nur für Mitglieder, aber gegen moderate 4 € finden auch Nicht-Mitglieder Einlass) befindet sich in einer schönen riesigen Wohnung in Mitte. Gehen Sie auf einen gemütlichen Cocktail hin oder lassen Sie sich telefonisch über die Parties und Events der Woche informieren.

Fréquenté par le petit monde de l'art et de la mode, ce club privé hyper tendance (avec une entrée très démocratique à 4 € pour les non-membres) s'est installé dans un sublime et vaste appartement de Mitte. Allez-y pour un cocktail intime entre amis, ou téléphonez pour obtenir le programme des soirées et des événements de la semaine.

Münzstraße 23
10178 Berlin (Mitte)
Tel. +49 (0)30 2809 6807
www.munzsalon.net

HOTELS

Dorint am Gendarmenmarkt Berlin

Karl Lagerfeld stays here, so why not you? This hotel boasts a modern interior, intimate atmosphere and great views across the Gendarmenmarkt from the rooms as well as from the exceptional health spa.

Hier steigt Karl Lagerfeld ab, warum also nicht auch Sie? Bietet modernes Interieur, intime Atmosphäre und einen schönen Blick auf den Gendarmenmarkt – sowohl aus den Zimmern wie auch aus dem erstklassigen Spa.

Karl Lagerfeld y descend, alors pourquoi pas vous ? Décoration intérieure moderne, atmosphère intime et vue imprenable sur Gendarmenmarkt depuis toutes les chambres, sans mentionner un exceptionnel centre de remise en forme.

Charlottenstraße 50–52
10117 Berlin
Tel. +49 (0)30 2037 50
www.dorint.de/berlin-Gendarmenmarkt

Art'otel Ermelerhaus Berlin

Art'otel dedicates its space to original works of art by Georg Baselitz, A. R. Penck and Andy Warhol. From the Philippe Starck bathrooms to the Rococo dining rooms, the Art'otel is all about the fusion of old and new.

An den Wänden hängen Originale von Georg Baselitz, A. R. Penck und Andy Warhol. Und von den Philippe-Starck-Bädern bis zu den Rokoko-Speiseräumen steht das Art'otel für die ultramoderne Fusion von Alt und Neu.

L'Art'otel consacre ses murs à des œuvres de Georg Baselitz, A. R. Penck et Andy Warhol. Des salles de bains conçues par Philippe Starck aux salons rococo, cet hôtel est entièrement placé sous le signe de la fusion entre l'ancien et le moderne.

Wallstraße 70–73
10179 Berlin
Tel. +49 (0)30 2406 20
www.artotel.de

Adlon Kempinski Hotel

After a full-glitz makeover in 1997, this landmark luxury hotel is the favourite for politicians and celebs like Michael Jackson alike. It boasts a serene wellness spa, and sits right in front of the famed Brandenburg Gates.

Nach der gründlichen Totalüberholung 1997 gilt das berühmte Luxushotel als Lieblingsherberge von Politikern und Promis wie Michael Jackson. Man rühmt sich seines beschaulichen Wellness-Spas und genießt die Lage direkt neben dem Brandenburger Tor.

Depuis sa brillante rénovation en 1997, cet incontournable hôtel de luxe est devenu le préféré des hommes politiques et des célébrités, notamment Michael Jackson. Il possède un espace forme et bien-être à l'ambiance sereine et se trouve juste en face de la célèbre porte de Brandebourg.

Unter den Linden 77
10117 Berlin
Tel. +49 (0)30 2261 0
www.hotel-adlon.de

AIRPORTS

Berlin-Schönefeld

12521 Berlin

Berlin-Tegel

13405 Berlin

Berlin Tempelhof

12101 Berlin

All airports are served by a centralised call centre and website (the latter mainly in German).

Alle drei Flughäfen betreiben ein zentrales Callcenter und eine gemeinsame Website.

Tous les aéroports berlinois sont reliés à un centre d'appels et à un site Web (principalement rédigé en allemand).

Tel. +49 (0)180 5000 186
www.berlin-airport.de

What makes Florence special to you? Aside from being 'unique' to me because it was where I was born, Florence is a very special place. Around every corner there is a small surprise, it is food for one's inspiration and fantasy Where is the best place to stay in Florence? The best place in my opinion is Villa San. Michele in Fiesole. It used to be a monastery, which adds to its charm, and it has an incredible view of Florence. If you prefer something in town there is always The Savoy located on the historical Piazza della Reppublica, close to Brunelleschi's Duomo. Where is your favourite place to eat in Florence? Probably the best place for dinner is my house with my family. I also recommend a visit the Giacosa Cafè, the historical tea house of the city that I have restored and personalised with my designs. Where is your favourite place to shop in Florence? Obviously, the Roberto Cavalli Boutique at Via Tornabuoni 83! ROBERTO CAVALLI

FLORENCE

TEXT BY ELENA MORETTI

Global nomads passing through Florence seek out three attractions: Brunelleschi's stunning cupola, an exciting shopping experience and the glamorous atmosphere provided by the sophisticated lifestyles of its inhabitants. After a long period of lethargy, it seems that the revival of Florence has finally occurred. The Tuscan tourist magnet is trying to expand beyond its traditional image as a city-museum and has rediscovered its talent for experimentation and research. High-quality private and public designs – by renowned names including Norman Foster, Jean Nouvel and Michele Bonan – trace the outline of a new city, and the biannual Pitti Immagine Uomo menswear event not only showcases men's apparel for the seasons to come, but also what's new on the retail scene for luxury houses and designer labels. In short, the 'city of Art' is fast becoming a 'city of Style'. The Salvatore Ferragamo fashion group was one of the first to move in this direction, introducing an innovative concept to hospitality with its Lungarno Hotels; in the brand's showroom-store, Lungarno Details Shop, visitors can choose furnishings and accessories they have seen in the hotel buildings. Sophisticated lighting and interior design abound in Florence, particularly on the glitziest shopping streets – basically Via de' Tornabuoni, Via della Vigna Nuova and Via Roma. Sink your feet into the magnificent carpet of the Casadei boutique, then flop into one of the lush seats and have an assistant bring you heaps of spiky heels in a multitude of colours and shapes. Try out Emilio Pucci's patterned silk frocks and spangled and sequinned jeans by Roberto Cavalli. In Florence, the ultimate consumer experience is to be found in narrow medieval streets where fashion thrives alongside artisan and handcraft shops and, of course, the best art galleries in the world. Florence now offers 21st century design and an awesome cultural and artistic history, side by side.

Kosmopoliten, die heute durch Florenz streifen, haben drei Attraktionen im Sinn: die atemberaubend schöne Kuppel von Brunelleschi, ein Einkaufserlebnis der absoluten Spitzenklasse und die glamouröse Atmosphäre des neuesten In-Viertels. Nach einer langen Phase der Lethargie erlebt Florenz endlich eine Renaissance. Man versucht das althergebrachte Image von der Museumsstadt loszuwerden und Geschmack an Experimenten und neuen Entdeckungen zu finden. Bestes Design im privaten wie im öffentlichen Bereich – von bekannten Namen wie Norman Foster, Jean Nouvel und Michele Bonan – prägen das Antlitz einer Stadt, die eine neue, ihrer kulturellen Bedeutung entsprechende Identität sucht. Daher ist die zweimal jährlich stattfindende Messe Pitti Immagine Uomo nicht nur ein Schaufenster für die Herrenkleidung der kommenden Saison, sondern auch Neuigkeitenbörse für die Einzelhandelsszene der Luxus- und Designerlabels. Die Devise lautet im Moment, die „Stadt der Kunst" in die „Stadt des Stils" zu verwandeln. Der Modekonzern Salvatore Ferragamo war einer der Ersten auf dem Weg in diese Richtung: In seinen Lungarno-Hotels führte man ein innovatives Konzept zur Gastlichkeit ein, und auch in dem historischen Häuserblock hinter dem Ponte Vecchio arbeitete man an einer Metamorphose. In dem Schauraum-Laden namens Lungarno Detail Shop können Kunden sich Möbel und Accessoires aussuchen, die sie in den Hotels gesehen haben. Raffinierte Beleuchtung und Inneneinrichtung im Überfluss prägen auch die eleganten Boutiquen und trendigen Spezialgeschäfte in den belebtesten Einkaufsstraßen –

vor allem in der Via de' Tornabuoni, Via della Vigna Nuova und Via Roma. Hier werden Sie oft merken, dass alles in weichen, dezenten Luxus gehüllt ist. Lassen Sie etwa Ihre Füße in den prächtigen Teppich der Boutique Casadei sinken, lassen Sie sich sodann in einem der ausladenden Sessel nieder und lassen Sie sich von einer Verkäuferin haufenweise hochhackige Schuhe in unzähligen Farben und Formen bringen. Probieren Sie auch eines der gemusterten Seidenkleider von Emilio Pucci, und falls Ihnen der Sinn nach einem Paar Jeans steht, etwa von Roberto Cavalli, achten Sie darauf, dass dieses mit Pailletten und Glitzer versehen ist. Abgesehen von diesem kosmopolitischen Mikrokosmos erleben Sie natürlich auch die schmalen, mittelalterlichen Gassen, die zauberhaften Kunstgewerbeläden am linken Ufer des Flusses, die ihre Waren nach wie vor von Hand herstellen. Und all das ist geprägt von der stillen, zurückhaltenden Eleganz der echten florentinischen Gemütsverfassung. Perfektes Design im Herzen der Tradition.

Les nomades du monde qui passent par Florence y viennent désormais pour trois attractions principales : la magnifique coupole de Brunelleschi, une profusion de boutiques hors pair et l'atmosphère glamour qui se dégage du nouveau quartier de la mode. Après une longue période de léthargie, Florence vit enfin son renouveau tant attendu. En cherchant à se débarrasser de son image historique de ville-musée, elle a redécouvert le goût de l'expérimentation et de la recherche. Les grands travaux de premier plan signés par d'illustres noms tels que Norman Foster, Jean Nouvel et Michele Bonan dessinent la carte d'une nouvelle ville, en quête d'une identité à la hauteur de son rôle culturel. En conséquence, le salon bisannuel Pitti Immagine Uomo présente non seulement les collections masculines des saisons à venir, mais également les nouveautés florentines à l'attention des maisons de luxe et des griffes de créateurs. Actuellement, le but consiste à transformer la « cité de l'Art » en « cité du Style ». Le groupe Salvatore Ferragamo a été l'un des premiers à prendre cette direction en lançant un concept hôtelier innovant avec ses hôtels Lungarno qui métamorphosent un très ancien bloc d'immeubles derrière le Ponte Vecchio. Dans la boutique showroom Lungarno Details Shop, les visiteurs peuvent acheter les meubles et les objets de décoration qu'ils ont repérés dans ces hôtels. La sophistication de l'éclairage et du design d'intérieur s'applique également aux boutiques raffinées et autres espaces de vente individuels très tendance, situés dans les rues commerçantes les plus chic, principalement Via de' Tornabuoni, Via della Vigna Nuova et Via Roma. Ici, vous remarquerez que tout semble enveloppé d'un luxe sobre et discret. Enfoncez vos pieds dans la sublime moquette de la boutique Casadei, puis plongez dans l'un de leurs luxueux fauteuils et demandez à un vendeur de vous apporter des tas de talons aiguilles déclinés dans une multitude de couleurs et de formes. Puis essayez l'une des robes en soie à motifs d'Emilio Pucci, et si vous cherchez un jean, par exemple de Roberto Cavalli, assurez-vous qu'il soit orné de paillettes et de strass. A côté d'un microcosme aussi cosmopolite, vous découvrirez également les étroites et minuscules rues médiévales, les merveilleux ateliers d'artisans de la rive gauche qui fabriquent encore eux-mêmes leurs produits, dans un monde où tout partage l'élégance tranquille de la véritable ambiance florentine : un havre du design en plein cœur de la tradition.

FASHION SHOWS AND FAIRS

Pitti Immagine Uomo

The first and most complete Italian exhibition dedicated to menswear, which takes place twice a year – in mid-January and late June – at the Fortezza da Basso. An extraordinary world preview of clothing and accessories collections hosted by Pitti Immagine in a design dimension of continuous research, and promoted by the Centro di Firenze per la Moda Italiana.

Die erste und umfassendste Messe für italienische Herrenmode, die zweimal jährlich – Mitte Januar und Ende Juni – in der Fortezza da Basso stattfindet. Diese außergewöhnliche Weltpremiere von Kleider- und Accessoirekollektionen wird von Pitti Immagine in einer sich ständig weiterentwickelnden Designdimension präsentiert, gefördert vom Centro di Firenze per la Moda Italiana.

Le premier salon et le plus complet d'Italie dédié à la mode pour homme, organisé deux fois par an (mi-janvier et fin juin) à la Fortezza da Basso. Une avant-première mondiale des collections de vêtements et d'accessoires organisée par Pitti Immagine dans un esprit créatif de recherche continue et dont la promotion est assurée par le Centro di Firenze per la Moda Italiana.

Pitti Immagine Bimbo

The fair is the international leader in medium-high and high fashion childrenswear. This world premier of clothing and accessories collections for children and teens (0 to 18 years), maternity wear, and childcare products, is held in January and early July at the Fortezza da Basso, and it usually includes a range of fashion shows.

Diese Messe ist führend im Bereich Kindermode der gehobenen und höchsten Preislage. Die Weltpremiere für Kleider- und Accessoirekollektionen für Kinder und Teens (0–18 Jahre), Umstandsmode und diverse Produkte für Kinder findet jeweils im Januar und Anfang Juli in der Fortezza da Basso und begleitet von diversen Modenschauen statt.

Ce salon est le leader mondial de la mode milieu de gamme et haut de gamme pour enfant. Organisée en janvier et début juin à la Fortezza da Basso, cette avant-première internationale des collections de mode et d'accessoires pour les enfants et les adolescents (de 0 à 18 ans), de vêtements de grossesse et de produits de soin pour enfant s'accompagne généralement de toute une série de défilés de mode.

Pitti Immagine Filati

Twice a year – in early February and July – this exhibition of yarn collections for the knitting industry holds a key position on the international trade fair calendar, and continues to vigorously support quality, selection, trends and the avant-garde.

Zweimal jährlich – Anfang Februar und im Juli – findet diese Messe für Garnkollektionen der Strickwarenindustrie statt und belegt ihre Schlüsselposition im internationalen Messekalender. Qualität, Vielfalt, Trends und Avantgarde finden hier seit Jahren tatkräftige Unterstützung.

Deux fois par an, début février et en juillet, ce salon du fil dédié à l'industrie de la maille démontre son positionnement clé en tant qu'événement de référence et de prestige sur le calendrier international des salons professionnels et continue à promouvoir avec conviction la qualité, le luxe, les tendances et l'avant-garde.

Pitti Immagine Fragranze

Fragranze is the only show of its kind in Europe dedicated to the world's finest makers of perfumes and fragrances. Held in mid-September in the striking venue of the Limonaie of Giardino Corsini, it is organized by Pitti Immagine.

Inzwischen findet die Fragranze schon zum dritten Mal statt. Die einzige Messe ihrer Art in ganz Europa für die besten Parfümeure und Dufthersteller der Welt. Das Ganze ereignet sich Mitte September im imposanten Limonaie des Giardino Corsini unter der Regie von Pitti Immagine.

Aujourd'hui à sa troisième édition, Fragranze est le seul salon européen consacré aux plus grands fabricants de fragrances et parfumeurs du monde. Organisé mi-septembre par Pitti Immagine dans les sublimes Limonaie du Giardino Corsini.

Pitti Immagine
Via Faenza, 111
50123 Florence
Tel. +39 055 36931
www.pittimmagine.com

Prato Expo

The most prestigious firms in the Prato area present their collections to a selected, qualified clientele at Prato Expo, an international trade fair for the textile sector. It is held twice a year at the Fortezza da Basso.

Bei dieser internationalen Textilmesse präsentieren die angesehensten Firmen aus dem Raum Prato ihre Kollektionen einem ausgesuchten Publikum von Experten. Der Event findet zweimal jährlich, jeweils für die Frühjahr/Sommer- und die Herbst/Winter-Kollektion in der Fortezza da Basso statt. Seine Bedeutung wird noch dadurch unterstrichen, dass sich hier eine wichtige Industrieregion, die vor allem von kleinen und mittleren Unternehmen geprägt wird, darstellt.

Les sociétés les plus prestigieuses de Prato présentent leurs collections devant une clientèle triée sur le volet lors de Prato Expo, salon international du secteur textile. Il a lieu deux fois par an à la Fortezza da Basso, d'abord pour les collections printemps/été puis pour les collections automne/hiver. Il est d'autant plus important qu'il offre une plate-forme d'expression aux petites et moyennes entreprises qui composent cet important secteur industriel.

Prato Expo
Via Valentini,14
59100 Prato
Tel. +39 0574455280
www.pratoexpo.com

The Vintage Selection

The fair features a great selection of the most important Italian and foreign vintage – clothing, accessories as well as furnishing items. The event is held concurrently with Pitti Filati and its organized by the Stazione Leopolda srl in collaboration with A. N. G. E. L. O.

Diese Messe zeigt eine riesige Auswahl der wichtigsten italienischen und ausländischen Vintage-Mode, Vintage-Accessoires und auch alter Einrichtungsgegenstände. Das Ganze findet parallel zu Pitti Filati statt und wird von der Stazione Leopolda srl in Zusammenarbeit mit A. N. G. E. L. O. veranstaltet.

Ce salon présente une sélection des meilleurs spécialistes de la mode vintage (vêtements, accessoires et meubles) italiens et étrangers. Organisé par Stazione Leopolda srl en collaboration avec A. N. G. E. L. O., l'événement a lieu en même temps que Pitti Filati.

Via Faenza, 113
50123 Florence
Tel. +39 055 212622
www.stazione-leopolda.com

FASHION SCHOOLS

Polimoda

International institute of fashion design and marketing
Polimoda organizes specialised courses in design, production, commercialisation and marketing, with the aim to create a close collaboration between the academic and production worlds, besides providing a constant comparison with the international scene. Founded on the initiative of the City Halls of Florence and Prato, in collaboration with the Fashion Institute of Technology of the State University of New York.

Polimoda veranstaltet spezielle Kurse für Design, Produktion, Vermarktung und Marketing mit dem Ziel einer engen Verknüpfung zwischen akademischem Bereich und Produktion. Außerdem sieht man sich in ständigem Wettstreit mit der internationalen Modeschulszene. Gegründet wurde die Schule auf Initiative der Rathäuser von Florenz und Prato, in Zusammenarbeit mit dem Fashion Institute of Technology der State University of New York.

Polimoda propose des cours spécialisés en création, production, commercialisation et marketing de la mode et vise à développer une étroite collaboration entre les mondes universitaire et professionnel tout en assurant une comparaison constante avec le panorama international. L'école a été fondée à l'initiative et grâce au soutien financier des Villes de Florence et de Prato, en collaboration avec le Fashion Institute of Technology de l'université de l'Etat de New York.

Villa Strozzi – Via Pisana, 77
50143 Florence
Tel. +39 055 739961/7399631/717173
www.polimoda.com

Accademia Italiana

A fashion school since 1984, Accademia Italiana offers professional courses and academic programs, as well as master courses at university level. The summer courses are moreover particularly indicated for those who wish to spend their vacation in a profitable manner, acquiring new knowledge and skills. Among the courses available: Italian language, drawing and painting, fashion design, window display design.

Die 1984 gegründete Modeschule bietet professionelle Kurse und Vorlesungen sowie Master-Studiengänge auf Hochschulniveau. Die Sommerkurse sind für Leute gedacht, die ihre Ferien sinnvoll nutzen wollen, um sich neue Kenntnisse und Fertigkeiten anzueignen. Die angebotenen Kurse umfassen u. a. Italienisch, Zeichnen und Malerei, Modedesign und Schaufenstergestaltung.

Ecole de mode depuis 1984, Accademia Italiana propose des formations professionnelles, des programmes d'enseignement et des Masters de niveau universitaire. Les cours d'été sont particulièrement recommandés à ceux qui souhaitent profiter de leurs vacances pour acquérir de nouvelles connaissances et compétences. Parmi les spécialités disponibles: langue italienne, dessin et peinture, création de mode et création de vitrines.

Piazza Pitti, 15
50125 Florence
Tel. +39 055 211619
www.accademiaitaliana.com

L'Atelier

The Atelier is specialised in teaching fashion, jewellery and interior design to international students who aspire to participate in a study abroad experience in Florence. Everyone will have the opportunity to fully understand Italian style and to create a personal collection through the study of fabrics, fashion techniques and costume history.

Das Atelier hat sich auf Lehrveranstaltungen in Mode, Schmuck- und Einrichtungsdesign für internationale Studenten spezialisiert, die in Florenz ausländische Studienerfahrung sammeln wollen. Hier hat jeder Gelegenheit, italienische Eleganz von Grund auf kennen zu lernen und sich mit Hilfe des Studiums von Stoffen, Techniken und Kostümgeschichte eine individuelle Kollektion zu erarbeiten.

L'Atelier propose des cours de mode, de bijouterie et de design d'intérieur aux étudiants internationaux qui souhaitent participer à un programme d'études à l'étranger à Florence. Tous y ont la possibilité de mieux comprendre le style italien et de réaliser une collection personnelle en étudiant les tissus, les techniques de couture et l'histoire du costume.

Via de' Bardi, 46
50125 Florence
Tel. +39 055 2657962
www.atelierfirenze.it

FASHION MUSEUMS AND GALLERIES

The Costume Gallery
The Costume Gallery occupies a wing of the Pitti Palace overlooking the Boboli Gardens. Its collection comprises six thousand items including costumes and accessories dating from the 16th to the 20th centuries. It is the only museum of the history of fashion in Italy and one of the most important in the world. A selection is exhibited in rotation every two years. There are frequent special exhibitions devoted to particular aspects of the collection.

The Costume Gallery nimmt einen Flügel des Palazzo Pitti mit Blick auf die Boboli-Gärten ein. Die Sammlung umfasst 6000 Exponate, Kleidung und Accessoires vom 16. bis 20. Jahrhundert. Es ist das einzige Museum für Modegeschichte in ganz Italien und eines der wichtigsten der Welt. Alle zwei Jahre wird die Auswahl der gezeigten Stücke im Rotationsprinzip ausgetauscht. Oft gibt es auch Sonderausstellungen zu besonderen Aspekten der Sammlung.

La Costume Gallery occupe toute une aile du palais Pitti qui donne sur les jardins de Boboli. Sa collection comprend six mille pièces, notamment des costumes et des accessoires du XVIᵉ au XXᵉ siècle. C'est le seul et unique musée d'histoire de la mode en Italie mais également l'un des plus importants au monde. Il expose une sélection de sa collection en rotation tous les deux ans et organise souvent des expositions spéciales autour d'un thème particulier de sa collection.

Piazza Pitti, 1
50125 Firenze
Tel. +39 055 2388763
www.uffizi.firenze.it

The Salvatore Ferragamo Museum
Besides photographs, patents, sketches, magazines and wooden lasts of famous feet, the museum hosts a collection of over 10,000 shoes designed by Salvatore Ferragamo from the end of the '20s until 1960, the year of his death.

Neben Fotografien, Urkunden, Zeichnungen, Zeitschriften und hölzernen Leisten berühmter Füße besitzt das Museum eine Sammlung von mehr als 10 000 von Salvatore Ferragamo entworfenen Schuhen, von Ende der 1920er Jahre bis zum Sterbejahr des Designers 1960.

Outre les photos, les brevets, les esquisses, les magazines et les formes en bois de pieds célèbres, le musée expose une collection de plus de 10 000 chaussures conçus par Salvatore Ferragamo en personne, de la fin des années 20 jusqu'en 1960, l'année de sa mort.

Palazzo Spini Feroni
Via de' Tornabuoni, 2
50123 Florence
http://www.museoferragamo.it

The Textile Museum of Prato
This first museum preserves more than six thousand samples of fabric datable from the 5th century A. D. up to the present day. The museum includes a contemporary textile section, deriving from constant contact between the museum and the local companies.

Passenderweise in einer Stadt, die seit dem Mittelalter ihren Ruf der Textilherstellung verdankt, hütet dieses Museum einen Schatz aus über 6000 Proben von Stoffen, die ältesten aus dem 5. Jahrhundert n. Chr., die jüngsten aus der Gegenwart. Das Museum umfasst auch eine moderne Textilwerkstatt, die sich dem engen Kontakt zu den ortsansässigen Firmen verdankt.

Installé dans une ville qui entretient sa vocation pour l'industrie textile depuis le Moyen Age, ce museum conserve plus de 6000 échantillons de tissu datant du Vᵉ siècle avant J.-C. jusqu'à aujourd'hui. Le circuit du musée inclut une section dédiée aux textiles contemporains, née de la collaboration permanente entre le musée et les entreprises locales.

Via Santa Chiara, 24
59100 Prato
Tel. +39 0574 611503
http://www.po-net.prato.it

FASHION SHOPS

BP Studio
In the heart of the elegant via della Vigna, BP Studio displays a truly amazing range of luxury cashmere knitwear, from soft twin sets to geometric, high-necked sweaters, to fancy accessories. Alongside the cashmere collection, you'll find a limited selection of garments by Paul Smith, Alberto Biani and Pringle of Scotland.

Mitten auf der eleganten Via della Vigna präsentiert BP Studio eine wahrlich erstaunliche Auswahl luxuriöser Kaschmir-Strickwaren. Von weichen Twinsets über geometrische Rollkragenpullover bis hin zu hübschen Accessoires. Neben der Kaschmirkollektion finden Sie hier auch eine Auswahl von Kreationen von Paul Smith, Alberto Biani und Pringle of Scotland.

Au cœur de l'élégante Via della Vigna, BP Studio présente une sélection de maille en cachemire de luxe vraiment incroyable : twin-sets tout doux, pulls géométriques à col montant et accessoires originaux. A côté de la collection en cachemire, vous trouverez une petite sélection de vêtements griffés Paul Smith, Alberto Biani ou Pringle of Scotland.

Via della Vigna Nuova, 15r
50123 Florence
Tel. +39 055 213243
www.bpstudio.it

Gerard Company
A mixture of shop labels, up-to-the-minute and exclusive brands – among others, Helmut Lang, Chloé, Marc Jacobs, Alexander McQueen – just metres from the ancient Piazza della Signoria. This is one of the most popular stores in town, and has opened a sister shop dedicated to vintage and childrenswear.

Eine Mischung aus topaktuellen und exklusiven Labels – darunter Helmut Lang, Chloé, Marc Jacobs und Alexander McQueen – und das nur ein paar Schritte von der historischen Piazza della Signoria entfernt. Einer der beliebtesten Läden der Stadt. Inzwischen gibt es schon einen Ableger für Vintage und Youngwear.

Un mélange entre griffes de créateurs d'avant-garde et marques de luxe, entre autres Helmut Lang, Chloé, Marc Jacobs et Alexander McQueen, à deux pas de l'antique Piazza della Signoria. Cette boutique, l'une des plus courues de la ville, a ouvert un second espace de vente dédié au vintage et au « youngwear ».

Via Vacchereccia, 18r
50122 Florence
Tel. +39 055 215942

Guya
If you aren't in the slightest bit enamoured of ladylike elegance, you'll probably love the mix-and-unmatched mood favoured by this shop. Boho chic, with a blend of offbeat designer names.

Wenn Sie mit damenhafter Eleganz nichts anfangen können, dann wird ihnen die kunterbunte Kombinationslust dieses ganz anderen Ladens bestimmt zusagen. Einen Schritt weiter als Boho Chic und mit einem Potpourri ausgefallener Designer.

Si vous ne vous sentez pas concerné par tous ces débats sur l'élégance féminine, vous allez probablement adorer le détonant métissage des genres prôné par cette boutique. Une alternative au chic bohème, avec un pot-pourri de créateurs excentriques.

Via Calimala, 29r
50122 Florence
Tel. +39 055 219163

Luisa Via Roma
Shocking windows, two floors, and all the labels shopaholics die for: Chloé, Dolce & Gabbana, Yohji Yamamoto, Antonio Marras, Rick Owens and more. An extraordinary accessories selection – including Luella and Balenciaga – is curated by eclectic owner Andrea Panconesi.

Schockierende Schaufenster, ein paar Mikrokosmen auf zwei Etagen und genau die Labels, für die Shopaholics alles tun würden: Chloé, Dolce & Gabbana, Yohji Yamamoto, Antonio Marras, Rick Owens und andere. Dazu noch eine außerordentliche Auswahl an Accessoires – von Luella und Balenciaga –, höchstpersönlich zusammengestellt von der vielseitigen Geschäftsinhaberin Andrea Panconesi.

Vitrines choquantes, deux étages divisés en petits microcosmes avec toutes les griffes pour lesquelles les accros du shopping sont prêtes à tuer : Chloé, Dolce & Gabbana, Yohji Yamamoto, Antonio Marras, Rick Owens et bien d'autres encore. Une sélection d'accessoires absolument extraordinaires (Luella, Balenciaga) choisis avec soin par Andrea Panconesi, l'éclectique propriétaire des lieux.

Via Roma, 19–21r
50123 Florence
Tel. +39 055 217826/7
www.luisaviaroma.com

Officina Profumo-Farmaceutica di Santa Maria Novella
Even if you're not exactly interested in purchasing essences, it is nevertheless worthwhile walking through the doors of one of the oldest pharmacies in the world. Founded in 1612 and still graced with frescoes and antiques, this stunning store stocks creams, scents and soaps made from

old recipes formulated by the Dominican monks.

Selbst wenn Sie eigentlich gar keine Duftessenzen kaufen wollen, lohnt sich ein Besuch in einer der ältesten Apotheken der Welt. Der 1612 gegründete, freskenverzierte und mit Antiquitäten eingerichtete Laden führt Cremes, Düfte und Seifen, die nach alten Rezepten der Dominikanermönche hergestellt sind.

Cette ex-pharmacie, l'une des plus anciennes du monde, vaut vraiment le détour même si vous n'êtes pas particulièrement intéressé par les essences. Fondée en 1612 et toujours décorée de fresques et d'antiquités, cette boutique très originale propose des crèmes, des parfums et des savons fabriqués à partir de formules ancestrales inventées par des moines dominicains.

Via della Scala, 16
50123 Florence
Tel. +39 055 216276
www.smnovella.it

Principe

Located on the corner of via Tornabuoni, this historic clothing emporium has dressed generations of Florentines. Now it offers high quality clothes and accessories for men, women and children, and a made-to-measure service with a wide range of fabrics.

Das historische Bekleidungshaus an der Ecke der Via Tornabuoni hat schon Generationen von Florentinern angezogen, mit seinem englisch beeinflussten Stil, der inzwischen zeitgemäß modernisiert wurde. Heute werden dort Kleider und Accessoires höchster Qualität für Herren, Damen und Kinder feilgeboten. Außerdem gibt es ein Maßatelier mit einer großen Auswahl Stoffen.

Situé au coin de la Via Tornabuoni, cet historique emporium de la mode a déjà habillé des générations entières de Florentins dans un style d'inspiration british et néanmoins moderne. Aujourd'hui, Principe propose des vêtements et des accessoires de grande qualité pour homme, pour femme et pour enfant, ainsi qu'un service de coupe sur mesure dans un large choix de tissus.

Via del Sole, 2
50123 Florence
Tel. +39 055 2399068
http://www.principedifirenze.com

Raspini

Frequently packed with celebrities and aristocrats, alongside its great range of some of the finest Italian labels (Prada, Fendi, Blumarine, Marni) Raspini displays a well-edited shoe collection. It has two other shops in Florence.

Oft wimmelt es hier von Prominenten und Aristokraten. Und neben der breiten Auswahl bester italienischer Marken (Prada, Fendi, Blumarine, Marni) bietet Raspini auch eine gut sortierte Schuhkollektion. Das Haus betreibt zwei Filialen in Florenz.

Souvent rempli de célébrités et d'aristocrates: Aux côtés de certaines des meilleures griffes italiennes (Prada, Fendi, Blumarine, Marni), Raspini propose aussi un choix de chaussures sélectionnées avec soin et possède deux autres boutiques à Florence.

Via Roma, 25–29r
Tel. +39 055 213077
50123 Firenze
www.raspini.com

Space

A veritable Mecca for fashion people and aesthetes. Search for garments with a strong urban character, or check out the stunning white space-pod store anyway, just for the sheer fun of it.

Ein echtes Mekka für Fashion-People und Ästheten. Stöbern Sie in Kleidern mit ausgeprägt urbanem Charakter, oder besuchen Sie die strahlend weiße Raumkapsel einfach nur zum Spaß.

La Mecque des fashion victims et autres esthètes. Vous y trouverez des vêtements au style très urbain, mais faites-y un tour de toutes façons, ne serait-ce que pour le simple plaisir de découvrir le décor de navette spatiale de cette étonnante boutique toute blanche.

Via de' Tornabuoni, 17r
50123 Florence
Tel. +39 055 216943

Spazio A

Six display windows looking out on the old and glamorous via Porta Rossa, an interior decoration minimalist in style, creating an innovative concept in stores. Technically speaking, this is a multi-designer-label, single-brand (Aeffe) store where you can find the best of Alberta Ferretti and Philosophy, Jean Paul Gaultier, Narciso Rodriguez and Moschino.

Sechs Schaufenster an der altehrwürdigen Via Porta Rossa, eine minimalistische Inneneinrichtung, die für ein innovatives Ladenkonzept sorgt. Genau betrachtet handelt es sich um einen Multi-Designer-Laden einer einzigen Marke – Aeffe. Hier finden Sie das Beste von Alberta Ferretti und Philosophy, Jean Paul Gaultier, Narciso Rodriguez und Moschino.

Six vitrines donnant sur la vénérable et glamour Via Porta Rossa et une décoration intérieure au style minimaliste produisent un concept innovant en matière d'espace de vente. Techniquement parlant, cette boutique multimarques appartient à une seule

griffe: Aeffe, où vous trouverez le meilleur d'Alberta Ferretti, Philosophy, Jean Paul Gaultier, Narciso Rodriguez et Moschino.

Via Porta Rossa, 103–115
50123 Florence
Tel. +39 055 212995

VINTAGE FASHION SHOPS

Elio Ferraro Gallery/Store

Walking in here is like stepping inside the glass displays at the Victoria & Albert Museum in London; you can actually touch original pieces by Hermès, Dior, Chanel and many others from the '30s onwards. No wonder creative teams from Calvin Klein and Emilio Pucci have visited in search of inspiration.

Wer hier hereinkommt, hat das Gefühl, eine Vitrine des Londoner Victoria & Albert Museums zu betreten. Hier kann man die Originale von Hermès, Dior, Chanel und vielen anderen Marken ab den 1930er Jahren tatsächlich berühren. Kein Wunder, dass die Kreativteams von Calvin Klein und Emilio Pucci hier schon nach Inspiration gesucht haben.

Entrer dans cette boutique revient à pénétrer dans les vitrines du Victoria & Albert Museum de Londres, sauf qu'ici on a le droit de toucher les pièces originales griffées Hermès, Dior, Chanel et bien d'autres, des années 30 à nos jours. Rien d'étonnant à ce que les équipes créatives de Calvin Klein et d'Emilio Pucci y passent régulièrement en quête d'inspiration.

Via del Parione, 47r
50123 Florence
Tel. +39 055 290425
www.elioferraro.com

Gerard Loft

Best known for must-have sportswear and funky denim from Levi's Red Line, Evisu, Vintage and Stone Island. Beside basic shop labels and new discoveries, you can comb the tiny corner dedicated to vintage garments.

Am bekanntesten ist der Laden für unverzichtbare Sportswear und unkonventionellen Denim von Levi's Red Line, Evisu, Vintage und Stone Island. Neben den wichtigsten Marken und neuen Entdeckungen gibt es noch eine kleine Ecke mit Vintage-Kleidung zum Stöbern.

Une boutique surtout connue pour ses pièces sportswear très recherchées et ses jeans funky griffés Levi's Red Line, Evisu, Vintage et Stone Island. Aux côtés des marques habituelles et des nouvelles découvertes, vous pourrez fouiller le minuscule stand dédié aux vêtements vintage.

Via de' Pecori, 34–40r
50123 Florence
Tel. +39 055 282491

FLEA MARKETS

San Lorenzo Market

From Piazza S. Lorenzo to Via dell'Ariento, all around the Basilica of San Lorenzo, winds the most important market in the city. A busy street market where you can purchase some excellent leather goods, jewellery and clothing, and there are usually some pretty designer-label accessories at low prices. In winter it is closed on Sundays and Mondays.

Von der Piazza S. Lorenzo bis zur Via dell'Ariento und rund um die Basilika San Lorenzo erstreckt sich der wichtigste Markt der Stadt. Ein geschäftiger Straßenmarkt, auf dem man hervorragende Lederwaren, Schmuck und Kleidung erstehen kann. Für gewöhnlich gibt es auch einige hübsche Designer-Accessoires zu günstigen Preisen. Im Winter bleibt der Markt Sonntags und Montags geschlossen.

De la Piazza S. Lorenzo à la Via dell'Ariento, le plus important marché de la ville rayonne autour de la basilique de San Lorenzo. Un marché de rue bruyant et bondé où vous pourrez acheter des articles de maroquinerie, des bijoux et des vêtements exceptionnels. On y trouve souvent certains accessoires de créateurs à prix modérés. Fermé le dimanche et le lundi en hiver.

Piazza S. Lorenzo
50123 Florence

Cascine Park

Probably the biggest and cheapest market in town. Every Tuesday morning (from 8am to 2pm), this market, which is situated in the Cascine Park along the A. Lincoln Avenue, is where Florentines go to buy bargain-priced clothes and shoes.

Der wahrscheinlich größte und günstigste Markt der Stadt. Jeden Dienstag (von 8 bis 14h) besuchen die Florentiner diesen Markt im Cascine Park an der Viale A. Lincoln, um preiswerte Kleider und Schuhe zu kaufen.

Probablement le plus vaste marché de la ville mais aussi le moins cher. Chaque mardi matin (de 8 à 14 heures), les Florentins vont marchander des vêtements et des chaussures à bon prix dans ce marché installé dans le parc Cascine le long de l'A. Lincoln Avenue.

Viale A. Lincoln
50144 Florence

Piazza dei Ciompi Market

Small daily flea market which is situated in Piazza dei Ciompi. If you're lucky to be here on the last Sunday of every month you'll see stalls running into the surrounding streets. There you can find furniture and objects from the past, prints, coins and cutlery, as well as affordable treasures amidst the bric-a-brac and dusty books.

Kleiner täglicher Markt auf der Piazza dei Ciompi. Wenn Sie das Glück haben, am letzten Sonntag des Monats hier zu sein, dann erstrecken sich die Stände bis in die Straßen rundherum. Hier entdeckt man Möbel und Objekte aus vergangenen Zeiten, Grafiken, Münzen und Besteck sowie bezahlbare Schätze zwischen viel Krimskrams und verstaubten Büchern.

Mini-marché aux puces quotidien situé Piazza dei Ciompi. Si vous avez la chance de vous y trouver le dernier dimanche du mois, vous pourrez voir ses stands déborder dans les rues du quartier. Au milieu du bric-à-brac et des livres poussiéreux, vous y trouverez des meubles et des objets anciens, des gravures, des pièces de monnaie, des couverts et autres trésors à prix abordable.

Piazza dei Ciompi
50122 Florence
Tel. +39 055 3283515

RESTAURANTS

Beccofino

Located on Lungarno Guicciardini, this is a hot spot with young Florentines. You can sip at the bar and then try a vaguely adventurous style of cooking. Chef Francesco Berardinelli is considered one of the new stars of Italian cuisine, revising Tuscan recipes with a twist. The great wine list is a good opportunity to try some lesser-known but fine blends.

Das Lokal am Lungarno Guicciardini ist ein gefragter Treffpunkt junger Florentiner. Man kann an der Bar einen Drink nehmen und dann die etwas abenteuerlustige Küche probieren. Küchenchef Francesco Berardinelli gilt als einer der neuen Stars der italienischen Gastronomie. Er versieht traditionelle toskanische Rezepte mit einem modernen Touch. Die großartige Weinkarte ist eine gute Gelegenheit, einmal weniger bekannte, aber edle Tropfen zu kosten.

Situé dans Lungarno Guicciardini, c'est l'un des repaires de prédilection de la jeunesse florentine. Vous pouvez siroter un cocktail au bar avant de déguster des plats plus ou moins audacieux. Considéré comme l'une des étoiles montantes de la cuisine italienne, le chef Francesco Berardinelli aime apporter sa touche décalée aux classiques toscans. La superbe carte de vins offre une bonne opportunité de goûter de bons crus moins connus.

Piazza degli Scarlatti, 1r – Lungarno
Guicciardini
50125 Florence
Tel. +39 055 290076

Il Cibrèo

Fabio Picchi, the owner, does not believe in serving pasta as a first course, but you won't miss it. Cibrèo is a gastronomic oasis, combining an elegant restaurant with a trattoria at its back door, and an exciting bar across the street. No table cloths or fine glassware at the trattoria, also known as the "poorman's" Cibrèo, and a limited, delicious version of the same menu.

Der Besitzer Fabio Picchi hält nichts von Pasta als erstem Gang, aber die werden Sie auch nicht vermissen. Das Cibrèo ist eine kulinarische Oase, die aus einem eleganten Restaurant mit Trattoria am Hintereingang und einer aufregenden Bar gleich gegenüber besteht. In der Trattoria, auch Cibrèo für Arme genannt, gibt es keine Tischdecken oder Gläser mit Stiel, dafür eine zwar begrenzte, aber ebenso köstliche Auswahl an Gerichten aus derselben Karte.

Le patron Fabio Picchi n'est pas fan de la tradition qui consiste à servir des pâtes en entrée, mais cela ne vous manquera pas. Cibrèo est un véritable oasis gastronomique avec un élégant restaurant, une trattoria dans l'arrière-cour et un bar très sympa de l'autre côté de la rue. Pas de nappes ni de verres à pied à la Trattoria, également connue comme le « Cibrèo du pauvre », avec une version limitée mais délicieuse du même menu.

Via Andrea del Verrocchio, 8r
50122 Florence
Tel. +39 055 2341100

Finisterrae

Restaurant and tapas bar in the Santa Croce area, Finisterrae is a homage to the variety of Mediterranean cuisine. An intriguing ambience in the heart of an antique palazzo is the starting point for a gastronomic voyage. From the authentic flavours of the Italian coast to spicy Lebanese cuisine, passing through the best that the tables of Spain and Portugal have to offer.

Restaurant und Tapas-Bar in der Gegend von Santa Croce. Das Finisterrae ist ein Geschenk der Vielfalt der Mittelmeerküche. Das ansprechende Ambiente mitten in einem historischen Palazzo ist der Ausgangspunkt einer gastronomischen Reise. Von den authentischen Aromen der italienischen Küste bis hin zur scharfen Küche des Libanon, vorbei am Besten, was Spanien und Portugal kulinarisch zu bieten haben.

Restaurant et bar à tapas dans le quartier de Santa Croce, Finisterrae est un hommage à la diversité de la cuisine méditerranéenne. Une ambiance captivante en plein cœur d'un palazzo ancien constitue le point de départ de votre voyage gastrono-

mique, des saveurs authentiques de la côte italienne aux plats libanais épicés en passant par le meilleur de la cuisine espagnole et portugaise.

Via de'Pepi, 5–7r
50122 Florence
Tel. +39 055 2638675

l'Garga

One of Florence's artsy hangouts. The interior has been decorated by Giuliano Gargani and his Canadian-born wife, Sharon Oddson. It's a frenzy of surrealist images and colour and the food reflects the artistic touches. International cuisine along with Sicilian dishes: great food in a fun atmosphere.

Einer der Künstlertreffs von Florenz. Die Einrichtung stammt von Giuliano Gargani und seiner in Kanada geborenen Ehefrau Sharon Oddson. Ein Rausch surrealistischer Bilder und Farben, und selbst das Essen hat einen künstlerischen Touch. Internationale und sizilianische Küche: prima Essen in witziger Atmosphäre.

L'un des repaires du petit monde artistique de Florence. L'intérieur a été décoré par Giuliano Gargani et son épouse canadienne Sharon Oddson. C'est un délire d'images et de couleurs surréalistes et le menu reflète ces touches artistiques. Plats internationaux et siciliens : excellente cuisine et atmosphère originale.

Via del Moro, 48
50123 Florence
Tel. +39 055 2398898

Momoyama

Technically operating as a club, this place touts itself as a sushi bar offering "inventive food". It is an original dining experience for Florence, with its bare minimalist ochre-coloured decor and tables spread over floors reaching well into the back. As you enter you will see a Japanese chef preparing sashimi and tekkamaki right in front of you.

Offiziell ein Club, wirbt dieses Lokal jedoch als Sushibar mit „kreativer Küche" für sich. In Florenz eine einzigartige Möglichkeit zum Abendessen. Das Dekor ist ockerfarben und minimalistisch, die niedrigen Tische sind weit bis in den hinteren Teil des Lokals verteilt. Wer eintritt, sieht als erstes einen japanischen Küchenchef, der Sashimi und Tekkamaki vor den Augen der Gäste zubereitet.

Fonctionnant techniquement comme un club, cet endroit se targue d'être un bar à sushi proposant une « cuisine inventive ». C'est un lieu original pour dîner à Florence, avec son décor dépouillé et minimaliste couleur ocre et ses innombrables tables. En entrant, vous découvrirez un chef japonais en train de préparer sashimi et tekkamaki juste sous vos yeux.

Borgo San Frediano, 10r
50124 Florence
Tel. +39 055 291840

Trattoria delle Belledonne

Just a few metres from via Tornabuoni, this is a real osteria where the menu is explained to you by the host. The ceramic-tiled tables, the menu written on a blackboard, all set the scene for Florence's version of a bistro. It was once a well kept secret, but has been popular with Americans since being featured in Bon Appetit magazine.

Nur ein paar Schritte von der Via Tornabuoni entfernt, stößt man auf diese echte Trattoria, in der die Speisenfolge vom Wirt persönlich vorgestellt wird. Gekachelte Tische, die Karte auf einer Schiefertafel, eben die florentinische Version eines Bistros. Das Lokal war ein Geheimtipp, bis es sich nach einem Porträt in der Zeitschrift Bon Appetit zum Lieblingslokal amerikanischer Touristen mauserte.

A quelques mètres de la Via Tornabuoni, voici une authentique osteria où le patron ne rechigne pas à vous traduire le menu. Tables en céramique, menu écrit à la craie sur un tableau noir : tous les ingrédients sont réunis pour en faire un bistrot version florentine. Autrefois uniquement connu des initiés, le restaurant accueille aujourd'hui beaucoup d'Américains depuis qu'il a bénéficié d'une critique dans le magazine Bon Appétit.

Via delle Belledonne, 16r
50123 Florence
Tel. +39 055 2382609

Trattoria Quattro Leoni

A corner of Old Florence not on the map. Only true Florentines know about this place, which is between via dello Sprone, via de' Vellutini and via Toscanella, at one time a house of tolerance. A classic for traditional Tuscan fare, but you might meet Sting or Dustin Hoffmann at one of the tables.

Ein Stückchen altes Florenz, wie man es auf keinem Stadtplan findet. Nur echte Florentiner kennen dieses ehemalige Bordell zwischen Via dello Sprone, Via de' Vellutini and Via Toscanella. Ein Klassiker für traditionelle toskanische Küche, allerdings kann es Ihnen passieren, dass Sting oder Dustin Hoffmann an einem der Tische sitzt.

Une adresse du Vieux Florence que vous ne trouverez pas sur la carte. Seuls les vrais Florentins connaissent cette ancienne maison close transformée en trattoria, située entre la Via dello Sprone, Via de' Vellutini et Via Toscanella. Un classique de la cuisine toscane traditionnelle, mais vous y croiserez peut-être Sting ou Dustin Hoffmann en train de dîner.

Via de' Vellutini, 1r – Piazza della Passera
50125 Florence
Tel. +39 055 218562

BARS

Caffè Giacosa by Roberto Cavalli

Plucky businessmen, informed tourists, elegant young ladies from the haute couture maisons, all gather together here for lunch. Right in the middle of Florence's flashiest shopping street, it's worth it just to catch the scene and see the beautifully laid out coffee-service.

Beherzte Geschäftsleute, gut informierte Touristen und elegante junge Damen aus den Haute-Couture-Salons treffen sich hier zum Mittagessen. Auf der schicksten Shopping-Meile von Florenz lohnt es sich schon, nur die Leute zu beobachten und den wunderbar servierten Kaffee zu genießen. Es gibt auch köstliche Schokolade.

Hommes d'affaires aux dents longues, touristes bien informés et élégantes jeunes femmes des maisons de haute couture, tous se retrouvent ici pour déjeuner. En plein cœur de la rue des boutiques les plus luxueuses de Florence, cette adresse vaut le détour pour observer sa faune et découvrir son service à café magnifiquement présenté. De plus, les chocolats sont délicieux.

Via della Spada, 10
50123 Florence
Tel. +39 055 2776328

Capocaccia

Thanks to its location on the banks of the river Arno, this is already the bellwether of trend-setting in town. At cocktail hour, tasty treats are served to chill-out and lounge music in a characteristic setting featuring Portuguese tiles. Sunday morning charming brunch buffet.

Schon allein wegen seiner Lage am Ufer des Arno ist dieses Lokal eine Art Trend-Barometer der Stadt. Zur Cocktailstunde werden köstliche Kleinigkeiten begleitet von Chill-Out- und Lounge-Music serviert. Das Ambiente prägen portugiesische Keramikkacheln. Zauberhaftes Brunch-Buffet am Sonntagmorgen.

Grâce à son emplacement sur les rives de l'Arno, cet endroit est depuis déjà un certain temps la plate-forme de lancement des tendances de la ville. A l'heure de l'apéritif, on y sirote de délicieux cocktails aux sons d'une musique lounge dans un décor d'azulejos, les fameux carreaux portugais. Excellent buffet pour le brunch du dimanche.

Lungarno Corsini, 12–14a
50123 Florence
Tel. +39 055 210751
http://www.capocaccia.com/

Frescobaldino

It's not your old-style vinaio where you belly up to the bar and have a shot glass of red with a rustic sandwich of fennel salami. Here you sit in a decorated room and take your choice from a vast selection of wines by the glass, and a menu which holds a place of honour for some savoury regional dishes.

Dies ist kein altmodischer Vinaio, wo Sie sich zur Bar durchboxen, um ein Glas Roten zu kippen und ein Panino mit Fenchelsalami zu verputzen. Hier sitzt man in einem hübsch dekorierten Lokal und wählt aus einer riesigen Palette glasweise angebotener Weine und einer Speisekarte, auf der einige regionale Spezialitäten in Ehren gehalten werden.

Ce n'est pas le genre de caviste à l'ancienne où l'on se cramponne au bar pour boire un verre de rouge accompagné d'un sandwich rustique de salami au fenouil. Ici, vous êtes assis à table dans une salle joliment décorée et faites votre choix parmi une vaste sélection de vins proposés au verre, avec un menu qui met à l'honneur certains plats régionaux très savoureux.

Via de' Magazzini 2–4r
50122 Florence
Tel. +39 055 284724

Porfirio Rubirosa

Manhattan-style design and party-like atmosphere at this posh spot just across the Fortezza area. The real draw is the fashionable Florentine crowd, especially dense before and after dinner for cocktails prepared by an expert barman.

Design à la Manhattan und Party-Atmosphäre bestimmen diesen schicken Treffpunkt gleich gegenüber der Fortezza-Gegend. Die wahre Attraktion sind die eleganten Einheimischen. Besonders voll ist es vor und nach dem Abendessen, wenn die Leute hier ihre Cocktails nehmen, die ein erfahrener Barkeeper mixt.

Design à la Manhattan et ambiance de fête dans ce bar très chic situé juste en face de la Fortezza. Sa véritable attraction réside dans sa faune de Florentins fashion, particulièrement dense avant et après le dîner en raison des cocktails préparés par son barman expert.

Viale F. Strozzi, 18–20r
50129 Florence
Tel. +39 055 490965

Procacci

The green marble used for the bar and table-tops is the same used in the city's great monuments. Here the chefs have for a century been tickling local – and quite a few foreign – palates with their "panini al tartufo": not so much a nutritional exercise as a ritual. You can also buy wine and foodstuffs, including truffles, to take away.

Der grüne Marmor von Bar und Tischplatten ist der gleiche wie bei den großartigen Monumenten der Stadt. Seit hundert Jahren kitzeln hier die Küchenchefs die Gaumen der Einheimischen – und ganz weniger Fremder – mit ihren Panini al Tartufo – wobei es hier weniger um Nahrungsaufnahme als um das Ritual geht. Wein und Lebensmittel, inklusive Trüffel, werden auch zum Mitnehmen verkauft.

Le bar et les dessus de table sont taillés dans le même marbre vert que celui des grands monuments de la ville. Ici, les chefs ravissent depuis un siècle les palais des Florentins, et de certains étrangers, avec leurs « panini al tartufo » : plus un rituel qu'un exercice nutritionnel. Il est également possible d'acheter du vin et des plats à emporter, notamment des truffes.

Via de' Tornabuoni 64r
50123 Florence
Tel. +39 055 211656

Rose's Café

Very popular for light lunch with an international clientele. The bar is open all day and serves everything, from a Viennese cappuccino to the standard Cosmopolitan made with real cranberry juice. Evenings, it becomes the city's coolest sushi bar.

Bei einer internationalen Kundschaft für ein leichtes Mittagessen beliebt. Die Bar ist den ganzen Tag über geöffnet und serviert praktisch alles, vom Wiener Kapuziner bis zum Cosmopolitan (sogar mit echtem Cranberry Juice). Abends die coolste Sushibar der Stadt.

Très prisé pour déjeuner léger et clientèle internationale. Le bar reste ouvert toute la journée et propose de tout, du cappuccino à la viennoise au cosmopolitan standard à base de vrai jus de canneberge. Le soir, il devient le bar à sushi le plus cool de la ville.

Via del Parione, 26r
50123 Florence
Tel. +39 055 287090

HOTELS

Continentale Contemporary Pleasing Hotel

An elegant habitat that joins atmosphere and scents inspired by Italian design of the '50s – a tribute to Salvatore Ferragamo's creativity – with a precise idea of contemporary comfort. Try the exclusive solarium with a stunning view over the hills and the city.

Elegantes Biotop, das die Atmosphäre und die vom italienischen Design der 1950er Jahre gelegten Fährten – ein Tribut an den Schöpfergeist von Salvatore Ferragamo – mit einer ganz präzisen Vorstellung von zeitgemäßem Komfort verbindet. Sehr zu empfehlen ist die exklusive Sonnenterrasse mit überwältigendem Blick über die Stadt und die Hügel.

Un hôtel élégant à l'atmosphère unique, avec ses touches déco inspirées du design italien des années 50, un hommage à la créativité de Salvatore Ferragamo et une idée bien précise du confort contemporain. Visitez son luxueux solarium avec vue imprenable sur les collines et sur la ville.

Vicolo dell'Oro, 6
50123 Florence
Tel. +39 055 27262
www.lungarnohotels.com

Gallery Hotel Art

More than a hotel, this spot quickly became a laboratory and meeting point for events connected with modern art. Inside, the Fusion Bar Shozan Gallery, is constantly developing projects in contemporary gastronomy.

Dieser Ort ist mehr als ein Hotel und avancierte rasch zu einer Art Labor und Treffpunkt für Events im Bereich moderner Kunst. Die Fusion-Bar Shozan Gallery entwickelt ständig Projekte zeitgemäßer Gastronomie.

Plus qu'un hôtel, ce lieu s'est rapidement imposé comme un laboratoire expérimental et un point de ralliement pour des événements liés à l'art moderne. A l'intérieur, le Fusion Bar Shozan Gallery ne cesse d'innover en matière de gastronomie contemporaine.

Vicolo dell'Oro, 5
50123 Florence
Tel. +39 055 27263
www.lungarnohotels.com

Grand Hotel

An antique fresco uncovered during restoration work is now the focal point for the Grand Hotel's lobby. At the heart of this historical building, designed in the late 1400s by Brunelleschi is the Winter Garden, reserved for VIP parties and theme events.

Ein antikes Fresko, das bei Renovierungsarbeiten zum Vorschein kam, ist nun Mittelpunkt der Lobby. Im Herzen dieses historischen Bauwerks, das Brunelleschi im späten 15. Jahrhundert entworfen hat, liegt der für VIP-Parties und themenbezogene Events reservierte Wintergarten.

Une fresque de l'Antiquité mise à jour pendant les travaux de restauration constitue aujourd'hui la principale attraction du hall d'entrée du Grand Hotel. En plein cœur de cet immeuble historique, conçu par Brunelleschi à la fin du XVe siècle, se cache le jardin d'hiver, réservé aux soirées VIP et autres manifestations à thème.

Piazza Ognissanti, 1
50123 Florence
Tel. +39 055 27163826
www.starwood.com

J. K. PLACE

It is immediately clear that this place could never be ordinary, as the sounds of the city fade away and a slower, more thoughtful rhythm prevails. British touches, rarefied décor, an understated display, calm and luxurious. There are only 20 rooms. Try the refined cuisine of the glamorous "Lounge".

Man bemerkt sofort, dass dies kein gewöhnliches Haus ist, während der Lärm der Stadt verklingt und ein langsamerer, gedankenverlorener Rhythmus vorherrscht. Spuren britischer Lebensart, sparsames Dekor, Zurückhaltung, Ruhe und Luxus. Es gibt nur 20 Zimmer. Versuchen Sie einmal die exquisite Küche des glamourösen Restaurants „The Lounge".

On comprend d'emblée que l'endroit n'a rien d'ordinaire, alors que les clameurs de la ville s'estompent et que s'installe un rythme plus lent, plus propice à la méditation. Touches british, décor dépouillé, sobriété et discrétion, tout n'y est que luxe, calme et volupté. L'hôtel propose 20 chambres et un restaurant glamour, « The Lounge », qui sert une la cuisine raffinée.

Piazza Santa Maria Novella, 7
50123 Florence
Tel. +39 055 2645181
www.jkplace.com

Lungarno

Designed by architect Michele Bonan, guests are greeted by a smart interiors with clean lines; exquisite furnishings and materials that merge beauty with well-being.

Das exklusive Hotelrestaurant „Borgo San Jacopo", gestaltet vom Architekten Michele Bonan, gilt als brandneuer Speisesaal des Modekonzerns Salvatore Ferragamo am Fluss. Die Gäste erwartet ein intelligenter Look mit klaren Linien. Exquisite Möbel und Materialien ergeben die perfekte Verbindung von Schönheit und Wohlfühlen.

Conçu par l'architecte Michele Bonan, son luxueux restaurant « Borgo San Jacopo » est le dernier-né des établissements ouverts par le groupe Salvatore Ferragamo sur les rives de l'Arno. Les clients sont accueillis dans un environnement classe aux lignes épurées, où la décoration et le mobilier exquis réussissent à conjuguer beauté et bien-être.

Borgo San Jacopo, 14
50123 Florence
Tel. +39 055 27261
www.lungarnohotels.com

Tornabuoni 1

Privileged view of the historical centre of Florence, hotel de charme, just a few rooms with customized service. All this is to be had at Antica Torre Tornabuoni, prestigious turn-of-the-century residence. Don't miss the spacious terrace with a breathtaking 360° vista over the city.

Dieses zauberhafte Hotel mit wenigen Zimmern und individuellem Service bietet eine privilegierte Aussicht auf die historische Altstadt von Florenz. Zu genießen im Antica Torre Tornabuoni, dem prachtvollen Palazzo der Jahrhundertwende. Lassen Sie sich die großzügige Terrasse, umgeben von den zinnenbewehrten Mauern des Guelfenturms, mit 360-Grad-Blick über die Stadt nicht entgehen.

Vue imprenable sur le centre historique de Florence dans ce petit hôtel de charme proposant seulement quelques chambres et un service personnalisé. Le tout dans l'Antica Torre Tornabuoni, prestigieuse résidence d'époque. Ne manquez pas de visiter sa spacieuse terrasse entourée de remparts à créneaux guelfes, avec vue panoramique à couper le souffle sur toute la ville.

Via de' Tornabuoni, 1
50123 Florence
Tel. +39 055 2658161
www.tornabuoni1.com

AIRPORT

Amerigo Vespucci Airport / Aeroporto di Firenze (FLR)

Located just 3 miles north-west of central Florence, between the "Firenze Nord" exits from the superhighway and Florence's industrial area near Prato. It is connected to the city's highway system and railway network. This small airport handles mainly domestic flights. Florence airport is open to the public from 05:30 to 23:00 and deals with daily flights to and from many domestic and some international airports, including London Gatwick in the UK.

Nur 5 km nordwestlich vom Stadtzentrum, zwischen den Superstrada-Ausfahrten Firenze Nord und der Industrieregion um Prato. Es besteht Anschluss an das Autobahnsystem und das Eisenbahnnetz der Stadt, allerdings treffen auf diesem kleinen Flughafen hauptsächlich Inlandsflüge ein. Der Flughafen von Florenz ist von 5.30 bis 23 h geöffnet, und es gibt tägliche Verbindungen zu vielen inländischen und einigen ausländischen Destinationen, etwa nach London Gatwick.

Situé à seulement cinq kilomètres au nord-est du centre de Florence, entre la sortie « Firenze Nord » de l'autoroute et la zone industrielle de la ville près de Prato. Relié au réseau autoroutier et ferroviaire de la ville, ce petit aéroport assure principalement des vols nationaux. L'aéroport de Florence est ouvert au public de 05h30 à 23h00 et assure des vols quotidiens à destination et en provenance de nombreux aéroports italiens et de quelques aéroports internationaux, notamment London Gatwick au Royaume-Uni.

Via del Termine, 11
50127 Florence
Tel. +39 055 3061300/055 3061702/055 3061700
Fax. +39 055 315874
www.aeroporto.firenze.it

What makes London special to you? I always wanted to live in England because I like the people here and there is lots to do. I do wish it was a bit cleaner though and that people would do more recycling **Where is the best place to stay in London?** I've never stayed in a nice hotel in London, only those cheap ones in Bayswater. After one of our shows we went for tea at the Basil Street Hotel in Knightsbridge which is lovely. I think I would like to stay there **Where is your favourite place to eat in London?** I mostly eat at home and I am most happy on the days when I get gravy. When my agents come from Japan they always take us to Japanese restaurants, which I love. There are lots that are good, but I like Yanbaru in Harcourt Street **Where is your favourite place to shop in London?** I like b store in Conduit Street. They sell my clothes and they're really nice. I also like Skandium in Marylebone High Street. They sell lots of different Scandinavian design products and you can buy liquorice there. PETER JENSEN

LONDON

TEXT BY DAN JONES

Beyond the slippery jellied eels, leftover punks and Waterloo sunsets, London remains one of the most exciting and creative fashion cities in the world. The heady swirl around London Fashion Week is as strong as ever, even if its star attractions have decamped in recent years. The city's undeniable strength is its wealth of younger off-schedule designers, specialist boutiques, huge department stores, countless vintage clothing emporiums and crackling bar and club scene. London has never lost its cocky, underground edge. For a city so aware of its own iconic history, it has a firm grasp of creative modernity and youthful, brave design. This clash of opposites is everywhere: from the major British designers secretly commissioned to tweak the collections of hugely popular high street brands to the arrival of Dover Street Market, a raw, urban space housing an eclectic, exclusive mix of bleeding-edge fashion. As new concept stores reanimate the city's ancient bespoke tailoring district, Savile Row, they revel in a tradition of stifling personal service. Approached territorially, fashion's sharpest edge – at least on the wallet – is still the west; the quiet decadence of Sloane Street and Brompton Road spreads into Kensington and, finally, Bond Street. Soho and Covent Garden are also innovative areas, dominated by designer-mix boutiques and streetwear stores linked through the back streets of the busier, cheaper heart of the city. Sprawling markets are a weekend institution with dubious back alleys and scorchingly colourful street-level stalls. Portobello and its nearby boutiques are still trawled by major designers and stylists searching for vintage couture and one-off originals. In the east, Brick Lane, Bethnal Green and Shoreditch are a little more satisfying: quite filthy and full of dark, damp treasures, these areas have seen a large collection of bars, clubs, galleries and today scruffy fashion kids populate the area in recent years.

Abgesehen von glibberigem Aal in Gelee, übrig gebliebenen Punkern und Waterloo Sunsets ist London nach wie vor eine der aufregendsten und kreativsten Modemetropolen der Welt. Der Wahnsinnswirbel um die London Fashion Week ist so groß wie noch nie, auch wenn deren Stars in den letzten Jahren ihre Zelte hier abgebrochen haben. Unbestreitbare Stärken der Stadt sind ihre Vielzahl jüngerer, unkonventioneller Designer, die vielen Spezialgeschäfte, die riesigen Kaufhäuser, zahllose Secondhand-Läden sowie die spannende Bar- und Clubszene. London hat seinen frechen Untergrund-Charme nie verloren. Bei einer Stadt, die sich ihrer historischen Bedeutung dermaßen bewusst ist, staunt man über so viel kreative Modernität, Jugendlichkeit und mutiges Design. Das Aufeinanderprallen der Gegensätze ist allgegenwärtig: Bei den gesetzten Kaufhäusern, die noch völlig unbekannte DJs buchen, oder bei den großen britischen Designern, die heimlich beauftragt werden, die Kollektionen von landesweit extrem populären Marken zu entwerfen. Nachdem neue Concept Stores begonnen haben, das legendäre alte Schneiderviertel Savile Row in der City neu zu beleben, schwelgt man dort im etwas angestaubten persönlichen Service. Geografisch und was die Preise angeht liegt der Westen der Stadt nach wie vor modisch unangefochten vorn. Die leise Dekadenz von Sloane Street und Bromp-

ton Road breitet sich bis nach Kensington aus und erreicht schließlich die Bond Street. Soho und Covent Garden sind modisch ebenfalls innovativ. Hier dominieren Boutiquen, die verschiedene Designer und Streetwear führen. Und dann gibt es noch die abgelegeneren Straßen des geschäftigeren, preiswerteren Stadtzentrums. An den Wochenenden sind ausgedehnte Märkte eine Institution; zu ihnen gehören auch zweifelhafte Nebenstraßen und kreischend bunte Stände. Portobello und die Boutiquen rundherum werden nach wie vor von den großen Designern und Stylisten durchstreift, die dort Vintage-Couture und Off-off-Unikate suchen. Im Osten ist die Gegen um die Brick Lane, Bethnal Green und Shoreditch vielversprechend: Ziemlich heruntergekommen, aber voll mit düsteren, modrigen Schätzen. Hier trifft man auch auf jede Menge Bars, Clubs, Galerien und die Schmuddelkinder der Modebranche, die diese Gegend in den letzten Jahren für sich entdeckt haben.

Au-delà des anguilles en gelée, des rares punks survivants et des couchers de soleil de Waterloo, Londres reste l'une des capitales de la mode les plus créatives et les plus stimulantes. Le tourbillon entêtant de la London Fashion Week est toujours aussi vivace, bien que ses stars aient décampé ces dernières années. La force de la ville réside indéniablement dans son nombre impressionnant d'aspirants créateurs, de boutiques spécialisées, de grands magasins et de surplus vintage, mais également dans ses bars et sa scène club en pleine effervescence. L'underground londonien n'a rien perdu de son insolence. Assumant parfaitement son statut de symbole historique, la ville reste pourtant fermement ancrée à l'avant-garde d'une création jeune et pleine d'audace. Ce choc des contraires transparaît partout : des plus grands créateurs britanniques auxquels on demande secrètement de concevoir les collections des marques de grande distribution, à l'arrivée du Dover Street Market, espace urbain brut qui accueille un mélange luxueux et éclectique de griffes plus que pointues. Quant aux nouvelles boutiques concept qui ont redonné vie à Savile Row, ancien quartier des tailleurs sur mesure, elles reprennent avec bonheur la tradition du service personnalisé à façon. D'un point de vue géographique, la mode la plus pointue – du moins pour le portefeuille – se trouve toujours à l'ouest ; la décadence tranquille de Sloane Street et Brompton Road touche aujourd'hui Kensington et Bond Street. Soho et Covent Garden jouent aussi la carte de l'innovation, dominés par des boutiques de créateurs et des magasins de streetwear tous reliés via les bas quartiers du cœur, plus grouillant et meilleur marché, de la ville. Avec leurs ruelles louches et leurs stands multicolores tentaculaires posés à même le sol, les marchés aux puces sont devenus une véritable institution du week-end. Portobello et les boutiques environnantes restent investis par les grands créateurs et les stylistes de magazine en quête de pièces haute couture vintage et de modèles originaux uniques. A l'est, les quartiers de Brick Lane, Bethnal Green et Shoreditch offrent un peu plus de satisfaction : plutôt louches et crades mais recelant d'innombrables trésors, ils ont vu s'ouvrir ces dernières années un large éventail de bars, de clubs et de galeries d'art envahis par une faune de kids grungy et branchés.

FASHION SHOWS AND FAIRS

Fashion East
Championing London's new style visionaries, Fashion East steps in where lack of funding and disregard for commercial gain can cause small businesses to fall at the first hurdle. For autumn/winter 2005, FE showcased Richard Nicoll and Husam El Odeh alongside i-D Contributor Gareth Pugh. Past designers include Jonathan Saunders, Ebru Ercon and Alastair Carr. An exciting launch pad for future names.

Als Tummelplatz für Londons neue Stilvisionäre springt Fashion East dort ein, wo kleine Firmen wegen zu schwacher finanzieller Ausstattung oder Vernachlässigung des kommerziellen Aspekts schon an der ersten Hürde scheitern würden. Eine spannende Startrampe für künftige bekannte Namen.

Défenseur des nouveaux visionnaires de la mode londonienne, Fashion East intervient quand le manque de financement et de succès commercial risque d'obliger les petites entreprises à fermer leurs portes au premier obstacle venu. Pour l'automne/hiver 2005, FE a présenté le travail de Richard Nicoll et Husam El Odeh aux côtés du styliste d'i-D Gareth Pugh. L'événement a précédemment vu défiler des créateurs tels que Jonathan Saunders, Ebru Ercon et Alastair Carr. Une superbe plate-forme de lancement pour les nouveaux talents.

www.fashioneast.co.uk

London Fashion Week
Organised and owned by the British Fashion Council, Fashion Week showcases the cream of the crop of London's design talent, alongside the Saint Martins MA graduate collection. For the up-to-date schedule info check out www.londonfashionweek.co.uk

Auf der Londoner Fashion Week, die das British Fashion Council veranstaltet, präsentiert sich die Crème de la Crème von Londons Designtalenten. Außerdem wir die Kollektion der Absolventen des Saint Martins gezeigt. Den aktuellen Veranstaltungskalender finden Sie auf der Website www.londonfashionweek.co.uk

Organisée par le British Fashion Council, la Fashion Week présente la crème de la crème des créateurs londoniens ainsi que les collections de fin d'études des étudiants en MA de Central Saint Martins. Pour connaître le programme, rendez-vous sur le site www.londonfashionweek.co.uk

Battersea Park
Chelsea Bridge Entrance
Queenstown Road
London SW11

Off Schedule
Championing the newest underground design talent Blow PR takes care of London's 'Off Schedule' each season. For the latest information and updates on off schedule shows and static presentations check out www.blow.co.uk

Blow PR kümmert sich in jeder Saison um die neuesten Underground-Designtalente. Aktuelle Informationen, Daten und Orte von Schauen „abseits des offiziellen Kalenders" und Ausstellungen findet man unter www.blow.co.uk

Pour faire connaître les tout derniers talents de la mode underground, Blow PR organise chaque saison les défilés « Off Schedule » de Londres. Pour consulter les dernières actualités du circuit off et les photos des défilés, visitez le site www.blow.co.uk

Frieze Art Fair
Focusing on the most dynamic established galleries working today, and presented alongside a varied schedule of talks, artists' commissions and music showcases, the Frieze Art Fair (alongside its little sister fair, Zoo) has fast become essential London viewing.

Veranstaltet von den dynamischsten etablierten Galerien der Gegenwart, ist die Frieze Art Fair (zusammen mit ihrer kleinen Schwester-Messe Zoo) schnell zu einer unverzichtbaren Attraktion Londons geworden. Zum Programm gehören auch Diskussionen, Kunstaktionen und Live-Musik.

Spécialisé dans les galeries d'art les plus dynamiques du moment et accompagné d'un programme varié de débats, d'interventions d'artistes et de performances musicales, le salon Frieze Art (aux côtés de sa petite sœur, le salon Zoo) s'est rapidement imposé comme un rendez-vous londonien à ne pas manquer.

www.friezeartfair.com
www.zooartfair.com

FASHION SCHOOLS

Central Saint Martins College of Art and Design
John Galliano, Hussein Chalayan and Alexander McQueen all studied here at London's famous fashion training camp. Churning out Brit design greats is second nature to its staff.

John Galliano, Hussein Chalayan und Alexander McQueen – sie alle haben in Londons zentraler Designerschmiede, Mode studiert. Am laufenden Band neue Talente des Designs hervorzubringen, ist den Lehrkräften hier schon in Fleisch und Blut übergegangen.

John Galliano, Hussein Chalayan et Alexander McQueen ont tous étudié dans ce célèbre camp retranché de la mode. Ici, la production en série de grands couturiers britanniques est une seconde nature.

107–109 Charing Cross Road
London WC2
Tel. +44 (0)20 7514 7000
www.csm.linst.ac.uk

Royal College of Art
The RCA's fashion school set a new precedent upon its creation in 1949 and has established a reputation for pure excellence ever since. Enjoying a healthy rivalry with Saint Martins, alumni have included Philip Treacy and glam-fashion star Julien Macdonald.

Die Modeschule des RCA hat mit ihrer Gründung 1949 neue Maßstäbe gesetzt und genießt seither einen exzellenten Ruf. Man steht in gesunder Konkurrenz zu Central Saint Martins. Unter anderem haben Philip Treacy und der Glam-Fashion-Star Julien Macdonald hier studiert.

Depuis sa création en 1949, le département Mode du Royal College of Art a établi de nouvelles références et n'a jamais failli à sa réputation d'excellence. Entretenant une saine rivalité avec Central Saint Martins, ses ex-diplômés incluent Philip Treacy et le roi du glam Julien Macdonald.

Kensington Gore
London SW7
Tel. +44 (0)20 7590 4444
www.rca.ac.uk

London College of Fashion
An integral part of one of the largest creative educational institutions in the world (the London Institute), LCF offers a rightly industry-based, practical education.

Als integraler Bestandteil einer der weltweit größten Ausbildungsinstitutionen im kreativen Bereich (des London Institute) bietet das LCF ein auf die Textilindustrie zugeschnittenes, praxisorientiertes Studium.

Intégré à l'une des institutions d'enseignement les plus créatives au monde (le London Institute), le LCF dispense une formation pratique qui reflète concrètement l'industrie de la mode.

20 John Prince's Street
London W1
Tel. +44 (0)20 7514 7400
www.lcf.linst.ac.uk

FASHION MUSEUMS AND GALLERIES

Tate Modern
An imposingly huge former power station on the South Bank of the Thames, Tate Modern was opened in 1999 to house the nation's collections of 20th and 21st century art, with international exhibitions and events running late into the night. The best art and photography bookshop in London.

In dem imposanten ehemaligen Kraftwerk am Südufer der Themse wurde 1999 dieses Museum für die staatlichen Sammlungen der Kunst des 20. und 21. Jahrhunderts eröffnet. Bis spätabends kann man hier internationale Ausstellungen und Events besuchen. Zum Museum gehört auch die beste Buchhandlung Londons.

Sur la rive sud de la Tamise, cette ancienne centrale électrique aux dimensions gigantesques a ouvert ses portes en 1999 pour accueillir les collections nationales d'art des XXe et XXIe siècles, des expositions internationales et même des soirées. Le Tate Modern possède également la meilleure librairie de Londres pour les livres d'art et de photo.

Bankside
London SE1
Tel. +44 (0)20 7887 8008
www.tate.org.uk

Victoria & Albert Museum
Set in grand surroundings, the V&A features decorative and applied arts, historical and contemporary, fashion and textiles, sculpture, silver and jewellery, furniture and photography. As with all UK public museums, admission to the main collections is free.

In eindrucksvollem Ambiente präsentiert das Victoria & Albert Museum dekorative und angewandte Kunst aus Vergangenheit und Gegenwart, Mode und Textilien, Skulpturen, Silber und Schmuck, Möbel und Fotografien. Wie bei allen öffentlichen Museen Großbritanniens ist der Eintritt zu den Hauptsammlungen frei.

Situé dans un cadre grandiose, le Victoria & Albert Museum est spécialisé dans les arts décoratifs et appliqués d'hier et d'aujourd'hui. Il présente également des expositions de mode, de textiles, de sculpture, des collections d'argenterie et de bijoux, de mobilier et de photographie. Comme dans tous les musées publics du Royaume-Uni, l'accès aux collections permanentes est gratuit.

Cromwell Road
London SW7
Tel. +44 (0)20 7942 2000
www.vam.ac.uk

Interim Art
Opened in 1984 by Maureen Paley, this space has a reputation for showing intelligent and impressive contemporary art and photography, including Gillian Wearing and Wolfgang Tillmans.

Die 1984 von Maureen Paley gegründete Galerie ist bekannt für die Präsentation eindrucksvoller moderner Kunst und Fotografie, etwa von Gillian Wearing und Wolfgang Tillmans.

Ouvert en 1984 par Maureen Paley, cet espace expose des photos et des œuvres d'art contemporain réputées intelligentes et impressionnantes, notamment le travail de Gillian Wearing et Wolfgang Tillmans.

10 Vyner Street
London E2
Tel. +44 (0)20 8980 7742
www.modernartinc.com

Sadie Coles HQ
A showcase of young British artists and international contemporary names, including photographer Jeff Burton and Raf Simons' collaborator Simon Periton.

Ein Schaufenster junger britischer und zeitgenössischer internationaler Künstler, darunter etwa der Fotograf Jeff Burton und Simon Periton, der mit Raf Simons zusammenarbeitet.

Expositions de jeunes artistes britanniques et de grands noms contemporains internationaux tels que le photographe Jeff Burton et Simon Periton, collaborateur de Raf Simons.

35 Heddon Street
London W1
Tel. +44 (0)20 7434 2227
www.sadiecoles.com

White Cube
Jay Jopling's acclaimed contemporary art gallery in Hoxton Square is the spiritual home of Brit Art: those represented here include Tracey Emin, Damien Hirst, Gary Hume and Jopling's wife Sam Taylor Wood.

Jay Joplings berühmte Galerie moderner Kunst an Hoxton Square ist die geistige Heimat der Brit Art: Zu den hier vertretenen Künstlern zählen Tracey Emin, Damien Hirst, Gary Hume und Joplings Ehefrau Sam Taylor Wood.

La célèbre galerie d'art contemporain de Jay Jopling sur Hoxton Square est le berceau spirituel de l'art britannique d'aujourd'hui : parmi les artistes exposés ici, on peut citer Tracey Emin, Damien Hirst, Gary Hume et Sam Taylor Wood, la femme de Jopling.

48 Hoxton Square
London N1
Tel. +44 (0)20 7930 5373
www.whitecube.com

Modern Art
Further east from its original Shoreditch premises but no less impressive, Stuart Shave's gallery has an eclectic stable of young and established art stars including Juergen Teller, Eva Rothschild, Tim Noble and Sue Webster.

Etwas weiter östlich als die alten Räumlichkeiten in Shoreditch, aber ebenso eindrucksvoll bietet Stuart Shaves Galerie einer eklektischen Mischung junger und etablierter Stars

der Kunstszene wie Jürgen Teller, Eva Rothschild, Tim Noble und Sue Webster ein Zuhause.

Située un peu plus à l'est que son premier établissement de Shoreditch mais tout aussi impressionnante, la galerie de Stuart Shave expose une sélection éclectique d'étoiles de l'art connues et moins connues, parmi lesquelles Juergen Teller, Eva Rothschild, Tim Noble et Sue Webster.

Modern Art
10 Vyner Street
London E2
Tel. +44 (0)20 8980 7743
www.modernartinc.com

FASHION SHOPS

Agent Provocateur
Seductively filthy lingerie, perfume, scented candles and fuck-me shoes for the sauciest boudoir by Vivienne Westwood's son Joseph Corre and wife Serena Rees, located in the darkest depths of Soho.

In den dunklen Tiefen von Soho bieten Vivienne Westwoods Sohn Joseph Corre und dessen Frau Serena Rees verführerische Reizwäsche, Parfüms, Duftkerzen und Come-fuck-me-Schuhe für die verruchtesten Boudoirs feil.

Lingerie scandaleuse, fragrances, bougies parfumées et chaussures « pousse au viol » dans ce boudoir coquin du fin fond de Soho ouvert par Serena Rees et Joseph Corre, le fils de Vivienne Westwood.

6 Broadwick Street
London W1
Tel. +44 (0)20 7439 0229
www.agentprovocateur.com

The World According To…
When Max Karie and Pippa Brooks decided to close their cult shop, 'Shop' on Brewer St exactly ten years after its initial inception, a whole host of London's prettiest stars cried into their Tocca pillows. But the sadness didn't last for long as the duo decided to shut up shop and open bigger and better than before. The basement shop now houses Eley Kishimoto, Marc by Marc Jacobs, Silas and Missy Elliott's Adidas range, whilst the painted horse, direct from a fairground carousel, commands centre stage.

Als Max Karie und Pippa Brooks beschlossen, ihren kultigen Laden namens Shop an der Brewer Street genau zehn Jahre nach seiner Eröffnung zu schließen, weinte ein ganzes Heer der hübschesten Londoner Stars in seine Tocca-Kissen. Aber die Trauer hielt nicht lange an, denn das Duo entschied, etwas Größeres und Besseres aufzumachen. Im neuen Souterrain-Laden werden Eley Kishimoto, Marc by Marc Jacobs, Silas und Missy Elliots Adidas-Kollektion

geführt, während das bemalte Karussellpferd im Mittelpunkt steht.

Quand Max Karie et Pippa Brooks ont fermé « Shop », leur boutique culte de Brewer Street, exactement dix ans après son ouverture, une belle brochette de stars londoniennes ont pleuré toute la nuit sur leurs oreillers griffés Tocca. Mais elles ont vite ravalé leurs larmes, car le duo a décidé d'ouvrir une nouvelle boutique encore plus grande et encore plus belle : installée en sous-sol, elle présente des créations Eley Kishimoto, Marc by Marc Jacobs, Silas et la collection Adidas de Missy Elliott autour de l'attraction centrale de la boutique, un cheval de bois déniché sur un vieux carrousel.

76 Brewer Street
London W1
Tel. +44 (0)20 7437 3540

B-Store
Championing graduates alongside more established avant-garde designers, buyer Matthew Murphy has created a singular vision modern boutique. The corridor-like space houses Bernhard Willhelm, Bless, Frank Leder, Siv Støldal, Cosmic Wonder, and Ute Ploier – an interesting bunch expertly chosen so even the most outrageous pieces easily slot into your day-to-day wardrobe.

Mit einer Mischung aus frischgebackenen Absolventen und eher etablierteren Avantgarde-Designern betreibt der Einkäufer Matthew Murphy eine moderne Boutique mit einzigartiger Vision. In dem korridorartigen Raum finden Bernhard Willhelm, Bless, Frank Leder, Siv Støldal, Cosmic Wonder und Ute Ploier Platz – eine spannende Truppe, mit sicherer Hand ausgewählt, so dass selbst die außergewöhnlichsten Stücke sich mühelos in Ihre alltägliche Garderobe einfügen.

Présentant les créations de jeunes diplômés à côté de celles de couturiers d'avant-garde déjà établis, l'acheteur Matthew Murphy a créé une boutique moderne à la vision singulière. Cet espace en forme de couloir accueille des vêtements griffés Bernhard Willhelm, Bless, Frank Leder, Siv Støldal, Cosmic Wonder et Ute Ploier : grâce à une sélection méticuleuse, même les pièces les plus originales trouveront facilement leur place dans votre garde-robe quotidienne.

6 Conduit Street
Mayfair
London W1S 2XE
Tel. +44 (0)20 7499 6628

Browns and Browns Focus
Together Browns and Browns Focus form one of London's most respected style emporiums. Opposite one another in the heart of the city's top end retail area. Browns stocks the

likes of Christian Dior, Dolce & Gabbana, Marni, Jil Sander and Raf Simons. Browns Focus is the kid sibling, showcasing young, sharp design in a concept boutique and carrying pieces from AF Vandevorst, Véronique Branquinho, Hussein Chalayan and Jessica Ogden.

Browns und Browns Focus bilden gemeinsam eines der geachtetsten Modeimperien Londons. Die Läden liegen sich im Herzen der nobelsten Einkaufsgegend direkt gegenüber. Bei Browns werden Marken wie Christian Dior, Dolce & Gabbana, Marni, Jil Sander und Raf Simons geführt. Browns Focus ist sozusagen das kleine Geschwisterchen und präsentiert junges, radikales Design als Konzeptboutique mit Kreationen von AF Vandevorst, Véronique Branquinho, Hussein Chalayan und Jessica Ogden.

Ensemble, Browns et Browns Focus constituent l'un des empires de la mode les plus respectés de Londres. Ils se font face en plein cœur du quartier des boutiques de luxe de la ville. Browns vend les créations de Christian Dior, Dolce & Gabbana, Marni, Jil Sander et Raf Simons, tandis que son petit frère Browns Focus présente une mode jeune plus pointue au sein d'une boutique concept, avec des pièces AF Vandevorst, Véronique Branquinho, Hussein Chalayan et Jessica Ogden.

23–27 South Molton Street
London W1
Tel. +44 (0)20 7491 7833
Browns Focus
Tel. +44 (0)20 7514 0063

Burberry London
Three floors of iconic Burberry designs, showcasing collections for men, women and children, accessories, homewear and a made-to-measure service in this beautifully refurbished fashion flagship.

Im wunderschön renovierten Flagship Store des Labels findet man auf drei Etagen im typischen Burberry-Design Kollektionen für Herren, Damen und Kinder, Accessoires, Homewear und eine Maßschneiderei.

Une référence incontournable de Londres. Superbement rénovés, les trois étages 100 % pur Burberry présentent les collections pour homme, pour femme et pour enfant, les accessoires et le homewear, ainsi qu'un service de coupe sur mesure.

21–23 Bond Street
London W1
Tel. +44 (0)20 7889 5222

Dover Street Market
An entirely new retail concept from Comme des Garçons' Rei Kawakubo, this impressive six floor 'marketplace' features a rolling list of new and established designers including

Undercover, Judy Blame, Junya Watanabe, Anne-Valerie Hash and Lanvin. A trek to the top floor is rewarded with cakes and tea courtesy of Rose Bakery.

Als ganz neues Einzelhandelskonzept Rei Kawakubos von Comme des Garçons funktioniert dieser eindrucksvolle „Markt" auf sechs Etagen. Hier werden nach dem Rotationsprinzip neue und etablierte Designer wie Undercover, Judy Blame, Junya Watanabe, Anne-Valerie Hash und Lanvin präsentiert. Die Reise in den obersten Stock wird mit Tee und Kuchen aus der Rose Bakery belohnt.

Tout nouveau concept de vente lancé par Rei Kawakubo de Comme des Garçons, cet impressionnant « marché » sur six étages accueille une longue liste de jeunes créateurs et de griffes réputées, notamment Undercover, Judy Blame, Junya Watanabe, Anne-Valerie Hash et Lanvin. Si vous faites l'effort de monter jusqu'au dernier étage, vous serez récompensé par des gâteaux et une tasse de thé de chez Rose Bakery.

Dover Street Market
17–18 Dover Street
London W1
Tel. +44 (0)20 7518 0680

Harvey Nichols
London's most applauded and glamorous department store with sprawling classic collections and contemporary designs including Chloé, Marc Jacobs, Rick Owens and Balenciaga. The fifth floor houses an acclaimed restaurant and food market.

Londons meistgelobtes und glamourösestes Kaufhaus bietet neben zahlreichen klassischen Kollektionen auch zeitgenössisches Design u. a. von Chloé, Marc Jacobs, Rick Owens und Balenciaga. Im fünften Stock befinden sich ein beliebtes Restaurant und eine Lebensmittelabteilung.

Le grand magasin le plus glamour et le plus applaudi de Londres. Collections classiques et griffes de jeunes créateurs comme Chloé, Marc Jacobs, Rick Owens et Balenciaga. Le cinquième étage accueille un restaurant et un marché très prisés.

109–125 Knightsbridge
London SW1
Tel. +44 (0)20 7235 5000
www.harveynichols.com

Hideout
London's one-stop streetwear shop with the most discerning customers in town. Labels stocked in the wooden shed-like space are particular and precise, with Neighborhood, Supreme, Visvim, PAM and Headporter sharing billing. Exclusives and constant limited edition collaborations ensure a hardcore squad of well-dressed enthusiasts.

Londons authentischster Streetwear Shop mit den auffälligsten Kunden der Stadt. Die Label, die in dem Holzhütten-ähnlichen Raum geführt werden, sind etwas Besonderes und in ihrem Stil äußerst präzise, wie z.B. Neighborhood, Supreme, Visvim, PAM und Headporter. Exklusives und Kooperationen in stets limitierten Auflagen sorgen für eine Hardcore-Truppe gut gekleideter Enthusiasten.

La meilleure boutique streetwear de Londres accueille les clients les plus exigeants. Les griffes présentées dans ce décor de cabane en bois ne sont pas n'importe lesquelles : Neighborhood, Supreme, Visvim, PAM et Headporter. Des exclusivités et des collaborations sur la sortie d'éditions limitées garantissent la satisfaction d'une clientèle pointue et enthousiaste.

7 Upper James Street
London W1
Tel. +44 (0)20 7437 4929

Kokon To Zai
Bang in the middle of Soho, boutique Kokon To Zai is tiny in stature but huge in inspiration. Run by designers Marjan Pejoski and Sasha Bezovski, the store houses the duo's recently launched menswear range KTZ, alongside Marjan's own label, Raf Simons, Bernhard Willhelm and the hottest graduate collections.

Die Boutique mitten im Herzen von Soho ist winzig, aber riesig in ihrer Inspirationskraft. Der Laden unter der Leitung der Designer Marjan Pejoski und Sasha Bezovski führt die kürzlich entwickelte Herrenlinie KTZ des Designer-Duos, außerdem Marjans eigenes Label, Raf Simons, Bernhard Willhelm sowie die Kollektionen der angesagtesten Modeschulabsolventen.

En plein cœur de Soho, la minuscule boutique Kokon To Zai ne manque pas d'inspiration. Gérée par les créateurs Marjan Pejoski et Sasha Bezovski, elle accueille la ligne pour homme KTZ récemment lancée par le duo, mais aussi la griffe éponyme de Pejoski, les créations de Raf Simons, de Bernhard Willhelm et les meilleures collections de jeunes diplômés.

57 Greek Street
London W1
Tel. +44 (0)20 7434 1316

Maison Martin Margiela
Considered a genius by many in the fashion world, Belgian designer Martin Margiela now has his own London outlet, tucked discreetly around the corner from the bright lights of Bond Street. Typically guarded, the store has little signage and a plastic sheet to separate the stark clinical brilliance of the architecture from the prying eyes of passing trade. Shop assistants wear doctor's coats and openly encourage customers to scrawl on

the white walls, which complements the classic-with-a-twist aesthetic championed by the label.

Viele in der Welt der Mode halten ihn für ein Genie. Inzwischen hat der belgische Designer seinen eigenen Laden in London, diskret gelegen, abseits der grellen Lichter der Bond Street. Typisch abgeschirmt, gibt es kaum Hinweise auf den Laden, und eine Plastikplane schützt die geradezu klinisch weiße Architektur vor den neugierigen Blicken der Passanten. Das Verkaufspersonal trägt Arztkittel und ermutigt die Kundschaft ganz offen, auf den weißen Wänden herumzukritzeln. Diese spiegeln die bevorzugte Ästhetik des Labels – klassisch, aber mit den gewissen Etwas.

Généralement considéré comme un génie par le petit monde de la mode, le créateur belge Martin Margiela possède désormais sa propre boutique londonienne. Discrètement installée non loin des lumières de Bond Street, c'est à peine si l'on remarque son enseigne. Un simple film de plastique cache le côté brillant, cru et clinique de son architecture aux regards indiscrets des passants. Les vendeurs portent des blouses de docteur et encouragent ouvertement les clients à gribouiller les murs blancs, histoire de parfaire l'esthétique classique et décalée défendue par la griffe.

1–9 Bruton Place
Mayfair
London W1J 6NE
Tel. +44 (0)20 7629 2682

Manolo Blahnik
Blahnik's first and only UK store is styled rather decadently as a disused Sicilian palazzo. An indulgent paradise for the shoe fetishists of Chelsea and surrounding areas.

Blahniks erster und einziger Laden in Großbritannien ist wie ein verlassener sizilianischer Palazzo eingerichtet. Ein Paradies für Schuhfetischisten aus Chelsea und Umgebung.

Le style de la première et unique boutique de Blahnik au Royaume-Uni évoque la décadence d'un palazzo sicilien laissé à l'abandon. Un paradis des plaisirs couru par les fétichistes de la chaussure de Chelsea et des quartiers environnants.

49–51 Old Church Street
London SW3
Tel. +44 (0)20 7352 3863

Paul Smith
The Mac Daddy of British fashion, (Sir) Paul Smith's entrepreneurial approach and eclectic English clothing have won him international acclaim and a knighthood. His Westbourne Grove store mixes vintage couture with modern made-to-measure pieces, antiques and homeware alongside his own signature collections.

Der Mac Daddy der britischen Mode, (Sir) Paul Smith, hat mit seinem eklektischen englischen Stil und seiner Unternehmensphilosophie nicht nur internationale Anerkennung, sondern auch einen Adelstitel eingeheimst. Sein Laden in Westbourne Grove mischt Vintage-Couture mit moderner Maßkleidung, Antiquitäten und Homewear mit den Kollektionen, die seinen Namen tragen.

Le génie commercial et la mode éclectique typiquement british de (Sir) Paul Smith lui ont valu un succès international et le titre de Chevalier de l'Empire Britannique. Dans sa boutique de Westbourne Grove, ses collections éponymes sont présentées aux côtés de pièces vintage, de créations contemporaines taillées sur mesure, d'antiquités et d'une ligne de homeware.

Westbourne House
122 and 120 Kensington Park Road
London W11
Tel. +44 (0)20 7727 3553
www.paulsmith.co.uk

Selfridges
Huge, future-focused department store stocking contemporary names such as Alexander McQueen, Miu Miu, Louis Vuitton, Prada and Helmut Lang alongside champagne bars, a food hall, vintage concessions, festival events and a dimly-lit technology zone.

Riesiges zukunftsorientiertes Kaufhaus mit vielen zeitgenössischen Designerlabels wie Alexander McQueen, Miu Miu, Louis Vuitton, Prada und Helmut Lang. Dazu kommen noch Champagner-Bars, eine Markthalle, Vintage-Läden, Events und eine schummrig beleuchtete Technology Zone.

Grand magasin immense et futuriste présentant des griffes contemporaines, notamment Alexander McQueen, Miu Miu, Louis Vuitton, Prada et Helmut Lang. On y trouve aussi des bars à champagne, un marché, des enseignes vintage et un espace technologique sobrement éclairé.

400 Oxford Street
London W1
Tel. +44 (0)20 7629 1234
www.selfridges.com

Topshop
The flagship store for this amazingly successful high street label – the largest of its kind in Europe. Always busy, its appeal spans all ages and backgrounds. Guest designers – recently including Markus Lupfer and Walé Adeyemi – are invited to create exclusive capsule collections. A hushed favourite for even the most respected fashion celebrities.

Der Flagship Store der gleichnamigen, überaus erfolgreichen Kette –

der größten ihrer Art in Europa. Hier gibt es immer etwas Neues, das Modefans aller Altersgruppen und Schichten anlockt. Gastdesigner – wie vor kurzem Markus Lupfer und Walé Adeyemi – entwerfen exklusive Mini-Kollektionen. Eine geflüsterte Lieblingsadresse der angesehensten Stars der Modebranche.

Boutique phare de la plus grande chaîne d'habillement d'Europe. Attirant toujours une clientèle de tous âges et de tous milieux sociaux. Top Shop invite régulièrement des stylistes renommés – récemment Markus Lupfer et Walé Adeyemi – à créer des mini-collections exclusives pour la chaîne. Une griffe que tout le monde adore en secret, même les stars les plus respectées de la mode.

Oxford Circus
London W1
Tel. +44 (0)20 7636 7700

Vivienne Westwood
Westwood is a national treasure. Her inspired, very British style has consistently challenged and influenced fashion design for over two decades. This is the World's End shop where it all began…

Westwood ist eine Art Nationalheiligtum. Ihr origineller, sehr britischer Stil stellt seit mehr als zwei Jahrzehnten Herausforderung und Vorbild zugleich dar. World's End ist der Laden, in dem alles begann …

Vivienne Westwood est un trésor national. Depuis plus de vingt ans, son style inspiré et très british ne cesse de remettre en question et d'influencer la mode. Et c'est là que tout a commencé pour elle, dans la boutique World's End…

430 King's Road
London SW10
Tel. +44 (0)20 7352 6551
www.viviennewestwood.com

VINTAGE FASHION SHOPS

Bang Bang
Celebrating its fifth year and recently refitted, Bang Bang stocks a diverse collection of unique vintage, high street and designer clothing. From Westwood corsets to Ossie Clark smocks and vintage Givenchy, along with jewellery and accessories from Dead Egg, Average Jo, and the shop's own designers through to second hand H&M, Bang Bang has it all.

Bang Bang feierte schon fünfjähriges Jubiläum und wurde kürzlich neu gestaltet. Der Laden führt eine vielfältige Kollektion aus Vintage-Unikaten, Nobelmeilen- und Designerkleidung. Von Westwood-Corsagen über Kittel von Ossie Clark bis hin zu Vintage-Givenchy. Dazu kommen Schmuck und Accessoires von Dead Egg, Average Jo und die hauseigenen Designer. Und das Sortiment reicht bis zu

Second Hand H&M. Bei Bang Bang gibt's schlichtweg alles.

Célébrant son cinquième anniversaire et récemment réaménagée, la boutique Bang Bang propose une sélection variée de pièces vintage uniques, de griffes commerciales et de créateurs respectés. Corsets Vivienne Westwood, caracos Ossie Clark, créations Givenchy vintage, bijoux et accessoires de chez Dead Egg et Average Jo, sans oublier les propres stylistes de la boutique et les vêtements H&M d'occasion : on trouve vraiment de tout chez Bang Bang.

21 Goodge Street
London W1T 2PJ
Tel. +44 (0)20 7631 4191

Beyond Retro
Beyond Retro sells a vast array of vintage clothing, shoes and accessories for men and women which have been carefully selected from North and Central America. The clothing dates back from the early '90s through to the current trends of today.

Beyond Retro verkauft eine riesige Auswahl an Vintage-Kleidung, -Schuhen und Accessoires für Herren und Damen, sorgfältig ausgewählt unter den Designern Nord- und Mittelamerikas. Die Sachen entstanden ab Anfang der 1990er Jahre, es sind aber auch aktuelle Trends vertreten.

Beyond Retro vend un large éventail de vêtements, de chaussures et d'accessoires vintage pour homme et pour femme, tous sélectionnés avec le plus grand soin en Amérique du Nord et en Amérique centrale. Les pièces proposées datent du début des années 90 jusqu'à aujourd'hui.

The Stables Market
Chalk Farm Road
London NW1 8AG
Tel. +44 (0)20 7267 8009

Rellik
Lovingly preserved garments from the '20s to more recent times are housed in this treasure chest just off Portobello Road. An emphasis on '70s designers like Zandra Rhodes, one-off originals and the largest vintage Westwood collection in the UK are also found here.

In dieser Schatztruhe gleich neben der Portobello Road stößt man auf liebevoll gehütete Kleider – von den 1920er Jahren bis in die jüngere Vergangenheit. Schwerpunkte bilden Designer der 1970er Jahre wie Zandra Rhodes, Einzelanfertigungen und die größte Kollektion von Westwood-Kreationen in ganz Großbritannien.

Des années 1920 à aujourd'hui, vêtements magnifiquement préservés dans ce petit écrin situé juste au bout de Portobello Road. Les créateurs des années 70 sont particulièrement

mis en valeur, notamment Zandra Rhodes. On y trouve aussi des originaux uniques et la plus grande collection de pièces Westwood vintage du Royaume-Uni.

8 Golborne Road
London W10
Tel. +44 (0)20 8962 0089

Steinberg & Tolkein
A London fashion institution, highly respected and much loved, Steinberg & Tolkein features two floors of sublime vintage couture, jewellery and lively kitsch discoveries from Victoriana to the 1990s. Accessories dominate the street level; the basement is dedicated to three rooms of clothing. Also has a concession in Selfridges.

Eine hoch geschätzte und heiß geliebte Londoner Institution mit zwei Etagen Second-Hand-Couture, Schmuck und Kitsch-Pretiosen aus allen Epochen zwischen viktorianischem Zeitalter und den 1990er Jahren. Im Erdgeschoss findet man vor allem Accessoires, im Untergeschoss auf drei Räume verteilt Kleidung. Es gibt auch eine Filiale bei Selfridges.

Véritable institution de la mode londonienne, respectée et adorée, la boutique Steinberg & Tolkein présente sur deux niveaux de sublimes pièces couture vintage, des bijoux et de réjouissantes trouvailles kitsch, de l'époque victorienne aux années 1990. Le rez-de-chaussée est consacré aux accessoires tandis que le sous-sol accueille trois salles remplies de vêtements. Possède également un stand chez Selfridges.

193 King's Road
London SW3
Tel. +44 (0)20 7376 3660

Virginia Antiques
Virginia's has been a haunt of designers and stylists since the '60s, with shrewd magpie eyes hunting for vintage perfection.

Seit den 1960er Jahren ein Lieblingsladen von Designern und Stylisten, die hier mit Argusaugen nach perfekter Vintage-Mode Ausschau halten.

Depuis les années 60, Virginia attire comme des mouches les couturiers et les stylistes à l'œil aiguisé en quête de perfection vintage.

98 Portland Road
London W11
Tel. +44 (0)20 7727 9908

FLEA MARKETS

Brick Lane Market
Sundays only – this local market has expanded in recent years to sell clothes, modern antiques, scuffed retro furniture and assorted rubbish. The nearby bars, clubs, cafés and galleries fuel a relaxed but close-knit fashion-conscious community.

Nur sonntags werden auf diesem in den letzten Jahren immer größer gewordenen Markt Kleider, Trödel, abgewohnte Retro-Möbel und aller möglicher Kram verkauft. In den Bars, Clubs, Cafés und Galerien der Umgebung trifft man auf ein legeres, aber eng miteinander verbundenes, modebewusstes Volk.

Ces dernières années, ce marché local ouvert seulement le dimanche s'est diversifié dans les vêtements, les objets décoratifs modernes, les meubles rétro éraflés et autre camelote. Dans le quartier, les bars, les clubs, les cafés et les galeries d'art accueillent une communauté fashion mais très soudée.

Brick Lane
London E2

Camden Lock Market
The Lock is the central dedicated market site in Camden. Spread over winding, twisting levels and rumbling railway arches, it has a strong emphasis on secondhand clothing, crafts and accessories. Friendly, lively and packed at weekends.

The Lock ist der Marktplatz im Zentrum von Camden. Über gewundene, verschlungene Ebenen und weitläufige Eisenbahnüberführungen erstreckt sich der Flohmarkt, auf dem vor allem Kleidung, Kunsthandwerk und Accessoires angeboten werden. Freundliche, lebendige Atmosphäre, an den Wochenenden allerdings ziemlich überlaufen.

Le Lock est la zone centrale de Camden dédiée aux puces. Il s'étale sur plusieurs niveaux sous les arcades grondantes du métro. Spécialisé dans les vêtements d'occasion, l'artisanat et les accessoires. Ambiance chaleureuse et très vivante. Bondé le week-end.

54–56 Camden Lock Place
Chalk Farm Road
London NW1
Tel. +44 (0)20 7284 2084

Old Spitalfields Market
Historic covered market allowing young designers and importers an essential outlet. Popular and eclectic, selling secondhand garments and innovative accessories alongside a gallery space in what is normally a sports centre – a friendly, community feel, closed on Saturdays, busiest on Sundays.

Der historische überdachte Markt ist eine wichtige Verkaufsgelegenheit für junge Designer und Importeure. Auf dem beliebten Markt wird eine eklektische Mischung aus Second-Hand-Kleidern und originellen Accessoires feilgeboten. Außerdem gibt es in einer Turnhalle Platz für Ausstellungen. Es herrscht ein freundliches Gemeinschaftsgefühl. Sonntags ist am meisten los, samstags bleibt der Markt geschlossen.

Marché couvert d'époque, point de vente important pour les jeunes créateurs et les importateurs. Populaire et éclectique, on y trouve des vêtements d'occasion et des accessoires originaux à côté d'un centre sportif transformé pour l'occasion en espace d'exposition. Ambiance communautaire et chaleureuse. Fermé le dimanche, plein à craquer le samedi.

65 Brushfield Street
London E1
Tel. +44 (0)20 7247 8556

Portobello Market

Fridays and Saturdays (although Fridays are best), this is west London's near-glamorous antique and vintage market. The surrounding boutiques, bars and clubs are very much part of a unique, fashionable scene.

Jeden Freitag (dem besten Tag) und Samstag findet hier in West London der beinahe schon glamouröse Antiquitäten- und Vintage-Markt statt. Die Boutiquen, Bars und Clubs der Umgebung sind Teil dieser einzigartigen modebewussten Szene.

A West London, le vendredi et le samedi (mais mieux le vendredi). Marché d'antiquités et de pièces vintage pas tout à fait glamour mais presque. Les boutiques, bars et clubs du coin grouillent d'une faune branchée et unique.

Portobello Road
London W11

RESTAURANTS

Baltic

Cuisine from Polish cured meats to meatballs and Georgian hot pots, flavoured vodka and a great wine list make Baltic London's best Eastern European restaurant, and a top eatery south of the river. The setting of an old coach-works has been renovated with a coolly modern décor. A 'wall of amber' bar and a glass roof top the restaurant and beautiful staff complete the package.

Eine Küche mit polnischen geräucherten Fleischbällchen, georgischen Eintöpfen, aromatisiertem Wodka und einer tollen Weinkarte macht das Baltic zum besten osteuropäischen Restaurant und einem Spitzenlokal südlich der Themse. Die alte Waggonfabrik wurde mit kühl-modernem Dekor renoviert. Eine Bar mit Bernsteinwand, ein Glasdach über dem Restaurant und ausgesucht freundliches Personal komplettieren das Ganze.

Viande séchée de Pologne, boulettes de viande et ragoûts de Géorgie, vodka aromatisée et une superbe carte de vins font du Baltic le meilleur restaurant londonien de cuisine d'Europe de l'Est et une adresse incon-

tournable au sud de la Tamise. Cette ancienne carrosserie a été rénovée avec un décor moderne plus épuré. Un bar tout en ambre, un toit en verre transparent et un personnel irréprochable viennent compléter le tableau.

74 Blackfriars Road
London SE1 8HA
Tel. +44 (0)20 7928 1111

E&O

Will Rickers' informal pan-Asian restaurant features an eclectic Oriental menu and good value in a chic setting. Popular with west London fashion folk.

Will Rickers' informelles panasiatisches Restaurant bietet eine gemischt orientalische Speisekarte zu vernünftigen Preisen in schickem Ambiente. Beliebt bei der Modeszene von West London.

Le restaurant asiatique informel de Will Rickers propose un menu oriental éclectique à bon rapport qualité-prix dans un décor chic. Très prisé par les branchés du West London.

14 Blenheim Crescent
London W11
Tel. +44 (0)20 7229 5454

The Ivy

London's most famous celebrity institution with perfectly classic British and modern European cuisine, a good wine list, wood panelling and conspicuously placed power tables. There's a typically healthy waiting list for reservations, although spaces might appear at the mention of the right name.

Londons berühmtestes Prominentenlokal mit klassischer britischer und moderner europäischer Küche, einer guten Weinkarte, Holzvertäfelungen und auffällig platzierten Tischen für die allerwichtigsten Gäste. Hier läuft natürlich nichts ohne die obligatorische Warteliste für Reservierungen. Erwähnt man allerdings den richtigen Namen, ist manchmal auch spontan etwas frei.

Institution people la plus célèbre de Londres. Cuisine anglaise parfaitement classique et nouvelle cuisine européenne, bonne carte de vins. Murs lambrissés et tables stratégiques placées en bonne vue. Longue liste d'attente pour les réservations, mais sachez qu'une table peut parfois se libérer miraculeusement quand on cite le nom qu'il faut.

1 West Street
London WC2
Tel. +44 (0)20 7836 4751

J Sheekey

Market-fresh fish and crustaceans dominate the menu at this intimate restaurant in four small rooms. If you can't secure a table at The Ivy, this close relative is a perfect alternative. Discreet with friendly, attentive service.

Fangfrische Fische und Meeresfrüchte dominieren die Speisekarte dieses gemütlichen Restaurants mit seinen vier kleinen Räumen. Wenn es Ihnen nicht gelingt, einen Tisch im Ivy zu ergattern, ist dies die perfekte Alternative. Diskret, mit freundlichem, aufmerksamem Service.

Poissons frais et crustacés du marché dominent la carte de ce restaurant intimiste composé de quatre petites salles. Si vous n'arrivez pas à réserver à l'Ivy, ce proche parent constitue l'alternative idéale. Service cordial et attentif.

28–32 St Martin's Court
London WC2
Tel. +44 (0)20 7240 2565

Les Trois Garçons

This celebrated French-run restaurant in a converted East End boozer is heralded by flaming torches outside and crammed with oddities (the décor) and camp, attractive objects (the clientele). Taxidermy and tiaras.

Dies berühmte Restaurant unter französischer Führung in einer ehemaligen Kneipe im East End macht von außen mit Fackeln auf sich aufmerksam. Drinnen steckt es voller Kuriositäten und Kitsch – was das Dekor betrifft – und attraktiver Objekte – unter den Gästen. Ausgestopfte Tiere und Diademe.

Géré par un Français et installé dans un bistrot reconverti de l'East End, l'entrée de ce restaurant plébiscité est annoncée à la flamme de ses torches. Plein de bizarreries (le décor) et d'objets attirants et maniérés (la clientèle). Très « diadèmes et taxidermie ».

1 Club Row
London E1
Tel. +44 (0)20 7613 1924

Nobu

Matsuhisa Nobuyuki's American/Japanese cuisine draws an exclusive and attractive celebrity crowd in this dark, sexy space. Perfect sushi.

Matsuhisa Nobuyukis amerikanisch-japanische Küche lockt ein exklusives und attraktives Publikum inklusive zahlreicher Berühmtheiten in dieses schummrige, verführerische Lokal. Perfektes Sushi.

La cuisine américano-japonaise de Matsuhisa Nobuyuki attire une faune exclusive et séduisante de célébrités en tout genre dans cet espace sombre et sexy. Les sushi sont parfaits.

Metropolitan Hotel
19 Old Park Lane
London W1
Tel. +44 (0)20 7447 4747

St John Restaurant

Favoured by London's art scene, St John is light and airy, specialising

in carnivorous British cooking: meat, game and seafood – as well as inspired salads for the less flesh-inclined.

Das helle, luftige Lieblingslokal der Londoner Kunstszene hat sich auf die fleischlichen Genüsse der britischen Küche spezialisiert: Fleisch, Wild und Meeresfrüchte. Wer es eher vegetarisch liebt, bekommt aber auch originelle Salate.

Chouchou du petit monde artistique de Londres, le St John est spécialisé dans la cuisine anglaise carnivore : viandes, gibier et crustacés, mais aussi des salades inspirées pour végétariens égarés.

26 St John Street
London EC1
Tel. +44 (0)20 7251 0848

The Rivington Grill

Slap-bang in the middle of Hoxton, this restaurant boasts a great location and a solid menu of British classics including its signature dish, The Sunday Roast.

Direkt im Zentrum von Hoxton kann dieses Restaurant mit seiner fantastischen Lage und einer soliden Speisekarte mit britischen Traditionsgerichten aufwarten. Aushängeschild ist „the sunday roast" – der Sonntagsbraten.

En plein cœur de Hoxton, ce restaurant bénéficie d'un superbe emplacement et propose un solide menu de classiques anglais, dont la spécialité du chef : le bon vieux rôti du dimanche.

28–30 Rivington Street
London EC2A
Tel. +44 (0)20 7729 7053

The Wolseley

Thirteen different champagnes, many different types of caviar and oysters on the menu, and all the cake you can you eat. You get the picture. In the style of the best Parisian cafés of yore, and situated in the swankiest destination on the Monopoly board, The Wolseley is a place to indulge in elegance.

Dreizehn verschiedene Champagnersorten, viele verschiedene Sorten Kaviar und Austern auf der Karte und jedes nur erdenkliche Gebäck. Das sollte zur Orientierung genügen. Im Stil der besten Pariser Cafés vergangener Zeiten ist das Wolseley der Ort schlechthin, um in Eleganz zu schwelgen.

Trente champagnes différents, plusieurs sortes de caviar et d'huîtres au menu, et gâteaux à volonté. Juste pour vous donner une idée. Dans le style des meilleurs cafés parisiens d'autrefois et situé dans le quartier le plus convoité au Monopoly, The Wolseley est le restaurant idéal pour s'adonner avec élégance aux plaisirs de la table.

160 Piccadilly
Mayfair
London W1J 9EB
Tel. +44 (0)20 7499 6996

Zuma

Designed by Japanese design team, Super Potato, Zuma is a restaurant that gleams with contemporary style. Polished marble, glass, and wood frame the moneyed, post-SATC clientele. From dynamite spider rolls from the Sushi menu, to whole native lobster tempura, the contemporary Japanese menu is appropriately chic.

Das vom japanischen Designteam Super Potato entworfene Restaurant erstrahlt in moderner Eleganz. Polierter Marmor, Glas und Holz umgeben die betuchte post-Sex-and-the-City-Klientel. Von Dynamite Spider Rolls aus der Sushi-Karte bis hin zu Tempura aus naturbelassenem Hummer erweist sich die moderne japanische Karte als adäquat chic.

Conçu par l'équipe de designers japonais Super Potato, Zuma est un restaurant au style résolument contemporain. Marbre poli, verre et bois encadrent une clientèle fortunée post-Sex & The City. Des makis explosifs du menu sushi au tempura de homard entier, on y déguste une cuisine japonaise moderne du dernier chic.

5 Raphael Street
London SW7 1DL
Tel. +44 (0)20 7584 1010

BARS

Bistrotheque

Down the unlikeliest of alleys is east London's hottest new fashion hangout, run by former House of Jazz designer Pablo Flack. Housing several bars and a top-class restaurant, the venue's tranny lip-synching contests are a particular delight.

In einer der unscheinbarsten Gassen befindet sich East Londons heißester und neuester Treff der Modeszene. Geführt wird das Lokal vom ehemaligen House-of-Jazz-Designer Pablo Flack. Die dort ausgetragenen Karaoke-Wettbewerbe von Transsexuellen sind ein besonderes Vergnügen.

Géré par Pablo Flack, ex-créateur de la griffe House of Jazz, le dernier endroit dont on parle se trouve au fond de la plus improbable des allées de l'East London. Accueillant plusieurs bars et un restaurant ultra-classe, on y vient notamment pour assister aux concours de play-back réservés aux transsexuels.

Bistrotheque
23–27 Wadeson St
London E2
(Tel. +44 (0)20 8983 7900

Blue Bar

This intimate and inviting Wedgwood-blue hotel bar always has a comfortable private corner to whisper secrets or spread gossip. Impeccably served drinks in rather elegant surrounds.

In der intimen, einladenden Hotelbar in Wedgewood-Blau findet man immer eine gemütliche, stille Ecke, um Geheimnisse oder den neuesten Klatsch auszutauschen. Tadellos servierte Drinks in ziemlich eleganter Umgebung.

Avec sa déco bleue style porcelaine de Wedgwood, ce bar d'hôtel intime et accueillant recèle de nombreux coins privés et confortables pour échanger des secrets ou répandre les derniers potins. Service impeccable et déco plutôt classe.

Berkley Hotel
Wilton Place
London SW1
Tel. +44 (0)20 7235 6000

Coach And Horses

This old haunt of writers and actors was once a great example of the tits'n'ass sleaze of Soho before it earned its international reputation of cool. Now the favoured drinking place of fashion students and a few old Soho relics.

Dieser traditionelle Treffpunkt von Schriftstellern und Schauspielern war einst ein Paradebeispiel für das verkommene, verruchte Soho – bevor das Viertel den internationalen Ruf einer hippen Gegend bekam. Heute ist es die Lieblingskneipe von Modestudenten und wenigen Relikten des alten Soho.

Cet ancien repaire d'écrivains et de comédiens offrait autrefois un bon échantillon de la faune sexuellement louche de Soho, avant qu'il gagne sa réputation internationale de quartier cool. C'est aujourd'hui le bar préféré des étudiants en mode et des rares reliques de l'ancien Soho.

29 Greek Street
London W1
Tel. +44 (0)20 7437 5920

George & Dragon

Still the central locus for east London's art and fashion crowd (with a slight stress on boys who like other boys), this boozer is still holding its own, in every sense.

Nach wie vor der Treffpunkt schlechthin für die Kunst- und Modeszene East Londons (leicht bevorzugt von Männern, die Männer mögen). Die Kneipe hat sich in jeder Hinsicht ihren Charakter bewahrt.

Restant le point d'attraction du petit monde de l'art et de la mode de l'East London (avec une clientèle plutôt gay), ce bar est toujours à la hauteur de sa réputation.

2 Hackney Road
London E2

Loungelover

Ignoring the bankers and city boys lurking at the bar, this place is a kitsch Cocteau-esque fantasy realised in an East End aircraft hangar. Fabulous with a very capital 'F'.

Wenn man sich die Banker und anderen Jungs aus der City wegdenkt, die an der Bar rumhängen, ist das die wahr gewordene Kitschfantasie à la Cocteau in einem Flugzeughangar im East End. Märchenhaft mit sehr großem M.

Ignorant les banquiers et les garçons de la City qui rôdent autour du bar, le Loungelover est une sorte de fantaisie kitsch à la Cocteau installée dans un hangar aérien de l'East End. Fabuleux de chez fabuleux.

Loungelover
1 Whitby Street
London E2
Tel. +44 (0)208713 326749

Old Blue Last

Until recently this Hoxton boozer was the haunt of cabaret singers and toothless old men. Then the team behind Vice magazine took some spit and polish to it, uncovering flocked wall paper, leather sofas stacked in the basement, and restored the faded glory of the 1950s. Now The Old Blue Last is one of hip east London's most favoured hang outs. There are visiting DJs, bands, and the promise of karaoke from 2005.

Bis vor kurzem war diese Kneipe in Hoxton das Lieblingslokal von tingelnden Sängerinnen und zahnlosen alten Männern. Dann brachte das Team der Zeitschrift Vice etwas Geduld und Spucke auf, um Textiltapeten wieder zum Vorschein zu bringen, die im Keller gestapelten Ledersofas zu entdecken und den verblichenen Glanz der 1950er Jahre wiederherzustellen. Heute gilt The Old Blue Last als eines der Lieblingslokale des hippen East London. Es gibt Gast-DJs, Band-Auftritte und für 2005 ist Karaoke angekündigt.

Il n'y a pas si longtemps, ce troquet était le repaire des chanteuses de cabaret et des vieux messieurs édentés. Puis, l'équipe du magazine Vice a décidé de retrousser ses manches pour restaurer la gloire passée des années 50 en découvrant le papier peint en velours floqué sur les murs et en ressortant les canapés en cuir oubliés dans la cave. Aujourd'hui, l'Old Blue Last est l'un des rendezvous favoris des branchés de l'East London. Les propriétaires y font venir des DJ, des groupes et promettent même un karaoké pour 2005.

39 Great Eastern Road
London EC2A 3ES
Tel. +44 (0)20 7739 5793

Prince Bonaparte

A busy, bright and spacious west London pub with an interesting but relaxed fashion crowd.

Ein gut besuchter, heller und geräumiger Pub in West London mit vielen interessanten, aber lockeren Modeleuten.

Dans le West London, ce pub lumineux et spacieux accueille une clientèle branchée et insolite qui ne se prend pas au sérieux.

80 Chepstow Road
London W2
Tel. +44 (0)20 7313 9491

CLUBS

The Key

Taking up the premises left vacant by '90s rave paradise, Bagleys, The Key serves up a five star platter of premium European and international techno, house, disco and punk. Proof comes from Berlin boys of the moment, Tiefschwarz, having selected it for their '05 London Issst residency.

In den Räumen von Bagleys, dem inzwischen leerstehenden Rave-Paradies der 1990er Jahre, serviert The Key eine Fünf-Sterne-Platte mit bestem europäischem und internationalem Techno, House, Disco und Punk. Bestätigt wurde diese Einschätzung von den angesagtesten Berliner Jungs, von Tiefschwarz, die den Club zu ihrer ersten Station von '05 London machten.

Installé dans les anciens locaux de Bagleys, ex-paradis des raveurs dans les années 90, The Key présente un plateau cinq étoiles de la meilleure musique techno, house, disco et punk européenne comme internationale. En témoigne les membres de Tiefschwarz, sensation berlinoise du moment, qui en ont fait leur résidence du « London Issst » pour 2005.

Lazer road, off York Way
Kings Cross
London N1 9AA
info@thekeylondon.com
Tel. +44 (0)20 7837 1027

The Ghetto

West End's premier queens and kings of trash assemble here to spray glitter everywhere, get dressed up and messed up. Home to London's original electroclash nightclub Nag Nag Nag, the Ghetto also homes London's smashing gay punky-tronica party, The Cock.

Die besten Trash Queens and Kings des West End versammeln sich hier, um Glitzer zu versprühen, sich aufzurüschen und einen drauf zu machen. Hier ist nicht nur Londons echter electroclash Nightclub Nag Nag Nag zu Hause, sondern auch die umwerfende Gay Punky-Tronica Party namens The Cock findet im Ghetto statt.

Les rois et reines du trash du West End se retrouvent ici pour répandre la bonne parole du glitter, se déguiser et partir en vrille. Résidence du Nag Nag Nag, premier club électroclash de Londres, le Ghetto accueille également la soirée The Cock prisée par les gays de la formidable scène punk électronique de Londres.

The Ghetto
Falconberg Court
London W1

Fabric
Amaze at the maze-like superclub situated in London's meat packing district. Three floors and loads of rooms, all playing host to those at the top of their game. Expect techno, house, hip-hop, drum and bass and grime taking you so close to the edge you'll feel like a lemming.

Staunen Sie über den labyrinthischen Superclub im Londoner Meat Packing District. Drei Stockwerke und jede Menge Räume, die allesamt Erstklassiges zu bieten haben. Rechnen Sie mit Techno, House, Hip-Hop, Drum and Bass und Grime, die Sie so in ihren Bann ziehen werden, dass Sie sich wie ein Lemming vorkommen.

Enorme club labyrinthique situé dans le quartier des abattoirs de Londres. Ses trois étages et ses nombreuses salles accueillent les meilleurs DJ du moment. Attendez-vous à transpirer avec bonheur sur de la techno, de la house, du hip-hop ou de la drum & bass.

77a Charterhouse Street
London EC1M 3HN

HOTELS

Claridges
The epitome of the grand old English-style hotel, Claridges has attracted a younger crowd of late, banking in on its 100 years of luxurious, debauched living. Rather pricey, it's often assumed to be dry and stuffy but in fact is welcoming and relaxed.

Der Inbegriff eines Grandhotels im altenglischen Stil lockt in letzter Zeit auch jüngere Leute an, die der hundertjährigen Tradition eines luxuriös-ausschweifenden Lebensstils vertrauen. Relativ teuer, aber nicht die Spur verknöchert oder verstaubt, sondern einladend und entspannt.

Symbole de la grande hôtellerie britannique à l'ancienne, le Claridges attire depuis peu une clientèle plus jeune en misant sur ses 100 ans de vie de débauche et de luxe. Plutôt cher, on dit souvent que l'accueil y est froid et rigide mais c'est faux : le

personne y est sympathique et décontracté.

55 Brook Street
London W1
Tel. +44 (0)20 7629 8860
www.savoy-group.co.uk/claridges

Covent Garden Hotel
A classical and modern interior: dark wood floors give the hotel a gentrified country life feel. Popular with a fashion crowd who enjoy a more peaceful space in the centre of the city.

Ein Haus mit klassisch-moderner Einrichtung: Die dunklen Holzböden verleihen dem Hotel das Flair von adeligem Landleben. Beliebt bei den Leuten aus der Modebranche, die es ruhiger mögen als mitten in der Stadt.

Décoration intérieure à la fois classique et moderne : le plancher de bois sombre donne à l'hôtel un côté « manoir de gentleman farmer ». En plein centre-ville, il accueille une clientèle branchée en quête d'un havre de paix.

10 Monmouth Street
London WC2
Tel. +44 (0)20 7836 4100

Great Eastern Hotel
The Victorian railway-station hotel opened in 1884, but was refurbished beautifully in 2000. The site offers five Conran restaurants, a private members bar and frenetic fashion club nights in the ballroom.

Das viktorianische Bahnhofshotel wurde 1884 eröffnet und 2000 wunderschön renoviert. Zum Haus gehören fünf Conran-Restaurants, eine intime Bar nur für Mitglieder und wilde Club Nights der Modeszene im Ballsaal.

Ouvert en 1884, cet hôtel de gare de l'époque victorienne a été entièrement rénové en l'an 2000. Le complexe regroupe cinq restaurants Conran et un bar privé. La salle de bal accueille des soirées fashion et frénétiques.

40 Liverpool Street
London EC2
Tel. +44 (0)20 7618 5000
www.great-eastern-hotel.co.uk

Portobello Hotel
Eccentric, off-beat and friendly – the atmosphere is intimate in this small, special hotel, a world away from bland super-chains, complimentary showercaps and an in-room trouser press. Unusual, sexy rooms that feel more like a home than a hotel.

Exzentrisch, anders und freundlich. In diesem kleinen, besonderen Hotel herrscht eine intime Atmosphäre – Welten entfernt von langweiligen Hotelketten mit Gratis-Duschhauben

und Hosenbügelautomat im Zimmer. In den kuscheligen Räumen fühlt man sich nicht wie in einem Hotel, sondern fast wie zu Hause.

Excentrique, décalé et accueillant, ce petit hôtel pas comme les autres se distingue par son atmosphère intimiste, à des années lumière des grandes chaînes hôtelières standardisées, des bonnets de douche gratuits et des chambres avec pressing intégré. Chambres insolites et sexy qui vous donnent l'impression d'être chez quelqu'un, pas à l'hôtel.

22 Stanley Gardens
London W11
Tel. +44 (0)20 7727 2777
www.portobello-hotel.co.uk

St Martin's Lane
Just off Trafalgar Square, St Martin's Lane is a coolly conceptual space. Ian Schrager and Philippe Starck offer a minimalist interior with the chain's typically excellent service. Floor to ceiling windows in every room with panoramic views of London.

Ganz nah am Trafalgar Square liegt dieses cool durchgestylte Hotel. Ian Schrager und Philippe Starck bieten minimalistisches Interieur und den bekannt ausgezeichneten Service der Kette. In jedem Zimmer kann man durch raumhohe Fenster die Aussicht auf London genießen.

Tout au bout de Trafalgar Square, le St Martin's Lane est un hôtel concept au décor plutôt froid et minimaliste conçu par Philippe Starck. Service excellent, comme dans tous les hôtels de la chaîne Ian Schrager. Fenêtres du sol au plafond dans toutes les chambres, avec vue panoramique sur Londres.

45 St Martin's Lane
London WC2
Tel. +44 (0)20 7300 5501
www.ianschragerhotels.com

The Sanderson
The Sanderson sets entirely new industry standards. Another Schrager/Starck collaboration, the hotel is a totally unconventional space with beautiful rooms.

Das Sanderson setzt vollkommen neue Maßstäbe in der Hotelbranche. Als weiteres Projekt von Schrager und Starck besticht es durch absolute Unkonventionalität und herrliche Zimmer.

Le Sanderson révolutionne le marché de l'hôtellerie. Né d'une énième collaboration Schrager/Starck, cet endroit complètement hors norme propose des chambres superbes.

50 Berners Street
London W1
Tel. +44 (0)20 7300 9500
www.ianschragerhotels.com

The Metropolitan Hotel
The original 'hip' hotel still flaunts a large celebrity following as the traditional default choice for the late night drinking A-to-D list. A central location, its fresh, innovative rooms overlook Hyde Park.

Das erste wirklich hippe Hotel hat immer noch eine große Fangemeinde als traditionelle Absacker-Location für Prominente der Kategorien A bis D. Dazu kommen noch die Zentrale Lage und die frischen, innovativen Zimmer mit Blick auf den Hyde Park.

Le premier hôtel « jet-set » remporte toujours autant de succès auprès des stars et autres membres de la crème qui en ont fait leur bar de nuit par défaut. Emplacement central, nouvelles chambres originales avec vue sur Hyde Park.

Old Park Lane
London W1
Tel. +44 (0)20 7447 1000

AIRPORTS

London City Airport
Royal Docks
London E16
Tel. +44 (0)20 7646 0088
www.londoncityairport.com

London Gatwick Airport
West Sussex RH6 0NP
Tel. +44 (0)8700002468
www.baa.co.uk

London Heathrow Airport
Heathrow Point West
234 Bath Road, Harlington
Middlesex UB3 5AP
Tel. +44 (0)87000 01234
www.baa.co.uk

London Stansted Airport
Bassingbourne Road
Essex CM24 1QW
Tel. +44 (0)8700000303
www.baa.co.uk

INTERNATIONAL RAIL CONNECTION

Waterloo International
Home to Eurostar and its high-speed passenger trains: Brussels, Lille and the centre of Paris in just three hours.

Wo der Eurostar zu Hause ist. Von hier aus kommt man in nur drei Stunden nach Brüssel, Lille oder ins Zentrum von Paris.

Terminus de l'Eurostar et de ses trains à grande vitesse : relie Bruxelles, Lille et le centre de Paris en moins de trois heures.

Waterloo Station
London SE1
Tel. ++44 (0)870 160 6600
www.eurostar.com

LOS ANGELES

TEXT BY ED PERRY

Square grids etched in the desert, stretching over mountains, flowing north and south along the long glistening line of the Pacific. The smog is a kind of smoke-screen, concealing the crazy fiction of the city below. Not only is Los Angeles built on fiction, it is even a kind of fiction in itself, a dream-city built on borrowed water and living on borrowed time. Here is the world centre of entertainment, the capital of tall stories and sleazy secrets, home to the Olympian few who reside in the hills and gaze upon the mad masses who go about the infinite grids in search of the American Dream. And they can be mad. The American Empire, like all Empires, follows the setting sun, and sooner or later every drug-crazed drop-out, every conspiracy nut and Vietnam vet, every deranged poet or acid-headed hipster, every Gulf-War syndrome'd philosopher or just plain kook ends up on Venice beach watching the sun set. The bards of LA, like the Chili Peppers, sing about it, the scribes like Chandler write about it, and the film-makers, actors, writers, wannabe producers and budding porn stars live it. The city is a swirling mass of corruption, ambition, big-money and spoiled lives – the beauty and the beast in all of us. And it lives on fiction. Nowhere in the world do so many people reinvent themselves down to every last detail. Thus the fashion here is about reinvention. Very often it's the façade of fake glamour and the imitation of success, or it's the rock star anti-fashion fashion, or sometimes it's just plain sex, but here you don't come looking for the cutting edge, here you come looking for the Fantasy. Whole lives get swallowed up by the Fantasy, and the fiction becomes reality. But Los Angeles is a city of stories, and secrets, of lives spread out in one of the most stunning locations in the world. It is a city to lose yourself in among the lost Angels and beautiful dreamers – the only thing like it in the history of the world.

In den Wüstensand geätzte quadratische Gitternetze erstrecken sich über Berge und nach Norden und Süden entlang der langen glitzernden Pazifikküste. Der Smog verhüllt wie ein Nebelvorhang die verrückte Märchenwelt der Stadt. Los Angeles gründet sich nicht nur auf Fiktion, sondern ist sogar selbst eine Art Fiktion – eine Traumstadt, auf geborgtes Wasser gebaut und von gestundeter Zeit lebend. Hier befindet sich das Zentrum der weltweiten Unterhaltung, in der Hauptstadt der großen Stories und schmutzigen Geheimnisse, das Zuhause der Wenigen, die in den Hügeln wie auf dem Olymp residieren und auf die verrückten Massen hinabschauen, die das unendliche Gitternetz auf der Suche nach dem American Dream durchstreifen. Manche von ihnen sind tatsächlich verrückt. Das amerikanische Imperium folgt wie alle Reiche der untergehenden Sonne, und früher oder später endet jeder mit Drogen zugedröhnte Aussteiger, jeder Verschwörungstheoretiker und Vietnamveteran, jeder gestörte Poet oder Hipster mit Ecstacy im Blut, jeder Philosoph mit Golfkriegs-Syndrom und jeder ganz normale Verrückte am Venice Beach, um den Sonnenuntergang zu betrachten. Die Barden von LA, wie die Chili Peppers, singen darüber, Schriftsteller wie Chandler schreiben darüber, und Filmemacher, Schauspieler, Möchtegern-Produzenten und aufstrebende Pornostars leben es. Die Stadt ist ein Wirbel aus Korruption, Ehrgeiz, dem großen Geld und verpfuschten Leben – den Licht- und Schattenseiten, die wir alle in uns haben. Und sie lebt von der Fiktion. Nirgendwo sonst auf der Welt legen sich die Leute eine bis ins Detail neue Biografie zu. Folglich geht es auch in der Mode darum, sich neu zu erfinden. Sehr oft dient sie als Fassade für falschen Glamour und geheuchelten Erfolg, oder es ist die Anti-Mode der Rockstars, manchmal auch nur der pure Sex. Man kommt allerdings auch nicht nach LA, um die brandneuen Trends zu finden, sondern auf der Suche nach Fantasie. Der fallen gelegentlich ganze Leben zum Opfer, und die Fiktion wird zur Realität. Los Angeles ist aber auch eine Stadt der Geschichten und Geheimnissen, der Leben an einem der aufregendsten Orte der Welt. Eine Stadt, in der man sich unter den gefallenen Engeln und wundervollen Träumern selbst verlieren kann – einzigartig in der gesamten Weltgeschichte.

Le quadrillage des routes semble comme gravé dans le désert, s'étalant sur les montagnes et poussant vers le nord et le sud le long de l'interminable côte étincelante du Pacifique. Le smog agit comme un écran de fumée qui masquerait les folles fictions se déroulant dans la ville en dessous. Los Angeles ne se contente pas d'être construit sur la fiction, c'est un genre de fiction à part entière, une ville de rêve bâtie à crédit et destinée un jour à sombrer dans l'océan. Bienvenue dans la capitale mondiale de l'entertainment, celle des grandes histoires et des secrets d'alcôve, patrie des dieux de l'Olympe qui vivent sur les hauteurs de la ville, avec vue imprenable sur les masses détraquées qui parcourent ses routes sans fin à la poursuite du rêve américain. Et elles ont toutes les raisons du monde d'être détraquées. L'Empire américain, comme tous les empires, a le regard tourné vers l'Ouest. Tôt ou tard, tous ses diplômés friands de drogues dures, tous ses paranos de la théorie du complot, ses vétérans du Vietnam, ses poètes dérangés, ses branchés sous acide, tous ses philosophes souffrant du syndrome de la guerre du Golfe et même ses simples tarés finissent sur la plage de Venice pour admirer le coucher du soleil. Un spectacle chanté par les Red Hot Chili Peppers et autres bardes de LA, décrit par des écrivains tels que Chandler, mais réellement vécu par les réalisateurs de film, les acteurs, les scénaristes, les aspirants producteurs et les futures stars du porno. La ville est une masse tourbillonnante de corruption, d'ambition, de gros sous et de vies gâchées, à l'image des contradictions que nous portons en chacun de nous. Elle vit de la fiction. C'est l'unique endroit sur terre où tant de gens se réinventent jusque dans les moindres détails. Ainsi, la mode produite par LA ne parle que de réinvention. Très souvent, elle présente la façade d'un glamour de pacotille et l'imitation du succès; il y a aussi la mode des stars de rock anti-fashion et parfois il ne s'agit que de sexe, mais on ne vient pas ici pour l'avant-garde, on vient y chercher le fantasme. Des vies entières sont avalées par le fantasme, et la fiction devient réalité. Mais Los Angeles est d'abord une ville d'histoires, de vies et de secrets racontés dans l'un des endroits les plus fascinants du monde. Une ville dans laquelle il faut se perdre parmi les anges déchus et les doux rêveurs, un lieu absolument unique dans l'histoire de l'humanité.

FASHION SHOPS

Prada

Epicentre of cool. Everything one would expect from Mrs. Prada: more avant-garde art gallery than clothes horse. Mannequins are spied through floor portholes. The stairway has legs and the changing rooms change from opaque to clear – don't forget to press the button, or you'll be shopping in your own Vanessa Beecroft-inspired installation.

Epizentrum der Coolness. Alles, was man von Signora Prada erwartet: mehr avantgardistische Kunstgalerie als Kleiderladen. Durch Bullaugen im Boden kann man Mannequins beobachten. Die Rolltreppe hat Beine, und die Umkleiden sind mal durchsichtig, mal opak – vergessen Sie also nicht den Knopf zu drücken, sonst kaufen Sie in Ihrer eigenen Installation à la Vanessa Beecroft ein.

L'épicentre du cool présente tout ce que l'on est en droit d'attendre de Madame Prada, dans une boutique qui ressemble plutôt à une galerie d'art avant-gardiste. On épie les mannequins à travers les hublots du plancher, l'escalier possède des jambes et les cabines d'essayage passent de l'opaque au transparent : n'oubliez pas d'appuyer sur le bouton, sinon vous finirez votre shopping dans votre propre installation artistique à la Vanessa Beecroft.

343 N. Rodeo Drive
Beverly Hills, CA 90210
Tel. +1 310 278 8661

Theodore

This is actually the last remaining independently owned store on Rodeo Drive. It stocks Ann Demeulemeester, Alexander McQueen and People of the Labyrinth. If you like to support independents then this is your only bet on this famous strip.

Dies ist tatsächlich der letzte Laden am Rodeo Drive in Privatbesitz. Er führt Ann Demeulemeester, Alexander McQueen und People of the Labyrinth. Wenn Sie Unabhängigkeit unterstützen wollen, dann ist das Ihre einzige Gelegenheit auf diesem berühmten Strip.

C'est en fait la dernière boutique indépendante de Rodeo Drive. Elle vend les créations d'Ann Demeulemeester, Alexander McQueen et People of the Labyrinth. Si vous tenez à soutenir les indépendants, alors ce sera votre seule et unique destination de shopping sur ce fameux boulevard.

453 N. Rodeo Drive
Beverly Hills, CA 90210
Tel. +1 310 276 9691

Barney's New York in LA

Barney's stocks some of the best fashion in New York, and in LA it's more of the same. The very best from the very established to the very cream of the cutting edge.

Barney's führt in New York einige der besten Modemarken, und in LA ist das nicht anders. Vom Allerbesten der sehr Etablierten bis hin zur Elite der Avantgardisten.

A New York, Barney's propose ce que la mode a de mieux à offrir, et c'est à peu près pareil dans son magasin de LA. On y trouve le meilleur des griffes bien établies aux côtés de la crème de la crème de l'avant-garde.

9570 Wiltshire Blvd.
Beverly Hills CA 90212
Tel. +1 310 276 4400
www.barneys.com

Fred Segal

Before Barney's came to LA from New York there was Fred Segal, and it's been going now for thirty years. A low slung and ivy clad cluster of boutiques, beauty cognescenti will trek here for hard-to-find treats like Lorac and Paula Dorf, and it is still the most name-checked store for the hoards of Hollywood hotties who shop here. The staff are thankfully hands-off in their approach and generally unpretentious.

Bevor Barney's aus New York nach LA kam, gab es hier schon seit inzwischen dreißig Jahren Fred Segal. Eine niedrige, efeuumrankte Ansammlung von Boutiquen. Beauty-Experten spüren hier schwer zu bekommende Marken wie Lorac und Paula Dorf auf. Und es ist nach wie vor der meistgenannte Laden der Horden von Hollywood-Sternchen, die hier shoppen gehen. Das Personal ist angenehm zurückhaltend und grundsätzlich unprätentiös.

Avant que le Barney's new-yorkais s'installe à LA, il y avait Fred Segal, une histoire qui dure depuis trente ans. Dans ce complexe commercial bas de plafond aux murs décorés de lierre, les connaisseurs sont à la recherche de pièces presque introuvables de Lorac et Paula Dorf. Ça reste l'espace de vente le plus cité par les hordes de stars hollywoodiennes qui y font leur shopping. Heureusement, le personnel sans prétention n'a pas tendance à vous harceler comme ailleurs.

8100 Melrose Ave/cross street North Crescent Heights Blvd.
Los Angeles, CA 90046
Tel. +1 323 651 4129

Marc Jacobs

The man has fans. Legions of them. And his LA store is there for his West Coast admirers, who are many. The store is suitably romantic, and with the ivy growing up the side looks like it's been there longer than it really has (it opened 2005). Conveniently, the Marc by Marc Jacobs store is just across the street.

Der Mann hat Fans. Scharenweise. Und sein Laden in LA ist für seine Bewunderer an der Westküste gedacht, von denen es reichlich gibt. Das Geschäft ist angemessen romantisch und wirkt dank des Efeus, der es umrankt, als sei es schon lange dort (tatsächlich wurde es erst 2005 eröffnet). Praktischerweise liegt der Marc by Marc Jacobs Store gleich gegenüber.

Cet homme-là compte des légions de fans. Et sa boutique de LA vient réaliser les rêves de ses nombreux admirateurs de la côte ouest. Avec son ambiance romantique, le lierre qui pousse le long des murs donne l'impression que la boutique est là depuis longtemps (alors qu'elle n'a ouvert qu'en 2005). Très pratique, la boutique Marc by Marc Jacobs se trouve juste de l'autre côté de la rue.

8409 Melrose Place
Los Angeles, CA 90069
Tel. +1 323 866 8255

Curve

Curve is a well edited store, but the sizes tend to be thin, thin and thinner. The collection at Curve highlights lesser-known designers that step outside the Gap-Banana Republic box.

Curve ist ein gut sortierter Laden, nur leider sind die Größen klein, kleiner und noch kleiner. Man stellt eher weniger bekannte Designer in den Vordergrund, die nicht ins Gap/Banana Republic-Schema passen.

Curve est une boutique bien achalandée, mais la taille des vêtements a tendance à rétrécir chaque saison. La sélection met en valeur des créateurs moins connus, à l'opposé des standards Gap ou Banana Republic.

54 N Robertson Blvd
Los Angeles, CA 90048
Tel. +1 310 360 8008

Beige

Local designers Louis Verdad and Michelle Mason along with the line of Beige's co-owner Tina Webb hang here. As do Seven and Frankie B jeans and James Coviello.

Hier hängen Kreationen der einheimischen Designer Louis Verdad und Michelle Mason und die Kollektion der Miteigentümerin Tina Webb. Außerdem Seven, Jeans von Frankie B und James Coviello.

Une boutique qui vend les vêtements des créateurs locaux Louis Verdad et Michelle Mason, à côté de la ligne de Tina Webb, co-gérante de Beige, des jeans Seven et Frankie B, et des créations James Coviello.

7274 Beverly Blvd
Los Angeles, CA 90036
Tel. +1 323 549 0064
Poinsettia Ave

Noni

Blending fashion, art exhibitions and music, this is a hip and cultured environment in which to find your newly favourite LA or San Francisco-based designer.

Der Mix aus Mode, Kunstausstellung und Musik macht aus diesem Laden einen angesagten, kultivierten Ort, an dem man neue Lieblingsdesigner aus LA oder San Francisco entdecken kann.

Mêlant mode, expositions artistiques et musique, voilà un environnement branché et cultivé idéal pour découvrir votre futur créateur préféré de LA ou de San Francisco.

225 N. Larchmont Blvd
Los Angeles, CA 90004
Tel. +1 323 469 3239

Brick Lane

A local shop in the increasingly too-cool-for-school Abbott Kinney. As the name suggests, this is an outlet in LA for young hip Brit labels.

Ein kleiner Laden am immer cooler werdenden Abbott Kinney. Wie der Name schon vermuten lässt, ein Outlet für junge, hippe Brit-Labels.

Boutique locale au beau milieu du boulevard Abbott Kinney ultra-cool. Comme son nom l'indique, c'est l'adresse de choix pour trouver les jeunes griffes anglaises du moment.

1132 Abbot Kinney Blvd
Venice, CA 90291
Tel. +1 310 392 2525

Planet Blue

Large space, cute staff, hip brands. There's also a Planet Blue Essentials that does home stuff.

Viel Platz, süßes Personal, hippe Marken. Außerdem gibt es einen Planet Blue Essentials für Homeware.

Boutique spacieuse, personnel charmant, marques branchées. Il existe également un espace Planet Blue Essentials qui vend du homewear.

3835 Cross Creek Rd # 13a
Malibu, CA 90265
Tel. +1 310 317 8566

Wolf

Men's clothes to the left, children's clothes to the right. Men's is a well-put-together mix of boho-hobo chic, and the kid's stuff is desirable and expensive vintage for hipster tots.

Männersachen zur Linken, Kindersachen zur Rechten. Für die Herren ein gut sortierter Mix aus Boho-Hobo-Chic; für den Hipster-Nachwuchs gibt's begehrte, teure Vintage-Sachen.

Vêtements pour homme à gauche, vêtements pour enfant à droite. La sélection masculine présente un mix étudié de créations bobo chic, tandis que la zone enfant inclut de superbes pièces vintage hors de prix pour les bébés à la mode.

1323 Abbot Kinney Blvd
Venice, CA 90291
Tel. +1 310 392 8551

B.N.Y

Limited edition trainers, stockist of Yohji Yamamoto, Undercover, Margiela, etc. Think very cool and very expensive. Great unpretentious staff.

Sneakers aus limitierten Auflagen. Außerdem führt man hier Yohji Yamamoto, Undercover, Margiela u. a. Sehr cool und sehr teuer, aber mit nettem, unkompliziertem Personal.

Survêtements en édition limitée, créations Yohji Yamamoto, Undercover, Margiela, etc. Sélection très cool et très chère. Personnel sympa et sans prétention.

2449 Main Street
Santa Monica, CA 90405
Tel. +1 310 396 1616

Undefeated

Trainer whores have been known to camp outside for their special limited editions.

Turnschuh-Fanatiker sollen wegen der limitierten Sondereditionen schon vor dem Laden campiert haben.

Les fanas du survêtement vont jusqu'à camper à l'extérieur pour être les premiers à rafler les éditions limitées d'Undefeated.

2654 Main Street # b
Santa Monica, CA 90405
Tel. +1 310 264 6124

OTHER SHOPS

Lost and Found

Children's clothes. Superb place for gifts. Yucca has plenty of other shops and is worth a visit anyway.

Kinderklamotten. Toll für Geschenke. Yucca hat noch jede Menge anderer Läden zu bieten und lohnt auf jeden Fall einen Besuch.

Vêtements pour enfant. Un endroit idéal pour les cadeaux. Sur Yucca, on trouve plein d'autres boutiques et la rue vaut le détour de toutes façons.

Lost & Found
6314 Yucca Street
Los Angeles, CA 90028
Tel. +1 323 856 0921

Taschen Book Store

Designed by Philippe Starck, the TASCHEN book store presents an excellent selection of illustrated books on art, architecture, photography, fashion and sex.

Der TASCHEN Buchladen wurde von Philippe Starck gestaltet und präsen-

tiert eine hervorragende Auswahl an Bildbänden zu den Themen Kunst, Architektur, Fotografie, Mode und Sex.

Conçue par Philippe Starck, la librairie TASCHEN présente une excellente sélection de livres illustrés sur l'art, l'architecture, la photographie, la mode et le sexe.

354 North Beverly Drive
Beverly Hills, CA 90210
Tel. +1 323 463 4441

Book Soup

Still holding on in the face of Barnes & Noble and Borders. One of LA's most celebrated book stores, this is a landmark among writers and booklovers all over the city. Wall to wall books, personal recommendations, right in the heart of West Hollywood.

Noch bietet man Barnes & Noble und Borders die Stirn. Eine der berühmtesten Buchhandlungen von LA. Ein Treffpunkt von Schriftstellern und Bibliophilen der ganzen Stadt. Bücher von oben bis unten, persönliche Empfehlungen, mitten im Herzen von West Hollywood.

La boutique fait toujours de la résistance face à Barnes & Noble et Borders. Cette librairie, l'une des préférées de LA, reste une adresse incontournable auprès des écrivains et des amateurs de littérature. Des murs entiers de livres et des conseils personnalisés, en plein cœur de West Hollywood.

8818 Sunset Blvd
Los Angeles, CA 90069
Tel. +1 310 659 3110

Zipper

A great place for gifts, in a really nice area to mooch about in. Zipper has a little of everything from cardboard rocking chairs (strangely comfy) to baby heads shaped out of chocolate (just plain strange).

Toller Geschenkeladen in einer netten Gegend zum Bummeln. Zipper führt ein bisschen von allem, angefangen bei Schaukelstühlen aus Pappe (erstaunlich bequem) bis hin zu Babyköpfen aus Schokolade (einfach nur seltsam).

Une adresse géniale pour les cadeaux, et un quartier agréable pour se promener. Zipper propose un peu de tout, des fauteuils à bascule en carton (étonnamment confortables) aux têtes de bébé en chocolat (vraiment étranges).

8316 West Third St
Los Angeles, CA 90048

Equator

Excellent and very arty book store with fine first editions and signed copies, specialising in American literature. Also features photographic or art exhibitions.

Ausgezeichnete und sehr ambitionierte Buchhandlung mit edlen Erstausgaben und signierten Exemplaren. Spezialisiert auf amerikanische Literatur. Hier finden auch Foto- und andere Kunstausstellungen statt.

Excellente librairie très arty spécialisée en littérature américaine. On y trouve des éditions originales et des livres dédicacés. Elle organise également des expositions d'art ou de photos.

1103 Abbot Kinney Blvd
Venice, CA 90291
Tel. +1 310 399 5544

Surfing Cowboys

Fine vintage furniture store, with great old movie posters and their own line of trendy shirts ('Charlie Don't Surf'). Get one!

Edler Laden für Vintage-Möbel mit tollen alten Filmplakaten und einer eigenen trendigen T-Shirt-Kollektion („Charlie Don't Surf"). Kaufen Sie sich eins!

Boutique de meubles vintage haut de gamme, avec de superbes affiches de vieux films et sa propre ligne de t-shirts tendance (« Charlie Don't Surf »). Il vous en faut absolument un !

1624 Abbot Kinney
Venice, CA 90291
Tel. +1 310 450 4891

VINTAGE FASHION SHOPS

Polkadots and Moonbeams

This shoebox-sized shop has been going 20 years. It has mushroomed from a treasure tucked off the beaten track to a celeb-encrusted gem on a very eclectic stretch of shops.

Diesen Laden von der Größe einer Schuhschachtel gibt es schon seit zwanzig Jahren. Er hat sich von einer verborgenen Schatztruhe fernab der ausgetretenen Wege zum von Promis belagerten Juwel in einer sehr gemischten Einkaufsstraße gemausert.

Cette boutique grande comme une boîte à chaussures existe depuis 20 ans. Au milieu d'une zone de boutiques éclectiques, ce petit trésor déniché hors des sentiers battus est désormais très prisé par les célébrités.

8367 W. 3rd St
Los Angeles, CA 90048
Tel. +1 323 651 1746

Decades

This is vintage, red carpet style. Owner Cameron Silver is not satisfied with having a shop, so she has created a 'salon'. Her efforts are rewarded with an Oscar-winning entourage of supporters. But don't come to rubber-neck – it is usually the celeb's stylist who does the shopping, not the head-honcho herself.

Vintage mit rotem Teppich. Die Eigentümerin Cameron Silver wollte sich nicht damit begnügen, einen Laden zu besitzen, also erschuf sie einen Salon. Ihre Mühen wurden mit einer Entourage aus Oscar-Gewinnern belohnt. Sie brauchen allerdings nicht herkommen, um sich die Nase platt zu drücken – üblicherweise gehen nämlich die Stylisten einkaufen, nicht die Stars selbst.

Ici, on trouve du vintage à porter sur les tapis rouges. La propriétaire Cameron Silver ne se contentant pas d'avoir une boutique, elle a créé un « salon ». Ses efforts sont récompensés par une base de supporters maintes fois primés aux Oscars. Mais inutile d'y passer pour voir des people : généralement les stars ne se déplacent pas et préfèrent envoyer leurs stylistes faire du shopping à leur place.

8214 1/2 Melrose Ave
Los Angeles, CA 90046
Tel. +1 323 655 0223

SquaresVille

Apparently the uber-trendiness of Vermont Avenue has not spoilt SquaresVille's reputation for carrying great vintage at Salvation Army prices.

Offensichtlich hat die Mega-Trendigkeit der Vermont Avenue dem Ruf von SquaresVille als Laden für tolle Vintage-Sachen zu Preisen wie bei der Heilsarmee nichts anhaben können.

Apparemment, le côté over-tendance de Vermont Avenue n'a pas encore gâché la réputation de SquaresVille, qui continue à proposer de belles trouvailles vintage à des prix dignes de l'Armée du salut.

1800 N. Vermont Ave
Tel. +1 323 669 8464

Luxe de Ville

One of the better shops on this stretch and a favourite haunt of stylists with a retro theme in mind.

Einer der besseren Läden auf dieser Einkaufsmeile und Anziehungspunkt für Stylisten, die an ein Retrothema denken.

L'une des meilleures boutiques du boulevard et le repaire favori des stylistes qui préparent un shooting photo à thème rétro.

2157 Sunset Blvd
Los Angeles, CA 90026
Tel. +1 213 353 0135

Jet Rag

This vintage store has a $1 Sunday sale, so if you've one buck left – splurge.

Dieser Vintage Store macht sonntags 1$-Ausverkauf. Wenn Sie also einen

Dollar übrig haben – verprassen Sie ihn!

Cette boutique vintage organise des soldes à 1 dollar le dimanche, alors s'il vous en reste un, foncez !

825 N. La Brea Ave
Los Angeles, CA 90038
Tel. +1 323 939 0528

AArdvark's Odd Ark
This is the granddaddy of LA's vintage. It's a chain of stores that sell a predictable assortment of Amerikana. The best stuff is high on hooks and tends to be pretty pricey.

Dies ist der Opa unter den Vintage-Läden von LA. Genau genommen handelt es sich um eine Kette, die ein vorhersehbares Sortiment von Amerikana verkauft. Die besten Sachen hängen ziemlich hoch und sind recht teuer.

C'est l'ancêtre du vintage à LA. Cette chaîne de magasins vend un assortiment pas très original de vêtements Western. Les meilleures pièces sont accrochées en hauteur et ont tendance à être un peu trop chères.

7579 Melrose Ave
Los Angeles, CA 90046
Tel. +1 323 655 6769

It's a Wrap
Ever wondered what happens to the cast offs of the studios' wardrobe departments? Well, some of it ends up here. So if you fancy wearing a bit of the backlot, that's barely been worn, drop by on your way to the obligatory studio tour.

Haben Sie schon mal überlegt, was die Filmstudios mit den ausrangierten Kostümen machen? Nun, ein Teil davon endet hier. Wenn Sie sich also vorstellen können, ein bisschen was aus dem Studiofundus anzuziehen, das kaum getragen wurde, dann schauen Sie doch auf dem Weg zur obligatorischen Studio-Tour hier vorbei.

Vous vous êtes déjà demandé où finissaient les vieux costumes des studios hollywoodiens ? Et bien, une partie d'entre eux atterrit ici. Alors si vous avez envie de vous offrir un petit bout de cinéma à peine porté, passez dans cette boutique quand vous irez faire la sacro-sainte visite des studios.

3315 W. Magnolia Blvd
Burbank, CA 91505
Tel. +1 818 567 7375

Wasteland
Most of the stores on the Third Street Promenade are slim pickings for fashionistas – with the exception of the Mac store obviously – but just off the Third Street Promenade walk street, is this vintage shop that has a mixed bag of offerings – well worth a rummage.

Die meisten Läden auf der Promenade der Third Street haben – abgesehen von Mac natürlich – Fashionistas kaum etwas zu bieten. In der Fußgängerstraße gleich neben der Third Street Promenade stößt man jedoch auf diesen Vintage-Laden mit bunt gemischtem Angebot. Reinschauen lohnt sich auf jeden Fall.

La plupart des boutiques sur Third Street Promenade ne combleront pas les attentes des fashion victims, à l'exception de Mac, évidemment. Mais en continuant à pied jusqu'au bout, vous tomberez sur cette boutique vintage et sa sélection variée qui valent largement quelques minutes de marche.

1338 4th Street
Santa Monica, CA 90401
Tel. +1 310 395 2620

Re Mix
'Death stock' sounds like a medieval torture but actually refers to never-been-worn vintage. It comes at a premium. Re-mix sells 'death stock' shoes for men and women.

„Death stock" klingt nach mittelalterlicher Folter, dabei bezeichnet es nur ungetragene Vintage-Mode. Die Sachen befinden sich in tadellosem Zustand. Re Mix verkauft „death stock" Schuhe für Herren und Damen.

L'expression « death stock » sonne comme une torture médiévale, mais en fait elle décrit les pièces vintage jamais portées, et donc de première qualité. Re-mix vend justement des « stocks morts » de chaussures pour homme et pour femme.

7605 1/2 Beverly Blvd
Los Angeles, CA 90036
Tel. +1 323 936 6210

PLACES TO SHOP

Hollywood Boulevard
Hollywood Boulevard has been reborn and now houses the Hollywood costume museum, it cost $615 million, and is a beacon of glitz in an area that still has an air of sleaziness. On Hollywood Boulevard is Mann's Chinese Theatre (6925 Hollywood Boulevard, between Highland and La Brea Avenues, +13234613331; +13234648111), where you'll find the famous courtyard where movie greats have made imprints of their hands and feet. Take a camera!

Am rundererneuerten Hollywood Boulevard befindet sich das Kostümmuseum von Hollywood, das 615 Millionen Dollar gekostet hat und einen Leuchtturm des Glitters in einer nach wie vor leicht anrüchigen Gegend darstellt. Ebenfalls am Hollywood Boulevard liegt Mann's Chinese Theatre (6925 Hollywood Boulevard, zwischen Highland und La Brea Avenues, +13234613331; +13234648111), mit

dem berühmten Innenhof, auf dem Filmstars Abdrücke ihrer Hände und Füße verewigt haben. Vergessen Sie Ihre Kamera nicht!

La résurrection de Hollywood Boulevard a coûté 615 millions de dollars. Il accueille désormais le musée du costume de Hollywood et brille de mille paillettes dans un quartier qui a pourtant gardé son côté crasseux. Visitez donc le Mann's Chinese Theatre (6925 Hollywood Boulevard, entre Highland et La Brea Avenues, +13234613331 ; +13234648111), vous y trouverez le célèbre trottoir où les grands du cinéma ont laissé l'empreinte de leurs mains et de leurs pieds. N'oubliez pas votre appareil photo !

The Grove
Right next to the Farmer's Market. Like the Third Street Promenade in Santa Monica it is an outdoor mall, popular with Angelenos and tourists alike for the convenience of having every big name store you can think of, in a car-free walking-zone.

Gleich neben Farmer's Market. Wie die Third Street Promenade in Santa Monica ist dies eine Mall im Freien. Bei Einheimischen wie bei Touristen beliebt, weil man hier Läden aller großen Labels bequem in einer autofreien Fußgängerzone findet.

Juste à côté du Farmer's Market. Comme la Third Street Promenade de Santa Monica, c'est un centre commercial en plein air couru par les habitants de LA comme par les touristes car on y trouve toutes les grandes enseignes qu'on peut imaginer, dans une zone piétonne interdite aux voitures.

189 the Grove Drive
Tel. +1 323 900 8000

Rodeo Drive
This institution continues to attract the haute couture clothing lines in three blocks of prime real estate. Slightly less expensive stores spill onto Robertson Boulevard between Beverly Boulevard and Third Street. Speaking of which...

Diese Institution lockt nach wie vor die Haute-Couture-Linien in drei Blocks in bester Lage. Geringfügig günstigere Läden findet man am Robertson Boulevard zwischen Beverly Boulevard und Third Street. Der Rest ist bekannt ...

Cette institution continue à attirer les collections de haute couture sur trois blocs immobiliers de première classe. Vous trouverez des boutiques légèrement plus abordables sur Robertson Boulevard entre Beverly Boulevard et Third Street. Justement, à propos de Robertson Boulevard...

Beverly Hills Visitors Bureau
Tel. +1 310 271 8174

South Robertson
This stretch of shops and boutiques contains the Ivy, where you may spot Hollywood honchos doing lunch. It also has loads of fun shops with a girly flavour. More expensive and glamorous than...

Zu diesem Abschnitt von Läden und Boutiquen gehört das Ivy, wo Sie mit Glück Hollywoodgrößen beim Lunch entdecken können. Es gibt auch einen Haufen Spaßgeschäfte mit Girly-Flair. Etwas teurer und glamouröser als ...

C'est sur ce boulevard commerçant que se trouve l'Ivy, où vous repérerez peut-être quelques magnats de Hollywood en plein déjeuner. Il accueille aussi des tas de boutiques marrantes qui vendent des vêtements très girly. Plus cher et plus glamour que...

Third Street
Really eclectic mix of shops you can walk to. Stretching from the colossus of the Beverly Centre to the Farmer's Market and The Grove, you'll find plenty of gems and several great places to have lunch. It's a great day's mooching, and not even Angelenos necessarily appreciate its richness. Another area that dispels the myth that you can't walk in LA.

Ein wahrhaft eklektischer Mix aus Läden, die Sie zu Fuß erreichen können. Die Straße reicht vom Koloss des Beverly Center bis zum Farmer's Market und The Grove. Dort finden Sie zahlreiche Juweliere und einige tolle Lokale zum Mittagessen. Toll für einen ganzen Tag zum Bummeln, was nicht einmal alle Angelenos wissen. Eine weitere Gegend, die den Mythos, man könne in LA nicht zu Fuß gehen, Lügen straft.

Mélange très excentrique de boutiques, à visiter à pied. S'étendant depuis le colosse du Beverly Centre jusqu'au Farmer's Market et au Grove, vous y trouverez de vrais petits bijoux et plusieurs très bons restaurants pour déjeuner. Un lieu de promenade idéal, et les Angelenos ne sont pas les seuls à apprécier la richesse de l'endroit. Un autre quartier qui met fin au mythe selon lequel on ne peut pas se promener à pied dans LA.

Melrose Avenue (between La Brea and Fairfax)
If you are looking for funky, with a bit of punk thrown in, then this is your zone. You know what you'll find in Beverly Hills: Dior, Chanel, Gucci, Prada. In contrast, Melrose and Beverly Boulevards, parallel shopping streets, offer some surprises with less-established, cutting-edge designers. More surprises await when you glance at price tags only a smidgen

less lofty than their Rodeo Drive counterparts. Apparently, it costs money to look glam. Costume Nationale, Daryl K, Miu Miu and Liza Bruce make their homes in this midtown neighborhood.

Falls Sie Funkiges mit einer Spur Punk suchen, dann sind Sie hier richtig. Was Sie in Beverly Hills finden, ist klar: Dior, Chanel, Gucci, Prada. Im Gegensatz dazu bieten die Einkaufsstraßen von Melrose und Beverly Boulevard einige Überraschungen mit weniger etablierten, topaktuellen Designern. Noch mehr Überraschungen erwarten Sie, wenn Sie einen Blick auf die Preisschilder werfen, die nur eine Spur einladender sind als am Rodeo Drive. Ganz offensichtlich kostet es ordentlich Geld, glamourös auszusehen. Costume Nationale, Daryl K, Miu Miu und Liza Bruce sind in dieser Gegend von Mid-Town zu Hause.

Si vous recherchez une ambiance funky avec une touche de punk, alors ce quartier est le vôtre. Car vous savez déjà ce que vous trouverez à Beverly Hills : Dior, Chanel, Gucci, Prada. Par contraste, les boulevards de Melrose et de Beverly, rues commerçantes parallèles, recèlent certaines surprises avec des créateurs d'avant-garde moins connus. Vous serez encore plus étonné en regardant les prix sur les étiquettes, à peine moins prohibitifs que leurs homologues de Rodeo Drive. Apparamment, s'offrir un look glamour coûte cher. Costume National, Daryl K, Miu Miu et Liza Bruce ont élu domicile dans ce quartier central.

Silver lake
Silver Lake, Echo Park and Los Feliz, LA's 'East Side' have become an artist's haven. It's a boho scene of rarified funkiness, with wealthy musicians, celebs and 'creatives' calling it home. The neighbourhood's shops, restaurants, bars and clubs reflect its residents, but what was, until recently, a genuinely eclectic enclave is becoming a self-conscious 'hot-spot'.

Silver Lake, Echo Park und Los Feliz, die East Side von LA, haben sich zum Künstlerrefugium entwickelt. Es ist eine Bohème-Szene mit gehobener Flippigkeit, aus wohlhabenden Musikern, VIPs und „Kreativen", die sich hier zu Hause fühlen. Die Läden, Restaurants, Bars und Clubs des Viertels entsprechen den Bewohnern. Allerdings ist die bis vor kurzem wirklich bunt gemischte Enklave dadurch zum selbstbewussten Hot-Spot geworden.

L'East Side de LA, avec Silver Lake, Echo Park et Los Feliz, est devenu le paradis des artistes. C'est une scène bobo mais encore un peu funky, avec les musiciens fortunés, les célébrités et autres « créatifs » qui y ont élu domicile. Les boutiques, les restaurants, les bars et les clubs du quartier

sont à l'image de ses habitants, mais ce qui était encore récemment une enclave authentiquement éclectique est en train de devenir le dernier coin à la mode et fier de l'être.

Venice Beach
Still truly bohemian – Venice is the most political area of Los Angeles. Amazingly, the residents are still fighting the attempts of city councilors to change the unique character of this idiosyncratic place. If they ever do change it to line the beach with Starbucks and Coffee Beans it will be a tragedy for the city. Abbot Kinney is a truly trendy hotspot for eaters and drinkers in the evenings, but the shops that line the street in the day are all independently owned – not a chain amongst them.

Noch echt Bohème, ist Venice das politischste Viertel von Los Angeles. Erstaunlicherweise kämpfen die Bewohner noch wie vor gegen die Versuche der Stadtverwaltung, dessen einzigartigen Charakter zu ändern. Sollte es ihr je gelingen, den Strand mit Starbucks und Coffee Beans zu pflastern, wäre das eine Tragödie für die ganze Stadt. Abbot Kinney ist ein wirklich trendiger Treffpunkt, um abends zum Essen oder auf einen Drink zu gehen, und die Läden, die die Straße säumen, sind alle selbstständig – keine einzige Filiale einer Handelskette.

Toujours très bohème, Venice est la zone la plus politisée de Los Angeles. Ses habitants luttent encore contre les tentatives des conseillers municipaux qui cherchent à transformer le caractère unique de ce lieu pas comme les autres. Et s'ils arrivent à leurs fins en bordant la plage de Starbucks et de Coffee Beans, ce sera une véritable tragédie pour la ville. Le soir, le boulevard Abbot Kinney accueille les dîneurs et autres noceurs dans ses bars et ses restaurants ultra tendance. Il faut savoir que les boutiques de la rue appartiennent toutes à des propriétaires indépendants : pas une seule chaîne parmi eux.

MARKETS
Many neighbourhoods close their streets to host a Farmer's Market once a week: the one on Hollywood is good and the one on Main Street (Sunday) in Santa Monica is excellent.

Viele Viertel sperren einmal pro Woche die Straßen für einen Wochenmarkt. Der in Hollywood ist gut, der auf der Main Street (sonntags) in Santa Monica ist exzellent.

Une fois par semaine, de nombreux quartiers deviennent piétons pour accueillir un marché : celui de Hollywood Boulevard est très bien, mais celui de Main Street (le dimanche) à Santa Monica est encore mieux.

Peddler on the Roof
A new weekly rooftop sample-sale and fleamarket featuring independent designers and hot boutiques.

Ein neuer wöchentlicher Flohmarkt und Musterverkauf auf einem Dach, mit Kreationen unabhängiger Designer und gefragter Boutiquen.

Sur les toits, un nouveau marché aux puces hebdomadaire présente des créateurs indépendants et des boutiques branchées.

Sunset Gower Studios
1423 North Gordon Street
Los Angeles, CA 90028
Tel. +1 323 467 3094

NIGHTLIFE

Cahuenga Corridor
This has become THE place to go: This previously sketchy area off Hollywood Boulevard has emerged as host LA's glitzy nightlife destinations: Concorde, XES, Tokio, White Lotus, Burgundy Room and the snappily named La Velvet Margarita Cantina (very Tarantino-esque).

DIE angesagte Gegend zum Ausgehen: Diese früher unsichere Gegend abseits vom Hollywood Boulevard beherbergt LAs glamouröseste Nachtlokale: Concorde, XES, Tokio, White Lotus, Burgundy Room und besonders schmissig getauft – La Velvet Margarita Cantina (sehr Tarantino-esque).

C'est devenu LE lieu où passer ses soirées : ce quartier autrefois sans intérêt au bout de Hollywood Boulevard accueille aujourd'hui les destinations nocturnes les plus paillettes de LA : Concorde, XES, Tokio, White Lotus, Burgundy Room et la bien nommée La Velvet Margarita Cantina (ambiance très Tarantino).

Beauty Bar
It's very LA: manicure and a martini for $10!

Das ist typisch LA: Maniküre und ein Martini für 10 Dollar!

Un bar très LA : manucure et cocktail pour 10 dollars !

1638 N. Cahuenga Blvd
Hollywood, CA 90028
Tel. +1 323 464 7676

The Room
Located down a dark alley with an unmarked sign, The Room is more like a hallway, but its intimacy is what has made it a favourite among people too young to have seen it in Swingers. It's the ultimate in true hipness to even find the place.

Am Ende einer dunklen Straße hat The Room mehr Ähnlichkeit mit einem Korridor, doch dank seiner Intimität ist es ein Favorit vieler Leute, die noch zu jung sind, um das aus dem „Swingers" zu kennen. Wahrhaft

hip ist man allerdings schon, wenn man das Lokal überhaupt findet.

Situé au fond d'une allée obscure, The Room ressemble à un couloir mais son côté intime en a fait l'un des bars préférés des gens trop jeunes pour l'avoir vu dans Swingers. Le comble de la branchitude, c'est déjà de réussir à trouver l'endroit.

1626 N. Cahuenga Blvd
Hollywood, CA 90028
Tel. +1 323 462 7196

Hotel Cafe
An essential part of LA's new folk scene – a cool music venue with a hip crowd.

Ein unverzichtbarer Teil der neuen Folk-Szene von LA – ein cooles Musiklokal mit witzigem Publikum.

Un lieu incontournable de la nouvelle scène folk de LA : bar musical sympa et faune branchée.

1623 1/2 N Cahuenga Blvd
Hollywood, CA 90028
Tel. +1 323 461 2040

Bar Marmont
Still without question your best bet to spot a celebrity in its natural habitat.

Ohne Frage nach wie vor der beste Ort, um einen Prominenten in seinem natürlichen Lebensraum zu beobachten.

De loin votre meilleure chance d'observer une célébrité dans son cadre de vie naturel.

8171 W. Sunset Blvd
West Hollywood, CA 90046
Tel. +1 323 650 0575

El Carmen
A small bar decorated with Mexican wrestler masks and serving 270 varieties of tequila. You have to taste their Margarita before you leave LA.

Eine kleine Bar, dekoriert mit mexikanischen Ringkämpfermasken, in der man Tequila in 270 Variationen serviert. Bevor Sie abreisen, müssen Sie die Margarita probieren.

Un petit bar décoré de masques de lutteurs mexicains qui propose 270 sortes de tequila différentes : ne quittez pas LA sans avoir goûté leur Margarita.

8138 W. Third Street
Los Angeles, CA 90048
Tel. +1 213 852 1556

Musso and Franks
No explanation needed. Oldest restaurant in Hollywood and it is still the same place where Fitzgerald drank all those damn martinis. Noir!

Erklärungen überflüssig. Das älteste Restaurant Hollywoods und genau der Ort, wo Fitzgerald all die verdammten Martinis getrunken hat. Noir!

Est-il encore nécessaire de présenter ce restaurant ? C'est le plus vieux de Hollywood et rien n'a changé depuis l'époque où Fitzgerald y ingurgitait cocktail sur cocktail. Ambiance très film noir !

6667 Hollywood Blvd
Hollywood, CA 90028
Tel. +1 323 467 778

Daddy's
Seriously dimly lit, great jukebox. Mix of hipsters, rock-stars, and industry-types.

Richtig gedämpftes Licht, klasse Jukebox. Eine Mischung aus Hipstern, Rockstars und Industrietypen.

Eclairage plus que subtil, jukebox génial. Faune bigarrée entre branchés, stars du rock et industrie de l'entertainment.

1610 N. Vine Street
Hollywood, CA 90028
Tel. +1 323 463 7777

Boardner's
Refreshingly unpretentious dive-bar where you still may spot the odd celebrity. Go here if you go to bars to drink.

Erfrischend unprätentiöse Kneipe, wo man auch den einen oder anderen Prominenten entdecken kann. Falls Sie zum Trinken in Bars gehen, sind Sie hier richtig.

Bar rafraîchissant et sans prétention, encore une adresse où vous pourrez croiser une star en goguette. Allez-y si vous aimez les bars avant tout pour boire.

1652 N. Cherokee Ave
Los Angeles, CA 90028
Tel. +1 323 462 9621

CULTURE

John Paul Getty Museum
This world-class venue is justly famous: the complex alone is worth a visit. The permanent collection is very good, and there is always an interesting temporary exhibit. Think twice before shelling out for the audio guides, however, which are a little disappointing.

Dieses Weltklasse-Museum ist zu Recht berühmt: Das Gebäude selbst ist einen Besuch wert. Die Dauerausstellung ist sehr gut, und es gibt immer spannende aktuelle Schauen. Ob Sie einen Audio-Guide benutzen wollen, sollten Sie sich allerdings gut überlegen. Der Service ist etwas enttäuschend.

Ce musée n'a pas volé sa réputation internationale : le complexe à lui seul vaut déjà le détour. La collection permanente est magnifique, et il y a toujours une exposition temporaire intéressante à voir. Toutefois, réfléchissez à deux fois avant de casquer pour les

guides audio, ils sont un peu décevants.

The Getty Center
1200 Getty Center Drive
Los Angeles, CA 90049
Tel. +1 310 440 7300

Museum of Neon Art
The great American beer sign and other under-appreciated icons of cocktail culture get illuminated in this cool exhibition.

Das Schild „Great American Beer" und andere unterschätzte Ikonen der Cocktail-Kultur werden in dieser coolen Ausstellung illuminiert.

La fameuse enseigne de bière américaine et autres icônes sous-estimées de la culture des bars ont trouvé la place qui leur revient dans ce musée très sympa.

501 W Olympic Boulevard
Los Angeles, CA 90015
Tel. +1 213 489 9918

Los Angeles County Museum of Art
The LACMA is a good bet if you're mired in the midst of Hollywood and going nuts.

Das LACMA ist ein Supertipp, wenn Sie mitten in Hollywood stecken und gerade die Krise kriegen.

Si vous sentez que Hollywood commence à vous rendre complètement dingue, allez donc vous ressourcer au LACMA.

5905 Wilshire Boulevard, 90036
Los Angeles, CA 90036
Tel. +1 213 857 6000

Museum of Contemporary Art (MOCA)
Located Downtown, this cheesily-acronymed gem houses one of the world's best collections of contemporary art, organised accessibly with an informal atmosphere.

Diese in Downtown gelegene, mit einem Augenzwinkern abgekürzte Schatztruhe birgt eine der weltbesten Sammlungen zeitgenössischer Kunst, die gut zugänglich in lockerer Atmosphäre präsentiert wird.

A Downtown, cet écrin baptisé d'un acronyme un peu neuneu accueille l'une des meilleures collections d'art contemporain au monde, présentée de façon accessible à tous au sein d'une atmosphère informelle.

250 S. Grand Ave
Los Angeles, CA 90012
Tel. +1 213 626 6222

Moca Pacific Design Centre
A West side division of the Museum of Contemporary Art, focusing on architecture and design, but with excellent lithographs, graphic design and photography as well.

Ein Westside-Ableger des Museum of Contemporary Art mit den Schwerpunkten Architektur und Design, aber auch mit hervorragenden Lithografien, Grafikdesigns und Fotografien.

Département du Museum of Contemporary Art à l'est de LA, spécialisé en architecture et en design, mais qui présente aussi d'excellentes lithographies, photos et œuvres graphiques.

8687 Melrose Ave
West Hollywood, CA 90067
Tel. +1 310 289 5223

Griffith Park
Griffith Park (East Side) is five times the size of New York's Central Park and is the largest city-run park in the US. The famous Griffith Park Observatory (4800 Western Heritage Way, +1 323 664 1181), is undergoing a three-year renovation project and until it's completed no visitors are allowed to sample the magnificent dusk views of this James Dean spot.

Der Griffith Park (East Side) ist fünfmal so groß wie der New Yorker Central Park und die größte städtische Grünanlage der USA. Das berühmte Griffith Park Observatorium (4800 Western Heritage Way, +1 323 664 1181), steckt gerade in einer dreijährigen Renovierungsphase. Und bis die nicht beendet ist, kann kein Besucher die prächtigen, dämmrigen Ansichten dieses James-Dean-Schauplatzes bewundern.

Griffith Park (East Side) fait cinq fois la taille du Central Park de New York et c'est le plus grand parc municipal des Etats-Unis. Le célèbre observatoire de Griffith Park (4800 Western Heritage Way, +1 323 664 1181) est actuellement en rénovation pour une durée de trois ans. En attendant, aucun visiteur n'est autorisé à profiter des sublimes vues nocturnes de ce lieu mythique devenu synonyme de James Dean.

The Hollywood Sign
The best places to see 'that sign' (all 15 metres of it) are from the corner of Sunset Boulevard and Bronson Avenue or from Paramount Studios at Melrose Avenue and Gower Street.

Die besten Plätze, um „das Zeichen" (mit seinen ganzen 15 Metern) zu sehen, sind an der Ecke Sunset Boulevard und Bronson Avenue oder bei den Paramount Studios an der Melrose Avenue und Gower Street.

Les meilleurs emplacements pour admirer les lettres « HOLLYWOOD » (et leurs 15 mètres de haut) se trouvent au coin de Sunset Boulevard et Bronson Avenue, ou aux studios Paramount au croisement de Melrose Avenue et Gower Street.

The West Side (Beaches)
The West Side is not the place for night-time shenanigans, but it does

host the glorious coast, and from the bright young playthings on Manhattan Beach, past the hip and hippy sleaziness of Venice Beach, up to the Santa Monica pier and beyond to Malibu's Surfrider Beach and Zuma, this is what the California lifestyle is all about.

Die West Side ist nicht der ideale Ort für Nachtschwärmer, aber hier gibt es die herrliche Küste, und angefangen bei den jungen Dingern am Manhattan Beach, vorbei an der hippen und zugleich leicht anrüchigen Hippie-Meile Venice Beach bis hinauf zum Santa Monica Pier und weiter zu Malibu Surfrider Beach und Zuma ist dies ein Symbol für den Californian Way of Life.

Le West Side n'est pas le lieu des folies nocturnes : des jeunes beautés de Manhattan Beach en passant par la crasse hippie branchée de Venice Beach jusqu'à la jetée de Santa Monica et au-delà vers les plages Surfrider Beach et Zuma de Malibu, la glorieuse côte symbolise par excellence le style de vie californien.

RESTAURANTS

Sushi-Nozawa
By far the best in town, maybe the country. You get what chef Nozawa picks out for you and you can keep it coming, but don't plan on lingering – he kicked out Charlize Theron and Stuart Townsend because they had been there too long. Totally unassuming decor and tucked anonymously into a strip mall – the "Trust Me Special" is famous.

Das mit Abstand beste Sushi-Lokal der Stadt, vielleicht sogar des Landes. Man bekommt, was Küchenchef Nozawa einem zuteilt, und darf immer weiter essen. Denken Sie aber nicht, dass Sie dort herumlungern könnten. Charlize Theron und Stuart Townsend wurden hinausgeworfen, weil sie sich zu viel Zeit ließen. Völlig unspektakuläres Dekor und sehr versteckt in einer kleinen Mall gelegen. Das „Trust Me Special" ist berühmt.

De loin le meilleur restaurant japonais de la ville, voire du pays. Vous mangez ce que le chef Nozawa a choisi pour vous et pouvez vous resservir, mais n'envisagez pas de traîner trop longtemps : il a déjà mis dehors Charlize Theron et Stuart Townsend parce qu'ils avaient tendance à s'éterniser. Décor totalement modeste et niché de façon anonyme dans un centre commercial : goûtez donc le « Trust Me Special », vous n'aurez pas à le regretter.

11288 Ventura Blvd, Unit C
Studio City, CA 91604
Tel. +1 818 508 7017

The Little Door
No sign, just a door. Therefore: very cool. If you can't get a table, go for a pre- dinner drink – the patio is lovely.

It might be French but the no smoking rule still applies inside.

Kein Schild, nur eine Tür. Und deshalb sehr cool. Wenn Sie keinen Tisch bekommen, nehmen Sie einen Aperitif – der Patio ist sehr hübsch. Die Küche mag französisch sein, trotzdem gilt drinnen Rauchverbot.

Pas d'enseigne, juste une porte. Comprenez : donc très cool. Si vous n'arrivez pas à obtenir une table, allez-y boire un verre avant dîner, le patio est charmant. Restaurant français, mais 100 % non fumeur à l'intérieur.

8164 W 3rd Street
Los Angeles, CA 90048
Tel. +1 323 951 1210

Pedals
Pedals at Shutters on the beach is a real find for brunch. The decor is not very promising but the terrace outside lets you sit with a view of the beach and the food is excellent.

Das Pedals im Shutters on the Beach ist ein Geheimtipp zum Brunch. Die Einrichtung ist nicht gerade eine Offenbarung, aber auf der Terrasse sitzt man mit Blick auf den Strand, und das Essen ist ausgezeichnet.

Dans l'hôtel Shutters on the Beach, Pedals est une vraie trouvaille pour le brunch. Le décor n'est pas très prometteur, mais la terrasse extérieure vous permet de déguster une cuisine excellente en admirant la plage.

One Pico Blvd
Santa Monica, CA 90405
Tel. +1 310 458 0030

Chi Restaurant
Owned by Justin Timberlake, situated in the Hyatt, and staffed with what appear to be Justin's former back-up dancers. Great oriental food with a red-leather decor.

Das Lokal gehört Justin Timberlake, liegt im Hyatt, und das Personal sieht aus, als hätte es zu Justins Hintergrund-Tänzern gehört. Tolles orientalisches Essen in rotem Lederambiente.

Appartenant à Justin Timberlake et installé dans le Hyatt. Les serveurs du restaurant sont aussi appétissants que les danseurs de Justin. Excellente cuisine orientale dans un décor de cuir rouge.

8401 Sunset Boulevard
West Hollywood, CA 90069
Tel. +1 323 848 3884

Cobras & Matadors
Scrumptious tapas in a hip-yet-unpretentious neo-industrial space. Cool or what?

Leckere Tapas in hippem, aber unprätentiösem Lokal mit Fabrikcharme. Cool, was sonst?

Succulents tapas dans un espace néo-industriel branché mais pas snob. On ne peut plus cool.

7615 Beverly Blvd
Los Angeles, CA 90027
Tel. +1 323 932 6178

Musso & Franks Grill
Musso & Franks Grill is Hollywood's oldest restaurant. The building may have been modernised but the restaurant still attracts Hollywood luminaries and tourists from around the world ever since opening its doors in 1919.

Das älteste Restaurant Hollywoods. Das Haus wurde zwar schon mal renoviert, dennoch lockt es seit seiner Eröffnung im Jahre 1919 Hollywoodstars und Touristen aus aller Welt an.

Musso & Franks Grill est le plus ancien restaurant de Hollywood. L'immeuble a été modernisé, mais le restaurant attire toujours les grands de Hollywood et les touristes du monde entier depuis son ouverture en 1919.

6667 Hollywood Blvd
Los Angeles, CA 90028
Tel. +1 900 28 6220

Figaro Brasserie
This is a little Parisian gem. Sidewalk café/boulangerie is attached. All meals daily.

Ein kleines Pariser Juwel. Sidewalk Café mit angeschlossener Boulangrie. Ganztägig warme Küche.

Un vrai petit bijou parisien. Un café-boulangerie en annexe. Ouvert toute la journée, tous les jours.

West Vermont Ave
Hollywood, CA 90069
Tel. +1 323 662 1587

Pacific Dining Car
Open 24 hours a day. It's the place to go if you need a rare steak at 3 a.m.

Rund um die Uhr geöffnet. Genau der richtige Ort, wenn Sie um drei Uhr morgens ein blutig gebratenes Steak brauchen.

Ouvert 24 heures sur 24. L'adresse idéale si vous avez envie d'un steak à 3 heures du matin.

1310 W. Sixth Street
Los Angeles, CA 90017
Tel. +1 213 483 6000

Jin Pastry Boutique and Tea Garden
Superb, if pricy, teas and tasty treats in a zenned-out little garden with soft seats, and all to a world-music chill-out soundtrack.

Phantastische, wenn auch teure Tees und leckere Kleinigkeiten in einem kleinen Garten mit Zen-Charakter.

Dazu weiche Sessel und ein Weltmusik Chillout-Soundtrack.

Thés et gâteaux chers mais excellents, servis dans un petit jardin très zen aux sièges confortables, sur fond de musique du monde plutôt down tempo.

1202 Abbot Kinney Blvd
Los Angeles, CA 90921
Tel. +1 310 399 8801

Chaya Venice
Cavernous, arty establishment with delicious California cuisine (blending French and Asian). Excellent service and a terrific sushi bar make this very popular spot an excellent choice if you're hungry out west.

Kellerartiger Künstlertreff mit köstlicher kalifornischer Küche (ein Mix aus Französisch und Asiatisch). Perfekter Service und eine unglaubliche Sushi-Bar machen dieses extrem beliebte Lokal zur idealen Wahl, wenn Sie richtig ausgehungert sind.

Sorte de caverne bohème servant une délicieuse cuisine californienne (fusion de plats français et asiatiques). Le service impeccable et le superbe sushi-bar font de cette adresse très courue un excellent choix si vous avez envie de manger dans la partie ouest de LA.

110 Navy Street @ Main
Venice, CA 90291
Tel. +1 310 396 1179

Urth Cafe
Brunch, lunch or tea time this is yummy. Good organic food, teas and coffees, in an upmarket-yet-relaxed atmosphere. There's one in Beverly Hills, too, which tends to be a little crowded and 'industrified'. This one's more chilled, and you can walk it off at the beach afterward! The Beverly Hills one is 8565 Melrose Ave. It is always packed with a crème de la crème crowd so if you can't get a table try the Pain Quotidien opposite (8607 Melrose Ave).

Ob zum Brunch, zum Lunch oder zur Teatime – hier schmeckt's immer. Gutes Bio-Essen, Tee und Kaffee in gehobener, aber trotzdem entspannter Atmosphäre. Es gibt auch ein Filiale in Beverly Hills, wo es oft etwas voller ist und man ein bisschen abgefertigt wird. Hier geht es ruhiger zu, und Sie können anschließend gleich am Strand spazieren gehen. Im Ableger in Beverly Hills, 8565 Melrose Ave, wimmelt es immer von Prominenten, aber falls Sie dort keinen Tisch bekommen, versuchen Sie es mal gegenüber im Pain Quotidien (8607 Melrose Ave).

Pour le brunch, le déjeuner ou à l'heure du thé, tout est délicieux. Excellents plats, thés et cafés bio dans une ambiance haut de gamme mais décontractée. Il y a aussi un

Urth Café à Beverly Hills, mais il a tendance à être toujours bondé et un peu trop « industrialisé ». Celui-ci est plus tranquille et vous pourrez faire un petit tour à la plage en sortant ! Celui de Beverly Hills, situé au 8565 Melrose Ave, est toujours rempli par la crème de la crème, donc si vous n'arrivez pas à obtenir une table, traversez la rue et essayez Pain Quotidien (8607 Melrose Ave).

2327 Main Street
Santa Monica, CA 90405
Tel. +1 310 314 7040

Joan's on Third
Fantastic deli with fine meats, cheeses, pastries and that type of thing. Great choice if you're in Park La Brea, perhaps cruising 3rd, and want a quick-but-delicious lunch. Not cheap.

Phantastischer Deli mit gutem Fleisch, Käste, Pasteten und ähnlichem. Tolle Idee, wenn Sie gerade in Park La Brea sind, vielleicht auf der 3rd Street bummeln und Lust auf ein schnelles, aber feines Mittagessen haben. Nicht billig.

Fantastique déli proposant notamment des viandes, des fromages et des pâtisseries de grande qualité. Un choix idéal si vous êtes dans Park La Brea en train de remonter 3rd Street et que vous avez envie d'un délicieux déjeuner sur le pouce. Pas vraiment bon marché.

8350 W 3rd Street
Los Angeles, CA 90048
Tel. +1 323 655 2285

Abbot's Pizza Company
Best pizza in LA. Standing room only. Features the bagel-crust pizza and loud, enthusiastic pizza-chefs!

Die beste Pizza von LA. Nur ein Stehimbiss. Hier gibt's Pizza mit Bagelkruste und lärmende, gutgelaunte Pizzabäcker!

La meilleure pizzeria de LA. Pas de tables, on mange uniquement debout. Les chefs bruyants et enthousiastes préparent notamment une pizza en croûte de bagel !

1407 Abbot Kinney Blvd
Venice, CA 90291
Tel. +1 310 396 7334

Brother's Sushi
Popular valley sushi joint for real sushi-at-the-counter sushi.

Beliebtes Sushi-Lokal im Valley. Es wird klassisch am Tresen serviert.

Dans la vallée, restaurant de sushi à succès, pour un repas au comptoir comme au Japon.

21418 Ventura Blvd
Woodland Hills, CA 91364
Tel. +1 818 992 1284

In and Out Burger

Hefty debate among Angelenos has selected this as the most often celebrated contender for that coveted crown 'best burger'. It's a privately-owned company, with no plans to franchise, and maybe that's why they have such a proud and loyal fan base in their West coast home turf. There are 18 outlets in the LA area.

Nach heftigen Debatten haben die einheimischen Angelenos das Lokal zum meistgepriesenen Bewerber um den begehrten Titel „Best Burger" gewählt. Es handelt sich um einen Laden in Privatbesitz, ohne Franchise-Ambitionen, und vielleicht hat man gerade deshalb eine so stolze und loyale Fangemeinde hier im heimischen Revier an der Westcoast. Im Raum LA gibt es 18 Filialen.

Après un débat les Angelenos ont élu ce restaurant comme le meilleur prétendant au titre très convoité de « meilleur burger » de la ville. C'est une entreprise indépendante et privée qui n'a aucune intention de lancer des franchises, et c'est sans doute la raison pour laquelle elle revendique un moyan de fans aussi fier et fidèle dans son restau de la côte ouest. In and Out Burger compte 18 points de vente dans la région de LA.

7009 Sunset Blvd
Hollywood, CA 90028
www.in-n-out.com

HOTELS

Chateau Marmont

Everybody has stayed here since 1930, from Greta Garbo to John Lennon. Johnny Depp used to live here, and many celebrities still do. Some die here too. John Belushi died of a drugs overdose in one of the bungalows and Jim Morrison fell out of a window once. A lot of the staff are waiting to be discovered. There are cottage 'villas' with their own private entrance. The 24-hour heated pool allows for night swims. Beautiful garden with lovely hedges full of paparazzi. The junior suites offer the most value for money.

Seit 1930 hat hier, von Greta Garbo bis John Lennon, alles übernachtet, was Rang und Namen hat. Johnny Depp wohnte eine Zeitlang hier, und viele Prominente tun das nach wie vor. Manche sterben sogar hier. John Belushi erlag in einem der Bungalows einer Überdosis Drogen, und Jim Morrison stürzte einmal aus dem Fenster. Viele Leute vom Personal hoffen darauf, entdeckt zu werden. Es gibt kleine „Villas" mit eigenem Eingang. Der rund um die Uhr beheizte Pool empfiehlt sich für nächtliches Schwimmen. Wunderschöner Garten mit hübschen Hecken

voller Paparazzi. Bei den Junior-Suiten ist das Preis-Leistungs-Verhältnis am besten.

Depuis 1930, tout le monde a séjourné ici un jour ou l'autre, de Greta Garbo à John Lennon. Johnny Depp a vécu et de nombreuses célébrités y habitent encore. Certaines y sont même mortes. John Belushi est décédé d'une overdose dans l'un des bungalows de l'hôtel et Jim Morrison est un jour tombé d'une fenêtre. Parmi les membres du personnel, nombreux sont ceux qui espèrent être repérés par un producteur. L'hôtel propose aussi des « villas » avec jardin et entrée privative. Piscine chauffée 24 heures sur 24 pour les baignades de nuit et magnifique jardin cerné de charmantes haies remplies de paparazzi. Les junior suites offrent le meilleur rapport qualité/prix.

8221 Sunset Blvd
West Hollywood, CA 90046
Tel. +1 323 656 1010

Avalon

A hip and stylish hotel-motel once home to Marilyn Monroe. Extremely central Beverly Hills location. The kidney-shaped pool is perfect for sitting back on a lounger with a cocktail. Expect to see the next Marilyn flitting through the corridors.

Ein angesagtes, schickes Motel, in dem einst Marilyn Monroe wohnte. Absolut zentral in Beverly Hills gelegen. Der nierenförmige Pool ist perfekt, um sich dort mit einem Cocktail zurückzulehnen. Rechnen Sie damit, die nächste Marilyn über die Flure huschen zu sehen.

Un hôtel-motel branché et élégant où Marilyn Monroe a résidé. Emplacement on ne peut plus central dans Beverly Hills. La piscine en forme de haricot est idéale pour se relaxer dans une chaise longue en sirotant un cocktail. Attendez-vous à croiser la future Marilyn dans les couloirs.

9400 West Olympic Blvd
Beverly Hills, CA 90212
Tel. +1 310 277 5221

Best Western Hollywood

Above the hipster hangout 101 diner. A lot of stylists, art directors and music folks staying in LA on the cheap, i.e. without an expense account, do it here. It's a Best Western but it's a good location at a bargain price.

Noch besser als der Hipster-Treff 101 Diner. Viele Stylisten, Artdirektoren und Leute aus der Musikbranche, die günstig, also nicht auf Spesen, in LA wohnen wollen, tun das hier. Es ist zwar ein Best Western, aber in guter Lage zu moderaten Preisen.

Au-dessus du très branché 101 Diner. Beaucoup de stylistes, de directeurs artistiques et de gens de la musique qui séjournent à LA « on the cheap », c'est-à-dire sans se faire rembourser leurs notes de frais, s'installent ici. L'hôtel appartient à la chaîne Best Western mais reste une bonne adresse aux tarifs abordables.

6141 Franklin Ave
Los Angeles, CA 90028
Tel. +1 888 203 9319

Beverly Laurel Motor Hotel

Situated above the famously hip Swingers diner. It's a slightly divey-but-cool motel-hotel: what is called in LA a no-tell motel. A number of rooms have two ambiguous double beds and the rooms can be accessed discreetly from the garage without passing a lobby. Nevertheless, in that location, it's a steal. One of the best deals in town.

Gleich über dem berühmten In-Lokal Swingers. Ein etwas spelunkenhaftes, aber cooles Motel: In LA nennt man so was ein „no-tell motel". Viele Zimmer haben zwei zweideutige Doppelbetten und sind diskret über die Garage zugänglich, ohne dass man durch die Lobby müsste. In dieser Lage ein absoluter Glücksfall. Eine der günstigsten Unterkünfte der Stadt.

Situé au-dessus du fameux restaurant Swingers. Un hôtel-motel légèrement louche mais cool : ce qu'on appelle à LA un « no-tell motel ». Certaines chambres incluent des doubles lits qui prêtent à l'équivoque. On peut accéder aux chambres discrètement depuis le garage sans passer par la réception. Dans ce quartier, ça reste une très bonne affaire. Même l'une des meilleures de la ville.

8018 Beverly Blvd
Los Angeles, CA 90048
Tel. +1 213 651 2441

The Argyle

This 1929 Art-Deco masterpiece offers a real flavour of old Los Angeles. Recently refurbished, and situated right in the heart of Sunset Strip, it has interesting artworks on the wall, a terrific view of Los Angeles, and a decadent atmosphere.

Dieses Art-Deco-Meisterwerk von 1929 versetzt einen ins alte Los Angeles. Kürzlich renoviert und mitten auf dem Sunset Strip gelegen, hat es spannende Kunst an den Wänden, eine Wahnsinns-Aussicht auf Los Angeles sowie eine leicht dekadente Atmosphäre zu bieten.

Ce chef d'œuvre Art Déco de 1929 évoque avec authenticité le vieux Los Angeles. Récemment réaménagé et situé en plein cœur du Sunset Strip,

ses murs présentent des œuvres d'art intéressantes. L'hôtel offre une incroyable vue sur Los Angeles et une atmosphère délicieusement décadente.

8358 W. Sunset Blvd
Los Angeles, CA 90069
Tel. +1 323 654 7100

The Viceroy

This arty, designer-friendly space is one of the newest additions to the hip-hotel scene in LA. It's also one of the best. A great pool area, good bar, and terrific location just minutes from the beach make this a good bet if you come to LA and want the best of all worlds.

Das künstlerische, designerfreundliche Haus ist einer der Neuzugänge der Hip-Hotel-Szene von LA. Noch dazu einer der besten. Eine tolle Pool-Landschaft, gute Bar und die Wahnsinnslage nur ein paar Minuten vom Strand entfernt machen es zu einer guten Wahl, wenn Sie nach LA kommen und sich das Allerbeste wünschen.

Cet espace design et arty est l'un des nouveaux venus sur la scène hôtelière branchée de LA. C'est également l'un des meilleurs. Une piscine géniale, un bar sympa et un emplacement de rêve à quelques minutes de la plage en font une adresse de choix, si vous venez à LA en quête du meilleur des mondes.

1819 Ocean Ave
Santa Monica, CA 90401
Tel. +1 310 260 7500

Channel Road Inn

A romantic B&B getaway in Santa Monica but close enough to the canyons and to Malibu to feel tucked away. Lovely breakfast and a warm welcome. Perfect for a weekend rendezvous.

Ein romantisch verstecktes Bed & Breakfast in Santa Monica, aber dennoch nah genug an den Canyons und an Malibu, um sich nicht weit ab vom Schuss zu fühlen. Schönes Frühstück und herzliche Atmosphäre. Perfekt für ein Wochenende zu zweit.

Bed & Breakfast romantique dans Santa Monica mais assez proche des canyons et de Malibu pour être dépaysé. Excellent petit déjeuner et accueil chaleureux. Idéal pour un week-end en amoureux.

219 West Channel Road
Santa Monica, CA 90402
Tel. +1 310 459 1920

<u>What makes Milan special to you?</u> It's the city where we both live and work, and it's one of the world's fashion and design capitals. It's definitely the most cosmopolitan Italian city, which means that you can find practically whatever the world offers, from entertainment to food and culture, but most of all shopping! <u>Where is the best place to stay in Milan?</u> The Four Seasons Hotel <u>Where is your favourite place to eat in Milan?</u> Insalateria delle Langhe, Da Giacomo and Antica Osteria della Pesa, places where you can taste excellent Italian food <u>Where is your favourite place to shop in Milan?</u> Fiorucci Love Therapy, Messaggerie Musicali for magazines, books and CDs, Nilufar for rare and unusual furniture. DOLCE & GABBANA

MILAN

TEXT BY GIANLUCA LONGO

Milan is still seen as the world capital of fashion and design. During the '80s, when the economic boom was at its height, the big names of Armani, Versace, Ferré, Max Mara and Gucci started to impose their Italian style all over the world from here. Today, these labels remain the power behind this northern city: few other capitals can afford the density of designer boutiques to be found in Milan's quadrilatero della moda, which cuts right into the city's heart, from Via Montenapoleone to Via della Spiga. Many of the reasons why Milan has become a world leader in fashion can be traced back to the 1960s. Milan then was a pivotal centre for industrial design, thanks to its legendary manufacturing industry. The transition to ready-to-wear clothing process was a natural progression. If not generally known for its absolute creativity, the Milanese fashion industry relies on the sheer quality of its product – and a hugely successful business has been built on this reputation. As a city, Milan doesn't appeal immediately to the aesthetic senses. It hasn't got the charm of Venice or the beauty of Rome. But the Milanese have a natural style all their own: appearances have always counted here and still do. A Milanese woman never rushes to the supermarket without full make-up, while the men pride themselves on being the best dressed in Europe – with a keen eye on their waistline. That said, outsiders often remark on how conservative fashion can be in Milan. The Milanese are hard-headed working types: the ties loosen up and the heels slip off only at the time of the aperitivo (a cultural institution). But herein lies the city's allure. In Milan, Italian style has reached its peak: the shops – be they fashion, furniture or food – the restaurants and the art galleries are simply and undeniably chic.

Mailand gilt nach wie vor als die Welthauptstadt von Mode und Design. Während der 1980er Jahre, auf dem Höhepunkt des Wirtschaftsbooms, begannen große Namen wie Armani, Versace, Ferré, Max Mara und Gucci von hier aus ihren italienischen Stil über die ganze Welt zu verbreiten. Bis heute haben diese Marken Macht über die norditalienische Stadt: Nur wenige andere Großstädte können sich eine solche Dichte von Designerboutiquen leisten, wie man sie im Mailänder Viertel „quadrilatero della moda" findet, das zwischen Via Montenapoleone und Via della Spiga mitten im Zentrum liegt. Viele Gründe für Mailands führende Rolle in der Mode lassen sich bis in die 1960er Jahre zurückverfolgen. Wegen ihrer legendären Manufakturen war die Stadt damals ein Zentrum des Industriedesigns. Der Übergang zur Herstellung von Prêt-à-Porter-Mode war daher ein ganz logischer Entwicklungsschritt. Wo es nicht um geniale Kreativität geht, kann sich die Mailänder Modeindustrie auf die pure Qualität ihrer Erzeugnisse verlassen – und allein auf dieser Reputation basiert das überaus erfolgreiche Geschäft. Die Ästhetik der Stadt an sich spricht den Besucher nicht gerade unmittelbar an. Den Zauber Venedigs oder die Schönheit Roms wird man hier vergeblich suchen. Doch besitzen dafür die Mailänder eine ganz eigene natürliche Eleganz: Die äußere Erscheinung war hier schon immer wichtig und ist es bis heute. So würde eine echte Mailänderin niemals ohne vollständiges Make-up mal rasch in den Supermarkt laufen; die Männer sind stolz darauf, als bestangezogene Vertreter ihres Geschlechts in Europa zu gelten – und achten deshalb streng auf ihre Linie. Unter diesen Umständen staunen Außenstehende immer wieder über den Konservativismus der Mailänder Mode. Die Mailänder arbeiten hart: Erst zur Stunde des „aperitivo", einer gesellschaftlichen Institution, werden Krawatten gelockert und High Heels abgestreift. Aber genau darin liegt auch der Reiz dieser Stadt. Mailand verkörpert italienische Eleganz in ihrer höchsten Form: Die Läden – ob sie nun Mode, Möbel oder Delikatessen verkaufen –, die Restaurants und die Kunstgalerien sind allesamt schlicht, aber zugleich unglaublich chic.

Milan est toujours considérée comme la capitale mondiale de la mode et du design. Pendant le boom économique des années 80, c'est depuis Milan que des noms tels qu'Armani, Versace, Ferré, Max Mara et Gucci commencent à imposer le style italien dans le monde entier. Aujourd'hui, ces griffes sont toujours le moteur de la ville du Nord: peu d'autres capitales présentent une telle densité de boutiques, notamment dans le « quadrilatero della moda », au cœur de la ville, de la Via Montenapoleone à la Via della Spiga. Dans une large mesure, les raisons qui ont permis à Milan de devenir un leader mondial de la mode remontent aux années 60. A cette époque, la ville occupait l'avant-garde du design industriel grâce à son industrie de fabrication légendaire. La transition vers le prêt-à-porter s'est effectuée naturellement. Si elle ne brille pas par son génie créatif, l'industrie de la mode milanaise est admirée pour la grande qualité de ses produits, une réputation qui a permis de développer un marché extrêmement porteur. La ville de Milan ne se distingue pas immédiatement par son esthétique. Elle n'a pas le charme de Venise ni la beauté de Rome. Mais les Milanais ont un style naturel bien à eux: ici, l'apparence extérieure a toujours revêtu une importance cruciale et c'est encore le cas aujourd'hui. Une Milanaise ne sortira jamais faire ses courses au supermarché sans être parfaitement maquillée. Quant aux hommes, ils se targuent d'être les mieux habillés d'Europe et gardent un œil attentif sur leur tour de taille. Ceci étant dit, les outsiders reprochent souvent à Milan le conservatisme de sa mode. Les Milanais sont des travailleurs acharnés: ce n'est qu'au moment de « l'aperitivo » (une institution dans la culture italienne) que les cravates se dénouent et qu'on retire les talons hauts. Mais c'est là que réside toute l'attitude de la ville. A Milan, le style italien atteint son zénith: les boutiques de mode, de meubles ou d'alimentation, les restaurants et les galeries d'art sont tout simplement et indéniablement chic.

FASHION SHOWS AND FAIRS

Milan Fashion Week

All you want or need to know about Milan Fashion Week: schedules, press contacts and information available from www.cameramoda.it.

Alles, was Sie über die Mailänder Modewoche wissen wollen oder müssen: Termine, Pressekontakte und sonstige Informationen finden Sie unter www.cameramoda.it.

Tout ce que vous avez besoin de savoir sur la Milan Fashion Week : programmes, contacts presse et informations diverses disponibles sur le site www.cameramoda.it.

Camera Nazionale della Moda Italiana
Via Morone, 6
Milan
Tel. +39 02 7771 081

Micam Modacalzature

Shoe fair and exhibition for traders and press.

Schuhmesse und -ausstellung für Händler und Presse.

Salon de la chaussure et expositions pour les acheteurs et la presse.

Fiera di Milano
Piazza Sei Febbraio
Milan
Tel. +39 02 8954 6251
www.micamonline.com

Mipel

Leather bags and accessories fair and exhibition for traders and press.

Messe und Ausstellung für Ledertaschen und -accessoires für Händler und Presse.

Salon des sacs et des accessoires en cuir et expositions pour les acheteurs et la presse.

Fiera di Milano
Piazza Sei Febbraio
Milan
Tel. +39 02 5845 11
www.mipel.com

Momi Moda Milano

The main fashion exhibition for traders and press, held during Milan Fashion Week.

Die wichtigste Modeausstellung für Händler und Presse während der Mailänder Modewoche.

Principal salon de la mode pour les acheteurs et la presse, organisé pendant la Milan Fashion Week.

Fiera di Milano
Piazza Sei Febbraio
Milan
Tel. +39 02 6411 041
www.momimodamilano.it

Sistema Moda Italia

Viale Sarca, 223
Milan
Tel. +39 02 661 03391
www.sistemamodaitalia.it

MVM MilanoVendeModa

The most "commercial" of the Milanese fairs, it represents the heart of the trade in Italian fashion.

Die „kommerziellste" unter den Mailänder Messen repräsentiert den Inbegriff des Handels mit italienischer Mode.

Le plus « commercial » des salons milanais représente le cœur du marché de la mode italienne.

Expo Cts
Via G. G. Covone 66
Tel. +39 02 3498 41
www.milanovendemoda.it

White

This salon is the perfect showcase for young and new designers, and runs during Milan Fashion Week. Since its relatively recent beginnings, it has been attracting more and more attention from both press and buyers.

Dieser Salon ist das perfekte Schaufenster für junge und neue Designer während der Mailänder Modewoche. Von Beginn an erregte diese noch relativ junge Veranstaltung mehr und mehr die Aufmerksamkeit von Presse und Einkäufern.

Organisé pendant la Milan Fashion Week, ce salon constitue la plateforme de présentation idéale pour les nouveaux jeunes créateurs. Lancé récemment avec succès, il attire de plus en plus d'acheteurs et de membres de la presse.

Viale Sarca, 223
Tel. +39 02 661 631
www.whitemilano.it

FASHION SCHOOLS

Facoltà del Design – Politecnico di Milano

The prestigious Milanese polytechnic offers a degree course in Design for Fashion and a Masters in Fashion and Design.

Das angesehene Mailänder Polytechnikum bietet ein Graduiertenkolleg in Modedesign sowie Master-Studiengänge in Mode und Design an.

La prestigieuse école polytechnique de Milan propose un cursus diplômant en création de mode ainsi qu'un Masters en mode et en design.

Via Durando, 38
Milan
Tel. +39 02 2399 5976

Istituto Europeo di Design

One of the main privately-owned fashion schools in Italy offers several courses: Fashion Design, Textile Design and Jewellery Design, together with fashion public relations and fashion retail and management.

Eine der wichtigsten privaten Modeschulen Italiens offeriert diverse Studienrichtungen: Modedesign, Textildesign und Schmuckdesign, außerdem Mode-PR sowie Mode-Einzelhandel und -Management.

L'une des principales écoles de mode privées d'Italie propose différents cursus en création de mode, création textile et création joaillière, ainsi que des cours en relations publiques, en distribution et gestion d'entreprise.

Via Sciesa, 4
Milan
Tel. +39 02 5519 4802

Istituto Marangoni

The best school for fashion designers, pattern cutters and print specialists, possibly the most comprehensive in all Italy. Courses vary from Fashion Business, Styling and Design, to Home Collection, Design and Production. The school now offers Advanced Masters courses in brand management, fashion buying, fashion promotion.

Die wahrscheinlich beste Modeschule Italiens für Modedesign, Zuschnitt und Textildruck. Das Kursangebot umfasst Mode-Business, Styling and Design, Home Collection, Design und Produktion. Inzwischen gibt es auch Postgraduiertenkurse in Markenmanagement, Modeeinkauf und Mode-Promotion.

La meilleure école pour les créateurs de mode, les traceurs de patrons et les spécialistes des imprimés. Probablement les cours les plus complets d'Italie, spécialisés en gestion, stylisme et création de mode, mais également en conception et production de mobilier. L'école propose désormais des Advanced Masters en gestion de marque, achat et promotion de produits de mode.

Via M Gonzaga, 6
Milan
Tel. +39 02 8610 90

Italian Fashion School

Supported by the Camera Nazionale della Moda, the school offers post graduate courses for the fashion industry: from fashion design to communication and management to CAD specialist courses in jewellery.

Mit Unterstützung der Camera Nazionale della Moda bietet die Schule Postgraduiertenkurse für die Modeindustrie an: von Modedesign bis Kommunikation und von Management bis hin zu CAD für Schmuckdesign.

Soutenue par la Camera Nazionale della Moda, l'école propose des troisièmes cycles spécialisés dans l'industrie de la mode : de la création de mode à la communication, de la gestion aux cours de CAO spécialisés en bijouterie.

Via Santa Marta, 18
Milan
Tel. +39 02 7771 081

SDA Bocconi

The prestigious Business University has specialised degree courses in fashion: its postgraduate Fashion Management and Design is among the best in the industry.

Die angesehene Wirtschaftsuniversität hat spezielle Postgraduiertenkurse im Bereich Mode im Angebot: Die Seminare für Mode-Management und Design gehören mit zum Besten, was diese Branche zu bieten hat.

La prestigieuse université de gestion propose des cursus diplômants spécialisés en mode : son programme de troisième cycle en gestion et création de mode figure parmi les meilleurs de l'industrie.

Fashion School Management
Via Bocconi, 8
Milan
Tel. +39 02 5836 31

Università IULM

The public relations school has just launched a new degree course in the marketing of luxury and fashion products.

Diese PR-Schule hat gerade ein neues Postgraduiertenstudium für das Marketing von Luxus- und Modeartikeln in sein Programm aufgenommen.

Cette école de relations publiques vient de lancer un nouveau cursus diplômant en marketing des produits de luxe et de mode.

Via San Marco, 46
Milan
Tel. +39 02 6571 656

FASHION MUSEUMS AND GALLERIES

Fabbrica EOS

A disused warehouse functions as an exhibition space, focusing on the fusion of photography, music, design and fashion. 'Eliminating all superficiality to reach the essence of art' is their motto.

In diesen Räumen eines ehemaligen Lagerhauses hat man sich auf das Zusammenspiel von Fotografie, Musik, Design und Mode spezialisiert. Alle Oberflächlichkeit verbannen, um zum Kern der Kunst vorzudringen – so lautet das Motto.

Cet entrepôt désaffecté a été reconverti en espace d'exposition et se spécialise dans la fusion entre photographie, musique, design et mode. Sa devise : « Eliminer toute superficialité pour atteindre l'essence de l'art ».

Piazza Baiamonti, 2
Milan
Tel. +39 02 6596532
www.inforel.it/fabbricaeos

Fondazione Nicola Trussardi

The exhibition space is located on the upper floors of the Trussardi Palace, while the ground floor is dedicated to shopping, and the first to a café-restaurant with a view of la Scala.

Die Galerie befindet sich in den oberen Stockwerken des Palazzo der Firma Trussardi. Im Erdgeschoss kann man einkaufen, während sich im ersten Stock ein Café-Restaurant mit Blick auf die Scala befindet.

Cet espace d'exposition est installé dans les étages supérieurs du Palais Trussardi, le rez-de-chaussée étant réservé aux boutiques et le premier étage accueillant un café-restaurant avec vue sur la Scala.

Palazzo Marino alla Scala
Piazza della Scala, 5
Milan
Tel. +39 02 8068821
www.fondazionenicolatrussardi.com

Fondazione Prada

Anish Kapoor, Louise Bourgeois and Marc Quinn have all shown their works in this amazing space, at the invitation of Miuccia Prada and her husband. An important window for the international contemporary art world – despite showing only two exclusive exhibitions a year.

Anish Kapoor, Louise Bourgeois und Marc Quinn haben auf Einladung von Miuccia Prada und ihrem Ehemann in diesen aufregenden Räumen bereits ihre Werke präsentiert. Die Galerie ist ein wichtiges Schaufenster der internationalen zeitgenössischen Kunst – auch wenn es nur zwei exklusive Ausstellungen pro Jahr gibt.

Anish Kapoor, Louise Bourgeois et Marc Quinn ont tous exposé dans cet espace impressionnant à l'invitation de Miuccia Prada et de son mari. Vitrine incontournable de la scène internationale de l'art contemporain, bien qu'elle ne présente que deux expositions par an.

Via Fogazzaro, 36
Milan
Tel. +39 02 5467 0515
www.fondazioneprada.org

Galleria Carla Sozzani

Based on the first floor of the most stylish shop in Milan – 10 Corso Como – this gallery exhibits work by the world's most important photographers, from Helmut Newton to David LaChapelle. The vernissages are the most sought after in town.

Im ersten Stock der elegantesten Einkaufsadresse Mailands – im 10 Corso Como – stellt diese Galerie Arbeiten der bedeutendsten Fotografen der

Welt aus, von Helmut Newton bis David LaChapelle. Die Vernissagen gelten als die begehrtesten der Stadt.

Installée au premier étage de la boutique la plus branchée de Milan, 10 Corso Como, cette galerie expose les œuvres des plus grands photographes du monde, de Helmut Newton à David LaChapelle. Ses vernissages sont particulièrement courus.

Corso Como, 10
Milan
Tel. +39 02 653531
www.galleriacarlasozzani.org

Photology

The most prestigious photography gallery in Milan.

Die angesehenste Fotogalerie Mailands.

La galerie de photo la plus prestigieuse de Milan.

Via Moscova, 25
Milan
Tel. +39 02 6595285
www.photology.com

Triennale di Milano

This 1933 building hosts some interesting shows, from fashion and architecture to industrial design.

In diesem Gebäude von 1933 finden immer wieder interessante Ausstellungen über Mode, Architektur und Industriedesign statt.

Cet immeuble de 1933 accueille des expositions intéressantes sur la mode, l'architecture et le design industriel.

Palazzo dell'Arte
Via Alemagna, 6
Milan
Tel. +39 02 724341

FASHION SHOPS

10 Corso Como

Opened ten years ago by Carla Sozzani, this is still a fascinating bazaar: ultra hip fashion, quirky accessories, rare CDs, precious homeware and anything else you can think of, sourced from all over the world.

Dieser vor zehn Jahren von Carla Sozzani eröffnete Bazar hat bis heute nichts von seiner Faszination eingebüßt: ultrahippe Mode, verrückte Accessoires, gesuchte CDs, kostbare Homeware und alles, was man sich sonst noch vorstellen kann – aus aller Welt.

Ouvert il y a dix ans par Carla Sozzani, ce grand bazar de la mode est toujours aussi fascinant : mode ultra-branchée, accessoires insolites, CD introuvables et objets précieux pour la maison, importés du monde entier.

Corso Como, 10
Milan
Tel. +39 02 2900 2674

Banner

The second shop in the Biffi family features the most refined fashion available. Ralph Lauren and Yohji Yamamoto are among the favourites.

Der zweite Laden der Familie Biffi präsentiert Mode der elegantesten Sorte. Ralph Lauren und Yohji Yamamoto zählen zu den Lieblingsdesignern.

La seconde boutique de la famille Biffi présente le meilleur de la mode élégante. Ralph Lauren et Yohji Yamamoto y sont en bonne place.

Via Sant'Andrea, 8
Milan
Tel. +39 02 7600 4609

B-Fly

This small shop is quite a challenge in a city where fashion is spelt with a capital F. All the merchandise here comes from emerging talent, often sourced directly from European fashion schools.

Der kleine Laden ist eine ziemliche Herausforderung in einer Stadt, wo Mode eine dermaßen herausragende Rolle spielt. Alles, was man hier findet, stammt von jungen Talenten, oft direkt von den Modeschulen Europas.

Cette petite boutique est un vrai défi dans une ville où la mode s'écrit avec un grand M. Ici, tous les vêtements sont créés par de jeunes talents, souvent directement repérés dans les écoles de mode d'Europe.

Corso di Porta Ticinese
Milan
Tel. +39 02 8942 3178

Biffi

This Milanese institution still sells the established designers, but always with attention given to the trendiest T-shirt maker and the coolest jeans brand.

Diese Mailänder Institution verkauft zwar nach wie vor etablierte Designermarken, führt aber immer auch die trendigsten T-Shirts und die coolsten Jeansmarken.

Cette véritable institution milanaise vend toujours les créations de couturiers bien établis, tout en réservant une place de choix au dernier créateur de t-shirts en vogue et à la marque de jeans la plus tendance du moment.

Corso Genova, 6
Milan
Tel. +39 02 8324 1228

Dantone

For avant-garde, new and up-and-coming designers, together with super fashionable labels from all over the world.

Für avantgardistische, neue und aufstrebende Designer. Außerdem findet

man hier super-angesagte Labels aus aller Welt.

Cette boutique présente les créations de nouveaux créateurs avant-gardistes, à côté de griffes hyper tendance venues du monde entier.

Corso Matteotti, 20
Milan
Tel. +39 02 7600 2098

Fiorucci

Since 1970, Fiorucci has always entertained the eyes of kitsch lovers and colour fanatics, and still presents an explosion of fancy fashion and funky gadgets today.

Seit 1970 erfreut Fiorucci die Herzen von Kitschfans und Farbenfanatikern. Das Label beeindruckt bis heute mit einem Feuerwerk ausgefallener Mode und verrückter Kinkerlitzchen.

Depuis 1970, Fiorucci séduit les amateurs de kitsch et les fanatiques de la couleur. La boutique présente toujours une explosion de mode fantaisiste et de gadgets funky.

Galleria Passerella, 1
Milan
Tel. +39 02 7602 3276

Frette

The chic-est and most refined Italian bedlinen. In crisp cotton, linen and even silk.

Die schickste und edelste Bettwäsche Italiens. Aus frischer Baumwolle, Leinen und sogar Seide.

Les articles de literie les plus chic et les plus raffinés d'Italie, en coton, en lin et même en soie.

Via Montenapoleone, 21
Milan
Tel. +39 02 7600 3791

La Vetrina di Beryl

The hippest shoe shop in town, loved by stylists and fashion editors.

Angesagtestes Schuhgeschäft der Stadt, das insbesondere Stylisten und Modejournalistinnen lieben.

Le magasin de chaussures le plus branché de la ville, chouchou des stylistes et des journalistes de mode.

Via Statuto, 4
Milan
Tel. +39 02 654278

VINTAGE FASHION SHOPS

Cavalli e Nastri

A genuine vintage store with pieces by Yves Saint Laurent, old Balenciaga, Emilio Pucci and more. A little pricey, but the condition of the clothes is pristine. Very unique.

Ein echter Vintage Store mit Kreationen von Yves Saint Laurent, alten Schätzen von Balenciaga, Emilio Pucci und anderen. Etwas teurer, aber dafür sind die Kleider meist praktisch ungetragen. Ein einzigartiger Laden.

Un vrai magasin vintage qui propose des pièces Yves Saint Laurent, Balenciaga, Emilio Pucci et bien d'autres encore. Un peu cher, mais les vêtements sont toujours en parfait état. Absolument unique.

Via Arena
Milan
Tel. +39 02 7200 0449

Il Salvagente
The Salvagente's huge and constant turnover of merchandise makes it an interesting visit, with leftovers of past seasons and surplus odds from every Italian designer label.

Das riesige und ständig wechselnde Angebot macht jeden Besuch hier interessant. Man entdeckt Restbestände vergangener Saisons und Überschüsse jeder italienischen Designermarke.

Une adresse à visiter régulièrement en raison de l'important roulement de son stock, avec les invendus des saisons passées et les fins de série de toutes les griffes italiennes.

Via Fratelli Bronzetti, 16
Milan
Tel. +39 02 7611 0328

L'Armadio di Laura
Great bargains, particularly for women.

Tolle Schnäppchen, vor allem für Damen.

De très bonnes affaires, particulièrement pour les femmes.

Via Voghera, 25
Milan
Tel. +39 02 8360 606

FLEA MARKETS

Mercato di San Donato
Around the metro station San Donato on Sundays.

Sonntags, rund um die Metrostation San Donato.

Autour de la station de métro San Donato, le dimanche.

Mercato di Senigallia
In Viale Papiniano, on the docks, on Saturdays.

Samstags, auf den Kais in der Viale Papiniano.

Dans le Viale Papiniano, sur les quais, le samedi.

RESTAURANTS

Altro
The open kitchen of this contemporary Italian restaurant is the main feature of Altro, based on the first floor of SpazioStrato, a homeware products showroom. The abstract white

paintings on the walls and the stainless steel tables perfectly fit with the modern and bold presentation of the food: Italian classics, revisited. The best choice when looking for an adventurous menu.

Die offene Küche dieses modernen italienischen Restaurants ist die Hauptattraktion des Altro, das sich im ersten Stock des SpazioStrato, einem Showroom für Homeware, befindet. Die abstrakten weißen Gemälde an den Wänden und die Edelstahltische passen perfekt zur modernen und zugleich bodenständigen Präsentation des Essens: italienische Klassiker, neu aufgetischt. Die beste Wahl, wenn Sie auf ein spannendes Menü aus sind.

Installé au premier étage de SpazioStrato, showroom d'articles pour la maison, ce restaurant italien contemporain se distingue par sa cuisine ouverte à la vue des clients. Les tableaux abstraits blancs accrochés aux murs et les tables en acier inoxydable reflètent fidèlement la présentation moderne et audacieuse des plats proposés : des classiques italiens revisités. L'adresse qui s'impose pour ceux qui recherchent un menu hors du commun.

Via Burlamacchi, 5
Milan
Tel. +39 02 54121804

Bagutta
Perfectly hidden in the quietest street of the buzzy shopping area, this restaurant offers a good selection of traditional Italian dishes. The atmosphere is very oldfashioned, with waiters who will always remember you. Great for a quick lunch in between appointments in town.

Perfekt versteckt in der stillsten Gasse des quirligen Einkaufsviertels, bietet dieses Restaurant eine gute Auswahl traditioneller italienischer Gerichte. Die Atmosphäre ist sehr altmodisch, mit Kellnern, die sich ewig an Sie erinnern werden. Perfekt für ein schnelles Mittagessen zwischen zwei Terminen in der Stadt.

Caché dans la rue la plus calme du bruyant quartier commerçant, ce restaurant propose une belle sélection de plats italiens traditionnels. L'atmosphère est vraiment à l'ancienne et ses serveurs n'oublient jamais le visage d'un client. Idéal pour déjeuner sur le pouce entre deux rendez-vous en ville.

Via Bagutta, 14
Milan
Tel. +39 02 7600 902

Bice
Bice is one of the most traditional of Milanese restaurants: its mushroom risotto is renowned as the best in town. Always busy, but worth the wait.

Eines der traditionsreichsten Mailänder Restaurants: Das Pilzrisotto gilt als das beste der Stadt. Immer voll, aber das Warten lohnt sich.

Bice est l'un des restaurants les plus traditionnels de Milan : son risotto aux champignons est réputé comme le meilleur de la ville. Toujours plein, mais vaut largement quelques minutes d'attente.

Via Borgospesso, 12
Milan
Tel. +39 02 7600 2572

Da Giacomo
This anonymous suburban trattoria attracts the Milan fashion crowd: designers, journalists and editors all seem to end up here at least once a week.

In diese anonyme Vorstadt-Trattoria zieht es die Mailänder Modeszene: Designer, Journalisten und Redakteurinnen kehren hier mindestens einmal pro Woche ein.

Cette trattoria anonyme aux abords de la ville attire le petit monde de la mode milanaise : créateurs, journalistes et rédacteurs semblent tous s'y retrouver au moins une fois par semaine.

Via Sottocorno, 6
Milan
Tel. +39 02 7602 3313

EDA
The trendy restaurant has been designed in a warehouse within a courtyard, and combines industrial cool with contemporary chic. The food is 'fancy' Italian; experimental but delicious.

Das trendige Restaurant wurde in einem Lagerhaus innerhalb eines Hofes eingerichtet und verbindet Industriekühle mit zeitgemäßem Schick. Die Küche ist „aufgemotzt" italienisch, experimentierfreudig, aber lecker.

Ce restaurant branché s'est installé dans la cour d'un ancien entrepôt qui combine design industriel et chic contemporain. Il propose une cuisine italienne originale, expérimentale mais délicieuse.

Via Filippino Lippi, 7
Milan
Tel. +39 02 2668 1962

Lucca
This restaurant remains a favourite spot for Tuscan food lovers. Always busy.

Nach wie vor ein Lieblingsrestaurant für alle Freunde der toskanischen Küche. Immer gut besucht.

Cette adresse reste incontournable pour tous les amoureux de la cuisine toscane. Toujours plein.

Via Panfilo Castaldi, 33
Milan
Tel. +39 02 2952 6668

Milch
This intimate restaurant always offers a warm atmosphere for a younger crowd. Simple food and good wines at a reasonable price. And all organic.

Ein gemütliches Restaurant mit stets freundlicher Atmosphäre für ein jüngeres Publikum. Einfaches Essen und gute Weine zu moderaten Preisen. Alles aus biologischem Anbau.

Ce restaurant intime accueille aujourd'hui une clientèle plus jeune, toujours dans une ambiance chaleureuse. Cuisine simple et bons vins à prix raisonnables. Cerise sur le gâteau : tout est bio.

Via Petrella, 19
Milan
Tel. +39 02 2940 5870

Nobu@Armani
This is the Italian version of De Niro's Nobu in NYC and London. Very good sushi, in a very chic environment.

Die italienische Variante von De Niros Nobu in NYC und London. Sehr gutes Sushi in sehr schickem Ambiente.

C'est la version italienne du Nobu de Robert De Niro à New York et Londres. Pour déguster d'excellents sushi dans un décor très chic.

Armani Store
Via Pisoni, 1
Milan
Tel. +39 02 7231 8645

Santa Lucia
One of the oldest pizzerias in Milan in a decadent chandeliered room. Still a favourite for the Milanese world of culture.

Eine der ältesten Pizzerien Mailands in einem dekadenten Lokal mit Kronleuchtern. Nach wie vor ein beliebter Treffpunkt der Mailänder Kulturszene.

L'une des plus vieilles pizzerias de Milan, avec une salle aux chandeliers des plus décadentes. Toujours l'une des adresses préférées du petit monde culturel de la ville.

Via San Pietro all'Orto, 3
Milan
Tel. +39 02 7602 3155

Shambala
The place to see and to be seen, offering a good fusion menu. The big terrace is ideal for summer dining.

Das richtige Lokal, um bei guter Fusion-Cuisine zu sehen und gesehen zu werden. Die große Terrasse lädt im Sommer zum Dinieren im Freien ein.

Le dernier endroit à voir et où il faut être vu propose un bon menu qui fusionne diverses cuisines. La grande terrasse est idéale pour dîner en été.

Via Ripamonti, 337
Milan
Tel. +39 02 5520 194

Taverna Morigi

Rustic and basic, la Taverna Morigi boasts one of the biggest selections of Italian wines, vintage or otherwise. To be tasted with their selection of salami and grissini.

Die rustikale und bodenständige Taverna Morigi kann sich einer der umfassendsten Kollektionen italienischer Weine rühmen, darunter echte Spitzenjahrgänge. Man degustiert mit verschiedenen Salamisorten und Grissini.

Simple et rustique, la Taverna Morigi propose l'un des plus vastes choix de vins italiens, notamment des grands crus. A déguster avec leur sélection de salamis et de gressins.

Via Morigi, 8
Milan
Tel. +39 02 8645 0880

Trattoria Le Langhe

The popular restaurant serves delicacies from the Piemonte region, famous for truffles, Barolo red wine and the bagna cauda, a dish of raw vegetables dipped in a sauce of butter, garlic, and chopped anchovies.

Das beliebte Restaurant serviert Spezialitäten aus der Region Piemont, die berühmt ist für Trüffel, Barolo und bagna cauda – Rohkost, die in einen Dip aus Butter, Knoblauch und gehackten Anchovis getaucht wird.

Ce restaurant populaire propose des spécialités du Piémont, une région réputée pour ses truffes, son vin rouge Barolo et la bagna cauda, un plat de légumes crus que l'on trempe dans une sauce à base de beurre, d'ail et d'anchois émincés.

Corso Como, 6
Milan
Tel. +39 02 6554 279

Trattoria della Pesa

This restaurant was opened 125 years ago, and still keeps the perfect standard of the pure Milanese cuisine, with a great selection of Italian wines. Here the ossobuco is the best in town.

Dieses Restaurant wurde vor 125 Jahren eröffnet und hält nach wie vor den perfekten Standard der klassischen Mailänder Küche. Hinzu kommt eine großartige Auswahl italienischer Weine. Das Ossobucco ist das beste der Stadt.

Ouvert il y a 125 ans, ce restaurant continue à respecter les plus hauts standards de la cuisine milanaise et

propose une superbe sélection de vins italiens. On y mange le meilleur osso-buco de la ville.

Via Pasubio, 10
Milan
Tel. +39 02 6555 741

BARS

Absolut Ice Bar

Everyone is provided with a thermal cape when entering this trendy bar: from the chairs to the shelves, it is all made of ice! And what better than Absolut vodka for drinks. Pure or mixed.

Wer diese trendige Bar betritt, erhält sofort einen wärmenden Umhang: von den Stühlen bis zu den Regalen besteht hier alles aus Eis! Und was könnte man hier Passenderes trinken als Absolut Wodka. Pur oder gemixt.

En entrant dans ce bar branché, tout le monde se voit remettre une couverture thermique : en effet, des chaises aux étagères, tout est en glace ! Le lieu idéal pour siroter un verre de vodka Absolut, pure ou en cocktail.

Piazza Gerusalemme, 12
Milan
Tel. +39 02 8907 8513

ATM

The arty and intellectual crowd meets at ATM for their aperitif: best outside, even in winter. Still a very 'fashion' bar.

Künstler und Intellektuelle treffen sich im ATM zum Aperitif – am liebsten draußen, selbst im Winter. Nach wie vor ein Mode-Bar.

Une clientèle arty et intello se retrouve chez ATM à l'heure de l'apéritif : plus sympa à l'extérieur, même en hiver. Un bar toujours très fashion.

Bastioni di Porta Volta, 15
Milan
Tel. +39 02 6552 365

Bar Bianco

Deep in the heart of the giardini, this bar is popular during the summer season for its outdoor tables and aperitifs. Open until late, when the young Milanese meet.

Diese Bar im Herzen der Giardini erfreut sich im Sommer wegen ihrer Tische und Aperitifs im Freien großer Beliebtheit. Die langen Öffnungszeiten nutzen vor allem die jungen Mailänder.

Niché au cœur d'un jardin public, ce bar est très fréquenté en été pour ses tables en extérieur et ses apéritifs. Reste ouvert tard, lieu de rendez-vous des jeunes Milanais.

Giardini Publicci, Via Gadio entrance
Milan
Tel. +39 02 2952 3354

Corso Como Caffè

The zen surroundings make this bar a hotspot of Milan. Great for cocktails too.

Das Zen-Ambiente macht diese Bar zu einem der angesagtesten Treffs von Mailand. Es gibt auch phantastische Cocktails.

Son ambiance zen en fait l'un des bars les plus courus de Milan. Idéal pour les cocktails.

Corso Como, 10
Milan
Tel. +39 02 654 831

Cuore

Maybe the smallest bar in Milan, with a charming and warm atmosphere. Not easy to find for first timers!

Die vielleicht kleinste Bar Mailands mit zauberhafter, freundlicher Atmosphäre. Beim ersten Besuch nicht ganz leicht zu finden!

Sans doute le plus petit bar de la ville, atmosphère chaleureuse et pleine de charme. Pas facile à trouver la première fois !

Via C. C. Mora, 3
Milan
+39 02 5810 5126

Da Claudio

The famous fish shop of the Brera area transforms itself to a cool bar at seven every night: the best aperitivo of Mediterranean sushi and chilled white wine. Loved by understated fashion folk.

Das berühmte Fischgeschäft des Viertels Brera verwandelt sich jeden Abend um sieben in eine coole Bar: mit den besten Mittelmeer-Sushi und kühlem Weißwein. Die auf Understatement eingeschworene Modeszene liebt dieses Lokal.

Tous les soirs à dix-neuf heures, la célèbre poissonnerie du quartier de Brera se transforme en bar branché et propose le meilleur des apéritifs : sushi de Méditerranée et vin blanc frais. Le rendez-vous des amateurs de mode discrète.

Via Ponte Vetero, 16
Milan

Dar el Yacout

This new Moroccan-decorated bar and restaurant has got a see-through Plexiglas dance floor with fountains and a pond underneath. The amazing food is served in a traditional style. Check for the belly dancing shows.

Zu diesem neuen Lokal mit Bar und Restaurant in marokkanischem Stil gehört eine durchsichtige Tanzfläche aus Plexiglas, unter der Springbrunnen und ein Teich zu sehen sind. Das ausgezeichnete Essen wird auf traditionelle Weise serviert. Erkundigen

Sie sich nach den Terminen der Bauchtanz-Vorführungen.

Ce nouveau bar-restaurant décoré à la marocaine possède un dancefloor en Plexiglas transparent donnant sur des fontaines et sur une petite mare. Cuisine exceptionnelle et service à l'ancienne. A ne pas rater : les spectacles de danse du ventre.

Via Cadore, 23
Milan
Tel. +39 02 5462 230

Frantoi Celletti

All about olives and olive oils. The aperitifs here are served with bruschetta (to be tried with flavoured oils), olive all'ascolana (stuffed giant olives) and mini sandwiches with olive creams. The décor itself is reminiscent of a traditional country-style olive oil factory.

Alles rund um Oliven und Olivenöle. Die Aperitifs serviert man hier mit Bruschetta (die man mit aromatisierten Ölen isst), Oliven all'ascolana (gefüllte Riesenoliven) und kleinen Broten mit Olivenpaste. Die Dekoration erinnert an eine traditionelle ländliche Olivenölmühle.

Olives et huiles d'olive à l'honneur : ici, les apéritifs sont servis avec une *bruschetta* (à essayer avec arômes d'huile d'olive), des olive all'ascolana (olives géantes fourrées) et des mini-sandwiches à la crème d'olive. Même le décor rappelle les manufactures d'huile d'olive traditionnelles qu'on trouve dans les campagnes.

Via Zuccoli, 6
Milan
Tel. +39 02 6698 3712

G-Lounge

The newest and chicest bar in town. Loved by the fashion crowd, it offers sushi for aperitifs and late night dancing on the lower ground floor. In summer the outdoor tables are very popular, alongside the alternative – sitting on your Vespa.

Eine der neueren und schicksten Bars der Stadt. Bei den Modeleuten extrem beliebt. Zu den Aperitifs gibt es Sushi, und nachts wird im Souterrain getanzt. Die Tische im Freien sind im Sommer heiß begehrt – wenn man nicht ohnehin auf seiner Vespa sitzt.

Flambant neuf, ce bar est le plus chic de la ville. Prisé par le monde de la mode, on peut y manger des sushi à l'apéritif. Dancing au sous-sol, ouvert tard dans la nuit. En été, les tables en terrasse sont toutes prises – reste donc l'alternative typiquement italienne : rester assis sur sa Vespa.

Via Larga 12
Milan

Just Cavalli Café

The best spot for fashionistas and friends, to see and to be seen, in a very Milanese way. And in typical Roberto Cavalli style: animal and rose prints for cushions, curtains and table cloths! Plus colourful, and tastefully lethal, cocktails.

Der beste Ort für Fashionistas und Co., um zu sehen und gesehen zu werden. Ein für Mailand und den Stil von Roberto Cavalli ganz typisches Lokal: Raubtier- und Rosenmotive auf Kissen, Vorhängen und Tischdecken! Dazu kommen bunte und tödlich leckere Cocktails.

Le dernier rendez-vous des fashion victims et de leurs amis, pour voir et être vus à la façon typiquement milanaise. Le tout dans le style inimitable de Roberto Cavalli : imprimés d'animaux et de roses sur les coussins, les rideaux et les nappes ! Sans oublier les cocktails multicolores délicieusement dangereux.

V. le Camoens
Milan
Tel. +39 02 311 8 17

Luminal

The big round club is the trendy spot of the year. Every Friday is "pretend to be a DJ" night, with surprise performers: designers Alessandro dell'Acqua, Antonio Berardi and model Michelle Hicks have all done it.

Der große runde Club ist der angesagteste Treffpunkt des Jahres. Jeden Samstag findet hier die „Pretend to be DJ"-Night mit erstaunlichen Protagonisten statt: Die Designer Alessandro dell Acqua, Antonio Berardi und das Model Michelle Hicks haben hier allesamt schon Platten aufgelegt.

Ce grand club tout rond apparaît comme l'adresse la plus branchée de l'année. Chaque vendredi, la soirée « Pretend to be DJ » reçoit des invités surprise : les créateurs Alessandro dell'Acqua, Antonio Berardi et la model Michelle Hicks sont tous passés derrière les platines.

Via Monte Grappa, 14
Milan
Tel. +39 02 3652 4841

HOTELS

Antica Locanda dei Mercanti

This charming little hotel is located in the very heart of Milan. There are fresh flowers in each room every day, and the three rooms at the top floor have private terraces.

Dieses bezaubernde kleine Hotel liegt mitten im Zentrum Mailands. In allen Zimmern gibt es täglich frische Blumen, und die drei Zimmer im obersten Stock haben sogar eigene Terrassen.

Ce petit hôtel de charme se trouve en plein cœur de Milan. Bouquets de fleurs changés chaque jour dans toutes les chambres. Les trois chambres du dernier étage bénéficient d'une terrasse privée.

Via San Tommaso, 6
Milan
Tel. +39 02 8054 080
www.locanda.it

Ariston

This newly-decorated hotel is the place for eco-lovers: breakfast is one hundred percent organic and even the water for the tea is purified. Very chic and comfortable.

Das frisch renovierte Hotel ist perfekt für Öko-Fans: Das Frühstück ist zu hundert Prozent bio, und selbst das Teewasser wird gefiltert. Sehr chic und komfortabel.

Cet hôtel récemment redécoré est l'adresse préférée des écolos : le petit déjeuner est 100 % bio, même l'eau du thé est purifiée. Très chic et tout confort.

Largo Carrobbio, 2
Milan
Tel. +39 02 7200 0556
www.brerahotels.com

Bulgari Hotel

Hidden in a private street in the Brera area, this chic hotel is the best on offer for visiting VIPs: soon after its opening Elizabeth Hurley and Naomi Campbell made it their Milanese home. The sleek décor and the warm tones of the lobby make the hotel very welcoming, and the prestigious restaurant is also critically acclaimed.

Versteckt in einer Privatstraße des Viertels Brera, empfiehlt sich dieses schicke Hotel als ideale Wahl für VIPs: Kurz nach der Eröffnung machten Elizabeth Hurley und Naomi Campbell es zu ihrem Mailänder Domizil. Die elegante Einrichtung und die warmen Farbtöne der Lobby sorgen für eine einladende Atmosphäre, und das bekannte Restaurant wird auch von Gourmetkritikern gepriesen.

Caché dans une voie privée du quartier de Brera, cet hôtel chic a tout pour combler les attentes des VIP en visite : peu de temps après son ouverture, Elizabeth Hurley et Naomi Campbell en ont fait leur résidence milanaise. Le décor épuré et les couleurs chaudes du hall d'entrée rendent l'hôtel très accueillant, sans oublier son prestigieux restaurant plébiscité par les critiques culinaires.

Via Fratelli Gabba, 7
Milan
Tel. +39 02 8058 051

Corso Como Hotel

Displaying a very sleek sense of style, this hotel has a very definite New York look. The rooms are well appointed and its location, in the up-and-coming Isola quarter, is ideal for restaurants and shops.

Das schnittige Design dieses Hotels erinnert eindeutig an New York. Die Zimmer sind gut ausgestattet, und das aufstrebende Viertel Isola eignet sich perfekt zum Essengehen und Einkaufen.

Design épuré dans le plus grand style new-yorkais. Les chambres sont bien équipées et l'hôtel, situé en plein milieu du nouveau quartier branché d'Isola, se trouve à deux pas des restaurants et des boutiques.

Via Tocqueville, 7
Milan
Tel. +39 02 6207 1

Diana

Art nouveau in design, The Diana has its own particular charm. Once the site of the first public swimming pool in Milan, the hotel has now opened its garden to the public for one of the most stylish aperitivi in town.

Das Jugendstil-Hotel Diana besitzt einen ganz eigenen Charme. Einst besaß man hier das erste öffentliche Schwimmbad der Stadt. Heute ist auch der Garten öffentlich zugänglich und Schauplatz eines der elegantesten „aperitivi" Mailands.

Avec son design Art Nouveau, le Diana possède un charme bien particulier. Autrefois le site de la première piscine municipale de Milan, l'hôtel ouvre désormais son jardin au public pour l'un des « aperitivi » les plus classe de la ville.

Viale Piave, 42
Milan
Tel. ++39 02 2058 1
www.sheraton.com/dianamajestic

Excelsior Gallia

Next to the magnificent all-white fascist building that is the Stazione Centrale, this hotel is a landmark of '30s architecture with a distinctive Art Deco interior. All the rooms are spacious and pleasingly retro.

Neben der bombastischen schneeweißen Stazione Centrale aus der faschistischen Ära gelegen, stellt dieses Hotel einen Meilenstein der Architektur der 1930er Jahre mit typischer Art-Deco-Einrichtung dar. Alle Zimmer sind geräumig und in gefälligem Retro-Stil gehalten.

A côté de l'imposant bâtiment fasciste tout blanc de la Stazione Centrale, cet hôtel apparaît comme un chef-d'œuvre de l'architecture des années 30, avec sa décoration intérieure Art Déco originale. Toutes les chambres sont spacieuses et séduisent les clients grâce à leur style rétro.

Piazza Duca d'Aosta, 9
Milan
Tel. +39 02 6785

Four Seasons

The Four Seasons is housed in a 15th century convent, and has kept the original frescos and the beautiful porch in the garden. Loved by celebrities and big fashion names, this is the most expensive hotel in Milan.

Das Hotel befindet sich in einem ehemaligen Kloster aus dem 15. Jahrhundert. Einige Fresken und die wundervollen Arkaden im Innenhof sind erhalten geblieben. Das teuerste Haus am Platze erfreut sich bei Prominenten – nicht nur aus der Modebranche – größter Beliebtheit.

Installé dans un couvent du XVe siècle, le Four Seasons a conservé les fresques d'époque et le magnifique porche du jardin. Couru par les célébrités et les grands noms de la mode, c'est aussi l'hôtel le plus cher de Milan.

Via Gesù, 8
Milan
Tel. +39 02 77088
www.fourseasons.com/milan

Grand Hotel de Milan

An elegant 1863 palazzo, situated in the very heart of Milan. The history of this hotel includes Wagner, Hemingway and Verdi, who all spent their time here. Two minutes away from La Scala.

Ein eleganter Palazzo aus dem Jahre 1863 im Herzen von Mailand gelegen. Zur Geschichte dieses Hotels gehören Namen wie Wagner, Hemingway und Verdi, die alle hier logierten. Zwei Minuten von der Scala entfernt.

Cet élégant palazzo construit en 1863 se trouve en plein cœur de la ville. Wagner, Hemingway et Verdi y ont tous séjourné. A deux minutes de La Scala.

Via Manzoni, 29
Milan
Tel. +39 02 7231 41
www.grandhoteletdemilan.it

Hotel Manzoni

In the middle of the fashion quadrilatero d'oro, Milan's chicest district, this hotel offers good rooms at a moderate price.

Mitten im Modeviertel „quadrilatero d'oro", Mailands schickster Gegend, bietet dieses Hotel anständige Zimmer zu moderaten Preisen.

Au cœur du quartier de la mode quadrilatero d'oro, le coin le plus chic de Milan, cet hôtel propose de belles chambres à prix modéré.

Via Santo Spirito, 20
Milan
Tel. +39 02 7600 5700
www.hotelmanzoni.com

Principe di Savoia

Once considered 'the' hotel for rich tourists, the Principe is now populated with a new, more fashionable clientele. The bar on the ground floor serves the best cocktails in the area and attracts the crowds during Milan Fashion Week.

Einst das Hotel schlechthin für reiche Touristen, wird das Principe heute von einer neuen, modebewussten Klientel frequentiert. Die Bar im Erdgeschoss serviert die besten Cocktails der ganzen Gegend und zieht damit unter anderem die Besucher der Mailänder Modewoche an.

Autrefois considéré comme l'hôtel des touristes fortunés, le Principe accueille aujourd'hui une nouvelle clientèle plus branchée. Le bar du rez-de-chaussée sert les meilleurs cocktails du coin et attire les foules pendant la Milan Fashion Week.

Piazza della Repubblica, 17
Milan
Tel. +39 02 6230 1

Straf Hotel
This hotel, just minutes away from the Duomo, is an inspired fusion of Italian fashion, original design and elegance. Vincenzo de Cootis, designer of avant-garde fashion label Haute, has chosen unusual materials for the 66 rooms: scratched mirrors, black stones and burnished brass. The lounge bar is the perfect hang-out for stylish Milanese.

Nur wenige Minuten vom Dom entfernt, stellt dieses Hotel eine gelungene Mischung aus italienischer Mode, originellem Design und Eleganz dar. Vincenzo de Cootis, Designer des Avantgarde-Labels Haute, wählte für die Einrichtung der 66 Zimmer ungewöhnliche Materialien: zerkratzte Spiegel, schwarzen Stein und poliertes Messing. Die Bar in der Lounge ist der perfekte Treff für stilbewusste Mailänder.

A quelques minutes du Dôme, cet hôtel propose une fusion inspirée entre mode italienne, design original et élégance. Vincenzo de Cootis, créateur de la griffe d'avant-garde Haute, a choisi des matières inhabituelles pour décorer les 66 chambres : miroirs rayés, pierres noires et cuivre poli. Le bar lounge est un rendez-vous idéal pour les élégants de Milan.

Via San Raffaele, 3
Milan
Tel. +39 02 8050 81

The Gray
The 21 rooms in this boutique hotel are all different: some have private gyms, some overlook the fashionable Galleria and some have ostrich leather bed heads! The all black and white restaurant, Le Noir, has a creatively revisited Mediterranean cuisine, perfect for brunch.

Die 21 Zimmer dieses Boutique-Hotels sind alle verschieden: Manche haben eigene Fitnessräume, manche bieten einem Blick auf die angesagte Galleria, und in wieder anderen sind die Kopfteile der Betten mit Straußenleder überzogen. Das ganz in Schwarzweiß gehalten Restaurant Le Noir bietet eine kreativ modernisierte Version der Mittelmeerküche und ist perfekt zum Brunchen.

Les 21 chambres de cet hôtel design sont toutes différentes : certaines possèdent leur propre salle de gym, d'autres donnent sur la Galleria ou présentent des têtes de lit en cuir d'autruche ! Le Noir, restaurant entièrement décoré en noir et blanc, sert une cuisine méditerranéenne revisitée avec créativité, idéale pour le brunch.

Via San Raffaele, 6
Milan
Tel. +39 02 7208 951

Three Rooms
The Three Rooms B&B is the essence of minimal Milan chic. Each individual apartment features 20th century classics, from Arne Jacobsen's Swan and Egg chairs to the Noguchi sofa to the crystal tables designed by Chris Ruhs. Bang & Olufsen systems keep the guests entertained, along with a choice of 24 kinds of teas and 13 different coffees.

Das Bed & Breakfast Three Rooms ist der Inbegriff des minimalistischen Mailänder Chics. In jedem der individuell eingerichteten Apartments trifft man auf Klassiker des 20. Jahrhunderts – von Arne Jacobsens Swan- und Egg-Stühlen bis hin zu Noguchi-Sofas oder Kristalltischen von Chris Ruhs. Anlagen von Bang & Olufsen sorgen neben 24 Tee- und 13 Kaffeesorten für die Unterhaltung der Gäste.

Ce « bed & breakfast » est le symbole même du chic minimaliste propre à Milan. Chaque appartement individuel présente des classiques du XXe siècle, des chaises Cygne et Œuf d'Arne Jacobsen au canapé de Noguchi en passant par les tables en cristal conçues par Chris Ruhs. Les clients peuvent profiter des systèmes Bang & Olufsen installés dans leurs chambres, sans oublier un choix de 24 sortes de thé et de 13 cafés différents.

Corso Como, 10
Milan
Tel. +39 02 6261 63

AIRPORTS

Linate (International)
Tel. +39 02 7485 2200
www.sea-aeroportimilano.it

Malpensa (Intercontinental)
Tel. +39 02 7485 2200
www.sea-aeroportimilano.it

MOSCOW

TEXT BY HELLIN KAY

Expanding at an unbelievable pace, Moscow continues to be one of the most exciting cities on the planet. Over the past few years, it has strived, and succeeded, in making itself an essential fashion destination – if not in terms of production then certainly when considering consumption levels. Whilst the Moscow fashion market had previously been limited to the output of GUM (the government-owned department store on Red Square), the city now boasts an impressive collection of luxury brand boutiques. Furthermore, the city has also developed a stable of young, up-and-coming designers, some of whom have outgrown Moscow and moved onto London, Milan and Paris; Nina Donis, Daria Razhumihina and Denis Simachev are amongst those who have already begun to pop up on the fashion pages of the International Herald Tribune. Meanwhile Moscow itself continues to be a city of endless talent and inspiration, maintaining its long, affable history with the avant-garde. The Russians have always appreciated the new and innovative, explaining the speed at which Moscow's fashion industry has grown. Nowadays, GUM is still on Red Square but it is no longer government owned nor stocked with minimal, drab goods – it now sells everything from Louis Vuitton to Sportmax. Across the street from the highly-desirable Tretyakovsy Proezd, there is also TSUM, the recently-renovated department store sister to GUM. Transformed it now boasts wares from Chloé and Alexander McQueen through to Miu Miu and Marni. GUM's output is perhaps rivalled only by Stoleshnikov Pereoulok, which in five years has gone from an empty alley to the hottest luxury location in Moscow. Within two years the usual luxury boutique suspects will be housed in a brand new St. Moritz-style village adjacent to Zhukova, on the outskirts of Moscow, where Abramovich and Putin both have their Dachas. The Moscow underground has developed a style and manner distinctly its own, as has its unique – and very wild – club scene.

Das in unglaublichem Tempo expandierende Moskau ist nach wie vor eine der aufregendsten Städte dieses Planeten. Im Laufe der letzten Jahre hat die Metropole darum gekämpft und es geschafft, sich als bedeutender Modestandort zu etablieren – wenn vielleicht auch nicht im Hinblick auf die Produktion, so doch sicher im Bereich Konsum. Einst beschränkte sich der Moskauer Modemarkt auf das Angebot des GUM (das Kaufhaus am Roten Platz gehörte dem Staat), während die Stadt sich heute einer imposanten Ansammlung von Luxusboutiquen diverser Marken rühmen kann, durch die alle bedeutenden Designer der Welt hier vertreten sind. Darüber hinaus bringt die Stadt zahlreiche junge, aufstrebende Designer hervor. Einigen von ihnen ist Moskau bereits zu klein geworden, so dass sie nach London, Mailand und Paris weitergezogen sind. Nina Donis, Daria Razhumihina und Denis Simachev etwa gehören zu denen, die während der internationalen Modewochen in Europa bereits auf den Seiten des International Herald Tribune aufscheinen. Moskau ist unterdessen weiterhin eine Stadt der grenzenlosen Begabung und Inspiration, die ihre lange, erfreuliche Geschichte der Avantgarde fortschreibt. Die Russen schätzten schon immer das Neue und Innovative, was auch das Tempo erklärt, in dem die Moskauer Modeindustrie gewachsen ist. Das GUM steht noch heute auf dem Roten Platz, aber es ist kein Staatseigentum mehr und hat auch kein beschränktes, eher

freudloses Sortiment mehr – inzwischen ist dort von Louis Vuitton bis hin zu Sportmax schlichtweg alles zu haben. Gleich gegenüber auf dem noblen Tretjakovskaja Proezd liegt das TSUM, das kürzlich renovierte Filial-Kaufhaus des GUM. Das Möchtegern-Harrods (noch nicht ganz so berühmt wie das Original) schmückt sich mit Designerkreationen von Chloé bis Alexander McQueen und von Miu Miu bis Marni. Mit dem Angebot des GUM kann es eigentlich nur die Stoleshnikov Pereoulok aufnehmen, die sich in nur fünf Jahren von einer leeren Gasse zu einer der heißesten Luxus-Locations Moskaus entwickelt hat. In den nächsten zwei Jahren sollen sich die üblichen Verdächtigen unter den Nobelboutiquen in einem St-Moritz-ähnlichen Dorf am Rande von Zhukova einfinden, dem absolut elegantesten Viertel der Moskauer Peripherie, wo auch Abramovich und Putin ihre Datschen haben. Die Moskauer Underground-Szene hat einen ganz eigenständigen Stil hervorgebracht, wie auch eine einzigartige – ziemlich wilde – Club-Landschaft.

Moscou se développe à un rythme incroyable et reste l'une des villes les plus fascinantes de la planète. Ces dernières années, elle a tout fait pour devenir une destination incontournable du monde de la mode et a atteint son objectif, peut-être pas en termes de production mais certainement en termes de consommation. Alors que le marché de la mode moscovite est longtemps resté confiné aux produits de GUM (le grand magasin d'Etat sur la place Rouge), la ville revendique aujourd'hui une impressionnante collection de boutiques de luxe où tous les grands créateurs du monde sont représentés. Par ailleurs, Moscou a également produit sa propre écurie de jeunes talents prometteurs qui, dans certains cas, ont quitté la capitale russe pour s'installer à Londres, Milan ou Paris ; Nina Donis, Daria Razhumihina et Denis Simachev ne sont que quelques-uns des nombreux créateurs présentés dans les pages du International Herald Tribune pendant les semaines de la mode en Europe. Parallèlement, Moscou reste une ville au talent infini, vibrante d'inspiration et avec une belle et longue tradition historique de l'avant-garde. En effet, les Russes ont toujours su apprécier la nouveauté et l'innovation, une qualité qui explique pourquoi l'industrie de la mode moscovite s'est développée aussi rapidement. Aujourd'hui, GUM trône toujours sur la place Rouge mais n'appartient plus à l'Etat. Le grand magasin ne se contente plus de proposer de tristes marchandises de première consommation : on y trouve désormais toutes sortes de marques, de Louis Vuitton à Sportmax. Récemment rénové, le grand magasin TSUM, petit frère de GUM, se trouve en face du très chic passage de Tretyakovsky Proyezd. Aspirant à devenir le Harrods russe (bien qu'il ne soit pas encore aussi fabuleux), il présente désormais des créations de Chloé, Alexander McQueen, Miu Miu ou Marni. Le seul concurrent potentiel de GUM est peut-être Stoleshnikov Pereoulok, galerie autrefois déserte qui en l'espace de cinq ans s'est transformée en destination de luxe la plus courue de Moscou. D'ici deux ans, les boutiques haut de gamme s'installeront dans un village flambant neuf au style très St. Moritz situé non loin de Zhukova, dernier quartier à la mode des abords de la ville où Abramovich et Poutine ont tous deux leurs datchas. L'underground moscovite s'est forgé une attitude et un style bien distincts, tout comme sa scène club unique et totalement déchaînée.

FASHION SHOWS AND FAIRS

Russian Fashion Week

Moscow holds its own fashion week annually, taking place after the conclusion of Paris fashion week in March. Organised by ArteFact Communications' Alexander Shumsky, the kingpin of fashion week has spent much time and energy convincing some of the world's hottest designers to come and show alongside Moscow's budding crop.

Moskau veranstaltet einmal jährlich, nach der Pariser Modewoche im März, seine eigene Fashion Week. Organisiert wird das Ganze von Alexander Shumskys ArteFact Communication. Der König der Modewoche hat Unmengen Zeit und Energie darauf verwendet, einige der heißesten Designer dazu zu bringen, hier neben den aufblühenden Moskauer Talenten zu präsentieren.

Moscou tient sa propre Semaine de la Mode une fois par an, après la fin des défilés parisiens en mars. Organisée par Alexander Shumsky d'Arte-Fact Communications, le caïd de la semaine de la mode a investi beaucoup de temps et d'énergie pour convaincre certains des créateurs internationaux les plus prisés de venir défiler à Moscou aux côtés des jeunes stylistes du cru.

www.rfw.ru
info@artefact.ru

FASHION SCHOOL

Moscow Textile Academy

The Textile Academy is the closest thing to a fashion school in Moscow, with a great emphasis on the technical science of textiles. It has spawned many a Russian talent including Nina Donis.

Die Textilakademie ist die Moskauer Institution, die einer Modeschule am nächsten kommt. Hier legt man großen Wert auf die technischen Aspekte von Textilien. Die Schule hat schon viele russische Talente, wie zum Beispiel Nina Donis, hervorgebracht.

La Textile Academy est l'institution moscovite qui s'apparente le plus à une école de mode, bien que l'accent y soit davantage mis sur la science technique des textiles. De nombreux talents russes y ont été formés, notamment Nina Donis.

Malaya Kaluzhskaya Ulitsa, 1
Moscow

FASHION SHOPS

James Boutique

Housed in a clean, modern space, James Boutique sells a mixture of great designers including Ann Demeulemeester, Yohji Yamamoto, Dries Van Noten and Alexander McQueen. A reading room provides an opportunity to catch up with the latest international fashion magazines.

Der gepflegte, moderne Laden verkauft eine Mischung berühmter Designer, darunter Ann Demeulemeester, Yohji Yamamoto, Dries van Noten und Alexander McQueen. In einem Lesezimmer hat man Gelegenheit, sich mit den aktuellen Ausgaben der internationalen Modemagazine auf den neuesten Stand zu bringen.

Installée dans un espace très moderne, James Boutique propose des pièces de grands créateurs, notamment Ann Demeulemeester, Yohji Yamamoto, Dries Van Noten et Alexander McQueen. Une salle de lecture vous permet de rester informé des nouvelles tendances grâce aux derniers numéros des magazines de mode du monde entier.

Tverskaya Ulitsa, 28
Moscow
Tel. +7 (0)95 9379 447

Le Form

One of the oldest surviving boutiques, Le Form tends to leave merchandise from several seasons ago on the shelves and mark them down until they sell, meaning that everything from Junya Watanabe to Helmut Lang can be found at very low prices. Recently, it has also started to carry Russian designers such as Denis Simachev.

Eine der ältesten Boutiquen, die überlebt haben. Stücke aus älteren Kollektionen werden hier so lange heruntergesetzt, bis sie sich verkaufen. So bekommt man hier alle möglichen Kreationen von Junya Watanabe bis Helmut Lang zu sehr günstigen Preisen. Seit kurzer Zeit führt man auch russische Designer wie Denis Simachev.

Le Form est l'une des rares boutiques qui ont survécu à l'ère communiste. Les propriétaires ont tendance à laisser les vêtements des saisons passées en linéaire et baissent régulièrement les prix jusqu'à ce qu'ils se vendent. Autrement dit, on peut trouver les créations de Junya Watanabe ou Helmut Lang à des prix défiant toute concurrence. Récemment, la boutique a commencé à soutenir les stylistes russes, dont Denis Simachev.

Povarskaya Ulitsa
House 35/28
Moscow
Tel. +7 (0)95 2918 220
www.leform.ru

Podium

A great little boutique that carries Alberta Ferretti, Ralph Lauren, Pucci, Plein Sud, Roberto Cavalli, Narciso Rodriguez, Chloé and Jean Paul Gaultier.

Eine großartige kleine Boutique, die Alberta Ferretti, Ralph Lauren, Pucci, Plein Sud, Roberto Cavalli, Narciso Rodriguez, Chloé und Jean Paul Gaultier führt.

Cette petite boutique très intéressante propose des pièces d'Alberta Ferretti, Ralph Lauren, Pucci, Plein Sud, Roberto Cavalli, Narcisco Rodriguez, Chloé et Jean Paul Gaultier.

Novinsky Boulevard, 18
Moscow
Tel. +7 (0)95 2024 686

Red Code

A good place to find everything from Martin Margiela to Paul Smith and Joseph: an eclectic mix with fantastic sales.

Ein genialer Laden, um alles mögliche von Martin Margiela bis Paul Smith und Joseph zu finden – eine eklektische Mischung mit phantastischen Sonderangeboten.

Un endroit idéal où l'on trouve de tout, de Martin Margiela à Paul Smith en passant par Joseph : sélection éclectique et soldes fantastiques.

GUM Shopping Center
Place Rouge
Moscow
Tel. +7 (0)95 9293 406

Seventh Element

A boutique with everything from McQueen and Versus to Philip Treacy hats, alongside selected Russian designers.

Eine Boutique mit einem Sortiment von McQueen und Versus bis hin zu Hüten von Philip Treacy. Dazu kommen ausgesuchte russische Designer.

Cette boutique présente une sélection variée, de McQueen à Versus en passant par les chapeaux de Philip Treacy, sans oublier les créations de stylistes russes.

Smolenskaya Ploshid
House 2
Moscow
Tel. +7 (0)95 2413 022

Soho Boutique

Soho Boutique is run by one of Moscow's most beautiful and well-known It girls. Julia Vyzgalina and her husband Alexander have single-handedly supplanted Moscow's penchant for Gucci in favour of Marc Jacobs, Mathew Williamson, Lanvin and Jimmy Choo. Soho Boutique is located only a few blocks from the original Gucci and Dolce shops on Kutuzovsky Prospect.

Die Soho Boutique wird von einem der hübschesten und bekanntesten It-Girls der besseren Moskauer Gesellschaft geführt. Julia Vyzgalina und ihr Ehemann Alexander haben auf eigene Faust die bekannte Moskauer Vorliebe für Gucci zugunsten von Marc Jacobs, Mathew Williamson, Lanvin und Jimmy Choo verändert. Noch dazu ist die Soho Boutique nur ein paar Häuserblocks von den Gucci- und Dolce-Shops am Kutuzovsky Prospekt entfernt.

Soho Boutique est gérée par l'une des plus belles mondaines de la jet-set de Moscou. Julia Vyzgalina et son mari Alexander ont réussi à supplanter le célèbre penchant des Moscovites pour Gucci en faveur de Marc Jacobs, Matthew Williamson, Lanvin et Jimmy Choo. Le magasin se trouve à quelques blocs des boutiques Gucci et Dolce sur Kutuzovsky Prospekt.

Kutuzovsky Prospekt, 23
Tel. +7 095 2495 826

Trading House Moscow

The original and best shopping centre in Moscow houses boutiques from Gucci, Dolce & Gabbana, Fendi, Chanel and Jil Sander. Expect prices to be higher than those in Milan or New York.

Die erste und beste Einkaufspassage der Stadt beherbergt Filialen von Gucci, Dolce & Gabbana, Fendi, Chanel und Jil Sander. Rechnen Sie mit Preisen, die über denen von Mailand oder New York liegen.

La meilleure galerie marchande de Moscou accueille les boutiques de Gucci, Dolce & Gabbana, Fendi, Chanel et Jil Sander. Attendez-vous à des prix plus élevés qu'à Milan ou à New York.

Kytyzovski Prospekt
House 31
Moscow
Tel. +7 (0)95 9333 034

Versace

The first high-end designer boutique to establish itself in Moscow, and still guaranteed to sell out of stock.

Die erste Nobeldesigner-Boutique Moskaus, die ihre Bestände nach wie vor komplett ausverkauft.

La première boutique haut de gamme à s'être installée à Moscou remporte un immense succès et écoule ses stocks à vitesse grand V.

Kyznetskii Most, 19
Moscow
Tel. +7 (0)95 9215 971

Vrema +

A high end boutique with an eclectic mix of Missoni, Paul Smith, Moschino, Versus and Yohji Yamamoto.

Nobelboutique mit einem eklektischen Mix aus Gucci, Dolce & Gabbana, Fendi, Chanel und Jil Sander.

Boutique de luxe présentant un choix éclectique de pièces Missoni, Paul Smith, Moschino, Versus et Yohji Yamamoto.

Malaya Bronaya, 10
Moscow
Tel. +7 (0)95 2916 691

VINTAGE FASHION SHOPS

Vtoroya Dihaneye/Second Breath

Prices may be relatively high, but you can find everything from vintage Dolce & Gabbana pants to a brand new Gucci bag at Second Breath.

Die Preise sind zwar relativ hoch, aber dafür kann man hier praktisch alles finden – von der Second-Hand-Hose aus dem Hause Dolce & Gabbana bis hin zur brandneuen Gucci-Tasche.

Les prix restent relativement élevés, mais vous pourrez tout y trouver, des pantalons vintage Dolce & Gabbana aux derniers sacs Gucci.

Pyatnitskaya Ulitsa, 2
Moscow
Tel. +7 (0)95 9513 161

Second Hand

Selling clothes by the weight at $6 per kilo, Second Hand offers a lucky dip of goods, both eclectic and down-home.

Hier werden Kleider nach Gewicht verkauft – für 6 Dollar das Kilo. Was man dafür bekommt, ist Glückssache, aber in jedem Fall bunt gemischt und authentisch.

Vendant les vêtements au poids à 6 dollars le kilo, Second Hand propose toutes sortes d'articles éclectiques, du chic à l'ordinaire.

Protopopovskii Pereoulok, 9
Moscow
Tel. +7 (0)95 2842 514

RESTAURANTS

Galleria

Arkady Novikov has become the star of Moscow's restaurant world. Galleria is but one of dozens of his restaurants in Moscow. Two years after its opening, however, it remains the hottest, trendiest spot for dinner in town. On any given night it is packed with the rich and over-fed, flanked by their blonde and underfed arm candy. Go for the food and people watching.

Arkady Novikov ist gegenwärtig der Star der Moskauer Restaurantszene. Galleria ist nur eines seiner Dutzende Restaurants in der Stadt. Selbst zwei Jahre nach seiner Eröffnung gilt es noch als die angesagteste, Dinner-Location. Hier ist es jeden Abend gerammelt voll. Es wimmelt von Reichen und Überfütterten mit ihren blonden, unterernährten, reizenden Begleiterinnen. Man geht wegen des Essens und zum Leute-Schauen hin.

Arkady Novikov est devenu la star de la restauration à Moscou. Galleria n'est que l'un de la bonne dizaine de

restaurants qu'il possède. Deux ans après son ouverture, Galleria reste l'adresse la plus tendance et la plus courue pour dîner en ville. Peuplé tous les soirs de riches et de nantis accompagnés de leurs blondes sous-alimentées. A tester pour la cuisine et le plaisir d'observer les gens.

Petrovka, 27
Moscow
Tel. +7 (0)95 9374 544

Bosco Café

This café sits right on Red Square, close enough to Lenin's tomb to hear the old fellow turning over in his glass casket. Great food (Caesar's salad, the freshest parmesan this side of the Kremlin), great coffee and deserts – and, again, great people watching.

Dieses Café direkt am Roten Platz befindet sich so nahe an Lenins Mausoleum, dass man den alten Mann in seinem Glassarg rotieren hört. Tolles Essen (Caesar's salad und der frischeste Parmesan diesseits der Kremlmauern), guter Kaffee, feine Desserts – und auch dies ein guter Platz, um Leute zu beobachten.

Ce café se trouve juste sur la place Rouge, assez près du mausolée de Lénine pour entendre le vieux lascar se retourner dans sa tombe de verre. Cuisine excellente (salade César, le parmesan le plus frais de ce côté du Kremlin), café et desserts succulents – un site d'observation idéal.

Place Rouge
Moscow
Tel. +7 (0)95 9293 182

Correa's Café

Isaac Correa, Moscow's premier chef, has recently opened up his own café, which serves a perfect blend of fresh and fantastic food. The crowd from Galleria and Vogue come for brunch and lunch. On any given Saturday, you will find the remnants of last night's party scene gathered here, still hung over and soothing their pain with the best coffee in Moscow.

Isaac Correa, der beste Küchenchef Moskaus, hat kürzlich sein eigenes Café eröffnet, wo er eine perfekte Mischung aus frischer und phantasievoller Küche serviert. Die Leute aus der Galeria und von der Vogue kommen zum Brunchen und Lunchen hierher. An jedem beliebigen Samstag stoßen Sie hier auf die versammelten Übriggebliebenen der Freitagnacht-Partys. Übernächtigt lindern sie ihre Kopfschmerzen mit dem besten Kaffee der Stadt.

Isaac Correa, le plus grand chef de Moscou, vient d'ouvrir son propre café où il sert un mélange parfait entre produits frais et cuisine fantastique. Les clients du Galleria et les gens de Vogue s'y retrouvent pour bruncher ou déjeuner. Chaque

samedi, on y croise les fêtards de la veille en train de soigner leurs gueules de bois avec le meilleur café de Moscou.

Bolshaya Gruzinskaya, 32
Moscow
Tel. +7 095 2059 100

Petrovich

A classic members-only haunt of the fashionable 'intelligentsia', decorated in tongue-in-cheek Soviet style. Great Russian food, the best horseradish vodka and live Russian music. Guests usually include top TV newscasters, magazine editors and the occasional politician.

Ein klassischer Treffpunkt der angesagten Intelligenzia – nur für Eingeweihte, versteht sich. Das Dekor ist ironischer Sowjetstil. Köstliche russische Küche mit dem besten Rettich-Wodka und Live-Musik. Zu den Gästen zählen üblicherweise bekannte Nachrichtensprecher aus dem Fernsehen, Journalisten und der eine oder andere Politiker.

Fréquenté par la nouvelle intelligentsia branchée, ce lieu classique réservé aux membres du club est décoré dans un style soviétique caricatural. Excellente cuisine russe, la meilleure vodka au raifort et groupes russes en direct. Parmi les habitués, on trouve des présentateurs de JT, des journalistes et parfois des hommes politiques.

Myasnitskaya Ulitsa, 24/7
Moscow
Tel. +7 (0)95 9230 082

Pushkin

Decorated in the old Russian style with lots of grand antiques and carpets, this is hands-down one of the best places in Moscow for Russian food cooked and served in the Tsarist tradition. High prices, great vodka and caviar.

Ein im alten russischen Stil eingerichtetes Restaurant mit vielen tollen Antiquitäten und Teppichen. Wirklich eine der besten Moskauer Adressen, um in echter Zarentradition zu speisen. Teuer, aber mit großartigem Wodka und Kaviar.

Décoré dans le style de l'ancienne Russie avec moult antiquités et nombreux tapis, c'est de loin l'une des meilleures adresses de Moscou pour déguster des plats russes préparés et servis dans la plus pure tradition tsariste. Prix élevés, vodka et caviar de premier choix.

Tverskoii Boulevard, 26-a
Moscow
Tel. +7 (0)95 2295 590

Vogue Café

Just a two-minute walk from Vogue's offices and Stoleshnikov Pereoulok (Moscow's Madison Avenue), this place is always packed with editors,

moguls and businessmen of every category. Another Arkady Novikov venue, the food is a blend of classic Soviet fare (with very modern prices) mixed with classic fusion and Eurocusine. Always good, always pricey.

Nur zwei Gehminuten von den Büros der Vogue und dem Stoleshnikov Pereoulok (Moskaus Pendant zur New Yorker Madison Avenue) entfernt, wimmelt es hier ständig von Journalistinnen, Wirtschaftsbonzen und Geschäftsleuten jeglicher Kategorie. Es handelt sich um ein weiteres Lokal von Arkady Novikov; die Küche ist ein Mix aus traditioneller Sowjetkost (den sehr modernen Preisen entsprechend aufgemotzt), klassischer internationaler und europäischer Cuisine. Immer gut, immer kostspielig.

A deux minutes de marche des bureaux de Vogue et de Stoleshnikov Pereoulok (la Madison Avenue de Moscou), ce restaurant est toujours plein de journalistes, de nababs et d'hommes d'affaires. Cette autre adresse d'Arkady Novikov propose un mélange entre plats soviétiques classiques (mais à des prix bien d'aujourd'hui), menu « fusion » et cuisine européenne traditionnelle. Toujours bon, toujours cher.

Kuznetsky Most, 7/9
Moscow
Tel. +7 (0)95 9231 701

BARS

Bar 30/7

The perfect place for a pre- or post-dinner drink, Bar 30/7 is open 24 hours a day and reminiscent of NYC drinking dens such as VON or The Whiskey Bar. It is strictly a bar only, but if you are hungry for food, the bartenders can provide you with a few menus from neighbouring joints, which will happily deliver within 15 minutes. Very NY style.

Der perfekte Ort für einen Drink vor oder nach dem Abendessen, denn die Bar 30/7 ist rund um die Uhr geöffnet und erinnert an Kneipen wie das VON oder The Whiskey Bar in New York. Es handelt sich zwar um eine reine Bar, aber wenn Sie unbedingt etwas essen möchten, bekommen Sie von den Barkeepern die Speisekarten einiger umliegender Lokale, die angenehmerweise innerhalb von 15 Minuten liefern. Sehr New-Yorkisch.

Idéal pour prendre un verre avant ou après dîner, le Bar 30/7 reste ouvert 24 heures sur 24 et rappelle les comptoirs de New York tels que VON ou le Whiskey Bar. On n'y sert que des boissons, mais si vous avez un petit creux, les barmen peuvent vous proposer les menus des restaurants d'à côté, qui se feront une joie de vous livrer en moins de 15 minutes. A la new-yorkaise.

Petrovka, 30/7
Moscow
Tel. +7 (0)95 2095 951

First

Decorated a decadent white, this venue remains one of the best clubs in Moscow. In the wintertime everyone packs into the bar in the back to dance, whilst in the summertime a huge tent is erected outside with a separate bar and dance floor (and the inevitable $1,000 tables which can be reserved ahead of time). Ever hear about the party where hundreds of wild butterflies were released onto the dance floor? This is the place.

In dekadentem Weiß dekoriert, ist dies nach wie vor einer der besten Moskauer Clubs. Im Winter drängelt sich alles hinten in der Bar, um zu tanzen, während im Sommer ein riesiges Zelt im Freien errichtet wird, mit eigener Bar und Tanzfläche (und mit den unvermeidlichen 1.000-Dollar-Tischen, die man im voraus reservieren kann). Haben Sie je von der Party gehört, bei der Hunderte Schmetterlinge auf der Tanzfläche freigelassen wurden? – Sie fand hier statt.

Avec son décor blanc décadent, cet endroit reste l'un des meilleurs clubs de Moscou. En hiver, tout le monde se retrouve au bar du fond pour danser, tandis qu'en été les patrons dressent une énorme tente à l'extérieur avec son propre bar et un dancefloor (et les inévitables tables à 1 000 dollars réservées à l'avance). Vous avez déjà entendu parler de cette fête où des centaines de papillons sauvages avaient été lâchés sur la piste de danse ? C'était là.

Sofiiskaya Naberezhnaya, 34
Moscow
Tel. +7 (0)95 951 3598

Fabrique

If you want to dance, come to Fabrique. Always packed with the hottest young guys and girls in the city, it also features excellent DJs from Europe and NYC. The perfect place to streetcast a photo shoot.

Wenn Sie tanzen möchten, kommen Sie in die Fabrique. Hier wimmelt es stets von den heißesten Jungs und Mädels der Stadt, außerdem legen auch ausgezeichnete DJs aus ganz Europa und New York auf. Der perfekte Ort, um für ein Fotoshooting zu casten.

Si vous voulez danser, rendez-vous chez Fabrique. Toujours prisé par la jeunesse dorée de la ville, ce bar fait également venir d'excellents DJ d'Europe et de New York. L'adresse idéale pour un casting sauvage.

Sadovnicheskaya Ulitsa, 33
Moscow
Tel. +7 (0)95 9536 576

Milk & Honey

Designed by London's Hassan Abdullah, this newest addition to Moscow's scene is the quintessential chill lounge. Owned by Ceawlin Thynn and his three partners, the place opened with a bang and remains an ideal spot to put away a fine bottle of wine or the perfect Mojito.

Vom Londoner Hassan Abdullah designt, ist dieser Neuzugang zur Moskauer Szene der Inbegriff einer Chill Lounge. Das Lokal gehört Ceawlin Thynn und seinen drei Partnern. Die Eröffnung war ein Knaller. Und bis heute ist dies der ideale Ort, um eine gute Flasche Wein oder einen perfekten Mojito zu trinken.

Conçu par le Londonien Hassan Abdullah, ce nouveau venu sur la scène moscovite symbolise la quintessence même du bar lounge. Appartenant à Ceawlin Thynn et à ses trois associés, son ouverture a fait grand bruit. L'endroit rêvé pour descendre une bouteille de bon vin ou siroter un mojito.

Myasnitskaya Ulitsa, 38
Moscow
Tel. +7 (0)95 9289 947
www.milkandhoney.ru

Osene

The latest in a line of super trendy clubs from the same people who put together ZIMA and LETO, this place represents the ultimate Moscow experience; hot girls, rich guys, obnoxious and overzealous 'face control' and very overpriced, underdone drinks. Great music is their saviour however.

Der jüngste in einer Reihe supertrendiger Clubs. Organisiert von denselben Leuten, die das ZIMA und das LETO auf die Beine gestellt haben, liefert dieser Ort die ultimative Moskau-Erfahrung: heiße Mädchen, reiche Typen, unangenehme und übereifrige Gesichtskontrolle und extrem überteuerte, nachlässig gemachte Drinks. Die großartige Musik reißt es jedoch raus.

Dernier-né des clubs branchés lancés par l'équipe qui a ouvert ZIMA et LETO, ce lieu incarne le top du « Moscou by night » : belles filles, riches hommes d'affaires, videurs odieux et trop zélés, cocktails ratés et hors de prix. Heureusement, la programmation musicale sauve l'endroit.

Teatralny Proezd, 3
Moscow
Tel. +7 (0)95 9219 888

Propaganda

Everyone from the richest kids to the poorest students will eventually find themselves here on any given night (Tuesdays and Thursdays are the most crowded), dancing to specially flown-in DJs from Berlin, Amsterdam, London and New York.

An jedem beliebigen Abend (am vollsten ist es dienstags und donnerstags) findet man hier ein total gemischtes Publikum – von den reichsten Kids bis zu den ärmsten Studenten. Getanzt wird zur Musik von extra eingeflogenen DJs aus Berlin, Amsterdam, London und New York.

Des fils à papa aux étudiants fauchés, tout le monde se retrouve dans ce bar ouvert tous les soirs (le mardi et le jeudi étant les plus courus) pour danser sur les sets de DJ spécialement venus de Berlin, d'Amsterdam, de Londres et de New York.

Bolshoi Zlatoistinski Pereoulok, 7
Moscow
Tel. +7 (0)95 9245 732

HOTELS

Ararat Park Hyatt

Hands down the coolest hotel in Moscow right now. With a gorgeous design and beautiful modern rooms, this is where all the visiting fashion PR people and designers stay. The hotel also houses a fabulous bar on its eleventh floor with absolutely the best views of Moscow. Gorgeous outdoor patio in the summertime and beautiful snow-covered rooftop view in the winter twilight.

Im Moment das mit Abstand coolste Hotel Moskaus. Mit tollem Design und wunderbar modernen Zimmern. Deshalb logieren hier alle Designer und PR-Leute aus der Modebranche. Zum Hotel gehört auch eine traumhafte Bar im elften Stock mit der absolut besten Aussicht über die Stadt. Großartiger Patio im Sommer und ein hübscher Blick auf das schneebedeckte Dach in der winterlichen Dämmerung.

L'hôtel le plus cool de Moscou à l'heure actuelle. Avec son design somptueux et ses belles chambres modernes, c'est ici que séjournent les RP de la mode et les créateurs de passage dans la capitale. Le bar fabuleux du onzième étage offre les plus belles vues sur la ville. Sublime patio en plein air l'été, et magnifique vue sur les toits enneigés l'hiver.

Neglinnaya Street, 4
Moscow
Tel. +7 (0)95 (or 501) 7831 234

The Baltschug Kempinski

Often playing host to visiting movie stars and divas, the Baltschug Kempinski sits on the edge of the River Moskva, a few minutes walk from Red Square. It boasts a large pool and casino, with a legendary buffet breakfast that includes all-you-can-eat champagne and caviar.

Im Kempinski am Ufer der Moskwa und nur wenige Gehminuten vom Roten Platz entfernt steigen oft Filmstars und andere Diven ab. Das Haus kann sich eines großen Pools, eines Casinos und eines legendären Frühstücksbuffets mit Champagner und Kaviar in unbegrenzter Menge rühmen.

Pied-à-terre des stars du cinéma et du show-biz de passage à Moscou, le Baltschug Kempinski borde les rives de la Moskova, à quelques minutes de marche de la place Rouge. Grande piscine et casino. Buffet de petit déjeuner légendaire, avec champagne et caviar à volonté.

Baltschug, 1
Moscow
Tel. +7 (0)95 2306 500

Metropol

This remains one of the few real Russian hotels on a high-end scale, sitting right on Red Square. Rooms are moderate to high in price. The hotel was reconstructed in the early 1900s and again in the late 1980s. No two rooms look alike and the antique interior is unique.

Eines der wenigen echt russischen Nobelhotels direkt am Roten Platz. Die Preise variieren zwischen moderat und hoch. Das Haus wurde zu Beginn des 20. Jahrhunderts und dann noch einmal Ende der 1980er Jahre renoviert. Jedes Zimmer ist individuell eingerichtet, was nicht zuletzt an den kostbaren Antiquitäten liegt.

Cet édifice reste l'un des rares témoins de la grande époque russe. Il se trouve juste sur la place Rouge et offre différentes catégories de chambres, à prix modéré ou très élevé. L'hôtel a été rénové au début du XXe siècle et à la fin des années 1980. On n'y trouve pas deux chambres identiques et la décoration intérieure d'époque vaut vraiment le détour.

Teatralnaya Ploshid
Moscow
Tel. +7 (0)95 9276 000

AIRPORT

Sheremyetev Airport

Tel. +7 (0)95 9379 090

What makes New York special to you? New York is a special place for me because of the friends I've met and have grown to love and respect Where is the best place to stay in NYC? The Abingdon Bed & Breakfast, 13 Eighth Avenue Where is your favourite place to eat in NYC? Cho Dang Gol on West 35th Street, a Korean restaurant that make their own tofu and have the best stews Where is your favourite place to shop in NYC? Cobblestones, 314 East Ninth street, a thrift store with great accessories and shoes TESS GIBERSON

NEW YORK

TEXT BY LEE CARTER

The only major fashion capital outside Europe's lavishly fringed borders, the megalopolis of New York stands as a glittering monument to future-is-now modernism and gimme-gimme glambition. In the vertical city of glass and steel, cash is king, Anna Wintour queen and cinched-up socialites parade as court jesters. Tradition is a weekly shopping spree at Barneys, lineage is cut by Studio 54 wannabes and history is anything in last month's trinity of glossies: Vogue, W and Harper's Bazaar. To whom does New York owe its wealth and opportunity? Its street culture. Seventh Avenue CEOs intersect with Madison Avenue advertising execs and Wall Street investment bankers in a well-oiled convergence of designer know-how, marketing chutzpah and bullish wealth. From Halston's disco decadence of the '70s, through to Calvin Klein's celebrity obsessions, to the well-heeled visions of American style by the likes of Ralph Lauren and Michael Kors today, success on the New York fashion stage has meant manufacturing, bottling and selling the cult of personality. But an entirely different, yet equally influential, seamscape exists on the streets below 14th Street, where designers of the downtown persuasion are digging in their non-heels in the fight against conformity. The ever-rebellious As Four collective and their doppelgangers breeze through lower Manhattan eschewing anything resembling a trend; art types prowl the Meatpacking District decked in the dark stylings of new menswear label Cloak; and the hip-haunted streets of Williamsburg are awash with Markus Huemer and the naughty T-shirts of Pleasure Principle. All the while, underground favourites like United Bamboo, Tess Giberson, Imitation of Christ and Benjamin Cho have become fixtures on the fashion map. Together, uptown and downtown designers have the city covered.

Als einzige größere Modemetropole außerhalb Europas wirkt die Riesenstadt New York wie ein glitzerndes Monument von „Die Zukunft ist jetzt"-Modernismus, „Haben wollen"-Glamour und Ehrgeiz. Zwischen den Wolkenkratzern aus Glas und Stahl steht Geld an erster Stelle, Anna Wintour an zweiter, und ihre aufgerüschte, prominente Entourage fungiert als Ansammlung von Hofnarren. Die allwöchentliche Einkaufsorgie bei Barneys ist Tradition. Herkunft zählt unter Studio-54-Imitatoren rein gar nichts, und Geschichte ist alles, was die Dreifaltigkeit der Hochglanzmagazine – Vogue, W und Harper's Bazaar – im letzten Monat verkündet hat. Wem verdankt New York seinen Reichtum und seine Chancen? Seiner Street Culture. CEOs von der Seventh Avenue mischen sich unter Werbeleute aus der Madison Avenue und Investmentbanker von der Wall Street. Das Ganze läuft dank des gut geölten Zusammenspiels von Designer-Know-how, Marketing-Chuzpe und neuem Geld. Von Halstons Disco-Dekadenz der 1970er Jahre über die Promi-Obsession von Calvin Klein bis hin zu den gut betuchten Visionen des amerikanischen Stils von Leuten wie Ralph Lauren und Michael Kors in unseren Tagen bestand Erfolg in der New Yorker Modeszene

schon immer darin, einen Persönlichkeitskult zu erschaffen und zu verkaufen. Eine ganz andere, aber ebenso erfolgreiche Modepolitik wird unterhalb der 14. Straße verfolgt, wo Downtown-Designer im Kampf gegen Konformität in Billigsachen schwelgen. Das von jeher rebellische Kollektiv As Four und seine Doppelgänger streifen durch Lower Manhattan und scheuen alles, was auch nur von Ferne einem Trend ähnelt. Künstlertypen schleichen in den dunklen Outfits des neuen Männerlabels Cloak durch den Meatpacking District, während die Straßen des von hippen Menschen heimgesuchten Williamsburg von Markus Huemer und frechen Pleasure-Principle-T-Shirts überflutet werden. Underground-Stars wie United Bamboo, Tess Giberson, Imitation of Christ und Benjamin Cho sind bereits zu Fixpunkten auf der modischen Landkarte geworden. Gemeinsam überziehen die Designer von Up- und Downtown die gesamte Stadt.

Seule grande capitale de la mode hors des frontières scintillantes de l'Europe, la mégalopole de New York est un étincelant monument dressé à la gloire du modernisme sous le signe de « le futur c'est maintenant » et d'une ambition attrape-tout. Dans la cité verticale de verre et d'acier, l'argent est roi et Anna Wintour tandis que reine les mondaines paradent sanglées dans leurs atours tels les bouffons de la Cour. La tradition exige de faire une descente hebdomadaire chez Barneys, la hiérarchie sociale est déterminée par les wanna-be's du Studio 54 et l'histoire se résume à ce que l'on a lu dans la trinité mensuelle sur papier glacé: Vogue, W et Harper's Bazaar. Mais à quoi New York doit-elle sa richesse et ses privilèges? A sa culture de la rue si variée. Les P-DG de la Septième Avenue se mêlent aux publicitaires de Madison Avenue et aux banquiers d'affaires de Wall Street dans une convergence bien huilée entre savoir-faire des stylistes, chutzpah marketing et richesse agressive. De la décadence disco de Halston dans les années 70 et des obsessions de célébrité de Calvin Klein aux visions fortunées du style américain proposées par Ralph Lauren et Michael Kors aujourd'hui, le succès sur la scène de la mode new-yorkaise revenait à fabriquer, mettre en bouteille et vendre le culte de la personnalité. Mais le paysage d'une couture entièrement différente et tout aussi influente apparaît au sud de 14th Street, où les créateurs de downtown se battent à grands coups de talons plats contre le conformisme. Le collectif rebelle As Four et ses clones parcourent le Lower Manhattan en fuyant tout ce qui ressemble de près ou de loin à une tendance. Une faune artistique rôde dans l'ancien quartier des abattoirs en arborant les sombres créations de Cloak, la nouvelle griffe pour homme. Quant aux rues de Williamsburg bondées de jeunes branchés, elles fourmillent d'œuvres de Markus Huemer et de t-shirts grivois de Pleasure Principle. Parallèlement, les favoris de l'underground comme United Bamboo, Tess Giberson, Imitation of Christ et Benjamin Cho sont devenus de petits étendards sur la carte de la mode. Ensemble, les créateurs d'uptown et de downtown ont quadrillé la ville.

FASHION SHOWS AND FAIRS

New York Fashion Week

At the same time as marquee names like Ralph Lauren, Donna Karan and Tommy Hilfiger pull out all the stops, smaller designers across Manhattan boycott 'the tents' (Sixth Avenue between 41st and 42nd Streets) in favour of offbeat and out-of-the-way venues, hoping to attract New York's anti-establishment and become the Next Big Thing.

Wenn die großen Marken wie Ralph Lauren, Donna Karan und Tommy Hilfiger alle Register ziehen, boykottieren kleinere Designer in ganz Manhattan „die Zelte" (an der Sixth Avenue zwischen 41st und 42nd Street) und locken das New Yorker Anti-Establishment an ausgefallene und entlegene Orte. So hofft man, Newcomer-Star der nächsten Saison zu werden.

Tandis que les noms d'enseignes comme Ralph Lauren, Donna Karan et Tommy Hilfiger accaparent tous les regards, les créateurs plus modestes de Manhattan boycottent les « tentes » (sur Sixth Avenue entre 41st et 42nd Streets) pour organiser des défilés et des shows très off et souvent loin de tout dans l'espoir d'attirer l'anti-establishment new-yorkais et de devenir enfin ceux dont on va parler.

Council of Fashion Designers of America
Seventh On Sixth
1412 Broadway
New York, NY 10018
Tel. +1212 302 1821

FASHION SCHOOLS

Fashion Institute of Technology

Of the two main fashion campuses of Manhattan, FIT teaches the nuts-and-bolts of the fashion trade, offering hundreds of practical courses to full- and part-time students from its Chelsea location.

Von den beiden wichtigsten Modeschulen Manhattans ist das FIT in Chelsea diejenige, die in Hunderten von Praxisseminaren für Voll- und Teilzeitstudierende das Modegeschäft von der Pike auf lehrt.

L'un des deux principaux campus de mode à Manhattan. Le FIT enseigne plutôt les rouages de l'industrie et propose des centaines de cours pratiques à des étudiants à temps complet ou partiel dans son établissement de Chelsea.

7th Avenue at 27th Street
New York, NY 10001
Tel. +1212 217 7999
www.fitnyc.suny.edu/html/dynamic.html

Parsons School of Design

Part of the New School of Social Research, the other major fashion school of Manhattan, Parsons School of Design offers an Ivy League-like curriculum of conceptual fashion courses from its low-key Greenwich Village campus.

Die zweite große Modeschule Manhattans gehört zur New School of Social Research. Sie bietet ihren Studierenden auf dem bescheidenen Campus in Greenwich Village einen hochkarätigen Lehrplan, u. a. mit konzeptionellen Modekursen.

Appartenant à la New School of Social Research, l'autre grande école de mode de Manhattan offre au sein de son modeste campus de Greenwich Village un programme digne de l'Ivy League, notamment des cours de mode conceptuelle.

2 West 13th Street
New York, NY 10011
Tel. +1212 229 8910
www.parsons.edu/html/splash.html

FASHION MUSEUMS AND GALLERIES

Costume Institute at the Metropolitan Museum of Art

Here new curator Harold Koda is elevating fashion to gilded and marbled status. Recent exhibits at the venerable New York museum range from a gala tribute to Jackie Kennedy to a show examining the distorting effects of fashion through all times and cultures.

Der Kurator Harold Koda hat der Mode hier endlich den gebührenden Platz eingeräumt. Die bisherigen Ausstellungen in diesem ehrwürdigen New Yorker Museum reichten von einer Gala-Hommage an Jackie Kennedy bis zu einer Schau über die entstellenden Auswirkungen von Mode in verschiedenen Epochen und Kulturen.

Ici, le nouveau conservateur Harold Koda donne toutes ses lettres de noblesse à la mode. Parmi les récents projets de ce vénérable musée new-yorkais figuraient un hommage mondain à Jackie Kennedy et une exposition sur les effets déformants de la mode à travers l'histoire et les cultures.

1000 Fifth Avenue
New York, NY 10028
Tel. +1212 879 5500

Cooper-Hewitt National Design Museum

Located in the former Andrew Carnegie mansion, the Cooper-Hewitt Museum houses one of the largest collections of design artefacts in the world. A day's romp, for sure.

Das in der ehemaligen Villa von Andrew Carnegie untergebrachte Museum besitzt eine der größten Design-Sammlungen weltweit. Genug zu sehen für einen ganzen Tag.

Installé dans l'ancien hôtel particulier d'Andrew Carnegie, le Cooper-Hewitt Museum abrite l'une des plus vastes collections de design du monde entier. Prévoir une journée, minimum.

2 East 91st Street
New York, NY 10128
Tel. +1212 849 8400

The Museum at Fashion Institute of Technology

The Fashion Institute of Technology's museum is its best feature, drawing the city's fashion curious to shows ranging from a Bonnie Cashin retrospective to a very scene-y „Visionaire" exhibit.

Das Museum des Fashion Institute of Technology ist fast das Beste am ganzen Institut. Es lockt Modeinteressierte New Yorker in Ausstellungen wie die Bonnie-Cashin-Retrospektive oder die extrem szenige Schau ‚Visionaire'.

Le musée du Fashion Institute of Technology est de loin sa pièce maîtresse. Il attire les fanas de mode de la ville grâce à des manifestations qui vont d'une rétrospective Bonnie Cashin à l'exposition « Visionaire » très dans l'esprit du temps.

Seventh Avenue at West 27th Street
New York, NY 10001
Tel. +1212 217 7999

Visionaire Gallery

By day, this small gallery space – launched by the talented names on the 'Visionaire' masthead – showcases new artists and designers. By night, plenty of chi-chi parties take place here too.

Tagsüber präsentiert diese kleine Galerie, von talentierten Köpfen des „Visionaire"-Projekts geführt, neue Künstler und Designer. Abends finden hier auch viele todschicke Parties statt.

Le jour, cette petite galerie d'art lancée par les talents figurant dans l'ours de « Visionaire » présente les œuvres de nouveaux artistes et designers. Le soir, on y donne également de nombreuses soirées extrêmement chic.

11 Mercer Street
New York, NY 10013
Tel. +1212 274 8959

FASHION SHOPS

Barneys New York

New York's quintessential shopping experience, featuring an impeccably curated selection of global brands and home-grown favourites alike. Every August and February, Barneys throws the city's most famous designer sale at its downtown warehouse, where queues are known to wrap around the block. Barneys also has two free-standing Co-op stores, one on West 18th Street and the other in SoHo, where myriad diffusion ranges and small labels are available.

Das Einkaufserlebnis schlechthin mit einer tadellosen Auswahl internationaler Marken und angesagter Labels. Jedes Jahr im August und Februar findet im Kaufhaus Downtown der berühmteste New Yorker Designer-Ausverkauf statt. Aus diesem Anlass bilden sich Schlangen, die sich um den ganzen Häuserblock winden. Es gibt außerdem zwei unabhängige Läden, einen in der West 18th Street und einen weiteren in SoHo. In beiden findet man unzählige Nebenlinien großer Designer und zahllose kleine Labels.

Le haut lieu du shopping new-yorkais présente une sélection impeccable de marques internationales aux cotés des principales griffes locales. En février et en août, Barneys organise ses célèbres soldes de créateurs dans son entrepôt de downtown, où les files d'attente font souvent le tour du bloc. Barneys possède également deux points de vente sur West 18th Street et à SoHo, où l'on trouve des myriades de marques de grande diffusion et de griffes moins connues.

660 Madison Avenue
New York, NY 10021
Tel. +1212 826 8900
www.barneys.com

Jeffrey

The original retail pioneer of the Meatpacking District, this large one-floor department store carries everything from Gucci and Pucci to Karan and Lauren, but the shop's real draw is a near inexhaustible selection of men's and women's footwear.

Als eigentlicher Pionier des Einzelhandels im Meatpacking District führt dieses große Kaufhaus auf einer einzigen Etage alle namhaften Marken, von Gucci und Pucci bis Karan und Lauren. Besonders gefragt ist jedoch die schier unerschöpfliche Auswahl an Damen- und Herrenschuhen.

Pionnier du Meatpacking District, quartier des anciens abattoirs, ce grand magasin sur un seul niveau propose tout, de Gucci à Pucci et de Donna Karan à Ralph Lauren. Sa véritable attraction réside toutefois dans une sélection de chaussures pratiquement infinie pour homme comme pour femme.

449 West 14th Street
New York, NY 10014
Tel. +1212 206 3928

Seven New York

Once nestled among the old schmatte peddlers of the Lower East Side, Seven has recently moved to SoHo, where it will continue to sell men's and women's fare from the world's most directional designers including Raf Simons, Boudicca, As Four, Preen, AF Vandevorst and Cosmic Wonder.

Der vormals an der Lower East Side angesiedelte Laden ist kürzlich nach SoHo umgezogen. Man findet dort aber weiterhin Männer- und Damenmode der progressivsten Designer wie Raf Simons, Boudicca, As Four, AF Vandevorst und Cosmic Wonder.

Autrefois niché au milieu des anciens vendeurs de fripes du Lower East Side, Seven vient de déménager à SoHo. La boutique continue de vendre les vêtements pour homme et pour femme des créateurs les plus innovants au monde, tels que Raf Simons, Boudicca, As Four, Preen, AF Vandevorst et Cosmic Wonder.

110 Mercer Street
New York, NY 10012
Tel. +1 212 646 5400
www.sevennewyork.com

Opening Ceremony
Modelled after the Olympics, each year Opening Ceremony sells designer wares from one spot on the globe, for example, Brazil, Germany, Hong Kong, in addition to local New York favourites such as Cloak, Rachel Comey, Indigo People and Mary Ping. London is the latest to receive the spotlight.

Nach dem Vorbild der Olympischen Spiele verkauft Opening Ceremony jedes Jahr Designerkleidung aus einem bestimmten Land oder einer Stadt wie z. B. Brasilien, Deutschland oder Hongkong. Dazu kommen einheimische New Yorker Lieblingslabels wie Cloak, Rachel Comey, Indigo People und Mary Ping. Als nächstes steht London im Rampenlicht.

Inspirée par les Jeux olympiques, la boutique Opening Ceremony vend chaque année les vêtements de créateurs venus d'un endroit particulier dans le monde, par exemple du Brésil, d'Allemagne ou de Hong-Kong, en plus des chouchous new-yorkais tels que Cloak, Rachel Comey, Indigo People et Mary Ping. Récemment, la ville de Londres a été mise à l'honneur.

35 Howard Street
New York, NY 10013
Tel. +1 212 219 2688
www.openingceremony.us

Kirna Zabête
This cheery two-storey SoHo boutique carries a wide range of unabashedly girly merchandise – including hard-to-find pieces by Lulu Guinness, Anya Hindmarch and New York's own Alice Roi – and reflects the quirky-cool personalities of its owners, Sarah Easley and Elizabeth Shepherd.

Die fröhliche zweistöckige Boutique in SoHo führt ein breites Sortiment frecher Girly-Mode. Darunter schwer zu findende Teile von Lulu Guinness, Anya Hindmarch und der New Yorkerin Alice Roi. Das Ganze entspricht dem eigenwillig coolen Geschmack der Ladenbesitzerinnen Sarah Easley und Elizabeth Shepherd.

Répartie sur deux niveaux, cette joyeuse boutique de SoHo réalise sans complexe le rêve de toutes les filles avec son large choix de vêtements, notamment des pièces introuvables ailleurs de Lulu Guinness, Anya Hindmarch et de la new-yorkaise Alice Roi, à l'image des personnalités cool et complexes de ses propriétaires Sarah Easley et Elizabeth Shepherd.

96 Greene Street
New York, NY 10012
Tel. +1 212 941 9656
www.kirnazabete.com

Century 21
Situated across from where the World Trade Center once stood, Century 21 was forced to close its doors on 9/11 before making a triumphant return nine months later. The beloved discount department store is where the sartorially obsessed make a bee-line when one of its personal shoppers calls with new arrivals from, say, Alexander McQueen, Dolce & Gabbana or Helmut Lang.

Gleich gegenüber vom Standort des ehemaligen World Trade Centers gelegen, war Century 21 gezwungen, seine Tore am 11. September 2002 zu schließen. Die Wiedereröffnung neun Monate später war ein Triumph. In diese heiß geliebte Institution pilgern Fashion-Addict wenn einer ihrer Personal Shoppers Neuzugänge etwa von Alexander McQueen, Dolce & Gabbana oder Helmut Lang vermeldet.

Située en face de l'ex-World Trade Center, la boutique Century 21 a fermé ses portes le 11 septembre avant de faire un retour triomphant neuf mois plus tard. Ce soldeur est particulièrement prisé par les obsédés de la couture qui s'y précipitent dès qu'un des acheteurs de la boutique les prévient de l'arrivée de nouveaux stocks Alexander McQueen, Dolce & Gabbana ou Helmut Lang, entre autres.

22 Cortlandt Street
New York, NY 10007
Tel. +1 212 227 9092

Comme des Garçons
Beyond its funky funnel-like entryway lies a cavernous and curved-wall interior echoing Rei Kawakubo's familiar off-beat approach where all her warped colour and fabric combos can be found. Also available are Comme's popular unisex fragrances.

Hinter dem außergewöhnlichen trichterförmigen Eingang stößt man auf ein höhlenartiges Inneres mit gewölbten Wänden, das Rei Kawakubos bekanntem Stil entspricht. Man findet hier all ihre eigenwilligen Farb- und Materialkombinationen. Auch die beliebten Unisex-Düfte sind erhältlich.

Derrière son entrée funky en forme d'entonnoir, on découvre une caverne toute en courbes qui reflète l'approche décalée familière de Rei Kawakubo et propose toutes ses couleurs et combinaisons de tissus bizarres. On y trouve également les célèbres parfums unisexe de Comme des Garçons.

520 West 22nd Street
New York, NY 10012
Tel. +1 212 604 9200

Prada
Created by design darling Rem Koolhaas, this space is a virtual theme park with not only the complete Prada collections to browse through, but favourite vintage pieces, plus video monitors, digital catalogues and adjustable changing rooms to complete the experience.

Der vom Designer-Liebling Rem Koolhaas entworfene Raum ist genau genommen ein virtueller Vergnügungspark, in dem man nicht nur durch die komplette Prada-Kollektion streifen kann. Begehrte Vintage-Stücke, Videobildschirme, digitale Kataloge und flexible Umkleidekabinen machen das Einkaufserlebnis perfekt.

Conçu par l'architecte chéri Rem Koolhaas, cet espace est une sorte de parc à thème où l'on a non seulement droit au panorama complet des collections Prada, mais aussi à des pièces vintage très recherchées, le tout au milieu d'écrans vidéo, de catalogues numériques et de cabines d'essayage modulables.

575 Broadway
New York, NY 10012
Tel. +1 212 334 8888

Zero
It's all about the pluses at Zero, a sparse shop launched by designer Maria Cornejo after moving to New York from London with her husband, photographer Mark Borthwick. Pieces hang unhindered on well-spaced racks, leaving most of the store open so the mind can roam free.

Diesen schlichten Laden eröffnete die Designerin Maria Cornejo, nachdem sie mit ihrem Mann, dem Fotografen Mark Borthwick, von London nach New York gezogen war. Die Kleider hängen frei auf wohlplatzierten Ständern und lassen den Großteil der Verkaufsfläche frei. So kann man seine Gedanken ungehindert schweifen lassen.

C'est l'idée de plus qui compte pour cette austère boutique lancée par la créatrice Maria Cornejo venue de Londres avec son époux, le photographe Mark Borthwick. Les vêtements sont accrochés librement sur des portants bien espacés, laissant la majeure partie du lieu ouverte à la méditation.

225 Mott Street
New York, NY 10036
Tel. +1 212 925 3849

VINTAGE FASHION SHOPS

Cherry
Cherry boasts an eclectic mix of high-end designer goods with wearable art and expensive vintage leathers. Treasures line the walls, and it isn't uncommon for top designers to pop in for a little secret research every now and then.

Hier findet man eine eklektische Mischung aus hochwertigen Designerwaren, Kunst zum Anziehen und teuren Second-Hand-Stücken aus Leder. Schätze säumen die Wände, und es ist nichts Ungewöhnliches, wenn immer mal wieder Designer von Weltruf reinschauen, um ein wenig Feldforschung zu betreiben.

Cherry affiche un mélange éclectique de pièces de créateurs haut de gamme, d'œuvres d'art portables ou de cuirs vintage à prix d'or. Des trésors s'alignent sur les murs et on y croise de temps en temps des stylistes connus en pleine recherche secrète.

19 Eighth Avenue
New York, NY 10014
Tel. +1 212 924 1410

Resurrection
This secondhand spot is serious about vintage, offering precious pieces by the likes of Ossie Clark, Emilio Pucci, Halston and Rudi Gernreich.

In diesem Second-Hand-Laden gibt es kostbare Stücke von Ossie Clark, Emilio Pucci, Halston und Rudi Gernreich.

Cette boutique de vêtements d'occasion ne rigole pas avec le vintage : elle propose de précieuses créations d'Ossie Clark, Emilio Pucci, Halston et Rudi Gernreich.

217 Mott Street
New York, 10012
Tel. +1 212 625 1374

What Comes Around Goes Around
Flogging more Western looks than high-end designer duds, this SoHo store with antler chandeliers specializes in denim and leather goods.

Der Laden in SoHo mit Lampen aus Geweihen verkauft eher Westernmode als edle Designerklamotten und hat sich auf Jeans und Ledersachen spezialisiert.

Plus axée sur les looks Western que sur les perles des créateurs de luxe, cette boutique de SoHo aux chandeliers en bois se spécialise dans le jean et le cuir.

351 West Broadway
New York, NY 10013
Tel. +1 212 343 9303

FLEA MARKETS

Chelsea Flea Market

(Annex Antique Fair and Flea Market)
The sprawling Chelsea Flea Markets
are packed with fashion insiders each
and every weekend. Among the
10,000 bargain-hunters who flock
here, designers are often spotted in
shades rummaging for inspiration.

Auf diesem weitläufigen Flohmarkt
tummeln sich jedes Wochenende
zahllose Insider aus der Modebranche. Unter den 10 000 Schnäppchen-
jägern entdeckt man oft Designer mit
großen Sonnenbrillen, die hier nach
neuer Inspiration suchen.

Ces marchés aux puces de Chelsea
qui s'étendent sans cesse sont envahis par les groupies de la mode
chaque week-end. Parmi les 10 000
farfouilleurs qui s'y précipitent, on
croise souvent des créateurs en quête
d'inspiration qui espèrent passer inco-
gnito sous leurs lunettes noires.

6th Avenue between 24th Street and
26th Street
New York, NY 10116
Tel. +1 212 243 5343

RESTAURANTS

Schiller's Liquor Bar

Restaurateur Keith McNally (Pastis,
Balthazar) continues to impress with
this atmospheric, low-key bistro in the
Lower East Side. French comfort food
in the form of steak frites, an iron skil-
let of garlic shrimps and a penne al'
arrabiata can be had here. Perfect for
a quick bite any time of the day.

Der Gastronom Keith McNally (Pastis,
Balthazar) macht sich auch mit diesem schlichten, gemütlichen Bistro
an der Lower East Side alle Ehre.
Man serviert hier schnelle französische Küche wie Steak frites oder ein
Eisenpfännchen mit Knoblauch-
Shrimps, aber auch Penne al'Arrabiata. Perfekt für einen schnellen Happen zu jeder Tageszeit.

Le restaurateur Keith McNally (Pastis,
Balthazar) continue à nous impressionner avec ce bistrot discret mais
chaleureux du Lower East Side. Il propose de la bonne vieille cuisine française sous forme de steak frites, une
poêlée de crevettes à l'ail ou des
penne à l'arrabiata. Le lieu idéal pour
satisfaire un petit creux à n'importe
quelle heure de la journée.

131 Rivington Street
New York, NY 10002
Tel. +1 212 260 4555

Bottino

The art crowd routinely pit stops at
Bottino during the synchronized
exhibit openings of the flourishing
Chelsea gallery scene. With an

uncomplicated menu, it cleans the
palette of the art patron who just
gobbled up a Damien Hirst or a Julian
Schnabel.

Die Kunstbranche kehrt während der
terminlich aufeinander abgestimmten
Vernissagen in der florierenden Gale-
rienszene von Chelsea hier ein. Die
schlichte Speisekarte sorgt bei dem
Kunstliebhaber, der gerade einen
Damien Hirst oder Julian Schnabel
gekauft hat, für einen klaren Kopf.

Le milieu de l'art vient par habitude
chez Bottino lors des vernissages
groupés des galeries d'un Chelsea en
plein essor. Grâce à sa carte sans chi-
chi, il réussit à déculpabiliser le
mécène qui vient de dépenser une
fortune sur un Damien Hirst ou un
Julian Schnabel.

246 Tenth Avenue
New York, NY 10001
Tel. +1 212 206 6766
www.bottinonyc.com

Da Silvano

The scenester's Italian restaurant of
choice, Da Silvano has been the pin-
nacle of New York dining (read media-
elite ogling) for over twenty years.
Anna Wintour and her Voguettes are
often spotted preening at outdoor
tables while a stream of media giants
eagerly put their names on the block-
long waiting list.

Der Lieblingsitaliener schlechthin der
Szenegänger und seit über zwanzig
Jahren der Fels in der New Yorker
Brandung (insbesondere für die
Medienelite). Man sieht Anna Wintour und ihre Voguetten sich oft an
einem der Tische im Freien putzen,
während Prominente aus der Medien-
branche sich darum reißen, ihre
Namen auf die ellenlange Warteliste
zu setzen.

Restaurant italien terriblement à la
mode, Da Silvano est le lieu préféré
des dîneurs new-yorkais (comprenez
l'élite médiatique) depuis plus de
vingt ans. Anna Wintour et ses
Voguettes y sont souvent repérées
en train de faire les belles en terrasse, tandis que les célébrités des
médias viennent ajouter leur nom sur
une liste d'attente assez longue pour
faire le tour du bloc.

260 Sixth Avenue
New York, NY 10014
Tel. +1 212 982 2343
www.dasilvano.com

Nobu

New York's fascination with Japanese
fusion isn't anywhere close to over.
Nobu, with its South American- and
Italian-tinted menu, is the latest of
these restaurants with a chef,
Nobuyuki Matsuhisa, at least as
famous as the celebrities who try to
slip in for a bit of take-out without
being noticed by the gawking diners.

Die Begeisterung der New Yorker
für eine Mischung aus italienischer
und japanischer Küche ist ungebrochen. Das Nobu mit seiner südame-
rikanisch und italienisch gefärbten
Karte ist das jüngste Restaurant dieser Art. Der Küchenchef Nobuyuki
Matsuhisa ist mindestens ebenso
berühmt wie die Stars, die versuchen hereinzuschleichen und etwas
zum Mitnehmen abzuholen, ohne
von den lästigen Gästen bemerkt
zu werden.

La fascination de New York pour la
cuisine fusion japonaise n'est pas
près de passer. Nobu, avec sa carte
teintée de cuisine sud-américaine et
italienne, est le dernier-né de ces restaurants et bénéficie d'un chef,
Nobuyuki Matsuhisa, au moins aussi
connu que les innombrables célébrités qui essaient de s'y glisser discrètement pour prendre des plats à
emporter sans être remarquées par
les clients indiscrets.

105 Hudson Street
New York, NY 10013
Tel. +1 212 219 0500

Café Gitane

A NoLIta institution, little Café Gitane
is like the coffeehouses you used to
frequent as a student to be seen
reading Jean-Paul Sartre while smoking like a chimney. Except the coffee
and French-Moroccan fare at this late-
night spot are truly excellent, as is
the locals-watching.

Als Institution von NoLIta erinnert
das kleine Café Gitane an die Lokale
der eigenen Studentenzeit. Als man
demonstrativ Jean-Paul Sartre las
und dazu wie ein Schlot rauchte. Nur
dass der Kaffee und die kleinen fran-
zösisch-marokkanischen Gerichte hier
ebenso gut sind wie die Gelegenheit,
Einheimische zu beobachten.

Institution de NoLIta, ce petit Café
Gitane rappelle ces cafétérias dans
lesquelles vous passiez votre temps
à l'université pour être vu en train
de lire du Jean-Paul Sartre tout en
fumant comme un pompier. Sauf que
dans ce bar de nuit, le café et la cuisine franco-marocaine sont vraiment
excellents. Tout comme le défilé des
habitués.

242 Mott Street
New York, NY 10012
Tel. +1 212 334 9552

BARS

Bungalow 8

Bungalow 8's claim to fame is its passion for pampering. Though located
in a "developing" part of Chelsea,
inside it feels like an Egyptian oasis.
You'll imbibe like a pharaoh, and you
can even order a helicopter if you've
had one too many – just the kind of
star treatment that has lured the fashion flock since day one.

Bungalow 8 ist berühmt dafür, seine
Gäste zu verwöhnen. Die Bar liegt
zwar in einem noch unterentwickel-
ten Teil von Chelsea, doch fühlt man
sich darin wie in einer ägyptischen
Oase. Sie können bechern wie ein
Pharao und sich sogar von einem
Helikopter abholen lassen, wenn Sie
ein Glas zu viel erwischt haben.
Genau die Art von Starbehandlung,
die die Modemeute seit dem ersten
Tag hierher lockt.

Bungalow 8 prétend être connu pour
sa passion du service. Bien que situé
dans une zone « en développement »
de Chelsea, on s'y sent comme dans
une oasis égyptienne. Vous y boirez
comme un pharaon, et pourrez même
commander un hélicoptère si vous
avez bu un verre de trop : voilà le
genre de traitement qui attire les
gens de la mode depuis le jour de
l'ouverture.

515 West 27th Street
New York, NY 10001
Tel. +1 212 629 3333

Dark Room

In the new LES (that's Lower East
Side, natch), this stonework basement bar is leading the way. In one
room, old-school locals croon to
Johnny Cash and his ilk, while in the
other room, the glossy fashion set
gets down to the sounds of dirty rock.

An der neuen LES (steht natürlich für
Lower East Side) begründet diese
gemauerte Kellerbar einen Trend. In
einem Raum gröhlen Einheimische
der alten Garde zu Johnny Cash und
Konsorten, während sich in einem
anderen die Hochglanz-Modemagazin-
Menschen zum Sound von schmutzi-
ger Rockmusik entspannen.

Dans le nouveau « L.E.S. » (Lower
East Side, bien évidemment), ce bar
en sous-sol ouvre la voie. Dans une
salle, les vieux habitués reprennent
les chansons de Johnny Cash et de
sa troupe, tandis que dans une autre,
la scène fashion se lâche aux
rythmes d'un rock crasseux.

165 Ludlow Street
New York, NY 10002
Tel. +1 212 353 0536

Happy Ending

Once a brothel for those of the Asian
persuasion, Happy Ending (a name
taken from the way in which the previous tenants would finish a massage) has reemerged as Chinatown's
bar of choice for residents of the gen-
trifying neighbourhood and late-night
shoppers of area boutiques.

Das ehemalige asiatische Bordell
(Happy Ending nannten die Vormieter
das Ende einer Massage) hat sich zu
Chinatowns Bar der Wahl sowohl bei
den Einheimischen des aufgewerte-
ten Viertels als auch bei den späten
Kunden der Boutiquen rundum entwickelt.

Ancien bordel de Chinatown dédié aux amateurs de beautés asiatiques, Happy Ending (un nom inspiré par la façon dont les précédents propriétaires clôturaient leurs massages) renaît comme le bar de choix des habitants de ce quartier en voie d'embourgeoisement et des clients nocturnes des boutiques du coin.

302 Broome Street
New York, NY 10002
Tel. +1 212 334 9676
www.happyendinglounge.com

Passerby
Attached to the Gavin Brown gallery, this insider hang-out that's the size of a postage stamp attracts art students, underground music enthusiasts and the fashion faithful alike, none too cool to kick up their heels on the lit-up dance floor.

Gleich neben der Galerie Gavin Brown lockt dieser briefmarkengroße Insidertreff Kunststudenten, Fans von Underground Music und Modeverrückte an, die sich nicht zu cool sind, auf der beleuchteten Tanzfläche ihre High Heels wegzukicken.

Rattaché à la galerie Gavin Brown, étudiants en art, fans de musique underground et fidèles de la mode n'hésitent pas à faire claquer leurs talons hauts sur le dancefloor lumineux de ce repaire de connaisseurs à peine plus grand qu'un timbre-poste.

436 West 15th Street
New York, NY 10011
Tel. +1 212 206 6847

HOTELS

Chelsea Hotel
The legendary haunt where William S. Burroughs wrote 'Naked Lunch', this one-time home to Jimi Hendrix, Janis Joplin, Andy Warhol, Tennessee Williams, Patti Smith, Allen Ginsberg and, tragically, Sid Vicious and Nancy Spungen still attracts the city's more bohemian passers-through.

Dies ist der legendäre Schlupfwinkel, wo William S. Burroughs „Naked Lunch" schrieb. Nach wie vor zieht das einstige Zuhause von Jimi Hendrix, Janis Joplin, Andy Warhol, Tennessee Williams, Patti Smith, Allen Ginsberg und tragischerweise auch Sid Vicious sowie Nancy Spungen eher die Bohemiens unter den Durchreisenden an.

Lieu légendaire où William Burroughs a écrit « Le Festin Nu », cet hôtel a vu défiler Jimi Hendrix, Janis Joplin, Andy Warhol, Tennessee Williams,

Patti Smith et Allen Ginsberg. Sans parler du souvenir tragique laissé par Sid Vicious et Nancy Spungen. Aujourd'hui, il attire toujours les visiteurs les plus bohèmes de la ville.

222 West 23rd Street
New York, NY 10011
Tel. +1 212 243 3700
www.hotelchelsea.com

Maritime Hotel
With its perfectly round windows overlooking the Hudson river, the Maritime Hotel is kitsch raised to an art form. Teak furniture and green-tiled bathrooms typify the over-the-top retro sheen of the rooms. To boot, its two restaurants and its Japanese-themed bar-club, Hiro, are among the city's preferred places to throw back a few.

Mit seinen kreisrunden Fenstern hinaus auf den Hudson hat das Maritime Hotel Kitsch zur Kunstform erhoben. Teakholzmöbel und grün geflieste Bäder kennzeichnen den übersteigerten Retro-Chic der Zimmer. Obendrein zählen die zwei Hotelrestaurants und die Club-Bar im japanischen Stil zu den bevorzugten Retrolokalen der Stadt.

Avec ses fenêtres toutes rondes donnant sur l'Hudson, le Maritime Hotel hisse le kitsch au rang d'art à part entière. Meubles en teck et salles de bains à carrelage vert caractérisent le lustre rétro surchargé de ses chambres. Par-dessus le marché, ses deux restaurants et Hiro, son bar-club japonais, comptent parmi les adresses préférées de la ville.

88 Ninth Avenue
New York, NY 10011
Tel. +1 212 243 3888
www.themaritimehotel.com

Hotel Gansevoort
Named after the old Dutch street onto which it looks, the monolithic Hotel Gansevoort is anything but Old World. The newest resident of the Meatpacking District boasts minimalist-catering features from a metal exterior to granite ceramic floors on the interior. The rooftop swimming pool is a must.

Das monolithische Hotel ist zwar nach der alten holländischen Straße benannt, auf die es blickt, ist aber nichts weniger als ein Vertreter der Alten Welt. Die jüngste Errungenschaft des Meatpacking District ist vielmehr stolz auf ihren Minimalismus, angefangen bei der Metallfassade bis hin zu den Granit-Keramik-

Fußböden. Der Pool auf dem Dach ist ein Muss.

Baptisé du nom hollandais de la vieille rue sur laquelle il donne, le monolithique Gansevoort n'a vraiment rien d'un hôtel à l'ancienne. Le tout nouveau résident du quartier des anciens abattoirs affiche tous les attributs du minimalisme hôtelier, de ses extérieurs en métal à ses sols carrelés de granite. A voir absolument : la piscine sur le toit.

18 Ninth Avenue
New York, NY 10014
Tel. +1 212 206 6700
www.hotelgansevoort.com

The Mercer
Built inside a landmark 19th century building in SoHo, this sister hotel to The Standard in Los Angeles serves as the temporary home to models, designers and a slew of Hollywood-variety celebrities. Don't check out before dining at the Mercer Kitchen in the basement.

Das in einem Wahrzeichen SoHos aus dem 19. Jahrhundert untergebrachte Partnerhotel von The Standard in Los Angeles dient Models, Designern und einem Haufen Hollywood-Prominenz als zweites Zuhause. Vor dem Auschecken unbedingt einmal in der Mercer Kitchen im Untergeschoss zu Abend essen.

Aménagé dans un immeuble classé du XIXᵉ siècle en plein SoHo, cet hôtel est le petit frère du Standard de Los Angeles. Mannequins, créateurs de mode et autres célébrités hollywoodiennes en ont fait leur pied-à-terre new-yorkais. Ne partez pas sans avoir dîné au restaurant Mercer Kitchen du sous-sol.

147 Mercer Street
New York, NY 10012
Tel. +1 212 966 6060
www.mercerhotel.com

Soho Grand
This industrial, steel-clad SoHo outpost features spacious rooms and penthouses with possibly the best views in all of Lower Manhattan. Better still, travellers who just can't part with their pets can procure grooming, day care, veterinarian services and limos for their pampered little darlings.

Das stahlverkleidete Haus im Industriedesign ist ein Außenposten in SoHo und präsentiert sich mit geräumigen Zimmern und Penthouses mit der wahrscheinlich besten Aussicht

über ganz Lower Manhattan. Noch dazu können Reisende, die sich nicht von ihren Haustieren trennen wollen, Hundefriseur, Betreuung, Tierarzt und Limousinen für ihre verhätschelten Lieblinge bestellen.

Habillé d'acier, cet hôtel de style industriel à SoHo possède des chambres spacieuses et ses penthouses offrent les plus belles vues sur le sud de Manhattan. Le plus : le client qui ne peut laisser son animal domestique chez lui se voit proposer divers services de toilettage et soins quotidiens, l'assistance d'un vétérinaire et même des limousines pour promener son toutou adoré.

310 West Broadway
New York, NY 10013
Tel. +1 212 965 3000
www.sohogrand.com

60 Thompson
Designed by Thomas O'Brien, also responsible for homes for Giorgio Armani and Ralph Lauren, this Mediterranean-tinged hotel in SoHo has an open and breezy feel that sets it far apart from the city's other, overly designed mainstays.

Das Design dieses mediterran angehauchten Hotels in SoHo stammt von Thomas O'Brien, der auch die Privathäuser von Giorgio Armani und Ralph Lauren eingerichtet hat. Das offene, luftige Ambiente grenzt es deutlich von den anderen übertrieben designten Hauptquartieren der Stadt ab.

Conçu par Thomas O'Brien, à qui l'on doit également les résidences de Giorgio Armani et de Ralph Lauren, cet hôtel de SoHo au style méditerranéen dégage un sentiment d'ouverture et d'élégance éthérée qui le distingue d'autres hôtels trop tape-à-l'œil de la ville.

60 Thompson Street
New York, NY 10012
Tel. +1 212 431 0400
www.60thompson.com

AIRPORTS

John F. Kennedy International Airport
Jamaica, NY 11430
Tel. +1 718 244 4444

Newark International Airport
Newark, NJ 07114
Tel. +1 973 961 6000

La Guardia Airport
Flushing, NY 11371
Tel. +1 718 533 3400

<u>Where is the best place to stay in Paris?</u> Azzedine Alaïa 'Trois Chambres'
<u>Where is your favourite place to eat in Paris?</u> Le Voltaire, especially in the Madame Picot space!
<u>Where is your favourite place to shop in Paris?</u> The Bosquet golf shop JEAN TOUITOU

PARIS

TEXT BY TEDDY CZOPP

In 2005, Paris is reinventing and rejuvenating its grand history; within the city's fashion industry, the legendary luxury brands are leading the way. Stronger and more confident, iconic houses like Chanel, Dior, Cartier and Louis Vuitton have lately been revamping their stores and further embellishing their images. Some might say that one result of the prevailing conservatism in Paris is that now is not a good time for young designers, in comparison with those in New York, Milan or London, where emerging talents are proudly celebrated. In any case, it is the right moment for France to cherish its national treasures. This phenomenon also applies to social and night life. Today, it is de rigueur to meet up and go out to old-fashioned cult places such as Maxim's or Castel, two magnificent venues in Paris that have recently hosted successful fashion parties. It's not only tourists that find these kind of places exciting – Parisians, too, are appreciating their heritage. Looking back to a certain simplicity, clubbing has seen new places like Le Baron or Truskel coming out as the coolest places to hang out; cabarets and revues like Le Lido or Le Crazy Horse are also hot again. For eating out, typical bistros and brasseries are preferred to fancy restaurants. Classy? Yes, Paris is a classy city but, today, that is exactly what Parisians like about it.

Im Jahr 2005 ist Paris dabei, seine großartige Geschichte neu zu schreiben und zu verjüngen. In der Modebranche geben dabei die legendären Luxuslabels den Ton an. Erstarkt und selbstbewusster denn je haben Kultmarken wie Chanel, Dior, Cartier und Louis Vuitton in jüngster Zeit ihre Läden aufpoliert und ihr Image weiter verbessert. Man könnte behaupten, eine der Folgen des in Paris vorherrschenden Konservativismus sei, dass junge Designer es hier momentan schwerer haben als etwa in New York, Mailand oder London, wo aufstrebende Talente stolz gefeiert werden. Wie auch immer es aber bestimmt der rechte Augenblick für Frankreich, um seine nationalen Aushängeschilder zu hegen. Dieses Phänomen gilt auch für das gesellschaftliche und das Nachtleben. Heute ist es Pflicht, gemeinsam altmodische legendäre Lokale wie das Maxim's oder Castel zu besuchen. An diesen beiden prachtvollen Schauplätzen fanden in jüngster Zeit gelungene Modepartys statt. Und es sind nicht nur die Touristen, die solche Orte aufregend finden – auch die Pariser schätzen diese Vermächtnisse. Gemäß dem Trend hin zu einer gewissen Schlichtheit sind beim Clubbing neue Lokale wie Le Baron oder Truskel als die coolsten Orte zum Abhängen gefragt. Aber auch Cabarets und Revue-Lokale wie Le Lido oder Le Crazy Horse sind wieder angesagt. Zum Essengehen gibt man typischen Bistros und Brasserien den Vorzug vor schicken Restaurants. Klassenbewusst? Ja, Paris ist wohl klassenbewusst, aber genau das lieben die Pariser heute an ihrer Stadt.

En 2005, Paris réinvente et rajeunit son illustre passé, et au sein de l'industrie de la mode, les légendaires marques de luxe ouvrent la voie. Plus fortes et plus confiantes, des maisons phares telles que Chanel, Dior, Cartier et Louis Vuitton ont récemment revu la conception de leurs boutiques et retravaillé leur image. D'aucuns diront que face au conservatisme qui prévaut à Paris, la période n'est pas des plus propices pour les jeunes créateurs, du moins par rapport à ceux de New York, Milan ou Londres où les talents émergents sont célébrés avec fierté. En tout cas, la France chérit actuellement ses trésors nationaux, un phénomène qui s'applique aussi à la vie sociale et nocturne. Aujourd'hui, la tendance veut qu'on sorte dans des lieux cultes et démodés comme Maxim's ou Castel, deux superbes adresses parisiennes qui depuis peu organisent avec succès des soirées très fashion. Ces endroits ne séduisent pas que les touristes : les Parisiens aussi savent apprécier leur héritage. Revenant à une certaine simplicité, la scène du clubbing voit de nouveaux rendez-vous, tels que Le Baron ou Le Truskel, s'imposer comme les bars les plus cool du moment ; les revues des cabarets du Lido ou du Crazy Horse bénéficient également d'un retour en grâce. Pour dîner, les Parisiens délaissent les restaurants de luxe et préfèrent se retrouver dans des bistrots et des brasseries plus typiques. Chic ? Oui, Paris reste une ville chic, mais c'est justement la raison pour laquelle ses habitants l'aiment autant aujourd'hui.